M000275283

Saint Thomas Aquinas

Summa Theologiae
Prima Pars, 1–49

Translated by Fr. Laurence Shapcote, OP

Summa Theologiae

Volume 13
Latin/English Edition of the Works of St. Thomas Aquinas

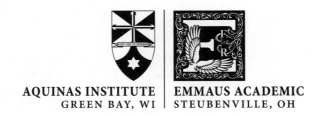

AQUINAS INSTITUTE | EMMAUS ACADEMIC
GREEN BAY, WI | STEUBENVILLE, OH

We would like to thank Kevin Bergdorf, Patricia Lynch, Josh and Holly Harnisch, Fr. Brian McMaster, Dr. Brian Cutter, and the Studentate Community of the Dominican Province of St. Albert the Great, USA, for their support. This series is dedicated to Marcus Berquist, Rose Johanna Trumbull, John and Mary Deignan, Thomas and Eleanor Sullivan, Ann C. Arcidi, the Very Rev. Romanus Cessario, OP, STM, and Fr. John T. Feeney and his sister Mary.

Published with the ecclesiastical approval of
The Most Reverend Paul D. Etienne, DD, STL
Bishop of Cheyenne
Given on November 10, 2012

Copyright © 2012
Aquinas Institute, Inc.
Green Bay, Wisconsin
www.aquinasinstitute.org

Printed in the United States of America

Third Printing 2021

Publisher's Cataloging-in-Publication Data

Thomas Aquinas, St., 1225?–1274
  Summa Theologiae Prima Pars, 1–49 / Saint Thomas Aquinas; edited by The Aquinas Institute;
  translated by Fr. Laurence Shapcote, OP
  p. 528 cm.
  ISBN 978-1-62340-006-4

1. Thomas, Aquinas, Saint, 1225?–1274 — Summa theologiae — Prima Pars — 1–49. 2. Catholic Church — Doctrines
—Early works to 1800. 3. Theology, Doctrinal — Early works to 1800. I. Title. II. Series

BX1749.T512 2012
230´.2--dc23   2012953831

Notes on the Text

Latin Text of St. Thomas

The Latin text used in this volume is based on the Corpus Thomisticum text of the Fundación Tomás de Aquino <www.corpusthomisticum.org>. This text is based on the Leonine Edition, transcribed by Fr. Roberto Busa SJ, and revised by Dr. Enrique Alarcón and other editors and collaborators of this bilingual edition. © 2012 Fundación Tomás de Aquino, Pamplona. Used with permission.

English Translation of St. Thomas

The English translation of the *Summa Theologiae* was prepared by Fr. Laurence Shapcote, O.P. (1864-1947), of the English Dominican Province. It has been edited and revised by The Aquinas Institute and its collaborators.

The Aquinas Institute requests your assistance in the continued perfection of these texts.
If you discover any errors, please send a note to us by e-mail: admin@theaquinasinstitute.org.

DEDICATED WITH LOVE TO
OUR LADY OF MT. CARMEL

Contents

Summa Theologiae
Prima Pars, 1-49

PROLOGUE

Quia Catholicae veritatis doctor non solum provectos debet instruere, sed ad eum pertinet etiam incipientes erudire, secundum illud apostoli I ad Corinth. III, *tanquam parvulis in Christo, lac vobis potum dedi, non escam*; propositum nostrae intentionis in hoc opere est, ea quae ad Christianam religionem pertinent, eo modo tradere, secundum quod congruit ad eruditionem incipientium. Consideravimus namque huius doctrinae novitios, in his quae a diversis conscripta sunt, plurimum impediri, partim quidem propter multiplicationem inutilium quaestionum, articulorum et argumentorum; partim etiam quia ea quae sunt necessaria talibus ad sciendum, non traduntur secundum ordinem disciplinae, sed secundum quod requirebat librorum expositio, vel secundum quod se praebebat occasio disputandi; partim quidem quia eorundem frequens repetitio et fastidium et confusionem generabat in animis auditorum.

Haec igitur et alia huiusmodi evitare studentes, tentabimus, cum confidentia divini auxilii, ea quae ad sacram doctrinam pertinent, breviter ac dilucide prosequi, secundum quod materia patietur.

Because the Master of Catholic Truth ought not only to teach the proficient, but also to instruct beginners, according to the Apostle: *As Unto Little Ones in Christ, I Gave You Milk to Drink, Not Meat* (1 Cor 3:1–2), we purpose in this book to treat of whatever belongs to the Christian Religion, in such a way as may tend to the instruction of beginners. We have considered that students in this Science have not seldom been hampered by what they have found written by other authors, partly on account of the multiplication of useless questions, articles, and arguments; partly also because those things that are needful for them to know are not taught according to the order of the subject-matter, but according as the plan of the book might require, or the occasion of the argument offer; partly, too, because frequent repetition brought weariness and confusion to the minds of the readers.

Endeavoring to avoid these and other like faults, we shall try, by God's help, to set forth whatever is included in this Sacred Science as briefly and clearly as the matter itself may allow.

QUESTION 1

THE NATURE OF SACRED DOCTRINE

Et ut intentio nostra sub aliquibus certis limitibus comprehendatur, necessarium est primo investigare de ipsa sacra doctrina, qualis sit, et ad quae se extendat.

Circa quae quaerenda sunt decem.

Primo, de necessitate huius doctrinae.

Secundo, utrum sit scientia.

Tertio, utrum sit una vel plures.

Quarto, utrum sit speculativa vel practica.

Quinto, de comparatione eius ad alias scientias.

Sexto, utrum sit sapientia.

Septimo, quid sit subiectum eius.

Octavo, utrum sit argumentativa.

Nono, utrum uti debeat metaphoricis vel symbolicis locutionibus.

Decimo, utrum Scriptura sacra huius doctrinae sit secundum plures sensus exponenda.

To place our purpose within proper limits, we first endeavor to investigate the nature and extent of this sacred doctrine.

Concerning this there are ten points of inquiry:

(1) Whether it is necessary?

(2) Whether it is a science?

(3) Whether it is one or many?

(4) Whether it is speculative or practical?

(5) How it is compared with other sciences?

(6) Whether it is the same as wisdom?

(7) Whether God is its subject-matter?

(8) Whether it is a matter of argument?

(9) Whether it rightly employs metaphors and similes?

(10) Whether the Sacred Scripture of this doctrine may be expounded in different senses?

Article 1

Whether, besides Philosophy, any Further Doctrine Is Required?

AD PRIMUM SIC PROCEDITUR. Videtur quod non sit necessarium, praeter philosophicas disciplinas, aliam doctrinam haberi. Ad ea enim quae supra rationem sunt, homo non debet conari, secundum illud Eccli. III, *altiora te ne quaesieris*. Sed ea quae rationi subduntur, sufficienter traduntur in philosophicis disciplinis. Superfluum igitur videtur, praeter philosophicas disciplinas, aliam doctrinam haberi.

PRAETEREA, doctrina non potest esse nisi de ente, nihil enim scitur nisi verum, quod cum ente convertitur. Sed de omnibus entibus tractatur in philosophicis disciplinis, et etiam de Deo, unde quaedam pars philosophiae dicitur theologia, sive scientia divina, ut patet per philosophum in VI Metaphys. Non fuit igitur necessarium, praeter philosophicas disciplinas, aliam doctrinam haberi.

SED CONTRA est quod dicitur II ad Tim. III, *omnis Scriptura divinitus inspirata utilis est ad docendum, ad arguendum, ad corripiendum, ad erudiendum ad iustitiam.* Scriptura autem divinitus inspirata non pertinet ad philosophicas disciplinas, quae sunt secundum rationem humanam inventae. Utile igitur est, praeter philosophicas disciplinas, esse aliam scientiam divinitus inspiratam.

OBJECTION 1: It seems that, besides philosophical science, we have no need of any further knowledge. For man should not seek to know what is above reason: *Seek not the things that are too high for thee* (Eccl 3:22). But whatever is not above reason is fully treated of in philosophical science. Therefore any other knowledge besides philosophical science is superfluous.

OBJ. 2: Further, knowledge can be concerned only with being, for nothing can be known, save what is true; and all that is, is true. But everything that is, is treated of in philosophical science—even God Himself; so that there is a part of philosophy called theology, or the divine science, as Aristotle has proved (*Metaph.* vi). Therefore, besides philosophical science, there is no need of any further knowledge.

ON THE CONTRARY, It is written (2 Tim 3:16): *All Scripture inspired of God is profitable to teach, to reprove, to correct, to instruct in justice.* Now Scripture, inspired of God, is no part of philosophical science, which has been built up by human reason. Therefore it is useful that besides philosophical science, there should be other knowledge, i.e., inspired of God.

3

RESPONDEO dicendum quod necessarium fuit ad humanam salutem, esse doctrinam quandam secundum revelationem divinam, praeter philosophicas disciplinas, quae ratione humana investigantur. Primo quidem, quia homo ordinatur ad Deum sicut ad quendam finem qui comprehensionem rationis excedit, secundum illud Isaiae LXIV, *oculus non vidit Deus absque te, quae praeparasti diligentibus te.* Finem autem oportet esse praecognitum hominibus, qui suas intentiones et actiones debent ordinare in finem. Unde necessarium fuit homini ad salutem, quod ei nota fierent quaedam per revelationem divinam, quae rationem humanam excedunt. Ad ea etiam quae de Deo ratione humana investigari possunt, necessarium fuit hominem instrui revelatione divina. Quia veritas de Deo, per rationem investigata, a paucis, et per longum tempus, et cum admixtione multorum errorum, homini proveniret, a cuius tamen veritatis cognitione dependet tota hominis salus, quae in Deo est. Ut igitur salus hominibus et convenientius et certius proveniat, necessarium fuit quod de divinis per divinam revelationem instruantur. Necessarium igitur fuit, praeter philosophicas disciplinas, quae per rationem investigantur, sacram doctrinam per revelationem haberi.

AD PRIMUM ergo dicendum quod, licet ea quae sunt altiora hominis cognitione, non sint ab homine per rationem inquirenda, sunt tamen, a Deo revelata, suscipienda per fidem. Unde et ibidem subditur, *plurima supra sensum hominum ostensa sunt tibi.* Et in huiusmodi sacra doctrina consistit.

AD SECUNDUM dicendum quod diversa ratio cognoscibilis diversitatem scientiarum inducit. Eandem enim conclusionem demonstrat astrologus et naturalis, puta quod terra est rotunda, sed astrologus per medium mathematicum, idest a materia abstractum; naturalis autem per medium circa materiam consideratum. Unde nihil prohibet de eisdem rebus, de quibus philosophicae disciplinae tractant secundum quod sunt cognoscibilia lumine naturalis rationis, et aliam scientiam tractare secundum quod cognoscuntur lumine divinae revelationis. Unde theologia quae ad sacram doctrinam pertinet, differt secundum genus ab illa theologia quae pars philosophiae ponitur.

I ANSWER THAT, It was necessary for man's salvation that there should be a knowledge revealed by God besides philosophical science built up by human reason. First, indeed, because man is directed to God, as to an end that surpasses the grasp of his reason: *The eye hath not seen, O God, besides Thee, what things Thou hast prepared for them that wait for Thee* (Isa 66:4). But the end must first be known by men who are to direct their thoughts and actions to the end. Hence it was necessary for the salvation of man that certain truths which exceed human reason should be made known to him by divine revelation. Even as regards those truths about God which human reason could have discovered, it was necessary that man should be taught by a divine revelation; because the truth about God such as reason could discover, would only be known by a few, and that after a long time, and with the admixture of many errors. Whereas man's whole salvation, which is in God, depends upon the knowledge of this truth. Therefore, in order that the salvation of men might be brought about more fitly and more surely, it was necessary that they should be taught divine truths by divine revelation. It was therefore necessary that besides philosophical science built up by reason, there should be a sacred science learned through revelation.

REPLY OBJ. 1: Although those things which are beyond man's knowledge may not be sought for by man through his reason, nevertheless, once they are revealed by God, they must be accepted by faith. Hence the sacred text continues, *For many things are shown to thee above the understanding of man* (Eccl 3:25). And in this, the sacred science consists.

REPLY OBJ. 2: Sciences are differentiated according to the various means through which knowledge is obtained. For the astronomer and the physicist both may prove the same conclusion: that the earth, for instance, is round: the astronomer by means of mathematics (i.e., abstracting from matter), but the physicist by means of matter itself. Hence there is no reason why those things which may be learned from philosophical science, so far as they can be known by natural reason, may not also be taught us by another science so far as they fall within revelation. Hence theology included in sacred doctrine differs in kind from that theology which is part of philosophy.

Article 2

Whether Sacred Doctrine Is a Science?

AD SECUNDUM SIC PROCEDITUR. Videtur quod sacra doctrina non sit scientia. Omnis enim scientia procedit ex principiis per se notis. Sed sacra doctrina procedit ex articulis fidei, qui non sunt per se noti, cum non ab omnibus concedantur, *non enim omnium est fides,* ut

OBJECTION 1: It seems that sacred doctrine is not a science. For every science proceeds from self-evident principles. But sacred doctrine proceeds from articles of faith which are not self-evident, since their truth is not admitted

dicitur II Thessalon. III. Non igitur sacra doctrina est scientia.

Praeterea, scientia non est singularium. Sed sacra doctrina tractat de singularibus, puta de gestis Abrahae, Isaac et Iacob, et similibus. Ergo sacra doctrina non est scientia.

Sed contra est quod Augustinus dicit, XIV de Trinitate, *huic scientiae attribuitur illud tantummodo quo fides saluberrima gignitur, nutritur, defenditur, roboratur.* Hoc autem ad nullam scientiam pertinet nisi ad sacram doctrinam. Ergo sacra doctrina est scientia.

Respondeo dicendum sacram doctrinam esse scientiam. Sed sciendum est quod duplex est scientiarum genus. Quaedam enim sunt, quae procedunt ex principiis notis lumine naturali intellectus, sicut arithmetica, geometria, et huiusmodi. Quaedam vero sunt, quae procedunt ex principiis notis lumine superioris scientiae, sicut perspectiva procedit ex principiis notificatis per geometriam, et musica ex principiis per arithmeticam notis. Et hoc modo sacra doctrina est scientia, quia procedit ex principiis notis lumine superioris scientiae, quae scilicet est scientia Dei et beatorum. Unde sicut musica credit principia tradita sibi ab arithmetico, ita doctrina sacra credit principia revelata sibi a Deo.

Ad primum ergo dicendum quod principia cuiuslibet scientiae vel sunt nota per se, vel reducuntur ad notitiam superioris scientiae. Et talia sunt principia sacrae doctrinae, ut dictum est.

Ad secundum dicendum quod singularia traduntur in sacra doctrina, non quia de eis principaliter tractetur, sed introducuntur tum in exemplum vitae, sicut in scientiis moralibus; tum etiam ad declarandum auctoritatem virorum per quos ad nos revelatio divina processit, super quam fundatur sacra Scriptura seu doctrina.

by all: *For all men have not faith* (2 Thess 3:2). Therefore sacred doctrine is not a science.

Obj. 2: Further, no science deals with individual facts. But this sacred science treats of individual facts, such as the deeds of Abraham, Isaac and Jacob and such like. Therefore sacred doctrine is not a science.

On the contrary, Augustine says (*De Trin.* xiv, 1) *to this science alone belongs that whereby saving faith is begotten, nourished, protected and strengthened.* But this can be said of no science except sacred doctrine. Therefore sacred doctrine is a science.

I answer that, Sacred doctrine is a science. We must bear in mind that there are two kinds of sciences. There are some which proceed from a principle known by the natural light of intelligence, such as arithmetic and geometry and the like. There are some which proceed from principles known by the light of a higher science: thus the science of perspective proceeds from principles established by geometry, and music from principles established by arithmetic. So it is that sacred doctrine is a science because it proceeds from principles established by the light of a higher science, namely, the science of God and the blessed. Hence, just as the musician accepts on authority the principles taught him by the mathematician, so sacred science is established on principles revealed by God.

Reply Obj. 1: The principles of any science are either in themselves self-evident, or reducible to the conclusions of a higher science; and such, as we have said, are the principles of sacred doctrine.

Reply Obj. 2: Individual facts are treated of in sacred doctrine, not because it is concerned with them principally, but they are introduced rather both as examples to be followed in our lives (as in moral sciences) and in order to establish the authority of those men through whom the divine revelation, on which this sacred scripture or doctrine is based, has come down to us.

Article 3

Whether Sacred Doctrine Is One Science?

Ad tertium sic proceditur. Videtur quod sacra doctrina non sit una scientia. Quia secundum philosophum in I Poster., *una scientia est quae est unius generis subiecti.* Creator autem et creatura, de quibus in sacra doctrina tractatur, non continentur sub uno genere subiecti. Ergo sacra doctrina non est una scientia.

Praeterea, in sacra doctrina tractatur de Angelis, de creaturis corporalibus, de moribus hominum. Huiusmodi autem ad diversas scientias philosophicas pertinent. Igitur sacra doctrina non est una scientia.

Objection 1: It seems that sacred doctrine is not one science; for according to the Philosopher (*Poster.* i) *that science is one which treats only of one class of subjects.* But the creator and the creature, both of whom are treated of in sacred doctrine, cannot be grouped together under one class of subjects. Therefore sacred doctrine is not one science.

Obj. 2: Further, in sacred doctrine we treat of angels, corporeal creatures and human morality. But these belong to separate philosophical sciences. Therefore sacred doctrine cannot be one science.

SED CONTRA est quod sacra Scriptura de ea loquitur sicut de una scientia, dicitur enim Sap. X, *dedit illi scientiam sanctorum.*

RESPONDEO dicendum sacram doctrinam unam scientiam esse. Est enim unitas potentiae et habitus consideranda secundum obiectum, non quidem materialiter, sed secundum rationem formalem obiecti, puta homo, asinus et lapis conveniunt in una formali ratione colorati, quod est obiectum visus. Quia igitur sacra Scriptura considerat aliqua secundum quod sunt divinitus revelata, secundum quod dictum est, omnia quaecumque sunt divinitus revelabilia, communicant in una ratione formali obiecti huius scientiae. Et ideo comprehenduntur sub sacra doctrina sicut sub scientia una.

AD PRIMUM ergo dicendum quod sacra doctrina non determinat de Deo et de creaturis ex aequo, sed de Deo principaliter, et de creaturis secundum quod referuntur ad Deum, ut ad principium vel finem. Unde unitas scientiae non impeditur.

AD SECUNDUM dicendum quod nihil prohibet inferiores potentias vel habitus diversificari circa illas materias, quae communiter cadunt sub una potentia vel habitu superiori, quia superior potentia vel habitus respicit obiectum sub universaliori ratione formali. Sicut obiectum sensus communis est sensibile, quod comprehendit sub se visibile et audibile, unde sensus communis, cum sit una potentia, extendit se ad omnia obiecta quinque sensuum. Et similiter ea quae in diversis scientiis philosophicis tractantur, potest sacra doctrina, una existens, considerare sub una ratione, inquantum scilicet sunt divinitus revelabilia, ut sic sacra doctrina sit velut quaedam impressio divinae scientiae, quae est una et simplex omnium.

ON THE CONTRARY, Holy Scripture speaks of it as one science: *Wisdom gave him the knowledge of holy things* (Wis 10:10).

I ANSWER THAT, Sacred doctrine is one science. The unity of a faculty or habit is to be gauged by its object, not indeed, in its material aspect, but as regards the precise formality under which it is an object. For example, man, ass, stone agree in the one precise formality of being colored; and color is the formal object of sight. Therefore, because Sacred Scripture considers things precisely under the formality of being divinely revealed, whatever has been divinely revealed possesses the one precise formality of the object of this science; and therefore is included under sacred doctrine as under one science.

REPLY OBJ. 1: Sacred doctrine does not treat of God and creatures equally, but of God primarily, and of creatures only so far as they are referable to God as their beginning or end. Hence the unity of this science is not impaired.

REPLY OBJ. 2: Nothing prevents inferior faculties or habits from being differentiated by something which falls under a higher faculty or habit as well; because the higher faculty or habit regards the object in its more universal formality, as the object of the common sense is whatever affects the senses, including, therefore, whatever is visible or audible. Hence the common sense, although one faculty, extends to all the objects of the five senses. Similarly, objects which are the subject-matter of different philosophical sciences can yet be treated of by this one single sacred science under one aspect precisely so far as they can be included in revelation. So that in this way, sacred doctrine bears, as it were, the stamp of the divine science which is one and simple, yet extends to everything.

Article 4

Whether Sacred Doctrine Is a Practical Science?

AD QUARTUM SIC PROCEDITUR. Videtur quod sacra doctrina sit scientia practica. Finis enim practicae est operatio, secundum philosophum in II Metaphys. Sacra autem doctrina ad operationem ordinatur, secundum illud Iac. I, *estote factores verbi, et non auditores tantum.* Ergo sacra doctrina est practica scientia.

PRAETEREA, sacra doctrina dividitur per legem veterem et novam. Lex autem pertinet ad scientiam moralem, quae est scientia practica. Ergo sacra doctrina est scientia practica.

SED CONTRA, omnis scientia practica est de rebus operabilibus ab homine; ut moralis de actibus hominum, et aedificativa de aedificiis. Sacra autem doctrina

OBJECTION 1: It seems that sacred doctrine is a practical science; for a practical science is that which ends in action according to the Philosopher (*Metaph.* ii). But sacred doctrine is ordained to action: *Be ye doers of the word, and not hearers only* (Jas 1:22). Therefore sacred doctrine is a practical science.

OBJ. 2: Further, sacred doctrine is divided into the Old and the New Law. But law implies a moral science which is a practical science. Therefore sacred doctrine is a practical science.

ON THE CONTRARY, Every practical science is concerned with human operations; as moral science is concerned with human acts, and architecture with buildings. But sacred doctrine is chiefly concerned with God, whose

est principaliter de Deo, cuius magis homines sunt opera. Non ergo est scientia practica, sed magis speculativa.

RESPONDEO dicendum quod sacra doctrina, ut dictum est, una existens, se extendit ad ea quae pertinent ad diversas scientias philosophicas, propter rationem formalem quam in diversis attendit, scilicet prout sunt divino lumine cognoscibilia. Unde licet in scientiis philosophicis alia sit speculativa et alia practica, sacra tamen doctrina comprehendit sub se utramque; sicut et Deus eadem scientia se cognoscit, et ea quae facit. Magis tamen est speculativa quam practica, quia principalius agit de rebus divinis quam de actibus humanis; de quibus agit secundum quod per eos ordinatur homo ad perfectam Dei cognitionem, in qua aeterna beatitudo consistit.

ET PER HOC patet responsio ad obiecta.

handiwork is especially man. Therefore it is not a practical but a speculative science.

I ANSWER THAT, Sacred doctrine, being one, extends to things which belong to different philosophical sciences because it considers in each the same formal aspect, namely, so far as they can be known through divine revelation. Hence, although among the philosophical sciences one is speculative and another practical, nevertheless sacred doctrine includes both; as God, by one and the same science, knows both Himself and His works. Still, it is speculative rather than practical because it is more concerned with divine things than with human acts; though it does treat even of these latter, inasmuch as man is ordained by them to the perfect knowledge of God in which consists eternal bliss.

THIS IS A SUFFICIENT answer to the Objections.

Article 5

Whether Sacred Doctrine Is Nobler than Other Sciences?

AD QUINTUM SIC PROCEDITUR. Videtur quod sacra doctrina non sit dignior aliis scientiis. Certitudo enim pertinet ad dignitatem scientiae. Sed aliae scientiae, de quarum principiis dubitari non potest, videntur esse certiores sacra doctrina, cuius principia, scilicet articuli fidei, dubitationem recipiunt. Aliae igitur scientiae videntur ista digniores.

PRAETEREA, inferioris scientiae est a superiori accipere, sicut musicus ab arithmetico. Sed sacra doctrina accipit aliquid a philosophicis disciplinis, dicit enim Hieronymus in epistola ad magnum oratorem urbis Romae, quod *doctores antiqui intantum philosophorum doctrinis atque sententiis suos resperserunt libros, ut nescias quid in illis prius admirari debeas, eruditionem saeculi, an scientiam Scripturarum.* Ergo sacra doctrina est inferior aliis scientiis.

SED CONTRA est quod aliae scientiae dicuntur ancillae huius, Prov. IX, *misit ancillas suas vocare ad arcem.*

RESPONDEO dicendum quod, cum ista scientia quantum ad aliquid sit speculativa, et quantum ad aliquid sit practica, omnes alias transcendit tam speculativas quam practicas. Speculativarum enim scientiarum una altera dignior dicitur, tum propter certitudinem, tum propter dignitatem materiae. Et quantum ad utrumque, haec scientia alias speculativas scientias excedit. Secundum certitudinem quidem, quia aliae scientiae certitudinem habent ex naturali lumine rationis humanae, quae potest errare, haec autem certitudinem habet ex lumine divinae scientiae, quae decipi non potest. Secundum dignitatem vero materiae, quia ista scientia est principaliter de his quae sua altitudine rationem transcendunt, aliae vero

OBJECTION 1: It seems that sacred doctrine is not nobler than other sciences; for the nobility of a science depends on the certitude it establishes. But other sciences, the principles of which cannot be doubted, seem to be more certain than sacred doctrine; for its principles—namely, articles of faith—can be doubted. Therefore other sciences seem to be nobler.

OBJ. 2: Further, it is the sign of a lower science to depend upon a higher; as music depends on arithmetic. But sacred doctrine does in a sense depend upon philosophical sciences; for Jerome observes, in his Epistle to Magnus, that *the ancient doctors so enriched their books with the ideas and phrases of the philosophers, that thou knowest not what more to admire in them, their profane erudition or their scriptural learning.* Therefore sacred doctrine is inferior to other sciences.

ON THE CONTRARY, Other sciences are called the handmaidens of this one: *Wisdom sent her maids to invite to the tower* (Prov 9:3).

I ANSWER THAT, Since this science is partly speculative and partly practical, it transcends all others speculative and practical. Now one speculative science is said to be nobler than another, either by reason of its greater certitude, or by reason of the higher worth of its subject-matter. In both these respects this science surpasses other speculative sciences; in point of greater certitude, because other sciences derive their certitude from the natural light of human reason, which can err; whereas this derives its certitude from the light of divine knowledge, which cannot be misled: in point of the higher worth of its subject-matter because this science treats chiefly of those things which by their sublimity transcend human reason; while other sciences

scientiae considerant ea tantum quae rationi subduntur. Practicarum vero scientiarum illa dignior est, quae ad ulteriorem finem ordinatur, sicut civilis militari, nam bonum exercitus ad bonum civitatis ordinatur. Finis autem huius doctrinae inquantum est practica, est beatitudo aeterna, ad quam sicut ad ultimum finem ordinantur omnes alii fines scientiarum practicarum. Unde manifestum est, secundum omnem modum, eam digniorem esse aliis.

AD PRIMUM ergo dicendum quod nihil prohibet id quod est certius secundum naturam, esse quoad nos minus certum, propter debilitatem intellectus nostri, *qui se habet ad manifestissima naturae, sicut oculus noctuae ad lumen solis*, sicut dicitur in II Metaphys. Unde dubitatio quae accidit in aliquibus circa articulos fidei, non est propter incertitudinem rei, sed propter debilitatem intellectus humani. Et tamen minimum quod potest haberi de cognitione rerum altissimarum, desiderabilius est quam certissima cognitio quae habetur de minimis rebus, ut dicitur in XI de animalibus.

AD SECUNDUM dicendum quod haec scientia accipere potest aliquid a philosophicis disciplinis, non quod ex necessitate eis indigeat, sed ad maiorem manifestationem eorum quae in hac scientia traduntur. Non enim accipit sua principia ab aliis scientiis, sed immediate a Deo per revelationem. Et ideo non accipit ab aliis scientiis tanquam a superioribus, sed utitur eis tanquam inferioribus et ancillis; sicut architectonicae utuntur subministrantibus, ut civilis militari. Et hoc ipsum quod sic utitur eis, non est propter defectum vel insufficientiam eius, sed propter defectum intellectus nostri; qui ex his quae per naturalem rationem (ex qua procedunt aliae scientiae) cognoscuntur, facilius manuducitur in ea quae sunt supra rationem, quae in hac scientia traduntur.

consider only those things which are within reason's grasp. Of the practical sciences, that one is nobler which is ordained to a further purpose, as political science is nobler than military science; for the good of the army is directed to the good of the State. But the purpose of this science, in so far as it is practical, is eternal bliss; to which as to an ultimate end the purposes of every practical science are directed. Hence it is clear that from every standpoint, it is nobler than other sciences.

REPLY OBJ. 1: It may well happen that what is in itself the more certain may seem to us the less certain on account of the weakness of our intelligence, *which is dazzled by the clearest objects of nature; as the owl is dazzled by the light of the sun* (*Metaph.* ii, lect. i). Hence the fact that some happen to doubt about articles of faith is not due to the uncertain nature of the truths, but to the weakness of human intelligence; yet the slenderest knowledge that may be obtained of the highest things is more desirable than the most certain knowledge obtained of lesser things, as is said in de Animalibus xi.

REPLY OBJ. 2: This science can in a sense depend upon the philosophical sciences, not as though it stood in need of them, but only in order to make its teaching clearer. For it accepts its principles not from other sciences, but immediately from God, by revelation. Therefore it does not depend upon other sciences as upon the higher, but makes use of them as of the lesser, and as handmaidens: even so the master sciences make use of the sciences that supply their materials, as political of military science. That it thus uses them is not due to its own defect or insufficiency, but to the defect of our intelligence, which is more easily led by what is known through natural reason (from which proceed the other sciences) to that which is above reason, such as are the teachings of this science.

Article 6

Whether This Doctrine Is the Same as Wisdom?

AD SEXTUM SIC PROCEDITUR. Videtur quod haec doctrina non sit sapientia. Nulla enim doctrina quae supponit sua principia aliunde, digna est nomine sapientiae, *quia sapientis est ordinare, et non ordinari* (I Metaphys.). Sed haec doctrina supponit principia sua aliunde, ut ex dictis patet. Ergo haec doctrina non est sapientia.

PRAETEREA, ad sapientiam pertinet probare principia aliarum scientiarum, unde ut caput dicitur scientiarum, ut VI Ethic. patet. Sed haec doctrina non probat principia aliarum scientiarum. Ergo non est sapientia.

PRAETEREA, haec doctrina per studium acquiritur. Sapientia autem per infusionem habetur, unde inter

OBJECTION 1: It seems that this doctrine is not the same as wisdom. For no doctrine which borrows its principles is worthy of the name of wisdom; seeing that *the wise man directs, and is not directed* (*Metaph.* i). But this doctrine borrows its principles. Therefore this science is not wisdom.

OBJ. 2: Further, it is a part of wisdom to prove the principles of other sciences. Hence it is called the chief of sciences, as is clear in *Ethic.* vi. But this doctrine does not prove the principles of other sciences. Therefore it is not the same as wisdom.

OBJ. 3: Further, this doctrine is acquired by study, whereas wisdom is acquired by God's inspiration; so that

septem dona spiritus sancti connumeratur, ut patet Isaiae XI. Ergo haec doctrina non est sapientia.

SED CONTRA est quod dicitur Deut. IV, in principio legis, *haec est nostra sapientia et intellectus coram populis.*

RESPONDEO dicendum quod haec doctrina maxime sapientia est inter omnes sapientias humanas, non quidem in aliquo genere tantum, sed simpliciter. Cum enim sapientis sit ordinare et iudicare, iudicium autem per altiorem causam de inferioribus habeatur; ille sapiens dicitur in unoquoque genere, qui considerat causam altissimam illius generis. Ut in genere aedificii, artifex qui disponit formam domus, dicitur sapiens et architector, respectu inferiorum artificum, qui dolant ligna vel parant lapides, unde dicitur I Cor. III, *ut sapiens architector fundamentum posui.* Et rursus, in genere totius humanae vitae, prudens sapiens dicitur, inquantum ordinat humanos actus ad debitum finem, unde dicitur Prov. X, *sapientia est viro prudentia.* Ille igitur qui considerat simpliciter altissimam causam totius universi, quae Deus est, maxime sapiens dicitur, unde et sapientia dicitur esse divinorum cognitio, ut patet per Augustinum, XII de Trinitate. Sacra autem doctrina propriissime determinat de Deo secundum quod est altissima causa, quia non solum quantum ad illud quod est per creaturas cognoscibile (quod philosophi cognoverunt, ut dicitur Rom. I, *quod notum est Dei, manifestum est illis*); sed etiam quantum ad id quod notum est sibi soli de seipso, et aliis per revelationem communicatum. Unde sacra doctrina maxime dicitur sapientia.

AD PRIMUM ergo dicendum quod sacra doctrina non supponit sua principia ab aliqua scientia humana, sed a scientia divina, a qua, sicut a summa sapientia, omnis nostra cognitio ordinatur.

AD SECUNDUM dicendum quod aliarum scientiarum principia vel sunt per se nota, et probari non possunt, vel per aliquam rationem naturalem probantur in aliqua alia scientia. Propria autem huius scientiae cognitio est, quae est per revelationem, non autem quae est per naturalem rationem. Et ideo non pertinet ad eam probare principia aliarum scientiarum, sed solum iudicare de eis, quidquid enim in aliis scientiis invenitur veritati huius scientiae repugnans, totum condemnatur ut falsum, unde dicitur II Cor. X, *consilia destruentes, et omnem altitudinem extollentem se adversus scientiam Dei.*

AD TERTIUM dicendum quod, cum iudicium ad sapientem pertineat, secundum duplicem modum iudicandi, dupliciter sapientia accipitur. Contingit enim aliquem iudicare, uno modo per modum inclinationis, sicut qui habet habitum virtutis, recte iudicat de his quae sunt secundum virtutem agenda, inquantum ad illa inclinatur, unde et in X Ethic. dicitur quod virtuosus est mensura et regula actuum humanorum. Alio modo, per modum cognitionis, sicut aliquis instructus in scientia morali, posset iudicare de actibus virtutis, etiam si

it is numbered among the gifts of the Holy Spirit (Isa 11:2). Therefore this doctrine is not the same as wisdom.

ON THE CONTRARY, It is written (Deut 4:6): *This is your wisdom and understanding in the sight of nations.*

I ANSWER THAT, This doctrine is wisdom above all human wisdom; not merely in any one order, but absolutely. For since it is the part of a wise man to arrange and to judge, and since lesser matters should be judged in the light of some higher principle, he is said to be wise in any one order who considers the highest principle in that order: thus in the order of building, he who plans the form of the house is called wise and architect, in opposition to the inferior laborers who trim the wood and make ready the stones: *As a wise architect, I have laid the foundation* (1 Cor 3:10). Again, in the order of all human life, the prudent man is called wise, inasmuch as he directs his acts to a fitting end: *Wisdom is prudence to a man* (Prov 10: 23). Therefore he who considers absolutely the highest cause of the whole universe, namely God, is most of all called wise. Hence wisdom is said to be the knowledge of divine things, as Augustine says (*De Trin.* xii, 14). But sacred doctrine essentially treats of God viewed as the highest cause—not only so far as He can be known through creatures just as philosophers knew Him—*That which is known of God is manifest in them* (Rom 1:19)—but also as far as He is known to Himself alone and revealed to others. Hence sacred doctrine is especially called wisdom.

REPLY OBJ. 1: Sacred doctrine derives its principles not from any human knowledge, but from the divine knowledge, through which, as through the highest wisdom, all our knowledge is set in order.

REPLY OBJ. 2: The principles of other sciences either are evident and cannot be proved, or are proved by natural reason through some other science. But the knowledge proper to this science comes through revelation and not through natural reason. Therefore it has no concern to prove the principles of other sciences, but only to judge of them. Whatsoever is found in other sciences contrary to any truth of this science must be condemned as false: *Destroying counsels and every height that exalteth itself against the knowledge of God* (2 Cor 10:4–5).

REPLY OBJ. 3: Since judgment appertains to wisdom, the twofold manner of judging produces a twofold wisdom. A man may judge in one way by inclination, as whoever has the habit of a virtue judges rightly of what concerns that virtue by his very inclination towards it. Hence it is the virtuous man, as we read (*Ethic.* X), who is the measure and rule of human acts. In another way, by knowledge, just as a man learned in moral science might be able to judge rightly about virtuous acts, though he had not the virtue. The first manner of judging divine things belongs to

virtutem non haberet. Primus igitur modus iudicandi de rebus divinis, pertinet ad sapientiam quae ponitur donum spiritus sancti secundum illud I Cor. II, *spiritualis homo iudicat omnia*, etc., et Dionysius dicit, II cap. de divinis nominibus, *Hierotheus doctus est non solum discens, sed et patiens divina.* Secundus autem modus iudicandi pertinet ad hanc doctrinam, secundum quod per studium habetur; licet eius principia ex revelatione habeantur.

that wisdom which is set down among the gifts of the Holy Spirit: *The spiritual man judgeth all things* (1 Cor 2:15). And Dionysius says (*Div. Nom.* ii): *Hierotheus is taught not by mere learning, but by experience of divine things.* The second manner of judging belongs to this doctrine which is acquired by study, though its principles are obtained by revelation.

Article 7

Whether God Is the Object of This Science?

AD SEPTIMUM SIC PROCEDITUR. Videtur quod Deus non sit subiectum huius scientiae. In qualibet enim scientia oportet supponere de subiecto quid est, secundum philosophum in I Poster. Sed haec scientia non supponit de Deo quid est, dicit enim Damascenus, *in Deo quid est, dicere impossibile est.* Ergo Deus non est subiectum huius scientiae.

PRAETEREA, omnia quae determinantur in aliqua scientia, comprehenduntur sub subiecto illius scientiae. Sed in sacra Scriptura determinatur de multis aliis quam de Deo, puta de creaturis, et de moribus hominum. Ergo Deus non est subiectum huius scientiae.

SED CONTRA, illud est subiectum scientiae, de quo est sermo in scientia. Sed in hac scientia fit sermo de Deo, dicitur enim theologia, quasi sermo de Deo. Ergo Deus est subiectum huius scientiae.

RESPONDEO dicendum quod Deus est subiectum huius scientiae. Sic enim se habet subiectum ad scientiam, sicut obiectum ad potentiam vel habitum. Proprie autem illud assignatur obiectum alicuius potentiae vel habitus, sub cuius ratione omnia referuntur ad potentiam vel habitum, sicut homo et lapis referuntur ad visum inquantum sunt colorata, unde coloratum est proprium obiectum visus. Omnia autem pertractantur in sacra doctrina sub ratione Dei, vel quia sunt ipse Deus; vel quia habent ordinem ad Deum, ut ad principium et finem. Unde sequitur quod Deus vere sit subiectum huius scientiae. Quod etiam manifestum fit ex principiis huius scientiae, quae sunt articuli fidei, quae est de Deo, idem autem est subiectum principiorum et totius scientiae, cum tota scientia virtute contineatur in principiis. Quidam vero, attendentes ad ea quae in ista scientia tractantur, et non ad rationem secundum quam considerantur, assignaverunt aliter subiectum huius scientiae, vel res et signa; vel opera reparationis; vel totum Christum, idest

OBJECTION 1: It seems that God is not the object of this science. For in every science, the nature of its object is presupposed. But this science cannot presuppose the essence of God, for Damascene says (*De Fide Orth.* i, iv): *It is impossible to define the essence of God.* Therefore God is not the object of this science.

OBJ. 2: Further, whatever conclusions are reached in any science must be comprehended under the object of the science. But in Holy Writ we reach conclusions not only concerning God, but concerning many other things, such as creatures and human morality. Therefore God is not the object of this science.

ON THE CONTRARY, The object of the science is that of which it principally treats. But in this science, the treatment is mainly about God; for it is called theology, as treating of God. Therefore God is the object of this science.

I ANSWER THAT, God is the object of this science. The relation between a science and its object is the same as that between a habit or faculty and its object. Now properly speaking, the object of a faculty or habit is the thing under the aspect of which all things are referred to that faculty or habit, as man and stone are referred to the faculty of sight in that they are colored. Hence colored things are the proper objects of sight. But in sacred science, all things are treated of under the aspect of God: either because they are God Himself or because they refer to God as their beginning and end. Hence it follows that God is in very truth the object of this science. This is clear also from the principles of this science, namely, the articles of faith, for faith is about God. The object of the principles and of the whole science must be the same, since the whole science is contained virtually in its principles. Some, however, looking to what is treated of in this science, and not to the aspect under which it is treated, have asserted the object of this science to be something other than God—that is, either things and signs;

caput et membra. De omnibus enim istis tractatur in ista scientia, sed secundum ordinem ad Deum.

AD PRIMUM ergo dicendum quod, licet de Deo non possimus scire quid est, utimur tamen eius effectu, in hac doctrina, vel naturae vel gratiae, loco definitionis, ad ea quae de Deo in hac doctrina considerantur, sicut et in aliquibus scientiis philosophicis demonstratur aliquid de causa per effectum, accipiendo effectum loco definitionis causae.

AD SECUNDUM dicendum quod omnia alia quae determinantur in sacra doctrina, comprehenduntur sub Deo, non ut partes vel species vel accidentia, sed ut ordinata aliqualiter ad ipsum.

or the works of salvation; or the whole Christ, as the head and members. Of all these things, in truth, we treat in this science, but so far as they have reference to God.

REPLY OBJ. 1: Although we cannot know in what consists the essence of God, nevertheless in this science we make use of His effects, either of nature or of grace, in place of a definition, in regard to whatever is treated of in this science concerning God; even as in some philosophical sciences we demonstrate something about a cause from its effect, by taking the effect in place of a definition of the cause.

REPLY OBJ. 2: Whatever other conclusions are reached in this sacred science are comprehended under God, not as parts or species or accidents but as in some way related to Him.

Article 8

Whether Sacred Doctrine is a Matter of Argument?

AD OCTAVUM SIC PROCEDITUR. Videtur quod haec doctrina non sit argumentativa. Dicit enim Ambrosius in libro I de fide Catholica, *tolle argumenta, ubi fides quaeritur*. Sed in hac doctrina praecipue fides quaeritur, unde dicitur Ioan. XX, *haec scripta sunt ut credatis*. Ergo sacra doctrina non est argumentativa.

PRAETEREA, si sit argumentativa, aut argumentatur ex auctoritate, aut ex ratione. Si ex auctoritate, non videtur hoc congruere eius dignitati, nam locus ab auctoritate est infirmissimus, secundum Boetium. Si etiam ex ratione, hoc non congruit eius fini, quia secundum Gregorium in homilia, *fides non habet meritum, ubi humana ratio praebet experimentum*. Ergo sacra doctrina non est argumentativa.

SED CONTRA est quod dicitur ad Titum I, de episcopo, *amplectentem eum qui secundum doctrinam est, fidelem sermonem, ut potens sit exhortari in doctrina sana, et eos qui contradicunt arguere*.

RESPONDEO dicendum quod, sicut aliae scientiae non argumentantur ad sua principia probanda, sed ex principiis argumentantur ad ostendendum alia in ipsis scientiis; ita haec doctrina non argumentatur ad sua principia probanda, quae sunt articuli fidei; sed ex eis procedit ad aliquid aliud ostendendum; sicut apostolus, I ad Cor. XV, ex resurrectione Christi argumentatur ad resurrectionem communem probandam. Sed tamen considerandum est in scientiis philosophicis, quod inferiores scientiae nec probant sua principia, nec contra negantem principia disputant, sed hoc relinquunt superiori scientiae, suprema vero inter eas, scilicet metaphysica, disputat contra negantem sua principia, si adversarius aliquid concedit, si autem nihil concedit, non potest cum eo disputare, potest tamen solvere rationes ipsius. Unde

OBJECTION 1: It seems this doctrine is not a matter of argument. For Ambrose says (*De Fide* 1): *Put arguments aside where faith is sought*. But in this doctrine, faith especially is sought: *But these things are written that you may believe* (John 20:31). Therefore sacred doctrine is not a matter of argument.

OBJ. 2: Further, if it is a matter of argument, the argument is either from authority or from reason. If it is from authority, it seems unbefitting its dignity, for the proof from authority is the weakest form of proof. But if it is from reason, this is unbefitting its end, because, according to Gregory (*Hom.* 26), *faith has no merit in those things of which human reason brings its own experience*. Therefore sacred doctrine is not a matter of argument.

ON THE CONTRARY, The Scripture says that a bishop should *embrace that faithful word which is according to doctrine, that he may be able to exhort in sound doctrine and to convince the gainsayers* (Titus 1:9).

I ANSWER THAT, As other sciences do not argue in proof of their principles, but argue from their principles to demonstrate other truths in these sciences: so this doctrine does not argue in proof of its principles, which are the articles of faith, but from them it goes on to prove something else; as the Apostle from the resurrection of Christ argues in proof of the general resurrection (1 Cor 15). However, it is to be borne in mind, in regard to the philosophical sciences, that the inferior sciences neither prove their principles nor dispute with those who deny them, but leave this to a higher science; whereas the highest of them, viz. metaphysics, can dispute with one who denies its principles, if only the opponent will make some concession; but if he concede nothing, it can have no dispute with him, though it can answer his objections. Hence Sacred Scripture, since it has no science

sacra Scriptura, cum non habeat superiorem, disputat cum negante sua principia, argumentando quidem, si adversarius aliquid concedat eorum quae per divinam revelationem habentur; sicut per auctoritates sacrae doctrinae disputamus contra haereticos, et per unum articulum contra negantes alium. Si vero adversarius nihil credat eorum quae divinitus revelantur, non remanet amplius via ad probandum articulos fidei per rationes, sed ad solvendum rationes, si quas inducit, contra fidem. Cum enim fides infallibili veritati innitatur, impossibile autem sit de vero demonstrari contrarium, manifestum est probationes quae contra fidem inducuntur, non esse demonstrationes, sed solubilia argumenta.

AD PRIMUM ergo dicendum quod, licet argumenta rationis humanae non habeant locum ad probandum quae fidei sunt, tamen ex articulis fidei haec doctrina ad alia argumentatur, ut dictum est.

AD SECUNDUM dicendum quod argumentari ex auctoritate est maxime proprium huius doctrinae, eo quod principia huius doctrinae per revelationem habentur, et sic oportet quod credatur auctoritati eorum quibus revelatio facta est. Nec hoc derogat dignitati huius doctrinae, nam licet locus ab auctoritate quae fundatur super ratione humana, sit infirmissimus; locus tamen ab auctoritate quae fundatur super revelatione divina, est efficacissimus. Utitur tamen sacra doctrina etiam ratione humana, non quidem ad probandum fidem, quia per hoc tolleretur meritum fidei; sed ad manifestandum aliqua alia quae traduntur in hac doctrina. Cum enim gratia non tollat naturam, sed perficiat, oportet quod naturalis ratio subserviat fidei; sicut et naturalis inclinatio voluntatis obsequitur caritati. Unde et apostolus dicit, II ad Cor. X, *in captivitatem redigentes omnem intellectum in obsequium Christi.* Et inde est quod etiam auctoritatibus philosophorum sacra doctrina utitur, ubi per rationem naturalem veritatem cognoscere potuerunt; sicut Paulus, actuum XVII, inducit verbum Arati, dicens, *sicut et quidam poetarum vestrorum dixerunt, genus Dei sumus.* Sed tamen sacra doctrina huiusmodi auctoritatibus utitur quasi extraneis argumentis, et probabilibus. Auctoritatibus autem canonicae Scripturae utitur proprie, ex necessitate argumentando. Auctoritatibus autem aliorum doctorum Ecclesiae, quasi arguendo ex propriis, sed probabiliter. Innititur enim fides nostra revelationi apostolis et prophetis factae, qui canonicos libros scripserunt, non autem revelationi, si qua fuit aliis doctoribus facta. Unde dicit Augustinus, in epistola ad Hieronymum, *solis eis Scripturarum libris qui canonici appellantur, didici hunc honorem deferre, ut nullum auctorem eorum in scribendo errasse aliquid firmissime credam. Alios autem ita lego, ut, quantalibet sanctitate doctrinaque praepolleant, non ideo verum putem, quod ipsi ita senserunt vel scripserunt.*

above itself, can dispute with one who denies its principles only if the opponent admits some at least of the truths obtained through divine revelation; thus we can argue with heretics from texts in Holy Writ, and against those who deny one article of faith, we can argue from another. If our opponent believes nothing of divine revelation, there is no longer any means of proving the articles of faith by reasoning, but only of answering his objections—if he has any—against faith. Since faith rests upon infallible truth, and since the contrary of a truth can never be demonstrated, it is clear that the arguments brought against faith cannot be demonstrations, but are difficulties that can be answered.

REPLY OBJ. 1: Although arguments from human reason cannot avail to prove what must be received on faith, nevertheless, this doctrine argues from articles of faith to other truths.

REPLY OBJ. 2: This doctrine is especially based upon arguments from authority, inasmuch as its principles are obtained by revelation: thus we ought to believe on the authority of those to whom the revelation has been made. Nor does this take away from the dignity of this doctrine, for although the argument from authority based on human reason is the weakest, yet the argument from authority based on divine revelation is the strongest. But sacred doctrine makes use even of human reason, not, indeed, to prove faith (for thereby the merit of faith would come to an end), but to make clear other things that are put forward in this doctrine. Since therefore grace does not destroy nature but perfects it, natural reason should minister to faith as the natural bent of the will ministers to charity. Hence the Apostle says: *Bringing into captivity every understanding unto the obedience of Christ* (2 Cor 10:5). Hence sacred doctrine makes use also of the authority of philosophers in those questions in which they were able to know the truth by natural reason, as Paul quotes a saying of Aratus: *As some also of your own poets said: For we are also His offspring* (Acts 17:28). Nevertheless, sacred doctrine makes use of these authorities as extrinsic and probable arguments; but properly uses the authority of the canonical Scriptures as an incontrovertible proof, and the authority of the doctors of the Church as one that may properly be used, yet merely as probable. For our faith rests upon the revelation made to the apostles and prophets who wrote the canonical books, and not on the revelations (if any such there are) made to other doctors. Hence Augustine says (*Epis. ad Hieron.* xix, 1): *Only those books of Scripture which are called canonical have I learned to hold in such honor as to believe their authors have not erred in any way in writing them. But other authors I so read as not to deem everything in their works to be true, merely on account of their having so thought and written, whatever may have been their holiness and learning.*

Article 9

Whether Holy Scripture Should Use Metaphors?

AD NONUM SIC PROCEDITUR. Videtur quod sacra Scriptura non debeat uti metaphoris. Illud enim quod est proprium infimae doctrinae, non videtur competere huic scientiae, quae inter alias tenet locum supremum, ut iam dictum est. Procedere autem per similitudines varias et repraesentationes, est proprium poeticae, quae est infima inter omnes doctrinas. Ergo huiusmodi similitudinibus uti, non est conveniens huic scientiae.

PRAETEREA, haec doctrina videtur esse ordinata ad veritatis manifestationem, unde et manifestatoribus eius praemium promittitur, Eccli. XXIV, *qui elucidant me, vitam aeternam habebunt.* Sed per huiusmodi similitudines veritas occultatur. Non ergo competit huic doctrinae divina tradere sub similitudine corporalium rerum.

PRAETEREA, quanto aliquae creaturae sunt sublimiores, tanto magis ad divinam similitudinem accedunt. Si igitur aliquae ex creaturis transumerentur ad Deum, tunc oporteret talem transumptionem maxime fieri ex sublimioribus creaturis, et non ex infimis. Quod tamen in Scripturis frequenter invenitur.

SED CONTRA est quod dicitur Osee XII, *ego visionem multiplicavi eis, et in manibus prophetarum assimilatus sum.* Tradere autem aliquid sub similitudine, est metaphoricum. Ergo ad sacram doctrinam pertinet uti metaphoris.

RESPONDEO dicendum quod conveniens est sacrae Scripturae divina et spiritualia sub similitudine corporalium tradere. Deus enim omnibus providet secundum quod competit eorum naturae. Est autem naturale homini ut per sensibilia ad intelligibilia veniat, quia omnis nostra cognitio a sensu initium habet. Unde convenienter in sacra Scriptura traduntur nobis spiritualia sub metaphoris corporalium. Et hoc est quod dicit Dionysius, I cap. caelestis hierarchiae, *impossibile est nobis aliter lucere divinum radium, nisi varietate sacrorum velaminum circumvelatum.* Convenit etiam sacrae Scripturae, quae communiter omnibus proponitur (secundum illud ad Rom. I, *sapientibus et insipientibus debitor sum*), ut spiritualia sub similitudinibus corporalium proponantur; ut saltem vel sic rudes eam capiant, qui ad intelligibilia secundum se capienda non sunt idonei.

AD PRIMUM ergo dicendum quod poeta utitur metaphoris propter repraesentationem, repraesentatio enim naturaliter homini delectabilis est. Sed sacra doctrina utitur metaphoris propter necessitatem et utilitatem, ut dictum est.

AD SECUNDUM dicendum quod radius divinae revelationis non destruitur propter figuras sensibiles quibus circumvelatur, ut dicit Dionysius, sed remanet in sua

OBJECTION 1: It seems that Holy Scripture should not use metaphors. For that which is proper to the lowest science seems not to befit this science, which holds the highest place of all. But to proceed by the aid of various similitudes and figures is proper to poetry, the least of all the sciences. Therefore it is not fitting that this science should make use of such similitudes.

OBJ. 2: Further, this doctrine seems to be intended to make truth clear. Hence a reward is held out to those who manifest it: *They that explain me shall have life everlasting* (Eccl 24:31). But by such similitudes truth is obscured. Therefore, to put forward divine truths by likening them to corporeal things does not befit this science.

OBJ. 3: Further, the higher creatures are, the nearer they approach to the divine likeness. If therefore any creature be taken to represent God, this representation ought chiefly to be taken from the higher creatures, and not from the lower; yet this is often found in Scriptures.

ON THE CONTRARY, It is written (Hos 12:10): *I have multiplied visions, and I have used similitudes by the ministry of the prophets.* But to put forward anything by means of similitudes is to use metaphors. Therefore this sacred science may use metaphors.

I ANSWER THAT, It is befitting Holy Writ to put forward divine and spiritual truths by means of comparisons with material things. For God provides for everything according to the capacity of its nature. Now it is natural to man to attain to intellectual truths through sensible objects, because all our knowledge originates from sense. Hence in Holy Writ, spiritual truths are fittingly taught under the likeness of material things. This is what Dionysius says (*Coel. Hier.* i): *We cannot be enlightened by the divine rays except they be hidden within the covering of many sacred veils.* It is also befitting Holy Writ, which is proposed to all without distinction of persons—'To the wise and to the unwise I am a debtor' (Rom 1:14)—that spiritual truths be expounded by means of figures taken from corporeal things, in order that thereby even the simple who are unable by themselves to grasp intellectual things may be able to understand it.

REPLY OBJ. 1: Poetry makes use of metaphors to produce a representation, for it is natural to man to be pleased with representations. But sacred doctrine makes use of metaphors as both necessary and useful.

REPLY OBJ. 2: The ray of divine revelation is not extinguished by the sensible imagery wherewith it is veiled, as Dionysius says (*Coel. Hier.* i); and its truth so far remains

veritate; ut mentes quibus fit revelatio, non permittat in similitudinibus permanere, sed elevet eas ad cognitionem intelligibilium; et per eos quibus revelatio facta est, alii etiam circa haec instruantur. Unde ea quae in uno loco Scripturae traduntur sub metaphoris, in aliis locis expressius exponuntur. Et ipsa etiam occultatio figurarum utilis est, ad exercitium studiosorum, et contra irrisiones infidelium, de quibus dicitur, Matth. VII, *nolite sanctum dare canibus.*

AD TERTIUM dicendum quod, sicut docet Dionysius, cap. II Cael. Hier., magis est conveniens quod divina in Scripturis tradantur sub figuris vilium corporum, quam corporum nobilium. Et hoc propter tria. Primo, quia per hoc magis liberatur humanus animus ab errore. Manifestum enim apparet quod haec secundum proprietatem non dicuntur de divinis, quod posset esse dubium, si sub figuris nobilium corporum describerentur divina; maxime apud illos qui nihil aliud a corporibus nobilius excogitare noverunt. Secundo, quia hic modus convenientior est cognitioni quam de Deo habemus in hac vita. Magis enim manifestatur nobis de ipso quid non est, quam quid est, et ideo similitudines illarum rerum quae magis elongantur a Deo, veriorem nobis faciunt aestimationem quod sit supra illud quod de Deo dicimus vel cogitamus. Tertio, quia per huiusmodi, divina magis occultantur indignis.

that it does not allow the minds of those to whom the revelation has been made, to rest in the metaphors, but raises them to the knowledge of truths; and through those to whom the revelation has been made others also may receive instruction in these matters. Hence those things that are taught metaphorically in one part of Scripture, in other parts are taught more openly. The very hiding of truth in figures is useful for the exercise of thoughtful minds and as a defense against the ridicule of the impious, according to the words *Give not that which is holy to dogs* (Matt 7:6).

REPLY OBJ. 3: As Dionysius says, (*Coel. Hier.* i) it is more fitting that divine truths should be expounded under the figure of less noble than of nobler bodies, and this for three reasons. First, because thereby men's minds are the better preserved from error. For then it is clear that these things are not literal descriptions of divine truths, which might have been open to doubt had they been expressed under the figure of nobler bodies, especially for those who could think of nothing nobler than bodies. Second, because this is more befitting the knowledge of God that we have in this life. For what He is not is clearer to us than what He is. Therefore similitudes drawn from things farthest away from God form within us a truer estimate that God is above whatsoever we may say or think of Him. Third, because thereby divine truths are the better hidden from the unworthy.

Article 10

Whether in Holy Scripture a Word May Have Several Senses?

AD DECIMUM SIC PROCEDITUR. Videtur quod sacra Scriptura sub una littera non habeat plures sensus, qui sunt historicus vel litteralis, allegoricus, tropologicus sive moralis, et anagogicus. Multiplicitas enim sensuum in una Scriptura parit confusionem et deceptionem, et tollit arguendi firmitatem, unde ex multiplicibus propositionibus non procedit argumentatio, sed secundum hoc aliquae fallaciae assignantur. Sacra autem Scriptura debet esse efficax ad ostendendam veritatem absque omni fallacia. Ergo non debent in ea sub una littera plures sensus tradi.

PRAETEREA, Augustinus dicit in libro de utilitate credendi, quod *Scriptura quae testamentum vetus vocatur, quadrifariam traditur, scilicet, secundum historiam, secundum aetiologiam, secundum analogiam, secundum allegoriam.* Quae quidem quatuor a quatuor praedictis videntur esse aliena omnino. Non igitur conveniens videtur quod eadem littera sacrae Scripturae secundum quatuor sensus praedictos exponatur.

OBJECTION 1: It seems that in Holy Writ a word cannot have several senses, historical or literal, allegorical, tropological or moral, and anagogical. For many different senses in one text produce confusion and deception and destroy all force of argument. Hence no argument, but only fallacies, can be deduced from a multiplicity of propositions. But Holy Writ ought to be able to state the truth without any fallacy. Therefore in it there cannot be several senses to a word.

OBJ. 2: Further, Augustine says (*De util. cred.* iii) that *the Old Testament has a fourfold division as to history, etiology, analogy and allegory.* Now these four seem altogether different from the four divisions mentioned in the first objection. Therefore it does not seem fitting to explain the same word of Holy Writ according to the four different senses mentioned above.

Praeterea, praeter praedictos sensus, invenitur sensus parabolicus, qui inter illos sensus quatuor non continetur.

Sed contra est quod dicit Gregorius, XX Moralium, *sacra Scriptura omnes scientias ipso locutionis suae more transcendit, quia uno eodemque sermone, dum narrat gestum, prodit mysterium.*

Respondeo dicendum quod auctor sacrae Scripturae est Deus, in cuius potestate est ut non solum voces ad significandum accommodet (quod etiam homo facere potest), sed etiam res ipsas. Et ideo, cum in omnibus scientiis voces significent, hoc habet proprium ista scientia, quod ipsae res significatae per voces, etiam significant aliquid. Illa ergo prima significatio, qua voces significant res, pertinet ad primum sensum, qui est sensus historicus vel litteralis. Illa vero significatio qua res significatae per voces, iterum res alias significant, dicitur sensus spiritualis; qui super litteralem fundatur, et eum supponit. Hic autem sensus spiritualis trifariam dividitur. Sicut enim dicit apostolus, ad Hebr. VII, *lex vetus figura est novae legis,* et *ipsa nova lex,* ut dicit Dionysius in ecclesiastica hierarchia, *est figura futurae gloriae,* in nova etiam lege, ea quae in capite sunt gesta, sunt signa eorum quae nos agere debemus. Secundum ergo quod ea quae sunt veteris legis, significant ea quae sunt novae legis, est sensus allegoricus, secundum vero quod ea quae in Christo sunt facta, vel in his quae Christum significant, sunt signa eorum quae nos agere debemus, est sensus moralis, prout vero significant ea quae sunt in aeterna gloria, est sensus anagogicus. Quia vero sensus litteralis est, quem auctor intendit, auctor autem sacrae Scripturae Deus est, qui omnia simul suo intellectu comprehendit, non est inconveniens, ut dicit Augustinus XII confessionum, si etiam secundum litteralem sensum in una littera Scripturae plures sint sensus.

Ad primum ergo dicendum quod multiplicitas horum sensuum non facit aequivocationem, aut aliam speciem multiplicitatis, quia, sicut iam dictum est, sensus isti non multiplicantur propter hoc quod una vox multa significet; sed quia ipsae res significatae per voces, aliarum rerum possunt esse signa. Et ita etiam nulla confusio sequitur in sacra Scriptura, cum omnes sensus fundentur super unum, scilicet litteralem; ex quo solo potest trahi argumentum, non autem ex his quae secundum allegoriam dicuntur, ut dicit Augustinus in epistola contra Vincentium Donatistam. Non tamen ex hoc aliquid deperit sacrae Scripturae, quia nihil sub spirituali sensu continetur fidei necessarium, quod Scriptura per litteralem sensum alicubi manifeste non tradat.

Ad secundum dicendum quod illa tria, historia, aetiologia, analogia, ad unum litteralem sensum pertinent. Nam historia est, ut ipse Augustinus exponit, cum simpliciter aliquid proponitur, aetiologia vero, cum causa dicti assignatur, sicut cum dominus assignavit causam

Obj. 3: Further, besides these senses, there is the parabolical, which is not one of these four.

On the contrary, Gregory says (*Moral.* xx, 1): *Holy Writ by the manner of its speech transcends every science, because in one and the same sentence, while it describes a fact, it reveals a mystery.*

I answer that, The author of Holy Writ is God, in whose power it is to signify His meaning, not by words only (as man also can do), but also by things themselves. So, whereas in every other science things are signified by words, this science has the property, that the things signified by the words have themselves also a signification. Therefore that first signification whereby words signify things belongs to the first sense, the historical or literal. That signification whereby things signified by words have themselves also a signification is called the spiritual sense, which is based on the literal, and presupposes it. Now this spiritual sense has a threefold division. For as the Apostle says (Heb 10:1), *the Old Law is a figure of the New Law,* and Dionysius says (*Coel. Hier.* i) *the New Law itself is a figure of future glory.* Again, in the New Law, whatever our Head has done is a type of what we ought to do. Therefore, so far as the things of the Old Law signify the things of the New Law, there is the allegorical sense; so far as the things done in Christ, or so far as the things which signify Christ, are types of what we ought to do, there is the moral sense. But so far as they signify what relates to eternal glory, there is the anagogical sense. Since the literal sense is that which the author intends, and since the author of Holy Writ is God, Who by one act comprehends all things by His intellect, it is not unfitting, as Augustine says (*Confess.* xii), if, even according to the literal sense, one word in Holy Writ should have several senses.

Reply Obj. 1: The multiplicity of these senses does not produce equivocation or any other kind of multiplicity, seeing that these senses are not multiplied because one word signifies several things, but because the things signified by the words can be themselves types of other things. Thus in Holy Writ no confusion results, for all the senses are founded on one—the literal—from which alone can any argument be drawn, and not from those intended in allegory, as Augustine says (*Epis.* 48). Nevertheless, nothing of Holy Scripture perishes on account of this, since nothing necessary to faith is contained under the spiritual sense which is not elsewhere put forward by the Scripture in its literal sense.

Reply Obj. 2: These three—history, etiology, analogy—are grouped under the literal sense. For it is called history, as Augustine expounds (*Epis.* 48), whenever anything is simply related; it is called etiology when its cause is assigned, as when Our Lord gave the reason why Moses

quare Moyses permisit licentiam repudiandi uxores, scilicet propter duritiam cordis ipsorum, Matt. XIX, analogia vero est, cum veritas unius Scripturae ostenditur veritati alterius non repugnare. Sola autem allegoria, inter illa quatuor, pro tribus spiritualibus sensibus ponitur. Sicut et Hugo de sancto Victore sub sensu allegorico etiam anagogicum comprehendit, ponens in tertio suarum sententiarum solum tres sensus, scilicet historicum, allegoricum et tropologicum.

AD TERTIUM dicendum quod sensus parabolicus sub litterali continetur, nam per voces significatur aliquid proprie, et aliquid figurative; nec est litteralis sensus ipsa figura, sed id quod est figuratum. Non enim cum Scriptura nominat Dei brachium, est litteralis sensus quod in Deo sit membrum huiusmodi corporale, sed id quod per hoc membrum significatur, scilicet virtus operativa. In quo patet quod sensui litterali sacrae Scripturae nunquam potest subesse falsum.

allowed the putting away of wives—namely, on account of the hardness of men's hearts; it is called analogy whenever the truth of one text of Scripture is shown not to contradict the truth of another. Of these four, allegory alone stands for the three spiritual senses. Thus Hugh of St. Victor (*Sacram.* iv, 4 Prolog.) includes the anagogical under the allegorical sense, laying down three senses only—the historical, the allegorical, and the tropological.

REPLY OBJ. 3: The parabolical sense is contained in the literal, for by words things are signified properly and figuratively. Nor is the figure itself, but that which is figured, the literal sense. When Scripture speaks of God's arm, the literal sense is not that God has such a member, but only what is signified by this member, namely operative power. Hence it is plain that nothing false can ever underlie the literal sense of Holy Writ.

QUESTION 2

THE EXISTENCE OF GOD

Quia igitur principalis intentio huius sacrae doctrinae est Dei cognitionem tradere, et non solum secundum quod in se est, sed etiam secundum quod est principium rerum et finis earum, et specialiter rationalis creaturae, ut ex dictis est manifestum; ad huius doctrinae expositionem intendentes, primo tractabimus de Deo; secundo, de motu rationalis creaturae in Deum; tertio, de Christo, qui, secundum quod homo, via est nobis tendendi in Deum.

Consideratio autem de Deo tripartita erit. Primo namque considerabimus ea quae ad essentiam divinam pertinent; secundo, ea quae pertinent ad distinctionem personarum; tertio, ea quae pertinent ad processum creaturarum ab ipso.

Circa essentiam vero divinam, primo considerandum est an Deus sit; secundo, quomodo sit, vel potius quomodo non sit; tertio considerandum erit de his quae ad operationem ipsius pertinent, scilicet de scientia et de voluntate et potentia.

Circa primum quaeruntur tria.

Primo, utrum Deum esse sit per se notum.

Secundo, utrum sit demonstrabile.

Tertio, an Deus sit.

Because the chief aim of sacred doctrine is to teach the knowledge of God, not only as He is in Himself, but also as He is the beginning of things and their last end, and especially of rational creatures, as is clear from what has been already said, therefore, in our endeavor to expound this science, we shall treat: (1) Of God; (2) Of the rational creature's advance towards God; (3) Of Christ, Who as man, is our way to God.

In treating of God there will be a threefold division, for we shall consider: (1) Whatever concerns the Divine Essence; (2) Whatever concerns the distinctions of Persons; (3) Whatever concerns the procession of creatures from Him.

Concerning the Divine Essence, we must consider: (1) Whether God exists? (2) The manner of His existence, or, rather, what is not the manner of His existence; (3) Whatever concerns His operations—namely, His knowledge, will, power.

Concerning the first, there are three points of inquiry:

(1) Whether the proposition *God exists* is self-evident?

(2) Whether it is demonstrable?

(3) Whether God exists?

Article 1

Whether the Existence of God Is Self-Evident?

AD PRIMUM SIC PROCEDITUR. Videtur quod Deum esse sit per se notum. Illa enim nobis dicuntur per se nota, quorum cognitio nobis naturaliter inest, sicut patet de primis principiis. Sed, sicut dicit Damascenus in principio libri sui, *omnibus cognitio existendi Deum naturaliter est inserta*. Ergo Deum esse est per se notum.

PRAETEREA, illa dicuntur esse per se nota, quae statim, cognitis terminis, cognoscuntur, quod philosophus attribuit primis demonstrationis principiis, in I Poster., scito enim quid est totum et quid pars, statim scitur quod omne totum maius est sua parte. Sed intellecto quid significet hoc nomen Deus, statim habetur quod Deus est. Significatur enim hoc nomine id quo maius significari non potest, maius autem est quod est in re et intellectu, quam quod est in intellectu tantum, unde

OBJECTION 1: It seems that the existence of God is self-evident. Now those things are said to be self-evident to us the knowledge of which is naturally implanted in us, as we can see in regard to first principles. But as Damascene says (*De Fide Orth.* i, 1,3), *the knowledge of God is naturally implanted in all.* Therefore the existence of God is self-evident.

OBJ. 2: Further, those things are said to be self-evident which are known as soon as the terms are known, which the Philosopher (*1 Poster.* iii) says is true of the first principles of demonstration. Thus, when the nature of a whole and of a part is known, it is at once recognized that every whole is greater than its part. But as soon as the signification of the word *God* is understood, it is at once seen that God exists. For by this word is signified that thing than which nothing greater can be conceived. But that which

cum, intellecto hoc nomine Deus, statim sit in intellectu, sequitur etiam quod sit in re. Ergo Deum esse est per se notum.

PRAETEREA, veritatem esse est per se notum, quia qui negat veritatem esse, concedit veritatem esse, si enim veritas non est, verum est veritatem non esse. Si autem est aliquid verum, oportet quod veritas sit. Deus autem est ipsa veritas, Ioann. XIV, *ego sum via, veritas et vita*. Ergo Deum esse est per se notum.

SED CONTRA, nullus potest cogitare oppositum eius quod est per se notum ut patet per philosophum, in IV Metaphys. et I Poster., circa prima demonstrationis principia. Cogitari autem potest oppositum eius quod est Deum esse, secundum illud Psalmi LII, *dixit insipiens in corde suo, non est Deus*. Ergo Deum esse non est per se notum.

RESPONDEO dicendum quod contingit aliquid esse per se notum dupliciter, uno modo, secundum se et non quoad nos; alio modo, secundum se et quoad nos. Ex hoc enim aliqua propositio est per se nota, quod praedicatum includitur in ratione subiecti, ut homo est animal, nam animal est de ratione hominis. Si igitur notum sit omnibus de praedicato et de subiecto quid sit, propositio illa erit omnibus per se nota, sicut patet in primis demonstrationum principiis, quorum termini sunt quaedam communia quae nullus ignorat, ut ens et non ens, totum et pars, et similia. Si autem apud aliquos notum non sit de praedicato et subiecto quid sit, propositio quidem quantum in se est, erit per se nota, non tamen apud illos qui praedicatum et subiectum propositionis ignorant. Et ideo contingit, ut dicit Boetius in libro de hebdomadibus, quod *quaedam sunt communes animi conceptiones et per se notae, apud sapientes tantum, ut incorporalia in loco non esse*. Dico ergo quod haec propositio, Deus est, quantum in se est, per se nota est, quia praedicatum est idem cum subiecto; Deus enim est suum esse, ut infra patebit. Sed quia nos non scimus de Deo quid est, non est nobis per se nota, sed indiget demonstrari per ea quae sunt magis nota quoad nos, et minus nota quoad naturam, scilicet per effectus.

AD PRIMUM ergo dicendum quod cognoscere Deum esse in aliquo communi, sub quadam confusione, est nobis naturaliter insertum, inquantum scilicet Deus est hominis beatitudo, homo enim naturaliter desiderat beatitudinem, et quod naturaliter desideratur ab homine, naturaliter cognoscitur ab eodem. Sed hoc non est simpliciter cognoscere Deum esse; sicut cognoscere venientem, non est cognoscere Petrum, quamvis sit Petrus veniens, multi enim perfectum hominis bonum, quod est beatitudo, existimant divitias; quidam vero voluptates; quidam autem aliquid aliud.

exists actually and mentally is greater than that which exists only mentally. Therefore, since as soon as the word *God* is understood it exists mentally, it also follows that it exists actually. Therefore the proposition *God exists* is self-evident.

OBJ. 3: Further, the existence of truth is self-evident. For whoever denies the existence of truth grants that truth does not exist: and, if truth does not exist, then the proposition *Truth does not exist* is true: and if there is anything true, there must be truth. But God is truth itself: *I am the way, the truth, and the life* (John 14:6). Therefore *God exists* is self-evident.

ON THE CONTRARY, No one can mentally admit the opposite of what is self-evident; as the Philosopher (*Metaph.* iv, lect. vi) states concerning the first principles of demonstration. But the opposite of the proposition *God is* can be mentally admitted: *The fool said in his heart, There is no God* (Ps 52:1). Therefore, that God exists is not self-evident.

I ANSWER THAT, A thing can be self-evident in either of two ways: on the one hand, self-evident in itself, though not to us; on the other, self-evident in itself, and to us. A proposition is self-evident because the predicate is included in the essence of the subject, as *Man is an animal*, for animal is contained in the essence of man. If, therefore the essence of the predicate and subject be known to all, the proposition will be self-evident to all; as is clear with regard to the first principles of demonstration, the terms of which are common things that no one is ignorant of, such as being and non-being, whole and part, and such like. If, however, there are some to whom the essence of the predicate and subject is unknown, the proposition will be self-evident in itself, but not to those who do not know the meaning of the predicate and subject of the proposition. Therefore, it happens, as Boethius says (*Hebdom.*), *there are some mental concepts self-evident only to the learned, as that incorporeal substances are not in space*. Therefore I say that this proposition, *God exists*, of itself is self-evident, for the predicate is the same as the subject, because God is His own existence as will be hereafter shown (Q. 3, Art. 4). Now because we do not know the essence of God, the proposition is not self-evident to us; but needs to be demonstrated by things that are more known to us, though less known in their nature—namely, by effects.

REPLY OBJ. 1: To know that God exists in a general and confused way is implanted in us by nature, inasmuch as God is man's beatitude. For man naturally desires happiness, and what is naturally desired by man must be naturally known to him. This, however, is not to know absolutely that God exists; just as to know that someone is approaching is not the same as to know that Peter is approaching, even though it is Peter who is approaching; for many there are who imagine that man's perfect good which is happiness, consists in riches, and others in pleasures, and others in something else.

AD SECUNDUM dicendum quod forte ille qui audit hoc nomen Deus, non intelligit significari aliquid quo maius cogitari non possit, cum quidam crediderint Deum esse corpus. Dato etiam quod quilibet intelligat hoc nomine Deus significari hoc quod dicitur, scilicet illud quo maius cogitari non potest; non tamen propter hoc sequitur quod intelligat id quod significatur per nomen, esse in rerum natura; sed in apprehensione intellectus tantum. Nec potest argui quod sit in re, nisi daretur quod sit in re aliquid quo maius cogitari non potest, quod non est datum a ponentibus Deum non esse.

AD TERTIUM dicendum quod veritatem esse in communi, est per se notum, sed primam veritatem esse, hoc non est per se notum quoad nos.

REPLY OBJ. 2: Perhaps not everyone who hears this word *God* understands it to signify something than which nothing greater can be thought, seeing that some have believed God to be a body. Yet, granted that everyone understands that by this word *God* is signified something than which nothing greater can be thought, nevertheless, it does not therefore follow that he understands that what the word signifies exists actually, but only that it exists mentally. Nor can it be argued that it actually exists, unless it be admitted that there actually exists something than which nothing greater can be thought; and this precisely is not admitted by those who hold that God does not exist.

REPLY OBJ. 3: The existence of truth in general is self-evident but the existence of a Primal Truth is not self-evident to us.

Article 2

Whether It Can Be Demonstrated That God Exists?

AD SECUNDUM SIC PROCEDITUR. Videtur quod Deum esse non sit demonstrabile. Deum enim esse est articulus fidei. Sed ea quae sunt fidei, non sunt demonstrabilia, quia demonstratio facit scire, fides autem de non apparentibus est, ut patet per apostolum, ad Hebr. XI. Ergo Deum esse non est demonstrabile.

PRAETEREA, medium demonstrationis est quod quid est. Sed de Deo non possumus scire quid est, sed solum quid non est, ut dicit Damascenus. Ergo non possumus demonstrare Deum esse.

PRAETEREA, si demonstraretur Deum esse, hoc non esset nisi ex effectibus eius. Sed effectus eius non sunt proportionati ei, cum ipse sit infinitus, et effectus finiti; finiti autem ad infinitum non est proportio. Cum ergo causa non possit demonstrari per effectum sibi non proportionatum, videtur quod Deum esse non possit demonstrari.

SED CONTRA est quod apostolus dicit, ad Rom. I, *invisibilia Dei per ea quae facta sunt, intellecta, conspiciuntur.* Sed hoc non esset, nisi per ea quae facta sunt, posset demonstrari Deum esse, primum enim quod oportet intelligi de aliquo, est an sit.

RESPONDEO dicendum quod duplex est demonstratio. Una quae est per causam, et dicitur propter quid, et haec est per priora simpliciter. Alia est per effectum, et dicitur demonstratio quia, et haec est per ea quae sunt priora quoad nos, cum enim effectus aliquis nobis est manifestior quam sua causa, per effectum procedimus ad cognitionem causae. Ex quolibet autem effectu potest demonstrari propriam causam eius esse (si tamen eius

OBJECTION 1: It seems that the existence of God cannot be demonstrated. For it is an article of faith that God exists. But what is of faith cannot be demonstrated, because a demonstration produces scientific knowledge; whereas faith is of the unseen (Heb 11:1). Therefore it cannot be demonstrated that God exists.

OBJ. 2: Further, the essence is the middle term of demonstration. But we cannot know in what God's essence consists, but solely in what it does not consist; as Damascene says (*De Fide Orth.* i, 4). Therefore we cannot demonstrate that God exists.

OBJ. 3: Further, if the existence of God were demonstrated, this could only be from His effects. But His effects are not proportionate to Him, since He is infinite and His effects are finite; and between the finite and infinite there is no proportion. Therefore, since a cause cannot be demonstrated by an effect not proportionate to it, it seems that the existence of God cannot be demonstrated.

ON THE CONTRARY, The Apostle says: *The invisible things of Him are clearly seen, being understood by the things that are made* (Rom 1:20). But this would not be unless the existence of God could be demonstrated through the things that are made; for the first thing we must know of anything is whether it exists.

I ANSWER THAT, Demonstration can be made in two ways: One is through the cause, and is called a priori, and this is to argue from what is prior absolutely. The other is through the effect, and is called a demonstration a posteriori; this is to argue from what is prior relatively only to us. When an effect is better known to us than its cause, from the effect we proceed to the knowledge of the cause. And from every effect the existence of its proper cause can be

effectus sint magis noti quoad nos), quia, cum effectus dependeant a causa, posito effectu necesse est causam praeexistere. Unde Deum esse, secundum quod non est per se notum quoad nos, demonstrabile est per effectus nobis notos.

AD PRIMUM ergo dicendum quod Deum esse, et alia huiusmodi quae per rationem naturalem nota possunt esse de Deo, ut dicitur Rom. I non sunt articuli fidei, sed praeambula ad articulos, sic enim fides praesupponit cognitionem naturalem, sicut gratia naturam, et ut perfectio perfectibile. Nihil tamen prohibet illud quod secundum se demonstrabile est et scibile, ab aliquo accipi ut credibile, qui demonstrationem non capit.

AD SECUNDUM dicendum quod cum demonstratur causa per effectum, necesse est uti effectu loco definitionis causae, ad probandum causam esse, et hoc maxime contingit in Deo. Quia ad probandum aliquid esse, necesse est accipere pro medio quid significet nomen non autem quod quid est, quia quaestio quid est, sequitur ad quaestionem an est. Nomina autem Dei imponuntur ab effectibus, ut postea ostendetur, unde, demonstrando Deum esse per effectum, accipere possumus pro medio quid significet hoc nomen Deus.

AD TERTIUM dicendum quod per effectus non proportionatos causae, non potest perfecta cognitio de causa haberi, sed tamen ex quocumque effectu potest manifeste nobis demonstrari causam esse, ut dictum est. Et sic ex effectibus Dei potest demonstrari Deum esse, licet per eos non perfecte possimus eum cognoscere secundum suam essentiam.

demonstrated, so long as its effects are better known to us; because since every effect depends upon its cause, if the effect exists, the cause must pre-exist. Hence the existence of God, in so far as it is not self-evident to us, can be demonstrated from those of His effects which are known to us.

REPLY OBJ. 1: The existence of God and other like truths about God, which can be known by natural reason, are not articles of faith, but are preambles to the articles; for faith presupposes natural knowledge, even as grace presupposes nature, and perfection supposes something that can be perfected. Nevertheless, there is nothing to prevent a man, who cannot grasp a proof, accepting, as a matter of faith, something which in itself is capable of being scientifically known and demonstrated.

REPLY OBJ. 2: When the existence of a cause is demonstrated from an effect, this effect takes the place of the definition of the cause in proof of the cause's existence. This is especially the case in regard to God, because, in order to prove the existence of anything, it is necessary to accept as a middle term the meaning of the word, and not its essence, for the question of its essence follows on the question of its existence. Now the names given to God are derived from His effects; consequently, in demonstrating the existence of God from His effects, we may take for the middle term the meaning of the word *God*.

REPLY OBJ. 3: From effects not proportionate to the cause no perfect knowledge of that cause can be obtained. Yet from every effect the existence of the cause can be clearly demonstrated, and so we can demonstrate the existence of God from His effects; though from them we cannot perfectly know God as He is in His essence.

Article 3

Whether God Exists?

AD TERTIUM SIC PROCEDITUR. Videtur quod Deus non sit. Quia si unum contrariorum fuerit infinitum, totaliter destruetur aliud. Sed hoc intelligitur in hoc nomine Deus, scilicet quod sit quoddam bonum infinitum. Si ergo Deus esset, nullum malum inveniretur. Invenitur autem malum in mundo. Ergo Deus non est.

PRAETEREA, quod potest compleri per pauciora principia, non fit per plura. Sed videtur quod omnia quae apparent in mundo, possunt compleri per alia principia, supposito quod Deus non sit, quia ea quae sunt naturalia, reducuntur in principium quod est natura; ea vero quae sunt a proposito, reducuntur in principium quod est ratio humana vel voluntas. Nulla igitur necessitas est ponere Deum esse.

OBJECTION 1: It seems that God does not exist; because if one of two contraries be infinite, the other would be altogether destroyed. But the word *God* means that He is infinite goodness. If, therefore, God existed, there would be no evil discoverable; but there is evil in the world. Therefore God does not exist.

OBJ. 2: Further, it is superfluous to suppose that what can be accounted for by a few principles has been produced by many. But it seems that everything we see in the world can be accounted for by other principles, supposing God did not exist. For all natural things can be reduced to one principle which is nature; and all voluntary things can be reduced to one principle which is human reason, or will. Therefore there is no need to suppose God's existence.

Sed contra est quod dicitur Exodi III, ex persona Dei, *ego sum qui sum.*

Respondeo dicendum quod Deum esse quinque viis probari potest.

Prima autem et manifestior via est, quae sumitur ex parte motus. Certum est enim, et sensu constat, aliqua moveri in hoc mundo. Omne autem quod movetur, ab alio movetur. Nihil enim movetur, nisi secundum quod est in potentia ad illud ad quod movetur, movet autem aliquid secundum quod est actu. Movere enim nihil aliud est quam educere aliquid de potentia in actum, de potentia autem non potest aliquid reduci in actum, nisi per aliquod ens in actu, sicut calidum in actu, ut ignis, facit lignum, quod est calidum in potentia, esse actu calidum, et per hoc movet et alterat ipsum. Non autem est possibile ut idem sit simul in actu et potentia secundum idem, sed solum secundum diversa, quod enim est calidum in actu, non potest simul esse calidum in potentia, sed est simul frigidum in potentia. Impossibile est ergo quod, secundum idem et eodem modo, aliquid sit movens et motum, vel quod moveat seipsum. Omne ergo quod movetur, oportet ab alio moveri. Si ergo id a quo movetur, moveatur, oportet et ipsum ab alio moveri et illud ab alio. Hic autem non est procedere in infinitum, quia sic non esset aliquod primum movens; et per consequens nec aliquod aliud movens, quia moventia secunda non movent nisi per hoc quod sunt mota a primo movente, sicut baculus non movet nisi per hoc quod est motus a manu. Ergo necesse est devenire ad aliquod primum movens, quod a nullo movetur, et hoc omnes intelligunt Deum.

Secunda via est ex ratione causae efficientis. Invenimus enim in istis sensibilibus esse ordinem causarum efficientium, nec tamen invenitur, nec est possibile, quod aliquid sit causa efficiens sui ipsius; quia sic esset prius seipso, quod est impossibile. Non autem est possibile quod in causis efficientibus procedatur in infinitum. Quia in omnibus causis efficientibus ordinatis, primum est causa medii, et medium est causa ultimi, sive media sint plura sive unum tantum, remota autem causa, removetur effectus, ergo, si non fuerit primum in causis efficientibus, non erit ultimum nec medium. Sed si procedatur in infinitum in causis efficientibus, non erit prima causa efficiens, et sic non erit nec effectus ultimus, nec causae efficientes mediae, quod patet esse falsum. Ergo est necesse ponere aliquam causam efficientem primam, quam omnes Deum nominant.

Tertia via est sumpta ex possibili et necessario, quae talis est. Invenimus enim in rebus quaedam quae sunt possibilia esse et non esse, cum quaedam inveniantur

On the contrary, It is said in the person of God: *I am Who am.* (Ex 3:14)

I answer that, The existence of God can be proved in five ways.

The first and more manifest way is the argument from motion. It is certain, and evident to our senses, that in the world some things are in motion. Now whatever is in motion is put in motion by another, for nothing can be in motion except it is in potentiality to that towards which it is in motion; whereas a thing moves inasmuch as it is in act. For motion is nothing else than the reduction of something from potentiality to actuality. But nothing can be reduced from potentiality to actuality, except by something in a state of actuality. Thus that which is actually hot, as fire, makes wood, which is potentially hot, to be actually hot, and thereby moves and changes it. Now it is not possible that the same thing should be at once in actuality and potentiality in the same respect, but only in different respects. For what is actually hot cannot simultaneously be potentially hot; but it is simultaneously potentially cold. It is therefore impossible that in the same respect and in the same way a thing should be both mover and moved, i.e., that it should move itself. Therefore, whatever is in motion must be put in motion by another. If that by which it is put in motion be itself put in motion, then this also must needs be put in motion by another, and that by another again. But this cannot go on to infinity, because then there would be no first mover, and, consequently, no other mover; seeing that subsequent movers move only inasmuch as they are put in motion by the first mover; as the staff moves only because it is put in motion by the hand. Therefore it is necessary to arrive at a first mover, put in motion by no other; and this everyone understands to be God.

The second way is from the nature of the efficient cause. In the world of sense we find there is an order of efficient causes. There is no case known (neither is it, indeed, possible) in which a thing is found to be the efficient cause of itself; for so it would be prior to itself, which is impossible. Now in efficient causes it is not possible to go on to infinity, because in all efficient causes following in order, the first is the cause of the intermediate cause, and the intermediate is the cause of the ultimate cause, whether the intermediate cause be several, or only one. Now to take away the cause is to take away the effect. Therefore, if there be no first cause among efficient causes, there will be no ultimate, nor any intermediate cause. But if in efficient causes it is possible to go on to infinity, there will be no first efficient cause, neither will there be an ultimate effect, nor any intermediate efficient causes; all of which is plainly false. Therefore it is necessary to admit a first efficient cause, to which everyone gives the name of God.

The third way is taken from possibility and necessity, and runs thus. We find in nature things that are possible to be and not to be, since they are found to be generated,

generari et corrumpi, et per consequens possibilia esse et non esse. Impossibile est autem omnia quae sunt, talia esse, quia quod possibile est non esse, quandoque non est. Si igitur omnia sunt possibilia non esse, aliquando nihil fuit in rebus. Sed si hoc est verum, etiam nunc nihil esset, quia quod non est, non incipit esse nisi per aliquid quod est; si igitur nihil fuit ens, impossibile fuit quod aliquid inciperet esse, et sic modo nihil esset, quod patet esse falsum. Non ergo omnia entia sunt possibilia, sed oportet aliquid esse necessarium in rebus. Omne autem necessarium vel habet causam suae necessitatis aliunde, vel non habet. Non est autem possibile quod procedatur in infinitum in necessariis quae habent causam suae necessitatis, sicut nec in causis efficientibus, ut probatum est. Ergo necesse est ponere aliquid quod sit per se necessarium, non habens causam necessitatis aliunde, sed quod est causa necessitatis aliis, quod omnes dicunt Deum.

Quarta via sumitur ex gradibus qui in rebus inveniuntur. Invenitur enim in rebus aliquid magis et minus bonum, et verum, et nobile, et sic de aliis huiusmodi. Sed magis et minus dicuntur de diversis secundum quod appropinquant diversimode ad aliquid quod maxime est, sicut magis calidum est, quod magis appropinquat maxime calido. Est igitur aliquid quod est verissimum, et optimum, et nobilissimum, et per consequens maxime ens, nam quae sunt maxime vera, sunt maxime entia, ut dicitur II Metaphys. Quod autem dicitur maxime tale in aliquo genere, est causa omnium quae sunt illius generis, sicut ignis, qui est maxime calidus, est causa omnium calidorum, ut in eodem libro dicitur. Ergo est aliquid quod omnibus entibus est causa esse, et bonitatis, et cuiuslibet perfectionis, et hoc dicimus Deum.

Quinta via sumitur ex gubernatione rerum. Videmus enim quod aliqua quae cognitione carent, scilicet corpora naturalia, operantur propter finem, quod apparet ex hoc quod semper aut frequentius eodem modo operantur, ut consequantur id quod est optimum; unde patet quod non a casu, sed ex intentione perveniunt ad finem. Ea autem quae non habent cognitionem, non tendunt in finem nisi directa ab aliquo cognoscente et intelligente, sicut sagitta a sagittante. Ergo est aliquid intelligens, a quo omnes res naturales ordinantur ad finem, et hoc dicimus Deum.

AD PRIMUM ergo dicendum quod, sicut dicit Augustinus in Enchiridio, *Deus, cum sit summe bonus, nullo modo sineret aliquid mali esse in operibus suis, nisi esset adeo omnipotens et bonus, ut bene faceret etiam de malo.* Hoc ergo ad infinitam Dei bonitatem pertinet, ut esse permittat mala, et ex eis eliciat bona.

and to corrupt, and consequently, they are possible to be and not to be. But it is impossible for these always to exist, for that which is possible not to be at some time is not. Therefore, if everything is possible not to be, then at one time there could have been nothing in existence. Now if this were true, even now there would be nothing in existence, because that which does not exist only begins to exist by something already existing. Therefore, if at one time nothing was in existence, it would have been impossible for anything to have begun to exist; and thus even now nothing would be in existence—which is absurd. Therefore, not all beings are merely possible, but there must exist something the existence of which is necessary. But every necessary thing either has its necessity caused by another, or not. Now it is impossible to go on to infinity in necessary things which have their necessity caused by another, as has been already proved in regard to efficient causes. Therefore we cannot but postulate the existence of some being having of itself its own necessity, and not receiving it from another, but rather causing in others their necessity. This all men speak of as God.

The fourth way is taken from the gradation to be found in things. Among beings there are some more and some less good, true, noble and the like. But more and less are predicated of different things, according as they resemble in their different ways something which is the maximum, as a thing is said to be hotter according as it more nearly resembles that which is hottest; so that there is something which is truest, something best, something noblest and, consequently, something which is uttermost being; for those things that are greatest in truth are greatest in being, as it is written in *Metaph.* ii. Now the maximum in any genus is the cause of all in that genus; as fire, which is the maximum heat, is the cause of all hot things. Therefore there must also be something which is to all beings the cause of their being, goodness, and every other perfection; and this we call God.

The fifth way is taken from the governance of the world. We see that things which lack intelligence, such as natural bodies, act for an end, and this is evident from their acting always, or nearly always, in the same way, so as to obtain the best result. Hence it is plain that not fortuitously, but designedly, do they achieve their end. Now whatever lacks intelligence cannot move towards an end, unless it be directed by some being endowed with knowledge and intelligence; as the arrow is shot to its mark by the archer. Therefore some intelligent being exists by whom all natural things are directed to their end; and this being we call God.

REPLY OBJ. 1: As Augustine says (*Enchiridion* xi): *Since God is the highest good, He would not allow any evil to exist in His works, unless His omnipotence and goodness were such as to bring good even out of evil.* This is part of the infinite goodness of God, that He should allow evil to exist, and out of it produce good.

AD SECUNDUM dicendum quod, cum natura propter determinatum finem operetur ex directione alicuius superioris agentis, necesse est ea quae a natura fiunt, etiam in Deum reducere, sicut in primam causam. Similiter etiam quae ex proposito fiunt, oportet reducere in aliquam altiorem causam, quae non sit ratio et voluntas humana, quia haec mutabilia sunt et defectibilia; oportet autem omnia mobilia et deficere possibilia reduci in aliquod primum principium immobile et per se necessarium, sicut ostensum est.

REPLY OBJ. 2: Since nature works for a determinate end under the direction of a higher agent, whatever is done by nature must needs be traced back to God, as to its first cause. So also whatever is done voluntarily must also be traced back to some higher cause other than human reason or will, since these can change or fail; for all things that are changeable and capable of defect must be traced back to an immovable and self-necessary first principle, as was shown in the body of the Article.

QUESTION 3

THE SIMPLICITY OF GOD

Cognito de aliquo an sit, inquirendum restat quomodo sit, ut sciatur de eo quid sit. Sed quia de Deo scire non possumus quid sit, sed quid non sit, non possumus considerare de Deo quomodo sit, sed potius quomodo non sit. Primo ergo considerandum est quomodo non sit; secundo, quomodo a nobis cognoscatur; tertio, quomodo nominetur.

Potest autem ostendi de Deo quomodo non sit, removendo ab eo ea quae ei non conveniunt, utpote compositionem, motum, et alia huiusmodi. Primo ergo inquiratur de simplicitate ipsius, per quam removetur ab eo compositio. Et quia simplicia in rebus corporalibus sunt imperfecta et partes, secundo inquiretur de perfectione ipsius; tertio, de infinitate eius; quarto, de immutabilitate; quinto, de unitate.

Circa primum quaeruntur octo.

Primo, utrum Deus sit corpus.

Secundo, utrum sit in eo compositio formae et materiae.

Tertio, utrum sit in eo compositio quidditatis, sive essentiae, vel naturae, et subiecti.

Quarto, utrum sit in eo compositio quae est ex essentia et esse.

Quinto, utrum sit in eo compositio generis et differentiae.

Sexto, utrum sit in eo compositio subiecti et accidentis.

Septimo, utrum sit quocumque modo compositus, vel totaliter simplex.

Octavo, utrum veniat in compositionem cum aliis.

When the existence of a thing has been ascertained there remains the further question of the manner of its existence, in order that we may know its essence. Now, because we cannot know what God is, but rather what He is not, we have no means for considering how God is, but rather how He is not. Therefore, we must consider: (1) How He is not; (2) How He is known by us; (3) How He is named.

Now it can be shown how God is not, by denying Him whatever is opposed to the idea of Him, viz. composition, motion, and the like. Therefore (1) we must discuss His simplicity, whereby we deny composition in Him; and because whatever is simple in material things is imperfect and a part of something else, we shall discuss (2) His perfection; (3) His infinity; (4) His immutability; (5) His unity.

Concerning His simplicity, there are eight points of inquiry:

(1) Whether God is a body?

(2) Whether He is composed of matter and form?

(3) Whether in Him there is composition of quiddity, essence or nature, and subject?

(4) Whether He is composed of essence and existence?

(5) Whether He is composed of genus and difference?

(6) Whether He is composed of subject and accident?

(7) Whether He is in any way composite, or wholly simple?

(8) Whether He enters into composition with other things?

Article 1

Whether God Is a Body?

AD PRIMUM SIC PROCEDITUR. Videtur quod Deus sit corpus. Corpus enim est quod habet trinam dimensionem. Sed sacra Scriptura attribuit Deo trinam dimensionem, dicitur enim Iob XI, *excelsior caelo est, et quid facies? Profundior Inferno, et unde cognosces? Longior terra mensura eius, et latior mari.* Ergo Deus est corpus.

PRAETEREA, omne figuratum est corpus, cum figura sit qualitas circa quantitatem. Sed Deus videtur esse

OBJECTION 1: It seems that God is a body. For a body is that which has the three dimensions. But Holy Scripture attributes the three dimensions to God, for it is written: *He is higher than Heaven, and what wilt thou do? He is deeper than Hell, and how wilt thou know? The measure of Him is longer than the earth and broader than the sea* (Job 11:8, 9). Therefore God is a body.

OBJ. 2: Further, everything that has figure is a body, since figure is a quality of quantity. But God seems to have

figuratus, cum scriptum sit Gen. I, *faciamus hominem ad imaginem et similitudinem nostram*, figura enim imago dicitur, secundum illud Hebr. I, *cum sit splendor gloriae, et figura substantiae eius*, idest imago. Ergo Deus est corpus.

PRAETEREA, omne quod habet partes corporeas, est corpus. Sed Scriptura attribuit Deo partes corporeas, dicitur enim Iob XL, *si habes brachium ut Deus*; et in Psalmo, *oculi domini super iustos; et, dextera domini fecit virtutem*. Ergo Deus est corpus.

PRAETEREA, situs non convenit nisi corpori. Sed ea quae ad situm pertinent, in Scripturis dicuntur de Deo, dicitur enim Isaiae VI, *vidi dominum sedentem*; et Isaiae III, *stat ad iudicandum dominus*. Ergo Deus est corpus.

PRAETEREA, nihil potest esse terminus localis a quo vel ad quem, nisi sit corpus vel aliquod corporeum. Sed Deus in Scriptura dicitur esse terminus localis ut ad quem, secundum illud Psalmi, *accedite ad eum, et illuminamini*; et ut a quo, secundum illud Hierem. XVII, *recedentes a te in terra scribentur*. Ergo Deus est corpus.

SED CONTRA est quod dicitur Ioan. IV, *spiritus est Deus*.

RESPONDEO dicendum absolute Deum non esse corpus. Quod tripliciter ostendi potest. Primo quidem, quia nullum corpus movet non motum, ut patet inducendo per singula. Ostensum est autem supra quod Deus est primum movens immobile. Unde manifestum est quod Deus non est corpus. Secundo, quia necesse est id quod est primum ens, esse in actu, et nullo modo in potentia. Licet enim in uno et eodem quod exit de potentia in actum, prius sit potentia quam actus tempore, simpliciter tamen actus prior est potentia, quia quod est in potentia, non reducitur in actum nisi per ens actu. Ostensum est autem supra quod Deus est primum ens. Impossibile est igitur quod in Deo sit aliquid in potentia. Omne autem corpus est in potentia, quia continuum, inquantum huiusmodi, divisibile est in infinitum. Impossibile est igitur Deum esse corpus. Tertio, quia Deus est id quod est nobilissimum in entibus, ut ex dictis patet. Impossibile est autem aliquod corpus esse nobilissimum in entibus. Quia corpus aut est vivum, aut non vivum. Corpus autem vivum, manifestum est quod est nobilius corpore non vivo. Corpus autem vivum non vivit inquantum corpus, quia sic omne corpus viveret, oportet igitur quod vivat per aliquid aliud, sicut corpus nostrum vivit per animam. Illud autem per quod vivit corpus, est nobilius quam corpus. Impossibile est igitur Deum esse corpus.

AD PRIMUM ergo dicendum quod, sicut supra dictum est, sacra Scriptura tradit nobis spiritualia et divina sub similitudinibus corporalium. Unde, cum trinam dimensionem Deo attribuit, sub similitudine quantitatis corporeae, quantitatem virtualem ipsius designat, utpote

figure, for it is written: *Let us make man to our image and likeness* (Gen 1:26). Now a figure is called an image, according to the text: *Who being the brightness of His glory and the figure*, i.e., the image, *of His substance* (Heb 1:3). Therefore God is a body.

OBJ. 3: Further, whatever has corporeal parts is a body. Now Scripture attributes corporeal parts to God. *Hast thou an arm like God?* (Job 40:4); and *The eyes of the Lord are upon the just* (Ps 33:16); and *The right hand of the Lord hath wrought strength* (Ps 117:16). Therefore God is a body.

OBJ. 4: Further, posture belongs only to bodies. But something which supposes posture is said of God in the Scriptures: *I saw the Lord sitting* (Isa 6:1), and *He standeth up to judge* (Isa 3:13). Therefore God is a body.

OBJ. 5: Further, only bodies or things corporeal can be a local term wherefrom or whereto. But in the Scriptures God is spoken of as a local term whereto, according to the words, *Come ye to Him and be enlightened* (Ps 33:6), and as a term wherefrom: *All they that depart from Thee shall be written in the earth* (Jer 17:13). Therefore God is a body.

ON THE CONTRARY, It is written in the Gospel of St. John (John 4:24): *God is a spirit*.

I ANSWER THAT, It is absolutely true that God is not a body; and this can be shown in three ways. First, because no body is in motion unless it be put in motion, as is evident from induction. Now it has been already proved (Q. 2, A. 3) that God is the First Mover, and is Himself unmoved. Therefore it is clear that God is not a body. Second, because the first being must of necessity be in act, and in no way in potentiality. For although in any single thing that passes from potentiality to actuality, the potentiality is prior in time to the actuality; nevertheless, absolutely speaking, actuality is prior to potentiality; for whatever is in potentiality can be reduced into actuality only by some being in actuality. Now it has been already proved that God is the First Being. It is therefore impossible that in God there should be any potentiality. But every body is in potentiality because the continuous, as such, is divisible to infinity; it is therefore impossible that God should be a body. Third, because God is the most noble of beings. Now it is impossible for a body to be the most noble of beings; for a body must be either animate or inanimate; and an animate body is manifestly nobler than any inanimate body. But an animate body is not animate precisely as body; otherwise all bodies would be animate. Therefore its animation depends upon some other thing, as our body depends for its animation on the soul. Hence that by which a body becomes animated must be nobler than the body. Therefore it is impossible that God should be a body.

REPLY OBJ. 1: As we have said above (Q. 1, A. 9), Holy Writ puts before us spiritual and divine things under the comparison of corporeal things. Hence, when it attributes to God the three dimensions under the comparison of corporeal quantity, it implies His virtual quantity; thus, by

per profunditatem, virtutem ad cognoscendum occulta; per altitudinem, excellentiam virtutis super omnia; per longitudinem, durationem sui esse; per latitudinem, affectum dilectionis ad omnia. Vel, ut dicit Dionysius, cap. IX de Div. Nom., per profunditatem Dei intelligitur incomprehensibilitas ipsius essentiae; per longitudinem, processus virtutis eius, omnia penetrantis; per latitudinem vero, superextensio eius ad omnia, inquantum scilicet sub eius protectione omnia continentur.

Ad secundum dicendum quod homo dicitur esse ad imaginem Dei, non secundum corpus, sed secundum id quo homo excellit alia animalia, unde, Gen. I, postquam dictum est, *faciamus hominem ad imaginem et similitudinem nostram*, subditur, *ut praesit piscibus maris*, et cetera. Excellit autem homo omnia animalia quantum ad rationem et intellectum. Unde secundum intellectum et rationem, quae sunt incorporea, homo est ad imaginem Dei.

Ad tertium dicendum quod partes corporeae attribuuntur Deo in Scripturis ratione suorum actuum, secundum quandam similitudinem. Sicut actus oculi est videre, unde oculus de Deo dictus, significat virtutem eius ad videndum modo intelligibili, non sensibili. Et simile est de aliis partibus.

Ad quartum dicendum quod etiam ea quae ad situm pertinent, non attribuuntur Deo nisi secundum quandam similitudinem, sicut dicitur sedens, propter suam immobilitatem et auctoritatem; et stans, propter suam fortitudinem ad debellandum omne quod adversatur.

Ad quintum dicendum quod ad Deum non acceditur passibus corporalibus, cum ubique sit, sed affectibus mentis, et eodem modo ab eo receditur. Et sic accessus et recessus, sub similitudine localis motus, designant spiritualem affectum.

depth, it signifies His power of knowing hidden things; by height, the transcendence of His excelling power; by length, the duration of His existence; by breadth, His act of love for all. Or, as says Dionysius (*Div. Nom.* ix), by the depth of God is meant the incomprehensibility of His essence; by length, the procession of His all-pervading power; by breadth, His overspreading all things, inasmuch as all things lie under His protection.

Reply Obj. 2: Man is said to be after the image of God, not as regards his body, but as regards that whereby he excels other animals. Hence, when it is said, *Let us make man to our image and likeness*, it is added, *And let him have dominion over the fishes of the sea* (Gen 1:26). Now man excels all animals by his reason and intelligence; hence it is according to his intelligence and reason, which are incorporeal, that man is said to be according to the image of God.

Reply Obj. 3: Corporeal parts are attributed to God in Scripture on account of His actions, and this is owing to a certain parallel. For instance the act of the eye is to see; hence the eye attributed to God signifies His power of seeing intellectually, not sensibly; and so on with the other parts.

Reply Obj. 4: Whatever pertains to posture, also, is only attributed to God by some sort of parallel. He is spoken of as sitting, on account of His unchangeableness and dominion; and as standing, on account of His power of overcoming whatever withstands Him.

Reply Obj. 5: We draw near to God by no corporeal steps, since He is everywhere, but by the affections of our soul, and by the actions of that same soul do we withdraw from Him; thus, to draw near to or to withdraw from signifies merely spiritual actions based on the metaphor of local motion.

Article 2

Whether God Is Composed of Matter and Form?

Ad secundum sic proceditur. Videtur quod in Deo sit compositio formae et materiae. Omne enim quod habet animam, est compositum ex materia et forma, quia anima est forma corporis. Sed Scriptura attribuit animam Deo, introducitur enim ad Hebr. X, ex persona Dei, *iustus autem meus ex fide vivit; quod si subtraxerit se, non placebit animae meae*. Ergo Deus est compositus ex materia et forma.

Praeterea, ira, gaudium, et huiusmodi, sunt passiones coniuncti, ut dicitur I de anima. Sed huiusmodi attribuuntur Deo in Scriptura dicitur enim in Psalmo,

Objection 1: It seems that God is composed of matter and form. For whatever has a soul is composed of matter and form; since the soul is the form of the body. But Scripture attributes a soul to God; for it is mentioned in Hebrews (Heb 10:38), where God says: *But My just man liveth by faith; but if he withdraw himself, he shall not please My soul.* Therefore God is composed of matter and form.

Obj. 2: Further, anger, joy and the like are passions of the composite. But these are attributed to God in Scripture:

iratus est furore dominus in populum suum. Ergo Deus ex materia et forma est compositus.

PRAETEREA, materia est principium individuationis. Sed Deus videtur esse individuum, non enim de multis praedicatur. Ergo est compositus ex materia et forma.

SED CONTRA, omne compositum ex materia et forma est corpus, quantitas enim dimensiva est quae primo inhaeret materiae. Sed Deus non est corpus, ut ostensum est. Ergo Deus non est compositus ex materia et forma.

RESPONDEO dicendum quod impossibile est in Deo esse materiam. Primo quidem, quia materia est id quod est in potentia. Ostensum est autem quod Deus est purus actus, non habens aliquid de potentialitate. Unde impossibile est quod Deus sit compositus ex materia et forma. Secundo, quia omne compositum ex materia et forma est perfectum et bonum per suam formam, unde oportet quod sit bonum per participationem, secundum quod materia participat formam. Primum autem quod est bonum et optimum, quod Deus est, non est bonum per participationem, quia bonum per essentiam, prius est bono per participationem. Unde impossibile est quod Deus sit compositus ex materia et forma. Tertio, quia unumquodque agens agit per suam formam, unde secundum quod aliquid se habet ad suam formam, sic se habet ad hoc quod sit agens. Quod igitur primum est et per se agens, oportet quod sit primo et per se forma. Deus autem est primum agens, cum sit prima causa efficiens, ut ostensum est. Est igitur per essentiam suam forma; et non compositus ex materia et forma.

AD PRIMUM ergo dicendum quod anima attribuitur Deo per similitudinem actus. Quod enim volumus aliquid nobis, ex anima nostra est, unde illud dicitur esse placitum animae Dei, quod est placitum voluntati ipsius.

AD SECUNDUM dicendum quod ira et huiusmodi attribuuntur Deo secundum similitudinem effectus, quia enim proprium est irati punire, ira eius punitio metaphorice vocatur.

AD TERTIUM dicendum quod formae quae sunt receptibiles in materia individuantur per materiam, quae non potest esse in alio, cum sit primum subiectum substans, forma vero, quantum est de se, nisi aliquid aliud impediat, recipi potest a pluribus. Sed illa forma quae non est receptibilis in materia, sed est per se subsistens, ex hoc ipso individuatur, quod non potest recipi in alio, et huiusmodi forma est Deus. Unde non sequitur quod habeat materiam.

The Lord was exceeding angry with His people (Ps 105:40). Therefore God is composed of matter and form.

OBJ. 3: Further, matter is the principle of individualization. But God seems to be individual, for He cannot be predicated of many. Therefore He is composed of matter and form.

ON THE CONTRARY, Whatever is composed of matter and form is a body; for dimensive quantity is the first property of matter. But God is not a body as proved in the preceding Article; therefore He is not composed of matter and form.

I ANSWER THAT, It is impossible that matter should exist in God. First, because matter is in potentiality. But we have shown (Q. 2, A. 3) that God is pure act, without any potentiality. Hence it is impossible that God should be composed of matter and form. Second, because everything composed of matter and form owes its perfection and goodness to its form; therefore its goodness is participated, inasmuch as matter participates the form. Now the first good and the best—viz. God—is not a participated good, because the essential good is prior to the participated good. Hence it is impossible that God should be composed of matter and form. Third, because every agent acts by its form; hence the manner in which it has its form is the manner in which it is an agent. Therefore whatever is primarily and essentially an agent must be primarily and essentially form. Now God is the first agent, since He is the first efficient cause. He is therefore of His essence a form; and not composed of matter and form.

REPLY OBJ. 1: A soul is attributed to God because His acts resemble the acts of a soul; for, that we will anything, is due to our soul. Hence what is pleasing to His will is said to be pleasing to His soul.

REPLY OBJ. 2: Anger and the like are attributed to God on account of a similitude of effect. Thus, because to punish is properly the act of an angry man, God's punishment is metaphorically spoken of as His anger.

REPLY OBJ. 3: Forms which can be received in matter are individualized by matter, which cannot be in another as in a subject since it is the first underlying subject; although form of itself, unless something else prevents it, can be received by many. But that form which cannot be received in matter, but is self-subsisting, is individualized precisely because it cannot be received in a subject; and such a form is God. Hence it does not follow that matter exists in God.

Article 3

Whether God is the Same as His Essence or Nature?

AD TERTIUM SIC PROCEDITUR. Videtur quod non sit idem Deus quod sua essentia vel natura. Nihil enim est in seipso. Sed essentia vel natura Dei, quae est deitas, dicitur esse in Deo. Ergo videtur quod Deus non sit idem quod sua essentia vel natura.

PRAETEREA, effectus assimilatur suae causae, quia omne agens agit sibi simile. Sed in rebus creatis non est idem suppositum quod sua natura, non enim idem est homo quod sua humanitas. Ergo nec Deus est idem quod sua deitas.

CONTRA, de Deo dicitur quod est vita, et non solum quod est vivens, ut patet Ioan. XIV, *ego sum via, veritas et vita*. Sicut autem se habet vita ad viventem, ita deitas ad Deum. Ergo Deus est ipsa deitas.

RESPONDEO dicendum quod Deus est idem quod sua essentia vel natura. Ad cuius intellectum sciendum est, quod in rebus compositis ex materia et forma, necesse est quod differant natura vel essentia et suppositum. Quia essentia vel natura comprehendit in se illa tantum quae cadunt in definitione speciei, sicut humanitas comprehendit in se ea quae cadunt in definitione hominis, his enim homo est homo, et hoc significat humanitas, hoc scilicet quo homo est homo. Sed materia individualis, cum accidentibus omnibus individuantibus ipsam, non cadit in definitione speciei, non enim cadunt in definitione hominis hae carnes et haec ossa, aut albedo vel nigredo, vel aliquid huiusmodi. Unde hae carnes et haec ossa, et accidentia designantia hanc materiam, non concluduntur in humanitate. Et tamen in eo quod est homo, includuntur, unde id quod est homo, habet in se aliquid quod non habet humanitas. Et propter hoc non est totaliter idem homo et humanitas, sed humanitas significatur ut pars formalis hominis; quia principia definientia habent se formaliter, respectu materiae individuantis. In his igitur quae non sunt composita ex materia et forma, in quibus individuatio non est per materiam individualem, idest per hanc materiam, sed ipsae formae per se individuantur, oportet quod ipsae formae sint supposita subsistentia. Unde in eis non differt suppositum et natura. Et sic, cum Deus non sit compositus ex materia et forma, ut ostensum est, oportet quod Deus sit sua deitas, sua vita, et quidquid aliud sic de Deo praedicatur.

AD PRIMUM ergo dicendum quod de rebus simplicibus loqui non possumus, nisi per modum compositorum, a quibus cognitionem accipimus. Et ideo, de Deo loquentes, utimur nominibus concretis, ut significemus eius subsistentiam, quia apud nos non subsistunt nisi composita, et utimur nominibus abstractis,

OBJECTION 1: It seems that God is not the same as His essence or nature. For nothing can be in itself. But the substance or nature of God—i.e., the Godhead—is said to be in God. Therefore it seems that God is not the same as His essence or nature.

OBJ. 2: Further, the effect is assimilated to its cause; for every agent produces its like. But in created things the suppositum is not identical with its nature; for a man is not the same as his humanity. Therefore God is not the same as His Godhead.

ON THE CONTRARY, It is said of God that He is life itself, and not only that He is a living thing: *I am the way, the truth, and the life* (John 14:6). Now the relation between Godhead and God is the same as the relation between life and a living thing. Therefore God is His very Godhead.

I ANSWER THAT, God is the same as His essence or nature. To understand this, it must be noted that in things composed of matter and form, the nature or essence must differ from the suppositum, because the essence or nature connotes only what is included in the definition of the species; as, humanity connotes all that is included in the definition of man, for it is by this that man is man, and it is this that humanity signifies, that, namely, whereby man is man. Now individual matter, with all the individualizing accidents, is not included in the definition of the species. For this particular flesh, these bones, this blackness or whiteness, etc., are not included in the definition of a man. Therefore this flesh, these bones, and the accidental qualities distinguishing this particular matter, are not included in humanity; and yet they are included in the thing which is man. Hence the thing which is a man has something more in it than has humanity. Consequently humanity and a man are not wholly identical; but humanity is taken to mean the formal part of a man, because the principles whereby a thing is defined are regarded as the formal constituent in regard to the individualizing matter. On the other hand, in things not composed of matter and form, in which individualization is not due to individual matter—that is to say, to this matter—the very forms being individualized of themselves—it is necessary the forms themselves should be subsisting supposita. Therefore suppositum and nature in them are identified. Since God then is not composed of matter and form, He must be His own Godhead, His own Life, and whatever else is thus predicated of Him.

REPLY OBJ. 1: We can speak of simple things only as though they were like the composite things from which we derive our knowledge. Therefore in speaking of God, we use concrete nouns to signify His subsistence, because with us only those things subsist which are composite; and we use abstract nouns to signify His simplicity. In saying therefore

ut significemus eius simplicitatem. Quod ergo dicitur deitas vel vita, vel aliquid huiusmodi, esse in Deo, referendum est ad diversitatem quae est in acceptione intellectus nostri; et non ad aliquam diversitatem rei.

AD SECUNDUM dicendum quod effectus Dei imitantur ipsum, non perfecte, sed secundum quod possunt. Et hoc ad defectum imitationis pertinet, quod id quod est simplex et unum, non potest repraesentari nisi per multa, et sic accidit in eis compositio, ex qua provenit quod in eis non est idem suppositum quod natura.

that Godhead, or life, or the like are in God, we indicate the composite way in which our intellect understands, but not that there is any composition in God.

REPLY OBJ. 2: The effects of God do not imitate Him perfectly, but only as far as they are able; and the imitation is here defective, precisely because what is simple and one, can only be represented by diverse things; consequently, composition is accidental to them, and therefore, in them suppositum is not the same as nature.

Article 4

Whether Essence and Existence Are the Same in God?

AD QUARTUM SIC PROCEDITUR. Videtur quod in Deo non sit idem essentia et esse. Si enim hoc sit, tunc ad esse divinum nihil additur. Sed esse cui nulla fit additio, est esse commune quod de omnibus praedicatur, sequitur ergo quod Deus sit ens commune praedicabile de omnibus. Hoc autem est falsum, secundum illud Sap. XIV, *incommunicabile nomen lignis et lapidibus imposuerunt*. Ergo esse Dei non est eius essentia.

PRAETEREA, de Deo scire possumus an sit, ut supra dictum est. Non autem possumus scire quid sit. Ergo non est idem esse Dei, et quod quid est eius, sive quidditas vel natura.

SED CONTRA est quod Hilarius dicit in VII de Trin., *esse non est accidens in Deo, sed subsistens veritas*. Id ergo quod subsistit in Deo, est suum esse.

RESPONDEO dicendum quod Deus non solum est sua essentia, ut ostensum est, sed etiam suum esse. Quod quidem multipliciter ostendi potest. Primo quidem, quia quidquid est in aliquo quod est praeter essentiam eius, oportet esse causatum vel a principiis essentiae, sicut accidentia propria consequentia speciem, ut risibile consequitur hominem et causatur ex principiis essentialibus speciei; vel ab aliquo exteriori, sicut calor in aqua causatur ab igne. Si igitur ipsum esse rei sit aliud ab eius essentia, necesse est quod esse illius rei vel sit causatum ab aliquo exteriori, vel a principiis essentialibus eiusdem rei. Impossibile est autem quod esse sit causatum tantum ex principiis essentialibus rei, quia nulla res sufficit quod sit sibi causa essendi, si habeat esse causatum. Oportet ergo quod illud cuius esse est aliud ab essentia sua, habeat esse causatum ab alio. Hoc autem non potest dici de Deo, quia Deum dicimus esse primam causam efficientem. Impossibile est ergo quod in Deo sit aliud esse, et aliud eius essentia. Secundo, quia esse est actualitas omnis formae vel naturae, non enim bonitas vel humanitas significatur in actu, nisi prout significamus eam esse. Oportet igitur quod ipsum esse comparetur ad

OBJECTION 1: It seems that essence and existence are not the same in God. For if it be so, then the divine being has nothing added to it. Now being to which no addition is made is universal being which is predicated of all things. Therefore it follows that God is being in general which can be predicated of everything. But this is false: *For men gave the incommunicable name to stones and wood* (Wis 14:21). Therefore God's existence is not His essence.

OBJ. 2: Further, we can know whether God exists as said above (Q. 2, A. 2); but we cannot know what He is. Therefore God's existence is not the same as His essence—that is, as His quiddity or nature.

ON THE CONTRARY, Hilary says (*Trin.* vii): *In God existence is not an accidental quality, but subsisting truth*. Therefore what subsists in God is His existence.

I ANSWER THAT, God is not only His own essence, as shown in the preceding article, but also His own existence. This may be shown in several ways. First, whatever a thing has besides its essence must be caused either by the constituent principles of that essence (like a property that necessarily accompanies the species—as the faculty of laughing is proper to a man—and is caused by the constituent principles of the species), or by some exterior agent—as heat is caused in water by fire. Therefore, if the existence of a thing differs from its essence, this existence must be caused either by some exterior agent or by its essential principles. Now it is impossible for a thing's existence to be caused by its essential constituent principles, for nothing can be the sufficient cause of its own existence, if its existence is caused. Therefore that thing, whose existence differs from its essence, must have its existence caused by another. But this cannot be true of God; because we call God the first efficient cause. Therefore it is impossible that in God His existence should differ from His essence. Second, existence is that which makes every form or nature actual; for goodness and humanity are spoken of as actual, only because they are spoken of as existing. Therefore existence must be

essentiam quae est aliud ab ipso, sicut actus ad potentiam. Cum igitur in Deo nihil sit potentiale, ut ostensum est supra, sequitur quod non sit aliud in eo essentia quam suum esse. Sua igitur essentia est suum esse. Tertio, quia sicut illud quod habet ignem et non est ignis, est ignitum per participationem, ita illud quod habet esse et non est esse, est ens per participationem. Deus autem est sua essentia, ut ostensum est. Si igitur non sit suum esse, erit ens per participationem, et non per essentiam. Non ergo erit primum ens, quod absurdum est dicere. Est igitur Deus suum esse, et non solum sua essentia.

AD PRIMUM ergo dicendum quod aliquid cui non fit additio potest intelligi dupliciter. Uno modo, ut de ratione eius sit quod non fiat ei additio; sicut de ratione animalis irrationalis est, ut sit sine ratione. Alio modo intelligitur aliquid cui non fit additio, quia non est de ratione eius quod sibi fiat additio, sicut animal commune est sine ratione, quia non est de ratione animalis communis ut habeat rationem; sed nec de ratione eius est ut careat ratione. Primo igitur modo, esse sine additione, est esse divinum, secundo modo, esse sine additione, est esse commune.

AD SECUNDUM dicendum quod esse dupliciter dicitur, uno modo, significat actum essendi; alio modo, significat compositionem propositionis, quam anima adinvenit coniungens praedicatum subiecto. Primo igitur modo accipiendo esse, non possumus scire esse Dei, sicut nec eius essentiam, sed solum secundo modo. Scimus enim quod haec propositio quam formamus de Deo, cum dicimus Deus est, vera est. Et hoc scimus ex eius effectibus, ut supra dictum est.

compared to essence, if the latter is a distinct reality, as actuality to potentiality. Therefore, since in God there is no potentiality, as shown above (A. 1), it follows that in Him essence does not differ from existence. Therefore His essence is His existence. Third, because, just as that which has fire, but is not itself fire, is on fire by participation; so that which has existence but is not existence, is a being by participation. But God is His own essence, as shown above (A. 3); if, therefore, He is not His own existence He will be not essential, but participated being. He will not therefore be the first being—which is absurd. Therefore God is His own existence, and not merely His own essence.

REPLY OBJ. 1: A thing that has nothing added to it can be of two kinds. Either its essence precludes any addition; thus, for example, it is of the essence of an irrational animal to be without reason. Or we may understand a thing to have nothing added to it, inasmuch as its essence does not require that anything should be added to it; thus the genus animal is without reason, because it is not of the essence of animal in general to have reason; but neither is it to lack reason. And so the divine being has nothing added to it in the first sense; whereas universal being has nothing added to it in the second sense.

REPLY OBJ. 2: *To be* can mean either of two things. It may mean the act of essence, or it may mean the composition of a proposition effected by the mind in joining a predicate to a subject. Taking *to be* in the first sense, we cannot understand God's existence nor His essence; but only in the second sense. We know that this proposition which we form about God when we say *God is*, is true; and this we know from His effects (Q. 2, A. 2).

Article 5

Whether God Is Contained in a Genus?

AD QUINTUM SIC PROCEDITUR. Videtur quod Deus sit in genere aliquo. Substantia enim est ens per se subsistens. Hoc autem maxime convenit Deo. Ergo Deus est in genere substantiae.

PRAETEREA, unumquodque mensuratur per aliquid sui generis; sicut longitudines per longitudinem, et numeri per numerum. Sed Deus est mensura omnium substantiarum, ut patet per Commentatorem, X Metaphys. Ergo Deus est in genere substantiae.

SED CONTRA, genus est prius, secundum intellectum, eo quod in genere continetur. Sed nihil est prius Deo, nec secundum rem, nec secundum intellectum. Ergo Deus non est in aliquo genere.

RESPONDEO dicendum quod aliquid est in genere dupliciter. Uno modo simpliciter et proprie; sicut

OBJECTION 1: It seems that God is contained in a genus. For a substance is a being that subsists of itself. But this is especially true of God. Therefore God is in a genus of substance.

OBJ. 2: Further, nothing can be measured save by something of its own genus; as length is measured by length and numbers by number. But God is the measure of all substances, as the Commentator shows (*Metaph.* x). Therefore God is in the genus of substance.

ON THE CONTRARY, In the mind, genus is prior to what it contains. But nothing is prior to God either really or mentally. Therefore God is not in any genus.

I ANSWER THAT, A thing can be in a genus in two ways; either absolutely and properly, as a species contained

species, quae sub genere continentur. Alio modo, per reductionem, sicut principia et privationes, sicut punctus et unitas reducuntur ad genus quantitatis, sicut principia; caecitas autem, et omnis privatio, reducitur ad genus sui habitus. Neutro autem modo Deus est in genere. Quod enim non possit esse species alicuius generis, tripliciter ostendi potest. Primo quidem, quia species constituitur ex genere et differentia. Semper autem id a quo sumitur differentia constituens speciem, se habet ad illud unde sumitur genus, sicut actus ad potentiam. Animal enim sumitur a natura sensitiva per modum concretionis; hoc enim dicitur animal, quod naturam sensitivam habet, rationale vero sumitur a natura intellectiva, quia rationale est quod naturam intellectivam habet, intellectivum autem comparatur ad sensitivum, sicut actus ad potentiam. Et similiter manifestum est in aliis. Unde, cum in Deo non adiungatur potentia actui, impossibile est quod sit in genere tanquam species. Secundo, quia, cum esse Dei sit eius essentia, ut ostensum est, si Deus esset in aliquo genere, oporteret quod genus eius esset ens, nam genus significat essentiam rei, cum praedicetur in eo quod quid est. Ostendit autem philosophus in III Metaphys., quod ens non potest esse genus alicuius, omne enim genus habet differentias quae sunt extra essentiam generis; nulla autem differentia posset inveniri, quae esset extra ens; quia non ens non potest esse differentia. Unde relinquitur quod Deus non sit in genere. Tertio, quia omnia quae sunt in genere uno, communicant in quidditate vel essentia generis, quod praedicatur de eis in eo quod quid est. Differunt autem secundum esse, non enim idem est esse hominis et equi, nec huius hominis et illius hominis. Et sic oportet quod quaecumque sunt in genere, differant in eis esse et quod quid est, idest essentia. In Deo autem non differt, ut ostensum est. Unde manifestum est quod Deus non est in genere sicut species. Et ex hoc patet quod non habet genus, neque differentias; neque est definitio ipsius; neque demonstratio, nisi per effectum, quia definitio est ex genere et differentia, demonstrationis autem medium est definitio. Quod autem Deus non sit in genere per reductionem ut principium, manifestum est ex eo quod principium quod reducitur in aliquod genus, non se extendit ultra genus illud, sicut punctum non est principium nisi quantitatis continuae, et unitas quantitatis discretae. Deus autem est principium totius esse, ut infra ostendetur. Unde non continetur in aliquo genere sicut principium.

AD PRIMUM ergo dicendum quod substantiae nomen non significat hoc solum quod est per se esse, quia hoc quod est esse, non potest per se esse genus, ut ostensum est. Sed significat essentiam cui competit sic esse, idest per se esse, quod tamen esse non est ipsa eius essentia. Et sic patet quod Deus non est in genere substantiae.

under a genus; or as being reducible to it, as principles and privations. For example, a point and unity are reduced to the genus of quantity, as its principles; while blindness and all other privations are reduced to the genus of habit. But in neither way is God in a genus. That He cannot be a species of any genus may be shown in three ways. First, because a species is constituted of genus and difference. Now that from which the difference constituting the species is derived, is always related to that from which the genus is derived, as actuality is related to potentiality. For animal is derived from sensitive nature, by concretion as it were, for that is animal, which has a sensitive nature. Rational being, on the other hand, is derived from intellectual nature, because that is rational, which has an intellectual nature, and intelligence is compared to sense, as actuality is to potentiality. The same argument holds good in other things. Hence since in God actuality is not added to potentiality, it is impossible that He should be in any genus as a species. Second, since the existence of God is His essence, if God were in any genus, He would be the genus being, because, since genus is predicated as an essential it refers to the essence of a thing. But the Philosopher has shown (*Metaph.* iii) that being cannot be a genus, for every genus has differences distinct from its generic essence. Now no difference can exist distinct from being; for non-being cannot be a difference. It follows then that God is not in a genus. Third, because all in one genus agree in the quiddity or essence of the genus which is predicated of them as an essential, but they differ in their existence. For the existence of man and of horse is not the same; as also of this man and that man: thus in every member of a genus, existence and quiddity—i.e., essence—must differ. But in God they do not differ, as shown in the preceding article. Therefore it is plain that God is not in a genus as if He were a species. From this it is also plain that He has no genus nor difference, nor can there be any definition of Him; nor, save through His effects, a demonstration of Him: for a definition is from genus and difference; and the mean of a demonstration is a definition. That God is not in a genus, as reducible to it as its principle, is clear from this, that a principle reducible to any genus does not extend beyond that genus; as, a point is the principle of continuous quantity alone; and unity, of discontinuous quantity. But God is the principle of all being. Therefore He is not contained in any genus as its principle.

REPLY OBJ. 1: The word substance signifies not only what exists of itself—for existence cannot of itself be a genus, as shown in the body of the article; but, it also signifies an essence that has the property of existing in this way—namely, of existing of itself; this existence, however, is not its essence. Thus it is clear that God is not in the genus of substance.

AD SECUNDUM dicendum quod obiectio illa procedit de mensura proportionata, hanc enim oportet esse homogeneam mensurato. Deus autem non est mensura proportionata alicui. Dicitur tamen mensura omnium, ex eo quod unumquodque tantum habet de esse, quantum ei appropinquat.

REPLY OBJ. 2: This objection turns upon proportionate measure which must be homogeneous with what is measured. Now, God is not a measure proportionate to anything. Still, He is called the measure of all things, in the sense that everything has being only according as it resembles Him.

Article 6

Whether in God There Are Any Accidents?

AD SEXTUM SIC PROCEDITUR. Videtur quod in Deo sint aliqua accidentia. Substantia enim nulli est accidens, ut dicitur in I Physic. Quod ergo in uno est accidens, non potest in alio esse substantia, sicut probatur quod calor non sit forma substantialis ignis, quia in aliis est accidens. Sed sapientia, virtus, et huiusmodi, quae in nobis sunt accidentia, Deo attribuuntur. Ergo et in Deo sunt accidentia.

PRAETEREA, in quolibet genere est unum primum. Multa autem sunt genera accidentium. Si igitur prima illorum generum non sunt in Deo, erunt multa prima extra Deum, quod est inconveniens.

SED CONTRA, omne accidens in subiecto est. Deus autem non potest esse subiectum, quia *forma simplex non potest esse subiectum*, ut dicit Boetius in Lib. de Trin. Ergo in Deo non potest esse accidens.

RESPONDEO dicendum quod, secundum praemissa, manifeste apparet quod in Deo accidens esse non potest. Primo quidem, quia subiectum comparatur ad accidens, sicut potentia ad actum, subiectum enim secundum accidens est aliquo modo in actu. Esse autem in potentia, omnino removetur a Deo, ut ex praedictis patet. Secundo, quia Deus est suum esse, et, ut Boetius dicit in Lib. de Hebdomad., *licet id quod est, aliquid aliud possit habere adiunctum, tamen ipsum esse nihil aliud adiunctum habere potest*, sicut quod est calidum, potest habere aliquid extraneum quam calidum, ut albedinem; sed ipse calor nihil habet praeter calorem. Tertio, quia omne quod est per se, prius est eo quod est per accidens. Unde, cum Deus sit simpliciter primum ens, in eo non potest esse aliquid per accidens. Sed nec accidentia per se in eo esse possunt, sicut risibile est per se accidens hominis. Quia huiusmodi accidentia causantur ex principiis subiecti, in Deo autem nihil potest esse causatum, cum sit causa prima. Unde relinquitur quod in Deo nullum sit accidens.

AD PRIMUM ergo dicendum quod virtus et sapientia non univoce dicuntur de Deo et de nobis, ut infra patebit. Unde non sequitur quod accidentia sint in Deo, sicut in nobis.

AD SECUNDUM dicendum quod, cum substantia sit prior accidentibus, principia accidentium reducuntur in

OBJECTION 1: It seems that there are accidents in God. For substance cannot be an accident, as Aristotle says (*Phys.* i). Therefore that which is an accident in one, cannot, in another, be a substance. Thus it is proved that heat cannot be the substantial form of fire, because it is an accident in other things. But wisdom, virtue, and the like, which are accidents in us, are attributes of God. Therefore in God there are accidents.

OBJ. 2: Further, in every genus there is a first principle. But there are many genera of accidents. If, therefore, the primal members of these genera are not in God, there will be many primal beings other than God—which is absurd.

ON THE CONTRARY, Every accident is in a subject. But God cannot be a subject, for *no simple form can be a subject*, as Boethius says (*De Trin.*). Therefore in God there cannot be any accident.

I ANSWER THAT, From all we have said, it is clear there can be no accident in God. First, because a subject is compared to its accidents as potentiality to actuality; for a subject is in some sense made actual by its accidents. But there can be no potentiality in God, as was shown (Q. 2, A. 3). Second, because God is His own existence; and as Boethius says (*Hebdom.*), *although every essence may have something superadded to it, this cannot apply to absolute being*: thus a heated substance can have something extraneous to heat added to it, as whiteness, nevertheless absolute heat can have nothing else than heat. Third, because what is essential is prior to what is accidental. Whence as God is absolute primal being, there can be in Him nothing accidental. Neither can He have any essential accidents (as the capability of laughing is an essential accident of man), because such accidents are caused by the constituent principles of the subject. Now there can be nothing caused in God, since He is the first cause. Hence it follows that there is no accident in God.

REPLY OBJ. 1: Virtue and wisdom are not predicated of God and of us univocally. Hence it does not follow that there are accidents in God as there are in us.

REPLY OBJ. 2: Since substance is prior to its accidents, the principles of accidents are reducible to the principles of

principia substantiae sicut in priora. Quamvis Deus non sit primum contentum in genere substantiae, sed primum extra omne genus, respectu totius esse.

the substance as to that which is prior; although God is not first as if contained in the genus of substance; yet He is first in respect to all being, outside of every genus.

Article 7

Whether God Is Altogether Simple?

AD SEPTIMUM SIC PROCEDITUR. Videtur quod Deus non sit omnino simplex. Ea enim quae sunt a Deo, imitantur ipsum, unde a primo ente sunt omnia entia, et a primo bono sunt omnia bona. Sed in rebus quae sunt a Deo, nihil est omnino simplex. Ergo Deus non est omnino simplex.

PRAETEREA, omne quod est melius, Deo attribuendum est. Sed, apud nos, composita sunt meliora simplicibus, sicut corpora mixta elementis, et elementa suis partibus. Ergo non est dicendum quod Deus sit omnino simplex.

SED CONTRA est quod Augustinus dicit, VI de Trin., quod *Deus vere et summe simplex est.*

RESPONDEO dicendum quod Deum omnino esse simplicem, multipliciter potest esse manifestum. Primo quidem per supradicta. Cum enim in Deo non sit compositio, neque quantitativarum partium, quia corpus non est; neque compositio formae et materiae, neque in eo sit aliud natura et suppositum; neque aliud essentia et esse, neque in eo sit compositio generis et differentiae; neque subiecti et accidentis, manifestum est quod Deus nullo modo compositus est, sed est omnino simplex. Secundo, quia omne compositum est posterius suis componentibus, et dependens ex eis. Deus autem est primum ens, ut supra ostensum est. Tertio, quia omne compositum causam habet, quae enim secundum se diversa sunt, non conveniunt in aliquod unum nisi per aliquam causam adunantem ipsa. Deus autem non habet causam, ut supra ostensum est, cum sit prima causa efficiens. Quarto, quia in omni composito oportet esse potentiam et actum, quod in Deo non est, quia vel una partium est actus respectu alterius; vel saltem omnes partes sunt sicut in potentia respectu totius. Quinto, quia omne compositum est aliquid quod non convenit alicui suarum partium. Et quidem in totis dissimilium partium, manifestum est, nulla enim partium hominis est homo, neque aliqua partium pedis est pes. In totis vero similium partium, licet aliquid quod dicitur de toto, dicatur de parte, sicut pars aeris est aer, et aquae aqua; aliquid tamen dicitur de toto, quod non convenit alicui partium, non enim si tota aqua est bicubita, et pars eius. Sic igitur in omni composito est aliquid quod non est ipsum. Hoc autem etsi possit dici de habente formam, quod scilicet

OBJECTION 1: It seems that God is not altogether simple. For whatever is from God must imitate Him. Thus from the first being are all beings; and from the first good is all good. But in the things which God has made, nothing is altogether simple. Therefore neither is God altogether simple.

OBJ. 2: Further, whatever is best must be attributed to God. But with us that which is composite is better than that which is simple; thus, chemical compounds are better than simple elements, and animals than the parts that compose them. Therefore it cannot be said that God is altogether simple.

ON THE CONTRARY, Augustine says (*De Trin.* iv, 6,7): *God is truly and absolutely simple.*

I ANSWER THAT, The absolute simplicity of God may be shown in many ways. First, from the previous articles of this question. For there is neither composition of quantitative parts in God, since He is not a body; nor composition of matter and form; nor does His nature differ from His suppositum; nor His essence from His existence; neither is there in Him composition of genus and difference, nor of subject and accident. Therefore, it is clear that God is nowise composite, but is altogether simple. Second, because every composite is posterior to its component parts, and is dependent on them; but God is the first being, as shown above (Q. 2, A. 3). Third, because every composite has a cause, for things in themselves different cannot unite unless something causes them to unite. But God is uncaused, as shown above (Q. 2, A. 3), since He is the first efficient cause. Fourth, because in every composite there must be potentiality and actuality; but this does not apply to God; for either one of the parts actuates another, or at least all the parts are potential to the whole. Fifth, because nothing composite can be predicated of any single one of its parts. And this is evident in a whole made up of dissimilar parts; for no part of a man is a man, nor any of the parts of the foot, a foot. But in wholes made up of similar parts, although something which is predicated of the whole may be predicated of a part (as a part of the air is air, and a part of water, water), nevertheless certain things are predicable of the whole which cannot be predicated of any of the parts; for instance, if the whole volume of water is two cubits, no part of it can be two cubits. Thus in every composite there is something which is not it itself. But, even if this could

habeat aliquid quod non est ipsum (puta in albo est aliquid quod non pertinet ad rationem albi), tamen in ipsa forma nihil est alienum. Unde, cum Deus sit ipsa forma, vel potius ipsum esse, nullo modo compositus esse potest. Et hanc rationem tangit Hilarius, VII de Trin., dicens, *Deus, qui virtus est, ex infirmis non continetur, neque qui lux est, ex obscuris coaptatur.*

AD PRIMUM ergo dicendum quod ea quae sunt a Deo, imitantur Deum sicut causata primam causam. Est autem hoc de ratione causati, quod sit aliquo modo compositum, quia ad minus esse eius est aliud quam quod quid est, ut infra patebit.

AD SECUNDUM dicendum quod apud nos composita sunt meliora simplicibus, quia perfectio bonitatis creaturae non invenitur in uno simplici, sed in multis. Sed perfectio divinae bonitatis invenitur in uno simplici, ut infra ostendetur.

be said of whatever has a form, viz. that it has something which is not it itself, as in a white object there is something which does not belong to the essence of white; nevertheless in the form itself, there is nothing besides itself. And so, since God is absolute form, or rather absolute being, He can be in no way composite. Hilary implies this argument, when he says (*De Trin.* vii): *God, Who is strength, is not made up of things that are weak; nor is He Who is light, composed of things that are dim.*

REPLY OBJ. 1: Whatever is from God imitates Him, as caused things imitate the first cause. But it is of the essence of a thing to be in some sort composite; because at least its existence differs from its essence, as will be shown hereafter (Q. 4, A. 3).

REPLY OBJ. 2: With us composite things are better than simple things, because the perfections of created goodness cannot be found in one simple thing, but in many things. But the perfection of divine goodness is found in one simple thing (QQ. 4, A. 1, and 6, A. 2).

Article 8

Whether God Enters into the Composition of Other Things?

AD OCTAVUM SIC PROCEDITUR. Videtur quod Deus in compositionem aliorum veniat. Dicit enim Dionysius, IV cap. Cael. Hier., *esse omnium est, quae super esse est deitas.* Sed esse omnium intrat compositionem uniuscuiusque. Ergo Deus in compositionem aliorum venit.

PRAETEREA, Deus est forma, dicit enim Augustinus, in libro de verbis domini, quod *verbum Dei (quod est Deus) est forma quaedam non formata.* Sed forma est pars compositi. Ergo Deus est pars alicuius compositi.

PRAETEREA, quaecumque sunt et nullo modo differunt, sunt idem. Sed Deus et materia prima sunt, et nullo modo differunt. Ergo penitus sunt idem. Sed materia prima intrat compositionem rerum. Ergo et Deus. Probatio mediae, quaecumque differunt, aliquibus differentiis differunt, et ita oportet ea esse composita; sed Deus et materia prima sunt omnino simplicia; ergo nullo modo differunt.

SED CONTRA est quod dicit Dionysius, II cap. de Div. Nom., quod neque tactus est eius (scilicet Dei), *neque alia quaedam ad partes commiscendi communio.*

PRAETEREA, dicitur in libro de causis, quod *causa prima regit omnes res, praeterquam commisceatur eis.*

RESPONDEO dicendum quod circa hoc fuerunt tres errores. Quidam enim posuerunt quod Deus esset anima mundi, ut patet per Augustinum in Lib. VII de civitate

OBJECTION 1: It seems that God enters into the composition of other things, for Dionysius says (*Coel. Hier.* iv): *The being of all things is that which is above being—the Godhead.* But the being of all things enters into the composition of everything. Therefore God enters into the composition of other things.

OBJ. 2: Further, God is a form; for Augustine says (*De Verb. Dom.* Serm. xxxviii) that, *the word of God, which is God, is an uncreated form.* But a form is part of a compound. Therefore God is part of some compound.

OBJ. 3: Further, whatever things exist, in no way differing from each other, are the same. But God and primary matter exist, and in no way differ from each other. Therefore they are absolutely the same. But primary matter enters into the composition things. Therefore also does God. Proof of the minor—whatever things differ, they differ by some differences, and therefore must be composite. But God and primary matter are altogether simple. Therefore they nowise differ from each other.

ON THE CONTRARY, Dionysius says (*Div. Nom.* ii): *There can be no touching Him*, i.e., God, *nor any other union with Him by mingling part with part.*

Further, *the first cause rules all things without commingling with them*, as the Philosopher says (*De Causis*).

I ANSWER THAT, On this point there have been three errors. Some have affirmed that God is the world-soul, as is clear from Augustine (*De Civ. Dei* vii, 6). This is practically

Dei, et ad hoc etiam reducitur, quod quidam dixerunt Deum esse animam primi caeli. Alii autem dixerunt Deum esse principium formale omnium rerum. Et haec dicitur fuisse opinio Almarianorum. Sed tertius error fuit David de Dinando, qui stultissime posuit Deum esse materiam primam. Omnia enim haec manifestam continent falsitatem, neque est possibile Deum aliquo modo in compositionem alicuius venire, nec sicut principium formale, nec sicut principium materiale. Primo quidem, quia supra diximus Deum esse primam causam efficientem. Causa autem efficiens cum forma rei factae non incidit in idem numero, sed solum in idem specie, homo enim generat hominem. Materia vero cum causa efficiente non incidit in idem numero, nec in idem specie, quia hoc est in potentia, illud vero in actu. Secundo, quia cum Deus sit prima causa efficiens, eius est primo et per se agere. Quod autem venit in compositionem alicuius, non est primo et per se agens, sed magis compositum, non enim manus agit, sed homo per manum; et ignis calefacit per calorem. Unde Deus non potest esse pars alicuius compositi. Tertio, quia nulla pars compositi potest esse simpliciter prima in entibus; neque etiam materia et forma, quae sunt primae partes compositorum. Nam materia est in potentia, potentia autem est posterior actu simpliciter, ut ex dictis patet. Forma autem quae est pars compositi, est forma participata, sicut autem participans est posterius eo quod est per essentiam, ita et ipsum participatum; sicut ignis in ignitis est posterior eo quod est per essentiam. Ostensum est autem quod Deus est primum ens simpliciter.

AD PRIMUM ergo dicendum quod deitas dicitur esse omnium effective et exemplariter, non autem per essentiam.

AD SECUNDUM dicendum quod verbum est forma exemplaris, non autem forma quae est pars compositi.

AD TERTIUM dicendum quod simplicia non differunt aliquibus aliis differentiis, hoc enim compositorum est. Homo enim et equus differunt rationali et irrationali differentiis, quae quidem differentiae non differunt amplius ab invicem aliis differentiis. Unde, si fiat vis in verbo, non proprie dicuntur differre, sed diversa esse, nam, secundum philosophum X Metaphys., *diversum absolute dicitur, sed omne differens aliquo differt.* Unde, si fiat vis in verbo, materia prima et Deus non differunt, sed sunt diversa seipsis. Unde non sequitur quod sint idem.

the same as the opinion of those who assert that God is the soul of the highest heaven. Again, others have said that God is the formal principle of all things; and this was the theory of the Almaricians. The third error is that of David of Dinant, who most absurdly taught that God was primary matter. Now all these contain manifest untruth; since it is not possible for God to enter into the composition of anything, either as a formal or a material principle. First, because God is the first efficient cause. Now the efficient cause is not identical numerically with the form of the thing caused, but only specifically: for man begets man. But primary matter can be neither numerically nor specifically identical with an efficient cause; for the former is merely potential, while the latter is actual. Second, because, since God is the first efficient cause, to act belongs to Him primarily and essentially. But that which enters into composition with anything does not act primarily and essentially, but rather the composite so acts; for the hand does not act, but the man by his hand; and, fire warms by its heat. Hence God cannot be part of a compound. Third, because no part of a compound can be absolutely primal among beings—not even matter, nor form, though they are the primal parts of every compound. For matter is merely potential; and potentiality is absolutely posterior to actuality, as is clear from the foregoing (Q. 3, A. 1): while a form which is part of a compound is a participated form; and as that which participates is posterior to that which is essential, so likewise is that which is participated; as fire in ignited objects is posterior to fire that is essentially such. Now it has been proved that God is absolutely primal being (Q. 2, A. 3).

REPLY OBJ. 1: The Godhead is called the being of all things, as their efficient and exemplar cause, but not as being their essence.

REPLY OBJ. 2: The Word is an exemplar form; but not a form that is part of a compound.

REPLY OBJ. 3: Simple things do not differ by added differences—for this is the property of compounds. Thus man and horse differ by their differences, rational and irrational; which differences, however, do not differ from each other by other differences. Hence, to be quite accurate, it is better to say that they are, not different, but diverse. Hence, according to the Philosopher (*Metaph.* x), *things which are diverse are absolutely distinct, but things which are different differ by something.* Therefore, strictly speaking, primary matter and God do not differ, but are by their very being, diverse. Hence it does not follow they are the same.

QUESTION 4

THE PERFECTION OF GOD

Post considerationem divinae simplicitatis, de perfectione ipsius Dei dicendum est.

Et quia unumquodque, secundum quod perfectum est, sic dicitur bonum, primo agendum est de perfectione divina; secundo de eius bonitate.

Circa primum quaeruntur tria.

Primo, utrum Deus sit perfectus.

Secundo, utrum Deus sit universaliter perfectus omnium in se perfectiones habens.

Tertio, utrum creaturae similes Deo dici possint.

Having considered the divine simplicity, we treat next of God's perfection.

Now because everything in so far as it is perfect is called good, we shall speak first of the divine perfection; second of the divine goodness.

Concerning the first there are three points of inquiry:

(1) Whether God is perfect?

(2) Whether God is perfect universally, as having in Himself the perfections of all things?

(3) Whether creatures can be said to be like God?

Article 1

Whether God is Perfect?

AD PRIMUM SIC PROCEDITUR. Videtur quod esse perfectum non conveniat Deo. Perfectum enim dicitur quasi totaliter factum. Sed Deo non convenit esse factum. Ergo nec esse perfectum.

PRAETEREA, Deus est primum rerum principium. Sed principia rerum videntur esse imperfecta, semen enim est principium animalium et plantarum. Ergo Deus est imperfectus.

PRAETEREA, ostensum est supra quod essentia Dei est ipsum esse. Sed ipsum esse videtur esse imperfectissimum, cum sit communissimum, et recipiens omnium additiones. Ergo Deus est imperfectus.

SED CONTRA est quod dicitur Matt. V, *estote perfecti, sicut et pater vester caelestis perfectus est.*

RESPONDEO dicendum quod, sicut philosophus narrat in XII Metaphys., quidam antiqui philosophi, scilicet Pythagorici et Speusippus, non attribuerunt optimum et perfectissimum primo principio. Cuius ratio est, quia philosophi antiqui consideraverunt principium materiale tantum, primum autem principium materiale imperfectissimum est. Cum enim materia, inquantum huiusmodi, sit in potentia, oportet quod primum principium materiale sit maxime in potentia; et ita maxime imperfectum. Deus autem ponitur primum principium, non materiale, sed in genere causae efficientis, et hoc oportet esse perfectissimum. Sicut enim materia, inquantum huiusmodi, est in potentia; ita agens, inquantum huiusmodi, est in actu. Unde primum principium activum

OBJECTION 1: It seems that perfection does not belong to God. For we say a thing is perfect if it is completely made. But it does not befit God to be made. Therefore He is not perfect.

OBJ. 2: Further, God is the first beginning of things. But the beginnings of things seem to be imperfect, as seed is the beginning of animal and vegetable life. Therefore God is imperfect.

OBJ. 3: Further, as shown above (Q. 3, A. 4), God's essence is existence. But existence seems most imperfect, since it is most universal and receptive of all modification. Therefore God is imperfect.

ON THE CONTRARY, It is written: *Be you perfect as also your heavenly Father is perfect* (Matt 5:48).

I ANSWER THAT, As the Philosopher relates (*Metaph.* xii), some ancient philosophers, namely, the Pythagoreans and Leucippus, did not predicate *best* and *most perfect* of the first principle. The reason was that the ancient philosophers considered only a material principle; and a material principle is most imperfect. For since matter as such is merely potential, the first material principle must be simply potential, and thus most imperfect. Now God is the first principle, not material, but in the order of efficient cause, which must be most perfect. For just as matter, as such, is merely potential, an agent, as such, is in the state of actuality. Hence, the first active principle must needs be most actual, and therefore most perfect; for a thing is perfect in proportion to its state of actuality, because we call

oportet maxime esse in actu, et per consequens maxime esse perfectum. Secundum hoc enim dicitur aliquid esse perfectum, secundum quod est actu, nam perfectum dicitur, cui nihil deest secundum modum suae perfectionis.

AD PRIMUM ergo dicendum quod, sicut dicit Gregorius, *balbutiendo ut possumus, excelsa Dei resonamus, quod enim factum non est, perfectum proprie dici non potest.* Sed quia in his quae fiunt, tunc dicitur esse aliquid perfectum, cum de potentia educitur in actum; transumitur hoc nomen perfectum ad significandum omne illud cui non deest esse in actu, sive hoc habeat per modum factionis, sive non.

AD SECUNDUM dicendum quod principium materiale, quod apud nos imperfectum invenitur, non potest esse simpliciter primum, sed praeceditur ab alio perfecto. Nam semen, licet sit principium animalis generati ex semine, tamen habet ante se animal vel plantam unde deciditur. Oportet enim ante id quod est in potentia, esse aliquid actu, cum ens in potentia non reducatur in actum, nisi per aliquod ens in actu.

AD TERTIUM dicendum quod ipsum esse est perfectissimum omnium, comparatur enim ad omnia ut actus. Nihil enim habet actualitatem, nisi inquantum est, unde ipsum esse est actualitas omnium rerum, et etiam ipsarum formarum. Unde non comparatur ad alia sicut recipiens ad receptum, sed magis sicut receptum ad recipiens. Cum enim dico esse hominis, vel equi, vel cuiuscumque alterius, ipsum esse consideratur ut formale et receptum, non autem ut illud cui competit esse.

that perfect which lacks nothing of the mode of its perfection.

REPLY OBJ. 1: As Gregory says (*Moral.* v, 26,29): *Though our lips can only stammer, we yet chant the high things of God.* For that which is not made is improperly called perfect. Nevertheless because created things are then called perfect, when from potentiality they are brought into actuality, this word *perfect* signifies whatever is not wanting in actuality, whether this be by way of perfection or not.

REPLY OBJ. 2: The material principle which with us is found to be imperfect, cannot be absolutely primal; but must be preceded by something perfect. For seed, though it be the principle of animal life reproduced through seed, has previous to it, the animal or plant from which is came. Because, previous to that which is potential, must be that which is actual; since a potential being can only be reduced into act by some being already actual.

REPLY OBJ. 3: Existence is the most perfect of all things, for it is compared to all things as that by which they are made actual; for nothing has actuality except so far as it exists. Hence existence is that which actuates all things, even their forms. Therefore it is not compared to other things as the receiver is to the received; but rather as the received to the receiver. When therefore I speak of the existence of man, or horse, or anything else, existence is considered a formal principle, and as something received; and not as that which exists.

Article 2

Whether the Perfections of All Things Are in God?

AD SECUNDUM SIC PROCEDITUR. Videtur quod in Deo non sint perfectiones omnium rerum. Deus enim simplex est, ut ostensum est. Sed perfectiones rerum sunt multae et diversae. Ergo in Deo non sunt omnes perfectiones rerum.

PRAETEREA, opposita non possunt esse in eodem. Sed perfectiones rerum sunt oppositae, unaquaeque enim species perficitur per suam differentiam specificam; differentiae autem quibus dividitur genus et constituuntur species, sunt oppositae. Cum ergo opposita non possint simul esse in eodem, videtur quod non omnes rerum perfectiones sint in Deo.

PRAETEREA, vivens est perfectius quam ens, et sapiens quam vivens, ergo et vivere est perfectius quam esse, et sapere quam vivere. Sed essentia Dei est ipsum

OBJECTION 1: It seems that the perfections of all things are not in God. For God is simple, as shown above (Q. 3, A. 7); whereas the perfections of things are many and diverse. Therefore the perfections of all things are not in God.

OBJ. 2: Further, opposites cannot coexist. Now the perfections of things are opposed to each other, for each thing is perfected by its specific difference. But the differences by which genera are divided, and species constituted, are opposed to each other. Therefore because opposites cannot coexist in the same subject, it seems that the perfections of all things are not in God.

OBJ. 3: Further, a living thing is more perfect than what merely exists; and an intelligent thing than what merely lives. Therefore life is more perfect than existence; and knowledge than life. But the essence of God is existence

esse. Ergo non habet in se perfectionem vitae et sapientiae, et alias huiusmodi perfectiones.

SED CONTRA est quod dicit Dionysius, cap. V de Div. Nom., quod *Deus in uno existentia omnia praehabet.*

RESPONDEO dicendum quod in Deo sunt perfectiones omnium rerum. Unde et dicitur universaliter perfectus, quia non deest ei aliqua nobilitas quae inveniatur in aliquo genere, ut dicit Commentator in V Metaphys. Et hoc quidem ex duobus considerari potest. Primo quidem, per hoc quod quidquid perfectionis est in effectu, oportet inveniri in causa effectiva, vel secundum eandem rationem, si sit agens univocum, ut homo generat hominem; vel eminentiori modo, si sit, agens aequivocum, sicut in sole est similitudo eorum quae generantur per virtutem solis. Manifestum est enim quod effectus praeexistit virtute in causa agente, praeexistere autem in virtute causae agentis, non est praeexistere imperfectiori modo, sed perfectiori; licet praeexistere in potentia causae materialis, sit praeexistere imperfectiori modo, eo quod materia, inquantum huiusmodi, est imperfecta; agens vero, inquantum huiusmodi, est perfectum. Cum ergo Deus sit prima causa effectiva rerum, oportet omnium rerum perfectiones praeexistere in Deo secundum eminentiorem modum. Et hanc rationem tangit Dionysius, cap. V de Div. Nom., dicens de Deo quod *non hoc quidem est, hoc autem non est, sed omnia est, ut omnium causa.* Secundo vero, ex hoc quod supra ostensum est, quod Deus est ipsum esse per se subsistens, ex quo oportet quod totam perfectionem essendi in se contineat. Manifestum est enim quod, si aliquod calidum non habeat totam perfectionem calidi, hoc ideo est, quia calor non participatur secundum perfectam rationem, sed si calor esset per se subsistens, non posset ei aliquid deesse de virtute caloris. Unde, cum Deus sit ipsum esse subsistens, nihil de perfectione essendi potest ei deesse. Omnium autem perfectiones pertinent ad perfectionem essendi, secundum hoc enim aliqua perfecta sunt, quod aliquo modo esse habent. Unde sequitur quod nullius rei perfectio Deo desit. Et hanc etiam rationem tangit Dionysius, cap. V de Div. Nom., dicens quod *Deus non quodammodo est existens, sed simpliciter et incircumscripte totum in seipso uniformiter esse praeaccipit,* et postea subdit quod *ipse est esse subsistentibus.*

AD PRIMUM ergo dicendum quod, *sicut sol,* ut dicit Dionysius, cap. V de Div. Nom., *sensibilium substantias et qualitates multas et differentes, ipse unus existens et uniformiter lucendo, in seipso uniformiter praeaccipit; ita multo magis in causa omnium necesse est praeexistere omnia secundum naturalem unionem.* Et sic, quae sunt diversa et opposita in seipsis, in Deo praeexistunt ut unum, absque detrimento simplicitatis ipsius.

ET PER HOC patet solutio ad secundum.

AD TERTIUM dicendum quod, sicut in eodem capite idem Dionysius dicit, licet ipsum esse sit perfectius

itself. Therefore He has not the perfections of life, and knowledge, and other similar perfections.

ON THE CONTRARY, Dionysius says (*Div. Nom.* v) that *God in His one existence prepossesses all things.*

I ANSWER THAT, All created perfections are in God. Hence He is spoken of as universally perfect, because He lacks not (says the Commentator, *Metaph.* v) any excellence which may be found in any genus. This may be seen from two considerations. First, because whatever perfection exists in an effect must be found in the effective cause: either in the same formality, if it is a univocal agent—as when man reproduces man; or in a more eminent degree, if it is an equivocal agent—thus in the sun is the likeness of whatever is generated by the sun's power. Now it is plain that the effect pre-exists virtually in the efficient cause: and although to pre-exist in the potentiality of a material cause is to pre-exist in a more imperfect way, since matter as such is imperfect, and an agent as such is perfect; still to pre-exist virtually in the efficient cause is to pre-exist not in a more imperfect, but in a more perfect way. Since therefore God is the first effective cause of things, the perfections of all things must pre-exist in God in a more eminent way. Dionysius implies the same line of argument by saying of God (*Div. Nom.* v): *It is not that He is this and not that, but that He is all, as the cause of all.* Second, from what has been already proved, God is existence itself, of itself subsistent (Q. 3, A. 4). Consequently, He must contain within Himself the whole perfection of being. For it is clear that if some hot thing has not the whole perfection of heat, this is because heat is not participated in its full perfection; but if this heat were self-subsisting, nothing of the virtue of heat would be wanting to it. Since therefore God is subsisting being itself, nothing of the perfection of being can be wanting to Him. Now all created perfections are included in the perfection of being; for things are perfect, precisely so far as they have being after some fashion. It follows therefore that the perfection of no one thing is wanting to God. This line of argument, too, is implied by Dionysius (*Div. Nom.* v), when he says that, *God exists not in any single mode, but embraces all being within Himself, absolutely, without limitation, uniformly;* and afterwards he adds that, *He is the very existence to subsisting things.*

REPLY OBJ. 1: *Even as the sun,* as Dionysius remarks, (*Div. Nom.* v), *while remaining one and shining uniformly, contains within itself first and uniformly the substances of sensible things, and many and diverse qualities; a fortiori should all things in a kind of natural unity pre-exist in the cause of all things;* and thus things diverse and in themselves opposed to each other, pre-exist in God as one, without injury to His simplicity.

THIS SUFFICES for the Reply to the Second Objection.

REPLY OBJ. 3: The same Dionysius says (*Div. Nom.* v) that, although existence is more perfect than life, and life

quam vita, et ipsa vita quam ipsa sapientia, si considerentur secundum quod distinguuntur ratione, tamen vivens est perfectius quam ens tantum, quia vivens etiam est ens; et sapiens est ens et vivens. Licet igitur ens non includat in se vivens et sapiens, quia non oportet quod illud quod participat esse, participet ipsum secundum omnem modum essendi, tamen ipsum esse Dei includit in se vitam et sapientiam; quia nulla de perfectionibus essendi potest deesse ei quod est ipsum esse subsistens.

than wisdom, if they are considered as distinguished in idea; nevertheless, a living thing is more perfect than what merely exists, because living things also exist and intelligent things both exist and live. Although therefore existence does not include life and wisdom, because that which participates in existence need not participate in every mode of existence; nevertheless God's existence includes in itself life and wisdom, because nothing of the perfection of being can be wanting to Him who is subsisting being itself.

Article 3

Whether Any Creature Can Be Like God?

AD TERTIUM SIC PROCEDITUR. Videtur quod nulla creatura possit esse similis Deo. Dicitur enim in Psalmo, *non est similis tui in diis, domine.* Sed inter omnes creaturas, excellentiores sunt quae dicuntur dii participative. Multo ergo minus aliae creaturae possunt dici Deo similes.

PRAETEREA, similitudo est comparatio quaedam. Non est autem comparatio eorum quae sunt diversorum generum; ergo nec similitudo, non enim dicimus quod dulcedo sit similis albedini. Sed nulla creatura est eiusdem generis cum Deo, cum Deus non sit in genere, ut supra ostensum est. Ergo nulla creatura est similis Deo.

PRAETEREA, similia dicuntur quae conveniunt in forma. Sed nihil convenit cum Deo in forma, nullius enim rei essentia est ipsum esse, nisi solius Dei. Ergo nulla creatura potest esse similis Deo.

PRAETEREA, in similibus est mutua similitudo, nam simile est simili simile. Si igitur aliqua creatura est similis Deo, et Deus erit similis alicui creaturae. Quod est contra id quod dicitur Isaiae XL, *cui similem fecistis Deum?*

SED CONTRA est quod dicitur Gen. I, *faciamus hominem ad imaginem et similitudinem nostram*; et I Ioann. III, *cum apparuerit, similes ei erimus.*

RESPONDEO dicendum quod, cum similitudo attendatur secundum convenientiam vel communicationem in forma, multiplex est similitudo, secundum multos modos communicandi in forma. Quaedam enim dicuntur similia, quae communicant in eadem forma secundum eandem rationem, et secundum eundem modum, et haec non solum dicuntur similia, sed aequalia in sua similitudine; sicut duo aequaliter alba, dicuntur similia in albedine. Et haec est perfectissima similitudo. Alio modo dicuntur similia, quae communicant in forma secundum eandem rationem, et non secundum eundem modum, sed secundum magis et minus; ut minus album dicitur simile magis albo. Et haec est similitudo imperfecta. Tertio modo dicuntur aliqua similia, quae communicant in eadem forma, sed non secundum eandem

OBJECTION 1: It seems that no creature can be like God. For it is written (Ps 85:8): *There is none among the gods like unto Thee, O Lord.* But of all creatures the most excellent are those which are called by participation gods. Therefore still less can other creatures be said to be like God.

OBJ. 2: Further, likeness implies comparison. But there can be no comparison between things in a different genus. Therefore neither can there be any likeness. Thus we do not say that sweetness is like whiteness. But no creature is in the same genus as God: since God is no genus, as shown above (Q. 3, A. 5). Therefore no creature is like God.

OBJ. 3: Further, we speak of those things as like which agree in form. But nothing can agree with God in form; for, save in God alone, essence and existence differ. Therefore no creature can be like to God.

OBJ. 4: Further, among like things there is mutual likeness; for like is like to like. If therefore any creature is like God, God will be like some creature, which is against what is said by Isaias: *To whom have you likened God?* (Isa 40:18).

ON THE CONTRARY, It is written: *Let us make man to our image and likeness* (Gen 1:26), and: *When He shall appear we shall be like to Him* (1 John 3:2).

I ANSWER THAT, Since likeness is based upon agreement or communication in form, it varies according to the many modes of communication in form. Some things are said to be like, which communicate in the same form according to the same formality, and according to the same mode; and these are said to be not merely like, but equal in their likeness; as two things equally white are said to be alike in whiteness; and this is the most perfect likeness. In another way, we speak of things as alike which communicate in form according to the same formality, though not according to the same measure, but according to more or less, as something less white is said to be like another thing more white; and this is imperfect likeness. In a third way some things are said to be alike which communicate in the same form, but not according to the same formality; as we

rationem; ut patet in agentibus non univocis. Cum enim omne agens agat sibi simile inquantum est agens, agit autem unumquodque secundum suam formam, necesse est quod in effectu sit similitudo formae agentis. Si ergo agens sit contentum in eadem specie cum suo effectu, erit similitudo inter faciens et factum in forma, secundum eandem rationem speciei; sicut homo generat hominem. Si autem agens non sit contentum in eadem specie, erit similitudo, sed non secundum eandem rationem speciei, sicut ea quae generantur ex virtute solis, accedunt quidem ad aliquam similitudinem solis, non tamen ut recipiant formam solis secundum similitudinem speciei, sed secundum similitudinem generis. Si igitur sit aliquod agens, quod non in genere contineatur, effectus eius adhuc magis accedent remote ad similitudinem formae agentis, non tamen ita quod participent similitudinem formae agentis secundum eandem rationem speciei aut generis, sed secundum aliqualem analogiam, sicut ipsum esse est commune omnibus. Et hoc modo illa quae sunt a Deo, assimilantur ei inquantum sunt entia, ut primo et universali principio totius esse.

AD PRIMUM ergo dicendum quod, sicut dicit Dionysius cap. IX de Div. Nom., cum sacra Scriptura dicit aliquid non esse simile Deo, *non est contrarium assimilationi ad ipsum. Eadem enim sunt similia Deo, et dissimilia, similia quidem secundum quod imitantur ipsum, prout contingit eum imitari qui non perfecte imitabilis est dissimilia vero, secundum quod deficiunt a sua causa*; non solum secundum intensionem et remissionem, sicut minus album deficit a magis albo; sed quia non est convenientia nec secundum speciem nec secundum genus.

AD SECUNDUM dicendum quod Deus non se habet ad creaturas sicut res diversorum generum, sed sicut id quod est extra omne genus, et principium omnium generum.

AD TERTIUM dicendum quod non dicitur esse similitudo creaturae ad Deum propter communicantiam in forma secundum eandem rationem generis et speciei, sed secundum analogiam tantum; prout scilicet Deus est ens per essentiam, et alia per participationem.

AD QUARTUM dicendum quod, licet aliquo modo concedatur quod creatura sit similis Deo, nullo tamen modo concedendum est quod Deus sit similis creaturae, quia, ut dicit Dionysius cap. IX de Div. Nom., *in his quae unius ordinis sunt, recipitur mutua similitudo, non autem in causa et causato*, dicimus enim quod imago sit similis homini, et non e converso. Et similiter dici potest aliquo modo quod creatura sit similis Deo, non tamen quod Deus sit similis creaturae.

see in non-univocal agents. For since every agent reproduces itself so far as it is an agent, and everything acts according to the manner of its form, the effect must in some way resemble the form of the agent. If therefore the agent is contained in the same species as its effect, there will be a likeness in form between that which makes and that which is made, according to the same formality of the species; as man reproduces man. If, however, the agent and its effect are not contained in the same species, there will be a likeness, but not according to the formality of the same species; as things generated by the sun's heat may be in some sort spoken of as like the sun, not as though they received the form of the sun in its specific likeness, but in its generic likeness. Therefore if there is an agent not contained in any genus, its effect will still more distantly reproduce the form of the agent, not, that is, so as to participate in the likeness of the agent's form according to the same specific or generic formality, but only according to some sort of analogy; as existence is common to all. In this way all created things, so far as they are beings, are like God as the first and universal principle of all being.

REPLY OBJ. 1: As Dionysius says (*Div. Nom.* ix), when Holy Writ declares that nothing is like God, it does not mean to deny all likeness to Him. For, *the same things can be like and unlike to God: like, according as they imitate Him, as far as He, Who is not perfectly imitable, can be imitated; unlike according as they fall short of their cause*, not merely in intensity and remission, as that which is less white falls short of that which is more white; but because they are not in agreement, specifically or generically.

REPLY OBJ. 2: God is not related to creatures as though belonging to a different genus, but as transcending every genus, and as the principle of all genera.

REPLY OBJ. 3: Likeness of creatures to God is not affirmed on account of agreement in form according to the formality of the same genus or species, but solely according to analogy, inasmuch as God is essential being, whereas other things are beings by participation.

REPLY OBJ. 4: Although it may be admitted that creatures are in some sort like God, it must nowise be admitted that God is like creatures; because, as Dionysius says (*Div. Nom.* ix): *A mutual likeness may be found between things of the same order, but not between a cause and that which is caused*. For, we say that a statue is like a man, but not conversely; so also a creature can be spoken of as in some sort like God; but not that God is like a creature.

QUESTION 5

GOODNESS IN GENERAL

Deinde quaeritur de bono,

et primo de bono in communi; secundo de bonitate Dei.

Circa primum quaeruntur sex.

Primo, utrum bonum et ens sint idem secundum rem.

Secundo, supposito quod differant ratione tantum, quid sit prius secundum rationem, utrum bonum vel ens.

Tertio, supposito quod ens sit prius, utrum omne ens sit bonum.

Quarto, ad quam causam ratio boni reducatur.

Quinto, utrum ratio boni consistat in modo, specie et ordine.

Sexto, quomodo dividatur bonum in honestum, utile et delectabile.

We next consider goodness:

First, goodness in general. Second, the goodness of God.

Under the first head there are six points of inquiry:

(1) Whether goodness and being are the same really?

(2) Granted that they differ only in idea, which is prior in thought?

(3) Granted that being is prior, whether every being is good?

(4) To what cause should goodness be reduced?

(5) Whether goodness consists in mode, species, and order?

(6) Whether goodness is divided into the virtuous, the useful, and the pleasant?

Article 1

Whether Goodness Differs Really from Being?

AD PRIMUM SIC PROCEDITUR. Videtur quod bonum differat secundum rem ab ente. Dicit enim Boethius, in libro de Hebdom., *intueor in rebus aliud esse quod sunt bona, et aliud esse quod sunt.* Ergo bonum et ens differunt secundum rem.

PRAETEREA, nihil informatur seipso. *Sed bonum dicitur per informationem entis*, ut habetur in commento libri de causis. Ergo bonum differt secundum rem ab ente.

PRAETEREA, bonum suscipit magis et minus. Esse autem non suscipit magis et minus. Ergo bonum differt secundum rem ab ente.

SED CONTRA est quod Augustinus dicit, in libro de doctrina Christiana, quod *inquantum sumus, boni sumus.*

RESPONDEO dicendum quod bonum et ens sunt idem secundum rem, sed differunt secundum rationem tantum. Quod sic patet. Ratio enim boni in hoc consistit, quod aliquid sit appetibile, unde philosophus, in I Ethic., dicit quod *bonum est quod omnia appetunt.* Manifestum est autem quod unumquodque est appetibile secundum quod est perfectum, nam omnia appetunt suam perfectionem. Intantum est autem perfectum unumquodque, inquantum est actu, unde manifestum est quod intantum est aliquid bonum, inquantum est ens, esse enim

OBJECTION 1: It seems that goodness differs really from being. For Boethius says (*De Hebdom.*): *I perceive that in nature the fact that things are good is one thing: that they are is another.* Therefore goodness and being really differ.

OBJ. 2: Further, nothing can be its own form. *But that is called good which has the form of being,* according to the commentary on *De Causis.* Therefore goodness differs really from being.

OBJ. 3: Further, goodness can be more or less. But being cannot be more or less. Therefore goodness differs really from being.

ON THE CONTRARY, Augustine says (*De Doctr. Christ.* i, 42) that, *inasmuch as we exist we are good.*

I ANSWER THAT, Goodness and being are really the same, and differ only in idea; which is clear from the following argument. The essence of goodness consists in this, that it is in some way desirable. Hence the Philosopher says (*Ethic.* i): *Goodness is what all desire.* Now it is clear that a thing is desirable only in so far as it is perfect; for all desire their own perfection. But everything is perfect so far as it is actual. Therefore it is clear that a thing is perfect so far as it exists; for it is existence that makes all things actual, as is clear from the foregoing (Q. 3, A. 4; Q. 4, A. 1). Hence

est actualitas omnis rei, ut ex superioribus patet. Unde manifestum est quod bonum et ens sunt idem secundum rem, sed bonum dicit rationem appetibilis, quam non dicit ens.

AD PRIMUM ergo dicendum quod, licet bonum et ens sint idem secundum rem, quia tamen differunt secundum rationem, non eodem modo dicitur aliquid ens simpliciter, et bonum simpliciter. Nam cum ens dicat aliquid proprie esse in actu; actus autem proprie ordinem habet ad potentiam; secundum hoc simpliciter aliquid dicitur ens, secundum quod primo discernitur ab eo quod est in potentia tantum. Hoc autem est esse substantiale rei uniuscuiusque; unde per suum esse substantiale dicitur unumquodque ens simpliciter. Per actus autem superadditos, dicitur aliquid esse secundum quid, sicut esse album significat esse secundum quid, non enim esse album aufert esse in potentia simpliciter, cum adveniat rei iam praeexistenti in actu. Sed bonum dicit rationem perfecti, quod est appetibile, et per consequens dicit rationem ultimi. Unde id quod est ultimo perfectum, dicitur bonum simpliciter. Quod autem non habet ultimam perfectionem quam debet habere, quamvis habeat aliquam perfectionem inquantum est actu, non tamen dicitur perfectum simpliciter, nec bonum simpliciter, sed secundum quid. Sic ergo secundum primum esse, quod est substantiale, dicitur aliquid ens simpliciter et bonum secundum quid, idest inquantum est ens, secundum vero ultimum actum dicitur aliquid ens secundum quid, et bonum simpliciter. Sic ergo quod dicit Boetius, quod *in rebus aliud est quod sunt bona, et aliud quod sunt*, referendum est ad esse bonum et ad esse simpliciter, quia secundum primum actum est aliquid ens simpliciter; et secundum ultimum, bonum simpliciter. Et tamen secundum primum actum est quodammodo bonum, et secundum ultimum actum est quodammodo ens.

AD SECUNDUM dicendum quod bonum dicitur per informationem, prout accipitur bonum simpliciter, secundum ultimum actum.

ET SIMILITER dicendum ad tertium, quod bonum dicitur secundum magis et minus, secundum actum supervenientem; puta secundum scientiam vel virtutem.

it is clear that goodness and being are the same really. But goodness presents the aspect of desirableness, which being does not present.

REPLY OBJ. 1: Although goodness and being are the same really, nevertheless since they differ in thought, they are not predicated of a thing absolutely in the same way. Since being properly signifies that something actually is, and actuality properly correlates to potentiality; a thing is, in consequence, said simply to have being, accordingly as it is primarily distinguished from that which is only in potentiality; and this is precisely each thing's substantial being. Hence by its substantial being, everything is said to have being simply; but by any further actuality it is said to have being relatively. Thus to be white implies relative being, for to be white does not take a thing out of simply potential being; because only a thing that actually has being can receive this mode of being. But goodness signifies perfection which is desirable; and consequently of ultimate perfection. Hence that which has ultimate perfection is said to be simply good; but that which has not the ultimate perfection it ought to have (although, in so far as it is at all actual, it has some perfection), is not said to be perfect simply nor good simply, but only relatively. In this way, therefore, viewed in its primal (i.e., substantial) being a thing is said to be simply, and to be good relatively (i.e., in so far as it has being) but viewed in its complete actuality, a thing is said to be relatively, and to be good simply. Hence the saying of Boethius (*De Hebdom.*), *I perceive that in nature the fact that things are good is one thing; that they are is another*, is to be referred to a thing's goodness simply, and having being simply. Because, regarded in its primal actuality, a thing simply exists; and regarded in its complete actuality, it is good simply—in such sort that even in its primal actuality, it is in some sort good, and even in its complete actuality, it in some sort has being.

REPLY OBJ. 2: Goodness is a form so far as absolute goodness signifies complete actuality.

REPLY OBJ. 3: Again, goodness is spoken of as more or less according to a thing's superadded actuality, for example, as to knowledge or virtue.

Article 2

Whether Goodness Is Prior in Idea to Being?

AD SECUNDUM SIC PROCEDITUR. Videtur quod bonum secundum rationem sit prius quam ens. Ordo enim nominum est secundum ordinem rerum significatarum per nomina. Sed Dionysius, inter alia nomina Dei, prius

OBJECTION 1: It seems that goodness is prior in idea to being. For names are arranged according to the arrangement of the things signified by the names. But Dionysius (*Div. Nom.* iii) assigned the first place, amongst the other

ponit bonum quam ens, ut patet, in III cap. de Div. Nom. Ergo bonum secundum rationem est prius quam ens.

PRAETEREA, illud est prius secundum rationem, quod ad plura se extendit. Sed bonum ad plura se extendit quam ens, quia, ut dicit Dionysius, V cap. de Div. Nom., *bonum se extendit ad existentia et non existentia, ens vero ad existentia tantum.* Ergo bonum est prius secundum rationem quam ens.

PRAETEREA, quod est universalius, est prius secundum rationem. Sed bonum videtur universalius esse quam ens, quia bonum habet rationem appetibilis; quibusdam autem appetibile est ipsum non esse; dicitur enim, Matth. XXVI, de Iuda, *bonum erat ei, si natus non fuisset* et cetera. Ergo bonum est prius quam ens, secundum rationem.

PRAETEREA, non solum esse est appetibile, sed et vita et sapientia, et multa huiusmodi, et sic videtur quod esse sit quoddam particulare appetibile, et bonum, universale. Bonum ergo simpliciter est prius secundum rationem quam ens.

SED CONTRA est quod dicitur in libro de causis, quod *prima rerum creatarum est esse.*

RESPONDEO dicendum quod ens secundum rationem est prius quam bonum. Ratio enim significata per nomen, est id quod concipit intellectus de re, et significat illud per vocem, illud ergo est prius secundum rationem, quod prius cadit in conceptione intellectus. Primo autem in conceptione intellectus cadit ens, quia secundum hoc unumquodque cognoscibile est, inquantum est actu, ut dicitur in IX Metaphys. Unde ens est proprium obiectum intellectus, et sic est primum intelligibile, sicut sonus est primum audibile. Ita ergo secundum rationem prius est ens quam bonum.

AD PRIMUM ergo dicendum quod Dionysius determinat de divinis nominibus secundum quod important circa Deum habitudinem causae, nominamus enim Deum, ut ipse dicit, ex creaturis, sicut causam ex effectibus. Bonum autem, cum habeat rationem appetibilis, importat habitudinem causae finalis, cuius causalitas prima est, quia agens non agit nisi propter finem, et ab agente materia movetur ad formam, unde dicitur quod finis est causa causarum. Et sic, in causando, bonum est prius quam ens, sicut finis quam forma, et hac ratione, inter nomina significantia causalitatem divinam, prius ponitur bonum quam ens. Et iterum quia, secundum Platonicos, qui, materiam a privatione non distinguentes, dicebant materiam esse non ens, ad plura se extendit participatio boni quam participatio entis. Nam materia prima participat bonum, cum appetat ipsum (nihil autem appetit nisi simile sibi), non autem participat ens, cum ponatur non ens. Et ideo dicit Dionysius quod *bonum extenditur ad non existentia.*

names of God, to His goodness rather than to His being. Therefore in idea goodness is prior to being.

OBJ. 2: Further, that which is the more extensive is prior in idea. But goodness is more extensive than being, because, as Dionysius notes (*Div. Nom.* v), *goodness extends to things both existing and non-existing; whereas existence extends to existing things alone.* Therefore goodness is in idea prior to being.

OBJ. 3: Further, what is the more universal is prior in idea. But goodness seems to be more universal than being, since goodness has the aspect of desirable; whereas to some non-existence is desirable; for it is said of Judas: *It were better for him, if that man had not been born* (Matt 26:24). Therefore in idea goodness is prior to being.

OBJ. 4: Further, not only is existence desirable, but life, knowledge, and many other things besides. Thus it seems that existence is a particular appetible, and goodness a universal appetible. Therefore, absolutely, goodness is prior in idea to being.

ON THE CONTRARY, It is said by Aristotle (*De Causis*) that *the first of created things is being.*

I ANSWER THAT, In idea being is prior to goodness. For the meaning signified by the name of a thing is that which the mind conceives of the thing and intends by the word that stands for it. Therefore, that is prior in idea, which is first conceived by the intellect. Now the first thing conceived by the intellect is being; because everything is knowable only inasmuch as it is in actuality. Hence, being is the proper object of the intellect, and is primarily intelligible; as sound is that which is primarily audible. Therefore in idea being is prior to goodness.

REPLY OBJ. 1: Dionysius discusses the Divine Names (*Div. Nom.* i, iii) as implying some causal relation in God; for we name God, as he says, from creatures, as a cause from its effects. But goodness, since it has the aspect of desirable, implies the idea of a final cause, the causality of which is first among causes, since an agent does not act except for some end; and by an agent matter is moved to its form. Hence the end is called the cause of causes. Thus goodness, as a cause, is prior to being, as is the end to the form. Therefore among the names signifying the divine causality, goodness precedes being. Again, according to the Platonists, who, through not distinguishing primary matter from privation, said that matter was non-being, goodness is more extensively participated than being; for primary matter participates in goodness as tending to it, for all seek their like; but it does not participate in being, since it is presumed to be non-being. Therefore Dionysius says that *goodness extends to non-existence* (*Div. Nom.* v).

UNDE PATET solutio ad secundum. Vel dicendum quod bonum extenditur ad existentia et non existentia, non secundum praedicationem, sed secundum causalitatem, ut per non existentia intelligamus, non ea simpliciter quae penitus non sunt, sed ea quae sunt in potentia et non in actu, quia bonum habet rationem finis, in quo non solum quiescunt quae sunt in actu, sed ad ipsum etiam ea moventur quae in actu non sunt sed in potentia tantum. Ens autem non importat habitudinem causae nisi formalis tantum, vel inhaerentis vel exemplaris, cuius causalitas non se extendit nisi ad ea quae sunt in actu.

AD TERTIUM dicendum quod non esse secundum se non est appetibile, sed per accidens, inquantum scilicet ablatio alicuius mali est appetibilis, quod malum quidem aufertur per non esse. Ablatio vero mali non est appetibilis, nisi inquantum per malum privatur quodam esse. Illud igitur quod per se est appetibile, est esse, non esse vero per accidens tantum, inquantum scilicet quoddam esse appetitur, quo homo non sustinet privari. Et sic etiam per accidens non esse dicitur bonum.

AD QUARTUM dicendum quod vita et scientia, et alia huiusmodi, sic appetuntur ut sunt in actu, unde in omnibus appetitur quoddam esse. Et sic nihil est appetibile nisi ens, et per consequens nihil est bonum nisi ens.

REPLY OBJ. 2: The same solution is applied to this objection. Or it may be said that goodness extends to existing and non-existing things, not so far as it can be predicated of them, but so far as it can cause them—if, indeed, by non-existence we understand not simply those things which do not exist, but those which are potential, and not actual. For goodness has the aspect of the end, in which not only actual things find their completion, but also towards which tend even those things which are not actual, but merely potential. Now being implies the habitude of a formal cause only, either inherent or exemplar; and its causality does not extend save to those things which are actual.

REPLY OBJ. 3: Non-being is desirable, not of itself, but only relatively—i.e., inasmuch as the removal of an evil, which can only be removed by non-being, is desirable. Now the removal of an evil cannot be desirable, except so far as this evil deprives a thing of some being. Therefore being is desirable of itself; and non-being only relatively, inasmuch as one seeks some mode of being of which one cannot bear to be deprived; thus even non-being can be spoken of as relatively good.

REPLY OBJ. 4: Life, wisdom, and the like, are desirable only so far as they are actual. Hence, in each one of them some sort of being is desired. And thus nothing can be desired except being; and consequently nothing is good except being.

Article 3

Whether Every Being Is Good?

AD TERTIUM SIC PROCEDITUR. Videtur quod non omne ens sit bonum. Bonum enim addit supra ens, ut ex dictis patet. Ea vero quae addunt aliquid supra ens, contrahunt ipsum, sicut substantia, quantitas, qualitas, et alia huiusmodi. Ergo bonum contrahit ens. Non igitur omne ens est bonum.

PRAETEREA, nullum malum est bonum, Isaiae V, *vae qui dicitis malum bonum, et bonum malum*. Sed aliquod ens dicitur malum. Ergo non omne ens est bonum.

PRAETEREA, bonum habet rationem appetibilis. Sed materia prima non habet rationem appetibilis, sed appetentis tantum. Ergo materia prima non habet rationem boni. Non igitur omne ens est bonum.

PRAETEREA, philosophus dicit, in III Metaphys., quod *in mathematicis non est bonum*. Sed mathematica sunt quaedam entia, alioquin de eis non esset scientia. Ergo non omne ens est bonum.

SED CONTRA, omne ens quod non est Deus, est Dei creatura. Sed omnis creatura Dei est bona, ut dicitur I ad

OBJECTION 1: It seems that not every being is good. For goodness is something superadded to being, as is clear from A. 1. But whatever is added to being limits it; as substance, quantity, quality, etc. Therefore goodness limits being. Therefore not every being is good.

OBJ. 2: Further, no evil is good: *Woe to you that call evil good and good evil* (Isa 5:20). But some things are called evil. Therefore not every being is good.

OBJ. 3: Further, goodness implies desirability. Now primary matter does not imply desirability, but rather that which desires. Therefore primary matter does not contain the formality of goodness. Therefore not every being is good.

OBJ. 4: Further, the Philosopher notes (*Metaph.* iii) that *in mathematics goodness does not exist*. But mathematics are entities; otherwise there would be no science of mathematics. Therefore not every being is good.

ON THE CONTRARY, Every being that is not God is God's creature. Now every creature of God is good

Tim., IV cap., *Deus vero est maxime bonus*. Ergo omne ens est bonum.

RESPONDEO dicendum quod omne ens, inquantum est ens, est bonum. Omne enim ens, inquantum est ens, est in actu, et quodammodo perfectum, quia omnis actus perfectio quaedam est. Perfectum vero habet rationem appetibilis et boni, ut ex dictis patet. Unde sequitur omne ens, inquantum huiusmodi, bonum esse.

AD PRIMUM ergo dicendum quod substantia, quantitas et qualitas, et ea quae sub eis continentur, contrahunt ens applicando ens ad aliquam quidditatem seu naturam. Sic autem non addit aliquid bonum super ens, sed rationem tantum appetibilis et perfectionis, quod convenit ipsi esse in quacumque natura sit. Unde bonum non contrahit ens.

AD SECUNDUM dicendum quod nullum ens dicitur malum inquantum est ens, sed inquantum caret quodam esse, sicut homo dicitur malus inquantum caret esse virtutis, et oculus dicitur malus inquantum caret acumine visus.

AD TERTIUM dicendum quod materia prima, sicut non est ens nisi in potentia, ita nec bonum nisi in potentia. Licet, secundum Platonicos, dici possit quod materia prima est non ens, propter privationem adiunctam. Sed tamen participat aliquid de bono, scilicet ipsum ordinem vel aptitudinem ad bonum. Et ideo non convenit sibi quod sit appetibile, sed quod appetat.

AD QUARTUM dicendum quod mathematica non subsistunt separata secundum esse, quia si subsisterent, esset in eis bonum, scilicet ipsum esse ipsorum. Sunt autem mathematica separata secundum rationem tantum, prout abstrahuntur a motu et a materia, et sic abstrahuntur a ratione finis, qui habet rationem moventis. Non est autem inconveniens quod in aliquo ente secundum rationem non sit bonum vel ratio boni, cum ratio entis sit prior quam ratio boni, sicut supra dictum est.

(1 Tim 4:4): and *God is the greatest good*. Therefore every being is good.

I ANSWER THAT, Every being, as being, is good. For all being, as being, has actuality and is in some way perfect; since every act implies some sort of perfection; and perfection implies desirability and goodness, as is clear from A. 1. Hence it follows that every being as such is good.

REPLY OBJ. 1: Substance, quantity, quality, and everything included in them, limit being by applying it to some essence or nature. Now in this sense, goodness does not add anything to being beyond the aspect of desirability and perfection, which is also proper to being, whatever kind of nature it may be. Hence goodness does not limit being.

REPLY OBJ. 2: No being can be spoken of as evil, formally as being, but only so far as it lacks being. Thus a man is said to be evil, because he lacks some virtue; and an eye is said to be evil, because it lacks the power to see well.

REPLY OBJ. 3: As primary matter has only potential being, so it is only potentially good. Although, according to the Platonists, primary matter may be said to be a non-being on account of the privation attaching to it, nevertheless, it does participate to a certain extent in goodness, viz. by its relation to, or aptitude for, goodness. Consequently, to be desirable is not its property, but to desire.

REPLY OBJ. 4: Mathematical entities do not subsist as realities; because they would be in some sort good if they subsisted; but they have only logical existence, inasmuch as they are abstracted from motion and matter; thus they cannot have the aspect of an end, which itself has the aspect of moving another. Nor is it repugnant that there should be in some logical entity neither goodness nor form of goodness; since the idea of being is prior to the idea of goodness, as was said in the preceding article.

Article 4

Whether Goodness Has the Aspect of a Final Cause?

AD QUARTUM SIC PROCEDITUR. Videtur quod bonum non habeat rationem causae finalis, sed magis aliarum. Ut enim dicit Dionysius, IV cap. de Div. Nom., *bonum laudatur ut pulchrum*. Sed pulchrum importat rationem causae formalis. Ergo bonum habet rationem causae formalis.

PRAETEREA, bonum est diffusivum sui esse, ut ex verbis Dionysii accipitur, quibus dicit quod *bonum est ex quo omnia subsistunt et sunt*. Sed esse diffusivum importat rationem causae efficientis. Ergo bonum habet rationem causae efficientis.

OBJECTION 1: It seems that goodness has not the aspect of a final cause, but rather of the other causes. For, as Dionysius says (*Div. Nom.* iv), *Goodness is praised as beauty*. But beauty has the aspect of a formal cause. Therefore goodness has the aspect of a formal cause.

OBJ. 2: Further, goodness is self-diffusive; for Dionysius says (*Div. Nom.* iv) that *goodness is that whereby all things subsist, and are*. But to be self-giving implies the aspect of an efficient cause. Therefore goodness has the aspect of an efficient cause.

Praeterea, dicit Augustinus in I de Doctr. Christ., quod *quia Deus bonus est, nos sumus.* Sed ex Deo sumus sicut ex causa efficiente. Ergo bonum importat rationem causae efficientis.

Sed contra est quod philosophus dicit, in II Physic., quod *illud cuius causa est, est sicut finis et bonum aliorum.* Bonum ergo habet rationem causae finalis.

Respondeo dicendum quod, cum bonum sit quod omnia appetunt, hoc autem habet rationem finis; manifestum est quod bonum rationem finis importat. Sed tamen ratio boni praesupponit rationem causae efficientis, et rationem causae formalis. Videmus enim quod id quod est primum in causando, ultimum est in causato, ignis enim primo calefacit quam formam ignis inducat, cum tamen calor in igne consequatur formam substantialem. In causando autem, primum invenitur bonum et finis, qui movet efficientem; secundo, actio efficientis, movens ad formam; tertio advenit forma. Unde e converso esse oportet in causato, quod primum sit ipsa forma, per quam est ens; secundo consideratur in ea virtus effectiva, secundum quod est perfectum in esse (quia unumquodque tunc perfectum est, quando potest sibi simile facere, ut dicit philosophus in IV Meteor.); tertio consequitur ratio boni, per quam in ente perfectio fundatur.

Ad primum ergo dicendum quod pulchrum et bonum in subiecto quidem sunt idem, quia super eandem rem fundantur, scilicet super formam, et propter hoc, bonum laudatur ut pulchrum. Sed ratione differunt. Nam bonum proprie respicit appetitum, est enim bonum quod omnia appetunt. Et ideo habet rationem finis, nam appetitus est quasi quidam motus ad rem. Pulchrum autem respicit vim cognoscitivam, pulchra enim dicuntur quae visa placent. Unde pulchrum in debita proportione consistit, quia sensus delectatur in rebus debite proportionatis, sicut in sibi similibus; nam et sensus ratio quaedam est, et omnis virtus cognoscitiva. Et quia cognitio fit per assimilationem, similitudo autem respicit formam, pulchrum proprie pertinet ad rationem causae formalis.

Ad secundum dicendum quod bonum dicitur diffusivum sui esse, eo modo quo finis dicitur movere.

Ad tertium dicendum quod quilibet habens voluntatem, dicitur bonus inquantum habet bonam voluntatem, quia per voluntatem utimur omnibus quae in nobis sunt. Unde non dicitur bonus homo, qui habet bonum intellectum, sed qui habet bonam voluntatem. Voluntas autem respicit finem ut obiectum proprium, et sic, quod dicitur, *quia Deus est bonus, sumus,* refertur ad causam finalem.

Obj. 3: Further, Augustine says (*De Doctr. Christ.* i, 31) that *we exist because God is good.* But we owe our existence to God as the efficient cause. Therefore goodness implies the aspect of an efficient cause.

On the contrary, The Philosopher says (*Phys.* ii) that *that is to be considered as the end and the good of other things, for the sake of which something is.* Therefore goodness has the aspect of a final cause.

I answer that, Since goodness is that which all things desire, and since this has the aspect of an end, it is clear that goodness implies the aspect of an end. Nevertheless, the idea of goodness presupposes the idea of an efficient cause, and also of a formal cause. For we see that what is first in causing, is last in the thing caused. Fire, e.g., heats first of all before it reproduces the form of fire; though the heat in the fire follows from its substantial form. Now in causing, goodness and the end come first, both of which move the agent to act; second, the action of the agent moving to the form; third, comes the form. Hence in that which is caused the converse ought to take place, so that there should be first, the form whereby it is a being; second, we consider in it its effective power, whereby it is perfect in being, for a thing is perfect when it can reproduce its like, as the Philosopher says (*Meteor.* iv); third, there follows the formality of goodness which is the basic principle of its perfection.

Reply Obj. 1: Beauty and goodness in a thing are identical fundamentally; for they are based upon the same thing, namely, the form; and consequently goodness is praised as beauty. But they differ logically, for goodness properly relates to the appetite (goodness being what all things desire); and therefore it has the aspect of an end (the appetite being a kind of movement towards a thing). On the other hand, beauty relates to the cognitive faculty; for beautiful things are those which please when seen. Hence beauty consists in due proportion; for the senses delight in things duly proportioned, as in what is after their own kind—because even sense is a sort of reason, just as is every cognitive faculty. Now since knowledge is by assimilation, and similarity relates to form, beauty properly belongs to the nature of a formal cause.

Reply Obj. 2: Goodness is described as self-diffusive in the sense that an end is said to move.

Reply Obj. 3: He who has a will is said to be good, so far as he has a good will; because it is by our will that we employ whatever powers we may have. Hence a man is said to be good, not by his good understanding; but by his good will. Now the will relates to the end as to its proper object. Thus the saying, *we exist because God is good* has reference to the final cause.

Article 5

Whether the Essence of Goodness Consists in Mode, Species and Order?

AD QUINTUM SIC PROCEDITUR. Videtur quod ratio boni non consistat in modo, specie et ordine. Bonum enim et ens ratione differunt, ut supra dictum est. Sed modus, species et ordo pertinere ad rationem entis videntur, quia, sicut dicitur Sap. XI, *omnia in numero, pondere et mensura disposuisti*, ad quae tria reducuntur species, modus et ordo, quia, ut dicit Augustinus, IV super Gen. ad litteram, *mensura omni rei modum praefigit, et numerus omni rei speciem praebet, et pondus omnem rem ad quietem et stabilitatem trahit*. Ergo ratio boni non consistit in modo, specie et ordine.

PRAETEREA, ipse modus, species et ordo bona quaedam sunt. Si ergo ratio boni consistit in modo, specie et ordine, oportet etiam quod modus habeat modum, speciem et ordinem, et similiter species et ordo. Ergo procederetur in infinitum.

PRAETEREA, malum est privatio modi et speciei et ordinis. Sed malum non tollit totaliter bonum. Ergo ratio boni non consistit in modo, specie et ordine.

PRAETEREA, illud in quo consistit ratio boni, non potest dici malum. Sed dicitur malus modus, mala species, malus ordo. Ergo ratio boni non consistit in modo, specie et ordine.

PRAETEREA, modus, species et ordo ex pondere, numero et mensura causantur, ut ex auctoritate Augustini inducta patet. Non autem omnia bona habent pondus, numerum et mensuram, dicit enim Ambrosius, in Hexaemeron, quod *lucis natura est, ut non in numero, non in pondere, non in mensura creata sit*. Non ergo ratio boni consistit in modo, specie et ordine.

SED CONTRA est quod dicit Augustinus, in libro de natura boni, *haec tria, modus, species et ordo, tanquam generalia bona sunt in rebus a Deo factis, et ita, haec tria ubi magna sunt, magna bona sunt; ubi parva, parva bona sunt; ubi nulla, nullum bonum est*. Quod non esset, nisi ratio boni in eis consisteret. Ergo ratio boni consistit in modo, specie et ordine.

RESPONDEO dicendum quod unumquodque dicitur bonum, inquantum est perfectum, sic enim est appetibile, ut supra dictum est. Perfectum autem dicitur, cui nihil deest secundum modum suae perfectionis. Cum autem unumquodque sit id quod est, per suam formam; forma autem praesupponit quaedam, et quaedam ad ipsam ex necessitate consequuntur; ad hoc quod aliquid sit perfectum et bonum, necesse est quod formam habeat, et ea quae praeexiguntur ad eam, et ea quae consequuntur ad ipsam. Praeexigitur autem ad formam determinatio sive commensuratio principiorum, seu materialium,

OBJECTION 1: It seems that the essence of goodness does not consist in mode, species and order. For goodness and being differ logically. But mode, species and order seem to belong to the nature of being, for it is written: *Thou hast ordered all things in measure, and number, and weight* (Wis 11:21). And to these three can be reduced species, mode and order, as Augustine says (*Gen ad lit.* iv, 3): *Measure fixes the mode of everything, number gives it its species, and weight gives it rest and stability*. Therefore the essence of goodness does not consist in mode, species and order.

OBJ. 2: Further, mode, species and order are themselves good. Therefore if the essence of goodness consists in mode, species and order, then every mode must have its own mode, species and order. The same would be the case with species and order in endless succession.

OBJ. 3: Further, evil is the privation of mode, species and order. But evil is not the total absence of goodness. Therefore the essence of goodness does not consist in mode, species and order.

OBJ. 4: Further, that wherein consists the essence of goodness cannot be spoken of as evil. Yet we can speak of an evil mode, species and order. Therefore the essence of goodness does not consist in mode, species and order.

OBJ. 5: Further, mode, species and order are caused by weight, number and measure, as appears from the quotation from Augustine. But not every good thing has weight, number and measure; for Ambrose says (Hexam. i, 9): *It is of the nature of light not to have been created in number, weight and measure*. Therefore the essence of goodness does not consist in mode, species and order.

ON THE CONTRARY, Augustine says (De Nat. Boni. iii): *These three—mode, species and order—as common good things, are in everything God has made; thus, where these three abound the things are very good; where they are less, the things are less good; where they do not exist at all, there can be nothing good*. But this would not be unless the essence of goodness consisted in them. Therefore the essence of goodness consists in mode, species and order.

I ANSWER THAT, Everything is said to be good so far as it is perfect; for in that way only is it desirable (as shown above, AA. 1, 3). Now a thing is said to be perfect if it lacks nothing according to the mode of its perfection. But since everything is what it is by its form (and since the form presupposes certain things, and from the form certain things necessarily follow), in order for a thing to be perfect and good it must have a form, together with all that precedes and follows upon that form. Now the form presupposes determination or commensuration of its principles, whether material or efficient, and this is signified by the

seu efficientium ipsam, et hoc significatur per modum, unde dicitur quod mensura modum praefigit. Ipsa autem forma significatur per speciem, quia per formam unumquodque in specie constituitur. Et propter hoc dicitur quod numerus speciem praebet, quia definitiones significantes speciem sunt sicut numeri, secundum philosophum in VIII Metaphys.; sicut enim unitas addita vel subtracta variat speciem numeri, ita in definitionibus differentia apposita vel subtracta. Ad formam autem consequitur inclinatio ad finem, aut ad actionem, aut ad aliquid huiusmodi, quia unumquodque, inquantum est actu, agit, et tendit in id quod sibi convenit secundum suam formam. Et hoc pertinet ad pondus et ordinem. Unde ratio boni, secundum quod consistit in perfectione, consistit etiam in modo, specie et ordine.

AD PRIMUM ergo dicendum quod ista tria non consequuntur ens, nisi inquantum est perfectum, et secundum hoc est bonum.

AD SECUNDUM dicendum quod modus, species et ordo eo modo dicuntur bona, sicut et entia, non quia ipsa sint quasi subsistentia, sed quia eis alia sunt et entia et bona. Unde non oportet quod ipsa habeant aliqua alia, quibus sint bona. Non enim sic dicuntur bona, quasi formaliter aliis sint bona; sed quia ipsis formaliter aliqua sunt bona; sicut albedo non dicitur ens quia ipsa aliquo sit, sed quia ipsa aliquid est secundum quid, scilicet album.

AD TERTIUM dicendum quod quodlibet esse est secundum formam aliquam, unde secundum quodlibet esse rei, consequuntur ipsam modus, species et ordo, sicut homo habet speciem, modum et ordinem, inquantum est homo; et similiter inquantum est albus, habet similiter modum, speciem et ordinem; et inquantum est virtuosus, et inquantum est sciens, et secundum omnia quae de ipso dicuntur. Malum autem privat quodam esse, sicut caecitas privat esse visus, unde non tollit omnem modum, speciem et ordinem; sed solum modum, speciem et ordinem quae consequuntur esse visus.

AD QUARTUM dicendum quod, sicut dicit Augustinus in libro de natura boni, *omnis modus, inquantum modus, bonus est* (et sic potest dici de specie et ordine), *sed malus modus, vel mala species, vel malus ordo, aut ideo dicuntur quia minora sunt quam esse debuerunt; aut quia non his rebus accommodantur, quibus accommodanda sunt; ut ideo dicantur mala, quia sunt aliena et incongrua.*

AD QUINTUM dicendum quod natura lucis dicitur esse sine numero et pondere et mensura, non simpliciter, sed per comparationem ad corporalia, quia virtus lucis ad omnia corporalia se extendit, inquantum est qualitas activa primi corporis alterantis, scilicet caeli.

mode: hence it is said that the measure marks the mode. But the form itself is signified by the species; for everything is placed in its species by its form. Hence the number is said to give the species, for definitions signifying species are like numbers, according to the Philosopher (*Metaph.* x); for as a unit added to, or taken from a number, changes its species, so a difference added to, or taken from a definition, changes its species. Further, upon the form follows an inclination to the end, or to an action, or something of the sort; for everything, in so far as it is in act, acts and tends towards that which is in accordance with its form; and this belongs to weight and order. Hence the essence of goodness, so far as it consists in perfection, consists also in mode, species and order.

REPLY OBJ. 1: These three only follow upon being, so far as it is perfect, and according to this perfection is it good.

REPLY OBJ. 2: Mode, species and order are said to be good, and to be beings, not as though they themselves were subsistences, but because it is through them that other things are both beings and good. Hence they have no need of other things whereby they are good: for they are spoken of as good, not as though formally constituted so by something else, but as formally constituting others good: thus whiteness is not said to be a being as though it were by anything else; but because, by it, something else has accidental being, as an object that is white.

REPLY OBJ. 3: Every being is due to some form. Hence, according to every being of a thing is its mode, species, order. Thus, a man has a mode, species and order as he is white, virtuous, learned and so on; according to everything predicated of him. But evil deprives a thing of some sort of being, as blindness deprives us of that being which is sight; yet it does not destroy every mode, species and order, but only such as follow upon the being of sight.

REPLY OBJ. 4: Augustine says (*De Nat. Boni.* xxiii), *Every mode, as mode, is good* (and the same can be said of species and order). *But an evil mode, species and order are so called as being less than they ought to be, or as not belonging to that which they ought to belong. Therefore they are called evil, because they are out of place and incongruous.*

REPLY OBJ. 5: The nature of light is spoken of as being without number, weight and measure, not absolutely, but in comparison with corporeal things, because the power of light extends to all corporeal things; inasmuch as it is an active quality of the first body that causes change, i.e., the heavens.

Article 6

Whether Goodness Is Rightly Divided into the Virtuous, the Useful and the Pleasant?

AD SEXTUM SIC PROCEDITUR. Videtur quod non convenienter dividatur bonum per honestum, utile et delectabile. Bonum enim, sicut dicit philosophus in I Ethic., dividitur per decem praedicamenta. Honestum autem, utile et delectabile inveniri possunt in uno praedicamento. Ergo non convenienter per haec dividitur bonum.

PRAETEREA, omnis divisio fit per opposita. Sed haec tria non videntur esse opposita, nam honesta sunt delectabilia, nullumque inhonestum est utile (quod tamen oportet, si divisio fieret per opposita, ut opponerentur honestum et utile), ut etiam dicit Tullius, in libro de officiis. Ergo praedicta divisio non est conveniens.

PRAETEREA, ubi unum propter alterum, ibi unum tantum est. Sed utile non est bonum nisi propter delectabile vel honestum. Ergo non debet utile dividi contra delectabile et honestum.

SED CONTRA est quod Ambrosius, in libro de officiis, utitur ista divisione boni.

RESPONDEO dicendum quod haec divisio proprie videtur esse boni humani. Si tamen altius et communius rationem boni consideremus, invenitur haec divisio proprie competere bono, secundum quod bonum est. Nam bonum est aliquid, inquantum est appetibile, et terminus motus appetitus. Cuius quidem motus terminatio considerari potest ex consideratione motus corporis naturalis. Terminatur autem motus corporis naturalis, simpliciter quidem ad ultimum; secundum quid autem etiam ad medium, per quod itur ad ultimum quod terminat motum, et dicitur aliquis terminus motus, inquantum aliquam partem motus terminat. Id autem quod est ultimus terminus motus, potest accipi dupliciter, vel ipsa res in quam tenditur, utpote locus vel forma; vel quies in re illa. Sic ergo in motu appetitus, id quod est appetibile terminans motum appetitus secundum quid, ut medium per quod tenditur in aliud, vocatur utile. Id autem quod appetitur ut ultimum, terminans totaliter motum appetitus, sicut quaedam res in quam per se appetitus tendit, vocatur honestum, quia honestum dicitur quod per se desideratur. Id autem quod terminat motum appetitus ut quies in re desiderata, est delectatio.

AD PRIMUM ergo dicendum quod bonum, inquantum est idem subiecto cum ente, dividitur per decem praedicamenta, sed secundum propriam rationem, competit sibi ista divisio.

OBJECTION 1: It seems that goodness is not rightly divided into the virtuous, the useful and the pleasant. For goodness is divided by the ten predicaments, as the Philosopher says (*Ethic.* i). But the virtuous, the useful and the pleasant can be found under one predicament. Therefore goodness is not rightly divided by them.

OBJ. 2: Further, every division is made by opposites. But these three do not seem to be opposites; for the virtuous is pleasing, and no wickedness is useful; whereas this ought to be the case if the division were made by opposites, for then the virtuous and the useful would be opposed; and Tully speaks of this (*De Offic.* ii). Therefore this division is incorrect.

OBJ. 3: Further, where one thing is on account of another, there is only one thing. But the useful is not goodness, except so far as it is pleasing and virtuous. Therefore the useful ought not to be divided against the pleasant and the virtuous.

ON THE CONTRARY, Ambrose makes use of this division of goodness (*De Offic.* i, 9).

I ANSWER THAT, This division properly concerns human goodness. But if we consider the nature of goodness from a higher and more universal point of view, we shall find that this division properly concerns goodness as such. For everything is good so far as it is desirable, and is a term of the movement of the appetite; the term of whose movement can be seen from a consideration of the movement of a natural body. Now the movement of a natural body is terminated by the end absolutely; and relatively by the means through which it comes to the end, where the movement ceases; so a thing is called a term of movement, so far as it terminates any part of that movement. Now the ultimate term of movement can be taken in two ways, either as the thing itself towards which it tends, e.g., a place or form; or a state of rest in that thing. Thus, in the movement of the appetite, the thing desired that terminates the movement of the appetite relatively, as a means by which something tends towards another, is called the useful; but that sought after as the last thing absolutely terminating the movement of the appetite, as a thing towards which for its own sake the appetite tends, is called the virtuous; for the virtuous is that which is desired for its own sake; but that which terminates the movement of the appetite in the form of rest in the thing desired, is called the pleasant.

REPLY OBJ. 1: Goodness, so far as it is identical with being, is divided by the ten predicaments. But this division belongs to it according to its proper formality.

AD SECUNDUM dicendum quod haec divisio non est per oppositas res, sed per oppositas rationes. Dicuntur tamen illa proprie delectabilia, quae nullam habent aliam rationem appetibilitatis nisi delectationem, cum aliquando sint et noxia et inhonesta. Utilia vero dicuntur, quae non habent in se unde desiderentur; sed desiderantur solum ut sunt ducentia in alterum, sicut sumptio medicinae amarae. Honesta vero dicuntur, quae in seipsis habent unde desiderentur.

AD TERTIUM dicendum quod bonum non dividitur in ista tria sicut univocum aequaliter de his praedicatum, sed sicut analogum, quod praedicatur secundum prius et posterius. Per prius enim praedicatur de honesto; et secundario de delectabili; tertio de utili.

REPLY OBJ. 2: This division is not by opposite things; but by opposite aspects. Now those things are called pleasing which have no other formality under which they are desirable except the pleasant, being sometimes hurtful and contrary to virtue. Whereas the useful applies to such as have nothing desirable in themselves, but are desired only as helpful to something further, as the taking of bitter medicine; while the virtuous is predicated of such as are desirable in themselves.

REPLY OBJ. 3: Goodness is not divided into these three as something univocal to be predicated equally of them all; but as something analogical to be predicated of them according to priority and posteriority. Hence it is predicated chiefly of the virtuous; then of the pleasant; and lastly of the useful.

Question 6

The Goodness of God

Deinde quaeritur de bonitate Dei. Et circa hoc quaeruntur quatuor.

Primo, utrum esse bonum conveniat Deo.

Secundo, utrum Deus sit summum bonum.

Tertio, utrum ipse solus sit bonus per suam essentiam.

Quarto, utrum omnia sint bona bonitate divina.

We next consider the goodness of God; under which head there are four points of inquiry:

(1) Whether goodness belongs to God?

(2) Whether God is the supreme good?

(3) Whether He alone is essentially good?

(4) Whether all things are good by the divine goodness?

Article 1

Whether God is Good?

Ad primum sic proceditur. Videtur quod esse bonum non conveniat Deo. Ratio enim boni consistit in modo, specie et ordine. Haec autem non videntur Deo convenire, cum Deus immensus sit, et ad aliquid non ordinetur. Ergo esse bonum non convenit Deo.

Praeterea, bonum est quod omnia appetunt. Sed Deum non omnia appetunt, quia non omnia cognoscunt ipsum, nihil autem appetitur nisi notum. Ergo esse bonum non convenit Deo.

Sed contra est quod dicitur Thren. III, *bonus est dominus sperantibus in eum, animae quaerenti illum.*

Respondeo dicendum quod bonum esse praecipue Deo convenit. Bonum enim aliquid est, secundum quod est appetibile. Unumquodque autem appetit suam perfectionem. Perfectio autem et forma effectus est quaedam similitudo agentis, cum omne agens agat sibi simile. Unde ipsum agens est appetibile, et habet rationem boni, hoc enim est quod de ipso appetitur, ut eius similitudo participetur. Cum ergo Deus sit prima causa effectiva omnium, manifestum est quod sibi competit ratio boni et appetibilis. Unde Dionysius, in libro de Div. Nom., attribuit bonum Deo sicut primae causae efficienti, dicens quod bonus dicitur Deus, *sicut ex quo omnia subsistunt.*

Ad primum ergo dicendum quod habere modum, speciem et ordinem, pertinet ad rationem boni causati. Sed bonum in Deo est sicut in causa, unde ad eum pertinet imponere aliis modum, speciem et ordinem. Unde ista tria sunt in Deo sicut in causa.

Ad secundum dicendum quod omnia, appetendo proprias perfectiones, appetunt ipsum Deum, inquantum perfectiones omnium rerum sunt quaedam

Objection 1: It seems that to be good does not belong to God. For goodness consists in mode, species and order. But these do not seem to belong to God; since God is immense and is not ordered to anything else. Therefore to be good does not belong to God.

Obj. 2: Further, the good is what all things desire. But all things do not desire God, because all things do not know Him; and nothing is desired unless it is known. Therefore to be good does not belong to God.

On the contrary, It is written (Lam 3:25): *The Lord is good to them that hope in Him, to the soul that seeketh Him.*

I answer that, To be good belongs pre-eminently to God. For a thing is good according to its desirableness. Now everything seeks after its own perfection; and the perfection and form of an effect consist in a certain likeness to the agent, since every agent makes its like; and hence the agent itself is desirable and has the nature of good. For the very thing which is desirable in it is the participation of its likeness. Therefore, since God is the first effective cause of all things, it is manifest that the aspect of good and of desirableness belong to Him; and hence Dionysius (*Div. Nom.* iv) attributes good to God as to the first efficient cause, saying that, God is called good *as by Whom all things subsist.*

Reply Obj. 1: To have mode, species and order belongs to the essence of caused good; but good is in God as in its cause, and hence it belongs to Him to impose mode, species and order on others; wherefore these three things are in God as in their cause.

Reply Obj. 2: All things, by desiring their own perfection, desire God Himself, inasmuch as the perfections of all things are so many similitudes of the divine being;

similitudines divini esse, ut ex dictis patet. Et sic eorum quae Deum appetunt, quaedam cognoscunt ipsum secundum seipsum, quod est proprium creaturae rationalis. Quaedam vero cognoscunt aliquas participationes suae bonitatis, quod etiam extenditur usque ad cognitionem sensibilem. Quaedam vero appetitum naturalem habent absque cognitione, utpote inclinata ad suos fines ab alio superiori cognoscente.

as appears from what is said above (Q. 4, A. 3). And so of those things which desire God, some know Him as He is Himself, and this is proper to the rational creature; others know some participation of His goodness, and this belongs also to sensible knowledge; others have a natural desire without knowledge, as being directed to their ends by a higher intelligence.

Article 2

Whether God Is the Supreme Good?

Ad secundum sic proceditur. Videtur quod Deus non sit summum bonum. Summum enim bonum addit aliquid supra bonum, alioquin omni bono conveniret. Sed omne quod se habet ex additione ad aliquid, est compositum. Ergo summum bonum est compositum. Sed Deus est summe simplex, ut supra ostensum est. Ergo Deus non est summum bonum.

Praeterea, *bonum est quod omnia appetunt,* ut dicit philosophus. Sed nihil aliud est quod omnia appetunt, nisi solus Deus, qui est finis omnium. Ergo nihil aliud est bonum nisi Deus. Quod etiam videtur per id quod dicitur Matth. XIX, *nemo bonus nisi solus Deus.* Sed summum dicitur in comparatione aliorum; sicut summum calidum in comparatione ad omnia calida. Ergo Deus non potest dici summum bonum.

Praeterea, summum comparationem importat. Sed quae non sunt unius generis, non sunt comparabilia; sicut dulcedo inconvenienter dicitur maior vel minor quam linea. Cum igitur Deus non sit in eodem genere cum aliis bonis, ut ex superioribus patet, videtur quod Deus non possit dici summum bonum respectu eorum.

Sed contra est quod dicit Augustinus, I de Trin., quod *Trinitas divinarum personarum est summum bonum, quod purgatissimis mentibus cernitur.*

Respondeo dicendum quod Deus est summum bonum simpliciter, et non solum in aliquo genere vel ordine rerum. Sic enim bonum Deo attribuitur, ut dictum est, inquantum omnes perfectiones desideratae effluunt ab eo, sicut a prima causa. Non autem effluunt ab eo sicut ab agente univoco, ut ex superioribus patet, sed sicut ab agente quod non convenit cum suis effectibus, neque in ratione speciei, nec in ratione generis. Similitudo autem effectus in causa quidem univoca invenitur uniformiter, in causa autem aequivoca invenitur excellentius, sicut calor excellentiori modo est in sole quam in igne. Sic ergo oportet quod cum bonum sit in Deo sicut in prima causa omnium non univoca, quod sit in eo excellentissimo modo. Et propter hoc dicitur summum bonum.

Objection 1: It seems that God is not the supreme good. For the supreme good adds something to good; otherwise it would belong to every good. But everything which is an addition to anything else is a compound thing: therefore the supreme good is a compound. But God is supremely simple; as was shown above (Q. 3, A. 7). Therefore God is not the supreme good.

Obj. 2: Further, *Good is what all desire,* as the Philosopher says (*Ethic.* i, 1). Now what all desire is nothing but God, Who is the end of all things: therefore there is no other good but God. This appears also from what is said (Luke 18:19): *None is good but God alone.* But we use the word supreme in comparison with others, as e.g., supreme heat is used in comparison with all other heats. Therefore God cannot be called the supreme good.

Obj. 3: Further, supreme implies comparison. But things not in the same genus are not comparable; as, sweetness is not properly greater or less than a line. Therefore, since God is not in the same genus as other good things, as appears above (QQ. 3, A. 5; 4, A. 3) it seems that God cannot be called the supreme good in relation to others.

On the contrary, Augustine says (*De Trin.* ii) that, the Trinity of the divine persons is *the supreme good, discerned by purified minds.*

I answer that, God is the supreme good simply, and not only as existing in any genus or order of things. For good is attributed to God, as was said in the preceding article, inasmuch as all desired perfections flow from Him as from the first cause. They do not, however, flow from Him as from a univocal agent, as shown above (Q. 4, A. 2); but as from an agent which does not agree with its effects either in species or genus. Now the likeness of an effect in the univocal cause is found uniformly; but in the equivocal cause it is found more excellently, as heat is in the sun more excellently than it is in fire. Therefore as good is in God as in the first, but not the univocal, cause of all things, it must be in Him in a most excellent way; and therefore He is called the supreme good.

AD PRIMUM ergo dicendum quod summum bonum addit super bonum, non rem aliquam absolutam, sed relationem tantum. Relatio autem qua aliquid de Deo dicitur relative ad creaturas, non est realiter in Deo, sed in creatura; in Deo vero secundum rationem; sicut scibile relative dicitur ad scientiam, non quia ad ipsam referatur, sed quia scientia refertur ad ipsum. Et sic non oportet quod in summo bono sit aliqua compositio, sed solum quod alia deficiant ab ipso.

AD SECUNDUM dicendum quod, cum dicitur *bonum est quod omnia appetunt*, non sic intelligitur quasi unumquodque bonum ab omnibus appetatur, sed quia quidquid appetitur, rationem boni habet. Quod autem dicitur, *nemo bonus nisi solus Deus*, intelligitur de bono per essentiam, ut post dicetur.

AD TERTIUM dicendum quod ea quae non sunt in eodem genere, si quidem sint in diversis generibus contenta, nullo modo comparabilia sunt. De Deo autem negatur esse in eodem genere cum aliis bonis, non quod ipse sit in quodam alio genere; sed quia ipse est extra genus, et principium omnis generis. Et sic comparatur ad alia per excessum. Et huiusmodi comparationem importat summum bonum.

REPLY OBJ. 1: The supreme good does not add to good any absolute thing, but only a relation. Now a relation of God to creatures, is not a reality in God, but in the creature; for it is in God in our idea only: as, what is knowable is so called with relation to knowledge, not that it depends on knowledge, but because knowledge depends on it. Thus it is not necessary that there should be composition in the supreme good, but only that other things are deficient in comparison with it.

REPLY OBJ. 2: When we say that *good is what all desire*, it is not to be understood that every kind of good thing is desired by all; but that whatever is desired has the nature of good. And when it is said, *None is good but God alone*, this is to be understood of essential goodness, as will be explained in the next article.

REPLY OBJ. 3: Things not of the same genus are in no way comparable to each other if indeed they are in different genera. Now we say that God is not in the same genus with other good things; not that He is any other genus, but that He is outside genus, and is the principle of every genus; and thus He is compared to others by excess, and it is this kind of comparison the supreme good implies.

Article 3

Whether to Be Essentially Good Belongs to God Alone?

AD TERTIUM SIC PROCEDITUR. Videtur quod esse bonum per essentiam non sit proprium Dei. Sicut enim unum convertitur cum ente, ita et bonum, ut supra habitum est. Sed omne ens est unum per suam essentiam, ut patet per philosophum in IV Metaphys. Ergo omne ens est bonum per suam essentiam.

PRAETEREA, si bonum est quod omnia appetunt, cum ipsum esse sit desideratum ab omnibus, ipsum esse cuiuslibet rei est eius bonum. Sed quaelibet res est ens per suam essentiam. Ergo quaelibet res est bona per suam essentiam.

PRAETEREA, omnis res per suam bonitatem est bona. Si igitur aliqua res est quae non sit bona per suam essentiam, oportebit quod eius bonitas non sit sua essentia. Illa ergo bonitas, cum sit ens quoddam, oportet quod sit bona, et si quidem alia bonitate, iterum de illa bonitate quaeretur. Aut ergo erit procedere in infinitum, aut venire ad aliquam bonitatem quae non erit bona per aliam bonitatem. Eadem ergo ratione standum est in primo. Res igitur quaelibet est bona per suam essentiam.

SED CONTRA est quod dicit Boetius, in libro de Hebdomad., quod *alia omnia a Deo sunt bona per participationem*. Non igitur per essentiam.

OBJECTION 1: It seems that to be essentially good does not belong to God alone. For as one is convertible with being, so is good; as we said above (Q. 5, A. 1). But every being is one essentially, as appears from the Philosopher (*Metaph.* iv); therefore every being is good essentially.

OBJ. 2: Further, if good is what all things desire, since being itself is desired by all, then the being of each thing is its good. But everything is a being essentially; therefore every being is good essentially.

OBJ. 3: Further, everything is good by its own goodness. Therefore if there is anything which is not good essentially, it is necessary to say that its goodness is not its own essence. Therefore its goodness, since it is a being, must be good; and if it is good by some other goodness, the same question applies to that goodness also; therefore we must either proceed to infinity, or come to some goodness which is not good by any other goodness. Therefore the first supposition holds good. Therefore everything is good essentially.

ON THE CONTRARY, Boethius says (*De Hebdom.*) that *all things but God are good by participation*. Therefore they are not good essentially.

RESPONDEO dicendum quod solus Deus est bonus per suam essentiam. Unumquodque enim dicitur bonum, secundum quod est perfectum. Perfectio autem alicuius rei triplex est. Prima quidem, secundum quod in suo esse constituitur. Secunda vero, prout ei aliqua accidentia superadduntur, ad suam perfectam operationem necessaria. Tertia vero perfectio alicuius est per hoc, quod aliquid aliud attingit sicut finem. Utpote prima perfectio ignis consistit in esse, quod habet per suam formam substantialem, secunda vero eius perfectio consistit in caliditate, levitate et siccitate, et huiusmodi, tertia vero perfectio eius est secundum quod in loco suo quiescit. Haec autem triplex perfectio nulli creato competit secundum suam essentiam, sed soli Deo, cuius solius essentia est suum esse; et cui non adveniunt aliqua accidentia; sed quae de aliis dicuntur accidentaliter, sibi conveniunt essentialiter, ut esse potentem, sapientem, et huiusmodi, sicut ex dictis patet. Ipse etiam ad nihil aliud ordinatur sicut ad finem, sed ipse est ultimus finis omnium rerum. Unde manifestum est quod solus Deus habet omnimodam perfectionem secundum suam essentiam. Et ideo ipse solus est bonus per suam essentiam.

AD PRIMUM ergo dicendum quod unum non importat rationem perfectionis, sed indivisionis tantum, quae unicuique rei competit secundum suam essentiam. Simplicium autem essentiae sunt indivisae et actu et potentia, compositorum vero essentiae sunt indivisae secundum actum tantum. Et ideo oportet quod quaelibet res sit una per suam essentiam, non autem bona, ut ostensum est.

AD SECUNDUM dicendum quod, licet unumquodque sit bonum inquantum habet esse, tamen essentia rei creatae non est ipsum esse, et ideo non sequitur quod res creata sit bona per suam essentiam.

AD TERTIUM dicendum quod bonitas rei creatae non est ipsa eius essentia, sed aliquid superadditum; vel ipsum esse eius, vel aliqua perfectio superaddita, vel ordo ad finem. Ipsa tamen bonitas sic superaddita dicitur bona sicut et ens, hac autem ratione dicitur ens, quia ea est aliquid, non quia ipsa aliquo alio sit. Unde hac ratione dicitur bona, quia ea est aliquid bonum, non quia ipsa habeat aliquam aliam bonitatem, qua sit bona.

I ANSWER THAT, God alone is good essentially. For everything is called good according to its perfection. Now perfection of a thing is threefold: first, according to the constitution of its own being; second, in respect of any accidents being added as necessary for its perfect operation; third, perfection consists in the attaining to something else as the end. Thus, for instance, the first perfection of fire consists in its existence, which it has through its own substantial form; its secondary perfection consists in heat, lightness and dryness, and the like; its third perfection is to rest in its own place. This triple perfection belongs to no creature by its own essence; it belongs to God only, in Whom alone essence is existence; in Whom there are no accidents; since whatever belongs to others accidentally belongs to Him essentially; as, to be powerful, wise and the like, as appears from what is stated above (Q. 3, A. 6); and He is not directed to anything else as to an end, but is Himself the last end of all things. Hence it is manifest that God alone has every kind of perfection by His own essence; therefore He Himself alone is good essentially.

REPLY OBJ. 1: *One* does not include the idea of perfection, but only of indivision, which belongs to everything according to its own essence. Now the essences of simple things are undivided both actually and potentially, but the essences of compounds are undivided only actually; and therefore everything must be one essentially, but not good essentially, as was shown above.

REPLY OBJ. 2: Although everything is good in that it has being, yet the essence of a creature is not very being; and therefore it does not follow that a creature is good essentially.

REPLY OBJ. 3: The goodness of a creature is not its very essence, but something superadded; it is either its existence, or some added perfection, or the order to its end. Still, the goodness itself thus added is good, just as it is being. But for this reason is it called being because by it something has being, not because it itself has being through something else: hence for this reason is it called good because by it something is good, and not because it itself has some other goodness whereby it is good.

Article 4

Whether All Things Are Good by the Divine Goodness?

AD QUARTUM SIC PROCEDITUR. Videtur quod omnia sint bona bonitate divina. Dicit enim Augustinus, VII de Trin., *bonum hoc et bonum illud, tolle hoc et tolle illud, et vide ipsum bonum, si potes, ita Deum videbis, non*

OBJECTION 1: It seems that all things are good by the divine goodness. For Augustine says (*De Trin.* viii), *This and that are good; take away this and that, and see good itself if thou canst; and so thou shalt see God, good not by*

alio bono bonum, sed bonum omnis boni. Sed unumquodque est bonum suo bono. Ergo unumquodque est bonum ipso bono quod est Deus.

PRAETEREA, sicut dicit Boetius, in libro de Hebdomad., omnia dicuntur bona inquantum ordinantur ad Deum, et hoc ratione bonitatis divinae. Ergo omnia sunt bona bonitate divina.

SED CONTRA est quod omnia sunt bona inquantum sunt. Sed non dicuntur omnia entia per esse divinum, sed per esse proprium. Ergo non omnia sunt bona bonitate divina, sed bonitate propria.

RESPONDEO dicendum quod nihil prohibet in his quae relationem important, aliquid ab extrinseco denominari; sicut aliquid denominatur locatum a loco, et mensuratum a mensura. Circa vero ea quae absolute dicuntur, diversa fuit opinio. Plato enim posuit omnium rerum species separatas; et quod ab eis individua denominantur, quasi species separatas participando; ut puta quod Socrates dicitur homo secundum ideam hominis separatam. Et sicut ponebat ideam hominis et equi separatam, quam vocabat per se hominem et per se equum, ita ponebat ideam entis et ideam unius separatam, quam dicebat per se ens et per se unum, et eius participatione unumquodque dicitur ens vel unum. Hoc autem quod est per se bonum et per se unum, ponebat esse summum Deum, a quo omnia dicuntur bona per modum participationis.

Et quamvis haec opinio irrationabilis videatur quantum ad hoc, quod ponebat species rerum naturalium separatas per se subsistentes, ut Aristoteles multipliciter probat; tamen hoc absolute verum est, quod est aliquod unum per essentiam suam bonum, quod dicimus Deum, ut ex superioribus patet. Huic etiam sententiae concordat Aristoteles. A primo igitur per suam essentiam ente et bono, unumquodque potest dici bonum et ens, inquantum participat ipsum per modum cuiusdam assimilationis, licet remote et deficienter, ut ex superioribus patet.

Sic ergo unumquodque dicitur bonum bonitate divina, sicut primo principio exemplari, effectivo et finali totius bonitatis. Nihilominus tamen unumquodque dicitur bonum similitudine divinae bonitatis sibi inhaerente, quae est formaliter sua bonitas denominans ipsum. Et sic est bonitas una omnium; et etiam multae bonitates.

ET PER HOC patet responsio ad obiecta.

any other good, but the good of every good. But everything is good by its own good; therefore everything is good by that very good which is God.

OBJ. 2: Further, as Boethius says (*De Hebdom.*), all things are called good, accordingly as they are directed to God, and this is by reason of the divine goodness; therefore all things are good by the divine goodness.

ON THE CONTRARY, All things are good, inasmuch as they have being. But they are not called beings through the divine being, but through their own being; therefore all things are not good by the divine goodness, but by their own goodness.

I ANSWER THAT, As regards relative things, we must admit extrinsic denomination; as, a thing is denominated *placed* from *place*, and *measured* from *measure*. But as regards absolute things opinions differ. Plato held the existence of separate ideas (Q. 84, A. 4) of all things, and that individuals were denominated by them as participating in the separate ideas; for instance, that Socrates is called man according to the separate idea of man. Now just as he laid down separate ideas of man and horse which he called absolute man and absolute horse, so likewise he laid down separate ideas of *being* and of *one*, and these he called absolute being and absolute oneness; and by participation of these, everything was called *being* or *one*; and what was thus absolute being and absolute one, he said was the supreme good. And because good is convertible with being, as one is also; he called God the absolute good, from whom all things are called good by way of participation.

Although this opinion appears to be unreasonable in affirming separate ideas of natural things as subsisting of themselves—as Aristotle argues in many ways—still, it is absolutely true that there is first something which is essentially being and essentially good, which we call God, as appears from what is shown above (Q. 2, A. 3), and Aristotle agrees with this. Hence from the first being, essentially such, and good, everything can be called good and a being, inasmuch as it participates in it by way of a certain assimilation which is far removed and defective; as appears from the above (Q. 4, A. 3).

Everything is therefore called good from the divine goodness, as from the first exemplary effective and final principle of all goodness. Nevertheless, everything is called good by reason of the similitude of the divine goodness belonging to it, which is formally its own goodness, whereby it is denominated good. And so of all things there is one goodness, and yet many goodnesses.

THIS IS A SUFFICIENT Reply to the Objections.

QUESTION 7

THE INFINITY OF GOD

Post considerationem divinae perfectionis, considerandum est de eius infinitate, et de existentia eius in rebus, attribuitur enim Deo quod sit ubique et in omnibus rebus, inquantum est incircumscriptibilis et infinitus.

Circa primum quaeruntur quatuor.

Primo, utrum Deus sit infinitus.

Secundo, utrum aliquid praeter ipsum sit infinitum secundum essentiam.

Tertio, utrum aliquid possit esse infinitum secundum magnitudinem.

Quarto, utrum possit esse infinitum in rebus secundum multitudinem.

After considering the divine perfection we must consider the divine infinity, and God's existence in things: for God is everywhere, and in all things, inasmuch as He is boundless and infinite.

Concerning the first, there are four points of inquiry:

(1) Whether God is infinite?

(2) Whether anything besides Him is infinite in essence?

(3) Whether anything can be infinitude in magnitude?

(4) Whether an infinite multitude can exist?

Article 1

Whether God Is Infinite?

AD PRIMUM SIC PROCEDITUR. Videtur quod Deus non sit infinitus. Omne enim infinitum est imperfectum, quia habet rationem partis et materiae, ut dicitur in III Physic. Sed Deus est perfectissimus. Ergo non est infinitus.

PRAETEREA, secundum philosophum in I Physic., finitum et infinitum conveniunt quantitati. Sed in Deo non est quantitas, cum non sit corpus, ut supra ostensum est. Ergo non competit sibi esse infinitum.

PRAETEREA, quod ita est hic quod non alibi, est finitum secundum locum, ergo quod ita est hoc quod non est aliud, est finitum secundum substantiam. Sed Deus est hoc, et non est aliud, non enim est lapis nec lignum. Ergo Deus non est infinitus secundum substantiam.

SED CONTRA est quod dicit Damascenus, quod *Deus est infinitus et aeternus et incircumscriptibilis.*

RESPONDEO dicendum quod omnes antiqui philosophi attribuunt infinitum primo principio, ut dicitur in III Physic., et hoc rationabiliter, considerantes res effluere a primo principio in infinitum. Sed quia quidam erraverunt circa naturam primi principii, consequens fuit ut errarent circa infinitatem ipsius. Quia enim ponebant primum principium materiam, consequenter attribuerunt primo principio infinitatem materialem; dicentes aliquod corpus infinitum esse primum principium rerum.

OBJECTION 1: It seems that God is not infinite. For everything infinite is imperfect, as the Philosopher says; because it has parts and matter, as is said in *Phys.* iii. But God is most perfect; therefore He is not infinite.

OBJ. 2: Further, according to the Philosopher (*Phys.* i), finite and infinite belong to quantity. But there is no quantity in God, for He is not a body, as was shown above (Q. 3, A. 1). Therefore it does not belong to Him to be infinite.

OBJ. 3: Further, what is here in such a way as not to be elsewhere, is finite according to place. Therefore that which is a thing in such a way as not to be another thing, is finite according to substance. But God is this, and not another; for He is not a stone or wood. Therefore God is not infinite in substance.

ON THE CONTRARY, Damascene says (*De Fide Orth.* i, 4) that *God is infinite and eternal, and boundless.*

I ANSWER THAT, All the ancient philosophers attribute infinitude to the first principle, as is said (*Phys.* iii), and with reason; for they considered that things flow forth infinitely from the first principle. But because some erred concerning the nature of the first principle, as a consequence they erred also concerning its infinity; forasmuch as they asserted that matter was the first principle; consequently they attributed to the first principle a material infinity to the effect that some infinite body was the first principle of things.

Considerandum est igitur quod infinitum dicitur aliquid ex eo quod non est finitum. Finitur autem quodammodo et materia per formam, et forma per materiam. Materia quidem per formam, inquantum materia, antequam recipiat formam, est in potentia ad multas formas, sed cum recipit unam, terminatur per illam. Forma vero finitur per materiam, inquantum forma, in se considerata, communis est ad multa, sed per hoc quod recipitur in materia, fit forma determinate huius rei. Materia autem perficitur per formam per quam finitur, et ideo infinitum secundum quod attribuitur materiae, habet rationem imperfecti; est enim quasi materia non habens formam. Forma autem non perficitur per materiam, sed magis per eam eius amplitudo contrahitur, unde infinitum secundum quod se tenet ex parte formae non determinatae per materiam, habet rationem perfecti. Illud autem quod est maxime formale omnium, est ipsum esse, ut ex superioribus patet. Cum igitur esse divinum non sit esse receptum in aliquo, sed ipse sit suum esse subsistens, ut supra ostensum est; manifestum est quod ipse Deus sit infinitus et perfectus.

Et per hoc patet responsio ad primum.

Ad secundum dicendum quod terminus quantitatis est sicut forma ipsius, cuius signum est, quod figura, quae consistit in terminatione quantitatis, est quaedam forma circa quantitatem. Unde infinitum quod competit quantitati, est infinitum quod se tenet ex parte materiae, et tale infinitum non attribuitur Deo, ut dictum est.

Ad tertium dicendum quod, ex hoc ipso quod esse Dei est per se subsistens non receptum in aliquo, prout dicitur infinitum, distinguitur ab omnibus aliis, et alia removentur ab eo, sicut, si esset albedo subsistens, ex hoc ipso quod non esset in alio, differret ab omni albedine existente in subiecto.

We must consider therefore that a thing is called infinite because it is not finite. Now matter is in a way made finite by form, and the form by matter. Matter indeed is made finite by form, inasmuch as matter, before it receives its form, is in potentiality to many forms; but on receiving a form, it is terminated by that one. Again, form is made finite by matter, inasmuch as form, considered in itself, is common to many; but when received in matter, the form is determined to this one particular thing. Now matter is perfected by the form by which it is made finite; therefore infinite as attributed to matter, has the nature of something imperfect; for it is as it were formless matter. On the other hand, form is not made perfect by matter, but rather is contracted by matter; and hence the infinite, regarded on the part of the form not determined by matter, has the nature of something perfect. Now being is the most formal of all things, as appears from what is shown above (Q. 4, A. 1, Obj. 3). Since therefore the divine being is not a being received in anything, but He is His own subsistent being as was shown above (Q. 3, A. 4), it is clear that God Himself is infinite and perfect.

From this appears the Reply to the First Objection.

Reply Obj. 2: Quantity is terminated by its form, which can be seen in the fact that a figure which consists in quantity terminated, is a kind of quantitative form. Hence the infinite of quantity is the infinite of matter; such a kind of infinite cannot be attributed to God; as was said above, in this article.

Reply Obj. 3: The fact that the being of God is self-subsisting, not received in any other, and is thus called infinite, shows Him to be distinguished from all other beings, and all others to be apart from Him. Even so, were there such a thing as a self-subsisting whiteness, the very fact that it did not exist in anything else, would make it distinct from every other whiteness existing in a subject.

Article 2

Whether Anything but God Can Be Essentially Infinite?

Ad secundum sic proceditur. Videtur quod aliquid aliud quam Deus possit esse infinitum per essentiam. Virtus enim rei proportionatur essentiae eius. Si igitur essentia Dei est infinita, oportet quod eius virtus sit infinita. Ergo potest producere effectum infinitum, cum quantitas virtutis per effectum cognoscatur.

Praeterea, quidquid habet virtutem infinitam, habet essentiam infinitam. Sed intellectus creatus habet virtutem infinitam, apprehendit enim universale, quod se potest extendere ad infinita singularia. Ergo omnis substantia intellectualis creata est infinita.

Objection 1: It seems that something else besides God can be essentially infinite. For the power of anything is proportioned to its essence. Now if the essence of God is infinite, His power must also be infinite. Therefore He can produce an infinite effect, since the extent of a power is known by its effect.

Obj. 2: Further, whatever has infinite power, has an infinite essence. Now the created intellect has an infinite power; for it apprehends the universal, which can extend itself to an infinitude of singular things. Therefore every created intellectual substance is infinite.

PRAETEREA, materia prima aliud est a Deo, ut supra ostensum est. Sed materia prima est infinita. Ergo aliquid aliud praeter Deum potest esse infinitum.

SED CONTRA est quod infinitum non potest esse ex principio aliquo, ut dicitur in III Physic. Omne autem quod est praeter Deum, est ex Deo sicut ex primo principio. Ergo nihil quod est praeter Deum, potest esse infinitum.

RESPONDEO dicendum quod aliquid praeter Deum potest esse infinitum secundum quid, sed non simpliciter. Si enim loquamur de infinito secundum quod competit materiae, manifestum est quod omne existens in actu, habet aliquam formam, et sic materia eius est terminata per formam. Sed quia materia, secundum quod est sub una forma substantiali, remanet in potentia ad multas formas accidentales; quod est finitum simpliciter, potest esse infinitum secundum quid, utpote lignum est finitum secundum suam formam, sed tamen est infinitum secundum quid, inquantum est in potentia ad figuras infinitas. Si autem loquamur de infinito secundum quod convenit formae, sic manifestum est quod illa quorum formae sunt in materia, sunt simpliciter finita, et nullo modo infinita. Si autem sint aliquae formae creatae non receptae in materia, sed per se subsistentes, ut quidam de Angelis opinantur, erunt quidem infinitae secundum quid, inquantum huiusmodi formae non terminantur neque contrahuntur per aliquam materiam, sed quia forma creata sic subsistens habet esse, et non est suum esse, necesse est quod ipsum eius esse sit receptum et contractum ad determinatam naturam. Unde non potest esse infinitum simpliciter.

AD PRIMUM ergo dicendum quod hoc est contra rationem facti, quod essentia rei sit ipsum esse eius, quia esse subsistens non est esse creatum, unde contra rationem facti est, quod sit simpliciter infinitum. Sicut ergo Deus, licet habeat potentiam infinitam, non tamen potest facere aliquid non factum (hoc enim esset contradictoria esse simul); ita non potest facere aliquid infinitum simpliciter.

AD SECUNDUM dicendum quod hoc ipsum quod virtus intellectus extendit se quodammodo ad infinita, procedit ex hoc quod intellectus est forma non in materia; sed vel totaliter separata, sicut sunt substantiae Angelorum; vel ad minus potentia intellectiva, quae non est actus alicuius organi, in anima intellectiva corpori coniuncta.

AD TERTIUM dicendum quod materia prima non existit in rerum natura per seipsam, cum non sit ens in actu, sed potentia tantum, unde magis est aliquid concreatum, quam creatum. Nihilominus tamen materia prima, etiam secundum potentiam, non est infinita simpliciter, sed secundum quid, quia eius potentia non se extendit nisi ad formas naturales.

OBJ. 3: Further, primary matter is something other than God, as was shown above (Q. 3, A. 8). But primary matter is infinite. Therefore something besides God can be infinite.

ON THE CONTRARY, The infinite cannot have a beginning, as said in *Phys.* iii. But everything outside God is from God as from its first principle. Therefore besides God nothing can be infinite.

I ANSWER THAT, Things other than God can be relatively infinite, but not absolutely infinite. For with regard to infinite as applied to matter, it is manifest that everything actually existing possesses a form; and thus its matter is determined by form. But because matter, considered as existing under some substantial form, remains in potentiality to many accidental forms, that which is absolutely finite can be relatively infinite; as, for example, wood is finite according to its own form, but still it is relatively infinite, inasmuch as it is in potentiality to an infinite number of shapes. But if we speak of the infinite in reference to form, it is manifest that those things, the forms of which are in matter, are absolutely finite, and in no way infinite. If, however, any created forms are not received into matter, but are self-subsisting, as some think is the case with angels, these will be relatively infinite, inasmuch as such kinds of forms are not terminated, nor contracted by any matter. But because a created form thus subsisting has being, and yet is not its own being, it follows that its being is received and contracted to a determinate nature. Hence it cannot be absolutely infinite.

REPLY OBJ. 1: It is against the nature of a made thing for its essence to be its existence; because subsisting being is not a created being; hence it is against the nature of a made thing to be absolutely infinite. Therefore, as God, although He has infinite power, cannot make a thing to be not made (for this would imply that two contradictories are true at the same time), so likewise He cannot make anything to be absolutely infinite.

REPLY OBJ. 2: The fact that the power of the intellect extends itself in a way to infinite things, is because the intellect is a form not in matter, but either wholly separated from matter, as is the angelic substance, or at least an intellectual power, which is not the act of any organ, in the intellectual soul joined to a body.

REPLY OBJ. 3: Primary matter does not exist by itself in nature, since it is not actually being, but potentially only; hence it is something concreated rather than created. Nevertheless, primary matter even as a potentiality is not absolutely infinite, but relatively, because its potentiality extends only to natural forms.

Article 3

Whether an Actually Infinite Magnitude Can Exist?

AD TERTIUM SIC PROCEDITUR. Videtur quod possit esse aliquid infinitum actu secundum magnitudinem. In scientiis enim mathematicis non invenitur falsum, *quia abstrahentium non est mendacium*, ut dicitur in II Physic. Sed scientiae mathematicae utuntur infinito secundum magnitudinem, dicit enim geometra in suis demonstrationibus, sit linea talis infinita. Ergo non est impossibile aliquid esse infinitum secundum magnitudinem.

PRAETEREA, id quod non est contra rationem alicuius, non est impossibile convenire sibi. Sed esse infinitum non est contra rationem magnitudinis, sed magis finitum et infinitum videntur esse passiones quantitatis. Ergo non est impossibile aliquam magnitudinem esse infinitam.

PRAETEREA, magnitudo divisibilis est in infinitum, sic enim definitur continuum, quod est in infinitum divisibile, ut patet in III Physic. Sed contraria nata sunt fieri circa idem. Cum ergo divisioni opponatur additio, et diminutioni augmentum, videtur quod magnitudo possit crescere in infinitum. Ergo possibile est esse magnitudinem infinitam.

PRAETEREA, motus et tempus habent quantitatem et continuitatem a magnitudine super quam transit motus, ut dicitur in IV Physic. Sed non est contra rationem temporis et motus quod sint infinita, cum unumquodque indivisibile signatum in tempore et motu circulari, sit principium et finis. Ergo nec contra rationem magnitudinis erit quod sit infinita.

SED CONTRA, omne corpus superficiem habet. Sed omne corpus superficiem habens est finitum, quia superficies est terminus corporis finiti. Ergo omne corpus est finitum. Et similiter potest dici de superficie et linea. Nihil est ergo infinitum secundum magnitudinem.

RESPONDEO dicendum quod aliud est esse infinitum secundum suam essentiam, et secundum magnitudinem. Dato enim quod esset aliquod corpus infinitum secundum magnitudinem, utpote ignis vel aer, non tamen esset infinitum secundum essentiam, quia essentia sua esset terminata ad aliquam speciem per formam, et ad aliquod individuum per materiam. Et ideo, habito ex praemissis quod nulla creatura est infinita secundum essentiam, adhuc restat inquirere utrum aliquid creatum sit infinitum secundum magnitudinem.

Sciendum est igitur quod corpus, quod est magnitudo completa, dupliciter sumitur, scilicet mathematice, secundum quod consideratur in eo sola quantitas; et naturaliter, secundum quod consideratur in eo materia et forma.

Et de corpore quidem naturali, quod non possit esse infinitum in actu, manifestum est. Nam omne corpus

OBJECTION 1: It seems that there can be something actually infinite in magnitude. For in mathematics there is no error, since *there is no lie in things abstract*, as the Philosopher says (*Phys.* ii). But mathematics uses the infinite in magnitude; thus, the geometrician in his demonstrations says, *Let this line be infinite*. Therefore it is not impossible for a thing to be infinite in magnitude.

OBJ. 2: Further, what is not against the nature of anything, can agree with it. Now to be infinite is not against the nature of magnitude; but rather both the finite and the infinite seem to be properties of quantity. Therefore it is not impossible for some magnitude to be infinite.

OBJ. 3: Further, magnitude is infinitely divisible, for the continuous is defined that which is infinitely divisible, as is clear from *Phys.* iii. But contraries are concerned about one and the same thing. Since therefore addition is opposed to division, and increase opposed to diminution, it appears that magnitude can be increased to infinity. Therefore it is possible for magnitude to be infinite.

OBJ. 4: Further, movement and time have quantity and continuity derived from the magnitude over which movement passes, as is said in *Phys.* iv. But it is not against the nature of time and movement to be infinite, since every determinate indivisible in time and circular movement is both a beginning and an end. Therefore neither is it against the nature of magnitude to be infinite.

ON THE CONTRARY, Every body has a surface. But every body which has a surface is finite; because surface is the term of a finite body. Therefore all bodies are finite. The same applies both to surface and to a line. Therefore nothing is infinite in magnitude.

I ANSWER THAT, It is one thing to be infinite in essence, and another to be infinite in magnitude. For granted that a body exists infinite in magnitude, as fire or air, yet this could not be infinite in essence, because its essence would be terminated in a species by its form, and confined to individuality by matter. And so assuming from these premises that no creature is infinite in essence, it still remains to inquire whether any creature can be infinite in magnitude.

We must therefore observe that a body, which is a complete magnitude, can be considered in two ways; mathematically, in respect to its quantity only; and naturally, as regards its matter and form.

Now it is manifest that a natural body cannot be actually infinite. For every natural body has some determined

naturale aliquam formam substantialem habet determinatam, cum igitur ad formam substantialem consequantur accidentia, necesse est quod ad determinatam formam consequantur determinata accidentia; inter quae est quantitas. Unde omne corpus naturale habet determinatam quantitatem et in maius et in minus. Unde impossibile est aliquod corpus naturale infinitum esse. Hoc etiam ex motu patet. Quia omne corpus naturale habet aliquem motum naturalem. Corpus autem infinitum non posset habere aliquem motum naturalem, nec rectum, quia nihil movetur naturaliter motu recto, nisi cum est extra suum locum, quod corpori infinito accidere non posset; occuparet enim omnia loca, et sic indifferenter quilibet locus esset locus eius. Et similiter etiam neque secundum motum circularem. Quia in motu circulari oportet quod una pars corporis transferatur ad locum in quo fuit alia pars; quod in corpore circulari, si ponatur infinitum, esse non posset, quia duae lineae protractae a centro, quanto longius protrahuntur a centro, tanto longius distant ab invicem; si ergo corpus esset infinitum, in infinitum lineae distarent ab invicem, et sic una nunquam posset pervenire ad locum alterius.

De corpore etiam mathematico eadem ratio est. Quia si imaginemur corpus mathematicum existens actu, oportet quod imaginemur ipsum sub aliqua forma, quia nihil est actu nisi per suam formam. Unde, cum forma quanti, inquantum huiusmodi, sit figura, oportebit quod habeat aliquam figuram. Et sic erit finitum, est enim figura, quae termino vel terminis comprehenditur.

AD PRIMUM ergo dicendum quod geometer non indiget sumere aliquam lineam esse infinitam actu, sed indiget accipere aliquam lineam finitam actu, a qua possit subtrahi quantum necesse est, et hanc nominat lineam infinitam.

AD SECUNDUM dicendum quod, licet infinitum non sit contra rationem magnitudinis in communi, est tamen contra rationem cuiuslibet speciei eius, scilicet contra rationem magnitudinis bicubitae vel tricubitae, sive circularis vel triangularis, et similium. Non autem est possibile in genere esse quod in nulla specie est. Unde non est possibile esse aliquam magnitudinem infinitam, cum nulla species magnitudinis sit infinita.

AD TERTIUM dicendum quod infinitum quod convenit quantitati, ut dictum est, se tenet ex parte materiae. Per divisionem autem totius acceditur ad materiam, nam partes se habent in ratione materiae, per additionem autem acceditur ad totum, quod se habet in ratione formae. Et ideo non invenitur infinitum in additione magnitudinis, sed in divisione tantum.

AD QUARTUM dicendum quod motus et tempus non sunt secundum totum in actu, sed successive, unde habent potentiam permixtam actui. Sed magnitudo est tota in actu. Et ideo infinitum quod convenit quantitati, et se tenet ex parte materiae, repugnat totalitati magnitudinis,

substantial form. Since therefore the accidents follow upon the substantial form, it is necessary that determinate accidents should follow upon a determinate form; and among these accidents is quantity. So every natural body has a greater or smaller determinate quantity. Hence it is impossible for a natural body to be infinite. The same appears from movement; because every natural body has some natural movement; whereas an infinite body could not have any natural movement; neither direct, because nothing moves naturally by a direct movement unless it is out of its place; and this could not happen to an infinite body, for it would occupy every place, and thus every place would be indifferently its own place. Neither could it move circularly; forasmuch as circular motion requires that one part of the body is necessarily transferred to a place occupied by another part, and this could not happen as regards an infinite circular body: for if two lines be drawn from the centre, the farther they extend from the centre, the farther they are from each other; therefore, if a body were infinite, the lines would be infinitely distant from each other; and thus one could never occupy the place belonging to any other.

The same applies to a mathematical body. For if we imagine a mathematical body actually existing, we must imagine it under some form, because nothing is actual except by its form; hence, since the form of quantity as such is figure, such a body must have some figure, and so would be finite; for figure is confined by a term or boundary.

REPLY OBJ. 1: A geometrician does not need to assume a line actually infinite, but takes some actually finite line, from which he subtracts whatever he finds necessary; which line he calls infinite.

REPLY OBJ. 2: Although the infinite is not against the nature of magnitude in general, still it is against the nature of any species of it; thus, for instance, it is against the nature of a bicubical or tricubical magnitude, whether circular or triangular, and so on. Now what is not possible in any species cannot exist in the genus; hence there cannot be any infinite magnitude, since no species of magnitude is infinite.

REPLY OBJ. 3: The infinite in quantity, as was shown above, belongs to matter. Now by division of the whole we approach to matter, forasmuch as parts have the aspect of matter; but by addition we approach to the whole which has the aspect of a form. Therefore the infinite is not in the addition of magnitude, but only in division.

REPLY OBJ. 4: Movement and time are whole, not actually but successively; hence they have potentiality mixed with actuality. But magnitude is an actual whole; therefore the infinite in quantity refers to matter, and does not agree with the totality of magnitude; yet it agrees with the totality

non autem totalitati temporis vel motus, esse enim in potentia convenit materiae.

of time and movement: for it is proper to matter to be in potentiality.

Article 4

Whether an Infinite Multitude Can Exist?

AD QUARTUM SIC PROCEDITUR. Videtur quod possibile sit esse multitudinem infinitam secundum actum. Non enim est impossibile id quod est in potentia reduci ad actum. Sed numerus est in infinitum multiplicabilis. Ergo non est impossibile esse multitudinem infinitam in actu.

PRAETEREA, cuiuslibet speciei possibile est esse aliquod individuum in actu. Sed species figurae sunt infinitae. Ergo possibile est esse infinitas figuras in actu.

PRAETEREA, ea quae non opponuntur ad invicem, non impediunt se invicem. Sed, posita aliqua multitudine rerum, adhuc possunt fieri alia multa quae eis non opponuntur, ergo non est impossibile aliqua iterum simul esse cum eis, et sic in infinitum. Ergo possibile est esse infinita in actu.

SED CONTRA est quod dicitur Sap. XI, *omnia in pondere, numero et mensura disposuisti.*

RESPONDEO dicendum quod circa hoc fuit duplex opinio. Quidam enim, sicut Avicenna et Algazel, dixerunt quod impossibile est esse multitudinem actu infinitam per se, sed infinitam per accidens multitudinem esse, non est impossibile. Dicitur enim multitudo esse infinita per se, quando requiritur ad aliquid ut multitudo infinita sit. Et hoc est impossibile esse, quia sic oporteret quod aliquid dependeret ex infinitis; unde eius generatio nunquam compleretur, cum non sit infinita pertransire.

Per accidens autem dicitur multitudo infinita, quando non requiritur ad aliquid infinitas multitudinis, sed accidit ita esse. Et hoc sic manifestari potest in operatione fabri, ad quam quaedam multitudo requiritur per se, scilicet quod sit ars in anima, et manus movens, et martellus. Et si haec in infinitum multiplicarentur, nunquam opus fabrile compleretur, quia dependeret ex infinitis causis. Sed multitudo martellorum quae accidit ex hoc quod unum frangitur et accipitur aliud, est multitudo per accidens, accidit enim quod multis martellis operetur; et nihil differt utrum uno vel duobus vel pluribus operetur, vel infinitis, si infinito tempore operaretur. Per hunc igitur modum, posuerunt quod possibile est esse actu multitudinem infinitam per accidens.

Sed hoc est impossibile. Quia omnem multitudinem oportet esse in aliqua specie multitudinis. Species autem multitudinis sunt secundum species numerorum. Nulla

OBJECTION 1: It seems that an actually infinite multitude is possible. For it is not impossible for a potentiality to be made actual. But number can be multiplied to infinity. Therefore it is possible for an infinite multitude actually to exist.

OBJ. 2: Further, it is possible for any individual of any species to be made actual. But the species of figures are infinite. Therefore an infinite number of actual figures is possible.

OBJ. 3: Further, things not opposed to each other do not obstruct each other. But supposing a multitude of things to exist, there can still be many others not opposed to them. Therefore it is not impossible for others also to coexist with them, and so on to infinite; therefore an actual infinite number of things is possible.

ON THE CONTRARY, It is written, *Thou hast ordered all things in measure, and number, and weight* (Wis 11:21).

I ANSWER THAT, A twofold opinion exists on this subject. Some, as Avicenna and Algazel, said that it was impossible for an actually infinite multitude to exist absolutely; but that an accidentally infinite multitude was not impossible. A multitude is said to be infinite absolutely, when an infinite multitude is necessary that something may exist. Now this is impossible; because it would entail something dependent on an infinity for its existence; and hence its generation could never come to be, because it is impossible to pass through an infinite medium.

A multitude is said to be accidentally infinite when its existence as such is not necessary, but accidental. This can be shown, for example, in the work of a carpenter requiring a certain absolute multitude; namely, art in the soul, the movement of the hand, and a hammer; and supposing that such things were infinitely multiplied, the carpentering work would never be finished, forasmuch as it would depend on an infinite number of causes. But the multitude of hammers, inasmuch as one may be broken and another used, is an accidental multitude; for it happens by accident that many hammers are used, and it matters little whether one or two, or many are used, or an infinite number, if the work is carried on for an infinite time. In this way they said that there can be an accidentally infinite multitude.

This, however, is impossible; since every kind of multitude must belong to a species of multitude. Now the species of multitude are to be reckoned by the species of numbers.

autem species numeri est infinita, quia quilibet numerus est multitudo mensurata per unum. Unde impossibile est esse multitudinem infinitam actu, sive per se, sive per accidens. Item, multitudo in rerum natura existens est creata, et omne creatum sub aliqua certa intentione creantis comprehenditur, non enim in vanum agens aliquod operatur. Unde necesse est quod sub certo numero omnia creata comprehendantur. Impossibile est ergo esse multitudinem infinitam in actu, etiam per accidens. Sed esse multitudinem infinitam in potentia, possibile est. Quia augmentum multitudinis consequitur divisionem magnitudinis, quanto enim aliquid plus dividitur, tanto plura secundum numerum resultant. Unde, sicut infinitum invenitur in potentia in divisione continui, quia proceditur ad materiam, ut supra ostensum est; eadem ratione etiam infinitum invenitur in potentia in additione multitudinis.

AD PRIMUM ergo dicendum quod unumquodque quod est in potentia, reducitur in actum secundum modum sui esse, dies enim non reducitur in actum ut sit tota simul, sed successive. Et similiter infinitum multitudinis non reducitur in actum ut sit totum simul, sed successive, quia post quamlibet multitudinem, potest sumi alia multitudo in infinitum.

AD SECUNDUM dicendum quod species figurarum habent infinitatem ex infinitate numeri, sunt enim species figurarum, trilaterum, quadrilaterum, et sic inde. Unde, sicut multitudo infinita numerabilis non reducitur in actum quod sit tota simul, ita nec multitudo figurarum.

AD TERTIUM dicendum quod, licet, quibusdam positis, alia poni non sit eis oppositum; tamen infinita poni opponitur cuilibet speciei multitudinis. Unde non est possibile esse aliquam multitudinem actu infinitam.

But no species of number is infinite; for every number is multitude measured by one. Hence it is impossible for there to be an actually infinite multitude, either absolute or accidental. Likewise multitude in nature is created; and everything created is comprehended under some clear intention of the Creator; for no agent acts aimlessly. Hence everything created must be comprehended in a certain number. Therefore it is impossible for an actually infinite multitude to exist, even accidentally. But a potentially infinite multitude is possible; because the increase of multitude follows upon the division of magnitude; since the more a thing is divided, the greater number of things result. Hence, as the infinite is to be found potentially in the division of the continuous, because we thus approach matter, as was shown in the preceding article, by the same rule, the infinite can be also found potentially in the addition of multitude.

REPLY OBJ. 1: Every potentiality is made actual according to its mode of being; for instance, a day is reduced to act successively, and not all at once. Likewise the infinite in multitude is reduced to act successively, and not all at once; because every multitude can be succeeded by another multitude to infinity.

REPLY OBJ. 2: Species of figures are infinite by infinitude of number. Now there are various species of figures, such as trilateral, quadrilateral and so on; and as an infinitely numerable multitude is not all at once reduced to act, so neither is the multitude of figures.

REPLY OBJ. 3: Although the supposition of some things does not preclude the supposition of others, still the supposition of an infinite number is opposed to any single species of multitude. Hence it is not possible for an actually infinite multitude to exist.

QUESTION 8

THE EXISTENCE OF GOD IN THINGS

Quia vero infinito convenire videtur quod ubique et in omnibus sit, considerandum est utrum hoc Deo conveniat. Et circa hoc quaeruntur quatuor.

Primo, utrum Deus sit in omnibus rebus.

Secundo, utrum Deus sit ubique.

Tertio, utrum Deus sit ubique per essentiam et potentiam et praesentiam.

Quarto, utrum esse ubique sit proprium Dei.

Since it evidently belongs to the infinite to be present everywhere, and in all things, we now consider whether this belongs to God; and concerning this there arise four points of inquiry:

(1) Whether God is in all things?

(2) Whether God is everywhere?

(3) Whether God is everywhere by essence, power, and presence?

(4) Whether to be everywhere belongs to God alone?

Article 1

Whether God Is in All Things?

AD PRIMUM SIC PROCEDITUR. Videtur quod Deus non sit in omnibus rebus. Quod enim est supra omnia, non est in omnibus rebus. Sed Deus est supra omnia, secundum illud Psalmi, *excelsus super omnes gentes dominus*, et cetera. Ergo Deus non est in omnibus rebus.

PRAETEREA, quod est in aliquo, continetur ab eo. Sed Deus non continetur a rebus, sed magis continet res. Ergo Deus non est in rebus, sed magis res sunt in eo. Unde Augustinus, in libro octoginta trium quaest., dicit quod *in ipso potius sunt omnia, quam ipse alicubi*.

PRAETEREA, quanto aliquod agens est virtuosius, tanto ad magis distans eius actio procedit. Sed Deus est virtuosissimum agens. Ergo eius actio pertingere potest ad ea etiam quae ab ipso distant, nec oportet quod sit in omnibus.

PRAETEREA, Daemones res aliquae sunt. Nec tamen Deus est in Daemonibus, non enim est conventio lucis ad tenebras, ut dicitur II ad Cor. VI. Ergo Deus non est in omnibus rebus.

SED CONTRA, ubicumque operatur aliquid, ibi est. Sed Deus operatur in omnibus, secundum illud Isaiae XXVI, *omnia opera nostra operatus es in nobis, domine*. Ergo Deus est in omnibus rebus.

RESPONDEO dicendum quod Deus est in omnibus rebus, non quidem sicut pars essentiae, vel sicut accidens, sed sicut agens adest ei in quod agit. Oportet enim omne agens coniungi ei in quod immediate agit, et sua virtute illud contingere, unde in VII Physic. probatur quod motum et movens oportet esse simul. Cum autem Deus sit ipsum esse per suam essentiam, oportet quod esse creatum sit proprius effectus eius; sicut ignire

OBJECTION 1: It seems that God is not in all things. For what is above all things is not in all things. But God is above all, according to the Psalm (Ps 112:4), *The Lord is high above all nations*, etc. Therefore God is not in all things.

OBJ. 2: Further, what is in anything is thereby contained. Now God is not contained by things, but rather does He contain them. Therefore God is not in things but things are rather in Him. Hence Augustine says (*Octog. Tri. Quaest.* qu. 20), that *in Him things are, rather than He is in any place.*

OBJ. 3: Further, the more powerful an agent is, the more extended is its action. But God is the most powerful of all agents. Therefore His action can extend to things which are far removed from Him; nor is it necessary that He should be in all things.

OBJ. 4: Further, the demons are beings. But God is not in the demons; for there is no fellowship between light and darkness (2 Cor 6:14). Therefore God is not in all things.

ON THE CONTRARY, A thing is wherever it operates. But God operates in all things, according to Isa. 26:12, *Lord . . . Thou hast wrought all our works in us*. Therefore God is in all things.

I ANSWER THAT, God is in all things; not, indeed, as part of their essence, nor as an accident, but as an agent is present to that upon which it works. For an agent must be joined to that wherein it acts immediately and touch it by its power; hence it is proved in *Phys.* vii that the thing moved and the mover must be joined together. Now since God is very being by His own essence, created being must be His proper effect; as to ignite is the proper effect of fire.

est proprius effectus ignis. Hunc autem effectum causat Deus in rebus, non solum quando primo esse incipiunt, sed quandiu in esse conservantur; sicut lumen causatur in aere a sole quandiu aer illuminatus manet. Quandiu igitur res habet esse, tandiu oportet quod Deus adsit ei, secundum modum quo esse habet. Esse autem est illud quod est magis intimum cuilibet, et quod profundius omnibus inest, cum sit formale respectu omnium quae in re sunt, ut ex supra dictis patet. Unde oportet quod Deus sit in omnibus rebus, et intime.

AD PRIMUM ergo dicendum quod Deus est supra omnia per excellentiam suae naturae, et tamen est in omnibus rebus, ut causans omnium esse, ut supra dictum est.

AD SECUNDUM dicendum quod, licet corporalia dicantur esse in aliquo sicut in continente, tamen spiritualia continent ea in quibus sunt, sicut anima continet corpus. Unde et Deus est in rebus sicut continens res. Tamen, per quandam similitudinem corporalium, dicuntur omnia esse in Deo, inquantum continentur ab ipso.

AD TERTIUM dicendum quod nullius agentis, quantumcumque virtuosi, actio procedit ad aliquid distans, nisi inquantum in illud per media agit. Hoc autem ad maximam virtutem Dei pertinet, quod immediate in omnibus agit. Unde nihil est distans ab eo, quasi in se illud Deum non habeat. Dicuntur tamen res distare a Deo per dissimilitudinem naturae vel gratiae, sicut et ipse est super omnia per excellentiam suae naturae.

AD QUARTUM dicendum quod in Daemonibus intelligitur et natura, quae est a Deo, et deformitas culpae, quae non est ab ipso. Et ideo non est absolute concedendum quod Deus sit in Daemonibus, sed cum hac additione, inquantum sunt res quaedam. In rebus autem quae nominant naturam non deformatam, absolute dicendum est Deum esse.

Now God causes this effect in things not only when they first begin to be, but as long as they are preserved in being; as light is caused in the air by the sun as long as the air remains illuminated. Therefore as long as a thing has being, God must be present to it, according to its mode of being. But being is innermost in each thing and most fundamentally inherent in all things since it is formal in respect of everything found in a thing, as was shown above (Q. 7, A. 1). Hence it must be that God is in all things, and innermostly.

REPLY OBJ. 1: God is above all things by the excellence of His nature; nevertheless, He is in all things as the cause of the being of all things; as was shown above in this article.

REPLY OBJ. 2: Although corporeal things are said to be in another as in that which contains them, nevertheless, spiritual things contain those things in which they are; as the soul contains the body. Hence also God is in things containing them; nevertheless, by a certain similitude to corporeal things, it is said that all things are in God; inasmuch as they are contained by Him.

REPLY OBJ. 3: No action of an agent, however powerful it may be, acts at a distance, except through a medium. But it belongs to the great power of God that He acts immediately in all things. Hence nothing is distant from Him, as if it could be without God in itself. But things are said to be distant from God by the unlikeness to Him in nature or grace; as also He is above all by the excellence of His own nature.

REPLY OBJ. 4: In the demons there is their nature which is from God, and also the deformity of sin which is not from Him; therefore, it is not to be absolutely conceded that God is in the demons, except with the addition, *inasmuch as they are beings*. But in things not deformed in their nature, we must say absolutely that God is.

Article 2

Whether God Is Everywhere?

AD SECUNDUM SIC PROCEDITUR. Videtur quod Deus non sit ubique. Esse enim ubique significat esse in omni loco. Sed esse in omni loco non convenit Deo, cui non convenit esse in loco, nam *incorporalia*, ut dicit Boetius, in libro de Hebdomad., *non sunt in loco*. Ergo Deus non est ubique.

PRAETEREA, sicut se habet tempus ad successiva, ita se habet locus ad permanentia. Sed unum indivisibile actionis vel motus, non potest esse in diversis temporibus. Ergo nec unum indivisibile in genere rerum permanentium, potest esse in omnibus locis. Esse autem divinum

OBJECTION 1: It seems that God is not everywhere. For to be everywhere means to be in every place. But to be in every place does not belong to God, to Whom it does not belong to be in place at all; for *incorporeal things*, as Boethius says (*De Hebdom.*), *are not in a place*. Therefore God is not everywhere.

OBJ. 2: Further, the relation of time to succession is the same as the relation of place to permanence. But one indivisible part of action or movement cannot exist in different times; therefore neither can one indivisible part in the genus of permanent things be in every place. Now the divine

non est successivum, sed permanens. Ergo Deus non est in pluribus locis. Et ita non est ubique.

PRAETEREA, quod est totum alicubi, nihil eius est extra locum illum. Sed Deus, si est in aliquo loco, totus est ibi, non enim habet partes. Ergo nihil eius est extra locum illum. Ergo Deus non est ubique.

SED CONTRA est quod dicitur Ierem. XXIII, *caelum et terram ego impleo.*

RESPONDEO dicendum quod, cum locus sit res quaedam, esse aliquid in loco potest intelligi dupliciter, vel per modum aliarum rerum, idest sicut dicitur aliquid esse in aliis rebus quocumque modo, sicut accidentia loci sunt in loco; vel per modum proprium loci, sicut locata sunt in loco. Utroque autem modo, secundum aliquid, Deus est in omni loco, quod est esse ubique. Primo quidem, sicut est in omnibus rebus, ut dans eis esse et virtutem et operationem, sic enim est in omni loco, ut dans ei esse et virtutem locativam. Item, locata sunt in loco inquantum replent locum, et Deus omnem locum replet. Non sicut corpus, corpus enim dicitur replere locum, inquantum non compatitur secum aliud corpus; sed per hoc quod Deus est in aliquo loco, non excluditur quin alia sint ibi, imo per hoc replet omnia loca, quod dat esse omnibus locatis, quae replent omnia loca.

AD PRIMUM ergo dicendum quod incorporalia non sunt in loco per contactum quantitatis dimensivae, sicut corpora, sed per contactum virtutis.

AD SECUNDUM dicendum quod indivisibile est duplex. Unum quod est terminus continui, ut punctus in permanentibus, et momentum in successivis. Et huiusmodi indivisibile, in permanentibus, quia habet determinatum situm, non potest esse in pluribus partibus loci, vel in pluribus locis, et similiter indivisibile actionis vel motus, quia habet determinatum ordinem in motu vel actione, non potest esse in pluribus partibus temporis. Aliud autem indivisibile est, quod est extra totum genus continui, et hoc modo substantiae incorporeae, ut Deus, Angelus et anima, dicuntur esse indivisibiles. Tale igitur indivisibile non applicatur ad continuum sicut aliquid eius, sed inquantum contingit illud sua virtute. Unde secundum quod virtus sua se potest extendere ad unum vel multa, ad parvum vel magnum, secundum hoc est in uno vel pluribus locis, et in loco parvo vel magno.

AD TERTIUM dicendum quod totum dicitur respectu partium. Est autem duplex pars, scilicet pars essentiae, ut forma et materia dicuntur partes compositi, et genus et differentia partes speciei; et etiam pars quantitatis, in quam scilicet dividitur aliqua quantitas. Quod ergo est totum in aliquo loco totalitate quantitatis, non potest esse extra locum illum, quia quantitas locati commensuratur quantitati loci, unde non est totalitas quantitatis, si non sit totalitas loci. Sed totalitas essentiae non commensuratur totalitati loci. Unde non oportet quod illud quod est totum totalitate essentiae in aliquo, nullo

being is not successive but permanent. Therefore God is not in many places; and thus He is not everywhere.

OBJ. 3: Further, what is wholly in any one place is not in part elsewhere. But if God is in any one place He is all there; for He has no parts. No part of Him then is elsewhere; and therefore God is not everywhere.

ON THE CONTRARY, It is written, *I fill heaven and earth* (Jer 23:24).

I ANSWER THAT, Since place is a thing, to be in place can be understood in a twofold sense; either by way of other things—i.e., as one thing is said to be in another no matter how; and thus the accidents of a place are in place; or by a way proper to place; and thus things placed are in a place. Now in both these senses, in some way God is in every place; and this is to be everywhere. First, as He is in all things giving them being, power and operation; so He is in every place as giving it existence and locative power. Again, things placed are in place, inasmuch as they fill place; and God fills every place; not, indeed, like a body, for a body is said to fill place inasmuch as it excludes the co-presence of another body; whereas by God being in a place, others are not thereby excluded from it; indeed, by the very fact that He gives being to the things that fill every place, He Himself fills every place.

REPLY OBJ. 1: Incorporeal things are in place not by contact of dimensive quantity, as bodies are, but by contact of power.

REPLY OBJ. 2: The indivisible is twofold. One is the term of the continuous; as a point in permanent things, and as a moment in succession; and this kind of the indivisible in permanent things, forasmuch as it has a determinate site, cannot be in many parts of place, or in many places; likewise the indivisible of action or movement, forasmuch as it has a determinate order in movement or action, cannot be in many parts of time. Another kind of the indivisible is outside of the whole genus of the continuous; and in this way incorporeal substances, like God, angel and soul, are called indivisible. Such a kind of indivisible does not belong to the continuous, as a part of it, but as touching it by its power; hence, according as its power can extend itself to one or to many, to a small thing, or to a great one, in this way it is in one or in many places, and in a small or large place.

REPLY OBJ. 3: A whole is so called with reference to its parts. Now part is twofold: viz. a part of the essence, as the form and the matter are called parts of the composite, while genus and difference are called parts of species. There is also part of quantity into which any quantity is divided. What therefore is whole in any place by totality of quantity, cannot be outside of that place, because the quantity of anything placed is commensurate to the quantity of the place; and hence there is no totality of quantity without totality of place. But totality of essence is not commensurate to the totality of place. Hence it is not necessary for that which

modo sit extra illud. Sicut apparet etiam in formis accidentalibus, quae secundum accidens quantitatem habent, albedo enim est tota in qualibet parte superficiei, si accipiatur totalitas essentiae, quia secundum perfectam rationem suae speciei invenitur in qualibet parte superficiei, si autem accipiatur totalitas secundum quantitatem, quam habet per accidens, sic non est tota in qualibet parte superficiei. In substantiis autem incorporeis non est totalitas, nec per se nec per accidens, nisi secundum perfectam rationem essentiae. Et ideo, sicut anima est tota in qualibet parte corporis, ita Deus totus est in omnibus et singulis.

is whole by totality of essence in a thing, not to be at all outside of it. This appears also in accidental forms which have accidental quantity; as an example, whiteness is whole in each part of the surface if we speak of its totality of essence; because according to the perfect idea of its species it is found to exist in every part of the surface. But if its totality be considered according to quantity which it has accidentally, then it is not whole in every part of the surface. On the other hand, incorporeal substances have no totality either of themselves or accidentally, except in reference to the perfect idea of their essence. Hence, as the soul is whole in every part of the body, so is God whole in all things and in each one.

Article 3

Whether God Is Everywhere by Essence, Presence and Power?

AD TERTIUM SIC PROCEDITUR. Videtur quod male assignentur modi existendi Deum in rebus, cum dicitur quod Deus est in omnibus rebus per essentiam, potentiam et praesentiam. Id enim per essentiam est in aliquo, quod essentialiter est in eo. Deus autem non est essentialiter in rebus, non enim est de essentia alicuius rei. Ergo non debet dici quod Deus sit in rebus per essentiam, praesentiam et potentiam.

PRAETEREA, hoc est esse praesentem alicui rei, scilicet non deesse illi. Sed hoc est Deum esse per essentiam in rebus, scilicet non deesse alicui rei. Ergo idem est esse Deum in omnibus per essentiam et praesentiam. Superfluum ergo fuit dicere quod Deus sit in rebus per essentiam, praesentiam et potentiam.

PRAETEREA, sicut Deus est principium omnium rerum per suam potentiam, ita per scientiam et voluntatem. Sed non dicitur Deus esse in rebus per scientiam et voluntatem. Ergo nec per potentiam.

PRAETEREA, sicut gratia est quaedam perfectio superaddita substantiae rei, ita multae sunt aliae perfectiones superadditae. Si ergo Deus dicitur esse speciali modo in quibusdam per gratiam, videtur quod secundum quamlibet perfectionem debeat accipi specialis modus essendi Deum in rebus.

SED CONTRA est quod Gregorius dicit, super Cant. Cantic., quod *Deus communi modo est in omnibus rebus praesentia, potentia et substantia, tamen familiari modo dicitur esse in aliquibus per gratiam.*

RESPONDEO dicendum quod Deus dicitur esse in re aliqua dupliciter. Uno modo, per modum causae agentis, et sic est in omnibus rebus creatis ab ipso. Alio modo, sicut obiectum operationis est in operante, quod proprium est in operationibus animae, secundum quod cognitum

OBJECTION 1: It seems that the mode of God's existence in all things is not properly described by way of essence, presence and power. For what is by essence in anything, is in it essentially. But God is not essentially in things; for He does not belong to the essence of anything. Therefore it ought not to be said that God is in things by essence, presence and power.

OBJ. 2: Further, to be present in anything means not to be absent from it. Now this is the meaning of God being in things by His essence, that He is not absent from anything. Therefore the presence of God in all things by essence and presence means the same thing. Therefore it is superfluous to say that God is present in things by His essence, presence and power.

OBJ. 3: Further, as God by His power is the principle of all things, so He is the same likewise by His knowledge and will. But it is not said that He is in things by knowledge and will. Therefore neither is He present by His power.

OBJ. 4: Further, as grace is a perfection added to the substance of a thing, so many other perfections are likewise added. Therefore if God is said to be in certain persons in a special way by grace, it seems that according to every perfection there ought to be a special mode of God's existence in things.

ON THE CONTRARY, A gloss on the Canticle of Canticles (5) says that, *God by a common mode is in all things by His presence, power and substance; still He is said to be present more familiarly in some by grace.*

I ANSWER THAT, God is said to be in a thing in two ways; in one way after the manner of an efficient cause; and thus He is in all things created by Him; in another way he is in things as the object of operation is in the operator; and this is proper to the operations of the soul, according as the

est in cognoscente, et desideratum in desiderante. Hoc igitur secundo modo, Deus specialiter est in rationali creatura, quae cognoscit et diligit illum actu vel habitu. Et quia hoc habet rationalis creatura per gratiam, ut infra patebit, dicitur esse hoc modo in sanctis per gratiam.

In rebus vero aliis ab ipso creatis quomodo sit, considerandum est ex his quae in rebus humanis esse dicuntur. Rex enim dicitur esse in toto regno suo per suam potentiam, licet non sit ubique praesens. Per praesentiam vero suam, dicitur aliquid esse in omnibus quae in prospectu ipsius sunt; sicut omnia quae sunt in aliqua domo, dicuntur esse praesentia alicui, qui tamen non est secundum substantiam suam in qualibet parte domus. Secundum vero substantiam vel essentiam, dicitur aliquid esse in loco in quo eius substantia habetur. Fuerunt ergo aliqui, scilicet Manichaei, qui dixerunt divinae potestati subiecta spiritualia esse et incorporalia, visibilia vero et corporalia subiecta esse dicebant potestati principii contrarii. Contra hos ergo oportet dicere quod Deus sit in omnibus per potentiam suam.

Fuerunt vero alii, qui licet crederent omnia esse subiecta divinae potentiae, tamen providentiam divinam usque ad haec inferiora corpora non extendebant, ex quorum persona dicitur Iob XXII, *circa cardines caeli perambulat, nec nostra considerat.* Et contra hos oportuit dicere quod sit in omnibus per suam praesentiam.

Fuerunt vero alii, qui licet dicerent omnia ad Dei providentiam pertinere, tamen posuerunt omnia non immediate esse a Deo creata, sed quod immediate creavit primas creaturas, et illae creaverunt alias. Et contra hos oportet dicere quod sit in omnibus per essentiam.

Sic ergo est in omnibus per potentiam, inquantum omnia eius potestati subduntur. Est per praesentiam in omnibus, inquantum omnia nuda sunt et aperta oculis eius. Est in omnibus per essentiam, inquantum adest omnibus ut causa essendi, sicut dictum est.

AD PRIMUM ergo dicendum quod Deus dicitur esse in omnibus per essentiam, non quidem rerum, quasi sit de essentia earum, sed per essentiam suam, quia substantia sua adest omnibus ut causa essendi, sicut dictum est.

AD SECUNDUM dicendum quod aliquid potest dici praesens alicui, inquantum subiacet eius conspectui, quod tamen distat ab eo secundum suam substantiam, ut dictum est. Et ideo oportuit duos modos poni, scilicet per essentiam, et praesentiam.

AD TERTIUM dicendum quod de ratione scientiae et voluntatis est, quod scitum sit in sciente, et volitum in volente, unde secundum scientiam et voluntatem, magis res sunt in Deo, quam Deus in rebus. Sed de ratione potentiae est, quod sit principium agendi in aliud, unde secundum potentiam agens comparatur et applicatur rei

thing known is in the one who knows; and the thing desired in the one desiring. In this second way God is especially in the rational creature which knows and loves Him actually or habitually. And because the rational creature possesses this prerogative by grace, as will be shown later (Q. 12), He is said to be thus in the saints by grace.

But how He is in other things created by Him, may be considered from human affairs. A king, for example, is said to be in the whole kingdom by his power, although he is not everywhere present. Again a thing is said to be by its presence in other things which are subject to its inspection; as things in a house are said to be present to anyone, who nevertheless may not be in substance in every part of the house. Lastly, a thing is said to be by way of substance or essence in that place in which its substance may be. Now there were some (the Manichees) who said that spiritual and incorporeal things were subject to the divine power; but that visible and corporeal things were subject to the power of a contrary principle. Therefore against these it is necessary to say that God is in all things by His power.

But others, though they believed that all things were subject to the divine power, still did not allow that divine providence extended to these inferior bodies, and in the person of these it is said, *He walketh about the poles of the heavens; and He doth not consider our things* (Job 22:14). Against these it is necessary to say that God is in all things by His presence.

Further, others said that, although all things are subject to God's providence, still all things are not immediately created by God; but that He immediately created the first creatures, and these created the others. Against these it is necessary to say that He is in all things by His essence.

Therefore, God is in all things by His power, inasmuch as all things are subject to His power; He is by His presence in all things, as all things are bare and open to His eyes; He is in all things by His essence, inasmuch as He is present to all as the cause of their being.

REPLY OBJ. 1: God is said to be in all things by essence, not indeed by the essence of the things themselves, as if He were of their essence; but by His own essence; because His substance is present to all things as the cause of their being.

REPLY OBJ. 2: A thing can be said to be present to another, when in its sight, though the thing may be distant in substance, as was shown in this article; and therefore two modes of presence are necessary; viz. by essence and by presence.

REPLY OBJ. 3: Knowledge and will require that the thing known should be in the one who knows, and the thing willed in the one who wills. Hence by knowledge and will things are more truly in God than God in things. But power is the principle of acting on another; hence by power

exteriori. Et sic per potentiam potest dici agens esse in altero.

AD QUARTUM dicendum quod nulla alia perfectio superaddita substantiae, facit Deum esse in aliquo sicut obiectum cognitum et amatum, nisi gratia, et ideo sola gratia facit singularem modum essendi Deum in rebus. Est autem alius singularis modus essendi Deum in homine per unionem, de quo modo suo loco agetur.

the agent is related and applied to an external thing; thus by power an agent may be said to be present to another.

REPLY OBJ. 4: No other perfection, except grace, added to substance, renders God present in anything as the object known and loved; therefore only grace constitutes a special mode of God's existence in things. There is, however, another special mode of God's existence in man by union, which will be treated of in its own place (Part III).

Article 4

Whether to Be Everywhere Belongs to God Alone?

AD QUARTUM SIC PROCEDITUR. Videtur quod esse ubique non sit proprium Dei. Universale enim, secundum philosophum, est ubique et semper, materia etiam prima, cum sit in omnibus corporibus, est ubique. Neutrum autem horum est Deus, ut ex praemissis patet. Ergo esse ubique non est proprium Dei.

PRAETEREA, numerus est in numeratis. Sed totum universum est constitutum in numero, ut patet Sap. XI. Ergo aliquis numerus est, qui est in toto universo, et ita ubique.

PRAETEREA, totum universum est quoddam *totum corpus perfectum*, ut dicitur in I caeli et mundi. Sed totum universum est ubique, quia extra ipsum nullus locus est. Non ergo solus Deus est ubique.

PRAETEREA, si aliquod corpus esset infinitum, nullus locus esset extra ipsum. Ergo esset ubique. Et sic, esse ubique non videtur proprium Dei.

PRAETEREA, *anima*, ut dicit Augustinus, in VI de Trin., *est tota in toto corpore, et tota in qualibet eius parte*. Si ergo non esset in mundo nisi unum solum animal, anima eius esset ubique. Et sic, esse ubique non est proprium Dei.

PRAETEREA, ut Augustinus dicit in epistola ad Volusianum, *anima ubi videt, ibi sentit; et ubi sentit, ibi vivit; et ubi vivit, ibi est*. Sed anima videt quasi ubique, quia successive videt etiam totum caelum. Ergo anima est ubique.

SED CONTRA est quod Ambrosius dicit, in libro de spiritu sancto, *quis audeat creaturam dicere spiritum sanctum, qui in omnibus et ubique et semper est; quod utique divinitatis est proprium?*

RESPONDEO dicendum quod esse ubique primo et per se, est proprium Dei. Dico autem esse ubique primo, quod secundum se totum est ubique. Si quid enim esset ubique, secundum diversas partes in diversis locis existens, non esset primo ubique, quia quod convenit alicui

OBJECTION 1: It seems that to be everywhere does not belong to God alone. For the universal, according to the Philosopher (*Poster.* i), is everywhere, and always; primary matter also, since it is in all bodies, is everywhere. But neither of these is God, as appears from what is said above (Q. 3). Therefore to be everywhere does not belong to God alone.

OBJ. 2: Further, number is in things numbered. But the whole universe is constituted in number, as appears from the Book of Wisdom (Wis 11:21). Therefore there is some number which is in the whole universe, and is thus everywhere.

OBJ. 3: Further, the universe is a kind of *whole perfect body* (*Coel. et Mund.* i). But the whole universe is everywhere, because there is no place outside it. Therefore to be everywhere does not belong to God alone.

OBJ. 4: Further, if any body were infinite, no place would exist outside of it, and so it would be everywhere. Therefore to be everywhere does not appear to belong to God alone.

OBJ. 5: Further, *the soul*, as Augustine says (*De Trin.* vi, 6), is *whole in the whole body, and whole in every one of its parts*. Therefore if there was only one animal in the world, its soul would be everywhere; and thus to be everywhere does not belong to God alone.

OBJ. 6: Further, as Augustine says (Ep. 137), *The soul feels where it sees, and lives where it feels, and is where it lives*. But the soul sees as it were everywhere: for in a succession of glances it comprehends the entire space of the heavens in its sight. Therefore the soul is everywhere.

ON THE CONTRARY, Ambrose says (*De Spir. Sanct.* i, 7): *Who dares to call the Holy Spirit a creature, Who in all things, and everywhere, and always is, which assuredly belongs to the divinity alone?*

I ANSWER THAT, To be everywhere primarily and absolutely, is proper to God. Now to be everywhere primarily is said of that which in its whole self is everywhere; for if a thing were everywhere according to its parts in different places, it would not be primarily everywhere, forasmuch as

ratione partis suae, non convenit ei primo; sicut si homo est albus dente, albedo non convenit primo homini, sed denti. Esse autem ubique per se dico id cui non convenit esse ubique per accidens, propter aliquam suppositionem factam, quia sic granum milii esset ubique, supposito quod nullum aliud corpus esset. Per se igitur convenit esse ubique alicui, quando tale est quod, qualibet positione facta, sequitur illud esse ubique. Et hoc proprie convenit Deo. Quia quotcumque loca ponantur, etiam si ponerentur infinita praeter ista quae sunt, oporteret in omnibus esse Deum, quia nihil potest esse nisi per ipsum. Sic igitur esse ubique primo et per se convenit Deo, et est proprium eius, quia quotcumque loca ponantur, oportet quod in quolibet sit Deus, non secundum partem, sed secundum seipsum.

AD PRIMUM ergo dicendum quod universale et materia prima sunt quidem ubique, sed non secundum idem esse.

AD SECUNDUM dicendum quod numerus, cum sit accidens, non est per se sed per accidens, in loco. Nec est totus in quolibet numeratorum, sed secundum partem. Et sic non sequitur quod sit primo et per se ubique.

AD TERTIUM dicendum quod totum corpus universi est ubique, sed non primo, quia non totum est in quolibet loco, sed secundum suas partes. Nec iterum per se, quia si ponerentur aliqua alia loca, non esset in eis.

AD QUARTUM dicendum quod, si esset corpus infinitum, esset ubique; sed secundum suas partes.

AD QUINTUM dicendum quod, si esset unum solum animal, anima eius esset ubique primo quidem, sed per accidens.

AD SEXTUM dicendum quod, cum dicitur anima alicubi videre, potest intelligi dupliciter. Uno modo, secundum quod hoc adverbium alicubi determinat actum videndi ex parte obiecti. Et sic verum est quod, dum caelum videt, in caelo videt, et eadem ratione in caelo sentit. Non tamen sequitur quod in caelo vivat vel sit, quia vivere et esse non important actum transeuntem in exterius obiectum. Alio modo potest intelligi secundum quod adverbium determinat actum videntis, secundum quod exit a vidente. Et sic verum est quod anima ubi sentit et videt, ibi est et vivit, secundum istum modum loquendi. Et ita non sequitur quod sit ubique.

what belongs to anything according to part does not belong to it primarily; thus if a man has white teeth, whiteness belongs primarily not to the man but to his teeth. But a thing is everywhere absolutely when it does not belong to it to be everywhere accidentally, that is, merely on some supposition; as a grain of millet would be everywhere, supposing that no other body existed. It belongs therefore to a thing to be everywhere absolutely when, on any supposition, it must be everywhere; and this properly belongs to God alone. For whatever number of places be supposed, even if an infinite number be supposed besides what already exist, it would be necessary that God should be in all of them; for nothing can exist except by Him. Therefore to be everywhere primarily and absolutely belongs to God and is proper to Him: because whatever number of places be supposed to exist, God must be in all of them, not as to a part of Him, but as to His very self.

REPLY OBJ. 1: The universal, and also primary matter are indeed everywhere; but not according to the same mode of existence.

REPLY OBJ. 2: Number, since it is an accident, does not, of itself, exist in place, but accidentally; neither is the whole but only part of it in each of the things numbered; hence it does not follow that it is primarily and absolutely everywhere.

REPLY OBJ. 3: The whole body of the universe is everywhere, but not primarily; forasmuch as it is not wholly in each place, but according to its parts; nor again is it everywhere absolutely, because, supposing that other places existed besides itself, it would not be in them.

REPLY OBJ. 4: If an infinite body existed, it would be everywhere; but according to its parts.

REPLY OBJ. 5: Were there one animal only, its soul would be everywhere primarily indeed, but only accidentally.

REPLY OBJ. 6: When it is said that the soul sees anywhere, this can be taken in two senses. In one sense the adverb *anywhere* determines the act of seeing on the part of the object; and in this sense it is true that while it sees the heavens, it sees in the heavens; and in the same way it feels in the heavens; but it does not follow that it lives or exists in the heavens, because to live and to exist do not import an act passing to an exterior object. In another sense it can be understood according as the adverb determines the act of the seer, as proceeding from the seer; and thus it is true that where the soul feels and sees, there it is, and there it lives according to this mode of speaking; and thus it does not follow that it is everywhere.

QUESTION 9

THE IMMUTABILITY OF GOD

Consequenter considerandum est de immutabilitate et aeternitate divina, quae immutabilitatem consequitur. Circa immutabilitatem vero quaeruntur duo.

Primo, utrum Deus sit omnino immutabilis.
Secundo, utrum esse immutabile sit proprium Dei.

We next consider God's immutability, and His eternity following on His immutability.

On the immutability of God there are two points of inquiry:

(1) Whether God is altogether immutable?
(2) Whether to be immutable belongs to God alone?

Article 1

Whether God is Altogether Immutable?

AD PRIMUM SIC PROCEDITUR. Videtur quod Deus non sit omnino immutabilis. Quidquid enim movet seipsum, est aliquo modo mutabile. Sed, sicut dicit Augustinus, VIII super Genesim ad litteram, *spiritus creator movet se nec per tempus nec per locum*. Ergo Deus est aliquo modo mutabilis.

PRAETEREA, Sap. VII dicitur de sapientia quod est *mobilior omnibus mobilibus*. Sed Deus est ipsa sapientia. Ergo Deus est mobilis.

PRAETEREA, appropinquari et elongari motum significant. Huiusmodi autem dicuntur de Deo in Scriptura, Iac. IV, *appropinquate Deo, et appropinquabit vobis*. Ergo Deus est mutabilis.

SED CONTRA est quod dicitur Malach. III, *ego Deus, et non mutor*.

RESPONDEO dicendum quod ex praemissis ostenditur Deum esse omnino immutabilem. Primo quidem, quia supra ostensum est esse aliquod primum ens, quod Deum dicimus, et quod huiusmodi primum ens oportet esse purum actum absque permixtione alicuius potentiae, eo quod potentia simpliciter est posterior actu. Omne autem quod quocumque modo mutatur, est aliquo modo in potentia. Ex quo patet quod impossibile est Deum aliquo modo mutari. Secundo, quia omne quod movetur, quantum ad aliquid manet, et quantum ad aliquid transit, sicut quod movetur de albedine in nigredinem, manet secundum substantiam. Et sic in omni eo quod movetur, attenditur aliqua compositio. Ostensum est autem supra quod in Deo nulla est compositio, sed est omnino simplex. Unde manifestum est quod Deus moveri non potest. Tertio, quia omne quod movetur, motu suo aliquid acquirit, et pertingit ad illud ad quod prius non pertingebat. Deus autem, cum sit infinitus, comprehendens in se omnem plenitudinem perfectionis totius esse, non potest aliquid acquirere, nec extendere

OBJECTION 1: It seems that God is not altogether immutable. For whatever moves itself is in some way mutable. But, as Augustine says (Gen ad lit, viii, 20), *The Creator Spirit moves Himself neither by time, nor by place.* Therefore God is in some way mutable.

OBJ. 2: Further, it is said of Wisdom, that *it is more mobile than all things active* (Wis 7:24). But God is wisdom itself; therefore God is movable.

OBJ. 3: Further, to approach and to recede signify movement. But these are said of God in Scripture, *Draw nigh to God and He will draw nigh to you* (Jas 4:8). Therefore God is mutable.

ON THE CONTRARY, It is written, *I am the Lord, and I change not* (Mal 3:6).

I ANSWER THAT, From what precedes, it is shown that God is altogether immutable. First, because it was shown above that there is some first being, whom we call God; and that this first being must be pure act, without the admixture of any potentiality, for the reason that, absolutely, potentiality is posterior to act. Now everything which is in any way changed, is in some way in potentiality. Hence it is evident that it is impossible for God to be in any way changeable. Second, because everything which is moved, remains as it was in part, and passes away in part; as what is moved from whiteness to blackness, remains the same as to substance; thus in everything which is moved, there is some kind of composition to be found. But it has been shown above (Q. 3, A. 7) that in God there is no composition, for He is altogether simple. Hence it is manifest that God cannot be moved. Third, because everything which is moved acquires something by its movement, and attains to what it had not attained previously. But since God is infinite, comprehending in Himself all the plenitude of perfection of all being, He cannot acquire anything new, nor extend Himself to

se in aliquid ad quod prius non pertingebat. Unde nullo modo sibi competit motus. Et inde est quod quidam antiquorum, quasi ab ipsa veritate coacti, posuerunt primum principium esse immobile.

AD PRIMUM ergo dicendum quod Augustinus ibi loquitur secundum modum quo Plato dicebat primum movens movere seipsum, omnem operationem nominans motum; secundum quod etiam ipsum intelligere et velle et amare motus quidam dicuntur. Quia ergo Deus intelligit et amat seipsum, secundum hoc dixerunt quod Deus movet seipsum, non autem secundum quod motus et mutatio est existentis in potentia, ut nunc loquimur de mutatione et motu.

AD SECUNDUM dicendum quod sapientia dicitur mobilis esse similitudinarie, secundum quod suam similitudinem diffundit usque ad ultima rerum. Nihil enim esse potest, quod non procedat a divina sapientia per quandam imitationem, sicut a primo principio effectivo et formali; prout etiam artificiata procedunt a sapientia artificis. Sic igitur inquantum similitudo divinae sapientiae gradatim procedit a supremis, quae magis participant de eius similitudine, usque ad infima rerum, quae minus participant dicitur esse quidam processus et motus divinae sapientiae in res, sicut si dicamus solem procedere usque ad terram, inquantum radius luminis eius usque ad terram pertingit. Et hoc modo exponit Dionysius, cap. I Cael. Hier., dicens quod *omnis processus divinae manifestationis venit ad nos a patre luminum moto.*

AD TERTIUM dicendum quod huiusmodi dicuntur de Deo in Scripturis metaphorice. Sicut enim dicitur sol intrare domum vel exire, inquantum radius eius pertingit ad domum; sic dicitur Deus appropinquare ad nos vel recedere a nobis, inquantum percipimus influentiam bonitatis ipsius, vel ab eo deficimus.

anything whereto He was not extended previously. Hence movement in no way belongs to Him. So, some of the ancients, constrained, as it were, by the truth, decided that the first principle was immovable.

REPLY OBJ. 1: Augustine there speaks in a similar way to Plato, who said that the first mover moves Himself; calling every operation a movement, even as the acts of understanding, and willing, and loving, are called movements. Therefore because God understands and loves Himself, in that respect they said that God moves Himself, not, however, as movement and change belong to a thing existing in potentiality, as we now speak of change and movement.

REPLY OBJ. 2: Wisdom is called mobile by way of similitude, according as it diffuses its likeness even to the outermost of things; for nothing can exist which does not proceed from the divine wisdom by way of some kind of imitation, as from the first effective and formal principle; as also works of art proceed from the wisdom of the artist. And so in the same way, inasmuch as the similitude of the divine wisdom proceeds in degrees from the highest things, which participate more fully of its likeness, to the lowest things which participate of it in a lesser degree, there is said to be a kind of procession and movement of the divine wisdom to things; as when we say that the sun proceeds to the earth, inasmuch as the ray of light touches the earth. In this way Dionysius (*Coel. Hier.* i) expounds the matter, that every procession of the divine manifestation comes to us from the movement of the Father of light.

REPLY OBJ. 3: These things are said of God in Scripture metaphorically. For as the sun is said to enter a house, or to go out, according as its rays reach the house, so God is said to approach to us, or to recede from us, when we receive the influx of His goodness, or decline from Him.

Article 2

Whether to Be Immutable Belongs to God Alone?

AD SECUNDUM SIC PROCEDITUR. Videtur quod esse immutabile non sit proprium Dei. Dicit enim philosophus, in II Metaphys., quod *materia est in omni eo quod movetur.* Sed substantiae quaedam creatae, sicut Angeli et animae, non habent materiam, ut quibusdam videtur. Ergo esse immutabile non est proprium Dei.

PRAETEREA, omne quod movetur, movetur propter aliquem finem, quod ergo iam pervenit ad ultimum finem, non movetur. Sed quaedam creaturae iam pervenerunt ad ultimum finem, sicut omnes beati. Ergo aliquae creaturae sunt immobiles.

OBJECTION 1: It seems that to be immutable does not belong to God alone. For the Philosopher says (*Metaph.* ii) that *matter is in everything which is moved*. But, according to some, certain created substances, as angels and souls, have not matter. Therefore to be immutable does not belong to God alone.

OBJ. 2: Further, everything in motion moves to some end. What therefore has already attained its ultimate end, is not in motion. But some creatures have already attained to their ultimate end; as all the blessed in heaven. Therefore some creatures are immovable.

PRAETEREA, omne quod est mutabile, est variabile. Sed formae sunt invariabiles, dicitur enim in libro sex principiorum, quod *forma est simplici et invariabili essentia consistens*. Ergo non est solius Dei proprium esse immutabile.

SED CONTRA est quod dicit Augustinus, in libro de natura boni, *solus Deus immutabilis est; quae autem fecit, quia ex nihilo sunt, mutabilia sunt.*

RESPONDEO dicendum quod solus Deus est omnino immutabilis, omnis autem creatura aliquo modo est mutabilis. Sciendum est enim quod mutabile potest aliquid dici dupliciter, uno modo, per potentiam quae in ipso est; alio modo, per potentiam quae in altero est. Omnes enim creaturae, antequam essent, non erant possibiles esse per aliquam potentiam creatam, cum nullum creatum sit aeternum, sed per solam potentiam divinam, inquantum Deus poterat eas in esse producere. Sicut autem ex voluntate Dei dependet quod res in esse producit, ita ex voluntate eius dependet quod res in esse conservat, non enim aliter eas in esse conservat, quam semper eis esse dando; unde si suam actionem eis subtraheret, omnia in nihilum redigerentur, ut patet per Augustinum, IV super Gen. ad Litt. Sicut igitur in potentia creatoris fuit ut res essent, antequam essent in seipsis, ita in potentia creatoris est, postquam sunt in seipsis, ut non sint. Sic igitur per potentiam quae est in altero, scilicet in Deo, sunt mutabiles, inquantum ab ipso ex nihilo potuerunt produci in esse, et de esse possunt reduci in non esse.

Si autem dicatur aliquid mutabile per potentiam in ipso existentem, sic etiam aliquo modo omnis creatura est mutabilis. Est enim in creatura duplex potentia, scilicet activa et passiva. Dico autem potentiam passivam, secundum quam aliquid assequi potest suam perfectionem, vel in essendo vel in consequendo finem. Si igitur attendatur mutabilitas rei secundum potentiam ad esse, sic non in omnibus creaturis est mutabilitas, sed in illis solum in quibus illud quod est possibile in eis, potest stare cum non esse. Unde in corporibus inferioribus est mutabilitas et secundum esse substantiale, quia materia eorum potest esse cum privatione formae substantialis ipsorum, et quantum ad esse accidentale, si subiectum compatiatur secum privationem accidentis; sicut hoc subiectum, homo, compatitur secum non album, et ideo potest mutari de albo in non album. Si vero sit tale accidens quod consequatur principia essentialia subiecti, privatio illius accidentis non potest stare cum subiecto, unde subiectum non potest mutari secundum illud accidens, sicut nix non potest fieri nigra. In corporibus vero caelestibus, materia non compatitur secum privationem formae, quia forma perficit totam potentialitatem materiae, et ideo non sunt mutabilia secundum esse substantiale; sed secundum esse locale, quia subiectum compatitur secum privationem huius loci vel illius. Substantiae

OBJ. 3: Further, everything which is mutable is variable. But forms are invariable; for it is said (Sex Princip. i) that *form is essence consisting of the simple and invariable.* Therefore it does not belong to God alone to be immutable.

ON THE CONTRARY, Augustine says (De Nat. Boni. i), *God alone is immutable; and whatever things He has made, being from nothing, are mutable.*

I ANSWER THAT, God alone is altogether immutable; whereas every creature is in some way mutable. Be it known therefore that a mutable thing can be called so in two ways: by a power in itself; and by a power possessed by another. For all creatures before they existed, were possible, not by any created power, since no creature is eternal, but by the divine power alone, inasmuch as God could produce them into existence. Thus, as the production of a thing into existence depends on the will of God, so likewise it depends on His will that things should be preserved; for He does not preserve them otherwise than by ever giving them existence; hence if He took away His action from them, all things would be reduced to nothing, as appears from Augustine (*Gen ad lit.* iv, 12). Therefore as it was in the Creator's power to produce them before they existed in themselves, so likewise it is in the Creator's power when they exist in themselves to bring them to nothing. In this way therefore, by the power of another—namely, of God—they are mutable, inasmuch as they are producible from nothing by Him, and are by Him reducible from existence to non-existence.

If, however, a thing is called mutable by a power in itself, thus also in some manner every creature is mutable. For every creature has a twofold power, active and passive; and I call that power passive which enables anything to attain its perfection either in being, or in attaining to its end. Now if the mutability of a thing be considered according to its power for being, in that way all creatures are not mutable, but those only in which what is potential in them is consistent with non-being. Hence, in the inferior bodies there is mutability both as regards substantial being, inasmuch as their matter can exist with privation of their substantial form, and also as regards their accidental being, supposing the subject to coexist with privation of accident; as, for example, this subject man can exist with not-whiteness and can therefore be changed from white to not-white. But supposing the accident to be such as to follow on the essential principles of the subject, then the privation of such an accident cannot coexist with the subject. Hence the subject cannot be changed as regards that kind of accident; as, for example, snow cannot be made black. Now in the celestial bodies matter is not consistent with privation of form, because the form perfects the whole potentiality of the matter; therefore these bodies are not mutable as to substantial being, but only as to locality, because the subject is consistent with privation of this or that place.

vero incorporeae, quia sunt ipsae formae subsistentes, quae tamen se habent ad esse ipsarum sicut potentia ad actum, non compatiuntur secum privationem huius actus, quia esse consequitur formam, et nihil corrumpitur nisi per hoc quod amittit formam. Unde in ipsa forma non est potentia ad non esse, et ideo huiusmodi substantiae sunt immutabiles et invariabiles secundum esse. Et hoc est quod dicit Dionysius, IV cap. de Div. Nom., quod *substantiae intellectuales creatae mundae sunt a generatione et ab omni variatione, sicut incorporales et immateriales.* Sed tamen remanet in eis duplex mutabilitas. Una secundum quod sunt in potentia ad finem, et sic est in eis mutabilitas secundum electionem de bono in malum, ut Damascenus dicit. Alia secundum locum, inquantum virtute sua finita possunt attingere quaedam loca quae prius non attingebant, quod de Deo dici non potest, qui sua infinitate omnia loca replet, ut supra dictum est.

Sic igitur in omni creatura est potentia ad mutationem, vel secundum esse substantiale, sicut corpora corruptibilia; vel secundum esse locale tantum, sicut corpora caelestia, vel secundum ordinem ad finem et applicationem virtutis ad diversa, sicut in Angelis. Et universaliter omnes creaturae communiter sunt mutabiles secundum potentiam creantis, in cuius potestate est esse et non esse earum. Unde, cum Deus nullo istorum modorum sit mutabilis, proprium eius est omnino immutabilem esse.

AD PRIMUM ergo dicendum quod obiectio illa procedit de eo quod est mutabile secundum esse substantiale vel accidentale, de tali enim motu philosophi tractaverunt.

AD SECUNDUM dicendum quod Angeli boni, supra immutabilitatem essendi, quae competit eis secundum naturam, habent immutabilitatem electionis ex divina virtute, tamen remanet in eis mutabilitas secundum locum.

AD TERTIUM dicendum quod formae dicuntur invariabiles, quia non possunt esse subiectum variationis, subiiciuntur tamen variationi, inquantum subiectum secundum eas variatur. Unde patet quod secundum quod sunt, sic variantur, non enim dicuntur entia quasi sint subiectum essendi, sed quia eis aliquid est.

On the other hand, incorporeal substances, being subsistent forms which, although with respect to their own existence are as potentiality to act, are not consistent with the privation of this act; forasmuch as existence is consequent upon form, and nothing corrupts except it lose its form. Hence in the form itself there is no power to non-existence; and so these kinds of substances are immutable and invariable as regards their existence. Wherefore Dionysius says (*Div. Nom.* iv) that *intellectual created substances are pure from generation and from every variation, as also are incorporeal and immaterial substances.* Still, there remains in them a twofold mutability: one as regards their potentiality to their end; and in that way there is in them a mutability according to choice from good to evil, as Damascene says (*De Fide* ii, 3,4); the other as regards place, inasmuch as by their finite power they attain to certain fresh places—which cannot be said of God, who by His infinity fills all places, as was shown above (Q. 8, A. 2).

Thus in every creature there is a potentiality to change either as regards substantial being as in the case of things corruptible; or as regards locality only, as in the case of the celestial bodies; or as regards the order to their end, and the application of their powers to diverse objects, as in the case with the angels; and universally all creatures generally are mutable by the power of the Creator, in Whose power is their existence and non-existence. Hence since God is in none of these ways mutable, it belongs to Him alone to be altogether immutable.

REPLY OBJ. 1: This objection proceeds from mutability as regards substantial or accidental being; for philosophers treated of such movement.

REPLY OBJ. 2: The good angels, besides their natural endowment of immutability of being, have also immutability of election by divine power; nevertheless there remains in them mutability as regards place.

REPLY OBJ. 3: Forms are called invariable, forasmuch as they cannot be subjects of variation; but they are subject to variation because by them their subject is variable. Hence it is clear that they vary in so far as they are; for they are not called beings as though they were the subject of being, but because through them something has being.

QUESTION 10

THE ETERNITY OF GOD

Deinde quaeritur de aeternitate. Et circa hoc quaeruntur sex.

Primo, quid sit aeternitas.

Secundo, utrum Deus sit aeternus.

Tertio, utrum esse aeternum sit proprium Dei.

Quarto, utrum aeternitas differat a tempore.

Quinto, de differentia aevi et temporis.

Sexto, utrum sit unum aevum tantum, sicut est unum tempus et una aeternitas.

We must now consider the eternity of God, concerning which arise six points of inquiry:

(1) What is eternity?

(2) Whether God is eternal?

(3) Whether to be eternal belongs to God alone?

(4) Whether eternity differs from time?

(5) The difference of aeviternity and of time.

(6) Whether there is only one aeviternity, as there is one time, and one eternity?

Article 1

Whether This Is a Good Definition of Eternity, The Simultaneously-Whole and Perfect Possession of Interminable Life?

AD PRIMUM SIC PROCEDITUR. Videtur quod non sit conveniens definitio aeternitatis, quam Boetius ponit V de consolatione, dicens quod *aeternitas est interminabilis vitae tota simul et perfecta possessio.* Interminabile enim negative dicitur. Sed negatio non est de ratione nisi eorum quae sunt deficientia, quod aeternitati non competit. Ergo in definitione aeternitatis non debet poni interminabile.

PRAETEREA, aeternitas durationem quandam significat. Duratio autem magis respicit esse quam vitam. Ergo non debuit poni in definitione aeternitatis vita, sed magis esse.

PRAETEREA, totum dicitur quod habet partes. Hoc autem aeternitati non convenit, cum sit simplex. Ergo inconvenienter dicitur tota.

PRAETEREA, plures dies non possunt esse simul, nec plura tempora. Sed in aeternitate pluraliter dicuntur dies et tempora, dicitur enim Micheae V, *egressus eius ab initio, a diebus aeternitatis*; et ad Rom., XVI cap., *secundum revelationem mysterii temporibus aeternis taciti.* Ergo aeternitas non est tota simul.

PRAETEREA, totum et perfectum sunt idem. Posito igitur quod sit tota, superflue additur quod sit perfecta.

PRAETEREA, possessio ad durationem non pertinet. Aeternitas autem quaedam duratio est. Ergo aeternitas non est possessio.

RESPONDEO dicendum quod, sicut in cognitionem simplicium oportet nos venire per composita, ita in cognitionem aeternitatis oportet nos venire per tempus; quod nihil aliud est quam numerus motus secundum

OBJECTION 1: It seems that the definition of eternity given by Boethius (*De Consol.* v) is not a good one: *Eternity is the simultaneously-whole and perfect possession of interminable life.* For the word *interminable* is a negative one. But negation only belongs to what is defective, and this does not belong to eternity. Therefore in the definition of eternity the word *interminable* ought not to be found.

OBJ. 2: Further, eternity signifies a certain kind of duration. But duration regards existence rather than life. Therefore the word *life* ought not to come into the definition of eternity; but rather the word *existence.*

OBJ. 3: Further, a whole is what has parts. But this is alien to eternity which is simple. Therefore it is improperly said to be *whole.*

OBJ. 4: Many days cannot occur together, nor can many times exist all at once. But in eternity, days and times are in the plural, for it is said, *His going forth is from the beginning, from the days of eternity* (Mic 5:2); and also it is said, *According to the revelation of the mystery hidden from eternity* (Rom 16:25). Therefore eternity is not omni-simultaneous.

OBJ. 5: Further, the whole and the perfect are the same thing. Supposing, therefore, that it is *whole*, it is superfluously described as *perfect.*

OBJ. 6: Further, duration does not imply *possession.* But eternity is a kind of duration. Therefore eternity is not possession.

I ANSWER THAT, As we attain to the knowledge of simple things by way of compound things, so must we reach to the knowledge of eternity by means of time, which is nothing but the numbering of movement by before and after.

prius et posterius. Cum enim in quolibet motu sit successio, et una pars post alteram, ex hoc quod numeramus prius et posterius in motu, apprehendimus tempus; quod nihil aliud est quam numerus prioris et posterioris in motu. In eo autem quod caret motu, et semper eodem modo se habet, non est accipere prius et posterius. Sicut igitur ratio temporis consistit in numeratione prioris et posterioris in motu, ita in apprehensione uniformitatis eius quod est omnino extra motum, consistit ratio aeternitatis.

Item, ea dicuntur tempore mensurari, quae principium et finem habent in tempore, ut dicitur in IV Physic., et hoc ideo, quia in omni eo quod movetur est accipere aliquod principium et aliquem finem. Quod vero est omnino immutabile, sicut nec successionem, ita nec principium aut finem habere potest.

Sic ergo ex duobus notificatur aeternitas. Primo, ex hoc quod id quod est in aeternitate, est interminabile, idest principio et fine carens (ut terminus ad utrumque referatur). Secundo, per hoc quod ipsa aeternitas successione caret, tota simul existens.

AD PRIMUM ergo dicendum quod simplicia consueverunt per negationem definiri, sicut punctus est cuius pars non est. Quod non ideo est, quod negatio sit de essentia eorum, sed quia intellectus noster, qui primo apprehendit composita, in cognitionem simplicium pervenire non potest, nisi per remotionem compositionis.

AD SECUNDUM dicendum quod illud quod est vere aeternum, non solum est ens, sed vivens, et ipsum vivere se extendit quodammodo ad operationem, non autem esse. Protensio autem durationis videtur attendi secundum operationem, magis quam secundum esse, unde et tempus est numerus motus.

AD TERTIUM dicendum quod aeternitas dicitur tota, non quia habet partes, sed inquantum nihil ei deest.

AD QUARTUM dicendum quod, sicut Deus, cum sit incorporeus, nominibus rerum corporalium metaphorice in Scripturis nominatur, sic aeternitas, tota simul existens, nominibus temporalibus successivis.

AD QUINTUM dicendum quod in tempore est duo considerare, scilicet ipsum tempus, quod est successivum; et nunc temporis, quod est imperfectum. Dicit ergo tota simul, ad removendum tempus, et perfecta, ad excludendum nunc temporis.

AD SEXTUM dicendum quod illud quod possidetur, firmiter et quiete habetur. Ad designandam ergo immutabilitatem et indeficientiam aeternitatis, usus est nomine possessionis.

For since succession occurs in every movement, and one part comes after another, the fact that we reckon before and after in movement, makes us apprehend time, which is nothing else but the measure of before and after in movement. Now in a thing bereft of movement, which is always the same, there is no before or after. As therefore the idea of time consists in the numbering of before and after in movement; so likewise in the apprehension of the uniformity of what is outside of movement, consists the idea of eternity.

Further, those things are said to be measured by time which have a beginning and an end in time, because in everything which is moved there is a beginning, and there is an end. But as whatever is wholly immutable can have no succession, so it has no beginning, and no end.

Thus eternity is known from two sources: first, because what is eternal is interminable—that is, has no beginning nor end (that is, no term either way); second, because eternity has no succession, being simultaneously whole.

REPLY OBJ. 1: Simple things are usually defined by way of negation; as *a point is that which has no parts*. Yet this is not to be taken as if the negation belonged to their essence, but because our intellect which first apprehends compound things, cannot attain to the knowledge of simple things except by removing the opposite.

REPLY OBJ. 2: What is truly eternal, is not only being, but also living; and life extends to operation, which is not true of being. Now the protraction of duration seems to belong to operation rather than to being; hence time is the numbering of movement.

REPLY OBJ. 3: Eternity is called whole, not because it has parts, but because it is wanting in nothing.

REPLY OBJ. 4: As God, although incorporeal, is named in Scripture metaphorically by corporeal names, so eternity though simultaneously whole, is called by names implying time and succession.

REPLY OBJ. 5: Two things are to be considered in time: time itself, which is successive; and the *now* of time, which is imperfect. Hence the expression *simultaneously-whole* is used to remove the idea of time, and the word *perfect* is used to exclude the *now* of time.

REPLY OBJ. 6: Whatever is possessed, is held firmly and quietly; therefore to designate the immutability and permanence of eternity, we use the word *possession*.

Article 2

Whether God is Eternal?

AD SECUNDUM SIC PROCEDITUR. Videtur quod Deus non sit aeternus. Nihil enim factum potest dici de Deo. Sed aeternitas est aliquid factum, dicit enim Boetius quod *nunc fluens facit tempus, nunc stans facit aeternitatem*; et Augustinus dicit, in libro octoginta trium quaest., quod Deus est auctor aeternitatis. Ergo Deus non est aeternus.

PRAETEREA, quod est ante aeternitatem et post aeternitatem, non mensuratur aeternitate. Sed Deus est ante aeternitatem, ut dicitur in libro de causis, et post aeternitatem; dicitur enim Exod. XV, quod *dominus regnabit in aeternum et ultra*. Ergo esse aeternum non convenit Deo.

PRAETEREA, aeternitas mensura quaedam est. Sed Deo non convenit esse mensuratum. Ergo non competit ei esse aeternum.

PRAETEREA, in aeternitate non est praesens, praeteritum vel futurum cum sit tota simul, ut dictum est. Sed de Deo dicuntur in Scripturis verba praesentis temporis, praeteriti vel futuri. Ergo Deus non est aeternus.

SED CONTRA est quod dicit Athanasius, *aeternus pater, aeternus filius, aeternus Spiritus Sanctus*.

RESPONDEO dicendum quod ratio aeternitatis consequitur immutabilitatem, sicut ratio temporis consequitur motum, ut ex dictis patet. Unde, cum Deus sit maxime immutabilis, sibi maxime competit esse aeternum. Nec solum est aeternus, sed est sua aeternitas, cum tamen nulla alia res sit sua duratio, quia non est suum esse. Deus autem est suum esse uniforme, unde, sicut est sua essentia, ita est sua aeternitas.

AD PRIMUM ergo dicendum quod nunc stans dicitur facere aeternitatem, secundum nostram apprehensionem. Sicut enim causatur in nobis apprehensio temporis, eo quod apprehendimus fluxum ipsius nunc, ita causatur in nobis apprehensio aeternitatis, inquantum apprehendimus nunc stans. Quod autem dicit Augustinus, quod *Deus est auctor aeternitatis*, intelligitur de aeternitate participata, eo enim modo communicat Deus suam aeternitatem aliquibus, quo et suam immutabilitatem.

ET PER HOC patet solutio ad secundum. Nam Deus dicitur esse ante aeternitatem, prout participatur a substantiis immaterialibus. Unde et ibidem dicitur, quod *intelligentia parificatur aeternitati*. Quod autem dicitur in Exodo, *dominus regnabit in aeternum et ultra* sciendum quod aeternum accipitur ibi pro saeculo, sicut habet alia translatio. Sic igitur dicitur quod regnabit ultra aeternum, quia durat ultra quodcumque saeculum, idest ultra quamcumque durationem datam, nihil est enim

OBJECTION 1: It seems that God is not eternal. For nothing made can be predicated of God; for Boethius says (*De Trin.* iv) that, *The now that flows away makes time, the now that stands still makes eternity*; and Augustine says (*Octog. Tri. Quaest.* qu. 28) *that God is the author of eternity*. Therefore God is not eternal.

OBJ. 2: Further, what is before eternity, and after eternity, is not measured by eternity. But, as Aristotle says (*De Causis*), *God is before eternity and He is after eternity*: for it is written that *the Lord shall reign for eternity, and beyond* (Exod 15:18). Therefore to be eternal does not belong to God.

OBJ. 3: Further, eternity is a kind of measure. But to be measured belongs not to God. Therefore it does not belong to Him to be eternal.

OBJ. 4: Further, in eternity, there is no present, past or future, since it is simultaneously whole; as was said in the preceding article. But words denoting present, past and future time are applied to God in Scripture. Therefore God is not eternal.

ON THE CONTRARY, Athanasius says in his Creed: *The Father is eternal, the Son is eternal, the Holy Spirit is eternal.*

I ANSWER THAT, The idea of eternity follows immutability, as the idea of time follows movement, as appears from the preceding article. Hence, as God is supremely immutable, it supremely belongs to Him to be eternal. Nor is He eternal only; but He is His own eternity; whereas, no other being is its own duration, as no other is its own being. Now God is His own uniform being; and hence as He is His own essence, so He is His own eternity.

REPLY OBJ. 1: The *now* that stands still, is said to make eternity according to our apprehension. As the apprehension of time is caused in us by the fact that we apprehend the flow of the *now*, so the apprehension of eternity is caused in us by our apprehending the *now* standing still. When Augustine says that *God is the author of eternity*, this is to be understood of participated eternity. For God communicates His eternity to some in the same way as He communicates His immutability.

REPLY OBJ. 2: From this appears the answer to the Second Objection. For God is said to be before eternity, according as it is shared by immaterial substances. Hence, also, in the same book, it is said that *intelligence is equal to eternity*. In the words of Exodus, *The Lord shall reign for eternity, and beyond*, eternity stands for age, as another rendering has it. Thus it is said that the Lord will reign beyond eternity, inasmuch as He endures beyond every age, i.e., beyond every kind of duration. For age is nothing more than

aliud saeculum quam periodus cuiuslibet rei, ut dicitur in libro I de caelo. Vel dicitur etiam ultra aeternum regnare, quia, si etiam aliquid aliud semper esset (ut motus caeli secundum quosdam philosophos), tamen Deus ultra regnat, inquantum eius regnum est totum simul.

AD TERTIUM dicendum quod aeternitas non est aliud quam ipse Deus. Unde non dicitur Deus aeternus, quasi sit aliquo modo mensuratus, sed accipitur ibi ratio mensurae secundum apprehensionem nostram tantum.

AD QUARTUM dicendum quod verba diversorum temporum attribuuntur Deo, inquantum eius aeternitas omnia tempora includit, non quod ipse varietur per praesens, praeteritum et futurum.

the period of each thing, as is said in the book De Coelo i. Or to reign beyond eternity can be taken to mean that if any other thing were conceived to exist for ever, as the movement of the heavens according to some philosophers, then God would still reign beyond, inasmuch as His reign is simultaneously whole.

REPLY OBJ. 3: Eternity is nothing else but God Himself. Hence God is not called eternal, as if He were in any way measured; but the idea of measurement is there taken according to the apprehension of our mind alone.

REPLY OBJ. 4: Words denoting different times are applied to God, because His eternity includes all times; not as if He Himself were altered through present, past and future.

Article 3

Whether to Be Eternal Belongs to God Alone?

AD TERTIUM SIC PROCEDITUR. Videtur quod esse aeternum non sit soli Deo proprium. Dicitur enim Danielis XII, quod *qui ad iustitiam erudiunt plurimos, erunt quasi stellae in perpetuas aeternitates.* Non autem essent plures aeternitates, si solus Deus esset aeternus. Non igitur solus Deus est aeternus.

PRAETEREA, Matth. XXV dicitur, *ite, maledicti, in ignem aeternum.* Non igitur solus Deus est aeternus.

PRAETEREA, omne necessarium est aeternum. Sed multa sunt necessaria; sicut omnia principia demonstrationis, et omnes propositiones demonstrativae. Ergo non solus Deus est aeternus.

SED CONTRA est quod dicit Hieronymus, ad Marcellam, *Deus solus est qui exordium non habet.* Quidquid autem exordium habet, non est aeternum. Solus ergo Deus est aeternus.

RESPONDEO dicendum quod aeternitas vere et proprie in solo Deo est. Quia aeternitas immutabilitatem consequitur, ut ex dictis patet. Solus autem Deus est omnino immutabilis, ut est superius ostensum. Secundum tamen quod aliqua ab ipso immutabilitatem percipiunt, secundum hoc aliqua eius aeternitatem participant. Quaedam ergo quantum ad hoc immutabilitatem sortiuntur a Deo, quod nunquam esse desinunt, et secundum hoc dicitur Eccle. I de terra, *quod in aeternum stat.* Quaedam etiam aeterna in Scripturis dicuntur propter diuturnitatem durationis, licet corruptibilia sint, sicut in Psalmo dicuntur *montes aeterni;* et Deuter. XXXIII etiam dicitur, *de pomis collium aeternorum.* Quaedam autem amplius participant de ratione aeternitatis, inquantum habent intransmutabilitatem vel secundum esse, vel ulterius secundum operationem, sicut Angeli et beati, qui verbo fruuntur, quia *quantum ad illam visionem verbi,*

OBJECTION 1: It seems that it does not belong to God alone to be eternal. For it is written that *those who instruct many to justice,* shall be *as stars unto perpetual eternities* (Dan 12:3). Now if God alone were eternal, there could not be many eternities. Therefore God alone is not the only eternal.

OBJ. 2: Further, it is written *Depart, ye cursed into eternal fire* (Matt 25:41). Therefore God is not the only eternal.

OBJ. 3: Further, every necessary thing is eternal. But there are many necessary things; as, for instance, all principles of demonstration and all demonstrative propositions. Therefore God is not the only eternal.

ON THE CONTRARY, Jerome says (Ep. ad Damasum, xv) that *God is the only one who has no beginning.* Now whatever has a beginning, is not eternal. Therefore God is the only one eternal.

I ANSWER THAT, Eternity truly and properly so called is in God alone, because eternity follows on immutability; as appears from the first article. But God alone is altogether immutable, as was shown above (Q. 9, A. 1). Accordingly, however, as some receive immutability from Him, they share in His eternity. Thus some receive immutability from God in the way of never ceasing to exist; in that sense it is said of the earth, *it standeth for ever* (Eccl. 1:4). Again, some things are called eternal in Scripture because of the length of their duration, although they are in nature corruptible; thus (Ps 75:5) the hills are called *eternal* and we read *of the fruits of the eternal hills.* (Deut 33:15). Some again, share more fully than others in the nature of eternity, inasmuch as they possess unchangeableness either in being or further still in operation; like the angels, and the blessed, who enjoy the Word, because *as regards that vision of the Word, no changing thoughts exist in the Saints,* as Augustine says

non sunt in sanctis volubiles cogitationes, ut dicit Augustinus, XV de Trin. Unde et videntes Deum dicuntur habere vitam aeternam, secundum illud Ioann. XVII, *haec est vita aeterna, ut cognoscant* et cetera.

AD PRIMUM ergo dicendum quod dicuntur multae aeternitates, secundum quod sunt multi participantes aeternitatem ex ipsa Dei contemplatione.

AD SECUNDUM dicendum quod ignis Inferni dicitur aeternus propter interminabilitatem tantum. Est tamen in poenis eorum transmutatio, secundum illud Iob XXIV, *ad nimium calorem transibunt ab aquis nivium*. Unde in Inferno non est vera aeternitas, sed magis tempus; secundum illud Psalmi, *erit tempus eorum in saecula*.

AD TERTIUM dicendum quod necessarium significat quendam modum veritatis. Verum autem, secundum philosophum, VI Metaphys., est in intellectu. Secundum hoc igitur vera et necessaria sunt aeterna, quia sunt in intellectu aeterno, qui est intellectus divinus solus. Unde non sequitur quod aliquid extra Deum sit aeternum.

(*De Trin.* xv). Hence those who see God are said to have eternal life; according to that text, *This is eternal life, that they may know Thee the only true God*, etc. (John 17:3).

REPLY OBJ. 1: There are said to be many eternities, accordingly as many share in eternity, by the contemplation of God.

REPLY OBJ. 2: The fire of hell is called eternal, only because it never ends. Still, there is change in the pains of the lost, according to the words *To extreme heat they will pass from snowy waters* (Job 24:19). Hence in hell true eternity does not exist, but rather time; according to the text of the Psalm *Their time will be for ever* (Ps 80:16).

REPLY OBJ. 3: Necessary means a certain mode of truth; and truth, according to the Philosopher (*Metaph.* vi), is in the mind. Therefore in this sense the true and necessary are eternal, because they are in the eternal mind, which is the divine intellect alone; hence it does not follow that anything beside God is eternal.

Article 4

Whether Eternity Differs from Time?

AD QUARTUM SIC PROCEDITUR. Videtur quod aeternitas non sit aliud a tempore. Impossibile est enim duas esse mensuras durationis simul, nisi una sit pars alterius, non enim sunt simul duo dies vel duae horae; sed dies et hora sunt simul, quia hora est pars diei. Sed aeternitas et tempus sunt simul, quorum utrumque mensuram quandam durationis importat. Cum igitur aeternitas non sit pars temporis, quia aeternitas excedit tempus et includit ipsum; videtur quod tempus sit pars aeternitatis, et non aliud ab aeternitate.

PRAETEREA, secundum philosophum in IV Physic., nunc temporis manet idem in toto tempore. Sed hoc videtur constituere rationem aeternitatis, quod sit idem indivisibiliter se habens in toto decursu temporis. Ergo aeternitas est nunc temporis. Sed nunc temporis non est aliud secundum substantiam a tempore. Ergo aeternitas non est aliud secundum substantiam a tempore.

PRAETEREA, sicut mensura primi motus est mensura omnium motuum, ut dicitur in IV Physic., ita videtur quod mensura primi esse sit mensura omnis esse. Sed aeternitas est mensura primi esse, quod est esse divinum. Ergo aeternitas est mensura omnis esse. Sed esse rerum corruptibilium mensuratur tempore. Ergo tempus vel est aeternitas, vel aliquid aeternitatis.

OBJECTION 1: It seems that eternity does not differ from time. For two measures of duration cannot exist together, unless one is part of the other; for instance two days or two hours cannot be together; nevertheless, we may say that a day or an hour are together, considering hour as part of a day. But eternity and time occur together, each of which imports a certain measure of duration. Since therefore eternity is not a part of time, forasmuch as eternity exceeds time, and includes it, it seems that time is a part of eternity, and is not a different thing from eternity.

OBJ. 2: Further, according to the Philosopher (*Phys.* iv), the *now* of time remains the same in the whole of time. But the nature of eternity seems to be that it is the same indivisible thing in the whole space of time. Therefore eternity is the *now* of time. But the *now* of time is not substantially different from time. Therefore eternity is not substantially different from time.

OBJ. 3: Further, as the measure of the first movement is the measure of every movement, as said in *Phys.* iv, it thus appears that the measure of the first being is that of every being. But eternity is the measure of the first being—that is, of the divine being. Therefore eternity is the measure of every being. But the being of things corruptible is measured by time. Time therefore is either eternity or is a part of eternity.

SED CONTRA est quod aeternitas est tota simul, in tempore autem est prius et posterius. Ergo tempus et aeternitas non sunt idem.

RESPONDEO dicendum quod manifestum est tempus et aeternitatem non esse idem. Sed huius diversitatis rationem quidam assignaverunt ex hoc quod aeternitas caret principio et fine, tempus autem habet principium et finem. Sed haec est differentia per accidens, et non per se. Quia dato quod tempus semper fuerit et semper futurum sit, secundum positionem eorum qui motum caeli ponunt sempiternum, adhuc remanebit differentia inter aeternitatem et tempus, ut dicit Boetius in libro de Consolat., ex hoc quod aeternitas est tota simul, quod tempori non convenit, quia aeternitas est mensura esse permanentis, tempus vero est mensura motus. Si tamen praedicta differentia attendatur quantum ad mensurata, et non quantum ad mensuras, sic habet aliquam rationem, quia solum illud mensuratur tempore, quod habet principium et finem in tempore, ut dicitur in IV Physic. Unde si motus caeli semper duraret, tempus non mensuraret ipsum secundum suam totam durationem, cum infinitum non sit mensurabile; sed mensuraret quamlibet circulationem, quae habet principium et finem in tempore.

Potest tamen et aliam rationem habere ex parte istarum mensurarum, si accipiatur finis et principium in potentia. Quia etiam dato quod tempus semper duret, tamen possibile est signare in tempore et principium et finem, accipiendo aliquas partes ipsius, sicut dicimus principium et finem diei vel anni, quod non contingit in aeternitate. Sed tamen istae differentiae consequuntur eam quae est per se et primo, differentiam, per hoc quod aeternitas est tota simul, non autem tempus.

AD PRIMUM ergo dicendum quod ratio illa procederet, si tempus et aeternitas essent mensurae unius generis, quod patet esse falsum, ex his quorum est tempus et aeternitas mensura.

AD SECUNDUM dicendum quod nunc temporis est idem subiecto in toto tempore, sed differens ratione, eo quod, sicut tempus respondet motui, ita nunc temporis respondet mobili; mobile autem est idem subiecto in toto decursu temporis, sed differens ratione, inquantum est hic et ibi. Et ista alternatio est motus. Similiter fluxus ipsius nunc, secundum quod alternatur ratione, est tempus. Aeternitas autem manet eadem et subiecto et ratione. Unde aeternitas non est idem quod nunc temporis.

AD TERTIUM dicendum quod, sicut aeternitas est propria mensura ipsius esse, ita tempus est propria mensura motus. Unde secundum quod aliquod esse recedit a permanentia essendi et subditur transmutationi, secundum hoc recedit ab aeternitate et subditur tempori. Esse ergo rerum corruptibilium, quia est transmutabile, non mensuratur aeternitate, sed tempore. Tempus

ON THE CONTRARY, Eternity is simultaneously whole. But time has a *before* and an *after*. Therefore time and eternity are not the same thing.

I ANSWER THAT, It is manifest that time and eternity are not the same. Some have founded this difference on the fact that eternity has neither beginning nor an end; whereas time has a beginning and an end. This, however, makes a merely accidental, and not an absolute difference because, granted that time always was and always will be, according to the idea of those who think the movement of the heavens goes on for ever, there would yet remain a difference between eternity and time, as Boethius says (*De Consol.* v), arising from the fact that eternity is simultaneously whole; which cannot be applied to time: for eternity is the measure of a permanent being; while time is a measure of movement. Supposing, however, that the aforesaid difference be considered on the part of the things measured, and not as regards the measures, then there is some reason for it, inasmuch as that alone is measured by time which has beginning and end in time. Hence, if the movement of the heavens lasted always, time would not be of its measure as regards the whole of its duration, since the infinite is not measurable; but it would be the measure of that part of its revolution which has beginning and end in time.

Another reason for the same can be taken from these measures in themselves, if we consider the end and the beginning as potentialities; because, granted also that time always goes on, yet it is possible to note in time both the beginning and the end, by considering its parts: thus we speak of the beginning and the end of a day or of a year; which cannot be applied to eternity. Still these differences follow upon the essential and primary differences, that eternity is simultaneously whole, but that time is not so.

REPLY OBJ. 1: Such a reason would be a valid one if time and eternity were the same kind of measure; but this is seen not to be the case when we consider those things of which the respective measures are time and eternity.

REPLY OBJ. 2: The *now* of time is the same as regards its subject in the whole course of time, but it differs in aspect; for inasmuch as time corresponds to movement, its *now* corresponds to what is movable; and the thing movable has the same one subject in all time, but differs in aspect as being here and there; and such alteration is movement. Likewise the flow of the *now* as alternating in aspect is time. But eternity remains the same according to both subject and aspect; and hence eternity is not the same as the *now* of time.

REPLY OBJ. 3: As eternity is the proper measure of permanent being, so time is the proper measure of movement; and hence, according as any being recedes from permanence of being, and is subject to change, it recedes from eternity, and is subject to time. Therefore the being of things corruptible, because it is changeable, is not measured by eternity, but by time; for time measures not only

enim mensurat non solum quae transmutantur in actu, sed quae sunt transmutabilia. Unde non solum mensurat motum, sed etiam quietem; quae est eius quod natum est moveri, et non movetur.

things actually changed, but also things changeable; hence it not only measures movement but it also measures repose, which belongs to whatever is naturally movable, but is not actually in motion.

Article 5

The Difference of Aeviternity and Time

AD QUINTUM SIC PROCEDITUR. Videtur quod aevum non sit aliud a tempore. Dicit enim Augustinus, VIII super Gen. ad Litt., quod *Deus movet creaturam spiritualem per tempus*. Sed aevum dicitur esse mensura spiritualium substantiarum. Ergo tempus non differt ab aevo.

PRAETEREA, de ratione temporis est quod habeat prius et posterius, de ratione vero aeternitatis est quod sit tota simul, ut dictum est. Sed aevum non est aeternitas, dicitur enim Eccli. I, quod *sapientia aeterna est ante aevum*. Ergo non est totum simul, sed habet prius et posterius, et ita est tempus.

PRAETEREA, si in aevo non est prius et posterius, sequitur quod in aeviternis non differat esse vel fuisse vel futurum esse. Cum igitur sit impossibile aeviterna non fuisse, sequitur quod impossibile sit ea non futura esse. Quod falsum est, cum Deus possit ea reducere in nihilum.

PRAETEREA, cum duratio aeviternorum sit infinita ex parte post, si aevum sit totum simul, sequitur quod aliquod creatum sit infinitum in actu, quod est impossibile. Non igitur aevum differt a tempore.

SED CONTRA est quod dicit Boetius, *qui tempus ab aevo ire iubes.*

RESPONDEO dicendum quod aevum differt a tempore et ab aeternitate, sicut medium existens inter illa. Sed horum differentiam aliqui sic assignant, dicentes quod aeternitas principio et fine caret; aevum habet principium, sed non finem; tempus autem habet principium et finem. Sed haec differentia est per accidens, sicut supra dictum est, quia si etiam semper aeviterna fuissent et semper futura essent, ut aliqui ponunt; vel etiam si quandoque deficerent, quod Deo possibile esset, adhuc aevum distingueretur ab aeternitate et tempore.

Alii vero assignant differentiam inter haec tria, per hoc quod aeternitas non habet prius et posterius; tempus autem habet prius et posterius cum innovatione et veteratione; aevum habet prius et posterius sine innovatione et veteratione. Sed haec positio implicat contradictoria. Quod quidem manifeste apparet, si innovatio et veteratio

OBJECTION 1: It seems that aeviternity is the same as time. For Augustine says (*Gen ad lit.* viii, 20, 22, 23), that *God moves the spiritual through time*. But aeviternity is said to be the measure of spiritual substances. Therefore time is the same as aeviternity.

OBJ. 2: Further, it is essential to time to have *before* and *after*; but it is essential to eternity to be simultaneously whole, as was shown above in the first article. Now aeviternity is not eternity; for it is written (Sir 1:1) that eternal *Wisdom is before age*. Therefore it is not simultaneously whole but has *before* and *after*; and thus it is the same as time.

OBJ. 3: Further, if there is no *before* and *after* in aeviternity, it follows that in aeviternal things there is no difference between being, having been, or going to be. Since then it is impossible for aeviternal things not to have been, it follows that it is impossible for them not to be in the future; which is false, since God can reduce them to nothing.

OBJ. 4: Further, since the duration of aeviternal things is infinite as to subsequent duration, if aeviternity is simultaneously whole, it follows that some creature is actually infinite; which is impossible. Therefore aeviternity does not differ from time.

ON THE CONTRARY, Boethius says (*De Consol.* iii) *Who commandest time to be separate from aeviternity.*

I ANSWER THAT, Aeviternity differs from time, and from eternity, as the mean between them both. This difference is explained by some to consist in the fact that eternity has neither beginning nor end, aeviternity, a beginning but no end, and time both beginning and end. This difference, however, is but an accidental one, as was shown above, in the preceding article; because even if aeviternal things had always been, and would always be, as some think, and even if they might sometimes fail to be, which is possible to God to allow; even granted this, aeviternity would still be distinguished from eternity, and from time.

Others assign the difference between these three to consist in the fact that eternity has no *before* and *after*; but that time has both, together with innovation and veteration; and that aeviternity has *before* and *after* without innovation and veteration. This theory, however, involves a contradiction; which manifestly appears if innovation and veteration be

referantur ad ipsam mensuram. Cum enim prius et posterius durationis non possint esse simul, si aevum habet prius et posterius, oportet quod, priore parte aevi recedente, posterior de novo adveniat, et sic erit innovatio in ipso aevo, sicut in tempore. Si vero referantur ad mensurata, adhuc sequitur inconveniens. Ex hoc enim res temporalis inveteratur tempore, quod habet esse transmutabile, et ex transmutabilitate mensurati, est prius et posterius in mensura, ut patet ex IV Physic. Si igitur ipsum aeviternum non sit inveterabile nec innovabile, hoc erit quia esse eius est intransmutabile. Mensura ergo eius non habebit prius et posterius. Est ergo dicendum quod, cum aeternitas sit mensura esse permanentis, secundum quod aliquid recedit a permanentia essendi, secundum hoc recedit ab aeternitate. Quaedam autem sic recedunt a permanentia essendi, quod esse eorum est subiectum transmutationis, vel in transmutatione consistit, et huiusmodi mensurantur tempore; sicut omnis motus, et etiam esse omnium corruptibilium. Quaedam vero recedunt minus a permanentia essendi, quia esse eorum nec in transmutatione consistit, nec est subiectum transmutationis, tamen habent transmutationem adiunctam, vel in actu vel in potentia. Sicut patet in corporibus caelestibus, quorum esse substantiale est intransmutabile; tamen esse intransmutabile habent cum transmutabilitate secundum locum. Et similiter patet de Angelis, quod habent esse intransmutabile cum transmutabilitate secundum electionem, quantum ad eorum naturam pertinet; et cum transmutabilitate intelligentiarum et affectionum, et locorum suo modo. Et ideo huiusmodi mensurantur aevo, quod est medium inter aeternitatem et tempus. Esse autem quod mensurat aeternitas, nec est mutabile, nec mutabilitati adiunctum. Sic ergo tempus habet prius et posterius, aevum autem non habet in se prius et posterius, sed ei coniungi possunt, aeternitas autem non habet prius neque posterius, neque ea compatitur.

AD PRIMUM ergo dicendum quod creaturae spirituales, quantum ad affectiones et intelligentias, in quibus est successio, mensurantur tempore. Unde et Augustinus ibidem dicit quod per tempus moveri, est per affectiones moveri. Quantum vero ad eorum esse naturale, mensurantur aevo. Sed quantum ad visionem gloriae, participant aeternitatem.

AD SECUNDUM dicendum quod aevum est totum simul, non tamen est aeternitas, quia compatitur secum prius et posterius.

AD TERTIUM dicendum quod in ipso esse Angeli in se considerato, non est differentia praeteriti et futuri, sed solum secundum adiunctas mutationes. Sed quod dicimus Angelum esse vel fuisse vel futurum esse, differt secundum acceptionem intellectus nostri, qui accipit esse Angeli per comparationem ad diversas partes temporis. Et cum dicit Angelum esse vel fuisse, supponit aliquid

referred to the measure itself. For since *before* and *after* of duration cannot exist together, if aeviternity has *before* and *after*, it must follow that with the receding of the first part of aeviternity, the after part of aeviternity must newly appear; and thus innovation would occur in aeviternity itself, as it does in time. And if they be referred to the things measured, even then an incongruity would follow. For a thing which exists in time grows old with time, because it has a changeable existence, and from the changeableness of a thing measured, there follows *before* and *after* in the measure, as is clear from Physic. iv. Therefore the fact that an aeviternal thing is neither inveterate, nor subject to innovation, comes from its changelessness; and consequently its measure does not contain *before* and *after*. We say then that since eternity is the measure of a permanent being, in so far as anything recedes from permanence of being, it recedes from eternity. Now some things recede from permanence of being, so that their being is subject to change, or consists in change; and these things are measured by time, as are all movements, and also the being of all things corruptible. But others recede less from permanence of being, forasmuch as their being neither consists in change, nor is the subject of change; nevertheless they have change annexed to them either actually or potentially. This appears in the heavenly bodies, the substantial being of which is unchangeable; and yet with unchangeable being they have changeableness of place. The same applies to the angels, who have an unchangeable being as regards their nature with changeableness as regards choice; moreover they have changeableness of intelligence, of affections and of places in their own degree. Therefore these are measured by aeviternity which is a mean between eternity and time. But the being that is measured by eternity is not changeable, nor is it annexed to change. In this way time has *before* and *after*; aeviternity in itself has no *before* and *after*, which can, however, be annexed to it; while eternity has neither *before* nor *after*, nor is it compatible with such at all.

REPLY OBJ. 1: Spiritual creatures as regards successive affections and intelligences are measured by time. Hence also Augustine says (*Gen ad lit.* viii, 20, 22, 23) that to be moved through time, is to be moved by affections. But as regards their nature they are measured by aeviternity; whereas as regards the vision of glory, they have a share of eternity.

REPLY OBJ. 2: Aeviternity is simultaneously whole; yet it is not eternity, because *before* and *after* are compatible with it.

REPLY OBJ. 3: In the very being of an angel considered absolutely, there is no difference of past and future, but only as regards accidental change. Now to say that an angel was, or is, or will be, is to be taken in a different sense according to the acceptation of our intellect, which apprehends the angelic existence by comparison with different parts of time. But when we say that an angel is, or was, we suppose

cum quo eius oppositum non subditur divinae potentiae, cum vero dicit futurum esse, nondum supponit aliquid. Unde, cum esse et non esse Angeli subsit divinae potentiae, absolute considerando, potest Deus facere quod esse Angeli non sit futurum, tamen non potest facere quod non sit dum est, vel quod non fuerit postquam fuit.

AD QUARTUM dicendum quod duratio aevi est infinita, quia non finitur tempore. Sic autem esse aliquod creatum infinitum, quod non finiatur quodam alio, non est inconveniens.

something, which being supposed, its opposite is not subject to the divine power. Whereas when we say he will be, we do not as yet suppose anything. Hence, since the existence and non-existence of an angel considered absolutely is subject to the divine power, God can make the existence of an angel not future; but He cannot cause him not to be while he is, or not to have been, after he has been.

REPLY OBJ. 4: The duration of aeviternity is infinite, forasmuch as it is not finished by time. Hence, there is no incongruity in saying that a creature is infinite, inasmuch as it is not ended by any other creature.

Article 6

Whether There Is Only One Aeviternity?

AD SEXTUM SIC PROCEDITUR. Videtur quod non sit tantum unum aevum. Dicitur enim in apocryphis Esdrae, *maiestas et potestas aevorum est apud te, domine.*

PRAETEREA, diversorum generum diversae sunt mensurae. Sed quaedam aeviterna sunt in genere corporalium, scilicet corpora caelestia, quaedam vero sunt spirituales substantiae, scilicet Angeli. Non ergo est unum aevum tantum.

PRAETEREA, cum aevum sit nomen durationis, quorum est unum aevum, est una duratio. Sed non omnium aeviternorum est una duratio, quia quaedam post alia esse incipiunt, ut maxime patet in animabus humanis. Non est ergo unum aevum tantum.

PRAETEREA, ea quae non dependent ab invicem, non videntur habere unam mensuram durationis, propter hoc enim omnium temporalium videtur esse unum tempus, quia omnium motuum quodammodo causa est primus motus, qui prius tempore mensuratur. Sed aeviterna non dependent ab invicem, quia unus Angelus non est causa alterius. Non ergo est unum aevum tantum.

SED CONTRA, aevum est simplicius tempore, et propinquius se habens ad aeternitatem. Sed tempus est unum tantum. Ergo multo magis aevum.

RESPONDEO dicendum quod circa hoc est duplex opinio, quidam enim dicunt quod est unum aevum tantum; quidam quod multa. Quid autem horum verius sit, oportet considerare ex causa unitatis temporis, in cognitionem enim spiritualium per corporalia devenimus.

Dicunt autem quidam esse unum tempus omnium temporalium, propter hoc quod est unus numerus omnium numeratorum, cum tempus sit numerus, secundum philosophum. Sed hoc non sufficit, quia tempus non est numerus ut abstractus extra numeratum, sed ut in numerato existens, alioquin non esset continuus; quia decem ulnae panni continuitatem habent, non ex numero, sed ex numerato. Numerus autem in numerato

OBJECTION 1: It seems that there is not only one aeviternity; for it is written in the apocryphal books of Esdras: *Majesty and power of ages are with Thee, O Lord.*

OBJ. 2: Further, different genera have different measures. But some aeviternal things belong to the corporeal genus, as the heavenly bodies; and others spiritual substances, as are the angels. Therefore there is not only one aeviternity.

OBJ. 3: Further, since aeviternity is a term of duration, where there is one aeviternity, there is also one duration. But not all aeviternal things have one duration, for some begin to exist after others; as appears in the case especially of human souls. Therefore there is not only one aeviternity.

OBJ. 4: Further, things not dependent on each other do not seem to have one measure of duration; for there appears to be one time for all temporal things; since the first movement, measured by time, is in some way the cause of all movement. But aeviternal things do not depend on each other, for one angel is not the cause of another angel. Therefore there is not only one aeviternity.

ON THE CONTRARY, Aeviternity is a more simple thing than time, and is nearer to eternity. But time is one only. Therefore much more is aeviternity one only.

I ANSWER THAT, A twofold opinion exists on this subject. Some say there is only one aeviternity; others that there are many aeviternities. Which of these is true, may be considered from the cause why time is one; for we can rise from corporeal things to the knowledge of spiritual things.

Now some say that there is only one time for temporal things, forasmuch as one number exists for all things numbered; as time is a number, according to the Philosopher (*Physic.* iv). This, however, is not a sufficient reason; because time is not a number abstracted from the thing numbered, but existing in the thing numbered; otherwise it would not be continuous; for ten ells of cloth are continuous not by reason of the number, but by reason of the thing

existens non est idem omnium, sed diversus diversorum. Unde alii assignant causam unitatis temporis ex unitate aeternitatis, quae est principium omnis durationis. Et sic, omnes durationes sunt unum, si consideretur earum principium, sunt vero multae, si consideretur diversitas eorum quae recipiunt durationem ex influxu primi principii. Alii vero assignant causam unitatis temporis ex parte materiae primae, quae est primum subiectum motus, cuius mensura est tempus. Sed neutra assignatio sufficiens videtur, quia ea quae sunt unum principio vel subiecto, et maxime remoto, non sunt unum simpliciter sed secundum quid. Est ergo ratio unitatis temporis, unitas primi motus, secundum quem, cum sit simplicissimus, omnes alii mensurantur, ut dicitur in X Metaphys. Sic ergo tempus ad illum motum comparatur non solum ut mensura ad mensuratum, sed etiam ut accidens ad subiectum; et sic ab eo recipit unitatem. Ad alios autem motus comparatur solum ut mensura ad mensuratum. Unde secundum eorum multitudinem non multiplicatur, quia una mensura separata multa mensurari possunt.

Hoc igitur habito, sciendum quod de substantiis spiritualibus duplex fuit opinio. Quidam enim dixerunt quod omnes processerunt a Deo in quadam aequalitate, ut Origenes dixit; vel etiam multae earum, ut quidam posuerunt. Alii vero dixerunt quod omnes substantiae spirituales processerunt a Deo quodam gradu et ordine et hoc videtur sentire Dionysius, qui dicit, cap. X Cael. Hier., quod inter substantias spirituales sunt primae, mediae et ultimae, etiam in uno ordine Angelorum. Secundum igitur primam opinionem, necesse est dicere quod sunt plura aeva, secundum quod sunt plura aeviterna prima aequalia. Secundum autem secundam opinionem, oportet dicere quod sit unum aevum tantum, quia, cum unumquodque mensuretur simplicissimo sui generis, ut dicitur in X Metaphys., oportet quod esse omnium aeviternorum mensuretur esse primi aeviterni, quod tanto est simplicius, quanto prius. Et quia secunda opinio verior est, ut infra ostendetur, concedimus ad praesens unum esse aevum tantum.

AD PRIMUM ergo dicendum quod aevum aliquando accipitur pro saeculo, quod est periodus durationis alicuius rei, et sic dicuntur multa aeva, sicut multa saecula.

AD SECUNDUM dicendum quod, licet corpora caelestia et spiritualia differant in genere naturae, tamen conveniunt in hoc, quod habent esse intransmutabile. Et sic mensurantur aevo.

AD TERTIUM dicendum quod nec omnia temporalia simul incipiunt, et tamen omnium est unum tempus, propter primum quod mensuratur tempore. Et sic omnia aeviterna habent unum aevum propter primum, etiam si non omnia simul incipiant.

numbered. Now number as it exists in the thing numbered, is not the same for all; but it is different for different things. Hence, others assert that the unity of eternity as the principle of all duration is the cause of the unity of time. Thus all durations are one in that view, in the light of their principle, but are many in the light of the diversity of things receiving duration from the influx of the first principle. On the other hand others assign primary matter as the cause why time is one; as it is the first subject of movement, the measure of which is time. Neither of these reasons, however, is sufficient; forasmuch as things which are one in principle, or in subject, especially if distant, are not one absolutely, but accidentally. Therefore the true reason why time is one, is to be found in the oneness of the first movement by which, since it is most simple, all other movements are measured (*Metaph.* X). Therefore time is referred to that movement, not only as a measure is to the thing measured, but also as accident is to subject; and thus receives unity from it. Whereas to other movements it is compared only as the measure is to the thing measured. Hence it is not multiplied by their multitude, because by one separate measure many things can be measured.

This being established, we must observe that a twofold opinion existed concerning spiritual substances. Some said that all proceeded from God in a certain equality, as Origen said (*Peri Archon.* i); or at least many of them, as some others thought. Others said that all spiritual substances proceeded from God in a certain degree and order; and Dionysius (*Coel. Hier.* x) seems to have thought so, when he said that among spiritual substances there are the first, the middle and the last; even in one order of angels. Now according to the first opinion, it must be said that there are many aeviternities as there are many aeviternal things of first degree. But according to the second opinion, it would be necessary to say that there is one aeviternity only; because since each thing is measured by the most simple element of its genus, it must be that the existence of all aeviternal things should be measured by the existence of the first aeviternal thing, which is all the more simple the nearer it is to the first. Wherefore because the second opinion is truer, as will be shown later (Q. 47, A. 2); we concede at present that there is only one aeviternity.

REPLY OBJ. 1: Aeviternity is sometimes taken for age, that is, a space of a thing's duration; and thus we say many aeviternities when we mean ages.

REPLY OBJ. 2: Although the heavenly bodies and spiritual things differ in the genus of their nature, still they agree in having a changeless being, and are thus measured by aeviternity.

REPLY OBJ. 3: All temporal things did not begin together; nevertheless there is one time for all of them, by reason of the first measured by time; and thus all aeviternal things have one aeviternity by reason of the first, though all did not begin together.

AD QUARTUM dicendum quod ad hoc quod aliqua mensurentur per aliquod unum, non requiritur quod illud unum sit causa omnium eorum; sed quod sit simplicius.

REPLY OBJ. 4: For things to be measured by one, it is not necessary that the one should be the cause of all, but that it be more simple than the rest.

QUESTION 11

THE UNITY OF GOD

Post praemissa, considerandum est de divina unitate. Et circa hoc quaeruntur quatuor.

Primo, utrum unum addat aliquid supra ens.
Secundo, utrum opponantur unum et multa.
Tertio, utrum Deus sit unus.
Quarto, utrum sit maxime unus.

After the foregoing, we consider the divine unity; concerning which there are four points of inquiry:

(1) Whether *one* adds anything to *being*?
(2) Whether *one* and *many* are opposed to each other?
(3) Whether God is one?
(4) Whether He is in the highest degree one?

Article 1

Whether One Adds Anything to Being?

AD PRIMUM SIC PROCEDITUR. Videtur quod unum addat aliquid supra ens. Omne enim quod est in aliquo genere determinato, se habet ex additione ad ens, quod circuit omnia genera. Sed unum est in genere determinato, est enim principium numeri, qui est species quantitatis. Ergo unum addit aliquid supra ens.

PRAETEREA, quod dividit aliquod commune, se habet ex additione ad illud. Sed ens dividitur per unum et multa. Ergo unum addit aliquid supra ens.

PRAETEREA, si unum non addit supra ens, idem esset dicere unum et ens. Sed nugatorie dicitur ens ens. Ergo nugatio esset dicere ens unum, quod falsum est. Addit igitur unum supra ens.

SED CONTRA est quod dicit Dionysius, ult. cap. de Div. Nom., *nihil est existentium non participans uno,* quod non esset, si unum adderet supra ens quod contraheret ipsum. Ergo unum non habet se ex additione ad ens.

RESPONDEO dicendum quod unum non addit supra ens rem aliquam, sed tantum negationem divisionis, unum enim nihil aliud significat quam ens indivisum. Et ex hoc ipso apparet quod unum convertitur cum ente. Nam omne ens aut est simplex, aut compositum. Quod autem est simplex, est indivisum et actu et potentia. Quod autem est compositum, non habet esse quandiu partes eius sunt divisae, sed postquam constituunt et componunt ipsum compositum. Unde manifestum est quod esse cuiuslibet rei consistit in indivisione. Et inde est quod unumquodque, sicut custodit suum esse, ita custodit suam unitatem.

AD PRIMUM igitur dicendum quod quidam, putantes idem esse unum quod convertitur cum ente, et quod est principium numeri, divisi sunt in contrarias positiones. Pythagoras enim et Plato, videntes quod

OBJECTION 1: It seems that *one* adds something to *being*. For everything is in a determinate genus by addition to being, which penetrates all genera. But *one* is a determinate genus, for it is the principle of number, which is a species of quantity. Therefore *one* adds something to *being*.

OBJ. 2: Further, what divides a thing common to all, is an addition to it. But *being* is divided by *one* and by *many*. Therefore *one* is an addition to *being*.

OBJ. 3: Further, if *one* is not an addition to *being*, one and *being* must have the same meaning. But it would be nugatory to call *being* by the name of *being*; therefore it would be equally so to call being *one*. Now this is false. Therefore *one* is an addition to *being*.

ON THE CONTRARY, Dionysius says (*Div. Nom.* 5, ult.): *Nothing which exists is not in some way one*, which would be false if *one* were an addition to *being*, in the sense of limiting it. Therefore *one* is not an addition to *being*.

I ANSWER THAT, One does not add any reality to *being*; but is only a negation of division; for *one* means undivided *being*. This is the very reason why *one* is the same as *being*. Now every being is either simple or compound. But what is simple is undivided, both actually and potentially. Whereas what is compound, has not being whilst its parts are divided, but after they make up and compose it. Hence it is manifest that the being of anything consists in undivision; and hence it is that everything guards its unity as it guards its being.

REPLY OBJ. 1: Some, thinking that the *one* convertible with *being* is the same as the *one* which is the principle of number, were divided into contrary opinions. Pythagoras and Plato, seeing that the *one* convertible with *being* did

unum quod convertitur cum ente, non addit aliquam rem supra ens, sed significat substantiam entis prout est indivisa, existimaverunt sic se habere de uno quod est principium numeri. Et quia numerus componitur ex unitatibus, crediderunt quod numeri essent substantiae omnium rerum. E contrario autem Avicenna, considerans quod unum quod est principium numeri, addit aliquam rem supra substantiam entis (alias numerus ex unitatibus compositus non esset species quantitatis), credidit quod unum quod convertitur cum ente, addat rem aliquam supra substantiam entis, sicut album supra hominem. Sed hoc manifeste falsum est, quia quaelibet res est una per suam substantiam. Si enim per aliquid aliud esset una quaelibet res, cum illud iterum sit unum, si esset iterum unum per aliquid aliud, esset abire in infinitum. Unde standum est in primo. Sic igitur dicendum est quod unum quod convertitur cum ente, non addit aliquam rem supra ens, sed unum quod est principium numeri, addit aliquid supra ens, ad genus quantitatis pertinens.

AD SECUNDUM dicendum quod nihil prohibet id quod est uno modo divisum, esse alio modo indivisum; sicut quod est divisum numero, est indivisum secundum speciem, et sic contingit aliquid esse uno modo unum, alio modo multa. Sed tamen si sit indivisum simpliciter; vel quia est indivisum secundum id quod pertinet ad essentiam rei, licet sit divisum quantum ad ea quae sunt extra essentiam rei, sicut quod est unum subiecto et multa secundum accidentia; vel quia est indivisum in actu, et divisum in potentia, sicut quod est unum toto et multa secundum partes, huiusmodi erit unum simpliciter, et multa secundum quid. Si vero aliquid e converso sit indivisum secundum quid, et divisum simpliciter; utpote quia est divisum secundum essentiam, et indivisum secundum rationem, vel secundum principium sive causam, erit multa simpliciter, et unum secundum quid; ut quae sunt multa numero et unum specie, vel unum principio. Sic igitur ens dividitur per unum et multa, quasi per unum simpliciter, et multa secundum quid. Nam et ipsa multitudo non contineretur sub ente, nisi contineretur aliquo modo sub uno. Dicit enim Dionysius, ult. cap. de Div. Nom., quod *non est multitudo non participans uno, sed quae sunt multa partibus, sunt unum toto; et quae sunt multa accidentibus, sunt unum subiecto; et quae sunt multa numero, sunt unum specie; et quae sunt speciebus multa, sunt unum genere; et quae sunt multa processibus, sunt unum principio.*

AD TERTIUM dicendum quod ideo non est nugatio cum dicitur ens unum, quia unum addit aliquid secundum rationem supra ens.

not add any reality to *being*, but signified the substance of *being* as undivided, thought that the same applied to the *one* which is the principle of number. And because number is composed of unities, they thought that numbers were the substances of all things. Avicenna, however, on the contrary, considering that *one* which is the principle of number, added a reality to the substance of *being* (otherwise number made of unities would not be a species of quantity), thought that the *one* convertible with *being* added a reality to the substance of beings; as *white* to *man*. This, however, is manifestly false, inasmuch as each thing is *one* by its substance. For if a thing were *one* by anything else but by its substance, since this again would be *one*, supposing it were again *one* by another thing, we should be driven on to infinity. Hence we must adhere to the former statement; therefore we must say that the *one* which is convertible with *being*, does not add a reality to being; but that the *one* which is the principle of number, does add a reality to *being*, belonging to the genus of quantity.

REPLY OBJ. 2: There is nothing to prevent a thing which in one way is divided, from being another way undivided; as what is divided in number, may be undivided in species; thus it may be that a thing is in one way *one*, and in another way *many*. Still, if it is absolutely undivided, either because it is so according to what belongs to its essence, though it may be divided as regards what is outside its essence, as what is one in subject may have many accidents; or because it is undivided actually, and divided potentially, as what is *one* in the whole, and is *many* in parts; in such a case a thing will be *one* absolutely and *many* accidentally. On the other hand, if it be undivided accidentally, and divided absolutely, as if it were divided in essence and undivided in idea or in principle or cause, it will be *many* absolutely and *one* accidentally; as what are *many* in number and *one* in species or *one* in principle. Hence in that way, being is divided by *one* and by *many*; as it were by *one* absolutely and by *many* accidentally. For multitude itself would not be contained under *being*, unless it were in some way contained under *one*. Thus Dionysius says (*Div. Nom.*, cap. ult.) that *there is no kind of multitude that is not in a way one. But what are many in their parts, are one in their whole; and what are many in accidents, are one in subject; and what are many in number, are one in species; and what are many in species, are one in genus; and what are many in processions, are one in principle.*

REPLY OBJ. 3: It does not follow that it is nugatory to say *being* is *one*; forasmuch as *one* adds an idea to *being*.

Article 2

Whether One and Many Are Opposed to Each Other?

Ad secundum sic proceditur. Videtur quod unum et multa non opponantur. Nullum enim oppositum praedicatur de suo opposito. Sed omnis multitudo est quodammodo unum, ut ex praedictis patet. Ergo unum non opponitur multitudini.

Praeterea, nullum oppositum constituitur ex suo opposito. Sed unum constituit multitudinem. Ergo non opponitur multitudini.

Praeterea, unum uni est oppositum. Sed multo opponitur paucum. Ergo non opponitur ei unum.

Praeterea, si unum opponitur multitudini, opponitur ei sicut indivisum diviso, et sic opponetur ei ut privatio habitui. Hoc autem videtur inconveniens, quia sequeretur quod unum sit posterius multitudine, et definiatur per eam; cum tamen multitudo definiatur per unum. Unde erit circulus in definitione, quod est inconveniens. Non ergo unum et multa sunt opposita.

Sed contra, quorum rationes sunt oppositae, ipsa sunt opposita. Sed ratio unius consistit in indivisibilitate, ratio vero multitudinis divisionem continet. Ergo unum et multa sunt opposita.

Respondeo dicendum quod unum opponitur multis, sed diversimode. Nam unum quod est principium numeri, opponitur multitudini quae est numerus, ut mensura mensurato, unum enim habet rationem primae mensurae, et numerus est multitudo mensurata per unum, ut patet ex X Metaphys. Unum vero quod convertitur cum ente, opponitur multitudini per modum privationis, ut indivisum diviso.

Ad primum ergo dicendum quod nulla privatio tollit totaliter esse, quia privatio est *negatio in subiecto*, secundum philosophum. Sed tamen omnis privatio tollit aliquod esse. Et ideo in ente, ratione suae communitatis, accidit quod privatio entis fundatur in ente, quod non accidit in privationibus formarum specialium, ut visus vel albedinis, vel alicuius huiusmodi. Et sicut est de ente, ita est de uno et bono, quae convertuntur cum ente, nam privatio boni fundatur in aliquo bono, et similiter remotio unitatis fundatur in aliquo uno. Et exinde contingit quod multitudo est quoddam unum, et malum est quoddam bonum, et non ens est quoddam ens. Non tamen oppositum praedicatur de opposito, quia alterum horum est simpliciter, et alterum secundum quid. Quod enim secundum quid est ens, ut in potentia, est non ens simpliciter, idest actu, vel quod est ens simpliciter in genere substantiae, est non ens secundum quid, quantum ad aliquod esse accidentale. Similiter ergo quod est bonum secundum quid, est malum simpliciter; vel e converso.

Objection 1: It seems that *one* and *many* are not mutually opposed. For no opposite thing is predicated of its opposite. But every multitude is in a certain way one, as appears from the preceding article. Therefore *one* is not opposed to *multitude*.

Obj. 2: Further, no opposite thing is constituted by its opposite. But multitude is constituted by one. Therefore it is not opposed to *multitude*.

Obj. 3: Further, *one* is opposed to *one*. But the idea of *few* is opposed to *many*. Therefore *one* is not opposed to *many*.

Obj. 4: Further, if *one* is opposed to *multitude*, it is opposed as the undivided is to the divided; and is thus opposed to it as privation is to habit. But this appears to be incongruous; because it would follow that *one* comes after *multitude*, and is defined by it; whereas, on the contrary, *multitude* is defined by *one*. Hence there would be a vicious circle in the definition; which is inadmissible. Therefore *one* and *many* are not opposed.

On the contrary, Things which are opposed in idea, are themselves opposed to each other. But the idea of *one* consists in indivisibility; and the idea of *multitude* contains division. Therefore *one* and *many* are opposed to each other.

I answer that, One is opposed to *many*, but in various ways. The one which is the principle of number is opposed to multitude which is number, as the measure is to the thing measured. For *one* implies the idea of a primary measure; and number is multitude measured by one, as is clear from *Metaph.* x. But the one which is convertible with being is opposed to multitude by way of privation; as the undivided is to the thing divided.

Reply Obj. 1: No privation entirely takes away the being of a thing, inasmuch as privation means *negation in the subject*, according to the Philosopher (*Categor.* viii). Nevertheless every privation takes away some being; and so in being, by reason of its universality, the privation of being has its foundation in being; which is not the case in privations of special forms, as of sight, or of whiteness and the like. And what applies to being applies also to one and to good, which are convertible with being, for the privation of good is founded in some good; likewise the removal of unity is founded in some one thing. Hence it happens that multitude is some one thing; and evil is some good thing, and non-being is some kind of being. Nevertheless, opposite is not predicated of opposite; forasmuch as one is absolute, and the other is relative; for what is relative being (as a potentiality) is non-being absolutely, i.e., actually; or what is absolute being in the genus of substance is non-being relatively as regards some accidental being. In the same way, what is relatively good is absolutely bad, or vice versa;

Et similiter quod est unum simpliciter, est multa secundum quid; et e converso.

AD SECUNDUM dicendum quod duplex est totum, quoddam homogeneum, quod componitur ex similibus partibus; quoddam vero heterogeneum, quod componitur ex dissimilibus partibus. In quolibet autem toto homogeneo, totum constituitur ex partibus habentibus formam totius, sicut quaelibet pars aquae est aqua, et talis est constitutio continui ex suis partibus. In quolibet autem toto heterogeneo, quaelibet pars caret forma totius, nulla enim pars domus est domus, nec aliqua pars hominis est homo. Et tale totum est multitudo. Inquantum ergo pars eius non habet formam multitudinis, componitur multitudo ex unitatibus, sicut domus ex non domibus, non quod unitates constituant multitudinem secundum id quod habent de ratione indivisionis, prout opponuntur multitudini; sed secundum hoc quod habent de entitate, sicut et partes domus constituunt domum per hoc quod sunt quaedam corpora, non per hoc quod sunt non domus.

AD TERTIUM dicendum quod multum accipitur dupliciter. Uno modo, absolute, et sic opponitur uni. Alio modo, secundum quod importat excessum quendam, et sic opponitur pauco. Unde primo modo duo sunt multa; non autem secundo.

AD QUARTUM dicendum quod unum opponitur privative multis, inquantum in ratione multorum est quod sint divisa. Unde oportet quod divisio sit prius unitate, non simpliciter, sed secundum rationem nostrae apprehensionis. Apprehendimus enim simplicia per composita, unde definimus punctum, cuius pars non est, vel principium lineae. Sed multitudo, etiam secundum rationem, consequenter se habet ad unum, quia divisa non intelligimus habere rationem multitudinis, nisi per hoc quod utrique divisorum attribuimus unitatem. Unde unum ponitur in definitione multitudinis, non autem multitudo in definitione unius. Sed divisio cadit in intellectu ex ipsa negatione entis. Ita quod primo cadit in intellectu ens; secundo, quod hoc ens non est illud ens, et sic secundo apprehendimus divisionem; tertio, unum; quarto, multitudinem.

likewise what is absolutely one is relatively many, and vice versa.

REPLY OBJ. 2: A whole is twofold. In one sense it is homogeneous, composed of like parts; in another sense it is heterogeneous, composed of dissimilar parts. Now in every homogeneous whole, the whole is made up of parts having the form of the whole; as, for instance, every part of water is water; and such is the constitution of a continuous thing made up of its parts. In every heterogeneous whole, however, every part is wanting in the form belonging to the whole; as, for instance, no part of a house is a house, nor is any part of a man a man. Now multitude is such a kind of a whole. Therefore inasmuch as its part has not the form of the multitude, the latter is composed of unities, as a house is composed of not houses; not, indeed, as if unities constituted multitude so far as they are undivided, in which way they are opposed to multitude; but so far as they have being, as also the parts of a house make up the house by the fact that they are beings, not by the fact that they are not houses.

REPLY OBJ. 3: *Many* is taken in two ways: absolutely, and in that sense it is opposed to *one*; in another way as importing some kind of excess, in which sense it is opposed to *few*; hence in the first sense two are many but not in the second sense.

REPLY OBJ. 4: *One* is opposed to *many* privatively, inasmuch as the idea of *many* involves division. Hence division must be prior to unity, not absolutely in itself, but according to our way of apprehension. For we apprehend simple things by compound things; and hence we define a point to be, *what has no part*, or *the beginning of a line*. Multitude also, in idea, follows on *one*; because we do not understand divided things to convey the idea of multitude except by the fact that we attribute unity to every part. Hence *one* is placed in the definition of *multitude*; but *multitude* is not placed in the definition of *one*. But division comes to be understood from the very negation of being: so what first comes to mind is being; second, that this being is not that being, and thus we apprehend division as a consequence; third, comes the notion of one; fourth, the notion of multitude.

Article 3

Whether God Is One?

AD TERTIUM SIC PROCEDITUR. Videtur quod Deus non sit unus. Dicitur enim I ad Cor. VIII, *siquidem sunt dii multi et domini multi*.

PRAETEREA, unum quod est principium numeri, non potest praedicari de Deo, cum nulla quantitas de Deo praedicetur. Similiter nec unum quod convertitur

OBJECTION 1: It seems that God is not one. For it is written *For there be many gods and many lords* (1 Cor 8:5).

OBJ. 2: Further, *One*, as the principle of number, cannot be predicated of God, since quantity is not predicated of God; likewise, neither can *one* which is convertible with

cum ente, quia importat privationem, et omnis privatio imperfectio est, quae Deo non competit. Non est igitur dicendum quod Deus sit unus.

Sed contra est quod dicitur Deut. VI, *audi, Israel, dominus Deus tuus unus est.*

Respondeo dicendum quod Deum esse unum, ex tribus demonstratur. Primo quidem ex eius simplicitate. Manifestum est enim quod illud unde aliquod singulare est hoc aliquid, nullo modo est multis communicabile. Illud enim unde Socrates est homo, multis communicari potest, sed id unde est hic homo, non potest communicari nisi uni tantum. Si ergo Socrates per id esset homo, per quod est hic homo, sicut non possunt esse plures Socrates, ita non possent esse plures homines. Hoc autem convenit Deo, nam ipse Deus est sua natura, ut supra ostensum est. Secundum igitur idem est Deus, et hic Deus. Impossibile est igitur esse plures deos.

Secundo vero, ex infinitate eius perfectionis. Ostensum est enim supra quod Deus comprehendit in se totam perfectionem essendi. Si ergo essent plures dii, oporteret eos differre. Aliquid ergo conveniret uni, quod non alteri. Et si hoc esset privatio, non esset simpliciter perfectus, si autem hoc esset perfectio, alteri eorum deesset. Impossibile est ergo esse plures deos. Unde et antiqui philosophi, quasi ab ipsa coacti veritate, ponentes principium infinitum, posuerunt unum tantum principium.

Tertio, ab unitate mundi. Omnia enim quae sunt, inveniuntur esse ordinata ad invicem, dum quaedam quibusdam deserviunt. Quae autem diversa sunt, in unum ordinem non convenirent, nisi ab aliquo uno ordinarentur. Melius enim multa reducuntur in unum ordinem per unum, quam per multa, quia per se unius unum est causa, et multa non sunt causa unius nisi per accidens, inquantum scilicet sunt aliquo modo unum. Cum igitur illud quod est primum, sit perfectissimum et per se, non per accidens, oportet quod primum reducens omnia in unum ordinem, sit unum tantum. Et hoc est Deus.

Ad primum ergo dicendum quod dicuntur dii multi secundum errorem quorundam qui multos deos colebant, existimantes planetas et alias stellas esse deos, vel etiam singulas partes mundi. Unde subdit, *nobis autem unus Deus*, et cetera.

Ad secundum dicendum quod unum secundum quod est principium numeri, non praedicatur de Deo; sed solum de his quae habent esse in materia. Unum enim quod est principium numeri, est de genere mathematicorum; quae habent esse in materia, sed sunt secundum rationem a materia abstracta. Unum vero quod convertitur cum ente, est quoddam metaphysicum,

being be predicated of God, because it imports privation, and every privation is an imperfection, which cannot apply to God. Therefore God is not one.

On the contrary, It is written *Hear, O Israel, the Lord our God is one Lord* (Deut 6:4).

I answer that, It can be shown from these three sources that God is one. First from His simplicity. For it is manifest that the reason why any singular thing is *this particular thing* is because it cannot be communicated to many: since that whereby Socrates is a man, can be communicated to many; whereas, what makes him this particular man, is only communicable to one. Therefore, if Socrates were a man by what makes him to be this particular man, as there cannot be many Socrates, so there could not in that way be many men. Now this belongs to God alone; for God Himself is His own nature, as was shown above (Q. 3, A. 3). Therefore, in the very same way God is God, and He is this God. Impossible is it therefore that many Gods should exist.

Second, this is proved from the infinity of His perfection. For it was shown above (Q. 4, A. 2) that God comprehends in Himself the whole perfection of being. If then many gods existed, they would necessarily differ from each other. Something therefore would belong to one which did not belong to another. And if this were a privation, one of them would not be absolutely perfect; but if a perfection, one of them would be without it. So it is impossible for many gods to exist. Hence also the ancient philosophers, constrained as it were by truth, when they asserted an infinite principle, asserted likewise that there was only one such principle.

Third, this is shown from the unity of the world. For all things that exist are seen to be ordered to each other since some serve others. But things that are diverse do not harmonize in the same order, unless they are ordered thereto by one. For many are reduced into one order by one better than by many: because one is the per se cause of one, and many are only the accidental cause of one, inasmuch as they are in some way one. Since therefore what is first is most perfect, and is so per se and not accidentally, it must be that the first which reduces all into one order should be only one. And this one is God.

Reply Obj. 1: Gods are called many by the error of some who worshipped many deities, thinking as they did that the planets and other stars were gods, and also the separate parts of the world. Hence the Apostle adds: *Our God is one*, etc.

Reply Obj. 2: *One* which is the principle of number is not predicated of God, but only of material things. For *one* the principle of number belongs to the genus of mathematics, which are material in being, and abstracted from matter only in idea. But *one* which is convertible with being is a metaphysical entity and does not depend on matter in its being. And although in God there is no privation, still,

quod secundum esse non dependet a materia. Et licet in Deo non sit aliqua privatio, tamen, secundum modum apprehensionis nostrae, non cognoscitur a nobis nisi per modum privationis et remotionis. Et sic nihil prohibet aliqua privative dicta de Deo praedicari; sicut quod est incorporeus, infinitus. Et similiter de Deo dicitur quod sit unus.

according to the mode of our apprehension, He is known to us by way only of privation and remotion. Thus there is no reason why a certain kind of privation should not be predicated of God; for instance, that He is incorporeal and infinite; and in the same way it is said of God that He is one.

Article 4

Whether God Is Supremely One?

AD QUARTUM SIC PROCEDITUR. Videtur quod Deus non sit maxime unus. Unum enim dicitur secundum privationem divisionis. Sed privatio non recipit magis et minus. Ergo Deus non dicitur magis unus quam alia quae sunt unum.

PRAETEREA, nihil videtur esse magis indivisibile quam id quod est indivisibile actu et potentia, cuiusmodi est punctus et unitas. Sed intantum dicitur aliquid magis unum, inquantum est indivisibile. Ergo Deus non est magis unum quam unitas et punctus.

PRAETEREA, quod est per essentiam bonum, est maxime bonum, ergo quod est per essentiam suam unum, est maxime unum. Sed omne ens est unum per suam essentiam, ut patet per philosophum in IV Metaphys. Ergo omne ens est maxime unum. Deus igitur non est magis unum quam alia entia.

SED CONTRA est quod dicit Bernardus, quod *inter omnia quae unum dicuntur, arcem tenet unitas divinae Trinitatis.*

RESPONDEO dicendum quod, cum unum sit ens indivisum, ad hoc quod aliquid sit maxime unum, oportet quod sit et maxime ens et maxime indivisum. Utrumque autem competit Deo. Est enim maxime ens, inquantum est non habens aliquod esse determinatum per aliquam naturam cui adveniat, sed est ipsum esse subsistens, omnibus modis indeterminatum. Est autem maxime indivisum, inquantum neque dividitur actu neque potentia, secundum quemcunque modum divisionis, cum sit omnibus modis simplex, ut supra ostensum est. Unde manifestum est quod Deus est maxime unus.

AD PRIMUM ergo dicendum quod, licet privatio secundum se non recipiat magis et minus, tamen secundum quod eius oppositum recipit magis et minus, etiam ipsa privativa dicuntur secundum magis et minus. Secundum igitur quod aliquid est magis divisum vel divisibile, vel minus, vel nullo modo, secundum hoc aliquid dicitur magis et minus vel maxime unum.

AD SECUNDUM dicendum quod punctus et unitas quae est principium numeri, non sunt maxime entia, cum non habeant esse nisi in subiecto aliquo. Unde

OBJECTION 1: It seems that God is not supremely one. For *one* is so called from the privation of division. But privation cannot be greater or less. Therefore God is not more *one* than other things which are called *one.*

OBJ. 2: Further, nothing seems to be more indivisible than what is actually and potentially indivisible; such as a point and unity. But a thing is said to be more *one* according as it is indivisible. Therefore God is not more one than unity is one and a point is one.

OBJ. 3: Further, what is essentially good is supremely good. Therefore what is essentially one is supremely one. But every being is essentially one, as the Philosopher says (*Metaph.* iv). Therefore every being is supremely one; and therefore God is not one more than any other being is one.

ON THE CONTRARY, Bernard says (*De Consid.* v): *Among all things called one, the unity of the Divine Trinity holds the first place.*

I ANSWER THAT, Since one is an undivided being, if anything is supremely one it must be supremely being, and supremely undivided. Now both of these belong to God. For He is supremely being, inasmuch as His being is not determined by any nature to which it is adjoined; since He is being itself, subsistent, absolutely undetermined. But He is supremely undivided inasmuch as He is divided neither actually nor potentially, by any mode of division; since He is altogether simple, as was shown above (Q. 3, A. 7). Hence it is manifest that God is one in the supreme degree.

REPLY OBJ. 1: Although privation considered in itself is not susceptive of more or less, still according as its opposite is subject to more or less, privation also can be considered itself in the light of more and less. Therefore according as a thing is more divided, or is divisible, either less or not at all, in the degree it is called more, or less, or supremely, one.

REPLY OBJ. 2: A point and unity which is the principle of number, are not supremely being, inasmuch as they have being only in some subject. Hence neither of them can be

neutrum eorum est maxime unum. Sicut enim subiectum non est maxime unum, propter diversitatem accidentis et subiecti, ita nec accidens.

AD TERTIUM dicendum quod, licet omne ens sit unum per suam substantiam, non tamen se habet aequaliter substantia cuiuslibet ad causandam unitatem, quia substantia quorundam est ex multis composita, quorundam vero non.

supremely one. For as a subject cannot be supremely one, because of the difference within it of accident and subject, so neither can an accident.

REPLY OBJ. 3: Although every being is one by its substance, still every such substance is not equally the cause of unity; for the substance of some things is compound and of others simple.

QUESTION 12

HOW GOD IS KNOWN BY US

Quia in superioribus consideravimus qualiter Deus sit secundum seipsum, restat considerandum qualiter sit in cognitione nostra, idest quomodo cognoscatur a creaturis. Et circa hoc quaeruntur tredecim.

Primo, utrum aliquis intellectus creatus possit videre essentiam Dei.

Secundo, utrum Dei essentia videatur ab intellectu per aliquam speciem creatam.

Tertio, utrum oculo corporeo Dei essentia possit videri.

Quarto, utrum aliqua substantia intellectualis creata ex suis naturalibus sufficiens sit videre Dei essentiam.

Quinto, utrum intellectus creatus ad videndam Dei essentiam indigeat aliquo lumine creato.

Sexto, utrum videntium essentiam Dei unus alio perfectius videat.

Septimo, utrum aliquis intellectus creatus possit comprehendere Dei essentiam.

Octavo, utrum intellectus creatus videns Dei essentiam, omnia in ipsa cognoscat.

Nono, utrum ea quae ibi cognoscit, per aliquas similitudines cognoscat.

Decimo, utrum simul cognoscat omnia quae in Deo videt.

Undecimo, utrum in statu huius vitae possit aliquis homo essentiam Dei videre.

Duodecimo, utrum per rationem naturalem Deum in hac vita possimus cognoscere.

Tertiodecimo, utrum, supra cognitionem naturalis rationis, sit in praesenti vita aliqua cognitio Dei per gratiam.

As hitherto we have considered God as He is in Himself, we now go on to consider in what manner He is in the knowledge of creatures; concerning which there are thirteen points of inquiry:

(1) Whether any created intellect can see the essence of God?

(2) Whether the essence of God is seen by the intellect through any created image?

(3) Whether the essence of God can be seen by the corporeal eye?

(4) Whether any created intellectual substance is sufficient by its own natural powers to see the essence of God?

(5) Whether the created intellect needs any created light in order to see the essence of God?

(6) Whether of those who see God, one sees Him more perfectly than another?

(7) Whether any created intellect can comprehend the essence of God?

(8) Whether the created intellect seeing the essence of God, knows all things in it?

(9) Whether what is there known is known by any similitudes?

(10) Whether the created intellect knows at once what it sees in God?

(11) Whether in the state of this life any man can see the essence of God?

(12) Whether by natural reason we can know God in this life?

(13) Whether there is in this life any knowledge of God through grace above the knowledge of natural reason?

Article 1

Whether Any Created Intellect Can See the Essence of God?

AD PRIMUM SIC PROCEDITUR. Videtur quod nullus intellectus creatus possit Deum per essentiam videre. Chrysostomus enim, super Ioannem, exponens illud quod dicitur Ioan. I, *Deum nemo vidit unquam*, sic dicit, *ipsum quod est Deus, non solum prophetae, sed nec Angeli viderunt nec Archangeli, quod enim creabilis est*

OBJECTION 1: It seems that no created intellect can see the essence of God. For Chrysostom (*Hom. xiv. in Joan.*) commenting on John 1:18, *No man hath seen God at any time*, says: *Not prophets only, but neither angels nor archangels have seen God. For how can a creature see what is increatable?* Dionysius also says (*Div. Nom.* i), speaking of God:

99

naturae, qualiter videre poterit quod increabile est? Dionysius etiam, I cap. de Div. Nom., loquens de Deo, dicit, *neque sensus est eius, neque phantasia, neque opinio, nec ratio, nec scientia.*

PRAETEREA, omne infinitum, inquantum huiusmodi, est ignotum. Sed Deus est infinitus, ut supra ostensum est. Ergo secundum se est ignotus.

PRAETEREA, intellectus creatus non est cognoscitivus nisi existentium, primum enim quod cadit in apprehensione intellectus, est ens. Sed Deus non est existens, sed supra existentia. Ut dicit Dionysius. Ergo non est intelligibilis; sed est supra omnem intellectum.

PRAETEREA, cognoscentis ad cognitum oportet esse aliquam proportionem, cum cognitum sit perfectio cognoscentis. Sed nulla est proportio intellectus creati ad Deum, quia in infinitum distant. Ergo intellectus creatus non potest videre essentiam Dei.

SED CONTRA est quod dicitur I Ioan. III, *videbimus eum sicuti est.*

RESPONDEO dicendum quod, cum unumquodque sit cognoscibile secundum quod est in actu, Deus, qui est actus purus absque omni permixtione potentiae, quantum in se est, maxime cognoscibilis est. Sed quod est maxime cognoscibile in se, alicui intellectui cognoscibile non est, propter excessum intelligibilis supra intellectum, sicut sol, qui est maxime visibilis, videri non potest a vespertilione, propter excessum luminis.

Hoc igitur attendentes, quidam posuerunt quod nullus intellectus creatus essentiam Dei videre potest. Sed hoc inconvenienter dicitur. Cum enim ultima hominis beatitudo in altissima eius operatione consistat, quae est operatio intellectus, si nunquam essentiam Dei videre potest intellectus creatus, vel nunquam beatitudinem obtinebit, vel in alio eius beatitudo consistet quam in Deo. Quod est alienum a fide. In ipso enim est ultima perfectio rationalis creaturae, quia est ei principium essendi, intantum enim unumquodque perfectum est, inquantum ad suum principium attingit. Similiter etiam est praeter rationem. Inest enim homini naturale desiderium cognoscendi causam, cum intuetur effectum; et ex hoc admiratio in hominibus consurgit. Si igitur intellectus rationalis creaturae pertingere non possit ad primam causam rerum, remanebit inane desiderium naturae.

Unde simpliciter concedendum est quod beati Dei essentiam videant.

AD PRIMUM ergo dicendum quod utraque auctoritas loquitur de visione comprehensionis. Unde praemittit Dionysius immediate ante verba proposita, dicens, *omnibus ipse est universaliter incomprehensibilis, et nec sensus est*, et cetera. Et Chrysostomus parum post verba

Neither is there sense, nor image, nor opinion, nor reason, nor knowledge of Him.

OBJ. 2: Further, everything infinite, as such, is unknown. But God is infinite, as was shown above (Q. 7, A. 1). Therefore in Himself He is unknown.

OBJ. 3: Further, the created intellect knows only existing things. For what falls first under the apprehension of the intellect is being. Now God is not something existing; but He is rather super-existence, as Dionysius says (*Div. Nom.* iv). Therefore God is not intelligible; but above all intellect.

OBJ. 4: Further, there must be some proportion between the knower and the known, since the known is the perfection of the knower. But no proportion exists between the created intellect and God; for there is an infinite distance between them. Therefore the created intellect cannot see the essence of God.

ON THE CONTRARY, It is written: *We shall see Him as He is* (1 John 2:2).

I ANSWER THAT, Since everything is knowable according as it is actual, God, Who is pure act without any admixture of potentiality, is in Himself supremely knowable. But what is supremely knowable in itself, may not be knowable to a particular intellect, on account of the excess of the intelligible object above the intellect; as, for example, the sun, which is supremely visible, cannot be seen by the bat by reason of its excess of light.

Therefore some who considered this, held that no created intellect can see the essence of God. This opinion, however, is not tenable. For as the ultimate beatitude of man consists in the use of his highest function, which is the operation of his intellect; if we suppose that the created intellect could never see God, it would either never attain to beatitude, or its beatitude would consist in something else beside God; which is opposed to faith. For the ultimate perfection of the rational creature is to be found in that which is the principle of its being; since a thing is perfect so far as it attains to its principle. Further the same opinion is also against reason. For there resides in every man a natural desire to know the cause of any effect which he sees; and thence arises wonder in men. But if the intellect of the rational creature could not reach so far as to the first cause of things, the natural desire would remain void.

Hence it must be absolutely granted that the blessed see the essence of God.

REPLY OBJ. 1: Both of these authorities speak of the vision of comprehension. Hence Dionysius premises immediately before the words cited, *He is universally to all incomprehensible*, etc. Chrysostom likewise after the words quoted says: *He says this of the most certain vision of the*

praedicta subdit, *visionem hic dicit certissimam patris considerationem et comprehensionem, tantam quantam pater habet de filio.*

Ad secundum dicendum quod infinitum quod se tenet ex parte materiae non perfectae per formam, ignotum est secundum se, quia omnis cognitio est per formam. Sed infinitum quod se tenet ex parte formae non limitatae per materiam, est secundum se maxime notum. Sic autem Deus est infinitus, et non primo modo, ut ex superioribus patet.

Ad tertium dicendum quod Deus non sic dicitur non existens, quasi nullo modo sit existens, sed quia est supra omne existens, inquantum est suum esse. Unde ex hoc non sequitur quod nullo modo possit cognosci, sed quod omnem cognitionem excedat, quod est ipsum non comprehendi.

Ad quartum dicendum quod proportio dicitur dupliciter. Uno modo, certa habitudo unius quantitatis ad alteram; secundum quod duplum, triplum et aequale sunt species proportionis. Alio modo, quaelibet habitudo unius ad alterum proportio dicitur. Et sic potest esse proportio creaturae ad Deum, inquantum se habet ad ipsum ut effectus ad causam, et ut potentia ad actum. Et secundum hoc, intellectus creatus proportionatus esse potest ad cognoscendum Deum.

Father, which is such a perfect consideration and comprehension as the Father has of the Son.

Reply Obj. 2: The infinity of matter not made perfect by form, is unknown in itself, because all knowledge comes by the form; whereas the infinity of the form not limited by matter, is in itself supremely known. God is Infinite in this way, and not in the first way: as appears from what was said above (Q. 7, A. 1).

Reply Obj. 3: God is not said to be not existing as if He did not exist at all, but because He exists above all that exists; inasmuch as He is His own existence. Hence it does not follow that He cannot be known at all, but that He exceeds every kind of knowledge; which means that He is not comprehended.

Reply Obj. 4: Proportion is twofold. In one sense it means a certain relation of one quantity to another, according as double, treble and equal are species of proportion. In another sense every relation of one thing to another is called proportion. And in this sense there can be a proportion of the creature to God, inasmuch as it is related to Him as the effect of its cause, and as potentiality to its act; and in this way the created intellect can be proportioned to know God.

Article 2

Whether the Essence of God Is Seen by the Created Intellect Through an Image?

Ad secundum sic proceditur. Videtur quod essentia Dei ab intellectu creato per aliquam similitudinem videatur. Dicitur enim I Ioan. III, *scimus quoniam, cum apparuerit, similes ei erimus, et videbimus eum sicuti est.*

Praeterea, Augustinus dicit, IX de Trin., *cum Deum novimus, fit aliqua Dei similitudo in nobis.*

Praeterea, intellectus in actu est intelligibile in actu, sicut sensus in actu est sensibile in actu. Hoc autem non est nisi inquantum informatur sensus similitudine rei sensibilis, et intellectus similitudine rei intellectae. Ergo, si Deus ab intellectu creato videtur in actu, oportet quod per aliquam similitudinem videatur.

Sed contra est quod dicit Augustinus, XV de Trin., quod cum apostolus dicit *videmus nunc per speculum et in aenigmate, speculi et aenigmatis nomine, quaecumque similitudines ab ipso significatae intelligi possunt, quae accommodatae sunt ad intelligendum Deum.* Sed videre Deum per essentiam non est visio aenigmatica vel specularis, sed contra eam dividitur. Ergo divina essentia non videtur per similitudines.

Objection 1: It seems that the essence of God is seen through an image by the created intellect. For it is written: *We know that when He shall appear, we shall be like to Him, and we shall see Him as He is* (1 John 3:2).

Obj. 2: Further, Augustine says (*De Trin.* v): *When we know God, some likeness of God is made in us.*

Obj. 3: Further, the intellect in act is the actual intelligible; as sense in act is the actual sensible. But this comes about inasmuch as sense is informed with the likeness of the sensible object, and the intellect with the likeness of the thing understood. Therefore, if God is seen by the created intellect in act, it must be that He is seen by some similitude.

On the contrary, Augustine says (*De Trin.* xv) that when the Apostle says, *We see through a glass and in an enigma*, by the terms 'glass' and 'enigma' certain similitudes are signified by him, which are accommodated to the vision of God. But to see the essence of God is not an enigmatic nor a speculative vision, but is, on the contrary, of an opposite kind. Therefore the divine essence is not seen through a similitude.

RESPONDEO dicendum quod ad visionem, tam sensibilem quam intellectualem, duo requiruntur, scilicet virtus visiva, et unio rei visae cum visu, non enim fit visio in actu, nisi per hoc quod res visa quodammodo est in vidente. Et in rebus quidem corporalibus, apparet quod res visa non potest esse in vidente per suam essentiam, sed solum per suam similitudinem, sicut similitudo lapidis est in oculo, per quam fit visio in actu, non autem ipsa substantia lapidis. Si autem esset una et eadem res, quae esset principium visivae virtutis, et quae esset res visa, oporteret videntem ab illa re et virtutem visivam habere, et formam per quam videret.

Manifestum est autem quod Deus et est auctor intellectivae virtutis, et ab intellectu videri potest. Et cum ipsa intellectiva virtus creaturae non sit Dei essentia, relinquitur quod sit aliqua participata similitudo ipsius, qui est primus intellectus. Unde et virtus intellectualis creaturae lumen quoddam intelligibile dicitur, quasi a prima luce derivatum, sive hoc intelligatur de virtute naturali, sive de aliqua perfectione superaddita gratiae vel gloriae. Requiritur ergo ad videndum Deum aliqua Dei similitudo ex parte visivae potentiae, qua scilicet intellectus sit efficax ad videndum Deum. Sed ex parte visae rei, quam necesse est aliquo modo uniri videnti per nullam similitudinem creatam Dei essentia videri potest. Primo quidem, quia, sicut dicit Dionysius, I cap. de Div. Nom., *per similitudines inferioris ordinis rerum nullo modo superiora possunt cognosci*, sicut per speciem corporis non potest cognosci essentia rei incorporeae. Multo igitur minus per speciem creatam quamcumque potest essentia Dei videri. Secundo, quia essentia Dei est ipsum esse eius, ut supra ostensum est, quod nulli formae creatae competere potest. Non potest igitur aliqua forma creata esse similitudo repraesentans videnti Dei essentiam. Tertio, quia divina essentia est aliquod incircumscriptum, continens in se supereminenter quidquid potest significari vel intelligi ab intellectu creato. Et hoc nullo modo per aliquam speciem creatam repraesentari potest, quia omnis forma creata est determinata secundum aliquam rationem vel sapientiae, vel virtutis, vel ipsius esse, vel alicuius huiusmodi. Unde dicere Deum per similitudinem videri, est dicere divinam essentiam non videri, quod est erroneum.

Dicendum ergo quod ad videndum Dei essentiam requiritur aliqua similitudo ex parte visivae potentiae, scilicet lumen gloriae, confortans intellectum ad videndum Deum, de quo dicitur in Psalmo, *in lumine tuo videbimus lumen*. Non autem per aliquam similitudinem creatam Dei essentia videri potest, quae ipsam divinam essentiam repraesentet ut in se est.

AD PRIMUM ergo dicendum quod auctoritas illa loquitur de similitudine quae est per participationem luminis gloriae.

I ANSWER THAT, Two things are required both for sensible and for intellectual vision—viz. power of sight, and union of the thing seen with the sight. For vision is made actual only when the thing seen is in a certain way in the seer. Now in corporeal things it is clear that the thing seen cannot be by its essence in the seer, but only by its likeness; as the similitude of a stone is in the eye, whereby the vision is made actual; whereas the substance of the stone is not there. But if the principle of the visual power and the thing seen were one and the same thing, it would necessarily follow that the seer would receive both the visual power and the form whereby it sees, from that one same thing.

Now it is manifest both that God is the author of the intellectual power, and that He can be seen by the intellect. And since the intellective power of the creature is not the essence of God, it follows that it is some kind of participated likeness of Him who is the first intellect. Hence also the intellectual power of the creature is called an intelligible light, as it were, derived from the first light, whether this be understood of the natural power, or of some perfection superadded of grace or of glory. Therefore, in order to see God, there must be some similitude of God on the part of the visual faculty, whereby the intellect is made capable of seeing God. But on the part of the object seen, which must necessarily be united to the seer, the essence of God cannot be seen by any created similitude. First, because as Dionysius says (*Div. Nom.* i), *by the similitudes of the inferior order of things, the superior can in no way be known*; as by the likeness of a body the essence of an incorporeal thing cannot be known. Much less therefore can the essence of God be seen by any created likeness whatever. Second, because the essence of God is His own very existence, as was shown above (Q. 3, A. 4), which cannot be said of any created form; and so no created form can be the similitude representing the essence of God to the seer. Third, because the divine essence is uncircumscribed, and contains in itself super-eminently whatever can be signified or understood by the created intellect. Now this cannot in any way be represented by any created likeness; for every created form is determined according to some aspect of wisdom, or of power, or of being itself, or of some like thing. Hence to say that God is seen by some similitude, is to say that the divine essence is not seen at all; which is false.

Therefore it must be said that to see the essence of God, there is required some similitude in the visual faculty, namely, the light of glory strengthening the intellect to see God, which is spoken of in the Psalm (35:10), *In Thy light we shall see light*. The essence of God, however, cannot be seen by any created similitude representing the divine essence itself as it really is.

REPLY OBJ. 1: That authority speaks of the similitude which is caused by participation of the light of glory.

Ad secundum dicendum quod Augustinus ibi loquitur de cognitione Dei quae habetur in via.

Ad tertium dicendum quod divina essentia est ipsum esse. Unde, sicut aliae formae intelligibiles quae non sunt suum esse, uniuntur intellectui secundum aliquod esse quo informant ipsum intellectum et faciunt ipsum in actu; ita divina essentia unitur intellectui creato ut intellectum in actu, per seipsam faciens intellectum in actu.

Reply Obj. 2: Augustine speaks of the knowledge of God here on earth.

Reply Obj. 3: The divine essence is existence itself. Hence as other intelligible forms which are not their own existence are united to the intellect by means of some entity, whereby the intellect itself is informed, and made in act; so the divine essence is united to the created intellect, as the object actually understood, making the intellect in act by and of itself.

Article 3

Whether the Essence of God Can Be Seen with the Bodily Eye?

Ad tertium sic proceditur. Videtur quod essentia Dei videri possit oculo corporali. Dicitur enim Iob XIX, *in carne mea videbo Deum*, etc.; et XLII, *auditu auris audivi te, nunc autem oculus meus videt te.*

Praeterea, Augustinus dicit, ultimo de civitate Dei, cap. XXIX, *vis itaque praepollentior oculorum erit illorum* (scilicet glorificatorum), *non ut acutius videant quam quidam perhibentur videre serpentes vel aquilae (quantalibet enim acrimonia cernendi eadem animalia vigeant, nihil aliud possunt videre quam corpora), sed ut videant et incorporalia.* Quicumque autem potest videre incorporalia, potest elevari ad videndum Deum. Ergo oculus glorificatus potest videre Deum.

Praeterea, Deus potest videri ab homine visione imaginaria, dicitur enim Isaiae VI, *vidi dominum sedentem super solium*, et cetera. Sed visio imaginaria a sensu originem habet, *phantasia enim est motus factus a sensu secundum actum*, ut dicitur in III de anima. Ergo Deus sensibili visione videri potest.

Sed contra est quod dicit Augustinus, in libro de videndo Deum ad Paulinam, *Deum nemo vidit unquam, vel in hac vita, sicut ipse est; vel in Angelorum vita, sicut visibilia ista quae corporali visione cernuntur.*

Respondeo dicendum quod impossibile est Deum videri sensu visus, vel quocumque alio sensu aut potentia sensitivae partis. Omnis enim potentia huiusmodi est actus corporalis organi, ut infra dicetur. Actus autem proportionatur ei cuius est actus. Unde nulla huiusmodi potentia potest se extendere ultra corporalia. Deus autem incorporeus est, ut supra ostensum est. Unde nec sensu nec imaginatione videri potest, sed solo intellectu.

Ad primum ergo dicendum quod, cum dicitur *in carne mea videbo Deum, salvatorem meum*, non intelligitur quod oculo carnis sit Deum visurus, sed quod in carne existens, post resurrectionem, visurus sit Deum. Similiter quod dicitur, *nunc oculus meus videt te*, intelligitur de oculo mentis, sicut Ephes. I dicit apostolus, *det*

Objection 1: It seems that the essence of God can be seen by the corporeal eye. For it is written (Job 19:26): *In my flesh I shall see . . . God*, and (Job 42:5), *With the hearing of the ear I have heard Thee, but now my eye seeth Thee.*

Obj. 2: Further, Augustine says (*De Civ. Dei* xxix, 29): *Those eyes* (namely the glorified) *will therefore have a greater power of sight, not so much to see more keenly, as some report of the sight of serpents or of eagles (for whatever acuteness of vision is possessed by these creatures, they can see only corporeal things) but to see even incorporeal things.* Now whoever can see incorporeal things, can be raised up to see God. Therefore the glorified eye can see God.

Obj. 3: Further, God can be seen by man through a vision of the imagination. For it is written: *I saw the Lord sitting upon a throne*, etc. (Isa 6:1). But an imaginary vision originates from sense; for the imagination is moved by sense to act. Therefore God can be seen by a vision of sense.

On the contrary, Augustine says (De Vid. Deum, Ep. cxlvii): *No one has ever seen God either in this life, as He is, nor in the angelic life, as visible things are seen by corporeal vision.*

I answer that, It is impossible for God to be seen by the sense of sight, or by any other sense, or faculty of the sensitive power. For every such kind of power is the act of a corporeal organ, as will be shown later (Q. 78). Now act is proportional to the nature which possesses it. Hence no power of that kind can go beyond corporeal things. For God is incorporeal, as was shown above (Q. 3, A. 1). Hence He cannot be seen by the sense or the imagination, but only by the intellect.

Reply Obj. 1: The words, *In my flesh I shall see God my Savior*, do not mean that God will be seen with the eye of the flesh, but that man existing in the flesh after the resurrection will see God. Likewise the words, *Now my eye seeth Thee*, are to be understood of the mind's eye, as the Apostle says: *May He give unto you the spirit of wisdom . . . in the*

vobis spiritum sapientiae in agnitione eius, illuminatos oculos cordis vestri.

AD SECUNDUM dicendum quod Augustinus loquitur inquirendo in verbis illis, et sub conditione. Quod patet ex hoc quod praemittitur, longe itaque potentiae alterius erunt (scilicet oculi glorificati), si per eos videbitur incorporea illa natura. Sed postmodum hoc determinat, dicens, *valde credibile est sic nos visuros mundana tunc corpora caeli novi et terrae novae, ut Deum ubique praesentem, et universa etiam corporalia gubernantem, clarissima perspicuitate videamus; non sicut nunc invisibilia Dei per ea quae facta sunt intellecta conspiciuntur; sed sicut homines, inter quos viventes motusque vitales exerentes vivimus, mox ut aspicimus, non credimus vivere, sed videmus.* Ex quo patet quod hoc modo intelligit oculos glorificatos Deum visuros, sicut nunc oculi nostri vident alicuius vitam. Vita autem non videtur oculo corporali, sicut per se visibile, sed sicut sensibile per accidens, quod quidem a sensu non cognoscitur, sed statim cum sensu ab aliqua alia virtute cognoscitiva. Quod autem statim, visis corporibus, divina praesentia ex eis cognoscatur per intellectum, ex duobus contingit, scilicet ex perspicacitate intellectus; et ex refulgentia divinae claritatis in corporibus innovatis.

AD TERTIUM dicendum quod in visione imaginaria non videtur Dei essentia, sed aliqua forma in imaginatione formatur, repraesentans Deum secundum aliquem modum similitudinis, prout in Scripturis divinis divina per res sensibiles metaphorice describuntur.

knowledge of Him, that the eyes of your heart may be *enlightened* (Eph 1:17, 18).

REPLY OBJ. 2: Augustine speaks as one inquiring, and conditionally. This appears from what he says previously: *Therefore they will have an altogether different power (viz. the glorified eyes), if they shall see that incorporeal nature;* and afterwards he explains this, saying: *It is very credible, that we shall so see the mundane bodies of the new heaven and the new earth, as to see most clearly God everywhere present, governing all corporeal things, not as we now see the invisible things of God as understood by what is made; but as when we see men among whom we live, living and exercising the functions of human life, we do not believe they live, but see it.* Hence it is evident how the glorified eyes will see God, as now our eyes see the life of another. But life is not seen with the corporeal eye, as a thing in itself visible, but as the indirect object of the sense; which indeed is not known by sense, but at once, together with sense, by some other cognitive power. But that the divine presence is known by the intellect immediately on the sight of, and through, corporeal things, happens from two causes—viz. from the perspicuity of the intellect, and from the refulgence of the divine glory infused into the body after its renovation.

REPLY OBJ. 3: The essence of God is not seen in a vision of the imagination; but the imagination receives some form representing God according to some mode of similitude; as in the divine Scripture divine things are metaphorically described by means of sensible things.

Article 4

Whether Any Created Intellect by Its Natural Powers Can See the Divine Essence?

AD QUARTUM SIC PROCEDITUR. Videtur quod aliquis intellectus creatus per sua naturalia divinam essentiam videre possit. Dicit enim Dionysius, cap. IV de Div. Nom., quod Angelus est speculum purum, clarissimum, *suscipiens totam, si fas est dicere, pulchritudinem Dei.* Sed unumquodque videtur dum videtur eius speculum. Cum igitur Angelus per sua naturalia intelligat seipsum, videtur quod etiam per sua naturalia intelligat divinam essentiam.

PRAETEREA, illud quod est maxime visibile, fit minus visibile nobis propter defectum nostri visus, vel corporalis vel intellectualis. Sed intellectus Angeli non patitur aliquem defectum. Cum ergo Deus secundum se sit maxime intelligibilis, videtur quod ab Angelo sit maxime intelligibilis. Si igitur alia intelligibilia per sua naturalia intelligere potest, multo magis Deum.

PRAETEREA, sensus corporeus non potest elevari ad intelligendam substantiam incorpoream, quia est supra

OBJECTION 1: It seems that a created intellect can see the Divine essence by its own natural power. For Dionysius says (*Div. Nom.* iv): *An angel is a pure mirror, most clear, receiving, if it is right to say so, the whole beauty of God.* But if a reflection is seen, the original thing is seen. Therefore since an angel by his natural power understands himself, it seems that by his own natural power he understands the Divine essence.

OBJ. 2: Further, what is supremely visible, is made less visible to us by reason of our defective corporeal or intellectual sight. But the angelic intellect has no such defect. Therefore, since God is supremely intelligible in Himself, it seems that in like manner He is supremely so to an angel. Therefore, if he can understand other intelligible things by his own natural power, much more can he understand God.

OBJ. 3: Further, corporeal sense cannot be raised up to understand incorporeal substance, which is above its

eius naturam. Si igitur videre Deum per essentiam sit supra naturam cuiuslibet intellectus creati, videtur quod nullus intellectus creatus ad videndum Dei essentiam pertingere possit, quod est erroneum, ut ex supradictis patet. Videtur ergo quod intellectui creato sit naturale divinam essentiam videre.

SED CONTRA est quod dicitur Rom. VI, *gratia Dei vita aeterna.* Sed vita aeterna consistit in visione divinae essentiae, secundum illud Ioan. XVII, *haec est vita aeterna, ut cognoscant te solum verum Deum,* et cetera. Ergo videre Dei essentiam convenit intellectui creato per gratiam, et non per naturam.

RESPONDEO dicendum quod impossibile est quod aliquis intellectus creatus per sua naturalia essentiam Dei videat. Cognitio enim contingit secundum quod cognitum est in cognoscente. Cognitum autem est in cognoscente secundum modum cognoscentis. Unde cuiuslibet cognoscentis cognitio est secundum modum suae naturae. Si igitur modus essendi alicuius rei cognitae excedat modum naturae cognoscentis, oportet quod cognitio illius rei sit supra naturam illius cognoscentis. Est autem multiplex modus essendi rerum. Quaedam enim sunt, quorum natura non habet esse nisi in hac materia individuali, et huiusmodi sunt omnia corporalia. Quaedam vero sunt, quorum naturae sunt per se subsistentes, non in materia aliqua, quae tamen non sunt suum esse, sed sunt esse habentes, et huiusmodi sunt substantiae incorporeae, quas Angelos dicimus.

Solius autem Dei proprius modus essendi est, ut sit suum esse subsistens. Ea igitur quae non habent esse nisi in materia individuali, cognoscere est nobis connaturale, eo quod anima nostra, per quam cognoscimus, est forma alicuius materiae. Quae tamen habet duas virtutes cognoscitivas. Unam, quae est actus alicuius corporei organi. Et huic connaturale est cognoscere res secundum quod sunt in materia individuali, unde sensus non cognoscit nisi singularia. Alia vero virtus cognoscitiva eius est intellectus, qui non est actus alicuius organi corporalis. Unde per intellectum connaturale est nobis cognoscere naturas, quae quidem non habent esse nisi in materia individuali; non tamen secundum quod sunt in materia individuali, sed secundum quod abstrahuntur ab ea per considerationem intellectus. Unde secundum intellectum possumus cognoscere huiusmodi res in universali, quod est supra facultatem sensus.

Intellectui autem angelico connaturale est cognoscere naturas non in materia existentes. Quod est supra naturalem facultatem intellectus animae humanae, secundum statum praesentis vitae, quo corpori unitur. Relinquitur ergo quod cognoscere ipsum esse subsistens, sit connaturale soli intellectui divino, et quod sit supra facultatem naturalem cuiuslibet intellectus creati, quia nulla creatura est suum esse, sed habet esse participatum. Non igitur potest intellectus creatus Deum per

nature. Therefore if to see the essence of God is above the nature of every created intellect, it follows that no created intellect can reach up to see the essence of God at all. But this is false, as appears from what is said above (A. 1). Therefore it seems that it is natural for a created intellect to see the Divine essence.

ON THE CONTRARY, It is written: *The grace of God is life everlasting* (Rom 6:23). But life everlasting consists in the vision of the Divine essence, according to the words: *This is eternal life, that they may know Thee the only true God*, etc. (John 17:3). Therefore to see the essence of God is possible to the created intellect by grace, and not by nature.

I ANSWER THAT, It is impossible for any created intellect to see the essence of God by its own natural power. For knowledge is regulated according as the thing known is in the knower. But the thing known is in the knower according to the mode of the knower. Hence the knowledge of every knower is ruled according to its own nature. If therefore the mode of anything's being exceeds the mode of the knower, it must result that the knowledge of the object is above the nature of the knower. Now the mode of being of things is manifold. For some things have being only in this one individual matter; as all bodies. But others are subsisting natures, not residing in matter at all, which, however, are not their own existence, but receive it; and these are the incorporeal beings, called angels.

But to God alone does it belong to be His own subsistent being. Therefore what exists only in individual matter we know naturally, forasmuch as our soul, whereby we know, is the form of certain matter. Now our soul possesses two cognitive powers; one is the act of a corporeal organ, which naturally knows things existing in individual matter; hence sense knows only the singular. But there is another kind of cognitive power in the soul, called the intellect; and this is not the act of any corporeal organ. Wherefore the intellect naturally knows natures which exist only in individual matter; not as they are in such individual matter, but according as they are abstracted therefrom by the considering act of the intellect; hence it follows that through the intellect we can understand these objects as universal; and this is beyond the power of the sense.

Now the angelic intellect naturally knows natures that are not in matter; but this is beyond the power of the intellect of our soul in the state of its present life, united as it is to the body. It follows therefore that to know self-subsistent being is natural to the divine intellect alone; and this is beyond the natural power of any created intellect; for no creature is its own existence, forasmuch as its existence is participated. Therefore the created intellect cannot see the

essentiam videre, nisi inquantum Deus per suam gratiam se intellectui creato coniungit, ut intelligibile ab ipso.

AD PRIMUM ergo dicendum quod iste modus cognoscendi Deum, est Angelo connaturalis, ut scilicet cognoscat eum per similitudinem eius in ipso Angelo refulgentem. Sed cognoscere Deum per aliquam similitudinem creatam, non est cognoscere essentiam Dei, ut supra ostensum est. Unde non sequitur quod Angelus per sua naturalia possit cognoscere essentiam Dei.

AD SECUNDUM dicendum quod intellectus Angeli non habet defectum, si defectus accipiatur privative, ut scilicet careat eo quod habere debet. Si vero accipiatur negative, sic quaelibet creatura invenitur deficiens, Deo comparata, dum non habet illam excellentiam quae invenitur in Deo.

AD TERTIUM dicendum quod sensus visus, quia omnino materialis est, nullo modo elevari potest ad aliquid immateriale. Sed intellectus noster vel angelicus, quia secundum naturam a materia aliqualiter elevatus est, potest ultra suam naturam per gratiam ad aliquid altius elevari. Et huius signum est, quia visus nullo modo potest in abstractione cognoscere id quod in concretione cognoscit, nullo enim modo potest percipere naturam, nisi ut hanc. Sed intellectus noster potest in abstractione considerare quod in concretione cognoscit. Etsi enim cognoscat res habentes formam in materia, tamen resolvit compositum in utrumque, et considerat ipsam formam per se. Et similiter intellectus Angeli, licet connaturale sit ei cognoscere esse concretum in aliqua natura, tamen potest ipsum esse secernere per intellectum, dum cognoscit quod aliud est ipse, et aliud est suum esse. Et ideo, cum intellectus creatus per suam naturam natus sit apprehendere formam concretam et esse concretum in abstractione, per modum resolutionis cuiusdam, potest per gratiam elevari ut cognoscat substantiam separatam subsistentem, et esse separatum subsistens.

essence of God, unless God by His grace unites Himself to the created intellect, as an object made intelligible to it.

REPLY OBJ. 1: This mode of knowing God is natural to an angel—namely, to know Him by His own likeness refulgent in the angel himself. But to know God by any created similitude is not to know the essence of God, as was shown above (A. 2). Hence it does not follow that an angel can know the essence of God by his own power.

REPLY OBJ. 2: The angelic intellect is not defective, if defect be taken to mean privation, as if it were without anything which it ought to have. But if the defect be taken negatively, in that sense every creature is defective, when compared with God; forasmuch as it does not possess the excellence which is in God.

REPLY OBJ. 3: The sense of sight, as being altogether material, cannot be raised up to immateriality. But our intellect, or the angelic intellect, inasmuch as it is elevated above matter in its own nature, can be raised up above its own nature to a higher level by grace. The proof is, that sight cannot in any way know abstractedly what it knows concretely; for in no way can it perceive a nature except as this one particular nature; whereas our intellect is able to consider abstractedly what it knows concretely. Now although it knows things which have a form residing in matter, still it resolves the composite into both of these elements; and it considers the form separately by itself. Likewise, also, the intellect of an angel, although it naturally knows the concrete in any nature, still it is able to separate that existence by its intellect; since it knows that the thing itself is one thing, and its existence is another. Since therefore the created intellect is naturally capable of apprehending the concrete form, and the concrete being abstractedly, by way of a kind of resolution of parts; it can by grace be raised up to know separate subsisting substance, and separate subsisting existence.

Article 5

Whether the Created Intellect Needs Any Created Light in Order to See the Essence of God?

AD QUINTUM SIC PROCEDITUR. Videtur quod intellectus creatus ad videndum essentiam Dei aliquo lumine creato non indigeat. Illud enim quod est per se lucidum in rebus sensibilibus, alio lumine non indiget ut videatur, ergo nec in intelligibilibus. Sed Deus est lux intelligibilis. Ergo non videtur per aliquod lumen creatum.

PRAETEREA, cum Deus videtur per medium, non videtur per suam essentiam. Sed cum videtur per aliquod lumen creatum, videtur per medium. Ergo non videtur per suam essentiam.

OBJECTION 1: It seems that the created intellect does not need any created light in order to see the essence of God. For what is of itself lucid in sensible things does not require any other light in order to be seen. Therefore the same applies to intelligible things. Now God is intelligible light. Therefore He is not seen by means of any created light.

OBJ. 2: Further, if God is seen through a medium, He is not seen in His essence. But if seen by any created light, He is seen through a medium. Therefore He is not seen in His essence.

Praeterea, illud quod est creatum, nihil prohibet alicui creaturae esse naturale. Si ergo per aliquod lumen creatum Dei essentia videtur, poterit illud lumen esse naturale alicui creaturae. Et ita illa creatura non indigebit aliquo alio lumine ad videndum Deum, quod est impossibile. Non est ergo necessarium quod omnis creatura ad videndum Dei essentiam lumen superadditum requirat.

Sed contra est quod dicitur in Psalmo, *in lumine tuo videbimus lumen.*

Respondeo dicendum quod omne quod elevatur ad aliquid quod excedit suam naturam, oportet quod disponatur aliqua dispositione quae sit supra suam naturam, sicut, si aer debeat accipere formam ignis, oportet quod disponatur aliqua dispositione ad talem formam. Cum autem aliquis intellectus creatus videt Deum per essentiam, ipsa essentia Dei fit forma intelligibilis intellectus. Unde oportet quod aliqua dispositio supernaturalis ei superaddatur, ad hoc quod elevetur in tantam sublimitatem. Cum igitur virtus naturalis intellectus creati non sufficiat ad Dei essentiam videndam, ut ostensum est, oportet quod ex divina gratia superaccrescat ei virtus intelligendi. Et hoc augmentum virtutis intellectivae illuminationem intellectus vocamus; sicut et ipsum intelligibile vocatur lumen vel lux. Et istud est lumen de quo dicitur Apoc. XXI, *quod claritas Dei illuminabit eam,* scilicet societatem beatorum Deum videntium. Et secundum hoc lumen efficiuntur deiformes, idest Deo similes; secundum illud I Ioan. III, *cum apparuerit, similes ei erimus, et videbimus eum sicuti est.*

Ad primum ergo dicendum quod lumen creatum est necessarium ad videndum Dei essentiam, non quod per hoc lumen Dei essentia intelligibilis fiat, quae secundum se intelligibilis est, sed ad hoc quod intellectus fiat potens ad intelligendum, per modum quo potentia fit potentior ad operandum per habitum, sicut etiam et lumen corporale necessarium est in visu exteriori, inquantum facit medium transparens in actu, ut possit moveri a colore.

Ad secundum dicendum quod lumen istud non requiritur ad videndum Dei essentiam quasi similitudo in qua Deus videatur, sed quasi perfectio quaedam intellectus, confortans ipsum ad videndum Deum. Et ideo potest dici quod non est medium in quo Deus videatur, sed sub quo videtur. Et hoc non tollit immediatam visionem Dei.

Ad tertium dicendum quod dispositio ad formam ignis non potest esse naturalis nisi habenti formam ignis. Unde lumen gloriae non potest esse naturale creaturae, nisi creatura esset naturae divinae, quod est impossibile. Per hoc enim lumen fit creatura rationalis deiformis, ut dictum est.

Obj. 3: Further, what is created can be natural to some creature. Therefore if the essence of God is seen through any created light, such a light can be made natural to some other creature; and thus, that creature would not need any other light to see God; which is impossible. Therefore it is not necessary that every creature should require a superadded light in order to see the essence of God.

On the contrary, It is written: *In Thy light we shall see light* (Ps 35:10).

I answer that, Everything which is raised up to what exceeds its nature, must be prepared by some disposition above its nature; as, for example, if air is to receive the form of fire, it must be prepared by some disposition for such a form. But when any created intellect sees the essence of God, the essence of God itself becomes the intelligible form of the intellect. Hence it is necessary that some supernatural disposition should be added to the intellect in order that it may be raised up to such a great and sublime height. Now since the natural power of the created intellect does not avail to enable it to see the essence of God, as was shown in the preceding article, it is necessary that the power of understanding should be added by divine grace. Now this increase of the intellectual powers is called the illumination of the intellect, as we also call the intelligible object itself by the name of light of illumination. And this is the light spoken of in the Apocalypse (Rev 21:23): *The glory of God hath enlightened it*—viz. the society of the blessed who see God. By this light the blessed are made *deiform*—i.e., like to God, according to the saying: *When He shall appear we shall be like to Him, and we shall see Him as He is* (1 John 2:2).

Reply Obj. 1: The created light is necessary to see the essence of God, not in order to make the essence of God intelligible, which is of itself intelligible, but in order to enable the intellect to understand in the same way as a habit makes a power abler to act. Even so corporeal light is necessary as regards external sight, inasmuch as it makes the medium actually transparent, and susceptible of color.

Reply Obj. 2: This light is required to see the divine essence, not as a similitude in which God is seen, but as a perfection of the intellect, strengthening it to see God. Therefore it may be said that this light is to be described not as a medium in which God is seen, but as one by which He is seen; and such a medium does not take away the immediate vision of God.

Reply Obj. 3: The disposition to the form of fire can be natural only to the subject of that form. Hence the light of glory cannot be natural to a creature unless the creature has a divine nature; which is impossible. But by this light the rational creature is made deiform, as is said in this article.

Article 6

Whether of Those Who See the Essence of God, One Sees More Perfectly Than Another?

AD SEXTUM SIC PROCEDITUR. Videtur quod videntium essentiam Dei unus alio perfectius non videat. Dicitur enim I Ioan. III, *videbimus eum sicuti est*. Sed ipse uno modo est. Ergo uno modo videbitur ab omnibus. Non ergo perfectius et minus perfecte.

PRAETEREA, Augustinus dicit, in libro octoginta trium qq., quod *unam rem non potest unus alio plus intelligere*. Sed omnes videntes Deum per essentiam, intelligunt Dei essentiam, intellectu enim videtur Deus, non sensu, ut supra habitum est. Ergo videntium divinam essentiam unus alio non clarius videt.

PRAETEREA, quod aliquid altero perfectius videatur, ex duobus contingere potest, vel ex parte obiecti visibilis; vel ex parte potentiae visivae videntis. Ex parte autem obiecti, per hoc quod obiectum perfectius in vidente recipitur, scilicet secundum perfectiorem similitudinem. Quod in proposito locum non habet, Deus enim non per aliquam similitudinem, sed per eius essentiam praesens est intellectui essentiam eius videnti. Relinquitur ergo quod, si unus alio perfectius eum videat, quod hoc sit secundum differentiam potentiae intellectivae. Et ita sequitur quod cuius potentia intellectiva naturaliter est sublimior, clarius eum videat. Quod est inconveniens, cum hominibus promittatur in beatitudine aequalitas Angelorum.

SED CONTRA est quod vita aeterna in visione Dei consistit, secundum illud Ioan. XVII, *haec est vita aeterna*, et cetera. Ergo, si omnes aequaliter Dei essentiam vident, in vita aeterna omnes erunt aequales. Cuius contrarium dicit apostolus, I Cor. XV, *stella differt a stella in claritate*.

RESPONDEO dicendum quod videntium Deum per essentiam unus alio perfectius eum videbit. Quod quidem non erit per aliquam Dei similitudinem perfectiorem in uno quam in alio, cum illa visio non sit futura per aliquam similitudinem, ut ostensum est. Sed hoc erit per hoc, quod intellectus unius habebit maiorem virtutem seu facultatem ad videndum Deum, quam alterius. Facultas autem videndi Deum non competit intellectui creato secundum suam naturam, sed per lumen gloriae, quod intellectum in quadam deiformitate constituit, ut ex superioribus patet.

Unde intellectus plus participans de lumine gloriae, perfectius Deum videbit. Plus autem participabit de lumine gloriae, qui plus habet de caritate, quia ubi est maior caritas, ibi est maius desiderium; et desiderium quodammodo facit desiderantem aptum et paratum ad

OBJECTION 1: It seems that of those who see the essence of God, one does not see more perfectly than another. For it is written (1 John 3:2): *We shall see Him as He is*. But He is only in one way. Therefore He will be seen by all in one way only; and therefore He will not be seen more perfectly by one and less perfectly by another.

OBJ. 2: Further, Augustine says (*Octog. Tri. Quaest.* qu. xxxii): *One person cannot see one and the same thing more perfectly than another*. But all who see the essence of God, understand the Divine essence, for God is seen by the intellect and not by sense, as was shown above (A. 3). Therefore of those who see the divine essence, one does not see more clearly than another.

OBJ. 3: Further, That anything be seen more perfectly than another can happen in two ways: either on the part of the visible object, or on the part of the visual power of the seer. On the part of the object, it may so happen because the object is received more perfectly in the seer, that is, according to the greater perfection of the similitude; but this does not apply to the present question, for God is present to the intellect seeing Him not by way of similitude, but by His essence. It follows then that if one sees Him more perfectly than another, this happens according to the difference of the intellectual power; thus it follows too that the one whose intellectual power is higher, will see Him the more clearly; and this is incongruous; since equality with angels is promised to men as their beatitude.

ON THE CONTRARY, Eternal life consists in the vision of God, according to John 17:3: *This is eternal life, that they may know Thee the only true God*, etc. Therefore if all saw the essence of God equally in eternal life, all would be equal; the contrary to which is declared by the Apostle: *Star differs from star in glory* (1 Cor 15:41).

I ANSWER THAT, Of those who see the essence of God, one sees Him more perfectly than another. This, indeed, does not take place as if one had a more perfect similitude of God than another, since that vision will not spring from any similitude; but it will take place because one intellect will have a greater power or faculty to see God than another. The faculty of seeing God, however, does not belong to the created intellect naturally, but is given to it by the light of glory, which establishes the intellect in a kind of *deiformity*, as appears from what is said above, in the preceding article.

Hence the intellect which has more of the light of glory will see God the more perfectly; and he will have a fuller participation of the light of glory who has more charity; because where there is the greater charity, there is the more desire; and desire in a certain degree makes the one desiring apt and prepared to receive the object desired. Hence

susceptionem desiderati. Unde qui plus habebit de caritate, perfectius Deum videbit, et beatior erit.

Ad primum ergo dicendum quod, cum dicitur *videbimus eum sicuti est*, hoc adverbium sicuti determinat modum visionis ex parte rei visae ut sit sensus, videbimus eum ita esse sicuti est, quia ipsum esse eius videbimus, quod est eius essentia. Non autem determinat modum visionis ex parte videntis, ut sit sensus, quod ita erit perfectus modus videndi, sicut est in Deo perfectus modus essendi.

Et per hoc etiam patet solutio ad secundum. Cum enim dicitur quod rem unam unus alio melius non intelligit, hoc habet veritatem si referatur ad modum rei intellectae, quia quicumque intelligit rem esse aliter quam sit, non vere intelligit. Non autem si referatur ad modum intelligendi, quia intelligere unius est perfectius quam intelligere alterius.

Ad tertium dicendum quod diversitas videndi non erit ex parte obiecti, quia idem obiectum omnibus praesentabitur, scilicet Dei essentia, nec ex diversa participatione obiecti per differentes similitudines, sed erit per diversam facultatem intellectus, non quidem naturalem, sed gloriosam, ut dictum est.

he who possesses the more charity, will see God the more perfectly, and will be the more beatified.

Reply Obj. 1: In the words, *We shall see Him as He is*, the conjunction *as* determines the mode of vision on the part of the object seen, so that the meaning is, we shall see Him to be as He is, because we shall see His existence, which is His essence. But it does not determine the mode of vision on the part of the one seeing; as if the meaning was that the mode of seeing God will be as perfect as is the perfect mode of God's existence.

Thus appears the answer to the Second Objection. For when it is said that one intellect does not understand one and the same thing better than another, this would be true if referred to the mode of the thing understood, for whoever understands it otherwise than it really is, does not truly understand it, but not if referred to the mode of understanding, for the understanding of one is more perfect than the understanding of another.

Reply Obj. 3: The diversity of seeing will not arise on the part of the object seen, for the same object will be presented to all—viz. the essence of God; nor will it arise from the diverse participation of the object seen by different similitudes; but it will arise on the part of the diverse faculty of the intellect, not, indeed, the natural faculty, but the glorified faculty.

Article 7

Whether Those Who See the Essence of God Comprehend Him?

Ad septimum sic proceditur. Videtur quod videntes Deum per essentiam ipsum comprehendant. Dicit enim apostolus, Philipp. III, *sequor autem si quo modo comprehendam.* Non autem frustra sequebatur, dicit enim ipse, I Cor. IX, *sic curro, non quasi in incertum.* Ergo ipse comprehendit, et eadem ratione alii, quos ad hoc invitat, dicens, *sic currite, ut comprehendatis.*

Praeterea, ut dicit Augustinus in libro de videndo Deum ad Paulinam, *illud comprehenditur, quod ita totum videtur, ut nihil eius lateat videntem.* Sed si Deus per essentiam videtur, totus videtur, et nihil eius latet videntem; cum Deus sit simplex. Ergo a quocumque videtur per essentiam, comprehenditur.

Si dicatur quod videtur totus, sed non totaliter, contra, totaliter vel dicit modum videntis, vel modum rei visae. Sed ille qui videt Deum per essentiam, videt eum totaliter, si significetur modus rei visae, quia videt eum sicuti est, ut dictum est. Similiter videt eum totaliter, si significetur modus videntis, quia tota virtute sua intellectus Dei essentiam videbit. Quilibet ergo videns

Objection 1: It seems that those who see the divine essence, comprehend God. For the Apostle says (Phil 3:12): *But I follow after, if I may by any means comprehend.* But the Apostle did not follow in vain; for he said (1 Cor 9:26): *I . . . so run, not as at an uncertainty.* Therefore he comprehended; and in the same way, others also, whom he invites to do the same, saying: *So run that you may comprehend.*

Obj. 2: Further, Augustine says (De Vid. Deum, Ep. cxlvii): *That is comprehended which is so seen as a whole, that nothing of it is hidden from the seer.* But if God is seen in His essence, He is seen whole, and nothing of Him is hidden from the seer, since God is simple. Therefore whoever sees His essence, comprehends Him.

Obj. 3: Further, if we say that He is seen as a *whole*, but not *wholly*, it may be contrarily urged that *wholly* refers either to the mode of the seer, or to the mode of the thing seen. But he who sees the essence of God, sees Him wholly, if the mode of the thing seen is considered; forasmuch as he sees Him as He is; also, likewise, he sees Him wholly if the mode of the seer is meant, forasmuch as the intellect

Deum per essentiam, totaliter eum videbit. Ergo eum comprehendet.

SED CONTRA est quod dicitur Ierem. XXXII, *fortissime, magne, potens, dominus exercituum nomen tibi; magnus consilio, et incomprehensibilis cogitatu.* Ergo comprehendi non potest.

RESPONDEO dicendum quod comprehendere Deum impossibile est cuicumque intellectui creato, *attingere vero mente Deum qualitercumque, magna est beatitudo,* ut dicit Augustinus.

Ad cuius evidentiam, sciendum est quod illud comprehenditur, quod perfecte cognoscitur. Perfecte autem cognoscitur, quod tantum cognoscitur, quantum est cognoscibile. Unde si id quod est cognoscibile per scientiam demonstrativam, opinione teneatur ex aliqua ratione probabili concepta, non comprehenditur. Puta, si hoc quod est triangulum habere tres angulos aequales duobus rectis, aliquis sciat per demonstrationem, comprehendit illud, si vero aliquis eius opinionem accipiat probabiliter, per hoc quod a sapientibus vel pluribus ita dicitur, non comprehendet ipsum, quia non pertingit ad illum perfectum modum cognitionis, quo cognoscibilis est. Nullus autem intellectus creatus pertingere potest ad illum perfectum modum cognitionis divinae essentiae, quo cognoscibilis est. Quod sic patet. Unumquodque enim sic cognoscibile est, secundum quod est ens actu. Deus igitur, cuius esse est infinitum, ut supra ostensum est, infinite cognoscibilis est. Nullus autem intellectus creatus potest Deum infinite cognoscere. Intantum enim intellectus creatus divinam essentiam perfectius vel minus perfecte cognoscit, inquantum maiori vel minori lumine gloriae perfunditur. Cum igitur lumen gloriae creatum, in quocumque intellectu creato receptum, non possit esse infinitum, impossibile est quod aliquis intellectus creatus Deum infinite cognoscat. Unde impossibile est quod Deum comprehendat.

AD PRIMUM ergo dicendum quod comprehensio dicitur dupliciter. Uno modo, stricte et proprie, secundum quod aliquid includitur in comprehendente. Et sic nullo modo Deus comprehenditur, nec intellectu nec aliquo alio, quia, cum sit infinitus, nullo finito includi potest, ut aliquid finitum eum infinite capiat, sicut ipse infinite est. Et sic de comprehensione nunc quaeritur. Alio modo comprehensio largius sumitur, secundum quod comprehensio insecutioni opponitur. Qui enim attingit aliquem, quando iam tenet ipsum, comprehendere eum dicitur. Et sic Deus comprehenditur a beatis, secundum illud Cant. III, *tenui eum, nec dimittam.* Et sic intelliguntur auctoritates apostoli de comprehensione. Et hoc modo comprehensio est una de tribus dotibus animae, quae respondet spei; sicut visio fidei, et fruitio caritati. Non enim, apud nos, omne quod videtur, iam tenetur vel habetur, quia videntur interdum distantia, vel quae non

will with its full power see the Divine essence. Therefore all who see the essence of God see Him wholly; therefore they comprehend Him.

ON THE CONTRARY, It is written: *O most mighty, great, and powerful, the Lord of hosts is Thy Name. Great in counsel, and incomprehensible in thought* (Jer 32:18,19). Therefore He cannot be comprehended.

I ANSWER THAT, It is impossible for any created intellect to comprehend God; yet *for the mind to attain to God in some degree is great beatitude,* as Augustine says (De Verb. Dom., Serm. xxxviii).

In proof of this we must consider that what is comprehended is perfectly known; and that is perfectly known which is known so far as it can be known. Thus, if anything which is capable of scientific demonstration is held only by an opinion resting on a probable proof, it is not comprehended; as, for instance, if anyone knows by scientific demonstration that a triangle has three angles equal to two right angles, he comprehends that truth; whereas if anyone accepts it as a probable opinion because wise men or most men teach it, he cannot be said to comprehend the thing itself, because he does not attain to that perfect mode of knowledge of which it is intrinsically capable. But no created intellect can attain to that perfect mode of the knowledge of the Divine intellect whereof it is intrinsically capable. Which thus appears—Everything is knowable according to its actuality. But God, whose being is infinite, as was shown above (Q. 7), is infinitely knowable. Now no created intellect can know God infinitely. For the created intellect knows the Divine essence more or less perfectly in proportion as it receives a greater or lesser light of glory. Since therefore the created light of glory received into any created intellect cannot be infinite, it is clearly impossible for any created intellect to know God in an infinite degree. Hence it is impossible that it should comprehend God.

REPLY OBJ. 1: *Comprehension* is twofold: in one sense it is taken strictly and properly, according as something is included in the one comprehending; and thus in no way is God comprehended either by intellect, or in any other way; forasmuch as He is infinite and cannot be included in any finite being; so that no finite being can contain Him infinitely, in the degree of His own infinity. In this sense we now take comprehension. But in another sense *comprehension* is taken more largely as opposed to *non-attainment*; for he who attains to anyone is said to comprehend him when he attains to him. And in this sense God is comprehended by the blessed, according to the words, *I held him, and I will not let him go* (Cant. 3:4); in this sense also are to be understood the words quoted from the Apostle concerning comprehension. And in this way *comprehension* is one of the three prerogatives of the soul, responding to hope, as vision responds to faith, and fruition responds to charity.

sunt in potestate nostra. Neque iterum omnibus quae habemus, fruimur, vel quia non delectamur in eis; vel quia non sunt ultimus finis desiderii nostri, ut desiderium nostrum impleant et quietent. Sed haec tria habent beati in Deo, quia et vident ipsum; et videndo, tenent sibi praesentem, in potestate habentes semper eum videre; et tenentes, fruuntur sicut ultimo fine desiderium implente.

AD SECUNDUM dicendum quod non propter hoc Deus incomprehensibilis dicitur, quasi aliquid eius sit quod non videatur, sed quia non ita perfecte videtur, sicut visibilis est. Sicut cum aliqua demonstrabilis propositio per aliquam probabilem rationem cognoscitur, non est aliquid eius quod non cognoscatur, nec subiectum, nec praedicatum, nec compositio, sed tota non ita perfecte cognoscitur, sicut cognoscibilis est. Unde Augustinus, definiendo comprehensionem, dicit quod *totum comprehenditur videndo, quod ita videtur, ut nihil eius lateat videntem; aut cuius fines circumspici possunt*, tunc enim fines alicuius circumspiciuntur, quando ad finem in modo cognoscendi illam rem pervenitur.

AD TERTIUM dicendum quod totaliter dicit modum obiecti, non quidem ita quod totus modus obiecti non cadat sub cognitione; sed quia modus obiecti non est modus cognoscentis. Qui igitur videt Deum per essentiam, videt hoc in eo, quod infinite existit, et infinite cognoscibilis est, sed hic infinitus modus non competit ei, ut scilicet ipse infinite cognoscat, sicut aliquis probabiliter scire potest aliquam propositionem esse demonstrabilem, licet ipse eam demonstrative non cognoscat.

For even among ourselves not everything seen is held or possessed, forasmuch as things either appear sometimes afar off, or they are not in our power of attainment. Neither, again, do we always enjoy what we possess; either because we find no pleasure in them, or because such things are not the ultimate end of our desire, so as to satisfy and quell it. But the blessed possess these three things in God; because they see Him, and in seeing Him, possess Him as present, having the power to see Him always; and possessing Him, they enjoy Him as the ultimate fulfilment of desire.

REPLY OBJ. 2: God is called incomprehensible not because anything of Him is not seen; but because He is not seen as perfectly as He is capable of being seen; thus when any demonstrable proposition is known by probable reason only, it does not follow that any part of it is unknown, either the subject, or the predicate, or the composition; but that it is not as perfectly known as it is capable of being known. Hence Augustine, in his definition of comprehension, says *the whole is comprehended when it is seen in such a way that nothing of it is hidden from the seer, or when its boundaries can be completely viewed or traced*; for the boundaries of a thing are said to be completely surveyed when the end of the knowledge of it is attained.

REPLY OBJ. 3: The word *wholly* denotes a mode of the object; not that the whole object does not come under knowledge, but that the mode of the object is not the mode of the one who knows. Therefore he who sees God's essence, sees in Him that He exists infinitely, and is infinitely knowable; nevertheless, this infinite mode does not extend to enable the knower to know infinitely; thus, for instance, a person can have a probable opinion that a proposition is demonstrable, although he himself does not know it as demonstrated.

Article 8

Whether Those Who See the Essence of God See All in God?

AD OCTAVUM SIC PROCEDITUR. Videtur quod videntes Deum per essentiam omnia in Deo videant. Dicit enim Gregorius, in IV Dialog. *quid est quod non videant, qui videntem omnia vident?* Sed Deus est videns omnia. Ergo qui vident Deum, omnia vident.

ITEM, quicumque videt speculum, videt ea quae in speculo resplendent. Sed omnia quaecumque fiunt vel fieri possunt, in Deo resplendent sicut in quodam speculo, ipse enim omnia in seipso cognoscit. Ergo quicumque videt Deum, videt omnia quae sunt et quae fieri possunt.

PRAETEREA, qui intelligit id quod est maius, potest intelligere minima, ut dicitur III de anima. Sed omnia quae Deus facit vel facere potest, sunt minus quam eius

OBJECTION 1: It seems that those who see the essence of God see all things in God. For Gregory says (*Dialog.* iv): *What do they not see, who see Him Who sees all things?* But God sees all things. Therefore those who see God see all things.

OBJ. 2: Further, whoever sees a mirror, sees what is reflected in the mirror. But all actual or possible things shine forth in God as in a mirror; for He knows all things in Himself. Therefore whoever sees God, sees all actual things in Him, and also all possible things.

OBJ. 3: Further, whoever understands the greater, can understand the least, as is said in *De Anima* iii. But all that God does, or can do, are less than His essence. Therefore

essentia. Ergo quicumque intelligit Deum, potest intelligere omnia quae Deus facit vel facere potest.

PRAETEREA, rationalis creatura omnia naturaliter scire desiderat. Si igitur videndo Deum non omnia sciat, non quietatur eius naturale desiderium, et ita, videndo Deum non erit beata. Quod est inconveniens. Videndo igitur Deum, omnia scit.

SED CONTRA est quod Angeli vident Deum per essentiam, et tamen non omnia sciunt. *Inferiores enim Angeli purgantur a superioribus a nescientia*, ut dicit Dionysius, VII cap. Cael. Hier. Ipsi etiam nesciunt futura contingentia et cogitationes cordium, hoc enim solius Dei est. Non ergo quicumque vident Dei essentiam, vident omnia.

RESPONDEO dicendum quod intellectus creatus, videndo divinam essentiam, non videt in ipsa omnia quae facit Deus vel facere potest. Manifestum est enim quod sic aliqua videntur in Deo, secundum quod sunt in ipso. Omnia autem alia sunt in Deo, sicut effectus sunt virtute in sua causa. Sic igitur videntur alia in Deo, sicut effectus in sua causa. Sed manifestum est quod quanto aliqua causa perfectius videtur, tanto plures eius effectus in ipsa videri possunt. Qui enim habet intellectum elevatum, statim uno principio demonstrativo proposito, ex ipso multarum conclusionum cognitionem accipit, quod non convenit ei qui debilioris intellectus est, sed oportet quod ei singula explanentur. Ille igitur intellectus potest in causa cognoscere omnes causae effectus, et omnes rationes effectuum, qui causam totaliter comprehendit. Nullus autem intellectus creatus totaliter Deum comprehendere potest, ut ostensum est. Nullus igitur intellectus creatus, videndo Deum, potest cognoscere omnia quae Deus facit vel potest facere, hoc enim esset comprehendere eius virtutem. Sed horum quae Deus facit vel facere potest, tanto aliquis intellectus plura cognoscit, quanto perfectius Deum videt.

AD PRIMUM ergo dicendum quod Gregorius loquitur quantum ad sufficientiam obiecti, scilicet Dei, quod, quantum in se est, sufficienter continet omnia et demonstrat. Non tamen sequitur quod unusquisque videns Deum omnia cognoscat, quia non perfecte comprehendit ipsum.

AD SECUNDUM dicendum quod videns speculum, non est necessarium quod omnia in speculo videat, nisi speculum visu suo comprehendat.

AD TERTIUM dicendum quod, licet maius sit videre Deum quam omnia alia, tamen maius est videre sic Deum quod omnia in eo cognoscantur, quam videre sic ipsum quod non omnia, sed pauciora vel plura cognoscantur in eo. Iam enim ostensum est quod multitudo cognitorum in Deo, consequitur modum videndi ipsum vel magis perfectum vel minus perfectum.

whoever understands God, can understand all that God does, or can do.

OBJ. 4: Further, the rational creature naturally desires to know all things. Therefore if in seeing God it does not know all things, its natural desire will not rest satisfied; thus, in seeing God it will not be fully happy; which is incongruous. Therefore he who sees God knows all things.

ON THE CONTRARY, The angels see the essence of God; and yet do not know all things. For as Dionysius says (*Coel. Hier.* vii), *the inferior angels are cleansed from ignorance by the superior angels.* Also they are ignorant of future contingent things, and of secret thoughts; for this knowledge belongs to God alone. Therefore whosoever sees the essence of God, does not know all things.

I ANSWER THAT, The created intellect, in seeing the divine essence, does not see in it all that God does or can do. For it is manifest that things are seen in God as they are in Him. But all other things are in God as effects are in the power of their cause. Therefore all things are seen in God as an effect is seen in its cause. Now it is clear that the more perfectly a cause is seen, the more of its effects can be seen in it. For whoever has a lofty understanding, as soon as one demonstrative principle is put before him can gather the knowledge of many conclusions; but this is beyond one of a weaker intellect, for he needs things to be explained to him separately. And so an intellect can know all the effects of a cause and the reasons for those effects in the cause itself, if it comprehends the cause wholly. Now no created intellect can comprehend God wholly, as shown above (A. 7). Therefore no created intellect in seeing God can know all that God does or can do, for this would be to comprehend His power; but of what God does or can do any intellect can know the more, the more perfectly it sees God.

REPLY OBJ. 1: Gregory speaks as regards the object being sufficient, namely, God, who in Himself sufficiently contains and shows forth all things; but it does not follow that whoever sees God knows all things, for he does not perfectly comprehend Him.

REPLY OBJ. 2: It is not necessary that whoever sees a mirror should see all that is in the mirror, unless his glance comprehends the mirror itself.

REPLY OBJ. 3: Although it is more to see God than to see all things else, still it is a greater thing to see Him so that all things are known in Him, than to see Him in such a way that not all things, but the fewer or the more, are known in Him. For it has been shown in this article that the more things are known in God according as He is seen more or less perfectly.

Ad quartum dicendum quod naturale desiderium rationalis creaturae est ad sciendum omnia illa quae pertinent ad perfectionem intellectus; et haec sunt species et genera rerum, et rationes earum, quae in Deo videbit quilibet videns essentiam divinam. Cognoscere autem alia singularia, et cogitata et facta eorum, non est de perfectione intellectus creati, nec ad hoc eius naturale desiderium tendit, nec iterum cognoscere illa quae nondum sunt, sed fieri a Deo possunt. Si tamen solus Deus videretur, qui est fons et principium totius esse et veritatis, ita repleret naturale desiderium sciendi, quod nihil aliud quaereretur, et beatus esset. Unde dicit Augustinus, V Confess., *infelix homo qui scit omnia illa (scilicet creaturas), te autem nescit, beatus autem qui te scit, etiam si illa nesciat. Qui vero te et illa novit, non propter illa beatior est, sed propter te solum beatus.*

Reply Obj. 4: The natural desire of the rational creature is to know everything that belongs to the perfection of the intellect, namely, the species and the genera of things and their types, and these everyone who sees the Divine essence will see in God. But to know other singulars, their thoughts and their deeds does not belong to the perfection of the created intellect nor does its natural desire go out to these things; neither, again, does it desire to know things that exist not as yet, but which God can call into being. Yet if God alone were seen, Who is the fount and principle of all being and of all truth, He would so fill the natural desire of knowledge that nothing else would be desired, and the seer would be completely beatified. Hence Augustine says (*Confess.* v): *Unhappy the man who knoweth all these* (i.e., all creatures) *and knoweth not Thee! but happy whoso knoweth Thee although he know not these. And whoso knoweth both Thee and them is not the happier for them, but for Thee alone.*

Article 9

Whether What Is Seen in God by Those Who See the Divine Essence, Is Seen Through Any Similitude?

Ad nonum sic proceditur. Videtur quod ea quae videntur in Deo, a videntibus divinam essentiam per aliquas similitudines videantur. Omnis enim cognitio est per assimilationem cognoscentis ad cognitum, sic enim intellectus in actu fit intellectum in actu, et sensus in actu sensibile in actu, inquantum eius similitudine informatur, ut pupilla similitudine coloris. Si igitur intellectus videntis Deum per essentiam intelligat in Deo aliquas creaturas, oportet quod earum similitudinibus informetur.

Praeterea, ea quae prius vidimus, memoriter tenemus. Sed Paulus, videns in raptu essentiam Dei, ut dicit Augustinus XII super Gen. ad litteram, postquam desiit essentiam Dei videre, recordatus est multorum quae in illo raptu viderat, unde ipse dicit quod *audivit arcana verba, quae non licet homini loqui,* II Cor. XII. Ergo oportet dicere quod aliquae similitudines eorum quae recordatus est, in eius intellectu remanserint. Et eadem ratione, quando praesentialiter videbat Dei essentiam, eorum quae in ipsa videbat, aliquas similitudines vel species habebat.

Sed contra est quod per unam speciem videtur speculum, et ea quae in speculo apparent. Sed omnia sic videntur in Deo sicut in quodam speculo intelligibili. Ergo, si ipse Deus non videtur per aliquam similitudinem, sed per suam essentiam; nec ea quae in ipso videntur, per aliquas similitudines sive species videntur.

Respondeo dicendum quod videntes Deum per essentiam, ea quae in ipsa essentia Dei vident, non

Objection 1: It seems that what is seen in God by those who see the Divine essence, is seen by means of some similitude. For every kind of knowledge comes about by the knower being assimilated to the object known. For thus the intellect in act becomes the actual intelligible, and the sense in act becomes the actual sensible, inasmuch as it is informed by a similitude of the object, as the eye by the similitude of color. Therefore if the intellect of one who sees the Divine essence understands any creatures in God, it must be informed by their similitudes.

Obj. 2: Further, what we have seen, we keep in memory. But Paul, seeing the essence of God whilst in ecstasy, when he had ceased to see the Divine essence, as Augustine says (*Gen ad lit.* ii, 28,34), remembered many of the things he had seen in the rapture; hence he said: *I have heard secret words which it is not granted to man to utter* (2 Cor 12:4). Therefore it must be said that certain similitudes of what he remembered, remained in his mind; and in the same way, when he actually saw the essence of God, he had certain similitudes or ideas of what he actually saw in it.

On the contrary, A mirror and what is in it are seen by means of one likeness. But all things are seen in God as in an intelligible mirror. Therefore if God Himself is not seen by any similitude but by His own essence, neither are the things seen in Him seen by any similitudes or ideas.

I answer that, Those who see the divine essence see what they see in God not by any likeness, but by the

vident per aliquas species, sed per ipsam essentiam divinam intellectui eorum unitam. Sic enim cognoscitur unumquodque, secundum quod similitudo eius est in cognoscente. Sed hoc contingit dupliciter. Cum enim quaecumque uni et eidem sunt similia, sibi invicem sint similia, virtus cognoscitiva dupliciter assimilari potest alicui cognoscibili. Uno modo, secundum se, quando directe eius similitudine informatur, et tunc cognoscitur illud secundum se. Alio modo, secundum quod informatur specie alicuius quod est ei simile, et tunc non dicitur res cognosci in seipsa, sed in suo simili. Alia enim est cognitio qua cognoscitur aliquis homo in seipso, et alia qua cognoscitur in sua imagine. Sic ergo, cognoscere res per earum similitudines in cognoscente existentes, est cognoscere eas in seipsis, seu in propriis naturis, sed cognoscere eas prout earum similitudines praeexistunt in Deo, est videre eas in Deo. Et hae duae cognitiones differunt. Unde secundum illam cognitionem qua res cognoscuntur a videntibus Deum per essentiam in ipso Deo, non videntur per aliquas similitudines alias; sed per solam essentiam divinam intellectui praesentem, per quam et Deus videtur.

AD PRIMUM ergo dicendum quod intellectus videntis Deum assimilatur rebus quae videntur in Deo, inquantum unitur essentiae divinae, in qua rerum omnium similitudines praeexistunt.

AD SECUNDUM dicendum quod aliquae potentiae cognoscitivae sunt, quae ex speciebus primo conceptis alias formare possunt. Sicut imaginatio ex praeconceptis speciebus montis et auri, format speciem montis aurei, et intellectus ex praeconceptis speciebus generis et differentiae, format rationem speciei. Et similiter ex similitudine imaginis formare possumus in nobis similitudinem eius cuius est imago. Et sic Paulus, vel quicumque alius videns Deum, ex ipsa visione essentiae divinae potest formare in se similitudines rerum quae in essentia divina videntur, quae remanserunt in Paulo etiam postquam desiit Dei essentiam videre. Ista tamen visio, qua videntur res per huiusmodi species sic conceptas, est alia a visione qua videntur res in Deo.

divine essence itself united to their intellect. For each thing is known in so far as its likeness is in the one who knows. Now this takes place in two ways. For as things which are like one and the same thing are like to each other, the cognitive faculty can be assimilated to any knowable object in two ways. In one way it is assimilated by the object itself, when it is directly informed by a similitude, and then the object is known in itself. In another way when informed by a similitude which resembles the object; and in this way, the knowledge is not of the thing in itself, but of the thing in its likeness. For the knowledge of a man in himself differs from the knowledge of him in his image. Hence to know things thus by their likeness in the one who knows, is to know them in themselves or in their own nature; whereas to know them by their similitudes pre-existing in God, is to see them in God. Now there is a difference between these two kinds of knowledge. Hence, according to the knowledge whereby things are known by those who see the essence of God, they are seen in God Himself not by any other similitudes but by the Divine essence alone present to the intellect; by which also God Himself is seen.

REPLY OBJ. 1: The created intellect of one who sees God is assimilated to what is seen in God, inasmuch as it is united to the Divine essence, in which the similitudes of all things pre-exist.

REPLY OBJ. 2: Some of the cognitive faculties form other images from those first conceived; thus the imagination from the preconceived images of a mountain and of gold can form the likeness of a golden mountain; and the intellect, from the preconceived ideas of genus and difference, forms the idea of species; in like manner from the similitude of an image we can form in our minds the similitude of the original of the image. Thus Paul, or any other person who sees God, by the very vision of the divine essence, can form in himself the similitudes of what is seen in the divine essence, which remained in Paul even when he had ceased to see the essence of God. Still this kind of vision whereby things are seen by this likeness thus conceived, is not the same as that whereby things are seen in God.

Article 10

Whether Those Who See the Essence of God See All They See in It at the Same Time?

AD DECIMUM SIC PROCEDITUR. Videtur quod videntes Deum per essentiam non simul videant omnia quae in ipso vident. Quia, secundum philosophum, *contingit multa scire, intelligere vero unum.* Sed ea quae videntur in Deo, intelliguntur, intellectu enim videtur Deus. Ergo non contingit a videntibus Deum simul multa videri in Deo.

OBJECTION 1: It seems that those who see the essence of God do not see all they see in Him at one and the same time. For according to the Philosopher (*Topic.* ii): *It may happen that many things are known, but only one is understood.* But what is seen in God, is understood; for God is seen by the intellect. Therefore those who see God do not see all in Him at the same time.

Praeterea, Augustinus dicit, VIII super Gen. ad litteram, quod *Deus movet creaturam spiritualem per tempus*, hoc est per intelligentiam et affectionem. Sed creatura spiritualis est Angelus, qui Deum videt. Ergo videntes Deum, successive intelligunt et afficiuntur, tempus enim successionem importat.

Sed contra est quod Augustinus dicit, ultimo de Trin., *non erunt volubiles nostrae cogitationes, ab aliis in alia euntes atque redeuntes; sed omnem scientiam nostram uno simul conspectu videbimus.*

Respondeo dicendum quod ea quae videntur in verbo, non successive, sed simul videntur. Ad cuius evidentiam considerandum est, quod ideo nos simul non possumus multa intelligere, quia multa per diversas species intelligimus; diversis autem speciebus non potest intellectus unus simul actu informari ad intelligendum per eas, sicut nec unum corpus potest simul diversis figuris figurari. Unde contingit quod, quando aliqua multa una specie intelligi possunt, simul intelliguntur, sicut diversae partes alicuius totius, si singulae propriis speciebus intelligantur, successive intelliguntur, et non simul; si autem omnes intelligantur una specie totius, simul intelliguntur. Ostensum est autem quod ea quae videntur in Deo, non videntur singula per suas similitudines, sed omnia per unam essentiam Dei. Unde simul, et non successive videntur.

Ad primum ergo dicendum quod sic unum tantum intelligimus, inquantum una specie intelligimus. Sed multa una specie intellecta simul intelliguntur, sicut in specie hominis intelligimus animal et rationale, et in specie domus parietem et tectum.

Ad secundum dicendum quod Angeli, quantum ad cognitionem naturalem qua cognoscunt res per species diversas eis inditas, non simul omnia cognoscunt, et sic moventur, secundum intelligentiam, per tempus. Sed secundum quod vident res in Deo, simul eas vident.

Obj. 2: Further, Augustine says (*Gen ad lit.* viii, 22, 23), *God moves the spiritual creature according to time*—i.e., by intelligence and affection. But the spiritual creature is the angel who sees God. Therefore those who see God understand and are affected successively; for time means succession.

On the contrary, Augustine says (*De Trin.* xvi): *Our thoughts will not be unstable, going to and fro from one thing to another; but we shall see all we know at one glance.*

I answer that, What is seen in the Word is seen not successively, but at the same time. In proof whereof, we ourselves cannot know many things all at once, forasmuch as we understand many things by means of many ideas. But our intellect cannot be actually informed by many diverse ideas at the same time, so as to understand by them; as one body cannot bear different shapes simultaneously. Hence, when many things can be understood by one idea, they are understood at the same time; as the parts of a whole are understood successively, and not all at the same time, if each one is understood by its own idea; whereas if all are understood under the one idea of the whole, they are understood simultaneously. Now it was shown above that things seen in God, are not seen singly by their own similitude; but all are seen by the one essence of God. Hence they are seen simultaneously, and not successively.

Reply Obj. 1: We understand one thing only when we understand by one idea; but many things understood by one idea are understood simultaneously, as in the idea of a man we understand *animal* and *rational*; and in the idea of a house we understand the wall and the roof.

Reply Obj. 2: As regards their natural knowledge, whereby they know things by diverse ideas given them, the angels do not know all things simultaneously, and thus they are moved in the act of understanding according to time; but as regards what they see in God, they see all at the same time.

Article 11

Whether Anyone in This Life Can See the Essence of God?

Ad undecimum sic proceditur. Videtur quod aliquis in hac vita possit Deum per essentiam videre. Dicit enim Iacob, Gen. XXXII, *vidi Deum facie ad faciem*. Sed videre facie ad faciem, est videre per essentiam, ut patet per illud quod dicitur I Cor. XIII, *videmus nunc per speculum et in aenigmate, tunc autem facie ad faciem*. Ergo Deus in hac vita per essentiam videri potest.

Praeterea, Num. XII dicit dominus de Moyse, *ore ad os loquor ei, et palam, et non per aenigmata et figuras, videt Deum*. Sed hoc est videre Deum per essentiam.

Objection 1: It seems that one can in this life see the Divine essence. For Jacob said: *I have seen God face to face* (Gen 32:30). But to see Him face to face is to see His essence, as appears from the words: *We see now in a glass and in a dark manner, but then face to face* (1 Cor 13:12). Therefore God can be seen through his essence in this life.

Obj. 2: Further, the Lord said to Moses: *I speak to him mouth to mouth, and plainly, and not by riddles and figures doth he see the Lord* (Num 12:8); but this is to see God in

Ergo aliquis in statu huius vitae potest Deum per essentiam videre.

PRAETEREA, illud in quo alia omnia cognoscimus, et per quod de aliis iudicamus, est nobis secundum se notum. Sed omnia etiam nunc in Deo cognoscimus. Dicit enim Augustinus, XII Conf., *si ambo videmus verum esse quod dicis, et ambo videmus verum esse quod dico, ubi quaeso illud videmus? Nec ego in te, nec tu in me, sed ambo in ipsa quae supra mentes nostras est, incommutabili veritate.* Idem etiam, in libro de vera religione, dicit quod secundum veritatem divinam de omnibus iudicamus. Et XII de Trin. dicit quod *rationis est iudicare de istis corporalibus secundum rationes incorporales et sempiternas, quae nisi supra mentem essent, incommutabiles profecto non essent.* Ergo et in hac vita ipsum Deum videmus.

PRAETEREA, secundum Augustinum, XII super Gen. ad Litt., visione intellectuali videntur ea quae sunt in anima per suam essentiam. Sed visio intellectualis est de rebus intelligibilibus, non per aliquas similitudines, sed per suas essentias, ut ipse ibidem dicit. Ergo, cum Deus sit per essentiam suam in anima nostra, per essentiam suam videtur a nobis.

SED CONTRA est quod dicitur Exod. XXXIII, *non videbit me homo et vivet.* Glossa, *quandiu hic mortaliter vivitur, videri per quasdam imagines Deus potest; sed per ipsam naturae suae speciem non potest.*

RESPONDEO dicendum quod ab homine puro Deus videri per essentiam non potest, nisi ab hac vita mortali separetur. Cuius ratio est quia, sicut supra dictum est, modus cognitionis sequitur modum naturae rei cognoscentis. Anima autem nostra, quandiu in hac vita vivimus, habet esse in materia corporali, unde naturaliter non cognoscit aliqua nisi quae habent formam in materia, vel quae per huiusmodi cognosci possunt. Manifestum est autem quod per naturas rerum materialium divina essentia cognosci non potest. Ostensum est enim supra quod cognitio Dei per quamcumque similitudinem creatam, non est visio essentiae ipsius. Unde impossibile est animae hominis secundum hanc vitam viventis, essentiam Dei videre. Et huius signum est, quod anima nostra, quanto magis a corporalibus abstrahitur, tanto intelligibilium abstractorum fit capacior. Unde in somniis et alienationibus a sensibus corporis, magis divinae revelationes percipiuntur, et praevisiones futurorum. Quod ergo anima elevetur usque ad supremum intelligibilium, quod est essentia divina, esse non potest quandiu hac mortali vita utitur.

AD PRIMUM ergo dicendum quod, secundum Dionysium, IV cap. Cael. Hier., sic in Scripturis dicitur aliquis Deum vidisse, inquantum formatae sunt aliquae figurae, vel sensibiles vel imaginariae, secundum aliquam similitudinem aliquod divinum repraesentantes. Quod ergo dicit Iacob, *vidi Deum facie ad faciem,* referendum

His essence. Therefore it is possible to see the essence of God in this life.

OBJ. 3: Further, that wherein we know all other things, and whereby we judge of other things, is known in itself to us. But even now we know all things in God; for Augustine says (*Confess.* viii): *If we both see that what you say is true, and we both see that what I say is true; where, I ask, do we see this? neither I in thee, nor thou in me; but both of us in the very incommutable truth itself above our minds.* He also says (*De Vera Relig.* xxx) that, *We judge of all things according to the divine truth*; and (*De Trin.* xii) that, *it is the duty of reason to judge of these corporeal things according to the incorporeal and eternal ideas; which unless they were above the mind could not be incommutable.* Therefore even in this life we see God Himself.

OBJ. 4: Further, according to Augustine (*Gen ad lit.* xii, 24, 25), those things that are in the soul by their essence are seen by intellectual vision. But intellectual vision is of intelligible things, not by similitudes, but by their very essences, as he also says (*Gen ad lit.* xiii, 24, 25). Therefore since God is in our soul by His essence, it follows that He is seen by us in His essence.

ON THE CONTRARY, It is written, *Man shall not see Me, and live* (Exod 32:20), and a gloss upon this says, *In this mortal life God can be seen by certain images, but not by the likeness itself of His own nature.*

I ANSWER THAT, God cannot be seen in His essence by a mere human being, except he be separated from this mortal life. The reason is because, as was said above (A. 4), the mode of knowledge follows the mode of the nature of the knower. But our soul, as long as we live in this life, has its being in corporeal matter; hence naturally it knows only what has a form in matter, or what can be known by such a form. Now it is evident that the Divine essence cannot be known through the nature of material things. For it was shown above (AA. 2, 9) that the knowledge of God by means of any created similitude is not the vision of His essence. Hence it is impossible for the soul of man in this life to see the essence of God. This can be seen in the fact that the more our soul is abstracted from corporeal things, the more it is capable of receiving abstract intelligible things. Hence in dreams and alienations of the bodily senses divine revelations and foresight of future events are perceived the more clearly. It is not possible, therefore, that the soul in this mortal life should be raised up to the supreme of intelligible objects, i.e., to the divine essence.

REPLY OBJ. 1: According to Dionysius (*Coel. hier.* iv) a man is said in the Scriptures to see God in the sense that certain figures are formed in the senses or imagination, according to some similitude representing in part the divinity. So when Jacob says, *I have seen God face to face,* this does not mean the Divine essence, but some figure

est, non ad ipsam divinam essentiam, sed ad figuram in qua repraesentabatur Deus. Et hoc ipsum ad quandam prophetiae eminentiam pertinet, ut videatur persona Dei loquentis, licet imaginaria visione, ut infra patebit, cum de gradibus prophetiae loquemur. Vel hoc dicit Iacob ad designandam quandam eminentiam intelligibilis contemplationis, supra communem statum.

Ad secundum dicendum quod, sicut Deus miraculose aliquid supernaturaliter in rebus corporeis operatur, ita etiam et supernaturaliter, et praeter communem ordinem, mentes aliquorum in hac carne viventium, sed non sensibus carnis utentium, usque ad visionem suae essentiae elevavit; ut dicit Augustinus, XII super Genes. ad Litt., et in libro de videndo Deum de Moyse, qui fuit magister Iudaeorum, et Paulo, qui fuit magister gentium. Et de hoc plenius tractabitur, cum de raptu agemus.

Ad tertium dicendum quod omnia dicimur in Deo videre, et secundum ipsum de omnibus iudicare, inquantum per participationem sui luminis omnia cognoscimus et diiudicamus, nam et ipsum lumen naturale rationis participatio quaedam est divini luminis; sicut etiam omnia sensibilia dicimus videre et iudicare in sole, idest per lumen solis. Unde dicit Augustinus, I Soliloquiorum, *disciplinarum spectamina videri non possunt, nisi aliquo velut suo sole illustrentur, videlicet Deo.* Sicut ergo ad videndum aliquid sensibiliter, non est necesse quod videatur substantia solis, ita ad videndum aliquid intelligibiliter, non est necessarium quod videatur essentia Dei.

Ad quartum dicendum quod visio intellectualis est eorum quae sunt in anima per suam essentiam sicut intelligibilia in intellectu. Sic autem Deus est in anima beatorum, non autem in anima nostra; sed per praesentiam, essentiam, et potentiam.

representing God. And this is to be referred to some high mode of prophecy, so that God seems to speak, though in an imaginary vision; as will later be explained (II-II, Q. 174) in treating of the degrees of prophecy. We may also say that Jacob spoke thus to designate some exalted intellectual contemplation, above the ordinary state.

Reply Obj. 2: As God works miracles in corporeal things, so also He does supernatural wonders above the common order, raising the minds of some living in the flesh beyond the use of sense, even up to the vision of His own essence; as Augustine says (*Gen ad lit.* xii, 26, 27, 28) of Moses, the teacher of the Jews; and of Paul, the teacher of the Gentiles. This will be treated more fully in the question of rapture (II-II, Q. 175).

Reply Obj. 3: All things are said to be seen in God and all things are judged in Him, because by the participation of His light, we know and judge all things; for the light of natural reason itself is a participation of the divine light; as likewise we are said to see and judge of sensible things in the sun, i.e., by the sun's light. Hence Augustine says (*Soliloq.* i, 8), *The lessons of instruction can only be seen as it were by their own sun*, namely God. As therefore in order to see a sensible object, it is not necessary to see the substance of the sun, so in like manner to see any intelligible object, it is not necessary to see the essence of God.

Reply Obj. 4: Intellectual vision is of the things which are in the soul by their essence, as intelligible things are in the intellect. And thus God is in the souls of the blessed; not thus is He in our soul, but by presence, essence and power.

Article 12

Whether God Can Be Known in This Life by Natural Reason?

Ad duodecimum sic proceditur. Videtur quod per naturalem rationem Deum in hac vita cognoscere non possimus. Dicit enim Boetius, in libro de Consol., quod *ratio non capit simplicem formam.* Deus autem maxime est simplex forma, ut supra ostensum est. Ergo ad eius cognitionem ratio naturalis pervenire non potest.

Praeterea, ratione naturali sine phantasmate nihil intelligit anima, ut dicitur in III de anima. Sed Dei, cum sit incorporeus, phantasma in nobis esse non potest. Ergo cognosci non potest a nobis cognitione naturali.

Praeterea, cognitio quae est per rationem naturalem, communis est bonis et malis, sicut natura eis communis est. Sed cognitio Dei competit tantum bonis, dicit

Objection 1: It seems that by natural reason we cannot know God in this life. For Boethius says (*De Consol.* v) that *reason does not grasp simple form.* But God is a supremely simple form, as was shown above (Q. 3, A. 7). Therefore natural reason cannot attain to know Him.

Obj. 2: Further, the soul understands nothing by natural reason without the use of the imagination. But we cannot have an imagination of God, Who is incorporeal. Therefore we cannot know God by natural knowledge.

Obj. 3: Further, the knowledge of natural reason belongs to both good and evil, inasmuch as they have a common nature. But the knowledge of God belongs only to the

enim Augustinus, I de Trin., quod *mentis humanae acies in tam excellenti luce non figitur, nisi per iustitiam fidei emundetur.* Ergo Deus per rationem naturalem cognosci non potest.

SED CONTRA est quod dicitur Rom. I, *quod notum est Dei, manifestum est in illis,* idest, quod cognoscibile est de Deo per rationem naturalem.

RESPONDEO dicendum quod naturalis nostra cognitio a sensu principium sumit, unde tantum se nostra naturalis cognitio extendere potest, inquantum manuduci potest per sensibilia. Ex sensibilibus autem non potest usque ad hoc intellectus noster pertingere, quod divinam essentiam videat, quia creaturae sensibiles sunt effectus Dei virtutem causae non adaequantes. Unde ex sensibilium cognitione non potest tota Dei virtus cognosci, et per consequens nec eius essentia videri. Sed quia sunt eius effectus a causa dependentes, ex eis in hoc perduci possumus, ut cognoscamus de Deo an est; et ut cognoscamus de ipso ea quae necesse est ei convenire secundum quod est prima omnium causa, excedens omnia sua causata.

Unde cognoscimus de ipso habitudinem ipsius ad creaturas, quod scilicet omnium est causa; et differentiam creaturarum ab ipso, quod scilicet ipse non est aliquid eorum quae ab eo causantur; et quod haec non removentur ab eo propter eius defectum, sed quia superexcedit.

AD PRIMUM ergo dicendum quod ratio ad formam simplicem pertingere non potest, ut sciat de ea quid est, potest tamen de ea cognoscere, ut sciat an est.

AD SECUNDUM dicendum quod Deus naturali cognitione cognoscitur per phantasmata effectus sui.

AD TERTIUM dicendum quod cognitio Dei per essentiam, cum sit per gratiam, non competit nisi bonis, sed cognitio eius quae est per rationem naturalem, potest competere bonis et malis. Unde dicit Augustinus, in libro Retractationum, *non approbo quod in oratione dixi, Deus, qui non nisi mundos verum scire voluisti, responderi enim potest, multos etiam non mundos multa scire vera,* scilicet per rationem naturalem.

good; for Augustine says (*De Trin.* i): *The weak eye of the human mind is not fixed on that excellent light unless purified by the justice of faith.* Therefore God cannot be known by natural reason.

ON THE CONTRARY, It is written (Rom 1:19), *That which is known of God,* namely, what can be known of God by natural reason, *is manifest in them.*

I ANSWER THAT, Our natural knowledge begins from sense. Hence our natural knowledge can go as far as it can be led by sensible things. But our mind cannot be led by sense so far as to see the essence of God; because the sensible effects of God do not equal the power of God as their cause. Hence from the knowledge of sensible things the whole power of God cannot be known; nor therefore can His essence be seen. But because they are His effects and depend on their cause, we can be led from them so far as to know of God *whether He exists,* and to know of Him what must necessarily belong to Him, as the first cause of all things, exceeding all things caused by Him.

Hence we know that His relationship with creatures so far as to be the cause of them all; also that creatures differ from Him, inasmuch as He is not in any way part of what is caused by Him; and that creatures are not removed from Him by reason of any defect on His part, but because He superexceeds them all.

REPLY OBJ. 1: Reason cannot reach up to simple form, so as to know *what it is;* but it can know *whether it is.*

REPLY OBJ. 2: God is known by natural knowledge through the images of His effects.

REPLY OBJ. 3: As the knowledge of God's essence is by grace, it belongs only to the good; but the knowledge of Him by natural reason can belong to both good and bad; and hence Augustine says (*Retract.* i), retracting what he had said before: *I do not approve what I said in prayer, 'God who willest that only the pure should know truth.' For it can be answered that many who are not pure can know many truths,* i.e., by natural reason.

Article 13

Whether by Grace a Higher Knowledge of God Can Be Obtained Than by Natural Reason?

AD DECIMUMTERTIUM SIC PROCEDITUR. Videtur quod per gratiam non habeatur altior cognitio Dei, quam ea quae habetur per naturalem rationem. Dicit enim Dionysius, in libro de mystica theologia, quod ille qui melius unitur Deo in hac vita, unitur ei sicut omnino ignoto, quod etiam de Moyse dicit, qui tamen excellentiam quandam obtinuit in gratiae cognitione. Sed

OBJECTION 1: It seems that by grace a higher knowledge of God is not obtained than by natural reason. For Dionysius says (*De Mystica Theol.* i) that whoever is the more united to God in this life, is united to Him as to one entirely unknown. He says the same of Moses, who nevertheless obtained a certain excellence by the knowledge conferred by grace. But to be united to God while ignoring of Him *what*

coniungi Deo ignorando de eo quid est, hoc contingit etiam per rationem naturalem. Ergo per gratiam non plenius cognoscitur a nobis Deus, quam per rationem naturalem.

Praeterea, per rationem naturalem in cognitionem divinorum pervenire non possumus, nisi per phantasmata, sic etiam nec secundum cognitionem gratiae. Dicit enim Dionysius, I cap. de Cael. Hier., quod *impossibile est nobis aliter lucere divinum radium, nisi varietate sacrorum velaminum circumvelatum.* Ergo per gratiam non plenius cognoscimus Deum, quam per rationem naturalem.

Praeterea, intellectus noster per gratiam fidei Deo adhaeret. Fides autem non videtur esse cognitio, dicit enim Gregorius, in Homil., quod *ea quae non videntur fidem habent, et non agnitionem.* Ergo per gratiam non additur nobis aliqua excellentior cognitio de Deo.

Sed contra est quod dicit apostolus, I Cor. II, *nobis revelavit Deus per spiritum suum,* illa scilicet quae nemo principum huius saeculi novit, idest philosophorum, ut exponit Glossa.

Respondeo dicendum quod per gratiam perfectior cognitio de Deo habetur a nobis, quam per rationem naturalem. Quod sic patet. Cognitio enim quam per naturalem rationem habemus, duo requirit, scilicet, phantasmata ex sensibilibus accepta, et lumen naturale intelligibile, cuius virtute intelligibiles conceptiones ab eis abstrahimus.

Et quantum ad utrumque, iuvatur humana cognitio per revelationem gratiae. Nam et lumen naturale intellectus confortatur per infusionem luminis gratuiti. Et interdum etiam phantasmata in imaginatione hominis formantur divinitus, magis exprimentia res divinas, quam ea quae naturaliter a sensibilibus accipimus; sicut apparet in visionibus prophetalibus. Et interdum etiam aliquae res sensibiles formantur divinitus, aut etiam voces, ad aliquid divinum exprimendum; sicut in Baptismo visus est Spiritus Sanctus in specie columbae, et vox patris audita est, *hic est filius meus dilectus.*

Ad primum ergo dicendum quod, licet per revelationem gratiae in hac vita non cognoscamus de Deo quid est, et sic ei quasi ignoto coniungamur; tamen plenius ipsum cognoscimus, inquantum plures et excellentiores effectus eius nobis demonstrantur; et inquantum ei aliqua attribuimus ex revelatione divina, ad quae ratio naturalis non pertingit, ut Deum esse trinum et unum.

Ad secundum dicendum quod ex phantasmatibus, vel a sensu acceptis secundum naturalem ordinem, vel divinitus in imaginatione formatis, tanto excellentior cognitio intellectualis habetur, quanto lumen intelligibile

He is, comes about also by natural reason. Therefore God is not more known to us by grace than by natural reason.

Obj. 2: Further, we can acquire the knowledge of divine things by natural reason only through the imagination; and the same applies to the knowledge given by grace. For Dionysius says (*Coel. Hier.* i) that *it is impossible for the divine ray to shine upon us except as screened round about by the many colored sacred veils.* Therefore we cannot know God more fully by grace than by natural reason.

Obj. 3: Further, our intellect adheres to God by grace of faith. But faith does not seem to be knowledge; for Gregory says (*Hom. xxvi in Ev.*) that *things not seen are the objects of faith, and not of knowledge.* Therefore there is not given to us a more excellent knowledge of God by grace.

On the contrary, The Apostle says that *God hath revealed to us His spirit,* what *none of the princes of this world knew* (1 Cor 2:10), namely, the philosophers, as the gloss expounds.

I answer that, We have a more perfect knowledge of God by grace than by natural reason. Which is proved thus. The knowledge which we have by natural reason contains two things: images derived from the sensible objects; and the natural intelligible light, enabling us to abstract from them intelligible conceptions.

Now in both of these, human knowledge is assisted by the revelation of grace. For the intellect's natural light is strengthened by the infusion of gratuitous light; and sometimes also the images in the human imagination are divinely formed, so as to express divine things better than those do which we receive from sensible objects, as appears in prophetic visions; while sometimes sensible things, or even voices, are divinely formed to express some divine meaning; as in the Baptism, the Holy Spirit was seen in the shape of a dove, and the voice of the Father was heard, *This is My beloved Son* (Matt 3:17).

Reply Obj. 1: Although by the revelation of grace in this life we cannot know of God *what He is,* and thus are united to Him as to one unknown; still we know Him more fully according as many and more excellent of His effects are demonstrated to us, and according as we attribute to Him some things known by divine revelation, to which natural reason cannot reach, as, for instance, that God is Three and One.

Reply Obj. 2: From the images either received from sense in the natural order, or divinely formed in the imagination, we have so much the more excellent intellectual knowledge, the stronger the intelligible light is in man; and

in homine fortius fuerit. Et sic per revelationem ex phantasmatibus plenior cognitio accipitur, ex infusione divini luminis.

AD TERTIUM dicendum quod fides cognitio quaedam est, inquantum intellectus determinatur per fidem ad aliquod cognoscibile. Sed haec determinatio ad unum non procedit ex visione credentis, sed a visione eius cui creditur. Et sic, inquantum deest visio, deficit a ratione cognitionis quae est in scientia, nam scientia determinat intellectum ad unum per visionem et intellectum primorum principiorum.

thus through the revelation given by the images a fuller knowledge is received by the infusion of the divine light.

REPLY OBJ. 3: Faith is a kind of knowledge, inasmuch as the intellect is determined by faith to some knowable object. But this determination to one object does not proceed from the vision of the believer, but from the vision of Him who is believed. Thus as far as faith falls short of vision, it falls short of the knowledge which belongs to science, for science determines the intellect to one object by the vision and understanding of first principles.

QUESTION 13

THE NAMES OF GOD

Consideratis his quae ad divinam cognitionem pertinent, procedendum est ad considerationem divinorum nominum, unumquodque enim nominatur a nobis, secundum quod ipsum cognoscimus.

Circa hoc ergo quaeruntur duodecim.

Primo, utrum Deus sit nominabilis a nobis.

Secundo, utrum aliqua nomina dicta de Deo, praedicentur de ipso substantialiter.

Tertio, utrum aliqua nomina dicta de Deo, proprie dicantur de ipso; an omnia attribuantur ei metaphorice.

Quarto, utrum multa nomina dicta de Deo, sint synonyma.

Quinto, utrum nomina aliqua dicantur de Deo et creaturis univoce, vel aequivoce.

Sexto, supposito quod dicantur analogice, utrum dicantur de Deo per prius, vel de creaturis.

Septimo, utrum aliqua nomina dicantur de Deo ex tempore.

Octavo, utrum hoc nomen Deus sit nomen naturae, vel operationis.

Nono, utrum hoc nomen Deus sit nomen communicabile.

Decimo, utrum accipiatur univoce vel aequivoce, secundum quod significat Deum per naturam, et per participationem, et secundum opinionem.

Undecimo, utrum hoc nomen qui est sit maxime proprium nomen Dei.

Duodecimo, utrum propositiones affirmativae possint formari de Deo.

After the consideration of those things which belong to the divine knowledge, we now proceed to the consideration of the divine names. For everything is named by us according to our knowledge of it.

Under this head, there are twelve points for inquiry:

(1) Whether God can be named by us?

(2) Whether any names applied to God are predicated of Him substantially?

(3) Whether any names applied to God are said of Him literally, or are all to be taken metaphorically?

(4) Whether any names applied to God are synonymous?

(5) Whether some names are applied to God and to creatures univocally or equivocally?

(6) Whether, supposing they are applied analogically, they are applied first to God or to creatures?

(7) Whether any names are applicable to God from time?

(8) Whether this name *God* is a name of nature, or of the operation?

(9) Whether this name *God* is a communicable name?

(10) Whether it is taken univocally or equivocally as signifying God, by nature, by participation, and by opinion?

(11) Whether this name, *Who is*, is the supremely appropriate name of God?

(12) Whether affirmative propositions can be formed about God?

Article 1

Whether a Name Can Be Given to God?

Ad primum sic proceditur. Videtur quod nullum nomen Deo conveniat. Dicit enim Dionysius, I cap. de Div. Nom., quod neque nomen eius est, neque opinio. Et Prov. XXX dicitur, *quod nomen eius, et quod nomen filii eius, si nosti?*

Praeterea, omne nomen aut dicitur in abstracto, aut in concreto. Sed nomina significantia in concreto, non competunt Deo, cum simplex sit, neque nomina significantia in abstracto, quia non significant aliquid perfectum subsistens. Ergo nullum nomen potest dici de Deo.

Objection 1: It seems that no name can be given to God. For Dionysius says (*Div. Nom.* i) that, *Of Him there is neither name, nor can one be found of Him*; and it is written: *What is His name, and what is the name of His Son, if thou knowest?* (Prov 30:4).

Obj. 2: Further, every name is either abstract or concrete. But concrete names do not belong to God, since He is simple, nor do abstract names belong to Him, forasmuch as they do not signify any perfect subsisting thing. Therefore no name can be said of God.

PRAETEREA, nomina significant substantiam cum qualitate; verba autem et participia significant cum tempore; pronomina autem cum demonstratione vel relatione. Quorum nihil competit Deo, quia sine qualitate est et sine omni accidente, et sine tempore; et sentiri non potest, ut demonstrari possit; nec relative significari, cum relativa sint aliquorum antedictorum recordativa, vel nominum, vel participiorum, vel pronominum demonstrativorum. Ergo Deus nullo modo potest nominari a nobis.

SED CONTRA est quod dicitur Exod. XV, *dominus quasi vir pugnator, omnipotens nomen eius.*

RESPONDEO dicendum quod, secundum philosophum, voces sunt signa intellectuum, et intellectus sunt rerum similitudines. Et sic patet quod voces referuntur ad res significandas, mediante conceptione intellectus. Secundum igitur quod aliquid a nobis intellectu cognosci potest, sic a nobis potest nominari. Ostensum est autem supra quod Deus in hac vita non potest a nobis videri per suam essentiam; sed cognoscitur a nobis ex creaturis, secundum habitudinem principii, et per modum excellentiae et remotionis. Sic igitur potest nominari a nobis ex creaturis, non tamen ita quod nomen significans ipsum, exprimat divinam essentiam secundum quod est, sicut hoc nomen homo exprimit sua significatione essentiam hominis secundum quod est, significat enim eius definitionem, declarantem eius essentiam; ratio enim quam significat nomen, est definitio.

AD PRIMUM ergo dicendum quod ea ratione dicitur Deus non habere nomen, vel esse supra nominationem, quia essentia eius est supra id quod de Deo intelligimus et voce significamus.

AD SECUNDUM dicendum quod, quia ex creaturis in Dei cognitionem venimus, et ex ipsis eum nominamus, nomina quae Deo attribuimus, hoc modo significant, secundum quod competit creaturis materialibus, quarum cognitio est nobis connaturalis, ut supra dictum est. Et quia in huiusmodi creaturis, ea quae sunt perfecta et subsistentia sunt composita; forma autem in eis non est aliquid completum subsistens, sed magis quo aliquid est, inde est quod omnia nomina a nobis imposita ad significandum aliquid completum subsistens, significant in concretione, prout competit compositis; quae autem imponuntur ad significandas formas simplices, significant aliquid non ut subsistens, sed ut quo aliquid est, sicut albedo significat ut quo aliquid est album. Quia igitur et Deus simplex est, et subsistens est, attribuimus ei et nomina abstracta, ad significandam simplicitatem eius; et nomina concreta, ad significandum subsistentiam et perfectionem ipsius, quamvis utraque nomina deficiant a modo ipsius, sicut intellectus noster non cognoscit eum ut est, secundum hanc vitam.

AD TERTIUM dicendum quod significare substantiam cum qualitate, est significare suppositum cum natura vel

OBJ. 3: Further, nouns are taken to signify substance with quality; verbs and participles signify substance with time; pronouns the same with demonstration or relation. But none of these can be applied to God, for He has no quality, nor accident, nor time; moreover, He cannot be felt, so as to be pointed out; nor can He be described by relation, inasmuch as relations serve to recall a thing mentioned before by nouns, participles, or demonstrative pronouns. Therefore God cannot in any way be named by us.

ON THE CONTRARY, It is written (Exod 15:3): *The Lord is a man of war, Almighty is His name.*

I ANSWER THAT, Since according to the Philosopher (*Peri Herm.* i), words are signs of ideas, and ideas the similitude of things, it is evident that words relate to the meaning of things signified through the medium of the intellectual conception. It follows therefore that we can give a name to anything in as far as we can understand it. Now it was shown above (Q. 12, AA. 11, 12) that in this life we cannot see the essence of God; but we know God from creatures as their principle, and also by way of excellence and remotion. In this way therefore He can be named by us from creatures, yet not so that the name which signifies Him expresses the divine essence in itself. Thus the name *man* expresses the essence of man in himself, since it signifies the definition of man by manifesting his essence; for the idea expressed by the name is the definition.

REPLY OBJ. 1: The reason why God has no name, or is said to be above being named, is because His essence is above all that we understand about God, and signify in word.

REPLY OBJ. 2: Because we know and name God from creatures, the names we attribute to God signify what belongs to material creatures, of which the knowledge is natural to us. And because in creatures of this kind what is perfect and subsistent is compound; whereas their form is not a complete subsisting thing, but rather is that whereby a thing is; hence it follows that all names used by us to signify a complete subsisting thing must have a concrete meaning as applicable to compound things; whereas names given to signify simple forms, signify a thing not as subsisting, but as that whereby a thing is; as, for instance, whiteness signifies that whereby a thing is white. And as God is simple, and subsisting, we attribute to Him abstract names to signify His simplicity, and concrete names to signify His substance and perfection, although both these kinds of names fail to express His mode of being, forasmuch as our intellect does not know Him in this life as He is.

REPLY OBJ. 3: To signify substance with quality is to signify the suppositum with a nature or determined form

forma determinata in qua subsistit. Unde, sicut de Deo dicuntur aliqua in concretione, ad significandum subsistentiam et perfectionem ipsius, sicut iam dictum est, ita dicuntur de Deo nomina significantia substantiam cum qualitate. Verba vero et participia consignificantia tempus dicuntur de ipso, ex eo quod aeternitas includit omne tempus, sicut enim simplicia subsistentia non possumus apprehendere et significare nisi per modum compositorum, ita simplicem aeternitatem non possumus intelligere vel voce exprimere, nisi per modum temporalium rerum; et hoc propter connaturalitatem intellectus nostri ad res compositas et temporales. Pronomina vero demonstrativa dicuntur de Deo, secundum quod faciunt demonstrationem ad id quod intelligitur, non ad id quod sentitur, secundum enim quod a nobis intelligitur, secundum hoc sub demonstratione cadit. Et sic, secundum illum modum quo nomina et participia et pronomina demonstrativa de Deo dicuntur, secundum hoc et pronominibus relativis significari potest.

in which it subsists. Hence, as some things are said of God in a concrete sense, to signify His subsistence and perfection, so likewise nouns are applied to God signifying substance with quality. Further, verbs and participles which signify time, are applied to Him because His eternity includes all time. For as we can apprehend and signify simple subsistences only by way of compound things, so we can understand and express simple eternity only by way of temporal things, because our intellect has a natural affinity to compound and temporal things. But demonstrative pronouns are applied to God as describing what is understood, not what is sensed. For we can only describe Him as far as we understand Him. Thus, according as nouns, participles and demonstrative pronouns are applicable to God, so far can He be signified by relative pronouns.

Article 2

Whether Any Name Can Be Applied to God Substantially?

Ad secundum sic proceditur. Videtur quod nullum nomen dicatur de Deo substantialiter. Dicit enim Damascenus, *oportet singulum eorum quae de Deo dicuntur, non quid est secundum substantiam significare, sed quid non est ostendere, aut habitudinem quandam, aut aliquid eorum quae assequuntur naturam vel operationem.*

Praeterea, dicit Dionysius, I cap. de Div. Nom., *omnem sanctorum theologorum hymnum invenies, ad bonos thearchiae processus, manifestative et laudative Dei nominationes dividentem,* et est sensus, quod nomina quae in divinam laudem sancti doctores assumunt, secundum processus ipsius Dei distinguuntur. Sed quod significat processum alicuius rei, nihil significat ad eius essentiam pertinens. Ergo nomina dicta de Deo, non dicuntur de ipso substantialiter.

Praeterea, secundum hoc nominatur aliquid a nobis, secundum quod intelligitur. Sed non intelligitur Deus a nobis in hac vita secundum suam substantiam. Ergo nec aliquod nomen impositum a nobis, dicitur de Deo secundum suam substantiam.

Sed contra est quod dicit Augustinus, VI de Trin., *Deo hoc est esse, quod fortem esse vel sapientem esse, et si quid de illa simplicitate dixeris, quo eius substantia significatur.* Ergo omnia nomina huiusmodi significant divinam substantiam.

Respondeo dicendum quod de nominibus quae de Deo dicuntur negative, vel quae relationem ipsius ad

Objection 1: It seems that no name can be applied to God substantially. For Damascene says (*De Fide Orth.* i, 9): *Everything said of God signifies not His substance, but rather shows forth what He is not; or expresses some relation, or something following from His nature or operation.*

Obj. 2: Further, Dionysius says (*Div. Nom.* i): *You will find a chorus of holy doctors addressed to the end of distinguishing clearly and praiseworthily the divine processions in the denomination of God.* Thus the names applied by the holy doctors in praising God are distinguished according to the divine processions themselves. But what expresses the procession of anything, does not signify its essence. Therefore the names applied to God are not said of Him substantially.

Obj. 3: Further, a thing is named by us according as we understand it. But God is not understood by us in this life in His substance. Therefore neither is any name we can use applied substantially to God.

On the contrary, Augustine says (*De Trin.* vi): *The being of God is the being strong, or the being wise, or whatever else we may say of that simplicity whereby His substance is signified.* Therefore all names of this kind signify the divine substance.

I answer that, Negative names applied to God, or signifying His relation to creatures manifestly do not at all

creaturam significant, manifestum est quod substantiam eius nullo modo significant; sed remotionem alicuius ab ipso, vel relationem eius ad alium, vel potius alicuius ad ipsum.

Sed de nominibus quae absolute et affirmative de Deo dicuntur, sicut bonus, sapiens, et huiusmodi, multipliciter aliqui sunt opinati. Quidam enim dixerunt quod haec omnia nomina, licet affirmative de Deo dicantur, tamen magis inventa sunt ad aliquid removendum a Deo, quam ad aliquid ponendum in ipso. Unde dicunt quod, cum dicimus Deum esse viventem, significamus quod Deus non hoc modo est, sicut res inanimatae, et similiter accipiendum est in aliis. Et hoc posuit Rabbi Moyses. Alii vero dicunt quod haec nomina imposita sunt ad significandum habitudinem eius ad creata, ut, cum dicimus Deus est bonus, sit sensus, Deus est causa bonitatis in rebus. Et eadem ratio est in aliis.

Sed utrumque istorum videtur esse inconveniens, propter tria. Primo quidem, quia secundum neutram harum positionum posset assignari ratio quare quaedam nomina magis de Deo dicerentur quam alia. Sic enim est causa corporum, sicut est causa bonorum, unde, si nihil aliud significatur, cum dicitur Deus est bonus, nisi Deus est causa bonorum, poterit similiter dici quod Deus est corpus, quia est causa corporum. Item, per hoc quod dicitur quod est corpus, removetur quod non sit ens in potentia tantum, sicut materia prima. Secundo, quia sequeretur quod omnia nomina dicta de Deo, per posterius dicerentur de ipso, sicut sanum per posterius dicitur de medicina, eo quod significat hoc tantum quod sit causa sanitatis in animali, quod per prius dicitur sanum. Tertio, quia hoc est contra intentionem loquentium de Deo. Aliud enim intendunt dicere, cum dicunt Deum viventem, quam quod sit causa vitae nostrae, vel quod differat a corporibus inanimatis.

Et ideo aliter dicendum est, quod huiusmodi quidem nomina significant substantiam divinam, et praedicantur de Deo substantialiter, sed deficiunt a repraesentatione ipsius. Quod sic patet. Significant enim sic nomina Deum, secundum quod intellectus noster cognoscit ipsum. Intellectus autem noster, cum cognoscat Deum ex creaturis, sic cognoscit ipsum, secundum quod creaturae ipsum repraesentant. Ostensum est autem supra quod Deus in se praehabet omnes perfectiones creaturarum, quasi simpliciter et universaliter perfectus. Unde quaelibet creatura intantum eum repraesentat, et est ei similis, inquantum perfectionem aliquam habet, non tamen ita quod repraesentet eum sicut aliquid eiusdem speciei vel generis, sed sicut excellens principium, a cuius forma effectus deficiunt, cuius tamen aliqualem similitudinem effectus consequuntur; sicut formae corporum inferiorum repraesentant virtutem solarem. Et hoc supra expositum est, cum de perfectione divina agebatur.

signify His substance, but rather express the distance of the creature from Him, or His relation to something else, or rather, the relation of creatures to Himself.

But as regards absolute and affirmative names of God, as *good*, *wise*, and the like, various and many opinions have been given. For some have said that all such names, although they are applied to God affirmatively, nevertheless have been brought into use more to express some remotion from God, rather than to express anything that exists positively in Him. Hence they assert that when we say that God lives, we mean that God is not like an inanimate thing; and the same in like manner applies to other names; and this was taught by Rabbi Moses. Others say that these names applied to God signify His relationship towards creatures: thus in the words, *God is good*, we mean, God is the cause of goodness in things; and the same rule applies to other names.

Both of these opinions, however, seem to be untrue for three reasons. First because in neither of them can a reason be assigned why some names more than others are applied to God. For He is assuredly the cause of bodies in the same way as He is the cause of good things; therefore if the words *God is good*, signified no more than, *God is the cause of good things*, it might in like manner be said that God is a body, inasmuch as He is the cause of bodies. So also to say that He is a body implies that He is not a mere potentiality, as is primary matter. Second, because it would follow that all names applied to God would be said of Him by way of being taken in a secondary sense, as healthy is secondarily said of medicine, forasmuch as it signifies only the cause of the health in the animal which primarily is called healthy. Third, because this is against the intention of those who speak of God. For in saying that God lives, they assuredly mean more than to say that He is the cause of our life, or that He differs from inanimate bodies.

Therefore we must hold a different doctrine—viz. that these names signify the divine substance, and are predicated substantially of God, although they fall short of a full representation of Him. Which is proved thus. For these names express God, so far as our intellects know Him. Now since our intellect knows God from creatures, it knows Him as far as creatures represent Him. Now it is shown above (Q. 4, A. 2) that God prepossesses in Himself all the perfections of creatures, being Himself simply and universally perfect. Hence every creature represents Him, and is like Him so far as it possesses some perfection; yet it represents Him not as something of the same species or genus, but as the excelling principle of whose form the effects fall short, although they derive some kind of likeness thereto, even as the forms of inferior bodies represent the power of the sun. This was explained above (Q. 4, A. 3), in treating of the divine perfection. Therefore the aforesaid names signify the divine substance, but in an imperfect manner, even as

Sic igitur praedicta nomina divinam substantiam significant, imperfecte tamen, sicut et creaturae imperfecte eam repraesentant. Cum igitur dicitur Deus est bonus, non est sensus, Deus est causa bonitatis, vel Deus non est malus, sed est sensus, id quod bonitatem dicimus in creaturis, praeexistit in Deo, et hoc quidem secundum modum altiorem. Unde ex hoc non sequitur quod Deo competat esse bonum inquantum causat bonitatem, sed potius e converso, quia est bonus, bonitatem rebus diffundit, secundum illud Augustini, de Doct. Christ., *inquantum bonus est, sumus.*

Ad primum ergo dicendum quod Damascenus ideo dicit quod haec nomina non significant quid est Deus, quia a nullo istorum nominum exprimitur quid est Deus perfecte, sed unumquodque imperfecte eum significat, sicut et creaturae imperfecte eum repraesentant.

Ad secundum dicendum quod in significatione nominum, aliud est quandoque a quo imponitur nomen ad significandum, et id ad quod significandum nomen imponitur, sicut hoc nomen lapis imponitur ab eo quod laedit pedem, non tamen imponitur ad hoc significandum quod significet laedens pedem, sed ad significandam quandam speciem corporum; alioquin omne laedens pedem esset lapis. Sic igitur dicendum est quod huiusmodi divina nomina imponuntur quidem a processibus deitatis, sicut enim secundum diversos processus perfectionum, creaturae Deum repraesentant, licet imperfecte; ita intellectus noster, secundum unumquemque processum, Deum cognoscit et nominat. Sed tamen haec nomina non imponit ad significandum ipsos processus, ut, cum dicitur Deus est vivens, sit sensus, ab eo procedit vita, sed ad significandum ipsum rerum principium, prout in eo praeexistit vita, licet eminentiori modo quam intelligatur vel significetur.

Ad tertium dicendum quod essentiam Dei in hac vita cognoscere non possumus secundum quod in se est, sed cognoscimus eam secundum quod repraesentatur in perfectionibus creaturarum. Et sic nomina a nobis imposita eam significant.

creatures represent it imperfectly. So when we say, *God is good*, the meaning is not, *God is the cause of goodness*, or *God is not evil*; but the meaning is, *Whatever good we attribute to creatures, pre-exists in God*, and in a more excellent and higher way. Hence it does not follow that God is good, because He causes goodness; but rather, on the contrary, He causes goodness in things because He is good; according to what Augustine says (*De Doctr. Christ.* i, 32), *Because He is good, we are.*

Reply Obj. 1: Damascene says that these names do not signify what God is, forasmuch as by none of these names is perfectly expressed what He is; but each one signifies Him in an imperfect manner, even as creatures represent Him imperfectly.

Reply Obj. 2: In the significance of names, that from which the name is derived is different sometimes from what it is intended to signify, as for instance, this name *stone* is imposed from the fact that it hurts the foot, but it is not imposed to signify that which hurts the foot, but rather to signify a certain kind of body; otherwise everything that hurts the foot would be a stone. So we must say that these kinds of divine names are imposed from the divine processions; for as according to the diverse processions of their perfections, creatures are the representations of God, although in an imperfect manner; so likewise our intellect knows and names God according to each kind of procession; but nevertheless these names are not imposed to signify the procession themselves, as if when we say *God lives*, the sense were, *life proceeds from Him*; but to signify the principle itself of things, in so far as life pre-exists in Him, although it pre-exists in Him in a more eminent way than can be understood or signified.

Reply Obj. 3: We cannot know the essence of God in this life, as He really is in Himself; but we know Him accordingly as He is represented in the perfections of creatures; and thus the names imposed by us signify Him in that manner only.

Article 3

Whether Any Name Can Be Applied to God in Its Literal Sense?

Ad tertium sic proceditur. Videtur quod nullum nomen dicatur de Deo proprie. Omnia enim nomina quae de Deo dicimus, sunt a creaturis accepta, ut dictum est. Sed nomina creaturarum metaphorice dicuntur de Deo, sicut cum dicitur Deus est lapis, vel leo, vel aliquid huiusmodi. Ergo omnia nomina dicta de Deo, dicuntur metaphorice.

Objection 1: It seems that no name is applied literally to God. For all names which we apply to God are taken from creatures; as was explained above (A. 1). But the names of creatures are applied to God metaphorically, as when we say, God is a stone, or a lion, or the like. Therefore names are applied to God in a metaphorical sense.

Praeterea, nullum nomen proprie dicitur de aliquo, a quo verius removetur quam de eo praedicetur. Sed omnia huiusmodi nomina, bonus sapiens, et similia, verius removentur a Deo quam de eo praedicentur, ut patet per Dionysium, II cap. Cael. Hier. Ergo nullum istorum nominum proprie dicitur de Deo.

Praeterea, nomina corporum non dicuntur de Deo nisi metaphorice, cum sit incorporeus. Sed omnia huiusmodi nomina implicant quasdam corporales conditiones, significant enim cum tempore, et cum compositione, et cum aliis huiusmodi, quae sunt conditiones corporum. Ergo omnia huiusmodi nomina dicuntur de Deo metaphorice.

Sed contra est quod dicit Ambrosius, in Lib. II de fide, *sunt quaedam nomina, quae evidenter proprietatem divinitatis ostendunt; et quaedam quae perspicuam divinae maiestatis exprimunt veritatem; alia vero sunt, quae translative per similitudinem de Deo dicuntur.* Non igitur omnia nomina dicuntur de Deo metaphorice, sed aliqua dicuntur proprie.

Respondeo dicendum quod, sicut dictum est, Deum cognoscimus ex perfectionibus procedentibus in creaturas ab ipso; quae quidem perfectiones in Deo sunt secundum eminentiorem modum quam in creaturis. Intellectus autem noster eo modo apprehendit eas, secundum quod sunt in creaturis, et secundum quod apprehendit, ita significat per nomina. In nominibus igitur quae Deo attribuimus, est duo considerare, scilicet, perfectiones ipsas significatas, ut bonitatem, vitam, et huiusmodi; et modum significandi. Quantum igitur ad id quod significant huiusmodi nomina, proprie competunt Deo, et magis proprie quam ipsis creaturis, et per prius dicuntur de eo. Quantum vero ad modum significandi, non proprie dicuntur de Deo, habent enim modum significandi qui creaturis competit.

Ad primum ergo dicendum quod quaedam nomina significant huiusmodi perfectiones a Deo procedentes in res creatas, hoc modo quod ipse modus imperfectus quo a creatura participatur divina perfectio, in ipso nominis significato includitur, sicut lapis significat aliquid materialiter ens, et huiusmodi nomina non possunt attribui Deo nisi metaphorice. Quaedam vero nomina significant ipsas perfectiones absolute, absque hoc quod aliquis modus participandi claudatur in eorum significatione, ut ens, bonum vivens, et huiusmodi, et talia proprie dicuntur de Deo.

Ad secundum dicendum quod ideo huiusmodi nomina dicit Dionysius negari a Deo, quia id quod significatur per nomen, non convenit eo modo ei, quo nomen significat, sed excellentiori modo. Unde ibidem dicit Dionysius quod Deus est super omnem substantiam et vitam.

Ad tertium dicendum quod ista nomina quae proprie dicuntur de Deo important conditiones corporales,

Obj. 2: Further, no name can be applied literally to anything if it should be withheld from it rather than given to it. But all such names as *good*, *wise*, and the like are more truly withheld from God than given to Him; as appears from Dionysius says (*Coel. Hier.* ii). Therefore none of these names belong to God in their literal sense.

Obj. 3: Further, corporeal names are applied to God in a metaphorical sense only, since He is incorporeal. But all such names imply some kind of corporeal condition; for their meaning is bound up with time and composition and like corporeal conditions. Therefore all these names are applied to God in a metaphorical sense.

On the contrary, Ambrose says (*De Fide* ii), *Some names there are which express evidently the property of the divinity, and some which express the clear truth of the divine majesty, but others there are which are applied to God metaphorically by way of similitude.* Therefore not all names are applied to God in a metaphorical sense, but there are some which are said of Him in their literal sense.

I answer that, According to the preceding article, our knowledge of God is derived from the perfections which flow from Him to creatures, which perfections are in God in a more eminent way than in creatures. Now our intellect apprehends them as they are in creatures, and as it apprehends them it signifies them by names. Therefore as to the names applied to God—viz. the perfections which they signify, such as goodness, life and the like, and their mode of signification. As regards what is signified by these names, they belong properly to God, and more properly than they belong to creatures, and are applied primarily to Him. But as regards their mode of signification, they do not properly and strictly apply to God; for their mode of signification applies to creatures.

Reply Obj. 1: There are some names which signify these perfections flowing from God to creatures in such a way that the imperfect way in which creatures receive the divine perfection is part of the very signification of the name itself, as *stone* signifies a material being, and names of this kind can be applied to God only in a metaphorical sense. Other names, however, express these perfections absolutely, without any such mode of participation being part of their signification, as the words *being*, *good*, *living*, and the like, and such names can be literally applied to God.

Reply Obj. 2: Such names as these, as Dionysius shows, are denied of God for the reason that what the name signifies does not belong to Him in the ordinary sense of its signification, but in a more eminent way. Hence Dionysius says also that God is above all substance and all life.

Reply Obj. 3: These names which are applied to God literally imply corporeal conditions not in the thing

non in ipso significato nominis, sed quantum ad modum significandi. Ea vero quae metaphorice de Deo dicuntur, important conditionem corporalem in ipso suo significato.

signified, but as regards their mode of signification; whereas those which are applied to God metaphorically imply and mean a corporeal condition in the thing signified.

Article 4

Whether Names Applied to God Are Synonymous?

Ad quartum sic proceditur. Videtur quod ista nomina dicta de Deo, sint nomina synonyma. Synonyma enim nomina dicuntur, quae omnino idem significant. Sed ista nomina dicta de Deo, omnino idem significant in Deo, quia bonitas Dei est eius essentia, et similiter sapientia. Ergo ista nomina sunt omnino synonyma.

Si dicatur quod ista nomina significant idem secundum rem, sed secundum rationes diversas, contra, ratio cui non respondet aliquid in re, est vana; si ergo istae rationes sunt multae, et res est una, videtur quod rationes istae sint vanae.

Praeterea, magis est unum quod est unum re et ratione, quam quod est unum re et multiplex ratione. Sed Deus est maxime unus. Ergo videtur quod non sit unus re et multiplex ratione. Et sic nomina dicta de Deo non significant rationes diversas, et ita sunt synonyma.

Sed contra, omnia synonyma, sibi invicem adiuncta, nugationem adducunt, sicut si dicatur vestis indumentum. Si igitur omnia nomina dicta de Deo sunt synonyma, non posset convenienter dici Deus bonus, vel aliquid huiusmodi; cum tamen scriptum sit Ierem. XXXII, *fortissime, magne, potens, dominus exercituum nomen tibi.*

Respondeo dicendum quod huiusmodi nomina dicta de Deo, non sunt synonyma. Quod quidem facile esset videre, si diceremus quod huiusmodi nomina sunt inducta ad removendum, vel ad designandum habitudinem causae respectu creaturarum, sic enim essent diversae rationes horum nominum secundum diversa negata, vel secundum diversos effectus connotatos. Sed secundum quod dictum est huiusmodi nomina substantiam divinam significare, licet imperfecte, etiam plane apparet, secundum praemissa, quod habent rationes diversas. Ratio enim quam significat nomen, est conceptio intellectus de re significata per nomen. Intellectus autem noster, cum cognoscat Deum ex creaturis, format ad intelligendum Deum conceptiones proportionatas perfectionibus procedentibus a Deo in creaturas. Quae quidem perfectiones in Deo praeexistunt unite et simpliciter, in creaturis vero recipiuntur divise et multipliciter. Sicut igitur diversis perfectionibus creaturarum respondet unum simplex principium, repraesentatum per diversas

Objection 1: It seems that these names applied to God are synonymous names. For synonymous names are those which mean exactly the same. But these names applied to God mean entirely the same thing in God; for the goodness of God is His essence, and likewise it is His wisdom. Therefore these names are entirely synonymous.

Obj. 2: Further, if it be said these names signify one and the same thing in reality, but differ in idea, it can be objected that an idea to which no reality corresponds is a vain notion. Therefore if these ideas are many, and the thing is one, it seems also that all these ideas are vain notions.

Obj. 3: Further, a thing which is one in reality and in idea, is more one than what is one in reality and many in idea. But God is supremely one. Therefore it seems that He is not one in reality and many in idea; and thus the names applied to God do not signify different ideas; and thus they are synonymous.

On the contrary, All synonyms united with each other are redundant, as when we say, *vesture clothing.* Therefore if all names applied to God are synonymous, we cannot properly say *good God* or the like, and yet it is written, *O most mighty, great and powerful, the Lord of hosts is Thy name* (Jer 32:18).

I answer that, These names spoken of God are not synonymous. This would be easy to understand, if we said that these names are used to remove, or to express the relation of cause to creatures; for thus it would follow that there are different ideas as regards the diverse things denied of God, or as regards diverse effects connoted. But even according to what was said above (A. 2), that these names signify the divine substance, although in an imperfect manner, it is also clear from what has been said (AA. 1, 2) that they have diverse meanings. For the idea signified by the name is the conception in the intellect of the thing signified by the name. But our intellect, since it knows God from creatures, in order to understand God, forms conceptions proportional to the perfections flowing from God to creatures, which perfections pre-exist in God unitedly and simply, whereas in creatures they are received and divided and multiplied. As therefore, to the different perfections of creatures, there corresponds one simple principle represented by different perfections of creatures in a various and manifold manner,

perfectiones creaturarum varie et multipliciter; ita variis et multiplicibus conceptibus intellectus nostri respondet unum omnino simplex, secundum huiusmodi conceptiones imperfecte intellectum. Et ideo nomina Deo attributa, licet significent unam rem, tamen, quia significant eam sub rationibus multis et diversis, non sunt synonyma.

Et sic patet solutio ad primum, quia nomina synonyma dicuntur, quae significant unum secundum unam rationem. Quae enim significant rationes diversas unius rei, non primo et per se unum significant, quia nomen non significat rem, nisi mediante conceptione intellectus, ut dictum est.

AD SECUNDUM dicendum quod rationes plures horum nominum non sunt cassae et vanae, quia omnibus eis respondet unum quid simplex, per omnia huiusmodi multipliciter et imperfecte repraesentatum.

AD TERTIUM dicendum quod hoc ipsum ad perfectam Dei unitatem pertinet, quod ea quae sunt multipliciter et divisim in aliis, in ipso sunt simpliciter et unite. Et ex hoc contingit quod est unus re et plures secundum rationem, quia intellectus noster ita multipliciter apprehendit eum, sicut res multipliciter ipsum repraesentant.

so also to the various and multiplied conceptions of our intellect, there corresponds one altogether simple principle, according to these conceptions, imperfectly understood. Therefore although the names applied to God signify one thing, still because they signify that under many and different aspects, they are not synonymous.

Thus appears the solution of the First Objection, since synonymous terms signify one thing under one aspect; for words which signify different aspects of one thing, do not signify primarily and absolutely one thing; because the term only signifies the thing through the medium of the intellectual conception, as was said above.

REPLY OBJ. 2: The many aspects of these names are not empty and vain, for there corresponds to all of them one simple reality represented by them in a manifold and imperfect manner.

REPLY OBJ. 3: The perfect unity of God requires that what are manifold and divided in others should exist in Him simply and unitedly. Thus it comes about that He is one in reality, and yet multiple in idea, because our intellect apprehends Him in a manifold manner, as things represent Him.

Article 5

Whether What Is Said of God and of Creatures Is Univocally Predicated of Them?

AD QUINTUM SIC PROCEDITUR. Videtur quod ea quae dicuntur de Deo et creaturis, univoce de ipsis dicantur. Omne enim aequivocum reducitur ad univocum, sicut multa ad unum. Nam si hoc nomen canis aequivoce dicitur de latrabili et marino, oportet quod de aliquibus univoce dicatur, scilicet de omnibus latrabilibus, aliter enim esset procedere in infinitum. Inveniuntur autem quaedam agentia univoca, quae conveniunt cum suis effectibus in nomine et definitione, ut homo generat hominem; quaedam vero agentia aequivoca, sicut sol causat calidum, cum tamen ipse non sit calidus nisi aequivoce. Videtur igitur quod primum agens, ad quod omnia agentia reducuntur, sit agens univocum. Et ita, quae de Deo et creaturis dicuntur, univoce praedicantur.

PRAETEREA, secundum aequivoca non attenditur aliqua similitudo. Cum igitur creaturae ad Deum sit aliqua similitudo, secundum illud Genes. I, *faciamus hominem ad imaginem et similitudinem nostram*, videtur quod aliquid univoce de Deo et creaturis dicatur.

PRAETEREA, mensura est homogenea mensurato, ut dicitur in X Metaphys. Sed Deus est prima mensura

OBJECTION 1: It seems that the things attributed to God and creatures are univocal. For every equivocal term is reduced to the univocal, as many are reduced to one; for if the name *dog* be said equivocally of the barking dog, and of the dogfish, it must be said of some univocally—viz. of all barking dogs; otherwise we proceed to infinitude. Now there are some univocal agents which agree with their effects in name and definition, as man generates man; and there are some agents which are equivocal, as the sun which causes heat, although the sun is hot only in an equivocal sense. Therefore it seems that the first agent to which all other agents are reduced, is an univocal agent: and thus what is said of God and creatures, is predicated univocally.

OBJ. 2: Further, there is no similitude among equivocal things. Therefore as creatures have a certain likeness to God, according to the word of Genesis (Gen 1:26), *Let us make man to our image and likeness*, it seems that something can be said of God and creatures univocally.

OBJ. 3: Further, measure is homogeneous with the thing measured. But God is the first measure of all

omnium entium, ut ibidem dicitur. Ergo Deus est homogeneus creaturis. Et ita aliquid univoce de Deo et creaturis dici potest.

SED CONTRA, quidquid praedicatur de aliquibus secundum idem nomen et non secundum eandem rationem, praedicatur de eis aequivoce. Sed nullum nomen convenit Deo secundum illam rationem, secundum quam dicitur de creatura, nam sapientia in creaturis est qualitas, non autem in Deo; genus autem variatum mutat rationem, cum sit pars definitionis. Et eadem ratio est in aliis. Quidquid ergo de Deo et creaturis dicitur, aequivoce dicitur.

PRAETEREA, Deus plus distat a creaturis, quam quaecumque creaturae ab invicem. Sed propter distantiam quarundam creaturarum, contingit quod nihil univoce de eis praedicari potest; sicut de his quae non conveniunt in aliquo genere. Ergo multo minus de Deo et creaturis aliquid univoce praedicatur, sed omnia praedicantur aequivoce.

RESPONDEO dicendum quod impossibile est aliquid praedicari de Deo et creaturis univoce. Quia omnis effectus non adaequans virtutem causae agentis, recipit similitudinem agentis non secundum eandem rationem, sed deficienter, ita ut quod divisim et multipliciter est in effectibus, in causa est simpliciter et eodem modo; sicut sol secundum unam virtutem, multiformes et varias formas in istis inferioribus producit. Eodem modo, ut supra dictum est, omnes rerum perfectiones, quae sunt in rebus creatis divisim et multipliciter, in Deo praeexistunt unite. Sic igitur, cum aliquod nomen ad perfectionem pertinens de creatura dicitur, significat illam perfectionem ut distinctam secundum rationem definitionis ab aliis, puta cum hoc nomen sapiens de homine dicitur, significamus aliquam perfectionem distinctam ab essentia hominis, et a potentia et ab esse ipsius, et ab omnibus huiusmodi. Sed cum hoc nomen de Deo dicimus, non intendimus significare aliquid distinctum ab essentia vel potentia vel esse ipsius. Et sic, cum hoc nomen sapiens de homine dicitur, quodammodo circumscribit et comprehendit rem significatam, non autem cum dicitur de Deo, sed relinquit rem significatam ut incomprehensam, et excedentem nominis significationem. Unde patet quod non secundum eandem rationem hoc nomen sapiens de Deo et de homine dicitur. Et eadem ratio est de aliis. Unde nullum nomen univoce de Deo et creaturis praedicatur.

Sed nec etiam pure aequivoce, ut aliqui dixerunt. Quia secundum hoc, ex creaturis nihil posset cognosci de Deo, nec demonstrari; sed semper incideret fallacia aequivocationis. Et hoc est tam contra philosophos, qui multa demonstrative de Deo probant, quam etiam contra apostolum dicentem, Rom. I, *invisibilia Dei per ea quae facta sunt, intellecta, conspiciuntur*. Dicendum est

beings. Therefore God is homogeneous with creatures; and thus a word may be applied univocally to God and to creatures.

ON THE CONTRARY, whatever is predicated of various things under the same name but not in the same sense, is predicated equivocally. But no name belongs to God in the same sense that it belongs to creatures; for instance, wisdom in creatures is a quality, but not in God. Now a different genus changes an essence, since the genus is part of the definition; and the same applies to other things. Therefore whatever is said of God and of creatures is predicated equivocally.

FURTHER, God is more distant from creatures than any creatures are from each other. But the distance of some creatures makes any univocal predication of them impossible, as in the case of those things which are not in the same genus. Therefore much less can anything be predicated univocally of God and creatures; and so only equivocal predication can be applied to them.

I ANSWER THAT, Univocal predication is impossible between God and creatures. The reason of this is that every effect which is not an adequate result of the power of the efficient cause, receives the similitude of the agent not in its full degree, but in a measure that falls short, so that what is divided and multiplied in the effects resides in the agent simply, and in the same manner; as for example the sun by exercise of its one power produces manifold and various forms in all inferior things. In the same way, as said in the preceding article, all perfections existing in creatures divided and multiplied, pre-exist in God unitedly. Thus when any term expressing perfection is applied to a creature, it signifies that perfection distinct in idea from other perfections; as, for instance, by the term *wise* applied to man, we signify some perfection distinct from a man's essence, and distinct from his power and existence, and from all similar things; whereas when we apply to it God, we do not mean to signify anything distinct from His essence, or power, or existence. Thus also this term *wise* applied to man in some degree circumscribes and comprehends the thing signified; whereas this is not the case when it is applied to God; but it leaves the thing signified as incomprehended, and as exceeding the signification of the name. Hence it is evident that this term *wise* is not applied in the same way to God and to man. The same rule applies to other terms. Hence no name is predicated univocally of God and of creatures.

Neither, on the other hand, are names applied to God and creatures in a purely equivocal sense, as some have said. Because if that were so, it follows that from creatures nothing could be known or demonstrated about God at all; for the reasoning would always be exposed to the fallacy of equivocation. Such a view is against the philosophers, who proved many things about God, and also against what the Apostle says: *The invisible things of God are clearly seen*

igitur quod huiusmodi nomina dicuntur de Deo et creaturis secundum analogiam, idest proportionem.

Quod quidem dupliciter contingit in nominibus, vel quia multa habent proportionem ad unum, sicut sanum dicitur de medicina et urina, inquantum utrumque habet ordinem et proportionem ad sanitatem animalis, cuius hoc quidem signum est, illud vero causa; vel ex eo quod unum habet proportionem ad alterum, sicut sanum dicitur de medicina et animali, inquantum medicina est causa sanitatis quae est in animali. Et hoc modo aliqua dicuntur de Deo et creaturis analogice, et non aequivoce pure, neque univoce. Non enim possumus nominare Deum nisi ex creaturis, ut supra dictum est. Et sic, quidquid dicitur de Deo et creaturis, dicitur secundum quod est aliquis ordo creaturae ad Deum, ut ad principium et causam, in qua praeexistunt excellenter omnes rerum perfectiones. Et iste modus communitatis medius est inter puram aequivocationem et simplicem univocationem. Neque enim in his quae analogice dicuntur, est una ratio, sicut est in univocis; nec totaliter diversa, sicut in aequivocis; sed nomen quod sic multipliciter dicitur, significat diversas proportiones ad aliquid unum; sicut sanum, de urina dictum, significat signum sanitatis animalis, de medicina vero dictum, significat causam eiusdem sanitatis.

AD PRIMUM ergo dicendum quod, licet in praedicationibus oporteat aequivoca ad univoca reduci, tamen in actionibus agens non univocum ex necessitate praecedit agens univocum. Agens enim non univocum est causa universalis totius speciei, ut sol est causa generationis omnium hominum. Agens vero univocum non est causa agens universalis totius speciei (alioquin esset causa sui ipsius, cum sub specie contineatur), sed est causa particularis respectu huius individui, quod in participatione speciei constituit. Causa igitur universalis totius speciei non est agens univocum. Causa autem universalis est prior particulari. Hoc autem agens universale, licet non sit univocum, non tamen est omnino aequivocum, quia sic non faceret sibi simile; sed potest dici agens analogicum, sicut in praedicationibus omnia univoca reducuntur ad unum primum, non univocum, sed analogicum, quod est ens.

AD SECUNDUM dicendum quod similitudo creaturae ad Deum est imperfecta, quia etiam nec idem secundum genus repraesentat, ut supra dictum est.

AD TERTIUM dicendum quod Deus non est mensura proportionata mensuratis. Unde non oportet quod Deus et creaturae sub uno genere contineantur.

EA VERO quae sunt in contrarium, concludunt quod non univoce huiusmodi nomina de Deo et creaturis praedicentur, non autem quod aequivoce.

being understood by the things that are made (Rom 1:20). Therefore it must be said that these names are said of God and creatures in an analogous sense, i.e., according to proportion.

Now names are thus used in two ways: either according as many things are proportionate to one, thus for example *healthy* predicated of medicine and urine in relation and in proportion to health of a body, of which the former is the sign and the latter the cause: or according as one thing is proportionate to another, thus *healthy* is said of medicine and animal, since medicine is the cause of health in the animal body. And in this way some things are said of God and creatures analogically, and not in a purely equivocal nor in a purely univocal sense. For we can name God only from creatures (A. 1). Thus whatever is said of God and creatures, is said according to the relation of a creature to God as its principle and cause, wherein all perfections of things pre-exist excellently. Now this mode of community of idea is a mean between pure equivocation and simple univocation. For in analogies the idea is not, as it is in univocals, one and the same, yet it is not totally diverse as in equivocals; but a term which is thus used in a multiple sense signifies various proportions to some one thing; thus *healthy* applied to urine signifies the sign of animal health, and applied to medicine signifies the cause of the same health.

REPLY OBJ. 1: Although equivocal predications must be reduced to univocal, still in actions, the non-univocal agent must precede the univocal agent. For the non-univocal agent is the universal cause of the whole species, as for instance the sun is the cause of the generation of all men; whereas the univocal agent is not the universal efficient cause of the whole species (otherwise it would be the cause of itself, since it is contained in the species), but is a particular cause of this individual which it places under the species by way of participation. Therefore the universal cause of the whole species is not an univocal agent; and the universal cause comes before the particular cause. But this universal agent, whilst it is not univocal, nevertheless is not altogether equivocal, otherwise it could not produce its own likeness, but rather it is to be called an analogical agent, as all univocal predications are reduced to one first non-univocal analogical predication, which is being.

REPLY OBJ. 2: The likeness of the creature to God is imperfect, for it does not represent one and the same generic thing (Q. 4, A. 3).

REPLY OBJ. 3: God is not the measure proportioned to things measured; hence it is not necessary that God and creatures should be in the same genus.

THE ARGUMENTS adduced in the contrary sense prove indeed that these names are not predicated univocally of God and creatures; yet they do not prove that they are predicated equivocally.

Article 6

Whether Names Predicated of God Are Predicated Primarily of Creatures?

AD SEXTUM SIC PROCEDITUR. Videtur quod nomina per prius dicantur de creaturis quam de Deo. Secundum enim quod cognoscimus aliquid, secundum hoc illud nominamus; cum nomina, secundum philosophum, sint signa intellectuum. Sed per prius cognoscimus creaturam quam Deum. Ergo nomina a nobis imposita, per prius conveniunt creaturis quam Deo.

PRAETEREA, secundum Dionysium, in libro de Div. Nom., Deum ex creaturis nominamus. Sed nomina a creaturis translata in Deum, per prius dicuntur de creaturis quam de Deo; sicut leo, lapis, et huiusmodi. Ergo omnia nomina quae de Deo et de creaturis dicuntur, per prius de creaturis quam de Deo dicuntur.

PRAETEREA, omnia nomina quae communiter de Deo et creaturis dicuntur, dicuntur de Deo sicut de causa omnium, ut dicit Dionysius. Sed quod dicitur de aliquo per causam, per posterius de illo dicitur, per prius enim dicitur animal sanum quam medicina, quae est causa sanitatis. Ergo huiusmodi nomina per prius dicuntur de creaturis quam de Deo.

SED CONTRA est quod dicitur Ephes. III, *flecto genua mea ad patrem domini nostri Iesu, ex quo omnis paternitas in caelo et in terra nominatur.* Et eadem ratio videtur de nominibus aliis quae de Deo et creaturis dicuntur. Ergo huiusmodi nomina per prius de Deo quam de creaturis dicuntur.

RESPONDEO dicendum quod in omnibus nominibus quae de pluribus analogice dicuntur, necesse est quod omnia dicantur per respectum ad unum, et ideo illud unum oportet quod ponatur in definitione omnium. Et quia ratio quam significat nomen, est definitio, ut dicitur in IV Metaphys., necesse est quod illud nomen per prius dicatur de eo quod ponitur in definitione aliorum, et per posterius de aliis, secundum ordinem quo appropinquant ad illud primum vel magis vel minus, sicut sanum quod dicitur de animali, cadit in definitione sani quod dicitur de medicina, quae dicitur sana inquantum causat sanitatem in animali; et in definitione sani quod dicitur de urina, quae dicitur sana inquantum est signum sanitatis animalis. Sic ergo omnia nomina quae metaphorice de Deo dicuntur, per prius de creaturis dicuntur quam de Deo, quia dicta de Deo, nihil aliud significant quam similitudines ad tales creaturas. Sicut enim ridere, dictum de prato, nihil aliud significat quam quod pratum similiter se habet in decore cum floret, sicut homo cum ridet, secundum similitudinem proportionis; sic nomen leonis, dictum de Deo, nihil aliud significat quam quod Deus similiter se habet ut fortiter operetur in suis operibus, sicut leo in suis. Et sic patet quod, secundum quod dicuntur de Deo, eorum significatio definiri non potest,

OBJECTION 1: It seems that names are predicated primarily of creatures rather than of God. For we name anything accordingly as we know it, since *names*, as the Philosopher says, *are signs of ideas*. But we know creatures before we know God. Therefore the names imposed by us are predicated primarily of creatures rather than of God.

OBJ. 2: Further, Dionysius says (*Div. Nom.* i): *We name God from creatures.* But names transferred from creatures to God, are said primarily of creatures rather than of God, as *lion, stone,* and the like. Therefore all names applied to God and creatures are applied primarily to creatures rather than to God.

OBJ. 3: Further, all names equally applied to God and creatures, are applied to God as the cause of all creatures, as Dionysius says (De Mystica Theol.). But what is applied to anything through its cause, is applied to it secondarily, for *healthy* is primarily predicated of animal rather than of medicine, which is the cause of health. Therefore these names are said primarily of creatures rather than of God.

ON THE CONTRARY, It is written, *I bow my knees to the Father, of our Lord Jesus Christ, of Whom all paternity in heaven and earth is named* (Eph 3:14,15); and the same applies to the other names applied to God and creatures. Therefore these names are applied primarily to God rather than to creatures.

I ANSWER THAT, In names predicated of many in an analogical sense, all are predicated because they have reference to some one thing; and this one thing must be placed in the definition of them all. And since that expressed by the name is the definition, as the Philosopher says (*Metaph.* iv), such a name must be applied primarily to that which is put in the definition of such other things, and secondarily to these others according as they approach more or less to that first. Thus, for instance, *healthy* applied to animals comes into the definition of *healthy* applied to medicine, which is called healthy as being the cause of health in the animal; and also into the definition of *healthy* which is applied to urine, which is called healthy in so far as it is the sign of the animal's health. Thus all names applied metaphorically to God, are applied to creatures primarily rather than to God, because when said of God they mean only similitudes to such creatures. For as *smiling* applied to a field means only that the field in the beauty of its flowering is like the beauty of the human smile by proportionate likeness, so the name of *lion* applied to God means only that God manifests strength in His works, as a lion in his. Thus it is clear that applied to God the signification of names can be defined only from what is said of creatures. But to other names not applied to God in a metaphorical sense, the same rule

nisi per illud quod de creaturis dicitur. De aliis autem nominibus, quae non metaphorice dicuntur de Deo, esset etiam eadem ratio, si dicerentur de Deo causaliter tantum, ut quidam posuerunt. Sic enim. Cum dicitur Deus est bonus, nihil aliud esset quam Deus est causa bonitatis creaturae, et sic hoc nomen bonum, dictum de Deo, clauderet in suo intellectu bonitatem creaturae. Unde bonum per prius diceretur de creatura quam de Deo. Sed supra ostensum est quod huiusmodi nomina non solum dicuntur de Deo causaliter, sed etiam essentialiter. Cum enim dicitur Deus est bonus, vel sapiens, non solum significatur quod ipse sit causa sapientiae vel bonitatis, sed quod haec in eo eminentius praeexistunt. Unde, secundum hoc, dicendum est quod, quantum ad rem significatam per nomen, per prius dicuntur de Deo quam de creaturis, quia a Deo huiusmodi perfectiones in creaturas manant. Sed quantum ad impositionem nominis, per prius a nobis imponuntur creaturis, quas prius cognoscimus. Unde et modum significandi habent qui competit creaturis, ut supra dictum est.

AD PRIMUM ergo dicendum quod obiectio illa procedit quantum ad impositionem nominis.

AD SECUNDUM dicendum quod non est eadem ratio de nominibus quae metaphorice de Deo dicuntur, et de aliis, ut dictum est.

AD TERTIUM dicendum quod obiectio illa procederet, si huiusmodi nomina solum de Deo causaliter dicerentur et non essentialiter, sicut sanum de medicina.

would apply if they were spoken of God as the cause only, as some have supposed. For when it is said, *God is good*, it would then only mean *God is the cause of the creature's goodness*; thus the term good applied to God would include in its meaning the creature's goodness. Hence *good* would apply primarily to creatures rather than to God. But as was shown above (A. 2), these names are applied to God not as the cause only, but also essentially. For the words, *God is good*, or *wise*, signify not only that He is the cause of wisdom or goodness, but that these exist in Him in a more excellent way. Hence as regards what the name signifies, these names are applied primarily to God rather than to creatures, because these perfections flow from God to creatures; but as regards the imposition of the names, they are primarily applied by us to creatures which we know first. Hence they have a mode of signification which belongs to creatures, as said above (A. 3).

REPLY OBJ. 1: This objection refers to the imposition of the name.

REPLY OBJ. 2: The same rule does not apply to metaphorical and to other names, as said above.

REPLY OBJ. 3: This objection would be valid if these names were applied to God only as cause, and not also essentially, for instance as *healthy* is applied to medicine.

Article 7

Whether Names Which Imply Relation to Creatures Are Predicated of God Temporally?

AD SEPTIMUM SIC PROCEDITUR. Videtur quod nomina quae important relationem ad creaturas, non dicantur de Deo ex tempore. Omnia enim huiusmodi nomina significant divinam substantiam, ut communiter dicitur. Unde et Ambrosius dicit quod hoc nomen dominus est nomen potestatis, quae est divina substantia, et creator significat Dei actionem, quae est eius essentia. Sed divina substantia non est temporalis, sed aeterna. Ergo huiusmodi nomina non dicuntur de Deo ex tempore, sed ab aeterno.

PRAETEREA, cuicumque convenit aliquid ex tempore, potest dici factum, quod enim ex tempore est album, fit album. Sed Deo non convenit esse factum. Ergo de Deo nihil praedicatur ex tempore.

PRAETEREA, si aliqua nomina dicuntur de Deo ex tempore propter hoc quod important relationem ad creaturas, eadem ratio videtur de omnibus quae relationem ad creaturas important. Sed quaedam nomina importantia relationem ad creaturas, dicuntur de Deo ab

OBJECTION 1: It seems that names which imply relation to creatures are not predicated of God temporally. For all such names signify the divine substance, as is universally held. Hence also Ambrose says (*De Fide* i) that this name *Lord* is the name of power, which is the divine substance; and *Creator* signifies the action of God, which is His essence. Now the divine substance is not temporal, but eternal. Therefore these names are not applied to God temporally, but eternally.

OBJ. 2: Further, that to which something applies temporally can be described as made; for what is white temporally is made white. But to be made does not apply to God. Therefore nothing can be predicated of God temporally.

OBJ. 3: Further, if any names are applied to God temporally as implying relation to creatures, the same rule holds good of all things that imply relation to creatures. But some names are spoken of God implying relation of God to creatures from eternity; for from eternity He knew and loved

aeterno, ab aeterno enim scivit creaturam et dilexit, secundum illud Ierem. XXXI, *in caritate perpetua dilexi te.* Ergo et alia nomina quae important relationem ad creaturas, ut dominus et creator, dicuntur de Deo ab aeterno.

PRAETEREA, huiusmodi nomina relationem significant. Oportet igitur quod relatio illa vel sit aliquid in Deo, vel in creatura tantum. Sed non potest esse quod sit in creatura tantum, quia sic Deus denominaretur dominus a relatione opposita, quae est in creaturis; nihil autem denominatur a suo opposito. Relinquitur ergo quod relatio est etiam aliquid in Deo. Sed in Deo nihil potest esse ex tempore, cum ipse sit supra tempus. Ergo videtur quod huiusmodi nomina non dicantur de Deo ex tempore.

PRAETEREA, secundum relationem dicitur aliquid relative, puta secundum dominium dominus, sicut secundum albedinem albus. Si igitur relatio dominii non est in Deo secundum rem, sed solum secundum rationem, sequitur quod Deus non sit realiter dominus, quod patet esse falsum.

PRAETEREA, in relativis quae non sunt simul natura, unum potest esse, altero non existente, sicut scibile existit, non existente scientia, ut dicitur in praedicamentis. Sed relativa quae dicuntur de Deo et creaturis, non sunt simul natura. Ergo potest aliquid dici relative de Deo ad creaturam, etiam creatura non existente. Et sic huiusmodi nomina, dominus et creator, dicuntur de Deo ab aeterno, et non ex tempore.

SED CONTRA est quod dicit Augustinus, V de Trin., quod haec relativa appellatio dominus Deo convenit ex tempore.

RESPONDEO dicendum quod quaedam nomina importantia relationem ad creaturam, ex tempore de Deo dicuntur, et non ab aeterno.

Ad cuius evidentiam, sciendum est quod quidam posuerunt relationem non esse rem naturae, sed rationis tantum. Quod quidem apparet esse falsum, ex hoc quod ipsae res naturalem ordinem et habitudinem habent ad invicem. Veruntamen sciendum est quod, cum relatio requirat duo extrema, tripliciter se habere potest ad hoc quod sit res naturae et rationis. Quandoque enim ex utraque parte est res rationis tantum, quando scilicet ordo vel habitudo non potest esse inter aliqua, nisi secundum apprehensionem rationis tantum, utpote cum dicimus idem eidem idem. Nam secundum quod ratio apprehendit bis aliquod unum, statuit illud ut duo; et sic apprehendit quandam habitudinem ipsius ad seipsum. Et similiter est de omnibus relationibus quae sunt inter ens et non ens; quas format ratio, inquantum apprehendit non ens ut quoddam extremum. Et idem est de omnibus relationibus quae consequuntur actum rationis, ut genus et species, et huiusmodi.

the creature, according to the word: *I have loved thee with an everlasting love* (Jer 31:3). Therefore also other names implying relation to creatures, as *Lord* and *Creator*, are applied to God from eternity.

OBJ. 4: Further, names of this kind signify relation. Therefore that relation must be something in God, or in the creature only. But it cannot be that it is something in the creature only, for in that case God would be called *Lord* from the opposite relation which is in creatures; and nothing is named from its opposite. Therefore the relation must be something in God also. But nothing temporal can be in God, for He is above time. Therefore these names are not applied to God temporally.

OBJ. 5: Further, a thing is called relative from relation; for instance lord from lordship, as white from whiteness. Therefore if the relation of lordship is not really in God, but only in idea, it follows that God is not really Lord, which is plainly false.

OBJ. 6: Further, in relative things which are not simultaneous in nature, one can exist without the other; as a thing knowable can exist without the knowledge of it, as the Philosopher says (*Praedic.* v). But relative things which are said of God and creatures are not simultaneous in nature. Therefore a relation can be predicated of God to the creature even without the existence of the creature; and thus these names *Lord* and *Creator* are predicated of God from eternity, and not temporally.

ON THE CONTRARY, Augustine says (*De Trin.* v) that this relative appellation *Lord* is applied to God temporally.

I ANSWER THAT, The names which import relation to creatures are applied to God temporally, and not from eternity.

To see this we must learn that some have said that relation is not a reality, but only an idea. But this is plainly seen to be false from the very fact that things themselves have a mutual natural order and habitude. Nevertheless it is necessary to know that since relation has two extremes, it happens in three ways that a relation is real or logical. Sometimes from both extremes it is an idea only, as when mutual order or habitude can only go between things in the apprehension of reason; as when we say a thing *the same as itself*. For reason apprehending one thing twice regards it as two; thus it apprehends a certain habitude of a thing to itself. And the same applies to relations between being and non-being formed by reason, apprehending non-being as an extreme. The same is true of relations that follow upon an act of reason, as genus and species, and the like.

Quaedam vero relationes sunt, quantum ad utrumque extremum, res naturae, quando scilicet est habitudo inter aliqua duo secundum aliquid realiter conveniens utrique. Sicut patet de omnibus relationibus quae consequuntur quantitatem, ut magnum et parvum, duplum et dimidium, et huiusmodi, nam quantitas est in utroque extremorum. Et simile est de relationibus quae consequuntur actionem et passionem, ut motivum et mobile, pater et filius, et similia.

Quandoque vero relatio in uno extremorum est res naturae, et in altero est res rationis tantum. Et hoc contingit quandocumque duo extrema non sunt unius ordinis. Sicut sensus et scientia referuntur ad sensibile et scibile, quae quidem, inquantum sunt res quaedam in esse naturali existentes, sunt extra ordinem esse sensibilis et intelligibilis, et ideo in scientia quidem et sensu est relatio realis, secundum quod ordinantur ad sciendum vel sentiendum res; sed res ipsae in se consideratae, sunt extra ordinem huiusmodi. Unde in eis non est aliqua relatio realiter ad scientiam et sensum; sed secundum rationem tantum, inquantum intellectus apprehendit ea ut terminos relationum scientiae et sensus. Unde philosophus dicit, in V Metaphys., quod non dicuntur relative eo quod ipsa referantur ad alia, sed quia alia referuntur ad ipsa. Et similiter dextrum non dicitur de columna, nisi inquantum ponitur animali ad dextram, unde huiusmodi relatio non est realiter in columna, sed in animali.

Cum igitur Deus sit extra totum ordinem creaturae, et omnes creaturae ordinentur ad ipsum, et non e converso, manifestum est quod creaturae realiter referuntur ad ipsum Deum; sed in Deo non est aliqua realis relatio eius ad creaturas, sed secundum rationem tantum, inquantum creaturae referuntur ad ipsum. Et sic nihil prohibet huiusmodi nomina importantia relationem ad creaturam, praedicari de Deo ex tempore, non propter aliquam mutationem ipsius, sed propter creaturae mutationem; sicut columna fit dextera animali, nulla mutatione circa ipsam existente, sed animali translato.

AD PRIMUM ergo dicendum quod relativa quaedam sunt imposita ad significandum ipsas habitudines relativas, ut dominus, servus, pater et filius, et huiusmodi, et haec dicuntur relativa secundum esse. Quaedam vero sunt imposita ad significandas res quas consequuntur quaedam habitudines, sicut movens et motum, caput et capitatum, et alia huiusmodi, quae dicuntur relativa secundum dici. Sic igitur et circa nomina divina haec differentia est consideranda. Nam quaedam significant ipsam habitudinem ad creaturam, ut dominus. Et huiusmodi non significant substantiam divinam directe, sed indirecte, inquantum praesupponunt ipsam, sicut dominium praesupponit potestatem, quae est divina substantia. Quaedam vero significant directe essentiam divinam, et ex consequenti important habitudinem; sicut

Now there are other relations which are realities as regards both extremes, as when for instance a habitude exists between two things according to some reality that belongs to both; as is clear of all relations, consequent upon quantity; as great and small, double and half, and the like; for quantity exists in both extremes: and the same applies to relations consequent upon action and passion, as motive power and the movable thing, father and son, and the like.

Again, sometimes a relation in one extreme may be a reality, while in the other extreme it is an idea only; and this happens whenever two extremes are not of one order; as sense and science refer respectively to sensible things and to intellectual things; which, inasmuch as they are realities existing in nature, are outside the order of sensible and intellectual existence. Therefore in science and in sense a real relation exists, because they are ordered either to the knowledge or to the sensible perception of things; whereas the things looked at in themselves are outside this order, and hence in them there is no real relation to science and sense, but only in idea, inasmuch as the intellect apprehends them as terms of the relations of science and sense. Hence the Philosopher says (*Metaph.* v) that they are called relative, not forasmuch as they are related to other things, but as others are related to them. Likewise for instance, *on the right* is not applied to a column, unless it stands as regards an animal on the right side; which relation is not really in the column, but in the animal.

Since therefore God is outside the whole order of creation, and all creatures are ordered to Him, and not conversely, it is manifest that creatures are really related to God Himself; whereas in God there is no real relation to creatures, but a relation only in idea, inasmuch as creatures are referred to Him. Thus there is nothing to prevent these names which import relation to the creature from being predicated of God temporally, not by reason of any change in Him, but by reason of the change of the creature; as a column is on the right of an animal, without change in itself, but by change in the animal.

REPLY OBJ. 1: Some relative names are imposed to signify the relative habitudes themselves, as *master* and *servant*, *father*, and *son*, and the like, and these relatives are called predicamental. But others are imposed to signify the things from which ensue certain habitudes, as the mover and the thing moved, the head and the thing that has a head, and the like: and these relatives are called transcendental. Thus, there is the same two-fold difference in divine names. For some signify the habitude itself to the creature, as *Lord*, and these do not signify the divine substance directly, but indirectly, in so far as they presuppose the divine substance; as dominion presupposes power, which is the divine substance. Others signify the divine essence directly, and consequently the corresponding habitudes, as *Savior*, *Creator*, and suchlike; and these signify the action of God, which

salvator, creator, et huiusmodi, significant actionem Dei, quae est eius essentia. Utraque tamen nomina ex tempore de Deo dicuntur quantum ad habitudinem quam important, vel principaliter vel consequenter, non autem quantum ad hoc quod significant essentiam, vel directe vel indirecte.

AD SECUNDUM dicendum quod, sicut relationes quae de Deo dicuntur ex tempore, non sunt in Deo nisi secundum rationem, ita nec fieri nec factum esse dicitur de Deo, nisi secundum rationem, nulla mutatione circa ipsum existente, sicut est id, *domine refugium factus es nobis.*

AD TERTIUM dicendum quod operatio intellectus et voluntatis est in operante, et ideo nomina quae significant relationes consequentes actionem intellectus vel voluntatis, dicuntur de Deo ab aeterno. Quae vero consequuntur actiones procedentes, secundum modum intelligendi, ad exteriores effectus, dicuntur de Deo ex tempore, ut salvator, creator, et huiusmodi.

AD QUARTUM dicendum quod relationes significatae per huiusmodi nomina quae dicuntur de Deo ex tempore, sunt in Deo secundum rationem tantum, oppositae autem relationes in creaturis sunt secundum rem. Nec est inconveniens quod a relationibus realiter existentibus in re, Deus denominetur, tamen secundum quod cointelliguntur per intellectum nostrum oppositae relationes in Deo. Ut sic Deus dicatur relative ad creaturam, quia creatura refertur ad ipsum, sicut philosophus dicit, in V Metaphys., quod scibile dicitur relative, quia scientia refertur ad ipsum.

AD QUINTUM dicendum quod, cum ea ratione referatur Deus ad creaturam, qua creatura refertur ad ipsum; cum relatio subiectionis realiter sit in creatura, sequitur quod Deus non secundum rationem tantum, sed realiter sit dominus. Eo enim modo dicitur dominus, quo creatura ei subiecta est.

AD SEXTUM dicendum quod, ad cognoscendum utrum relativa sint simul natura vel non, non oportet considerare ordinem rerum de quibus relativa dicuntur, sed significationes ipsorum relativorum. Si enim unum in sui intellectu claudat aliud et e converso, tunc sunt simul natura, sicut duplum et dimidium, pater et filius, et similia. Si autem unum in sui intellectu claudat aliud, et non e converso, tunc non sunt simul natura. Et hoc modo se habent scientia et scibile. Nam scibile dicitur secundum potentiam, scientia autem secundum habitum, vel secundum actum. Unde scibile, secundum modum suae significationis, praeexistit scientiae. Sed si accipiatur scibile secundum actum, tunc est simul cum scientia secundum actum, nam scitum non est aliquid nisi sit eius scientia. Licet igitur Deus sit prior creaturis, quia tamen in significatione domini clauditur quod

is His essence. Yet both names are said of God temporally so far as they imply a habitude either principally or consequently, but not as signifying the essence, either directly or indirectly.

REPLY OBJ. 2: As relations applied to God temporally are only in God in our idea, so, *to become* or *to be made* are applied to God only in idea, with no change in Him, as for instance when we say, *Lord, Thou art become our refuge* (Ps 89:1).

REPLY OBJ. 3: The operation of the intellect and the will is in the operator; therefore names signifying relations following upon the action of the intellect or will, are applied to God from eternity; whereas those following upon the actions proceeding according to our mode of thinking to external effects are applied to God temporally, as *Savior*, *Creator*, and the like.

REPLY OBJ. 4: Relations signified by these names which are applied to God temporally, are in God only in idea; but the opposite relations in creatures are real. Nor is it incongruous that God should be denominated from relations really existing in the thing, yet so that the opposite relations in God should also be understood by us at the same time; in the sense that God is spoken of relatively to the creature, inasmuch as the creature is related to Him: thus the Philosopher says (*Metaph.* v) that the object is said to be knowable relatively because knowledge relates to it.

REPLY OBJ. 5: Since God is related to the creature for the reason that the creature is related to Him: and since the relation of subjection is real in the creature, it follows that God is Lord not in idea only, but in reality; for He is called Lord according to the manner in which the creature is subject to Him.

REPLY OBJ. 6: To know whether relations are simultaneous by nature or otherwise, it is not necessary to consider the order of things to which they belong but the meaning of the relations themselves. For if one in its idea includes another, and vice versa, then they are simultaneous by nature: as double and half, father and son, and the like. But if one in its idea includes another, and not vice versa, they are not simultaneous by nature. This applies to science and its object; for the object knowable is considered as a potentiality, and the science as a habit, or as an act. Hence the knowable object in its mode of signification exists before science, but if the same object is considered in act, then it is simultaneous with science in act; for the object known is nothing as such unless it is known. Thus, though God is prior to the creature, still because the signification of Lord includes the idea of a servant and vice versa, these two relative terms,

habeat servum, et e converso, ista duo relativa, dominus et servus, sunt simul natura. Unde Deus non fuit dominus, antequam haberet creaturam sibi subiectam.

Lord and *servant*, are simultaneous by nature. Hence, God was not *Lord* until He had a creature subject to Himself.

Article 8

Whether This Name God Is a Name of the Nature?

AD OCTAVUM SIC PROCEDITUR. Videtur quod hoc nomen Deus non sit nomen naturae. Dicit enim Damascenus, in I libro, quod *Deus dicitur a theein*, quod est currere, et fovere universa; *vel ab aethein, idest ardere (Deus enim noster ignis consumens est omnem malitiam); vel a theasthai*, quod est considerare, omnia. Haec autem omnia ad operationem pertinent. Ergo hoc nomen Deus operationem significat, et non naturam.

PRAETEREA, secundum hoc aliquid nominatur a nobis, secundum quod cognoscitur. Sed divina natura est nobis ignota. Ergo hoc nomen Deus non significat naturam divinam.

SED CONTRA est quod dicit Ambrosius, in libro I de fide, quod Deus est nomen naturae.

RESPONDEO dicendum quod non est semper idem id a quo imponitur nomen ad significandum, et id ad quod significandum nomen imponitur. Sicut enim substantiam rei ex proprietatibus vel operationibus eius cognoscimus, ita substantiam rei denominamus quandoque ab aliqua eius operatione vel proprietate, sicut substantiam lapidis denominamus ab aliqua actione eius, quia laedit pedem; non tamen hoc nomen impositum est ad significandum hanc actionem, sed substantiam lapidis. Si qua vero sunt quae secundum se sunt nota nobis, ut calor, frigus, albedo, et huiusmodi, non ab aliis denominantur. Unde in talibus idem est quod nomen significat, et id a quo imponitur nomen ad significandum.

Quia igitur Deus non est notus nobis in sui natura, sed innotescit nobis ex operationibus vel effectibus eius, ex his possumus eum nominare, ut supra dictum est. Unde hoc nomen Deus est nomen operationis, quantum ad id a quo imponitur ad significandum. Imponitur enim hoc nomen ab universali rerum providentia, omnes enim loquentes de Deo, hoc intendunt nominare Deum, quod habet providentiam universalem de rebus. Unde dicit Dionysius, XII cap. de Div. Nom., quod *deitas est quae omnia videt providentia et bonitate perfecta*. Ex hac autem operatione hoc nomen Deus assumptum, impositum est ad significandum divinam naturam.

AD PRIMUM ergo dicendum quod omnia quae posuit Damascenus, pertinent ad providentiam, a qua imponitur hoc nomen Deus ad significandum.

OBJECTION 1: It seems that this name, *God*, is not a name of the nature. For Damascene says (*De Fide Orth.* 1) that *God (Theos) is so called from theein which means to take care of, and to cherish all things; or from aithein that is, to burn, for our God is a fire consuming all malice; or from theasthai, which means to consider all things*. But all these names belong to operation. Therefore this name *God* signifies His operation and not His nature.

OBJ. 2: Further, a thing is named by us as we know it. But the divine nature is unknown to us. Therefore this name *God* does not signify the divine nature.

ON THE CONTRARY, Ambrose says (*De Fide* i) that *God* is a name of the nature.

I ANSWER THAT, Whence a name is imposed, and what the name signifies are not always the same thing. For as we know substance from its properties and operations, so we name substance sometimes for its operation, or its property; e.g., we name the substance of a stone from its act, as for instance that it hurts the foot; but still this name is not meant to signify the particular action, but the stone's substance. The things, on the other hand, known to us in themselves, such as heat, cold, whiteness and the like, are not named from other things. Hence as regards such things the meaning of the name and its source are the same.

Because therefore God is not known to us in His nature, but is made known to us from His operations or effects, we name Him from these, as said in A. 1; hence this name *God* is a name of operation so far as relates to the source of its meaning. For this name is imposed from His universal providence over all things; since all who speak of God intend to name God as exercising providence over all; hence Dionysius says (*Div. Nom.* ii), *The Deity watches over all with perfect providence and goodness*. But taken from this operation, this name *God* is imposed to signify the divine nature.

REPLY OBJ. 1: All that Damascene says refers to providence; which is the source of the signification of the name *God*.

AD SECUNDUM dicendum quod, secundum quod naturam alicuius rei ex eius proprietatibus et effectibus cognoscere possumus, sic eam nomine possumus significare. Unde, quia substantiam lapidis ex eius proprietate possumus cognoscere secundum seipsam, sciendo quid est lapis, hoc nomen lapis ipsam lapidis naturam, secundum quod in se est, significat, significat enim definitionem lapidis, per quam scimus quid est lapis. Ratio enim quam significat nomen, est definitio, ut dicitur in IV Metaphys. Sed ex effectibus divinis divinam naturam non possumus cognoscere secundum quod in se est, ut sciamus de ea quid est; sed per modum eminentiae et causalitatis et negationis, ut supra dictum est. Et sic hoc nomen Deus significat naturam divinam. Impositum est enim nomen hoc ad aliquid significandum supra omnia existens, quod est principium omnium, et remotum ab omnibus. Hoc enim intendunt significare nominantes Deum.

REPLY OBJ. 2: We can name a thing according to the knowledge we have of its nature from its properties and effects. Hence because we can know what stone is in itself from its property, this name *stone* signifies the nature of the stone itself; for it signifies the definition of stone, by which we know what it is, for the idea which the name signifies is the definition, as is said in *Metaph.* iv. Now from the divine effects we cannot know the divine nature in itself, so as to know what it is; but only by way of eminence, and by way of causality, and of negation as stated above (Q. 12, A. 12). Thus the name *God* signifies the divine nature, for this name was imposed to signify something existing above all things, the principle of all things and removed from all things; for those who name God intend to signify all this.

Article 9

Whether This Name God Is Communicable?

AD NONUM SIC PROCEDITUR. Videtur quod hoc nomen Deus sit communicabile. Cuicumque enim communicatur res significata per nomen, communicatur et nomen ipsum. Sed hoc nomen Deus, ut dictum est, significat divinam naturam, quae est communicabilis aliis, secundum illud II Pet. I, *magna et pretiosa promissa nobis donavit, ut per hoc efficiamur divinae consortes naturae.* Ergo hoc nomen Deus est communicabile.

PRAETEREA, sola nomina propria non sunt communicabilia. Sed hoc nomen Deus non est nomen proprium, sed appellativum, quod patet ex hoc quod habet plurale, secundum illud Psalmi LXXXI, *ego dixi, dii estis.* Ergo hoc nomen Deus est communicabile.

PRAETEREA, hoc nomen Deus imponitur ab operatione, ut dictum est. Sed alia nomina quae imponuntur Deo ab operationibus, sive ab effectibus, sunt communicabilia, ut bonus, sapiens et huiusmodi. Ergo et hoc nomen Deus est communicabile.

SED CONTRA est quod dicitur Sap. XIV, *incommunicabile nomen lignis et lapidibus imposuerunt*; et loquitur de nomine deitatis. Ergo hoc nomen Deus est nomen incommunicabile.

RESPONDEO dicendum quod aliquod nomen potest esse communicabile dupliciter, uno modo, proprie; alio modo, per similitudinem. Proprie quidem communicabile est, quod secundum totam significationem nominis, est communicabile multis. Per similitudinem autem communicabile est, quod est communicabile secundum aliquid eorum quae includuntur in nominis

OBJECTION 1: It seems that this name *God* is communicable. For whosoever shares in the thing signified by a name shares in the name itself. But this name *God* signifies the divine nature, which is communicable to others, according to the words, *He hath given us great and precious promises, that by these we may be made partakers of the divine nature* (2 Pet 1:4). Therefore this name *God* can be communicated to others.

OBJ. 2: Further, only proper names are not communicable. Now this name *God* is not a proper, but an appellative noun; which appears from the fact that it has a plural, according to the text, *I have said, You are gods* (Ps 81:6). Therefore this name *God* is communicable.

OBJ. 3: Further, this name *God* comes from operation, as explained. But other names given to God from His operations or effects are communicable; as *good, wise,* and the like. Therefore this name *God* is communicable.

ON THE CONTRARY, It is written: *They gave the incommunicable name to wood and stones* (Wis 14:21), in reference to the divine name. Therefore this name *God* is incommunicable.

I ANSWER THAT, A name is communicable in two ways: properly, and by similitude. It is properly communicable in the sense that its whole signification can be given to many; by similitude it is communicable according to something that is included in the signification of the name. For instance this name *lion* is properly communicable to all things of the same nature as *lion*; by similitude it is communicable to

significatione. Hoc enim nomen leo proprie communicatur omnibus illis in quibus invenitur natura quam significat hoc nomen leo, per similitudinem vero communicabile est illis qui participant aliquid leoninum, ut puta audaciam vel fortitudinem, qui metaphorice leones dicuntur.

Ad sciendum autem quae nomina proprie sunt communicabilia, considerandum est quod omnis forma in supposito singulari existens, per quod individuatur, communis est multis, vel secundum rem vel secundum rationem saltem, sicut natura humana communis est multis secundum rem et rationem, natura autem solis non est communis multis secundum rem, sed secundum rationem tantum; potest enim natura solis intelligi ut in pluribus suppositis existens. Et hoc ideo, quia intellectus intelligit naturam cuiuslibet speciei per abstractionem a singulari, unde esse in uno supposito singulari vel in pluribus, est praeter intellectum naturae speciei, unde, servato intellectu naturae speciei, potest intelligi ut in pluribus existens.

Sed singulare, ex hoc ipso quod est singulare, est divisum ab omnibus aliis. Unde omne nomen impositum ad significandum aliquod singulare, est incommunicabile et re et ratione, non enim potest nec in apprehensione cadere pluralitas huius individui. Unde nullum nomen significans aliquod individuum, est communicabile multis proprie, sed solum secundum similitudinem; sicut aliquis metaphorice potest dici Achilles, inquantum habet aliquid de proprietatibus Achillis, scilicet fortitudinem. Formae vero quae non individuantur per aliquod suppositum, sed per seipsas (quia scilicet sunt formae subsistentes), si intelligerentur secundum quod sunt in seipsis, non possent communicari nec re neque ratione; sed forte per similitudinem, sicut dictum est de individuis. Sed quia formas simplices per se subsistentes non possumus intelligere secundum quod sunt, sed intelligimus eas ad modum rerum compositarum habentium formas in materia; ideo, ut dictum est, imponimus eis nomina concreta significantia naturam in aliquo supposito. Unde, quantum pertinet ad rationem nominum, eadem ratio est de nominibus quae a nobis imponuntur ad significandum naturas rerum compositarum, et de nominibus quae a nobis imponuntur ad significandum naturas simplices subsistentes.

Unde, cum hoc nomen Deus impositum sit ad significandum naturam divinam, ut dictum est; natura autem divina multiplicabilis non est, ut supra ostensum est, sequitur quod hoc nomen Deus incommunicabile quidem sit secundum rem, sed communicabile sit secundum opinionem, quemadmodum hoc nomen sol esset communicabile secundum opinionem ponentium multos soles. Et secundum hoc dicitur Gal. IV, *his qui natura non sunt dii, serviebatis*; Glossa, *non sunt dii natura, sed opinione hominum*. Est nihilominus communicabile hoc

those who participate in the nature of a lion, as for instance by courage, or strength, and those who thus participate are called lions metaphorically.

To know, however, what names are properly communicable, we must consider that every form existing in the singular subject, by which it is individualized, is common to many either in reality, or in idea; as human nature is common to many in reality, and in idea; whereas the nature of the sun is not common to many in reality, but only in idea; for the nature of the sun can be understood as existing in many subjects; and the reason is because the mind understands the nature of every species by abstraction from the singular. Hence to be in one singular subject or in many is outside the idea of the nature of the species. So, given the idea of a species, it can be understood as existing in many.

But the singular, from the fact that it is singular, is divided off from all others. Hence every name imposed to signify any singular thing is incommunicable both in reality and idea; for the plurality of this individual thing cannot be; nor can it be conceived in idea. Hence no name signifying any individual thing is properly communicable to many, but only by way of similitude; as for instance a person can be called *Achilles* metaphorically, forasmuch as he may possess something of the properties of Achilles, such as strength. On the other hand, forms which are individualized not by any suppositum, but by and of themselves, as being subsisting forms, if understood as they are in themselves, could not be communicable either in reality or in idea; but only perhaps by way of similitude, as was said of individuals. Forasmuch as we are unable to understand simple self-subsisting forms as they really are, we understand them as compound things having forms in matter; therefore, as was said in the first article, we give them concrete names signifying a nature existing in some suppositum. Hence, so far as concerns images, the same rules apply to names we impose to signify the nature of compound things as to names given to us to signify simple subsisting natures.

Since, then, this name *God* is given to signify the divine nature as stated above (A. 8), and since the divine nature cannot be multiplied as shown above (Q. 11, A. 3), it follows that this name *God* is incommunicable in reality, but communicable in opinion; just in the same way as this name *sun* would be communicable according to the opinion of those who say there are many suns. Therefore, it is written: *You served them who by nature are not gods*, (Gal 4:8), and a gloss adds, *Gods not in nature, but in human opinion*. Nevertheless this name *God* is communicable, not in

nomen Deus, non secundum suam totam significationem, sed secundum aliquid eius, per quandam similitudinem, ut dii dicantur, qui participant aliquid divinum per similitudinem, secundum illud, *ego dixi, dii estis.*

Si vero esset aliquod nomen impositum ad significandum Deum non ex parte naturae, sed ex parte suppositi, secundum quod consideratur ut hoc aliquid, illud nomen esset omnibus modis incommunicabile, sicut forte est nomen tetragrammaton apud Hebraeos. Et est simile si quis imponeret nomen soli designans hoc individuum.

AD PRIMUM ergo dicendum quod natura divina non est communicabilis nisi secundum similitudinis participationem.

AD SECUNDUM dicendum quod hoc nomen Deus est nomen appellativum, et non proprium, quia significat naturam divinam ut in habente; licet ipse Deus, secundum rem, non sit nec universalis nec particularis. Nomina enim non sequuntur modum essendi qui est in rebus, sed modum essendi secundum quod in cognitione nostra est. Et tamen, secundum rei veritatem, est incommunicabile, secundum quod dictum est de hoc nomine sol.

AD TERTIUM dicendum quod haec nomina bonus, sapiens, et similia, imposita quidem sunt a perfectionibus procedentibus a Deo in creaturas, non tamen sunt imposita ad significandum divinam naturam, sed ad significandum ipsas perfectiones absolute. Et ideo etiam secundum rei veritatem sunt communicabilia multis. Sed hoc nomen Deus impositum est ab operatione propria Deo, quam experimur continue, ad significandum divinam naturam.

its whole signification, but in some part of it by way of similitude; so that those are called gods who share in divinity by likeness, according to the text, *I have said, You are gods* (Ps 81:6).

But if any name were given to signify God not as to His nature but as to His suppositum, accordingly as He is considered as *this something*, that name would be absolutely incommunicable; as, for instance, perhaps the Tetragrammaton among the Hebrew; and this is like giving a name to the sun as signifying this individual thing.

REPLY OBJ. 1: The divine nature is only communicable according to the participation of some similitude.

REPLY OBJ. 2: This name *God* is an appellative name, and not a proper name, for it signifies the divine nature in the possessor; although God Himself in reality is neither universal nor particular. For names do not follow upon the mode of being in things, but upon the mode of being as it is in our mind. And yet it is incommunicable according to the truth of the thing, as was said above concerning the name *sun*.

REPLY OBJ. 3: These names *good*, *wise*, and the like, are imposed from the perfections proceeding from God to creatures; but they do not signify the divine nature, but rather signify the perfections themselves absolutely; and therefore they are in truth communicable to many. But this name *God* is given to God from His own proper operation, which we experience continually, to signify the divine nature.

Article 10

Whether This Name God Is Applied to God Univocally by Nature, by Participation, and According to Opinion?

AD DECIMUM SIC PROCEDITUR. Videtur quod hoc nomen Deus univoce dicatur de Deo per naturam, et per participationem, et secundum opinionem. Ubi enim est diversa significatio, non est contradictio affirmantis et negantis, aequivocatio enim impedit contradictionem sed Catholicus dicens idolum non est Deus, contradicit Pagano dicenti idolum est Deus. Ergo Deus utrobique sumptum univoce dicitur.

PRAETEREA, sicut idolum est Deus secundum opinionem et non secundum veritatem, ita fruitio carnalium delectationum dicitur felicitas secundum opinionem, et non secundum veritatem. Sed hoc nomen

OBJECTION 1: It seems that this name *God* is applied to God univocally by nature, by participation, and according to opinion. For where a diverse signification exists, there is no contradiction of affirmation and negation; for equivocation prevents contradiction. But a Catholic who says: *An idol is not God*, contradicts a pagan who says: *An idol is God.* Therefore *God* in both senses is spoken of univocally.

OBJ. 2: Further, as an idol is God in opinion, and not in truth, so the enjoyment of carnal pleasures is called happiness in opinion, and not in truth. But this name *beatitude* is applied univocally to this supposed happiness, and also

beatitudo univoce dicitur de hac beatitudine opinata, et de hac beatitudine vera. Ergo et hoc nomen Deus univoce dicitur de Deo secundum veritatem, et de Deo secundum opinionem.

PRAETEREA, univoca dicuntur quorum est ratio una. Sed Catholicus, cum dicit unum esse Deum, intelligit nomine Dei rem omnipotentem, et super omnia venerandam, et hoc idem intelligit gentilis, cum dicit idolum esse Deum. Ergo hoc nomen Deus univoce dicitur utrobique.

SED CONTRA, illud quod est in intellectu, est similitudo eius quod est in re, ut dicitur in I Periherm. Sed animal, dictum de animali vero et de animali picto, aequivoce dicitur. Ergo hoc nomen Deus, dictum de Deo vero et de Deo secundum opinionem, aequivoce dicitur.

PRAETEREA, nullus potest significare id quod non cognoscit, sed gentilis non cognoscit naturam divinam, ergo, cum dicit idolum est Deus, non significat veram deitatem. Hanc autem significat Catholicus dicens unum esse Deum. Ergo hoc nomen Deus non dicitur univoce, sed aequivoce, de Deo vero, et de Deo secundum opinionem.

RESPONDEO dicendum quod hoc nomen Deus, in praemissis tribus significationibus, non accipitur neque univoce neque aequivoce, sed analogice. Quod ex hoc patet. Quia univocorum est omnino eadem ratio, aequivocorum est omnino ratio diversa, in analogicis vero, oportet quod nomen secundum unam significationem acceptum, ponatur in definitione eiusdem nominis secundum alias significationes accepti. Sicut ens de substantia dictum, ponitur in definitione entis secundum quod de accidente dicitur; et sanum dictum de animali, ponitur in definitione sani secundum quod dicitur de urina et de medicina; huius enim sani quod est in animali, urina est significativa, et medicina factiva.

Sic accidit in proposito. Nam hoc nomen Deus, secundum quod pro Deo vero sumitur, in ratione Dei sumitur secundum quod dicitur Deus secundum opinionem vel participationem. Cum enim aliquem nominamus Deum secundum participationem, intelligimus nomine Dei aliquid habens similitudinem veri Dei. Similiter cum idolum nominamus Deum, hoc nomine Deus intelligimus significari aliquid, de quo homines opinantur quod sit Deus. Et sic manifestum est quod alia et alia est significatio nominis, sed una illarum significationum clauditur in significationibus aliis. Unde manifestum est quod analogice dicitur.

AD PRIMUM ergo dicendum quod nominum multiplicitas non attenditur secundum nominis praedicationem, sed secundum significationem, hoc enim nomen homo, de quocumque praedicetur, sive vere sive false, dicitur uno modo. Sed tunc multipliciter diceretur, si per hoc nomen homo intenderemus significare diversa, puta, si unus intenderet significare per hoc nomen homo

to true happiness. Therefore also this name *God* is applied univocally to the true God, and to God also in opinion.

OBJ. 3: Further, names are called univocal because they contain one idea. Now when a Catholic says: *There is one God*, he understands by the name God an omnipotent being, and one venerated above all; while the heathen understands the same when he says: *An idol is God*. Therefore this name *God* is applied univocally to both.

ON THE CONTRARY, The idea in the intellect is the likeness of what is in the thing as is said in Peri Herm. i. But the word *animal* applied to a true animal, and to a picture of one, is equivocal. Therefore this name *God* applied to the true God and to God in opinion is applied equivocally.

FURTHER, No one can signify what he does not know. But the heathen does not know the divine nature. So when he says an idol is God, he does not signify the true Deity. On the other hand, a Catholic signifies the true Deity when he says that there is one God. Therefore this name *God* is not applied univocally, but equivocally to the true God, and to God according to opinion.

I ANSWER THAT, This name *God* in the three aforesaid significations is taken neither univocally nor equivocally, but analogically. This is apparent from this reason: Univocal terms mean absolutely the same thing, but equivocal terms absolutely different; whereas in analogical terms a word taken in one signification must be placed in the definition of the same word taken in other senses; as, for instance, *being* which is applied to *substance* is placed in the definition of being as applied to *accident*; and *healthy* applied to animal is placed in the definition of healthy as applied to urine and medicine. For urine is the sign of health in the animal, and medicine is the cause of health.

The same applies to the question at issue. For this name *God*, as signifying the true God, includes the idea of God when it is used to denote God in opinion, or participation. For when we name anyone god by participation, we understand by the name of god some likeness of the true God. Likewise, when we call an idol god, by this name god we understand and signify something which men think is God; thus it is manifest that the name has different meanings, but that one of them is comprised in the other significations. Hence it is manifestly said analogically.

REPLY OBJ. 1: The multiplication of names does not depend on the predication of the name, but on the signification: for this name *man*, of whomsoever it is predicated, whether truly or falsely, is predicated in one sense. But it would be multiplied if by the name *man* we meant to signify different things; for instance, if one meant to signify by this name *man* what man really is, and another meant to

id quod vere est homo, et alius intenderet significare eodem nomine lapidem, vel aliquid aliud. Unde patet quod Catholicus dicens idolum non esse Deum, contradicit Pagano hoc asserenti, quia uterque utitur hoc nomine Deus ad significandum verum Deum. Cum enim Paganus dicit idolum esse Deum, non utitur hoc nomine secundum quod significat Deum opinabilem, sic enim verum diceret, cum etiam Catholici interdum in tali significatione hoc nomine utantur, ut cum dicitur, *omnes dii gentium Daemonia.*

ET SIMILITER dicendum ad secundum et tertium. Nam illae rationes procedunt secundum diversitatem praedicationis nominis, et non secundum diversam significationem.

AD QUARTUM dicendum quod animal dictum de animali vero et de picto, non dicitur pure aequivoce; sed philosophus largo modo accipit aequivoca, secundum quod includunt in se analoga. Quia et ens, quod analogice dicitur, aliquando dicitur aequivoce praedicari de diversis praedicamentis.

AD QUINTUM dicendum quod ipsam naturam Dei prout in se est, neque Catholicus neque Paganus cognoscit, sed uterque cognoscit eam secundum aliquam rationem causalitatis vel excellentiae vel remotionis, ut supra dictum est. Et secundum hoc, in eadem significatione accipere potest gentilis hoc nomen Deus, cum dicit idolum est Deus, in qua accipit ipsum Catholicus dicens idolum non est Deus. Si vero aliquis esset qui secundum nullam rationem Deum cognosceret, nec ipsum nominaret, nisi forte sicut proferimus nomina quorum significationem ignoramus.

signify by the same name a stone, or something else. Hence it is evident that a Catholic saying that an idol is not God contradicts the pagan asserting that it is God; because each of them uses this name *God* to signify the true God. For when the pagan says an idol is God, he does not use this name as meaning God in opinion, for he would then speak the truth, as also Catholics sometimes use the name in that sense, as in the Psalm, *All the gods of the Gentiles are demons* (Ps 95:5).

THE SAME REMARK applies to the Second and Third Objections. For these reasons proceed from the different predication of the name, and not from its various significations.

REPLY OBJ. 4: The term *animal* applied to a true and a pictured animal is not purely equivocal; for the Philosopher takes equivocal names in a large sense, including analogous names; because also being, which is predicated analogically, is sometimes said to be predicated equivocally of different predicaments.

REPLY OBJ. 5 : Neither a Catholic nor a pagan knows the very nature of God as it is in itself; but each one knows it according to some idea of causality, or excellence, or remotion (Q. 12, A. 12). So a pagan can take this name *God* in the same way when he says an idol is God, as the Catholic does in saying an idol is not God. But if anyone should be quite ignorant of God altogether, he could not even name Him, unless, perhaps, as we use names the meaning of which we know not.

Article 11

Whether This Name, HE WHO IS, Is the Most Proper Name of God?

AD UNDECIMUM SIC PROCEDITUR. Videtur quod hoc nomen qui est non sit maxime proprium nomen Dei. Hoc enim nomen Deus est nomen incommunicabile, ut dictum est. Sed hoc nomen qui est non est nomen incommunicabile. Ergo hoc nomen qui est non est maxime proprium nomen Dei.

PRAETEREA, Dionysius dicit, III cap. de Div. Nom., quod *boni nominatio est manifestativa omnium Dei processionum.* Sed hoc maxime Deo convenit, quod sit universale rerum principium. Ergo hoc nomen bonum est maxime proprium Dei, et non hoc nomen qui est.

PRAETEREA, omne nomen divinum videtur importare relationem ad creaturas, cum Deus non cognoscatur a nobis nisi per creaturas. Sed hoc nomen qui est nullam importat habitudinem ad creaturas. Ergo hoc nomen qui est non est maxime proprium nomen Dei.

OBJECTION 1: It seems that this name HE WHO IS is not the most proper name of God. For this name *God* is an incommunicable name. But this name HE WHO IS, is not an incommunicable name. Therefore this name HE WHO IS is not the most proper name of God.

OBJ. 2: Further, Dionysius says (*Div. Nom.* iii) that *the name of good excellently manifests all the processions of God.* But it especially belongs to God to be the universal principle of all things. Therefore this name *good* is supremely proper to God, and not this name HE WHO IS.

OBJ. 3: Further, every divine name seems to imply relation to creatures, for God is known to us only through creatures. But this name HE WHO IS imports no relation to creatures. Therefore this name HE WHO IS is not the most applicable to God.

SED CONTRA est quod dicitur Exod. III, quod Moysi quaerenti, *si dixerint mihi, quod est nomen eius? Quid dicam eis?* Et respondit ei dominus, *sic dices eis, qui est misit me ad vos.* Ergo hoc nomen qui est est maxime proprium nomen Dei.

RESPONDEO dicendum quod hoc nomen qui est triplici ratione est maxime proprium nomen Dei.

Primo quidem, propter sui significationem. Non enim significat formam aliquam, sed ipsum esse. Unde, cum esse Dei sit ipsa eius essentia, et hoc nulli alii conveniat, ut supra ostensum est, manifestum est quod inter alia nomina hoc maxime proprie nominat Deum, unumquodque enim denominatur a sua forma.

Secundo, propter eius universalitatem. Omnia enim alia nomina vel sunt minus communia; vel, si convertantur cum ipso, tamen addunt aliqua supra ipsum secundum rationem; unde quodammodo informant et determinant ipsum. Intellectus autem noster non potest ipsam Dei essentiam cognoscere in statu viae, secundum quod in se est, sed quemcumque modum determinet circa id quod de Deo intelligit, deficit a modo quo Deus in se est. Et ideo, quanto aliqua nomina sunt minus determinata, et magis communia et absoluta, tanto magis proprie dicuntur de Deo a nobis. Unde et Damascenus dicit quod *principalius omnibus quae de Deo dicuntur nominibus, est qui est, totum enim in seipso comprehendens, habet ipsum esse velut quoddam pelagus substantiae infinitum et indeterminatum.* Quolibet enim alio nomine determinatur aliquis modus substantiae rei, sed hoc nomen qui est nullum modum essendi determinat, sed se habet indeterminate ad omnes; et ideo nominat ipsum *pelagus substantiae infinitum.*

Tertio vero, ex eius consignificatione. Significat enim esse in praesenti, et hoc maxime proprie de Deo dicitur, cuius esse non novit praeteritum vel futurum, ut dicit Augustinus in V de Trin.

AD PRIMUM ergo dicendum quod hoc nomen qui est est magis proprium nomen Dei quam hoc nomen Deus, quantum ad id a quo imponitur, scilicet ab esse, et quantum ad modum significandi et consignificandi, ut dictum est. Sed quantum ad id ad quod imponitur nomen ad significandum, est magis proprium hoc nomen Deus, quod imponitur ad significandum naturam divinam. Et adhuc magis proprium nomen est tetragrammaton, quod est impositum ad significandam ipsam Dei substantiam incommunicabilem, et, ut sic liceat loqui, singularem.

AD SECUNDUM dicendum quod hoc nomen bonum est principale nomen Dei inquantum est causa, non tamen simpliciter, nam esse absolute praeintelligitur causae.

AD TERTIUM dicendum quod non est necessarium quod omnia nomina divina important habitudinem ad

ON THE CONTRARY, It is written that when Moses asked, *If they should say to me, What is His name? what shall I say to them?* The Lord answered him, *Thus shalt thou say to them, HE WHO IS hath sent me to you* (Exod 3:13, 14). Therefore this name HE WHO IS most properly belongs to God.

I ANSWER THAT, This name HE WHO IS is most properly applied to God, for three reasons:

First, because of its signification. For it does not signify form, but simply existence itself. Hence since the existence of God is His essence itself, which can be said of no other (Q. 3, A. 4), it is clear that among other names this one specially denominates God, for everything is denominated by its form.

Second, on account of its universality. For all other names are either less universal, or, if convertible with it, add something above it at least in idea; hence in a certain way they inform and determine it. Now our intellect cannot know the essence of God itself in this life, as it is in itself, but whatever mode it applies in determining what it understands about God, it falls short of the mode of what God is in Himself. Therefore the less determinate the names are, and the more universal and absolute they are, the more properly they are applied to God. Hence Damascene says (*De Fide Orth.* i) that, *HE WHO IS, is the principal of all names applied to God; for comprehending all in itself, it contains existence itself as an infinite and indeterminate sea of substance.* Now by any other name some mode of substance is determined, whereas this name HE WHO IS, determines no mode of being, but is indeterminate to all; and therefore it denominates the *infinite ocean of substance.*

Third, from its consignification, for it signifies present existence; and this above all properly applies to God, whose existence knows not past or future, as Augustine says (*De Trin.* v).

REPLY OBJ. 1: This name HE WHO IS is the name of God more properly than this name *God*, as regards its source, namely, existence; and as regards the mode of signification and consignification, as said above. But as regards the object intended by the name, this name *God* is more proper, as it is imposed to signify the divine nature; and still more proper is the Tetragrammaton, imposed to signify the substance of God itself, incommunicable and, if one may so speak, singular.

REPLY OBJ. 2: This name *good* is the principal name of God in so far as He is a cause, but not absolutely; for existence considered absolutely comes before the idea of cause.

REPLY OBJ. 3: It is not necessary that all the divine names should import relation to creatures, but it suffices

creaturas; sed sufficit quod imponantur ab aliquibus perfectionibus procedentibus a Deo in creaturas. Inter quas prima est ipsum esse, a qua sumitur hoc nomen qui est.

that they be imposed from some perfections flowing from God to creatures. Among these the first is existence, from which comes this name, HE WHO IS.

Article 12

Whether Affirmative Propositions Can Be Formed About God?

AD DUODECIMUM SIC PROCEDITUR. Videtur quod propositiones affirmativae non possunt formari de Deo. Dicit enim Dionysius, II cap. Cael. Hier., quod *negationes de Deo sunt verae, affirmationes autem incompactae.*

PRAETEREA, Boetius dicit, in libro de Trin., quod *forma simplex subiectum esse non potest.* Sed Deus maxime est forma simplex, ut supra ostensum est. Ergo non potest esse subiectum. Sed omne illud de quo propositio affirmativa formatur, accipitur ut subiectum. Ergo de Deo propositio affirmativa formari non potest.

PRAETEREA, omnis intellectus intelligens rem aliter quam sit, est falsus. Sed Deus habet esse absque omni compositione, ut supra probatum est. Cum igitur omnis intellectus affirmativus intelligat aliquid cum compositione, videtur quod propositio affirmativa vere de Deo formari non possit.

SED CONTRA est quod fidei non subest falsum. Sed propositiones quaedam affirmativae subduntur fidei, utpote quod Deus est trinus et unus, et quod est omnipotens. Ergo propositiones affirmativae possunt vere formari de Deo.

RESPONDEO dicendum quod propositiones affirmativae possunt vere formari de Deo. Ad cuius evidentiam, sciendum est quod in qualibet propositione affirmativa vera, oportet quod praedicatum et subiectum significent idem secundum rem aliquo modo, et diversum secundum rationem. Et hoc patet tam in propositionibus quae sunt de praedicato accidentali, quam in illis quae sunt de praedicato substantiali. Manifestum est enim quod homo et albus sunt idem subiecto, et differunt ratione, alia enim est ratio hominis, et alia ratio albi. Et similiter cum dico homo est animal, illud enim ipsum quod est homo, vere animal est; in eodem enim supposito est et natura sensibilis, a qua dicitur animal, et rationalis, a qua dicitur homo. Unde hic etiam praedicatum et subiectum sunt idem supposito, sed diversa ratione. Sed et in propositionibus in quibus idem praedicatur de seipso, hoc aliquo modo invenitur; inquantum intellectus id quod ponit ex parte subiecti, trahit ad partem suppositi, quod vero ponit ex parte praedicati, trahit ad naturam formae in supposito existentis, secundum quod dicitur quod praedicata tenentur formaliter, et subiecta materialiter. Huic vero diversitati quae est secundum rationem,

OBJECTION 1: It seems that affirmative propositions cannot be formed about God. For Dionysius says (*Coel. Hier.* ii) that *negations about God are true; but affirmations are vague.*

OBJ. 2: Further, Boethius says (*De Trin.* ii) that *a simple form cannot be a subject.* But God is the most absolutely simple form, as shown (Q. 3): therefore He cannot be a subject. But everything about which an affirmative proposition is made is taken as a subject. Therefore an affirmative proposition cannot be formed about God.

OBJ. 3: Further, every intellect is false which understands a thing otherwise than as it is. But God has existence without any composition as shown above (Q. 3, A. 7). Therefore since every affirmative intellect understands something as compound, it follows that a true affirmative proposition about God cannot be made.

ON THE CONTRARY, What is of faith cannot be false. But some affirmative propositions are of faith; as that God is Three and One; and that He is omnipotent. Therefore true affirmative propositions can be formed about God.

I ANSWER THAT, True affirmative propositions can be formed about God. To prove this we must know that in every true affirmative proposition the predicate and the subject signify in some way the same thing in reality, and different things in idea. And this appears to be the case both in propositions which have an accidental predicate, and in those which have an essential predicate. For it is manifest that *man* and *white* are the same in subject, and different in idea; for the idea of man is one thing, and that of whiteness is another. The same applies when I say, *man is an animal*, since the same thing which is man is truly animal; for in the same suppositum there is sensible nature by reason of which he is called animal, and the rational nature by reason of which he is called man; hence here again predicate and subject are the same as to suppositum, but different as to idea. But in propositions where one same thing is predicated of itself, the same rule in some way applies, inasmuch as the intellect draws to the suppositum what it places in the subject; and what it places in the predicate it draws to the nature of the form existing in the suppositum; according to the saying that *predicates are to be taken formally, and subjects materially.* To this diversity in idea corresponds the

respondet pluralitas praedicati et subiecti, identitatem vero rei significat intellectus per ipsam compositionem.

Deus autem, in se consideratus, est omnino unus et simplex, sed tamen intellectus noster secundum diversas conceptiones ipsum cognoscit, eo quod non potest ipsum ut in seipso est, videre. Sed tamen, quamvis intelligat ipsum sub diversis conceptionibus, cognoscit tamen quod omnibus suis conceptionibus respondet una et eadem res simpliciter. Hanc ergo pluralitatem quae est secundum rationem, repraesentat per pluralitatem praedicati et subiecti, unitatem vero repraesentat intellectus per compositionem.

AD PRIMUM ergo dicendum quod Dionysius dicit affirmationes de Deo esse incompactas, vel inconvenientes secundum aliam translationem, inquantum nullum nomen Deo competit secundum modum significandi, ut supra dictum est.

AD SECUNDUM dicendum quod intellectus noster non potest formas simplices subsistentes secundum quod in seipsis sunt, apprehendere, sed apprehendit eas secundum modum compositorum, in quibus est aliquid quod subiicitur, et est aliquid quod inest. Et ideo apprehendit formam simplicem in ratione subiecti, et attribuit ei aliquid.

AD TERTIUM dicendum quod haec propositio, intellectus intelligens rem aliter quam sit, est falsus, est duplex, ex eo quod hoc adverbium aliter potest determinare hoc verbum intelligit ex parte intellecti, vel ex parte intelligentis. Si ex parte intellecti, sic propositio vera est, et est sensus, quicumque intellectus intelligit rem esse aliter quam sit, falsus est. Sed hoc non habet locum in proposito, quia intellectus noster, formans propositionem de Deo, non dicit eum esse compositum, sed simplicem. Si vero ex parte intelligentis, sic propositio falsa est. Alius est enim modus intellectus in intelligendo, quam rei in essendo. Manifestum est enim quod intellectus noster res materiales infra se existentes intelligit immaterialiter; non quod intelligat eas esse immateriales, sed habet modum immaterialem in intelligendo. Et similiter, cum intelligit simplicia quae sunt supra se, intelligit ea secundum modum suum, scilicet composite, non tamen ita quod intelligat ea esse composita. Et sic intellectus noster non est falsus, formans compositionem de Deo.

plurality of predicate and subject, while the intellect signifies the identity of the thing by the composition itself.

God, however, as considered in Himself, is altogether one and simple, yet our intellect knows Him by different conceptions because it cannot see Him as He is in Himself. Nevertheless, although it understands Him under different conceptions, it knows that one and the same simple object corresponds to its conceptions. Therefore the plurality of predicate and subject represents the plurality of idea; and the intellect represents the unity by composition.

REPLY OBJ. 1: Dionysius says that the affirmations about God are vague or, according to another translation, *incongruous*, inasmuch as no name can be applied to God according to its mode of signification.

REPLY OBJ. 2: Our intellect cannot comprehend simple subsisting forms, as they really are in themselves; but it apprehends them as compound things in which there is something taken as subject and something that is inherent. Therefore it apprehends the simple form as a subject, and attributes something else to it.

REPLY OBJ. 3: This proposition, *The intellect understanding anything otherwise than it is, is false*, can be taken in two senses, accordingly as this adverb *otherwise* determines the word *understanding* on the part of the thing understood, or on the part of the one who understands. Taken as referring to the thing understood, the proposition is true, and the meaning is: Any intellect which understands that the thing is otherwise than it is, is false. But this does not hold in the present case; because our intellect, when forming a proposition about God, does not affirm that He is composite, but that He is simple. But taken as referring to the one who understands, the proposition is false. For the mode of the intellect in understanding is different from the mode of the thing in its essence. Since it is clear that our intellect understands material things below itself in an immaterial manner; not that it understands them to be immaterial things; but its manner of understanding is immaterial. Likewise, when it understands simple things above itself, it understands them according to its own mode, which is in a composite manner; yet not so as to understand them to be composite things. And thus our intellect is not false in forming composition in its ideas concerning God.

QUESTION 14

GOD'S KNOWLEDGE

Post considerationem eorum quae ad divinam substantiam pertinent, restat considerandum de his quae pertinent ad operationem ipsius.

Et quia operatio quaedam est quae manet in operante, quaedam vero quae procedit in exteriorem effectum, primo agemus de scientia et voluntate (nam intelligere in intelligente est, et velle in volente); et postmodum de potentia Dei, quae consideratur ut principium operationis divinae in effectum exteriorem procedentis.

Quia vero intelligere quoddam vivere est, post considerationem divinae scientiae, considerandum erit de vita divina.

Et quia scientia verorum est, erit etiam considerandum de veritate et falsitate.

Rursum, quia omne cognitum in cognoscente est, rationes autem rerum secundum quod sunt in Deo cognoscente, ideae vocantur, cum consideratione scientiae erit etiam adiungenda consideratio de ideis.

Circa scientiam vero quaeruntur sexdecim.

Primo, utrum in Deo sit scientia.
Secundo, utrum Deus intelligat seipsum.
Tertio, utrum comprehendat se.
Quarto, utrum suum intelligere sit sua substantia.
Quinto, utrum intelligat alia a se.

Sexto, utrum habeat de eis propriam cognitionem.
Septimo, utrum scientia Dei sit discursiva.
Octavo, utrum scientia Dei sit causa rerum.

Nono, utrum scientia Dei sit eorum quae non sunt.

Decimo, utrum sit malorum.
Undecimo, utrum sit singularium.
Duodecimo, utrum sit infinitorum.
Decimotertio, utrum sit contingentium futurorum.
Decimoquarto, utrum sit enuntiabilium.
Decimoquinto, utrum scientia Dei sit variabilis.
Decimosexto, utrum Deus de rebus habeat speculativam scientiam vel practicam.

Having considered what belongs to the divine substance, we have now to treat of God's operation.

And since one kind of operation is immanent, and another kind of operation proceeds to the exterior effect, we treat first of knowledge and of will (for understanding abides in the intelligent agent, and will is in the one who wills); and afterwards of the power of God, the principle of the divine operation as proceeding to the exterior effect.

Now because to understand is a kind of life, after treating of the divine knowledge, we consider the divine life.

And as knowledge concerns truth, we consider truth and falsehood.

Further, as everything known is in the knower, and the types of things as existing in the knowledge of God are called ideas, to the consideration of knowledge will be added the treatment of ideas.

Concerning knowledge, there are sixteen points for inquiry:

(1) Whether there is knowledge in God?
(2) Whether God understands Himself?
(3) Whether He comprehends Himself?
(4) Whether His understanding is His substance?
(5) Whether He understands other things besides Himself?
(6) Whether He has a proper knowledge of them?
(7) Whether the knowledge of God is discursive?
(8) Whether the knowledge of God is the cause of things?
(9) Whether God has knowledge of non-existing things?
(10) Whether He has knowledge of evil?
(11) Whether He has knowledge of individual things?
(12) Whether He knows the infinite?
(13) Whether He knows future contingent things?
(14) Whether He knows enunciable things?
(15) Whether the knowledge of God is variable?
(16) Whether God has speculative or practical knowledge of things?

Article 1

Whether There Is Knowledge in God?

AD PRIMUM SIC PROCEDITUR. Videtur quod in Deo non sit scientia. Scientia enim habitus est, qui Deo non competit, cum sit medius inter potentiam et actum. Ergo scientia non est in Deo.

PRAETEREA, scientia, cum sit conclusionum, est quaedam cognitio ab alio causata, scilicet ex cognitione principiorum. Sed nihil causatum est in Deo. Ergo scientia non est in Deo.

PRAETEREA, omnis scientia vel universalis vel particularis est. Sed in Deo non est universale et particulare, ut ex superioribus patet; ergo in Deo non est scientia.

SED CONTRA est quod apostolus dicit Rom. XI, *o altitudo divitiarum sapientiae et scientiae Dei.*

RESPONDEO dicendum quod in Deo perfectissime est scientia. Ad cuius evidentiam, considerandum est quod cognoscentia a non cognoscentibus in hoc distinguuntur, quia non cognoscentia nihil habent nisi formam suam tantum; sed cognoscens natum est habere formam etiam rei alterius, nam species cogniti est in cognoscente. Unde manifestum est quod natura rei non cognoscentis est magis coarctata et limitata, natura autem rerum cognoscentium habet maiorem amplitudinem et extensionem. Propter quod dicit philosophus, III de anima, quod *anima est quodammodo omnia.* Coarctatio autem formae est per materiam. Unde et supra diximus quod formae, secundum quod sunt magis immateriales, secundum hoc magis accedunt ad quandam infinitatem. Patet igitur quod immaterialitas alicuius rei est ratio quod sit cognoscitiva; et secundum modum immaterialitatis est modus cognitionis. Unde in II de anima dicitur quod plantae non cognoscunt, propter suam materialitatem. Sensus autem cognoscitivus est, quia receptivus est specierum sine materia, et intellectus adhuc magis cognoscitivus, quia magis separatus est a materia et immixtus, ut dicitur in III de anima. Unde, cum Deus sit in summo immaterialitatis, ut ex superioribus patet, sequitur quod ipse sit in summo cognitionis.

AD PRIMUM ergo dicendum quod, quia perfectiones procedentes a Deo in creaturas, altiori modo sunt in Deo, ut supra dictum est, oportet quod, quandocumque aliquod nomen sumptum a quacumque perfectione creaturae Deo attribuitur, secludatur ab eius significatione omne illud quod pertinet ad imperfectum modum qui competit creaturae. Unde scientia non est qualitas in Deo vel habitus, sed substantia et actus purus.

AD SECUNDUM dicendum quod ea quae sunt divisim et multipliciter in creaturis, in Deo sunt simpliciter et unite, ut supra dictum est. Homo autem, secundum diversa cognita, habet diversas cognitiones, nam

OBJECTION 1: It seems that in God there is not knowledge. For knowledge is a habit; and habit does not belong to God, since it is the mean between potentiality and act. Therefore knowledge is not in God.

OBJ. 2: Further, since science is about conclusions, it is a kind of knowledge caused by something else which is the knowledge of principles. But nothing is caused in God; therefore science is not in God.

OBJ. 3: Further, all knowledge is universal or particular. But in God there is no universal or particular (Q. 3, A. 5). Therefore in God there is not knowledge.

ON THE CONTRARY, The Apostle says, *O the depth of the riches of the wisdom and of the knowledge of God* (Rom 11:33).

I ANSWER THAT, In God there exists the most perfect knowledge. To prove this, we must note that intelligent beings are distinguished from non-intelligent beings in that the latter possess only their own form; whereas the intelligent being is naturally adapted to have also the form of some other thing; for the idea of the thing known is in the knower. Hence it is manifest that the nature of a non-intelligent being is more contracted and limited; whereas the nature of intelligent beings has a greater amplitude and extension; therefore the Philosopher says (*De Anima* iii) that *the soul is in a sense all things.* Now the contraction of the form comes from the matter. Hence, as we have said above (Q. 7, A. 1), forms according as they are the more immaterial, approach more nearly to a kind of infinity. Therefore it is clear that the immateriality of a thing is the reason why it is cognitive; and according to the mode of immateriality is the mode of knowledge. Hence it is said in *De Anima* ii that plants do not know, because they are wholly material. But sense is cognitive because it can receive images free from matter, and the intellect is still further cognitive, because it is more separated from matter and unmixed, as said in *De Anima* iii. Since therefore God is in the highest degree of immateriality as stated above (Q. 7, A. 1), it follows that He occupies the highest place in knowledge.

REPLY OBJ. 1: Because perfections flowing from God to creatures exist in a higher state in God Himself (Q. 4, A. 2), whenever a name taken from any created perfection is attributed to God, it must be separated in its signification from anything that belongs to that imperfect mode proper to creatures. Hence knowledge is not a quality of God, nor a habit, but substance and pure act.

REPLY OBJ. 2: Whatever is divided and multiplied in creatures exists in God simply and unitedly (Q. 13, A. 4). Now man has different kinds of knowledge, according to the different objects of His knowledge. He has intelligence

secundum quod cognoscit principia, dicitur habere intelligentiam; scientiam vero, secundum quod cognoscit conclusiones; sapientiam, secundum quod cognoscit causam altissimam; consilium vel prudentiam, secundum quod cognoscit agibilia. Sed haec omnia Deus una et simplici cognitione cognoscit, ut infra patebit. Unde simplex Dei cognitio omnibus istis nominibus nominari potest, ita tamen quod ab unoquoque eorum, secundum quod in divinam praedicationem venit, secludatur quidquid imperfectionis est, et retineatur quidquid perfectionis est. Et secundum hoc dicitur Iob XII, *apud ipsum est sapientia et fortitudo; ipse habet consilium et intelligentiam.*

Ad tertium dicendum quod scientia est secundum modum cognoscentis, scitum enim est in sciente secundum modum scientis. Et ideo, cum modus divinae essentiae sit altior quam modus quo creaturae sunt, scientia divina non habet modum creatae scientiae, ut scilicet sit universalis vel particularis, vel in habitu vel in potentia, vel secundum aliquem talem modum disposita.

as regards the knowledge of principles; he has science as regards knowledge of conclusions; he has wisdom, according as he knows the highest cause; he has counsel or prudence, according as he knows what is to be done. But God knows all these by one simple act of knowledge, as will be shown (A. 7). Hence the simple knowledge of God can be named by all these names; in such a way, however, that there must be removed from each of them, so far as they enter into divine predication, everything that savors of imperfection; and everything that expresses perfection is to be retained in them. Hence it is said, *With Him is wisdom and strength, He hath counsel and understanding* (Job 12:13).

Reply Obj. 3: Knowledge is according to the mode of the one who knows; for the thing known is in the knower according to the mode of the knower. Now since the mode of the divine essence is higher than that of creatures, divine knowledge does not exist in God after the mode of created knowledge, so as to be universal or particular, or habitual, or potential, or existing according to any such mode.

Article 2

Whether God Understands Himself?

Ad secundum sic proceditur. Videtur quod Deus non intelligat se. Dicitur enim in libro de causis, quod *omnis sciens qui scit suam essentiam, est rediens ad essentiam suam reditione completa.* Sed Deus non exit extra essentiam suam, nec aliquo modo movetur, et sic non competit sibi redire ad essentiam suam. Ergo ipse non est sciens essentiam suam.

Praeterea, intelligere est quoddam pati et moveri, ut dicitur in III de anima, scientia etiam est assimilatio ad rem scitam, et scitum etiam est perfectio scientis. Sed nihil movetur, vel patitur, vel perficitur a seipso; neque similitudo sibi est, ut Hilarius dicit. Ergo Deus non est sciens seipsum.

Praeterea, praecipue Deo sumus similes secundum intellectum, quia secundum mentem sumus ad imaginem Dei, ut dicit Augustinus. Sed intellectus noster non intelligit se, nisi sicut intelligit alia, ut dicitur in III de anima. Ergo nec Deus intelligit se, nisi forte intelligendo alia.

Sed contra est quod dicitur I ad Cor. II, *quae sunt Dei, nemo novit nisi spiritus Dei.*

Respondeo dicendum quod Deus se per seipsum intelligit. Ad cuius evidentiam, sciendum est quod, licet in operationibus quae transeunt in exteriorem effectum, obiectum operationis, quod significatur ut terminus, sit aliquid extra operantem; tamen in operationibus quae

Objection 1: It seems that God does not understand Himself. For it is said by the Philosopher (*De Causis*), *Every knower who knows his own essence, returns completely to his own essence.* But God does not go out from His own essence, nor is He moved at all; thus He cannot return to His own essence. Therefore He does not know His own essence.

Obj. 2: Further, to understand is a kind of passion and movement, as the Philosopher says (*De Anima* iii); and knowledge also is a kind of assimilation to the object known; and the thing known is the perfection of the knower. But nothing is moved, or suffers, or is made perfect by itself, *nor*, as Hilary says (*De Trin.* iii), *is a thing its own likeness.* Therefore God does not understand Himself.

Obj. 3: Further, we are like to God chiefly in our intellect, because we are the image of God in our mind, as Augustine says (*Gen ad lit.* vi). But our intellect understands itself, only as it understands other things, as is said in *De Anima* iii. Therefore God understands Himself only so far perchance as He understands other things.

On the contrary, It is written: *The things that are of God no man knoweth, but the Spirit of God* (1 Cor 2:11).

I answer that, God understands Himself through Himself. In proof whereof it must be known that although in operations which pass to an external effect, the object of the operation, which is taken as the term, exists outside the operator; nevertheless in operations that remain in

sunt in operante, obiectum quod significatur ut terminus operationis, est in ipso operante; et secundum quod est in eo, sic est operatio in actu. Unde dicitur in libro de anima, quod sensibile in actu est sensus in actu, et intelligibile in actu est intellectus in actu. Ex hoc enim aliquid in actu sentimus vel intelligimus, quod intellectus noster vel sensus informatur in actu per speciem sensibilis vel intelligibilis. Et secundum hoc tantum sensus vel intellectus aliud est a sensibili vel intelligibili, quia utrumque est in potentia.

Cum igitur Deus nihil potentialitatis habeat, sed sit actus purus, oportet quod in eo intellectus et intellectum sint idem omnibus modis, ita scilicet, ut neque careat specie intelligibili, sicut intellectus noster cum intelligit in potentia; neque species intelligibilis sit aliud a substantia intellectus divini, sicut accidit in intellectu nostro, cum est actu intelligens; sed ipsa species intelligibilis est ipse intellectus divinus. Et sic seipsum per seipsum intelligit.

AD PRIMUM ergo dicendum quod redire ad essentiam suam nihil aliud est quam rem subsistere in seipsa. Forma enim, inquantum perficit materiam dando ei esse, quodammodo supra ipsam effunditur, inquantum vero in seipsa habet esse, in seipsam redit. Virtutes igitur cognoscitivae quae non sunt subsistentes, sed actus aliquorum organorum, non cognoscunt seipsas; sicut patet in singulis sensibus. Sed virtutes cognoscitivae per se subsistentes, cognoscunt seipsas. Et propter hoc dicitur in libro de causis, quod *sciens essentiam suam, redit ad essentiam suam*. Per se autem subsistere maxime convenit Deo. Unde secundum hunc modum loquendi, ipse est maxime rediens ad essentiam suam, et cognoscens seipsum.

AD SECUNDUM dicendum quod moveri et pati sumuntur aequivoce secundum quod intelligere dicitur esse quoddam moveri vel pati, ut dicitur in III de anima. Non enim intelligere est motus qui est actus imperfecti, qui est ab alio in aliud, sed actus perfecti, existens in ipso agente. Similiter etiam quod intellectus perficiatur ab intelligibili vel assimiletur ei, hoc convenit intellectui qui quandoque est in potentia, quia per hoc quod est in potentia, differt ab intelligibili, et assimilatur ei per speciem intelligibilem, quae est similitudo rei intellectae; et perficitur per ipsam, sicut potentia per actum. Sed intellectus divinus, qui nullo modo est in potentia, non perficitur per intelligibile, neque assimilatur ei, sed est sua perfectio et suum intelligibile.

AD TERTIUM dicendum quod esse naturale non est materiae primae, quae est in potentia, nisi secundum quod est reducta in actum per formam. Intellectus autem noster possibilis se habet in ordine intelligibilium,

the operator, the object signified as the term of operation, resides in the operator; and accordingly as it is in the operator, the operation is actual. Hence the Philosopher says (*De Anima* iii) that *the sensible in act is sense in act, and the intelligible in act is intellect in act*. For the reason why we actually feel or know a thing is because our intellect or sense is actually informed by the sensible or intelligible species. And because of this only, it follows that sense or intellect is distinct from the sensible or intelligible object, since both are in potentiality.

Since therefore God has nothing in Him of potentiality, but is pure act, His intellect and its object are altogether the same; so that He neither is without the intelligible species, as is the case with our intellect when it understands potentially; nor does the intelligible species differ from the substance of the divine intellect, as it differs in our intellect when it understands actually; but the intelligible species itself is the divine intellect itself, and thus God understands Himself through Himself.

REPLY OBJ. 1: Return to its own essence means only that a thing subsists in itself. Inasmuch as the form perfects the matter by giving it existence, it is in a certain way diffused in it; and it returns to itself inasmuch as it has existence in itself. Therefore those cognitive faculties which are not subsisting, but are the acts of organs, do not know themselves, as in the case of each of the senses; whereas those cognitive faculties which are subsisting, know themselves; hence it is said in *De Causis* that, *whoever knows his essence returns to it*. Now it supremely belongs to God to be self-subsisting. Hence according to this mode of speaking, He supremely returns to His own essence, and knows Himself.

REPLY OBJ. 2: Movement and passion are taken equivocally, according as to understand is described as a kind of movement or passion, as stated in *De Anima* iii. For to understand is not a movement that is an act of something imperfect passing from one to another, but it is an act, existing in the agent itself, of something perfect. Likewise that the intellect is perfected by the intelligible object, i.e., is assimilated to it, this belongs to an intellect which is sometimes in potentiality; because the fact of its being in a state of potentiality makes it differ from the intelligible object and assimilates it thereto through the intelligible species, which is the likeness of the thing understood, and makes it to be perfected thereby, as potentiality is perfected by act. On the other hand, the divine intellect, which is no way in potentiality, is not perfected by the intelligible object, nor is it assimilated thereto, but is its own perfection, and its own intelligible object.

REPLY OBJ. 3: Existence in nature does not belong to primary matter, which is a potentiality, unless it is reduced to act by a form. Now our passive intellect has the same relation to intelligible objects as primary matter has to

sicut materia prima in ordine rerum naturalium, eo quod est in potentia ad intelligibilia, sicut materia prima ad naturalia. Unde intellectus noster possibilis non potest habere intelligibilem operationem, nisi inquantum perficitur per speciem intelligibilem alicuius. Et sic intelligit seipsum per speciem intelligibilem, sicut et alia, manifestum est enim quod ex eo quod cognoscit intelligibile, intelligit ipsum suum intelligere, et per actum cognoscit potentiam intellectivam. Deus autem est sicut actus purus tam in ordine existentium, quam in ordine intelligibilium, et ideo per seipsum, seipsum intelligit.

natural things; for it is in potentiality as regards intelligible objects, just as primary matter is to natural things. Hence our passive intellect can be exercised concerning intelligible objects only so far as it is perfected by the intelligible species of something; and in that way it understands itself by an intelligible species, as it understands other things: for it is manifest that by knowing the intelligible object it understands also its own act of understanding, and by this act knows the intellectual faculty. But God is a pure act in the order of existence, as also in the order of intelligible objects; therefore He understands Himself through Himself.

Article 3

Whether God Comprehends Himself?

AD TERTIUM SIC PROCEDITUR. Videtur quod Deus non comprehendat seipsum. Dicit enim Augustinus, in libro octoginta trium quaest., quod id quod comprehendit se, finitum est sibi. Sed Deus est omnibus modis infinitus. Ergo non comprehendit se.

SI DICATUR quod Deus infinitus est nobis, sed sibi finitus, contra, verius est unumquodque secundum quod est apud Deum, quam secundum quod est apud nos. Si igitur Deus sibi ipsi est finitus, nobis autem infinitus, verius est Deum esse finitum, quam infinitum. Quod est contra prius determinata. Non ergo Deus comprehendit seipsum.

SED CONTRA est quod Augustinus dicit ibidem, *omne quod intelligit se, comprehendit se*. Sed Deus intelligit se. Ergo comprehendit se.

RESPONDEO dicendum quod Deus perfecte comprehendit seipsum. Quod sic patet. Tunc enim dicitur aliquid comprehendi, quando pervenitur ad finem cognitionis ipsius, et hoc est quando res cognoscitur ita perfecte, sicut cognoscibilis est. Sicut propositio demonstrabilis comprehenditur, quando scitur per demonstrationem, non autem quando cognoscitur per aliquam rationem probabilem. Manifestum est autem quod Deus ita perfecte cognoscit seipsum, sicut perfecte cognoscibilis est. Est enim unumquodque cognoscibile secundum modum sui actus, non enim cognoscitur aliquid secundum quod in potentia est, sed secundum quod est in actu, ut dicitur in IX Metaphys. Tanta est autem virtus Dei in cognoscendo, quanta est actualitas eius in existendo, quia per hoc quod actu est, et ab omni materia et potentia separatus, Deus cognoscitivus est, ut ostensum est. Unde manifestum est quod tantum seipsum cognoscit, quantum cognoscibilis est. Et propter hoc seipsum perfecte comprehendit.

OBJECTION 1: It seems that God does not comprehend Himself. For Augustine says (*Octog. Tri. Quaest.* xv), that *whatever comprehends itself is finite as regards itself*. But God is in all ways infinite. Therefore He does not comprehend Himself.

OBJ. 2: If it is said that God is infinite to us, and finite to Himself, it can be urged to the contrary, that everything in God is truer than it is in us. If therefore God is finite to Himself, but infinite to us, then God is more truly finite than infinite; which is against what was laid down above (Q. 7, A. 1). Therefore God does not comprehend Himself.

ON THE CONTRARY, Augustine says (*Octog. Tri. Quaest.* xv), that *Everything that understands itself, comprehends itself*. But God understands Himself. Therefore He comprehends Himself.

I ANSWER THAT, God perfectly comprehends Himself, as can be thus proved. A thing is said to be comprehended when the end of the knowledge of it is attained, and this is accomplished when it is known as perfectly as it is knowable; as, for instance, a demonstrable proposition is comprehended when known by demonstration, not, however, when it is known by some probable reason. Now it is manifest that God knows Himself as perfectly as He is perfectly knowable. For everything is knowable according to the mode of its own actuality, since a thing is not known according as it is in potentiality, but in so far as it is in actuality, as said in *Metaph.* ix. Now the power of God in knowing is as great as His actuality in existing; because it is from the fact that He is in act and free from all matter and potentiality, that God is cognitive, as shown above (AA. 1, 2). Whence it is manifest that He knows Himself as much as He is knowable; and for that reason He perfectly comprehends Himself.

AD PRIMUM ergo dicendum quod comprehendere, si proprie accipiatur, significat aliquid habens et includens alterum. Et sic oportet quod omne comprehensum sit finitum, sicut omne inclusum. Non sic autem comprehendi dicitur Deus a seipso, ut intellectus suus sit aliud quam ipse, et capiat ipsum et includat. Sed huiusmodi locutiones per negationem sunt exponendae. Sicut enim Deus dicitur esse in seipso, quia a nullo exteriori continetur; ita dicitur comprehendi a seipso, quia nihil est sui quod lateat ipsum dicit enim Augustinus, in libro de videndo Deum, quod *totum comprehenditur videndo, quod ita videtur, ut nihil eius lateat videntem.*

AD SECUNDUM dicendum quod, cum dicitur Deus finitus est sibi, intelligendum est secundum quandam similitudinem proportionis; quia sic se habet in non excedendo intellectum suum, sicut se habet aliquod finitum in non excedendo intellectum finitum. Non autem sic dicitur Deus sibi finitus, quod ipse intelligat se esse aliquid finitum.

REPLY OBJ. 1: The strict meaning of *comprehension* signifies that one thing holds and includes another; and in this sense everything comprehended is finite, as also is everything included in another. But God is not said to be comprehended by Himself in this sense, as if His intellect were a faculty apart from Himself, and as if it held and included Himself; for these modes of speaking are to be taken by way of negation. But as God is said to be in Himself, forasmuch as He is not contained by anything outside of Himself; so He is said to be comprehended by Himself, forasmuch as nothing in Himself is hidden from Himself. For Augustine says (*De Vid. Deum.* ep. cxii), *The whole is comprehended when seen, if it is seen in such a way that nothing of it is hidden from the seer.*

REPLY OBJ. 2: When it is said, *God is finite to Himself,* this is to be understood according to a certain similitude of proportion, because He has the same relation in not exceeding His intellect, as anything finite has in not exceeding finite intellect. But God is not to be called finite to Himself in this sense, as if He understood Himself to be something finite.

Article 4

Whether the Act of God's Intellect Is His Substance?

AD QUARTUM SIC PROCEDITUR. Videtur quod ipsum intelligere Dei non sit eius substantia. Intelligere enim est quaedam operatio. Operatio autem aliquid significat procedens ab operante. Ergo ipsum intelligere Dei non est ipsa Dei substantia.

PRAETEREA, cum aliquis intelligit se intelligere, hoc non est intelligere aliquid magnum vel principale intellectum, sed intelligere quoddam secundarium et accessorium. Si igitur Deus sit ipsum intelligere, intelligere Deum erit sicut cum intelligimus intelligere. Et sic non erit aliquid magnum intelligere Deum.

PRAETEREA, omne intelligere est aliquid intelligere. Cum ergo Deus intelligit se, si ipsemet non est aliud quam suum intelligere, intelligit se intelligere, et intelligere se intelligere se, et sic in infinitum. Non ergo ipsum intelligere Dei est eius substantia.

SED CONTRA est quod dicit Augustinus, Lib. VII de Trin., *Deo hoc est esse, quod sapientem esse.* Hoc autem est sapientem esse, quod intelligere. Ergo Deo hoc est esse, quod intelligere. Sed esse Dei est eius substantia, ut supra ostensum est. Ergo intelligere Dei est eius substantia.

RESPONDEO dicendum quod est necesse dicere quod intelligere Dei est eius substantia. Nam si intelligere Dei

OBJECTION 1: It seems that the act of God's intellect is not His substance. For to understand is an operation. But an operation signifies something proceeding from the operator. Therefore the act of God's intellect is not His substance.

OBJ. 2: Further, to understand one's act of understanding, is to understand something that is neither great nor chiefly understood, but secondary and accessory. If therefore God be his own act of understanding, His act of understanding will be as when we understand our act of understanding: and thus God's act of understanding will not be something great.

OBJ. 3: Further, every act of understanding means understanding something. When therefore God understands Himself, if He Himself is not distinct from this act of understanding, He understands that He understands Himself; and so on to infinity. Therefore the act of God's intellect is not His substance.

ON THE CONTRARY, Augustine says (*De Trin.* vii), *In God to be is the same as to be wise.* But to be wise is the same thing as to understand. Therefore in God to be is the same thing as to understand. But God's existence is His substance, as shown above (Q. 3, A. 4). Therefore the act of God's intellect is His substance.

I ANSWER THAT, It must be said that the act of God's intellect is His substance. For if His act of understanding were

sit aliud quam eius substantia, oporteret, ut dicit philosophus in XII Metaphys., quod aliquid aliud esset actus et perfectio substantiae divinae, ad quod se haberet substantia divina sicut potentia ad actum (quod est omnino impossibile), nam intelligere est perfectio et actus intelligentis. Hoc autem qualiter sit, considerandum est. Sicut enim supra dictum est, intelligere non est actio progrediens ad aliquid extrinsecum, sed manet in operante sicut actus et perfectio eius, prout esse est perfectio existentis, sicut enim esse consequitur formam, ita intelligere sequitur speciem intelligibilem. In Deo autem non est forma quae sit aliud quam suum esse, ut supra ostensum est. Unde, cum ipsa sua essentia sit etiam species intelligibilis, ut dictum est, ex necessitate sequitur quod ipsum eius intelligere sit eius essentia et eius esse.

Et sic patet ex omnibus praemissis quod in Deo intellectus, et id quod intelligitur, et species intelligibilis, et ipsum intelligere, sunt omnino unum et idem. Unde patet quod per hoc quod Deus dicitur intelligens, nulla multiplicitas ponitur in eius substantia.

AD PRIMUM ergo dicendum quod intelligere non est operatio exiens ab ipso operante, sed manens in ipso.

AD SECUNDUM dicendum quod, cum intelligitur illud intelligere quod non est subsistens, non intelligitur aliquid magnum; sicut cum intelligimus intelligere nostrum. Et ideo non est simile de ipso intelligere divino, quod est subsistens.

ET PER HOC patet responsio ad tertium. Nam intelligere divinum, quod est in seipso subsistens, est sui ipsius; et non alicuius alterius, ut sic oporteat procedere in infinitum.

other than His substance, then something else, as the Philosopher says (*Metaph.* xii), would be the act and perfection of the divine substance, to which the divine substance would be related, as potentiality is to act, which is altogether impossible; because the act of understanding is the perfection and act of the one understanding. Let us now consider how this is. As was laid down above (A. 2), to understand is not an act passing to anything extrinsic; for it remains in the operator as his own act and perfection; as existence is the perfection of the one existing: just as existence follows on the form, so in like manner to understand follows on the intelligible species. Now in God there is no form which is something other than His existence, as shown above (Q. 3). Hence as His essence itself is also His intelligible species, it necessarily follows that His act of understanding must be His essence and His existence.

Thus it follows from all the foregoing that in God, intellect, and the object understood, and the intelligible species, and His act of understanding are entirely one and the same. Hence when God is said to be understanding, no kind of multiplicity is attached to His substance.

REPLY OBJ. 1: To understand is not an operation proceeding out of the operator, but remaining in him.

REPLY OBJ. 2: When that act of understanding which is not subsistent is understood, something not great is understood; as when we understand our act of understanding; and so this cannot be likened to the act of the divine understanding which is subsistent.

THUS appears the Reply to the Third Objection. For the act of divine understanding subsists in itself, and belongs to its very self and is not another's; hence it need not proceed to infinity.

Article 5

Whether God Knows Things Other Than Himself?

AD QUINTUM SIC PROCEDITUR. Videtur quod Deus non cognoscat alia a se. Quaecumque enim sunt alia a Deo, sunt extra ipsum. Sed Augustinus dicit, in libro octoginta trium qu., quod *neque quidquam Deus extra seipsum intuetur.* Ergo non cognoscit alia a se.

PRAETEREA, intellectum est perfectio intelligentis. Si ergo Deus intelligat alia a se, aliquid aliud erit perfectio Dei, et nobilius ipso. Quod est impossibile.

PRAETEREA, ipsum intelligere speciem habet ab intelligibili, sicut et omnis alius actus a suo obiecto, unde et ipsum intelligere tanto est nobilius, quanto etiam nobilius est ipsum quod intelligitur. Sed Deus est ipsum suum intelligere, ut ex dictis patet. Si igitur Deus

OBJECTION 1: It seems that God does not know things besides Himself. For all other things but God are outside of God. But Augustine says (*Octog. Tri. Quaest.* qu. xlvi) that *God does not behold anything out of Himself.* Therefore He does not know things other than Himself.

OBJ. 2: Further, the object understood is the perfection of the one who understands. If therefore God understands other things besides Himself, something else will be the perfection of God, and will be nobler than He; which is impossible.

OBJ. 3: Further, the act of understanding is specified by the intelligible object, as is every other act from its own object. Hence the intellectual act is so much the nobler, the nobler the object understood. But God is His own intellectual act. If therefore God understands anything other than

intelligit aliquid aliud a se, ipse Deus specificatur per aliquid aliud a se, quod est impossibile. Non igitur intelligit alia a se.

SED CONTRA est quod dicitur Hebr. IV, *omnia nuda et aperta sunt oculis eius.*

RESPONDEO dicendum quod necesse est Deum cognoscere alia a se. Manifestum est enim quod seipsum perfecte intelligit, alioquin suum esse non esset perfectum, cum suum esse sit suum intelligere. Si autem perfecte aliquid cognoscitur, necesse est quod virtus eius perfecte cognoscatur. Virtus autem alicuius rei perfecte cognosci non potest, nisi cognoscantur ea ad quae virtus se extendit. Unde, cum virtus divina se extendat ad alia, eo quod ipsa est prima causa effectiva omnium entium, ut ex supradictis patet; necesse est quod Deus alia a se cognoscat. Et hoc etiam evidentius fit, si adiungatur quod ipsum esse causae agentis primae, scilicet Dei, est eius intelligere. Unde quicumque effectus praeexistunt in Deo sicut in causa prima, necesse est quod sint in ipso eius intelligere; et quod omnia in eo sint secundum modum intelligibilem, nam omne quod est in altero, est in eo secundum modum eius in quo est.

Ad sciendum autem qualiter alia a se cognoscat, considerandum est quod dupliciter aliquid cognoscitur, uno modo, in seipso; alio modo, in altero. In seipso quidem cognoscitur aliquid, quando cognoscitur per speciem propriam adaequatam ipsi cognoscibili, sicut cum oculus videt hominem per speciem hominis. In alio autem videtur id quod videtur per speciem continentis, sicut cum pars videtur in toto per speciem totius, vel cum homo videtur in speculo per speciem speculi, vel quocumque alio modo contingat aliquid in alio videri.

Sic igitur dicendum est quod Deus seipsum videt in seipso, quia seipsum videt per essentiam suam. Alia autem a se videt non in ipsis, sed in seipso, inquantum essentia sua continet similitudinem aliorum ab ipso.

AD PRIMUM ergo dicendum quod verbum Augustini dicentis quod Deus nihil extra se intuetur, non est sic intelligendum, quasi nihil quod sit extra se intueatur, sed quia id quod est extra seipsum, non intuetur nisi in seipso, ut dictum est.

AD SECUNDUM dicendum quod intellectum est perfectio intelligentis non quidem secundum suam substantiam, sed secundum suam speciem, secundum quam est in intellectu, ut forma et perfectio eius, *lapis enim non est in anima, sed species eius*, ut dicitur in III de anima. Ea vero quae sunt alia a Deo, intelliguntur a Deo inquantum essentia Dei continet species eorum, ut dictum est. Unde non sequitur quod aliquid aliud sit perfectio divini intellectus, quam ipsa essentia Dei.

AD TERTIUM dicendum quod ipsum intelligere non specificatur per id quod in alio intelligitur, sed per

Himself, then God Himself is specified by something else than Himself; which cannot be. Therefore He does not understand things other than Himself.

ON THE CONTRARY, It is written: *All things are naked and open to His eyes* (Heb 4:13).

I ANSWER THAT, God necessarily knows things other than Himself. For it is manifest that He perfectly understands Himself; otherwise His existence would not be perfect, since His existence is His act of understanding. Now if anything is perfectly known, it follows of necessity that its power is perfectly known. But the power of anything can be perfectly known only by knowing to what its power extends. Since therefore the divine power extends to other things by the very fact that it is the first effective cause of all things, as is clear from the aforesaid (Q. 2, A. 3), God must necessarily know things other than Himself. And this appears still more plainly if we add that the very existence of the first effective cause—viz., God—is His own act of understanding. Hence whatever effects pre-exist in God, as in the first cause, must be in His act of understanding, and all things must be in Him according to an intelligible mode: for everything which is in another, is in it according to the mode of that in which it is.

Now in order to know how God knows things other than Himself, we must consider that a thing is known in two ways: in itself, and in another. A thing is known in itself when it is known by the proper species adequate to the knowable object; as when the eye sees a man through the image of a man. A thing is seen in another through the image of that which contains it; as when a part is seen in the whole by the image of the whole; or when a man is seen in a mirror by the image in the mirror, or by any other mode by which one thing is seen in another.

So we say that God sees Himself in Himself, because He sees Himself through His essence; and He sees other things not in themselves, but in Himself, inasmuch as His essence contains the similitude of things other than Himself.

REPLY OBJ. 1: The passage of Augustine in which it is said that God *sees nothing outside Himself* is not to be taken in such a way, as if God saw nothing outside Himself, but in the sense that what is outside Himself He does not see except in Himself, as above explained.

REPLY OBJ. 2: The object understood is a perfection of the one understanding not by its substance, but by its image, according to which it is in the intellect, as its form and perfection, as is said in *De Anima* iii. For *a stone is not in the soul, but its image.* Now those things which are other than God are understood by God, inasmuch as the essence of God contains their images as above explained; hence it does not follow that there is any perfection in the divine intellect other than the divine essence.

REPLY OBJ. 3: The intellectual act is not specified by what is understood in another, but by the principal object

principale intellectum, in quo alia intelliguntur. Intantum enim ipsum intelligere specificatur per obiectum suum, inquantum forma intelligibilis est principium intellectualis operationis, nam omnis operatio specificatur per formam quae est principium operationis, sicut calefactio per calorem. Unde per illam formam intelligibilem specificatur intellectualis operatio, quae facit intellectum in actu. Et haec est species principalis intellecti, quae in Deo nihil est aliud quam essentia sua, in qua omnes species rerum comprehenduntur. Unde non oportet quod ipsum intelligere divinum, vel potius ipse Deus, specificetur per aliud quam per essentiam divinam.

understood in which other things are understood. For the intellectual act is specified by its object, inasmuch as the intelligible form is the principle of the intellectual operation: since every operation is specified by the form which is its principle of operation; as heating by heat. Hence the intellectual operation is specified by that intelligible form which makes the intellect in act. And this is the image of the principal thing understood, which in God is nothing but His own essence in which all images of things are comprehended. Hence it does not follow that the divine intellectual act, or rather God Himself, is specified by anything else than the divine essence itself.

Article 6

Whether God Knows Things Other Than Himself by Proper Knowledge?

AD SEXTUM SIC PROCEDITUR. Videtur quod Deus non cognoscat alia a se propria cognitione. Sic enim cognoscit alia a se, ut dictum est, secundum quod alia ab ipso in eo sunt. Sed alia ab eo sunt in ipso sicut in prima causa communi et universali. Ergo et alia cognoscuntur a Deo, sicut in causa prima et universali. Hoc autem est cognoscere in universali, et non secundum propriam cognitionem. Ergo Deus cognoscit alia a se in universali, et non secundum propriam cognitionem.

PRAETEREA, quantum distat essentia creaturae ab essentia divina, tantum distat essentia divina ab essentia creaturae. Sed per essentiam creaturae non potest cognosci essentia divina, ut supra dictum est. Ergo nec per essentiam divinam potest cognosci essentia creaturae. Et sic, cum Deus nihil cognoscat nisi per essentiam suam, sequitur quod non cognoscat creaturam secundum eius essentiam, ut cognoscat de ea quid est, quod est propriam cognitionem de re habere.

PRAETEREA, propria cognitio non habetur de re, nisi per propriam eius rationem. Sed cum Deus cognoscat omnia per essentiam suam, non videtur quod unumquodque per propriam rationem cognoscat, idem enim non potest esse propria ratio multorum et diversorum. Non ergo habet propriam cognitionem Deus de rebus, sed communem, nam cognoscere res non secundum propriam rationem, est cognoscere res solum in communi.

SED CONTRA, habere propriam cognitionem de rebus, est cognoscere res non solum in communi, sed secundum quod sunt ab invicem distinctae. Sic autem Deus cognoscit res. Unde dicitur Heb. IV, quod *pertingit usque ad divisionem spiritus et animae, compagum quoque et medullarum; et discretor cogitationum et intentionum cordis; et non est ulla creatura invisibilis in conspectu eius.*

OBJECTION 1: It seems that God does not know things other than Himself by proper knowledge. For, as was shown (A. 5), God knows things other than Himself, according as they are in Himself. But other things are in Him as in their common and universal cause, and are known by God as in their first and universal cause. This is to know them by general, and not by proper knowledge. Therefore God knows things besides Himself by general, and not by proper knowledge.

OBJ. 2: Further, the created essence is as distant from the divine essence, as the divine essence is distant from the created essence. But the divine essence cannot be known by the created essence, as said above (Q. 12, A. 2). Therefore neither can the created essence be known by the divine essence. Thus as God knows only by His essence, it follows that He does not know what the creature is in its essence, so as to know *what it is*, which is to have proper knowledge of it.

OBJ. 3: Further, proper knowledge of a thing can come only through its proper ratio. But as God knows all things by His essence, it seems that He does not know each thing by its proper ratio; for one thing cannot be the proper ratio of many and diverse things. Therefore God has not a proper knowledge of things, but a general knowledge; for to know things otherwise than by their proper ratio is to have only a common and general knowledge of them.

ON THE CONTRARY, To have a proper knowledge of things is to know them not only in general, but as they are distinct from each other. Now God knows things in that manner. Hence it is written that He reaches *even to the division of the soul and the spirit, of the joints also and the marrow, and is a discerner of thoughts and intents of the heart; neither is there any creature invisible in His sight* (Heb 4:12,13).

RESPONDEO dicendum quod circa hoc quidam erraverunt, dicentes quod Deus alia a se non cognoscit nisi in communi, scilicet inquantum sunt entia. Sicut enim ignis, si cognosceret seipsum ut est principium caloris, cognosceret naturam caloris, et omnia alia inquantum sunt calida; ita Deus, inquantum cognoscit se ut principium essendi, cognoscit naturam entis, et omnia alia inquantum sunt entia.

Sed hoc non potest esse. Nam intelligere aliquid in communi, et non in speciali, est imperfecte aliquid cognoscere. Unde intellectus noster, dum de potentia in actum reducitur, pertingit prius ad cognitionem universalem et confusam de rebus, quam ad propriam rerum cognitionem, sicut de imperfecto ad perfectum procedens, ut patet in I Physic. Si igitur cognitio Dei de rebus aliis a se, esset in universali tantum, et non in speciali, sequeretur quod eius intelligere non esset omnibus modis perfectum, et per consequens nec eius esse, quod est contra ea quae superius ostensa sunt. Oportet igitur dicere quod alia a se cognoscat propria cognitione; non solum secundum quod communicant in ratione entis, sed secundum quod unum ab alio distinguitur. Et ad huius evidentiam, considerandum est quod quidam, volentes ostendere quod Deus per unum cognoscit multa, utuntur quibusdam exemplis, ut puta quod, si centrum cognosceret seipsum, cognosceret omnes lineas progredientes a centro; vel lux, si cognosceret seipsam, cognosceret omnes colores.

Sed haec exempla, licet quantum ad aliquid similia sint, scilicet quantum ad universalem causalitatem; tamen deficiunt quantum ad hoc, quod multitudo et diversitas non causantur ab illo uno principio universali, quantum ad id quod principium distinctionis est, sed solum quantum ad id in quo communicant. Non enim diversitas colorum causatur ex luce solum, sed ex diversa dispositione diaphani recipientis, et similiter diversitas linearum ex diverso situ. Et inde est quod huiusmodi diversitas et multitudo non potest cognosci in suo principio secundum propriam cognitionem, sed solum in communi. Sed in Deo non sic est. Supra enim ostensum est quod quidquid perfectionis est in quacumque creatura, totum praeexistit et continetur in Deo secundum modum excellentem. Non solum autem id in quo creaturae communicant, scilicet ipsum esse, ad perfectionem pertinet; sed etiam ea per quae creaturae ad invicem distinguuntur, sicut vivere, et intelligere, et huiusmodi, quibus viventia a non viventibus, et intelligentia a non intelligentibus distinguuntur. Et omnis forma, per quam quaelibet res in propria specie constituitur, perfectio quaedam est. Et sic omnia in Deo praeexistunt, non solum quantum ad id quod commune est omnibus, sed etiam quantum ad ea secundum quae res distinguuntur. Et sic, cum Deus in se omnes perfectiones contineat, comparatur Dei essentia ad omnes rerum

I ANSWER THAT, Some have erred on this point, saying that God knows things other than Himself only in general, that is, only as beings. For as fire, if it knew itself as the principle of heat, would know the nature of heat, and all things else in so far as they are hot; so God, through knowing Himself as the principle of being, knows the nature of being, and all other things in so far as they are beings.

But this cannot be. For to know a thing in general and not in particular, is to have an imperfect knowledge. Hence our intellect, when it is reduced from potentiality to act, acquires first a universal and confused knowledge of things before it knows them in particular; as proceeding from the imperfect to the perfect, as is clear from *Phys.* i. If therefore the knowledge of God regarding things other than Himself is only universal and not special, it would follow that His understanding would not be absolutely perfect; therefore neither would His being be perfect; and this is against what was said above (Q. 4, A. 1). We must therefore hold that God knows things other than Himself with a proper knowledge; not only in so far as being is common to them, but in so far as one is distinguished from the other. In proof thereof we may observe that some wishing to show that God knows many things by one, bring forward some examples, as, for instance, that if the centre knew itself, it would know all lines that proceed from the centre; or if light knew itself, it would know all colors.

Now these examples, although similar in part, namely, as regards universal causality, nevertheless fail in this respect, that multitude and diversity are caused by the one universal principle, not as regards that which is the principle of distinction, but only as regards that in which they communicate. For the diversity of colors is not caused by the light only, but by the different disposition of the diaphanous medium which receives it; and likewise, the diversity of the lines is caused by their different position. Hence it is that this kind of diversity and multitude cannot be known in its principle by proper knowledge, but only in a general way. In God, however, it is otherwise. For it was shown above (Q. 4, A. 2) that whatever perfection exists in any creature, wholly pre-exists and is contained in God in an excelling manner. Now not only what is common to creatures—viz., being—belongs to their perfection, but also what makes them distinguished from each other; as living and understanding, and the like, whereby living beings are distinguished from the non-living, and the intelligent from the non-intelligent. Likewise every form whereby each thing is constituted in its own species, is a perfection; and thus all things pre-exist in God, not only as regards what is common to all, but also as regards what distinguishes one thing from another. And therefore as God contains all perfections in Himself, the essence of God is compared to all other essences of things, not as the common to the proper,

essentias, non sicut commune ad propria, ut unitas ad numeros, vel centrum ad lineas; sed sicut perfectus actus ad imperfectos, ut si dicerem, homo ad animal, vel senarius, qui est numerus perfectus, ad numeros imperfectos sub ipso contentos. Manifestum est autem quod per actum perfectum cognosci possunt actus imperfecti, non solum in communi, sed etiam propria cognitione. Sicut qui cognoscit hominem, cognoscit animal propria cognitione, et qui cognoscit senarium, cognoscit trinarium propria cognitione.

Sic igitur, cum essentia Dei habeat in se quidquid perfectionis habet essentia cuiuscumque rei alterius, et adhuc amplius, Deus in seipso potest omnia propria cognitione cognoscere. Propria enim natura uniuscuiusque consistit, secundum quod per aliquem modum divinam perfectionem participat. Non autem Deus perfecte seipsum cognosceret, nisi cognosceret quomodocumque participabilis est ab aliis sua perfectio, nec etiam ipsam naturam essendi perfecte sciret, nisi cognosceret omnes modos essendi. Unde manifestum est quod Deus cognoscit omnes res propria cognitione, secundum quod ab aliis distinguuntur.

AD PRIMUM ergo dicendum quod sic cognoscere aliquid sicut in cognoscente est, potest dupliciter intelligi. Uno modo, secundum quod hoc adverbium sic importat modum cognitionis ex parte rei cognitae. Et sic falsum est. Non enim semper cognoscens cognoscit cognitum secundum illud esse quod habet in cognoscente, oculus enim non cognoscit lapidem secundum esse quod habet in oculo; sed per speciem lapidis quam habet in se, cognoscit lapidem secundum esse quod habet extra oculum. Et si aliquis cognoscens cognoscat cognitum secundum esse quod habet in cognoscente, nihilominus cognoscit ipsum secundum esse quod habet extra cognoscentem, sicut intellectus cognoscit lapidem secundum esse intelligibile quod habet in intellectu, inquantum cognoscit se intelligere; sed nihilominus cognoscit esse lapidis in propria natura. Si vero intelligatur secundum quod hoc adverbium sic importat modum ex parte cognoscentis, verum est quod sic solum cognoscens cognoscit cognitum, secundum quod est in cognoscente, quia quanto perfectius est cognitum in cognoscente, tanto perfectior est modus cognitionis.

Sic igitur dicendum est quod Deus non solum cognoscit res esse in seipso; sed per id quod in seipso continet res, cognoscit eas in propria natura; et tanto perfectius, quanto perfectius est unumquodque in ipso.

AD SECUNDUM dicendum quod essentia creaturae comparatur ad essentiam Dei, ut actus imperfectus ad perfectum. Et ideo essentia creaturae non sufficienter ducit in cognitionem essentiae divinae, sed e converso.

AD TERTIUM dicendum quod idem non potest accipi ut ratio diversorum per modum adaequationis. Sed divina essentia est aliquid excedens omnes creaturas.

as unity is to numbers, or as the centre (of a circle) to the (radiating) lines; but as perfect acts to imperfect; as if I were to compare man to animal; or six, a perfect number, to the imperfect numbers contained under it. Now it is manifest that by a perfect act, imperfect acts can be known not only in general, but also by proper knowledge; thus, for example, whoever knows a man, knows an animal by proper knowledge; and whoever knows the number six, knows the number three also by proper knowledge.

As therefore the essence of God contains in itself all the perfection contained in the essence of any other being, and far more, God can know in Himself all of them with proper knowledge. For the nature proper to each thing consists in some degree of participation in the divine perfection. Now God could not be said to know Himself perfectly unless He knew all the ways in which His own perfection can be shared by others. Neither could He know the very nature of being perfectly, unless He knew all modes of being. Hence it is manifest that God knows all things with proper knowledge, in their distinction from each other.

REPLY OBJ. 1: So to know a thing as it is in the knower, may be understood in two ways. In one way this adverb *so* imports the mode of knowledge on the part of the thing known; and in that sense it is false. For the knower does not always know the object known according to the existence it has in the knower; since the eye does not know a stone according to the existence it has in the eye; but by the image of the stone which is in the eye, the eye knows the stone according to its existence outside the eye. And if any knower has a knowledge of the object known according to the (mode of) existence it has in the knower, the knower nevertheless knows it according to its (mode of) existence outside the knower; thus the intellect knows a stone according to the intelligible existence it has in the intellect, inasmuch as it knows that it understands; while nevertheless it knows what a stone is in its own nature. If however the adverb 'so' be understood to import the mode (of knowledge) on the part of the knower, in that sense it is true that only the knower has knowledge of the object known as it is in the knower; for the more perfectly the thing known is in the knower, the more perfect is the mode of knowledge.

We must say therefore that God not only knows that all things are in Himself; but by the fact that they are in Him, He knows them in their own nature and all the more perfectly, the more perfectly each one is in Him.

REPLY OBJ. 2: The created essence is compared to the essence of God as the imperfect to the perfect act. Therefore the created essence cannot sufficiently lead us to the knowledge of the divine essence, but rather the converse.

REPLY OBJ. 3: The same thing cannot be taken in an equal manner as the ratio of different things. But the divine essence excels all creatures. Hence it can be taken as the

Unde potest accipi ut propria ratio uniuscuiusque, secundum quod diversimode est participabilis vel imitabilis a diversis creaturis.

proper ratio of each thing according to the diverse ways in which diverse creatures participate in, and imitate it.

Article 7

Whether the Knowledge of God Is Discursive?

AD SEPTIMUM SIC PROCEDITUR. Videtur quod scientia Dei sit discursiva. Scientia enim Dei non est secundum scire in habitu, sed secundum intelligere in actu. Sed secundum philosophum, in II Topic., *scire in habitu contingit multa simul, sed intelligere actu unum tantum.* Cum ergo Deus multa cognoscat, quia et se et alia, ut ostensum est, videtur quod non simul omnia intelligat, sed de uno in aliud discurrat.

PRAETEREA, cognoscere effectum per causam est scire discurrentis. Sed Deus cognoscit alia per seipsum, sicut effectum per causam. Ergo cognitio sua est discursiva.

PRAETEREA, perfectius Deus scit unamquamque creaturam quam nos sciamus. Sed nos in causis creatis cognoscimus earum effectus, et sic de causis ad causata discurrimus. Ergo videtur similiter esse in Deo.

SED CONTRA est quod Augustinus dicit, in XV de Trin., quod *Deus non particulatim vel singillatim omnia videt, velut alternante conspectu hinc illuc, et inde huc; sed omnia videt simul.*

RESPONDEO dicendum quod in scientia divina nullus est discursus. Quod sic patet. In scientia enim nostra duplex est discursus. Unus secundum successionem tantum, sicut cum, postquam intelligimus aliquid in actu, convertimus nos ad intelligendum aliud. Alius discursus est secundum causalitatem, sicut cum per principia pervenimus in cognitionem conclusionum. Primus autem discursus Deo convenire non potest. Multa enim, quae successive intelligimus si unumquodque eorum in seipso consideretur, omnia simul intelligimus si in aliquo uno ea intelligamus, puta si partes intelligamus in toto, vel si diversas res videamus in speculo. Deus autem omnia videt in uno, quod est ipse, ut habitum est. Unde simul, et non successive omnia videt. Similiter etiam et secundus discursus Deo competere non potest. Primo quidem, quia secundus discursus praesupponit primum, procedentes enim a principiis ad conclusiones, non simul utrumque considerant. Deinde, quia discursus talis est procedentis de noto ad ignotum. Unde manifestum est quod, quando cognoscitur primum, adhuc ignoratur secundum. Et sic secundum non cognoscitur in primo, sed ex primo. Terminus vero discursus est, quando secundum videtur in primo, resolutis effectibus in causas,

OBJECTION 1: It seems that the knowledge of God is discursive. For the knowledge of God is not habitual knowledge, but actual knowledge. Now the Philosopher says (*Topic.* ii): *The habit of knowledge may regard many things at once; but actual understanding regards only one thing at a time.* Therefore as God knows many things, Himself and others, as shown above (AA. 2, 5), it seems that He does not understand all at once, but discourses from one to another.

OBJ. 2: Further, discursive knowledge is to know the effect through its cause. But God knows things through Himself, as an effect (is known) through its cause. Therefore His knowledge is discursive.

OBJ. 3: Further, God knows each creature more perfectly than we know it. But we know the effects in their created causes; and thus we go discursively from causes to things caused. Therefore it seems that the same applies to God.

ON THE CONTRARY, Augustine says (*De Trin.* xv), *God does not see all things in their particularity or separately, as if He saw alternately here and there; but He sees all things together at once.*

I ANSWER THAT, In the divine knowledge there is no discursion; the proof of which is as follows. In our knowledge there is a twofold discursion: one is according to succession only, as when we have actually understood anything, we turn ourselves to understand something else; while the other mode of discursion is according to causality, as when through principles we arrive at the knowledge of conclusions. The first kind of discursion cannot belong to God. For many things, which we understand in succession if each is considered in itself, we understand simultaneously if we see them in some one thing; if, for instance, we understand the parts in the whole, or see different things in a mirror. Now God sees all things in one (thing), which is Himself. Therefore God sees all things together, and not successively. Likewise the second mode of discursion cannot be applied to God. First, because this second mode of discursion presupposes the first mode; for whosoever proceeds from principles to conclusions does not consider both at once; second, because to discourse thus is to proceed from the known to the unknown. Hence it is manifest that when the first is known, the second is still unknown; and thus the second is known not in the first, but from the first. Now the term of discursive reasoning is attained when

et tunc cessat discursus. Unde, cum Deus effectus suos in seipso videat sicut in causa, eius cognitio non est discursiva.

AD PRIMUM ergo dicendum quod, licet sit unum tantum intelligere in seipso, tamen contingit multa intelligere in aliquo uno, ut dictum est.

AD SECUNDUM dicendum quod Deus non cognoscit per causam quasi prius cognitam, effectus incognitos, sed eos cognoscit in causa. Unde eius cognitio est sine discursu, ut dictum est.

AD TERTIUM dicendum quod effectus causarum creatarum videt quidem Deus in ipsis causis, multo melius quam nos, non tamen ita quod cognitio effectuum causetur in ipso ex cognitione causarum creatarum, sicut in nobis. Unde eius scientia non est discursiva.

the second is seen in the first, by resolving the effects into their causes; and then the discursion ceases. Hence as God sees His effects in Himself as their cause, His knowledge is not discursive.

REPLY OBJ. 1: Although there is only one act of understanding in itself, nevertheless many things may be understood in one (medium), as shown above.

REPLY OBJ. 2: God does not know by their cause, known, as it were previously, effects unknown; but He knows the effects in the cause; and hence His knowledge is not discursive, as was shown above.

REPLY OBJ. 3: God sees the effects of created causes in the causes themselves, much better than we can; but still not in such a manner that the knowledge of the effects is caused in Him by the knowledge of the created causes, as is the case with us; and hence His knowledge is not discursive.

Article 8

Whether the Knowledge of God Is the Cause of Things?

AD OCTAVUM SIC PROCEDITUR. Videtur quod scientia Dei non sit causa rerum. Dicit enim Origenes, super epistolam ad Rom., *non propterea aliquid erit, quia id scit Deus futurum; sed quia futurum est, ideo scitur a Deo antequam fiat.*

PRAETEREA, posita causa ponitur effectus. Sed scientia Dei est aeterna. Si ergo scientia Dei est causa rerum creatarum, videtur quod creaturae sint ab aeterno.

PRAETEREA, scibile est prius scientia, et mensura eius, ut dicitur in X Metaphys. Sed id quod est posterius et mensuratum, non potest esse causa. Ergo scientia Dei non est causa rerum.

SED CONTRA est quod dicit Augustinus, XV de Trin., *universas creaturas, et spirituales et corporales, non quia sunt, ideo novit Deus; sed ideo sunt, quia novit.*

RESPONDEO dicendum quod scientia Dei est causa rerum. Sic enim scientia Dei se habet ad omnes res creatas, sicut scientia artificis se habet ad artificiata. Scientia autem artificis est causa artificiatorum, eo quod artifex operatur per suum intellectum, unde oportet quod forma intellectus sit principium operationis, sicut calor est principium calefactionis. Sed considerandum est quod forma naturalis, inquantum est forma manens in eo cui dat esse, non nominat principium actionis; sed secundum quod habet inclinationem ad effectum. Et similiter forma intelligibilis non nominat principium actionis secundum quod est tantum in intelligente, nisi adiungatur ei inclinatio ad effectum, quae est per voluntatem. Cum enim forma intelligibilis ad opposita se habeat (cum sit eadem scientia oppositorum), non produceret

OBJECTION 1: It seems that the knowledge of God is not the cause of things. For Origen says, on Rom. 8:30, *Whom He called, them He also justified*, etc.: *A thing will happen not because God knows it as future; but because it is future, it is on that account known by God, before it exists.*

OBJ. 2: Further, given the cause, the effect follows. But the knowledge of God is eternal. Therefore if the knowledge of God is the cause of things created, it seems that creatures are eternal.

OBJ. 3: Further, *The thing known is prior to knowledge, and is its measure*, as the Philosopher says (*Metaph.* x). But what is posterior and measured cannot be a cause. Therefore the knowledge of God is not the cause of things.

ON THE CONTRARY, Augustine says (*De Trin.* xv), *Not because they are, does God know all creatures spiritual and temporal, but because He knows them, therefore they are.*

I ANSWER THAT, The knowledge of God is the cause of things. For the knowledge of God is to all creatures what the knowledge of the artificer is to things made by his art. Now the knowledge of the artificer is the cause of the things made by his art from the fact that the artificer works by his intellect. Hence the form of the intellect must be the principle of action, as heat is the principle of heating. Nevertheless, we must observe that a natural form, being a form that remains in that to which it gives existence, denotes a principle of action according only as it has an inclination to an effect; and likewise, the intelligible form does not denote a principle of action in so far as it resides in the one who understands unless there is added to it the inclination to an effect, which inclination is through the will. For since the intelligible form has a relation to opposite things

determinatum effectum, nisi determinaretur ad unum per appetitum, ut dicitur in IX Metaphys. Manifestum est autem quod Deus per intellectum suum causat res, cum suum esse sit suum intelligere. Unde necesse est quod sua scientia sit causa rerum, secundum quod habet voluntatem coniunctam. Unde scientia Dei, secundum quod est causa rerum, consuevit nominari scientia approbationis.

Ad primum ergo dicendum quod Origenes locutus est attendens rationem scientiae, cui non competit ratio causalitatis, nisi adiuncta voluntate, ut dictum est.

Sed quod dicit ideo praescire Deum aliqua, quia sunt futura, intelligendum est secundum causam consequentiae, non secundum causam essendi. Sequitur enim, si aliqua sunt futura, quod Deus ea praescierit, non tamen res futurae sunt causa quod Deus sciat.

Ad secundum dicendum quod scientia Dei est causa rerum, secundum quod res sunt in scientia. Non fuit autem in scientia Dei, quod res essent ab aeterno. Unde, quamvis scientia Dei sit aeterna, non sequitur tamen quod creaturae sint ab aeterno.

Ad tertium dicendum quod res naturales sunt mediae inter scientiam Dei et scientiam nostram, nos enim scientiam accipimus a rebus naturalibus, quarum Deus per suam scientiam causa est. Unde, sicut scibilia naturalia sunt priora quam scientia nostra, et mensura eius, ita scientia Dei est prior quam res naturales, et mensura ipsarum. Sicut aliqua domus est media inter scientiam artificis qui eam fecit, et scientiam illius qui eius cognitionem ex ipsa iam facta capit.

(inasmuch as the same knowledge relates to opposites), it would not produce a determinate effect unless it were determined to one thing by the appetite, as the Philosopher says (*Metaph.* ix). Now it is manifest that God causes things by His intellect, since His being is His act of understanding; and hence His knowledge must be the cause of things, in so far as His will is joined to it. Hence the knowledge of God as the cause of things is usually called the *knowledge of approbation*.

Reply Obj. 1: Origen spoke in reference to that aspect of knowledge to which the idea of causality does not belong unless the will is joined to it, as is said above.

But when he says the reason why God foreknows some things is because they are future, this must be understood according to the cause of consequence, and not according to the cause of essence. For if things are in the future, it follows that God knows them; but not that the futurity of things is the cause why God knows them.

Reply Obj. 2: The knowledge of God is the cause of things according as things are in His knowledge. Now that things should be eternal was not in the knowledge of God; hence although the knowledge of God is eternal, it does not follow that creatures are eternal.

Reply Obj. 3: Natural things are midway between the knowledge of God and our knowledge: for we receive knowledge from natural things, of which God is the cause by His knowledge. Hence, as the natural objects of knowledge are prior to our knowledge, and are its measure, so, the knowledge of God is prior to natural things, and is the measure of them; as, for instance, a house is midway between the knowledge of the builder who made it, and the knowledge of the one who gathers his knowledge of the house from the house already built.

Article 9

Whether God Has Knowledge of Things That Are Not?

Ad nonum sic proceditur. Videtur quod Deus non habeat scientiam non entium. Scientia enim Dei non est nisi verorum. Sed verum et ens convertuntur. Ergo scientia Dei non est non entium.

Praeterea, scientia requirit similitudinem inter scientem et scitum. Sed ea quae non sunt, non possunt habere aliquam similitudinem ad Deum, qui est ipsum esse. Ergo ea quae non sunt, non possunt sciri a Deo.

Praeterea, scientia Dei est causa scitorum ab ipso. Sed non est causa non entium, quia non ens non habet causam. Ergo Deus non habet scientiam de non entibus.

Sed contra est quod dicit apostolus ad Rom. IV, *qui vocat ea quae non sunt, tanquam ea quae sunt.*

Objection 1: It seems that God has not knowledge of things that are not. For the knowledge of God is of true things. But *truth* and *being* are convertible terms. Therefore the knowledge of God is not of things that are not.

Obj. 2: Further, knowledge requires likeness between the knower and the thing known. But those things that are not cannot have any likeness to God, Who is very being. Therefore what is not, cannot be known by God.

Obj. 3: Further, the knowledge of God is the cause of what is known by Him. But it is not the cause of things that are not, because a thing that is not, has no cause. Therefore God has no knowledge of things that are not.

On the contrary, The Apostle says: *Who . . . calleth those things that are not as those that are* (Rom 4:17).

RESPONDEO dicendum quod Deus scit omnia quaecumque sunt quocumque modo. Nihil autem prohibet ea quae non sunt simpliciter, aliquo modo esse. Simpliciter enim sunt, quae actu sunt. Ea vero quae non sunt actu, sunt in potentia vel ipsius Dei, vel creaturae; sive in potentia activa, sive in passiva, sive in potentia opinandi, vel imaginandi, vel quocumque modo significandi. Quaecumque igitur possunt per creaturam fieri vel cogitari vel dici, et etiam quaecumque ipse facere potest, omnia cognoscit Deus, etiam si actu non sint. Et pro tanto dici potest quod habet etiam non entium scientiam.

Sed horum quae actu non sunt, est attendenda quaedam diversitas. Quaedam enim, licet non sint nunc in actu, tamen vel fuerunt vel erunt, et omnia ista dicitur Deus scire scientia visionis. Quia, cum intelligere Dei, quod est eius esse, aeternitate mensuretur, quae sine successione existens totum tempus comprehendit, praesens intuitus Dei fertur in totum tempus, et in omnia quae sunt in quocumque tempore, sicut in subiecta sibi praesentialiter. Quaedam vero sunt, quae sunt in potentia Dei vel creaturae, quae tamen nec sunt nec erunt neque fuerunt. Et respectu horum non dicitur habere scientiam visionis, sed simplicis intelligentiae. Quod ideo dicitur, quia ea quae videntur apud nos, habent esse distinctum extra videntem.

AD PRIMUM ergo dicendum quod, secundum quod sunt in potentia, sic habent veritatem ea quae non sunt actu, verum est enim ea esse in potentia. Et sic sciuntur a Deo.

AD SECUNDUM dicendum quod, cum Deus sit ipsum esse, intantum unumquodque est, inquantum participat de Dei similitudine, sicut unumquodque intantum est calidum, inquantum participat calorem. Sic et ea quae sunt in potentia, etiam si non sunt in actu, cognoscuntur a Deo.

AD TERTIUM dicendum quod Dei scientia est causa rerum, voluntate adiuncta. Unde non oportet quod quaecumque scit Deus, sint vel fuerint vel futura sint, sed solum ea quae vult esse, vel permittit esse. Et iterum, non est in scientia Dei ut illa sint, sed quod esse possint.

I ANSWER THAT, God knows all things whatsoever that in any way are. Now it is possible that things that are not absolutely, should be in a certain sense. For things absolutely are which are actual; whereas things which are not actual, are in the power either of God Himself or of a creature, whether in active power, or passive; whether in power of thought or of imagination, or of any other manner of meaning whatsoever. Whatever therefore can be made, or thought, or said by the creature, as also whatever He Himself can do, all are known to God, although they are not actual. And in so far it can be said that He has knowledge even of things that are not.

Now a certain difference is to be noted in the consideration of those things that are not actual. For though some of them may not be in act now, still they were, or they will be; and God is said to know all these with the knowledge of vision: for since God's act of understanding, which is His being, is measured by eternity; and since eternity is without succession, comprehending all time, the present glance of God extends over all time, and to all things which exist in any time, as to objects present to Him. But there are other things in God's power, or the creature's, which nevertheless are not, nor will be, nor were; and as regards these He is said to have knowledge, not of vision, but of simple intelligence. This is so called because the things we see around us have distinct being outside the seer.

REPLY OBJ. 1: Those things that are not actual are true in so far as they are in potentiality; for it is true that they are in potentiality; and as such they are known by God.

REPLY OBJ. 2: Since God is very being, everything is, in so far as it participates in the likeness of God, as everything is hot in so far as it participates in heat. So, things in potentiality are known by God, although they are not in act.

REPLY OBJ. 3: The knowledge of God, joined to His will, is the cause of things. Hence it is not necessary that whatever God knows, is, or was, or will be; but only is this necessary as regards what He wills to be, or permits to be. Further, it is in the knowledge of God not that they be, but that they be possible.

Article 10

Whether God Knows Evil Things?

AD DECIMUM SIC PROCEDITUR. Videtur quod Deus non cognoscat mala. Dicit enim philosophus, in III de anima, quod intellectus qui non est in potentia, non cognoscit privationem. Sed *malum est privatio boni*, ut dicit Augustinus. Igitur, cum intellectus Dei nunquam sit

OBJECTION 1: It seems that God does not know evil things. For the Philosopher (*De Anima* iii) says that the intellect which is not in potentiality does not know privation. But *evil is the privation of good*, as Augustine says (*Confess.* iii, 7). Therefore, as the intellect of God is never in

in potentia, sed semper actu, ut ex dictis patet, videtur quod Deus non cognoscat mala.

PRAETEREA, omnis scientia vel est causa sciti, vel causatur ab eo. Sed scientia Dei non est causa mali, nec causatur a malo. Ergo scientia Dei non est malorum.

PRAETEREA, omne quod cognoscitur, cognoscitur per suam similitudinem, vel per suum oppositum. Quidquid autem cognoscit Deus, cognoscit per suam essentiam, ut ex dictis patet. Divina autem essentia neque est similitudo mali, neque ei malum opponitur, divinae enim essentiae nihil est contrarium, ut dicit Augustinus, XII de Civ. Dei. Ergo Deus non cognoscit mala.

PRAETEREA, quod cognoscitur non per seipsum, sed per aliud, imperfecte cognoscitur. Sed malum non cognoscitur a Deo per seipsum, quia sic oporteret quod malum esset in Deo; oportet enim cognitum esse in cognoscente. Si ergo cognoscitur per aliud, scilicet per bonum, imperfecte cognoscetur ab ipso, quod est impossibile, quia nulla cognitio Dei est imperfecta. Ergo scientia Dei non est malorum.

SED CONTRA est quod dicitur Proverb. XV, *Infernus et perditio coram Deo.*

RESPONDEO dicendum quod quicumque perfecte cognoscit aliquid, oportet quod cognoscat omnia quae possunt illi accidere. Sunt autem quaedam bona, quibus accidere potest ut per mala corrumpantur. Unde Deus non perfecte cognosceret bona, nisi etiam cognosceret mala. Sic autem est cognoscibile unumquodque, secundum quod est. Unde, cum hoc sit esse mali, quod est privatio boni, per hoc ipsum quod Deus cognoscit bona, cognoscit etiam mala; sicut per lucem cognoscuntur tenebrae. Unde dicit Dionysius, VII cap. de Div. Nom., quod *Deus per semetipsum tenebrarum accipit visionem, non aliunde videns tenebras quam a lumine.*

AD PRIMUM ergo dicendum quod verbum philosophi est sic intelligendum, quod intellectus qui non est in potentia, non cognoscit privationem per privationem in ipso existentem. Et hoc congruit cum eo quod supra dixerat, quod punctum et omne indivisibile per privationem divisionis cognoscitur. Quod contingit ex hoc, quia formae simplices et indivisibiles non sunt actu in intellectu nostro, sed in potentia tantum, nam si essent actu in intellectu nostro, non per privationem cognoscerentur. Et sic cognoscuntur simplicia a substantiis separatis. Deus igitur non cognoscit malum per privationem in se existentem, sed per bonum oppositum.

AD SECUNDUM dicendum quod scientia Dei non est causa mali, sed est causa boni, per quod cognoscitur malum.

AD TERTIUM dicendum quod, licet malum non opponatur essentiae divinae, quae non est corruptibilis per malum, opponitur tamen effectibus Dei; quos per

potentiality, but is always in act, as is clear from the foregoing (A. 2), it seems that God does not know evil things.

OBJ. 2: Further, all knowledge is either the cause of the thing known, or is caused by it. But the knowledge of God is not the cause of evil, nor is it caused by evil. Therefore God does not know evil things.

OBJ. 3: Further, everything known is known either by its likeness, or by its opposite. But whatever God knows, He knows through His essence, as is clear from the foregoing (A. 5). Now the divine essence neither is the likeness of evil, nor is evil contrary to it; for to the divine essence there is no contrary, as Augustine says (*De Civ. Dei* xii). Therefore God does not know evil things.

OBJ. 4: Further, what is known through another and not through itself, is imperfectly known. But evil is not known by God; for the thing known must be in the knower. Therefore if evil is known through another, namely, through good, it would be known by Him imperfectly; which cannot be, for the knowledge of God is not imperfect. Therefore God does not know evil things.

ON THE CONTRARY, It is written (Prov 15:11), *Hell and destruction are before God.*

I ANSWER THAT, Whoever knows a thing perfectly, must know all that can be accidental to it. Now there are some good things to which corruption by evil may be accidental. Hence God would not know good things perfectly, unless He also knew evil things. Now a thing is knowable in the degree in which it is; hence since this is the essence of evil that it is the privation of good, by the fact that God knows good things, He knows evil things also; as by light is known darkness. Hence Dionysius says (*Div. Nom.* vii): *God through Himself receives the vision of darkness, not otherwise seeing darkness except through light.*

REPLY OBJ. 1: The saying of the Philosopher must be understood as meaning that the intellect which is not in potentiality, does not know privation by privation existing in it; and this agrees with what he said previously, that a point and every indivisible thing are known by privation of division. This is because simple and indivisible forms are in our intellect not actually, but only potentially; for were they actually in our intellect, they would not be known by privation. It is thus that simple things are known by separate substances. God therefore knows evil, not by privation existing in Himself, but by the opposite good.

REPLY OBJ. 2: The knowledge of God is not the cause of evil; but is the cause of the good whereby evil is known.

REPLY OBJ. 3: Although evil is not opposed to the divine essence, which is not corruptible by evil, it is opposed

essentiam suam cognoscit, et eos cognoscens, mala opposita cognoscit.

AD QUARTUM dicendum quod cognoscere aliquid per aliud tantum, est imperfectae cognitionis, si illud sit cognoscibile per se. Sed malum non est per se cognoscibile, quia de ratione mali est, quod sit privatio boni. Et sic neque definiri, neque cognosci potest, nisi per bonum.

to the effects of God, which He knows by His essence; and knowing them, He knows the opposite evils.

REPLY OBJ. 4: To know a thing by something else only, belongs to imperfect knowledge, if that thing is of itself knowable; but evil is not of itself knowable, forasmuch as the very nature of evil means the privation of good; therefore evil can neither be defined nor known except by good.

Article 11

Whether God Knows Singular Things?

AD UNDECIMUM SIC PROCEDITUR. Videtur quod Deus non cognoscat singularia. Intellectus enim divinus immaterialior est quam intellectus humanus. Sed intellectus humanus, propter suam immaterialitatem, non cognoscit singularia, sed, sicut dicitur in II de anima, *ratio est universalium, sensus vero singularium.* Ergo Deus non cognoscit singularia.

PRAETEREA, illae solae virtutes in nobis sunt singularium cognoscitivae, quae recipiunt species non abstractas a materialibus conditionibus. Sed res in Deo sunt maxime abstractae ab omni materialitate. Ergo Deus non cognoscit singularia.

PRAETEREA, omnis cognitio est per aliquam similitudinem. Sed similitudo singularium, inquantum sunt singularia, non videtur esse in Deo, quia principium singularitatis est materia, quae, cum sit ens in potentia tantum, omnino est dissimilis Deo, qui est actus purus. Non ergo Deus potest cognoscere singularia.

SED CONTRA est quod dicitur, Proverb. XVI, *omnes viae hominum patent oculis eius.*

RESPONDEO dicendum quod Deus cognoscit singularia. Omnes enim perfectiones in creaturis inventae, in Deo praeexistunt secundum altiorem modum, ut ex dictis patet. Cognoscere autem singularia pertinet ad perfectionem nostram. Unde necesse est quod Deus singularia cognoscat. Nam et philosophus pro inconvenienti habet, quod aliquid cognoscatur a nobis, quod non cognoscatur a Deo. Unde contra Empedoclem arguit, in I de anima et in III Metaphys., quod accideret Deum esse insipientissimum, si discordiam ignoraret. Sed perfectiones quae in inferioribus dividuntur, in Deo simpliciter et unite existunt. Unde, licet nos per aliam potentiam cognoscamus universalia et immaterialia, et per aliam singularia et materialia; Deus tamen per suum simplicem intellectum utraque cognoscit.

Sed qualiter hoc esse possit, quidam manifestare volentes, dixerunt quod Deus cognoscit singularia per causas universales, nam nihil est in aliquo singularium, quod non ex aliqua causa oriatur universali. Et ponunt

OBJECTION 1: It seems that God does not know singular things. For the divine intellect is more immaterial than the human intellect. Now the human intellect by reason of its immateriality does not know singular things; but as the Philosopher says (*De Anima* ii), *reason has to do with universals, sense with singular things.* Therefore God does not know singular things.

OBJ. 2: Further, in us those faculties alone know the singular, which receive the species not abstracted from material conditions. But in God things are in the highest degree abstracted from all materiality. Therefore God does not know singular things.

OBJ. 3: Further, all knowledge comes about through the medium of some likeness. But the likeness of singular things in so far as they are singular, does not seem to be in God; for the principle of singularity is matter, which, since it is in potentiality only, is altogether unlike God, Who is pure act. Therefore God cannot know singular things.

ON THE CONTRARY, It is written (Prov 16:2), *All the ways of a man are open to His eyes.*

I ANSWER THAT, God knows singular things. For all perfections found in creatures pre-exist in God in a higher way, as is clear from the foregoing (Q. 4, A. 2). Now to know singular things is part of our perfection. Hence God must know singular things. Even the Philosopher considers it incongruous that anything known by us should be unknown to God; and thus against Empedocles he argues (*De Anima* i and *Metaph.* iii) that God would be most ignorant if He did not know discord. Now the perfections which are divided among inferior beings, exist simply and unitedly in God; hence, although by one faculty we know the universal and immaterial, and by another we know singular and material things, nevertheless God knows both by His simple intellect.

Now some, wishing to show how this can be, said that God knows singular things by universal causes. For nothing exists in any singular thing, that does not arise from some universal cause. They give the example of an astrologer who

exemplum, sicut si aliquis astrologus cognosceret omnes motus universales caeli, posset praenuntiare omnes eclipses futuras. Sed istud non sufficit. Quia singularia ex causis universalibus sortiuntur quasdam formas et virtutes, quae, quantumcumque ad invicem coniungantur, non individuantur nisi per materiam individualem. Unde qui cognosceret Socratem per hoc quod est albus vel Sophronisci filius, vel quidquid aliud sic dicatur, non cognosceret ipsum inquantum est hic homo. Unde secundum modum praedictum, Deus non cognosceret singularia in sua singularitate.

Alii vero dixerunt quod Deus cognoscit singularia, applicando causas universales ad particulares effectus. Sed hoc nihil est. Quia nullus potest applicare aliquid ad alterum, nisi illud praecognoscat, unde dicta applicatio non potest esse ratio cognoscendi particularia, sed cognitionem singularium praesupponit.

Et ideo aliter dicendum est, quod, cum Deus sit causa rerum per suam scientiam, ut dictum est, intantum se extendit scientia Dei, inquantum se extendit eius causalitas. Unde, cum virtus activa Dei se extendat non solum ad formas, a quibus accipitur ratio universalis, sed etiam usque ad materiam, ut infra ostendetur; necesse est quod scientia Dei usque ad singularia se extendat, quae per materiam individuantur. Cum enim sciat alia a se per essentiam suam, inquantum est similitudo rerum velut principium activum earum, necesse est quod essentia sua sit principium sufficiens cognoscendi omnia quae per ipsum fiunt, non solum in universali, sed etiam in singulari. Et esset simile de scientia artificis, si esset productiva totius rei, et non formae tantum.

AD PRIMUM ergo dicendum quod intellectus noster speciem intelligibilem abstrahit a principiis individuantibus, unde species intelligibilis nostri intellectus non potest esse similitudo principiorum individualium. Et propter hoc, intellectus noster singularia non cognoscit. Sed species intelligibilis divini intellectus, quae est Dei essentia, non est immaterialis per abstractionem, sed per seipsam, principium existens omnium principiorum quae intrant rei compositionem, sive sint principia speciei, sive principia individui. Unde per eam Deus cognoscit non solum universalia, sed etiam singularia.

AD SECUNDUM dicendum quod, quamvis species intellectus divini secundum esse suum non habeat conditiones materiales, sicut species receptae in imaginatione et sensu; tamen virtute se extendit ad immaterialia et materialia, ut dictum est.

AD TERTIUM dicendum quod materia, licet recedat a Dei similitudine secundum suam potentialitatem, tamen inquantum vel sic esse habet, similitudinem quandam retinet divini esse.

knows all the universal movements of the heavens, and can thence foretell all eclipses that are to come. This, however, is not enough; for singular things from universal causes attain to certain forms and powers which, however they may be joined together, are not individualized except by individual matter. Hence he who knows Socrates because he is white, or because he is the son of Sophroniscus, or because of something of that kind, would not know him in so far as he is this particular man. Hence according to the aforesaid mode, God would not know singular things in their singularity.

On the other hand, others have said that God knows singular things by the application of universal causes to particular effects. But this will not hold, forasmuch as no one can apply a thing to another unless he first knows that thing; hence the said application cannot be the reason of knowing the particular, for it presupposes the knowledge of singular things.

Therefore it must be said otherwise, that, since God is the cause of things by His knowledge, as stated above (A. 8), His knowledge extends as far as His causality extends. Hence as the active power of God extends not only to forms, which are the source of universality, but also to matter, as we shall prove further on (Q. 44, A. 2), the knowledge of God must extend to singular things, which are individualized by matter. For since He knows things other than Himself by His essence, as being the likeness of things, or as their active principle, His essence must be the sufficing principle of knowing all things made by Him, not only in the universal, but also in the singular. The same would apply to the knowledge of the artificer, if it were productive of the whole thing, and not only of the form.

REPLY OBJ. 1: Our intellect abstracts the intelligible species from the individualizing principles; hence the intelligible species in our intellect cannot be the likeness of the individual principles; and on that account our intellect does not know the singular. But the intelligible species in the divine intellect, which is the essence of God, is immaterial not by abstraction, but of itself, being the principle of all the principles which enter into the composition of things, whether principles of the species or principles of the individual; hence by it God knows not only universal, but also singular things.

REPLY OBJ. 2: Although as regards the species in the divine intellect its being has no material conditions like the images received in the imagination and sense, yet its power extends to both immaterial and material things.

REPLY OBJ. 3: Although matter as regards its potentiality recedes from likeness to God, yet, even in so far as it has being in this wise, it retains a certain likeness to the divine being.

Article 12
Whether God Can Know Infinite Things?

AD DUODECIMUM SIC PROCEDITUR. Videtur quod Deus non possit cognoscere infinita. Infinitum enim, secundum quod est infinitum, est ignotum, quia *infinitum est cuius quantitatem accipientibus semper est aliquid extra assumere*, ut dicitur in III Physic. Augustinus etiam dicit, XII de Civ. Dei, quod *quidquid scientia comprehenditur, scientis comprehensione finitur*. Sed infinita non possunt finiri. Ergo non possunt scientia Dei comprehendi.

SI DICATUR quod ea quae in se sunt infinita, scientiae Dei finita sunt, contra, ratio infiniti est quod sit impertransibile; et finiti quod sit pertransibile, ut dicitur in III Physic. Sed infinitum non potest transiri nec a finito, nec ab infinito, ut probatur in VI Physic. Ergo infinitum non potest esse finitum finito, neque etiam infinito. Et ita infinita non sunt finita scientiae Dei, quae est infinita.

PRAETEREA, scientia Dei est mensura scitorum. Sed contra rationem infiniti est, quod sit mensuratum. Ergo infinita non possunt sciri a Deo.

SED CONTRA est quod dicit Augustinus, XII de Civ. Dei, *quamvis infinitorum numerorum nullus sit numerus, non est tamen incomprehensibilis ei, cuius scientiae non est numerus.*

RESPONDEO dicendum quod, cum Deus sciat non solum ea quae sunt actu, sed etiam ea quae sunt in potentia vel sua vel creaturae, ut ostensum est; haec autem constat esse infinita; necesse est dicere quod Deus sciat infinita. Et licet scientia visionis, quae est tantum eorum quae sunt vel erunt vel fuerunt, non sit infinitorum, ut quidam dicunt, cum non ponamus mundum ab aeterno fuisse, nec generationem et motum in aeternum mansura, ut individua in infinitum multiplicentur, tamen, si diligentius consideretur, necesse est dicere quod Deus etiam scientia visionis sciat infinita. Quia Deus scit etiam cogitationes et affectiones cordium, quae in infinitum multiplicabuntur, creaturis rationalibus permanentibus absque fine.

Hoc autem ideo est, quia cognitio cuiuslibet cognoscentis se extendit secundum modum formae quae est principium cognitionis. Species enim sensibilis, quae est in sensu, est similitudo solum unius individui, unde per eam solum unum individuum cognosci potest. Species autem intelligibilis intellectus nostri est similitudo rei quantum ad naturam speciei, quae est participabilis a particularibus infinitis, unde intellectus noster per speciem intelligibilem hominis, cognoscit quodammodo homines infinitos. Sed tamen non inquantum

OBJECTION 1: It seems that God cannot know infinite things. For the infinite, as such, is unknown, since the infinite is that which, *to those who measure it, leaves always something more to be measured*, as the Philosopher says (*Phys.* iii). Moreover, Augustine says (*De Civ. Dei* xii) that *whatever is comprehended by knowledge, is bounded by the comprehension of the knower*. Now infinite things have no boundary. Therefore they cannot be comprehended by the knowledge of God.

OBJ. 2: Further, if we say that things infinite in themselves are finite in God's knowledge, against this it may be urged that the essence of the infinite is that it is untraversable, and the finite that it is traversable, as said in *Phys.* iii. But the infinite is not traversable either by the finite or by the infinite, as is proved in *Phys.* vi. Therefore the infinite cannot be bounded by the finite, nor even by the infinite; and so the infinite cannot be finite in God's knowledge, which is infinite.

OBJ. 3: Further, the knowledge of God is the measure of what is known. But it is contrary to the essence of the infinite that it be measured. Therefore infinite things cannot be known by God.

ON THE CONTRARY, Augustine says (*De Civ. Dei* xii), *Although we cannot number the infinite, nevertheless it can be comprehended by Him whose knowledge has no bounds.*

I ANSWER THAT, Since God knows not only things actual but also things possible to Himself or to created things, as shown above (A. 9), and as these must be infinite, it must be held that He knows infinite things. Although the knowledge of vision which has relation only to things that are, or will be, or were, is not of infinite things, as some say, for we do not say that the world is eternal, nor that generation and movement will go on for ever, so that individuals be infinitely multiplied; yet, if we consider more attentively, we must hold that God knows infinite things even by the knowledge of vision. For God knows even the thoughts and affections of hearts, which will be multiplied to infinity as rational creatures go on for ever.

The reason of this is to be found in the fact that the knowledge of every knower is measured by the mode of the form which is the principle of knowledge. For the sensible image in sense is the likeness of only one individual thing, and can give the knowledge of only one individual. But the intelligible species of our intellect is the likeness of the thing as regards its specific nature, which is participable by infinite particulars; hence our intellect by the intelligible species of man in a certain way knows infinite men; not however as distinguished from each other, but as

distinguuntur ab invicem, sed secundum quod communicant in natura speciei; propter hoc quod species intelligibilis intellectus nostri non est similitudo hominum quantum ad principia individualia, sed solum quantum ad principia speciei. Essentia autem divina, per quam intellectus divinus intelligit, est similitudo sufficiens omnium quae sunt vel esse possunt, non solum quantum ad principia communia, sed etiam quantum ad principia propria uniuscuiusque, ut ostensum est. Unde sequitur quod scientia Dei se extendat ad infinita, etiam secundum quod sunt ab invicem distincta.

AD PRIMUM ergo dicendum quod *infiniti ratio congruit quantitati*, secundum philosophum in I Physic. De ratione autem quantitatis est ordo partium. Cognoscere ergo infinitum secundum modum infiniti, est cognoscere partem post partem. Et sic nullo modo contingit cognosci infinitum, quia quantacumque quantitas partium accipiatur, semper remanet aliquid extra accipientem. Deus autem non sic cognoscit infinitum vel infinita, quasi enumerando partem post partem; cum cognoscat omnia simul, non successive, ut supra dictum est. Unde nihil prohibet ipsum cognoscere infinita.

AD SECUNDUM dicendum quod transitio importat quandam successionem in partibus, et inde est quod infinitum transiri non potest, neque a finito neque ab infinito. Sed ad rationem comprehensionis sufficit adaequatio, quia id comprehendi dicitur, cuius nihil est extra comprehendentem. Unde non est contra rationem infiniti, quod comprehendatur ab infinito. Et sic, quod in se est infinitum, potest dici finitum scientiae Dei, tanquam comprehensum, non tamen tanquam pertransibile.

AD TERTIUM dicendum quod scientia Dei est mensura rerum, non quantitativa, qua quidem mensura carent infinita; sed quia mensurat essentiam et veritatem rei. Unumquodque enim intantum habet de veritate suae naturae, inquantum imitatur Dei scientiam; sicut artificiatum inquantum concordat arti. Dato autem quod essent aliqua infinita actu secundum numerum, puta infiniti homines; vel secundum quantitatem continuam, ut si esset aer infinitus, ut quidam antiqui dixerunt, tamen manifestum est quod haberent esse determinatum et finitum, quia esse eorum esset limitatum ad aliquas determinatas naturas. Unde mensurabilia essent secundum scientiam Dei.

communicating in the nature of the species; and the reason is because the intelligible species of our intellect is the likeness of man not as to the individual principles, but as to the principles of the species. On the other hand, the divine essence, whereby the divine intellect understands, is a sufficing likeness of all things that are, or can be, not only as regards the universal principles, but also as regards the principles proper to each one, as shown above. Hence it follows that the knowledge of God extends to infinite things, even as distinct from each other.

REPLY OBJ. 1: The idea of the infinite pertains to quantity, as the Philosopher says (*Phys.* i). But the idea of quantity implies the order of parts. Therefore to know the infinite according to the mode of the infinite is to know part after part; and in this way the infinite cannot be known; for whatever quantity of parts be taken, there will always remain something else outside. But God does not know the infinite or infinite things as if He enumerated part after part, since He knows all things simultaneously, and not successively, as said above (A. 7). Hence there is nothing to prevent Him from knowing infinite things.

REPLY OBJ. 2: Transition imports a certain succession of parts; and hence it is that the infinite cannot be traversed by the finite, nor by the infinite. But equality suffices for comprehension, because that is said to be comprehended which has nothing outside the comprehender. Hence it is not against the idea of the infinite to be comprehended by the infinite. And so, what is infinite in itself can be called finite to the knowledge of God as comprehended; but not as if it were traversable.

REPLY OBJ. 3: The knowledge of God is the measure of things, not quantitatively, for the infinite is not subject to this kind of measure; but it is the measure of the essence and truth of things. For everything has truth of nature according to the degree in which it imitates the knowledge of God, as the thing made by art agrees with the art. Granted, however, an actually infinite number of things, for instance, an infinitude of men, or an infinitude in continuous quantity, as an infinitude of air, as some of the ancients held; yet it is manifest that these would have a determinate and finite being, because their being would be limited to some determinate nature. Hence they would be measurable as regards the knowledge of God.

Article 13

Whether the Knowledge of God Is of Future Contingent Things?

AD DECIMUMTERTIUM SIC PROCEDITUR. Videtur quod scientia Dei non sit futurorum contingentium. A causa enim necessaria procedit effectus

OBJECTION 1: It seems that the knowledge of God is not of future contingent things. For from a necessary cause proceeds a necessary effect. But the knowledge of God is

necessarius. Sed scientia Dei est causa scitorum, ut supra dictum est. Cum ergo ipsa sit necessaria, sequitur scita eius esse necessaria. Non ergo scientia Dei est contingentium.

PRAETEREA, omnis conditionalis cuius antecedens est necessarium absolute, consequens est necessarium absolute. Sic enim se habet antecedens ad consequens, sicut principia ad conclusionem, ex principiis autem necessariis non sequitur conclusio nisi necessaria, ut in I Poster. probatur. Sed haec est quaedam conditionalis vera, si Deus scivit hoc futurum esse, hoc erit, quia scientia Dei non est nisi verorum. Huius autem conditionalis antecedens est necessarium absolute, tum quia est aeternum; tum quia significatur ut praeteritum. Ergo et consequens est necessarium absolute. Igitur quidquid scitur a Deo, est necessarium. Et sic scientia Dei non est contingentium.

PRAETEREA, omne scitum a Deo necesse est esse, quia etiam omne scitum a nobis necesse est esse, cum tamen scientia Dei certior sit quam scientia nostra. Sed nullum contingens futurum necesse est esse. Ergo nullum contingens futurum est scitum a Deo.

SED CONTRA est quod dicitur in Psalmo XXXII, *qui finxit singillatim corda eorum, qui intelligit omnia opera eorum*, scilicet hominum. Sed opera hominum sunt contingentia, utpote libero arbitrio subiecta. Ergo Deus scit futura contingentia.

RESPONDEO dicendum quod, cum supra ostensum sit quod Deus sciat omnia non solum quae actu sunt, sed etiam quae sunt in potentia sua vel creaturae; horum autem quaedam sunt contingentia nobis futura; sequitur quod Deus contingentia futura cognoscat.

Ad cuius evidentiam, considerandum est quod contingens aliquod dupliciter potest considerari. Uno modo, in seipso, secundum quod iam actu est. Et sic non consideratur ut futurum, sed ut praesens, neque ut ad utrumlibet contingens, sed ut determinatum ad unum. Et propter hoc, sic infallibiliter subdi potest certae cognitioni, utpote sensui visus, sicut cum video Socratem sedere. Alio modo potest considerari contingens, ut est in sua causa. Et sic consideratur ut futurum, et ut contingens nondum determinatum ad unum, quia causa contingens se habet ad opposita. Et sic contingens non subditur per certitudinem alicui cognitioni. Unde quicumque cognoscit effectum contingentem in causa sua tantum, non habet de eo nisi coniecturalem cognitionem. Deus autem cognoscit omnia contingentia, non solum prout sunt in suis causis, sed etiam prout unumquodque eorum est actu in seipso. Et licet contingentia fiant in actu successive, non tamen Deus successive cognoscit contingentia, prout sunt in suo esse, sicut nos, sed simul. Quia sua cognitio mensuratur aeternitate, sicut etiam suum esse, aeternitas autem, tota simul existens, ambit

the cause of things known, as said above (A. 8). Since therefore that knowledge is necessary, what He knows must also be necessary. Therefore the knowledge of God is not of contingent things.

OBJ. 2: Further, every conditional proposition of which the antecedent is absolutely necessary must have an absolutely necessary consequent. For the antecedent is to the consequent as principles are to the conclusion: and from necessary principles only a necessary conclusion can follow, as is proved in Poster. i. But this is a true conditional proposition, *If God knew that this thing will be, it will be*, for the knowledge of God is only of true things. Now the antecedent conditional of this is absolutely necessary, because it is eternal, and because it is signified as past. Therefore the consequent is also absolutely necessary. Therefore whatever God knows, is necessary; and so the knowledge of God is not of contingent things.

OBJ. 3: Further, everything known by God must necessarily be, because even what we ourselves know, must necessarily be; and, of course, the knowledge of God is much more certain than ours. But no future contingent things must necessarily be. Therefore no contingent future thing is known by God.

ON THE CONTRARY, It is written (Ps 32:15), *He Who hath made the hearts of every one of them; Who understandeth all their works*, i.e., of men. Now the works of men are contingent, being subject to free will. Therefore God knows future contingent things.

I ANSWER THAT, Since as was shown above (A. 9), God knows all things; not only things actual but also things possible to Him and creatures; and since some of these are future contingent to us, it follows that God knows future contingent things.

In evidence of this, we must consider that a contingent thing can be considered in two ways; first, in itself, in so far as it is now in act: and in this sense it is not considered as future, but as present; neither is it considered as contingent (as having reference) to one of two terms, but as determined to one; and on account of this it can be infallibly the object of certain knowledge, for instance to the sense of sight, as when I see that Socrates is sitting down. In another way a contingent thing can be considered as it is in its cause; and in this way it is considered as future, and as a contingent thing not yet determined to one; forasmuch as a contingent cause has relation to opposite things: and in this sense a contingent thing is not subject to any certain knowledge. Hence, whoever knows a contingent effect in its cause only, has merely a conjectural knowledge of it. Now God knows all contingent things not only as they are in their causes, but also as each one of them is actually in itself. And although contingent things become actual successively, nevertheless God knows contingent things not successively, as they are in their own being, as we do; but simultaneously. The reason is because His knowledge is

totum tempus, ut supra dictum est. Unde omnia quae sunt in tempore, sunt Deo ab aeterno praesentia, non solum ea ratione qua habet rationes rerum apud se praesentes, ut quidam dicunt, sed quia eius intuitus fertur ab aeterno super omnia, prout sunt in sua praesentialitate. Unde manifestum est quod contingentia et infallibiliter a Deo cognoscuntur, inquantum subduntur divino conspectui secundum suam praesentialitatem, et tamen sunt futura contingentia, suis causis comparata.

Ad primum ergo dicendum quod, licet causa suprema sit necessaria, tamen effectus potest esse contingens, propter causam proximam contingentem, sicut germinatio plantae est contingens propter causam proximam contingentem, licet motus solis, qui est causa prima, sit necessarius. Et similiter scita a Deo sunt contingentia propter causas proximas, licet scientia Dei, quae est causa prima, sit necessaria.

Ad secundum dicendum quod quidam dicunt quod hoc antecedens, Deus scivit hoc contingens futurum, non est necessarium, sed contingens, quia, licet sit praeteritum, tamen importat respectum ad futurum. Sed hoc non tollit ei necessitatem, quia id quod habuit respectum ad futurum, necesse est habuisse, licet etiam futurum non sequatur quandoque. Alii vero dicunt hoc antecedens esse contingens, quia est compositum ex necessario et contingenti; sicut istud dictum est contingens, Socratem esse hominem album. Sed hoc etiam nihil est. Quia cum dicitur, Deus scivit esse futurum hoc contingens, contingens non ponitur ibi nisi ut materia verbi, et non sicut principalis pars propositionis, unde contingentia eius vel necessitas nihil refert ad hoc quod propositio sit necessaria vel contingens, vera vel falsa. Ita enim potest esse verum me dixisse hominem esse asinum, sicut me dixisse Socratem currere, vel Deum esse, et eadem ratio est de necessario et contingenti. Unde dicendum est quod hoc antecedens est necessarium absolute. Nec tamen sequitur, ut quidam dicunt, quod consequens sit necessarium absolute, quia antecedens est causa remota consequentis, quod propter causam proximam contingens est. Sed hoc nihil est. Esset enim conditionalis falsa, cuius antecedens esset causa remota necessaria, et consequens effectus contingens, ut puta si dicerem, si sol movetur, herba germinabit.

Et ideo aliter dicendum est, quod quando in antecedente ponitur aliquid pertinens ad actum animae, consequens est accipiendum non secundum quod in se est, sed secundum quod est in anima, aliud enim est esse rei in seipsa, et esse rei in anima. Ut puta, si dicam, si anima intelligit aliquid, illud est immateriale, intelligendum est quod illud est immateriale secundum quod est in intellectu, non secundum quod est in seipso. Et similiter si dicam, si Deus scivit aliquid, illud erit, consequens intelligendum est prout subest divinae scientiae, scilicet

measured by eternity, as is also His being; and eternity being simultaneously whole comprises all time, as said above (Q. 10, A. 2). Hence all things that are in time are present to God from eternity, not only because He has the types of things present within Him, as some say; but because His glance is carried from eternity over all things as they are in their presentiality. Hence it is manifest that contingent things are infallibly known by God, inasmuch as they are subject to the divine sight in their presentiality; yet they are future contingent things in relation to their own causes.

Reply Obj. 1: Although the supreme cause is necessary, the effect may be contingent by reason of the proximate contingent cause; just as the germination of a plant is contingent by reason of the proximate contingent cause, although the movement of the sun which is the first cause, is necessary. So likewise things known by God are contingent on account of their proximate causes, while the knowledge of God, which is the first cause, is necessary.

Reply Obj. 2: Some say that this antecedent, *God knew this contingent to be future*, is not necessary, but contingent; because, although it is past, still it imports relation to the future. This however does not remove necessity from it; for whatever has had relation to the future, must have had it, although the future sometimes does not follow. On the other hand some say that this antecedent is contingent, because it is a compound of necessary and contingent; as this saying is contingent, *Socrates is a white man*. But this also is to no purpose; for when we say, *God knew this contingent to be future*, contingent is used here only as the matter of the word, and not as the chief part of the proposition. Hence its contingency or necessity has no reference to the necessity or contingency of the proposition, or to its being true or false. For it may be just as true that I said a man is an ass, as that I said Socrates runs, or God is: and the same applies to necessary and contingent. Hence it must be said that this antecedent is absolutely necessary. Nor does it follow, as some say, that the consequent is absolutely necessary, because the antecedent is the remote cause of the consequent, which is contingent by reason of the proximate cause. But this is to no purpose. For the conditional would be false were its antecedent the remote necessary cause, and the consequent a contingent effect; as, for example, if I said, *if the sun moves, the grass will grow*.

Therefore we must reply otherwise, that when the antecedent contains anything belonging to an act of the soul, the consequent must be taken not as it is in itself, but as it is in the soul: for the existence of a thing in itself is different from the existence of a thing in the soul. For example, when I say, *What the soul understands is immaterial*, this is to be understood that it is immaterial as it is in the intellect, not as it is in itself. Likewise if I say, *If God knew anything, it will be*, the consequent must be understood as it is subject to the divine knowledge, i.e., as it is in its presentiality. And

prout est in sua praesentialitate. Et sic necessarium est, sicut et antecedens, *quia omne quod est, dum est, necesse est esse,* ut dicitur in I Periherm.

AD TERTIUM dicendum quod ea quae temporaliter in actum reducuntur, a nobis successive cognoscuntur in tempore, sed a Deo in aeternitate, quae est supra tempus. Unde nobis, quia cognoscimus futura contingentia inquantum talia sunt, certa esse non possunt, sed soli Deo, cuius intelligere est in aeternitate supra tempus. Sicut ille qui vadit per viam, non videt illos qui post eum veniunt, sed ille qui ab aliqua altitudine totam viam intuetur, simul videt omnes transeuntes per viam. Et ideo illud quod scitur a nobis, oportet esse necessarium etiam secundum quod in se est, quia ea quae in se sunt contingentia futura, a nobis sciri non possunt. Sed ea quae sunt scita a Deo, oportet esse necessaria secundum modum quo subsunt divinae scientiae, ut dictum est, non autem absolute, secundum quod in propriis causis considerantur. Unde et haec propositio, omne scitum a Deo necessarium est esse, consuevit distingui. Quia potest esse de re, vel de dicto. Si intelligatur de re, est divisa et falsa, et est sensus, omnis res quam Deus scit, est necessaria. Vel potest intelligi de dicto, et sic est composita et vera; et est sensus, hoc dictum, scitum a Deo esse, est necessarium.

Sed obstant quidam, dicentes quod ista distinctio habet locum in formis separabilibus a subiecto; ut si dicam, album possibile est esse nigrum. Quae quidem de dicto est falsa, et de re est vera, res enim quae est alba, potest esse nigra; sed hoc dictum, album esse nigrum, nunquam potest esse verum. In formis autem inseparabilibus a subiecto, non habet locum praedicta distinctio; ut si dicam, corvum nigrum possibile est esse album, quia in utroque sensu est falsa. Esse autem scitum a Deo, est inseparabile a re, quia quod est scitum a Deo, non potest esse non scitum. Haec autem instantia locum haberet, si hoc quod dico scitum, importaret aliquam dispositionem subiecto inhaerentem. Sed cum importet actum scientis, ipsi rei scitae, licet semper sciatur, potest aliquid attribui secundum se, quod non attribuitur ei inquantum stat sub actu sciendi, sicut esse materiale attribuitur lapidi secundum se, quod non attribuitur ei secundum quod est intelligibile.

thus it is necessary, as also is the antecedent: *For everything that is, while it is, must be necessarily be,* as the Philosopher says (*Peri Herm.* i).

REPLY OBJ. 3: Things reduced to act in time, as known by us successively in time, but by God (are known) in eternity, which is above time. Whence to us they cannot be certain, forasmuch as we know future contingent things as such; but (they are certain) to God alone, whose understanding is in eternity above time. Just as he who goes along the road, does not see those who come after him; whereas he who sees the whole road from a height, sees at once all travelling by the way. Hence what is known by us must be necessary, even as it is in itself; for what is future contingent in itself, cannot be known by us. Whereas what is known by God must be necessary according to the mode in which they are subject to the divine knowledge, as already stated, but not absolutely as considered in their own causes. Hence also this proposition, *Everything known by God must necessarily be,* is usually distinguished; for this may refer to the thing, or to the saying. If it refers to the thing, it is divided and false; for the sense is, *Everything which God knows is necessary.* If understood of the saying, it is composite and true; for the sense is, *This proposition, 'that which is known by God is' is necessary.*

Now some urge an objection and say that this distinction holds good with regard to forms that are separable from the subject; thus if I said, *It is possible for a white thing to be black,* it is false as applied to the saying, and true as applied to the thing: for a thing which is white, can become black; whereas this saying, *a white thing is black,* can never be true. But in forms that are inseparable from the subject, this distinction does not hold, for instance, if I said, *A black crow can be white;* for in both senses it is false. Now to be known by God is inseparable from the thing; for what is known by God cannot be not known. This objection, however, would hold if these words *that which is known* implied any disposition inherent to the subject; but since they import an act of the knower, something can be attributed to the thing known, in itself (even if it always be known), which is not attributed to it in so far as it stands under actual knowledge; thus material existence is attributed to a stone in itself, which is not attributed to it inasmuch as it is known.

Article 14

Whether God Knows Enunciable Things?

AD DECIMUMQUARTUM SIC PROCEDITUR. Videtur quod Deus non cognoscat enuntiabilia. Cognoscere enim enuntiabilia convenit intellectui nostro, secundum

OBJECTION 1: It seems that God does not know enunciable things. For to know enunciable things belongs to our intellect as it composes and divides. But in the divine

quod componit et dividit. Sed in intellectu divino nulla est compositio. Ergo Deus non cognoscit enuntiabilia.

PRAETEREA, omnis cognitio fit per aliquam similitudinem. Sed in Deo nulla est similitudo enuntiabilium, cum sit omnino simplex. Ergo Deus non cognoscit enuntiabilia.

SED CONTRA est quod dicitur in Psalmo XCIII, *dominus scit cogitationes hominum*. Sed enuntiabilia continentur in cogitationibus hominum. Ergo Deus cognoscit enuntiabilia.

RESPONDEO dicendum quod, cum formare enuntiabilia sit in potestate intellectus nostri; Deus autem scit quidquid est in potentia sua vel creaturae, ut supra dictum est; necesse est quod Deus sciat omnia enuntiabilia quae formari possunt.

Sed, sicut scit materialia immaterialiter, et composita simpliciter, ita scit enuntiabilia non per modum enuntiabilium, quasi scilicet in intellectu eius sit compositio vel divisio enuntiabilium; sed unumquodque cognoscit per simplicem intelligentiam, intelligendo essentiam uniuscuiusque. Sicut si nos in hoc ipso quod intelligimus quid est homo, intelligeremus omnia quae de homine praedicari possunt. Quod quidem in intellectu nostro non contingit, qui de uno in aliud discurrit, propter hoc quod species intelligibilis sic repraesentat unum, quod non repraesentat aliud. Unde, intelligendo quid est homo, non ex hoc ipso alia quae ei insunt, intelligimus; sed divisim, secundum quandam successionem. Et propter hoc, ea quae seorsum intelligimus, oportet nos in unum redigere per modum compositionis vel divisionis, enuntiationem formando. Sed species intellectus divini, scilicet eius essentia, sufficit ad demonstrandum omnia. Unde, intelligendo essentiam suam, cognoscit essentias omnium, et quaecumque eis accidere possunt.

AD PRIMUM ergo dicendum quod ratio illa procederet, si Deus cognosceret enuntiabilia per modum enuntiabilium.

AD SECUNDUM dicendum quod compositio enuntiabilis significat aliquod esse rei, et sic Deus per suum esse, quod est eius essentia, est similitudo omnium eorum quae per enuntiabilia significantur.

intellect, there is no composition. Therefore God does not know enunciable things.

OBJ. 2: Further, every kind of knowledge is made through some likeness. But in God there is no likeness of enunciable things, since He is altogether simple. Therefore God does not know enunciable things.

ON THE CONTRARY, It is written: *The Lord knoweth the thoughts of men* (Ps 93:11). But enunciable things are contained in the thoughts of men. Therefore God knows enunciable things.

I ANSWER THAT, Since it is in the power of our intellect to form enunciations, and since God knows whatever is in His own power or in that of creatures, as said above (A. 9), it follows of necessity that God knows all enunciations that can be formed.

Now just as He knows material things immaterially, and composite things simply, so likewise He knows enunciable things not after the manner of enunciable things, as if in His intellect there were composition or division of enunciations; for He knows each thing by simple intelligence, by understanding the essence of each thing; as if we by the very fact that we understand what man is, were to understand all that can be predicated of man. This, however, does not happen in our intellect, which discourses from one thing to another, forasmuch as the intelligible species represents one thing in such a way as not to represent another. Hence when we understand what man is, we do not forthwith understand other things which belong to him, but we understand them one by one, according to a certain succession. On this account the things we understand as separated, we must reduce to one by way of composition or division, by forming an enunciation. Now the species of the divine intellect, which is God's essence, suffices to represent all things. Hence by understanding His essence, God knows the essences of all things, and also whatever can be accidental to them.

REPLY OBJ. 1: This objection would avail if God knew enunciable things after the manner of enunciable things.

REPLY OBJ. 2: Enunciatory composition signifies some existence of a thing; and thus God by His existence, which is His essence, is the similitude of all those things which are signified by enunciation.

Article 15

Whether the Knowledge of God Is Variable?

AD DECIMUMQUINTUM SIC PROCEDITUR. Videtur quod scientia Dei sit variabilis. Scientia enim relative dicitur ad scibile. Sed ea quae important relationem ad creaturam, dicuntur de Deo ex tempore, et variantur

OBJECTION 1: It seems that the knowledge of God is variable. For knowledge is related to what is knowable. But whatever imports relation to the creature is applied to God from time, and varies according to the variation of

secundum variationem creaturarum. Ergo scientia Dei est variabilis, secundum variationem creaturarum.

Praeterea, quidquid potest Deus facere, potest scire. Sed Deus potest plura facere quam faciat. Ergo potest plura scire quam sciat. Et sic scientia sua potest variari secundum augmentum et diminutionem.

Praeterea, Deus scivit Christum nasciturum. Nunc autem nescit Christum nasciturum, quia Christus nasciturus non est. Ergo non quidquid Deus scivit, scit. Et ita scientia Dei videtur esse variabilis.

Sed contra est quod dicitur Iac. I, quod *apud Deum non est transmutatio, neque vicissitudinis obumbratio.*

Respondeo dicendum quod, cum scientia Dei sit eius substantia, ut ex dictis patet; sicut substantia eius est omnino immutabilis, ut supra ostensum est, ita oportet scientiam eius omnino invariabilem esse.

Ad primum ergo dicendum quod dominus et creator, et huiusmodi, important relationes ad creaturas secundum quod in seipsis sunt. Sed scientia Dei importat relationem ad creaturas secundum quod sunt in Deo, quia secundum hoc est unumquodque intellectum in actu quod est in intelligente. Res autem creatae sunt in Deo invariabiliter, in seipsis autem variabiliter. Vel aliter dicendum est, quod dominus et creator, et huiusmodi, important relationes quae consequuntur actus qui intelliguntur terminari ad ipsas creaturas secundum quod in seipsis sunt, et ideo huiusmodi relationes varie de Deo dicuntur, secundum variationem creaturarum. Sed scientia et amor, et huiusmodi, important relationes quae consequuntur actus qui intelliguntur in Deo esse, et ideo invariabiliter praedicantur de Deo.

Ad secundum dicendum quod Deus scit etiam ea quae potest facere et non facit. Unde ex hoc quod potest plura facere quam facit, non sequitur quod possit plura scire quam sciat, nisi hoc referatur ad scientiam visionis, secundum quam dicitur scire ea quae sunt in actu secundum aliquod tempus. Ex hoc tamen quod scit quod aliqua possunt esse quae non sunt, vel non esse quae sunt, non sequitur quod scientia sua sit variabilis, sed quod cognoscat rerum variabilitatem. Si tamen aliquid esset quod prius Deus nescivisset et postea sciret, esset eius scientia variabilis. Sed hoc esse non potest, quia quidquid est vel potest esse secundum aliquod tempus, Deus in aeterno suo scit. Et ideo ex hoc ipso quod ponitur aliquid esse secundum quodcumque tempus, oportet poni quod ab aeterno sit scitum a Deo. Et ideo non debet concedi quod Deus possit plura scire quam sciat, quia haec propositio implicat quod ante nesciverit et postea sciat.

creatures. Therefore the knowledge of God is variable according to the variation of creatures.

Obj. 2: Further, whatever God can make, He can know. But God can make more than He does. Therefore He can know more than He knows. Thus His knowledge can vary according to increase and diminution.

Obj. 3: Further, God knew that Christ would be born. But He does not know now that Christ will be born; because Christ is not to be born in the future. Therefore God does not know everything He once knew; and thus the knowledge of God is variable.

On the contrary, It is said, that in God *there is no change nor shadow of alteration* (Jas 1:17).

I answer that, Since the knowledge of God is His substance, as is clear from the foregoing (A. 4), just as His substance is altogether immutable, as shown above (Q. 9, A. 1), so His knowledge likewise must be altogether invariable.

Reply Obj. 1: *Lord*, *Creator* and the like, import relations to creatures in so far as they are in themselves. But the knowledge of God imports relation to creatures in so far as they are in God; because everything is actually understood according as it is in the one who understands. Now created things are in God in an invariable manner, while they exist variably in themselves. We may also say that *Lord*, *Creator* and the like, import the relations consequent upon the acts which are understood as terminating in the creatures themselves, as they are in themselves; and thus these relations are attributed to God variously, according to the variation of creatures. But *knowledge* and *love*, and the like, import relations consequent upon the acts which are understood to be in God; and therefore these are predicated of God in an invariable manner.

Reply Obj. 2: God knows also what He can make, and does not make. Hence from the fact that He can make more than He makes, it does not follow that He can know more than He knows, unless this be referred to the knowledge of vision, according to which He is said to know those things which are in act in some period of time. But from the fact that He knows some things might be which are not, or that some things might not be which are, it does not follow that His knowledge is variable, but rather that He knows the variability of things. If, however, anything existed which God did not previously know, and afterwards knew, then His knowledge would be variable. But this could not be; for whatever is, or can be in any period of time, is known by God in His eternity. Therefore from the fact that a thing exists in some period of time, it follows that it is known by God from eternity. Therefore it cannot be granted that God can know more than He knows; because such a proposition implies that first of all He did not know, and then afterwards knew.

AD TERTIUM dicendum quod antiqui nominales dixerunt idem esse enuntiabile, Christum nasci, et esse nasciturum, et esse natum, quia eadem res significatur per haec tria, scilicet nativitas Christi. Et secundum hoc sequitur quod Deus quidquid scivit, sciat, quia modo scit Christum natum, quod significat idem ei quod est Christum esse nasciturum. Sed haec opinio falsa est. Tum quia diversitas partium orationis diversitatem enuntiabilium causat. Tum etiam quia sequeretur quod propositio quae semel est vera, esset semper vera, quod est contra philosophum, qui dicit quod haec oratio, Socrates sedet, vera est eo sedente, et eadem falsa est, eo surgente. Et ideo concedendum est quod haec non est vera, quidquid Deus scivit, scit, si ad enuntiabilia referatur. Sed ex hoc non sequitur quod scientia Dei sit variabilis. Sicut enim absque variatione divinae scientiae est, quod sciat unam et eandem rem quandoque esse et quandoque non esse; ita absque variatione divinae scientiae est, quod scit aliquod enuntiabile quandoque esse verum, et quandoque esse falsum. Esset autem ex hoc scientia Dei variabilis, si enuntiabilia cognosceret per modum enuntiabilium, componendo et dividendo, sicut accidit in intellectu nostro. Unde cognitio nostra variatur, vel secundum veritatem et falsitatem, puta si, mutata re, eandem opinionem de re illa retineamus, vel secundum diversas opiniones, ut si primo opinemur aliquem sedere, et postea opinemur eum non sedere. Quorum neutrum potest esse in Deo.

REPLY OBJ. 3: The ancient Nominalists said that it was the same thing to say *Christ is born* and *will be born* and *was born*; because the same thing is signified by these three—viz., the nativity of Christ. Therefore it follows, they said, that whatever God knew, He knows; because now He knows that Christ is born, which means the same thing as that Christ will be born. This opinion, however, is false; both because the diversity in the parts of a sentence causes a diversity of enunciations; and because it would follow that a proposition which is true once would be always true; which is contrary to what the Philosopher lays down (*Categor.* iii) when he says that this sentence, *Socrates sits*, is true when he is sitting, and false when he rises up. Therefore, it must be conceded that this proposition is not true, *Whatever God knew He knows*, if referred to enunciable propositions. But because of this, it does not follow that the knowledge of God is variable. For as it is without variation in the divine knowledge that God knows one and the same thing sometime to be, and sometime not to be, so it is without variation in the divine knowledge that God knows an enunciable proposition is sometime true, and sometime false. The knowledge of God, however, would be variable if He knew enunciable things by way of enunciation, by composition and division, as occurs in our intellect. Hence our knowledge varies either as regards truth and falsity, for example, if when either as regards truth and falsity, for example, if when a thing suffers change we retained the same opinion about it; or as regards diverse opinions, as if we first thought that anyone was sitting, and afterwards thought that he was not sitting; neither of which can be in God.

Article 16

Whether God Has a Speculative Knowledge of Things?

AD DECIMUMSEXTUM SIC PROCEDITUR. Videtur quod Deus de rebus non habeat scientiam speculativam. Scientia enim Dei est causa rerum, ut supra ostensum est. Sed scientia speculativa non est causa rerum scitarum. Ergo scientia Dei non est speculativa.

PRAETEREA. Scientia speculativa est per abstractionem a rebus, quod divinae scientiae non competit. Ergo scientia Dei non est speculativa.

SED CONTRA, omne quod est nobilius, Deo est attribuendum. Sed scientia speculativa est nobilior quam practica, ut patet per philosophum, in principio Metaphys. Ergo Deus habet de rebus scientiam speculativam.

RESPONDEO dicendum quod aliqua scientia est speculativa tantum, aliqua practica tantum, aliqua vero secundum aliquid speculativa et secundum aliquid

OBJECTION 1: It seems that God has not a speculative knowledge of things. For the knowledge of God is the cause of things, as shown above (A. 8). But speculative knowledge is not the cause of the things known. Therefore the knowledge of God is not speculative.

OBJ. 2: Further, speculative knowledge comes by abstraction from things; which does not belong to the divine knowledge. Therefore the knowledge of God is not speculative.

ON THE CONTRARY, Whatever is the more excellent must be attributed to God. But speculative knowledge is more excellent than practical knowledge, as the Philosopher says in the beginning of Metaphysics. Therefore God has a speculative knowledge of things.

I ANSWER THAT, Some knowledge is speculative only; some is practical only; and some is partly speculative and partly practical. In proof whereof it must be observed that

practica. Ad cuius evidentiam, sciendum est quod aliqua scientia potest dici speculativa tripliciter. Primo, ex parte rerum scitarum, quae non sunt operabiles a sciente, sicut est scientia hominis de rebus naturalibus vel divinis. Secundo, quantum ad modum sciendi, ut puta si aedificator consideret domum definiendo et dividendo et considerando universalia praedicata ipsius. Hoc siquidem est operabilia modo speculativo considerare, et non secundum quod operabilia sunt, operabile enim est aliquid per applicationem formae ad materiam, non per resolutionem compositi in principia universalia formalia. Tertio, quantum ad finem, *nam intellectus practicus differt fine a speculativo*, sicut dicitur in III de anima. Intellectus enim practicus ordinatur ad finem operationis, finis autem intellectus speculativi est consideratio veritatis. Unde, si quis aedificator consideret qualiter posset fieri aliqua domus, non ordinans ad finem operationis, sed ad cognoscendum tantum, erit, quantum ad finem, speculativa consideratio, tamen de re operabili. Scientia igitur quae est speculativa ratione ipsius rei scitae, est speculativa tantum. Quae vero speculativa est vel secundum modum vel secundum finem, est secundum quid speculativa et secundum quid practica. Cum vero ordinatur ad finem operationis, est simpliciter practica.

Secundum hoc ergo, dicendum est quod Deus de seipso habet scientiam speculativam tantum, ipse enim operabilis non est. De omnibus vero aliis habet scientiam et speculativam et practicam. Speculativam quidem, quantum ad modum, quidquid enim in rebus nos speculative cognoscimus definiendo et dividendo, hoc totum Deus multo perfectius novit.

Sed de his quae potest quidem facere, sed secundum nullum tempus facit, non habet practicam scientiam, secundum quod practica scientia dicitur a fine. Sic autem habet practicam scientiam de his quae secundum aliquod tempus facit. Mala vero, licet ab eo non sint operabilia, tamen sub cognitione practica ipsius cadunt, sicut et bona, inquantum permittit vel impedit vel ordinat ea, sicut et aegritudines cadunt sub practica scientia medici, inquantum per artem suam curat eas.

AD PRIMUM ergo dicendum quod scientia Dei est causa, non quidem sui ipsius, sed aliorum, quorundam quidem actu, scilicet eorum quae secundum aliquod tempus fiunt; quorundam vero virtute, scilicet eorum quae potest facere, et tamen nunquam fiunt.

AD SECUNDUM dicendum quod scientiam esse acceptam a rebus scitis, non per se convenit scientiae speculativae, sed per accidens, inquantum est humana.

AD ID VERO quod in contrarium obiicitur, dicendum quod de operabilibus perfecta scientia non habetur, nisi sciantur inquantum operabilia sunt. Et ideo, cum scientia Dei sit omnibus modis perfecta, oportet quod sciat ea

knowledge can be called speculative in three ways: first, on the part of the things known, which are not operable by the knower; such is the knowledge of man about natural or divine things. Second, as regards the manner of knowing—as, for instance, if a builder consider a house by defining and dividing, and considering what belongs to it in general: for this is to consider operable things in a speculative manner, and not as practically operable; for operable means the application of form to matter, and not the resolution of the composite into its universal formal principles. Third, as regards the end; *for the practical intellect differs in its end from the speculative*, as the Philosopher says (*De Anima* iii). For the practical intellect is ordered to the end of the operation; whereas the end of the speculative intellect is the consideration of truth. Hence if a builder should consider how a house can be made, not ordering this to the end of operation, but only to know (how to do it), this would be only a speculative consideration as regards the end, although it concerns an operable thing. Therefore knowledge which is speculative by reason of the thing itself known, is merely speculative. But that which is speculative either in its mode or as to its end is partly speculative and partly practical: and when it is ordained to an operative end it is simply practical.

In accordance with this, therefore, it must be said that God has of Himself a speculative knowledge only; for He Himself is not operable. But of all other things He has both speculative and practical knowledge. He has speculative knowledge as regards the mode; for whatever we know speculatively in things by defining and dividing, God knows all this much more perfectly.

Now of things which He can make, but does not make at any time, He has not a practical knowledge, according as knowledge is called practical from the end. But He has a practical knowledge of what He makes in some period of time. And, as regards evil things, although they are not operable by Him, yet they fall under His practical knowledge, like good things, inasmuch as He permits, or impedes, or directs them; as also sicknesses fall under the practical knowledge of the physician, inasmuch as he cures them by his art.

REPLY OBJ. 1: The knowledge of God is the cause, not indeed of Himself, but of other things. He is actually the cause of some, that is, of things that come to be in some period of time; and He is virtually the cause of others, that is, of things which He can make, and which nevertheless are never made.

REPLY OBJ. 2: The fact that knowledge is derived from things known does not essentially belong to speculative knowledge, but only accidentally in so far as it is human.

IN ANSWER to what is objected on the contrary, we must say that perfect knowledge of operable things is obtainable only if they are known in so far as they are operable. Therefore, since the knowledge of God is in every way perfect,

quae sunt a se operabilia, inquantum huiusmodi, et non solum secundum quod sunt speculabilia. Sed tamen non receditur a nobilitate speculativae scientiae, quia omnia alia a se videt in seipso, seipsum autem speculative cognoscit; et sic in speculativa sui ipsius scientia, habet cognitionem et speculativam et practicam omnium aliorum.

He must know what is operable by Him, formally as such, and not only in so far as they are speculative. Nevertheless this does not impair the nobility of His speculative knowledge, forasmuch as He sees all things other than Himself in Himself, and He knows Himself speculatively; and so in the speculative knowledge of Himself, he possesses both speculative and practical knowledge of all other things.

QUESTION 15

Post considerationem de scientia Dei, restat considerare de ideis.

Et circa hoc quaeruntur tria.

Primo, an sint ideae.

Secundo, utrum sint plures, vel una tantum.

Tertio, utrum sint omnium quae cognoscuntur a Deo.

After considering the knowledge of God, it remains to consider ideas.

And about this there are three points of inquiry:

(1) Whether there are ideas?

(2) Whether they are many, or one only?

(3) Whether there are ideas of all things known by God?

Article 1

Whether There Are Ideas?

AD PRIMUM SIC PROCEDITUR. Videtur quod ideae non sint. Dicit enim Dionysius, VII cap. de Div. Nom., quod Deus non cognoscit res secundum ideam. Sed ideae non ponuntur ad aliud, nisi ut per eas cognoscantur res. Ergo ideae non sunt.

PRAETEREA, Deus in seipso cognoscit omnia, ut supra dictum est. Sed seipsum non cognoscit per ideam. Ergo nec alia.

PRAETEREA, idea ponitur ut principium cognoscendi et operandi. Sed essentia divina est sufficiens principium cognoscendi et operandi omnia. Non ergo necesse est ponere ideas.

SED CONTRA est quod dicit Augustinus, in libro octoginta trium quaest., *tanta vis in ideis constituitur, ut, nisi his intellectis, sapiens esse nemo possit.*

RESPONDEO dicendum quod necesse est ponere in mente divina ideas. Idea enim Graece, Latine forma dicitur, unde per ideas intelliguntur formae aliarum rerum, praeter ipsas res existentes. Forma autem alicuius rei praeter ipsam existens, ad duo esse potest, vel ut sit exemplar eius cuius dicitur forma; vel ut sit principium cognitionis ipsius, secundum quod formae cognoscibilium dicuntur esse in cognoscente. Et quantum ad utrumque est necesse ponere ideas. Quod sic patet.

In omnibus enim quae non a casu generantur, necesse est formam esse finem generationis cuiuscumque. Agens autem non ageret propter formam, nisi inquantum similitudo formae est in ipso. Quod quidem contingit dupliciter. In quibusdam enim agentibus praeexistit forma rei fiendae secundum esse naturale, sicut in his quae agunt per naturam; sicut homo generat hominem, et ignis ignem. In quibusdam vero secundum esse intelligibile, ut in his quae agunt per intellectum; sicut

OBJECTION 1: It seems that there are no ideas. For Dionysius says (*Div. Nom.* vii), that God does not know things by ideas. But ideas are for nothing else except that things may be known through them. Therefore there are no ideas.

OBJ. 2: Further, God knows all things in Himself, as has been already said (Q. 14, A. 5). But He does not know Himself through an idea; neither therefore other things.

OBJ. 3: Further, an idea is considered to be the principle of knowledge and action. But the divine essence is a sufficient principle of knowing and effecting all things. It is not therefore necessary to suppose ideas.

ON THE CONTRARY, Augustine says (*Octog. Tri. Quaest.* qu. xlvi), *Such is the power inherent in ideas, that no one can be wise unless they are understood.*

I ANSWER THAT, It is necessary to suppose ideas in the divine mind. For the Greek word Idea is in Latin Forma. Hence by ideas are understood the forms of things, existing apart from the things themselves. Now the form of anything existing apart from the thing itself can be for one of two ends: either to be the type of that of which it is called the form, or to be the principle of the knowledge of that thing, inasmuch as the forms of things knowable are said to be in him who knows them. In either case we must suppose ideas, as is clear for the following reason:

In all things not generated by chance, the form must be the end of any generation whatsoever. But an agent does not act on account of the form, except in so far as the likeness of the form is in the agent, as may happen in two ways. For in some agents the form of the thing to be made pre-exists according to its natural being, as in those that act by their nature; as a man generates a man, or fire generates fire. Whereas in other agents (the form of the thing to be made pre-exists) according to intelligible being, as in those that

similitudo domus praeexistit in mente aedificatoris. Et haec potest dici idea domus, quia artifex intendit domum assimilare formae quam mente concepit. Quia igitur mundus non est casu factus, sed est factus a Deo per intellectum agente, ut infra patebit, necesse est quod in mente divina sit forma, ad similitudinem cuius mundus est factus. Et in hoc consistit ratio ideae.

Ad primum ergo dicendum quod Deus non intelligit res secundum ideam extra se existentem. Et sic etiam Aristoteles improbat opinionem Platonis de ideis, secundum quod ponebat eas per se existentes, non in intellectu.

Ad secundum dicendum quod, licet Deus per essentiam suam se et alia cognoscat, tamen essentia sua est principium operativum aliorum, non autem sui ipsius, et ideo habet rationem ideae secundum quod ad alia comparatur, non autem secundum quod comparatur ad ipsum Deum.

Ad tertium dicendum quod Deus secundum essentiam suam est similitudo omnium rerum. Unde idea in Deo nihil est aliud quam Dei essentia.

act by the intellect; and thus the likeness of a house pre-exists in the mind of the builder. And this may be called the idea of the house, since the builder intends to build his house like to the form conceived in his mind. As then the world was not made by chance, but by God acting by His intellect, as will appear later (Q. 46, A. 1), there must exist in the divine mind a form to the likeness of which the world was made. And in this the notion of an idea consists.

Reply Obj. 1: God does not understand things according to an idea existing outside Himself. Thus Aristotle (*Metaph.* ix) rejects the opinion of Plato, who held that ideas existed of themselves, and not in the intellect.

Reply Obj. 2: Although God knows Himself and all else by His own essence, yet His essence is the operative principle of all things, except of Himself. It has therefore the nature of an idea with respect to other things; though not with respect to Himself.

Reply Obj. 3: God is the similitude of all things according to His essence; therefore an idea in God is identical with His essence.

Article 2

Whether Ideas Are Many?

Ad secundum sic proceditur. Videtur quod non sint plures ideae. Idea enim in Deo est eius essentia. Sed essentia Dei est una tantum. Ergo et idea est una.

Praeterea, sicut idea est principium cognoscendi et operandi, ita ars et sapientia. Sed in Deo non sunt plures artes et sapientiae. Ergo nec plures ideae.

Si dicatur quod ideae multiplicantur secundum respectus ad diversas creaturas, contra, pluralitas idearum est ab aeterno. Si ergo ideae sunt plures, creaturae autem sunt temporales, ergo temporale erit causa aeterni.

Praeterea, respectus isti aut sunt secundum rem in creaturis tantum, aut etiam in Deo. Si in creaturis tantum, cum creaturae non sint ab aeterno, pluralitas idearum non erit ab aeterno, si multiplicentur solum secundum huiusmodi respectus. Si autem realiter sunt in Deo, sequitur quod alia pluralitas realis sit in Deo quam pluralitas personarum, quod est contra Damascenum, dicentem quod in divinis omnia unum sunt, praeter ingenerationem, generationem et processionem. Sic igitur non sunt plures ideae.

Sed contra est quod dicit Augustinus, in libro octoginta trium quaest., *ideae sunt principales quaedam formae vel rationes rerum stabiles atque incommutabiles,*

Objection 1: It seems that ideas are not many. For an idea in God is His essence. But God's essence is one only. Therefore there is only one idea.

Obj. 2: Further, as the idea is the principle of knowing and operating, so are art and wisdom. But in God there are not several arts or wisdoms. Therefore in Him there is no plurality of ideas.

Obj. 3: Further, if it be said that ideas are multiplied according to their relations to different creatures, it may be argued on the contrary that the plurality of ideas is eternal. If, then, ideas are many, but creatures temporal, then the temporal must be the cause of the eternal.

Obj. 4: Further, these relations are either real in creatures only, or in God also. If in creatures only, since creatures are not from eternity, the plurality of ideas cannot be from eternity, if ideas are multiplied only according to these relations. But if they are real in God, it follows that there is a real plurality in God other than the plurality of Persons: and this is against the teaching of Damascene (*De Fide Orth.* i, 10), who says, in God all things are one, except *ingenerability, generation, and procession*. Ideas therefore are not many.

On the contrary, Augustine says (*Octog. Tri. Quaest.* qu. xlvi), *Ideas are certain principal forms, or permanent and immutable types of things, they themselves not being*

quia ipsae formatae non sunt, ac per hoc aeternae ac semper eodem modo se habentes, quae divina intelligentia continentur. Sed cum ipsae neque oriantur neque intereant, secundum eas tamen formari dicitur omne quod oriri et interire potest, et omne quod oritur et interit.

RESPONDEO dicendum quod necesse est ponere plures ideas. Ad cuius evidentiam, considerandum est quod in quolibet effectu illud quod est ultimus finis, proprie est intentum a principali agente; sicut ordo exercitus a duce. Illud autem quod est optimum in rebus existens, est bonum ordinis universi, ut patet per philosophum in XII Metaphys. Ordo igitur universi est proprie a Deo intentus, et non per accidens proveniens secundum successionem agentium, prout quidam dixerunt quod Deus creavit primum creatum tantum, quod creatum creavit secundum creatum, et sic inde quousque producta est tanta rerum multitudo, secundum quam opinionem, Deus non haberet nisi ideam primi creati. Sed si ipse ordo universi est per se creatus ab eo, et intentus ab ipso, necesse est quod habeat ideam ordinis universi. Ratio autem alicuius totius haberi non potest, nisi habeantur propriae rationes eorum ex quibus totum constituitur, sicut aedificator speciem domus concipere non posset, nisi apud ipsum esset propria ratio cuiuslibet partium eius. Sic igitur oportet quod in mente divina sint propriae rationes omnium rerum. Unde dicit Augustinus, in libro octoginta trium quaest., quod *singula propriis rationibus a Deo creata sunt.* Unde sequitur quod in mente divina sint plures ideae. Hoc autem quomodo divinae simplicitati non repugnet, facile est videre, si quis consideret ideam operati esse in mente operantis sicut quod intelligitur; non autem sicut species qua intelligitur, quae est forma faciens intellectum in actu. Forma enim domus in mente aedificatoris est aliquid ab eo intellectum, ad cuius similitudinem domum in materia format. Non est autem contra simplicitatem divini intellectus, quod multa intelligat, sed contra simplicitatem eius esset, si per plures species eius intellectus formaretur. Unde plures ideae sunt in mente divina ut intellectae ab ipso. Quod hoc modo potest videri. Ipse enim essentiam suam perfecte cognoscit, unde cognoscit eam secundum omnem modum quo cognoscibilis est. Potest autem cognosci non solum secundum quod in se est, sed secundum quod est participabilis secundum aliquem modum similitudinis a creaturis. Unaquaeque autem creatura habet propriam speciem, secundum quod aliquo modo participat divinae essentiae similitudinem. Sic igitur inquantum Deus cognoscit suam essentiam ut sic imitabilem a tali creatura, cognoscit eam ut propriam rationem et ideam huius creaturae. Et similiter de aliis. Et sic patet quod Deus intelligit plures rationes proprias plurium rerum; quae sunt plures ideae.

formed. Thus they are eternal, and existing always in the same manner, as being contained in the divine intelligence. Whilst, however, they themselves neither come into being nor decay, yet we say that in accordance with them everything is formed that can rise or decay, and all that actually does so.

I ANSWER THAT, It must necessarily be held that ideas are many. In proof of which it is to be considered that in every effect the ultimate end is the proper intention of the principal agent, as the order of an army (is the proper intention) of the general. Now the highest good existing in things is the good of the order of the universe, as the Philosopher clearly teaches in *Metaph.* xii. Therefore the order of the universe is properly intended by God, and is not the accidental result of a succession of agents, as has been supposed by those who have taught that God created only the first creature, and that this creature created the second creature, and so on, until this great multitude of beings was produced. According to this opinion God would have the idea of the first created thing alone; whereas, if the order itself of the universe was created by Him immediately, and intended by Him, He must have the idea of the order of the universe. Now there cannot be an idea of any whole, unless particular ideas are had of those parts of which the whole is made; just as a builder cannot conceive the idea of a house unless he has the idea of each of its parts. So, then, it must needs be that in the divine mind there are the proper ideas of all things. Hence Augustine says (*Octog. Tri. Quaest.* qu. xlvi), *that each thing was created by God according to the idea proper to it,* from which it follows that in the divine mind ideas are many. Now it can easily be seen how this is not repugnant to the simplicity of God, if we consider that the idea of a work is in the mind of the operator as that which is understood, and not as the image whereby he understands, which is a form that makes the intellect in act. For the form of the house in the mind of the builder is something understood by him, to the likeness of which he forms the house in matter. Now, it is not repugnant to the simplicity of the divine mind that it understand many things; though it would be repugnant to its simplicity were His understanding to be formed by a plurality of images. Hence many ideas exist in the divine mind, as things understood by it; as can be proved thus. Inasmuch as He knows His own essence perfectly, He knows it according to every mode in which it can be known. Now it can be known not only as it is in itself, but as it can be participated in by creatures according to some degree of likeness. But every creature has its own proper species, according to which it participates in some degree in likeness to the divine essence. So far, therefore, as God knows His essence as capable of such imitation by any creature, He knows it as the particular type and idea of that creature; and in like manner as regards other creatures. So it is clear that God understands many particular types of things and these are many ideas.

AD PRIMUM ergo dicendum quod idea non nominat divinam essentiam inquantum est essentia, sed inquantum est similitudo vel ratio huius vel illius rei. Unde secundum quod sunt plures rationes intellectae ex una essentia, secundum hoc dicuntur plures ideae.

AD SECUNDUM dicendum quod sapientia et ars significantur ut quo Deus intelligit, sed idea ut quod Deus intelligit. Deus autem uno intelligit multa; et non solum secundum quod in seipsis sunt, sed etiam secundum quod intellecta sunt; quod est intelligere plures rationes rerum. Sicut artifex, dum intelligit formam domus in materia, dicitur intelligere domum, dum autem intelligit formam domus ut a se speculatam, ex eo quod intelligit se intelligere eam, intelligit ideam vel rationem domus. Deus autem non solum intelligit multas res per essentiam suam, sed etiam intelligit se intelligere multa per essentiam suam. Sed hoc est intelligere plures rationes rerum; vel, plures ideas esse in intellectu eius ut intellectas.

AD TERTIUM dicendum quod huiusmodi respectus, quibus multiplicantur ideae, non causantur a rebus, sed ab intellectu divino, comparante essentiam suam ad res.

AD QUARTUM dicendum quod respectus multiplicantes ideas, non sunt in rebus creatis, sed in Deo. Non tamen sunt reales respectus, sicut illi quibus distinguuntur personae, sed respectus intellecti a Deo.

REPLY OBJ. 1: The divine essence is not called an idea in so far as it is that essence, but only in so far as it is the likeness or type of this or that thing. Hence ideas are said to be many, inasmuch as many types are understood through the self-same essence.

REPLY OBJ. 2: By wisdom and art we signify that by which God understands; but an idea, that which God understands. For God by one understands many things, and that not only according to what they are in themselves, but also according as they are understood, and this is to understand the several types of things. In the same way, an architect is said to understand a house, when he understands the form of the house in matter. But if he understands the form of a house, as devised by himself, from the fact that he understands that he understands it, he thereby understands the type or idea of the house. Now not only does God understand many things by His essence, but He also understands that He understands many things by His essence. And this means that He understands the several types of things; or that many ideas are in His intellect as understood by Him.

REPLY OBJ. 3: Such relations, whereby ideas are multiplied, are caused not by the things themselves, but by the divine intellect comparing its own essence with these things.

REPLY OBJ. 4: Relations multiplying ideas do not exist in created things, but in God. Yet they are not real relations, such as those whereby the Persons are distinguished, but relations understood by God.

Article 3

Whether There Are Ideas of All Things That God Knows?

AD TERTIUM SIC PROCEDITUR. Videtur quod non omnium quae cognoscit Deus, sint ideae in ipso. Mali enim idea non est in Deo, quia sequeretur malum esse in Deo. Sed mala cognoscuntur a Deo. Ergo non omnium quae cognoscuntur a Deo, sunt ideae.

PRAETEREA, Deus cognoscit ea quae nec sunt nec erunt nec fuerunt, ut supra dictum est. Sed horum non sunt ideae, quia dicit Dionysius, V cap. de Div. Nom., quod *exemplaria sunt divinae voluntates, determinativae et effectivae rerum*. Ergo non omnium quae a Deo cognoscuntur, sunt ideae in ipso.

PRAETEREA, Deus cognoscit materiam primam, quae non potest habere ideam, cum nullam habeat formam. Ergo idem quod prius.

PRAETEREA, constat quod Deus scit non solum species, sed etiam genera et singularia et accidentia. Sed horum non sunt ideae, secundum positionem Platonis, qui

OBJECTION 1: It seems that there are not ideas in God of all things that He knows. For the idea of evil is not in God; since it would follow that evil was in Him. But evil things are known by God. Therefore there are not ideas of all things that God knows.

OBJ. 2: Further, God knows things that neither are, nor will be, nor have been, as has been said above (A. 9). But of such things there are no ideas, since, as Dionysius says (*Div. Nom.* v): *Acts of the divine will are the determining and effective types of things.* Therefore there are not in God ideas of all things known by Him.

OBJ. 3: Further, God knows primary matter, of which there can be no idea, since it has no form. Hence the same conclusion.

OBJ. 4: Further, it is certain that God knows not only species, but also genera, singulars, and accidents. But there are not ideas of these, according to Plato's teaching, who first taught ideas, as Augustine says (*Octog. Tri. Quaest.*

primus ideas introduxit, ut dicit Augustinus. Non ergo omnium cognitorum a Deo sunt ideae in ipso.

SED CONTRA, ideae sunt rationes in mente divina existentes, ut per Augustinum patet. Sed omnium quae cognoscit, Deus habet proprias rationes. Ergo omnium quae cognoscit, habet ideam.

RESPONDEO dicendum quod, cum ideae a Platone ponerentur principia cognitionis rerum et generationis ipsarum, ad utrumque se habet idea, prout in mente divina ponitur. Et secundum quod est principium factionis rerum, exemplar dici potest, et ad practicam cognitionem pertinet. Secundum autem quod principium cognoscitivum est, proprie dicitur ratio; et potest etiam ad scientiam speculativam pertinere. Secundum ergo quod exemplar est, secundum hoc se habet ad omnia quae a Deo fiunt secundum aliquod tempus. Secundum vero quod principium cognoscitivum est, se habet ad omnia quae cognoscuntur a Deo, etiam si nullo tempore fiant; et ad omnia quae a Deo cognoscuntur secundum propriam rationem, et secundum quod cognoscuntur ab ipso per modum speculationis.

AD PRIMUM ergo dicendum quod malum cognoscitur a Deo non per propriam rationem, sed per rationem boni. Et ideo malum non habet in Deo ideam, neque secundum quod idea est exemplar, neque secundum quod est ratio.

AD SECUNDUM dicendum quod eorum quae neque sunt neque erunt neque fuerunt, Deus non habet practicam cognitionem, nisi virtute tantum. Unde respectu eorum non est idea in Deo, secundum quod idea significat exemplar, sed solum secundum quod significat rationem.

AD TERTIUM dicendum quod Plato, secundum quosdam, posuit materiam non creatam, et ideo non posuit ideam esse materiae, sed materiae concausam. Sed quia nos ponimus materiam creatam a Deo, non tamen sine forma, habet quidem materia ideam in Deo, non tamen aliam ab idea compositi. Nam materia secundum se neque esse habet, neque cognoscibilis est.

AD QUARTUM dicendum quod genera non possunt habere ideam aliam ab idea speciei, secundum quod idea significat exemplar, quia nunquam genus fit nisi in aliqua specie. Similiter etiam est de accidentibus quae inseparabiliter concomitantur subiectum, quia haec simul fiunt cum subiecto. Accidentia autem quae superveniunt subiecto, specialem ideam habent. Artifex enim per formam domus facit omnia accidentia quae a principio concomitantur domum, sed ea quae superveniunt domui iam factae, ut picturae vel aliquid aliud, facit per aliquam aliam formam. Individua vero, secundum Platonem, non habebant aliam ideam quam ideam speciei, tum quia singularia individuantur per materiam, quam ponebat esse increatam, ut quidam dicunt, et concausam

qu. xlvi). Therefore there are not ideas in God of all things known by Him.

ON THE CONTRARY, Ideas are types existing in the divine mind, as is clear from Augustine (*Octog. Tri. Quaest.* qu. xlvi). But God has the proper types of all things that He knows; and therefore He has ideas of all things known by Him.

I ANSWER THAT, As ideas, according to Plato, are principles of the knowledge of things and of their generation, an idea has this twofold office, as it exists in the mind of God. So far as the idea is the principle of the making of things, it may be called an *exemplar*, and belongs to practical knowledge. But so far as it is a principle of knowledge, it is properly called a *type*, and may belong to speculative knowledge also. As an exemplar, therefore, it has respect to everything made by God in any period of time; whereas as a principle of knowledge it has respect to all things known by God, even though they never come to be in time; and to all things that He knows according to their proper type, in so far as they are known by Him in a speculative manner.

REPLY OBJ. 1: Evil is known by God not through its own type, but through the type of good. Evil, therefore, has no idea in God, neither in so far as an idea is an *exemplar* nor as a *type*.

REPLY OBJ. 2: God has no practical knowledge, except virtually, of things which neither are, nor will be, nor have been. Hence, with respect to these there is no idea in God in so far as idea signifies an *exemplar* but only in so far as it denotes a *type*.

REPLY OBJ. 3: Plato is said by some to have considered matter as not created; and therefore he postulated not an idea of matter but a concause with matter. Since, however, we hold matter to be created by God, though not apart from form, matter has its idea in God; but not apart from the idea of the composite; for matter in itself can neither exist, nor be known.

REPLY OBJ. 4: Genus can have no idea apart from the idea of species, in so far as idea denotes an *exemplar*; for genus cannot exist except in some species. The same is the case with those accidents that inseparably accompany their subject; for these come into being along with their subject. But accidents which supervene to the subject, have their special idea. For an architect produces through the form of the house all the accidents that originally accompany it; whereas those that are superadded to the house when completed, such as painting, or any other such thing, are produced through some other form. Now individual things, according to Plato, have no other idea than that of species; both because particular things are individualized by matter, which, as some say, he held to be uncreated and the

ideae; tum quia intentio naturae consistit in speciebus, nec particularia producit, nisi ut in eis species salventur. Sed providentia divina non solum se extendit ad species, sed ad singularia, ut infra dicetur.

concause with the idea; and because the intention of nature regards the species, and produces individuals only that in them the species may be preserved. However, divine providence extends not merely to species, but to individuals as will be shown later (Q. 22, A. 3).

QUESTION 16

TRUTH

Quoniam autem scientia verorum est, post considerationem scientiae Dei, de veritate inquirendum est.

Circa quam quaeruntur octo.

Primo, utrum veritas sit in re, vel tantum in intellectu.

Secundo, utrum sit tantum in intellectu componente et dividente.

Tertio, de comparatione veri ad ens.

Quarto, de comparatione veri ad bonum.

Quinto, utrum Deus sit veritas.

Sexto, utrum omnia sint vera veritate una, vel pluribus.

Septimo, de aeternitate veritatis.

Octavo, de incommutabilitate ipsius.

Since knowledge is of things that are true, after the consideration of the knowledge of God, we must inquire concerning truth.

About this there are eight points of inquiry:

(1) Whether truth resides in the thing, or only in the intellect?

(2) Whether it resides only in the intellect composing and dividing?

(3) On the comparison of the true to being.

(4) On the comparison of the true to the good.

(5) Whether God is truth?

(6) Whether all things are true by one truth, or by many?

(7) On the eternity of truth.

(8) On the unchangeableness of truth.

Article 1

Whether Truth Resides Only in the Intellect?

AD PRIMUM SIC PROCEDITUR. Videtur quod veritas non sit tantum in intellectu, sed magis in rebus. Augustinus enim, in libro Soliloq., reprobat hanc notificationem veri, verum est id quod videtur, quia secundum hoc, lapides qui sunt in abditissimo terrae sinu, non essent veri lapides, quia non videntur. Reprobat etiam istam, verum est quod ita se habet ut videtur cognitori, si velit et possit cognoscere, quia secundum hoc sequeretur quod nihil esset verum, si nullus posset cognoscere. Et definit sic verum, verum est id quod est. Et sic videtur quod veritas sit in rebus, et non in intellectu.

PRAETEREA, quidquid est verum, veritate verum est. Si igitur veritas est in intellectu solo, nihil erit verum nisi secundum quod intelligitur, quod est error antiquorum philosophorum, qui dicebant omne quod videtur, esse verum. Ad quod sequitur contradictoria simul esse vera, cum contradictoria simul a diversis vera esse videantur.

Praeterea, propter quod unumquodque, et illud magis, ut patet I Poster. *Sed ex eo quod res est vel non est, est opinio vel oratio vera vel falsa,* secundum philosophum in praedicamentis. Ergo veritas magis est in rebus quam in intellectu.

SED CONTRA est quod philosophus dicit, VI Metaphys., quod *verum et falsum non sunt in rebus, sed in intellectu.*

OBJECTION 1: It seems that truth does not reside only in the intellect, but rather in things. For Augustine (*Soliloq.* ii, 5) condemns this definition of truth, *That is true which is seen,* since it would follow that stones hidden in the bosom of the earth would not be true stones, as they are not seen. He also condemns the following, *That is true which is as it appears to the knower, who is willing and able to know,* for hence it would follow that nothing would be true, unless someone could know it. Therefore he defines truth thus: *That is true which is.* It seems, then, that truth resides in things, and not in the intellect.

OBJ. 2: Further, whatever is true, is true by reason of truth. If, then, truth is only in the intellect, nothing will be true except in so far as it is understood. But this is the error of the ancient philosophers, who said that whatever seems to be true is so. Consequently mutual contradictories seem to be true as seen by different persons at the same time.

OBJ. 3: Further, *that, on account of which a thing is so, is itself more so,* as is evident from the Philosopher (*Poster.* i). But it is from the fact that a thing is or is not, that our thought or word is true or false, as the Philosopher teaches (Praedicam. iii). Therefore truth resides rather in things than in the intellect.

ON THE CONTRARY, The Philosopher says (*Metaph.* vi), *The true and the false reside not in things, but in the intellect.*

179

RESPONDEO dicendum quod, sicut bonum nominat id in quod tendit appetitus, ita verum nominat id in quod tendit intellectus. Hoc autem distat inter appetitum et intellectum, sive quamcumque cognitionem, quia cognitio est secundum quod cognitum est in cognoscente, appetitus autem est secundum quod appetens inclinatur in ipsam rem appetitam. Et sic terminus appetitus, quod est bonum, est in re appetibili, sed terminus cognitionis, quod est verum, est in ipso intellectu. Sicut autem bonum est in re, inquantum habet ordinem ad appetitum; et propter hoc ratio bonitatis derivatur a re appetibili in appetitum, secundum quod appetitus dicitur bonus, prout est boni, ita, cum verum sit in intellectu secundum quod conformatur rei intellectae, necesse est quod ratio veri ab intellectu ad rem intellectam derivetur, ut res etiam intellecta vera dicatur, secundum quod habet aliquem ordinem ad intellectum. Res autem intellecta ad intellectum aliquem potest habere ordinem vel per se, vel per accidens. Per se quidem habet ordinem ad intellectum a quo dependet secundum suum esse, per accidens autem ad intellectum a quo cognoscibilis est. Sicut si dicamus quod domus comparatur ad intellectum artificis per se, per accidens autem comparatur ad intellectum a quo non dependet.

Iudicium autem de re non sumitur secundum id quod inest ei per accidens, sed secundum id quod inest ei per se. Unde unaquaeque res dicitur vera absolute, secundum ordinem ad intellectum a quo dependet. Et inde est quod res artificiales dicuntur verae per ordinem ad intellectum nostrum, dicitur enim domus vera, quae assequitur similitudinem formae quae est in mente artificis; et dicitur oratio vera, inquantum est signum intellectus veri. Et similiter res naturales dicuntur esse verae, secundum quod assequuntur similitudinem specierum quae sunt in mente divina, dicitur enim verus lapis, qui assequitur propriam lapidis naturam, secundum praeconceptionem intellectus divini. Sic ergo veritas principaliter est in intellectu; secundario vero in rebus, secundum quod comparantur ad intellectum ut ad principium. Et secundum hoc, veritas diversimode notificatur. Nam Augustinus, in libro de vera Relig., dicit quod *veritas est, qua ostenditur id quod est.* Et Hilarius dicit quod *verum est declarativum aut manifestativum esse.* Et hoc pertinet ad veritatem secundum quod est in intellectu. Ad veritatem autem rei secundum ordinem ad intellectum, pertinet definitio Augustini in libro de vera Relig., *veritas est summa similitudo principii, quae sine ulla dissimilitudine est.* Et quaedam definitio Anselmi, *veritas est rectitudo sola mente perceptibilis*; nam rectum est, quod principio concordat. Et quaedam definitio Avicennae, *veritas uniuscuiusque rei est proprietas sui esse quod stabilitum est ei.* Quod autem dicitur quod veritas est adaequatio rei et intellectus potest ad utrumque pertinere.

I ANSWER THAT, As the good denotes that towards which the appetite tends, so the true denotes that towards which the intellect tends. Now there is this difference between the appetite and the intellect, or any knowledge whatsoever, that knowledge is according as the thing known is in the knower, whilst appetite is according as the desirer tends towards the thing desired. Thus the term of the appetite, namely good, is in the object desirable, and the term of the intellect, namely true, is in the intellect itself. Now as good exists in a thing so far as that thing is related to the appetite—and hence the aspect of goodness passes on from the desirable thing to the appetite, in so far as the appetite is called good if its object is good; so, since the true is in the intellect in so far as it is conformed to the object understood, the aspect of the true must needs pass from the intellect to the object understood, so that also the thing understood is said to be true in so far as it has some relation to the intellect. Now a thing understood may be in relation to an intellect either essentially or accidentally. It is related essentially to an intellect on which it depends as regards its essence; but accidentally to an intellect by which it is knowable; even as we may say that a house is related essentially to the intellect of the architect, but accidentally to the intellect upon which it does not depend.

Now we do not judge of a thing by what is in it accidentally, but by what is in it essentially. Hence, everything is said to be true absolutely, in so far as it is related to the intellect from which it depends; and thus it is that artificial things are said to be true as being related to our intellect. For a house is said to be true that expresses the likeness of the form in the architect's mind; and words are said to be true so far as they are the signs of truth in the intellect. In the same way natural things are said to be true in so far as they express the likeness of the species that are in the divine mind. For a stone is called true, which possesses the nature proper to a stone, according to the preconception in the divine intellect. Thus, then, truth resides primarily in the intellect, and secondarily in things according as they are related to the intellect as their principle. Consequently there are various definitions of truth. Augustine says (*De Vera Relig.* xxxvi), *Truth is that whereby is made manifest that which is*; and Hilary says (*De Trin.* v) that *Truth makes being clear and evident* and this pertains to truth according as it is in the intellect. As to the truth of things in so far as they are related to the intellect, we have Augustine's definition (*De Vera Relig.* xxxvi), *Truth is a supreme likeness without any unlikeness to a principle*: also Anselm's definition (De Verit. xii), *Truth is rightness, perceptible by the mind alone*; for that is right which is in accordance with the principle; also Avicenna's definition (*Metaph.* viii, 6), *The truth of each thing is a property of the essence which is immutably attached to it.* The definition that *Truth is the equation of thought and thing* is applicable to it under either aspect.

AD PRIMUM ergo dicendum quod Augustinus loquitur de veritate rei; et excludit a ratione huius veritatis, comparationem ad intellectum nostrum. Nam id quod est per accidens, ab unaquaque definitione excluditur.

AD SECUNDUM dicendum quod antiqui philosophi species rerum naturalium non dicebant procedere ab aliquo intellectu, sed eas provenire a casu, et quia considerabant quod verum importat comparationem ad intellectum, cogebantur veritatem rerum constituere in ordine ad intellectum nostrum. Ex quo inconvenientia sequebantur quae philosophus prosequitur in IV Metaphys. Quae quidem inconvenientia non accidunt, si ponamus veritatem rerum consistere in comparatione ad intellectum divinum.

AD TERTIUM dicendum quod, licet veritas intellectus nostri a re causetur, non tamen oportet quod in re per prius inveniatur ratio veritatis, sicut neque in medicina per prius invenitur ratio sanitatis quam in animali; virtus enim medicinae, non sanitas eius, causat sanitatem, cum non sit agens univocum. Et similiter esse rei, non veritas eius, causat veritatem intellectus. Unde philosophus dicit quod opinio et oratio vera est *ex eo quod res est, non ex eo quod res vera est.*

REPLY OBJ. 1: Augustine is speaking about the truth of things, and excludes from the notion of this truth, relation to our intellect; for what is accidental is excluded from every definition.

REPLY OBJ. 2: The ancient philosophers held that the species of natural things did not proceed from any intellect, but were produced by chance. But as they saw that truth implies relation to intellect, they were compelled to base the truth of things on their relation to our intellect. From this, conclusions result that are inadmissible, and which the Philosopher refutes (*Metaph.* iv). Such, however, do not follow, if we say that the truth of things consists in their relation to the divine intellect.

REPLY OBJ. 3: Although the truth of our intellect is caused by the thing, yet it is not necessary that truth should be there primarily, any more than that health should be primarily in medicine, rather than in the animal: for the virtue of medicine, and not its health, is the cause of health, for here the agent is not univocal. In the same way, the being of the thing, not its truth, is the cause of truth in the intellect. Hence the Philosopher says that a thought or a word is true *from the fact that a thing is, not because a thing is true.*

Article 2

Whether Truth Resides Only in the Intellect Composing and Dividing?

AD SECUNDUM SIC PROCEDITUR. Videtur quod veritas non sit solum in intellectu componente et dividente. Dicit enim philosophus, in III de anima, quod sicut sensus propriorum sensibilium semper veri sunt, ita et intellectus eius quod quid est. Sed compositio et divisio non est neque in sensu, neque in intellectu cognoscente quod quid est. Ergo veritas non solum est in compositione et divisione intellectus.

PRAETEREA, Isaac dicit, in libro de definitionibus, quod veritas est adaequatio rei et intellectus. Sed sicut intellectus complexorum potest adaequari rebus, ita intellectus incomplexorum, et etiam sensus sentiens rem ut est. Ergo veritas non est solum in compositione et divisione intellectus.

SED CONTRA est quod dicit philosophus, in VI Metaphys., quod circa simplicia et *quod quid est non est veritas, nec in intellectu neque in rebus.*

RESPONDEO dicendum quod verum, sicut dictum est, secundum sui primam rationem est in intellectu. Cum autem omnis res sit vera secundum quod habet propriam formam naturae suae, necesse est quod intellectus, inquantum est cognoscens, sit verus inquantum habet similitudinem rei cognitae, quae est forma eius

OBJECTION 1: It seems that truth does not reside only in the intellect composing and dividing. For the Philosopher says (*De Anima* iii) that as the senses are always true as regards their proper sensible objects, so is the intellect as regards *what a thing is.* Now composition and division are neither in the senses nor in the intellect knowing *what a thing is.* Therefore truth does not reside only in the intellect composing and dividing.

OBJ. 2: Further, Isaac says in his book On Definitions that truth is the equation of thought and thing. Now just as the intellect with regard to complex things can be equated to things, so also with regard to simple things; and this is true also of sense apprehending a thing as it is. Therefore truth does not reside only in the intellect composing and dividing.

ON THE CONTRARY, the Philosopher says (*Metaph.* vi) that with regard to simple things and *what a thing is, truth is found neither in the intellect nor in things.*

I ANSWER THAT, As stated before, truth resides, in its primary aspect, in the intellect. Now since everything is true according as it has the form proper to its nature, the intellect, in so far as it is knowing, must be true, in so far as it has the likeness of the thing known, this being its form, as knowing. For this reason truth is defined by the conformity

inquantum est cognoscens. Et propter hoc per conformitatem intellectus et rei veritas definitur. Unde conformitatem istam cognoscere, est cognoscere veritatem. Hanc autem nullo modo sensus cognoscit, licet enim visus habeat similitudinem visibilis, non tamen cognoscit comparationem quae est inter rem visam et id quod ipse apprehendit de ea. Intellectus autem conformitatem sui ad rem intelligibilem cognoscere potest, sed tamen non apprehendit eam secundum quod cognoscit de aliquo quod quid est; sed quando iudicat rem ita se habere sicut est forma quam de re apprehendit, tunc primo cognoscit et dicit verum. Et hoc facit componendo et dividendo, nam in omni propositione aliquam formam significatam per praedicatum, vel applicat alicui rei significatae per subiectum, vel removet ab ea. Et ideo bene invenitur quod sensus est verus de aliqua re, vel intellectus cognoscendo quod quid est, sed non quod cognoscat aut dicat verum. Et similiter est de vocibus complexis aut incomplexis. Veritas quidem igitur potest esse in sensu, vel in intellectu cognoscente quod quid est, ut in quadam re vera, non autem ut cognitum in cognoscente, quod importat nomen veri; perfectio enim intellectus est verum ut cognitum. Et ideo, proprie loquendo, veritas est in intellectu componente et dividente, non autem in sensu, neque in intellectu cognoscente quod quid est.

ET PER HOC patet solutio ad obiecta.

of intellect and thing; and hence to know this conformity is to know truth. But in no way can sense know this. For although sight has the likeness of a visible thing, yet it does not know the comparison which exists between the thing seen and that which itself apprehends concerning it. But the intellect can know its own conformity with the intelligible thing; yet it does not apprehend it by knowing of a thing *what a thing is*. When, however, it judges that a thing corresponds to the form which it apprehends about that thing, then first it knows and expresses truth. This it does by composing and dividing: for in every proposition it either applies to, or removes from the thing signified by the subject, some form signified by the predicate: and this clearly shows that the sense is true of any thing, as is also the intellect, when it knows *what a thing is*; but it does not thereby know or affirm truth. This is in like manner the case with complex or non-complex words. Truth therefore may be in the senses, or in the intellect knowing *what a thing is*, as in anything that is true; yet not as the thing known in the knower, which is implied by the word *truth*; for the perfection of the intellect is truth as known. Therefore, properly speaking, truth resides in the intellect composing and dividing; and not in the senses; nor in the intellect knowing *what a thing is*.

AND THUS the Objections given are solved.

Article 3

Whether the True and Being Are Convertible Terms?

AD TERTIUM SIC PROCEDITUR. Videtur quod verum et ens non convertantur. Verum enim est proprie in intellectu, ut dictum est. Ens autem proprie est in rebus. Ergo non convertuntur.

PRAETEREA, id quod se extendit ad ens et non ens, non convertitur cum ente. Sed verum se extendit ad ens et non ens, nam verum est quod est esse, et quod non est non esse. Ergo verum et ens non convertuntur.

PRAETEREA, quae se habent secundum prius et posterius, non videntur converti. Sed verum videtur prius esse quam ens, nam ens non intelligitur nisi sub ratione veri. Ergo videtur quod non sint convertibilia.

SED CONTRA est quod dicit philosophus, II Metaphys., quod eadem est dispositio rerum in esse et veritate.

RESPONDEO dicendum quod, sicut bonum habet rationem appetibilis, ita verum habet ordinem ad cognitionem. Unumquodque autem inquantum habet de esse, intantum est cognoscibile. Et propter hoc dicitur

OBJECTION 1: It seems that the true and being are not convertible terms. For the true resides properly in the intellect, as stated (A. 1); but being is properly in things. Therefore they are not convertible.

OBJ. 2: Further, that which extends to being and not-being is not convertible with being. But the true extends to being and not-being; for it is true that what is, is; and that what is not, is not. Therefore the true and being are not convertible.

OBJ. 3: Further, things which stand to each other in order of priority and posteriority seem not to be convertible. But the true appears to be prior to being; for being is not understood except under the aspect of the true. Therefore it seems they are not convertible.

ON THE CONTRARY, the Philosopher says (*Metaph*. ii) that there is the same disposition of things in being and in truth.

I ANSWER THAT, As good has the nature of what is desirable, so truth is related to knowledge. Now everything, in as far as it has being, so far is it knowable. Wherefore it is said in *De Anima* iii that *the soul is in some manner all*

in III de anima, quod anima est quodammodo omnia secundum sensum et intellectum. Et ideo, sicut bonum convertitur cum ente, ita et verum. Sed tamen, sicut bonum addit rationem appetibilis supra ens, ita et verum comparationem ad intellectum.

AD PRIMUM ergo dicendum quod verum est in rebus et in intellectu, ut dictum est. Verum autem quod est in rebus, convertitur cum ente secundum substantiam. Sed verum quod est in intellectu, convertitur cum ente, ut manifestativum cum manifestato. Hoc enim est de ratione veri, ut dictum est. Quamvis posset dici quod etiam ens est in rebus et in intellectu, sicut et verum; licet verum principaliter in intellectu, ens vero principaliter in rebus. Et hoc accidit propter hoc, quod verum et ens differunt ratione.

AD SECUNDUM dicendum quod non ens non habet in se unde cognoscatur, sed cognoscitur inquantum intellectus facit illud cognoscibile. Unde verum fundatur in ente, inquantum non ens est quoddam ens rationis, apprehensum scilicet a ratione.

AD TERTIUM dicendum quod, cum dicitur quod ens non potest apprehendi sine ratione veri, hoc potest dupliciter intelligi. Uno modo, ita quod non apprehendatur ens, nisi ratio veri assequatur apprehensionem entis. Et sic locutio habet veritatem. Alio modo posset sic intelligi, quod ens non posset apprehendi, nisi apprehenderetur ratio veri. Et hoc falsum est. Sed verum non potest apprehendi, nisi apprehendatur ratio entis, quia ens cadit in ratione veri. Et est simile sicut si comparemus intelligibile ad ens. Non enim potest intelligi ens, quin ens sit intelligibile, sed tamen potest intelligi ens, ita quod non intelligatur eius intelligibilitas. Et similiter ens intellectum est verum, non tamen intelligendo ens, intelligitur verum.

things, through the senses and the intellect. And therefore, as good is convertible with being, so is the true. But as good adds to being the notion of desirable, so the true adds relation to the intellect.

REPLY OBJ. 1: The true resides in things and in the intellect, as said before (A. 1). But the true that is in things is convertible with being as to substance; while the true that is in the intellect is convertible with being, as the manifestation with the manifested; for this belongs to the nature of truth, as has been said already (A. 1). It may, however, be said that being also is in things and in the intellect, as is the true; although truth is primarily in the intellect, while being is primarily in things; and this is so because truth and being differ in idea.

REPLY OBJ. 2: Not-being has nothing in itself whereby it can be known; yet it is known in so far as the intellect renders it knowable. Hence the true is based on being, inasmuch as not-being is a kind of logical being, apprehended, that is, by reason.

REPLY OBJ. 3: When it is said that being cannot be apprehended except under the notion of the true, this can be understood in two ways. In the one way so as to mean that being is not apprehended, unless the idea of the true follows apprehension of being; and this is true. In the other way, so as to mean that being cannot be apprehended unless the idea of the true be apprehended also; and this is false. But the true cannot be apprehended unless the idea of being be apprehended also, since being is included in the idea of the true. The case is the same if we compare the intelligible object with being. For being cannot be understood, unless being is intelligible. Yet being can be understood while its intelligibility is not understood. Similarly, being when understood is true, yet the true is not understood by understanding being.

Article 4

Whether Good Is Logically Prior to the True?

AD QUARTUM SIC PROCEDITUR. Videtur quod bonum secundum rationem sit prius quam verum. Quod enim est universalius, secundum rationem prius est, ut patet ex I Physic. Sed bonum est universalius quam verum, nam verum est quoddam bonum, scilicet intellectus. Ergo bonum prius est secundum rationem quam verum.

PRAETEREA, bonum est in rebus, verum autem in compositione et divisione intellectus, ut dictum est. Sed ea quae sunt in re, sunt priora his quae sunt in intellectu. Ergo prius est secundum rationem bonum quam verum.

OBJECTION 1: It seems that good is logically prior to the true. For what is more universal is logically prior, as is evident from *Phys.* i. But the good is more universal than the true, since the true is a kind of good, namely, of the intellect. Therefore the good is logically prior to the true.

OBJ. 2: Further, good is in things, but the true is in the intellect composing and dividing as said above (A. 2). But that which is in things is prior to that which is in the intellect. Therefore good is logically prior to the true.

PRAETEREA, veritas est quaedam species virtutis, ut patet in IV Ethic. Sed virtus continetur sub bono, est enim bona qualitas mentis, ut dicit Augustinus. Ergo bonum est prius quam verum.

SED CONTRA, quod est in pluribus, est prius secundum rationem. Sed verum est in quibusdam in quibus non est bonum, scilicet in mathematicis. Ergo verum est prius quam bonum.

RESPONDEO dicendum quod, licet bonum et verum supposito convertantur cum ente, tamen ratione differunt. Et secundum hoc verum, absolute loquendo, prius est quam bonum. Quod ex duobus apparet. Primo quidem ex hoc, quod verum propinquius se habet ad ens, quod est prius, quam bonum. Nam verum respicit ipsum esse simpliciter et immediate, ratio autem boni consequitur esse, secundum quod est aliquo modo perfectum; sic enim appetibile est. Secundo apparet ex hoc, quod cognitio naturaliter praecedit appetitum. Unde, cum verum respiciat cognitionem, bonum autem appetitum, prius erit verum quam bonum secundum rationem.

AD PRIMUM ergo dicendum quod voluntas et intellectus mutuo se includunt, nam intellectus intelligit voluntatem, et voluntas vult intellectum intelligere. Sic ergo inter illa quae ordinantur ad obiectum voluntatis, continentur etiam ea quae sunt intellectus; et e converso. Unde in ordine appetibilium, bonum se habet ut universale, et verum ut particulare, in ordine autem intelligibilium est e converso. Ex hoc ergo quod verum est quoddam bonum, sequitur quod bonum sit prius in ordine appetibilium, non autem quod sit prius simpliciter.

AD SECUNDUM dicendum quod secundum hoc est aliquid prius ratione, quod prius cadit in intellectu. Intellectus autem per prius apprehendit ipsum ens; et secundario apprehendit se intelligere ens; et tertio apprehendit se appetere ens. Unde primo est ratio entis, secundo ratio veri, tertio ratio boni, licet bonum sit in rebus.

AD TERTIUM dicendum quod virtus quae dicitur veritas, non est veritas communis, sed quaedam veritas secundum quam homo in dictis et factis ostendit se ut est. Veritas autem vitae dicitur particulariter, secundum quod homo in vita sua implet illud ad quod ordinatur per intellectum divinum, sicut etiam dictum est veritatem esse in ceteris rebus. Veritas autem iustitiae est secundum quod homo servat id quod debet alteri secundum ordinem legum. Unde ex his particularibus veritatibus non est procedendum ad veritatem communem.

OBJ. 3: Further, truth is a species of virtue, as is clear from *Ethic*. iv. But virtue is included under good; since, as Augustine says (*De Lib. Arbit.* ii, 19), it is a good quality of the mind. Therefore the good is prior to the true.

ON THE CONTRARY, What is in more things is prior logically. But the true is in some things wherein good is not, as, for instance, in mathematics. Therefore the true is prior to good.

I ANSWER THAT, Although the good and the true are convertible with being, as to suppositum, yet they differ logically. And in this manner the true, speaking absolutely, is prior to good, as appears from two reasons. First, because the true is more closely related to being than is good. For the true regards being itself simply and immediately; while the nature of good follows being in so far as being is in some way perfect; for thus it is desirable. Second, it is evident from the fact that knowledge naturally precedes appetite. Hence, since the true regards knowledge, but the good regards the appetite, the true must be prior in idea to the good.

REPLY OBJ. 1: The will and the intellect mutually include one another: for the intellect understands the will, and the will wills the intellect to understand. So then, among things directed to the object of the will, are comprised also those that belong to the intellect; and conversely. Whence in the order of things desirable, good stands as the universal, and the true as the particular; whereas in the order of intelligible things the converse is the case. From the fact, then, that the true is a kind of good, it follows that the good is prior in the order of things desirable; but not that it is prior absolutely.

REPLY OBJ. 2: A thing is prior logically in so far as it is prior to the intellect. Now the intellect apprehends primarily being itself; second, it apprehends that it understands being; and third, it apprehends that it desires being. Hence the idea of being is first, that of truth second, and the idea of good third, though good is in things.

REPLY OBJ. 3: The virtue which is called *truth* is not truth in general, but a certain kind of truth according to which man shows himself in deed and word as he really is. But truth as applied to *life* is used in a particular sense, inasmuch as a man fulfills in his life that to which he is ordained by the divine intellect, as it has been said that truth exists in other things (A. 1). Whereas the truth of *justice* is found in man as he fulfills his duty to his neighbor, as ordained by law. Hence we cannot argue from these particular truths to truth in general.

Article 5

Whether God Is Truth?

AD QUINTUM SIC PROCEDITUR. Videtur quod Deus non sit veritas. Veritas enim consistit in compositione et divisione intellectus. Sed in Deo non est compositio et divisio. Ergo non est ibi veritas.

PRAETEREA, veritas, secundum Augustinum, in libro de vera Relig., est similitudo principii. Sed Dei non est similitudo ad principium. Ergo in Deo non est veritas.

PRAETEREA, quidquid dicitur de Deo, dicitur de eo ut de prima causa omnium, sicut esse Dei est causa omnis esse, et bonitas eius est causa omnis boni. Si ergo in Deo sit veritas, ergo omne verum erit ab ipso. Sed aliquem peccare est verum. Ergo hoc erit a Deo. Quod patet esse falsum.

SED CONTRA est quod dicit dominus, Ioan. XIV, *ego sum via, veritas et vita.*

RESPONDEO dicendum quod, sicut dictum est, veritas invenitur in intellectu secundum quod apprehendit rem ut est, et in re secundum quod habet esse conformabile intellectui. Hoc autem maxime invenitur in Deo. Nam esse suum non solum est conforme suo intellectui, sed etiam est ipsum suum intelligere; et suum intelligere est mensura et causa omnis alterius esse, et omnis alterius intellectus; et ipse est suum esse et intelligere. Unde sequitur quod non solum in ipso sit veritas, sed quod ipse sit ipsa summa et prima veritas.

AD PRIMUM ergo dicendum quod, licet in intellectu divino non sit compositio et divisio, tamen secundum suam simplicem intelligentiam iudicat de omnibus, et cognoscit omnia complexa. Et sic in intellectu eius est veritas.

AD SECUNDUM dicendum quod verum intellectus nostri est secundum quod conformatur suo principio, scilicet rebus, a quibus cognitionem accipit. Veritas etiam rerum est secundum quod conformantur suo principio, scilicet intellectui divino. Sed hoc, proprie loquendo, non potest dici in veritate divina, nisi forte secundum quod veritas appropriatur filio, qui habet principium. Sed si de veritate essentialiter dicta loquamur, non potest intelligi, nisi resolvatur affirmativa in negativam, sicut cum dicitur, pater est a se, quia non est ab alio. Et similiter dici potest similitudo principii veritas divina, inquantum esse suum non est suo intellectui dissimile.

AD TERTIUM dicendum quod non ens et privationes non habent ex seipsis veritatem, sed solum ex apprehensione intellectus. Omnis autem apprehensio intellectus a Deo est, unde quidquid est veritatis in hoc quod dico, istum fornicari est verum, totum est a Deo. Sed si

OBJECTION 1: It seems that God is not truth. For truth consists in the intellect composing and dividing. But in God there is not composition and division. Therefore in Him there is not truth.

OBJ. 2: Further, truth, according to Augustine (*De Vera Relig.* xxxvi), is a *likeness to the principle*. But in God there is no likeness to a principle. Therefore in God there is not truth.

OBJ. 3: Further, whatever is said of God, is said of Him as of the first cause of all things; thus the being of God is the cause of all being, and His goodness the cause of all good. If therefore there is truth in God, all truth will be from Him. But it is true that someone sins. Therefore this will be from God; which is evidently false.

ON THE CONTRARY, Our Lord says, *I am the Way, the Truth, and the Life* (John 14:6).

I ANSWER THAT, As said above (A. 1), truth is found in the intellect according as it apprehends a thing as it is, and in things according as they have being conformable to an intellect. This is to the greatest degree found in God. For His being is not only conformed to His intellect, but it is the very act of His intellect; and His act of understanding is the measure and cause of every other being and of every other intellect, and He Himself is His own existence and act of understanding. Whence it follows not only that truth is in Him, but that He is truth itself, and the sovereign and first truth.

REPLY OBJ. 1: Although in the divine intellect there is neither composition nor division, yet in His simple act of intelligence He judges of all things and knows all things complex; and thus there is truth in His intellect.

REPLY OBJ. 2: The truth of our intellect is according to its conformity with its principle, that is to say, to the things from which it receives knowledge. The truth also of things is according to their conformity with their principle, namely, the divine intellect. Now this cannot be said, properly speaking, of divine truth; unless perhaps in so far as truth is appropriated to the Son, Who has a principle. But if we speak of divine truth in its essence, we cannot understand this unless the affirmative must be resolved into the negative, as when one says: *the Father is of Himself, because He is not from another*. Similarly, the divine truth can be called a *likeness to the principle*, inasmuch as His existence is not dissimilar to His intellect.

REPLY OBJ. 3: Not-being and privation have no truth of themselves, but only in the apprehension of the intellect. Now all apprehension of the intellect is from God. Hence all the truth that exists in the statement—'that a person commits fornication is true'—is entirely from God. But

arguatur, ergo istum fornicari est a Deo, est fallacia accidentis.

to argue, *Therefore that this person fornicates is from God*, is a fallacy of Accident.

Article 6

Whether There Is Only One Truth, According to Which All Things Are True?

AD SEXTUM SIC PROCEDITUR. Videtur quod una sola sit veritas, secundum quam omnia sunt vera. Quia, secundum Augustinum, nihil est maius mente humana, nisi Deus. Sed veritas est maior mente humana, alioquin mens iudicaret de veritate; nunc autem omnia iudicat secundum veritatem, et non secundum seipsam. Ergo solus Deus est veritas. Ergo non est alia veritas quam Deus.

PRAETEREA, Anselmus dicit, in libro de veritate, quod sicut tempus se habet ad temporalia, ita veritas ad res veras. Sed unum est tempus omnium temporalium. Ergo una est veritas, qua omnia vera sunt.

SED CONTRA est quod in Psalmo XI dicitur, *diminutae sunt veritates a filiis hominum.*

RESPONDEO dicendum quod quodammodo una est veritas, qua omnia sunt vera, et quodammodo non. Ad cuius evidentiam, sciendum est quod, quando aliquid praedicatur univoce de multis, illud in quolibet eorum secundum propriam rationem invenitur, sicut animal in qualibet specie animalis. Sed quando aliquid dicitur analogice de multis, illud invenitur secundum propriam rationem in uno eorum tantum, a quo alia denominantur. Sicut sanum dicitur de animali et urina et medicina, non quod sanitas sit nisi in animali tantum, sed a sanitate animalis denominatur medicina sana, inquantum est illius sanitatis effectiva, et urina, inquantum est illius sanitatis significativa. Et quamvis sanitas non sit in medicina neque in urina, tamen in utroque est aliquid per quod hoc quidem facit, illud autem significat sanitatem. Dictum est autem quod veritas per prius est in intellectu, et per posterius in rebus, secundum quod ordinantur ad intellectum divinum. Si ergo loquamur de veritate prout existit in intellectu, secundum propriam rationem, sic in multis intellectibus creatis sunt multae veritates; etiam in uno et eodem intellectu, secundum plura cognita. Unde dicit Glossa super illud Psalmi XI, *diminutae sunt veritates a filiis hominum* etc., quod sicut ab una facie hominis resultant plures similitudines in speculo, sic ab una veritate divina resultant plures veritates. Si vero loquamur de veritate secundum quod est in rebus, sic omnes sunt verae una prima veritate, cui unumquodque assimilatur secundum suam entitatem. Et sic, licet plures sint essentiae vel formae rerum, tamen una est veritas divini intellectus, secundum quam omnes res denominantur verae.

OBJECTION 1: It seems that there is only one truth, according to which all things are true. For according to Augustine (*De Trin.* xv, 1), *nothing is greater than the mind of man, except God.* Now truth is greater than the mind of man; otherwise the mind would be the judge of truth: whereas in fact it judges all things according to truth, and not according to its own measure. Therefore God alone is truth. Therefore there is no other truth but God.

OBJ. 2: Further, Anselm says (*De Verit.* xiv) that, *as is the relation of time to temporal things, so is that of truth to true things.* But there is only one time for all temporal things. Therefore there is only one truth, by which all things are true.

ON THE CONTRARY, it is written (Ps 11:2), *Truths are decayed from among the children of men.*

I ANSWER THAT, In one sense truth, whereby all things are true, is one, and in another sense it is not. In proof of which we must consider that when anything is predicated of many things univocally, it is found in each of them according to its proper nature; as animal is found in each species of animal. But when anything is predicated of many things analogically, it is found in only one of them according to its proper nature, and from this one the rest are denominated. So healthiness is predicated of animal, of urine, and of medicine, not that health is only in the animal; but from the health of the animal, medicine is called healthy, in so far as it is the cause of health, and urine is called healthy, in so far as it indicates health. And although health is neither in medicine nor in urine, yet in either there is something whereby the one causes, and the other indicates health. Now we have said (A. 1) that truth resides primarily in the intellect; and secondarily in things, according as they are related to the divine intellect. If therefore we speak of truth, as it exists in the intellect, according to its proper nature, then are there many truths in many created intellects; and even in one and the same intellect, according to the number of things known. Whence a gloss on Ps. 11:2, *Truths are decayed from among the children of men*, says: *As from one man's face many likenesses are reflected in a mirror, so many truths are reflected from the one divine truth.* But if we speak of truth as it is in things, then all things are true by one primary truth; to which each one is assimilated according to its own entity. And thus, although the essences or forms of things are many, yet the truth of the divine intellect is one, in conformity to which all things are said to be true.

AD PRIMUM ergo dicendum quod anima non secundum quamcumque veritatem iudicat de rebus omnibus; sed secundum veritatem primam, inquantum resultat in ea sicut in speculo, secundum prima intelligibilia. Unde sequitur quod veritas prima sit maior anima. Et tamen etiam veritas creata, quae est in intellectu nostro, est maior anima, non simpliciter, sed secundum quid, inquantum est perfectio eius; sicut etiam scientia posset dici maior anima. Sed verum est quod nihil subsistens est maius mente rationali, nisi Deus.

AD SECUNDUM dicendum quod dictum Anselmi veritatem habet, secundum quod res dicuntur verae per comparationem ad intellectum divinum.

REPLY OBJ. 1: The soul does not judge of things according to any kind of truth, but according to the primary truth, inasmuch as it is reflected in the soul, as in a mirror, by reason of the first principles of the understanding. It follows, therefore, that the primary truth is greater than the soul. And yet, even created truth, which resides in our intellect, is greater than the soul, not simply, but in a certain degree, in so far as it is its perfection; even as science may be said to be greater than the soul. Yet it is true that nothing subsisting is greater than the rational soul, except God.

REPLY OBJ. 2: The saying of Anselm is correct in so far as things are said to be true by their relation to the divine intellect.

Article 7

Whether Created Truth Is Eternal?

AD SEPTIMUM SIC PROCEDITUR. Videtur quod veritas creata sit aeterna. Dicit enim Augustinus, in libro de libero arbitrio, quod nihil est magis aeternum quam ratio circuli, et duo et tria esse quinque. Sed horum veritas est veritas creata. Ergo veritas creata est aeterna.

PRAETEREA, omne quod est semper, est aeternum. Sed universalia sunt ubique et semper. Ergo sunt aeterna. Ergo et verum, quod est maxime universale.

PRAETEREA, id quod est verum in praesenti, semper fuit verum esse futurum. Sed sicut veritas propositionis de praesenti est veritas creata, ita veritas propositionis de futuro. Ergo aliqua veritas creata est aeterna.

PRAETEREA, omne quod caret principio et fine, est aeternum. Sed veritas enuntiabilium caret principio et fine. Quia, si veritas incoepit cum ante non esset, verum erat veritatem non esse, et utique aliqua veritate verum erat, et sic veritas erat antequam inciperet. Et similiter si ponatur veritatem habere finem, sequitur quod sit postquam desierit, verum enim erit veritatem non esse. Ergo veritas est aeterna.

SED CONTRA est quod solus Deus est aeternus, ut supra habitum est.

RESPONDEO dicendum quod veritas enuntiabilium non est aliud quam veritas intellectus. Enuntiabile enim et est in intellectu, et est in voce. Secundum autem quod est in intellectu, habet per se veritatem. Sed secundum quod est in voce, dicitur verum enuntiabile, secundum quod significat aliquam veritatem intellectus; non propter aliquam veritatem in enuntiabili existentem sicut in subiecto. Sicut urina dicitur sana, non a sanitate quae in ipsa sit, sed a sanitate animalis, quam significat. Similiter etiam supra dictum est quod res denominantur verae a veritate intellectus. Unde si nullus intellectus esset

OBJECTION 1: It seems that created truth is eternal. For Augustine says (De Lib. Arbit. ii, 8) *Nothing is more eternal than the nature of a circle, and that two added to three make five.* But the truth of these is a created truth. Therefore created truth is eternal.

OBJ. 2: Further, that which is always, is eternal. But universals are always and everywhere; therefore they are eternal. So therefore is truth, which is the most universal.

OBJ. 3: Further, it was always true that what is true in the present was to be in the future. But as the truth of a proposition regarding the present is a created truth, so is that of a proposition regarding the future. Therefore some created truth is eternal.

OBJ. 4: Further, all that is without beginning and end is eternal. But the truth of enunciables is without beginning and end; for if their truth had a beginning, since it was not before, it was true that truth was not, and true, of course, by reason of truth; so that truth was before it began to be. Similarly, if it be asserted that truth has an end, it follows that it is after it has ceased to be, for it will still be true that truth is not. Therefore truth is eternal.

ON THE CONTRARY, God alone is eternal, as laid down before (Q. 10, Art. 3).

I ANSWER THAT, The truth of enunciations is no other than the truth of the intellect. For an enunciation resides in the intellect, and in speech. Now according as it is in the intellect it has truth of itself: but according as it is in speech, it is called enunciable truth, according as it signifies some truth of the intellect, not on account of any truth residing in the enunciation, as though in a subject. Thus urine is called healthy, not from any health within it but from the health of an animal which it indicates. In like manner it has been already said that things are called true from the truth of the intellect. Hence, if no intellect were eternal, no truth would

aeternus, nulla veritas esset aeterna. Sed quia solus intellectus divinus est aeternus, in ipso solo veritas aeternitatem habet. Nec propter hoc sequitur quod aliquid aliud sit aeternum quam Deus, quia veritas intellectus divini est ipse Deus, ut supra ostensum est.

AD PRIMUM ergo dicendum quod ratio circuli, et duo et tria esse quinque, habent aeternitatem in mente divina.

AD SECUNDUM dicendum quod aliquid esse semper et ubique, potest intelligi dupliciter. Uno modo, quia habet in se unde se extendat ad omne tempus et ad omnem locum, sicut Deo competit esse ubique et semper. Alio modo, quia non habet in se quo determinetur ad aliquem locum vel tempus, sicut materia prima dicitur esse una, non quia habet unam formam, sicut homo est unus ab unitate unius formae, sed per remotionem omnium formarum distinguentium. Et per hunc modum, quodlibet universale dicitur esse ubique et semper, inquantum universalia abstrahunt ab hic et nunc. Sed ex hoc non sequitur ea esse aeterna, nisi in intellectu, si quis sit aeternus.

AD TERTIUM dicendum quod illud quod nunc est, ex eo futurum fuit antequam esset, quia in causa sua erat ut fieret. Unde, sublata causa, non esset futurum illud fieri. Sola autem causa prima est aeterna. Unde ex hoc non sequitur quod ea quae sunt, semper fuerit verum ea esse futura, nisi quatenus in causa sempiterna fuit ut essent futura. Quae quidem causa solus Deus est.

AD QUARTUM dicendum quod, quia intellectus noster non est aeternus, nec veritas enuntiabilium quae a nobis formantur, est aeterna, sed quandoque incoepit. Et antequam huiusmodi veritas esset, non erat verum dicere veritatem talem non esse, nisi ab intellectu divino, in quo solum veritas est aeterna. Sed nunc verum est dicere veritatem tunc non fuisse. Quod quidem non est verum nisi veritate quae nunc est in intellectu nostro, non autem per aliquam veritatem ex parte rei. Quia ista est veritas de non ente; non ens autem non habet ex se ut sit verum, sed solummodo ex intellectu apprehendente ipsum. Unde intantum est verum dicere veritatem non fuisse, inquantum apprehendimus non esse ipsius ut praecedens esse eius.

be eternal. Now because only the divine intellect is eternal, in it alone truth has eternity. Nor does it follow from this that anything else but God is eternal, since the truth of the divine intellect is God Himself, as shown already (A. 5).

REPLY OBJ. 1: The nature of a circle, and the fact that two and three make five, have eternity in the mind of God.

REPLY OBJ. 2: That something is always and everywhere, can be understood in two ways. In one way, as having in itself the power of extension to all time and to all places, as it belongs to God to be everywhere and always. In the other way as not having in itself determination to any place or time, as primary matter is said to be one, not because it has one form, but by the absence of all distinguishing form. In this manner all universals are said to be everywhere and always, in so far as universals are independent of place and time. It does not, however, follow from this that they are eternal, except in an intellect, if one exists that is eternal.

REPLY OBJ. 3: That which now is, was future, before it (actually) was; because it was in its cause that it would be. Hence, if the cause were removed, that thing's coming to be was not future. But the first cause is alone eternal. Hence it does not follow that it was always true that what now is would be, except in so far as its future being was in the sempiternal cause; and God alone is such a cause.

REPLY OBJ. 4: Because our intellect is not eternal, neither is the truth of enuncible propositions which are formed by us, eternal, but it had a beginning in time. Now before such truth existed, it was not true to say that such a truth did exist, except by reason of the divine intellect, wherein alone truth is eternal. But it is true now to say that that truth did not then exist: and this is true only by reason of the truth that is now in our intellect; and not by reason of any truth in the things. For this is truth concerning not-being; and not-being has not truth of itself, but only so far as our intellect apprehends it. Hence it is true to say that truth did not exist, in so far as we apprehend its not-being as preceding its being.

Article 8

Whether Truth Is Immutable?

AD OCTAVUM SIC PROCEDITUR. Videtur quod veritas sit immutabilis. Dicit enim Augustinus, in libro II de libero arbitrio, quod *veritas non est aequalis menti, quia esset mutabilis, sicut et mens.*

OBJECTION 1: It seems that truth is immutable. For Augustine says (*De Lib. Arbit.* ii, 12), that *Truth and mind do not rank as equals, otherwise truth would be mutable, as the mind is.*

PRAETEREA, id quod remanet post omnem mutationem, est immutabile, sicut prima materia est ingenita et incorruptibilis, quia remanet post omnem generationem et corruptionem. Sed veritas remanet post omnem mutationem, quia post omnem mutationem verum est dicere esse vel non esse. Ergo veritas est immutabilis.

PRAETEREA, si veritas enuntiationis mutatur, maxime mutatur ad mutationem rei. Sed sic non mutatur. Veritas enim, secundum Anselmum, *est rectitudo quaedam*, inquantum aliquid implet id quod est de ipso in mente divina. Haec autem propositio, Socrates sedet, accipit a mente divina ut significet Socratem sedere, quod significat etiam eo non sedente. Ergo veritas propositionis nullo modo mutatur.

PRAETEREA, ubi est eadem causa, et idem effectus. Sed eadem res est causa veritatis harum trium propositionum Socrates sedet, sedebit, et sedit. Ergo eadem est harum veritas. Sed oportet quod alterum horum sit verum. Ergo veritas harum propositionum immutabiliter manet. Et eadem ratione cuiuslibet alterius propositionis.

SED CONTRA est quod dicitur in Psalmo XI, *diminutae sunt veritates a filiis hominum*.

RESPONDEO dicendum quod, sicut supra dictum est, veritas proprie est in solo intellectu, res autem dicuntur verae a veritate quae est in aliquo intellectu. Unde mutabilitas veritatis consideranda est circa intellectum. Cuius quidem veritas in hoc consistit, quod habeat conformitatem ad res intellectas. Quae quidem conformitas variari potest dupliciter, sicut et quaelibet alia similitudo, ex mutatione alterius extremi. Unde uno modo variatur veritas ex parte intellectus, ex eo quod de re eodem modo se habente aliquis aliam opinionem accipit, alio modo si, opinione eadem manente, res mutetur. Et utroque modo fit mutatio de vero in falsum. Si ergo sit aliquis intellectus in quo non possit esse alternatio opinionum, vel cuius acceptionem non potest subterfugere res aliqua, in eo est immutabilis veritas. Talis autem est intellectus divinus, ut ex superioribus patet. Unde veritas divini intellectus est immutabilis. Veritas autem intellectus nostri mutabilis est. Non quod ipsa sit subiectum mutationis, sed inquantum intellectus noster mutatur de veritate in falsitatem; sic enim formae mutabiles dici possunt. Veritas autem intellectus divini est secundum quam res naturales dicuntur verae, quae est omnino immutabilis.

AD PRIMUM ergo dicendum quod Augustinus loquitur de veritate divina.

AD SECUNDUM dicendum quod verum et ens sunt convertibilia. Unde, sicut ens non generatur neque corrumpitur per se, sed per accidens, inquantum hoc vel illud ens corrumpitur vel generatur, ut dicitur in I Physic.;

OBJ. 2: Further, what remains after every change is immutable; as primary matter is unbegotten and incorruptible, since it remains after all generation and corruption. But truth remains after all change; for after every change it is true to say that a thing is, or is not. Therefore truth is immutable.

OBJ. 3: Further, if the truth of an enunciation changes, it changes mostly with the changing of the thing. But it does not thus change. For truth, according to Anselm (De Verit. viii), *is a certain rightness* in so far as a thing answers to that which is in the divine mind concerning it. But this proposition that *Socrates sits*, receives from the divine mind the signification that Socrates does sit; and it has the same signification even though he does not sit. Therefore the truth of the proposition in no way changes.

OBJ. 4: Further, where there is the same cause, there is the same effect. But the same thing is the cause of the truth of the three propositions, *Socrates sits, will sit, sat*. Therefore the truth of each is the same. But one or other of these must be the true one. Therefore the truth of these propositions remains immutable; and for the same reason that of any other.

ON THE CONTRARY, It is written (Ps 11:2), *Truths are decayed from among the children of men*.

I ANSWER THAT, Truth, properly speaking, resides only in the intellect, as said before (A. 1); but things are called true in virtue of the truth residing in an intellect. Hence the mutability of truth must be regarded from the point of view of the intellect, the truth of which consists in its conformity to the thing understood. Now this conformity may vary in two ways, even as any other likeness, through change in one of the two extremes. Hence in one way truth varies on the part of the intellect, from the fact that a change of opinion occurs about a thing which in itself has not changed, and in another way, when the thing is changed, but not the opinion; and in either way there can be a change from true to false. If, then, there is an intellect wherein there can be no alternation of opinions, and the knowledge of which nothing can escape, in this is immutable truth. Now such is the divine intellect, as is clear from what has been said before (Q. 14, A. 15). Hence the truth of the divine intellect is immutable. But the truth of our intellect is mutable; not because it is itself the subject of change, but in so far as our intellect changes from truth to falsity, for thus forms may be called mutable. Whereas the truth of the divine intellect is that according to which natural things are said to be true, and this is altogether immutable.

REPLY OBJ. 1: Augustine is speaking of divine truth.

REPLY OBJ. 2: The true and being are convertible terms. Hence just as being is not generated nor corrupted of itself, but accidentally, in so far as this being or that is corrupted or generated, as is said in *Phys.* i, so does truth change, not

ita veritas mutatur, non quod nulla veritas remaneat, sed quia non remanet illa veritas quae prius erat.

AD TERTIUM dicendum quod propositio non solum habet veritatem sicut res aliae veritatem habere dicuntur, inquantum implent id quod de eis est ordinatum ab intellectu divino; sed dicitur habere veritatem quodam speciali modo, inquantum significat veritatem intellectus. Quae quidem consistit in conformitate intellectus et rei. Qua quidem subtracta, mutatur veritas opinionis, et per consequens veritas propositionis. Sic igitur haec propositio, Socrates sedet, eo sedente vera est et veritate rei, inquantum est quaedam vox significativa; et veritate significationis, inquantum significat opinionem veram. Socrate vero surgente, remanet prima veritas, sed mutatur secunda.

AD QUARTUM dicendum quod sessio Socratis, quae est causa veritatis huius propositionis, Socrates sedet, non eodem modo se habet dum Socrates sedet, et postquam sederit, et antequam sederet. Unde et veritas ab hoc causata, diversimode se habet; et diversimode significatur propositionibus de praesenti, praeterito et futuro. Unde non sequitur quod, licet altera trium propositionum sit vera, quod eadem veritas invariabilis maneat.

so as that no truth remains, but because that truth does not remain which was before.

REPLY OBJ. 3: A proposition not only has truth, as other things are said to have it, in so far, that is, as they correspond to that which is the design of the divine intellect concerning them; but it is said to have truth in a special way, in so far as it indicates the truth of the intellect, which consists in the conformity of the intellect with a thing. When this disappears, the truth of an opinion changes, and consequently the truth of the proposition. So therefore this proposition, *Socrates sits*, is true, as long as he is sitting, both with the truth of the thing, in so far as the expression is significative, and with the truth of signification, in so far as it signifies a true opinion. When Socrates rises, the first truth remains, but the second is changed.

REPLY OBJ. 4: The sitting of Socrates, which is the cause of the truth of the proposition, *Socrates sits*, has not the same meaning when Socrates sits, after he sits, and before he sits. Hence the truth which results varies, and is variously signified by these propositions concerning present, past, or future. Thus it does not follow, though one of the three propositions is true, that the same truth remains invariable.

QUESTION 17

FALSITY

Deinde quaeritur de falsitate.
Et circa hoc quaeruntur quatuor.
Primo, utrum falsitas sit in rebus.
Secundo, utrum sit in sensu.
Tertio, utrum sit in intellectu.
Quarto, de oppositione veri et falsi.

We next consider falsity.
About this, four points of inquiry arise:
(1) Whether falsity exists in things?
(2) Whether it exists in the sense?
(3) Whether it exists in the intellect?
(4) Concerning the opposition of the true and the false.

Article 1

Whether Falsity Exists in Things?

AD PRIMUM SIC PROCEDITUR. Videtur quod falsitas non sit in rebus. Dicit enim Augustinus, in libro Soliloq., *si verum est id quod est, falsum non esse uspiam concludetur, quovis repugnante.*

PRAETEREA, falsum dicitur a fallendo. Sed res non fallunt, ut dicit Augustinus in libro de vera Relig., *quia non ostendunt aliud quam suam speciem.* Ergo falsum in rebus non invenitur.

PRAETEREA, verum dicitur in rebus per comparationem ad intellectum divinum, ut supra dictum est. Sed quaelibet res, inquantum est, imitatur Deum. Ergo quaelibet res vera est, absque falsitate. Et sic nulla res est falsa.

SED CONTRA est quod dicit Augustinus, in libro de vera Relig., quod *omne corpus est verum corpus et falsa unitas*; quia imitatur unitatem, et non est unitas. Sed quaelibet res imitatur divinam bonitatem, et ab ea deficit. Ergo in omnibus rebus est falsitas.

RESPONDEO dicendum quod, cum verum et falsum opponantur; opposita autem sunt circa idem; necesse est ut ibi prius quaeratur falsitas, ubi primo veritas invenitur, hoc est in intellectu. In rebus autem neque veritas neque falsitas est, nisi per ordinem ad intellectum. Et quia unumquodque secundum id quod convenit ei per se, simpliciter nominatur; secundum autem id quod convenit ei per accidens, non nominatur nisi secundum quid; res quidem simpliciter falsa dici posset per comparationem ad intellectum a quo dependet, cui comparatur per se; in ordine autem ad alium intellectum, cui comparatur per accidens, non posset dici falsa nisi secundum quid. Dependent autem ab intellectu divino res naturales, sicut ab intellectu humano res artificiales. Dicuntur igitur res artificiales falsae simpliciter et secundum se,

OBJECTION 1: It appears that falsity does not exist in things. For Augustine says (*Soliloq.* ii, 8), *If the true is that which is, it will be concluded that the false exists nowhere; whatever reason may appear to the contrary.*

OBJ. 2: Further, false is derived from *fallere* (to deceive). But things do not deceive; for, as Augustine says (*De Vera Relig.* 33), they show nothing but their own species. Therefore the false is not found in things.

OBJ. 3: Further, the true is said to exist in things by conformity to the divine intellect, as stated above (Q. 16). But everything, in so far as it exists, imitates God. Therefore everything is true without admixture of falsity; and thus nothing is false.

ON THE CONTRARY, Augustine says (*De Vera Relig.* 34): *Every body is a true body and a false unity: for it imitates unity without being unity.* But everything imitates the divine unity yet falls short of it. Therefore in all things falsity exists.

I ANSWER THAT, Since true and false are opposed, and since opposites stand in relation to the same thing, we must needs seek falsity, where primarily we find truth; that is to say, in the intellect. Now, in things, neither truth nor falsity exists, except in relation to the intellect. And since every thing is denominated simply by what belongs to it per se, but is denominated relatively by what belongs to it accidentally, a thing indeed may be called false simply when compared with the intellect on which it depends, and to which it is compared per se; but may be called false relatively as directed to another intellect, to which it is compared accidentally. Now natural things depend on the divine intellect, as artificial things on the human. Wherefore artificial things are said to be false simply and in themselves, in so far as they fall short of the form of the art; whence a craftsman

191

inquantum deficiunt a forma artis, unde dicitur aliquis artifex opus falsum facere, quando deficit ab operatione artis.

Sic autem in rebus dependentibus a Deo, falsitas inveniri non potest per comparationem ad intellectum divinum, cum quidquid in rebus accidit, ex ordinatione divini intellectus procedat, nisi forte in voluntariis agentibus tantum, in quorum potestate est subducere se ab ordinatione divini intellectus; in quo malum culpae consistit, secundum quod ipsa peccata falsitates et mendacia dicuntur in Scripturis, secundum illud Psalmi IV, *ut quid diligitis vanitatem et quaeritis mendacium?* Sicut per oppositum operatio virtuosa veritas vitae nominatur, inquantum subditur ordini divini intellectus; sicut dicitur Ioan. III, *qui facit veritatem, venit ad lucem.*

Sed per ordinem ad intellectum nostrum, ad quem comparantur res naturales per accidens, possunt dici falsae, non simpliciter, sed secundum quid. Et hoc dupliciter. Uno modo, secundum rationem significati, ut dicatur illud esse falsum in rebus, quod significatur vel repraesentatur oratione vel intellectu falso. Secundum quem modum quaelibet res potest dici esse falsa, quantum ad id quod ei non inest, sicut si dicamus diametrum esse falsum commensurabile, ut dicit philosophus in V Metaphys.; et sicut dicit Augustinus, in libro Soliloq., quod *tragoedus est falsus Hector.* Sicut e contrario potest unumquodque dici verum, secundum id quod competit ei. Alio modo, per modum causae. Et sic dicitur res esse falsa, quae nata est facere de se opinionem falsam. Et quia innatum est nobis per ea quae exterius apparent de rebus iudicare, eo quod nostra cognitio a sensu ortum habet, qui primo et per se est exteriorum accidentium; ideo ea quae in exterioribus accidentibus habent similitudinem aliarum rerum, dicuntur esse falsa secundum illas res; sicut fel est falsum mel, et stannum est falsum argentum. Et secundum hoc dicit Augustinus, in libro Soliloq., quod *eas res falsas nominamus, quae verisimilia apprehendimus.* Et philosophus dicit, in V Metaphys., quod *falsa dicuntur quaecumque apta nata sunt apparere aut qualia non sunt, aut quae non sunt.* Et per hunc modum etiam dicitur homo falsus, inquantum est amativus falsarum opinionum vel locutionum. Non autem ex hoc quod potest eas confingere, quia sic etiam sapientes et scientes falsi dicerentur, ut dicitur in V Metaphys.

AD PRIMUM ergo dicendum quod res comparata ad intellectum, secundum id quod est, dicitur vera, secundum id quod non est, dicitur falsa. *Unde verus tragoedus est falsus Hector,* ut dicitur in II Soliloq. Sicut igitur in his quae sunt, invenitur quoddam non esse; ita in his quae sunt, invenitur quaedam ratio falsitatis.

AD SECUNDUM dicendum quod res per se non fallunt, sed per accidens. Dant enim occasionem falsitatis, eo quod similitudinem eorum gerunt, quorum non habent existentiam.

is said to produce a false work, if it falls short of the proper operation of his art.

In things that depend on God, falseness cannot be found, in so far as they are compared with the divine intellect; since whatever takes place in things proceeds from the ordinance of that intellect, unless perhaps in the case of voluntary agents only, who have it in their power to withdraw themselves from what is so ordained; wherein consists the evil of sin. Thus sins themselves are called untruths and lies in the Scriptures, according to the words of the text, *Why do you love vanity, and seek after lying?* (Ps 4:3): as on the other hand virtuous deeds are called the *truth of life* as being obedient to the order of the divine intellect. Thus it is said, *He that doth truth, cometh to the light* (John 3:21).

But in relation to our intellect, natural things which are compared thereto accidentally, can be called false; not simply, but relatively; and that in two ways. In one way according to the thing signified, and thus a thing is said to be false as being signified or represented by word or thought that is false. In this respect anything can be said to be false as regards any quality not possessed by it; as if we should say that a diameter is a false commensurable thing, as the Philosopher says (*Metaph.* v, 34). So, too, Augustine says (*Soliloq.* ii, 10): *The true tragedian is a false Hector*: even as, on the contrary, anything can be called true, in regard to that which is becoming to it. In another way a thing can be called false, by way of cause—and thus a thing is said to be false that naturally begets a false opinion. And whereas it is innate in us to judge things by external appearances, since our knowledge takes its rise from sense, which principally and naturally deals with external accidents, therefore those external accidents, which resemble things other than themselves, are said to be false with respect to those things; thus gall is falsely honey; and tin, false gold. Regarding this, Augustine says (*Soliloq.* ii, 6): *We call those things false that appear to our apprehension like the true*: and the Philosopher says (*Metaph.* v, 34): *Things are called false that are naturally apt to appear such as they are not, or what they are not.* In this way a man is called false as delighting in false opinions or words, and not because he can invent them; for in this way many wise and learned persons might be called false, as stated in *Metaph.* v, 34.

REPLY OBJ. 1: A thing compared with the intellect is said to be true in respect to what it is; and false in respect to what it is not. Hence, *The true tragedian is a false Hector*, as stated in *Soliloq.* ii, 6. As, therefore, in things that are is found a certain non-being, so in things that are is found a degree of falseness.

REPLY OBJ. 2: Things do not deceive by their own nature, but by accident. For they give occasion to falsity, by the likeness they bear to things which they actually are not.

AD TERTIUM dicendum quod per comparationem ad intellectum divinum non dicuntur res falsae, quod esset eas esse falsas simpliciter, sed per comparationem ad intellectum nostrum, quod est eas esse falsas secundum quid.

AD QUARTUM, quod in oppositum obiicitur, dicendum quod similitudo vel repraesentatio deficiens non inducit rationem falsitatis, nisi inquantum praestat occasionem falsae opinionis. Unde non ubicumque est similitudo, dicitur res falsa, sed ubicumque est talis similitudo, quae nata est facere opinionem falsam, non cuicumque, sed ut in pluribus.

REPLY OBJ. 3: Things are said to be false, not as compared with the divine intellect, in which case they would be false simply, but as compared with our intellect; and thus they are false only relatively.

TO THE ARGUMENT which is urged on the contrary, likeness or defective representation does not involve the idea of falsity except in so far as it gives occasion to false opinion. Hence a thing is not always said to be false, because it resembles another thing; but only when the resemblance is such as naturally to produce a false opinion, not in any one case, but in the majority of instances.

Article 2

Whether There Is Falsity in the Senses?

AD SECUNDUM SIC PROCEDITUR. Videtur quod in sensu non sit falsitas. Dicit enim Augustinus, in libro de vera Relig., *si omnes corporis sensus ita nuntiant ut afficiuntur, quid ab eis amplius exigere debemus, ignoro.* Et sic videtur quod ex sensibus non fallamur. Et sic falsitas in sensu non est.

PRAETEREA, philosophus dicit, in IV Metaphys., quod *falsitas non est propria sensui, sed phantasiae.*

PRAETEREA, in incomplexis non est verum nec falsum, sed solum in complexis. Sed componere et dividere non pertinet ad sensum. Ergo in sensu non est falsitas.

SED CONTRA est quod dicit Augustinus, in libro Soliloq., *apparet nos in omnibus sensibus similitudine lenocinante falli.*

RESPONDEO dicendum quod falsitas non est quaerenda in sensu, nisi sicut ibi est veritas. Veritas autem non sic est in sensu, ut sensus cognoscat veritatem; sed inquantum veram apprehensionem habet de sensibilibus, ut supra dictum est. Quod quidem contingit eo quod apprehendit res ut sunt. Unde contingit falsitatem esse in sensu, ex hoc quod apprehendit vel iudicat res aliter quam sint.

Sic autem se habet ad cognoscendum res, inquantum similitudo rerum est in sensu. Similitudo autem alicuius rei est in sensu tripliciter. Uno modo, primo et per se; sicut in visu est similitudo colorum et aliorum propriorum sensibilium. Alio modo, per se, sed non primo; sicut in visu est similitudo figurae vel magnitudinis, et aliorum communium sensibilium. Tertio modo, nec primo nec per se, sed per accidens; sicut in visu est similitudo hominis, non inquantum est homo, sed inquantum huic colorato accidit esse hominem.

OBJECTION 1: It seems that falsity is not in the senses. For Augustine says (*De Vera Relig.* 33): *If all the bodily senses report as they are affected, I do not know what more we can require from them.* Thus it seems that we are not deceived by the senses; and therefore that falsity is not in them.

OBJ. 2: Further, the Philosopher says (*Metaph.* iv, 24) that *falsity is not proper to the senses, but to the imagination.*

OBJ. 3: Further, in non-complex things there is neither true nor false, but in complex things only. But affirmation and negation do not belong to the senses. Therefore in the senses there is no falsity.

ON THE CONTRARY, Augustine says (*Soliloq.* ii, 6), *It appears that the senses entrap us into error by their deceptive similitudes.*

I ANSWER THAT, Falsity is not to be sought in the senses except as truth is in them. Now truth is not in them in such a way as that the senses know truth, but in so far as they apprehend sensible things truly, as said above (Q. 16, A. 2), and this takes place through the senses apprehending things as they are, and hence it happens that falsity exists in the senses through their apprehending or judging things to be otherwise than they really are.

The knowledge of things by the senses is in proportion to the existence of their likeness in the senses; and the likeness of a thing can exist in the senses in three ways. In the first way, primarily and of its own nature, as in sight there is the likeness of colors, and of other sensible objects proper to it. Second, of its own nature, though not primarily; as in sight there is the likeness of shape, size, and of other sensible objects common to more than one sense. Third, neither primarily nor of its own nature, but accidentally, as in sight, there is the likeness of a man, not as man, but in so far as it is accidental to the colored object to be a man.

Et circa propria sensibilia sensus non habet falsam cognitionem, nisi per accidens, et ut in paucioribus, ex eo scilicet quod, propter indispositionem organi, non convenienter recipit formam sensibilem, sicut et alia passiva, propter suam indispositionem, deficienter recipiunt impressionem agentium. Et inde est quod, propter corruptionem linguae, infirmis dulcia amara esse videntur. De sensibilibus vero communibus et per accidens, potest esse falsum iudicium etiam in sensu recte disposito, quia sensus non directe refertur ad illa, sed per accidens, vel ex consequenti, inquantum refertur ad alia.

AD PRIMUM ergo dicendum quod sensum affici, est ipsum eius sentire. Unde per hoc quod sensus ita nuntiant sicut afficiuntur, sequitur quod non decipiamur in iudicio quo iudicamus nos sentire aliquid. Sed ex eo quod sensus aliter afficitur interdum quam res sit, sequitur quod nuntiet nobis aliquando rem aliter quam sit. Et ex hoc fallimur per sensum circa rem, non circa ipsum sentire.

AD SECUNDUM dicendum quod falsitas dicitur non esse propria sensui, quia non decipitur circa proprium obiectum. Unde in alia translatione planius dicitur, quod *sensus proprii sensibilis falsus non est.* Phantasiae autem attribuitur falsitas, quia repraesentat similitudinem rei etiam absentis; unde quando aliquis convertitur ad similitudinem rei tanquam ad rem ipsam, provenit ex tali apprehensione falsitas. Unde etiam philosophus, in V Metaphys., dicit quod umbrae et picturae et somnia dicuntur falsa, inquantum non subsunt res quarum habent similitudinem.

AD TERTIUM dicendum quod ratio illa procedit, quod falsitas non sit in sensu sicut in cognoscente verum et falsum.

Sense, then, has no false knowledge about its proper objects, except accidentally and rarely, and then, because of the unsound organ it does not receive the sensible form rightly; just as other passive subjects because of their indisposition receive defectively the impressions of the agent. Hence, for instance, it happens that on account of an unhealthy tongue sweet seems bitter to a sick person. But as to common objects of sense, and accidental objects, even a rightly disposed sense may have a false judgment, because it is referred to them not directly, but accidentally, or as a consequence of being directed to other things.

REPLY OBJ. 1: The affection of sense is its sensation itself. Hence, from the fact that sense reports as it is affected, it follows that we are not deceived in the judgment by which we judge that we experience sensation. Since, however, sense is sometimes affected erroneously of that object, it follows that it sometimes reports erroneously of that object; and thus we are deceived by sense about the object, but not about the fact of sensation.

REPLY OBJ. 2: Falsity is said not to be proper to sense, since sense is not deceived as to its proper object. Hence in another translation it is said more plainly, *Sense, about its proper object, is never false.* Falsity is attributed to the imagination, as it represents the likeness of something even in its absence. Hence, when anyone perceives the likeness of a thing as if it were the thing itself, falsity results from such an apprehension; and for this reason the Philosopher says (*Metaph.* v, 34) that shadows, pictures, and dreams are said to be false inasmuch as they convey the likeness of things that are not present in substance.

REPLY OBJ. 3: This argument proves that the false is not in the sense, as in that which knows the true and the false.

Article 3

Whether Falsity Is in the Intellect?

AD TERTIUM SIC PROCEDITUR. Videtur quod falsitas non sit in intellectu. Dicit enim Augustinus, in libro octoginta trium quaest., *omnis qui fallitur, id in quo fallitur, non intelligit.* Sed falsum dicitur esse in aliqua cognitione, secundum quod per eam fallimur. Ergo in intellectu non est falsitas.

PRAETEREA, philosophus dicit, in III de anima, quod intellectus semper est rectus. Non ergo in intellectu est falsitas.

SED CONTRA est quod dicitur in III de anima, quod *ubi compositio intellectuum est, ibi verum et falsum est.* Sed compositio intellectuum est in intellectu. Ergo verum et falsum est in intellectu.

OBJECTION 1: It seems that falsity is not in the intellect. For Augustine says (*Qq. lxxxiii*, 32), *Everyone who is deceived, understands not that in which he is deceived.* But falsity is said to exist in any knowledge in so far as we are deceived therein. Therefore falsity does not exist in the intellect.

OBJ. 2: Further, the Philosopher says (*De Anima* iii, 51) that the intellect is always right. Therefore there is no falsity in the intellect.

ON THE CONTRARY, It is said in *De Anima* iii, 21, 22 that *where there is composition of objects understood, there is truth and falsehood.* But such composition is in the intellect. Therefore truth and falsehood exist in the intellect.

RESPONDEO dicendum quod, sicut res habet esse per propriam formam, ita virtus cognoscitiva habet cognoscere per similitudinem rei cognitae. Unde, sicut res naturalis non deficit ab esse quod sibi competit secundum suam formam, potest autem deficere ab aliquibus accidentalibus vel consequentibus; sicut homo ab hoc quod est habere duos pedes, non autem ab hoc quod est esse hominem, ita virtus cognoscitiva non deficit in cognoscendo respectu illius rei cuius similitudine informatur; potest autem deficere circa aliquid consequens ad ipsam, vel accidens ei. Sicut est dictum quod visus non decipitur circa sensibile proprium, sed circa sensibilia communia, quae consequenter se habent ad illud, et circa sensibilia per accidens. Sicut autem sensus informatur directe similitudine propriorum sensibilium, ita intellectus informatur similitudine quidditatis rei. Unde circa quod quid est intellectus non decipitur, sicut neque sensus circa sensibilia propria. In componendo vero vel dividendo potest decipi, dum attribuit rei cuius quidditatem intelligit, aliquid quod eam non consequitur, vel quod ei opponitur. Sic enim se habet intellectus ad iudicandum de huiusmodi, sicut sensus ad iudicandum de sensibilibus communibus vel per accidens. Hac tamen differentia servata, quae supra circa veritatem dicta est, quod falsitas in intellectu esse potest, non solum quia cognitio intellectus falsa est, sed quia intellectus eam cognoscit, sicut et veritatem, in sensu autem falsitas non est ut cognita, ut dictum est.

Quia vero falsitas intellectus per se solum circa compositionem intellectus est, per accidens etiam in operatione intellectus qua cognoscit quod quid est, potest esse falsitas, inquantum ibi compositio intellectus admiscetur. Quod potest esse dupliciter. Uno modo, secundum quod intellectus definitionem unius attribuit alteri; ut si definitionem circuli attribuat homini. Unde definitio unius rei est falsa de altera. Alio modo, secundum quod partes definitionis componit ad invicem, quae simul sociari non possunt, sic enim definitio non est solum falsa respectu alicuius rei, sed est falsa in se. Ut si formet talem definitionem, animal rationale quadrupes, falsus est intellectus sic definiendo, propterea quod falsus est in formando hanc compositionem, aliquod animal rationale est quadrupes. Et propter hoc, in cognoscendo quidditates simplices non potest esse intellectus falsus, sed vel est verus, vel totaliter nihil intelligit.

AD PRIMUM ergo dicendum quod, quia quidditas rei est proprium obiectum intellectus, propter hoc tunc proprie dicimur aliquid intelligere, quando, reducentes illud in quod quid est, sic de eo iudicamus, sicut accidit in demonstrationibus, in quibus non est falsitas. Et hoc modo intelligitur verbum Augustini, quod omnis qui fallitur, non intelligit id in quo fallitur, non autem ita, quod in nulla operatione intellectus aliquis fallatur.

I ANSWER THAT, Just as a thing has being by its proper form, so the knowing faculty has knowledge by the likeness of the thing known. Hence, as natural things cannot fall short of the being that belongs to them by their form, but may fall short of accidental or consequent qualities, even as a man may fail to possess two feet, but not fail to be a man; so the faculty of knowing cannot fail in knowledge of the thing with the likeness of which it is informed; but may fail with regard to something consequent upon that form, or accidental thereto. For it has been said (A. 2) that sight is not deceived in its proper sensible, but about common sensibles that are consequent to that object; or about accidental objects of sense. Now as the sense is directly informed by the likeness of its proper object, so is the intellect by the likeness of the essence of a thing. Hence the intellect is not deceived about the essence of a thing, as neither the sense about its proper object. But in affirming and denying, the intellect may be deceived, by attributing to the thing of which it understands the essence, something which is not consequent upon it, or is opposed to it. For the intellect is in the same position as regards judging of such things, as sense is as to judging of common, or accidental, sensible objects. There is, however, this difference, as before mentioned regarding truth (Q. 16, A. 2), that falsity can exist in the intellect not only because the knowledge of the intellect is false, but because the intellect is conscious of that knowledge, as it is conscious of truth; whereas in sense, falsity does not exist as known, as stated above (A. 2).

But because falsity of the intellect is concerned essentially only with the composition of the intellect, falsity occurs also accidentally in that operation of the intellect whereby it knows the essence of a thing, in so far as composition of the intellect is mixed up in it. This can take place in two ways. In one way, by the intellect applying to one thing the definition proper to another; as that of a circle to a man. Wherefore the definition of one thing is false of another. In another way, by composing a definition of parts which are mutually exclusive. For thus the definition is not only false of the thing, but false in itself. A definition such as *a reasonable four-footed animal* would be of this kind, and the intellect false in making it; for such a statement as *some reasonable animals are four-footed* is false in itself. For this reason the intellect cannot be false in its knowledge of simple essences; but it is either true, or it understands nothing at all.

REPLY OBJ. 1: Because the essence of a thing is the proper object of the intellect, we are properly said to understand a thing when we reduce it to its essence, and judge of it thereby; as takes place in demonstrations, in which there is no falsity. In this sense Augustine's words must be understood, *that he who is deceived, understands not that wherein he is deceived*; and not in the sense that no one is ever deceived in any operation of the intellect.

AD SECUNDUM dicendum quod intellectus semper est rectus, secundum quod intellectus est principiorum, circa quae non decipitur, ex eadem causa qua non decipitur circa quod quid est. Nam principia per se nota sunt illa quae statim, intellectis terminis, cognoscuntur, ex eo quod praedicatum ponitur in definitione subiecti.

REPLY OBJ. 2: The intellect is always right as regards first principles, since it is not deceived about them for the same reason that it is not deceived about what a thing is. For self-known principles are such as are known as soon as the terms are understood, from the fact that the predicate is contained in the definition of the subject.

Article 4

Whether True and False Are Contraries?

AD QUARTUM SIC PROCEDITUR. Videtur quod verum et falsum non sint contraria. Verum enim et falsum opponuntur sicut quod est et quod non est, *nam verum est id quod est*, ut dicit Augustinus. Sed quod est et quod non est, non opponuntur ut contraria. Ergo verum et falsum non sunt contraria.

PRAETEREA, unum contrariorum non est in alio. Sed falsum est in vero, quia, sicut dicit Augustinus in libro Soliloq., *tragoedus non esset falsus Hector, si non esset verus tragoedus*. Ergo verum et falsum non sunt contraria.

PRAETEREA, in Deo non est contrarietas aliqua, *nihil enim divinae substantiae est contrarium*, ut dicit Augustinus, XII de Civit. Dei. Sed Deo opponitur falsitas, nam idolum in Scriptura mendacium nominatur, Ierem. VIII, *apprehenderunt mendacium*; Glossa, *idest idola*. Ergo verum et falsum non sunt contraria.

SED CONTRA est quod dicit philosophus, in II Periherm., ponit enim falsam opinionem verae contrariam.

RESPONDEO dicendum quod verum et falsum opponuntur ut contraria, et non sicut affirmatio et negatio, ut quidam dixerunt. Ad cuius evidentiam, sciendum est quod negatio neque ponit aliquid, neque determinat sibi aliquod subiectum. Et propter hoc, potest dici tam de ente quam de non ente; sicut non videns, et non sedens. Privatio autem non ponit aliquid, sed determinat sibi subiectum. Est enim *negatio in subiecto*, ut dicitur IV Metaphys., caecum enim non dicitur nisi de eo quod est natum videre. Contrarium vero et aliquid ponit, et subiectum determinat, nigrum enim est aliqua species coloris. Falsum autem aliquid ponit. Est enim falsum, ut dicit philosophus, IV Metaphys., ex eo quod dicitur vel videtur aliquid esse quod non est, vel non esse quod est. Sicut enim verum ponit acceptionem adaequatam rei, ita falsum acceptionem rei non adaequatam. Unde manifestum est quod verum et falsum sunt contraria.

AD PRIMUM ergo dicendum quod id quod est in rebus, est veritas rei sed id quod est ut apprehensum, est verum intellectus, in quo primo est veritas. Unde et falsum est id quod non est ut apprehensum. Apprehendere autem esse et non esse, contrarietatem habet, sicut

OBJECTION 1: It seems that true and false are not contraries. For true and false are opposed, as that which is to that which is not; for *truth*, as Augustine says (*Soliloq.* ii, 5), *is that which is*. But that which is and that which is not are not opposed as contraries. Therefore true and false are not contrary things.

OBJ. 2: Further, one of two contraries is not in the other. But falsity is in truth, because, as Augustine says, (*Soliloq.* ii, 10), *A tragedian would not be a false Hector, if he were not a true tragedian.* Therefore true and false are not contraries.

OBJ. 3: Further, in God there is no contrariety, for *nothing is contrary to the Divine Substance*, as Augustine says (*De Civ. Dei* xii, 2). But falsity is opposed to God, for an idol is called in Scripture a lie, *They have laid hold on lying* (Jer 8:5), that is to say, *an idol*, as a gloss says. Therefore false and true are not contraries.

ON THE CONTRARY, The Philosopher says (*Peri Herm.* ii), that a false opinion is contrary to a true one.

I ANSWER THAT, True and false are opposed as contraries, and not, as some have said, as affirmation and negation. In proof of which it must be considered that negation neither asserts anything nor determines any subject, and can therefore be said of being as of not-being, for instance not-seeing or not-sitting. But privation asserts nothing, whereas it determines its subject, for it is *negation in a subject*, as stated in *Metaph.* iv, 4: v. 27; for blindness is not said except of one whose nature it is to see. Contraries, however, both assert something and determine the subject, for blackness is a species of color. Falsity asserts something, for a thing is false, as the Philosopher says (*Metaph.* iv, 27), inasmuch as something is said or seems to be something that it is not, or not to be what it really is. For as truth implies an adequate apprehension of a thing, so falsity implies the contrary. Hence it is clear that true and false are contraries.

REPLY OBJ. 1: What is in things is the truth of the thing; but what is apprehended, is the truth of the intellect, wherein truth primarily resides. Hence the false is that which is not as apprehended. To apprehend being, and not-being, implies contrariety; for, as the Philosopher proves

probat philosophus, in II Periherm., quod huic opinioni, bonum est bonum, contraria est, bonum non est bonum.

AD SECUNDUM dicendum quod falsum non fundatur in vero sibi contrario, sicut nec malum in bono sibi contrario; sed in eo quod sibi subiicitur. Et hoc ideo in utroque accidit, quia verum et bonum communia sunt, et convertuntur cum ente, unde, sicut omnis privatio fundatur in subiecto quod est ens, ita omne malum fundatur in aliquo bono, et omne falsum in aliquo vero.

AD TERTIUM dicendum quod, quia contraria et opposita privative nata sunt fieri circa idem, ideo Deo, prout in se consideratur, non est aliquid contrarium, neque ratione suae bonitatis, neque ratione suae veritatis, quia in intellectu eius non potest esse falsitas aliqua. Sed in apprehensione nostra habet aliquid contrarium, nam verae opinioni de ipso contrariatur falsa opinio. Et sic idola mendacia dicuntur opposita veritati divinae, inquantum falsa opinio de idolis contrariatur verae opinioni de unitate Dei.

(*Peri Herm.* ii), the contrary of this statement *God is good*, is, *God is not good*.

REPLY OBJ. 2: Falsity is not founded in the truth which is contrary to it, just as evil is not founded in the good which is contrary to it, but in that which is its proper subject. This happens in either, because true and good are universals, and convertible with being. Hence, as every privation is founded in a subject, that is a being, so every evil is founded in some good, and every falsity in some truth.

REPLY OBJ. 3: Because contraries, and opposites by way of privation, are by nature about one and the same thing, therefore there is nothing contrary to God, considered in Himself, either with respect to His goodness or His truth, for in His intellect there can be nothing false. But in our apprehension of Him contraries exist, for the false opinion concerning Him is contrary to the true. So idols are called lies, opposed to the divine truth, inasmuch as the false opinion concerning them is contrary to the true opinion of the divine unity.

QUESTION 18

THE LIFE OF GOD

Quoniam autem intelligere viventium est, post consi-derationem de scientia et intellectu divino, considerandum est de vita ipsius.

Et circa hoc quaeruntur quatuor.

Primo, quorum sit vivere.

Secundo, quid sit vita.

Tertio, utrum vita Deo conveniat.

Quarto, utrum omnia in Deo sint vita.

Since to understand belongs to living beings, after considering the divine knowledge and intellect, we must consider the divine life.

About this, four points of inquiry arise:

(1) To whom does it belong to live?

(2) What is life?

(3) Whether life is properly attributed to God?

(4) Whether all things in God are life?

Article 1

Whether to Live Belongs to All Natural Things?

AD PRIMUM SIC PROCEDITUR. Videtur quod omnium rerum naturalium sit vivere. Dicit enim philosophus, in VIII Physic., quod *motus est ut vita quaedam natura existentibus omnibus.* Sed omnes res naturales participant motum. Ergo omnes res naturales participant vitam.

PRAETEREA, plantae dicuntur vivere, inquantum habent in seipsis principium motus augmenti et decrementi. Sed motus localis est perfectior et prior secundum naturam quam motus augmenti et decrementi, ut probatur in VIII Physic. Cum igitur omnia corpora naturalia habeant aliquod principium motus localis, videtur quod omnia corpora naturalia vivant.

PRAETEREA, inter corpora naturalia imperfectiora sunt elementa. Sed eis attribuitur vita, dicuntur enim aquae vivae. Ergo multo magis alia corpora naturalia vitam habent.

SED CONTRA est quod dicit Dionysius, VI cap. de Div. Nom., quod *plantae secundum ultimam resonantiam vitae habent vivere,* ex quo potest accipi quod ultimum gradum vitae obtinent plantae. Sed corpora inanimata sunt infra plantas. Ergo eorum non est vivere.

RESPONDEO dicendum quod ex his quae manifeste vivunt, accipere possumus quorum sit vivere, et quorum non sit vivere. Vivere autem manifeste animalibus convenit, dicitur enim in libro de vegetabilibus, quod *vita in animalibus manifesta est.* Unde secundum illud oportet distinguere viventia a non viventibus secundum quod animalia dicuntur vivere. Hoc autem est in quo primo manifestatur vita, et in quo ultimo remanet. Primo autem dicimus animal vivere, quando incipit ex se motum habere; et tandiu iudicatur animal vivere, quandiu talis motus in eo apparet; quando vero iam ex se non habet

OBJECTION 1: It seems that to live belongs to all natural things. For the Philosopher says (*Phys.* viii, 1) that *Movement is like a kind of life possessed by all things existing in nature.* But all natural things participate in movement. Therefore all natural things partake of life.

OBJ. 2: Further, plants are said to live, inasmuch as they have in themselves a principle of movement of growth and decay. But local movement is naturally more perfect than, and prior to, movement of growth and decay, as the Philosopher shows (*Phys.* viii, 56, 57). Since then, all natural bodies have in themselves some principle of local movement, it seems that all natural bodies live.

OBJ. 3: Further, amongst natural bodies the elements are the less perfect. Yet life is attributed to them, for we speak of *living waters*. Much more, therefore, have other natural bodies life.

ON THE CONTRARY, Dionysius says (*Div. Nom.* vi, 1) that *The last echo of life is heard in the plants*, whereby it is inferred that their life is life in its lowest degree. But inanimate bodies are inferior to plants. Therefore they have not life.

I ANSWER THAT, We can gather to what things life belongs, and to what it does not, from such things as manifestly possess life. Now life manifestly belongs to animals, for it said in *De Vegetab.* i that in animals life is manifest. We must, therefore, distinguish living from lifeless things, by comparing them to that by reason of which animals are said to live: and this it is in which life is manifested first and remains last. We say then that an animal begins to live when it begins to move of itself: and as long as such movement appears in it, so long it is considered to be alive. When it no longer has any movement of itself, but is only moved

199

aliquem motum, sed movetur tantum ab alio tunc dicitur animal mortuum, per defectum vitae. Ex quo patet quod illa proprie sunt viventia, quae seipsa secundum aliquam speciem motus movent; sive accipiatur motus proprie, sicut motus dicitur actus imperfecti, idest existentis in potentia; sive motus accipiatur communiter, prout motus dicitur actus perfecti, prout intelligere et sentire dicitur moveri, ut dicitur in III de anima. Ut sic viventia dicantur quaecumque se agunt ad motum vel operationem aliquam, ea vero in quorum natura non est ut se agant ad aliquem motum vel operationem, viventia dici non possunt, nisi per aliquam similitudinem.

Ad primum ergo dicendum quod verbum illud philosophi potest intelligi vel de motu primo, scilicet corporum caelestium; vel de motu communiter. Et utroque modo motus dicitur quasi vita corporum naturalium, per similitudinem; et non per proprietatem. Nam motus caeli est in universo corporalium naturarum, sicut motus cordis in animali, quo conservatur vita. Similiter etiam quicumque motus naturalis hoc modo se habet ad res naturales, ut quaedam similitudo vitalis operationis. Unde, si totum universum corporale esset unum animal, ita quod iste motus esset a movente intrinseco, ut quidam posuerunt, sequeretur quod motus esset vita omnium naturalium corporum.

Ad secundum dicendum quod corporibus gravibus et levibus non competit moveri, nisi secundum quod sunt extra dispositionem suae naturae, utpote cum sunt extra locum proprium, cum enim sunt in loco proprio et naturali, quiescunt. Sed plantae et aliae res viventes moventur motu vitali, secundum hoc quod sunt in sua dispositione naturali, non autem in accedendo ad eam vel in recedendo ab ea, imo secundum quod recedunt a tali motu, recedunt a naturali dispositione. Et praeterea, corpora gravia et levia moventur a motore extrinseco, vel generante, qui dat formam, vel removente prohibens, ut dicitur in VIII Physic., et ita non movent seipsa, sicut corpora viventia.

Ad tertium dicendum quod aquae vivae dicuntur, quae habent continuum fluxum, aquae enim stantes, quae non continuantur ad principium continue fluens, dicuntur mortuae, ut aquae cisternarum et lacunarum. Et hoc dicitur per similitudinem, inquantum enim videntur se movere, habent similitudinem vitae. Sed tamen non est in eis vera ratio vitae, quia hunc motum non habent a seipsis, sed a causa generante eas; sicut accidit circa motum aliorum gravium et levium.

by another power, then its life is said to fail, and the animal to be dead. Whereby it is clear that those things are properly called living that move themselves by some kind of movement, whether it be movement properly so called, as the act of an imperfect being, i.e., of a thing in potentiality, is called movement; or movement in a more general sense, as when said of the act of a perfect thing, as understanding and feeling are called movement. Accordingly all things are said to be alive that determine themselves to movement or operation of any kind: whereas those things that cannot by their nature do so, cannot be called living, unless by a similitude.

Reply Obj. 1: These words of the Philosopher may be understood either of the first movement, namely, that of the celestial bodies, or of the movement in its general sense. In either way is movement called the life, as it were, of natural bodies, speaking by a similitude, and not attributing it to them as their property. The movement of the heavens is in the universe of corporeal natures as the movement of the heart, whereby life is preserved, is in animals. Similarly also every natural movement in respect to natural things has a certain similitude to the operations of life. Hence, if the whole corporeal universe were one animal, so that its movement came from an *intrinsic moving force*, as some in fact have held, in that case movement would really be the life of all natural bodies.

Reply Obj. 2: To bodies, whether heavy or light, movement does not belong, except in so far as they are displaced from their natural conditions, and are out of their proper place; for when they are in the place that is proper and natural to them, then they are at rest. Plants and other living things move with vital movement, in accordance with the disposition of their nature, but not by approaching thereto, or by receding from it, for in so far as they recede from such movement, so far do they recede from their natural disposition. Heavy and light bodies are moved by an extrinsic force, either generating them and giving them form, or removing obstacles from their way. They do not therefore move themselves, as do living bodies.

Reply Obj. 3: Waters are called living that have a continuous current: for standing waters, that are not connected with a continually flowing source, are called dead, as in cisterns and ponds. This is merely a similitude, inasmuch as the movement they are seen to possess makes them look as if they were alive. Yet this is not life in them in its real sense, since this movement of theirs is not from themselves but from the cause that generates them. The same is the case with the movement of other heavy and light bodies.

Article 2

Whether Life Is an Operation?

AD SECUNDUM SIC PROCEDITUR. Videtur quod vita sit quaedam operatio. Nihil enim dividitur nisi per ea quae sunt sui generis. Sed vivere dividitur per operationes quasdam, ut patet per philosophum in II libro de anima, qui distinguit vivere per quatuor, scilicet alimento uti, sentire, moveri secundum locum, et intelligere. Ergo vita est operatio quaedam.

PRAETEREA, vita activa dicitur alia esse a contemplativa. Sed contemplativi ab activis non diversificantur nisi secundum operationes quasdam. Ergo vita est quaedam operatio.

PRAETEREA, cognoscere Deum est operatio quaedam. Haec autem est vita, ut patet per illud Ioan. XVII, *haec est autem vita aeterna, ut cognoscant te solum verum Deum*. Ergo vita est operatio.

SED CONTRA est quod dicit philosophus, in II de anima, *vivere viventibus est esse*.

RESPONDEO dicendum quod, sicut ex dictis patet, intellectus noster, qui proprie est cognoscitivus quidditatis rei ut proprii obiecti, accipit a sensu, cuius propria obiecta sunt accidentia exteriora. Et inde est quod ex his quae exterius apparent de re, devenimus ad cognoscendam essentiam rei. Et quia sic nominamus aliquid sicut cognoscimus illud, ut ex supradictis patet, inde est quod plerumque a proprietatibus exterioribus imponuntur nomina ad significandas essentias rerum. Unde huiusmodi nomina quandoque accipiuntur proprie pro ipsis essentiis rerum, ad quas significandas principaliter sunt imposita, aliquando autem sumuntur pro proprietatibus a quibus imponuntur, et hoc minus proprie. Sicut patet quod hoc nomen corpus impositum est ad significandum quoddam genus substantiarum, ex eo quod in eis inveniuntur tres dimensiones, et ideo aliquando ponitur hoc nomen corpus ad significandas tres dimensiones, secundum quod corpus ponitur species quantitatis. Sic ergo dicendum est et de vita. Nam vitae nomen sumitur ex quodam exterius apparenti circa rem, quod est movere seipsum, non tamen est impositum hoc nomen ad hoc significandum, sed ad significandam substantiam cui convenit secundum suam naturam movere seipsam, vel agere se quocumque modo ad operationem. Et secundum hoc, vivere nihil aliud est quam esse in tali natura, et vita significat hoc ipsum, sed in abstracto; sicut hoc nomen cursus significat ipsum currere in abstracto.

Unde vivum non est praedicatum accidentale, sed substantiale. Quandoque tamen vita sumitur minus proprie pro operationibus vitae, a quibus nomen vitae assumitur; sicut dicit philosophus, IX Ethic., quod *vivere principaliter est sentire vel intelligere*.

OBJECTION 1: It seems that life is an operation. For nothing is divided except into parts of the same genus. But life is divided by certain operations, as is clear from the Philosopher (*De Anima* ii, 13), who distinguishes four kinds of life, namely, nourishment, sensation, local movement and understanding. Therefore life is an operation.

OBJ. 2: Further, the active life is said to be different from the contemplative. But the contemplative is only distinguished from the active by certain operations. Therefore life is an operation.

OBJ. 3: Further, to know God is an operation. But this is life, as is clear from the words of John 18:3, *Now this is eternal life, that they may know Thee, the only true God*. Therefore life is an operation.

ON THE CONTRARY, The Philosopher says (*De Anima* ii, 37), *In living things, to live is to be*.

I ANSWER THAT, As is clear from what has been said (Q. 17, A. 3), our intellect, which takes cognizance of the essence of a thing as its proper object, gains knowledge from sense, of which the proper objects are external accidents. Hence from external appearances we come to the knowledge of the essence of things. And because we name a thing in accordance with our knowledge of it, as is clear from what has already been said (Q. 13, A. 1), so from external properties names are often imposed to signify essences. Hence such names are sometimes taken strictly to denote the essence itself, the signification of which is their principal object; but sometimes, and less strictly, to denote the properties by reason of which they are imposed. And so we see that the word *body* is used to denote a genus of substances from the fact of their possessing three dimensions: and is sometimes taken to denote the dimensions themselves; in which sense body is said to be a species of quantity. The same must be said of life. The name is given from a certain external appearance, namely, self-movement, yet not precisely to signify this, but rather a substance to which self-movement and the application of itself to any kind of operation, belong naturally. To live, accordingly, is nothing else than to exist in this or that nature; and life signifies this, though in the abstract, just as the word *running* denotes *to run* in the abstract.

Hence *living* is not an accidental but an essential predicate. Sometimes, however, life is used less properly for the operations from which its name is taken, and thus the Philosopher says (*Ethic.* ix, 9) that to live is principally to sense or to understand.

AD PRIMUM ergo dicendum quod philosophus ibi accipit vivere pro operatione vitae. Vel dicendum est melius, quod sentire et intelligere, et huiusmodi, quandoque sumuntur pro quibusdam operationibus; quandoque autem pro ipso esse sic operantium. Dicitur enim IX Ethic., quod *esse est sentire vel intelligere*, idest habere naturam ad sentiendum vel intelligendum. Et hoc modo distinguit philosophus vivere per illa quatuor. Nam in istis inferioribus quatuor sunt genera viventium. Quorum quaedam habent naturam solum ad utendum alimento, et ad consequentia, quae sunt augmentum et generatio; quaedam ulterius ad sentiendum, ut patet in animalibus immobilibus, sicut sunt ostrea; quaedam vero, cum his, ulterius ad movendum se secundum locum, sicut animalia perfecta, ut quadrupedia et volatilia et huiusmodi; quaedam vero ulterius ad intelligendum, sicut homines.

AD SECUNDUM dicendum quod opera vitae dicuntur, quorum principia sunt in operantibus, ut seipsos inducant in tales operationes. Contingit autem aliquorum operum inesse hominibus non solum principia naturalia, ut sunt potentiae naturales; sed etiam quaedam superaddita, ut sunt habitus inclinantes ad quaedam operationum genera quasi per modum naturae, et facientes illas operationes esse delectabiles. Et ex hoc dicitur, quasi per quandam similitudinem, quod illa operatio quae est homini delectabilis, et ad quam inclinatur, et in qua conversatur, et ordinat vitam suam ad ipsam, dicitur vita hominis, unde quidam dicuntur agere vitam luxuriosam, quidam vitam honestam. Et per hunc modum vita contemplativa ab activa distinguitur. Et per hunc etiam modum cognoscere Deum dicitur vita aeterna.

UNDE PATET solutio ad tertium.

REPLY OBJ. 1: The Philosopher here takes *to live* to mean an operation of life. Or it would be better to say that sensation and intelligence and the like, are sometimes taken for the operations, sometimes for the existence itself of the operator. For he says (*Ethic*. ix, 9) that to live is to sense or to understand—in other words, to have a nature capable of sensation or understanding. Thus, then, he distinguishes life by the four operations mentioned. For in this lower world there are four kinds of living things. It is the nature of some to be capable of nothing more than taking nourishment, and, as a consequence, of growing and generating. Others are able, in addition, to sense, as we see in the case of shellfish and other animals without movement. Others have the further power of moving from place to place, as perfect animals, such as quadrupeds, and birds, and so on. Others, as man, have the still higher faculty of understanding.

REPLY OBJ. 2: By vital operations are meant those whose principles are within the operator, and in virtue of which the operator produces such operations of itself. It happens that there exist in men not merely such natural principles of certain operations as are their natural powers, but something over and above these, such as habits inclining them like a second nature to particular kinds of operations, so that the operations become sources of pleasure. Thus, as by a similitude, any kind of work in which a man takes delight, so that his bent is towards it, his time spent in it, and his whole life ordered with a view to it, is said to be the life of that man. Hence some are said to lead a life of self-indulgence, others a life of virtue. In this way the contemplative life is distinguished from the active, and thus to know God is said to be life eternal.

WHEREFORE the Reply to the Third Objection is clear.

Article 3

Whether Life Is Properly Attributed to God?

AD TERTIUM SIC PROCEDITUR. Videtur quod Deo non conveniat vita. Vivere enim dicuntur aliqua secundum quod movent seipsa, ut dictum est. Sed Deo non competit moveri. Ergo neque vivere.

PRAETEREA, in omnibus quae vivunt, est accipere aliquod vivendi principium, unde dicitur in II de anima, quod *anima est viventis corporis causa et principium*. Sed Deus non habet aliquod principium. Ergo sibi non competit vivere.

PRAETEREA, principium vitae in rebus viventibus quae apud nos sunt, est anima vegetabilis, quae non est nisi in rebus corporalibus. Ergo rebus incorporalibus non competit vivere.

OBJECTION 1: It seems that life is not properly attributed to God. For things are said to live inasmuch as they move themselves, as previously stated (A. 2). But movement does not belong to God. Neither therefore does life.

OBJ. 2: Further, in all living things we must needs suppose some principle of life. Hence it is said by the Philosopher (*De Anima* ii, 4) that *the soul is the cause and principle of the living body*. But God has no principle. Therefore life cannot be attributed to Him.

OBJ. 3: Further, the principle of life in the living things that exist among us is the vegetative soul. But this exists only in corporeal things. Therefore life cannot be attributed to incorporeal things.

SED CONTRA est quod dicitur in Psalmo LXXXIII, *cor meum et caro mea exultaverunt in Deum vivum.*

RESPONDEO dicendum quod vita maxime proprie in Deo est. Ad cuius evidentiam, considerandum est quod, cum vivere dicantur aliqua secundum quod operantur ex seipsis, et non quasi ab aliis mota; quanto perfectius competit hoc alicui, tanto perfectius in eo invenitur vita. In moventibus autem et motis tria per ordinem inveniuntur. Nam primo, finis movet agentem; agens vero principale est quod per suam formam agit; et hoc interdum agit per aliquod instrumentum, quod non agit ex virtute suae formae, sed ex virtute principalis agentis; cui instrumento competit sola executio actionis. Inveniuntur igitur quaedam, quae movent seipsa, non habito respectu ad formam vel finem, quae inest eis a natura, sed solum quantum ad executionem motus, sed forma per quam agunt, et finis propter quem agunt, determinantur eis a natura. Et huiusmodi sunt plantae, quae secundum formam inditam eis a natura, movent seipsas secundum augmentum et decrementum.

Quaedam vero ulterius movent seipsa, non solum habito respectu ad executionem motus, sed etiam quantum ad formam quae est principium motus, quam per se acquirunt. Et huiusmodi sunt animalia, quorum motus principium est forma non a natura indita, sed per sensum accepta. Unde quanto perfectiorem sensum habent, tanto perfectius movent seipsa. Nam ea quae non habent nisi sensum tactus, movent solum seipsa motu dilatationis et constrictionis, ut ostrea, parum excedentia motum plantae. Quae vero habent virtutem sensitivam perfectam, non solum ad cognoscendum coniuncta et tangentia, sed etiam ad cognoscendum distantia, movent seipsa in remotum motu processivo. Sed quamvis huiusmodi animalia formam quae est principium motus, per sensum accipiant, non tamen per seipsa praestituunt sibi finem suae operationis, vel sui motus; sed est eis inditus a natura, cuius instinctu ad aliquid agendum moventur per formam sensu apprehensam. Unde supra talia animalia sunt illa quae movent seipsa, etiam habito respectu ad finem, quem sibi praestituunt. Quod quidem non fit nisi per rationem et intellectum, cuius est cognoscere proportionem finis et eius quod est ad finem, et unum ordinare in alterum. Unde perfectior modus vivendi est eorum quae habent intellectum, haec enim perfectius movent seipsa. Et huius est signum, quod in uno et eodem homine virtus intellectiva movet potentias sensitivas; et potentiae sensitivae per suum imperium movent organa, quae exequuntur motum. Sicut etiam in artibus, videmus quod ars ad quam pertinet usus navis, scilicet ars gubernatoria, praecipit ei quae inducit formam navis, et haec praecipit illi quae habet executionem tantum, in disponendo materiam.

ON THE CONTRARY, It is said (Ps 83:3): *My heart and my flesh have rejoiced in the living God.*

I ANSWER THAT, Life is in the highest degree properly in God. In proof of which it must be considered that since a thing is said to live in so far as it operates of itself and not as moved by another, the more perfectly this power is found in anything, the more perfect is the life of that thing. In things that move and are moved, a threefold order is found. In the first place, the end moves the agent: and the principal agent is that which acts through its form, and sometimes it does so through some instrument that acts by virtue not of its own form, but of the principal agent, and does no more than execute the action. Accordingly there are things that move themselves, not in respect of any form or end naturally inherent in them, but only in respect of the executing of the movement; the form by which they act, and the end of the action being alike determined for them by their nature. Of this kind are plants, which move themselves according to their inherent nature, with regard only to executing the movements of growth and decay.

Other things have self-movement in a higher degree, that is, not only with regard to executing the movement, but even as regards to the form, the principle of movement, which form they acquire of themselves. Of this kind are animals, in which the principle of movement is not a naturally implanted form; but one received through sense. Hence the more perfect is their sense, the more perfect is their power of self-movement. Such as have only the sense of touch, as shellfish, move only with the motion of expansion and contraction; and thus their movement hardly exceeds that of plants. Whereas such as have the sensitive power in perfection, so as to recognize not only connection and touch, but also objects apart from themselves, can move themselves to a distance by progressive movement. Yet although animals of the latter kind receive through sense the form that is the principle of their movement, nevertheless they cannot of themselves propose to themselves the end of their operation, or movement; for this has been implanted in them by nature; and by natural instinct they are moved to any action through the form apprehended by sense. Hence such animals as move themselves in respect to an end they themselves propose are superior to these. This can only be done by reason and intellect; whose province it is to know the proportion between the end and the means to that end, and duly coordinate them. Hence a more perfect degree of life is that of intelligent beings; for their power of self-movement is more perfect. This is shown by the fact that in one and the same man the intellectual faculty moves the sensitive powers; and these by their command move the organs of movement. Thus in the arts we see that the art of using a ship, i.e., the art of navigation, rules the art of ship-designing; and this in its turn rules the art that is only concerned with preparing the material for the ship.

Sed quamvis intellectus noster ad aliqua se agat, tamen aliqua sunt ei praestituta a natura; sicut sunt prima principia, circa quae non potest aliter se habere, et ultimus finis, quem non potest non velle. Unde, licet quantum ad aliquid moveat se, tamen oportet quod quantum ad aliqua ab alio moveatur. Illud igitur cuius sua natura est ipsum eius intelligere, et cui id quod naturaliter habet, non determinatur ab alio, hoc est quod obtinet summum gradum vitae. Tale autem est Deus. Unde in Deo maxime est vita. Unde philosophus, in XII Metaphys., ostenso quod Deus sit intelligens, concludit quod habeat vitam perfectissimam et sempiternam, quia intellectus eius est perfectissimus, et semper in actu.

AD PRIMUM ergo dicendum quod, sicut dicitur in IX Metaphys., duplex est actio, una, quae transit in exteriorem materiam, ut calefacere et secare; alia, quae manet in agente, ut intelligere, sentire et velle. Quarum haec est differentia, quia prima actio non est perfectio agentis quod movet, sed ipsius moti; secunda autem actio est perfectio agentis. Unde, quia motus est actus mobilis, secunda actio, inquantum est actus operantis, dicitur motus eius; ex hac similitudine, quod, sicut motus est actus mobilis, ita huiusmodi actio est actus agentis; licet motus sit actus imperfecti, scilicet existentis in potentia, huiusmodi autem actio est actus perfecti, idest existentis in actu, ut dicitur in III de anima. Hoc igitur modo quo intelligere est motus, id quod se intelligit, dicitur se movere. Et per hunc modum etiam Plato posuit quod Deus movet seipsum, non eo modo quo motus est actus imperfecti.

AD SECUNDUM dicendum quod, sicut Deus est ipsum suum esse et suum intelligere, ita est suum vivere. Et propter hoc, sic vivit, quod non habet vivendi principium.

AD TERTIUM dicendum quod vita in istis inferioribus recipitur in natura corruptibili, quae indiget et generatione ad conservationem speciei, et alimento ad conservationem individui. Et propter hoc, in istis inferioribus non invenitur vita sine anima vegetabili. Sed hoc non habet locum in rebus incorruptibilibus.

But although our intellect moves itself to some things, yet others are supplied by nature, as are first principles, which it cannot doubt; and the last end, which it cannot but will. Hence, although with respect to some things it moves itself, yet with regard to other things it must be moved by another. Wherefore that being whose act of understanding is its very nature, and which, in what it naturally possesses, is not determined by another, must have life in the most perfect degree. Such is God; and hence in Him principally is life. From this the Philosopher concludes (*Metaph.* xii, 51), after showing God to be intelligent, that God has life most perfect and eternal, since His intellect is most perfect and always in act.

REPLY OBJ. 1: As stated in *Metaph.* ix, 16, action is twofold. Actions of one kind pass out to external matter, as to heat or to cut; whilst actions of the other kind remain in the agent, as to understand, to sense and to will. The difference between them is this, that the former action is the perfection not of the agent that moves, but of the thing moved; whereas the latter action is the perfection of the agent. Hence, because movement is an act of the thing in movement, the latter action, in so far as it is the act of the operator, is called its movement by this similitude: that as movement is an act of the thing moved, so an act of this kind is the act of the agent, although movement is an act of the imperfect, that is, of what is in potentiality; while this kind of act is an act of the perfect, that is to say, of what is in act as stated in *De Anima* iii, 28. In the sense, therefore, in which understanding is movement, that which understands itself is said to move itself. It is in this sense that Plato also taught that God moves Himself; not in the sense in which movement is an act of the imperfect.

REPLY OBJ. 2: As God is His own very existence and understanding, so is He His own life; and therefore He so lives that He has no principle of life.

REPLY OBJ. 3: Life in this lower world is bestowed on a corruptible nature, that needs generation to preserve the species, and nourishment to preserve the individual. For this reason life is not found here below apart from a vegetative soul: but this does not hold good with incorruptible natures.

Article 4

Whether All Things Are Life in God?

AD QUARTUM SIC PROCEDITUR. Videtur quod non omnia sint vita in Deo. Dicitur enim Act. XVII, *in ipso vivimus, movemur et sumus.* Sed non omnia in Deo sunt motus. Ergo non omnia in ipso sunt vita.

OBJECTION 1: It seems that not all things are life in God. For it is said (Acts 17:28), *In Him we live, and move, and be.* But not all things in God are movement. Therefore not all things are life in Him.

PRAETEREA, omnia sunt in Deo sicut in primo exemplari. Sed exemplata debent conformari exemplari. Cum igitur non omnia vivant in seipsis, videtur quod non omnia in Deo sint vita.

PRAETEREA, sicut Augustinus dicit in libro de vera Relig., substantia vivens est melior qualibet substantia non vivente. Si igitur ea quae in seipsis non vivunt, in Deo sunt vita, videtur quod verius sint res in Deo quam in seipsis. Quod tamen videtur esse falsum, cum in seipsis sint in actu, in Deo vero in potentia.

PRAETEREA, sicut sciuntur a Deo bona, et ea quae fiunt secundum aliquod tempus; ita mala, et ea quae Deus potest facere, sed nunquam fiunt. Si ergo omnia sunt vita in Deo, inquantum sunt scita ab ipso, videtur quod etiam mala, et quae nunquam fiunt, sunt vita in Deo, inquantum sunt scita ab eo. Quod videtur inconveniens.

SED CONTRA est quod dicitur Ioan. I, *quod factum est, in ipso vita erat*. Sed omnia praeter Deum facta sunt. Ergo omnia in Deo sunt vita.

RESPONDEO dicendum quod, sicut dictum est, vivere Dei est eius intelligere. In Deo autem est idem intellectus et quod intelligitur, et ipsum intelligere eius. Unde quidquid est in Deo ut intellectum, est ipsum vivere vel vita eius. Unde, cum omnia quae facta sunt a Deo, sint in ipso ut intellecta, sequitur quod omnia in ipso sunt ipsa vita divina.

AD PRIMUM ergo dicendum quod creaturae in Deo esse dicuntur dupliciter. Uno modo, inquantum continentur et conservantur virtute divina, sicut dicimus ea esse in nobis, quae sunt in nostra potestate. Et sic creaturae dicuntur esse in Deo, etiam prout sunt in propriis naturis. Et hoc modo intelligendum est verbum apostoli dicentis, *in ipso vivimus, movemur et sumus*, quia et nostrum vivere, et nostrum esse, et nostrum moveri causantur a Deo. Alio modo dicuntur res esse in Deo sicut in cognoscente. Et sic sunt in Deo per proprias rationes, quae non sunt aliud in Deo ab essentia divina. Unde res, prout sic in Deo sunt, sunt essentia divina. Et quia essentia divina est vita, non autem motus, inde est quod res, hoc modo loquendi, in Deo non sunt motus, sed vita.

AD SECUNDUM dicendum quod exemplata oportet conformari exemplari secundum rationem formae, non autem secundum modum essendi. Nam alterius modi esse habet quandoque forma in exemplari et in exemplato, sicut forma domus in mente artificis habet esse immateriale et intelligibile, in domo autem quae est extra animam, habet esse materiale et sensibile. Unde et rationes rerum quae in seipsis non vivunt, in mente divina sunt vita, quia in mente divina habent esse divinum.

AD TERTIUM dicendum quod, si de ratione rerum naturalium non esset materia, sed tantum forma, omnibus

OBJ. 2: Further, all things are in God as their first model. But things modeled ought to conform to the model. Since, then, not all things have life in themselves, it seems that not all things are life in God.

OBJ. 3: Further, as Augustine says (*De Vera Relig.* 29), a living substance is better than a substance that does not live. If, therefore, things which in themselves have not life, are life in God, it seems that things exist more truly in God than themselves. But this appears to be false; since in themselves they exist actually, but in God potentially.

OBJ. 4: Further, just as good things and things made in time are known by God, so are bad things, and things that God can make, but that never will be made. If, therefore, all things are life in God, inasmuch as known by Him, it seems that even bad things and things that will never be made are life in God, as known by Him, and this appears inadmissible.

ON THE CONTRARY, (John 1:3, 4), it is said, *What was made, in Him was life*. But all things were made, except God. Therefore all things are life in God.

I ANSWER THAT, In God to live is to understand, as before stated (A. 3). In God intellect, the thing understood, and the act of understanding, are one and the same. Hence whatever is in God as understood is the very living or life of God. Now, wherefore, since all things that have been made by God are in Him as things understood, it follows that all things in Him are the divine life itself.

REPLY OBJ. 1: Creatures are said to be in God in a twofold sense. In one way, so far are they are held together and preserved by the divine power; even as we say that things that are in our power are in us. And creatures are thus said to be in God, even as they exist in their own natures. In this sense we must understand the words of the Apostle when he says, *In Him we live, move, and be*; since our being, living, and moving are themselves caused by God. In another sense things are said to be in God, as in Him who knows them, in which sense they are in God through their proper ideas, which in God are not distinct from the divine essence. Hence things as they are in God are the divine essence. And since the divine essence is life and not movement, it follows that things existing in God in this manner are not movement, but life.

REPLY OBJ. 2: The thing modeled must be like the model according to the form, not the mode of being. For sometimes the form has being of another kind in the model from that which it has in the thing modelled. Thus the form of a house has in the mind of the architect immaterial and intelligible being; but in the house that exists outside his mind, material and sensible being. Hence the ideas of things, though not existing in themselves, are life in the divine mind, as having a divine existence in that mind.

REPLY OBJ. 3: If form only, and not matter, belonged to natural things, then in all respects natural things would

modis veriori modo essent res naturales in mente divina per suas ideas, quam in seipsis. Propter quod et Plato posuit quod homo separatus erat verus homo, homo autem materialis est homo per participationem. Sed quia de ratione rerum naturalium est materia, dicendum quod res naturales verius esse habent simpliciter in mente divina, quam in seipsis, quia in mente divina habent esse increatum, in seipsis autem esse creatum. Sed esse hoc, utpote homo vel equus, verius habent in propria natura quam in mente divina, quia ad veritatem hominis pertinet esse materiale, quod non habent in mente divina. Sicut domus nobilius esse habet in mente artificis, quam in materia, sed tamen verius dicitur domus quae est in materia, quam quae est in mente; quia haec est domus in actu, illa autem domus in potentia.

AD QUARTUM dicendum quod, licet mala sint in Dei scientia, inquantum sub Dei scientia comprehenduntur, non tamen sunt in Deo sicut creata a Deo vel conservata ab ipso, neque sicut habentia rationem in Deo, cognoscuntur enim a Deo per rationes bonorum. Unde non potest dici quod mala sint vita in Deo. Ea vero quae secundum nullum tempus sunt, possunt dici esse vita in Deo, secundum quod vivere nominat intelligere tantum, inquantum intelliguntur a Deo, non autem secundum quod vivere importat principium operationis.

exist more truly in the divine mind, by the ideas of them, than in themselves. For which reason, in fact, Plato held that the separate man was the true man; and that man as he exists in matter, is man only by participation. But since matter enters into the being of natural things, we must say that those things have simply being in the divine mind more truly than in themselves, because in that mind they have an uncreated being, but in themselves a created being: whereas this particular being, a man, or horse, for example, has this being more truly in its own nature than in the divine mind, because it belongs to human nature to be material, which, as existing in the divine mind, it is not. Even so a house has nobler being in the architect's mind than in matter; yet a material house is called a house more truly than the one which exists in the mind, since the former is actual, the latter only potential.

REPLY OBJ. 4: Although bad things are in God's knowledge, as being comprised under that knowledge, yet they are not in God as created by Him, or preserved by Him, or as having their type in Him. They are known by God through the types of good things. Hence it cannot be said that bad things are life in God. Those things that are not in time may be called life in God in so far as life means understanding only, and inasmuch as they are understood by God; but not in so far as life implies a principle of operation.

QUESTION 19

THE WILL OF GOD

Post considerationem eorum quae ad divinam scientiam pertinent, considerandum est de his quae pertinent ad voluntatem divinam,

ut sit prima consideratio de ipsa Dei voluntate; secunda, de his quae ad voluntatem absolute pertinent; tertia, de his quae ad intellectum in ordine ad voluntatem pertinent.

Circa ipsam autem voluntatem quaeruntur duodecim.

Primo, utrum in Deo sit voluntas.

Secundo, utrum Deus velit alia a se.

Tertio, utrum quidquid Deus vult, ex necessitate velit.

Quarto, utrum voluntas Dei sit causa rerum.

Quinto, utrum voluntatis divinae sit assignare aliquam causam.

Sexto, utrum voluntas divina semper impleatur.

Septimo, utrum voluntas Dei sit mutabilis.

Octavo, utrum voluntas Dei necessitatem rebus volitis imponat.

Nono, utrum in Deo sit voluntas malorum.

Decimo, utrum Deus habeat liberum arbitrium.

Undecimo, utrum sit distinguenda in Deo voluntas signi.

Duodecimo, utrum convenienter circa divinam voluntatem ponantur quinque signa.

After considering the things belonging to the divine knowledge, we consider what belongs to the divine will.

The first consideration is about the divine will itself; the second about what belongs strictly to His will; the third about what belongs to the intellect in relation to His will.

About His will itself there are twelve points of inquiry:

(1) Whether there is will in God?

(2) Whether God wills things apart from Himself?

(3) Whether whatever God wills, He wills necessarily?

(4) Whether the will of God is the cause of things?

(5) Whether any cause can be assigned to the divine will?

(6) Whether the divine will is always fulfilled?

(7) Whether the will of God is mutable?

(8) Whether the will of God imposes necessity on the things willed?

(9) Whether there is in God the will of evil?

(10) Whether God has free will?

(11) Whether the will of expression is distinguished in God?

(12) Whether five expressions of will are rightly assigned to the divine will?

Article 1

Whether There Is Will in God?

AD PRIMUM SIC PROCEDITUR. Videtur quod in Deo non sit voluntas. Obiectum enim voluntatis est finis et bonum. Sed Dei non est assignare aliquem finem. Ergo voluntas non est in Deo.

PRAETEREA, voluntas est appetitus quidam. Appetitus autem, cum sit rei non habitae, imperfectionem designat, quae Deo non competit. Ergo voluntas non est in Deo.

PRAETEREA, secundum philosophum, in III de anima, voluntas est movens motum. Sed Deus est primum movens immobile. Ut probatur VIII Physic. Ergo in Deo non est voluntas.

SED CONTRA est quod dicit apostolus, Rom. XII, *ut probetis quae sit voluntas Dei.*

OBJECTION 1: It seems that there is not will in God. For the object of will is the end and the good. But we cannot assign to God any end. Therefore there is not will in God.

OBJ. 2: Further, will is a kind of appetite. But appetite, as it is directed to things not possessed, implies imperfection, which cannot be imputed to God. Therefore there is not will in God.

OBJ. 3: Further, according to the Philosopher (*De Anima* iii, 54), the will moves, and is moved. But God is the first cause of movement, and Himself is unmoved, as proved in *Phys.* viii, 49. Therefore there is not will in God.

ON THE CONTRARY, The Apostle says (Rom 12:2): *That you may prove what is the will of God.*

RESPONDEO dicendum in Deo voluntatem esse, sicut et in eo est intellectus, voluntas enim intellectum consequitur. Sicut enim res naturalis habet esse in actu per suam formam, ita intellectus intelligens actu per suam formam intelligibilem. Quaelibet autem res ad suam formam naturalem hanc habet habitudinem, ut quando non habet ipsam, tendat in eam; et quando habet ipsam, quiescat in ea. Et idem est de qualibet perfectione naturali, quod est bonum naturae. Et haec habitudo ad bonum, in rebus carentibus cognitione, vocatur appetitus naturalis. Unde et natura intellectualis ad bonum apprehensum per formam intelligibilem, similem habitudinem habet, ut scilicet, cum habet ipsum, quiescat in illo; cum vero non habet, quaerat ipsum. Et utrumque pertinet ad voluntatem. Unde in quolibet habente intellectum, est voluntas; sicut in quolibet habente sensum, est appetitus animalis. Et sic oportet in Deo esse voluntatem, cum sit in eo intellectus. Et sicut suum intelligere est suum esse, ita suum velle.

AD PRIMUM ergo dicendum quod, licet nihil aliud a Deo sit finis Dei, tamen ipsemet est finis respectu omnium quae ab eo fiunt. Et hoc per suam essentiam, cum per suam essentiam sit bonus, ut supra ostensum est, finis enim habet rationem boni.

AD SECUNDUM dicendum quod voluntas in nobis pertinet ad appetitivam partem, quae licet ab appetendo nominetur, non tamen hunc solum habet actum, ut appetat quae non habet; sed etiam ut amet quod habet, et delectetur in illo. Et quantum ad hoc voluntas in Deo ponitur; quae semper habet bonum quod est eius obiectum, cum sit indifferens ab eo secundum essentiam, ut dictum est.

AD TERTIUM dicendum quod voluntas cuius obiectum principale est bonum quod est extra voluntatem, oportet quod sit mota ab aliquo. Sed obiectum divinae voluntatis est bonitas sua, quae est eius essentia. Unde, cum voluntas Dei sit eius essentia, non movetur ab alio a se, sed a se tantum, eo modo loquendi quo intelligere et velle dicitur motus. Et secundum hoc Plato dixit quod primum movens movet seipsum.

I ANSWER THAT, There is will in God, as there is intellect: since will follows upon intellect. For as natural things have actual existence by their form, so the intellect is actually intelligent by its intelligible form. Now everything has this aptitude towards its natural form, that when it has it not, it tends towards it; and when it has it, it is at rest therein. It is the same with every natural perfection, which is a natural good. This aptitude to good in things without knowledge is called natural appetite. Whence also intellectual natures have a like aptitude as apprehended through its intelligible form; so as to rest therein when possessed, and when not possessed to seek to possess it, both of which pertain to the will. Hence in every intellectual being there is will, just as in every sensible being there is animal appetite. And so there must be will in God, since there is intellect in Him. And as His intellect is His own existence, so is His will.

REPLY OBJ. 1: Although nothing apart from God is His end, yet He Himself is the end with respect to all things made by Him. And this by His essence, for by His essence He is good, as shown above (Q. 6, A. 3): for the end has the aspect of good.

REPLY OBJ. 2: Will in us belongs to the appetitive part, which, although named from appetite, has not for its only act the seeking what it does not possess; but also the loving and the delighting in what it does possess. In this respect will is said to be in God, as having always good which is its object, since, as already said, it is not distinct from His essence.

REPLY OBJ. 3: A will of which the principal object is a good outside itself, must be moved by another; but the object of the divine will is His goodness, which is His essence. Hence, since the will of God is His essence, it is not moved by another than itself, but by itself alone, in the same sense as understanding and willing are said to be movement. This is what Plato meant when he said that the first mover moves itself.

Article 2

Whether God Wills Things Apart from Himself?

AD SECUNDUM SIC PROCEDITUR. Videtur quod Deus non velit alia a se. Velle enim divinum est eius esse. Sed Deus non est aliud a se. Ergo non vult aliud a se.

PRAETEREA, volitum movet voluntatem, sicut appetibile appetitum, ut dicitur in III de anima. Si igitur Deus

OBJECTION 1: It seems that God does not will things apart from Himself. For the divine will is the divine existence. But God is not other than Himself. Therefore He does not will things other than Himself.

OBJ. 2: Further, the willed moves the willer, as the appetible the appetite, as stated in *De Anima* iii, 54. If, therefore,

velit aliquid aliud a se, movebitur eius voluntas ab aliquo alio, quod est impossibile.

PRAETEREA, cuicumque voluntati sufficit aliquod volitum, nihil quaerit extra illud. Sed Deo sufficit sua bonitas, et voluntas eius ex ea satiatur. Ergo Deus non vult aliquid aliud a se.

PRAETEREA, actus voluntatis multiplicatur secundum volita. Si igitur Deus velit se et alia a se, sequitur quod actus voluntatis eius sit multiplex, et per consequens eius esse, quod est eius velle. Hoc autem est impossibile. Non ergo vult alia a se.

SED CONTRA est quod apostolus dicit, I Thess. IV, *haec est voluntas Dei, sanctificatio vestra.*

RESPONDEO dicendum quod Deus non solum se vult, sed etiam alia a se. Quod apparet a simili prius introducto. Res enim naturalis non solum habet naturalem inclinationem respectu proprii boni, ut acquirat ipsum cum non habet, vel ut quiescat in illo cum habet; sed etiam ut proprium bonum in alia diffundat, secundum quod possibile est. Unde videmus quod omne agens, inquantum est actu et perfectum, facit sibi simile. Unde et hoc pertinet ad rationem voluntatis, ut bonum quod quis habet, aliis communicet, secundum quod possibile est. Et hoc praecipue pertinet ad voluntatem divinam, a qua, per quandam similitudinem, derivatur omnis perfectio. Unde, si res naturales, inquantum perfectae sunt, suum bonum aliis communicant, multo magis pertinet ad voluntatem divinam, ut bonum suum aliis per similitudinem communicet, secundum quod possibile est. Sic igitur vult et se esse, et alia. Sed se ut finem, alia vero ut ad finem, inquantum condecet divinam bonitatem etiam alia ipsam participare.

AD PRIMUM ergo dicendum quod, licet divinum velle sit eius esse secundum rem, tamen differt ratione, secundum diversum modum intelligendi et significandi, ut ex superioribus patet. In hoc enim quod dico Deum esse, non importatur habitudo ad aliquid, sicut in hoc quod dico Deum velle. Et ideo, licet non sit aliquid aliud a se, vult tamen aliquid aliud a se.

AD SECUNDUM dicendum quod in his quae volumus propter finem, tota ratio movendi est finis, et hoc est quod movet voluntatem. Et hoc maxime apparet in his quae volumus tantum propter finem. Qui enim vult sumere potionem amaram, nihil in ea vult nisi sanitatem, et hoc solum est quod movet eius voluntatem. Secus autem est in eo qui sumit potionem dulcem, quam non solum propter sanitatem, sed etiam propter se aliquis velle potest. Unde, cum Deus alia a se non velit nisi propter finem qui est sua bonitas, ut dictum est, non sequitur quod aliquid aliud moveat voluntatem eius nisi bonitas

God wills anything apart from Himself, His will must be moved by another; which is impossible.

OBJ. 3: Further, if what is willed suffices the willer, he seeks nothing beyond it. But His own goodness suffices God, and completely satisfies His will. Therefore God does not will anything apart from Himself.

OBJ. 4: Further, acts of will are multiplied in proportion to the number of their objects. If, therefore, God wills Himself and things apart from Himself, it follows that the act of His will is manifold, and consequently His existence, which is His will. But this is impossible. Therefore God does not will things apart from Himself.

ON THE CONTRARY, The Apostle says (1 Thess 4:3): *This is the will of God, your sanctification.*

I ANSWER THAT, God wills not only Himself, but other things apart from Himself. This is clear from the comparison which we made above (A. 1). For natural things have a natural inclination not only towards their own proper good, to acquire it if not possessed, and, if possessed, to rest therein; but also to spread abroad their own good amongst others, so far as possible. Hence we see that every agent, in so far as it is perfect and in act, produces its like. It pertains, therefore, to the nature of the will to communicate as far as possible to others the good possessed; and especially does this pertain to the divine will, from which all perfection is derived in some kind of likeness. Hence, if natural things, in so far as they are perfect, communicate their good to others, much more does it appertain to the divine will to communicate by likeness its own good to others as much as possible. Thus, then, He wills both Himself to be, and other things to be; but Himself as the end, and other things as ordained to that end, inasmuch as it befits the divine goodness that other things should be partakers therein.

REPLY OBJ. 1: The divine will is God's own existence essentially, yet they differ in aspect, according to the different ways of understanding them and expressing them, as is clear from what has already been said (Q. 13, A. 4). For when we say that God exists, no relation to any other object is implied, as we do imply when we say that God wills. Therefore, although He is not anything apart from Himself, yet He does will things apart from Himself.

REPLY OBJ. 2: In things willed for the sake of the end, the whole reason for our being moved is the end, and this it is that moves the will, as most clearly appears in things willed only for the sake of the end. He who wills to take a bitter draught, in doing so wills nothing else than health; and this alone moves his will. It is different with one who takes a draught that is pleasant, which anyone may will to do, not only for the sake of health, but also for its own sake. Hence, although God wills things apart from Himself only for the sake of the end, which is His own goodness, it does not follow that anything else moves His will, except His goodness. So, as He understands things apart from

sua. Et sic, sicut alia a se intelligit intelligendo essentiam suam, ita alia a se vult, volendo bonitatem suam.

AD TERTIUM dicendum quod ex hoc quod voluntati divinae sufficit sua bonitas, non sequitur quod nihil aliud velit, sed quod nihil aliud vult nisi ratione suae bonitatis. Sicut etiam intellectus divinus, licet sit perfectus ex hoc ipso quod essentiam divinam cognoscit, tamen in ea cognoscit alia.

AD QUARTUM dicendum quod, sicut intelligere divinum est unum, quia multa non videt nisi in uno; ita velle divinum est unum et simplex, quia multa non vult nisi per unum, quod est bonitas sua.

Himself by understanding His own essence, so He wills things apart from Himself by willing His own goodness.

REPLY OBJ. 3: From the fact that His own goodness suffices the divine will, it does not follow that it wills nothing apart from itself, but rather that it wills nothing except by reason of its goodness. Thus, too, the divine intellect, though its perfection consists in its very knowledge of the divine essence, yet in that essence knows other things.

REPLY OBJ. 4: As the divine intellect is one, as seeing the many only in the one, in the same way the divine will is one and simple, as willing the many only through the one, that is, through its own goodness.

Article 3

Whether Whatever God Wills He Wills Necessarily?

AD TERTIUM SIC PROCEDITUR. Videtur quod quidquid Deus vult, ex necessitate velit. Omne enim aeternum est necessarium. Sed quidquid Deus vult, ab aeterno vult, alias, voluntas eius esset mutabilis. Ergo quidquid vult, ex necessitate vult.

PRAETEREA, Deus vult alia a se, inquantum vult bonitatem suam. Sed Deus bonitatem suam ex necessitate vult. Ergo alia a se ex necessitate vult.

PRAETEREA, quidquid est Deo naturale, est necessarium, quia Deus est per se necesse esse, et principium omnis necessitatis, ut supra ostensum est. Sed naturale est ei velle quidquid vult, quia in Deo nihil potest esse praeter naturam, ut dicitur in V Metaphys. Ergo quidquid vult, ex necessitate vult.

PRAETEREA, non necesse esse, et possibile non esse, aequipollent. Si igitur non necesse est Deum velle aliquid eorum quae vult, possibile est eum non velle illud; et possibile est eum velle illud quod non vult. Ergo voluntas divina est contingens ad utrumlibet. Et sic imperfecta, quia omne contingens est imperfectum et mutabile.

PRAETEREA, ab eo quod est ad utrumlibet, non sequitur aliqua actio, nisi ab aliquo alio inclinetur ad unum, ut dicit Commentator, in II Physic. Si ergo voluntas Dei in aliquibus se habet ad utrumlibet, sequitur quod ab aliquo alio determinetur ad effectum. Et sic habet aliquam causam priorem.

PRAETEREA, quidquid Deus scit, ex necessitate scit. Sed sicut scientia divina est eius essentia, ita voluntas divina. Ergo quidquid Deus vult, ex necessitate vult.

OBJECTION 1: It seems that whatever God wills He wills necessarily. For everything eternal is necessary. But whatever God wills, He wills from eternity, for otherwise His will would be mutable. Therefore whatever He wills, He wills necessarily.

OBJ. 2: Further, God wills things apart from Himself, inasmuch as He wills His own goodness. Now God wills His own goodness necessarily. Therefore He wills things apart from Himself necessarily.

OBJ. 3: Further, whatever belongs to the nature of God is necessary, for God is of Himself necessary being, and the principle of all necessity, as above shown (Q. 2, A. 3). But it belongs to His nature to will whatever He wills; since in God there can be nothing over and above His nature as stated in *Metaph.* v, 6. Therefore whatever He wills, He wills necessarily.

OBJ. 4: Further, being that is not necessary, and being that is possible not to be, are one and the same thing. If, therefore, God does not necessarily will a thing that He wills, it is possible for Him not to will it, and therefore possible for Him to will what He does not will. And so the divine will is contingent upon one or the other of two things, and imperfect, since everything contingent is imperfect and mutable.

OBJ. 5: Further, on the part of that which is indifferent to one or the other of two things, no action results unless it is inclined to one or the other by some other power, as the Commentator says in *Phys.* ii. If, then, the Will of God is indifferent with regard to anything, it follows that His determination to act comes from another; and thus He has some cause prior to Himself.

OBJ. 6: Further, whatever God knows, He knows necessarily. But as the divine knowledge is His essence, so is the divine will. Therefore whatever God wills, He wills necessarily.

SED CONTRA est quod dicit apostolus, Ephes. I, *qui operatur omnia secundum consilium voluntatis suae.* Quod autem operamur ex consilio voluntatis, non ex necessitate volumus. Non ergo quidquid Deus vult, ex necessitate vult.

RESPONDEO dicendum quod necessarium dicitur aliquid dupliciter, scilicet absolute, et ex suppositione. Necessarium absolute iudicatur aliquid ex habitudine terminorum, utpote quia praedicatum est in definitione subiecti, sicut necessarium est hominem esse animal; vel quia subiectum est de ratione praedicati, sicut hoc est necessarium, numerum esse parem vel imparem. Sic autem non est necessarium Socratem sedere. Unde non est necessarium absolute, sed potest dici necessarium ex suppositione, supposito enim quod sedeat, necesse est eum sedere dum sedet. Circa divina igitur volita hoc considerandum est, quod aliquid Deum velle est necessarium absolute, non tamen hoc est verum de omnibus quae vult. Voluntas enim divina necessariam habitudinem habet ad bonitatem suam, quae est proprium eius obiectum. Unde bonitatem suam esse Deus ex necessitate vult; sicut et voluntas nostra ex necessitate vult beatitudinem. Sicut et quaelibet alia potentia necessariam habitudinem habet ad proprium et principale obiectum, ut visus ad colorem; quia de sui ratione est, ut in illud tendat. Alia autem a se Deus vult, inquantum ordinantur ad suam bonitatem ut in finem. Ea autem quae sunt ad finem, non ex necessitate volumus volentes finem, nisi sint talia, sine quibus finis esse non potest, sicut volumus cibum, volentes conservationem vitae; et navem, volentes transfretare. Non sic autem ex necessitate volumus ea sine quibus finis esse potest, sicut equum ad ambulandum, quia sine hoc possumus ire; et eadem ratio est in aliis. Unde, cum bonitas Dei sit perfecta, et esse possit sine aliis, cum nihil ei perfectionis ex aliis accrescat; sequitur quod alia a se eum velle, non sit necessarium absolute. Et tamen necessarium est ex suppositione, supposito enim quod velit, non potest non velle, quia non potest voluntas eius mutari.

AD PRIMUM ergo dicendum quod ex hoc quod Deus ab aeterno vult aliquid, non sequitur quod necesse est eum illud velle, nisi ex suppositione.

AD SECUNDUM dicendum quod, licet Deus ex necessitate velit bonitatem suam, non tamen ex necessitate vult ea quae vult propter bonitatem suam, quia bonitas eius potest esse sine aliis.

AD TERTIUM dicendum quod non est naturale Deo velle aliquid aliorum, quae non ex necessitate vult. Neque tamen innaturale, aut contra naturam, sed est voluntarium.

AD QUARTUM dicendum quod aliquando aliqua causa necessaria habet non necessariam habitudinem ad aliquem effectum, quod est propter defectum effectus,

ON THE CONTRARY, The Apostle says (Eph 1:11): *Who worketh all things according to the counsel of His will.* Now, what we work according to the counsel of the will, we do not will necessarily. Therefore God does not will necessarily whatever He wills.

I ANSWER THAT, There are two ways in which a thing is said to be necessary, namely, absolutely, and by supposition. We judge a thing to be absolutely necessary from the relation of the terms, as when the predicate forms part of the definition of the subject: thus it is absolutely necessary that man is an animal. It is the same when the subject forms part of the notion of the predicate; thus it is absolutely necessary that a number must be odd or even. In this way it is not necessary that Socrates sits: wherefore it is not necessary absolutely, though it may be so by supposition; for, granted that he is sitting, he must necessarily sit, as long as he is sitting. Accordingly as to things willed by God, we must observe that He wills something of absolute necessity: but this is not true of all that He wills. For the divine will has a necessary relation to the divine goodness, since that is its proper object. Hence God wills His own goodness necessarily, even as we will our own happiness necessarily, and as any other faculty has necessary relation to its proper and principal object, for instance the sight to color, since it tends to it by its own nature. But God wills things apart from Himself in so far as they are ordered to His own goodness as their end. Now in willing an end we do not necessarily will things that conduce to it, unless they are such that the end cannot be attained without them; as, we will to take food to preserve life, or to take a ship in order to cross the sea. But we do not necessarily will things without which the end is attainable, such as a horse for a journey which we can take on foot, for we can make the journey without one. The same applies to other means. Hence, since the goodness of God is perfect, and can exist without other things inasmuch as no perfection can accrue to Him from them, it follows that His willing things apart from Himself is not absolutely necessary. Yet it can be necessary by supposition, for supposing that He wills a thing, then He is unable not to will it, as His will cannot change.

REPLY OBJ. 1: From the fact that God wills from eternity whatever He wills, it does not follow that He wills it necessarily, except by supposition.

REPLY OBJ. 2: Although God necessarily wills His own goodness, He does not necessarily will things willed on account of His goodness; for it can exist without other things.

REPLY OBJ. 3: It is not natural to God to will any of those other things that He does not will necessarily; and yet it is not unnatural or contrary to His nature, but voluntary.

REPLY OBJ. 4: Sometimes a necessary cause has a non-necessary relation to an effect; owing to a deficiency in the effect, and not in the cause. Even so, the sun's power

et non propter defectum causae. Sicut virtus solis habet non necessariam habitudinem ad aliquid eorum quae contingenter hic eveniunt, non propter defectum virtutis solaris, sed propter defectum effectus non necessario ex causa provenientis. Et similiter, quod Deus non ex necessitate velit aliquid eorum quae vult, non accidit ex defectu voluntatis divinae, sed ex defectu qui competit volito secundum suam rationem, quia scilicet est tale, ut sine eo esse possit perfecta bonitas Dei. Qui quidem defectus consequitur omne bonum creatum.

AD QUINTUM ergo dicendum quod causa quae est ex se contingens, oportet quod determinetur ab aliquo exteriori ad effectum. Sed voluntas divina, quae ex se necessitatem habet, determinat seipsam ad volitum, ad quod habet habitudinem non necessariam.

AD SEXTUM dicendum quod, sicut divinum esse in se est necessarium, ita et divinum velle et divinum scire, sed divinum scire habet necessariam habitudinem ad scita, non autem divinum velle ad volita. Quod ideo est, quia scientia habetur de rebus, secundum quod sunt in sciente, voluntas autem comparatur ad res, secundum quod sunt in seipsis. Quia igitur omnia alia habent necessarium esse secundum quod sunt in Deo; non autem secundum quod sunt in seipsis, habent necessitatem absolutam ita quod sint per seipsa necessaria; propter hoc Deus quaecumque scit, ex necessitate scit, non autem quaecumque vult, ex necessitate vult.

has a non-necessary relation to some contingent events on this earth, owing to a defect not in the solar power, but in the effect that proceeds not necessarily from the cause. In the same way, that God does not necessarily will some of the things that He wills, does not result from defect in the divine will, but from a defect belonging to the nature of the thing willed, namely, that the perfect goodness of God can be without it; and such defect accompanies all created good.

REPLY OBJ. 5: A naturally contingent cause must be determined to act by some external power. The divine will, which by its nature is necessary, determines itself to will things to which it has no necessary relation.

REPLY OBJ. 6: As the divine essence is necessary of itself, so is the divine will and the divine knowledge; but the divine knowledge has a necessary relation to the thing known; not the divine will to the thing willed. The reason for this is that knowledge is of things as they exist in the knower; but the will is directed to things as they exist in themselves. Since then all other things have necessary existence inasmuch as they exist in God; but no absolute necessity so as to be necessary in themselves, in so far as they exist in themselves; it follows that God knows necessarily whatever He wills, but does not will necessarily whatever He wills.

Article 4

Whether the Will of God Is the Cause of Things?

AD QUARTUM SIC PROCEDITUR. Videtur quod voluntas Dei non sit causa rerum. Dicit enim Dionysius, cap. IV de Div. Nom., *sicut noster sol, non ratiocinans aut praeeligens, sed per ipsum esse illuminat omnia participare lumen ipsius valentia; ita et bonum divinum per ipsam essentiam omnibus existentibus immittit bonitatis suae radios.* Sed omne quod agit per voluntatem, agit ut ratiocinans et praeeligens. Ergo Deus non agit per voluntatem. Ergo voluntas Dei non est causa rerum.

PRAETEREA, id quod est per essentiam, est primum in quolibet ordine sicut in ordine ignitorum est primum, quod est ignis per essentiam sed Deus est primum agens. Ergo est agens per essentiam suam, quae est natura eius. Agit igitur per naturam, et non per voluntatem. Voluntas igitur divina non est causa rerum.

PRAETEREA, quidquid est causa alicuius per hoc quod est tale, est causa per naturam, et non per voluntatem, ignis enim causa est calefactionis, quia est calidus; sed artifex est causa domus, quia vult eam facere. Sed Augustinus dicit, in I de Doct. Christ., quod *quia Deus*

OBJECTION 1: It seems that the will of God is not the cause of things. For Dionysius says (*Div. Nom.* iv, 1): *As our sun, not by reason nor by pre-election, but by its very being, enlightens all things that can participate in its light, so the divine good by its very essence pours the rays of goodness upon everything that exists.* But every voluntary agent acts by reason and pre-election. Therefore God does not act by will; and so His will is not the cause of things.

OBJ. 2: Further, The first in any order is that which is essentially so, thus in the order of burning things, that comes first which is fire by its essence. But God is the first agent. Therefore He acts by His essence; and that is His nature. He acts then by nature, and not by will. Therefore the divine will is not the cause of things.

OBJ. 3: Further, Whatever is the cause of anything, through being such a thing, is the cause by nature, and not by will. For fire is the cause of heat, as being itself hot; whereas an architect is the cause of a house, because he wills to build it. Now Augustine says (*De Doctr. Christ.* i,

bonus est, sumus. Ergo Deus per suam naturam est causa rerum, et non per voluntatem.

PRAETEREA, unius rei una est causa. Sed rerum creatarum est causa scientia Dei, ut supra dictum est. Ergo voluntas Dei non debet poni causa rerum.

SED CONTRA est quod dicitur Sap. XI, *quomodo posset aliquid permanere, nisi tu voluisses?*

RESPONDEO dicendum quod necesse est dicere voluntatem Dei esse causam rerum, et Deum agere per voluntatem, non per necessitatem naturae, ut quidam existimaverunt.

Quod quidem apparere potest tripliciter. Primo quidem, ex ipso ordine causarum agentium. Cum enim propter finem agat et intellectus et natura, ut probatur in II Physic., necesse est ut agenti per naturam praedeterminetur finis, et media necessaria ad finem, ab aliquo superiori intellectu; sicut sagittae praedeterminatur finis et certus modus a sagittante. Unde necesse est quod agens per intellectum et voluntatem, sit prius agente per naturam. Unde, cum primum in ordine agentium sit Deus, necesse est quod per intellectum et voluntatem agat.

Secundo, ex ratione naturalis agentis, ad quod pertinet ut unum effectum producat, quia natura uno et eodem modo operatur, nisi impediatur. Et hoc ideo, quia secundum quod est tale, agit, unde, quandiu est tale, non facit nisi tale. Omne enim agens per naturam, habet esse determinatum. Cum igitur esse divinum non sit determinatum, sed contineat in se totam perfectionem essendi, non potest esse quod agat per necessitatem naturae, nisi forte causaret aliquid indeterminatum et infinitum in essendo; quod est impossibile, ut ex superioribus patet. Non igitur agit per necessitatem naturae sed effectus determinati ab infinita ipsius perfectione procedunt secundum determinationem voluntatis et intellectus ipsius.

Tertio, ex habitudine effectuum ad causam. Secundum hoc enim effectus procedunt a causa agente, secundum quod praeexistunt in ea, quia omne agens agit sibi simile. Praeexistunt autem effectus in causa secundum modum causae. Unde, cum esse divinum sit ipsum eius intelligere, praeexistunt in eo effectus eius secundum modum intelligibilem. Unde et per modum intelligibilem procedunt ab eo. Et sic, per consequens, per modum voluntatis, nam inclinatio eius ad agendum quod intellectu conceptum est, pertinet ad voluntatem. Voluntas igitur Dei est causa rerum.

AD PRIMUM ergo dicendum quod Dionysius per verba illa non intendit excludere electionem a Deo simpliciter, sed secundum quid, inquantum scilicet non

32), *Because God is good, we exist.* Therefore God is the cause of things by His nature, and not by His will.

OBJ. 4: Further, Of one thing there is one cause. But the cause of created things is the knowledge of God, as said before (Q. 14, A. 8). Therefore the will of God cannot be considered the cause of things.

ON THE CONTRARY, It is said (Wis 11:26), *How could anything endure, if Thou wouldst not?*

I ANSWER THAT, We must hold that the will of God is the cause of things; and that He acts by the will, and not, as some have supposed, by a necessity of His nature.

This can be shown in three ways: First, from the order itself of active causes. Since both intellect and nature act for an end, as proved in *Phys.* ii, 49, the natural agent must have the end and the necessary means predetermined for it by some higher intellect; as the end and definite movement is predetermined for the arrow by the archer. Hence the intellectual and voluntary agent must precede the agent that acts by nature. Hence, since God is first in the order of agents, He must act by intellect and will.

This is shown, second, from the character of a natural agent, of which the property is to produce one and the same effect; for nature operates in one and the same way unless it be prevented. This is because the nature of the act is according to the nature of the agent; and hence as long as it has that nature, its acts will be in accordance with that nature; for every natural agent has a determinate being. Since, then, the Divine Being is undetermined, and contains in Himself the full perfection of being, it cannot be that He acts by a necessity of His nature, unless He were to cause something undetermined and indefinite in being: and that this is impossible has been already shown (Q. 7, A. 2). He does not, therefore, act by a necessity of His nature, but determined effects proceed from His own infinite perfection according to the determination of His will and intellect.

Third, it is shown by the relation of effects to their cause. For effects proceed from the agent that causes them, in so far as they pre-exist in the agent; since every agent produces its like. Now effects pre-exist in their cause after the mode of the cause. Wherefore since the Divine Being is His own intellect, effects pre-exist in Him after the mode of intellect, and therefore proceed from Him after the same mode. Consequently, they proceed from Him after the mode of will, for His inclination to put in act what His intellect has conceived appertains to the will. Therefore the will of God is the cause of things.

REPLY OBJ. 1: Dionysius in these words does not intend to exclude election from God absolutely; but only in a certain sense, in so far, that is, as He communicates

quibusdam solum bonitatem suam communicat, sed omnibus, prout scilicet electio discretionem quandam importat.

AD SECUNDUM dicendum quod, quia essentia Dei est eius intelligere et velle, ex hoc ipso quod per essentiam suam agit, sequitur quod agat per modum intellectus et voluntatis.

AD TERTIUM dicendum quod bonum est obiectum voluntatis. Pro tanto ergo dicitur, quia Deus bonus est, sumus, inquantum sua bonitas est ei ratio volendi omnia alia, ut supra dictum est.

AD QUARTUM dicendum quod unius et eiusdem effectus, etiam in nobis, est causa scientia ut dirigens, qua concipitur forma operis, et voluntas ut imperans, quia forma, ut est in intellectu tantum, non determinatur ad hoc quod sit vel non sit in effectu, nisi per voluntatem. Unde intellectus speculativus nihil dicit de operando. Sed potentia est causa ut exequens, quia nominat immediatum principium operationis. Sed haec omnia in Deo unum sunt.

His goodness not merely to certain things, but to all; and as election implies a certain distinction.

REPLY OBJ. 2: Because the essence of God is His intellect and will, from the fact of His acting by His essence, it follows that He acts after the mode of intellect and will.

REPLY OBJ. 3: Good is the object of the will. The words, therefore, *Because God is good, we exist*, are true inasmuch as His goodness is the reason of His willing all other things, as said before (A. 2, ad 2).

REPLY OBJ. 4: Even in us the cause of one and the same effect is knowledge as directing it, whereby the form of the work is conceived, and will as commanding it, since the form as it is in the intellect only is not determined to exist or not to exist in the effect, except by the will. Hence, the speculative intellect has nothing to say to operation. But the power is cause, as executing the effect, since it denotes the immediate principle of operation. But in God all these things are one.

Article 5

Whether Any Cause Can Be Assigned to the Divine Will?

AD QUINTUM SIC PROCEDITUR. Videtur quod voluntatis divinae sit assignare aliquam causam. Dicit enim Augustinus, libro octoginta trium quaest., *quis audeat dicere Deum irrationabiliter omnia condidisse?* Sed agenti voluntario, quod est ratio operandi, est etiam causa volendi. Ergo voluntas Dei habet aliquam causam.

PRAETEREA, in his quae fiunt a volente qui propter nullam causam aliquid vult, non oportet aliam causam assignare nisi voluntatem volentis. Sed voluntas Dei est causa omnium rerum, ut ostensum est. Si igitur voluntatis eius non sit aliqua causa, non oportebit in omnibus rebus naturalibus aliam causam quaerere, nisi solam voluntatem divinam. Et sic omnes scientiae essent supervacuae, quae causas aliquorum effectuum assignare nituntur, quod videtur inconveniens. Est igitur assignare aliquam causam voluntatis divinae.

PRAETEREA, quod fit a volente non propter aliquam causam, dependet ex simplici voluntate eius. Si igitur voluntas Dei non habeat aliquam causam, sequitur quod omnia quae fiunt, dependeant ex simplici eius voluntate, et non habeant aliquam aliam causam. Quod est inconveniens.

SED CONTRA est quod dicit Augustinus, in libro octoginta trium quaest., *omnis causa efficiens maior est eo quod efficitur; nihil tamen maius est voluntate Dei; non ergo causa eius quaerenda est.*

OBJECTION 1: It seems that some cause can be assigned to the divine will. For Augustine says (Qq. lxxxiii, 46): *Who would venture to say that God made all things irrationally?* But to a voluntary agent, what is the reason of operating, is the cause of willing. Therefore the will of God has some cause.

OBJ. 2: Further, in things made by one who wills to make them, and whose will is influenced by no cause, there can be no cause assigned except by the will of him who wills. But the will of God is the cause of all things, as has been already shown (A. 4). If, then, there is no cause of His will, we cannot seek in any natural things any cause, except the divine will alone. Thus all science would be in vain, since science seeks to assign causes to effects. This seems inadmissible, and therefore we must assign some cause to the divine will.

OBJ. 3: Further, what is done by the willer, on account of no cause, depends simply on his will. If, therefore, the will of God has no cause, it follows that all things made depend simply on His will, and have no other cause. But this also is not admissible.

ON THE CONTRARY, Augustine says (Qq. lxxxiii, 28): *Every efficient cause is greater than the thing effected.* But nothing is greater than the will of God. We must not then seek for a cause of it.

RESPONDEO dicendum quod nullo modo voluntas Dei causam habet. Ad cuius evidentiam, considerandum est quod, cum voluntas sequatur intellectum, eodem modo contingit esse causam alicuius volentis ut velit, et alicuius intelligentis ut intelligat. In intellectu autem sic est quod, si seorsum intelligat principium, et seorsum conclusionem, intelligentia principii est causa scientiae conclusionis. Sed si intellectus in ipso principio inspiceret conclusionem, uno intuitu apprehendens utrumque, in eo scientia conclusionis non causaretur ab intellectu principiorum, quia idem non est causa sui ipsius. Sed tamen intelligeret principia esse causas conclusionis. Similiter est ex parte voluntatis, circa quam sic se habet finis ad ea quae sunt ad finem, sicut in intellectu principia ad conclusiones.

Unde, si aliquis uno actu velit finem, et alio actu ea quae sunt ad finem, velle finem erit ei causa volendi ea quae sunt ad finem. Sed si uno actu velit finem et ea quae sunt ad finem, hoc esse non poterit, quia idem non est causa sui ipsius. Et tamen erit verum dicere quod velit ordinare ea quae sunt ad finem, in finem. Deus autem, sicut uno actu omnia in essentia sua intelligit, ita uno actu vult omnia in sua bonitate. Unde, sicut in Deo intelligere causam non est causa intelligendi effectus, sed ipse intelligit effectus in causa; ita velle finem non est ei causa volendi ea quae sunt ad finem, sed tamen vult ea quae sunt ad finem, ordinari in finem. Vult ergo hoc esse propter hoc, sed non propter hoc vult hoc.

AD PRIMUM ergo dicendum quod voluntas Dei rationabilis est, non quod aliquid sit Deo causa volendi, sed inquantum vult unum esse propter aliud.

AD SECUNDUM dicendum quod, cum velit Deus effectus sic esse, ut ex causis certis proveniant, ad hoc quod servetur ordo in rebus; non est supervacuum, etiam cum voluntate Dei, alias causas quaerere. Esset tamen supervacuum, si aliae causae quaererentur ut primae, et non dependentes a divina voluntate. Et sic loquitur Augustinus in III de Trin., *placuit vanitati philosophorum etiam aliis causis effectus contingentes tribuere, cum omnino videre non possent superiorem ceteris omnibus causam, idest voluntatem Dei.*

AD TERTIUM dicendum quod, cum Deus velit effectus esse propter causas, quicumque effectus praesupponunt aliquem alium effectum, non dependent ex sola Dei voluntate, sed ex aliquo alio. Sed primi effectus ex sola divina voluntate dependent. Utpote si dicamus quod Deus voluit hominem habere manus, ut deservirent intellectui, operando diversa opera, et voluit eum habere intellectum, ad hoc quod esset homo, et voluit eum esse hominem, ut frueretur ipso, vel ad complementum

I ANSWER THAT, In no wise has the will of God a cause. In proof of which we must consider that, since the will follows from the intellect, there is cause of the will in the person who wills, in the same way as there is a cause of the understanding in the person that understands. The case with the understanding is this: that if the premise and its conclusion are understood separately from each other, the understanding the premise is the cause that the conclusion is known. If the understanding perceive the conclusion in the premise itself, apprehending both the one and the other at the same glance, in this case the knowing of the conclusion would not be caused by understanding the premises, since a thing cannot be its own cause; and yet, it would be true that the thinker would understand the premises to be the cause of the conclusion. It is the same with the will, with respect to which the end stands in the same relation to the means to the end, as do the premises to the conclusion with regard to the understanding.

Hence, if anyone in one act wills an end, and in another act the means to that end, his willing the end will be the cause of his willing the means. This cannot be the case if in one act he wills both end and means; for a thing cannot be its own cause. Yet it will be true to say that he wills to order to the end the means to the end. Now as God by one act understands all things in His essence, so by one act He wills all things in His goodness. Hence, as in God to understand the cause is not the cause of His understanding the effect, for He understands the effect in the cause, so, in Him, to will an end is not the cause of His willing the means, yet He wills the ordering of the means to the end. Therefore, He wills this to be as means to that; but does not will this on account of that.

REPLY OBJ. 1: The will of God is reasonable, not because anything is to God a cause of willing, but in so far as He wills one thing to be on account of another.

REPLY OBJ. 2: Since God wills effects to proceed from definite causes, for the preservation of order in the universe, it is not unreasonable to seek for causes secondary to the divine will. It would, however, be unreasonable to do so, if such were considered as primary, and not as dependent on the will of God. In this sense Augustine says (*De Trin.* iii, 2): *Philosophers in their vanity have thought fit to attribute contingent effects to other causes, being utterly unable to perceive the cause that is shown above all others, the will of God.*

REPLY OBJ. 3: Since God wills effects to come from causes, all effects that presuppose some other effect do not depend solely on the will of God, but on something else besides: but the first effect depends on the divine will alone. Thus, for example, we may say that God willed man to have hands to serve his intellect by their work, and intellect, that he might be man; and willed him to be man that he might enjoy Him, or for the completion of the universe. But this cannot be reduced to other created secondary ends. Hence

universi. Quae quidem non est reducere ad alios fines creatos ulteriores. Unde huiusmodi dependent ex simplici voluntate Dei, alia vero ex ordine etiam aliarum causarum.

such things depend on the simple will of God; but the others on the order of other causes.

Article 6

Whether the Will of God Is Always Fulfilled?

AD SEXTUM SIC PROCEDITUR. Videtur quod voluntas Dei non semper impleatur. Dicit enim apostolus, I ad Tim. II, quod *Deus vult omnes homines salvos fieri, et ad agnitionem veritatis venire.* Sed hoc non ita evenit. Ergo voluntas Dei non semper impletur.

PRAETEREA, sicut se habet scientia ad verum, ita voluntas ad bonum. Sed Deus scit omne verum. Ergo vult omne bonum. Sed non omne bonum fit, multa enim bona possunt fieri, quae non fiunt. Non ergo voluntas Dei semper impletur.

PRAETEREA, voluntas Dei, cum sit causa prima, non excludit causas medias, ut dictum est. Sed effectus causae primae potest impediri per defectum causae secundae, sicut effectus virtutis motivae impeditur propter debilitatem tibiae. Ergo et effectus divinae voluntatis potest impediri propter defectum secundarum causarum. Non ergo voluntas Dei semper impletur.

SED CONTRA est quod dicitur in Psalmo CXIII, *omnia quaecumque voluit Deus, fecit.*

RESPONDEO dicendum quod necesse est voluntatem Dei semper impleri. Ad cuius evidentiam, considerandum est quod, cum effectus conformetur agenti secundum suam formam, eadem ratio est in causis agentibus, quae est in causis formalibus. In formis autem sic est quod, licet aliquid possit deficere ab aliqua forma particulari, tamen a forma universali nihil deficere potest, potest enim esse aliquid quod non est homo vel vivum, non autem potest esse aliquid quod non sit ens. Unde et hoc idem in causis agentibus contingere oportet. Potest enim aliquid fieri extra ordinem alicuius causae particularis agentis, non autem extra ordinem alicuius causae universalis, sub qua omnes causae particulares comprehenduntur. Quia, si aliqua causa particularis deficiat a suo effectu, hoc est propter aliquam aliam causam particularem impedientem, quae continetur sub ordine causae universalis, unde effectus ordinem causae universalis nullo modo potest exire. Et hoc etiam patet in corporalibus. Potest enim impediri quod aliqua stella non inducat suum effectum, sed tamen quicumque effectus ex causa corporea impediente in rebus corporalibus consequatur, oportet quod reducatur per aliquas causas medias in universalem virtutem primi caeli. Cum igitur voluntas Dei sit universalis causa omnium rerum,

OBJECTION 1: It seems that the will of God is not always fulfilled. For the Apostle says (1 Tim 2:4): *God will have all men to be saved, and to come to the knowledge of the truth.* But this does not happen. Therefore the will of God is not always fulfilled.

OBJ. 2: Further, as is the relation of knowledge to truth, so is that of the will to good. Now God knows all truth. Therefore He wills all good. But not all good actually exists; for much more good might exist. Therefore the will of God is not always fulfilled.

OBJ. 3: Further, since the will of God is the first cause, it does not exclude intermediate causes. But the effect of a first cause may be hindered by a defect of a secondary cause; as the effect of the motive power may be hindered by the weakness of the limb. Therefore the effect of the divine will may be hindered by a defect of the secondary causes. The will of God, therefore, is not always fulfilled.

ON THE CONTRARY, It is said (Ps 113:11): *God hath done all things, whatsoever He would.*

I ANSWER THAT, The will of God must needs always be fulfilled. In proof of which we must consider that since an effect is conformed to the agent according to its form, the rule is the same with active causes as with formal causes. The rule in forms is this: that although a thing may fall short of any particular form, it cannot fall short of the universal form. For though a thing may fail to be, for example, a man or a living being, yet it cannot fail to be a being. Hence the same must happen in active causes. Something may fall outside the order of any particular active cause, but not outside the order of the universal cause; under which all particular causes are included: and if any particular cause fails of its effect, this is because of the hindrance of some other particular cause, which is included in the order of the universal cause. Therefore an effect cannot possibly escape the order of the universal cause. Even in corporeal things this is clearly seen. For it may happen that a star is hindered from producing its effects; yet whatever effect does result, in corporeal things, from this hindrance of a corporeal cause, must be referred through intermediate causes to the universal influence of the first heaven. Since, then, the will of God is the universal cause of all things, it is impossible that the divine will should not produce its effect. Hence that which seems to depart from the divine will in one order,

impossibile est quod divina voluntas suum effectum non consequatur. Unde quod recedere videtur a divina voluntate secundum unum ordinem, relabitur in ipsam secundum alium, sicut peccator, qui, quantum est in se, recedit a divina voluntate peccando, incidit in ordinem divinae voluntatis, dum per eius iustitiam punitur.

AD PRIMUM ergo dicendum quod illud verbum apostoli, quod Deus vult omnes homines salvos fieri etc., potest tripliciter intelligi. Uno modo, ut sit accommoda distributio, secundum hunc sensum, *Deus vult salvos fieri omnes homines qui salvantur, non quia nullus homo sit quem salvum fieri non velit, sed quia nullus salvus fit, quem non velit salvum fieri*, ut dicit Augustinus secundo potest intelligi, ut fiat distributio pro generibus singulorum, et non pro singulis generum, secundum hunc sensum, Deus vult de quolibet statu hominum salvos fieri, mares et feminas, Iudaeos et gentiles, parvos et magnos; non tamen omnes de singulis statibus. Tertio, secundum Damascenum, intelligitur de voluntate antecedente, non de voluntate consequente. Quae quidem distinctio non accipitur ex parte ipsius voluntatis divinae, in qua nihil est prius vel posterius; sed ex parte volitorum.

Ad cuius intellectum, considerandum est quod unumquodque, secundum quod bonum est, sic est volitum a Deo. Aliquid autem potest esse in prima sui consideratione, secundum quod absolute consideratur, bonum vel malum, quod tamen, prout cum aliquo adiuncto consideratur, quae est consequens consideratio eius, e contrario se habet. Sicut hominem vivere est bonum, et hominem occidi est malum, secundum absolutam considerationem, sed si addatur circa aliquem hominem, quod sit homicida, vel vivens in periculum multitudinis, sic bonum est eum occidi, et malum est eum vivere. Unde potest dici quod iudex iustus antecedenter vult omnem hominem vivere; sed consequenter vult homicidam suspendi. Similiter Deus antecedenter vult omnem hominem salvari; sed consequenter vult quosdam damnari, secundum exigentiam suae iustitiae. Neque tamen id quod antecedenter volumus, simpliciter volumus, sed secundum quid. Quia voluntas comparatur ad res, secundum quod in seipsis sunt, in seipsis autem sunt in particulari, unde simpliciter volumus aliquid, secundum quod volumus illud consideratis omnibus circumstantiis particularibus, quod est consequenter velle. Unde potest dici quod iudex iustus simpliciter vult homicidam suspendi, sed secundum quid vellet eum vivere, scilicet inquantum est homo. Unde magis potest dici velleitas, quam absoluta voluntas. Et sic patet quod quidquid Deus simpliciter vult, fit; licet illud quod antecedenter vult, non fiat.

AD SECUNDUM dicendum quod actus cognoscitivae virtutis est secundum quod cognitum est in cognoscente, actus autem virtutis appetitivae est ordinatus ad res,

returns into it in another order; as does the sinner, who by sin falls away from the divine will as much as lies in him, yet falls back into the order of that will, when by its justice he is punished.

REPLY OBJ. 1: The words of the Apostle, *God will have all men to be saved*, etc. can be understood in three ways. First, by a restricted application, in which case they would mean, as Augustine says (*De praed. sanct.* i, 8: *Enchiridion* 103), *God wills all men to be saved that are saved, not because there is no man whom He does not wish saved, but because there is no man saved whose salvation He does not will.* Second, they can be understood as applying to every class of individuals, not to every individual of each class; in which case they mean that God wills some men of every class and condition to be saved, males and females, Jews and Gentiles, great and small, but not all of every condition. Third, according to Damascene (*De Fide Orth.* ii, 29), they are understood of the antecedent will of God; not of the consequent will. This distinction must not be taken as applying to the divine will itself, in which there is nothing antecedent nor consequent, but to the things willed.

To understand this we must consider that everything, in so far as it is good, is willed by God. A thing taken in its primary sense, and absolutely considered, may be good or evil, and yet when some additional circumstances are taken into account, by a consequent consideration may be changed into the contrary. Thus that a man should live is good; and that a man should be killed is evil, absolutely considered. But if in a particular case we add that a man is a murderer or dangerous to society, to kill him is a good; that he live is an evil. Hence it may be said of a just judge, that antecedently he wills all men to live; but consequently wills the murderer to be hanged. In the same way God antecedently wills all men to be saved, but consequently wills some to be damned, as His justice exacts. Nor do we will simply, what we will antecedently, but rather we will it in a qualified manner; for the will is directed to things as they are in themselves, and in themselves they exist under particular qualifications. Hence we will a thing simply inasmuch as we will it when all particular circumstances are considered; and this is what is meant by willing consequently. Thus it may be said that a just judge wills simply the hanging of a murderer, but in a qualified manner he would will him to live, to wit, inasmuch as he is a man. Such a qualified will may be called a willingness rather than an absolute will. Thus it is clear that whatever God simply wills takes place; although what He wills antecedently may not take place.

REPLY OBJ. 2: An act of the cognitive faculty is according as the thing known is in the knower; while an act of the appetite faculty is directed to things as they exist in

secundum quod in seipsis sunt. Quidquid autem potest habere rationem entis et veri, totum est virtualiter in Deo; sed non totum existit in rebus creatis. Et ideo Deus cognoscit omne verum, non tamen vult omne bonum, nisi inquantum vult se, in quo virtualiter omne bonum existit.

Ad tertium dicendum quod causa prima tunc potest impediri a suo effectu per defectum causae secundae, quando non est universaliter prima, sub se omnes causas comprehendens, quia sic effectus nullo modo posset suum ordinem evadere. Et sic est de voluntate Dei, ut dictum est.

themselves. But all that can have the nature of being and truth virtually exists in God, though it does not all exist in created things. Therefore God knows all truth; but does not will all good, except in so far as He wills Himself, in Whom all good virtually exists.

Reply Obj. 3: A first cause can be hindered in its effect by deficiency in the secondary cause, when it is not the universal first cause, including within itself all causes; for then the effect could in no way escape its order. And thus it is with the will of God, as said above.

Article 7

Whether the Will of God Is Changeable?

Ad septimum sic proceditur. Videtur quod voluntas Dei sit mutabilis. Dicit enim dominus Genes. VI, *poenitet me fecisse hominem.* Sed quemcumque poenitet de eo quod fecit, habet mutabilem voluntatem. Ergo Deus habet mutabilem voluntatem.

Praeterea, Ierem. XVIII, ex persona domini dicitur, *loquar adversus gentem et adversus regnum, ut eradicem et destruam et disperdam illud; sed si poenitentiam egerit gens illa a malo suo, agam et ego poenitentiam super malo quod cogitavi ut facerem ei.* Ergo Deus habet mutabilem voluntatem.

Praeterea, quidquid Deus facit, voluntarie facit. Sed Deus non semper eadem facit, nam quandoque praecepit legalia observari, quandoque prohibuit. Ergo habet mutabilem voluntatem.

Praeterea, Deus non ex necessitate vult quod vult, ut supra dictum est. Ergo potest velle et non velle idem. Sed omne quod habet potentiam ad opposita, est mutabile, sicut quod potest esse et non esse, est mutabile secundum substantiam; et quod potest esse hic et non esse hic, est mutabile secundum locum. Ergo Deus est mutabilis secundum voluntatem.

Sed contra est quod dicitur Num. XXIII, *non est Deus, quasi homo, ut mentiatur; neque ut filius hominis, ut mutetur.*

Respondeo dicendum quod voluntas Dei est omnino immutabilis. Sed circa hoc considerandum est, quod aliud est mutare voluntatem; et aliud est velle aliquarum rerum mutationem. Potest enim aliquis, eadem voluntate immobiliter permanente, velle quod nunc fiat hoc, et postea fiat contrarium. Sed tunc voluntas mutaretur, si aliquis inciperet velle quod prius non voluit, vel desineret velle quod voluit. Quod quidem accidere non potest, nisi praesupposita mutatione vel ex parte cognitionis, vel circa dispositionem substantiae ipsius volentis. Cum

Objection 1: It seems that the will of God is changeable. For the Lord says (Gen 6:7): *It repenteth Me that I have made man.* But whoever repents of what he has done, has a changeable will. Therefore God has a changeable will.

Obj. 2: Further, it is said in the person of the Lord: *I will speak against a nation and against a kingdom, to root out, and to pull down, and to destroy it; but if that nation shall repent of its evil, I also will repent of the evil that I have thought to do to them* (Jer 18:7, 8). Therefore God has a changeable will.

Obj. 3: Further, whatever God does, He does voluntarily. But God does not always do the same thing, for at one time He ordered the law to be observed, and at another time forbade it. Therefore He has a changeable will.

Obj. 4: Further, God does not will of necessity what He wills, as said before (A. 3). Therefore He can both will and not will the same thing. But whatever can incline to either of two opposites, is changeable substantially; and that which can exist in a place or not in that place, is changeable locally. Therefore God is changeable as regards His will.

On the contrary, It is said: *God is not as a man, that He should lie, nor as the son of man, that He should be changed* (Num 23:19).

I answer that, The will of God is entirely unchangeable. On this point we must consider that to change the will is one thing; to will that certain things should be changed is another. It is possible to will a thing to be done now, and its contrary afterwards; and yet for the will to remain permanently the same: whereas the will would be changed, if one should begin to will what before he had not willed; or cease to will what he had willed before. This cannot happen, unless we presuppose change either in the knowledge or in the disposition of the substance of the willer. For since the will

enim voluntas sit boni, aliquis de novo dupliciter potest incipere aliquid velle. Uno modo sic, quod de novo incipiat sibi illud esse bonum. Quod non est absque mutatione eius, sicut adveniente frigore, incipit esse bonum sedere ad ignem, quod prius non erat. Alio modo sic, quod de novo cognoscat illud esse sibi bonum, cum prius hoc ignorasset, ad hoc enim consiliamur, ut sciamus quid nobis sit bonum. Ostensum est autem supra quod tam substantia Dei quam eius scientia est omnino immutabilis. Unde oportet voluntatem eius omnino esse immutabilem.

AD PRIMUM ergo dicendum quod illud verbum domini metaphorice intelligendum est, secundum similitudinem nostram, cum enim nos poenitet, destruimus quod fecimus. Quamvis hoc esse possit absque mutatione voluntatis, cum etiam aliquis homo, absque mutatione voluntatis, interdum velit aliquid facere, simul intendens postea illud destruere. Sic igitur Deus poenituisse dicitur, secundum similitudinem operationis, inquantum hominem quem fecerat, per diluvium a facie terrae delevit.

AD SECUNDUM dicendum quod voluntas Dei, cum sit causa prima et universalis, non excludit causas medias, in quarum virtute est ut aliqui effectus producantur. Sed quia omnes causae mediae non adaequant virtutem causae primae, multa sunt in virtute et scientia et voluntate divina, quae non continentur sub ordine causarum inferiorum; sicut resuscitatio Lazari. Unde aliquis respiciens ad causas inferiores, dicere poterat, Lazarus non resurget, respiciens vero ad causam primam divinam, poterat dicere, Lazarus resurget. Et utrumque horum Deus vult, scilicet quod aliquid quandoque sit futurum secundum causam inferiorem, quod tamen futurum non sit secundum causam superiorem; vel e converso. Sic ergo dicendum est quod Deus aliquando pronuntiat aliquid futurum, secundum quod continetur in ordine causarum inferiorum, ut puta secundum dispositionem naturae vel meritorum; quod tamen non fit, quia aliter est in causa superiori divina. Sicut cum praedixit Ezechiae, *dispone domui tuae, quia morieris et non vives*, ut habetur Isaiae XXXVIII; neque tamen ita evenit, quia ab aeterno aliter fuit in scientia et voluntate divina, quae immutabilis est. Propter quod dicit Gregorius, quod *Deus immutat sententiam, non tamen mutat consilium*, scilicet voluntatis suae. Quod ergo dicit, poenitentiam agam ego, intelligitur metaphorice dictum, nam homines quando non implent quod comminati sunt, poenitere videntur.

AD TERTIUM dicendum quod ex ratione illa non potest concludi quod Deus habeat mutabilem voluntatem; sed quod mutationem velit.

AD QUARTUM dicendum quod, licet Deum velle aliquid non sit necessarium absolute, tamen necessarium

regards good, a man may in two ways begin to will a thing. In one way when that thing begins to be good for him, and this does not take place without a change in him. Thus when the cold weather begins, it becomes good to sit by the fire; though it was not so before. In another way when he knows for the first time that a thing is good for him, though he did not know it before; hence we take counsel in order to know what is good for us. Now it has already been shown that both the substance of God and His knowledge are entirely unchangeable (QQ. 9, A. 1; 14, A. 15). Therefore His will must be entirely unchangeable.

REPLY OBJ. 1: These words of the Lord are to be understood metaphorically, and according to the likeness of our nature. For when we repent, we destroy what we have made; although we may even do so without change of will; as, when a man wills to make a thing, at the same time intending to destroy it later. Therefore God is said to have repented, by way of comparison with our mode of acting, in so far as by the deluge He destroyed from the face of the earth man whom He had made.

REPLY OBJ. 2: The will of God, as it is the first and universal cause, does not exclude intermediate causes that have power to produce certain effects. Since however all intermediate causes are inferior in power to the first cause, there are many things in the divine power, knowledge and will that are not included in the order of inferior causes. Thus in the case of the raising of Lazarus, one who looked only on inferior causes might have said: *Lazarus will not rise again*, but looking at the divine first cause might have said: *Lazarus will rise again*. And God wills both: that is, that in the order of the inferior cause a thing shall happen; but that in the order of the higher cause it shall not happen; or He may will conversely. We may say, then, that God sometimes declares that a thing shall happen according as it falls under the order of inferior causes, as of nature, or merit, which yet does not happen as not being in the designs of the divine and higher cause. Thus He foretold to Ezechias: *Take order with thy house, for thou shalt die, and not live* (Isa 38:1). Yet this did not take place, since from eternity it was otherwise disposed in the divine knowledge and will, which is unchangeable. Hence Gregory says (*Moral.* xvi, 5): *The sentence of God changes, but not His counsel*—that is to say, the counsel of His will. When therefore He says, *I also will repent*, His words must be understood metaphorically. For men seem to repent, when they do not fulfill what they have threatened.

REPLY OBJ. 3: It does not follow from this argument that God has a will that changes, but that He sometimes wills that things should change.

REPLY OBJ. 4: Although God's willing a thing is not by absolute necessity, yet it is necessary by supposition, on

est ex suppositione, propter immutabilitatem divinae voluntatis, ut supra dictum est.

account of the unchangeableness of the divine will, as has been said above (A. 3).

Article 8

Whether the Will of God Imposes Necessity on the Things Willed?

AD OCTAVUM SIC PROCEDITUR. Videtur quod voluntas Dei rebus volitis necessitatem imponat. Dicit enim Augustinus, in Enchirid., *nullus fit salvus, nisi quem Deus voluerit salvari. Et ideo rogandus est ut velit, quia necesse est fieri, si voluerit.*

PRAETEREA, omnis causa quae non potest impediri, ex necessitate suum effectum producit, quia *et natura semper idem operatur, nisi aliquid impediat,* ut dicitur in II Physic. Sed voluntas Dei non potest impediri, dicit enim apostolus, ad Rom. IX, *voluntati enim eius quis resistit?* Ergo voluntas Dei imponit rebus volitis necessitatem.

PRAETEREA, illud quod habet necessitatem ex priori, est necessarium absolute, sicut animal mori est necessarium, quia est ex contrariis compositum. Sed res creatae a Deo, comparantur ad voluntatem divinam sicut ad aliquid prius, a quo habent necessitatem, cum haec conditionalis sit vera, si aliquid Deus vult, illud est; omnis autem conditionalis vera est necessaria. Sequitur ergo quod omne quod Deus vult, sit necessarium absolute.

SED CONTRA, omnia bona quae fiunt, Deus vult fieri. Si igitur eius voluntas imponat rebus volitis necessitatem, sequitur quod omnia bona ex necessitate eveniunt. Et sic perit liberum arbitrium et consilium, et omnia huiusmodi.

RESPONDEO dicendum quod divina voluntas quibusdam volitis necessitatem imponit, non autem omnibus. Cuius quidem rationem aliqui assignare voluerunt ex causis mediis quia ea quae producit per causas necessarias, sunt necessaria; ea vero quae producit per causas contingentes, sunt contingentia.

Sed hoc non videtur sufficienter dictum, propter duo. Primo quidem, quia effectus alicuius primae causae est contingens propter causam secundam, ex eo quod impeditur effectus causae primae per defectum causae secundae; sicut virtus solis per defectum plantae impeditur. Nullus autem defectus causae secundae impedire potest quin voluntas Dei effectum suum producat. Secundo, quia, si distinctio contingentium a necessariis referatur solum in causas secundas, sequitur hoc esse praeter intentionem et voluntatem divinam, quod est inconveniens. Et ideo melius dicendum est, quod hoc contingit propter efficaciam divinae voluntatis. Cum enim aliqua causa efficax fuerit ad agendum, effectus

OBJECTION 1: It seems that the will of God imposes necessity on the things willed. For Augustine says (*Enchiridion* 103): *No one is saved, except whom God has willed to be saved. He must therefore be asked to will it; for if He wills it, it must necessarily be.*

OBJ. 2: Further, every cause that cannot be hindered, produces its effect necessarily, because, as the Philosopher says (*Phys.* ii, 84) *Nature always works in the same way, if there is nothing to hinder it.* But the will of God cannot be hindered. For the Apostle says (Rom 9:19): *Who resisteth His will?* Therefore the will of God imposes necessity on the things willed.

OBJ. 3: Further, whatever is necessary by its antecedent cause is necessary absolutely; it is thus necessary that animals should die, being compounded of contrary elements. Now things created by God are related to the divine will as to an antecedent cause, whereby they have necessity. For the conditional statement is true that if God wills a thing, it comes to pass; and every true conditional statement is necessary. It follows therefore that all that God wills is necessary absolutely.

ON THE CONTRARY, All good things that exist God wills to be. If therefore His will imposes necessity on things willed, it follows that all good happens of necessity; and thus there is an end of free will, counsel, and all other such things.

I ANSWER THAT, The divine will imposes necessity on some things willed but not on all. The reason of this some have chosen to assign to intermediate causes, holding that what God produces by necessary causes is necessary; and what He produces by contingent causes contingent.

This does not seem to be a sufficient explanation, for two reasons. First, because the effect of a first cause is contingent on account of the secondary cause, from the fact that the effect of the first cause is hindered by deficiency in the second cause, as the sun's power is hindered by a defect in the plant. But no defect of a secondary cause can hinder God's will from producing its effect. Second, because if the distinction between the contingent and the necessary is to be referred only to secondary causes, this must be independent of the divine intention and will; which is inadmissible. It is better therefore to say that this happens on account of the efficacy of the divine will. For when a cause is efficacious to act, the effect follows upon the cause, not only as

consequitur causam non tantum secundum id quod fit, sed etiam secundum modum fiendi vel essendi, ex debilitate enim virtutis activae in semine, contingit quod filius nascitur dissimilis patri in accidentibus, quae pertinent ad modum essendi. Cum igitur voluntas divina sit efficacissima, non solum sequitur quod fiant ea quae Deus vult fieri; sed quod eo modo fiant, quo Deus ea fieri vult. Vult autem quaedam fieri Deus necessario, et quaedam contingenter, ut sit ordo in rebus, ad complementum universi. Et ideo quibusdam effectibus aptavit causas necessarias, quae deficere non possunt, ex quibus effectus de necessitate proveniunt, quibusdam autem aptavit causas contingentes defectibiles, ex quibus effectus contingenter eveniunt. Non igitur propterea effectus voliti a Deo, eveniunt contingenter, quia causae proximae sunt contingentes, sed propterea quia Deus voluit eos contingenter evenire, contingentes causas ad eos praeparavit.

AD PRIMUM ergo dicendum quod per illud verbum Augustini intelligenda est necessitas in rebus volitis a Deo, non absoluta, sed conditionalis, necesse est enim hanc conditionalem veram esse, si Deus hoc vult, necesse est hoc esse.

AD SECUNDUM dicendum quod, ex hoc ipso quod nihil voluntati divinae resistit, sequitur quod non solum fiant ea quae Deus vult fieri; sed quod fiant contingenter vel necessario, quae sic fieri vult.

AD TERTIUM dicendum quod posteriora habent necessitatem a prioribus, secundum modum priorum. Unde et ea quae fiunt a voluntate divina, talem necessitatem habent, qualem Deus vult ea habere, scilicet, vel absolutam, vel conditionalem tantum. Et sic, non omnia sunt necessaria absolute.

to the thing done, but also as to its manner of being done or of being. Thus from defect of active power in the seed it may happen that a child is born unlike its father in accidental points, that belong to its manner of being. Since then the divine will is perfectly efficacious, it follows not only that things are done, which God wills to be done, but also that they are done in the way that He wills. Now God wills some things to be done necessarily, some contingently, to the right ordering of things, for the building up of the universe. Therefore to some effects He has attached necessary causes, that cannot fail; but to others defectible and contingent causes, from which arise contingent effects. Hence it is not because the proximate causes are contingent that the effects willed by God happen contingently, but because God prepared contingent causes for them, it being His will that they should happen contingently.

REPLY OBJ. 1: By the words of Augustine we must understand a necessity in things willed by God that is not absolute, but conditional. For the conditional statement that if God wills a thing it must necessarily be, is necessarily true.

REPLY OBJ. 2: From the very fact that nothing resists the divine will, it follows that not only those things happen that God wills to happen, but that they happen necessarily or contingently according to His will.

REPLY OBJ. 3: Consequents have necessity from their antecedents according to the mode of the antecedents. Hence things effected by the divine will have that kind of necessity that God wills them to have, either absolute or conditional. Not all things, therefore, are absolute necessities.

Article 9

Whether God Wills Evils?

AD NONUM SIC PROCEDITUR. Videtur quod voluntas Dei sit malorum. Omne enim bonum quod fit, Deus vult. Sed mala fieri bonum est, dicit enim Augustinus, in Enchirid., *quamvis ea quae mala sunt, inquantum mala sunt, non sint bona; tamen, ut non solum bona, sed etiam ut sint mala, bonum est.* Ergo Deus vult mala.

PRAETEREA, dicit Dionysius, IV cap. de Div. Nom., erit malum ad omnis (idest universi) perfectionem conferens. Et Augustinus dicit, in Enchirid., *ex omnibus consistit universitatis admirabilis pulchritudo; in qua etiam illud quod malum dicitur, bene ordinatum, et loco suo positum, eminentius commendat bona; ut magis placeant, et laudabiliora sint, dum comparantur malis.* Sed Deus vult omne illud quod pertinet ad perfectionem et decorem

OBJECTION 1: It seems that God wills evils. For every good that exists, God wills. But it is a good that evil should exist. For Augustine says (*Enchiridion* 95): *Although evil in so far as it is evil is not a good, yet it is good that not only good things should exist, but also evil things.* Therefore God wills evil things.

OBJ. 2: Further, Dionysius says (*Div. Nom.* iv, 23): *Evil would conduce to the perfection of everything,* i.e., the universe. And Augustine says (*Enchiridion* 10, 11): *Out of all things is built up the admirable beauty of the universe, wherein even that which is called evil, properly ordered and disposed, commends the good more evidently in that good is more pleasing and praiseworthy when contrasted with evil.* But God wills all that appertains to the perfection and

universi, quia hoc est quod Deus maxime vult in creaturis. Ergo Deus vult mala.

PRAETEREA, mala fieri, et non fieri, sunt contradictorie opposita. Sed Deus non vult mala non fieri, quia, cum mala quaedam fiant, non semper voluntas Dei impleretur. Ergo Deus vult mala fieri.

SED CONTRA est quod dicit Augustinus, in libro octoginta trium quaest., *nullo sapiente homine auctore, fit homo deterior; est autem Deus omni sapiente homine praestantior; multo igitur minus, Deo auctore, fit aliquis deterior. Illo autem auctore cum dicitur, illo volente dicitur.* Non ergo volente Deo, fit homo deterior. Constat autem quod quolibet malo fit aliquid deterius. Ergo Deus non vult mala.

RESPONDEO dicendum quod, cum ratio boni sit ratio appetibilis, ut supra dictum est, malum autem opponatur bono; impossibile est quod aliquod malum, inquantum huiusmodi, appetatur, neque appetitu naturali, neque animali, neque intellectuali, qui est voluntas. Sed aliquod malum appetitur per accidens, inquantum consequitur ad aliquod bonum. Et hoc apparet in quolibet appetitu. Non enim agens naturale intendit privationem vel corruptionem; sed formam, cui coniungitur privatio alterius formae; et generationem unius, quae est corruptio alterius. Leo etiam, occidens cervum, intendit cibum, cui coniungitur occisio animalis. Similiter fornicator intendit delectationem, cui coniungitur deformitas culpae. Malum autem quod coniungitur alicui bono, est privatio alterius boni. Nunquam igitur appeteretur malum, nec per accidens, nisi bonum cui coniungitur malum, magis appeteretur quam bonum quod privatur per malum. Nullum autem bonum Deus magis vult quam suam bonitatem, vult tamen aliquod bonum magis quam aliud quoddam bonum. Unde malum culpae, quod privat ordinem ad bonum divinum, Deus nullo modo vult. Sed malum naturalis defectus, vel malum poenae vult, volendo aliquod bonum, cui coniungitur tale malum, sicut, volendo iustitiam, vult poenam; et volendo ordinem naturae servari, vult quaedam naturaliter corrumpi.

AD PRIMUM ergo dicendum quod quidam dixerunt quod, licet Deus non velit mala, vult tamen mala esse vel fieri, quia, licet mala non sint bona, bonum tamen est mala esse vel fieri. Quod ideo dicebant, quia ea quae in se mala sunt, ordinantur ad aliquod bonum, quem quidem ordinem importari credebant in hoc quod dicitur, mala esse vel fieri. Sed hoc non recte dicitur. Quia malum non ordinatur ad bonum per se, sed per accidens. Praeter intentionem enim peccantis est, quod ex hoc sequatur aliquod bonum; sicut praeter intentionem tyrannorum fuit, quod ex eorum persecutionibus claresceret patientia martyrum. Et ideo non potest dici quod talis ordo ab

beauty of the universe, for this is what God desires above all things in His creatures. Therefore God wills evil.

OBJ. 3: Further, that evil should exist, and should not exist, are contradictory opposites. But God does not will that evil should not exist; otherwise, since various evils do exist, God's will would not always be fulfilled. Therefore God wills that evil should exist.

ON THE CONTRARY, Augustine says (Qq. 83,3): *No wise man is the cause of another man becoming worse. Now God surpasses all men in wisdom. Much less therefore is God the cause of man becoming worse; and when He is said to be the cause of a thing, He is said to will it.* Therefore it is not by God's will that man becomes worse. Now it is clear that every evil makes a thing worse. Therefore God wills not evil things.

I ANSWER THAT, Since the ratio of good is the ratio of appetibility, as said before (Q. 5, A. 1), and since evil is opposed to good, it is impossible that any evil, as such, should be sought for by the appetite, either natural, or animal, or by the intellectual appetite which is the will. Nevertheless evil may be sought accidentally, so far as it accompanies a good, as appears in each of the appetites. For a natural agent intends not privation or corruption, but the form to which is annexed the privation of some other form, and the generation of one thing, which implies the corruption of another. Also when a lion kills a stag, his object is food, to obtain which the killing of the animal is only the means. Similarly the fornicator has merely pleasure for his object, and the deformity of sin is only an accompaniment. Now the evil that accompanies one good, is the privation of another good. Never therefore would evil be sought after, not even accidentally, unless the good that accompanies the evil were more desired than the good of which the evil is the privation. Now God wills no good more than He wills His own goodness; yet He wills one good more than another. Hence He in no way wills the evil of sin, which is the privation of right order towards the divine good. The evil of natural defect, or of punishment, He does will, by willing the good to which such evils are attached. Thus in willing justice He wills punishment; and in willing the preservation of the natural order, He wills some things to be naturally corrupted.

REPLY OBJ. 1: Some have said that although God does not will evil, yet He wills that evil should be or be done, because, although evil is not a good, yet it is good that evil should be or be done. This they said because things evil in themselves are ordered to some good end; and this order they thought was expressed in the words *that evil should be or be done.* This, however, is not correct, since evil is not of itself ordered to good, but accidentally. For it is beside the intention of the sinner, that any good should follow from his sin; as it was beside the intention of tyrants that the patience of the martyrs should shine forth from all their persecutions. It cannot therefore be said that such an ordering

bonum importetur per hoc quod dicitur, quod malum esse vel fieri sit bonum, quia nihil iudicatur secundum illud quod competit ei per accidens, sed secundum illud quod competit ei per se.

AD SECUNDUM dicendum quod malum non operatur ad perfectionem et decorem universi nisi per accidens, ut dictum est. Unde et hoc quod dicit Dionysius, quod *malum est ad universi perfectionem conferens*, concludit inducendo quasi ad inconveniens.

AD TERTIUM dicendum quod, licet mala fieri, et mala non fieri, contradictorie opponantur; tamen velle mala fieri, et velle mala non fieri, non opponuntur contradictorie, cum utrumque sit affirmativum. Deus igitur neque vult mala fieri, neque vult mala non fieri, sed vult permittere mala fieri. Et hoc est bonum.

to good is implied in the statement that it is a good thing that evil should be or be done, since nothing is judged of by that which appertains to it accidentally, but by that which belongs to it essentially.

REPLY OBJ. 2: Evil does not operate towards the perfection and beauty of the universe, except accidentally, as said above (ad 1). Therefore Dionysius in saying that *evil would conduce to the perfection of the universe*, draws a conclusion by reduction to an absurdity.

REPLY OBJ. 3: The statements that evil exists, and that evil exists not, are opposed as contradictories; yet the statements that anyone wills evil to exist and that he wills it not to be, are not so opposed; since either is affirmative. God therefore neither wills evil to be done, nor wills it not to be done, but wills to permit evil to be done; and this is a good.

Article 10

Whether God Has Free-Will?

AD DECIMUM SIC PROCEDITUR. Videtur quod Deus non habeat liberum arbitrium. Dicit enim Hieronymus, in homilia de filio prodigo, *solus Deus est, in quem peccatum non cadit, nec cadere potest; cetera, cum sint liberi arbitrii, in utramque partem flecti possunt.*

PRAETEREA, liberum arbitrium est facultas rationis et voluntatis, qua bonum et malum eligitur. Sed Deus non vult malum, ut dictum est. Ergo liberum arbitrium non est in Deo.

SED CONTRA est quod dicit Ambrosius, in libro de fide, *Spiritus Sanctus dividit singulis prout vult, idest pro liberae voluntatis arbitrio, non necessitatis obsequio.*

RESPONDEO dicendum quod liberum arbitrium habemus respectu eorum quae non necessario volumus, vel naturali instinctu. Non enim ad liberum arbitrium pertinet quod volumus esse felices, sed ad naturalem instinctum. Unde et alia animalia, quae naturali instinctu moventur ad aliquid, non dicuntur libero arbitrio moveri. Cum igitur Deus ex necessitate suam bonitatem velit, alia vero non ex necessitate, ut supra ostensum est; respectu illorum quae non ex necessitate vult, liberum arbitrium habet.

AD PRIMUM ergo dicendum quod Hieronymus videtur excludere a Deo liberum arbitrium, non simpliciter, sed solum quantum ad hoc quod est deflecti in peccatum.

AD SECUNDUM dicendum quod, cum malum culpae dicatur per aversionem a bonitate divina, per quam Deus omnia vult, ut supra ostensum est, manifestum est quod impossibile est eum malum culpae velle. Et tamen ad opposita se habet, inquantum velle potest hoc esse vel

OBJECTION 1: It seems that God has not free-will. For Jerome says, in a homily on the prodigal son; *God alone is He who is not liable to sin, nor can be liable: all others, as having free-will, can be inclined to either side.*

OBJ. 2: Further, free-will is the faculty of the reason and will, by which good and evil are chosen. But God does not will evil, as has been said (A. 9). Therefore there is not free-will in God.

ON THE CONTRARY, Ambrose says (*De Fide* ii, 3): *The Holy Spirit divideth unto each one as He will, namely, according to the free choice of the will, not in obedience to necessity.*

I ANSWER THAT, We have free-will with respect to what we will not of necessity, nor by natural instinct. For our will to be happy does not appertain to free-will, but to natural instinct. Hence other animals, that are moved to act by natural instinct, are not said to be moved by free-will. Since then God necessarily wills His own goodness, but other things not necessarily, as shown above (A. 3), He has free will with respect to what He does not necessarily will.

REPLY OBJ. 1: Jerome seems to deny free-will to God not simply, but only as regards the inclination to sin.

REPLY OBJ. 2: Since the evil of sin consists in turning away from the divine goodness, by which God wills all things, as above shown, it is manifestly impossible for Him to will the evil of sin; yet He can make choice of one of two opposites, inasmuch as He can will a thing to be, or not to

non esse. Sicut et nos, non peccando, possumus velle sedere, et non velle sedere.

be. In the same way we ourselves, without sin, can will to sit down, and not will to sit down.

Article 11

Whether the Will of Expression Is to Be Distinguished in God?

AD UNDECIMUM SIC PROCEDITUR. Videtur quod non sit distinguenda in Deo voluntas signi. Sicut enim voluntas Dei est causa rerum, ita et scientia. Sed non assignantur aliqua signa ex parte divinae scientiae. Ergo neque debent assignari aliqua signa ex parte divinae voluntatis.

PRAETEREA, omne signum quod non concordat ei cuius est signum, est falsum. Si igitur signa quae assignantur circa voluntatem divinam, non concordant divinae voluntati, sunt falsa, si autem concordant, superflue assignantur. Non igitur sunt aliqua signa circa voluntatem divinam assignanda.

SED CONTRA est quod voluntas Dei est una, cum ipsa sit Dei essentia. Quandoque autem pluraliter significatur, ut cum dicitur, *magna opera domini, exquisita in omnes voluntates eius*. Ergo oportet quod aliquando signum voluntatis pro voluntate accipiatur.

RESPONDEO dicendum quod in Deo quaedam dicuntur proprie, et quaedam secundum metaphoram, ut ex supradictis patet. Cum autem aliquae passiones humanae in divinam praedicationem metaphorice assumuntur, hoc fit secundum similitudinem effectus, unde illud quod est signum talis passionis in nobis, in Deo nomine illius passionis metaphorice significatur. Sicut, apud nos, irati punire consueverunt, unde ipsa punitio est signum irae, et propter hoc, ipsa punitio nomine irae significatur, cum Deo attribuitur. Similiter id quod solet esse in nobis signum voluntatis, quandoque metaphorice in Deo voluntas dicitur. Sicut, cum aliquis praecipit aliquid, signum est quod velit illud fieri, unde praeceptum divinum quandoque metaphorice voluntas Dei dicitur, secundum illud Matth. VI, *fiat voluntas tua, sicut in caelo et in terra*. Sed hoc distat inter voluntatem et iram, quia ira de Deo nunquam proprie dicitur, cum in suo principali intellectu includat passionem, voluntas autem proprie de Deo dicitur. Et ideo in Deo distinguitur voluntas proprie, et metaphorice dicta. Voluntas enim proprie dicta, vocatur voluntas beneplaciti, voluntas autem metaphorice dicta, est voluntas signi, eo quod ipsum signum voluntatis voluntas dicitur.

AD PRIMUM ergo dicendum quod scientia non est causa eorum quae fiunt, nisi per voluntatem, non enim quae scimus facimus, nisi velimus. Et ideo signum non attribuitur scientiae, sicut attribuitur voluntati.

OBJECTION 1: It seems that the will of expression is not to be distinguished in God. For as the will of God is the cause of things, so is His wisdom. But no expressions are assigned to the divine wisdom. Therefore no expressions ought to be assigned to the divine will.

OBJ. 2: Further, every expression that is not in agreement with the mind of him who expresses himself, is false. If therefore the expressions assigned to the divine will are not in agreement with that will, they are false. But if they do agree, they are superfluous. No expressions therefore must be assigned to the divine will.

ON THE CONTRARY, The will of God is one, since it is the very essence of God. Yet sometimes it is spoken of as many, as in the words of Ps. 110:2: *Great are the works of the Lord, sought out according to all His wills.* Therefore sometimes the sign must be taken for the will.

I ANSWER THAT, Some things are said of God in their strict sense; others by metaphor, as appears from what has been said before (Q. 13, A. 3). When certain human passions are predicated of the Godhead metaphorically, this is done because of a likeness in the effect. Hence a thing that is in us a sign of some passion, is signified metaphorically in God under the name of that passion. Thus with us it is usual for an angry man to punish, so that punishment becomes an expression of anger. Therefore punishment itself is signified by the word anger, when anger is attributed to God. In the same way, what is usually with us an expression of will, is sometimes metaphorically called will in God; just as when anyone lays down a precept, it is a sign that he wishes that precept obeyed. Hence a divine precept is sometimes called by metaphor the will of God, as in the words: *Thy will be done on earth, as it is in heaven* (Matt 6:10). There is, however, this difference between will and anger, that anger is never attributed to God properly, since in its primary meaning it includes passion; whereas will is attributed to Him properly. Therefore in God there are distinguished will in its proper sense, and will as attributed to Him by metaphor. Will in its proper sense is called the will of good pleasure; and will metaphorically taken is the will of expression, inasmuch as the sign itself of will is called will.

REPLY OBJ. 1: Knowledge is not the cause of a thing being done, unless through the will. For we do not put into act what we know, unless we will to do so. Accordingly expression is not attributed to knowledge, but to will.

AD SECUNDUM dicendum quod signa voluntatis dicuntur voluntates divinae, non quia sint signa quod Deus velit, sed quia ea quae in nobis solent esse signa volendi, in Deo divinae voluntates dicuntur. Sicut punitio non est signum quod in Deo sit ira, sed punitio, ex eo ipso quod in nobis est signum irae, in Deo dicitur ira.

REPLY OBJ. 2: Expressions of will are called divine wills, not as being signs that God wills anything; but because what in us is the usual expression of our will, is called the divine will in God. Thus punishment is not a sign that there is anger in God; but it is called anger in Him, from the fact that it is an expression of anger in ourselves.

Article 12

Whether Five Expressions of Will Are Rightly Assigned to the Divine Will?

AD DUODECIMUM SIC PROCEDITUR. Videtur quod inconvenienter circa divinam voluntatem ponantur quinque signa, scilicet, prohibitio, praeceptum, consilium, operatio et permissio. Nam eadem quae nobis praecipit Deus vel consulit, in nobis quandoque operatur, et eadem quae prohibet, quandoque permittit. Ergo non debent ex opposito dividi.

PRAETEREA, nihil Deus operatur, nisi volens, ut dicitur Sap. XI. Sed voluntas signi distinguitur a voluntate beneplaciti. Ergo operatio sub voluntate signi comprehendi non debet.

PRAETEREA, operatio et permissio communiter ad omnes creaturas pertinent, quia in omnibus Deus operatur, et in omnibus aliquid fieri permittit. Sed praeceptum, consilium et prohibitio pertinent ad solam rationalem creaturam. Ergo non veniunt convenienter in unam divisionem, cum non sint unius ordinis.

PRAETEREA, malum pluribus modis contingit quam bonum, quia *bonum contingit uno modo, sed malum omnifariam*, ut patet per philosophum in II Ethic., et per Dionysium in IV cap. de Div. Nom. Inconvenienter igitur respectu mali assignatur unum signum tantum, scilicet prohibitio; respectu vero boni, duo signa, scilicet consilium et praeceptum.

RESPONDEO dicendum quod huiusmodi signa voluntatis dicuntur ea, quibus consuevimus demonstrare nos aliquid velle. Potest autem aliquis declarare se velle aliquid, vel per seipsum, vel per alium. Per seipsum quidem, inquantum facit aliquid, vel directe, vel indirecte et per accidens. Directe quidem, cum per se aliquid operatur, et quantum ad hoc, dicitur esse signum operatio. Indirecte autem, inquantum non impedit operationem, nam removens prohibens dicitur movens per accidens, ut dicitur in VIII Physic. Et quantum ad hoc, dicitur signum permissio. Per alium autem declarat se aliquid velle, inquantum ordinat alium ad aliquid faciendum; vel necessaria inductione, quod fit praecipiendo quod quis vult, et prohibendo contrarium; vel aliqua persuasoria inductione, quod pertinet ad consilium. Quia igitur his modis declaratur aliquem velle aliquid, propter hoc ista

OBJECTION 1: It seems that five expressions of will—namely, prohibition, precept, counsel, operation, and permission—are not rightly assigned to the divine will. For the same things that God bids us do by His precept or counsel, these He sometimes operates in us, and the same things that He prohibits, these He sometimes permits. They ought not therefore to be enumerated as distinct.

OBJ. 2: Further, God works nothing unless He wills it, as the Scripture says (Wis 11:26). But the will of expression is distinct from the will of good pleasure. Therefore operation ought not to be comprehended in the will of expression.

OBJ. 3: Further, operation and permission appertain to all creatures in common, since God works in them all, and permits some action in them all. But precept, counsel, and prohibition belong to rational creatures only. Therefore they do not come rightly under one division, not being of one order.

OBJ. 4: Further, evil happens in more ways than good, since *good happens in one way, but evil in all kinds of ways*, as declared by the Philosopher (*Ethic.* ii, 6), and Dionysius (*Div. Nom.* iv, 22). It is not right therefore to assign one expression only in the case of evil—namely, prohibition—and two—namely, counsel and precept—in the case of good.

I ANSWER THAT, By these signs we name the expression of will by which we are accustomed to show that we will something. A man may show that he wills something, either by himself or by means of another. He may show it by himself, by doing something either directly, or indirectly and accidentally. He shows it directly when he works in his own person; in that way the expression of his will is his own working. He shows it indirectly, by not hindering the doing of a thing; for what removes an impediment is called an accidental mover. In this respect the expression is called permission. He declares his will by means of another when he orders another to perform a work, either by insisting upon it as necessary by precept, and by prohibiting its contrary; or by persuasion, which is a part of counsel. Since in these ways the will of man makes itself known, the same five are sometimes denominated with regard to the divine will, as

quinque nominantur interdum nomine voluntatis divinae, tanquam signa voluntatis. Quod enim praeceptum, consilium et prohibitio dicantur Dei voluntas, patet per id quod dicitur Matth. VI *fiat voluntas tua, sicut in caelo et in terra.* Quod autem permissio vel operatio dicantur Dei voluntas patet per Augustinum, qui dicit in Enchirid., *nihil fit, nisi omnipotens fieri velit, vel sinendo ut fiat, vel faciendo.*

Vel potest dici quod permissio et operatio referuntur ad praesens permissio quidem ad malum, operatio vero ad bonum. Ad futurum vero, prohibitio, respectu mali; respectu vero boni necessarii, praeceptum; respectu vero superabundantis boni, consilium.

AD PRIMUM ergo dicendum quod nihil prohibet, circa eandem rem, aliquem diversimode declarare se aliquid velle, sicut inveniuntur multa nomina idem significantia. Unde nihil prohibet idem subiacere praecepto et consilio et operationi, et prohibitioni vel permissioni.

AD SECUNDUM dicendum quod, sicut Deus potest significari metaphorice velle id quod non vult voluntate proprie accepta, ita potest metaphorice significari velle id quod proprie vult. Unde nihil prohibet de eodem esse voluntatem beneplaciti, et voluntatem signi. Sed operatio semper est eadem cum voluntate beneplaciti, non autem praeceptum vel consilium, tum quia haec est de praesenti, illud de futuro; tum quia haec per se est effectus voluntatis, illud autem per alium, ut dictum est.

AD TERTIUM dicendum quod creatura rationalis est domina sui actus, et ideo circa ipsam specialia quaedam signa divinae voluntatis assignantur, inquantum rationalem creaturam Deus ordinat ad agendum voluntarie et per se. Sed aliae creaturae non agunt nisi motae ex operatione divina, et ideo circa alias non habent locum nisi operatio et permissio.

AD QUARTUM dicendum quod omne malum culpae, licet multipliciter contingat, tamen in hoc convenit, quod discordat a voluntate divina et ideo unum signum respectu malorum assignatur, scilicet prohibitio. Sed diversimode bona se habent ad bonitatem divinam. Quia quaedam sunt, sine quibus fruitionem divinae bonitatis consequi non possumus, et respectu horum est praeceptum. Quaedam vero sunt, quibus perfectius consequimur, et respectu horum est consilium. Vel dicendum quod consilium est non solum de melioribus bonis assequendis, sed etiam de minoribus malis vitandis.

the expression of that will. That precept, counsel, and prohibition are called the will of God is clear from the words of Matt. 6:10: *Thy will be done on earth as it is in heaven.* That permission and operation are called the will of God is clear from Augustine (*Enchiridion* 95), who says: *Nothing is done, unless the Almighty wills it to be done, either by permitting it, or by actually doing it.*

Or it may be said that permission and operation refer to present time, permission being with respect to evil, operation with regard to good. Whilst as to future time, prohibition is in respect to evil, precept to good that is necessary and counsel to good that is of supererogation.

REPLY OBJ. 1: There is nothing to prevent anyone declaring his will about the same matter in different ways; thus we find many words that mean the same thing. Hence there is no reason why the same thing should not be the subject of precept, operation, and counsel; or of prohibition or permission.

REPLY OBJ. 2: As God may by metaphor be said to will what by His will, properly speaking, He wills not; so He may by metaphor be said to will what He does, properly speaking, will. Hence there is nothing to prevent the same thing being the object of the will of good pleasure, and of the will of expression. But operation is always the same as the will of good pleasure; while precept and counsel are not; both because the former regards the present, and the two latter the future; and because the former is of itself the effect of the will; the latter its effect as fulfilled by means of another.

REPLY OBJ. 3: Rational creatures are masters of their own acts; and for this reason certain special expressions of the divine will are assigned to their acts, inasmuch as God ordains rational creatures to act voluntarily and of themselves. Other creatures act only as moved by the divine operation; therefore only operation and permission are concerned with these.

REPLY OBJ. 4: All evil of sin, though happening in many ways, agrees in being out of harmony with the divine will. Hence with regard to evil, only one expression is assigned, that of prohibition. On the other hand, good stands in various relations to the divine goodness, since there are good deeds without which we cannot attain to the fruition of that goodness, and these are the subject of precept; and there are others by which we attain to it more perfectly, and these are the subject of counsel. Or it may be said that counsel is not only concerned with the obtaining of greater good; but also with the avoiding of lesser evils.

QUESTION 20

GOD'S LOVE

Deinde considerandum est de his quae absolute ad voluntatem Dei pertinent.

In parte autem appetitiva inveniuntur in nobis et passiones animae, ut gaudium, amor, et huiusmodi; et habitus moralium virtutum, ut iustitia, fortitudo, et huiusmodi. Unde primo considerabimus de amore Dei; secundo, de iustitia Dei, et misericordia eius.

Circa primum quaeruntur quatuor.

Primo, utrum in Deo sit amor.

Secundo, utrum amet omnia.

Tertio, utrum magis amet unum quam aliud.

Quarto, utrum meliora magis amet.

We next consider those things that pertain absolutely to the will of God.

In the appetitive part of the soul there are found in ourselves both the passions of the soul, as joy, love, and the like; and the habits of the moral virtues, as justice, fortitude and the like. Hence we shall first consider the love of God, and second His justice and mercy.

About the first there are four points of inquiry:

(1) Whether love exists in God?

(2) Whether He loves all things?

(3) Whether He loves one thing more than another?

(4) Whether He loves more the better things?

Article 1

Whether Love Exists in God?

AD PRIMUM SIC PROCEDITUR. Videtur quod amor non sit in Deo. Nulla enim passio est in Deo. Amor est passio. Ergo amor non est in Deo.

PRAETEREA, amor, ira, tristitia, et huiusmodi, contra se dividuntur. Sed tristitia et ira non dicuntur de Deo nisi metaphorice. Ergo nec amor.

PRAETEREA, Dionysius dicit, IV cap. de Div. Nom., *amor est vis unitiva et concretiva*. Hoc autem in Deo locum habere non potest, cum sit simplex. Ergo in Deo non est amor.

SED CONTRA est quod dicitur I Ioan. IV, *Deus caritas est.*

RESPONDEO dicendum quod necesse est ponere amorem in Deo. Primus enim motus voluntatis, et cuiuslibet appetitivae virtutis, est amor. Cum enim actus voluntatis, et cuiuslibet appetitivae virtutis tendat in bonum et malum, sicut in propria obiecta; bonum autem principalius et per se est obiectum voluntatis et appetitus, malum autem secundario et per aliud, inquantum scilicet opponitur bono, oportet naturaliter esse priores actus voluntatis et appetitus qui respiciunt bonum, his qui respiciunt malum; ut gaudium quam tristitia, et amor quam odium. Semper enim quod est per se, prius est eo quod est per aliud. Rursus, quod est communius, naturaliter est prius, unde et intellectus per prius habet ordinem ad verum commune, quam ad particularia quaedam vera. Sunt autem quidam actus voluntatis et appetitus, respicientes bonum sub aliqua speciali

OBJECTION 1: It seems that love does not exist in God. For in God there are no passions. Now love is a passion. Therefore love is not in God.

OBJ. 2: Further, love, anger, sorrow and the like, are mutually divided against one another. But sorrow and anger are not attributed to God, unless by metaphor. Therefore neither is love attributed to Him.

OBJ. 3: Further, Dionysius says (*Div. Nom.* iv): *Love is a uniting and binding force*. But this cannot take place in God, since He is simple. Therefore love does not exist in God.

ON THE CONTRARY, It is written: *God is love* (1 John 4:16).

I ANSWER THAT, We must needs assert that in God there is love: because love is the first movement of the will and of every appetitive faculty. For since the acts of the will and of every appetitive faculty tend towards good and evil, as to their proper objects: and since good is essentially and especially the object of the will and the appetite, whereas evil is only the object secondarily and indirectly, as opposed to good; it follows that the acts of the will and appetite that regard good must naturally be prior to those that regard evil; thus, for instance, joy is prior to sorrow, love to hate: because what exists of itself is always prior to that which exists through another. Again, the more universal is naturally prior to what is less so. Hence the intellect is first directed to universal truth; and in the second place to particular and special truths. Now there are certain acts of the will and appetite that regard good under some special

conditione, sicut gaudium et delectatio est de bono praesenti et habito; desiderium autem et spes, de bono nondum adepto. Amor autem respicit bonum in communi, sive sit habitum, sive non habitum. Unde amor naturaliter est primus actus voluntatis et appetitus. Et propter hoc, omnes alii motus appetitivi praesupponunt amorem, quasi primam radicem. Nullus enim desiderat aliquid, nisi bonum amatum, neque aliquis gaudet, nisi de bono amato. Odium etiam non est nisi de eo quod contrariatur rei amatae. Et similiter tristitiam, et cetera huiusmodi, manifestum est in amorem referri, sicut in primum principium. Unde in quocumque est voluntas vel appetitus, oportet esse amorem, remoto enim primo, removentur alia. Ostensum est autem in Deo esse voluntatem. Unde necesse est in eo ponere amorem.

AD PRIMUM ergo dicendum quod vis cognitiva non movet, nisi mediante appetitiva. Et sicut in nobis ratio universalis movet mediante ratione particulari, ut dicitur in III de anima; ita appetitus intellectivus, qui dicitur voluntas, movet in nobis mediante appetitu sensitivo. Unde proximum motivum corporis in nobis est appetitus sensitivus. Unde semper actum appetitus sensitivi concomitatur aliqua transmutatio corporis; et maxime circa cor, quod est primum principium motus in animali. Sic igitur actus appetitus sensitivi, inquantum habent transmutationem corporalem annexam, passiones dicuntur, non autem actus voluntatis. Amor igitur et gaudium et delectatio, secundum quod significant actus appetitus sensitivi, passiones sunt, non autem secundum quod significant actus appetitus intellectivi. Et sic ponuntur in Deo. Unde dicit philosophus, in VII Ethic., quod *Deus una et simplici operatione gaudet.* Et eadem ratione, sine passione amat.

AD SECUNDUM dicendum quod in passionibus sensitivi appetitus, est considerare aliquid quasi materiale, scilicet corporalem transmutationem; et aliquid quasi formale, quod est ex parte appetitus. Sicut in ira, ut dicitur in I de anima, materiale est accensio sanguinis circa cor, vel aliquid huiusmodi; formale vero, appetitus vindictae. Sed rursus, ex parte eius quod est formale, in quibusdam horum designatur aliqua imperfectio; sicut in desiderio, quod est boni non habiti; et in tristitia, quae est mali habiti. Et eadem ratio est de ira, quae tristitiam supponit. Quaedam vero nullam imperfectionem designant, ut amor et gaudium. Cum igitur nihil horum Deo conveniat secundum illud quod est materiale in eis, ut dictum est; illa quae imperfectionem important etiam formaliter, Deo convenire non possunt nisi metaphorice, propter similitudinem effectus, ut supra dictum est. Quae autem imperfectionem non important, de Deo

condition, as joy and delight regard good present and possessed; whereas desire and hope regard good not as yet possessed. Love, however, regards good universally, whether possessed or not. Hence love is naturally the first act of the will and appetite; for which reason all the other appetite movements presuppose love, as their root and origin. For nobody desires anything nor rejoices in anything, except as a good that is loved: nor is anything an object of hate except as opposed to the object of love. Similarly, it is clear that sorrow, and other things like to it, must be referred to love as to their first principle. Hence, in whomsoever there is will and appetite, there must also be love: since if the first is wanting, all that follows is also wanting. Now it has been shown that will is in God (Q. 19, A. 1), and hence we must attribute love to Him.

REPLY OBJ. 1: The cognitive faculty does not move except through the medium of the appetitive: and just as in ourselves the universal reason moves through the medium of the particular reason, as stated in *De Anima* iii, 58, 75, so in ourselves the intellectual appetite, or the will as it is called, moves through the medium of the sensitive appetite. Hence, in us the sensitive appetite is the proximate motive-force of our bodies. Some bodily change therefore always accompanies an act of the sensitive appetite, and this change affects especially the heart, which, as the Philosopher says (*De part. animal.* iii, 4), is the first principle of movement in animals. Therefore acts of the sensitive appetite, inasmuch as they have annexed to them some bodily change, are called passions; whereas acts of the will are not so called. Love, therefore, and joy and delight are passions; in so far as they denote acts of the intellective appetite, they are not passions. It is in this latter sense that they are in God. Hence the Philosopher says (*Ethic.* vii): *God rejoices by an operation that is one and simple,* and for the same reason He loves without passion.

REPLY OBJ. 2: In the passions of the sensitive appetite there may be distinguished a certain material element—namely, the bodily change—and a certain formal element, which is on the part of the appetite. Thus in anger, as the Philosopher says (*De Anima* iii, 15, 63, 64), the material element is the kindling of the blood about the heart; but the formal, the appetite for revenge. Again, as regards the formal element of certain passions a certain imperfection is implied, as in desire, which is of the good we have not, and in sorrow, which is about the evil we have. This applies also to anger, which supposes sorrow. Certain other passions, however, as love and joy, imply no imperfection. Since therefore none of these can be attributed to God on their material side, as has been said (ad 1); neither can those that even on their formal side imply imperfection be attributed to Him; except metaphorically, and from likeness of effects, as already show (Q. 3, A. 2, ad 2; Q. 19, A. 11). Whereas,

proprie dicuntur, ut amor et gaudium, tamen sine passione, ut dictum est.

AD TERTIUM dicendum quod actus amoris semper tendit in duo, scilicet in bonum quod quis vult alicui; et in eum cui vult bonum. Hoc enim est proprie amare aliquem, velle ei bonum. Unde in eo quod aliquis amat se, vult bonum sibi. Et sic illud bonum quaerit sibi unire, inquantum potest. Et pro tanto dicitur amor vis unitiva, etiam in Deo, sed absque compositione, quia illud bonum quod vult sibi, non est aliud quam ipse, qui est per suam essentiam bonus, ut supra ostensum est. In hoc vero quod aliquis amat alium, vult bonum illi. Et sic utitur eo tanquam seipso, referens bonum ad illum, sicut ad seipsum. Et pro tanto dicitur amor vis concretiva, quia alium aggregat sibi habens se ad eum sicut ad seipsum. Et sic etiam amor divinus est vis concretiva, absque compositione quae sit in Deo, inquantum aliis bona vult.

those that do not imply imperfection, such as love and joy, can be properly predicated of God, though without attributing passion to Him, as said before (Q. 19, A. 11).

REPLY OBJ. 3: An act of love always tends towards two things; to the good that one wills, and to the person for whom one wills it: since to love a person is to wish that person good. Hence, inasmuch as we love ourselves, we wish ourselves good; and, so far as possible, union with that good. So love is called the unitive force, even in God, yet without implying composition; for the good that He wills for Himself, is no other than Himself, Who is good by His essence, as above shown (Q. 6, AA. 1, 3). And by the fact that anyone loves another, he wills good to that other. Thus he puts the other, as it were, in the place of himself; and regards the good done to him as done to himself. So far love is a binding force, since it aggregates another to ourselves, and refers his good to our own. And then again the divine love is a binding force, inasmuch as God wills good to others; yet it implies no composition in God.

Article 2

Whether God Loves All Things?

AD SECUNDUM SIC PROCEDITUR. Videtur quod Deus non omnia amet. Quia, secundum Dionysium, IV cap. de Div. Nom., amor amantem extra se ponit, et eum quodammodo in amatum transfert. Inconveniens autem est dicere quod Deus, extra se positus, in alia transferatur. Ergo inconveniens est dicere quod Deus alia a se amet.

PRAETEREA, amor Dei aeternus est. Sed ea quae sunt alia a Deo, non sunt ab aeterno nisi in Deo. Ergo Deus non amat ea nisi in seipso. Sed secundum quod sunt in eo, non sunt aliud ab eo. Ergo Deus non amat alia a seipso.

PRAETEREA, duplex est amor, scilicet concupiscentiae, et amicitiae. Sed Deus creaturas irrationales non amat amore concupiscentiae, quia nullius extra se eget, nec etiam amore amicitiae, quia non potest ad res irrationales haberi, ut patet per philosophum, in VIII Ethic. Ergo Deus non omnia amat.

PRAETEREA, in Psalmo dicitur, *odisti omnes qui operantur iniquitatem*. Nihil autem simul odio habetur et amatur. Ergo Deus non omnia amat.

SED CONTRA est quod dicitur Sap. XI, *diligis omnia quae sunt, et nihil odisti eorum quae fecisti*.

RESPONDEO dicendum quod Deus omnia existentia amat. Nam omnia existentia, inquantum sunt, bona sunt, ipsum enim esse cuiuslibet rei quoddam bonum

OBJECTION 1: It seems that God does not love all things. For according to Dionysius (*Div. Nom.* iv, 1), love places the lover outside himself, and causes him to pass, as it were, into the object of his love. But it is not admissible to say that God is placed outside of Himself, and passes into other things. Therefore it is inadmissible to say that God loves things other than Himself.

OBJ. 2: Further, the love of God is eternal. But things apart from God are not from eternity; except in God. Therefore God does not love anything, except as it exists in Himself. But as existing in Him, it is no other than Himself. Therefore God does not love things other than Himself.

OBJ. 3: Further, love is twofold—the love, namely, of desire, and the love of friendship. Now God does not love irrational creatures with the love of desire, since He needs no creature outside Himself. Nor with the love of friendship; since there can be no friendship with irrational creatures, as the Philosopher shows (*Ethic.* viii, 2). Therefore God does not love all things.

OBJ. 4: Further, it is written (Ps 5:7): *Thou hatest all the workers of iniquity*. Now nothing is at the same time hated and loved. Therefore God does not love all things.

ON THE CONTRARY, It is said (Wis 11:25): *Thou lovest all things that are, and hatest none of the things which Thou hast made*.

I ANSWER THAT, God loves all existing things. For all existing things, in so far as they exist, are good, since the existence of a thing is itself a good; and likewise,

est, et similiter quaelibet perfectio ipsius. Ostensum est autem supra quod voluntas Dei est causa omnium rerum et sic oportet quod intantum habeat aliquid esse, aut quodcumque bonum, inquantum est volitum a Deo. Cuilibet igitur existenti Deus vult aliquod bonum. Unde, cum amare nil aliud sit quam velle bonum alicui, manifestum est quod Deus omnia quae sunt, amat. Non tamen eo modo sicut nos. Quia enim voluntas nostra non est causa bonitatis rerum, sed ab ea movetur sicut ab obiecto, amor noster, quo bonum alicui volumus, non est causa bonitatis ipsius, sed e converso bonitas eius, vel vera vel aestimata, provocat amorem, quo ei volumus et bonum conservari quod habet, et addi quod non habet, et ad hoc operamur. Sed amor Dei est infundens et creans bonitatem in rebus.

AD PRIMUM ergo dicendum quod amans sic fit extra se in amatum translatus, inquantum vult amato bonum, et operatur per suam providentiam, sicut et sibi. Unde et Dionysius dicit, IV cap. de Div. Nom., *audendum est autem et hoc pro veritate dicere, quod et ipse omnium causa, per abundantiam amativae bonitatis, extra seipsum fit ad omnia existentia providentiis.*

AD SECUNDUM dicendum quod, licet creaturae ab aeterno non fuerint nisi in Deo, tamen per hoc quod ab aeterno in Deo fuerunt, ab aeterno Deus cognovit res in propriis naturis, et eadem ratione amavit. Sicut et nos per similitudines rerum, quae in nobis sunt, cognoscimus res in seipsis existentes.

AD TERTIUM dicendum quod amicitia non potest haberi nisi ad rationales creaturas, in quibus contingit esse redamationem, et communicationem in operibus vitae, et quibus contingit bene evenire vel male, secundum fortunam et felicitatem, sicut et ad eas proprie benevolentia est. Creaturae autem irrationales non possunt pertingere ad amandum Deum, neque ad communicationem intellectualis et beatae vitae, qua Deus vivit. Sic igitur Deus, proprie loquendo, non amat creaturas irrationales amore amicitiae, sed amore quasi concupiscentiae; inquantum ordinat eas ad rationales creaturas, et etiam ad seipsum; non quasi eis indigeat, sed propter suam bonitatem et nostram utilitatem. Concupiscimus enim aliquid et nobis et aliis.

AD QUARTUM dicendum quod nihil prohibet unum et idem secundum aliquid amari, et secundum aliquid odio haberi. Deus autem peccatores, inquantum sunt naturae quaedam, amat, sic enim et sunt, et ab ipso sunt. Inquantum vero peccatores sunt, non sunt, sed ab esse deficiunt, et hoc in eis a Deo non est. Unde secundum hoc ab ipso odio habentur.

whatever perfection it possesses. Now it has been shown above (Q. 19, A. 4) that God's will is the cause of all things. It must needs be, therefore, that a thing has existence, or any kind of good, only inasmuch as it is willed by God. To every existing thing, then, God wills some good. Hence, since to love anything is nothing else than to will good to that thing, it is manifest that God loves everything that exists. Yet not as we love. Because since our will is not the cause of the goodness of things, but is moved by it as by its object, our love, whereby we will good to anything, is not the cause of its goodness; but conversely its goodness, whether real or imaginary, calls forth our love, by which we will that it should preserve the good it has, and receive besides the good it has not, and to this end we direct our actions: whereas the love of God infuses and creates goodness.

REPLY OBJ. 1: A lover is placed outside himself, and made to pass into the object of his love, inasmuch as he wills good to the beloved; and works for that good by his providence even as he works for his own. Hence Dionysius says (*Div. Nom.* iv, 1): *On behalf of the truth we must make bold to say even this, that He Himself, the cause of all things, by His abounding love and goodness, is placed outside Himself by His providence for all existing things.*

REPLY OBJ. 2: Although creatures have not existed from eternity, except in God, yet because they have been in Him from eternity, God has known them eternally in their proper natures; and for that reason has loved them, even as we, by the images of things within us, know things existing in themselves.

REPLY OBJ. 3: Friendship cannot exist except towards rational creatures, who are capable of returning love, and communicating one with another in the various works of life, and who may fare well or ill, according to the changes of fortune and happiness; even as to them is benevolence properly speaking exercised. But irrational creatures cannot attain to loving God, nor to any share in the intellectual and beatific life that He lives. Strictly speaking, therefore, God does not love irrational creatures with the love of friendship; but as it were with the love of desire, in so far as He orders them to rational creatures, and even to Himself. Yet this is not because He stands in need of them; but only on account of His goodness, and of the services they render to us. For we can desire a thing for others as well as for ourselves.

REPLY OBJ. 4: Nothing prevents one and the same thing being loved under one aspect, while it is hated under another. God loves sinners in so far as they are existing natures; for they have existence and have it from Him. In so far as they are sinners, they have not existence at all, but fall short of it; and this in them is not from God. Hence under this aspect, they are hated by Him.

Article 3

Whether God Loves All Things Equally?

AD TERTIUM SIC PROCEDITUR. Videtur quod Deus aequaliter diligat omnia. Dicitur enim Sap. VI, *aequaliter est ei cura de omnibus.* Sed providentia Dei, quam habet de rebus, est ex amore quo amat res. Ergo aequaliter amat omnia.

PRAETEREA, amor Dei est eius essentia. Sed essentia Dei magis et minus non recipit. Ergo nec amor eius. Non igitur quaedam aliis magis amat.

PRAETEREA, sicut amor Dei se extendit ad res creatas, ita et scientia et voluntas. Sed Deus non dicitur scire quaedam magis quam alia, neque magis velle. Ergo nec magis quaedam aliis diligit.

SED CONTRA est quod dicit Augustinus, super Ioann., *omnia diligit Deus quae fecit; et inter ea magis diligit creaturas rationales; et de illis eas amplius, quae sunt membra unigeniti sui; et multo magis ipsum unigenitum suum.*

RESPONDEO dicendum quod, cum amare sit velle bonum alicui, duplici ratione potest aliquid magis vel minus amari. Uno modo, ex parte ipsius actus voluntatis, qui est magis vel minus intensus. Et sic Deus non magis quaedam aliis amat, quia omnia amat uno et simplici actu voluntatis, et semper eodem modo se habente. Alio modo, ex parte ipsius boni quod aliquis vult amato. Et sic dicimur aliquem magis alio amare, cui volumus maius bonum; quamvis non magis intensa voluntate. Et hoc modo necesse est dicere quod Deus quaedam aliis magis amat. Cum enim amor Dei sit causa bonitatis rerum, ut dictum est, non esset aliquid alio melius, si Deus non vellet uni maius bonum quam alteri.

AD PRIMUM ergo dicendum quod dicitur Deo aequaliter esse cura de omnibus, non quia aequalia bona sua cura omnibus dispenset; sed quia ex aequali sapientia et bonitate omnia administrat.

AD SECUNDUM dicendum quod ratio illa procedit de intensione amoris ex parte actus voluntatis, qui est divina essentia. Bonum autem quod Deus creaturae vult, non est divina essentia. Unde nihil prohibet illud intendi vel remitti.

AD TERTIUM dicendum quod intelligere et velle significant solum actus, non autem in sua significatione includunt aliqua obiecta, ex quorum diversitate possit dici Deus magis vel minus scire aut velle; sicut circa amorem dictum est.

OBJECTION 1: It seems that God loves all things equally. For it is said: *He hath equally care of all* (Wis 6:8). But God's providence over things comes from the love wherewith He loves them. Therefore He loves all things equally.

OBJ. 2: Further, the love of God is His essence. But God's essence does not admit of degree; neither therefore does His love. He does not therefore love some things more than others.

OBJ. 3: Further, as God's love extends to created things, so do His knowledge and will extend. But God is not said to know some things more than others; nor will one thing more than another. Neither therefore does He love some things more than others.

ON THE CONTRARY, Augustine says (*Tract. in Joan.* cx): *God loves all things that He has made, and amongst them rational creatures more, and of these especially those who are members of His only-begotten Son Himself.*

I ANSWER THAT, Since to love a thing is to will it good, in a twofold way anything may be loved more, or less. In one way on the part of the act of the will itself, which is more or less intense. In this way God does not love some things more than others, because He loves all things by an act of the will that is one, simple, and always the same. In another way on the part of the good itself that a person wills for the beloved. In this way we are said to love that one more than another, for whom we will a greater good, though our will is not more intense. In this way we must needs say that God loves some things more than others. For since God's love is the cause of goodness in things, as has been said (A. 2), no one thing would be better than another, if God did not will greater good for one than for another.

REPLY OBJ. 1: God is said to have equally care of all, not because by His care He deals out equal good to all, but because He administers all things with a like wisdom and goodness.

REPLY OBJ. 2: This argument is based on the intensity of love on the part of the act of the will, which is the divine essence. But the good that God wills for His creatures, is not the divine essence. Therefore there is no reason why it may not vary in degree.

REPLY OBJ. 3: To understand and to will denote the act alone, and do not include in their meaning objects from the diversity of which God may be said to know or will more or less, as has been said with respect to God's love.

Article 4

Whether God Always Loves More the Better Things?

AD QUARTUM SIC PROCEDITUR. Videtur quod Deus non semper magis diligat meliora. Manifestum est enim quod Christus est melior toto genere humano, cum sit Deus et homo. Sed Deus magis dilexit genus humanum quam Christum, quia dicitur Rom. VIII, *proprio filio suo non pepercit, sed pro nobis omnibus tradidit illum.* Ergo Deus non semper magis diligit meliora.

PRAETEREA, Angelus est melior homine, unde in Psalmo VIII dicitur de homine, *minuisti eum paulo minus ab Angelis.* Sed Deus plus dilexit hominem quam Angelum, dicitur enim Hebr. II, *nusquam Angelos apprehendit, sed semen Abrahae apprehendit.* Ergo Deus non semper magis diligit meliora.

PRAETEREA, Petrus fuit melior Ioanne, quia plus Christum diligebat. Unde dominus, sciens hoc esse verum, interrogavit Petrum, dicens, *Simon Ioannis, diligis me plus his?* Sed tamen Christus plus dilexit Ioannem quam Petrum, ut enim dicit Augustinus, super illud Ioan. XXI, *Simon Ioannis diligis me? Hoc ipso signo Ioannes a ceteris discipulis discernitur; non quod solum eum, sed quod plus eum ceteris diligebat.* Non ergo semper magis diligit meliora.

PRAETEREA, melior est innocens poenitente; *cum poenitentia sit secunda tabula post naufragium,* ut dicit Hieronymus. Sed Deus plus diligit poenitentem quam innocentem, quia plus de eo gaudet, dicitur enim Luc. XV, *dico vobis quod maius gaudium erit in caelo super uno peccatore poenitentiam agente, quam super nonaginta novem iustis, qui non indigent poenitentia.* Ergo Deus non semper magis diligit meliora.

PRAETEREA, melior est iustus praescitus, quam peccator praedestinatus. Sed Deus plus diligit peccatorem praedestinatum, quia vult ei maius bonum, scilicet vitam aeternam. Ergo Deus non semper magis diligit meliora.

SED CONTRA, unumquodque diligit sibi simile; ut patet per illud quod habetur Eccli. XIII, *omne animal diligit sibi simile.* Sed intantum aliquid est melius, inquantum est Deo similius. Ergo meliora magis diliguntur a Deo.

RESPONDEO dicendum quod necesse est dicere, secundum praedicta, quod Deus magis diligat meliora. Dictum est enim quod Deum diligere magis aliquid, nihil aliud est quam ei maius bonum velle, voluntas enim Dei est causa bonitatis in rebus. Et sic, ex hoc sunt aliqua meliora, quod Deus eis maius bonum vult. Unde sequitur quod meliora plus amet.

OBJECTION 1: It seems that God does not always love more the better things. For it is manifest that Christ is better than the whole human race, being God and man. But God loved the human race more than He loved Christ; for it is said: *He spared not His own Son, but delivered Him up for us all* (Rom 8:32). Therefore God does not always love more the better things.

OBJ. 2: Further, an angel is better than a man. Hence it is said of man: *Thou hast made him a little less than the angels* (Ps 8:6). But God loved men more than He loved the angels, for it is said: *Nowhere doth He take hold of the angels, but of the seed of Abraham He taketh hold* (Heb 2:16). Therefore God does not always love more the better things.

OBJ. 3: Further, Peter was better than John, since he loved Christ more. Hence the Lord, knowing this to be true, asked Peter, saying: *Simon, son of John, lovest thou Me more than these?* Yet Christ loved John more than He loved Peter. For as Augustine says, commenting on the words, *Simon, son of John, lovest thou Me?: By this very mark is John distinguished from the other disciples, not that He loved him only, but that He loved him more than the rest.* Therefore God does not always love more the better things.

OBJ. 4: Further, the innocent man is better than the repentant, since repentance is, as Jerome says (Cap. 3 in Isa.), *a second plank after shipwreck.* But God loves the penitent more than the innocent; since He rejoices over him the more. For it is said: *I say to you that there shall be joy in heaven upon the one sinner that doth penance, more than upon ninety-nine just who need not penance* (Luke 15:7). Therefore God does not always love more the better things.

OBJ. 5: Further, the just man who is foreknown is better than the predestined sinner. Now God loves more the predestined sinner, since He wills for him a greater good, life eternal. Therefore God does not always love more the better things.

ON THE CONTRARY, Everything loves what is like it, as appears from (Sir 13:19): *Every beast loveth its like.* Now the better a thing is, the more like is it to God. Therefore the better things are more loved by God.

I ANSWER THAT, It must needs be, according to what has been said before, that God loves more the better things. For it has been shown (AA. 2, 3), that God's loving one thing more than another is nothing else than His willing for that thing a greater good: because God's will is the cause of goodness in things; and the reason why some things are better than others, is that God wills for them a greater good. Hence it follows that He loves more the better things.

AD PRIMUM ergo dicendum quod Deus Christum diligit, non solum plus quam totum humanum genus, sed etiam magis quam totam universitatem creaturarum, quia scilicet ei maius bonum voluit, quia dedit ei nomen, quod est super omne nomen, ut verus Deus esset. Nec eius excellentiae deperiit ex hoc quod Deus dedit eum in mortem pro salute humani generis, quinimo ex hoc factus est victor gloriosus; *factus enim est principatus super humerum eius*, ut dicitur Isaiae IX.

AD SECUNDUM dicendum quod naturam humanam assumptam a Dei verbo in persona Christi, secundum praedicta, Deus plus amat quam omnes Angelos, et melior est, maxime ratione unionis. Sed loquendo de humana natura communiter, eam angelicae comparando, secundum ordinem ad gratiam et gloriam, aequalitas invenitur; cum eadem sit mensura hominis et Angeli, ut dicitur Apoc. XXI; ita tamen quod quidam Angeli quibusdam hominibus, et quidam homines quibusdam Angelis, quantum ad hoc, potiores inveniuntur. Sed quantum ad conditionem naturae, Angelus est melior homine. Nec ideo naturam humanam assumpsit Deus, quia hominem absolute plus diligeret, sed quia plus indigebat. Sicut bonus paterfamilias aliquid pretiosius dat servo aegrotanti, quod non dat filio sano.

AD TERTIUM dicendum quod haec dubitatio de Petro et Ioanne multipliciter solvitur. Augustinus namque refert hoc ad mysterium, dicens quod vita activa, quae significatur per Petrum, plus diligit Deum quam vita contemplativa, quae significatur per Ioannem, quia magis sentit praesentis vitae angustias, et aestuantius ab eis liberari desiderat, et ad Deum ire. Contemplativam vero vitam Deus plus diligit, quia magis eam conservat; non enim finitur simul cum vita corporis, sicut vita activa.

Quidam vero dicunt quod Petrus plus dilexit Christum in membris; et sic etiam a Christo plus fuit dilectus; unde ei Ecclesiam commendavit. Ioannes vero plus dilexit Christum in seipso; et sic etiam plus ab eo fuit dilectus; unde ei commendavit matrem. Alii vero dicunt quod incertum est quis horum plus Christum dilexerit amore caritatis, et similiter quem Deus plus dilexerit in ordine ad maiorem gloriam vitae aeternae. Sed Petrus dicitur plus dilexisse, quantum ad quandam promptitudinem vel fervorem, Ioannes vero plus dilectus, quantum ad quaedam familiaritatis indicia, quae Christus ei magis demonstrabat, propter eius iuventutem et puritatem. Alii vero dicunt quod Christus plus dilexit Petrum, quantum ad excellentius donum caritatis, Ioannem vero plus, quantum ad donum intellectus. Unde simpliciter Petrus fuit melior, et magis dilectus, sed Ioannes secundum quid. Praesumptuosum tamen videtur hoc diiudicare, quia, ut dicitur Prov. XVI, *spirituum ponderator est dominus*, et non alius.

REPLY OBJ. 1: God loves Christ not only more than He loves the whole human race, but more than He loves the entire created universe: because He willed for Him the greater good in giving Him *a name that is above all names*, in so far as He was true God. Nor did anything of His excellence diminish when God delivered Him up to death for the salvation of the human race; rather did He become thereby a glorious conqueror: *The government was placed upon His shoulder*, according to Isa. 9:6.

REPLY OBJ. 2: God loves the human nature assumed by the Word of God in the person of Christ more than He loves all the angels; for that nature is better, especially on the ground of the union with the Godhead. But speaking of human nature in general, and comparing it with the angelic, the two are found equal, in the order of grace and of glory: since according to Rev 21:17, the measure of a man and of an angel is the same. Yet so that, in this respect, some angels are found nobler than some men, and some men nobler than some angels. But as to natural condition an angel is better than a man. God therefore did not assume human nature because He loved man, absolutely speaking, more; but because the needs of man were greater; just as the master of a house may give some costly delicacy to a sick servant, that he does not give to his own son in sound health.

REPLY OBJ. 3: This doubt concerning Peter and John has been solved in various ways. Augustine interprets it mystically, and says that the active life, signified by Peter, loves God more than the contemplative signified by John, because the former is more conscious of the miseries of this present life, and therefore the more ardently desires to be freed from them, and depart to God. God, he says, loves more the contemplative life, since He preserves it longer. For it does not end, as the active life does, with the life of the body.

Some say that Peter loved Christ more in His members, and therefore was loved more by Christ also, for which reason He gave him the care of the Church; but that John loved Christ more in Himself, and so was loved more by Him; on which account Christ commended His mother to his care. Others say that it is uncertain which of them loved Christ more with the love of charity, and uncertain also which of them God loved more and ordained to a greater degree of glory in eternal life. Peter is said to have loved more, in regard to a certain promptness and fervor; but John to have been more loved, with respect to certain marks of familiarity which Christ showed to him rather than to others, on account of his youth and purity. While others say that Christ loved Peter more, from his more excellent gift of charity; but John more, from his gifts of intellect. Hence, absolutely speaking, Peter was the better and more beloved; but, in a certain sense, John was the better, and was loved the more. However, it may seem presumptuous to pass judgment on these matters; since *the Lord* and no other *is the weigher of spirits* (Prov 16:2).

Ad quartum dicendum quod poenitentes et innocentes se habent sicut excedentia et excessa. Nam sive sint innocentes, sive poenitentes, illi sunt meliores et magis dilecti, qui plus habent de gratia. Ceteris tamen paribus, innocentia dignior est et magis dilecta. Dicitur tamen Deus plus gaudere de poenitente quam de innocente, quia plerumque poenitentes cautiores, humiliores et ferventiores resurgunt. Unde Gregorius dicit ibidem, quod *dux in praelio eum militem plus diligit, qui post fugam conversus, fortiter hostem premit, quam qui nunquam fugit, nec unquam fortiter fecit.*

Vel, alia ratione, quia aequale donum gratiae plus est, comparatum poenitenti, qui meruit poenam, quam innocenti, qui non meruit. Sicut centum marcae maius donum est, si dentur pauperi, quam si dentur regi.

Ad quintum dicendum quod, cum voluntas Dei sit causa bonitatis in rebus, secundum illud tempus pensanda est bonitas eius qui amatur a Deo, secundum quod dandum est ei ex bonitate divina aliquod bonum. Secundum ergo illud tempus quo praedestinato peccatori dandum est ex divina voluntate maius bonum, melior est; licet secundum aliquod aliud tempus, sit peior; quia et secundum aliquod tempus, non est nec bonus neque malus.

Reply Obj. 4: The penitent and the innocent are related as exceeding and exceeded. For whether innocent or penitent, those are the better and better loved who have most grace. Other things being equal, innocence is the nobler thing and the more beloved. God is said to rejoice more over the penitent than over the innocent, because often penitents rise from sin more cautious, humble, and fervent. Hence Gregory commenting on these words (*Hom. 34 in Ev.*) says that, *In battle the general loves the soldier who after flight returns and bravely pursues the enemy, more than him who has never fled, but has never done a brave deed.*

Or it may be answered that gifts of grace, equal in themselves, are more as conferred on the penitent, who deserved punishment, than as conferred on the innocent, to whom no punishment was due; just as a hundred pounds are a greater gift to a poor man than to a king.

Reply Obj. 5: Since God's will is the cause of goodness in things, the goodness of one who is loved by God is to be reckoned according to the time when some good is to be given to him by divine goodness. According therefore to the time, when there is to be given by the divine will to the predestined sinner a greater good, the sinner is better; although according to some other time he is the worse; because even according to some time he is neither good nor bad.

QUESTION 21

THE JUSTICE AND MERCY OF GOD

Post considerationem divini amoris, de iustitia et misericordia eius agendum est.

Et circa hoc quaeruntur quatuor.

Primo, utrum in Deo sit iustitia.

Secundo, utrum iustitia eius veritas dici possit.

Tertio, utrum in Deo sit misericordia.

Quarto, utrum in omni opere Dei sit iustitia et misericordia.

After considering the divine love, we must treat of God's justice and mercy.

Under this head there are four points of inquiry:

(1) Whether there is justice in God?

(2) Whether His justice can be called truth?

(3) Whether there is mercy in God?

(4) Whether in every work of God there are justice and mercy?

Article 1

Whether There Is Justice in God?

AD PRIMUM SIC PROCEDITUR. Videtur quod in Deo non sit iustitia. Iustitia enim contra temperantiam dividitur. Temperantia autem non est in Deo. Ergo nec iustitia.

PRAETEREA, quicumque facit omnia pro libito suae voluntatis, non secundum iustitiam operatur. Sed, sicut dicit apostolus, ad Ephes. I, Deus *operatur omnia secundum consilium suae voluntatis.* Non ergo ei iustitia debet attribui.

PRAETEREA, actus iustitiae est reddere debitum. Sed Deus nulli est debitor. Ergo Deo non competit iustitia.

PRAETEREA, quidquid est in Deo, est eius essentia. Sed hoc non competit iustitiae, dicit enim Boetius, in libro de Hebdomad., quod *bonum essentiam, iustum vero actum respicit.* Ergo iustitia non competit Deo.

SED CONTRA est quod dicitur in Psalmo X, *iustus dominus, et iustitias dilexit.*

RESPONDEO dicendum quod duplex est species iustitiae. Una, quae consistit in mutua datione et acceptione, ut puta quae consistit in emptione et venditione, et aliis huiusmodi communicationibus vel commutationibus. Et haec dicitur a philosopho, in V Ethic., iustitia commutativa, vel directiva commutationum sive communicationum. Et haec non competit Deo, quia, ut dicit apostolus, Rom. XI, *quis prior dedit illi, et retribuetur ei?* Alia, quae consistit in distribuendo, et dicitur distributiva iustitia, secundum quam aliquis gubernator vel dispensator dat unicuique secundum suam dignitatem. Sicut igitur ordo congruus familiae, vel cuiuscumque multitudinis gubernatae, demonstrat huiusmodi iustitiam in gubernante; ita ordo universi, qui apparet tam in rebus naturalibus quam in rebus voluntariis, demonstrat

OBJECTION 1: It seems that there is not justice in God. For justice is divided against temperance. But temperance does not exist in God: neither therefore does justice.

OBJ. 2: Further, he who does whatsoever he wills and pleases does not work according to justice. But, as the Apostle says: *God worketh all things according to the counsel of His will* (Eph 1:11). Therefore justice cannot be attributed to Him.

OBJ. 3: Further, the act of justice is to pay what is due. But God is no man's debtor. Therefore justice does not belong to God.

OBJ. 4: Further, whatever is in God, is His essence. But justice cannot belong to this. For Boethius says (*De Hebdom.*): *Good regards the essence; justice the act.* Therefore justice does not belong to God.

ON THE CONTRARY, It is said (Ps 10:8): *The Lord is just, and hath loved justice.*

I ANSWER THAT, There are two kinds of justice. The one consists in mutual giving and receiving, as in buying and selling, and other kinds of intercourse and exchange. This the Philosopher (*Ethic.* v, 4) calls commutative justice, that directs exchange and intercourse of business. This does not belong to God, since, as the Apostle says: *Who hath first given to Him, and recompense shall be made him?* (Rom 11:35). The other consists in distribution, and is called distributive justice; whereby a ruler or a steward gives to each what his rank deserves. As then the proper order displayed in ruling a family or any kind of multitude evinces justice of this kind in the ruler, so the order of the universe, which is seen both in effects of nature and in effects of will, shows forth the justice of God. Hence Dionysius says (*Div. Nom.* viii, 4): *We must needs see that God is truly just, in seeing how He*

Dei iustitiam. Unde dicit Dionysius, VIII cap. de Div. Nom., *oportet videre in hoc veram Dei esse iustitiam, quod omnibus tribuit propria, secundum uniuscuiusque existentium dignitatem; et uniuscuiusque naturam in proprio salvat ordine et virtute.*

AD PRIMUM ergo dicendum quod virtutum moralium quaedam sunt circa passiones; sicut temperantia circa concupiscentias, fortitudo circa timores et audacias, mansuetudo circa iram. Et huiusmodi virtutes Deo attribui non possunt, nisi secundum metaphoram, quia in Deo neque passiones sunt, ut supra dictum est; neque appetitus sensitivus, in quo sunt huiusmodi virtutes sicut in subiecto, ut dicit philosophus in III Ethic. Quaedam vero virtutes morales sunt circa operationes; ut puta circa dationes et sumptus, ut iustitia et liberalitas et magnificentia; quae etiam non sunt in parte sensitiva, sed in voluntate. Unde nihil prohibet huiusmodi virtutes in Deo ponere, non tamen circa actiones civiles sed circa actiones Deo convenientes. Ridiculum est enim secundum virtutes politicas Deum laudare, ut dicit philosophus in X Ethic.

AD SECUNDUM dicendum quod, cum bonum intellectum sit obiectum voluntatis, impossibile est Deum velle nisi quod ratio suae sapientiae habet. Quae quidem est sicut lex iustitiae, secundum quam eius voluntas recta et iusta est. Unde quod secundum suam voluntatem facit, iuste facit, sicut et nos quod secundum legem facimus, iuste facimus. Sed nos quidem secundum legem alicuius superioris, Deus autem sibi ipsi est lex.

AD TERTIUM dicendum quod unicuique debetur quod suum est. Dicitur autem esse suum alicuius, quod ad ipsum ordinatur; sicut servus est domini, et non e converso; nam liberum est quod sui causa est. In nomine ergo debiti, importatur quidam ordo exigentiae vel necessitatis alicuius ad quod ordinatur. Est autem duplex ordo considerandus in rebus. Unus, quo aliquid creatum ordinatur ad aliud creatum, sicut partes ordinantur ad totum, et accidentia ad substantias, et unaquaeque res ad suum finem. Alius ordo, quo omnia creata ordinantur in Deum. Sic igitur et debitum attendi potest dupliciter in operatione divina, aut secundum quod aliquid debetur Deo; aut secundum quod aliquid debetur rei creatae. Et utroque modo Deus debitum reddit. Debitum enim est Deo, ut impleatur in rebus id quod eius sapientia et voluntas habet, et quod suam bonitatem manifestat, et secundum hoc iustitia Dei respicit decentiam ipsius, secundum quam reddit sibi quod sibi debetur. Debitum etiam est alicui rei creatae, quod habeat id quod ad ipsam ordinatur, sicut homini, quod habeat manus, et quod ei alia animalia serviant. Et sic etiam Deus operatur iustitiam, quando dat unicuique quod ei debetur secundum rationem suae naturae et conditionis. Sed hoc debitum dependet ex primo, quia hoc unicuique debetur, quod est ordinatum ad ipsum secundum ordinem divinae

gives to all existing things what is proper to the condition of each; and preserves the nature of each in the order and with the powers that properly belong to it.

REPLY OBJ. 1: Certain of the moral virtues are concerned with the passions, as temperance with concupiscence, fortitude with fear and daring, meekness with anger. Such virtues as these can only metaphorically be attributed to God; since, as stated above (Q. 20, A. 1), in God there are no passions; nor a sensitive appetite, which is, as the Philosopher says (*Ethic.* iii, 10), the subject of those virtues. On the other hand, certain moral virtues are concerned with works of giving and expending; such as justice, liberality, and magnificence; and these reside not in the sensitive faculty, but in the will. Hence, there is nothing to prevent our attributing these virtues to God; although not in civil matters, but in such acts as are not unbecoming to Him. For, as the Philosopher says (*Ethic.* x, 8), it would be absurd to praise God for His political virtues.

REPLY OBJ. 2: Since good as perceived by intellect is the object of the will, it is impossible for God to will anything but what His wisdom approves. This is, as it were, His law of justice, in accordance with which His will is right and just. Hence, what He does according to His will He does justly: as we do justly what we do according to law. But whereas law comes to us from some higher power, God is a law unto Himself.

REPLY OBJ. 3: To each one is due what is his own. Now that which is directed to a man is said to be his own. Thus the master owns the servant, and not conversely, for that is free which is its own cause. In the word debt, therefore, is implied a certain exigence or necessity of the thing to which it is directed. Now a twofold order has to be considered in things: the one, whereby one created thing is directed to another, as the parts of the whole, accident to substance, and all things whatsoever to their end; the other, whereby all created things are ordered to God. Thus in the divine operations debt may be regarded in two ways, as due either to God, or to creatures, and in either way God pays what is due. It is due to God that there should be fulfilled in creatures what His will and wisdom require, and what manifests His goodness. In this respect, God's justice regards what befits Him; inasmuch as He renders to Himself what is due to Himself. It is also due to a created thing that it should possess what is ordered to it; thus it is due to man to have hands, and that other animals should serve him. Thus also God exercises justice, when He gives to each thing what is due to it by its nature and condition. This debt however is derived from the former; since what is due to each thing is due to it as ordered to it according to the divine wisdom. And although God in this way pays each thing its due, yet He Himself is not the debtor, since

sapientiae. Et licet Deus hoc modo debitum alicui det, non tamen ipse est debitor, quia ipse ad alia non ordinatur, sed potius alia in ipsum. Et ideo iustitia quandoque dicitur in Deo condecentia suae bonitatis; quandoque vero retributio pro meritis. Et utrumque modum tangit Anselmus, dicens, *cum punis malos, iustum est, quia illorum meritis convenit; cum vero parcis malis, iustum est, quia bonitati tuae condecens est.*

Ad quartum dicendum quod, licet iustitia respiciat actum, non tamen per hoc excluditur quin sit essentia Dei, quia etiam id quod est de essentia rei, potest esse principium actionis. Sed bonum non semper respicit actum, quia aliquid dicitur esse bonum, non solum secundum quod agit, sed etiam secundum quod in sua essentia perfectum est. Et propter hoc ibidem dicitur quod bonum comparatur ad iustum, sicut generale ad speciale.

He is not directed to other things, but rather other things to Him. Justice, therefore, in God is sometimes spoken of as the fitting accompaniment of His goodness; sometimes as the reward of merit. Anselm touches on either view where he says (*Prosolog.* 10): *When Thou dost punish the wicked, it is just, since it agrees with their deserts; and when Thou dost spare the wicked, it is also just; since it befits Thy goodness.*

Reply Obj. 4: Although justice regards act, this does not prevent its being the essence of God; since even that which is of the essence of a thing may be the principle of action. But good does not always regard act; since a thing is called good not merely with respect to act, but also as regards perfection in its essence. For this reason it is said (*De Hebdom.*) that the good is related to the just, as the general to the special.

Article 2

Whether the Justice of God Is Truth?

Ad secundum sic proceditur. Videtur quod iustitia Dei non sit veritas. Iustitia enim est in voluntate, est enim rectitudo voluntatis, ut dicit Anselmus. Veritas autem est in intellectu, secundum philosophum in VI Metaphys. et in VI Ethic. Ergo iustitia non pertinet ad veritatem.

Praeterea, veritas, secundum philosophum in IV Ethic., est quaedam alia virtus a iustitia. Non ergo veritas pertinet ad rationem iustitiae.

Sed contra est quod in Psalmo LXXXIV dicitur, *misericordia et veritas obviaverunt sibi*; et ponitur ibi veritas pro iustitia.

Respondeo dicendum quod veritas consistit in adaequatione intellectus et rei, sicut supra dictum est. Intellectus autem qui est causa rei, comparatur ad ipsam sicut regula et mensura, e converso autem est de intellectu qui accipit scientiam a rebus. Quando igitur res sunt mensura et regula intellectus, veritas consistit in hoc, quod intellectus adaequatur rei, ut in nobis accidit, ex eo enim quod res est vel non est, opinio nostra et oratio vera vel falsa est. Sed quando intellectus est regula vel mensura rerum, veritas consistit in hoc, quod res adaequantur intellectui, sicut dicitur artifex facere verum opus, quando concordat arti.

Sicut autem se habent artificiata ad artem, ita se habent opera iusta ad legem cui concordant. Iustitia igitur Dei, quae constituit ordinem in rebus conformem rationi sapientiae suae, quae est lex eius, convenienter veritas nominatur. Et sic etiam dicitur in nobis veritas iustitiae.

Objection 1: It seems that the justice of God is not truth. For justice resides in the will; since, as Anselm says (*Dial.* Verit. 13), it is a rectitude of the will, whereas truth resides in the intellect, as the Philosopher says (*Metaph.* vi; *Ethic.* vi, 2,6). Therefore justice does not appertain to truth.

Obj. 2: Further, according to the Philosopher (*Ethic.* iv, 7), truth is a virtue distinct from justice. Truth therefore does not appertain to the idea of justice.

On the contrary, it is said (Ps 84:11): *Mercy and truth have met each other*: where truth stands for justice.

I answer that, Truth consists in the equation of mind and thing, as said above (Q. 16, A. 1). Now the mind, that is the cause of the thing, is related to it as its rule and measure; whereas the converse is the case with the mind that receives its knowledge from things. When therefore things are the measure and rule of the mind, truth consists in the equation of the mind to the thing, as happens in ourselves. For according as a thing is, or is not, our thoughts or our words about it are true or false. But when the mind is the rule or measure of things, truth consists in the equation of the thing to the mind; just as the work of an artist is said to be true, when it is in accordance with his art.

Now as works of art are related to art, so are works of justice related to the law with which they accord. Therefore God's justice, which establishes things in the order conformable to the rule of His wisdom, which is the law of His justice, is suitably called truth. Thus we also in human affairs speak of the truth of justice.

Ad primum ergo dicendum quod iustitia, quantum ad legem regulantem, est in ratione vel intellectu, sed quantum ad imperium, quo opera regulantur secundum legem, est in voluntate.

Ad secundum dicendum quod veritas illa de qua loquitur philosophus ibi, est quaedam virtus per quam aliquis demonstrat se talem in dictis vel factis, qualis est. Et sic consistit in conformitate signi ad significatum, non autem in conformitate effectus ad causam et regulam, sicut de veritate iustitiae dictum est.

Reply Obj. 1: Justice, as to the law that governs, resides in the reason or intellect; but as to the command whereby our actions are governed according to the law, it resides in the will.

Reply Obj. 2: The truth of which the Philosopher is speaking in this passage, is that virtue whereby a man shows himself in word and deed such as he really is. Thus it consists in the conformity of the sign with the thing signified; and not in that of the effect with its cause and rule: as has been said regarding the truth of justice.

Article 3

Whether Mercy Can Be Attributed to God?

Ad tertium sic proceditur. Videtur quod misericordia Deo non competat. Misericordia enim est species tristitiae, ut dicit Damascenus. Sed tristitia non est in Deo. Ergo nec misericordia.

Praeterea, misericordia est relaxatio iustitiae. Sed Deus non potest praetermittere id quod ad iustitiam suam pertinet. Dicitur enim II ad Tim. II, *si non credimus, ille fidelis permanet, seipsum negare non potest*, negaret autem seipsum, ut dicit Glossa ibidem, si dicta sua negaret. Ergo misericordia Deo non competit.

Sed contra est quod dicitur in Psalmo CX, *miserator et misericors dominus*.

Respondeo dicendum quod misericordia est Deo maxime attribuenda, tamen secundum effectum, non secundum passionis affectum. Ad cuius evidentiam, considerandum est quod misericors dicitur aliquis quasi habens miserum cor, quia scilicet afficitur ex miseria alterius per tristitiam, ac si esset eius propria miseria. Et ex hoc sequitur quod operetur ad depellendam miseriam alterius, sicut miseriam propriam, et hic est misericordiae effectus. Tristari ergo de miseria alterius non competit Deo, sed repellere miseriam alterius, hoc maxime ei competit, ut per miseriam quemcumque defectum intelligamus. Defectus autem non tolluntur, nisi per alicuius bonitatis perfectionem, prima autem origo bonitatis Deus est, ut supra ostensum est. Sed considerandum est quod elargiri perfectiones rebus, pertinet quidem et ad bonitatem divinam, et ad iustitiam, et ad liberalitatem, et misericordiam, tamen secundum aliam et aliam rationem. Communicatio enim perfectionum, absolute considerata, pertinet ad bonitatem, ut supra ostensum est. Sed inquantum perfectiones rebus a Deo dantur secundum earum proportionem, pertinet ad iustitiam, ut dictum est supra. Inquantum vero non attribuit rebus

Objection 1: It seems that mercy cannot be attributed to God. For mercy is a kind of sorrow, as Damascene says (*De Fide Orth.* ii, 14). But there is no sorrow in God; and therefore there is no mercy in Him.

Obj. 2: Further, mercy is a relaxation of justice. But God cannot remit what appertains to His justice. For it is said (2 Tim 2:13): *If we believe not, He continueth faithful: He cannot deny Himself.* But He would deny Himself, as a gloss says, if He should deny His words. Therefore mercy is not becoming to God.

On the contrary, it is said (Ps 110:4): *He is a merciful and gracious Lord.*

I answer that, Mercy is especially to be attributed to God, as seen in its effect, but not as an affection of passion. In proof of which it must be considered that a person is said to be merciful, as being, so to speak, sorrowful at heart; being affected with sorrow at the misery of another as though it were his own. Hence it follows that he endeavors to dispel the misery of this other, as if it were his; and this is the effect of mercy. To sorrow, therefore, over the misery of others belongs not to God; but it does most properly belong to Him to dispel that misery, whatever be the defect we call by that name. Now defects are not removed, except by the perfection of some kind of goodness; and the primary source of goodness is God, as shown above (Q. 6, A. 4). It must, however, be considered that to bestow perfections appertains not only to the divine goodness, but also to His justice, liberality, and mercy; yet under different aspects. The communicating of perfections, absolutely considered, appertains to goodness, as shown above (Q. 6, AA. 1, 4); in so far as perfections are given to things in proportion, the bestowal of them belongs to justice, as has been already said (A. 1); in so far as God does not bestow them for His own use, but only on account of His goodness, it belongs

perfectiones propter utilitatem suam, sed solum propter suam bonitatem, pertinet ad liberalitatem. Inquantum vero perfectiones datae rebus a Deo, omnem defectum expellunt, pertinet ad misericordiam.

AD PRIMUM igitur dicendum quod obiectio illa procedit de misericordia, quantum ad passionis affectum.

AD SECUNDUM dicendum quod Deus misericorditer agit, non quidem contra iustitiam suam faciendo, sed aliquid supra iustitiam operando, sicut si alicui cui debentur centum denarii, aliquis ducentos det de suo, tamen non contra iustitiam facit, sed liberaliter vel misericorditer operatur. Et similiter si aliquis offensam in se commissam remittat. Qui enim aliquid remittit, quodammodo donat illud, unde apostolus remissionem donationem vocat, Ephes. V, *donate invicem, sicut et Christus vobis donavit.* Ex quo patet quod misericordia non tollit iustitiam, sed est quaedam iustitiae plenitudo. Unde dicitur Iac. II, quod *misericordia superexaltat iudicium.*

to liberality; in so far as perfections given to things by God expel defects, it belongs to mercy.

REPLY OBJ. 1: This argument is based on mercy, regarded as an affection of passion.

REPLY OBJ. 2: God acts mercifully, not indeed by going against His justice, but by doing something more than justice; thus a man who pays another two hundred pieces of money, though owing him only one hundred, does nothing against justice, but acts liberally or mercifully. The case is the same with one who pardons an offense committed against him, for in remitting it he may be said to bestow a gift. Hence the Apostle calls remission a forgiving: *Forgive one another, as Christ has forgiven you* (Eph 4:32). Hence it is clear that mercy does not destroy justice, but in a sense is the fullness thereof. And thus it is said: *Mercy exalteth itself above judgment* (Jas 2:13).

Article 4

Whether in Every Work of God There Are Mercy and Justice?

AD QUARTUM SIC PROCEDITUR. Videtur quod non in omnibus Dei operibus sit misericordia et iustitia. Quaedam enim opera Dei attribuuntur misericordiae, ut iustificatio impii, quaedam vero iustitiae, ut damnatio impiorum. Unde dicitur Iac. II, *iudicium sine misericordia fiet ei qui non fecerit misericordiam.* Non ergo in omni opere Dei apparet misericordia et iustitia.

PRAETEREA, apostolus, ad Rom. XV, conversionem Iudaeorum attribuit iustitiae et veritati; conversionem autem gentium, misericordiae. Ergo non in quolibet opere Dei est iustitia et misericordia.

PRAETEREA, multi iusti in hoc mundo affliguntur. Hoc autem est iniustum. Non ergo in omni opere Dei est iustitia et misericordia.

PRAETEREA, iustitiae est reddere debitum, misericordiae autem sublevare miseriam, et sic tam iustitia quam misericordia aliquid praesupponit in suo opere. Sed creatio nihil praesupponit. Ergo in creatione neque misericordia est, neque iustitia.

SED CONTRA est quod dicitur in Psalmo XXIV, *omnes viae domini misericordia et veritas.*

RESPONDEO dicendum quod necesse est quod in quolibet opere Dei misericordia et veritas inveniantur; si tamen misericordia pro remotione cuiuscumque defectus accipiatur; quamvis non omnis defectus proprie possit dici miseria, sed solum defectus rationalis naturae, quam contingit esse felicem; nam miseria felicitati opponitur. Huius autem necessitatis ratio est, quia, cum debitum quod ex divina iustitia redditur, sit vel debitum

OBJECTION 1: It seems that not in every work of God are mercy and justice. For some works of God are attributed to mercy, as the justification of the ungodly; and others to justice, as the damnation of the wicked. Hence it is said: *Judgment without mercy to him that hath not done mercy* (Jas 2:13). Therefore not in every work of God do mercy and justice appear.

OBJ. 2: Further, the Apostle attributes the conversion of the Jews to justice and truth, but that of the Gentiles to mercy (Rom 15). Therefore not in every work of God are justice and mercy.

OBJ. 3: Further, many just persons are afflicted in this world; which is unjust. Therefore not in every work of God are justice and mercy.

OBJ. 4: Further, it is the part of justice to pay what is due, but of mercy to relieve misery. Thus both justice and mercy presuppose something in their works: whereas creation presupposes nothing. Therefore in creation neither mercy nor justice is found.

ON THE CONTRARY, It is said (Ps 24:10): *All the ways of the Lord are mercy and truth.*

I ANSWER THAT, Mercy and truth are necessarily found in all God's works, if mercy be taken to mean the removal of any kind of defect. Not every defect, however, can properly be called a misery; but only defect in a rational nature whose lot is to be happy; for misery is opposed to happiness. For this necessity there is a reason, because since a debt paid according to the divine justice is one due either to God, or to some creature, neither the one

Deo, vel debitum alicui creaturae, neutrum potest in aliquo opere Dei praetermitti. Non enim potest facere aliquid Deus, quod non sit conveniens sapientiae et bonitati ipsius; secundum quem modum diximus aliquid esse debitum Deo. Similiter etiam quidquid in rebus creatis facit, secundum convenientem ordinem et proportionem facit; in quo consistit ratio iustitiae. Et sic oportet in omni opere Dei esse iustitiam. Opus autem divinae iustitiae semper praesupponit opus misericordiae, et in eo fundatur. Creaturae enim non debetur aliquid, nisi propter aliquid in eo praeexistens, vel praeconsideratum, et rursus, si illud creaturae debetur, hoc erit propter aliquid prius. Et cum non sit procedere in infinitum, oportet devenire ad aliquid quod ex sola bonitate divinae voluntatis dependeat, quae est ultimus finis. Utpote si dicamus quod habere manus debitum est homini propter animam rationalem; animam vero rationalem habere, ad hoc quod sit homo; hominem vero esse, propter divinam bonitatem. Et sic in quolibet opere Dei apparet misericordia, quantum ad primam radicem eius. Cuius virtus salvatur in omnibus consequentibus; et etiam vehementius in eis operatur, sicut causa primaria vehementius influit quam causa secunda. Et propter hoc etiam ea quae alicui creaturae debentur, Deus, ex abundantia suae bonitatis, largius dispensat quam exigat proportio rei. Minus enim est quod sufficeret ad conservandum ordinem iustitiae, quam quod divina bonitas confert, quae omnem proportionem creaturae excedit.

AD PRIMUM ergo dicendum quod quaedam opera attribuuntur iustitiae et quaedam misericordiae, quia in quibusdam vehementius apparet iustitia, in quibusdam misericordia. Et tamen in damnatione reproborum apparet misericordia, non quidem totaliter relaxans, sed aliqualiter allevians, dum punit citra condignum.

Et in iustificatione impii apparet iustitia, dum culpas relaxat propter dilectionem, quam tamen ipse misericorditer infundit, sicut de Magdalena legitur, Luc. VII, *dimissa sunt ei peccata multa, quoniam dilexit multum.*

AD SECUNDUM dicendum quod iustitia et misericordia Dei apparet in conversione Iudaeorum et gentium, sed aliqua ratio iustitiae apparet in conversione Iudaeorum, quae non apparet in conversione gentium, sicut quod salvati sunt propter promissiones patribus factas.

AD TERTIUM dicendum quod in hoc etiam quod iusti puniuntur in hoc mundo, apparet iustitia et misericordia; inquantum per huiusmodi afflictiones aliqua levia in eis purgantur, et ab affectu terrenorum in Deum magis eriguntur; secundum illud Gregorii, *mala quae in hoc mundo nos premunt, ad Deum nos ire compellunt.*

AD QUARTUM dicendum quod, licet creationi non praesupponatur aliquid in rerum natura, praesupponitur tamen aliquid in Dei cognitione. Et secundum hoc

nor the other can be lacking in any work of God: because God can do nothing that is not in accord with His wisdom and goodness; and it is in this sense, as we have said, that anything is due to God. Likewise, whatever is done by Him in created things, is done according to proper order and proportion wherein consists the idea of justice. Thus justice must exist in all God's works. Now the work of divine justice always presupposes the work of mercy; and is founded thereupon. For nothing is due to creatures, except for something pre-existing in them, or foreknown. Again, if this is due to a creature, it must be due on account of something that precedes. And since we cannot go on to infinity, we must come to something that depends only on the goodness of the divine will—which is the ultimate end. We may say, for instance, that to possess hands is due to man on account of his rational soul; and his rational soul is due to him that he may be man; and his being man is on account of the divine goodness. So in every work of God, viewed at its primary source, there appears mercy. In all that follows, the power of mercy remains, and works indeed with even greater force; as the influence of the first cause is more intense than that of second causes. For this reason does God out of abundance of His goodness bestow upon creatures what is due to them more bountifully than is proportionate to their deserts: since less would suffice for preserving the order of justice than what the divine goodness confers; because between creatures and God's goodness there can be no proportion.

REPLY OBJ. 1: Certain works are attributed to justice, and certain others to mercy, because in some justice appears more forcibly and in others mercy. Even in the damnation of the reprobate mercy is seen, which, though it does not totally remit, yet somewhat alleviates, in punishing short of what is deserved.

In the justification of the ungodly, justice is seen, when God remits sins on account of love, though He Himself has mercifully infused that love. So we read of Magdalen: *Many sins are forgiven her, because she hath loved much* (Luke 7:47).

REPLY OBJ. 2: God's justice and mercy appear both in the conversion of the Jews and of the Gentiles. But an aspect of justice appears in the conversion of the Jews which is not seen in the conversion of the Gentiles; inasmuch as the Jews were saved on account of the promises made to the fathers.

REPLY OBJ. 3: Justice and mercy appear in the punishment of the just in this world, since by afflictions lesser faults are cleansed in them, and they are the more raised up from earthly affections to God. As to this Gregory says (*Moral.* xxvi, 9): *The evils that press on us in this world force us to go to God.*

REPLY OBJ. 4: Although creation presupposes nothing in the universe; yet it does presuppose something in the knowledge of God. In this way too the idea of justice is

etiam salvatur ibi ratio iustitiae, inquantum res in esse producitur, secundum quod convenit divinae sapientiae et bonitati. Et salvatur quodammodo ratio misericordiae, inquantum res de non esse in esse mutatur.

preserved in creation; by the production of beings in a manner that accords with the divine wisdom and goodness. And the idea of mercy, also, is preserved in the change of creatures from non-existence to existence.

Question 22

The Providence of God

Consideratis autem his quae ad voluntatem absolute pertinent, procedendum est ad ea quae respiciunt simul intellectum et voluntatem. Huiusmodi autem est providentia quidem respectu omnium; praedestinatio vero et reprobatio, et quae ad haec consequuntur, respectu hominum specialiter, in ordine ad aeternam salutem. Nam et post morales virtutes, in scientia morali, consideratur de prudentia, ad quam providentia pertinere videtur.

Circa providentiam autem Dei quaeruntur quatuor.

Primo, utrum Deo conveniat providentia.
Secundo, utrum omnia divinae providentiae subsint.
Tertio, utrum divina providentia immediate sit de omnibus.
Quarto, utrum providentia divina imponat necessitatem rebus provisis.

Having considered all that relates to the will absolutely, we must now proceed to those things which have relation to both the intellect and the will, namely providence, in respect to all created things; predestination and reprobation and all that is connected with these acts in respect especially of man as regards his eternal salvation. For in the science of morals, after the moral virtues themselves, comes the consideration of prudence, to which providence would seem to belong.

Concerning God's providence there are four points of inquiry:

(1) Whether providence is suitably assigned to God?
(2) Whether everything comes under divine providence?
(3) Whether divine providence is immediately concerned with all things?
(4) Whether divine providence imposes any necessity upon things foreseen?

Article 1

Whether Providence Can Suitably Be Attributed to God?

Ad primum sic proceditur. Videtur quod providentia Deo non conveniat. Providentia enim, secundum Tullium, est pars prudentiae. Prudentia autem, cum sit bene consiliativa, secundum philosophum in VI Ethic., Deo competere non potest, qui nullum dubium habet, unde eum consiliari oporteat. Ergo providentia Deo non competit.

Praeterea, quidquid est in Deo, est aeternum. Sed providentia non est aliquid aeternum, est enim circa existentia, quae non sunt aeterna, secundum Damascenum. Ergo providentia non est in Deo.

Praeterea, nullum compositum est in Deo. Sed providentia videtur esse aliquid compositum, quia includit in se voluntatem et intellectum. Ergo providentia non est in Deo.

Sed contra est quod dicitur Sap. XIV, *tu autem, pater, gubernas omnia providentia.*

Respondeo dicendum quod necesse est ponere providentiam in Deo. Omne enim bonum quod est in rebus, a Deo creatum est, ut supra ostensum est. In rebus autem invenitur bonum, non solum quantum ad substantiam rerum, sed etiam quantum ad ordinem earum

Objection 1: It seems that providence is not becoming to God. For providence, according to Tully (*De Invent.* ii), is a part of prudence. But prudence, since, according to the Philosopher (*Ethic.* vi, 5, 9, 18), it gives good counsel, cannot belong to God, Who never has any doubt for which He should take counsel. Therefore providence cannot belong to God.

Obj. 2: Further, whatever is in God, is eternal. But providence is not anything eternal, for it is concerned with existing things that are not eternal, according to Damascene (*De Fide Orth.* ii, 29). Therefore there is no providence in God.

Obj. 3: Further, there is nothing composite in God. But providence seems to be something composite, because it includes both the intellect and the will. Therefore providence is not in God.

On the contrary, It is said (Wis 14:3): *But Thou, Father, governest all things by providence.*

I answer that, It is necessary to attribute providence to God. For all the good that is in created things has been created by God, as was shown above (Q. 6, A. 4). In created things good is found not only as regards their substance, but also as regards their order towards an end and

243

in finem, et praecipue in finem ultimum, qui est bonitas divina, ut supra habitum est. Hoc igitur bonum ordinis in rebus creatis existens, a Deo creatum est. Cum autem Deus sit causa rerum per suum intellectum, et sic cuiuslibet sui effectus oportet rationem in ipso praeexistere, ut ex superioribus patet; necesse est quod ratio ordinis rerum in finem in mente divina praeexistat. Ratio autem ordinandorum in finem, proprie providentia est. Est enim principalis pars prudentiae, ad quam aliae duae partes ordinantur, scilicet memoria praeteritorum, et intelligentia praesentium; prout ex praeteritis memoratis, et praesentibus intellectis, coniectamus de futuris providendis. Prudentiae autem proprium est, secundum philosophum in VI Ethic., ordinare alia in finem; sive respectu sui ipsius, sicut dicitur homo prudens, qui bene ordinat actus suos ad finem vitae suae; sive respectu aliorum sibi subiectorum in familia vel civitate vel regno, secundum quem modum dicitur Matt. XXIV, *fidelis servus et prudens, quem constituit dominus super familiam suam.* Secundum quem modum prudentia vel providentia Deo convenire potest, nam in ipso Deo nihil est in finem ordinabile, cum ipse sit finis ultimus. Ipsa igitur ratio ordinis rerum in finem, providentia in Deo nominatur. Unde Boetius, IV de Consol., dicit quod *providentia est ipsa divina ratio in summo omnium principe constituta, quae cuncta disponit.* Dispositio autem potest dici tam ratio ordinis rerum in finem, quam ratio ordinis partium in toto.

AD PRIMUM ergo dicendum quod, secundum philosophum in VI Ethic., *prudentia proprie est praeceptiva eorum, de quibus eubulia recte consiliatur, et synesis recte iudicat.* Unde, licet consiliari non competat Deo, secundum quod consilium est inquisitio de rebus dubiis; tamen praecipere de ordinandis in finem, quorum rectam rationem habet, competit Deo, secundum illud Psalmi, *praeceptum posuit, et non praeteribit.* Et secundum hoc competit Deo ratio prudentiae et providentiae. Quamvis etiam dici possit, quod ipsa ratio rerum agendarum consilium in Deo dicitur; non propter inquisitionem, sed propter certitudinem cognitionis, ad quam consiliantes inquirendo perveniunt. Unde dicitur Ephes. I, *qui operatur omnia secundum consilium voluntatis suae.*

AD SECUNDUM dicendum quod ad curam duo pertinent, scilicet ratio ordinis, quae dicitur providentia et dispositio; et executio ordinis, quae dicitur gubernatio. Quorum primum est aeternum, secundum temporale.

AD TERTIUM dicendum quod providentia est in intellectu, sed praesupponit voluntatem finis, nullus enim praecipit de agendis propter finem, nisi velit finem.

especially their last end, which, as was said above, is the divine goodness (Q. 21, A. 4). This good of order existing in things created, is itself created by God. Since, however, God is the cause of things by His intellect, and thus it behooves that the type of every effect should pre-exist in Him, as is clear from what has gone before (Q. 19, A. 4), it is necessary that the type of the order of things towards their end should pre-exist in the divine mind: and the type of things ordered towards an end is, properly speaking, providence. For it is the chief part of prudence, to which two other parts are directed—namely, remembrance of the past, and understanding of the present; inasmuch as from the remembrance of what is past and the understanding of what is present, we gather how to provide for the future. Now it belongs to prudence, according to the Philosopher (*Ethic.* vi, 12), to direct other things towards an end whether in regard to oneself—as for instance, a man is said to be prudent, who orders well his acts towards the end of life—or in regard to others subject to him, in a family, city or kingdom; in which sense it is said (Matt 24:45), *a faithful and wise servant, whom his lord hath appointed over his family.* In this way prudence or providence may suitably be attributed to God. For in God Himself there can be nothing ordered towards an end, since He is the last end. This type of order in things towards an end is therefore in God called providence. Whence Boethius says (*De Consol.* iv, 6) that *Providence is the divine type itself, seated in the Supreme Ruler; which disposeth all things*: which disposition may refer either to the type of the order of things towards an end, or to the type of the order of parts in the whole.

REPLY OBJ. 1: According to the Philosopher (*Ethic.* vi, 9, 10), *Prudence is what, strictly speaking, commands all that 'ebulia' has rightly counselled and 'synesis' rightly judged.* Whence, though to take counsel may not be fitting to God, from the fact that counsel is an inquiry into matters that are doubtful, nevertheless to give a command as to the ordering of things towards an end, the right reason of which He possesses, does belong to God, according to Ps. 148:6: *He hath made a decree, and it shall not pass away.* In this manner both prudence and providence belong to God. Although at the same time it may be said that the very reason of things to be done is called counsel in God; not because of any inquiry necessitated, but from the certitude of the knowledge, to which those who take counsel come by inquiry. Whence it is said: *Who worketh all things according to the counsel of His will* (Eph 1:11).

REPLY OBJ. 2: Two things pertain to the care of providence—namely, the *reason of order*, which is called providence and disposition; and the execution of order, which is termed government. Of these, the first is eternal, and the second is temporal.

REPLY OBJ. 3: Providence resides in the intellect; but presupposes the act of willing the end. Nobody gives a precept about things done for an end; unless he will that end.

Unde et prudentia praesupponit virtutes morales, per quas appetitus se habet ad bonum, ut dicitur in VI Ethic. Et tamen si providentia ex aequali respiceret voluntatem et intellectum divinum, hoc esset absque detrimento divinae simplicitatis; cum voluntas et intellectus in Deo sint idem, ut supra dictum est.

Hence prudence presupposes the moral virtues, by means of which the appetitive faculty is directed towards good, as the Philosopher says. Even if Providence has to do with the divine will and intellect equally, this would not affect the divine simplicity, since in God both the will and intellect are one and the same thing, as we have said above (Q. 19).

Article 2

Whether Everything Is Subject to the Providence of God?

Ad secundum sic proceditur. Videtur quod non omnia sint subiecta divinae providentiae. Nullum enim provisum est fortuitum. Si ergo omnia sunt provisa a Deo, nihil erit fortuitum, et sic perit casus et fortuna. Quod est contra communem opinionem.

Praeterea, omnis sapiens provisor excludit defectum et malum, quantum potest, ab his quorum curam gerit. Videmus autem multa mala in rebus esse. Aut igitur Deus non potest ea impedire, et sic non est omnipotens, aut non de omnibus curam habet.

Praeterea, quae ex necessitate eveniunt, providentiam seu prudentiam non requirunt, unde, secundum philosophum in VI Ethic., *prudentia est recta ratio contingentium, de quibus est consilium et electio.* Cum igitur multa in rebus ex necessitate eveniant, non omnia providentiae subduntur.

Praeterea, quicumque dimittitur sibi, non subest providentiae alicuius gubernantis. Sed homines sibi ipsis dimittuntur a Deo, secundum illud Eccli. XV, *Deus ab initio constituit hominem, et reliquit eum in manu consilii sui;* et specialiter mali, secundum illud, *dimisit illos secundum desideria cordis eorum.* Non igitur omnia divinae providentiae subsunt.

Praeterea, apostolus, I Cor. IX, dicit quod *non est Deo cura de bobus,* et eadem ratione, de aliis creaturis irrationalibus. Non igitur omnia subsunt divinae providentiae.

Sed contra est quod dicitur Sap. VIII, de divina sapientia, quod *attingit a fine usque ad finem fortiter, et disponit omnia suaviter.*

Respondeo dicendum quod quidam totaliter providentiam negaverunt, sicut Democritus et Epicurei, ponentes mundum factum esse casu. Quidam vero posuerunt incorruptibilia tantum providentiae subiacere; corruptibilia vero, non secundum individua, sed secundum species; sic enim incorruptibilia sunt. Ex quorum persona dicitur Iob XXII, *nubes latibulum eius, et circa cardines caeli perambulat, neque nostra considerat.* A corruptibilium autem generalitate excepit Rabbi Moyses homines, propter splendorem intellectus, quem

Objection 1: It seems that everything is not subject to divine providence. For nothing foreseen can happen by chance. If then everything was foreseen by God, nothing would happen by chance. And thus hazard and luck would disappear; which is against common opinion.

Obj. 2: Further, a wise provider excludes any defect or evil, as far as he can, from those over whom he has a care. But we see many evils existing. Either, then, God cannot hinder these, and thus is not omnipotent; or else He does not have care for everything.

Obj. 3: Further, whatever happens of necessity does not require providence or prudence. Hence, according to the Philosopher (*Ethic.* vi, 5, 9, 10, 11): *Prudence is the right reason of things contingent concerning which there is counsel and choice.* Since, then, many things happen from necessity, everything cannot be subject to providence.

Obj. 4: Further, whatsoever is left to itself cannot be subject to the providence of a governor. But men are left to themselves by God in accordance with the words: *God made man from the beginning, and left him in the hand of his own counsel* (Sir 15:14). And particularly in reference to the wicked: *I let them go according to the desires of their heart* (Ps 80:13). Everything, therefore, cannot be subject to divine providence.

Obj. 5: Further, the Apostle says (1 Cor 9:9): *God doth not care for oxen*: and we may say the same of other irrational creatures. Thus everything cannot be under the care of divine providence.

On the contrary, It is said of Divine Wisdom: *She reacheth from end to end mightily, and ordereth all things sweetly* (Wis 8:1).

I answer that, Certain persons totally denied the existence of providence, as Democritus and the Epicureans, maintaining that the world was made by chance. Others taught that incorruptible things only were subject to providence and corruptible things not in their individual selves, but only according to their species; for in this respect they are incorruptible. They are represented as saying (Job 22:14): *The clouds are His covert; and He doth not consider our things; and He walketh about the poles of heaven.* Rabbi Moses, however, excluded men from the generality

participant, in aliis autem individuis corruptibilibus, aliorum opinionem est secutus.

Sed necesse est dicere omnia divinae providentiae subiacere, non in universali tantum, sed etiam in singulari. Quod sic patet. Cum enim omne agens agat propter finem, tantum se extendit ordinatio effectuum in finem, quantum se extendit causalitas primi agentis. Ex hoc enim contingit in operibus alicuius agentis aliquid provenire non ad finem ordinatum, quia effectus ille consequitur ex aliqua alia causa, praeter intentionem agentis. Causalitas autem Dei, qui est primum agens, se extendit usque ad omnia entia, non solum quantum ad principia speciei, sed etiam quantum ad individualia principia, non solum incorruptibilium, sed etiam corruptibilium. Unde necesse est omnia quae habent quocumque modo esse, ordinata esse a Deo in finem, secundum illud apostoli, ad Rom. XIII, *quae a Deo sunt, ordinata sunt.* Cum ergo nihil aliud sit Dei providentia quam ratio ordinis rerum in finem, ut dictum est, necesse est omnia, inquantum participant esse, intantum subdi divinae providentiae. Similiter etiam supra ostensum est quod Deus omnia cognoscit, et universalia et particularia. Et cum cognitio eius comparetur ad res sicut cognitio artis ad artificiata, ut supra dictum est, necesse est quod omnia supponantur suo ordini, sicut omnia artificiata subduntur ordini artis.

AD PRIMUM ergo dicendum quod aliter est de causa universali, et de causa particulari. Ordinem enim causae particularis aliquid potest exire, non autem ordinem causae universalis. Non enim subducitur aliquid ab ordine causae particularis, nisi per aliquam aliam causam particularem impedientem, sicut lignum impeditur a combustione per actionem aquae. Unde, cum omnes causae particulares concludantur sub universali causa, impossibile est aliquem effectum ordinem causae universalis effugere. Inquantum igitur aliquis effectus ordinem alicuius causae particularis effugit, dicitur esse casuale vel fortuitum, respectu causae particularis, sed respectu causae universalis, a cuius ordine subtrahi non potest, dicitur esse provisum. Sicut et concursus duorum servorum, licet sit casualis quantum ad eos, est tamen provisus a domino, qui eos scienter sic ad unum locum mittit, ut unus de alio nesciat.

AD SECUNDUM dicendum quod aliter de eo est qui habet curam alicuius particularis, et de provisore universali. Quia provisor particularis excludit defectum ab eo quod eius curae subditur, quantum potest, sed provisor universalis permittit aliquem defectum in aliquo particulari accidere, ne impediatur bonum totius. Unde corruptiones et defectus in rebus naturalibus, dicuntur

of things corruptible, on account of the excellence of the intellect which they possess, but in reference to all else that suffers corruption he adhered to the opinion of the others.

We must say, however, that all things are subject to divine providence, not only in general, but even in their own individual selves. This is made evident thus. For since every agent acts for an end, the ordering of effects towards that end extends as far as the causality of the first agent extends. Whence it happens that in the effects of an agent something takes place which has no reference towards the end, because the effect comes from a cause other than, and outside the intention of the agent. But the causality of God, Who is the first agent, extends to all being, not only as to constituent principles of species, but also as to the individualizing principles; not only of things incorruptible, but also of things corruptible. Hence all things that exist in whatsoever manner are necessarily directed by God towards some end; as the Apostle says: *Those things that are of God are well ordered* (Rom 13:1). Since, therefore, as the providence of God is nothing less than the type of the order of things towards an end, as we have said, it necessarily follows that all things, inasmuch as they participate in existence, must likewise be subject to divine providence. It has also been shown (Q. 14, AA. 6, 11) that God knows all things, both universal and particular. And since His knowledge may be compared to the things themselves, as the knowledge of art to the objects of art, all things must of necessity come under His ordering; as all things wrought by art are subject to the ordering of that art.

REPLY OBJ. 1: There is a difference between universal and particular causes. A thing can escape the order of a particular cause; but not the order of a universal cause. For nothing escapes the order of a particular cause, except through the intervention and hindrance of some other particular cause; as, for instance, wood may be prevented from burning, by the action of water. Since then, all particular causes are included under the universal cause, it could not be that any effect should take place outside the range of that universal cause. So far then as an effect escapes the order of a particular cause, it is said to be casual or fortuitous in respect to that cause; but if we regard the universal cause, outside whose range no effect can happen, it is said to be foreseen. Thus, for instance, the meeting of two servants, although to them it appears a chance circumstance, has been fully foreseen by their master, who has purposely sent them to meet at the one place, in such a way that the one knows not about the other.

REPLY OBJ. 2: It is otherwise with one who has care of a particular thing, and one whose providence is universal, because a particular provider excludes all defects from what is subject to his care as far as he can; whereas, one who provides universally allows some little defect to remain, lest the good of the whole should be hindered. Hence, corruption and defects in natural things are said to be contrary

esse contra naturam particularem; sed tamen sunt de intentione naturae universalis, inquantum defectus unius cedit in bonum alterius, vel etiam totius universi; nam corruptio unius est generatio alterius, per quam species conservatur. Cum igitur Deus sit universalis provisor totius entis, ad ipsius providentiam pertinet ut permittat quosdam defectus esse in aliquibus particularibus rebus, ne impediatur bonum universi perfectum. Si enim omnia mala impedirentur, multa bona deessent universo, non enim esset vita leonis, si non esset occisio animalium; nec esset patientia martyrum, si non esset persecutio tyrannorum. Unde dicit Augustinus in Enchirid. *Deus omnipotens nullo modo sineret malum aliquod esse in operibus suis, nisi usque adeo esset omnipotens et bonus, ut bene faceret etiam de malo.* Ex his autem duabus rationibus quas nunc solvimus, videntur moti fuisse, qui divinae providentiae subtraxerunt corruptibilia, in quibus inveniuntur casualia et mala.

AD TERTIUM dicendum quod homo non est institutor naturae, sed utitur in operibus artis et virtutis, ad suum usum, rebus naturalibus. Unde providentia humana non se extendit ad necessaria, quae ex natura proveniunt. Ad quae tamen se extendit providentia Dei, qui est auctor naturae. Et ex hac ratione videntur moti fuisse, qui cursum rerum naturalium subtraxerunt divinae providentiae, attribuentes ipsum necessitati materiae; ut Democritus, et alii naturales antiqui.

AD QUARTUM dicendum quod in hoc quod dicitur Deum hominem sibi reliquisse, non excluditur homo a divina providentia, sed ostenditur quod non praefigitur ei virtus operativa determinata ad unum, sicut rebus naturalibus; quae aguntur tantum, quasi ab altero directae in finem, non autem seipsa agunt, quasi se dirigentia in finem, ut creaturae rationales per liberum arbitrium, quo consiliantur et eligunt. Unde signanter dicit, *in manu consilii sui.* Sed quia ipse actus liberi arbitrii reducitur in Deum sicut in causam, necesse est ut ea quae ex libero arbitrio fiunt, divinae providentiae subdantur, providentia enim hominis continetur sub providentia Dei, sicut causa particularis sub causa universali. Hominum autem iustorum quodam excellentiori modo Deus habet providentiam quam impiorum, inquantum non permittit contra eos evenire aliquid, quod finaliter impediat salutem eorum, nam *diligentibus Deum omnia cooperantur in bonum,* ut dicitur Rom. VIII. Sed ex hoc ipso quod impios non retrahit a malo culpae, dicitur eos dimittere. Non tamen ita, quod totaliter ab eius providentia excludantur, alioquin in nihilum deciderent, nisi per eius providentiam conservarentur. Et ex hac ratione

to some particular nature; yet they are in keeping with the plan of universal nature; inasmuch as the defect in one thing yields to the good of another, or even to the universal good: for the corruption of one is the generation of another, and through this it is that a species is kept in existence. Since God, then, provides universally for all being, it belongs to His providence to permit certain defects in particular effects, that the perfect good of the universe may not be hindered, for if all evil were prevented, much good would be absent from the universe. A lion would cease to live, if there were no slaying of animals; and there would be no patience of martyrs if there were no tyrannical persecution. Thus Augustine says (*Enchiridion* 2): *Almighty God would in no wise permit evil to exist in His works, unless He were so almighty and so good as to produce good even from evil.* It would appear that it was on account of these two arguments to which we have just replied, that some were persuaded to consider corruptible things—e.g., casual and evil things—as removed from the care of divine providence.

REPLY OBJ. 3: Man is not the author of nature; but he uses natural things in applying art and virtue to his own use. Hence human providence does not reach to that which takes place in nature from necessity; but divine providence extends thus far, since God is the author of nature. Apparently it was this argument that moved those who withdrew the course of nature from the care of divine providence, attributing it rather to the necessity of matter, as Democritus, and others of the ancients.

REPLY OBJ. 4: When it is said that God left man to himself, this does not mean that man is exempt from divine providence; but merely that he has not a prefixed operating force determined to only the one effect; as in the case of natural things, which are only acted upon as though directed by another towards an end; and do not act of themselves, as if they directed themselves towards an end, like rational creatures, through the possession of free will, by which these are able to take counsel and make a choice. Hence it is significantly said: *In the hand of his own counsel.* But since the very act of free will is traced to God as to a cause, it necessarily follows that everything happening from the exercise of free will must be subject to divine providence. For human providence is included under the providence of God, as a particular under a universal cause. God, however, extends His providence over the just in a certain more excellent way than over the wicked; inasmuch as He prevents anything happening which would impede their final salvation. For *to them that love God, all things work together unto good* (Rom 8:28). But from the fact that He does not restrain the wicked from the evil of sin, He is said to abandon them: not that He altogether withdraws His providence

videtur motus fuisse Tullius, qui res humanas, de quibus consiliamur, divinae providentiae subtraxit.

Ad quintum dicendum quod, quia creatura rationalis habet per liberum arbitrium dominium sui actus, ut dictum est, speciali quodam modo subditur divinae providentiae; ut scilicet ei imputetur aliquid ad culpam vel ad meritum, et reddatur ei aliquid ut poena vel praemium. Et quantum ad hoc curam Dei apostolus a bobus removet. Non tamen ita quod individua irrationalium creaturarum ad Dei providentiam non pertineant, ut Rabbi Moyses existimavit.

from them; otherwise they would return to nothing, if they were not preserved in existence by His providence. This was the reason that had weight with Tully, who withdrew from the care of divine providence human affairs concerning which we take counsel.

Reply Obj. 5: Since a rational creature has, through its free will, control over its actions, as was said above (Q. 19, A. 10), it is subject to divine providence in an especial manner, so that something is imputed to it as a fault, or as a merit; and there is given it accordingly something by way of punishment or reward. In this way, the Apostle withdraws oxen from the care of God: not, however, that individual irrational creatures escape the care of divine providence; as was the opinion of the Rabbi Moses.

Article 3

Whether God Has Immediate Providence Over Everything?

Ad tertium sic proceditur. Videtur quod Deus non immediate omnibus provideat. Quidquid enim est dignitatis, Deo est attribuendum. Sed ad dignitatem alicuius regis pertinet, quod habeat ministros, quibus mediantibus subditis provideat. Ergo multo magis Deus non immediate omnibus provideat.

Praeterea, ad providentiam pertinet res in finem ordinare. Finis autem cuiuslibet rei est eius perfectio et bonum. Ad quamlibet autem causam pertinet effectum suum perducere ad bonum. Quaelibet igitur causa agens est causa effectus providentiae. Si igitur Deus omnibus immediate providet, subtrahuntur omnes causae secundae.

Praeterea, Augustinus dicit, in Enchirid., quod *melius est quaedam nescire quam scire, ut vilia*, et idem dicit philosophus, in XII Metaphys. Sed omne quod est melius, Deo est attribuendum. Ergo Deus non habet immediate providentiam quorundam vilium et malorum.

Sed contra est quod dicitur Iob XXXIV, *quem constituit alium super terram? Aut quem posuit super orbem quem fabricatus est?* Super quo dicit Gregorius, *mundum per seipsum regit, quem per seipsum condidit.*

Respondeo dicendum quod ad providentiam duo pertinent, scilicet ratio ordinis rerum provisarum in finem; et executio huius ordinis, quae gubernatio dicitur. Quantum igitur ad primum horum, Deus immediate omnibus providet. Quia in suo intellectu habet rationem omnium, etiam minimorum, et quascumque causas aliquibus effectibus praefecit, dedit eis virtutem ad illos effectus producendos. Unde oportet quod ordinem

Objection 1: It seems that God has not immediate providence over all things. For whatever is contained in the notion of dignity, must be attributed to God. But it belongs to the dignity of a king, that he should have ministers; through whose mediation he provides for his subjects. Therefore much less has God Himself immediate providence over all things.

Obj. 2: Further, it belongs to providence to order all things to an end. Now the end of everything is its perfection and its good. But it appertains to every cause to direct its effect to good; wherefore every active cause is a cause of the effect of providence. If therefore God were to have immediate providence over all things, all secondary causes would be withdrawn.

Obj. 3: Further, Augustine says (*Enchiridion* 17) that, *It is better to be ignorant of some things than to know them, for example, vile things*: and the Philosopher says the same (*Metaph.* xii, 51). But whatever is better must be assigned to God. Therefore He has not immediate providence over bad and vile things.

On the contrary, It is said (Job 34:13): *What other hath He appointed over the earth? or whom hath He set over the world which He made?* On which passage Gregory says (*Moral.* xxiv, 20): *Himself He ruleth the world which He Himself hath made.*

I answer that, Two things belong to providence—namely, the type of the order of things foreordained towards an end; and the execution of this order, which is called government. As regards the first of these, God has immediate providence over everything, because He has in His intellect the types of everything, even the smallest; and whatsoever causes He assigns to certain effects, He gives them the power to produce those effects. Whence it must

illorum effectuum in sua ratione praehabuerit. Quantum autem ad secundum, sunt aliqua media divinae providentiae. Quia inferiora gubernat per superiora; non propter defectum suae virtutis, sed propter abundantiam suae bonitatis, ut dignitatem causalitatis etiam creaturis communicet. Et secundum hoc excluditur opinio Platonis, quam narrat Gregorius Nyssenus, triplicem providentiam ponentis. Quarum prima est summi Dei, qui primo et principaliter providet rebus spiritualibus; et consequenter toti mundo, quantum ad genera, species et causas universales. Secunda vero providentia est, qua providetur singularibus generabilium et corruptibilium, et hanc attribuit diis qui circumeunt caelos, idest substantiis separatis, quae movent corpora caelestia circulariter. Tertia vero providentia est rerum humanarum, quam attribuebat Daemonibus, quos Platonici ponebant medios inter nos et deos, ut narrat Augustinus IX de Civ. Dei.

Ad primum ergo dicendum quod habere ministros executores suae providentiae, pertinet ad dignitatem regis, sed quod non habeat rationem eorum quae per eos agenda sunt, est ex defectu ipsius. Omnis enim scientia operativa tanto perfectior est, quanto magis particularia considerat, in quibus est actus.

Ad secundum dicendum quod per hoc quod Deus habet immediate providentiam de rebus omnibus, non excluduntur causae secundae, quae sunt executrices huius ordinis, ut ex supra dictis patet.

Ad tertium dicendum quod nobis melius est non cognoscere mala et vilia, inquantum per ea impedimur a consideratione meliorum, quia non possumus simul multa intelligere, et inquantum cogitatio malorum pervertit interdum voluntatem in malum. Sed hoc non habet locum in Deo, qui simul omnia uno intuitu videt, et cuius voluntas ad malum flecti non potest.

be that He has beforehand the type of those effects in His mind. As to the second, there are certain intermediaries of God's providence; for He governs things inferior by superior, not on account of any defect in His power, but by reason of the abundance of His goodness; so that the dignity of causality is imparted even to creatures. Thus Plato's opinion, as narrated by Gregory of Nyssa (*De Provid.* viii, 3), is exploded. He taught a threefold providence. First, one which belongs to the supreme Deity, Who first and foremost has provision over spiritual things, and thus over the whole world as regards genus, species, and universal causes. The second providence, which is over the individuals of all that can be generated and corrupted, he attributed to the divinities who circulate in the heavens; that is, certain separate substances, which move corporeal things in a circular direction. The third providence, over human affairs, he assigned to demons, whom the Platonic philosophers placed between us and the gods, as Augustine tells us (*De Civ. Dei*, 1, 2: viii, 14).

Reply Obj. 1: It pertains to a king's dignity to have ministers who execute his providence. But the fact that he has not the plan of those things which are done by them arises from a deficiency in himself. For every operative science is the more perfect, the more it considers the particular things with which its action is concerned.

Reply Obj. 2: God's immediate provision over everything does not exclude the action of secondary causes; which are the executors of His order, as was said above (Q. 19, AA. 5, 8).

Reply Obj. 3: It is better for us not to know low and vile things, because by them we are impeded in our knowledge of what is better and higher; for we cannot understand many things simultaneously; because the thought of evil sometimes perverts the will towards evil. This does not hold with God, Who sees everything simultaneously at one glance, and whose will cannot turn in the direction of evil.

Article 4

Whether Providence Imposes Any Necessity on Things Foreseen?

Ad quartum sic proceditur. Videtur quod divina providentia necessitatem rebus provisis imponat. Omnis enim effectus qui habet aliquam causam per se, quae iam est vel fuit, ad quam de necessitate sequitur, provenit ex necessitate, ut philosophus probat in VI Metaphys. Sed providentia Dei, cum sit aeterna, praeexistit; et ad eam sequitur effectus de necessitate; non enim potest divina providentia frustrari. Ergo providentia divina necessitatem rebus provisis imponit.

Praeterea, unusquisque provisor stabilit opus suum quantum potest, ne deficiat. Sed Deus est summe

Objection 1: It seems that divine providence imposes necessity upon things foreseen. For every effect that has a per se cause, either present or past, which it necessarily follows, happens from necessity; as the Philosopher proves (*Metaph.* vi, 7). But the providence of God, since it is eternal, pre-exists; and the effect flows from it of necessity, for divine providence cannot be frustrated. Therefore divine providence imposes a necessity upon things foreseen.

Obj. 2: Further, every provider makes his work as stable as he can, lest it should fail. But God is most powerful.

potens. Ergo necessitatis firmitatem rebus a se provisis tribuit.

Praeterea, Boetius dicit, IV de Consol., quod fatum, *ab immobilis providentiae proficiscens exordiis, actus fortunasque hominum indissolubili causarum connexione constringit.* Videtur ergo quod providentia necessitatem rebus provisis imponat.

Sed contra est quod dicit Dionysius, IV cap. de Div. Nom., quod *corrumpere naturam non est providentiae.* Hoc autem habet quarundam rerum natura, quod sint contingentia. Non igitur divina providentia necessitatem rebus imponit, contingentiam excludens.

Respondeo dicendum quod providentia divina quibusdam rebus necessitatem imponit, non autem omnibus, ut quidam crediderunt. Ad providentiam enim pertinet ordinare res in finem. Post bonitatem autem divinam, quae est finis a rebus separatus, principale bonum in ipsis rebus existens, est perfectio universi, quae quidem non esset, si non omnes gradus essendi invenirentur in rebus. Unde ad divinam providentiam pertinet omnes gradus entium producere. Et ideo quibusdam effectibus praeparavit causas necessarias, ut necessario evenirent; quibusdam vero causas contingentes, ut evenirent contingenter, secundum conditionem proximarum causarum.

Ad primum ergo dicendum quod effectus divinae providentiae non solum est aliquid evenire quocumque modo; sed aliquid evenire vel contingenter vel necessario. Et ideo evenit infallibiliter et necessario, quod divina providentia disponit evenire infallibiliter et necessario, et evenit contingenter, quod divinae providentiae ratio habet ut contingenter eveniat.

Ad secundum dicendum quod in hoc est immobilis et certus divinae providentiae ordo, quod ea quae ab ipso providentur, cuncta eveniunt eo modo quo ipse providet, sive necessario sive contingenter.

Ad tertium dicendum quod indissolubilitas illa et immutabilitas quam Boetius tangit, pertinet ad certitudinem providentiae, quae non deficit a suo effectu, neque a modo eveniendi quem providit, non autem pertinet ad necessitatem effectuum. Et considerandum est quod necessarium et contingens proprie consequuntur ens, inquantum huiusmodi. Unde modus contingentiae et necessitatis cadit sub provisione Dei, qui est universalis provisor totius entis, non autem sub provisione aliquorum particularium provisorum.

Therefore He assigns the stability of necessity to things provided.

Obj. 3: Further, Boethius says (*De Consol.* iv, 6): *Fate from the immutable source of providence binds together human acts and fortunes by the indissoluble connection of causes.* It seems therefore that providence imposes necessity upon things foreseen.

On the contrary, Dionysius says that (*Div. Nom.* iv, 23) *to corrupt nature is not the work of providence.* But it is in the nature of some things to be contingent. Divine providence does not therefore impose any necessity upon things so as to destroy their contingency.

I answer that, Divine providence imposes necessity upon some things; not upon all, as some formerly believed. For to providence it belongs to order things towards an end. Now after the divine goodness, which is an extrinsic end to all things, the principal good in things themselves is the perfection of the universe; which would not be, were not all grades of being found in things. Whence it pertains to divine providence to produce every grade of being. And thus it has prepared for some things necessary causes, so that they happen of necessity; for others contingent causes, that they may happen by contingency, according to the nature of their proximate causes.

Reply Obj. 1: The effect of divine providence is not only that things should happen somehow; but that they should happen either by necessity or by contingency. Therefore whatsoever divine providence ordains to happen infallibly and of necessity happens infallibly and of necessity; and that happens from contingency, which the plan of divine providence conceives to happen from contingency.

Reply Obj. 2: The order of divine providence is unchangeable and certain, so far as all things foreseen happen as they have been foreseen, whether from necessity or from contingency.

Reply Obj. 3: That indissolubility and unchangeableness of which Boethius speaks, pertain to the certainty of providence, which fails not to produce its effect, and that in the way foreseen; but they do not pertain to the necessity of the effects. We must remember that properly speaking *necessary* and *contingent* are consequent upon being, as such. Hence the mode both of necessity and of contingency falls under the foresight of God, who provides universally for all being; not under the foresight of causes that provide only for some particular order of things.

Question 23

Predestination

Post considerationem divinae providentiae, agendum est de praedestinatione, et de libro vitae.

Et circa praedestinationem quaeruntur octo.

Primo, utrum Deo conveniat praedestinatio.

Secundo, quid sit praedestinatio; et utrum ponat aliquid in praedestinato.

Tertio, utrum Deo competat reprobatio aliquorum hominum.

Quarto, de comparatione praedestinationis ad electionem; utrum scilicet praedestinati eligantur.

Quinto, utrum merita sint causa vel ratio praedestinationis, vel reprobationis, aut electionis.

Sexto, de certitudine praedestinationis; utrum scilicet praedestinati infallibiliter salventur.

Septimo, utrum numerus praedestinatorum sit certus.

Octavo, utrum praedestinatio possit iuvari precibus sanctorum.

After consideration of divine providence, we must treat of predestination and the book of life.

Concerning predestination there are eight points of inquiry:

(1) Whether predestination is suitably attributed to God?

(2) What is predestination, and whether it places anything in the predestined?

(3) Whether to God belongs the reprobation of some men?

(4) On the comparison of predestination to election; whether, that is to say, the predestined are chosen?

(5) Whether merits are the cause or reason of predestination, or reprobation, or election?

(6) Of the certainty of predestination; whether the predestined will infallibly be saved?

(7) Whether the number of the predestined is certain?

(8) Whether predestination can be furthered by the prayers of the saints?

Article 1

Whether Men Are Predestined by God?

Ad primum sic proceditur. Videtur quod homines non praedestinentur a Deo. Dicit enim Damascenus, in II libro, *oportet cognoscere quod omnia quidem praecognoscit Deus, non autem omnia praedeterminat. Praecognoscit enim ea quae in nobis sunt; non autem praedeterminat ea.* Sed merita et demerita humana sunt in nobis, inquantum sumus nostrorum actuum domini per liberum arbitrium. Ea ergo quae pertinent ad meritum vel demeritum, non praedestinantur a Deo. Et sic hominum praedestinatio tollitur.

Praeterea, omnes creaturae ordinantur ad suos fines per divinam providentiam, ut supra dictum est. Sed aliae creaturae non dicuntur praedestinari a Deo. Ergo nec homines.

Praeterea, Angeli sunt capaces beatitudinis, sicut et homines. Sed Angelis non competit praedestinari, ut videtur, cum in eis nunquam fuerit miseria; praedestinatio autem *est propositum miserendi,* ut dicit Augustinus. Ergo homines non praedestinantur.

Objection 1: It seems that men are not predestined by God, for Damascene says (*De Fide Orth.* ii, 30): *It must be borne in mind that God foreknows but does not predetermine everything, since He foreknows all that is in us, but does not predetermine it all.* But human merit and demerit are in us, forasmuch as we are the masters of our own acts by free will. All that pertains therefore to merit or demerit is not predestined by God; and thus man's predestination is done away.

Obj. 2: Further, all creatures are directed to their end by divine providence, as was said above (Q. 22, AA. 1, 2). But other creatures are not said to be predestined by God. Therefore neither are men.

Obj. 3: Further, the angels are capable of beatitude, as well as men. But predestination is not suitable to angels, since in them there never was any unhappiness; for predestination, as Augustine says (*De praedest. sanct.* 17), is the *purpose to take pity.* Therefore men are not predestined.

PRAETEREA, beneficia hominibus a Deo collata, per spiritum sanctum viris sanctis revelantur, secundum illud apostoli, I Cor. II, *nos autem non spiritum huius mundi accepimus, sed spiritum qui ex Deo est, ut sciamus quae a Deo donata sunt nobis.* Si ergo homines praedestinarentur a Deo, cum praedestinatio sit Dei beneficium, esset praedestinatis nota sua praedestinatio. Quod patet esse falsum.

SED CONTRA est quod dicitur Rom. VIII, *quos praedestinavit, hos et vocavit.*

RESPONDEO dicendum quod Deo conveniens est homines praedestinare. Omnia enim divinae providentiae subiacent, ut supra ostensum est. Ad providentiam autem pertinet res in finem ordinare, ut dictum est. Finis autem ad quem res creatae ordinantur a Deo, est duplex. Unus, qui excedit proportionem naturae creatae et facultatem, et hic finis est vita aeterna, quae in divina visione consistit, quae est supra naturam cuiuslibet creaturae, ut supra habitum est. Alius autem finis est naturae creatae proportionatus, quem scilicet res creata potest attingere secundum virtutem suae naturae. Ad illud autem ad quod non potest aliquid virtute suae naturae pervenire, oportet quod ab alio transmittatur; sicut sagitta a sagittante mittitur ad signum. Unde, proprie loquendo, rationalis creatura, quae est capax vitae aeternae, perducitur in ipsam quasi a Deo transmissa. Cuius quidem transmissionis ratio in Deo praeexistit; sicut et in eo est ratio ordinis omnium in finem, quam diximus esse providentiam. Ratio autem alicuius fiendi in mente actoris existens, est quaedam praeexistentia rei fiendae in eo. Unde ratio praedictae transmissionis creaturae rationalis in finem vitae aeternae, praedestinatio nominatur, nam destinare est mittere. Et sic patet quod praedestinatio, quantum ad obiecta, est quaedam pars providentiae.

AD PRIMUM ergo dicendum quod Damascenus nominat praedeterminationem impositionem necessitatis; sicut est in rebus naturalibus, quae sunt praedeterminatae ad unum. Quod patet ex eo quod subdit, *non enim vult malitiam, neque compellit virtutem.* Unde praedestinatio non excluditur.

AD SECUNDUM dicendum quod creaturae irrationales non sunt capaces illius finis qui facultatem humanae naturae excedit. Unde non proprie dicuntur praedestinari, etsi aliquando abusive praedestinatio nominetur respectu cuiuscumque alterius finis.

AD TERTIUM dicendum quod praedestinari convenit Angelis, sicut et hominibus, licet nunquam fuerint miseri. Nam motus non accipit speciem a termino a quo, sed a termino ad quem, nihil enim refert, quantum ad rationem dealbationis, utrum ille qui dealbatur, fuerit niger aut pallidus vel rubeus. Et similiter nihil refert ad rationem praedestinationis, utrum aliquis praedestinetur in vitam aeternam a statu miseriae, vel non. Quamvis

OBJ. 4: Further, the benefits God confers upon men are revealed by the Holy Spirit to holy men according to the saying of the Apostle (1 Cor 2:12): *Now we have received not the spirit of this world, but the Spirit that is of God: that we may know the things that are given us from God.* Therefore if man were predestined by God, since predestination is a benefit from God, his predestination would be made known to each predestined; which is clearly false.

ON THE CONTRARY, It is written (Rom 8:30): *Whom He predestined, them He also called.*

I ANSWER THAT, It is fitting that God should predestine men. For all things are subject to His providence, as was shown above (Q. 22, A. 2). Now it belongs to providence to direct things towards their end, as was also said (Q. 22, AA. 1, 2). The end towards which created things are directed by God is twofold; one which exceeds all proportion and faculty of created nature; and this end is life eternal, that consists in seeing God which is above the nature of every creature, as shown above (Q. 12, A. 4). The other end, however, is proportionate to created nature, to which end created being can attain according to the power of its nature. Now if a thing cannot attain to something by the power of its nature, it must be directed thereto by another; thus, an arrow is directed by the archer towards a mark. Hence, properly speaking, a rational creature, capable of eternal life, is led towards it, directed, as it were, by God. The reason of that direction pre-exists in God; as in Him is the type of the order of all things towards an end, which we proved above to be providence. Now the type in the mind of the doer of something to be done, is a kind of pre-existence in him of the thing to be done. Hence the type of the aforesaid direction of a rational creature towards the end of life eternal is called predestination. For to destine, is to direct or send. Thus it is clear that predestination, as regards its objects, is a part of providence.

REPLY OBJ. 1: Damascene calls predestination an imposition of necessity, after the manner of natural things which are predetermined towards one end. This is clear from his adding: *He does not will malice, nor does He compel virtue.* Whence predestination is not excluded by Him.

REPLY OBJ. 2: Irrational creatures are not capable of that end which exceeds the faculty of human nature. Whence they cannot be properly said to be predestined; although improperly the term is used in respect of any other end.

REPLY OBJ. 3: Predestination applies to angels, just as it does to men, although they have never been unhappy. For movement does not take its species from the term wherefrom but from the term whereto. Because it matters nothing, in respect of the notion of making white, whether he who is made white was before black, yellow or red. Likewise it matters nothing in respect of the notion of predestination whether one is predestined to life eternal from the state of

dici possit quod omnis collatio boni supra debitum eius cui confertur, ad misericordiam pertineat, ut supra dictum est.

AD QUARTUM dicendum quod, etiam si aliquibus ex speciali privilegio sua praedestinatio reveletur, non tamen convenit ut reveletur omnibus, quia sic illi qui non sunt praedestinati, desperarent; et securitas in praedestinatis negligentiam pareret.

misery or not. Although it may be said that every conferring of good above that which is due pertains to mercy; as was shown previously (Q. 21, AA. 3, 4).

REPLY OBJ. 4: Even if by a special privilege their predestination were revealed to some, it is not fitting that it should be revealed to everyone; because, if so, those who were not predestined would despair; and security would beget negligence in the predestined.

Article 2

Whether Predestination Places Anything in the Predestined?

AD SECUNDUM SIC PROCEDITUR. Videtur quod praedestinatio ponat aliquid in praedestinato. Omnis enim actio ex se passionem infert. Si ergo praedestinatio actio est in Deo, oportet quod praedestinatio passio sit in praedestinatis.

PRAETEREA, Origenes dicit, super illud Rom. I, *qui praedestinatus est etc., praedestinatio est eius qui non est, sed destinatio eius est qui est*. Sed Augustinus dicit, in libro de praedestinatione sanctorum, *quid est praedestinatio, nisi destinatio alicuius?* Ergo praedestinatio non est nisi alicuius existentis. Et ita ponit aliquid in praedestinato.

PRAETEREA, praeparatio est aliquid in praeparato. Sed praedestinatio est praeparatio beneficiorum Dei, ut dicit Augustinus, in libro de Praedest. Sanct. Ergo praedestinatio est aliquid in praedestinatis.

PRAETEREA, temporale non ponitur in definitione aeterni. Sed gratia, quae est aliquid temporale, ponitur in definitione praedestinationis, nam praedestinatio dicitur esse *praeparatio gratiae in praesenti, et gloriae in futuro*. Ergo praedestinatio non est aliquid aeternum. Et ita oportet quod non sit in Deo, sed in praedestinatis, nam quidquid est in Deo, est aeternum.

SED CONTRA est quod Augustinus dicit, quod *praedestinatio est praescientia beneficiorum Dei*. Sed praescientia non est in praescitis, sed in praesciente. Ergo nec praedestinatio est in praedestinatis, sed in praedestinante.

RESPONDEO dicendum quod praedestinatio non est aliquid in praedestinatis, sed in praedestinante tantum. Dictum est enim quod praedestinatio est quaedam pars providentiae providentia autem non est in rebus provisis; sed est quaedam ratio in intellectu provisoris, ut supra dictum est. Sed executio providentiae, quae gubernatio dicitur, passive quidem est in gubernatis; active autem est in gubernante. Unde manifestum est quod praedestinatio est quaedam ratio ordinis aliquorum in salutem aeternam, in mente divina existens. Executio

OBJECTION 1: It seems that predestination does place something in the predestined. For every action of itself causes passion. If therefore predestination is action in God, predestination must be passion in the predestined.

OBJ. 2: Further, Origen says on the text, *He who was predestined*, etc. (Rom 1:4): *Predestination is of one who is not; destination, of one who is.* And Augustine says (*De Praed. Sanct.*): *What is predestination but the destination of one who is?* Therefore predestination is only of one who actually exists; and it thus places something in the predestined.

OBJ. 3: Further, preparation is something in the thing prepared. But predestination is the preparation of God's benefits, as Augustine says (*De Praed. Sanct.* ii, 14). Therefore predestination is something in the predestined.

OBJ. 4: Further, nothing temporal enters into the definition of eternity. But grace, which is something temporal, is found in the definition of predestination. For predestination is the preparation of grace in the present; and of glory in the future. Therefore predestination is not anything eternal. So it must needs be that it is in the predestined, and not in God; for whatever is in Him is eternal.

ON THE CONTRARY, Augustine says (*De Praed. Sanct.* ii, 14) that *predestination is the foreknowledge of God's benefits*. But foreknowledge is not in the things foreknown, but in the person who foreknows them. Therefore, predestination is in the one who predestines, and not in the predestined.

I ANSWER THAT, Predestination is not anything in the predestined; but only in the person who predestines. We have said above that predestination is a part of providence. Now providence is not anything in the things provided for; but is a type in the mind of the provider, as was proved above (Q. 22, A. 1). But the execution of providence which is called government, is in a passive way in the thing governed, and in an active way in the governor. Whence it is clear that predestination is a kind of type of the ordering of some persons towards eternal salvation, existing in

autem huius ordinis est passive quidem in praedestinatis; active autem est in Deo. Est autem executio praedestinationis vocatio et magnificatio, secundum illud apostoli, ad Rom. VIII, *quos praedestinavit, hos et vocavit; et quos vocavit, hos et magnificavit.*

AD PRIMUM ergo dicendum quod actiones in exteriorem materiam transeuntes, inferunt ex se passionem, ut calefactio et secatio, non autem actiones in agente manentes, ut sunt intelligere et velle, ut supra dictum est. Et talis actio est praedestinatio. Unde praedestinatio non ponit aliquid in praedestinato. Sed executio eius, quae transit in exteriores res, ponit in eis aliquem effectum.

AD SECUNDUM dicendum quod destinatio aliquando sumitur pro reali missione alicuius ad aliquem terminum, et sic destinatio non est nisi eius quod est. Alio modo sumitur destinatio pro missione quam aliquis mente concipit, secundum quod dicimur destinare, quod mente firmiter proponimus, et hoc secundo modo dicitur II Machab. cap. VI, *Eleazarus destinavit non admittere illicita propter vitae amorem.* Et sic destinatio potest esse eius quod non est. Tamen praedestinatio, ratione antecessionis quam importat, potest esse eius quod non est, qualitercumque destinatio sumatur.

AD TERTIUM dicendum quod duplex est praeparatio. Quaedam patientis, ut patiatur, et haec praeparatio est in praeparato. Quaedam alia est agentis, ut agat, et haec est in agente. Et talis praeparatio est praedestinatio; prout aliquod agens per intellectum dicitur se praeparare ad agendum, inquantum praeconcipit rationem operis fiendi. Et sic Deus ab aeterno praeparavit praedestinando, concipiens rationem ordinis aliquorum in salutem.

AD QUARTUM dicendum quod gratia non ponitur in definitione praedestinationis, quasi aliquid existens de essentia eius, sed inquantum praedestinatio importat respectum ad gratiam, ut causae ad effectum, et actus ad obiectum. Unde non sequitur quod praedestinatio sit aliquid temporale.

the divine mind. The execution, however, of this order is in a passive way in the predestined, but actively in God. The execution of predestination is the calling and magnification; according to the Apostle (Rom 8:30): *Whom He predestined, them He also called and whom He called, them He also magnified.*

REPLY OBJ. 1: Actions passing out to external matter imply of themselves passion—for example, the actions of warming and cutting; but not so actions remaining in the agent, as understanding and willing, as said above (Q. 14, A. 2; Q. 18, A. 3, ad 1). Predestination is an action of this latter class. Wherefore, it does not put anything in the predestined. But its execution, which passes out to external things, has an effect in them.

REPLY OBJ. 2: Destination sometimes denotes a real mission of someone to a given end; thus, destination can only be said of someone actually existing. It is taken, however, in another sense for a mission which a person conceives in the mind; and in this manner we are said to destine a thing which we firmly propose in our mind. In this latter way it is said that Eleazar *determined not to do any unlawful things for the love of life* (2 Macc 6:20). Thus destination can be of a thing which does not exist. Predestination, however, by reason of the antecedent nature it implies, can be attributed to a thing which does not actually exist; in whatsoever way destination is accepted.

REPLY OBJ. 3: Preparation is twofold: of the patient in respect to passion, and this is in the thing prepared; and of the agent to action, and this is in the agent. Such a preparation is predestination, and as an agent by intellect is said to prepare itself to act, accordingly as it preconceives the idea of what is to be done. Thus, God from all eternity prepared by predestination, conceiving the idea of the order of some towards salvation.

REPLY OBJ. 4: Grace does not come into the definition of predestination, as something belonging to its essence, but inasmuch as predestination implies a relation to grace, as of cause to effect, and of act to its object. Whence it does not follow that predestination is anything temporal.

Article 3

Whether God Reprobates Any Man?

AD TERTIUM SIC PROCEDITUR. Videtur quod Deus nullum hominem reprobet. Nullus enim reprobat quem diligit. Sed Deus omnem hominem diligit, secundum illud Sap. XI, *diligis omnia quae sunt, et nihil odisti eorum quae fecisti.* Ergo Deus nullum hominem reprobat.

PRAETEREA, si Deus aliquem hominem reprobat, oportet quod sic se habeat reprobatio ad reprobatos,

OBJECTION 1: It seems that God reprobates no man. For nobody reprobates what he loves. But God loves every man, according to (Wis 11:25): *Thou lovest all things that are, and Thou hatest none of the things Thou hast made.* Therefore God reprobates no man.

OBJ. 2: Further, if God reprobates any man, it would be necessary for reprobation to have the same relation to

sicut praedestinatio ad praedestinatos. Sed praedestinatio est causa salutis praedestinatorum. Ergo reprobatio erit causa perditionis reproborum. Hoc autem est falsum, dicitur enim Osee XIII, *perditio tua, Israel, ex te est; tantummodo ex me auxilium tuum.* Non ergo Deus aliquem reprobat.

PRAETEREA, nulli debet imputari quod vitare non potest. Sed si Deus aliquem reprobat, non potest vitare quin ipse pereat, dicitur enim Eccle. VII, *considera opera Dei, quod nemo possit corrigere quem ipse despexerit.* Ergo non esset hominibus imputandum quod pereunt. Hoc autem est falsum. Non ergo Deus aliquem reprobat.

SED CONTRA est quod dicitur Malach. I, *Iacob dilexi, Esau autem odio habui.*

RESPONDEO dicendum quod Deus aliquos reprobat. Dictum enim est supra quod praedestinatio est pars providentiae. Ad providentiam autem pertinet permittere aliquem defectum in rebus quae providentiae subduntur, ut supra dictum est. Unde, cum per divinam providentiam homines in vitam aeternam ordinentur, pertinet etiam ad divinam providentiam, ut permittat aliquos ab isto fine deficere. Et hoc dicitur reprobare. Sic igitur, sicut praedestinatio est pars providentiae respectu eorum qui divinitus ordinantur in aeternam salutem; ita reprobatio est pars providentiae respectu illorum qui ab hoc fine decidunt. Unde reprobatio non nominat praescientiam tantum, sed aliquid addit secundum rationem, sicut et providentia, ut supra dictum est. Sicut enim praedestinatio includit voluntatem conferendi gratiam et gloriam, ita reprobatio includit voluntatem permittendi aliquem cadere in culpam, et inferendi damnationis poenam pro culpa.

AD PRIMUM ergo dicendum quod Deus omnes homines diligit, et etiam omnes creaturas, inquantum omnibus vult aliquod bonum, non tamen quodcumque bonum vult omnibus. Inquantum igitur quibusdam non vult hoc bonum quod est vita aeterna, dicitur eos habere odio, vel reprobare.

AD SECUNDUM dicendum quod aliter se habet reprobatio in causando, quam praedestinatio. Nam praedestinatio est causa et eius quod expectatur in futura vita a praedestinatis, scilicet gloriae; et eius quod percipitur in praesenti, scilicet gratiae. Reprobatio vero non est causa eius quod est in praesenti, scilicet culpae; sed est causa derelictionis a Deo. Est tamen causa eius quod redditur in futuro, scilicet poenae aeternae. Sed culpa provenit ex libero arbitrio eius qui reprobatur et a gratia deseritur. Et secundum hoc verificatur dictum prophetae, scilicet, *perditio tua, Israel, ex te.*

AD TERTIUM dicendum quod reprobatio Dei non subtrahit aliquid de potentia reprobati. Unde, cum dicitur quod reprobatus non potest gratiam adipisci, non est hoc intelligendum secundum impossibilitatem

the reprobates as predestination has to the predestined. But predestination is the cause of the salvation of the predestined. Therefore reprobation will likewise be the cause of the loss of the reprobate. But this false. For it is said (Hos 13:9): *Destruction is thy own, O Israel; Thy help is only in Me.* God does not, then, reprobate any man.

OBJ. 3: Further, to no one ought anything be imputed which he cannot avoid. But if God reprobates anyone, that one must perish. For it is said (Eccl 7:14): *Consider the works of God, that no man can correct whom He hath despised.* Therefore it could not be imputed to any man, were he to perish. But this is false. Therefore God does not reprobate anyone.

ON THE CONTRARY, It is said (Mal 1:2,3): *I have loved Jacob, but have hated Esau.*

I ANSWER THAT, God does reprobate some. For it was said above (A. 1) that predestination is a part of providence. To providence, however, it belongs to permit certain defects in those things which are subject to providence, as was said above (Q. 22, A. 2). Thus, as men are ordained to eternal life through the providence of God, it likewise is part of that providence to permit some to fall away from that end; this is called reprobation. Thus, as predestination is a part of providence, in regard to those ordained to eternal salvation, so reprobation is a part of providence in regard to those who turn aside from that end. Hence reprobation implies not only foreknowledge, but also something more, as does providence, as was said above (Q. 22, A. 1). Therefore, as predestination includes the will to confer grace and glory; so also reprobation includes the will to permit a person to fall into sin, and to impose the punishment of damnation on account of that sin.

REPLY OBJ. 1: God loves all men and all creatures, inasmuch as He wishes them all some good; but He does not wish every good to them all. So far, therefore, as He does not wish this particular good—namely, eternal life—He is said to hate or reprobate them.

REPLY OBJ. 2: Reprobation differs in its causality from predestination. This latter is the cause both of what is expected in the future life by the predestined—namely, glory—and of what is received in this life—namely, grace. Reprobation, however, is not the cause of what is in the present—namely, sin; but it is the cause of abandonment by God. It is the cause, however, of what is assigned in the future—namely, eternal punishment. But guilt proceeds from the free-will of the person who is reprobated and deserted by grace. In this way, the word of the prophet is true—namely, *Destruction is thy own, O Israel.*

REPLY OBJ. 3: Reprobation by God does not take anything away from the power of the person reprobated. Hence, when it is said that the reprobated cannot obtain grace, this must not be understood as implying absolute

absolutam, sed secundum impossibilitatem conditionatam, sicut supra dictum est quod praedestinatum necesse est salvari, necessitate conditionata, quae non tollit libertatem arbitrii. Unde, licet aliquis non possit gratiam adipisci qui reprobatur a Deo, tamen quod in hoc peccatum vel illud labatur, ex eius libero arbitrio contingit. Unde et merito sibi imputatur in culpam.

impossibility: but only conditional impossibility: as was said above (Q. 19, A. 3), that the predestined must necessarily be saved; yet a conditional necessity, which does not do away with the liberty of choice. Whence, although anyone reprobated by God cannot acquire grace, nevertheless that he falls into this or that particular sin comes from the use of his free-will. Hence it is rightly imputed to him as guilt.

Article 4

Whether the Predestined Are Chosen by God?

AD QUARTUM SIC PROCEDITUR. Videtur quod praedestinati non eligantur a Deo. Dicit enim Dionysius, IV cap. de Div. Nom., quod, sicut sol corporeus non eligendo omnibus corporibus lumen immittit, ita et Deus suam bonitatem. Sed bonitas divina communicatur praecipue aliquibus secundum participationem gratiae et gloriae. Ergo Deus absque electione gratiam et gloriam communicat. Quod ad praedestinationem pertinet.

PRAETEREA, electio est eorum quae sunt. Sed praedestinatio ab aeterno est etiam eorum quae non sunt. Ergo praedestinantur aliqui absque electione.

PRAETEREA, electio quandam discretionem importat. *Sed Deus vult omnes homines salvos fieri*, ut dicitur I Tim. II. Ergo praedestinatio, quae praeordinat homines in salutem, est absque electione.

SED CONTRA est quod dicitur Ephes. I, *elegit nos in ipso ante mundi constitutionem.*

RESPONDEO dicendum quod praedestinatio, secundum rationem, praesupponit electionem; et electio dilectionem. Cuius ratio est, quia praedestinatio, ut dictum est, est pars providentiae. Providentia autem, sicut et prudentia, est ratio in intellectu existens, praeceptiva ordinationis aliquorum in finem, ut supra dictum est. Non autem praecipitur aliquid ordinandum in finem, nisi praeexistente voluntate finis. Unde praedestinatio aliquorum in salutem aeternam, praesupponit, secundum rationem, quod Deus illorum velit salutem. Ad quod pertinet electio et dilectio. Dilectio quidem, inquantum vult eis hoc bonum salutis aeternae, nam diligere est velle alicui bonum, ut supra dictum est. Electio autem, inquantum hoc bonum aliquibus prae aliis vult, cum quosdam reprobet, ut supra dictum est. Electio tamen et dilectio aliter ordinantur in nobis et in Deo, eo quod in nobis voluntas diligendo non causat bonum; sed ex bono praeexistente incitamur ad diligendum. Et ideo eligimus aliquem, quem diligamus, et sic electio dilectionem praecedit in nobis. In Deo autem est e converso. Nam voluntas eius, qua vult bonum alicui diligendo, est causa quod illud bonum ab eo prae aliis habeatur. Et sic

OBJECTION 1: It seems that the predestined are not chosen by God. For Dionysius says (*Div. Nom.* iv, 1) that as the corporeal sun sends his rays upon all without selection, so does God His goodness. But the goodness of God is communicated to some in an especial manner through a participation of grace and glory. Therefore God without any selection communicates His grace and glory; and this belongs to predestination.

OBJ. 2: Further, election is of things that exist. But predestination from all eternity is also of things which do not exist. Therefore, some are predestined without election.

OBJ. 3: Further, election implies some discrimination. Now God *wills all men to be saved* (1 Tim 2:4). Therefore, predestination which ordains men towards eternal salvation, is without election.

ON THE CONTRARY, It is said (Eph 1:4): *He chose us in Him before the foundation of the world.*

I ANSWER THAT, Predestination presupposes election in the order of reason; and election presupposes love. The reason of this is that predestination, as stated above (A. 1), is a part of providence. Now providence, as also prudence, is the plan existing in the intellect directing the ordering of some things towards an end; as was proved above (Q. 22, A. 2). But nothing is directed towards an end unless the will for that end already exists. Whence the predestination of some to eternal salvation presupposes, in the order of reason, that God wills their salvation; and to this belong both election and love:—love, inasmuch as He wills them this particular good of eternal salvation; since to love is to wish well to anyone, as stated above (Q. 20, AA. 2 ,3):—election, inasmuch as He wills this good to some in preference to others; since He reprobates some, as stated above (A. 3). Election and love, however, are differently ordered in God, and in ourselves: because in us the will in loving does not cause good, but we are incited to love by the good which already exists; and therefore we choose someone to love, and so election in us precedes love. In God, however, it is the reverse. For His will, by which in loving He wishes good to someone, is the cause of that good possessed by

patet quod dilectio praesupponitur electioni, secundum rationem; et electio praedestinationi. Unde omnes praedestinati sunt electi et dilecti.

AD PRIMUM ergo dicendum quod, si consideretur communicatio bonitatis divinae in communi, absque electione bonitatem suam communicat; inquantum scilicet nihil est, quod non participet aliquid de bonitate eius, ut supra dictum est. Sed si consideretur communicatio istius vel illius boni, non absque electione tribuit, quia quaedam bona dat aliquibus, quae non dat aliis. Et sic in collatione gratiae et gloriae attenditur electio.

AD SECUNDUM dicendum quod, quando voluntas eligentis provocatur ad eligendum a bono in re praeexistente, tunc oportet quod electio sit eorum quae sunt; sicut accidit in electione nostra. Sed in Deo est aliter, ut dictum est. Et ideo, sicut dicit Augustinus, *eliguntur a Deo qui non sunt, neque tamen errat qui eligit.*

AD TERTIUM dicendum quod, sicut supra dictum est, Deus vult omnes homines salvos fieri antecedenter, quod non est simpliciter velle, sed secundum quid, non autem consequenter, quod est simpliciter velle.

some in preference to others. Thus it is clear that love precedes election in the order of reason, and election precedes predestination. Whence all the predestinate are objects of election and love.

REPLY OBJ. 1: If the communication of the divine goodness in general be considered, God communicates His goodness without election; inasmuch as there is nothing which does not in some way share in His goodness, as we said above (Q. 6, A. 4). But if we consider the communication of this or that particular good, He does not allot it without election; since He gives certain goods to some men, which He does not give to others. Thus in the conferring of grace and glory election is implied.

REPLY OBJ. 2: When the will of the person choosing is incited to make a choice by the good already pre-existing in the object chosen, the choice must needs be of those things which already exist, as happens in our choice. In God it is otherwise; as was said above (Q. 20, A. 2). Thus, as Augustine says (*De Verb. Ap. Serm.* 11): *Those are chosen by God, who do not exist; yet He does not err in His choice.*

REPLY OBJ. 3: God wills all men to be saved by His antecedent will, which is to will not simply but relatively; and not by His consequent will, which is to will simply.

Article 5

Whether the Foreknowledge of Merits Is the Cause of Predestination?

AD QUINTUM SIC PROCEDITUR. Videtur quod praescientia meritorum sit causa praedestinationis. Dicit enim apostolus, Rom. VIII, *quos praescivit, hos et praedestinavit.* Et Glossa Ambrosii, super illud Rom. IX, *miserebor cui miserebor* etc., dicit, *misericordiam illi dabo, quem praescio toto corde reversurum ad me.* Ergo videtur quod praescientia meritorum sit causa praedestinationis.

PRAETEREA, praedestinatio divina includit divinam voluntatem, quae irrationabilis esse non potest, cum praedestinatio sit propositum miserendi, ut Augustinus dicit. Sed nulla alia ratio potest esse praedestinationis nisi praescientia meritorum. Ergo praescientia meritorum est causa vel ratio praedestinationis.

PRAETEREA, *non est iniquitas apud Deum*, ut dicitur Rom. IX. Iniquum autem esse videtur, ut aequalibus inaequalia dentur. Omnes autem homines sunt aequales et secundum naturam, et secundum peccatum originale, attenditur autem in eis inaequalitas secundum merita vel demerita propriorum actuum. Non igitur inaequalia praeparat Deus hominibus, praedestinando et reprobando, nisi propter differentium meritorum praescientiam.

OBJECTION 1: It seems that foreknowledge of merits is the cause of predestination. For the Apostle says (Rom 8:29): *Whom He foreknew, He also predestined.* Again a gloss of Ambrose on Rom. 9:15: *I will have mercy upon whom I will have mercy* says: *I will give mercy to him who, I foresee, will turn to Me with his whole heart.* Therefore it seems the foreknowledge of merits is the cause of predestination.

OBJ. 2: Further, Divine predestination includes the divine will, which by no means can be irrational; since predestination is *the purpose to have mercy*, as Augustine says (*De Praed. Sanct.* ii, 17). But there can be no other reason for predestination than the foreknowledge of merits. Therefore it must be the cause of reason of predestination.

OBJ. 3: Further, *There is no injustice in God* (Rom 9:14). Now it would seem unjust that unequal things be given to equals. But all men are equal as regards both nature and original sin; and inequality in them arises from the merits or demerits of their actions. Therefore God does not prepare unequal things for men by predestinating and reprobating, unless through the foreknowledge of their merits and demerits.

SED CONTRA est quod dicit apostolus, ad Tit. III, *non ex operibus iustitiae, quae fecimus nos, sed secundum suam misericordiam salvos nos fecit.* Sicut autem salvos nos fecit, ita et praedestinavit nos salvos fieri. Non ergo praescientia meritorum est causa vel ratio praedestinationis.

RESPONDEO dicendum quod, cum praedestinatio includat voluntatem, ut supra dictum est, sic inquirenda est ratio praedestinationis, sicut inquiritur ratio divinae voluntatis. Dictum est autem supra quod non est assignare causam divinae voluntatis ex parte actus volendi; sed potest assignari ratio ex parte volitorum, inquantum scilicet Deus vult esse aliquid propter aliud. Nullus ergo fuit ita insanae mentis, qui diceret merita esse causam divinae praedestinationis, ex parte actus praedestinantis. Sed hoc sub quaestione vertitur, utrum ex parte effectus, praedestinatio habeat aliquam causam. Et hoc est quaerere, utrum Deus praeordinaverit se daturum effectum praedestinationis alicui, propter merita aliqua.

Fuerunt igitur quidam, qui dixerunt quod effectus praedestinationis praeordinatur alicui propter merita praeexistentia in alia vita. Et haec fuit positio Origenis, qui posuit animas humanas ab initio creatas, et secundum diversitatem suorum operum, diversos status eas sortiri in hoc mundo corporibus unitas. Sed hanc opinionem excludit apostolus, Rom. IX, dicens, *cum nondum nati fuissent, aut aliquid egissent boni vel mali, non ex operibus, sed ex vocante dictum est, quia maior serviet minori.*

Fuerunt ergo alii, qui dixerunt quod merita praeexistentia in hac vita sunt ratio et causa effectus praedestinationis. Posuerunt enim Pelagiani quod initium benefaciendi sit ex nobis, consummatio autem a Deo. Et sic, ex hoc contingit quod alicui datur praedestinationis effectus, et non alteri, quia unus initium dedit se praeparando, et non alius. Sed contra hoc est quod dicit apostolus, II Cor. III, quod *non sumus sufficientes cogitare aliquid a nobis, quasi ex nobis.* Nullum autem anterius principium inveniri potest quam cogitatio. Unde non potest dici quod aliquod in nobis initium existat, quod sit ratio effectus praedestinationis.

Unde fuerunt alii, qui dixerunt quod merita sequentia praedestinationis effectum, sunt ratio praedestinationis, ut intelligatur quod ideo Deus dat gratiam alicui, et praeordinavit se ei daturum, quia praescivit eum bene usurum gratia; sicut si rex det alicui militi equum, quem scit eo bene usurum. Sed isti videntur distinxisse inter id quod est ex gratia, et id quod est ex libero arbitrio, quasi non possit esse idem ex utroque. Manifestum est autem quod id quod est gratiae, est praedestinationis effectus, et hoc non potest poni ut ratio praedestinationis, cum hoc sub praedestinatione concludatur. Si igitur aliquid

ON THE CONTRARY, The Apostle says (Titus 3:5): *Not by works of justice which we have done, but according to His mercy He saved us.* But as He saved us, so He predestined that we should be saved. Therefore, foreknowledge of merits is not the cause or reason of predestination.

I ANSWER THAT, Since predestination includes will, as was said above (A. 4), the reason of predestination must be sought for in the same way as was the reason of the will of God. Now it was shown above (Q. 19, A. 5), that we cannot assign any cause of the divine will on the part of the act of willing; but a reason can be found on the part of the things willed; inasmuch as God wills one thing on account of something else. Wherefore nobody has been so insane as to say that merit is the cause of divine predestination as regards the act of the predestinator. But this is the question, whether, as regards the effect, predestination has any cause; or what comes to the same thing, whether God preordained that He would give the effect of predestination to anyone on account of any merits.

Accordingly there were some who held that the effect of predestination was pre-ordained for some on account of pre-existing merits in a former life. This was the opinion of Origen, who thought that the souls of men were created in the beginning, and according to the diversity of their works different states were assigned to them in this world when united with the body. The Apostle, however, rebuts this opinion where he says (Rom 9:11,12): *For when they were not yet born, nor had done any good or evil . . . not of works, but of Him that calleth, it was said of her: The elder shall serve the younger.*

Others said that pre-existing merits in this life are the reason and cause of the effect of predestination. For the Pelagians taught that the beginning of doing well came from us; and the consummation from God: so that it came about that the effect of predestination was granted to one, and not to another, because the one made a beginning by preparing, whereas the other did not. But against this we have the saying of the Apostle (2 Cor 3:5), that *we are not sufficient to think anything of ourselves as of ourselves.* Now no principle of action can be imagined previous to the act of thinking. Wherefore it cannot be said that anything begun in us can be the reason of the effect of predestination.

And so others said that merits following the effect of predestination are the reason of predestination; giving us to understand that God gives grace to a person, and preordains that He will give it, because He knows beforehand that He will make good use of that grace, as if a king were to give a horse to a soldier because he knows he will make good use of it. But these seem to have drawn a distinction between that which flows from grace, and that which flows from free will, as if the same thing cannot come from both. It is, however, manifest that what is of grace is the effect of predestination; and this cannot be considered as the reason

aliud ex parte nostra sit ratio praedestinationis, hoc erit praeter effectum praedestinationis. Non est autem distinctum quod est ex libero arbitrio, et ex praedestinatione; sicut nec est distinctum quod est ex causa secunda, et causa prima, divina enim providentia producit effectus per operationes causarum secundarum, ut supra dictum est. Unde et id quod est per liberum arbitrium, est ex praedestinatione.

Dicendum est ergo quod effectum praedestinationis considerare possumus dupliciter. Uno modo, in particulari. Et sic nihil prohibet aliquem effectum praedestinationis esse causam et rationem alterius, posteriorem quidem prioris, secundum rationem causae finalis; priorem vero posterioris, secundum rationem causae meritoriae, quae reducitur ad dispositionem materiae. Sicut si dicamus quod Deus praeordinavit se daturum alicui gloriam ex meritis; et quod praeordinavit se daturum alicui gratiam, ut mereretur gloriam. Alio modo potest considerari praedestinationis effectus in communi. Et sic impossibile est quod totus praedestinationis effectus in communi habeat aliquam causam ex parte nostra. Quia quidquid est in homine ordinans ipsum in salutem, comprehenditur totum sub effectu praedestinationis, etiam ipsa praeparatio ad gratiam, neque enim hoc fit nisi per auxilium divinum, secundum illud Thren. ultimi, *converte nos, domine, ad te, et convertemur.* Habet tamen hoc modo praedestinatio, ex parte effectus, pro ratione divinam bonitatem; ad quam totus effectus praedestinationis ordinatur ut in finem, et ex qua procedit sicut ex principio primo movente.

AD PRIMUM ergo dicendum quod usus gratiae praescitus, non est ratio collationis gratiae, nisi secundum rationem causae finalis, ut dictum est.

AD SECUNDUM dicendum quod praedestinatio habet rationem ex parte effectus, in communi, ipsam divinam bonitatem. In particulari autem, unus effectus est ratio alterius, ut dictum est.

AD TERTIUM dicendum quod ex ipsa bonitate divina ratio sumi potest praedestinationis aliquorum, et reprobationis aliorum. Sic enim Deus dicitur omnia propter suam bonitatem fecisse, ut in rebus divina bonitas repraesentetur. Necesse est autem quod divina bonitas, quae in se est una et simplex, multiformiter repraesentetur in rebus; propter hoc quod res creatae ad simplicitatem divinam attingere non possunt. Et inde est quod ad completionem universi requiruntur diversi gradus rerum, quarum quaedam altum, et quaedam infimum locum teneant in universo. Et ut multiformitas graduum conservetur in rebus, Deus permittit aliqua mala fieri, ne multa bona impediantur, ut supra dictum est. Sic igitur consideremus totum genus humanum, sicut totam

of predestination, since it is contained in the notion of predestination. Therefore, if anything else in us be the reason of predestination, it will be outside the effect of predestination. Now there is no distinction between what flows from free will, and what is of predestination; as there is not distinction between what flows from a secondary cause and from a first cause. For the providence of God produces effects through the operation of secondary causes, as was above shown (Q. 22, A. 3). Wherefore, that which flows from free-will is also of predestination.

We must say, therefore, that the effect of predestination may be considered in a twofold light—in one way, in particular; and thus there is no reason why one effect of predestination should not be the reason or cause of another; a subsequent effect being the reason of a previous effect, as its final cause; and the previous effect being the reason of the subsequent as its meritorious cause, which is reduced to the disposition of the matter. Thus we might say that God pre-ordained to give glory on account of merit, and that He pre-ordained to give grace to merit glory. In another way, the effect of predestination may be considered in general. Thus, it is impossible that the whole of the effect of predestination in general should have any cause as coming from us; because whatsoever is in man disposing him towards salvation, is all included under the effect of predestination; even the preparation for grace. For neither does this happen otherwise than by divine help, according to the prophet Jeremias (Lam 5:21): *convert us, O Lord, to Thee, and we shall be converted.* Yet predestination has in this way, in regard to its effect, the goodness of God for its reason; towards which the whole effect of predestination is directed as to an end; and from which it proceeds, as from its first moving principle.

REPLY OBJ. 1: The use of grace foreknown by God is not the cause of conferring grace, except after the manner of a final cause; as was explained above.

REPLY OBJ. 2: Predestination has its foundation in the goodness of God as regards its effects in general. Considered in its particular effects, however, one effect is the reason of another; as already stated.

REPLY OBJ. 3: The reason for the predestination of some, and reprobation of others, must be sought for in the goodness of God. Thus He is said to have made all things through His goodness, so that the divine goodness might be represented in things. Now it is necessary that God's goodness, which in itself is one and undivided, should be manifested in many ways in His creation; because creatures in themselves cannot attain to the simplicity of God. Thus it is that for the completion of the universe there are required different grades of being; some of which hold a high and some a low place in the universe. That this multiformity of grades may be preserved in things, God allows some evils, lest many good things should never happen, as was said above (Q. 22, A. 2). Let us then consider the whole of

rerum universitatem. Voluit igitur Deus in hominibus, quantum ad aliquos, quos praedestinat, suam repraesentare bonitatem per modum misericordiae, parcendo; et quantum ad aliquos, quos reprobat, per modum iustitiae, puniendo. Et haec est ratio quare Deus quosdam eligit, et quosdam reprobat. Et hanc causam assignat apostolus, ad Rom. IX, dicens, *volens Deus ostendere iram* (idest vindictam iustitiae), *et notam facere potentiam suam, sustinuit* (idest permisit) *in multa patientia, vasa irae apta in interitum, ut ostenderet divitias gloriae suae in vasa misericordiae, quae praeparavit in gloriam.* Et II Tim. II dicit, *in magna autem domo non solum sunt vasa aurea et argentea, sed etiam lignea et fictilia; et quaedam quidem in honorem, quaedam in contumeliam.* Sed quare hos elegit in gloriam, et illos reprobavit, non habet rationem nisi divinam voluntatem. Unde Augustinus dicit, super Ioannem, *quare hunc trahat, et illum non trahat, noli velle diiudicare, si non vis errare.* Sicut etiam in rebus naturalibus potest assignari ratio, cum prima materia tota sit in se uniformis, quare una pars eius est sub forma ignis, et alia sub forma terrae, a Deo in principio condita, ut scilicet sit diversitas specierum in rebus naturalibus. Sed quare haec pars materiae est sub ista forma, et illa sub alia, dependet ex simplici divina voluntate. Sicut ex simplici voluntate artificis dependet, quod ille lapis est in ista parte parietis, et ille in alia, quamvis ratio artis habeat quod aliqui sint in hac, et aliqui sint in illa. Neque tamen propter hoc est iniquitas apud Deum, si inaequalia non inaequalibus praeparat. Hoc enim esset contra iustitiae rationem, si praedestinationis effectus ex debito redderetur, et non daretur ex gratia. In his enim quae ex gratia dantur, potest aliquis pro libito suo dare cui vult, plus vel minus, dummodo nulli subtrahat debitum, absque praeiudicio iustitiae. Et hoc est quod dicit paterfamilias, Matt. XX, *tolle quod tuum est, et vade. An non licet mihi quod volo, facere?*

the human race, as we consider the whole universe. God wills to manifest His goodness in men; in respect to those whom He predestines, by means of His mercy, as sparing them; and in respect of others, whom he reprobates, by means of His justice, in punishing them. This is the reason why God elects some and rejects others. To this the Apostle refers, saying (Rom 9:22, 23): *What if God, willing to show His wrath, and to make His power known, endured with much patience vessels of wrath, fitted for destruction; that He might show the riches of His glory on the vessels of mercy, which He hath prepared unto glory* and (2 Tim 2:20): *But in a great house there are not only vessels of gold and silver; but also of wood and of earth; and some, indeed, unto honor, but some unto dishonor.* Yet why He chooses some for glory, and reprobates others, has no reason, except the divine will. Whence Augustine says (*Tract.* xxvi. in Joan.): *Why He draws one, and another He draws not, seek not to judge, if thou dost not wish to err.* Thus too, in the things of nature, a reason can be assigned, since primary matter is altogether uniform, why one part of it was fashioned by God from the beginning under the form of fire, another under the form of earth, that there might be a diversity of species in things of nature. Yet why this particular part of matter is under this particular form, and that under another, depends upon the simple will of God; as from the simple will of the artificer it depends that this stone is in part of the wall, and that in another; although the plan requires that some stones should be in this place, and some in that place. Neither on this account can there be said to be injustice in God, if He prepares unequal lots for not unequal things. This would be altogether contrary to the notion of justice, if the effect of predestination were granted as a debt, and not gratuitously. In things which are given gratuitously, a person can give more or less, just as he pleases (provided he deprives nobody of his due), without any infringement of justice. This is what the master of the house said: *Take what is thine, and go thy way. Is it not lawful for me to do what I will?* (Matt 20:14,15).

Article 6

Whether Predestination Is Certain?

Ad sextum sic proceditur. Videtur quod praedestinatio non sit certa. Quia super illud Apoc. III, *tene quod habes, ne alius accipiat coronam tuam,* dicit Augustinus, quod *alius non est accepturus, nisi iste perdiderit.* Potest ergo et acquiri et perdi corona, quae est praedestinationis effectus. Non est igitur praedestinatio certa.

Praeterea, posito possibili, nullum sequitur impossibile. Possibile est autem aliquem praedestinatum,

Objection 1: It seems that predestination is not certain. Because on the words *Hold fast that which thou hast, that no one take thy crown,* (Rev 3:11), Augustine says (*De Corr. et Grat.* 15): *Another will not receive, unless this one were to lose it.* Hence the crown which is the effect of predestination can be both acquired and lost. Therefore predestination cannot be certain.

Obj. 2: Further, granted what is possible, nothing impossible follows. But it is possible that one predestined—e.g.,

ut Petrum, peccare, et tunc occidi. Hoc autem posito, sequitur praedestinationis effectum frustrari. Hoc igitur non est impossibile. Non ergo est praedestinatio certa.

PRAETEREA, quidquid Deus potuit, potest. Sed potuit non praedestinare quem praedestinavit. Ergo nunc potest non praedestinare. Ergo praedestinatio non est certa.

SED CONTRA est quod super illud Rom. VIII, *quos praescivit, et praedestinavit* etc., dicit Glossa, *praedestinatio est praescientia et praeparatio beneficiorum Dei, qua certissime liberantur quicumque liberantur.*

RESPONDEO dicendum quod praedestinatio certissime et infallibiliter consequitur suum effectum, nec tamen imponit necessitatem, ut scilicet effectus eius ex necessitate proveniat. Dictum est enim supra quod praedestinatio est pars providentiae. Sed non omnia quae providentiae subduntur, necessaria sunt, sed quaedam contingenter eveniunt, secundum conditionem causarum proximarum, quas ad tales effectus divina providentia ordinavit. Et tamen providentiae ordo est infallibilis, ut supra ostensum est. Sic igitur et ordo praedestinationis est certus; et tamen libertas arbitrii non tollitur, ex qua contingenter provenit praedestinationis effectus. Ad hoc etiam consideranda sunt quae supra dicta sunt de divina scientia et de divina voluntate, quae contingentiam a rebus non tollunt, licet certissima et infallibilia sint.

AD PRIMUM ergo dicendum quod corona dicitur esse alicuius, dupliciter. Uno modo, ex praedestinatione divina, et sic nullus coronam suam amittit. Alio modo, ex merito gratiae, quod enim meremur, quodammodo nostrum est. Et sic suam coronam aliquis amittere potest per peccatum mortale sequens. Alius autem illam coronam amissam accipit, inquantum loco eius subrogatur. Non enim permittit Deus aliquos cadere, quin alios erigat, secundum illud Iob XXXIV, *conteret multos et innumerabiles, et stare faciet alios pro eis.* Sic enim in locum Angelorum cadentium substituti sunt homines; et in locum Iudaeorum, gentiles. Substitutus autem in statum gratiae, etiam quantum ad hoc coronam cadentis accipit, quod de bonis quae alius fecit, in aeterna vita gaudebit, in qua unusquisque gaudebit de bonis tam a se quam ab aliis factis.

AD SECUNDUM dicendum quod, licet sit possibile eum qui est praedestinatus, mori in peccato mortali, secundum se consideratum; tamen hoc est impossibile, posito (prout scilicet ponitur) eum esse praedestinatum. Unde non sequitur quod praedestinatio falli possit.

AD TERTIUM dicendum quod, cum praedestinatio includat divinam voluntatem, sicut supra dictum est quod Deum velle aliquid creatum est necessarium ex suppositione, propter immutabilitatem divinae voluntatis, non tamen absolute; ita dicendum est hic de

Peter—may sin and then be killed. But if this were so, it would follow that the effect of predestination would be thwarted. This then, is not impossible. Therefore predestination is not certain.

OBJ. 3: Further, whatever God could do in the past, He can do now. But He could have not predestined whom He hath predestined. Therefore now He is able not to predestine him. Therefore predestination is not certain.

ON THE CONTRARY, A gloss on Rom. 8:29: *Whom He foreknew, He also predestined,* says: *Predestination is the foreknowledge and preparation of the benefits of God, by which whosoever are freed will most certainly be freed.*

I ANSWER THAT, Predestination most certainly and infallibly takes effect; yet it does not impose any necessity, so that, namely, its effect should take place from necessity. For it was said above (A. 1), that predestination is a part of providence. But not all things subject to providence are necessary; some things happening from contingency, according to the nature of the proximate causes, which divine providence has ordained for such effects. Yet the order of providence is infallible, as was shown above (Q. 22, A. 4). So also the order of predestination is certain; yet free-will is not destroyed; whence the effect of predestination has its contingency. Moreover all that has been said about the divine knowledge and will (Q. 14, A. 13; Q. 19, A. 4) must also be taken into consideration; since they do not destroy contingency in things, although they themselves are most certain and infallible.

REPLY OBJ. 1: The crown may be said to belong to a person in two ways; first, by God's predestination, and thus no one loses his crown: second, by the merit of grace; for what we merit, in a certain way is ours; and thus anyone may lose his crown by mortal sin. Another person receives that crown thus lost, inasmuch as he takes the former's place. For God does not permit some to fall, without raising others; according to Job 34:24: *He shall break in pieces many and innumerable, and make others to stand in their stead.* Thus men are substituted in the place of the fallen angels; and the Gentiles in that of the Jews. He who is substituted for another in the state of grace, also receives the crown of the fallen in that in eternal life he will rejoice at the good the other has done, in which life he will rejoice at all good whether done by himself or by others.

REPLY OBJ. 2: Although it is possible for one who is predestined considered in himself to die in mortal sin; yet it is not possible, supposed, as in fact it is supposed, that he is predestined. Whence it does not follow that predestination can fall short of its effect.

REPLY OBJ. 3: Since predestination includes the divine will as stated above (A. 4): and the fact that God wills any created thing is necessary on the supposition that He so wills, on account of the immutability of the divine will, but is not necessary absolutely; so the same must be said of

praedestinatione. Unde non oportet dicere quod Deus possit non praedestinare quem praedestinavit, in sensu composito accipiendo; licet, absolute considerando, Deus possit praedestinare vel non praedestinare. Sed ex hoc non tollitur praedestinationis certitudo.

predestination. Wherefore one ought not to say that God is able not to predestinate one whom He has predestined, taking it in a composite sense, though, absolutely speaking, God can predestinate or not. But in this way the certainty of predestination is not destroyed.

Article 7

Whether the Number of the Predestined Is Certain?

AD SEPTIMUM SIC PROCEDITUR. Videtur quod numerus praedestinatorum non sit certus. Numerus enim cui potest fieri additio, non est certus. Sed numero praedestinatorum potest fieri additio, ut videtur, dicitur enim Deut. I, *dominus Deus noster addat ad hunc numerum multa millia*; Glossa, *idest definitum apud Deum, qui novit qui sunt eius.* Ergo numerus praedestinatorum non est certus.

PRAETEREA, non potest assignari ratio quare magis in hoc numero quam in alio, Deus homines praeordinet ad salutem. Sed nihil a Deo sine ratione disponitur. Ergo non est certus numerus salvandorum praeordinatus a Deo.

PRAETEREA, operatio Dei est perfectior quam operatio naturae. Sed in operibus naturae bonum invenitur ut in pluribus, defectus autem et malum ut in paucioribus. Si igitur a Deo institueretur numerus salvandorum, plures essent salvandi quam damnandi. Cuius contrarium ostenditur Matt. VII, ubi dicitur, *lata et spatiosa est via quae ducit ad perditionem, et multi sunt qui intrant per eam, angusta est porta, et arcta via, quae ducit ad vitam, et pauci sunt qui inveniunt eam.* Non ergo est praeordinatus a Deo numerus salvandorum.

SED CONTRA est quod Augustinus dicit, in libro de correptione et gratia, *certus est praedestinatorum numerus, qui neque augeri potest, neque minui.*

RESPONDEO dicendum quod numerus praedestinatorum est certus. Sed quidam dixerunt eum esse certum formaliter, sed non materialiter, ut puta si diceremus certum esse quod centum vel mille salventur, non autem quod hi vel illi. Sed hoc tollit certitudinem praedestinationis, de qua iam diximus. Et ideo oportet dicere quod numerus praedestinatorum sit certus Deo non solum formaliter, sed etiam materialiter. Sed advertendum est quod numerus praedestinatorum certus Deo dicitur, non solum ratione cognitionis, quia scilicet scit quot sunt salvandi (sic enim Deo certus est etiam numerus guttarum pluviae, et arenae maris); sed ratione electionis et definitionis cuiusdam. Ad cuius evidentiam, est sciendum quod omne agens intendit facere aliquid finitum, ut ex supradictis de infinito apparet. Quicumque

OBJECTION 1: It seems that the number of the predestined is not certain. For a number to which an addition can be made is not certain. But there can be an addition to the number of the predestined as it seems; for it is written (Deut 1:11): *The Lord God adds to this number many thousands*, and a gloss adds, *fixed by God, who knows those who belong to Him.* Therefore the number of the predestined is not certain.

OBJ. 2: Further, no reason can be assigned why God pre-ordains to salvation one number of men more than another. But nothing is arranged by God without a reason. Therefore the number to be saved pre-ordained by God cannot be certain.

OBJ. 3: Further, the operations of God are more perfect than those of nature. But in the works of nature, good is found in the majority of things; defect and evil in the minority. If, then, the number of the saved were fixed by God at a certain figure, there would be more saved than lost. Yet the contrary follows from Matt. 7:13,14: *For wide is the gate, and broad the way that leadeth to destruction, and many there are who go in thereat. How narrow is the gate, and strait is the way that leadeth to life; and few there are who find it!* Therefore the number of those pre-ordained by God to be saved is not certain.

ON THE CONTRARY, Augustine says (*De Corr. et Grat.* 13): *The number of the predestined is certain, and can neither be increased nor diminished.*

I ANSWER THAT, The number of the predestined is certain. Some have said that it was formally, but not materially certain; as if we were to say that it was certain that a hundred or a thousand would be saved; not however these or those individuals. But this destroys the certainty of predestination; of which we spoke above (A. 6). Therefore we must say that to God the number of the predestined is certain, not only formally, but also materially. It must, however, be observed that the number of the predestined is said to be certain to God, not by reason of His knowledge, because, that is to say, He knows how many will be saved (for in this way the number of drops of rain and the sands of the sea are certain to God); but by reason of His deliberate choice and determination. For the further evidence of which we must remember that every agent intends

autem intendit aliquam determinatam mensuram in suo effectu, excogitat aliquem numerum in partibus essentialibus eius, quae per se requiruntur ad perfectionem totius. Non enim per se eligit aliquem numerum in his quae non principaliter requiruntur, sed solum propter aliud, sed in tanto numero accipit huiusmodi, inquantum sunt necessaria propter aliud. Sicut aedificator excogitat determinatam mensuram domus, et etiam determinatum numerum mansionum quas vult facere in domo, et determinatum numerum mensurarum parietis vel tecti, non autem eligit determinatum numerum lapidum, sed accipit tot, quot sufficiunt ad explendam tantam mensuram parietis. Sic igitur considerandum est in Deo, respectu totius universitatis quae est eius effectus. Praeordinavit enim in qua mensura deberet esse totum universum, et quis numerus esset conveniens essentialibus partibus universi, quae scilicet habent aliquo modo ordinem ad perpetuitatem; quot scilicet sphaerae, quot stellae, quot elementa, quot species rerum. Individua vero corruptibilia non ordinantur ad bonum universi quasi principaliter, sed quasi secundario, inquantum in eis salvatur bonum speciei. Unde, licet Deus sciat numerum omnium individuorum, non tamen numerus vel boum vel culicum, vel aliorum huiusmodi, est per se praeordinatus a Deo, sed tot ex huiusmodi divina providentia produxit, quot sufficiunt ad specierum conservationem. Inter omnes autem creaturas, principalius ordinantur ad bonum universi creaturae rationales, quae, inquantum huiusmodi, incorruptibiles sunt; et potissime illae quae beatitudinem consequuntur, quae immediatius attingunt ultimum finem. Unde certus est Deo numerus praedestinatorum, non solum per modum cognitionis, sed etiam per modum cuiusdam principalis praefinitionis.

Non sic autem omnino est de numero reproborum; qui videntur esse praeordinati a Deo in bonum electorum, quibus *omnia cooperantur in bonum*. De numero autem omnium praedestinatorum hominum, quis sit, dicunt quidam quod tot ex hominibus salvabuntur, quot Angeli ceciderunt. Quidam vero, quod tot salvabuntur, quot Angeli remanserunt. Quidam vero, quod tot ex hominibus salvabuntur, quot Angeli ceciderunt, et insuper tot, quot fuerunt Angeli creati. Sed melius dicitur quod *soli Deo est cognitus numerus electorum in superna felicitate locandus*.

AD PRIMUM ergo dicendum quod verbum illud Deuteronomii est intelligendum de illis qui sunt praenotati a Deo respectu praesentis iustitiae. Horum enim numerus et augetur et minuitur, et non numerus praedestinatorum.

AD SECUNDUM dicendum quod ratio quantitatis alicuius partis, accipienda est ex proportione illius partis

to make something finite, as is clear from what has been said above when we treated of the infinite (Q. 7, AA. 2 ,3). Now whosoever intends some definite measure in his effect thinks out some definite number in the essential parts, which are by their very nature required for the perfection of the whole. For of those things which are required not principally, but only on account of something else, he does not select any definite number per se; but he accepts and uses them in such numbers as are necessary on account of that other thing. For instance, a builder thinks out the definite measurements of a house, and also the definite number of rooms which he wishes to make in the house; and definite measurements of the walls and roof; he does not, however, select a definite number of stones, but accepts and uses just so many as are sufficient for the required measurements of the wall. So also must we consider concerning God in regard to the whole universe, which is His effect. For He pre-ordained the measurements of the whole of the universe, and what number would befit the essential parts of that universe—that is to say, which have in some way been ordained in perpetuity; how many spheres, how many stars, how many elements, and how many species. Individuals, however, which undergo corruption, are not ordained as it were chiefly for the good of the universe, but in a secondary way, inasmuch as the good of the species is preserved through them. Whence, although God knows the total number of individuals, the number of oxen, flies and such like, is not pre-ordained by God per se; but divine providence produces just so many as are sufficient for the preservation of the species. Now of all creatures the rational creature is chiefly ordained for the good of the universe, being as such incorruptible; more especially those who attain to eternal happiness, since they more immediately reach the ultimate end. Whence the number of the predestined is certain to God; not only by way of knowledge, but also by way of a principal pre-ordination.

It is not exactly the same thing in the case of the number of the reprobate, who would seem to be pre-ordained by God for the good of the elect, in whose regard *all things work together unto good* (Rom 8:28). Concerning the number of all the predestined, some say that so many men will be saved as angels fell; some, so many as there were angels left; others, as many as the number of angels created by God. It is, however, better to say that, *to God alone is known the number for whom is reserved eternal happiness*

REPLY OBJ. 1: These words of Deuteronomy must be taken as applied to those who are marked out by God beforehand in respect to present righteousness. For their number is increased and diminished, but not the number of the predestined.

REPLY OBJ. 2: The reason of the quantity of any one part must be judged from the proportion of that part of the

ad totum. Sic enim est apud Deum ratio quare tot stellas fecerit, vel tot rerum species, et quare tot praedestinavit, ex proportione partium principalium ad bonum universi.

AD TERTIUM dicendum quod bonum proportionatum communi statui naturae, accidit ut in pluribus; et defectus ab hoc bono, ut in paucioribus. Sed bonum quod excedit communem statum naturae, invenitur ut in paucioribus; et defectus ab hoc bono, ut in pluribus. Sicut patet quod plures homines sunt qui habent sufficientem scientiam ad regimen vitae suae, pauciores autem qui hac scientia carent, qui moriones vel stulti dicuntur, sed paucissimi sunt, respectu aliorum, qui attingunt ad habendam profundam scientiam intelligibilium rerum. Cum igitur beatitudo aeterna, in visione Dei consistens, excedat communem statum naturae, et praecipue secundum quod est gratia destituta per corruptionem originalis peccati, pauciores sunt qui salvantur. Et in hoc etiam maxime misericordia Dei apparet, quod aliquos in illam salutem erigit, a qua plurimi deficiunt secundum communem cursum et inclinationem naturae.

whole. Thus in God the reason why He has made so many stars, or so many species of things, or predestined so many, is according to the proportion of the principal parts to the good of the whole universe.

REPLY OBJ. 3: The good that is proportionate to the common state of nature is to be found in the majority; and is wanting in the minority. The good that exceeds the common state of nature is to be found in the minority, and is wanting in the majority. Thus it is clear that the majority of men have a sufficient knowledge for the guidance of life; and those who have not this knowledge are said to be half-witted or foolish; but they who attain to a profound knowledge of things intelligible are a very small minority in respect to the rest. Since their eternal happiness, consisting in the vision of God, exceeds the common state of nature, and especially in so far as this is deprived of grace through the corruption of original sin, those who are saved are in the minority. In this especially, however, appears the mercy of God, that He has chosen some for that salvation, from which very many in accordance with the common course and tendency of nature fall short.

Article 8

Whether Predestination Can Be Furthered by the Prayers of the Saints?

AD OCTAVUM SIC PROCEDITUR. Videtur quod praedestinatio non possit iuvari precibus sanctorum. Nullum enim aeternum praeceditur ab aliquo temporali, et per consequens non potest temporale iuvare ad hoc quod aliquod aeternum sit. Sed praedestinatio est aeterna. Cum igitur preces sanctorum sint temporales, non possunt iuvare ad hoc quod aliquis praedestinetur. Non ergo praedestinatio iuvatur precibus sanctorum.

PRAETEREA, sicut nihil indiget consilio nisi propter defectum cognitionis, ita nihil indiget auxilio nisi propter defectum virtutis. Sed neutrum horum competit Deo praedestinanti, unde dicitur Rom. XI, *quis adiuvit spiritum domini? Aut quis consiliarius eius fuit?* Ergo praedestinatio non iuvatur precibus sanctorum.

PRAETEREA, eiusdem est adiuvari et impediri. Sed praedestinatio non potest aliquo impediri. Ergo non potest aliquo iuvari.

SED CONTRA est quod dicitur Genes. XXV, quod *Isaac rogavit Deum pro Rebecca uxore sua, et dedit conceptum Rebeccae.* Ex illo autem conceptu natus est Iacob, qui praedestinatus fuit. Non autem fuisset impleta praedestinatio, si natus non fuisset. Ergo praedestinatio iuvatur precibus sanctorum.

OBJECTION 1: It seems that predestination cannot be furthered by the prayers of the saints. For nothing eternal can be preceded by anything temporal; and in consequence nothing temporal can help towards making something else eternal. But predestination is eternal. Therefore, since the prayers of the saints are temporal, they cannot so help as to cause anyone to become predestined. Predestination therefore is not furthered by the prayers of the saints.

OBJ. 2: Further, as there is no need of advice except on account of defective knowledge, so there is no need of help except through defective power. But neither of these things can be said of God when He predestines. Whence it is said: *Who hath helped the Spirit of the Lord? Or who hath been His counsellor?* (Rom 11:34). Therefore predestination cannot be furthered by the prayers of the saints.

OBJ. 3: Further, if a thing can be helped, it can also be hindered. But predestination cannot be hindered by anything. Therefore it cannot be furthered by anything.

ON THE CONTRARY, It is said that *Isaac besought the Lord for his wife because she was barren; and He heard him and made Rebecca to conceive* (Gen 25:21). But from that conception Jacob was born, and he was predestined. Now his predestination would not have happened if he had never been born. Therefore predestination can be furthered by the prayers of the saints.

RESPONDEO dicendum quod circa hanc quaestionem diversi errores fuerunt. Quidam enim, attendentes certitudinem divinae praedestinationis, dixerunt superfluas esse orationes, vel quidquid aliud fiat ad salutem aeternam consequendam, quia his factis vel non factis, praedestinati consequuntur, reprobati non consequuntur. Sed contra hoc sunt omnes admonitiones sacrae Scripturae, exhortantes ad orationem, et ad alia bona opera.

Alii vero dixerunt quod per orationes mutatur divina praedestinatio. Et haec dicitur fuisse opinio Aegyptiorum, qui ponebant ordinationem divinam, quam fatum appellabant, aliquibus sacrificiis et orationibus impediri posse. Sed contra hoc etiam est auctoritas sacrae Scripturae. Dicitur enim I Reg. XV, porro *triumphator in Israel non parcet, neque poenitudine flectetur.* Et Rom. XI dicitur quod *sine poenitentia sunt dona Dei et vocatio.*

Et ideo aliter dicendum, quod in praedestinatione duo sunt consideranda, scilicet ipsa praeordinatio divina, et effectus eius. Quantum igitur ad primum, nullo modo praedestinatio iuvatur precibus sanctorum, non enim precibus sanctorum fit, quod aliquis praedestinetur a Deo. Quantum vero ad secundum, dicitur praedestinatio iuvari precibus sanctorum, et aliis bonis operibus, quia providentia, cuius praedestinatio est pars, non subtrahit causas secundas, sed sic providet effectus, ut etiam ordo causarum secundarum subiaceat providentiae. Sicut igitur sic providentur naturales effectus, ut etiam causae naturales ad illos naturales effectus ordinentur, sine quibus illi effectus non provenirent; ita praedestinatur a Deo salus alicuius, ut etiam sub ordine praedestinationis cadat quidquid hominem promovet in salutem, vel orationes propriae, vel aliorum, vel alia bona, vel quidquid huiusmodi, sine quibus aliquis salutem non consequitur. Unde praedestinatis conandum est ad bene operandum et orandum, quia per huiusmodi praedestinationis effectus certitudinaliter impletur. Propter quod dicitur II Petr. I, *satagite, ut per bona opera certam vestram vocationem et electionem faciatis.*

AD PRIMUM ergo dicendum quod ratio illa ostendit quod praedestinatio non iuvatur precibus sanctorum, quantum ad ipsam praeordinationem.

AD SECUNDUM dicendum quod aliquis dicitur adiuvari per alium, dupliciter. Uno modo, inquantum ab eo accipit virtutem, et sic adiuvari infirmi est, unde Deo non competit. Et sic intelligitur illud, *quis adiuvit spiritum domini?* Alio modo dicitur quis adiuvari per aliquem, per quem exequitur suam operationem, sicut dominus per ministrum. Et hoc modo Deus adiuvatur per nos, inquantum exequimur suam ordinationem, secundum illud I ad Cor. III, *Dei enim adiutores sumus.* Neque hoc est propter defectum divinae virtutis, sed

I ANSWER THAT, Concerning this question, there were different errors. Some, regarding the certainty of divine predestination, said that prayers were superfluous, as also anything else done to attain salvation; because whether these things were done or not, the predestined would attain, and the reprobate would not attain, eternal salvation. But against this opinion are all the warnings of Holy Scripture, exhorting us to prayer and other good works.

Others declared that the divine predestination was altered through prayer. This is stated to have the opinion of the Egyptians, who thought that the divine ordination, which they called fate, could be frustrated by certain sacrifices and prayers. Against this also is the authority of Scripture. For it is said: *But the triumpher in Israel will not spare and will not be moved to repentance* (1 Kgs 15:29); and that *the gifts and the calling of God are without repentance* (Rom 11:29).

Wherefore we must say otherwise that in predestination two things are to be considered—namely, the divine ordination; and its effect. As regards the former, in no possible way can predestination be furthered by the prayers of the saints. For it is not due to their prayers that anyone is predestined by God. As regards the latter, predestination is said to be helped by the prayers of the saints, and by other good works; because providence, of which predestination is a part, does not do away with secondary causes but so provides effects, that the order of secondary causes falls also under providence. So, as natural effects are provided by God in such a way that natural causes are directed to bring about those natural effects, without which those effects would not happen; so the salvation of a person is predestined by God in such a way, that whatever helps that person towards salvation falls under the order of predestination; whether it be one's own prayers or those of another; or other good works, and such like, without which one would not attain to salvation. Whence, the predestined must strive after good works and prayer; because through these means predestination is most certainly fulfilled. For this reason it is said: *Labor more that by good works you may make sure your calling and election* (2 Pet 1:10).

REPLY OBJ. 1: This argument shows that predestination is not furthered by the prayers of the saints, as regards the preordination.

REPLY OBJ. 2: One is said to be helped by another in two ways; in one way, inasmuch as he receives power from him: and to be helped thus belongs to the weak; but this cannot be said of God, and thus we are to understand, *Who hath helped the Spirit of the Lord?* In another way one is said to be helped by a person through whom he carries out his work, as a master through a servant. In this way God is helped by us; inasmuch as we execute His orders, according to 1 Cor. 3:9: *We are God's co-adjutors.* Nor is this on account of any defect in the power of God, but because He

quia utitur causis mediis, ut ordinis pulchritudo servetur in rebus, et ut etiam creaturis dignitatem causalitatis communicet.

AD TERTIUM dicendum quod secundae causae non possunt egredi ordinem causae primae universalis, ut supra dictum est; sed ipsum exequuntur. Et ideo praedestinatio per creaturas potest adiuvari, sed non impediri.

employs intermediary causes, in order that the beauty of order may be preserved in the universe; and also that He may communicate to creatures the dignity of causality.

REPLY OBJ. 3: Secondary causes cannot escape the order of the first universal cause, as has been said above (Q. 19, A. 6), indeed, they execute that order. And therefore predestination can be furthered by creatures, but it cannot be impeded by them.

Question 24

The Book of Life

Deinde considerandum est de libro vitae. Et circa hoc quaeruntur tria.

Primo, quid sit liber vitae.

Secundo, cuius vitae sit liber.

Tertio, utrum aliquis possit deleri de libro vitae.

We now consider the book of life; concerning which there are three points of inquiry:

(1) What is the book of life?

(2) Of what life is it the book?

(3) Whether anyone can be blotted out of the book of life?

Article 1

Whether the Book of Life Is the Same As Predestination?

Ad primum sic proceditur. Videtur quod liber vitae non sit idem quod praedestinatio. Dicitur enim Eccli. XXIV, *haec omnia liber vitae*; Glossa, *idest novum et vetus testamentum*. Hoc autem non est praedestinatio. Ergo liber vitae non est idem quod praedestinatio.

Praeterea, Augustinus, in libro XX de Civ. Dei, ait quod liber vitae est quaedam vis divina, qua fiet *ut cuique opera sua bona vel mala in memoriam reducantur*. Sed vis divina non videtur pertinere ad praedestinationem, sed magis ad attributum potentiae. Ergo liber vitae non est idem quod praedestinatio.

Praeterea, praedestinationi opponitur reprobatio. Si igitur liber vitae esset praedestinatio, inveniretur liber mortis, sicut liber vitae.

Sed contra est quod dicitur in Glossa, super illud Psalmi LXVIII, *deleantur de libro viventium, liber iste est notitia Dei, qua praedestinavit ad vitam, quos praescivit.*

Respondeo dicendum quod liber vitae in Deo dicitur metaphorice, secundum similitudinem a rebus humanis acceptam. Est enim consuetum apud homines, quod illi qui ad aliquid eliguntur, conscribuntur in libro; utpote milites vel consiliarii, qui olim dicebantur patres conscripti. Patet autem ex praemissis quod omnes praedestinati eliguntur a Deo ad habendum vitam aeternam. Ipsa ergo praedestinatorum conscriptio dicitur liber vitae. Dicitur autem metaphorice aliquid conscriptum in intellectu alicuius, quod firmiter in memoria tenet, secundum illud Prov. III, *ne obliviscaris legis meae, et praecepta mea cor tuum custodiat*; et post pauca sequitur, *describe illa in tabulis cordis tui*. Nam et in libris materialibus aliquid conscribitur ad succurrendum memoriae. Unde ipsa Dei notitia, qua firmiter retinet se aliquos praedestinasse ad vitam aeternam, dicitur liber

Objection 1: It seems that the book of life is not the same thing as predestination. For it is said, *All things are the book of life* (Sir 4:32)—i.e., the Old and New Testament according to a gloss. This, however, is not predestination. Therefore the book of life is not predestination.

Obj. 2: Further, Augustine says (*De Civ. Dei* xx, 14) that *the book of life is a certain divine energy, by which it happens that to each one his good or evil works are recalled to memory*. But divine energy belongs seemingly, not to predestination, but rather to divine power. Therefore the book of life is not the same thing as predestination.

Obj. 3: Further, reprobation is opposed to predestination. So, if the book of life were the same as predestination, there should also be a book of death, as there is a book of life.

On the contrary, It is said in a gloss upon Ps. 68:29, *Let them be blotted out of the book of the living*, This book is the knowledge of God, by which He hath predestined to life those whom He foreknew.

I answer that, The book of life is in God taken in a metaphorical sense, according to a comparison with human affairs. For it is usual among men that they who are chosen for any office should be inscribed in a book; as, for instance, soldiers, or counsellors, who formerly were called *conscript* fathers. Now it is clear from the preceding (Q. 23, A. 4) that all the predestined are chosen by God to possess eternal life. This conscription, therefore, of the predestined is called the book of life. A thing is said metaphorically to be written upon the mind of anyone when it is firmly held in the memory, according to Prov. 3:3: *Forget not My Law, and let thy heart keep My commandments*, and further on, *Write them in the tablets of thy heart*. For things are written down in material books to help the memory. Whence, the knowledge of God, by which He firmly remembers that He has predestined some to eternal life, is

vitae. Nam sicut Scriptura libri est signum eorum quae fienda sunt ita Dei notitia est quoddam signum apud ipsum, eorum qui sunt perducendi ad vitam aeternam; secundum illud II Tim. II, *firmum fundamentum Dei stat, habens signaculum hoc, novit dominus qui sunt eius.*

AD PRIMUM ergo dicendum quod liber vitae potest dici dupliciter. Uno modo, conscriptio eorum qui sunt electi ad vitam, et sic loquimur nunc de libro vitae. Alio modo potest dici liber vitae, conscriptio eorum quae ducunt in vitam. Et hoc dupliciter. Vel sicut agendorum, et sic novum et vetus testamentum dicitur liber vitae. Vel sicut iam factorum, et sic illa vis divina, qua fiet ut cuilibet in memoriam reducantur facta sua, dicitur liber vitae. Sicut etiam liber militiae potest dici, vel in quo scribuntur electi ad militiam, vel in quo traditur ars militaris, vel in quo recitantur facta militum.

UNDE PATET solutio ad secundum.

AD TERTIUM dicendum quod non est consuetum conscribi eos qui repudiantur, sed eos qui eliguntur. Unde reprobationi non respondet liber mortis, sicut praedestinationi liber vitae.

AD QUARTUM dicendum quod secundum rationem differt liber vitae a praedestinatione. Importat enim notitiam praedestinationis, sicut etiam ex Glossa inducta apparet.

called the book of life. For as the writing in a book is the sign of things to be done, so the knowledge of God is a sign in Him of those who are to be brought to eternal life, according to 2 Tim. 11:19: *The sure foundation of God standeth firm, having this seal; the Lord knoweth who are His.*

REPLY OBJ. 1: The book of life may be understood in two senses. In one sense as the inscription of those who are chosen to life; thus we now speak of the book of life. In another sense the inscription of those things which lead us to life may be called the book of life; and this also is twofold, either as of things to be done; and thus the Old and New Testament are called a book of life; or of things already done, and thus that divine energy by which it happens that to each one his deeds will be recalled to memory, is spoken of as the book of life. Thus that also may be called the book of war, whether it contains the names inscribed of those chosen for military service; or treats of the art of warfare, or relates the deeds of soldiers.

HENCE the solution of the Second Objection.

REPLY OBJ. 3: It is the custom to inscribe, not those who are rejected, but those who are chosen. Whence there is no book of death corresponding to reprobation, as the book of life to predestination.

REPLY OBJ. 4: Predestination and the book of life are different aspects of the same thing. For this latter implies the knowledge of predestination; as also is made clear from the gloss quoted above.

Article 2

Whether the Book of Life Regards Only the Life of Glory of the Predestined?

AD SECUNDUM SIC PROCEDITUR. Videtur quod liber vitae non sit solum respectu vitae gloriae praedestinatorum. Liber enim vitae est notitia vitae. Sed Deus per vitam suam cognoscit omnem aliam vitam. Ergo liber vitae praecipue dicitur respectu vitae divinae; et non solum respectu vitae praedestinatorum.

PRAETEREA, sicut vita gloriae est a Deo, ita vita naturae. Si igitur notitia vitae gloriae dicitur liber vitae, etiam notitia vitae naturae dicetur liber vitae.

PRAETEREA, aliqui eliguntur ad gratiam, qui non eliguntur ad vitam gloriae; ut patet per id quod dicitur Ioan. VI, *nonne duodecim vos elegi, et unus ex vobis Diabolus est?* Sed liber vitae est conscriptio electionis divinae, ut dictum est. Ergo etiam est respectu vitae gratiae.

SED CONTRA est quod liber vitae est notitia praedestinationis, ut dictum est. Sed praedestinatio non respicit vitam gratiae, nisi secundum quod ordinatur ad gloriam, non enim sunt praedestinati, qui habent gratiam

OBJECTION 1: It seems that the book of life does not only regard the life of glory of the predestined. For the book of life is the knowledge of life. But God, through His own life, knows all other life. Therefore the book of life is so called in regard to divine life; and not only in regard to the life of the predestined.

OBJ. 2: Further, as the life of glory comes from God, so also does the life of nature. Therefore, if the knowledge of the life of glory is called the book of life; so also should the knowledge of the life of nature be so called.

OBJ. 3: Further, some are chosen to the life of grace who are not chosen to the life of glory; as it is clear from what is said: *Have not I chosen you twelve, and one of you is a devil?* (John 6:71). But the book of life is the inscription of the divine election, as stated above (A. 1). Therefore it applies also to the life of grace.

ON THE CONTRARY, The book of life is the knowledge of predestination, as stated above (ibid.). But predestination does not regard the life of grace, except so far as it is directed to glory; for those are not predestined who have

et deficiunt a gloria. Liber igitur vitae non dicitur nisi respectu gloriae.

RESPONDEO dicendum quod liber vitae, ut dictum est, importat conscriptionem quandam sive notitiam electorum ad vitam. Eligitur autem aliquis ad id quod non competit sibi secundum suam naturam. Et iterum, id ad quod eligitur aliquis, habet rationem finis, non enim miles eligitur aut conscribitur ad hoc quod armetur, sed ad hoc quod pugnet; hoc enim est proprium officium ad quod militia ordinatur. Finis autem supra naturam existens, est vita gloriae, ut supra dictum est. Unde proprie liber vitae respicit vitam gloriae.

AD PRIMUM ergo dicendum quod vita divina, etiam prout est vita gloriosa, est Deo naturalis. Unde respectu eius non est electio, et per consequens neque liber vitae. Non enim dicimus quod aliquis homo eligatur ad habendum sensum, vel aliquid eorum quae consequuntur naturam.

Unde per hoc etiam patet solutio ad secundum. Respectu enim vitae naturalis non est electio, neque liber vitae.

AD TERTIUM dicendum quod vita gratiae non habet rationem finis, sed rationem eius quod est ad finem. Unde ad vitam gratiae non dicitur aliquis eligi, nisi inquantum vita gratiae ordinatur ad gloriam. Et propter hoc, illi qui habent gratiam et excidunt a gloria, non dicuntur esse electi simpliciter, sed secundum quid. Et similiter non dicuntur esse scripti simpliciter in libro vitae sed secundum quid; prout scilicet de eis in ordinatione et notitia divina existit, quod sint habituri aliquem ordinem ad vitam aeternam, secundum participationem gratiae.

grace and yet fail to obtain glory. The book of life altogether is only so called in regard to the life of glory.

I ANSWER THAT, The book of life, as stated above (A. 1), implies a conscription or a knowledge of those chosen to life. Now a man is chosen for something which does not belong to him by nature; and again that to which a man is chosen has the aspect of an end. For a soldier is not chosen or inscribed merely to put on armor, but to fight; since this is the proper duty to which military service is directed. But the life of glory is an end exceeding human nature, as said above (Q. 23, A. 1). Wherefore, strictly speaking, the book of life regards the life of glory.

REPLY OBJ. 1: The divine life, even considered as a life of glory, is natural to God; whence in His regard there is no election, and in consequence no book of life: for we do not say that anyone is chosen to possess the power of sense, or any of those things that are consequent on nature.

From this we gather the Reply to the Second Objection. For there is no election, nor a book of life, as regards the life of nature.

REPLY OBJ. 3: The life of grace has the aspect, not of an end, but of something directed towards an end. Hence nobody is said to be chosen to the life of grace, except so far as the life of grace is directed to glory. For this reason those who, possessing grace, fail to obtain glory, are not said to be chosen simply, but relatively. Likewise they are not said to be written in the book of life simply, but relatively; that is to say, that it is in the ordination and knowledge of God that they are to have some relation to eternal life, according to their participation in grace.

Article 3

Whether Anyone May Be Blotted Out of the Book of Life?

AD TERTIUM SIC PROCEDITUR. Videtur quod nullus deleatur de libro vitae. Dicit enim Augustinus, in XX de Civ. Dei, quod *praescientia Dei, quae non potest falli, liber vitae est*. Sed a praescientia Dei non potest aliquid subtrahi, similiter neque a praedestinatione. Ergo nec de libro vitae potest aliquis deleri.

PRAETEREA, quidquid est in aliquo, est in eo per modum eius in quo est. Sed liber vitae est quid aeternum et immutabile. Ergo quidquid est in eo, est ibi non temporaliter, sed immobiliter et indelebiliter.

PRAETEREA, deletio Scripturae opponitur. Sed aliquis non potest de novo scribi in libro vitae. Ergo neque inde deleri potest.

OBJECTION 1: It seems that no one may be blotted out of the book of life. For Augustine says (*De Civ. Dei* xx, 15): *God's foreknowledge, which cannot be deceived, is the book of life*. But nothing can be taken away from the foreknowledge of God, nor from predestination. Therefore neither can anyone be blotted out from the book of life.

OBJ. 2: Further, whatever is in a thing is in it according to the disposition of that thing. But the book of life is something eternal and immutable. Therefore whatsoever is written therein, is there not in a temporary way, but immovably, and indelibly.

OBJ. 3: Further, blotting out is the contrary to inscription. But nobody can be written a second time in the book of life. Neither therefore can he be blotted out.

SED CONTRA est quod dicitur in Psalmo LXVIII, *deleantur de libro viventium.*

RESPONDEO dicendum quod quidam dicunt quod de libro vitae nullus potest deleri secundum rei veritatem, potest tamen aliquis deleri secundum opinionem hominum. Est enim consuetum in Scripturis ut aliquid dicatur fieri, quando innotescit. Et secundum hoc, aliqui dicuntur esse scripti in libro vitae, inquantum homines opinantur eos ibi scriptos, propter praesentem iustitiam quam in eis vident. Sed quando apparet, vel in hoc seculo vel in futuro, quod ab hac iustitia exciderunt, dicuntur inde deleri. Et sic etiam exponitur in Glossa deletio talis, super illud Psalmi LXVIII, *deleantur de libro viventium.* Sed quia non deleri de libro vitae ponitur inter praemia iustorum, secundum illud Apoc. III, *qui vicerit, sic vestietur vestimentis albis, et non delebo nomen eius de libro vitae*; quod autem sanctis repromittitur, non est solum in hominum opinione; potest dici quod deleri vel non deleri de libro vitae, non solum ad opinionem hominum referendum est, sed etiam quantum ad rem. Est enim liber vitae conscriptio ordinatorum in vitam aeternam. Ad quam ordinatur aliquis ex duobus, scilicet ex praedestinatione divina, et haec ordinatio nunquam deficit; et ex gratia. Quicumque enim gratiam habet, ex hoc ipso est dignus vita aeterna. Et haec ordinatio deficit interdum, quia aliqui ordinati sunt ex gratia habita ad habendum vitam aeternam, a qua tamen deficiunt per peccatum mortale. Illi igitur qui sunt ordinati ad habendum vitam aeternam ex praedestinatione divina, sunt simpliciter scripti in libro vitae, quia sunt ibi scripti ut habituri vitam aeternam in seipsa. Et isti nunquam delentur de libro vitae. Sed illi qui sunt ordinati ad habendum vitam aeternam, non ex praedestinatione divina, sed solum ex gratia, dicuntur esse scripti in libro vitae, non simpliciter, sed secundum quid, quia sunt ibi scripti ut habituri vitam aeternam, non in seipsa, sed in sua causa. Et tales possunt deleri de libro vitae, ut deletio non referatur ad notitiam Dei, quasi Deus aliquid praesciat, et postea nesciat; sed ad rem scitam, quia scilicet Deus scit aliquem prius ordinari in vitam aeternam, et postea non ordinari, cum deficit a gratia.

AD PRIMUM ergo dicendum quod deletio, ut dictum est, non refertur ad librum vitae ex parte praescientiae, quasi in Deo sit aliqua mutabilitas, sed ex parte praescitorum, quae sunt mutabilia.

AD SECUNDUM dicendum quod, licet res in Deo sint immutabiliter, tamen in seipsis mutabiles sunt. Et ad hoc pertinet deletio libri vitae.

AD TERTIUM dicendum quod eo modo quo aliquis dicitur deleri de libro vitae, potest dici quod ibi scribatur de novo; vel secundum opinionem hominum, vel secundum quod de novo incipit habere ordinem ad vitam

ON THE CONTRARY, It is said, *Let them be blotted out from the book of the living* (Ps 68:29).

I ANSWER THAT, Some have said that none could be blotted out of the book of life as a matter of fact, but only in the opinion of men. For it is customary in the Scriptures to say that something is done when it becomes known. Thus some are said to be written in the book of life, inasmuch as men think they are written therein, on account of the present righteousness they see in them; but when it becomes evident, either in this world or in the next, that they have fallen from that state of righteousness, they are then said to be blotted out. And thus a gloss explains the passage: *Let them be blotted out of the book of the living.* But because not to be blotted out of the book of life is placed among the rewards of the just, according to the text, *He that shall overcome, shall thus be clothed in white garments, and I will not blot his name out of the book of life* (Rev 3:5) (and what is promised to holy men, is not merely something in the opinion of men), it can therefore be said that to be blotted out, and not blotted out, of the book of life is not only to be referred to the opinion of man, but to the reality of the fact. For the book of life is the inscription of those ordained to eternal life, to which one is directed from two sources; namely, from predestination, which direction never fails, and from grace; for whoever has grace, by this very fact becomes fitted for eternal life. This direction fails sometimes; because some are directed by possessing grace, to obtain eternal life, yet they fail to obtain it through mortal sin. Therefore those who are ordained to possess eternal life through divine predestination are written down in the book of life simply, because they are written therein to have eternal life in reality; such are never blotted out from the book of life. Those, however, who are ordained to eternal life, not through divine predestination, but through grace, are said to be written in the book of life not simply, but relatively, for they are written therein not to have eternal life in itself, but in its cause only. Yet though these latter can be said to be blotted out of the book of life, this blotting out must not be referred to God, as if God foreknew a thing, and afterwards knew it not; but to the thing known, namely, because God knows one is first ordained to eternal life, and afterwards not ordained when he falls from grace.

REPLY OBJ. 1: The act of blotting out does not refer to the book of life as regards God's foreknowledge, as if in God there were any change; but as regards things foreknown, which can change.

REPLY OBJ. 2: Although things are immutably in God, yet in themselves they are subject to change. To this it is that the blotting out of the book of life refers.

REPLY OBJ. 3: The way in which one is said to be blotted out of the book of life is that in which one is said to be written therein anew; either in the opinion of men, or because he begins again to have relation towards eternal life

aeternam per gratiam. Quod etiam sub divina notitia comprehenditur, licet non de novo.

through grace; which also is included in the knowledge of God, although not anew.

QUESTION 25

THE POWER OF GOD

Post considerationem divinae scientiae et voluntatis, et eorum quae ad hoc pertinent, restat considerandum de divina potentia.

Et circa hoc quaeruntur sex.

Primo, utrum in Deo sit potentia.

Secundo, utrum eius potentia sit infinita.

Tertio, utrum sit omnipotens.

Quarto, utrum possit facere quod ea quae sunt praeterita, non fuerint.

Quinto, utrum Deus possit facere quae non facit, vel praetermittere quae facit.

Sexto, utrum quae facit, possit facere meliora.

After considering the divine foreknowledge and will, and other things pertaining thereto, it remains for us to consider the power of God.

About this are six points of inquiry:

(1) Whether there is power in God?

(2) Whether His power is infinite?

(3) Whether He is almighty?

(4) Whether He could make the past not to have been?

(5) Whether He could do what He does not, or not do what He does?

(6) Whether what He makes He could make better?

Article 1

Whether There Is Power in God?

AD PRIMUM SIC PROCEDITUR. Videtur quod in Deo non sit potentia. Sicut enim prima materia se habet ad potentiam, ita Deus, qui est agens primum, se habet ad actum. Sed prima materia, secundum se considerata, est absque omni actu. Ergo agens primum, quod est Deus, est absque potentia.

PRAETEREA, secundum philosophum, in IX Metaphys., qualibet potentia melior est eius actus, nam forma est melior quam materia, et actio quam potentia activa; est enim finis eius. Sed nihil est melius eo quod est in Deo, quia quidquid est in Deo, est Deus, ut supra ostensum est. Ergo nulla potentia est in Deo.

PRAETEREA, potentia est principium operationis. Sed operatio divina est eius essentia, cum in Deo nullum sit accidens. Essentiae autem divinae non est aliquod principium. Ergo ratio potentiae Deo non convenit.

PRAETEREA, supra ostensum est quod scientia Dei et voluntas eius sunt causa rerum. Causa autem et principium idem sunt. Ergo non oportet in Deo assignare potentiam, sed solum scientiam et voluntatem.

SED CONTRA est quod dicitur in Psalmo LXXXVIII, *potens es, domine, et veritas tua in circuitu tuo.*

RESPONDEO dicendum quod duplex est potentia, scilicet passiva, quae nullo modo est in Deo; et activa, quam oportet in Deo summe ponere. Manifestum est enim quod unumquodque, secundum quod est actu et perfectum, secundum hoc est principium activum alicuius, patitur autem unumquodque, secundum quod

OBJECTION 1: It seems that power is not in God. For as primary matter is to power, so God, who is the first agent, is to act. But primary matter, considered in itself, is devoid of all act. Therefore, the first agent—namely, God—is devoid of power.

OBJ. 2: Further, according to the Philosopher (*Metaph.* vi, 19), better than every power is its act. For form is better than matter; and action than active power, since it is its end. But nothing is better than what is in God; because whatsoever is in God, is God, as was shown above (Q. 3, A. 3). Therefore, there is no power in God.

OBJ. 3: Further, Power is the principle of operation. But the divine power is God's essence, since there is nothing accidental in God: and of the essence of God there is no principle. Therefore there is no power in God.

OBJ. 4: Further, it was shown above (Q. 14, A. 8; Q. 19, A. 4) that God's knowledge and will are the cause of things. But the cause and principle of a thing are identical. We ought not, therefore, to assign power to God; but only knowledge and will.

ON THE CONTRARY, It is said: *Thou art mighty, O Lord, and Thy truth is round about Thee* (Ps 88:9).

I ANSWER THAT, Power is twofold—namely, passive, which exists not at all in God; and active, which we must assign to Him in the highest degree. For it is manifest that everything, according as it is in act and is perfect, is the active principle of something: whereas everything is passive according as it is deficient and imperfect. Now it was

est deficiens et imperfectum. Ostensum est autem supra quod Deus est purus actus, et simpliciter et universaliter perfectus; neque in eo aliqua imperfectio locum habet. Unde sibi maxime competit esse principium activum, et nullo modo pati. Ratio autem activi principii convenit potentiae activae. Nam potentia activa est principium agendi in aliud, potentia vero passiva est principium patiendi ab alio, ut philosophus dicit, V Metaphys. Relinquitur ergo quod in Deo maxime sit potentia activa.

Ad primum ergo dicendum quod potentia activa non dividitur contra actum, sed fundatur in eo, nam unumquodque agit secundum quod est actu. Potentia vero passiva dividitur contra actum, nam unumquodque patitur secundum quod est in potentia. Unde haec potentia excluditur a Deo, non autem activa.

Ad secundum dicendum quod, quandocumque actus est aliud a potentia, oportet quod actus sit nobilior potentia. Sed actio Dei non est aliud ab eius potentia, sed utrumque est essentia divina, quia nec esse eius est aliud ab eius essentia. Unde non oportet quod aliquid sit nobilius quam potentia Dei.

Ad tertium dicendum quod potentia in rebus creatis non solum est principium actionis, sed etiam effectus. Sic igitur in Deo salvatur ratio potentiae quantum ad hoc, quod est principium effectus, non autem quantum ad hoc, quod est principium actionis, quae est divina essentia. Nisi forte secundum modum intelligendi, prout divina essentia, quae in se simpliciter praehabet quidquid perfectionis est in rebus creatis, potest intelligi et sub ratione actionis, et sub ratione potentiae; sicut etiam intelligitur et sub ratione suppositi habentis naturam, et sub ratione naturae.

Ad quartum dicendum quod potentia non ponitur in Deo ut aliquid differens a scientia et voluntate secundum rem, sed solum secundum rationem; inquantum scilicet potentia importat rationem principii exequentis id quod voluntas imperat, et ad quod scientia dirigit; quae tria Deo secundum idem conveniunt. Vel dicendum quod ipsa scientia vel voluntas divina, secundum quod est principium effectivum, habet rationem potentiae. Unde consideratio scientiae et voluntatis praecedit in Deo considerationem potentiae, sicut causa praecedit operationem et effectum.

shown above (Q. 3, A. 2; Q. 4, AA. 1, 2), that God is pure act, simply and in all ways perfect, nor in Him does any imperfection find place. Whence it most fittingly belongs to Him to be an active principle, and in no way whatsoever to be passive. On the other hand, the notion of active principle is consistent with active power. For active power is the principle of acting upon something else; whereas passive power is the principle of being acted upon by something else, as the Philosopher says (*Metaph.* v, 17). It remains, therefore, that in God there is active power in the highest degree.

Reply Obj. 1: Active power is not contrary to act, but is founded upon it, for everything acts according as it is actual: but passive power is contrary to act; for a thing is passive according as it is potential. Whence this potentiality is not in God, but only active power.

Reply Obj. 2: Whenever act is distinct from power, act must be nobler than power. But God's action is not distinct from His power, for both are His divine essence; neither is His existence distinct from His essence. Hence it does not follow that there should be anything in God nobler than His power.

Reply Obj. 3: In creatures, power is the principle not only of action, but likewise of effect. Thus in God the idea of power is retained, inasmuch as it is the principle of an effect; not, however, as it is a principle of action, for this is the divine essence itself; except, perchance, after our manner of understanding, inasmuch as the divine essence, which pre-contains in itself all perfection that exists in created things, can be understood either under the notion of action, or under that of power; as also it is understood under the notion of suppositum possessing nature, and under that of nature. Accordingly the notion of power is retained in God in so far as it is the principle of an effect.

Reply Obj. 4: Power is predicated of God not as something really distinct from His knowledge and will, but as differing from them logically; inasmuch as power implies a notion of a principle putting into execution what the will commands, and what knowledge directs, which three things in God are identified. Or we may say, that the knowledge or will of God, according as it is the effective principle, has the notion of power contained in it. Hence the consideration of the knowledge and will of God precedes the consideration of His power, as the cause precedes the operation and effect.

Article 2

Whether the Power of God Is Infinite?

AD SECUNDUM SIC PROCEDITUR. Videtur quod potentia Dei non sit infinita. Omne enim infinitum est imperfectum, secundum philosophum, in III Physic. Sed potentia Dei non est imperfecta. Ergo non est infinita.

PRAETEREA, omnis potentia manifestatur per effectum, alias frustra esset. Si igitur potentia Dei esset infinita, posset facere effectum infinitum. Quod est impossibile.

PRAETEREA, philosophus probat in VIII Physic., quod si potentia alicuius corporis esset infinita, moveret in instanti. Deus autem non movet in instanti, sed movet creaturam spiritualem *per tempus, creaturam vero corporalem per locum et tempus*, secundum Augustinum, VIII super Genesim ad litteram. Non ergo est eius potentia infinita.

SED CONTRA est quod dicit Hilarius, VIII de Trin., quod *Deus est immensae virtutis, vivens, potens*. Omne autem immensum est infinitum. Ergo virtus divina est infinita.

RESPONDEO dicendum quod, sicut iam dictum est, secundum hoc potentia activa invenitur in Deo, secundum quod ipse actu est. Esse autem eius est infinitum, inquantum non est limitatum per aliquid recipiens; ut patet per ea quae supra dicta sunt, cum de infinitate divinae essentiae ageretur. Unde necesse est quod activa potentia Dei sit infinita. In omnibus enim agentibus hoc invenitur, quod quanto aliquod agens perfectius habet formam qua agit, tanto est maior eius potentia in agendo. Sicut quanto est aliquid magis calidum, tanto habet maiorem potentiam ad calefaciendum, et haberet utique potentiam infinitam ad calefaciendum, si eius calor esset infinitus. Unde, cum ipsa essentia divina, per quam Deus agit, sit infinita, sicut supra ostensum est, sequitur quod eius potentia sit infinita.

AD PRIMUM ergo dicendum quod philosophus loquitur de infinito quod est ex parte materiae non terminatae per formam; cuiusmodi est infinitum quod congruit quantitati. Sic autem non est infinita divina essentia, ut supra ostensum est; et per consequens nec eius potentia. Unde non sequitur quod sit imperfecta.

AD SECUNDUM dicendum quod potentia agentis univoci tota manifestatur in suo effectu, potentia enim generativa hominis nihil potest plus quam generare hominem. Sed potentia agentis non univoci non tota manifestatur in sui effectus productione, sicut potentia solis non tota manifestatur in productione alicuius animalis ex putrefactione generati. Manifestum est autem quod Deus non est agens univocum, nihil enim aliud potest cum eo convenire neque in specie, neque in genere, ut supra ostensum est. Unde relinquitur quod effectus eius

OBJECTION 1: It seems that the power of God is not infinite. For everything that is infinite is imperfect according to the Philosopher (*Phys.* iii, 6). But the power of God is far from imperfect. Therefore it is not infinite.

OBJ. 2: Further, every power is made known by its effect; otherwise it would be ineffectual. If, then, the power of God were infinite, it could produce an infinite effect, but this is impossible.

OBJ. 3: Further, the Philosopher proves (*Phys.* viii, 79) that if the power of any corporeal thing were infinite, it would cause instantaneous movement. God, however, does not cause instantaneous movement, but moves the spiritual creature in time, and the corporeal creature in place and time, as Augustine says (*Gen ad lit.* 20, 22, 23). Therefore, His power is not infinite.

ON THE CONTRARY, Hilary says (*De Trin.* viii), that *God's power is immeasurable. He is the living mighty one.* Now everything that is immeasurable is infinite. Therefore the power of God is infinite.

I ANSWER THAT, As stated above (A. 1), active power exists in God according to the measure in which He is actual. Now His existence is infinite, inasmuch as it is not limited by anything that receives it, as is clear from what has been said, when we discussed the infinity of the divine essence (Q. 7, A. 1). Wherefore, it is necessary that the active power in God should be infinite. For in every agent is it found that the more perfectly an agent has the form by which it acts, the greater its power to act. For instance, the hotter a thing is, the greater the power it has to give heat; and it would have infinite power to give heat, were its own heat infinite. Whence, since the divine essence, through which God acts, is infinite, as was shown above (Q. 7, A. 1), it follows that His power likewise is infinite.

REPLY OBJ. 1: The Philosopher is here speaking of an infinity in regard to matter not limited by any form; and such infinity belongs to quantity. But the divine essence is otherwise, as was shown above (Q. 7, A. 1); and consequently so also His power. It does not follow, therefore, that it is imperfect.

REPLY OBJ. 2: The power of a univocal agent is wholly manifested in its effect. The generative power of man, for example, is not able to do more than beget man. But the power of a non-univocal agent does not wholly manifest itself in the production of its effect: as, for example, the power of the sun does not wholly manifest itself in the production of an animal generated from putrefaction. Now it is clear that God is not a univocal agent. For nothing agrees with Him either in species or in genus, as was shown above (Q. 3, A. 5; Q. 4, A. 3). Whence it follows that His effect is

semper est minor quam potentia eius. Non ergo oportet quod manifestetur infinita potentia Dei in hoc, quod producat effectum infinitum. Et tamen, etiam si nullum effectum produceret, non esset Dei potentia frustra. Quia frustra est quod ordinatur ad finem, quem non attingit, potentia autem Dei non ordinatur ad effectum sicut ad finem, sed magis ipsa est finis sui effectus.

AD TERTIUM dicendum quod philosophus in VIII Physic., probat, quod si aliquod corpus haberet potentiam infinitam, quod moveret in non tempore. Et tamen ostendit, quod potentia motoris caeli est infinita, quia movere potest tempore infinito. Relinquitur ergo secundum eius intentionem, quod potentia infinita corporis si esset, moveret in non tempore, non autem potentia incorporei motoris. Cuius ratio est, quia corpus movens aliud corpus, est agens univocum. Unde oportet quod tota potentia agentis manifestetur in motu. Quia igitur quanto moventis corporis potentia est maior, tanto velocius movet, necesse est quod si fuerit infinita, moveat improportionabiliter citius, quod est movere in non tempore. Sed movens incorporeum est agens non univocum. Unde non oportet, quod tota virtus eius manifestetur in motu ita, quod moveat in non tempore. Et praesertim, quia movet secundum dispositionem suae voluntatis.

always less than His power. It is not necessary, therefore, that the infinite power of God should be manifested so as to produce an infinite effect. Yet even if it were to produce no effect, the power of God would not be ineffectual; because a thing is ineffectual which is ordained towards an end to which it does not attain. But the power of God is not ordered toward its effect as towards an end; rather, it is the end of the effect produced by it.

REPLY OBJ. 3: The Philosopher (*Phys.* viii, 79) proves that if a body had infinite power, it would cause a non-temporal movement. And he shows that the power of the mover of heaven is infinite, because it can move in an infinite time. It remains, therefore, according to his reckoning, that the infinite power of a body, if such existed, would move without time; not, however, the power of an incorporeal mover. The reason of this is that one body moving another is a univocal agent; wherefore it follows that the whole power of the agent is made known in its motion. Since then the greater the power of a moving body, the more quickly does it move; the necessary conclusion is that if its power were infinite, it would move beyond comparison faster, and this is to move without time. An incorporeal mover, however, is not a univocal agent; whence it is not necessary that the whole of its power should be manifested in motion, so as to move without time; and especially since it moves in accordance with the disposition of its will.

Article 3

Whether God Is Omnipotent?

AD TERTIUM SIC PROCEDITUR. Videtur quod Deus non sit omnipotens. Moveri enim et pati aliquid omnium est. Sed hoc Deus non potest, est enim immobilis, ut supra dictum est. Non igitur est omnipotens.

PRAETEREA, peccare aliquid agere est. Sed Deus non potest peccare, neque seipsum negare, ut dicitur II Tim. II. Ergo Deus non est omnipotens.

PRAETEREA, de Deo dicitur quod *omnipotentiam suam parcendo maxime et miserando manifestat.* Ultimum igitur quod potest divina potentia, est parcere et misereri. Aliquid autem est multo maius quam parcere et misereri; sicut creare alium mundum, vel aliquid huiusmodi. Ergo Deus non est omnipotens.

PRAETEREA, super illud I Cor. I, *stultam fecit Deus sapientiam huius mundi,* dicit Glossa, *sapientiam huius mundi fecit Deus stultam, ostendendo possibile, quod illa impossibile iudicabat.* Unde videtur quod non sit aliquid iudicandum possibile vel impossibile secundum inferiores causas, prout sapientia huius mundi iudicat; sed secundum potentiam divinam. Si igitur Deus sit omnipotens, omnia erunt possibilia. Nihil ergo impossibile.

OBJECTION 1: It seems that God is not omnipotent. For movement and passiveness belong to everything. But this is impossible with God, for He is immovable, as was said above (Q. 2, A. 3). Therefore He is not omnipotent.

OBJ. 2: Further, sin is an act of some kind. But God cannot sin, nor *deny Himself* as it is said in 2 Tim. 2:13. Therefore He is not omnipotent.

OBJ. 3: Further, it is said of God that He manifests His omnipotence *especially by sparing and having mercy.* Therefore the greatest act possible to the divine power is to spare and have mercy. There are things much greater, however, than sparing and having mercy; for example, to create another world, and the like. Therefore God is not omnipotent.

OBJ. 4: Further, upon the text, *God hath made foolish the wisdom of this world* (1 Cor 1:20), a gloss says: *God hath made the wisdom of this world foolish by showing those things to be possible which it judges to be impossible.* Whence it would seem that nothing is to be judged possible or impossible in reference to inferior causes, as the wisdom of this world judges them; but in reference to the divine power. If God, then, were omnipotent, all things would be

Sublato autem impossibili, tollitur necessarium, nam quod necesse est esse, impossibile est non esse. Nihil ergo erit necessarium in rebus, si Deus est omnipotens. Hoc autem est impossibile. Ergo Deus non est omnipotens.

SED CONTRA est quod dicitur Luc. I, *non erit impossibile apud Deum omne verbum.*

RESPONDEO dicendum quod communiter confitentur omnes Deum esse omnipotentem. Sed rationem omnipotentiae assignare videtur difficile. Dubium enim potest esse quid comprehendatur sub ista distributione, cum dicitur omnia posse Deum. Sed si quis recte consideret, cum potentia dicatur ad possibilia, cum Deus omnia posse dicitur, nihil rectius intelligitur quam quod possit omnia possibilia, et ob hoc omnipotens dicatur. Possibile autem dicitur dupliciter, secundum philosophum, in V Metaphys. Uno modo, per respectum ad aliquam potentiam, sicut quod subditur humanae potentiae, dicitur esse possibile homini. Non autem potest dici quod Deus dicatur omnipotens, quia potest omnia quae sunt possibilia naturae creatae, quia divina potentia in plura extenditur. Si autem dicatur quod Deus sit omnipotens, quia potest omnia quae sunt possibilia suae potentiae, erit circulatio in manifestatione omnipotentiae, hoc enim non erit aliud quam dicere quod Deus est omnipotens, quia potest omnia quae potest.

Relinquitur igitur quod Deus dicatur omnipotens, quia potest omnia possibilia absolute, quod est alter modus dicendi possibile. Dicitur autem aliquid possibile vel impossibile absolute, ex habitudine terminorum, possibile quidem, quia praedicatum non repugnat subiecto, ut Socratem sedere; impossibile vero absolute, quia praedicatum repugnat subiecto, ut hominem esse asinum.

Est autem considerandum quod, cum unumquodque agens agat sibi simile, unicuique potentiae activae correspondet possibile ut obiectum proprium, secundum rationem illius actus in quo fundatur potentia activa, sicut potentia calefactiva refertur, ut ad proprium obiectum, ad esse calefactibile. Esse autem divinum, super quod ratio divinae potentiae fundatur, est esse infinitum, non limitatum ad aliquod genus entis, sed praehabens in se totius esse perfectionem. Unde quidquid potest habere rationem entis, continetur sub possibilibus absolutis, respectu quorum Deus dicitur omnipotens. Nihil autem opponitur rationi entis, nisi non ens. Hoc igitur repugnat rationi possibilis absoluti, quod subditur divinae omnipotentiae, quod implicat in se esse et non esse simul. Hoc enim omnipotentiae non subditur,

possible; nothing, therefore impossible. But if we take away the impossible, then we destroy also the necessary; for what necessarily exists is impossible not to exist. Therefore there would be nothing at all that is necessary in things if God were omnipotent. But this is an impossibility. Therefore God is not omnipotent.

ON THE CONTRARY, It is said: *No word shall be impossible with God* (Luke 1:37).

I ANSWER THAT, All confess that God is omnipotent; but it seems difficult to explain in what His omnipotence precisely consists: for there may be doubt as to the precise meaning of the word 'all' when we say that God can do all things. If, however, we consider the matter aright, since power is said in reference to possible things, this phrase, *God can do all things,* is rightly understood to mean that God can do all things that are possible; and for this reason He is said to be omnipotent. Now according to the Philosopher (*Metaph.* v, 17), a thing is said to be possible in two ways. First in relation to some power, thus whatever is subject to human power is said to be possible to man. Second absolutely, on account of the relation in which the very terms stand to each other. Now God cannot be said to be omnipotent through being able to do all things that are possible to created nature; for the divine power extends farther than that. If, however, we were to say that God is omnipotent because He can do all things that are possible to His power, there would be a vicious circle in explaining the nature of His power. For this would be saying nothing else but that God is omnipotent, because He can do all that He is able to do.

It remains therefore, that God is called omnipotent because He can do all things that are possible absolutely; which is the second way of saying a thing is possible. For a thing is said to be possible or impossible absolutely, according to the relation in which the very terms stand to one another, possible if the predicate is not incompatible with the subject, as that Socrates sits; and absolutely impossible when the predicate is altogether incompatible with the subject, as, for instance, that a man is a donkey.

It must, however, be remembered that since every agent produces an effect like itself, to each active power there corresponds a thing possible as its proper object according to the nature of that act on which its active power is founded; for instance, the power of giving warmth is related as to its proper object to the being capable of being warmed. The divine existence, however, upon which the nature of power in God is founded, is infinite, and is not limited to any genus of being; but possesses within itself the perfection of all being. Whence, whatsoever has or can have the nature of being, is numbered among the absolutely possible things, in respect of which God is called omnipotent. Now nothing is opposed to the idea of being except non-being. Therefore, that which implies being and non-being at the same time is repugnant to the idea of an absolutely possible

non propter defectum divinae potentiae; sed quia non potest habere rationem factibilis neque possibilis. Quaecumque igitur contradictionem non implicant, sub illis possibilibus continentur, respectu quorum dicitur Deus omnipotens. Ea vero quae contradictionem implicant, sub divina omnipotentia non continentur, quia non possunt habere possibilium rationem. Unde convenientius dicitur quod non possunt fieri, quam quod Deus non potest ea facere. Neque hoc est contra verbum Angeli dicentis, *non erit impossibile apud Deum omne verbum.* Id enim quod contradictionem implicat, verbum esse non potest, quia nullus intellectus potest illud concipere.

AD PRIMUM ergo dicendum quod Deus dicitur omnipotens secundum potentiam activam, non secundum potentiam passivam, ut dictum est. Unde, quod non potest moveri et pati, non repugnat omnipotentiae.

AD SECUNDUM dicendum quod peccare est deficere a perfecta actione, unde posse peccare est posse deficere in agendo, quod repugnat omnipotentiae. Et propter hoc, Deus peccare non potest, qui est omnipotens. Quamvis philosophus dicat, in IV Topic., quod potest Deus et studiosus prava agere. Sed hoc intelligitur vel sub conditione cuius antecedens sit impossibile, ut puta si dicamus quod potest Deus prava agere si velit, nihil enim prohibet conditionalem esse veram, cuius antecedens et consequens est impossibile; sicut si dicatur, si homo est asinus, habet quatuor pedes. Vel ut intelligatur quod Deus potest aliqua agere, quae nunc prava videntur; quae tamen si ageret, bona essent. Vel loquitur secundum communem opinionem gentilium, qui homines dicebant transferri in deos, ut Iovem vel Mercurium.

AD TERTIUM dicendum quod Dei omnipotentia ostenditur maxime in parcendo et miserando, quia per hoc ostenditur Deum habere summam potestatem, quod libere peccata dimittit, eius enim qui superioris legi astringitur, non est libere peccata condonare. Vel quia, parcendo hominibus et miserando, perducit eos ad participationem infiniti boni, qui est ultimus effectus divinae virtutis. Vel quia, ut supra dictum est, effectus divinae misericordiae est fundamentum omnium divinorum operum, nihil enim debetur alicui nisi propter id quod est datum ei a Deo non debitum. In hoc autem maxime divina omnipotentia manifestatur, quod ad ipsam pertinet prima institutio omnium bonorum.

AD QUARTUM dicendum quod possibile absolutum non dicitur neque secundum causas superiores, neque secundum causas inferiores sed secundum seipsum. Possibile vero quod dicitur secundum aliquam potentiam, nominatur possibile secundum proximam

thing, within the scope of the divine omnipotence. For such cannot come under the divine omnipotence, not because of any defect in the power of God, but because it has not the nature of a feasible or possible thing. Therefore, everything that does not imply a contradiction in terms, is numbered amongst those possible things, in respect of which God is called omnipotent: whereas whatever implies contradiction does not come within the scope of divine omnipotence, because it cannot have the aspect of possibility. Hence it is better to say that such things cannot be done, than that God cannot do them. Nor is this contrary to the word of the angel, saying: *No word shall be impossible with God.* For whatever implies a contradiction cannot be a word, because no intellect can possibly conceive such a thing.

REPLY OBJ. 1: God is said to be omnipotent in respect to His active power, not to passive power, as was shown above (A. 1). Whence the fact that He is immovable or impassible is not repugnant to His omnipotence.

REPLY OBJ. 2: To sin is to fall short of a perfect action; hence to be able to sin is to be able to fall short in action, which is repugnant to omnipotence. Therefore it is that God cannot sin, because of His omnipotence. Nevertheless, the Philosopher says (*Topic.* iv, 3) that God can deliberately do what is evil. But this must be understood either on a condition, the antecedent of which is impossible—as, for instance, if we were to say that God can do evil things if He will. For there is no reason why a conditional proposition should not be true, though both the antecedent and consequent are impossible: as if one were to say: *If man is a donkey, he has four feet.* Or he may be understood to mean that God can do some things which now seem to be evil: which, however, if He did them, would then be good. Or he is, perhaps, speaking after the common manner of the heathen, who thought that men became gods, like Jupiter or Mercury.

REPLY OBJ. 3: God's omnipotence is particularly shown in sparing and having mercy, because in this is it made manifest that God has supreme power, that He freely forgives sins. For it is not for one who is bound by laws of a superior to forgive sins of his own free will. Or, because by sparing and having mercy upon men, He leads them on to the participation of an infinite good; which is the ultimate effect of the divine power. Or because, as was said above (Q. 21, A. 4), the effect of the divine mercy is the foundation of all the divine works. For nothing is due to anyone, except on account of something already given him gratuitously by God. In this way the divine omnipotence is particularly made manifest, because to it pertains the first foundation of all good things.

REPLY OBJ. 4: The absolute possible is not so called in reference either to higher causes, or to inferior causes, but in reference to itself. But the possible in reference to some power is named possible in reference to its proximate cause. Hence those things which it belongs to God alone to

causam. Unde ea quae immediate nata sunt fieri a Deo solo, ut creare, iustificare, et huiusmodi, dicuntur possibilia secundum causam superiorem, quae autem nata sunt fieri a causis inferioribus, dicuntur possibilia secundum causas inferiores. Nam secundum conditionem causae proximae, effectus habet contingentiam vel necessitatem, ut supra dictum est. In hoc autem reputatur stulta mundi sapientia, quod ea quae sunt impossibilia naturae, etiam Deo impossibilia iudicabat. Et sic patet quod omnipotentia Dei impossibilitatem et necessitatem a rebus non excludit.

do immediately—as, for example, to create, to justify, and the like—are said to be possible in reference to a higher cause. Those things, however, which are of such kind as to be done by inferior causes are said to be possible in reference to those inferior causes. For it is according to the condition of the proximate cause that the effect has contingency or necessity, as was shown above (Q. 14, A. 1, ad 2). Thus is it that the wisdom of the world is deemed foolish, because what is impossible to nature, it judges to be impossible to God. So it is clear that the omnipotence of God does not take away from things their impossibility and necessity.

Article 4

Whether God Can Make the Past Not to Have Been?

Ad quartum sic proceditur. Videtur quod Deus possit facere quod praeterita non fuerint. Quod enim est impossibile per se, magis est impossibile quam quod est impossibile per accidens. Sed Deus potest facere id quod est impossibile per se, ut caecum illuminare, vel mortuum resuscitare. Ergo multo magis potest Deus facere illud quod est impossibile per accidens. Sed praeterita non fuisse, est impossibile per accidens, accidit enim Socratem non currere esse impossibile, ex hoc quod praeteriit. Ergo Deus potest facere quod praeterita non fuerint.

Praeterea, quidquid Deus facere potuit, potest, cum eius potentia non minuatur. Sed Deus potuit facere, antequam Socrates curreret, quod non curreret. Ergo, postquam cucurrit, potest Deus facere quod non cucurrerit.

Praeterea, caritas est maior virtus quam virginitas. Sed Deus potest reparare caritatem amissam. Ergo et virginitatem. Ergo potest facere quod illa quae corrupta fuit, non fuerit corrupta.

Sed contra est quod Hieronymus dicit, *cum Deus omnia possit, non potest de corrupta facere incorruptam.* Ergo eadem ratione non potest facere de quocumque alio praeterito quod non fuerit.

Respondeo dicendum quod, sicut supra dictum est, sub omnipotentia Dei non cadit aliquid quod contradictionem implicat. Praeterita autem non fuisse, contradictionem implicat. Sicut enim contradictionem implicat dicere quod Socrates sedet et non sedet, ita, quod sederit et non sederit. Dicere autem quod sederit, est dicere quod sit praeteritum, dicere autem quod non sederit, est dicere quod non fuerit. Unde praeterita non fuisse, non subiacet divinae potentiae. Et hoc est quod Augustinus dicit, contra Faustum, *quisquis ita dicit, si Deus omnipotens est, faciat ut quae facta sunt, facta non fuerint, non*

Objection 1: It seems that God can make the past not to have been. For what is impossible in itself is much more impossible than that which is only impossible accidentally. But God can do what is impossible in itself, as to give sight to the blind, or to raise the dead. Therefore, and much more can He do what is only impossible accidentally. Now for the past not to have been is impossible accidentally: thus for Socrates not to be running is accidentally impossible, from the fact that his running is a thing of the past. Therefore God can make the past not to have been.

Obj. 2: Further, what God could do, He can do now, since His power is not lessened. But God could have effected, before Socrates ran, that he should not run. Therefore, when he has run, God could effect that he did not run.

Obj. 3: Further, charity is a more excellent virtue than virginity. But God can supply charity that is lost; therefore also lost virginity. Therefore He can so effect that what was corrupt should not have been corrupt.

On the contrary, Jerome says (*Ep. 22 ad Eustoch.*): *Although God can do all things, He cannot make a thing that is corrupt not to have been corrupted.* Therefore, for the same reason, He cannot effect that anything else which is past should not have been.

I answer that, As was said above (Q. 7, A. 2), there does not fall under the scope of God's omnipotence anything that implies a contradiction. Now that the past should not have been implies a contradiction. For as it implies a contradiction to say that Socrates is sitting, and is not sitting, so does it to say that he sat, and did not sit. But to say that he did sit is to say that it happened in the past. To say that he did not sit, is to say that it did not happen. Whence, that the past should not have been, does not come under the scope of divine power. This is what Augustine means when he says (*Contra Faust.* xxix, 5): *Whosoever*

videt hoc se dicere, si Deus omnipotens est, faciat ut ea quae vera sunt, eo ipso quod vera sunt, falsa sint. Et philosophus dicit, in VI Ethic., quod hoc solo privatur Deus, ingenita facere quae sunt facta.

AD PRIMUM ergo dicendum quod, licet praeterita non fuisse sit impossibile per accidens, si consideretur id quod est praeteritum, idest cursus Socratis; tamen, si consideretur praeteritum sub ratione praeteriti, ipsum non fuisse est impossibile non solum per se, sed absolute, contradictionem implicans. Et sic est magis impossibile quam mortuum resurgere, quod non implicat contradictionem, quod dicitur impossibile secundum aliquam potentiam, scilicet naturalem. Talia enim impossibilia divinae potentiae subduntur.

AD SECUNDUM dicendum quod sicut Deus, quantum est ad perfectionem divinae potentiae, omnia potest, sed quaedam non subiacent eius potentiae, quia deficiunt a ratione possibilium; ita, si attendatur immutabilitas divinae potentiae, quidquid Deus potuit, potest; aliqua tamen olim habuerunt rationem possibilium, dum erant fienda, quae iam deficiunt a ratione possibilium, dum sunt facta. Et sic dicitur Deus ea non posse, quia ea non possunt fieri.

AD TERTIUM dicendum quod omnem corruptionem mentis et corporis Deus auferre potest a muliere corrupta, hoc tamen ab ea removeri non poterit, quod corrupta non fuerit. Sicut etiam ab aliquo peccatore auferre non potest quod non peccaverit, et quod caritatem non amiserit.

says, *If God is almighty, let Him make what is done as if it were not done, does not see that this is to say: If God is almighty let Him effect that what is true, by the very fact that it is true, be false*: and the Philosopher says (*Ethic.* vi, 2): *Of this one thing alone is God deprived—namely, to make undone the things that have been done.*

REPLY OBJ. 1: Although it is impossible accidentally for the past not to have been, if one considers the past thing itself, as, for instance, the running of Socrates; nevertheless, if the past thing is considered as past, that it should not have been is impossible, not only in itself, but absolutely since it implies a contradiction. Thus, it is more impossible than the raising of the dead; in which there is nothing contradictory, because this is reckoned impossible in reference to some power, that is to say, some natural power; for such impossible things do come beneath the scope of divine power.

REPLY OBJ. 2: As God, in accordance with the perfection of the divine power, can do all things, and yet some things are not subject to His power, because they fall short of being possible; so, also, if we regard the immutability of the divine power, whatever God could do, He can do now. Some things, however, at one time were in the nature of possibility, whilst they were yet to be done, which now fall short of the nature of possibility, when they have been done. So is God said not to be able to do them, because they themselves cannot be done.

REPLY OBJ. 3: God can remove all corruption of the mind and body from a woman who has fallen; but the fact that she had been corrupt cannot be removed from her; as also is it impossible that the fact of having sinned or having lost charity thereby can be removed from the sinner.

Article 5

Whether God Can Do What He Does Not?

AD QUINTUM SIC PROCEDITUR. Videtur quod Deus non possit facere nisi ea quae facit. Deus enim non potest facere quae non praescivit et praeordinavit se facturum. Sed non praescivit neque praeordinavit se facturum, nisi ea quae facit. Ergo non potest facere nisi ea quae facit.

PRAETEREA, Deus non potest facere nisi quod debet, et quod iustum est fieri. Sed Deus non debet facere quae non facit, nec iustum est ut faciat quae non facit. Ergo Deus non potest facere nisi quae facit.

PRAETEREA, Deus non potest facere nisi quod bonum est, et conveniens rebus factis. Sed rebus factis a Deo non est bonum nec conveniens aliter esse quam sint. Ergo Deus non potest facere nisi quae facit.

OBJECTION 1: It seems that God cannot do other than what He does. For God cannot do what He has not foreknown and pre-ordained that He would do. But He neither foreknew nor pre-ordained that He would do anything except what He does. Therefore He cannot do except what He does.

OBJ. 2: Further, God can only do what ought to be done and what is right to be done. But God is not bound to do what He does not; nor is it right that He should do what He does not. Therefore He cannot do except what He does.

OBJ. 3: Further, God cannot do anything that is not good and befitting creation. But it is not good for creatures nor befitting them to be otherwise than as they are. Therefore God cannot do except what He does.

SED CONTRA est quod dicitur Matt. XXVI, *an non possum rogare patrem meum, et exhibebit mihi modo plus quam duodecim legiones Angelorum?* Neque autem ipse rogabat, neque pater exhibebat ad repugnandum Iudaeis. Ergo Deus potest facere quod non facit.

RESPONDEO dicendum quod circa hoc quidam dupliciter erraverunt. Quidam enim posuerunt Deum agere quasi ex necessitate naturae; ut sicut ex actione rerum naturalium non possunt alia provenire nisi quae eveniunt, utpote ex semine hominis homo, ex semine olivae oliva; ita ex operatione divina non possint aliae res, vel alius ordo rerum effluere, nisi sicut nunc est. Sed supra ostendimus Deum non agere quasi ex necessitate naturae, sed voluntatem eius esse omnium rerum causam; neque etiam ipsam voluntatem naturaliter et ex necessitate determinari ad has res. Unde nullo modo iste cursus rerum sic ex necessitate a Deo provenit, quod alia provenire non possent. Alii vero dixerunt quod potentia divina determinatur ad hunc cursum rerum, propter ordinem sapientiae et iustitiae divinae, sine quo Deus nihil operatur. Cum autem potentia Dei, quae est eius essentia, non sit aliud quam Dei sapientia, convenienter quidem dici potest quod nihil sit in Dei potentia, quod non sit in ordine divinae sapientiae, nam divina sapientia totum posse potentiae comprehendit. Sed tamen ordo a divina sapientia rebus inditus, in quo ratio iustitiae consistit, ut supra dictum est, non adaequat divinam sapientiam, sic ut divina sapientia limitetur ad hunc ordinem. Manifestum est enim quod tota ratio ordinis, quam sapiens rebus a se factis imponit, a fine sumitur. Quando igitur finis est proportionatus rebus propter finem factis, sapientia facientis limitatur ad aliquem determinatum ordinem. Sed divina bonitas est finis improportionabiliter excedens res creatas. Unde divina sapientia non determinatur ad aliquem certum ordinem rerum, ut non possit alius cursus rerum ab ipsa effluere. Unde dicendum est simpliciter quod Deus potest alia facere quam quae facit.

AD PRIMUM ergo dicendum quod in nobis, in quibus est aliud potentia et essentia a voluntate et intellectu, et iterum intellectus aliud a sapientia, et voluntas aliud a iustitia, potest esse aliquid in potentia, quod non potest esse in voluntate iusta, vel in intellectu sapiente. Sed in Deo est idem potentia et essentia et voluntas et intellectus et sapientia et iustitia. Unde nihil potest esse in potentia divina, quod non possit esse in voluntate iusta ipsius, et in intellectu sapiente eius. Tamen, quia voluntas non determinatur ex necessitate ad haec vel illa, nisi forte ex suppositione, ut supra dictum est; neque sapientia Dei et iustitia determinantur ad hunc ordinem, ut supra dictum est; nihil prohibet esse aliquid in potentia Dei, quod non vult, et quod non continetur sub ordine quem statuit rebus. Et quia potentia intelligitur

ON THE CONTRARY, It is said: *Thinkest thou that I cannot ask My Father, and He will give Me presently more than twelve legions of angels?* (Matt 26:53). But He neither asked for them, nor did His Father show them to refute the Jews. Therefore God can do what He does not.

I ANSWER THAT, In this matter certain persons erred in two ways. Some laid it down that God acts from natural necessity in such way that as from the action of nature nothing else can happen beyond what actually takes place—as, for instance, from the seed of man, a man must come, and from that of an olive, an olive; so from the divine operation there could not result other things, nor another order of things, than that which now is. But we showed above (Q. 19, A. 3) that God does not act from natural necessity, but that His will is the cause of all things; nor is that will naturally and from any necessity determined to those things. Whence in no way at all is the present course of events produced by God from any necessity, so that other things could not happen. Others, however, said that the divine power is restricted to this present course of events through the order of the divine wisdom and justice without which God does nothing. But since the power of God, which is His essence, is nothing else but His wisdom, it can indeed be fittingly said that there is nothing in the divine power which is not in the order of the divine wisdom; for the divine wisdom includes the whole potency of the divine power. Yet the order placed in creation by divine wisdom, in which order the notion of His justice consists, as said above (Q. 21, A. 2), is not so adequate to the divine wisdom that the divine wisdom should be restricted to this present order of things. Now it is clear that the whole idea of order which a wise man puts into things made by him is taken from their end. So, when the end is proportionate to the things made for that end, the wisdom of the maker is restricted to some definite order. But the divine goodness is an end exceeding beyond all proportion things created. Whence the divine wisdom is not so restricted to any particular order that no other course of events could happen. Wherefore we must simply say that God can do other things than those He has done.

REPLY OBJ. 1: In ourselves, in whom power and essence are distinct from will and intellect, and again intellect from wisdom, and will from justice, there can be something in the power which is not in the just will nor in the wise intellect. But in God, power and essence, will and intellect, wisdom and justice, are one and the same. Whence, there can be nothing in the divine power which cannot also be in His just will or in His wise intellect. Nevertheless, because His will cannot be determined from necessity to this or that order of things, except upon supposition, as was said above (Q. 19, A. 3), neither are the wisdom and justice of God restricted to this present order, as was shown above; so nothing prevents there being something in the divine power which He does not will, and which is not included in the order which He has placed in things. Again, because power

ut exequens, voluntas autem ut imperans, et intellectus et sapientia ut dirigens, quod attribuitur potentiae secundum se consideratae, dicitur Deus posse secundum potentiam absolutam. Et huiusmodi est omne illud in quo potest salvari ratio entis, ut supra dictum est. Quod autem attribuitur potentiae divinae secundum quod exequitur imperium voluntatis iustae, hoc dicitur Deus posse facere de potentia ordinata. Secundum hoc ergo, dicendum est quod Deus potest alia facere, de potentia absoluta, quam quae praescivit et praeordinavit se facturum, non tamen potest esse quod aliqua faciat, quae non praesciverit et praeordinaverit se facturum. Quia ipsum facere subiacet praescientiae et praeordinationi, non autem ipsum posse, quod est naturale. Ideo enim Deus aliquid facit, quia vult, non tamen ideo potest, quia vult, sed quia talis est in sua natura.

AD SECUNDUM dicendum quod Deus non debet aliquid alicui nisi sibi. Unde, cum dicitur quod Deus non potest facere nisi quod debet nihil aliud significatur nisi quod Deus non potest facere nisi quod ei est conveniens et iustum. Sed hoc quod dico conveniens et iustum, potest intelligi dupliciter. Uno modo, sic quod hoc quod dico conveniens et iustum, prius intelligatur coniungi cum hoc verbo est, ita quod restringatur ad standum pro praesentibus; et sic referatur ad potentiam. Et sic falsum est quod dicitur, est enim sensus, Deus non potest facere nisi quod modo conveniens est et iustum. Si vero prius coniungatur cum hoc verbo potest, quod habet vim ampliandi, et postmodum cum hoc verbo est, significabitur quoddam praesens confusum, et erit locutio vera, sub hoc sensu, Deus non potest facere nisi id quod, si faceret, esset conveniens et iustum.

AD TERTIUM dicendum quod, licet iste cursus rerum sit determinatus istis rebus quae nunc sunt, non tamen ad hunc cursum limitatur divina sapientia et potestas. Unde, licet istis rebus quae nunc sunt, nullus alius cursus esset bonus et conveniens, tamen Deus posset alias res facere, et alium eis imponere ordinem.

is considered as executing, the will as commanding, and the intellect and wisdom as directing; what is attributed to His power considered in itself, God is said to be able to do in accordance with His absolute power. Of such a kind is everything which has the nature of being, as was said above (A. 3). What is, however, attributed to the divine power, according as it carries into execution the command of a just will, God is said to be able to do by His ordinary power. In this manner, we must say that God can do other things by His absolute power than those He has foreknown and pre-ordained He would do. But it could not happen that He should do anything which He had not foreknown, and had not pre-ordained that He would do, because His actual doing is subject to His foreknowledge and pre-ordination, though His power, which is His nature, is not so. For God does things because He wills so to do; yet the power to do them does not come from His will, but from His nature.

REPLY OBJ. 2: God is bound to nobody but Himself. Hence, when it is said that God can only do what He ought, nothing else is meant by this than that God can do nothing but what is befitting to Himself, and just. But these words *befitting* and *just* may be understood in two ways: one, in direct connection with the verb *is*; and thus they would be restricted to the present order of things; and would concern His power. Then what is said in the objection is false; for the sense is that God can do nothing except what is now fitting and just. If, however, they be joined directly with the verb *can* (which has the effect of extending the meaning), and then second with *is*, the present will be signified, but in a confused and general way. The sentence would then be true in this sense: *God cannot do anything except that which, if He did it, would be suitable and just.*

REPLY OBJ. 3: Although this order of things be restricted to what now exists, the divine power and wisdom are not thus restricted. Whence, although no other order would be suitable and good to the things which now are, yet God can do other things and impose upon them another order.

Article 6

Whether God Can Do Better Than What He Does?

AD SEXTUM SIC PROCEDITUR. Videtur quod Deus non possit meliora facere ea quae facit. Quidquid enim Deus facit, potentissime et sapientissime facit. Sed tanto fit aliquid melius, quanto fit potentius et sapientius. Ergo Deus non potest aliquid facere melius quam facit.

PRAETEREA, Augustinus, contra Maximinum, sic argumentatur, *si Deus potuit, et noluit, gignere filium sibi aequalem, invidus fuit*. Eadem ratione, si Deus potuit res

OBJECTION 1: It seems that God cannot do better than He does. For whatever God does, He does in a most powerful and wise way. But a thing is so much the better done as it is more powerfully and wisely done. Therefore God cannot do anything better than He does.

OBJ. 2: Further, Augustine thus argues (*Contra Maximin.* iii, 8): *If God could, but would not, beget a Son His equal, He would have been envious.* For the same reason,

meliores facere quam fecerit, et noluit, invidus fuit. Sed invidia est omnino relegata a Deo. Ergo Deus unumquodque fecit optimum. Non ergo Deus potest aliquid facere melius quam fecit.

PRAETEREA, id quod est maxime et valde bonum, non potest melius fieri, quia maximo nihil est maius. Sed, sicut Augustinus dicit in Enchirid., *bona sunt singula quae Deus fecit, sed simul universa valde bona, quia ex omnibus consistit universitatis admirabilis pulchritudo.* Ergo bonum universi non potest melius fieri a Deo.

PRAETEREA, homo Christus est plenus gratia et veritate, et spiritum habet non ad mensuram, et sic non potest esse melior. Beatitudo etiam creata dicitur esse summum bonum, et sic non potest esse melius. Beata etiam virgo Maria est super omnes choros Angelorum exaltata, et sic non potest esse melior. Non igitur omnia quae fecit Deus, potest facere meliora.

SED CONTRA est quod dicitur ad Ephes. III, quod *Deus potens est omnia facere abundantius quam petimus aut intelligimus.*

RESPONDEO dicendum quod bonitas alicuius rei est duplex. Una quidem, quae est de essentia rei; sicut esse rationale est de essentia hominis. Et quantum ad hoc bonum, Deus non potest facere aliquam rem meliorem quam ipsa sit, licet possit facere aliquam aliam ea meliorem. Sicut etiam non potest facere quaternarium maiorem, quia, si esset maior, iam non esset quaternarius, sed alius numerus. Sic enim se habet additio differentiae substantialis in definitionibus, sicut additio unitatis in numeris, ut dicitur in VIII Metaphys. Alia bonitas est, quae est extra essentiam rei; sicut bonum hominis est esse virtuosum vel sapientem. Et secundum tale bonum, potest Deus res a se factas facere meliores. Simpliciter autem loquendo, qualibet re a se facta potest Deus facere aliam meliorem.

AD PRIMUM ergo dicendum quod, cum dicitur Deum posse aliquid facere melius quam facit, si ly melius sit nomen, verum est, qualibet enim re potest facere aliam meliorem. Eandem vero potest facere meliorem quodammodo, et quodammodo non, sicut dictum est. Si vero ly melius sit adverbium, et importet modum ex parte facientis, sic Deus non potest facere melius quam sicut facit, quia non potest facere ex maiori sapientia et bonitate. Si autem importet modum ex parte facti, sic potest facere melius, quia potest dare rebus a se factis meliorem modum essendi quantum ad accidentalia, licet non quantum ad essentialia.

AD SECUNDUM dicendum quod de ratione filii est quod aequetur patri, cum ad perfectum venerit, non est autem de ratione creaturae alicuius, quod sit melior quam a Deo facta est. Unde non est similis ratio.

if God could have made better things than He has done, but was not willing so to do, He would have been envious. But envy is far removed from God. Therefore God makes everything of the best. He cannot therefore make anything better than He does.

OBJ. 3: Further, what is very good and the best of all cannot be bettered; because nothing is better than the best. But as Augustine says (*Enchiridion* 10), *each thing that God has made is good, and, taken all together they are very good; because in them all consists the wondrous beauty of the universe.* Therefore the good in the universe could not be made better by God.

OBJ. 4: Further, Christ as man is full of grace and truth, and has the Spirit without measure; and so He cannot be better. Again created happiness is described as the highest good, and thus cannot be better. And the Blessed Virgin Mary is raised above all the choirs of angels, and so cannot be better than she is. God cannot therefore make all things better than He has made them.

ON THE CONTRARY, It is said (Eph 3:20): *God is able to do all things more abundantly than we desire or understand.*

I ANSWER THAT, The goodness of anything is twofold; one, which is of the essence of it—thus, for instance, to be rational pertains to the essence of man. As regards this good, God cannot make a thing better than it is itself; although He can make another thing better than it; even as He cannot make the number four greater than it is; because if it were greater it would no longer be four, but another number. For the addition of a substantial difference in definitions is after the manner of the addition of unity of numbers (*Metaph.* viii, 10). Another kind of goodness is that which is over and above the essence; thus, the good of a man is to be virtuous or wise. As regards this kind of goodness, God can make better the things He has made. Absolutely speaking, however, God can make something else better than each thing made by Him.

REPLY OBJ. 1: When it is said that God can make a thing better than He makes it, if *better* is taken substantively, this proposition is true. For He can always make something else better than each individual thing: and He can make the same thing in one way better than it is, and in another way not; as was explained above. If, however, *better* is taken as an adverb, implying the manner of the making; thus God cannot make anything better than He makes it, because He cannot make it from greater wisdom and goodness. But if it implies the manner of the thing done, He can make something better; because He can give to things made by Him a better manner of existence as regards the accidents, although not as regards the substance.

REPLY OBJ. 2: It is of the nature of a son that he should be equal to his father, when he comes to maturity. But it is not of the nature of anything created, that it should be better than it was made by God. Hence the comparison fails.

AD TERTIUM dicendum quod universum, suppositis istis rebus, non potest esse melius; propter decentissimum ordinem his rebus attributum a Deo, in quo bonum universi consistit. Quorum si unum aliquod esset melius, corrumperetur proportio ordinis, sicut, si una chorda plus debito intenderetur, corrumperetur citharae melodia. Posset tamen Deus alias res facere, vel alias addere istis rebus factis, et sic esset illud universum melius.

AD QUARTUM dicendum quod humanitas Christi ex hoc quod est unita Deo, et beatitudo creata ex hoc quod est fruitio Dei, et beata virgo ex hoc quod est mater Dei, habent quandam dignitatem infinitam, ex bono infinito quod est Deus. Et ex hac parte non potest aliquid fieri melius eis, sicut non potest aliquid melius esse Deo.

REPLY OBJ. 3: The universe, the present creation being supposed, cannot be better, on account of the most beautiful order given to things by God; in which the good of the universe consists. For if any one thing were bettered, the proportion of order would be destroyed; as if one string were stretched more than it ought to be, the melody of the harp would be destroyed. Yet God could make other things, or add something to the present creation; and then there would be another and a better universe.

REPLY OBJ. 4: The humanity of Christ, from the fact that it is united to the Godhead; and created happiness from the fact that it is the fruition of God; and the Blessed Virgin from the fact that she is the mother of God; have all a certain infinite dignity from the infinite good, which is God. And on this account there cannot be anything better than these; just as there cannot be anything better than God.

QUESTION 26

DIVINE BEATITUDE

Ultimo autem, post considerationem eorum quae ad divinae essentiae unitatem pertinent, considerandum est de divina beatitudine.

Et circa hoc quaeruntur quatuor.

Primo, utrum beatitudo Deo competat.

Secundo, secundum quid dicitur Deus esse beatus, utrum secundum actum intellectus.

Tertio, utrum sit essentialiter beatitudo cuiuslibet beati.

Quarto, utrum in eius beatitudine omnis beatitudo includatur.

After considering all that pertains to the unity of the divine essence, we come to treat of the divine beatitude.

Concerning this, there are four points of inquiry:

(1) Whether beatitude belongs to God?

(2) In regard to what is God called blessed; does this regard His act of intellect?

(3) Whether He is essentially the beatitude of each of the blessed?

(4) Whether all other beatitude is included in the divine beatitude?

Article 1

Whether Beatitude Belongs to God?

AD PRIMUM SIC PROCEDITUR. Videtur quod beatitudo Deo non conveniat. *Beatitudo enim*, secundum Boetium, in III de Consol., *est status omnium bonorum aggregatione perfectus.* Sed aggregatio bonorum non habet locum in Deo, sicut nec compositio. Ergo Deo non convenit beatitudo.

PRAETEREA, beatitudo, sive felicitas, est praemium virtutis, secundum philosophum, in I Ethic. Sed Deo non convenit praemium, sicut nec meritum. Ergo nec beatitudo.

SED CONTRA est quod dicit apostolus, I ad Tim. ultimo, *quem suis temporibus ostendet Deus beatus et solus potens, rex regum et dominus dominantium.*

RESPONDEO dicendum quod beatitudo maxime Deo competit. Nihil enim aliud sub nomine beatitudinis intelligitur, nisi bonum perfectum intellectualis naturae; cuius est suam sufficientiam cognoscere in bono quod habet; et cui competit ut ei contingat aliquid vel bene vel male, et sit suarum operationum domina. Utrumque autem istorum excellentissime Deo convenit, scilicet perfectum esse, et intelligentem. Unde beatitudo maxime convenit Deo.

AD PRIMUM ergo dicendum quod aggregatio bonorum est in Deo non per modum compositionis, sed per modum simplicitatis, quia quae in creaturis multiplicia sunt, in Deo praeexistunt simpliciter et unite, ut supra dictum est.

AD SECUNDUM dicendum quod esse praemium virtutis accidit beatitudini vel felicitati, inquantum aliquis

OBJECTION 1: It seems that beatitude does not belong to God. For beatitude according to Boethius (*De Consol.* iv) *is a state made perfect by the aggregation of all good things.* But the aggregation of goods has no place in God; nor has composition. Therefore beatitude does not belong to God.

OBJ. 2: Further, beatitude or happiness is the reward of virtue, according to the Philosopher (*Ethic.* i, 9). But reward does not apply to God; as neither does merit. Therefore neither does beatitude.

ON THE CONTRARY, The Apostle says: *Which in His times He shall show, who is the Blessed and only Almighty, the King of Kings and Lord of Lords* (1 Tim 6:15).

I ANSWER THAT, Beatitude belongs to God in a very special manner. For nothing else is understood to be meant by the term beatitude than the perfect good of an intellectual nature; which is capable of knowing that it has a sufficiency of the good which it possesses, to which it is competent that good or ill may befall, and which can control its own actions. All of these things belong in a most excellent manner to God, namely, to be perfect, and to possess intelligence. Whence beatitude belongs to God in the highest degree.

REPLY OBJ. 1: Aggregation of good is in God, after the manner not of composition, but of simplicity; for those things which in creatures is manifold, pre-exist in God, as was said above (Q. 4, A. 2; Q. 13, A. 4), in simplicity and unity.

REPLY OBJ. 2: It belongs as an accident to beatitude or happiness to be the reward of virtue, so far as anyone attains

beatitudinem acquirit, sicut esse terminum generationis accidit enti, inquantum exit de potentia in actum. Sicut igitur Deus habet esse, quamvis non generetur; ita habet beatitudinem, quamvis non mereatur.

to beatitude; even as to be the term of generation belongs accidentally to a being, so far as it passes from potentiality to act. As, then, God has being, though not begotten; so He has beatitude, although not acquired by merit.

Article 2

Whether God Is Called Blessed in Respect of His Intellect?

AD SECUNDUM SIC PROCEDITUR. Videtur quod Deus non dicatur beatus secundum intellectum. Beatitudo enim est summum bonum. Sed bonum dicitur in Deo secundum essentiam, quia bonum respicit esse, quod est secundum essentiam, secundum Boetium, in libro de Hebdomad. Ergo et beatitudo dicitur in Deo secundum essentiam, et non secundum intellectum.

PRAETEREA, beatitudo habet rationem finis. Finis autem est obiectum voluntatis, sicut et bonum. Ergo beatitudo dicitur in Deo secundum voluntatem, et non secundum intellectum.

SED CONTRA est quod Gregorius dicit, XXXII Moralium, *ipse gloriosus est, qui, dum seipso perfruitur, accedentis laudis indigens non est.* Esse autem gloriosum significat esse beatum. Cum igitur Deo fruamur secundum intellectum, quia *visio est tota merces,* ut dicit Augustinus, videtur quod beatitudo dicatur in Deo secundum intellectum.

RESPONDEO dicendum quod beatitudo, sicut dictum est, significat bonum perfectum intellectualis naturae. Et inde est quod, sicut unaquaeque res appetit suam perfectionem, ita et intellectualis natura naturaliter appetit esse beata. Id autem quod est perfectissimum in qualibet intellectuali natura, est intellectualis operatio, secundum quam capit quodammodo omnia. Unde cuiuslibet intellectualis naturae creatae beatitudo consistit in intelligendo. In Deo autem non est aliud esse et intelligere secundum rem, sed tantum secundum intelligentiae rationem. Attribuenda ergo est Deo beatitudo secundum intellectum, sicut et aliis beatis, qui per assimilationem ad beatitudinem ipsius, beati dicuntur.

AD PRIMUM ergo dicendum quod ex illa ratione probatur quod Deus sit beatus secundum suam essentiam, non autem quod beatitudo ei conveniat secundum rationem essentiae, sed magis secundum rationem intellectus.

AD SECUNDUM dicendum quod beatitudo, cum sit bonum, est obiectum voluntatis. Obiectum autem praeintelligitur actui potentiae. Unde, secundum modum intelligendi, prius est beatitudo divina, quam actus voluntatis in ea requiescentis. Et hoc non potest esse nisi actus intellectus. Unde in actu intellectus attenditur beatitudo.

OBJECTION 1: It seems that God is not called blessed in respect to His intellect. For beatitude is the highest good. But good is said to be in God in regard to His essence, because good has reference to being which is according to essence, according to Boethius (*De Hebdom.*). Therefore beatitude also is said to be in God in regard to His essence, and not to His intellect.

OBJ. 2: Further, Beatitude implies the notion of end. Now the end is the object of the will, as also is the good. Therefore beatitude is said to be in God with reference to His will, and not with reference to His intellect.

ON THE CONTRARY, Gregory says (*Moral.* xxxii, 7): *He is in glory, Who whilst He rejoices in Himself, needs not further praise.* To be in glory, however, is the same as to be blessed. Therefore, since we enjoy God in respect to our intellect, because *vision is the whole of the reward,* as Augustine says (*De Civ. Dei* xxii), it would seem that beatitude is said to be in God in respect of His intellect.

I ANSWER THAT, Beatitude, as stated above (A. 1), is the perfect good of an intellectual nature. Thus it is that, as everything desires the perfection of its nature, intellectual nature desires naturally to be happy. Now that which is most perfect in any intellectual nature is the intellectual operation, by which in some sense it grasps everything. Whence the beatitude of every intellectual nature consists in understanding. Now in God, to be and to understand are one and the same thing; differing only in the manner of our understanding them. Beatitude must therefore be assigned to God in respect of His intellect; as also to the blessed, who are called blessed by reason of the assimilation to His beatitude.

REPLY OBJ. 1: This argument proves that beatitude belongs to God; not that beatitude pertains essentially to Him under the aspect of His essence; but rather under the aspect of His intellect.

REPLY OBJ. 2: Since beatitude is a good, it is the object of the will; now the object is understood as prior to the act of a power. Whence in our manner of understanding, divine beatitude precedes the act of the will at rest in it. This cannot be other than the act of the intellect; and thus beatitude is to be found in an act of the intellect.

Article 3

Whether God Is the Beatitude of Each of the Blessed?

Ad tertium sic proceditur. Videtur quod Deus sit beatitudo cuiuslibet beati. Deus enim est summum bonum, ut supra ostensum est. Impossibile est autem esse plura summa bona, ut etiam ex superioribus patet. Cum igitur de ratione beatitudinis sit, quod sit summum bonum, videtur quod beatitudo non sit aliud quam Deus.

Praeterea, beatitudo est finis rationalis naturae ultimus. Sed esse ultimum finem rationalis naturae, soli Deo convenit. Ergo beatitudo cuiuslibet beati est solus Deus.

Sed contra, beatitudo unius est maior beatitudine alterius, secundum illud I Cor. XV, *stella differt a stella in claritate*. Sed Deo nihil est maius. Ergo beatitudo est aliquid aliud quam Deus.

Respondeo dicendum quod beatitudo intellectualis naturae consistit in actu intellectus. In quo duo possunt considerari, scilicet obiectum actus, quod est intelligibile; et ipse actus, qui est intelligere. Si igitur beatitudo consideretur ex parte ipsius obiecti, sic solus Deus est beatitudo, quia ex hoc solo est aliquis beatus, quod Deum intelligit; secundum illud Augustini, in V libro Confess., *beatus est qui te novit, etiam si alia ignoret*. Sed ex parte actus intelligentis, beatitudo est quid creatum in creaturis beatis, in Deo autem est etiam secundum hoc, aliquid increatum.

Ad primum ergo dicendum quod beatitudo, quantum ad obiectum, est summum bonum simpliciter, sed quantum ad actum, in creaturis beatis, est summum bonum, non simpliciter, sed in genere bonorum participabilium a creatura.

Ad secundum dicendum quod finis est duplex, scilicet cuius et quo, ut philosophus dicit, scilicet ipsa res, et usus rei, sicut avaro est finis pecunia, et acquisitio pecuniae. Creaturae igitur rationalis est quidem Deus finis ultimus ut res; beatitudo autem creata ut usus, vel magis fruitio, rei.

Objection 1: It seems that God is the beatitude of each of the blessed. For God is the supreme good, as was said above (Q. 6, AA. 2, 4). But it is quite impossible that there should be many supreme goods, as also is clear from what has been said above (Q. 11, A. 3). Therefore, since it is of the essence of beatitude that it should be the supreme good, it seems that beatitude is nothing else but God Himself.

Obj. 2: Further, beatitude is the last end of the rational nature. But to be the last end of the rational nature belongs only to God. Therefore the beatitude of every blessed is God alone.

On the contrary, The beatitude of one is greater than that of another, according to 1 Cor. 15:41: *Star differeth from star in glory*. But nothing is greater than God. Therefore beatitude is something different from God.

I answer that, The beatitude of an intellectual nature consists in an act of the intellect. In this we may consider two things, namely, the object of the act, which is the thing understood; and the act itself which is to understand. If, then, beatitude be considered on the side of the object, God is the only beatitude; for everyone is blessed from this sole fact, that he understands God, in accordance with the saying of Augustine (*Confess.* v, 4): *Blessed is he who knoweth Thee, though he know naught else.* But as regards the act of understanding, beatitude is a created thing in beatified creatures; but in God, even in this way, it is an uncreated thing.

Reply Obj. 1: Beatitude, as regards its object, is the supreme good absolutely, but as regards its act, in beatified creatures it is their supreme good, not absolutely, but in that kind of goods which a creature can participate.

Reply Obj. 2: End is twofold, namely, objective and subjective, as the Philosopher says (*Greater Ethics* i, 3), namely, the *thing itself* and *its use*. Thus to a miser the end is money, and its acquisition. Accordingly God is indeed the last end of a rational creature, as the thing itself; but created beatitude is the end, as the use, or rather fruition, of the thing.

Article 4

Whether All Other Beatitude Is Included in the Beatitude of God?

AD QUARTUM SIC PROCEDITUR. Videtur quod beatitudo divina non complectatur omnes beatitudines. Sunt enim quaedam beatitudines falsae. Sed in Deo nihil potest esse falsum. Ergo divina beatitudo non complectitur omnem beatitudinem.

PRAETEREA, quaedam beatitudo, secundum quosdam, consistit in rebus corporalibus, sicut in voluptatibus, divitiis, et huiusmodi, quae quidem Deo convenire non possunt, cum sit incorporeus. Ergo beatitudo eius non complectitur omnem beatitudinem.

SED CONTRA est quod beatitudo est perfectio quaedam. Divina autem perfectio complectitur omnem perfectionem, ut supra ostensum est. Ergo divina beatitudo complectitur omnem beatitudinem.

RESPONDEO dicendum quod quidquid est desiderabile in quacumque beatitudine, vel vera vel falsa, totum eminentius in divina beatitudine praeexistit. De contemplativa enim felicitate, habet continuam et certissimam contemplationem sui et omnium aliorum, de activa vero, gubernationem totius universi. De terrena vero felicitate, quae consistit in voluptate, divitiis, potestate, dignitate et fama, secundum Boetium, in III de Consol., habet gaudium de se et de omnibus aliis, pro delectatione, pro divitiis, habet omnimodam sufficientiam, quam divitiae promittunt, pro potestate, omnipotentiam, pro dignitate, omnium regimen, pro fama vero, admirationem totius creaturae.

AD PRIMUM ergo dicendum quod beatitudo aliqua secundum hoc est falsa, secundum quod deficit a ratione verae beatitudinis, et sic non est in Deo. Sed quidquid habet de similitudine, quantumcumque tenui, beatitudinis, totum praeexistit in divina beatitudine.

AD SECUNDUM dicendum quod bona quae sunt in corporalibus corporaliter, in Deo sunt spiritualiter, secundum modum suum.

Et haec dicta sufficiant de his quae pertinent ad divinae essentiae unitatem.

OBJECTION 1: It seems that the divine beatitude does not embrace all other beatitudes. For there are some false beatitudes. But nothing false can be in God. Therefore the divine beatitude does not embrace all other beatitudes.

OBJ. 2: Further, a certain beatitude, according to some, consists in things corporeal; as in pleasure, riches, and such like. Now none of these have to do with God, since He is incorporeal. Therefore His beatitude does not embrace all other beatitudes.

ON THE CONTRARY, Beatitude is a certain perfection. But the divine perfection embraces all other perfection, as was shown above (Q. 4, A. 2). Therefore the divine beatitude embraces all other beatitudes.

I ANSWER THAT, Whatever is desirable in whatsoever beatitude, whether true or false, pre-exists wholly and in a more eminent degree in the divine beatitude. As to contemplative happiness, God possesses a continual and most certain contemplation of Himself and of all things else; and as to that which is active, He has the governance of the whole universe. As to earthly happiness, which consists in delight, riches, power, dignity, and fame, according to Boethius (*De Consol.* iii, 10), He possesses joy in Himself and all things else for His delight; instead of riches He has that complete self-sufficiency, which is promised by riches; in place of power, He has omnipotence; for dignities, the government of all things; and in place of fame, He possesses the admiration of all creatures.

REPLY OBJ. 1: A particular kind of beatitude is false according as it falls short of the idea of true beatitude; and thus it is not in God. But whatever semblance it has, howsoever slight, of beatitude, the whole of it pre-exists in the divine beatitude.

REPLY OBJ. 2: The good that exists in things corporeal in a corporeal manner, is also in God, but in a spiritual manner.

We have now spoken enough concerning what pertains to the unity of the divine essence.

QUESTION 27

THE PROCESSION OF THE DIVINE PERSONS

Consideratis autem his quae ad divinae essentiae unitatem pertinent, restat considerare de his quae pertinent ad Trinitatem personarum in divinis.

Et quia personae divinae secundum relationes originis distinguuntur, secundum ordinem doctrinae prius considerandum est de origine, sive de processione, secundo, de relationibus originis; tertio, de personis.

Circa processionem quaeruntur quinque.

Primo, utrum processio sit in divinis.

Secundo, utrum aliqua processio in divinis generatio dici possit.

Tertio, utrum praeter generationem aliqua alia processio possit esse in divinis.

Quarto, utrum illa alia processio possit dici generatio.

Quinto, utrum in divinis sint plures processiones quam duae.

Having considered what belongs to the unity of the divine essence, it remains to treat of what belongs to the Trinity of the persons in God.

And because the divine Persons are distinguished from each other according to the relations of origin, the order of the doctrine leads us to consider first, the question of origin or procession; second, the relations of origin; third, the persons.

Concerning procession there are five points of inquiry:

(1) Whether there is procession in God?

(2) Whether any procession in God can be called generation?

(3) Whether there can be any other procession in God besides generation?

(4) Whether that other procession can be called generation?

(5) Whether there are more than two processions in God?

Article 1

Whether There Is Procession in God?

AD PRIMUM SIC PROCEDITUR. Videtur quod in Deo non possit esse aliqua processio. Processio enim significat motum ad extra. Sed in divinis nihil est mobile, neque extraneum. Ergo neque processio.

PRAETEREA, omne procedens est diversum ab eo a quo procedit. Sed in Deo non est aliqua diversitas, sed summa simplicitas. Ergo in Deo non est processio aliqua.

PRAETEREA, procedere ab alio videtur rationi primi principii repugnare. Sed Deus est primum principium, ut supra ostensum est. Ergo in Deo processio locum non habet.

SED CONTRA est quod dicit dominus, Ioan. VIII, *ego ex Deo processi.*

RESPONDEO dicendum quod divina Scriptura, in rebus divinis, nominibus ad processionem pertinentibus utitur. Hanc autem processionem diversi diversimode acceperunt. Quidam enim acceperunt hanc processionem secundum quod effectus procedit a causa. Et sic accepit Arius, dicens filium procedere a patre sicut primam eius creaturam, et spiritum sanctum procedere a patre et filio sicut creaturam utriusque. Et secundum hoc, neque filius neque Spiritus Sanctus esset verus Deus. Quod

OBJECTION 1: It would seem that there cannot be any procession in God. For procession signifies outward movement. But in God there is nothing mobile, nor anything extraneous. Therefore neither is there procession in God.

OBJ. 2: Further, everything which proceeds differs from that whence it proceeds. But in God there is no diversity; but supreme simplicity. Therefore in God there is no procession.

OBJ. 3: Further, to proceed from another seems to be against the nature of the first principle. But God is the first principle, as shown above (Q. 2, A. 3). Therefore in God there is no procession.

ON THE CONTRARY, Our Lord says, *From God I proceeded* (John 8:42).

I ANSWER THAT, Divine Scripture uses, in relation to God, names which signify procession. This procession has been differently understood. Some have understood it in the sense of an effect, proceeding from its cause; so Arius took it, saying that the Son proceeds from the Father as His primary creature, and that the Holy Spirit proceeds from the Father and the Son as the creature of both. In this sense neither the Son nor the Holy Spirit would be true God: and this is contrary to what is said of the Son, *That . . . we may*

est contra id quod dicitur de filio, I Ioan. ult., *ut simus in vero filio eius, hic est verus Deus.* Et de spiritu sancto dicitur, I Cor. VI, *nescitis quia membra vestra templum sunt spiritus sancti?* Templum autem habere solius Dei est. Alii vero hanc processionem acceperunt secundum quod causa dicitur procedere in effectum, inquantum vel movet ipsum, vel similitudinem suam ipsi imprimit. Et sic accepit Sabellius, dicens ipsum Deum patrem filium dici, secundum quod carnem assumpsit ex virgine. Et eundem dicit spiritum sanctum, secundum quod creaturam rationalem sanctificat, et ad vitam movet. Huic autem acceptioni repugnant verba domini de se dicentis, Ioan. V, *non potest facere a se filius quidquam*; et multa alia, per quae ostenditur quod non est ipse pater qui filius. Si quis autem diligenter consideret, uterque accepit processionem secundum quod est ad aliquid extra, unde neuter posuit processionem in ipso Deo. Sed, cum omnis processio sit secundum aliquam actionem, sicut secundum actionem quae tendit in exteriorem materiam, est aliqua processio ad extra; ita secundum actionem quae manet in ipso agente, attenditur processio quaedam ad intra. Et hoc maxime patet in intellectu, cuius actio, scilicet intelligere, manet in intelligente. Quicumque enim intelligit, ex hoc ipso quod intelligit, procedit aliquid intra ipsum, quod est conceptio rei intellectae, ex vi intellectiva proveniens, et ex eius notitia procedens. Quam quidem conceptionem vox significat, et dicitur verbum cordis, significatum verbo vocis.

Cum autem Deus sit super omnia, ea quae in Deo dicuntur, non sunt intelligenda secundum modum infimarum creaturarum, quae sunt corpora; sed secundum similitudinem supremarum creaturarum, quae sunt intellectuales substantiae; a quibus etiam similitudo accepta deficit a repraesentatione divinorum. Non ergo accipienda est processio secundum quod est in corporalibus, vel per motum localem, vel per actionem alicuius causae in exteriorem effectum, ut calor a calefaciente in calefactum; sed secundum emanationem intelligibilem, utpote verbi intelligibilis a dicente, quod manet in ipso. Et sic fides Catholica processionem ponit in divinis.

AD PRIMUM ergo dicendum quod obiectio illa procedit de processione quae est motus localis, vel quae est secundum actionem tendentem in exteriorem materiam, vel in exteriorem effectum, talis autem processio non est in divinis, ut dictum est.

AD SECUNDUM dicendum quod id quod procedit secundum processionem quae est ad extra, oportet esse diversum ab eo a quo procedit. Sed id quod procedit ad intra processu intelligibili, non oportet esse diversum, imo, quanto perfectius procedit, tanto magis est unum cum eo a quo procedit. Manifestum est enim quod quanto

be in His true Son. *This is true God* (1 John 5:20). Of the Holy Spirit it is also said, *Know you not that your members are the temple of the Holy Spirit?* (1 Cor 6:19). Now, to have a temple is God's prerogative. Others take this procession to mean the cause proceeding to the effect, as moving it, or impressing its own likeness on it; in which sense it was understood by Sabellius, who said that God the Father is called Son in assuming flesh from the Virgin, and that the Father also is called Holy Spirit in sanctifying the rational creature, and moving it to life. The words of the Lord contradict such a meaning, when He speaks of Himself, *The Son cannot of Himself do anything* (John 5:19); while many other passages show the same, whereby we know that the Father is not the Son. Careful examination shows that both of these opinions take procession as meaning an outward act; hence neither of them affirms procession as existing in God Himself; whereas, since procession always supposes action, and as there is an outward procession corresponding to the act tending to external matter, so there must be an inward procession corresponding to the act remaining within the agent. This applies most conspicuously to the intellect, the action of which remains in the intelligent agent. For whenever we understand, by the very fact of understanding there proceeds something within us, which is a conception of the object understood, a conception issuing from our intellectual power and proceeding from our knowledge of that object. This conception is signified by the spoken word; and it is called the word of the heart signified by the word of the voice.

As God is above all things, we should understand what is said of God, not according to the mode of the lowest creatures, namely bodies, but from the similitude of the highest creatures, the intellectual substances; while even the similitudes derived from these fall short in the representation of divine objects. Procession, therefore, is not to be understood from what it is in bodies, either according to local movement or by way of a cause proceeding forth to its exterior effect, as, for instance, heat from the agent to the thing made hot. Rather it is to be understood by way of an intelligible emanation, for example, of the intelligible word which proceeds from the speaker, yet remains in him. In that sense the Catholic Faith understands procession as existing in God.

REPLY OBJ. 1: This objection comes from the idea of procession in the sense of local motion, or of an action tending to external matter, or to an exterior effect; which kind of procession does not exist in God, as we have explained.

REPLY OBJ. 2: Whatever proceeds by way of outward procession is necessarily distinct from the source whence it proceeds, whereas, whatever proceeds within by an intelligible procession is not necessarily distinct; indeed, the more perfectly it proceeds, the more closely it is one with the source whence it proceeds. For it is clear that the

aliquid magis intelligitur, tanto conceptio intellectualis est magis intima intelligenti, et magis unum, nam intellectus secundum hoc quod actu intelligit, secundum hoc fit unum cum intellecto. Unde, cum divinum intelligere sit in fine perfectionis, ut supra dictum est, necesse est quod verbum divinum sit perfecte unum cum eo a quo procedit, absque omni diversitate.

AD TERTIUM dicendum quod procedere a principio ut extraneum et diversum, repugnat rationi primi principii, sed procedere ut intimum et absque diversitate, per modum intelligibilem, includitur in ratione primi principii. Cum enim dicimus aedificatorem principium domus, in ratione huius principii includitur conceptio suae artis, et includeretur in ratione primi principii, si aedificator esset primum principium. Deus autem, qui est primum principium rerum, comparatur ad res creatas ut artifex ad artificiata.

more a thing is understood, the more closely is the intellectual conception joined and united to the intelligent agent; since the intellect by the very act of understanding is made one with the object understood. Thus, as the divine intelligence is the very supreme perfection of God (Q. 14, A. 2), the divine Word is of necessity perfectly one with the source whence He proceeds, without any kind of diversity.

REPLY OBJ. 3: To proceed from a principle, so as to be something outside and distinct from that principle, is irreconcilable with the idea of a first principle; whereas an intimate and uniform procession by way of an intelligible act is included in the idea of a first principle. For when we call the builder the principle of the house, in the idea of such a principle is included that of his art; and it would be included in the idea of the first principle were the builder the first principle of the house. God, Who is the first principle of all things, may be compared to things created as the architect is to things designed.

Article 2

Whether Any Procession in God Can Be Called Generation?

AD SECUNDUM SIC PROCEDITUR. Videtur quod processio quae est in divinis, non possit dici generatio. Generatio enim est mutatio de non esse in esse, corruptioni opposita; et utriusque subiectum est materia. Sed nihil horum competit divinis. Ergo non potest generatio esse in divinis.

PRAETEREA, in Deo est processio secundum modum intelligibilem, ut dictum est. Sed in nobis talis processio non dicitur generatio. Ergo neque in Deo.

PRAETEREA, omne genitum accipit esse a generante. Esse ergo cuiuslibet geniti est esse receptum. Sed nullum esse receptum est per se subsistens. Cum igitur esse divinum sit esse per se subsistens, ut supra probatum est, sequitur quod nullius geniti esse sit esse divinum. Non est ergo generatio in divinis.

SED CONTRA est quod dicitur in Psalmo II, *ego hodie genui te.*

RESPONDEO dicendum quod processio verbi in divinis dicitur generatio. Ad cuius evidentiam, sciendum est quod nomine generationis dupliciter utimur. Uno modo, communiter ad omnia generabilia et corruptibilia, et sic generatio nihil aliud est quam mutatio de non esse ad esse. Alio modo, proprie in viventibus, et sic generatio significat originem alicuius viventis a principio vivente coniuncto. Et haec proprie dicitur nativitas. Non tamen omne huiusmodi dicitur genitum, sed proprie quod procedit secundum rationem similitudinis. Unde

OBJECTION 1: It would seem that no procession in God can be called generation. For generation is change from non-existence to existence, and is opposed to corruption; while matter is the subject of both. Nothing of all this belongs to God. Therefore generation cannot exist in God.

OBJ. 2: Further, procession exists in God, according to an intelligible mode, as above explained (A. 1). But such a process is not called generation in us; therefore neither is it to be so called in God.

OBJ. 3: Further, anything that is generated derives existence from its generator. Therefore such existence is a derived existence. But no derived existence can be a self-subsistence. Therefore, since the divine existence is self-subsisting (Q. 3, A. 4), it follows that no generated existence can be the divine existence. Therefore there is no generation in God.

ON THE CONTRARY, It is said (Ps 2:7): *This day have I begotten Thee.*

I ANSWER THAT, The procession of the Word in God is called generation. In proof whereof we must observe that generation has a twofold meaning: one common to everything subject to generation and corruption; in which sense generation is nothing but change from non-existence to existence. In another sense it is proper and belongs to living things; in which sense it signifies the origin of a living being from a conjoined living principle; and this is properly called birth. Not everything of that kind, however, is called begotten; but, strictly speaking, only what proceeds by way

pilus vel capillus non habet rationem geniti et filii, sed solum quod procedit secundum rationem similitudinis, non cuiuscumque, nam vermes qui generantur in animalibus, non habent rationem generationis et filiationis, licet sit similitudo secundum genus, sed requiritur ad rationem talis generationis, quod procedat secundum rationem similitudinis in natura eiusdem speciei, sicut homo procedit ab homine, et equus ab equo. In viventibus autem quae de potentia in actum vitae procedunt, sicut sunt homines et animalia, generatio utramque generationem includit. Si autem sit aliquod vivens cuius vita non exeat de potentia in actum, processio, si qua in tali vivente invenitur, excludit omnino primam rationem generationis; sed potest habere rationem generationis quae est propria viventium. Sic igitur processio verbi in divinis habet rationem generationis. Procedit enim per modum intelligibilis actionis, quae est operatio vitae, et a principio coniuncto, ut supra iam dictum est, et secundum rationem similitudinis, quia conceptio intellectus est similitudo rei intellectae, et in eadem natura existens, quia in Deo idem est intelligere et esse, ut supra ostensum est. Unde processio verbi in divinis dicitur generatio, et ipsum verbum procedens dicitur filius.

AD PRIMUM ergo dicendum quod obiectio illa procedit de generatione secundum rationem primam, prout importat exitum de potentia in actum. Et sic non invenitur in divinis, ut supra dictum est.

AD SECUNDUM dicendum quod intelligere in nobis non est ipsa substantia intellectus, unde verbum quod secundum intelligibilem operationem procedit in nobis, non est eiusdem naturae cum eo a quo procedit. Unde non proprie et complete competit sibi ratio generationis. Sed intelligere divinum est ipsa substantia intelligentis, ut supra ostensum est, unde verbum procedens procedit ut eiusdem naturae subsistens. Et propter hoc proprie dicitur genitum et filius. Unde et his quae pertinent ad generationem viventium, utitur Scriptura ad significandam processionem divinae sapientiae, scilicet conceptione et partu, dicitur enim ex persona divinae sapientiae, Proverb. VIII, *nondum erant abyssi, et ego iam concepta eram; ante colles ego parturiebar.* Sed in intellectu nostro utimur nomine conceptionis, secundum quod in verbo nostri intellectus invenitur similitudo rei intellectae, licet non inveniatur naturae identitas.

AD TERTIUM dicendum quod non omne acceptum est receptum in aliquo subiecto, alioquin non posset dici quod tota substantia rei creatae sit accepta a Deo, cum totius substantiae non sit aliquod subiectum receptivum. Sic igitur id quod est genitum in divinis, accipit esse a generante, non tanquam illud esse sit receptum in aliqua materia vel subiecto (quod repugnat subsistentiae divini esse); sed secundum hoc dicitur esse acceptum,

of similitude. Hence a hair has not the aspect of generation and sonship, but only that has which proceeds by way of a similitude. Nor will any likeness suffice; for a worm which is generated from animals has not the aspect of generation and sonship, although it has a generic similitude; for this kind of generation requires that there should be a procession by way of similitude in the same specific nature; as a man proceeds from a man, and a horse from a horse. So in living things, which proceed from potential to actual life, such as men and animals, generation includes both these kinds of generation. But if there is a being whose life does not proceed from potentiality to act, procession (if found in such a being) excludes entirely the first kind of generation; whereas it may have that kind of generation which belongs to living things. So in this manner the procession of the Word in God is generation; for He proceeds by way of intelligible action, which is a vital operation:—from a conjoined principle (as above described):—by way of similitude, inasmuch as the concept of the intellect is a likeness of the object conceived:—and exists in the same nature, because in God the act of understanding and His existence are the same, as shown above (Q. 14, A. 4). Hence the procession of the Word in God is called generation; and the Word Himself proceeding is called the Son.

REPLY OBJ. 1: This objection is based on the idea of generation in the first sense, importing the issuing forth from potentiality to act; in which sense it is not found in God.

REPLY OBJ. 2: The act of human understanding in ourselves is not the substance itself of the intellect; hence the word which proceeds within us by intelligible operation is not of the same nature as the source whence it proceeds; so the idea of generation cannot be properly and fully applied to it. But the divine act of intelligence is the very substance itself of the one who understands (Q. 14, A. 4). The Word proceeding therefore proceeds as subsisting in the same nature; and so is properly called begotten, and Son. Hence Scripture employs terms which denote generation of living things in order to signify the procession of the divine Wisdom, namely, conception and birth; as is declared in the person of the divine Wisdom, *The depths were not as yet, and I was already conceived; before the hills, I was brought forth.* (Prov 8:24). In our way of understanding we use the word *conception* in order to signify that in the word of our intellect is found the likeness of the thing understood, although there be no identity of nature.

REPLY OBJ. 3: Not everything derived from another has existence in another subject; otherwise we could not say that the whole substance of created being comes from God, since there is no subject that could receive the whole substance. So, then, what is generated in God receives its existence from the generator, not as though that existence were received into matter or into a subject (which would conflict with the divine self-subsistence); but when we

inquantum procedens ab alio habet esse divinum, non quasi aliud ab esse divino existens. In ipsa enim perfectione divini esse continetur et verbum intelligibiliter procedens, et principium verbi; sicut et quaecumque ad eius perfectionem pertinent, ut supra dictum est.

speak of His existence as received, we mean that He Who proceeds receives divine existence from another; not, however, as if He were other from the divine nature. For in the perfection itself of the divine existence are contained both the Word intelligibly proceeding and the principle of the Word, with whatever belongs to His perfection (Q. 4, A. 2).

Article 3

Whether Any Other Procession Exists in God Besides That of the Word?

AD TERTIUM SIC PROCEDITUR. Videtur quod non sit in divinis alia processio a generatione verbi. Eadem enim ratione erit aliqua alia processio ab illa alia processione, et sic procederetur in infinitum, quod est inconveniens. Standum est igitur in primo, ut sit una tantum processio in divinis.

PRAETEREA, in omni natura invenitur tantum unus modus communicationis illius naturae, et hoc ideo est, quia operationes secundum terminos habent unitatem et diversitatem. Sed processio in divinis non est nisi secundum communicationem divinae naturae. Cum igitur sit una tantum natura divina, ut supra ostensum est, relinquitur quod una sit tantum processio in divinis.

PRAETEREA, si sit in divinis alia processio ab intelligibili processione verbi, non erit nisi processio amoris, quae est secundum voluntatis operationem. Sed talis processio non potest esse alia a processione intellectus intelligibili, quia voluntas in Deo non est aliud ab intellectu, ut supra ostensum est. Ergo in Deo non est alia processio praeter processionem verbi.

SED CONTRA est quod Spiritus Sanctus procedit a patre, ut dicitur Ioan. XV. Ipse autem est alius a filio, secundum illud Ioan. XIV, *rogabo patrem meum, et alium Paracletum dabit vobis*. Ergo in divinis est alia processio praeter processionem verbi.

RESPONDEO dicendum quod in divinis sunt duae processiones, scilicet processio verbi, et quaedam alia.

Ad cuius evidentiam, considerandum est quod in divinis non est processio nisi secundum actionem quae non tendit in aliquid extrinsecum, sed manet in ipso agente. Huiusmodi autem actio in intellectuali natura est actio intellectus et actio voluntatis. Processio autem verbi attenditur secundum actionem intelligibilem. Secundum autem operationem voluntatis invenitur in nobis quaedam alia processio, scilicet processio amoris, secundum quam amatum est in amante, sicut per conceptionem verbi res dicta vel intellecta, est in intelligente. Unde et praeter processionem verbi, ponitur alia processio in divinis, quae est processio amoris.

AD PRIMUM ergo dicendum quod non est necessarium procedere in divinis processionibus in infinitum.

OBJECTION 1: It would seem that no other procession exists in God besides the generation of the Word. Because, for whatever reason we admit another procession, we should be led to admit yet another, and so on to infinitude; which cannot be. Therefore we must stop at the first, and hold that there exists only one procession in God.

OBJ. 2: Further, every nature possesses but one mode of self-communication; because operations derive unity and diversity from their terms. But procession in God is only by way of communication of the divine nature. Therefore, as there is only one divine nature (Q. 11, A. 4), it follows that only one procession exists in God.

OBJ. 3: Further, if any other procession but the intelligible procession of the Word existed in God, it could only be the procession of love, which is by the operation of the will. But such a procession is identified with the intelligible procession of the intellect, inasmuch as the will in God is the same as His intellect (Q. 19, A. 1). Therefore in God there is no other procession but the procession of the Word.

ON THE CONTRARY, The Holy Spirit proceeds from the Father (John 15:26); and He is distinct from the Son, according to the words, *I will ask My Father, and He will give you another Paraclete* (John 14:16). Therefore in God another procession exists besides the procession of the Word.

I ANSWER THAT, There are two processions in God; the procession of the Word, and another.

In evidence whereof we must observe that procession exists in God, only according to an action which does not tend to anything external, but remains in the agent itself. Such an action in an intellectual nature is that of the intellect, and of the will. The procession of the Word is by way of an intelligible operation. The operation of the will within ourselves involves also another procession, that of love, whereby the object loved is in the lover; as, by the conception of the word, the object spoken of or understood is in the intelligent agent. Hence, besides the procession of the Word in God, there exists in Him another procession called the procession of love.

REPLY OBJ. 1: There is no need to go on to infinitude in the divine processions; for the procession which

Processio enim quae est ad intra in intellectuali natura, terminatur in processione voluntatis.

AD SECUNDUM dicendum quod quidquid est in Deo, est Deus, ut supra ostensum est, quod non contingit in aliis rebus. Et ideo per quamlibet processionem quae non est ad extra, communicatur divina natura, non autem aliae naturae.

AD TERTIUM dicendum quod, licet in Deo non sit aliud voluntas et intellectus, tamen de ratione voluntatis et intellectus est, quod processiones quae sunt secundum actionem utriusque, se habeant secundum quendam ordinem. Non enim est processio amoris nisi in ordine ad processionem verbi, nihil enim potest voluntate amari, nisi sit in intellectu conceptum. Sicut igitur attenditur quidam ordo verbi ad principium a quo procedit, licet in divinis sit eadem substantia intellectus et conceptio intellectus; ita, licet in Deo sit idem voluntas et intellectus, tamen, quia de ratione amoris est quod non procedat nisi a conceptione intellectus, habet ordinis distinctionem processio amoris a processione verbi in divinis.

is accomplished within the agent in an intellectual nature terminates in the procession of the will.

REPLY OBJ. 2: All that exists in God, is God (Q. 3, AA. 3, 4); whereas the same does not apply to others. Therefore the divine nature is communicated by every procession which is not outward, and this does not apply to other natures.

REPLY OBJ. 3: Though will and intellect are not diverse in God, nevertheless the nature of will and intellect requires the processions belonging to each of them to exist in a certain order. For the procession of love occurs in due order as regards the procession of the Word; since nothing can be loved by the will unless it is conceived in the intellect. So as there exists a certain order of the Word to the principle whence He proceeds, although in God the substance of the intellect and its concept are the same; so, although in God the will and the intellect are the same, still, inasmuch as love requires by its very nature that it proceed only from the concept of the intellect, there is a distinction of order between the procession of love and the procession of the Word in God.

Article 4

Whether the Procession of Love in God Is Generation?

AD QUARTUM SIC PROCEDITUR. Videtur quod processio amoris in divinis sit generatio. Quod enim procedit in similitudine naturae in viventibus, dicitur generatum et nascens. Sed id quod procedit in divinis per modum amoris, procedit in similitudine naturae, alias esset extraneum a natura divina, et sic esset processio ad extra. Ergo quod procedit in divinis per modum amoris, procedit ut genitum et nascens.

PRAETEREA, sicut similitudo est de ratione verbi, ita est etiam de ratione amoris, unde dicitur Eccli. XIII, quod *omne animal diligit simile sibi.* Si igitur ratione similitudinis verbo procedenti convenit generari et nasci, videtur etiam quod amori procedenti convenit generari.

PRAETEREA, non est in genere quod non est in aliqua eius specie. Si igitur in divinis sit quaedam processio amoris, oportet quod, praeter hoc nomen commune, habeat aliquod nomen speciale. Sed non est aliud nomen dare nisi generatio. Ergo videtur quod processio amoris in divinis sit generatio.

SED CONTRA est quia secundum hoc sequeretur quod Spiritus Sanctus, qui procedit ut amor, procederet ut genitus. Quod est contra illud Athanasii, *Spiritus Sanctus a patre et filio non factus nec creatus nec genitus, sed procedens.*

RESPONDEO dicendum quod processio amoris in divinis non debet dici generatio. Ad cuius evidentiam,

OBJECTION 1: It would seem that the procession of love in God is generation. For what proceeds by way of likeness of nature among living things is said to be generated and born. But what proceeds in God by way of love proceeds in the likeness of nature; otherwise it would be extraneous to the divine nature, and would be an external procession. Therefore what proceeds in God by way of love, proceeds as generated and born.

OBJ. 2: Further, as similitude is of the nature of the word, so does it belong to love. Hence it is said, that *every beast loves its like* (Sir 13:19). Therefore if the Word is begotten and born by way of likeness, it seems becoming that love should proceed by way of generation.

OBJ. 3: Further, what is not in any species is not in the genus. So if there is a procession of love in God, there ought to be some special name besides this common name of procession. But no other name is applicable but generation. Therefore the procession of love in God is generation.

ON THE CONTRARY, Were this true, it would follow that the Holy Spirit Who proceeds as love, would proceed as begotten; which is against the statement of Athanasius: *The Holy Spirit is from the Father and the Son, not made, nor begotten, but proceeding.*

I ANSWER THAT, The procession of love in God ought not to be called generation. In evidence whereof we must

sciendum est quod haec est differentia inter intellectum et voluntatem, quod intellectus fit in actu per hoc quod res intellecta est in intellectu secundum suam similitudinem, voluntas autem fit in actu, non per hoc quod aliqua similitudo voliti sit in voluntate, sed ex hoc quod voluntas habet quandam inclinationem in rem volitam. Processio igitur quae attenditur secundum rationem intellectus, est secundum rationem similitudinis, et intantum potest habere rationem generationis, quia omne generans generat sibi simile. Processio autem quae attenditur secundum rationem voluntatis, non consideratur secundum rationem similitudinis, sed magis secundum rationem impellentis et moventis in aliquid.

Et ideo quod procedit in divinis per modum amoris, non procedit ut genitum vel ut filius, sed magis procedit ut spiritus, quo nomine quaedam vitalis motio et impulsio designatur, prout aliquis ex amore dicitur moveri vel impelli ad aliquid faciendum.

AD PRIMUM ergo dicendum quod quidquid est in divinis, est unum cum divina natura. Unde ex parte huius unitatis non potest accipi propria ratio huius processionis vel illius, secundum quam una distinguatur ab alia, sed oportet quod propria ratio huius vel illius processionis accipiatur secundum ordinem unius processionis ad aliam. Huiusmodi autem ordo attenditur secundum rationem voluntatis et intellectus. Unde secundum horum propriam rationem sortitur in divinis nomen utraque processio, quod imponitur ad propriam rationem rei significandam. Et inde est quod procedens per modum amoris et divinam naturam accipit, et tamen non dicitur natum.

AD SECUNDUM dicendum quod similitudo aliter pertinet ad verbum, et aliter ad amorem. Nam ad verbum pertinet inquantum ipsum est quaedam similitudo rei intellectae, sicut genitum est similitudo generantis, sed ad amorem pertinet, non quod ipse amor sit similitudo, sed inquantum similitudo est principium amandi. Unde non sequitur quod amor sit genitus, sed quod genitum sit principium amoris.

AD TERTIUM dicendum quod Deum nominare non possumus nisi ex creaturis, ut dictum est supra. Et quia in creaturis communicatio naturae non est nisi per generationem, processio in divinis non habet proprium vel speciale nomen nisi generationis. Unde processio quae non est generatio, remansit sine speciali nomine. Sed potest nominari spiratio, quia est processio spiritus.

consider that the intellect and the will differ in this respect, that the intellect is made actual by the object understood residing according to its own likeness in the intellect; whereas the will is made actual, not by any similitude of the object willed within it, but by its having a certain inclination to the thing willed. Thus the procession of the intellect is by way of similitude, and is called generation, because every generator begets its own like; whereas the procession of the will is not by way of similitude, but rather by way of impulse and movement towards an object.

So what proceeds in God by way of love, does not proceed as begotten, or as son, but proceeds rather as spirit; which name expresses a certain vital movement and impulse, accordingly as anyone is described as moved or impelled by love to perform an action.

REPLY OBJ. 1: All that exists in God is one with the divine nature. Hence the proper notion of this or that procession, by which one procession is distinguished from another, cannot be on the part of this unity: but the proper notion of this or that procession must be taken from the order of one procession to another; which order is derived from the nature of the will and intellect. Hence, each procession in God takes its name from the proper notion of will and intellect; the name being imposed to signify what its nature really is; and so it is that the Person proceeding as love receives the divine nature, but is not said to be born.

REPLY OBJ. 2: Likeness belongs in a different way to the word and to love. It belongs to the word as being the likeness of the object understood, as the thing generated is the likeness of the generator; but it belongs to love, not as though love itself were a likeness, but because likeness is the principle of loving. Thus it does not follow that love is begotten, but that the one begotten is the principle of love.

REPLY OBJ. 3: We can name God only from creatures (Q. 13, A. 1). As in creatures generation is the only principle of communication of nature, procession in God has no proper or special name, except that of generation. Hence the procession which is not generation has remained without a special name; but it can be called spiration, as it is the procession of the Spirit.

Article 5

Whether There Are More Than Two Processions in God?

AD QUINTUM SIC PROCEDITUR. Videtur quod sint plures processiones in divinis quam duae. Sicut enim scientia et voluntas attribuitur Deo, ita et potentia. Si igitur secundum intellectum et voluntatem accipiuntur in Deo duae processiones, videtur quod tertia sit accipienda secundum potentiam.

PRAETEREA, bonitas maxime videtur esse principium processionis, cum bonum dicatur diffusivum sui esse. Videtur igitur quod secundum bonitatem aliqua processio in divinis accipi debeat.

PRAETEREA, maior est fecunditatis virtus in Deo quam in nobis. Sed in nobis non est tantum una processio verbi, sed multae, quia ex uno verbo in nobis procedit aliud verbum; et similiter ex uno amore alius amor. Ergo et in Deo sunt plures processiones quam duae.

SED CONTRA est quod in Deo non sunt nisi duo procedentes, scilicet filius et Spiritus Sanctus. Ergo sunt ibi tantum duae processiones.

RESPONDEO dicendum quod processiones in divinis accipi non possunt nisi secundum actiones quae in agente manent. Huiusmodi autem actiones in natura intellectuali et divina non sunt nisi duae, scilicet intelligere et velle. Nam sentire, quod etiam videtur esse operatio in sentiente, est extra naturam intellectualem, neque totaliter est remotum a genere actionum quae sunt ad extra; nam sentire perficitur per actionem sensibilis in sensum. Relinquitur igitur quod nulla alia processio possit esse in Deo, nisi verbi et amoris.

AD PRIMUM ergo dicendum quod potentia est principium agendi in aliud, unde secundum potentiam accipitur actio ad extra. Et sic secundum attributum potentiae non accipitur processio divinae personae, sed solum processio creaturarum.

AD SECUNDUM dicendum quod bonum, sicut dicit Boetius in libro de Hebd., pertinet ad essentiam et non ad operationem, nisi forte sicut obiectum voluntatis.

Unde, cum processiones divinas secundum aliquas actiones necesse sit accipere, secundum bonitatem et huiusmodi alia attributa non accipiuntur aliae processiones nisi verbi et amoris, secundum quod Deus suam essentiam, veritatem et bonitatem intelligit et amat.

AD TERTIUM dicendum quod, sicut supra habitum est, Deus uno simplici actu omnia intelligit, et similiter omnia vult. Unde in eo non potest esse processio verbi ex verbo, neque amoris ex amore, sed est in eo solum

OBJECTION 1: It would seem that there are more than two processions in God. As knowledge and will are attributed to God, so is power. Therefore, if two processions exist in God, of intellect and will, it seems that there must also be a third procession of power.

OBJ. 2: Further, goodness seems to be the greatest principle of procession, since goodness is diffusive of itself. Therefore there must be a procession of goodness in God.

OBJ. 3: Further, in God there is greater power of fecundity than in us. But in us there is not only one procession of the word, but there are many: for in us from one word proceeds another; and also from one love proceeds another. Therefore in God there are more than two processions.

ON THE CONTRARY, In God there are not more than two who proceed—the Son and the Holy Spirit. Therefore there are in Him but two processions.

I ANSWER THAT, The divine processions can be derived only from the actions which remain within the agent. In a nature which is intellectual, and in the divine nature, these actions are two, the acts of intelligence and of will. The act of sensation, which also appears to be an operation within the agent, takes place outside the intellectual nature, nor can it be reckoned as wholly removed from the sphere of external actions; for the act of sensation is perfected by the action of the sensible object upon sense. It follows that no other procession is possible in God but the procession of the Word, and of Love.

REPLY OBJ. 1: Power is the principle whereby one thing acts on another. Hence it is that external action points to power. Thus the divine power does not imply the procession of a divine person; but is indicated by the procession therefrom of creatures.

REPLY OBJ. 2: As Boethius says (*De Hebdom.*), goodness belongs to the essence and not to the operation, unless considered as the object of the will.

Thus, as the divine processions must be denominated from certain actions, no other processions can be understood in God according to goodness and the like attributes except those of the Word and of Love, according as God understands and loves His own essence, truth and goodness.

REPLY OBJ. 3: As above explained (Q. 14, A. 5; Q. 19, A. 5), God understands all things by one simple act; and by one act also He wills all things. Hence there cannot exist in Him a procession of Word from Word, nor of Love from

unum verbum perfectum, et unus amor perfectus. Et in hoc eius perfecta fecunditas manifestatur.

Love: for there is in Him only one perfect Word, and one perfect Love; thereby being manifested His perfect fecundity.

QUESTION 28

THE DIVINE RELATIONS

Deinde considerandum est de relationibus divinis. Et circa hoc quaeruntur quatuor.

Primo, utrum in Deo sint aliquae relationes reales.

Secundo, utrum illae relationes sint ipsa essentia divina, vel sint extrinsecus affixae.

Tertio, utrum possint esse in Deo plures relationes realiter distinctae ab invicem.

Quarto, de numero harum relationum.

The divine relations are next to be considered, in four points of inquiry:

(1) Whether there are real relations in God?

(2) Whether those relations are the divine essence itself, or are extrinsic to it?

(3) Whether in God there can be several relations distinct from each other?

(4) The number of these relations.

Article 1

Whether There Are Real Relations in God?

AD PRIMUM SIC PROCEDITUR. Videtur quod in Deo non sint aliquae relationes reales. Dicit enim Boetius, in libro de Trin., quod *cum quis praedicamenta in divinam vertit praedicationem, cuncta mutantur in substantiam quae praedicari possunt; ad aliquid vero omnino non potest praedicari.* Sed quidquid est realiter in Deo, de ipso praedicari potest. Ergo relatio non est realiter in Deo.

PRAETEREA, dicit Boetius in eodem libro, quod *similis est relatio in Trinitate patris ad filium, et utriusque ad spiritum sanctum, ut eius quod est idem, ad id quod est idem.* Sed huiusmodi relatio est rationis tantum, quia omnis relatio realis exigit duo extrema realiter. Ergo relationes quae ponuntur in divinis, non sunt reales relationes, sed rationis tantum.

PRAETEREA, relatio paternitatis est relatio principii. Sed cum dicitur, Deus est principium creaturarum, non importatur aliqua relatio realis, sed rationis tantum. Ergo nec paternitas in divinis est relatio realis. Et eadem ratione nec aliae relationes quae ponuntur ibi.

PRAETEREA, generatio in divinis est secundum intelligibilis verbi processionem. Sed relationes quae consequuntur operationem intellectus, sunt relationes rationis. Ergo paternitas et filiatio, quae dicuntur in divinis secundum generationem, sunt relationes rationis tantum.

SED CONTRA est quod pater non dicitur nisi a paternitate, et filius a filiatione. Si igitur paternitas et filiatio non sunt in Deo realiter, sequitur quod Deus non sit realiter pater aut filius, sed secundum rationem intelligentiae tantum, quod est haeresis Sabelliana.

RESPONDEO dicendum quod relationes quaedam sunt in divinis realiter. Ad cuius evidentiam,

OBJECTION 1: It would seem that there are no real relations in God. For Boethius says (*De Trin.* iv), *All possible predicaments used as regards the Godhead refer to the substance; for nothing can be predicated relatively.* But whatever really exists in God can be predicated of Him. Therefore no real relation exists in God.

OBJ. 2: Further, Boethius says (*De Trin.* iv) that, *Relation in the Trinity of the Father to the Son, and of both to the Holy Spirit, is the relation of the same to the same.* But a relation of this kind is only a logical one; for every real relation requires and implies in reality two terms. Therefore the divine relations are not real relations, but are formed only by the mind.

OBJ. 3: Further, the relation of paternity is the relation of a principle. But to say that God is the principle of creatures does not import any real relation, but only a logical one. Therefore paternity in God is not a real relation; while the same applies for the same reason to the other relations in God.

OBJ. 4: Further, the divine generation proceeds by way of an intelligible word. But the relations following upon the operation of the intellect are logical relations. Therefore paternity and filiation in God, consequent upon generation, are only logical relations.

ON THE CONTRARY, The Father is denominated only from paternity; and the Son only from filiation. Therefore, if no real paternity or filiation existed in God, it would follow that God is not really Father or Son, but only in our manner of understanding; and this is the Sabellian heresy.

I ANSWER THAT, relations exist in God really; in proof whereof we may consider that in relations alone is found

considerandum est quod solum in his quae dicuntur ad aliquid, inveniuntur aliqua secundum rationem tantum, et non secundum rem. Quod non est in aliis generibus, quia alia genera, ut quantitas et qualitas, secundum propriam rationem significant aliquid alicui inhaerens. Ea vero quae dicuntur ad aliquid, significant secundum propriam rationem solum respectum ad aliud. Qui quidem respectus aliquando est in ipsa natura rerum; utpote quando aliquae res secundum suam naturam ad invicem ordinatae sunt, et invicem inclinationem habent. Et huiusmodi relationes oportet esse reales. Sicut in corpore gravi est inclinatio et ordo ad locum medium, unde respectus quidam est in ipso gravi respectu loci medii. Et similiter est de aliis huiusmodi. Aliquando vero respectus significatus per ea quae dicuntur ad aliquid, est tantum in ipsa apprehensione rationis conferentis unum alteri, et tunc est relatio rationis tantum; sicut cum comparat ratio hominem animali, ut speciem ad genus. Cum autem aliquid procedit a principio eiusdem naturae, necesse est quod ambo, scilicet procedens et id a quo procedit, in eodem ordine conveniant, et sic oportet quod habeant reales respectus ad invicem. Cum igitur processiones in divinis sint in identitate naturae, ut ostensum est, necesse est quod relationes quae secundum processiones divinas accipiuntur, sint relationes reales.

AD PRIMUM ergo dicendum quod ad aliquid dicitur omnino non praedicari in Deo, secundum propriam rationem eius quod dicitur ad aliquid; inquantum scilicet propria ratio eius quod ad aliquid dicitur, non accipitur per comparationem ad illud cui inest relatio, sed per respectum ad alterum. Non ergo per hoc excludere voluit quod relatio non esset in Deo, sed quod non praedicaretur per modum inhaerentis secundum propriam relationis rationem, sed magis per modum ad aliud se habentis.

AD SECUNDUM dicendum quod relatio quae importatur per hoc nomen idem, est relatio rationis tantum, si accipiatur simpliciter idem, quia huiusmodi relatio non potest consistere nisi in quodam ordine quem ratio adinvenit alicuius ad seipsum, secundum aliquas eius duas considerationes. Secus autem est, cum dicuntur aliqua eadem esse, non in numero, sed in natura generis sive speciei. Boetius igitur relationes quae sunt in divinis, assimilat relationi identitatis, non quantum ad omnia, sed quantum ad hoc solum, quod per huiusmodi relationes non diversificatur substantia, sicut nec per relationem identitatis.

AD TERTIUM dicendum quod, cum creatura procedat a Deo in diversitate naturae, Deus est extra ordinem totius creaturae, nec ex eius natura est eius habitudo ad creaturas. Non enim producit creaturas ex necessitate suae naturae, sed per intellectum et per voluntatem, ut supra dictum est. Et ideo in Deo non est realis relatio ad creaturas. Sed in creaturis est realis relatio ad Deum, quia creaturae continentur sub ordine divino, et

something which is only in the apprehension and not in reality. This is not found in any other genus; forasmuch as other genera, as quantity and quality, in their strict and proper meaning, signify something inherent in a subject. But relation in its own proper meaning signifies only what refers to another. Such regard to another exists sometimes in the nature of things, as in those things which by their own very nature are ordered to each other, and have a mutual inclination; and such relations are necessarily real relations; as in a heavy body is found an inclination and order to the centre; and hence there exists in the heavy body a certain respect in regard to the centre, and the same applies to other things. Sometimes, however, this regard to another, signified by relation, is to be found only in the apprehension of reason comparing one thing to another, and this is a logical relation only; as, for instance, when reason compares man to animal as the species to the genus. But when something proceeds from a principle of the same nature, then both the one proceeding and the source of procession, agree in the same order; and then they have real relations to each other. Therefore as the divine processions are in the identity of the same nature, as above explained (Q. 27, AA. 2, 4), these relations, according to the divine processions, are necessarily real relations.

REPLY OBJ. 1: Relationship is not predicated of God according to its proper and formal meaning, that is to say, in so far as its proper meaning denotes comparison to that in which relation is inherent, but only as denoting regard to another. Nevertheless Boethius did not wish to exclude relation in God; but he wished to show that it was not to be predicated of Him as regards the mode of inherence in Himself in the strict meaning of relation; but rather by way of relation to another.

REPLY OBJ. 2: The relation signified by the term *the same* is a logical relation only, if in regard to absolutely the same thing; because such a relation can exist only in a certain order observed by reason as regards the order of anything to itself, according to some two aspects thereof. The case is otherwise, however, when things are called the same, not numerically, but generically or specifically. Thus Boethius likens the divine relations to a relation of identity, not in every respect, but only as regards the fact that the substance is not diversified by these relations, as neither is it by relation of identity.

REPLY OBJ. 3: As the creature proceeds from God in diversity of nature, God is outside the order of the whole creation, nor does any relation to the creature arise from His nature; for He does not produce the creature by necessity of His nature, but by His intellect and will, as is above explained (Q. 14, AA. 3, 4; Q. 19, A. 8). Therefore there is no real relation in God to the creature; whereas in creatures there is a real relation to God; because creatures are

in earum natura est quod dependeant a Deo. Sed processiones divinae sunt in eadem natura. Unde non est similis ratio.

AD QUARTUM dicendum quod relationes quae consequuntur solam operationem intellectus in ipsis rebus intellectis, sunt relationes rationis tantum, quia scilicet eas ratio adinvenit inter duas res intellectas. Sed relationes quae consequuntur operationem intellectus, quae sunt inter verbum intellectualiter procedens et illud a quo procedit, non sunt relationes rationis tantum, sed rei, quia et ipse intellectus et ratio est quaedam res, et comparatur realiter ad id quod procedit intelligibiliter, sicut res corporalis ad id quod procedit corporaliter. Et sic paternitas et filiatio sunt relationes reales in divinis.

contained under the divine order, and their very nature entails dependence on God. On the other hand, the divine processions are in one and the same nature. Hence no parallel exists.

REPLY OBJ. 4: Relations which result from the mental operation alone in the objects understood are logical relations only, inasmuch as reason observes them as existing between two objects perceived by the mind. Those relations, however, which follow the operation of the intellect, and which exist between the word intellectually proceeding and the source whence it proceeds, are not logical relations only, but are real relations; inasmuch as the intellect and the reason are real things, and are really related to that which proceeds from them intelligibly; as a corporeal thing is related to that which proceeds from it corporeally. Thus paternity and filiation are real relations in God.

Article 2

Whether Relation in God Is the Same As His Essence?

AD SECUNDUM SIC PROCEDITUR. Videtur quod relatio in Deo non sit idem quod sua essentia. Dicit enim Augustinus, in V de Trin., quod *non omne quod dicitur in Deo, dicitur secundum substantiam. Dicitur enim ad aliquid, sicut pater ad filium, sed haec non secundum substantiam dicuntur.* Ergo relatio non est divina essentia.

PRAETEREA, Augustinus dicit, VII de Trin., *omnis res quae relative dicitur, est etiam aliquid excepto relativo; sicut homo dominus, et homo servus.* Si igitur relationes aliquae sunt in Deo, oportet esse in Deo aliquid aliud praeter relationes. Sed hoc aliud non potest esse nisi essentia. Ergo essentia est aliud a relationibus.

PRAETEREA, esse relativi est ad aliud se habere, ut dicitur in praedicamentis. Si igitur relatio sit ipsa divina essentia, sequitur quod esse divinae essentiae sit ad aliud se habere, quod repugnat perfectioni divini esse, quod est maxime absolutum et per se subsistens, ut supra ostensum est. Non igitur relatio est ipsa essentia divina.

SED CONTRA, omnis res quae non est divina essentia, est creatura. Sed relatio realiter competit Deo. Si ergo non est divina essentia, erit creatura, et ita ei non erit adoratio latriae exhibenda, contra quod in praefatione cantatur, *ut in personis proprietas, et in maiestate adoretur aequalitas.*

RESPONDEO dicendum quod circa hoc dicitur Gilbertus Porretanus errasse, sed errorem suum postmodum in Remensi Concilio revocasse. Dixit enim quod relationes in divinis sunt assistentes, sive extrinsecus affixae.

OBJECTION 1: It would seem that the divine relation is not the same as the divine essence. For Augustine says (*De Trin.* v) that *not all that is said of God is said of His substance, for we say some things relatively, as Father in respect of the Son: but such things do not refer to the substance.* Therefore the relation is not the divine essence.

OBJ. 2: Further, Augustine says (*De Trin.* vii) that, *every relative expression is something besides the relation expressed, as master is a man, and slave is a man.* Therefore, if relations exist in God, there must be something else besides relation in God. This can only be His essence. Therefore essence differs from relation.

OBJ. 3: Further, the essence of relation is the being referred to another, as the Philosopher says (*Praedic.* v). So if relation is the divine essence, it follows that the divine essence is essentially itself a relation to something else; whereas this is repugnant to the perfection of the divine essence, which is supremely absolute and self-subsisting (Q. 3, A. 4). Therefore relation is not the divine essence.

ON THE CONTRARY, Everything which is not the divine essence is a creature. But relation really belongs to God; and if it is not the divine essence, it is a creature; and it cannot claim the adoration of latria; contrary to what is sung in the Preface: *Let us adore the distinction of the Persons, and the equality of their Majesty.*

I ANSWER THAT, It is reported that Gilbert de la Porree erred on this point, but revoked his error later at the council of Rheims. For he said that the divine relations are assistant, or externally affixed.

Ad cuius evidentiam, considerandum est quod in quolibet novem generum accidentis est duo considerare. Quorum unum est esse quod competit unicuique ipsorum secundum quod est accidens. Et hoc communiter in omnibus est inesse subiecto, accidentis enim esse est inesse. Aliud quod potest considerari in unoquoque, est propria ratio uniuscuiusque illorum generum. Et in aliis quidem generibus a relatione, utpote quantitate et qualitate, etiam propria ratio generis accipitur secundum comparationem ad subiectum, nam quantitas dicitur mensura substantiae, qualitas vero dispositio substantiae. Sed ratio propria relationis non accipitur secundum comparationem ad illud in quo est, sed secundum comparationem ad aliquid extra. Si igitur consideremus, etiam in rebus creatis, relationes secundum id quod relationes sunt, sic inveniuntur esse assistentes, non intrinsecus affixae; quasi significantes respectum quodammodo contingentem ipsam rem relatam, prout ab ea tendit in alterum. Si vero consideretur relatio secundum quod est accidens, sic est inhaerens subiecto, et habens esse accidentale in ipso. Sed Gilbertus Porretanus consideravit relationem primo modo tantum.

Quidquid autem in rebus creatis habet esse accidentale, secundum quod transfertur in Deum, habet esse substantiale, nihil enim est in Deo ut accidens in subiecto, sed quidquid est in Deo, est eius essentia. Sic igitur ex ea parte qua relatio in rebus creatis habet esse accidentale in subiecto, relatio realiter existens in Deo habet esse essentiae divinae, idem omnino ei existens. In hoc vero quod ad aliquid dicitur, non significatur aliqua habitudo ad essentiam, sed magis ad suum oppositum.

Et sic manifestum est quod relatio realiter existens in Deo, est idem essentiae secundum rem; et non differt nisi secundum intelligentiae rationem, prout in relatione importatur respectus ad suum oppositum, qui non importatur in nomine essentiae. Patet ergo quod in Deo non est aliud esse relationis et esse essentiae, sed unum et idem.

AD PRIMUM ergo dicendum quod verba illa Augustini non pertinent ad hoc, quod paternitas, vel alia relatio quae est in Deo, secundum esse suum non sit idem quod divina essentia; sed quod non praedicatur secundum modum substantiae, ut existens in eo de quo dicitur, sed ut ad alterum se habens. Et propter hoc dicuntur duo tantum esse praedicamenta in divinis. Quia alia praedicamenta important habitudinem ad id de quo dicuntur, tam secundum suum esse, quam secundum proprii generis rationem, nihil autem quod est in Deo, potest habere habitudinem ad id in quo est, vel de quo dicitur, nisi habitudinem identitatis, propter summam Dei simplicitatem.

AD SECUNDUM dicendum quod, sicut in rebus creatis, in illo quod dicitur relative, non solum est invenire respectum ad alterum, sed etiam aliquid absolutum, ita

To perceive the error here expressed, we must consider that in each of the nine genera of accidents there are two points for remark. One is the nature belonging to each one of them considered as an accident; which commonly applies to each of them as inherent in a subject, for the essence of an accident is to inhere. The other point of remark is the proper nature of each one of these genera. In the genera, apart from that of relation, as in quantity and quality, even the true idea of the genus itself is derived from a respect to the subject; for quantity is called the measure of substance, and quality is the disposition of substance. But the true idea of relation is not taken from its respect to that in which it is, but from its respect to something outside. So if we consider even in creatures, relations formally as such, in that aspect they are said to be *assistant*, and not intrinsically affixed, for, in this way, they signify a respect which affects a thing related and tends from that thing to something else; whereas, if relation is considered as an accident, it inheres in a subject, and has an accidental existence in it. Gilbert de la Porree considered relation in the former mode only.

Now whatever has an accidental existence in creatures, when considered as transferred to God, has a substantial existence; for there is no accident in God; since all in Him is His essence. So, in so far as relation has an accidental existence in creatures, relation really existing in God has the existence of the divine essence in no way distinct therefrom. But in so far as relation implies respect to something else, no respect to the essence is signified, but rather to its opposite term.

Thus it is manifest that relation really existing in God is really the same as His essence and only differs in its mode of intelligibility; as in relation is meant that regard to its opposite which is not expressed in the name of essence. Thus it is clear that in God relation and essence do not differ from each other, but are one and the same.

REPLY OBJ. 1: These words of Augustine do not imply that paternity or any other relation which is in God is not in its very being the same as the divine essence; but that it is not predicated under the mode of substance, as existing in Him to Whom it is applied; but as a relation. So there are said to be two predicaments only in God, since other predicaments import habitude to that of which they are spoken, both in their generic and in their specific nature; but nothing that exists in God can have any relation to that wherein it exists or of whom it is spoken, except the relation of identity; and this by reason of God's supreme simplicity.

REPLY OBJ. 2: As the relation which exists in creatures involves not only a regard to another, but also something absolute, so the same applies to God, yet not in the same

et in Deo, sed tamen aliter et aliter. Nam id quod invenitur in creatura praeter id quod continetur sub significatione nominis relativi, est alia res, in Deo autem non est alia res, sed una et eadem, quae non perfecte exprimitur relationis nomine, quasi sub significatione talis nominis comprehensa. Dictum est enim supra, cum de divinis nominibus agebatur, quod plus continetur in perfectione divinae essentiae, quam aliquo nomine significari possit. Unde non sequitur quod in Deo, praeter relationem, sit aliquid aliud secundum rem; sed solum considerata nominum ratione.

AD TERTIUM dicendum quod, si in perfectione divina nihil plus contineretur quam quod significat nomen relativum, sequeretur quod esse eius esset imperfectum, utpote ad aliquid aliud se habens, sicut si non contineretur ibi plus quam quod nomine sapientiae significatur, non esset aliquid subsistens. Sed quia divinae essentiae perfectio est maior quam quod significatione alicuius nominis comprehendi possit, non sequitur, si nomen relativum, vel quodcumque aliud nomen dictum de Deo, non significat aliquid perfectum, quod divina essentia habeat esse imperfectum, quia divina essentia comprehendit in se omnium generum perfectionem, ut supra dictum est.

way. What is contained in the creature above and beyond what is contained in the meaning of relation, is something else besides that relation; whereas in God there is no distinction, but both are one and the same; and this is not perfectly expressed by the word *relation*, as if it were comprehended in the ordinary meaning of that term. For it was above explained (Q. 13, A. 2), in treating of the divine names, that more is contained in the perfection of the divine essence than can be signified by any name. Hence it does not follow that there exists in God anything besides relation in reality; but only in the various names imposed by us.

REPLY OBJ. 3: If the divine perfection contained only what is signified by relative names, it would follow that it is imperfect, being thus related to something else; as in the same way, if nothing more were contained in it than what is signified by the word *wisdom*, it would not in that case be a subsistence. But as the perfection of the divine essence is greater than can be included in any name, it does not follow, if a relative term or any other name applied to God signify something imperfect, that the divine essence is in any way imperfect; for the divine essence comprehends within itself the perfection of every genus (Q. 4, A. 2).

Article 3

Whether the Relations in God Are Really Distinguished from Each Other?

AD TERTIUM SIC PROCEDITUR. Videtur quod relationes quae sunt in Deo, realiter ab invicem non distinguantur. Quaecumque enim uni et eidem sunt eadem, sibi invicem sunt eadem. Sed omnis relatio in Deo existens est idem secundum rem cum divina essentia. Ergo relationes secundum rem ab invicem non distinguuntur.

PRAETEREA, sicut paternitas et filiatio secundum nominis rationem distinguuntur ab essentia divina, ita et bonitas et potentia. Sed propter huiusmodi rationis distinctionem non est aliqua realis distinctio bonitatis et potentiae divinae. Ergo neque paternitatis et filiationis.

PRAETEREA, in divinis non est distinctio realis nisi secundum originem. Sed una relatio non videtur oriri ex alia. Ergo relationes non distinguuntur realiter ab invicem.

SED CONTRA est quod dicit Boetius, in libro de Trin., quod *substantia in divinis continet unitatem, relatio multiplicat Trinitatem*. Si ergo relationes non distinguuntur ab invicem realiter, non erit in divinis Trinitas realis, sed rationis tantum, quod est Sabelliani erroris.

OBJECTION 1: It would seem that the divine relations are not really distinguished from each other. For things which are identified with the same, are identified with each other. But every relation in God is really the same as the divine essence. Therefore the relations are not really distinguished from each other.

OBJ. 2: Further, as paternity and filiation are by name distinguished from the divine essence, so likewise are goodness and power. But this kind of distinction does not make any real distinction of the divine goodness and power. Therefore neither does it make any real distinction of paternity and filiation.

OBJ. 3: Further, in God there is no real distinction but that of origin. But one relation does not seem to arise from another. Therefore the relations are not really distinguished from each other.

ON THE CONTRARY, Boethius says (*De Trin.*) that in God *the substance contains the unity; and relation multiplies the trinity*. Therefore, if the relations were not really distinguished from each other, there would be no real trinity in God, but only an ideal trinity, which is the error of Sabellius.

RESPONDEO dicendum quod ex eo quod aliquid alicui attribuitur, oportet quod attribuantur ei omnia quae sunt de ratione illius, sicut cuicumque attribuitur homo, oportet quod attribuatur ei esse rationale. De ratione autem relationis est respectus unius ad alterum, secundum quem aliquid alteri opponitur relative. Cum igitur in Deo realiter sit relatio, ut dictum est, oportet quod realiter sit ibi oppositio. Relativa autem oppositio in sui ratione includit distinctionem. Unde oportet quod in Deo sit realis distinctio, non quidem secundum rem absolutam, quae est essentia, in qua est summa unitas et simplicitas; sed secundum rem relativam.

AD PRIMUM ergo dicendum quod, secundum philosophum in III Physic., argumentum illud tenet, quod quaecumque uni et eidem sunt eadem, sibi invicem sunt eadem, in his quae sunt idem re et ratione, sicut tunica et indumentum, non autem in his quae differunt ratione. Unde ibidem dicit quod, licet actio sit idem motui, similiter et passio, non tamen sequitur quod actio et passio sint idem, quia in actione importatur respectus ut a quo est motus in mobili, in passione vero ut qui est ab alio. Et similiter, licet paternitas sit idem secundum rem cum essentia divina, et similiter filiatio, tamen haec duo in suis propriis rationibus important oppositos respectus. Unde distinguuntur ab invicem.

AD SECUNDUM dicendum quod potentia et bonitas non important in suis rationibus aliquam oppositionem, unde non est similis ratio.

AD TERTIUM dicendum quod, quamvis relationes, proprie loquendo, non oriantur vel procedant ab invicem, tamen accipiuntur per oppositum secundum processionem alicuius ab alio.

I ANSWER THAT, The attributing of anything to another involves the attribution likewise of whatever is contained in it. So when *man* is attributed to anyone, a rational nature is likewise attributed to him. The idea of relation, however, necessarily means regard of one to another, according as one is relatively opposed to another. So as in God there is a real relation (A. 1), there must also be a real opposition. The very nature of relative opposition includes distinction. Hence, there must be real distinction in God, not, indeed, according to that which is absolute—namely, essence, wherein there is supreme unity and simplicity—but according to that which is relative.

REPLY OBJ. 1: According to the Philosopher (*Phys.* iii), this argument holds, that whatever things are identified with the same thing are identified with each other, if the identity be real and logical; as, for instance, a tunic and a garment; but not if they differ logically. Hence in the same place he says that although action is the same as motion, and likewise passion; still it does not follow that action and passion are the same; because action implies reference as of something *from which* there is motion in the thing moved; whereas passion implies reference as of something *which is from* another. Likewise, although paternity, just as filiation, is really the same as the divine essence; nevertheless these two in their own proper idea and definitions import opposite respects. Hence they are distinguished from each other.

REPLY OBJ. 2: Power and goodness do not import any opposition in their respective natures; and hence there is no parallel argument.

REPLY OBJ. 3: Although relations, properly speaking, do not arise or proceed from each other, nevertheless they are considered as opposed according to the procession of one from another.

Article 4

Whether in God There Are Only Four Real Relations—Paternity, Filiation, Spiration, and Procession?

AD QUARTUM SIC PROCEDITUR. Videtur quod in Deo non sint tantum quatuor relationes reales, scilicet paternitas, filiatio, spiratio et processio. Est enim considerare in Deo relationes intelligentis ad intellectum, et volentis ad volitum, quae videntur esse relationes reales, neque sub praedictis continentur. Non ergo sunt solum quatuor relationes reales in Deo.

PRAETEREA, relationes reales accipiuntur in Deo secundum processionem intelligibilem verbi. Sed relationes intelligibiles multiplicantur in infinitum, ut Avicenna dicit. Ergo in Deo sunt infinitae relationes reales.

PRAETEREA, ideae sunt in Deo ab aeterno, ut supra dictum est. Non autem distinguuntur ab invicem nisi

OBJECTION 1: It would seem that in God there are not only four real relations—paternity, filiation, spiration and procession. For it must be observed that in God there exist the relations of the intelligent agent to the object understood; and of the one willing to the object willed; which are real relations not comprised under those above specified. Therefore there are not only four real relations in God.

OBJ. 2: Further, real relations in God are understood as coming from the intelligible procession of the Word. But intelligible relations are infinitely multiplied, as Avicenna says. Therefore in God there exists an infinite series of real relations.

OBJ. 3: Further, ideas in God are eternal (Q. 15, A. 1); and are only distinguished from each other by reason of

secundum respectum ad res, ut supra dictum est. Ergo in Deo sunt multo plures relationes aeternae.

PRAETEREA, aequalitas et similitudo et identitas sunt relationes quaedam; et sunt in Deo ab aeterno. Ergo plures relationes sunt ab aeterno in Deo, quam quae dictae sunt.

SED CONTRA, videtur quod sint pauciores. Quia secundum philosophum, in III Physic., *eadem via est de Athenis ad Thebas, et de Thebis ad Athenas*. Ergo videtur quod pari ratione eadem sit relatio de patre ad filium, quae dicitur paternitas, et de filio ad patrem, quae dicitur filiatio. Et sic non sunt quatuor relationes in Deo.

RESPONDEO dicendum quod, secundum philosophum, in V Metaphys., relatio omnis fundatur vel supra quantitatem, ut duplum et dimidium; vel supra actionem et passionem, ut faciens et factum, pater et filius, dominus et servus, et huiusmodi. Cum autem quantitas non sit in Deo (est enim sine quantitate magnus, ut dicit Augustinus). Relinquitur ergo quod realis relatio in Deo esse non possit, nisi super actionem fundata. Non autem super actiones secundum quas procedit aliquid extrinsecum a Deo, quia relationes Dei ad creaturas non sunt realiter in ipso, ut supra dictum est. Unde relinquitur quod relationes reales in Deo non possunt accipi, nisi secundum actiones secundum quas est processio in Deo, non extra, sed intra. Huiusmodi autem processiones sunt duae tantum, ut supra dictum est, quarum una accipitur secundum actionem intellectus, quae est processio verbi; alia secundum actionem voluntatis, quae est processio amoris. Secundum quamlibet autem processionem oportet duas accipere relationes oppositas, quarum una sit procedentis a principio, et alia ipsius principii. Processio autem verbi dicitur generatio, secundum propriam rationem qua competit rebus viventibus. Relatio autem principii generationis in viventibus perfectis dicitur paternitas, relatio vero procedentis a principio dicitur filiatio. Processio vero amoris non habet nomen proprium, ut supra dictum est, unde neque relationes quae secundum ipsam accipiuntur. Sed vocatur relatio principii huius processionis spiratio; relatio autem procedentis, processio; quamvis haec duo nomina ad ipsas processiones vel origines pertineant, et non ad relationes.

AD PRIMUM ergo dicendum quod in his in quibus differt intellectus et intellectum, volens et volitum, potest esse realis relatio et scientiae ad rem scitam, et volentis ad rem volitam. Sed in Deo est idem omnino intellectus et intellectum, quia intelligendo se intelligit omnia alia, et eadem ratione voluntas et volitum. Unde in Deo huiusmodi relationes non sunt reales, sicut neque relatio eiusdem ad idem. Sed tamen relatio ad verbum est realis,

their regard to things, as above stated. Therefore in God there are many more eternal relations.

OBJ. 4: Further, equality, and likeness, and identity are relations: and they are in God from eternity. Therefore several more relations are eternal in God than the above named.

OBJ. 5: Further, it may also contrariwise be said that there are fewer relations in God than those above named. For, according to the Philosopher (*Phys.* iii 24), *It is the same way from Athens to Thebes, as from Thebes to Athens*. By the same way of reasoning there is the same relation from the Father to the Son, that of paternity, and from the Son to the Father, that of filiation; and thus there are not four relations in God.

I ANSWER THAT, According to the Philosopher (*Metaph.* v), every relation is based either on quantity, as double and half; or on action and passion, as the doer and the deed, the father and the son, the master and the servant, and the like. Now as there is no quantity in God, for He is great without quantity, as Augustine says (*De Trin.* i, 1), it follows that a real relation in God can be based only on action. Such relations are not based on the actions of God according to any extrinsic procession, forasmuch as the relations of God to creatures are not real in Him (Q. 13, A. 7). Hence, it follows that real relations in God can be understood only in regard to those actions according to which there are internal, and not external, processions in God. These processions are two only, as above explained (Q. 27, A. 5), one derived from the action of the intellect, the procession of the Word; and the other from the action of the will, the procession of love. In respect of each of these processions two opposite relations arise; one of which is the relation of the person proceeding from the principle; the other is the relation of the principle Himself. The procession of the Word is called generation in the proper sense of the term, whereby it is applied to living things. Now the relation of the principle of generation in perfect living beings is called paternity; and the relation of the one proceeding from the principle is called filiation. But the procession of Love has no proper name of its own (Q. 27, A. 4); and so neither have the ensuing relations a proper name of their own. The relation of the principle of this procession is called spiration; and the relation of the person proceeding is called procession: although these two names belong to the processions or origins themselves, and not to the relations.

REPLY OBJ. 1: In those things in which there is a difference between the intellect and its object, and the will and its object, there can be a real relation, both of science to its object, and of the willer to the object willed. In God, however, the intellect and its object are one and the same; because by understanding Himself, God understands all other things; and the same applies to His will and the object that He wills. Hence it follows that in God these kinds

quia verbum intelligitur ut procedens per actionem intelligibilem, non autem ut res intellecta. Cum enim intelligimus lapidem, id quod ex re intellecta concipit intellectus, vocatur verbum.

Ad secundum dicendum quod in nobis relationes intelligibiles in infinitum multiplicantur, quia alio actu intelligit homo lapidem, et alio actu intelligit se intelligere lapidem, et alio etiam intelligit hoc intelligere, et sic in infinitum multiplicantur actus intelligendi, et per consequens relationes intellectae. Sed hoc in Deo non habet locum, quia uno actu tantum omnia intelligit.

Ad tertium dicendum quod respectus ideales sunt ut intellecti a Deo. Unde ex eorum pluralitate non sequitur quod sint plures relationes in Deo, sed quod Deus cognoscat plures relationes.

Ad quartum dicendum quod aequalitas et similitudo in Deo non sunt relationes reales, sed rationis tantum, ut infra patebit.

Ad quintum dicendum quod via est eadem ab uno termino ad alterum, et e converso; sed tamen respectus sunt diversi. Unde ex hoc non potest concludi quod eadem sit relatio patris ad filium, et e converso, sed posset hoc concludi de aliquo absoluto, si esset medium inter ea.

of relations are not real; as neither is the relation of a thing to itself. Nevertheless, the relation to the word is a real relation; because the word is understood as proceeding by an intelligible action; and not as a thing understood. For when we understand a stone, that which the intellect conceives from the thing understood, is called the word.

Reply Obj. 2: Intelligible relations in ourselves are infinitely multiplied, because a man understands a stone by one act, and by another act understands that he understands the stone, and again by another, understands that he understands this; thus the acts of understanding are infinitely multiplied, and consequently also the relations understood. This does not apply to God, inasmuch as He understands all things by one act alone.

Reply Obj. 3: Ideal relations exist as understood by God. Hence it does not follow from their plurality that there are many relations in God; but that God knows these many relations.

Reply Obj. 4: Equality and similitude in God are not real relations; but are only logical relations (Q. 42, A. 3, ad 4).

Reply Obj. 5: The way from one term to another and conversely is the same; nevertheless the mutual relations are not the same. Hence, we cannot conclude that the relation of the father to the son is the same as that of the son to the father; but we could conclude this of something absolute, if there were such between them.

QUESTION 29

THE DIVINE PERSONS

Praemissis autem his quae de processionibus et relationibus praecognoscenda videbantur, necessarium est aggredi de personis.

Et primo, secundum considerationem absolutam; et deinde secundum comparativam considerationem.

Oportet autem absolute de personis, primo quidem in communi considerare; deinde de singulis personis.

Ad communem autem considerationem personarum quatuor pertinere videntur, primo quidem, significatio huius nominis persona; secundo vero, numerus personarum; tertio, ea quae consequuntur numerum personarum, vel ei opponuntur, ut diversitas et solitudo, et huiusmodi; quarto vero, ea quae pertinent ad notitiam personarum.

Circa primum quaeruntur quatuor.

Primo, de definitione personae.

Secundo, de comparatione personae ad essentiam, subsistentiam et hypostasim.

Tertio, utrum nomen personae competat in divinis.

Quarto, quid ibi significet.

Having premised what have appeared necessary notions concerning the processions and the relations, we must now approach the subject of the persons.

First, we shall consider the persons absolutely, and then comparatively as regards each other.

We must consider the persons absolutely first in common; and then singly.

The general consideration of the persons seemingly involves four points: (1) The signification of this word *person*; (2) the number of the persons; (3) what is involved in the number of persons, or is opposed thereto; as diversity, and similitude, and the like; and (4) what belongs to our knowledge of the persons.

Four subjects of inquiry are comprised in the first point:
(1) The definition of *person*.
(2) The comparison of person to essence, subsistence, and hypostasis.
(3) Whether the name of person is becoming to God?
(4) What does it signify in Him?

Article 1

The Definition of Person

AD PRIMUM SIC PROCEDITUR. Videtur quod incompetens sit definitio personae quam Boetius assignat in libro de duabus naturis, quae talis est, *persona est rationalis naturae individua substantia.* Nullum enim singulare definitur. Sed persona significat quoddam singulare. Ergo persona inconvenienter definitur.

PRAETEREA, substantia, prout ponitur in definitione personae, aut sumitur pro substantia prima, aut pro substantia secunda. Si pro substantia prima, superflue additur individua, quia substantia prima est substantia individua. Si vero stat pro substantia secunda, falso additur, et est oppositio in adiecto, nam secundae substantiae dicuntur genera vel species. Ergo definitio est male assignata.

PRAETEREA, nomen intentionis non debet poni in definitione rei. Non enim esset bona assignatio, si quis diceret, homo est species animalis, homo enim est nomen rei, et species est nomen intentionis. Cum igitur persona sit nomen rei (significat enim substantiam

OBJECTION 1: It would seem that the definition of person given by Boethius (*De Duab. Nat.*) is insufficient—that is, *a person is an individual substance of a rational nature.* For nothing singular can be subject to definition. But *person* signifies something singular. Therefore person is improperly defined.

OBJ. 2: Further, substance as placed above in the definition of person, is either first substance, or second substance. If it is the former, the word *individual* is superfluous, because first substance is individual substance; if it stands for second substance, the word *individual* is false, for there is contradiction of terms; since second substances are the genera or species. Therefore this definition is incorrect.

OBJ. 3: Further, an intentional term must not be included in the definition of a thing. For to define a man as *a species of animal* would not be a correct definition; since man is the name of a thing, and species is a name of an intention. Therefore, since person is the name of a thing (for it

307

quandam rationalis naturae), inconvenienter indivi-duum, quod est nomen intentionis, in eius definitione ponitur.

PRAETEREA, *natura est principium motus et quietis in eo in quo est per se et non per accidens*, ut dicitur in II Physic. Sed persona est in rebus immobilibus, sicut in Deo et in Angelis. Non ergo in definitione personae debuit poni natura, sed magis essentia.

PRAETEREA, anima separata est rationalis naturae individua substantia. Non autem est persona. Inconve-nienter ergo persona sic definitur.

RESPONDEO dicendum quod, licet universale et particulare inveniantur in omnibus generibus, tamen speciali quodam modo individuum invenitur in genere substantiae. Substantia enim individuatur per seipsam, sed accidentia individuantur per subiectum, quod est substantia, dicitur enim haec albedo, inquantum est in hoc subiecto. Unde etiam convenienter individua sub-stantiae habent aliquod speciale nomen prae aliis, di-cuntur enim hypostases, vel primae substantiae.

Sed adhuc quodam speciaiori et perfectiori modo invenitur particulare et individuum in substantiis ratio-nalibus, quae habent dominium sui actus, et non solum aguntur, sicut alia, sed per se agunt, actiones autem in singularibus sunt. Et ideo etiam inter ceteras substantias quoddam speciale nomen habent singularia rationalis naturae. Et hoc nomen est persona.

Et ideo in praedicta definitione personae ponitur substantia individua, inquantum significat singulare in genere substantiae, additur autem rationalis naturae, in-quantum significat singulare in rationalibus substantiis.

AD PRIMUM ergo dicendum quod, licet hoc singu-lare vel illud definiri non possit, tamen id quod pertinet ad communem rationem singularitatis, definiri potest, et sic philosophus definit substantiam primam. Et hoc modo definit Boetius personam.

AD SECUNDUM dicendum quod, secundum quo-sdam, substantia in definitione personae ponitur pro substantia prima, quae est hypostasis. Neque tamen su-perflue additur individua. Quia nomine hypostasis vel substantiae primae, excluditur ratio universalis et partis (non enim dicimus quod homo communis sit hyposta-sis, neque etiam manus, cum sit pars), sed per hoc quod additur individuum, excluditur a persona ratio assump-tibilis; humana enim natura in Christo non est persona, quia est assumpta a digniori, scilicet a verbo Dei. Sed melius dicendum est quod substantia accipitur commu-niter, prout dividitur per primam et secundam, et per hoc quod additur individua, trahitur ad standum pro substantia prima.

signifies a substance of a rational nature), the word *individual* which is an intentional name comes improperly into the definition.

OBJ. 4: Further, *Nature is the principle of motion and rest, in those things in which it is essentially, and not acci-dentally*, as Aristotle says (*Phys.* ii). But person exists in things immovable, as in God, and in the angels. Therefore the word *nature* ought not to enter into the definition of person, but the word should rather be *essence*.

OBJ. 5: Further, the separated soul is an individual sub-stance of the rational nature; but it is not a person. There-fore person is not properly defined as above.

I ANSWER THAT, Although the universal and particu-lar exist in every genus, nevertheless, in a certain special way, the individual belongs to the genus of substance. For substance is individualized by itself; whereas the accidents are individualized by the subject, which is the substance; since this particular whiteness is called *this*, because it ex-ists in this particular subject. And so it is reasonable that the individuals of the genus substance should have a special name of their own; for they are called *hypostases*, or first substances.

Further still, in a more special and perfect way, the par-ticular and the individual are found in the rational sub-stances which have dominion over their own actions; and which are not only made to act, like others; but which can act of themselves; for actions belong to singulars. There-fore also the individuals of the rational nature have a spe-cial name even among other substances; and this name is *person*.

Thus the term *individual substance* is placed in the defi-nition of person, as signifying the singular in the genus of substance; and the term *rational nature* is added, as signify-ing the singular in rational substances.

REPLY OBJ. 1: Although this or that singular may not be definable, yet what belongs to the general idea of singu-larity can be defined; and so the Philosopher (*De Praedic.*, cap. De substantia) gives a definition of first substance; and in this way Boethius defines person.

REPLY OBJ. 2: In the opinion of some, the term *sub-stance* in the definition of person stands for first substance, which is the hypostasis; nor is the term *individual* superflu-ously added, forasmuch as by the name of hypostasis or first substance the idea of universality and of part is excluded. For we do not say that man in general is an hypostasis, nor that the hand is since it is only a part. But where *individual* is added, the idea of assumptibility is excluded from per-son; for the human nature in Christ is not a person, since it is assumed by a greater—that is, by the Word of God. It is, however, better to say that substance is here taken in a gen-eral sense, as divided into first and second, and when *indi-vidual* is added, it is restricted to first substance.

AD TERTIUM dicendum quod, quia substantiales differentiae non sunt nobis notae, vel etiam nominatae non sunt, oportet interdum uti differentiis accidentalibus loco substantialium, puta si quis diceret, ignis est corpus simplex, calidum et siccum, accidentia enim propria sunt effectus formarum substantialium, et manifestant eas. Et similiter nomina intentionum possunt accipi ad definiendum res, secundum quod accipiuntur pro aliquibus nominibus rerum quae non sunt posita. Et sic hoc nomen individuum ponitur in definitione personae, ad designandum modum subsistendi qui competit substantiis particularibus.

AD QUARTUM dicendum quod, secundum philosophum, in V Metaphys., nomen naturae primo impositum est ad significandam generationem viventium, quae dicitur nativitas. Et quia huiusmodi generatio est a principio intrinseco, extensum est hoc nomen ad significandum principium intrinsecum cuiuscumque motus. Et sic definitur natura in II Physic. Et quia huiusmodi principium est formale vel materiale, communiter tam materia quam forma dicitur natura. Et quia per formam completur essentia uniuscuiusque rei, communiter essentia uniuscuiusque rei, quam significat eius definitio, vocatur natura. Et sic accipitur hic natura. Unde Boetius in eodem libro dicit quod *natura est unumquodque informans specifica differentia*, specifica enim differentia est quae complet definitionem, et sumitur a propria forma rei. Et ideo convenientius fuit quod in definitione personae, quae est singulare alicuius generis determinati, uteretur nomine naturae, quam essentiae, quae sumitur ab esse, quod est communissimum.

AD QUINTUM dicendum quod anima est pars humanae speciei, et ideo, licet sit separata, quia tamen retinet naturam unibilitatis, non potest dici substantia individua quae est hypostasis vel substantia prima; sicut nec manus, nec quaecumque alia partium hominis. Et sic non competit ei neque definitio personae, neque nomen.

REPLY OBJ. 3: Substantial differences being unknown to us, or at least unnamed by us, it is sometimes necessary to use accidental differences in the place of substantial; as, for example, we may say that fire is a simple, hot, and dry body: for proper accidents are the effects of substantial forms, and make them known. Likewise, terms expressive of intention can be used in defining realities if used to signify things which are unnamed. And so the term *individual* is placed in the definition of person to signify the mode of subsistence which belongs to particular substances.

REPLY OBJ. 4: According to the Philosopher (*Metaph.* v, 5), the word *nature* was first used to signify the generation of living things, which is called nativity. And because this kind of generation comes from an intrinsic principle, this term is extended to signify the intrinsic principle of any kind of movement. In this sense he defines *nature* (*Phys.* ii, 3). And since this kind of principle is either formal or material, both matter and form are commonly called nature. And as the essence of anything is completed by the form; so the essence of anything, signified by the definition, is commonly called nature. And here nature is taken in that sense. Hence Boethius says (*De Duab. Nat.*) that, *nature is the specific difference giving its form to each thing*, for the specific difference completes the definition, and is derived from the special form of a thing. So in the definition of *person*, which means the singular in a determined genus, it is more correct to use the term *nature* than *essence*, because the latter is taken from being, which is most common.

REPLY OBJ. 5: The soul is a part of the human species; and so, although it may exist in a separate state, yet since it ever retains its nature of unibility, it cannot be called an individual substance, which is the hypostasis or first substance, as neither can the hand nor any other part of man; thus neither the definition nor the name of person belongs to it.

Article 2

Whether Person Is the Same As Hypostasis, Subsistence, and Essence?

AD SECUNDUM SIC PROCEDITUR. Videtur quod persona sit idem quod hypostasis, subsistentia et essentia. Dicit enim Boetius, in libro de Duab. Natur., quod *Graeci naturae rationalis individuam substantiam hypostaseos nomine vocaverunt*. Sed hoc etiam, apud nos, significat nomen personae. Ergo persona omnino idem est quod hypostasis.

PRAETEREA, sicut in divinis dicimus tres personas, ita in divinis dicimus tres subsistentias, quod non esset,

OBJECTION 1: It would seem that *person* is the same as *hypostasis*, *subsistence*, and *essence*. For Boethius says (*De Duab. Nat.*) that *the Greeks called the individual substance of the rational nature by the name hypostasis*. But this with us signifies *person*. Therefore *person* is altogether the same as *hypostasis*.

OBJ. 2: Further, as we say there are three persons in God, so we say there are three subsistences in God; which

nisi persona et subsistentia idem significarent. Ergo idem significant persona et subsistentia.

PRAETEREA, Boetius dicit, in commento praedicamentorum, quod usia, quod est idem quod essentia, significat compositum ex materia et forma. Id autem quod est compositum ex materia et forma, est individuum substantiae, quod et hypostasis et persona dicitur. Ergo omnia praedicta nomina idem significare videntur.

SED CONTRA est quod Boetius dicit, in libro de Duab. Natur., quod *genera et species subsistunt tantum; individua vero non modo subsistunt, verum etiam substant.* Sed a subsistendo dicuntur subsistentiae, sicut a substando substantiae vel hypostases. Cum igitur esse hypostases vel personas non conveniat generibus vel speciebus, hypostases vel personae non sunt idem quod subsistentiae.

PRAETEREA, Boetius dicit, in commento praedicamentorum, quod hypostasis dicitur materia, usiosis autem, idest subsistentia, dicitur forma. Sed neque forma neque materia potest dici persona. Ergo persona differt a praedictis.

RESPONDEO dicendum quod, secundum philosophum, in V Metaphys., substantia dicitur dupliciter. Uno modo dicitur substantia quidditas rei, quam significat definitio, secundum quod dicimus quod definitio significat substantiam rei, quam quidem substantiam Graeci usiam vocant, quod nos essentiam dicere possumus. Alio modo dicitur substantia subiectum vel suppositum quod subsistit in genere substantiae. Et hoc quidem, communiter accipiendo, nominari potest et nomine significante intentionem, et sic dicitur suppositum. Nominatur etiam tribus nominibus significantibus rem, quae quidem sunt res naturae, subsistentia et hypostasis, secundum triplicem considerationem substantiae sic dictae. Secundum enim quod per se existit et non in alio, vocatur subsistentia, illa enim subsistere dicimus, quae non in alio, sed in se existunt. Secundum vero quod supponitur alicui naturae communi, sic dicitur res naturae; sicut hic homo est res naturae humanae. Secundum vero quod supponitur accidentibus, dicitur hypostasis vel substantia. Quod autem haec tria nomina significant communiter in toto genere substantiarum, hoc nomen persona significat in genere rationalium substantiarum.

AD PRIMUM ergo dicendum quod hypostasis, apud Graecos, ex propria significatione nominis habet quod significet quodcumque individuum substantiae, sed ex usu loquendi habet quod sumatur pro individuo rationalis naturae, ratione suae excellentiae.

AD SECUNDUM dicendum quod, sicut nos dicimus in divinis pluraliter tres personas et tres subsistentias, ita Graeci dicunt tres hypostases. Sed quia nomen substantiae, quod secundum proprietatem significationis respondet hypostasi, aequivocatur apud nos, cum quandoque significet essentiam, quandoque hypostasim;

implies that *person* and *subsistence* have the same meaning. Therefore *person* and *subsistence* mean the same.

OBJ. 3: Further, Boethius says (*Com. Praed.*) that the Greek ousia, which means essence, signifies a being composed of matter and form. Now that which is composed of matter and form is the individual substance called *hypostasis* and *person*. Therefore all the aforesaid names seem to have the same meaning.

OBJ. 4: On the contrary, Boethius says (*De Duab. Nat.*) that genera and species only subsist; whereas individuals are not only subsistent, but also substand. But subsistences are so called from subsisting, as substance or hypostasis is so called from substanding. Therefore, since genera and species are not hypostases or persons, these are not the same as subsistences.

OBJ. 5: Further, Boethius says (*Com. Praed.*) that matter is called hypostasis, and form is called ousiosis—that is, subsistence. But neither form nor matter can be called person. Therefore person differs from the others.

I ANSWER THAT, According to the Philosopher (*Metaph.* v), substance is twofold. In one sense it means the quiddity of a thing, signified by its definition, and thus we say that the definition means the substance of a thing; in which sense substance is called by the Greeks ousia, what we may call *essence*. In another sense substance means a subject or suppositum, which subsists in the genus of substance. To this, taken in a general sense, can be applied a name expressive of an intention; and thus it is called suppositum. It is also called by three names signifying a reality—that is, *a thing of nature, subsistence*, and *hypostasis*, according to a threefold consideration of the substance thus named. For, as it exists in itself and not in another, it is called *subsistence*; as we say that those things subsist which exist in themselves, and not in another. As it underlies some common nature, it is called *a thing of nature*; as, for instance, this particular man is a human natural thing. As it underlies the accidents, it is called *hypostasis*, or *substance*. What these three names signify in common to the whole genus of substances, this name *person* signifies in the genus of rational substances.

REPLY OBJ. 1: Among the Greeks the term *hypostasis*, taken in the strict interpretation of the word, signifies any individual of the genus substance; but in the usual way of speaking, it means the individual of the rational nature, by reason of the excellence of that nature.

REPLY OBJ. 2: As we say *three persons* plurally in God, and *three subsistences*, so the Greeks say *three hypostases*. But because the word *substance*, which, properly speaking, corresponds in meaning to *hypostasis*, is used among us in an equivocal sense, since it sometimes means essence, and sometimes means hypostasis, in order to avoid any

ne possit esse erroris occasio, maluerunt pro hypostasi transferre subsistentiam, quam substantiam.

AD TERTIUM dicendum quod essentia proprie est id quod significatur per definitionem. Definitio autem complectitur principia speciei, non autem principia individualia. Unde in rebus compositis ex materia et forma, essentia significat non solum formam, nec solum materiam, sed compositum ex materia et forma communi, prout sunt principia speciei. Sed compositum ex hac materia et ex hac forma, habet rationem hypostasis et personae, anima enim et caro et os sunt de ratione hominis, sed haec anima et haec caro et hoc os sunt de ratione huius hominis. Et ideo hypostasis et persona addunt supra rationem essentiae principia individualia; neque sunt idem cum essentia in compositis ex materia et forma, ut supra dictum est, cum de simplicitate divina ageretur.

AD QUARTUM dicendum quod Boetius dicit genera et species subsistere, inquantum individuis aliquibus competit subsistere, ex eo quod sunt sub generibus et speciebus in praedicamento substantiae comprehensis, non quod ipsae species vel genera subsistant, nisi secundum opinionem Platonis, qui posuit species rerum separatim subsistere a singularibus. Substare vero competit eisdem individuis in ordine ad accidentia, quae sunt praeter rationem generum et specierum.

AD QUINTUM dicendum quod individuum compositum ex materia et forma, habet quod substet accidenti, ex proprietate materiae. Unde et Boetius dicit, in libro de Trin., *forma simplex subiectum esse non potest.* Sed quod per se subsistat, habet ex proprietate suae formae, quae non advenit rei subsistenti, sed dat esse actuale materiae, ut sic individuum subsistere possit. Propter hoc ergo hypostasim attribuit materiae, et usiosim, sive subsistentiam, formae, quia materia est principium substandi, et forma est principium subsistendi.

occasion of error, it was thought preferable to use *subsistence* for hypostasis, rather than *substance*.

REPLY OBJ. 3: Strictly speaking, the essence is what is expressed by the definition. Now, the definition comprises the principles of the species, but not the individual principles. Hence in things composed of matter and form, the essence signifies not only the form, nor only the matter, but what is composed of matter and the common form, as the principles of the species. But what is composed of this matter and this form has the nature of hypostasis and person. For soul, flesh, and bone belong to the nature of man; whereas this soul, this flesh and this bone belong to the nature of this man. Therefore hypostasis and person add the individual principles to the idea of essence; nor are these identified with the essence in things composed of matter and form, as we said above when treating of divine simplicity (Q. 3, A. 3).

REPLY OBJ. 4: Boethius says that genera and species subsist, inasmuch as it belongs to some individual things to subsist, from the fact that they belong to genera and species comprised in the predicament of substance, but not because the species and genera themselves subsist; except in the opinion of Plato, who asserted that the species of things subsisted separately from singular things. To substand, however, belongs to the same individual things in relation to the accidents, which are outside the essence of genera and species.

REPLY OBJ. 5: The individual composed of matter and form substands in relation to accident from the very nature of matter. Hence Boethius says (*De Trin.*): *A simple form cannot be a subject.* Its self-subsistence is derived from the nature of its form, which does not supervene to the things subsisting, but gives actual existence to the matter and makes it subsist as an individual. On this account, therefore, he ascribes hypostasis to matter, and ousiosis, or subsistence, to the form, because the matter is the principle of substanding, and form is the principle of subsisting.

Article 3

Whether the Word Person Should Be Said of God?

AD TERTIUM SIC PROCEDITUR. Videtur quod nomen personae non sit ponendum in divinis. Dicit enim Dionysius, in principio de Div. Nom. *universaliter non est audendum aliquid dicere nec cogitare de supersubstantiali occulta divinitate, praeter ea quae divinitus nobis ex sanctis eloquiis sunt expressa.* Sed nomen personae non exprimitur nobis in sacra Scriptura novi vel veteris testamenti. Ergo non est nomine personae utendum in divinis.

OBJECTION 1: It would seem that the name *person* should not be said of God. For Dionysius says (*Div. Nom.*): *No one should ever dare to say or think anything of the supersubstantial and hidden Divinity, beyond what has been divinely expressed to us by the oracles.* But the name *person* is not expressed to us in the Old or New Testament. Therefore *person* is not to be applied to God.

PRAETEREA, Boetius dicit, in libro de Duab. Natur., *nomen personae videtur traductum ex his personis quae in comoediis tragoediisque homines repraesentabant; persona enim dicta est a personando, quia concavitate ipsa maior necesse est ut volvatur sonus. Graeci vero has personas prosopa vocant, ab eo quod ponantur in facie, atque ante oculos obtegant vultum.* Sed hoc non potest competere in divinis, nisi forte secundum metaphoram. Ergo nomen personae non dicitur de Deo nisi metaphorice.

PRAETEREA, omnis persona est hypostasis. Sed nomen hypostasis non videtur Deo competere, cum, secundum Boetium, significet id quod subiicitur accidentibus, quae in Deo non sunt. Hieronymus etiam dicit quod in hoc nomine hypostasis, venenum latet sub melle. Ergo hoc nomen persona non est dicendum de Deo.

PRAETEREA, a quocumque removetur definitio, et definitum. Sed definitio personae supra posita non videtur Deo competere. Tum quia ratio importat discursivam cognitionem, quae non competit Deo, ut supra ostensum est, et sic Deus non potest dici rationalis naturae. Tum etiam quia Deus dici non potest individua substantia, cum principium individuationis sit materia, Deus autem immaterialis est; neque etiam accidentibus substat, ut substantia dici possit. Nomen ergo personae Deo attribui non debet.

SED CONTRA est quod dicitur in symbolo Athanasii, *alia est persona patris, alia filii, alia spiritus sancti.*

RESPONDEO dicendum quod persona significat id quod est perfectissimum in tota natura, scilicet subsistens in rationali natura. Unde, cum omne illud quod est perfectionis, Deo sit attribuendum, eo quod eius essentia continet in se omnem perfectionem; conveniens est ut hoc nomen persona de Deo dicatur. Non tamen eodem modo quo dicitur de creaturis, sed excellentiori modo; sicut et alia nomina quae, creaturis a nobis imposita, Deo attribuuntur; sicut supra ostensum est, cum de divinis nominibus ageretur.

AD PRIMUM ergo dicendum quod, licet nomen personae in Scriptura veteris vel novi testamenti non inveniatur dictum de Deo, tamen id quod nomen significat, multipliciter in sacra Scriptura invenitur assertum de Deo; scilicet quod est maxime per se ens, et perfectissime intelligens. Si autem oporteret de Deo dici solum illa, secundum vocem, quae sacra Scriptura de Deo tradit, sequeretur quod nunquam in alia lingua posset aliquis loqui de Deo, nisi in illa in qua primo tradita est Scriptura veteris vel novi testamenti. Ad inveniendum autem nova nomina, antiquam fidem de Deo significantia, coegit necessitas disputandi cum haereticis. Nec haec

OBJ. 2: Further, Boethius says (*De Duab. Nat.*): *The word person seems to be taken from those persons who represented men in comedies and tragedies. For person comes from sounding through, since a greater volume of sound is produced through the cavity in the mask. These persons or masks the Greeks called prosopa, as they were placed on the face and covered the features before the eyes.* This, however, can apply to God only in a metaphorical sense. Therefore the word *person* is only applied to God metaphorically.

OBJ. 3: Further, every person is a hypostasis. But the word *hypostasis* does not apply to God, since, as Boethius says (*De Duab. Nat.*), it signifies what is the subject of accidents, which do not exist in God. Jerome also says (*Ep. ad Damas.*) that, *in this word hypostasis, poison lurks in honey.* Therefore the word *person* should not be said of God.

OBJ. 4: Further, if a definition is denied of anything, the thing defined is also denied of it. But the definition of *person*, as given above, does not apply to God. Both because reason implies a discursive knowledge, which does not apply to God, as we proved above (Q. 14, A. 12); and thus God cannot be said to have *a rational nature*. And also because God cannot be called an individual substance, since the principle of individuation is matter; while God is immaterial: nor is He the subject of accidents, so as to be called a substance. Therefore the word *person* ought not to be attributed to God.

ON THE CONTRARY, In the Creed of Athanasius we say: *One is the person of the Father, another of the Son, another of the Holy Spirit.*

I ANSWER THAT, *Person* signifies what is most perfect in all nature—that is, a subsistent individual of a rational nature. Hence, since everything that is perfect must be attributed to God, forasmuch as His essence contains every perfection, this name *person* is fittingly applied to God; not, however, as it is applied to creatures, but in a more excellent way; as other names also, which, while giving them to creatures, we attribute to God; as we showed above when treating of the names of God (Q. 13, A. 2).

REPLY OBJ. 1: Although the word *person* is not found applied to God in Scripture, either in the Old or New Testament, nevertheless what the word signifies is found to be affirmed of God in many places of Scripture; as that He is the supreme self-subsisting being, and the most perfectly intelligent being. If we could speak of God only in the very terms themselves of Scripture, it would follow that no one could speak about God in any but the original language of the Old or New Testament. The urgency of confuting heretics made it necessary to find new words to express the ancient faith about God. Nor is such a kind of novelty to be shunned; since it is by no means profane, for it does

novitas vitanda est, cum non sit profana, utpote a Scripturarum sensu non discordans, docet autem apostolus profanas vocum novitates vitare, I ad Tim. ult.

AD SECUNDUM dicendum quod, quamvis hoc nomen persona non conveniat Deo quantum ad id a quo impositum est nomen, tamen quantum ad id ad quod significandum imponitur, maxime Deo convenit. Quia enim in comoediis et tragoediis repraesentabantur aliqui homines famosi, impositum est hoc nomen persona ad significandum aliquos dignitatem habentes. Unde consueverunt dici personae in Ecclesiis, quae habent aliquam dignitatem. Propter quod quidam definiunt personam, dicentes quod *persona est hypostasis proprietate distincta ad dignitatem pertinente.* Et quia magnae dignitatis est in rationali natura subsistere, ideo omne individuum rationalis naturae dicitur persona, ut dictum est. Sed dignitas divinae naturae excedit omnem dignitatem, et secundum hoc maxime competit Deo nomen personae.

AD TERTIUM dicendum quod nomen hypostasis non competit Deo quantum ad id a quo est impositum nomen, cum non substet accidentibus, competit autem ei quantum ad id, quod est impositum ad significandum rem subsistentem. Hieronymus autem dicit sub hoc nomine venenum latere, quia antequam significatio huius nominis esset plene nota apud Latinos, haeretici per hoc nomen simplices decipiebant, ut confiterentur plures essentias, sicut confitentur plures hypostases; propter hoc quod nomen substantiae, cui respondet in Graeco nomen hypostasis, communiter accipitur apud nos pro essentia.

AD QUARTUM dicendum quod Deus potest dici rationalis naturae, secundum quod ratio non importat discursum, sed communiter intellectualem naturam. Individuum autem Deo competere non potest quantum ad hoc quod individuationis principium est materia, sed solum secundum quod importat incommunicabilitatem. Substantia vero convenit Deo, secundum quod significat existere per se. Quidam tamen dicunt quod definitio superius a Boetio data, non est definitio personae secundum quod personas in Deo dicimus. Propter quod Ricardus de sancto Victore, corrigere volens hanc definitionem, dixit quod persona, secundum quod de Deo dicitur, est divinae naturae incommunicabilis existentia.

not lead us astray from the sense of Scripture. The Apostle warns us to avoid *profane novelties of words* (1 Tim 6:20).

REPLY OBJ. 2: Although this name *person* may not belong to God as regards the origin of the term, nevertheless it excellently belongs to God in its objective meaning. For as famous men were represented in comedies and tragedies, the name *person* was given to signify those who held high dignity. Hence, those who held high rank in the Church came to be called *persons*. Thence by some the definition of person is given as *hypostasis distinct by reason of dignity.* And because subsistence in a rational nature is of high dignity, therefore every individual of the rational nature is called a *person.* Now the dignity of the divine nature excels every other dignity; and thus the name *person* preeminently belongs to God.

REPLY OBJ. 3: The word *hypostasis* does not apply to God as regards its source of origin, since He does not underlie accidents; but it applies to Him in its objective sense, for it is imposed to signify the subsistence. Jerome said that *poison lurks in this word*, forasmuch as before it was fully understood by the Latins, the heretics used this term to deceive the simple, to make people profess many essences as they profess several hypostases, inasmuch as the word *substance*, which corresponds to hypostasis in Greek, is commonly taken amongst us to mean essence.

REPLY OBJ. 4: It may be said that God has a rational nature, if reason be taken to mean, not discursive thought, but in a general sense, an intelligent nature. But God cannot be called an *individual* in the sense that His individuality comes from matter; but only in the sense which implies incommunicability. *Substance* can be applied to God in the sense of signifying self-subsistence. There are some, however, who say that the definition of Boethius, quoted above (A. 1), is not a definition of person in the sense we use when speaking of persons in God. Therefore Richard of St. Victor amends this definition by adding that *Person* in God is *the incommunicable existence of the divine nature.*

Article 4

Whether This Word Person Signifies Relation?

AD QUARTUM SIC PROCEDITUR. Videtur quod hoc nomen persona non significet relationem, sed substantiam, in divinis. Dicit enim Augustinus, in VII de Trin.,

OBJECTION 1: It would seem that this word *person*, as applied to God, does not signify relation, but substance. For Augustine says (*De Trin.* vii, 6): *When we speak of the*

cum dicimus personam patris, non aliud dicimus quam substantiam patris; ad se quippe dicitur persona, non ad filium.

PRAETEREA, quid quaerit de essentia. Sed, sicut dicit Augustinus in eodem loco, cum dicitur, *tres sunt qui testimonium dant in caelo, pater, verbum et spiritus sanctus; et quaeritur, quid tres? Respondetur, tres personae.* Ergo hoc nomen persona significat essentiam.

PRAETEREA, secundum philosophum, IV Metaphys., id quod significatur per nomen, est eius definitio. Sed definitio personae est rationalis naturae individua substantia, ut dictum est. Ergo hoc nomen persona significat substantiam.

PRAETEREA, persona in hominibus et Angelis non significat relationem, sed aliquid absolutum. Si igitur in Deo significaret relationem, diceretur aequivoce de Deo et hominibus et Angelis.

SED CONTRA est quod dicit Boetius, in libro de Trin., quod omne nomen ad personas pertinens, relationem significat. Sed nullum nomen magis pertinet ad personas, quam hoc nomen persona. Ergo hoc nomen persona relationem significat.

RESPONDEO dicendum quod circa significationem huius nominis persona in divinis, difficultatem ingerit quod pluraliter de tribus praedicatur, praeter naturam essentialium nominum; neque etiam ad aliquid dicitur, sicut nomina quae relationem significant.

Unde quibusdam visum est quod hoc nomen persona simpliciter, ex virtute vocabuli, essentiam significet in divinis, sicut hoc nomen Deus, et hoc nomen sapiens, sed propter instantiam haereticorum, est accommodatum, ex ordinatione Concilii, ut possit poni pro relativis; et praecipue in plurali, vel cum nomine partitivo, ut cum dicimus tres personas, vel alia est persona patris, alia filii. In singulari vero potest sumi pro absoluto, et pro relativo. Sed haec non videtur sufficiens ratio. Quia si hoc nomen persona, ex vi suae significationis, non habet quod significet nisi essentiam in divinis; ex hoc quod dictum est tres personas, non fuisset haereticorum quietata calumnia, sed maioris calumniae data esset eis occasio. Et ideo alii dixerunt quod hoc nomen persona in divinis significat simul essentiam et relationem. Quorum quidam dixerunt quod significat essentiam in recto, et relationem in obliquo. Quia persona dicitur quasi per se una, unitas autem pertinet ad essentiam. Quod autem dicitur per se, implicat relationem oblique, intelligitur enim pater per se esse, quasi relatione distinctus a filio. Quidam vero dixerunt e converso, quod significat relationem in recto, et essentiam in obliquo, quia in definitione personae, natura ponitur in obliquo. Et isti propinquius ad veritatem accesserunt.

Ad evidentiam igitur huius quaestionis, considerandum est quod aliquid est de significatione minus

person of the Father, we mean nothing else but the substance of the Father, for person is said in regard to Himself, and not in regard to the Son.

OBJ. 2: Further, the interrogation *What?* refers to essence. But, as Augustine says: *When we say there are three who bear witness in heaven, the Father, the Word, and the Holy Spirit, and it is asked, Three what? the answer is, Three persons.* Therefore person signifies essence.

OBJ. 3: According to the Philosopher (*Metaph.* iv), the meaning of a word is its definition. But the definition of *person* is this: *The individual substance of the rational nature,* as above stated. Therefore *person* signifies substance.

OBJ. 4: Further, person in men and angels does not signify relation, but something absolute. Therefore, if in God it signified relation, it would bear an equivocal meaning in God, in man, and in angels.

ON THE CONTRARY, Boethius says (*De Trin.*) that *every word that refers to the persons signifies relation.* But no word belongs to person more strictly than the very word *person* itself. Therefore this word *person* signifies relation.

I ANSWER THAT, A difficulty arises concerning the meaning of this word *person* in God, from the fact that it is predicated plurally of the Three in contrast to the nature of the names belonging to the essence; nor does it in itself refer to another, as do the words which express relation.

Hence some have thought that this word *person* of itself expresses absolutely the divine essence; as this name *God* and this word *Wise*; but that to meet heretical attack, it was ordained by conciliar decree that it was to be taken in a relative sense, and especially in the plural, or with the addition of a distinguishing adjective; as when we say, *Three persons,* or, *one is the person of the Father, another of the Son,* etc. Used, however, in the singular, it may be either absolute or relative. But this does not seem to be a satisfactory explanation; for, if this word *person,* by force of its own signification, expresses the divine essence only, it follows that forasmuch as we speak of *three persons,* so far from the heretics being silenced, they had still more reason to argue. Seeing this, others maintained that this word *person* in God signifies both the essence and the relation. Some of these said that it signifies directly the essence, and relation indirectly, forasmuch as *person* means as it were *by itself one*; and unity belongs to the essence. And what is *by itself* implies relation indirectly; for the Father is understood to exist *by Himself,* as relatively distinct from the Son. Others, however, said, on the contrary, that it signifies relation directly; and essence indirectly; forasmuch as in the definition of *person* the term nature is mentioned indirectly; and these come nearer to the truth.

To determine the question, we must consider that something may be included in the meaning of a less common

communis, quod tamen non est de significatione magis communis, rationale enim includitur in significatione hominis, quod tamen non est de significatione animalis. Unde aliud est quaerere de significatione animalis, et aliud est quaerere de significatione animalis quod est homo. Similiter aliud est quaerere de significatione huius nominis persona in communi, et aliud de significatione personae divinae. Persona enim in communi significat substantiam individuam rationalis naturae, ut dictum est. Individuum autem est quod est in se indistinctum, ab aliis vero distinctum. Persona igitur, in quacumque natura, significat id quod est distinctum in natura illa sicut in humana natura significat has carnes et haec ossa et hanc animam, quae sunt principia individuantia hominem; quae quidem, licet non sint de significatione personae, sunt tamen de significatione personae humanae.

Distinctio autem in divinis non fit nisi per relationes originis, ut dictum est supra. Relatio autem in divinis non est sicut accidens inhaerens subiecto, sed est ipsa divina essentia, unde est subsistens, sicut essentia divina subsistit. Sicut ergo deitas est Deus, ita paternitas divina est Deus pater, qui est persona divina. Persona igitur divina significat relationem ut subsistentem. Et hoc est significare relationem per modum substantiae quae est hypostasis subsistens in natura divina; licet subsistens in natura divina non sit aliud quam natura divina. Et secundum hoc, verum est quod hoc nomen persona significat relationem in recto, et essentiam in obliquo, non tamen relationem inquantum est relatio, sed inquantum significatur per modum hypostasis. Similiter etiam significat essentiam in recto, et relationem in obliquo, inquantum essentia idem est quod hypostasis; hypostasis autem significatur in divinis ut relatione distincta; et sic relatio, per modum relationis significata, cadit in ratione personae in obliquo. Et secundum hoc etiam dici potest, quod haec significatio huius nominis persona non erat percepta ante haereticorum calumniam, unde non erat in usu hoc nomen persona, nisi sicut unum aliorum absolutorum. Sed postmodum accommodatum est hoc nomen persona ad standum pro relativo, ex congruentia suae significationis, ut scilicet hoc quod stat pro relativo, non solum habeat ex usu, ut prima opinio dicebat, sed etiam ex significatione sua.

AD PRIMUM ergo dicendum quod hoc nomen persona dicitur ad se, non ad alterum, quia significat relationem, non per modum relationis, sed per modum substantiae quae est hypostasis. Et secundum hoc Augustinus dicit quod significat essentiam, prout in Deo essentia est idem cum hypostasi, quia in Deo non differt quod est et quo est.

AD SECUNDUM dicendum quod quid quandoque quaerit de natura quam significat definitio; ut cum quaeritur, quid est homo? Et respondetur, animal rationale mortale. Quandoque vero quaerit suppositum; ut cum

term, which is not included in the more common term; as *rational* is included in the meaning of *man*, and not in the meaning of *animal*. So that it is one thing to ask the meaning of the word animal, and another to ask its meaning when the animal in question is man. Also, it is one thing to ask the meaning of this word *person* in general; and another to ask the meaning of *person* as applied to God. For *person* in general signifies the individual substance of a rational figure. The individual in itself is undivided, but is distinct from others. Therefore *person* in any nature signifies what is distinct in that nature: thus in human nature it signifies this flesh, these bones, and this soul, which are the individuating principles of a man, and which, though not belonging to *person* in general, nevertheless do belong to the meaning of a particular human person.

Now distinction in God is only by relation of origin, as stated above (Q. 28, AA. 2, 3), while relation in God is not as an accident in a subject, but is the divine essence itself; and so it is subsistent, for the divine essence subsists. Therefore, as the Godhead is God so the divine paternity is God the Father, Who is a divine person. Therefore a divine person signifies a relation as subsisting. And this is to signify relation by way of substance, and such a relation is a hypostasis subsisting in the divine nature, although in truth that which subsists in the divine nature is the divine nature itself. Thus it is true to say that the name *person* signifies relation directly, and the essence indirectly; not, however, the relation as such, but as expressed by way of a hypostasis. So likewise it signifies directly the essence, and indirectly the relation, inasmuch as the essence is the same as the hypostasis: while in God the hypostasis is expressed as distinct by the relation: and thus relation, as such, enters into the notion of the person indirectly. Thus we can say that this signification of the word *person* was not clearly perceived before it was attacked by heretics. Hence, this word *person* was used just as any other absolute term. But afterwards it was applied to express relation, as it lent itself to that signification, so that this word *person* means relation not only by use and custom, according to the first opinion, but also by force of its own proper signification.

REPLY OBJ. 1: This word *person* is said in respect to itself, not to another; forasmuch as it signifies relation not as such, but by way of a substance—which is a hypostasis. In that sense Augustine says that it signifies the essence, inasmuch as in God essence is the same as the hypostasis, because in God what He is, and whereby He is are the same.

REPLY OBJ. 2: The term *what* refers sometimes to the nature expressed by the definition, as when we ask, What is man? and we answer: A mortal rational animal. Sometimes it refers to the suppositum, as when we ask, What swims

quaeritur, quid natat in mari? Et respondetur, piscis. Et sic quaerentibus quid tres? Responsum est, tres personae.

AD TERTIUM dicendum quod in intellectu substantiae individuae, idest distinctae vel incommunicabilis, intelligitur in divinis relatio, ut dictum est.

AD QUARTUM dicendum quod diversa ratio minus communium non facit aequivocationem in magis communi. Licet enim sit alia propria definitio equi et asini, tamen univocantur in nomine animalis, quia communis definitio animalis convenit utrique. Unde non sequitur quod, licet in significatione personae divinae contineatur relatio, non autem in significatione angelicae personae vel humanae, quod nomen personae aequivoce dicatur. Licet nec etiam dicatur univoce, cum nihil univoce de Deo dici possit et de creaturis, ut supra ostensum est.

in the sea? and answer, A fish. So to those who ask, Three what? we answer, Three persons.

REPLY OBJ. 3: In God, the individual—i.e., distinct and incommunicable substance—includes the idea of relation, as above explained.

REPLY OBJ. 4: The different sense of the less common term does not produce equivocation in the more common. Although a horse and an ass have their own proper definitions, nevertheless they agree univocally in animal, because the common definition of animal applies to both. So it does not follow that, although relation is contained in the signification of divine person, but not in that of an angelic or of a human person, the word *person* is used in an equivocal sense. Though neither is it applied univocally, since nothing can be said univocally of God and creatures (Q. 13, A. 5).

QUESTION 30

THE PLURALITY OF PERSONS IN GOD

Deinde quaeritur de pluralitate personarum. Et circa hoc quaeruntur quatuor.

Primo, utrum sint plures personae in divinis.

Secundo, quot sunt.

Tertio, quid significent termini numerales in divinis.

Quarto, de communitate huius nominis persona.

We are now led to consider the plurality of the persons: about which there are four points of inquiry:

(1) Whether there are several persons in God?

(2) How many are they?

(3) What the numeral terms signify in God?

(4) The community of the term *person*.

Article 1

Whether There Are Several Persons in God?

AD PRIMUM SIC PROCEDITUR. Videtur quod non sit ponere plures personas in divinis. Persona enim est rationalis naturae individua substantia. Si ergo sunt plures personae in divinis, sequitur quod sint plures substantiae, quod videtur haereticum.

PRAETEREA, pluralitas proprietatum absolutarum non facit distinctionem personarum, neque in Deo neque in nobis, multo igitur minus pluralitas relationum. Sed in Deo non est alia pluralitas nisi relationum, ut supra dictum est. Ergo non potest dici quod in Deo sint plures personae.

PRAETEREA, Boetius dicit, de Deo loquens, quod hoc vere unum est, in quo nullus est numerus. Sed pluralitas importat numerum. Ergo non sunt plures personae in divinis.

PRAETEREA, ubicumque est numerus, ibi est totum et pars. Si igitur in Deo sit numerus personarum, erit in Deo ponere totum et partem, quod simplicitati divinae repugnat.

SED CONTRA est quod dicit Athanasius, *alia est persona patris, alia filii, alia spiritus sancti*. Ergo pater et filius et Spiritus Sanctus sunt plures personae.

RESPONDEO dicendum quod plures esse personas in divinis, sequitur ex praemissis. Ostensum est enim supra quod hoc nomen persona significat in divinis relationem, ut rem subsistentem in natura divina. Supra autem habitum est quod sunt plures relationes reales in divinis. Unde sequitur quod sint plures res subsistentes in divina natura. Et hoc est esse plures personas in divinis.

AD PRIMUM ergo dicendum quod substantia non ponitur in definitione personae secundum quod significat essentiam, sed secundum quod significat suppositum, quod patet ex hoc quod additur individua. Ad

OBJECTION 1: It would seem that there are not several persons in God. For person is *the individual substance of a rational nature*. If then there are several persons in God, there must be several substances; which appears to be heretical.

OBJ. 2: Further, Plurality of absolute properties does not make a distinction of persons, either in God, or in ourselves. Much less therefore is this effected by a plurality of relations. But in God there is no plurality but of relations (Q. 28, A. 3). Therefore there cannot be several persons in God.

OBJ. 3: Further, Boethius says of God (*De Trin.* i), that *this is truly one which has no number*. But plurality implies number. Therefore there are not several persons in God.

OBJ. 4: Further, where number is, there is whole and part. Thus, if in God there exist a number of persons, there must be whole and part in God; which is inconsistent with the divine simplicity.

ON THE CONTRARY, Athanasius says: *One is the person of the Father, another of the Son, another of the Holy Spirit.* Therefore the Father, and the Son, and the Holy Spirit are several persons.

I ANSWER THAT, It follows from what precedes that there are several persons in God. For it was shown above (Q. 29, A. 4) that this word *person* signifies in God a relation as subsisting in the divine nature. It was also established (Q. 28, A. 1) that there are several real relations in God; and hence it follows that there are also several realities subsistent in the divine nature; which means that there are several persons in God.

REPLY OBJ. 1: The definition of *person* includes *substance*, not as meaning the essence, but the suppositum which is made clear by the addition of the term *individual*. To signify the substance thus understood, the Greeks use

significandum autem substantiam sic dictam, habent Graeci nomen hypostasis, unde sicut nos dicimus tres personas, ita ipsi dicunt tres hypostases. Nos autem non consuevimus dicere tres substantias, ne intelligerentur tres essentiae, propter nominis aequivocationem.

AD SECUNDUM dicendum quod proprietates absolutae in divinis, ut bonitas et sapientia, non opponuntur ad invicem, unde neque realiter distinguuntur. Quamvis ergo eis conveniat subsistere, non tamen sunt plures res subsistentes, quod est esse plures personas. Proprietates autem absolutae in rebus creatis non subsistunt, licet realiter ab invicem distinguantur, ut albedo et dulcedo. Sed proprietates relativae in Deo et subsistunt, et realiter ab invicem distinguuntur, ut supra dictum est. Unde pluralitas talium proprietatum sufficit ad pluralitatem personarum in divinis.

AD TERTIUM dicendum quod a Deo, propter summam unitatem et simplicitatem, excluditur omnis pluralitas absolute dictorum; non autem pluralitas relationum. Quia relationes praedicantur de aliquo ut ad alterum; et sic compositionem in ipso de quo dicuntur non important, ut Boetius in eodem libro docet.

AD QUARTUM dicendum quod numerus est duplex, scilicet numerus simplex vel absolutus, ut duo et tria et quatuor; et numerus qui est in rebus numeratis, ut duo homines et duo equi. Si igitur in divinis accipiatur numerus absolute sive abstracte, nihil prohibet in eo esse totum et partem, et sic non est nisi in acceptione intellectus nostri; non enim numerus absolutus a rebus numeratis est nisi in intellectu. Si autem accipiamus numerum prout est in rebus numeratis, sic in rebus quidem creatis, unum est pars duorum, et duo trium, ut unus homo duorum, et duo trium, sed non est sic in Deo, quia tantus est pater quanta tota Trinitas, ut infra patebit.

the name *hypostasis*. So, as we say, *Three persons*, they say *Three hypostases*. We are not, however, accustomed to say three substances, lest we be understood to mean three essences or natures, by reason of the equivocal signification of the term.

REPLY OBJ. 2: The absolute properties in God, such as goodness and wisdom, are not mutually opposed; and hence, neither are they really distinguished from each other. Therefore, although they subsist, nevertheless they are not several subsistent realities—that is, several persons. But the absolute properties in creatures do not subsist, although they are really distinguished from each other, as whiteness and sweetness; on the other hand, the relative properties in God subsist, and are really distinguished from each other (Q. 28, A. 3). Hence the plurality of persons in God.

REPLY OBJ. 3: The supreme unity and simplicity of God exclude every kind of plurality of absolute things, but not plurality of relations, because relations are predicated relatively; and thus the relations do not import composition in that of which they are predicated, as Boethius teaches in the same book.

REPLY OBJ. 4: Number is twofold, simple or absolute, as two and three and four; and number as existing in things numbered, as two men and two horses. So, if number in God is taken absolutely or abstractedly, there is nothing to prevent whole and part from being in Him, and thus number in Him is only in our way of understanding; forasmuch as number regarded apart from things numbered exists only in the intellect. But if number be taken as it is in the things numbered, in that sense as existing in creatures, one is part of two, and two of three, as one man is part of two men, and two of three; but this does not apply to God, because the Father is of the same magnitude as the whole Trinity, as we shall show further on (Q. 42, AA. 1, 4).

Article 2

Whether There Are More Than Three Persons in God?

AD SECUNDUM SIC PROCEDITUR. Videtur quod in Deo sint plures personae quam tres. Pluralitas enim personarum in divinis est secundum pluralitatem proprietatum relativarum, ut dictum est. Sed quatuor sunt relationes in divinis, ut supra dictum est, scilicet paternitas, filiatio, communis spiratio et processio. Ergo quatuor personae sunt in divinis.

PRAETEREA, non plus differt natura a voluntate in Deo, quam natura ab intellectu. Sed in divinis est alia persona quae procedit per modum voluntatis, ut amor; et alia quae procedit per modum naturae, ut filius. Ergo est etiam alia quae procedit per modum intellectus, ut

OBJECTION 1: It would seem that there are more than three persons in God. For the plurality of persons in God arises from the plurality of the relative properties as stated above (A. 1). But there are four relations in God as stated above (Q. 28, A. 4), paternity, filiation, common spiration, and procession. Therefore there are four persons in God.

OBJ. 2: The nature of God does not differ from His will more than from His intellect. But in God, one person proceeds from the will, as love; and another proceeds from His nature, as Son. Therefore another proceeds from His intellect, as Word, besides the one Who proceeds from His

verbum; et alia quae procedit per modum naturae, ut filius. Et sic iterum sequitur quod non sunt tantum tres personae in divinis.

PRAETEREA, in rebus creatis quod excellentius est, plures habet operationes intrinsecas, sicut homo supra alia animalia habet intelligere et velle. Sed Deus in infinitum excedit omnem creaturam. Ergo non solum est ibi persona procedens per modum voluntatis et per modum intellectus, sed infinitis aliis modis. Ergo sunt infinitae personae in divinis.

PRAETEREA, ex infinita bonitate patris est, quod infinite seipsum communicet, producendo personam divinam. Sed etiam in spiritu sancto est infinita bonitas. Ergo Spiritus Sanctus producit divinam personam, et illa aliam, et sic in infinitum.

PRAETEREA, omne quod continetur sub determinato numero, est mensuratum, numerus enim mensura quaedam est. Sed personae divinae sunt immensae, ut patet per Athanasium, *immensus pater, immensus filius, immensus Spiritus Sanctus*. Non ergo sub numero ternario continentur.

SED CONTRA est quod dicitur I Ioan. ult., *tres sunt qui testimonium dant in caelo, pater, verbum et Spiritus Sanctus*. Quaerentibus autem, *quid tres*? Respondetur, *tres personae*, ut Augustinus dicit, in VII de Trin. Sunt igitur tres personae tantum in divinis.

RESPONDEO dicendum quod, secundum praemissa, necesse est ponere tantum tres personas in divinis. Ostensum est enim quod plures personae sunt plures relationes subsistentes, ab invicem realiter distinctae. Realis autem distinctio inter relationes divinas non est nisi in ratione oppositionis relativae. Ergo oportet duas relationes oppositas ad duas personas pertinere, si quae autem relationes oppositae non sunt, ad eandem personam necesse est eas pertinere. Paternitas ergo et filiatio, cum sint oppositae relationes, ad duas personas ex necessitate pertinent. Paternitas igitur subsistens est persona patris, et filiatio subsistens est persona filii. Aliae autem duae relationes ad neutram harum oppositionem habent, sed sibi invicem opponuntur. Impossibile est igitur quod ambae uni personae conveniant. Oportet ergo quod vel una earum conveniat utrique dictarum personarum, aut quod una uni, et alia alii. Non autem potest esse quod processio conveniat patri et filio, vel alteri eorum, quia sic sequeretur quod processio intellectus, quae est generatio in divinis, secundum quam accipitur paternitas et filiatio, prodiret ex processione amoris, secundum quam accipitur spiratio et processio, si persona generans et genita procederent a spirante, quod est contra praemissa. Relinquitur ergo quod spiratio conveniat et personae patris et personae filii, utpote nullam habens oppositionem relativam nec ad paternitatem nec ad filiationem. Et per consequens oportet quod conveniat processio alteri personae, quae dicitur persona spiritus sancti, quae per

nature, as Son; thus again it follows that there are not only three persons in God.

OBJ. 3: Further, the more perfect a creature is, the more interior operations it has; as a man has understanding and will beyond other animals. But God infinitely excels every creature. Therefore in God not only is there a person proceeding from the will, and another from the intellect, but also in an infinite number of ways. Therefore there are an infinite number of persons in God.

OBJ. 4: Further, it is from the infinite goodness of the Father that He communicates Himself infinitely in the production of a divine person. But also in the Holy Spirit is infinite goodness. Therefore the Holy Spirit produces a divine person; and that person another; and so to infinity.

OBJ. 5: Further, everything within a determinate number is measured, for number is a measure. But the divine persons are immense, as we say in the Creed of Athanasius: *The Father is immense, the Son is immense, the Holy Spirit is immense*. Therefore the persons are not contained within the number three.

ON THE CONTRARY, It is said: *There are three who bear witness in heaven, the Father, the Word, and the Holy Spirit* (1 John 5:7). To those who ask, *Three what?* we answer, with Augustine (*De Trin.* vii, 4), *Three persons*. Therefore there are but three persons in God.

I ANSWER THAT, As was explained above, there can be only three persons in God. For it was shown above that the several persons are the several subsisting relations really distinct from each other. But a real distinction between the divine relations can come only from relative opposition. Therefore two opposite relations must needs refer to two persons: and if any relations are not opposite they must needs belong to the same person. Since then paternity and filiation are opposite relations, they belong necessarily to two persons. Therefore the subsisting paternity is the person of the Father; and the subsisting filiation is the person of the Son. The other two relations are not opposed to each other; therefore these two cannot belong to one person: hence either one of them must belong to both of the aforesaid persons; or one must belong to one person, and the other to the other. Now, procession cannot belong to the Father and the Son, or to either of them; for thus it would follow that the procession of the intellect, which in God is generation, wherefrom paternity and filiation are derived, would issue from the procession of love, whence spiration and procession are derived, if the person generating and the person generated proceeded from the person spirating; and this is against what was laid down above (Q. 27, AA. 3, 4). We must consequently admit that spiration belongs to the person of the Father, and to the person of the Son, forasmuch as it has no relative opposition either to paternity or to filiation; and consequently that procession belongs to the other person who is called the person of the Holy Spirit,

modum amoris procedit, ut supra habitum est. Relinquitur ergo tantum tres personas esse in divinis, scilicet patrem et filium et spiritum sanctum.

AD PRIMUM ergo dicendum quod, licet sint quatuor relationes in divinis, tamen una earum, scilicet spiratio, non separatur a persona patris et filii, sed convenit utrique. Et sic, licet sit relatio, non tamen dicitur proprietas, quia non convenit uni tantum personae, neque est relatio personalis, idest constituens personam. Sed hae tres relationes, paternitas, filiatio et processio, dicuntur proprietates personales, quasi personas constituentes, nam paternitas est persona patris, filiatio persona filii, processio persona spiritus sancti procedentis.

AD SECUNDUM dicendum quod id quod procedit per modum intellectus, ut verbum, procedit secundum rationem similitudinis, sicut etiam id quod procedit per modum naturae, et ideo supra dictum est quod processio verbi divini est ipsa generatio per modum naturae. Amor autem, inquantum huiusmodi, non procedit ut similitudo illius a quo procedit (licet in divinis amor sit coessentialis inquantum est divinus), et ideo processio amoris non dicitur generatio in divinis.

AD TERTIUM dicendum quod homo, cum sit perfectior aliis animalibus, habet plures operationes intrinsecas quam alia animalia, quia eius perfectio est per modum compositionis. Unde in Angelis, qui sunt perfectiores et simpliciores, sunt pauciores operationes intrinsecae quam in homine, quia in eis non est imaginari, sentire, et huiusmodi. Sed in Deo, secundum rem, non est nisi una operatio, quae est sua essentia. Sed quomodo sunt duae processiones, supra ostensum est.

AD QUARTUM dicendum quod ratio illa procederet, si Spiritus Sanctus haberet aliam numero bonitatem a bonitate patris, oporteret enim quod, sicut pater per suam bonitatem producit personam divinam, ita et Spiritus Sanctus. Sed una et eadem bonitas patris est et spiritus sancti. Neque etiam est distinctio nisi per relationes personarum. Unde bonitas convenit spiritui sancto quasi habita ab alio, patri autem, sicut a quo communicatur alteri. Oppositio autem relationis non permittit ut cum relatione spiritus sancti sit relatio principii respectu divinae personae, quia ipse procedit ab aliis personis quae in divinis esse possunt.

AD QUINTUM dicendum quod numerus determinatus, si accipiatur numerus simplex, qui est tantum in acceptione intellectus, per unum mensuratur. Si vero accipiatur numerus rerum in divinis personis, sic non competit ibi ratio mensurati, quia eadem est magnitudo trium personarum, ut infra patebit; idem autem non mensuratur per idem.

who proceeds by way of love, as above explained. Therefore only three persons exist in God, the Father, the Son, and the Holy Spirit.

REPLY OBJ. 1: Although there are four relations in God, one of them, spiration, is not separated from the person of the Father and of the Son, but belongs to both; thus, although it is a relation, it is not called a property, because it does not belong to only one person; nor is it a personal relation—i.e., constituting a person. The three relations—paternity, filiation, and procession—are called personal properties, constituting as it were the persons; for paternity is the person of the Father, filiation is the person of the Son, procession is the person of the Holy Spirit proceeding.

REPLY OBJ. 2: That which proceeds by way of intelligence, as word, proceeds according to similitude, as also that which proceeds by way of nature; thus, as above explained (Q. 27, A. 3), the procession of the divine Word is the very same as generation by way of nature. But love, as such, does not proceed as the similitude of that whence it proceeds; although in God love is co-essential as being divine; and therefore the procession of love is not called generation in God.

REPLY OBJ. 3: As man is more perfect than other animals, he has more intrinsic operations than other animals, because his perfection is something composite. Hence the angels, who are more perfect and more simple, have fewer intrinsic operations than man, for they have no imagination, or feeling, or the like. In God there exists only one real operation—that is, His essence. How there are in Him two processions was above explained (Q. 27, AA. 1, 4).

REPLY OBJ. 4: This argument would prove if the Holy Spirit possessed another goodness apart from the goodness of the Father; for then if the Father produced a divine person by His goodness, the Holy Spirit also would do so. But the Father and the Holy Spirit have one and the same goodness. Nor is there any distinction between them except by the personal relations. So goodness belongs to the Holy Spirit, as derived from another; and it belongs to the Father, as the principle of its communication to another. The opposition of relation does not allow the relation of the Holy Spirit to be joined with the relation of principle of another divine person, because He Himself proceeds from the other persons who are in God.

REPLY OBJ. 5: A determinate number, if taken as a simple number, existing in the mind only, is measured by one. But when we speak of a number of things as applied to the persons in God, the notion of measure has no place, because the magnitude of the three persons is the same (Q. 42, AA. 1, 4), and the same is not measured by the same.

Article 3

Whether the Numeral Terms Denote Anything Real in God?

AD TERTIUM SIC PROCEDITUR. Videtur quod termini numerales ponant aliquid in divinis. Unitas enim divina est eius essentia. Sed omnis numerus est unitas repetita. Ergo omnis terminus numeralis in divinis significat essentiam. Ergo ponit aliquid in Deo.

PRAETEREA, quidquid dicitur de Deo et creaturis, eminentius convenit Deo quam creaturis. Sed termini numerales in creaturis aliquid ponunt. Ergo multo magis in Deo.

PRAETEREA, si termini numerales non ponunt aliquid in divinis, sed inducuntur ad removendum tantum, ut per pluralitatem removeatur unitas, et per unitatem pluralitas; sequitur quod sit circulatio in ratione, confundens intellectum et nihil certificans; quod est inconveniens. Relinquitur ergo quod termini numerales aliquid ponunt in divinis.

SED CONTRA est quod Hilarius dicit, in IV de Trin., *sustulit singularitatis ac solitudinis intelligentiam professio consortii,* quod est professio pluralitatis. Et Ambrosius dicit, in libro de fide *cum unum Deum dicimus, unitas pluralitatem excludit deorum, non quantitatem in Deo ponimus.* Ex quibus videtur quod huiusmodi nomina sunt inducta in divinis ad removendum, non ad ponendum aliquid.

RESPONDEO dicendum quod Magister, in sententiis, ponit quod termini numerales non ponunt aliquid in divinis, sed removent tantum. Alii vero dicunt contrarium.

Ad evidentiam igitur huius, considerandum est quod omnis pluralitas consequitur aliquam divisionem. Est autem duplex divisio. Una materialis, quae fit secundum divisionem continui, et hanc consequitur numerus qui est species quantitatis. Unde talis numerus non est nisi in rebus materialibus habentibus quantitatem. Alia est divisio formalis, quae fit per oppositas vel diversas formas, et hanc divisionem sequitur multitudo quae non est in aliquo genere, sed est de transcendentibus, secundum quod ens dividitur per unum et multa. Et talem multitudinem solam contingit esse in rebus immaterialibus.

Quidam igitur, non considerantes nisi multitudinem quae est species quantitatis discretae, quia videbant quod quantitas discreta non habet locum in divinis, posuerunt quod termini numerales non ponunt aliquid in Deo, sed removent tantum. Alii vero, eandem multitudinem considerantes, dixerunt quod, sicut scientia ponitur in Deo secundum rationem propriam scientiae, non autem secundum rationem sui generis, quia in Deo nulla est qualitas; ita numerus in Deo ponitur secundum propriam rationem numeri, non autem secundum rationem sui generis, quod est quantitas.

OBJECTION 1: It would seem that the numeral terms denote something real in God. For the divine unity is the divine essence. But every number is unity repeated. Therefore every numeral term in God signifies the essence; and therefore it denotes something real in God.

OBJ. 2: Further, whatever is said of God and of creatures, belongs to God in a more eminent manner than to creatures. But the numeral terms denote something real in creatures; therefore much more so in God.

OBJ. 3: Further, if the numeral terms do not denote anything real in God, and are introduced simply in a negative and removing sense, as plurality is employed to remove unity, and unity to remove plurality; it follows that a vicious circle results, confusing the mind and obscuring the truth; and this ought not to be. Therefore it must be said that the numeral terms denote something real in God.

ON THE CONTRARY, Hilary says (*De Trin.* iv): *If we admit companionship*—that is, plurality—*we exclude the idea of oneness and of solitude*; and Ambrose says (*De Fide* i): *When we say one God, unity excludes plurality of gods, and does not imply quantity in God.* Hence we see that these terms are applied to God in order to remove something; and not to denote anything positive.

I ANSWER THAT, The Master (*Sent.* i, D, 24) considers that the numeral terms do not denote anything positive in God, but have only a negative meaning. Others, however, assert the contrary.

In order to resolve this point, we may observe that all plurality is a consequence of division. Now division is twofold; one is material, and is division of the continuous; from this results number, which is a species of quantity. Number in this sense is found only in material things which have quantity. The other kind of division is called formal, and is effected by opposite or diverse forms; and this kind of division results in a multitude, which does not belong to a genus, but is transcendental in the sense in which being is divided by one and by many. This kind of multitude is found only in immaterial things.

Some, considering only that multitude which is a species of discrete quantity, and seeing that such kind of quantity has no place in God, asserted that the numeral terms do not denote anything real in God, but remove something from Him. Others, considering the same kind of multitude, said that as knowledge exists in God according to the strict sense of the word, but not in the sense of its genus (as in God there is no such thing as a quality), so number exists in God in the proper sense of number, but not in the sense of its genus, which is quantity.

Nos autem dicimus quod termini numerales, secundum quod veniunt in praedicationem divinam, non sumuntur a numero qui est species quantitatis; quia sic de Deo non dicerentur nisi metaphorice, sicut et aliae proprietates corporalium, sicut latitudo, longitudo, et similia, sed sumuntur a multitudine secundum quod est transcendens. Multitudo autem sic accepta hoc modo se habet ad multa de quibus praedicatur, sicut unum quod convertitur cum ente ad ens. Huiusmodi autem unum, sicut supra dictum est, cum de Dei unitate ageretur, non addit aliquid supra ens nisi negationem divisionis tantum, unum enim significat ens indivisum. Et ideo de quocumque dicatur unum, significatur illa res indivisa, sicut unum dictum de homine, significat naturam vel substantiam hominis non divisam. Et eadem ratione, cum dicuntur res multae, multitudo sic accepta significat res illas cum indivisione circa unamquamque earum.

Numerus autem qui est species quantitatis, ponit quoddam accidens additum supra ens, et similiter unum quod est principium numeri. Termini ergo numerales significant in divinis illa de quibus dicuntur, et super hoc nihil addunt nisi negationem, ut dictum est, et quantum ad hoc, veritatem dixit Magister in sententiis. Ut, cum dicimus, essentia est una, unum significat essentiam indivisam, cum dicimus, persona est una, significat personam indivisam, cum dicimus, personae sunt plures, significantur illae personae, et indivisio circa unamquamque earum; quia de ratione multitudinis est, quod ex unitatibus constet.

AD PRIMUM ergo dicendum quod unum, cum sit de transcendentibus, est communius quam substantia et quam relatio, et similiter multitudo. Unde potest stare in divinis et pro substantia et pro relatione, secundum quod competit his quibus adiungitur. Et tamen per huiusmodi nomina, supra essentiam vel relationem, additur, ex eorum significatione propria, negatio quaedam divisionis, ut dictum est.

AD SECUNDUM dicendum quod multitudo quae ponit aliquid in rebus creatis, est species quantitatis; quae non transumitur in divinam praedicationem; sed tantum multitudo transcendens, quae non addit supra ea de quibus dicitur, nisi indivisionem circa singula. Et talis multitudo dicitur de Deo.

AD TERTIUM dicendum quod unum non est remotivum multitudinis, sed divisionis, quae est prior, secundum rationem, quam unum vel multitudo. Multitudo autem non removet unitatem, sed removet divisionem circa unumquodque eorum ex quibus constat multitudo. Et haec supra exposita sunt, cum de divina unitate ageretur.

Sciendum tamen est quod auctoritates in oppositum inductae, non probant sufficienter propositum. Licet enim pluralitate excludatur solitudo, et unitate deorum pluralitas, non tamen sequitur quod his nominibus hoc

But we say that numeral terms predicated of God are not derived from number, a species of quantity, for in that sense they could bear only a metaphorical sense in God, like other corporeal properties, such as length, breadth, and the like; but that they are taken from multitude in a transcendent sense. Now multitude so understood has relation to the many of which it is predicated, as *one* convertible with *being* is related to being; which kind of oneness does not add anything to being, except a negation of division, as we saw when treating of the divine unity (Q. 11, A. 1); for *one* signifies undivided being. So, of whatever we say *one*, we imply its undivided reality: thus, for instance, *one* applied to man signifies the undivided nature or substance of a man. In the same way, when we speak of many things, multitude in this latter sense points to those things as being each undivided in itself.

But number, if taken as a species of quantity, denotes an accident added to being; as also does *one* which is the principle of that number. Therefore the numeral terms in God signify the things of which they are said, and beyond this they add negation only, as stated (*Sent.* i, D, 24); in which respect the Master was right (*Sent.* i, D, 24). So when we say the essence is one, the term *one* signifies the essence undivided; and when we say the person is one, it signifies the person undivided; and when we say the persons are many, we signify those persons, and their individual undividedness; for it is of the very nature of multitude that it should be composed of units.

REPLY OBJ. 1: One, as it is a transcendental, is wider and more general than substance and relation. And so likewise is multitude; hence in God it may mean both substance and relation, according to the context. Still, the very signification of such names adds a negation of division, beyond substance and relation; as was explained above.

REPLY OBJ. 2: Multitude, which denotes something real in creatures, is a species of quantity, and cannot be used when speaking of God: unlike transcendental multitude, which adds only indivision to those of which it is predicated. Such a kind of multitude is applicable to God.

REPLY OBJ. 3: *One* does not exclude multitude, but division, which logically precedes one or multitude. Multitude does not remove unity, but division from each of the individuals which compose the multitude. This was explained when we treated of the divine unity (Q. 11, A. 2).

It must be observed, nevertheless, that the opposite arguments do not sufficiently prove the point advanced. Although the idea of solitude is excluded by plurality, and the plurality of gods by unity, it does not follow that these terms

solum significetur. Albedine enim excluditur nigredo, non tamen nomine albedinis significatur sola nigredinis exclusio.

express this signification alone. For blackness is excluded by whiteness; nevertheless, the term whiteness does not signify the mere exclusion of blackness.

Article 4

Whether This Term Person Can Be Common to the Three Persons?

AD QUARTUM SIC PROCEDITUR. Videtur quod hoc nomen persona non possit esse commune tribus personis. Nihil enim est commune tribus personis nisi essentia. Sed hoc nomen persona non significat essentiam in recto. Ergo non est commune tribus.

PRAETEREA, commune opponitur incommunicabili. Sed de ratione personae est quod sit incommunicabilis, ut patet ex definitione Ricardi de s. Victore supra posita. Ergo hoc nomen persona non est commune tribus.

PRAETEREA, si est commune tribus, aut ista communitas attenditur secundum rem, aut secundum rationem. Sed non secundum rem, quia sic tres personae essent una persona. Nec iterum secundum rationem tantum, quia sic persona esset universale, in divinis autem non est universale et particulare, neque genus neque species, ut supra ostensum est. Non ergo hoc nomen persona est commune tribus.

SED CONTRA est quod dicit Augustinus, VII de Trin., quod cum quaereretur, *quid tres*? Responsum est, *tres personae*; quia commune est eis id quod est persona.

RESPONDEO dicendum quod ipse modus loquendi ostendit hoc nomen persona tribus esse commune, cum dicimus tres personas, sicut cum dicimus tres homines, ostendimus hominem esse commune tribus. Manifestum est autem quod non est communitas rei, sicut una essentia communis est tribus, quia sic sequeretur unam esse personam trium, sicut essentia est una.

Qualis autem sit communitas, investigantes diversimode locuti sunt. Quidam enim dixerunt quod est communitas negationis; propter hoc, quod in definitione personae ponitur incommunicabile. Quidam autem dixerunt quod est communitas intentionis, eo quod in definitione personae ponitur individuum; sicut si dicatur quod esse speciem est commune equo et bovi. Sed utrumque horum excluditur per hoc, quod hoc nomen persona non est nomen negationis neque intentionis, sed est nomen rei. Et ideo dicendum est quod etiam in rebus humanis hoc nomen persona est commune communitate rationis, non sicut genus vel species, sed sicut individuum vagum. Nomina enim generum vel specierum, ut homo vel animal, sunt imposita ad significandum ipsas naturas communes; non autem intentiones naturarum communium, quae significantur his nominibus genus

OBJECTION 1: It would seem that this term *person* cannot be common to the three persons. For nothing is common to the three persons but the essence. But this term *person* does not signify the essence directly. Therefore it is not common to all three.

OBJ. 2: Further, the common is the opposite to the incommunicable. But the very meaning of person is that it is incommunicable; as appears from the definition given by Richard of St. Victor (Q. 29, A. 3, ad 4). Therefore this term *person* is not common to all the three persons.

OBJ. 3: Further, if the name *person* is common to the three, it is common either really, or logically. But it is not so really; otherwise the three persons would be one person; nor again is it so logically; otherwise person would be a universal. But in God there is neither universal nor particular; neither genus nor species, as we proved above (Q. 3, A. 5). Therefore this term 'person' is not common to the three.

ON THE CONTRARY, Augustine says (*De Trin.* vii, 4) that when we ask, *Three what?* we say, *Three persons*, because what a person is, is common to them.

I ANSWER THAT, The very mode of expression itself shows that this term *person* is common to the three when we say *three persons*; for when we say *three men* we show that *man* is common to the three. Now it is clear that this is not community of a real thing, as if one essence were common to the three; otherwise there would be only one person of the three, as also one essence.

What is meant by such a community has been variously determined by those who have examined the subject. Some have called it a community of exclusion, forasmuch as the definition of *person* contains the word *incommunicable*. Others thought it to be a community of intention, as the definition of person contains the word *individual*; as we say that to be a species is common to horse and ox. Both of these explanations, however, are excluded by the fact that *person* is not a name of exclusion nor of intention, but the name of a reality. We must therefore resolve that even in human affairs this name *person* is common by a community of idea, not as genus or species, but as a vague individual thing. The names of genera and species, as man or animal, are given to signify the common natures themselves, but not the intentions of those common natures, signified by the terms genus or species. The vague individual thing, as *some man*,

vel species. Sed individuum vagum, ut aliquis homo, significat naturam communem cum determinato modo existendi qui competit singularibus, ut scilicet sit per se subsistens distinctum ab aliis. Sed in nomine singularis designati, significatur determinatum distinguens, sicut in nomine Socratis haec caro et hoc os. Hoc tamen interest, quod aliquis homo significat naturam, vel individuum ex parte naturae, cum modo existendi qui competit singularibus, hoc autem nomen persona non est impositum ad significandum individuum ex parte naturae, sed ad significandum rem subsistentem in tali natura. Hoc autem est commune secundum rationem omnibus personis divinis, ut unaquaeque earum subsistat in natura divina distincta ab aliis. Et sic hoc nomen persona, secundum rationem, est commune tribus personis divinis.

AD PRIMUM ergo dicendum quod ratio illa procedit de communitate rei.

AD SECUNDUM dicendum quod, licet persona sit incommunicabilis, tamen ipse modus existendi incommunicabiliter, potest esse pluribus communis.

AD TERTIUM dicendum quod, licet sit communitas rationis et non rei tamen non sequitur quod in divinis sit universale et particulare, vel genus vel species. Tum quia neque in rebus humanis communitas personae est communitas generis vel speciei. Tum quia personae divinae habent unum esse, genus autem et species, et quodlibet universale, praedicatur de pluribus secundum esse differentibus.

signifies the common nature with the determinate mode of existence of singular things—that is, something self-subsisting, as distinct from others. But the name of a designated singular thing signifies that which distinguishes the determinate thing; as the name Socrates signifies this flesh and this bone. But there is this difference—that the term *some man* signifies the nature, or the individual on the part of its nature, with the mode of existence of singular things; while this name *person* is not given to signify the individual on the part of the nature, but the subsistent reality in that nature. Now this is common in idea to the divine persons, that each of them subsists distinctly from the others in the divine nature. Thus this name *person* is common in idea to the three divine persons.

REPLY OBJ. 1: This argument is founded on a real community.

REPLY OBJ. 2: Although person is incommunicable, yet the mode itself of incommunicable existence can be common to many.

REPLY OBJ. 3: Although this community is logical and not real, yet it does not follow that in God there is universal or particular, or genus, or species; both because neither in human affairs is the community of person the same as community of genus or species; and because the divine persons have one being; whereas genus and species and every other universal are predicated of many which differ in being.

QUESTION 31

UNITY AND PLURALITY IN GOD

Post haec considerandum est de his quae ad unitatem vel pluralitatem pertinent in divinis. Et circa hoc quaeruntur quatuor.

Primo, de ipso nomine Trinitatis.

Secundo, utrum possit dici, filius est alius a patre.

Tertio, utrum dictio exclusiva, quae videtur alietatem excludere, possit adiungi nomini essentiali in divinis.

Quarto, utrum possit adiungi termino personali.

We now consider what belongs to the unity or plurality in God; which gives rise to four points of inquiry:

(1) Concerning the word 'Trinity.'
(2) Whether we can say that the Son is other than the Father?
(3) Whether an exclusive term, which seems to exclude otherness, can be joined to an essential name in God?
(4) Whether it can be joined to a personal term?

Article 1

Whether There Is Trinity in God?

AD PRIMUM SIC PROCEDITUR. Videtur quod non sit Trinitas in divinis. Omne enim nomen in divinis vel significat substantiam, vel relationem. Sed hoc nomen Trinitas non significat substantiam, praedicaretur enim de singulis personis. Neque significat relationem, quia non dicitur secundum nomen ad aliud. Ergo nomine Trinitatis non est utendum in divinis.

PRAETEREA, hoc nomen Trinitas videtur esse nomen collectivum, cum significet multitudinem. Tale autem nomen non convenit in divinis, cum unitas importata per nomen collectivum sit minima unitas, in divinis autem est maxima unitas. Ergo hoc nomen Trinitas non convenit in divinis.

PRAETEREA, omne trinum est triplex. Sed in Deo non est triplicitas, cum triplicitas sit species inaequalitatis. Ergo nec Trinitas.

PRAETEREA, quidquid est in Deo, est in unitate essentiae divinae, quia Deus est sua essentia. Si igitur Trinitas est in Deo, erit in unitate essentiae divinae. Et sic in Deo erunt tres essentiales unitates, quod est haereticum.

PRAETEREA, in omnibus quae dicuntur de Deo, concretum praedicatur de abstracto, deitas enim est Deus, et paternitas est pater. Sed Trinitas non potest dici trina, quia sic essent novem res in divinis, quod est erroneum. Ergo nomine Trinitatis non est utendum in divinis.

SED CONTRA est quod Athanasius dicit, quod *unitas in Trinitate, et Trinitas in unitate veneranda sit.*

RESPONDEO dicendum quod nomen Trinitatis in divinis significat determinatum numerum personarum.

OBJECTION 1: It would seem there is not trinity in God. For every name in God signifies substance or relation. But this name *Trinity* does not signify the substance; otherwise it would be predicated of each one of the persons: nor does it signify relation; for it does not express a name that refers to another. Therefore the word *Trinity* is not to be applied to God.

OBJ. 2: Further, this word *trinity* is a collective term, since it signifies multitude. But such a word does not apply to God; as the unity of a collective name is the least of unities, whereas in God there exists the greatest possible unity. Therefore this word *trinity* does not apply to God.

OBJ. 3: Further, every trine is threefold. But in God there is not triplicity; since triplicity is a kind of inequality. Therefore neither is there trinity in God.

OBJ. 4: Further, all that exists in God exists in the unity of the divine essence; because God is His own essence. Therefore, if Trinity exists in God, it exists in the unity of the divine essence; and thus in God there would be three essential unities; which is heresy.

OBJ. 5: Further, in all that is said of God, the concrete is predicated of the abstract; for Deity is God and paternity is the Father. But the Trinity cannot be called trine; otherwise there would be nine realities in God; which, of course, is erroneous. Therefore the word trinity is not to be applied to God.

ON THE CONTRARY, Athanasius says: *Unity in Trinity; and Trinity in Unity is to be revered.*

I ANSWER THAT, The name *Trinity* in God signifies the determinate number of persons. And so the plurality of

325

Sicut igitur ponitur pluralitas personarum in divinis, ita utendum est nomine Trinitatis, quia hoc idem quod significat pluralitas indeterminate, significat hoc nomen Trinitas determinate.

AD PRIMUM ergo dicendum quod hoc nomen Trinitas, secundum etymologiam vocabuli, videtur significare unam essentiam trium personarum, secundum quod dicitur Trinitas quasi trium unitas. Sed secundum proprietatem vocabuli, significat magis numerum personarum unius essentiae. Et propter hoc non possumus dicere quod pater sit Trinitas, quia non est tres personae. Non autem significat ipsas relationes personarum, sed magis numerum personarum ad invicem relatarum. Et inde est quod, secundum nomen, ad aliud non refertur.

AD SECUNDUM dicendum quod nomen collectivum duo importat, scilicet pluralitatem suppositorum, et unitatem quandam, scilicet ordinis alicuius, populus enim est multitudo hominum sub aliquo ordine comprehensorum. Quantum ergo ad primum, hoc nomen Trinitas convenit cum nominibus collectivis, sed quantum ad secundum differt, quia in divina Trinitate non solum est unitas ordinis, sed cum hoc est etiam unitas essentiae.

AD TERTIUM dicendum quod Trinitas absolute dicitur, significat enim numerum ternarium personarum. Sed triplicitas significat proportionem inaequalitatis, est enim species proportionis inaequalis, sicut patet per Boetium in arithmetica. Et ideo non est in Deo triplicitas, sed Trinitas.

AD QUARTUM dicendum quod in Trinitate divina intelligitur et numerus, et personae numeratae. Cum ergo dicimus Trinitatem in unitate, non ponimus numerum in unitate essentiae, quasi sit ter una, sed personas numeratas ponimus in unitate naturae, sicut supposita alicuius naturae dicuntur esse in natura illa. E converso autem dicimus unitatem in Trinitate, sicut natura dicitur esse in suis suppositis.

AD QUINTUM dicendum quod, cum dicitur, Trinitas est trina, ratione numeri importati significatur multiplicatio eiusdem numeri in seipsum, cum hoc quod dico trinum, importet distinctionem in suppositis illius de quo dicitur. Et ideo non potest dici quod Trinitas sit trina, quia sequeretur, si Trinitas esset trina, quod tria essent supposita Trinitatis; sicut cum dicitur, Deus est trinus, sequitur quod sunt tria supposita deitatis.

persons in God requires that we should use the word trinity; because what is indeterminately signified by plurality, is signified by trinity in a determinate manner.

REPLY OBJ. 1: In its etymological sense, this word *Trinity* seems to signify the one essence of the three persons, according as trinity may mean trine-unity. But in the strict meaning of the term it rather signifies the number of persons of one essence; and on this account we cannot say that the Father is the Trinity, as He is not three persons. Yet it does not mean the relations themselves of the Persons, but rather the number of persons related to each other; and hence it is that the word in itself does not express regard to another.

REPLY OBJ. 2: Two things are implied in a collective term, plurality of the supposita, and a unity of some kind of order. For *people* is a multitude of men comprehended under a certain order. In the first sense, this word *trinity* is like other collective words; but in the second sense it differs from them, because in the divine Trinity not only is there unity of order, but also with this there is unity of essence.

REPLY OBJ. 3: *Trinity* is taken in an absolute sense; for it signifies the threefold number of persons. *Triplicity* signifies a proportion of inequality; for it is a species of unequal proportion, according to Boethius (*Arith.* i, 23). Therefore in God there is not triplicity, but Trinity.

REPLY OBJ. 4: In the divine Trinity is to be understood both number and the persons numbered. So when we say, *Trinity in Unity*, we do not place number in the unity of the essence, as if we meant three times one; but we place the Persons numbered in the unity of nature; as the supposita of a nature are said to exist in that nature. On the other hand, we say *Unity in Trinity*; meaning that the nature is in its supposita.

REPLY OBJ. 5: When we say, *Trinity is trine*, by reason of the number implied, we signify the multiplication of that number by itself; since the word trine imports a distinction in the supposita of which it is spoken. Therefore it cannot be said that the Trinity is trine; otherwise it follows that, if the Trinity be trine, there would be three supposita of the Trinity; as when we say, *God is trine*, it follows that there are three supposita of the Godhead.

Article 2

Whether the Son Is Other Than the Father?

AD SECUNDUM SIC PROCEDITUR. Videtur quod filius non sit alius a patre. Alius enim est relativum diversitatis substantiae. Si igitur filius est alius a patre, videtur

OBJECTION 1: It would seem that the Son is not other than the Father. For *other* is a relative term implying diversity of substance. If, then, the Son is other than the Father,

quod sit a patre diversus. Quod est contra Augustinum, VII de Trin., ubi dicit quod, cum dicimus tres personas, non diversitatem intelligere volumus.

PRAETEREA, quicumque sunt alii ab invicem, aliquo modo ab invicem differunt. Si igitur filius est alius a patre, sequitur quod sit differens a patre. Quod est contra Ambrosium, in I de fide, ubi ait, *pater et filius deitate unum sunt, nec est ibi substantiae differentia, neque ulla diversitas.*

PRAETEREA, ab alio alienum dicitur. Sed filius non est alienus a patre, dicit enim Hilarius, in VII de Trin., quod in divinis personis nihil est diversum, nihil alienum, nihil separabile. Ergo filius non est alius a patre.

PRAETEREA, alius et aliud idem significant, sed sola generis consignificatione differunt. Si ergo filius est alius a patre, videtur sequi quod filius sit aliud a patre.

SED CONTRA est quod Augustinus dicit, in libro de fide ad Petrum, *una est enim essentia patris et filii et spiritus sancti, in qua non est aliud pater, aliud filius, aliud Spiritus Sanctus; quamvis personaliter sit alius pater, alius filius, alius Spiritus Sanctus.*

RESPONDEO dicendum quod, quia ex verbis inordinate prolatis incurritur haeresis, ut Hieronymus dicit, ideo cum de Trinitate loquimur, cum cautela et modestia est agendum, quia, ut Augustinus dicit, in I de Trin., *nec periculosius alicubi erratur, nec laboriosius aliquid quaeritur, nec fructuosius aliquid invenitur.* Oportet autem in his quae de Trinitate loquimur, duos errores oppositos cavere, temperate inter utrumque procedentes, scilicet errorem Arii, qui posuit cum Trinitate personarum Trinitatem substantiarum; et errorem Sabellii, qui posuit cum unitate essentiae unitatem personae.

Ad evitandum igitur errorem Arii, vitare debemus in divinis nomen diversitatis et differentiae, ne tollatur unitas essentiae, possumus autem uti nomine distinctionis, propter oppositionem relativam. Unde sicubi in aliqua Scriptura authentica diversitas vel differentia personarum invenitur, sumitur diversitas vel differentia pro distinctione. Ne autem tollatur simplicitas divinae essentiae, vitandum est nomen separationis et divisionis, quae est totius in partes. Ne autem tollatur aequalitas, vitandum est nomen disparitatis. Ne vero tollatur similitudo, vitandum est nomen alieni et discrepantis, dicit enim Ambrosius, in libro de fide, quod in patre et filio non est discrepans, sed una divinitas, et secundum Hilarium, ut dictum est, in divinis nihil est alienum, nihil separabile.

Ad vitandum vero errorem Sabellii, vitare debemus singularitatem, ne tollatur communicabilitas essentiae divinae, unde Hilarius dicit, VII de Trin., *patrem et filium singularem Deum praedicare, sacrilegum est.* Debemus

He must be different from the Father; which is contrary to what Augustine says (*De Trin.* vii), that when we speak of three persons, *we do not mean to imply diversity.*

OBJ. 2: Further, whosoever are other from one another, differ in some way from one another. Therefore, if the Son is other than the Father, it follows that He differs from the Father; which is against what Ambrose says (*De Fide* i), that *the Father and the Son are one in Godhead; nor is there any difference in substance between them, nor any diversity.*

OBJ. 3: Further, the term alien is taken from alius (other). But the Son is not alien from the Father, for Hilary says (*De Trin.* vii) that *in the divine persons there is nothing diverse, nothing alien, nothing separable.* Therefore the Son is not other than the Father.

OBJ. 4: Further, the terms *other person* and *other thing* have the same meaning, differing only in gender. So if the Son is another person from the Father, it follows that the Son is a thing apart from the Father.

ON THE CONTRARY, Augustine says: *There is one essence of the Father and Son and Holy Spirit, in which the Father is not one thing, the Son another, and the Holy Spirit another; although the Father is one person, the Son another, and the Holy Spirit another.*

I ANSWER THAT, Since, as Jerome remarks, a heresy arises from words wrongly used, when we speak of the Trinity we must proceed with care and with befitting modesty; because, as Augustine says (*De Trin.* i, 3), *Nowhere is error more harmful, the quest more toilsome, the finding more fruitful.* Now, in treating of the Trinity, we must beware of two opposite errors, and proceed cautiously between them—namely, the error of Arius, who placed a Trinity of substance with the Trinity of persons; and the error of Sabellius, who placed unity of person with the unity of essence.

Thus, to avoid the error of Arius we must shun the use of the terms diversity and difference in God, lest we take away the unity of essence: we may, however, use the term *distinction* on account of the relative opposition. Hence whenever we find terms of *diversity* or *difference* of Persons used in an authentic work, these terms of *diversity* or *difference* are taken to mean *distinction*. But lest the simplicity and singleness of the divine essence be taken away, the terms *separation* and *division*, which belong to the parts of a whole, are to be avoided: and lest equality be taken away, we avoid the use of the term *disparity*: and lest we remove similitude, we avoid the terms *alien* and *discrepant*. For Ambrose says (*De Fide* i) that *in the Father and the Son there is no discrepancy, but one Godhead*: and according to Hilary, as quoted above, *in God there is nothing alien, nothing separable.*

To avoid the heresy of Sabellius, we must shun the term *singularity*, lest we take away the communicability of the divine essence. Hence Hilary says (*De Trin.* vii): *It is sacrilege to assert that the Father and the Son are singular in*

etiam vitare nomen unici, ne tollatur numerus personarum, unde Hilarius in eodem libro dicit quod a Deo excluditur singularis atque unici intelligentia. Dicimus tamen unicum filium, quia non sunt plures filii in divinis. Neque tamen dicimus unicum Deum, quia pluribus deitas est communis vitamus etiam nomen confusi, ne tollatur ordo naturae a personis, unde Ambrosius dicit, I de fide, *neque confusum est quod unum est, neque multiplex esse potest quod indifferens est.* Vitandum est etiam nomen solitarii, ne tollatur consortium trium personarum, dicit enim Hilarius, in IV de Trin., *nobis neque solitarius, neque diversus Deus est confitendus.*

Hoc autem nomen alius, masculine sumptum, non importat nisi distinctionem suppositi. Unde convenienter dicere possumus quod filius est alius a patre, quia scilicet est aliud suppositum divinae naturae, sicut est alia persona, et alia hypostasis.

Ad primum ergo dicendum quod alius, quia est sicut quoddam particulare nomen, tenet se ex parte suppositi, unde ad eius rationem sufficit distinctio substantiae quae est hypostasis vel persona. Sed diversitas requirit distinctionem substantiae quae est essentia. Et ideo non possumus dicere quod filius sit diversus a patre, licet sit alius.

Ad secundum dicendum quod differentia importat distinctionem formae. Est autem tantum una forma in divinis, ut patet per id quod dicitur Philip. II, *qui cum in forma Dei esset.* Et ideo nomen differentis non proprie competit in divinis, ut patet per auctoritatem inductam. Utitur tamen Damascenus nomine differentiae in divinis personis, secundum quod proprietas relativa significatur per modum formae, unde dicit quod non differunt ab invicem hypostases secundum substantiam, sed secundum determinatas proprietates. Sed differentia sumitur pro distinctione, ut dictum est.

Ad tertium dicendum quod alienum est quod est extraneum et dissimile. Sed hoc non importatur cum dicitur alius. Et ideo dicimus filium alium a patre, licet non dicamus alienum.

Ad quartum dicendum quod neutrum genus est informe, masculinum autem est formatum et distinctum, et similiter femininum. Et ideo convenienter per neutrum genus significatur essentia communis, per masculinum autem et femininum, aliquod suppositum determinatum in communi natura. Unde etiam in rebus humanis, si quaeratur, quis est iste? Respondetur, Socrates, quod nomen est suppositi, si autem quaeratur, quid est iste? Respondetur, animal rationale et mortale. Et ideo, quia in divinis distinctio est secundum personas, non autem secundum essentiam, dicimus quod pater est alius a filio, sed non aliud, et e converso dicimus quod sunt unum, sed non unus.

Godhead. We must avoid the adjective *alone* lest we take away the number of persons. Hence Hilary says in the same book: *We exclude from God the idea of singularity or aloneness.* Nevertheless, we say *the only Son,* for in God there is no plurality of Sons. Yet, we do not say *the only God,* for the Deity is common to several. We avoid the word *confused,* lest we take away from the Persons the order of their nature. Hence Ambrose says (*De Fide* i): *What is one is not confused; and there is no multiplicity where there is no difference.* The word *solitary* is also to be avoided, lest we take away the society of the three persons; for, as Hilary says (*De Trin.* iv), *We confess neither a solitary nor a diverse God.*

This word *other,* however, in the masculine sense, means only a distinction of suppositum; and hence we can properly say that *the Son is other than the Father,* because He is another suppositum of the divine nature, as He is another person and another hypostasis.

Reply Obj. 1: *Other,* being like the name of a particular thing, refers to the suppositum; and so, there is sufficient reason for using it, where there is a distinct substance in the sense of hypostasis or person. But diversity requires a distinct substance in the sense of essence. Thus we cannot say that the Son is diverse from the Father, although He is another.

Reply Obj. 2: *Difference* implies distinction of form. There is one form in God, as appears from the text, *Who, when He was in the form of God* (Phil 2:6). Therefore the term *difference* does not properly apply to God, as appears from the authority quoted. Yet, Damascene (*De Fide Orth.* i, 5) employs the term *difference* in the divine persons, as meaning that the relative property is signified by way of form. Hence he says that the hypostases do not differ from each other in substance, but according to determinate properties. But *difference* is taken for *distinction,* as above stated.

Reply Obj. 3: The term *alien* means what is extraneous and dissimilar; which is not expressed by the term *other*; and therefore we say that the Son is *other* than the Father, but not that He is anything *alien.*

Reply Obj. 4: The neuter gender is formless; whereas the masculine is formed and distinct; and so is the feminine. So the common essence is properly and aptly expressed by the neuter gender, but by the masculine and feminine is expressed the determined subject in the common nature. Hence also in human affairs, if we ask, Who is this man? we answer, Socrates, which is the name of the suppositum; whereas, if we ask, What is he? we reply, A rational and mortal animal. So, because in God distinction is by the persons, and not by the essence, we say that the Father is other than the Son, but not something else; while conversely we say that they are one thing, but not one person.

Article 3

Whether the Exclusive Word Alone Should Be Added to the Essential Term in God?

AD TERTIUM SIC PROCEDITUR. Videtur quod dictio exclusiva *solus* non sit addenda termino essentiali in divinis. Quia secundum philosophum, in II Elench., *solus est qui cum alio non est.* Sed Deus est cum Angelis et sanctis animabus. Ergo non possumus dicere Deum solum.

PRAETEREA, quidquid adiungitur termino essentiali in divinis, potest praedicari de qualibet persona per se, et de omnibus simul, quia enim convenienter dicitur sapiens Deus, possumus dicere, pater est sapiens Deus, et Trinitas est sapiens Deus. Sed Augustinus, in VI de Trin., dicit, *consideranda est illa sententia, qua dicitur non esse patrem verum Deum solum.* Ergo non potest dici solus Deus.

PRAETEREA, si haec dictio *solus* adiungitur termino essentiali, aut hoc erit respectu praedicati personalis, aut respectu praedicati essentialis. Sed non respectu praedicati personalis, quia haec est falsa, solus Deus est pater, cum etiam homo sit pater. Neque etiam respectu praedicati essentialis. Quia si haec esset vera, solus Deus creat, videtur sequi quod haec esset vera, solus pater creat, quia quidquid dicitur de Deo, potest dici de patre. Haec autem est falsa, quia etiam filius est creator. Non ergo haec dictio *solus* potest in divinis adiungi termino essentiali.

SED CONTRA est quod dicitur I ad Tim. I, *regi saeculorum immortali, invisibili, soli Deo.*

RESPONDEO dicendum quod haec dictio *solus* potest accipi ut categorematica vel syncategorematica. Dicitur autem dictio categorematica, quae absolute ponit rem significatam circa aliquod suppositum; ut albus circa hominem, cum dicitur homo albus. Si ergo sic accipiatur haec dictio *solus*, nullo modo potest adiungi alicui termino in divinis, quia poneret solitudinem circa terminum cui adiungeretur, et sic sequeretur Deum esse solitarium; quod est contra praedicta. Dictio vero syncategorematica dicitur, quae importat ordinem praedicati ad subiectum, sicut haec dictio omnis, vel nullus. Et similiter haec dictio *solus*, quia excludit omne aliud suppositum a consortio praedicati. Sicut, cum dicitur, solus Socrates scribit, non datur intelligi quod Socrates sit solitarius; sed quod nullus sit ei consors in scribendo, quamvis cum eo multis existentibus. Et per hunc modum nihil prohibet hanc dictionem *solus* adiungere alicui essentiali termino in divinis, inquantum excluduntur omnia alia a Deo a consortio praedicati, ut si dicamus, solus Deus est aeternus, quia nihil praeter Deum est aeternum.

AD PRIMUM ergo dicendum quod, licet Angeli et animae sanctae semper sint cum Deo, tamen, si non esset pluralitas personarum in divinis, sequeretur, quod

OBJECTION 1: It would seem that the exclusive word *alone* is not to be added to an essential term in God. For, according to the Philosopher (*Elench.* ii, 3), *He is alone who is not with another.* But God is with the angels and the souls of the saints. Therefore we cannot say that God is alone.

OBJ. 2: Further, whatever is joined to the essential term in God can be predicated of every person per se, and of all the persons together; for, as we can properly say that God is wise, we can say the Father is a wise God; and the Trinity is a wise God. But Augustine says (*De Trin.* vi, 9): *We must consider the opinion that the Father is not true God alone.* Therefore God cannot be said to be alone.

OBJ. 3: Further if this expression *alone* is joined to an essential term, it would be so joined as regards either the personal predicate or the essential predicate. But it cannot be the former, as it is false to say, *God alone is Father*, since man also is a father; nor, again, can it be applied as regards the latter, for, if this saying were true, *God alone creates*, it would follow that the *Father alone creates*, as whatever is said of God can be said of the Father; and it would be false, as the Son also creates. Therefore this expression *alone* cannot be joined to an essential term in God.

ON THE CONTRARY, It is said, *To the King of ages, immortal, invisible, the only God* (1 Tim 1:17).

I ANSWER THAT, This term *alone* can be taken as a categorematical term, or as a syncategorematical term. A categorematical term is one which ascribes absolutely its meaning to a given suppositum; as, for instance, *white* to man, as when we say a *white man.* If the term *alone* is taken in this sense, it cannot in any way be joined to any term in God; for it would mean solitude in the term to which it is joined; and it would follow that God was solitary, against what is above stated (A. 2). A syncategorematical term imports the order of the predicate to the subject; as this expression *every one* or *no one*; and likewise the term *alone*, as excluding every other suppositum from the predicate. Thus, when we say, *Socrates alone writes*, we do not mean that Socrates is solitary, but that he has no companion in writing, though many others may be with him. In this way nothing prevents the term *alone* being joined to any essential term in God, as excluding the predicate from all things but God; as if we said *God alone is eternal*, because nothing but God is eternal.

REPLY OBJ. 1: Although the angels and the souls of the saints are always with God, nevertheless, if plurality of persons did not exist in God, He would be alone or solitary.

Deus esset solus vel solitarius. Non enim tollitur solitudo per associationem alicuius quod est extraneae naturae, dicitur enim aliquis solus esse in horto, quamvis sint ibi multae plantae et animalia. Et similiter diceretur Deus esse solus vel solitarius, Angelis et hominibus cum eo existentibus, si non essent in divinis personae plures. Consociatio igitur Angelorum et animarum non excludit solitudinem absolutam a divinis, et multo minus solitudinem respectivam, per comparationem ad aliquod praedicatum.

Ad secundum dicendum quod haec dictio solus, proprie loquendo, non ponitur ex parte praedicati, quod sumitur formaliter, respicit enim suppositum, inquantum excludit aliud suppositum ab eo cui adiungitur. Sed hoc adverbium tantum, cum sit exclusivum, potest poni ex parte subiecti, et ex parte praedicati, possumus enim dicere, tantum Socrates currit, idest nullus alius; et, Socrates currit tantum, idest nihil aliud facit. Unde non proprie dici potest, pater est solus Deus, vel, Trinitas est solus Deus, nisi forte ex parte praedicati intelligatur aliqua implicatio, ut dicatur, Trinitas est Deus qui est solus Deus. Et secundum hoc etiam posset esse vera ista, pater est Deus qui est solus Deus, si relativum referret praedicatum, et non suppositum. Augustinus autem, cum dicit patrem non esse solum Deum, sed Trinitatem esse solum Deum, loquitur expositive, ac si diceret, cum dicitur, regi saeculorum, invisibili, soli Deo, non est exponendum de persona patris, sed de sola Trinitate.

Ad tertium dicendum quod utroque modo potest haec dictio solus adiungi termino essentiali. Haec enim propositio, solus Deus est pater, est duplex. Quia ly pater potest praedicare personam patris, et sic est vera, non enim homo est illa persona. Vel potest praedicare relationem tantum, et sic est falsa, quia relatio paternitatis etiam in aliis invenitur, licet non univoce. Similiter haec est vera, solus Deus creat. Nec tamen sequitur, ergo solus pater, quia, ut sophistae dicunt, dictio exclusiva immobilitat terminum cui adiungitur, ut non possit fieri sub eo descensus pro aliquo suppositorum; non enim sequitur, solus homo est animal rationale mortale, ergo solus Socrates.

For solitude is not removed by association with anything that is extraneous in nature; thus anyone is said to be alone in a garden, though many plants and animals are with him in the garden. Likewise, God would be alone or solitary, though angels and men were with Him, supposing that several persons were not within Him. Therefore the society of angels and of souls does not take away absolute solitude from God; much less does it remove respective solitude, in reference to a predicate.

Reply Obj. 2: This expression *alone*, properly speaking, does not affect the predicate, which is taken formally, for it refers to the suppositum, as excluding any other suppositum from the one which it qualifies. But the adverb *only*, being exclusive, can be applied either to subject or predicate. For we can say, *Only Socrates*—that is, no one else—*runs*: and *Socrates runs only*—that is, he does nothing else. Hence it is not properly said that the Father is God alone, or the Trinity is God alone, unless some implied meaning be assumed in the predicate, as, for instance, *The Trinity is God Who alone is God*. In that sense it can be true to say that the Father is that God Who alone is God, if the relative be referred to the predicate, and not to the suppositum. So, when Augustine says that the Father is not God alone, but that the Trinity is God alone, he speaks expositively, as he might explain the words, *To the King of ages, invisible, the only God*, as applying not to the Father, but to the Trinity alone.

Reply Obj. 3: In both ways can the term *alone* be joined to an essential term. For this proposition, *God alone is Father*, can mean two things, because the word *Father* can signify the person of the Father; and then it is true; for no man is that person: or it can signify that relation only; and thus it is false, because the relation of paternity is found also in others, though not in a univocal sense. Likewise it is true to say God alone creates; nor, does it follow that *therefore the Father alone creates*, because, as logicians say, an exclusive diction so fixes the term to which it is joined that what is said exclusively of that term cannot be said exclusively of an individual contained in that term: for instance, from the premise, *Man alone is a mortal rational animal*, we cannot conclude, *Therefore Socrates alone is such*.

Article 4

Whether an Exclusive Diction Can Be Joined to the Personal Term?

Ad quartum sic proceditur. Videtur quod dictio exclusiva possit adiungi termino personali, etiam si praedicatum sit commune. Dicit enim dominus, ad patrem loquens, Ioan. XVII, *ut cognoscant te, solum Deum verum*. Ergo solus pater est Deus verus.

Objection 1: It would seem that an exclusive diction can be joined to the personal term, even though the predicate is common. For our Lord speaking to the Father, said: *That they may know Thee, the only true God* (John 17:3). Therefore the Father alone is true God.

Praeterea, Matth. XI dicitur, nemo novit filium nisi pater; quod idem significat ac si diceretur, solus pater novit filium. Sed nosse filium est commune. Ergo idem quod prius.

Praeterea, dictio exclusiva non excludit illud quod est de intellectu termini cui adiungitur, unde non excludit partem, neque universale, non enim sequitur, solus Socrates est albus, ergo manus eius non est alba; vel, ergo homo non est albus. Sed una persona est in intellectu alterius, sicut pater in intellectu filii, et e converso. Non ergo per hoc quod dicitur, solus pater est Deus, excluditur filius vel Spiritus Sanctus. Et sic videtur haec locutio esse vera.

Praeterea, ab Ecclesia cantatur, *tu solus altissimus, Iesu Christe.*

Sed contra, haec locutio, solus pater est Deus, habet duas expositivas, scilicet, pater est Deus, et, nullus alius a patre est Deus. Sed haec secunda est falsa, quia filius alius est a patre, qui est Deus. Ergo et haec est falsa, solus pater est Deus. Et sic de similibus.

Respondeo dicendum quod, cum dicimus, solus pater est Deus, haec propositio potest habere multiplicem intellectum. Si enim solus ponat solitudinem circa patrem, sic est falsa, secundum quod sumitur categorematice. Secundum vero quod sumitur syncategorematice, sic iterum potest intelligi multipliciter. Quia si excludat a forma subiecti, sic est vera, ut sit sensus, solus pater est Deus, idest, ille cum quo nullus alius est pater, est Deus. Et hoc modo exponit Augustinus, in VI de Trin., cum dicit, *solum patrem dicimus, non quia separatur a filio vel spiritu sancto; sed hoc dicentes, significamus quod illi simul cum eo non sunt pater.* Sed hic sensus non habetur ex consueto modo loquendi, nisi intellecta aliqua implicatione, ut si dicatur, ille qui solus dicitur pater, est Deus. Secundum vero proprium sensum, excludit a consortio praedicati. Et sic haec propositio est falsa, si excludit alium masculine, est autem vera, si excludit aliud neutraliter tantum, quia filius est alius a patre, non tamen aliud; similiter et Spiritus Sanctus. Sed quia haec dictio solus respicit proprie subiectum, ut dictum est, magis se habet ad excludendum alium quam aliud. Unde non est extendenda talis locutio; sed pie exponenda, sicubi inveniatur in authentica Scriptura.

Ad primum ergo dicendum quod, cum dicimus, te solum Deum verum, non intelligitur de persona patris, sed de tota Trinitate, ut Augustinus exponit. Vel, si intelligatur de persona patris, non excluduntur aliae personae, propter essentiae unitatem, prout ly solus excludit tantum aliud, ut dictum est.

Et similiter dicendum est ad secundum. Cum enim aliquid essentiale dicitur de patre, non excluditur

Obj. 2: Further, He said: *No one knows the Son but the Father* (Matt 11:27); which means that the Father alone knows the Son. But to know the Son is common (to the persons). Therefore the same conclusion follows.

Obj. 3: Further, an exclusive diction does not exclude what enters into the concept of the term to which it is joined. Hence it does not exclude the part, nor the universal; for it does not follow that if we say *Socrates alone is white*, that therefore *his hand is not white*, or that *man is not white*. But one person is in the concept of another; as the Father is in the concept of the Son; and conversely. Therefore, when we say, 'The Father alone is God,' we do not exclude the Son, nor the Holy Spirit; so that such a mode of speaking is true.

Obj. 4: Further, the Church sings: *Thou alone art Most High, O Jesus Christ.*

On the contrary, This proposition *The Father alone is God* includes two assertions—namely, that the Father is God, and that no other besides the Father is God. But this second proposition is false, for the Son is another from the Father, and He is God. Therefore this is false, The Father alone is God; and the same of the like sayings.

I answer that, When we say, *The Father alone is God*, such a proposition can be taken in several senses. If *alone* means solitude in the Father, it is false in a categorematical sense; but if taken in a syncategorematical sense it can again be understood in several ways. For if it exclude (all others) from the form of the subject, it is true, the sense being *the Father alone is God*—that is, *He who with no other is the Father, is God*. In this way Augustine expounds when he says (*De Trin.* vi, 6): *We say the Father alone, not because He is separate from the Son, or from the Holy Spirit, but because they are not the Father together with Him*. This, however, is not the usual way of speaking, unless we understand another implication, as though we said *He who alone is called the Father is God*. But in the strict sense the exclusion affects the predicate. And thus the proposition is false if it excludes another in the masculine sense; but true if it excludes it in the neuter sense; because the Son is another person than the Father, but not another thing; and the same applies to the Holy Spirit. But because this diction *alone*, properly speaking, refers to the subject, it tends to exclude another Person rather than other things. Hence such a way of speaking is not to be taken too literally, but it should be piously expounded, whenever we find it in an authentic work.

Reply Obj. 1: When we say, *Thee the only true God*, we do not understand it as referring to the person of the Father, but to the whole Trinity, as Augustine expounds (*De Trin.* vi, 9). Or, if understood of the person of the Father, the other persons are not excluded by reason of the unity of essence; in so far as the word *only* excludes another thing, as above explained.

The same Reply can be given to Obj. 2. For an essential term applied to the Father does not exclude the Son or

filius vel Spiritus Sanctus, propter essentiae unitatem. Tamen sciendum est quod in auctoritate praedicta, haec dictio nemo non idem est quod nullus homo, quod videtur significare vocabulum (non enim posset excipi persona patris), sed sumitur, secundum usum loquendi, distributive pro quacumque rationali natura.

AD TERTIUM dicendum quod dictio exclusiva non excludit illa quae sunt de intellectu termini cui adiungitur, si non differunt secundum suppositum, ut pars et universale. Sed filius differt supposito a patre, et ideo non est similis ratio.

AD QUARTUM dicendum quod non dicimus absolute quod solus filius sit altissimus, sed quod solus sit altissimus *cum spiritu sancto, in gloria Dei patris.*

the Holy Spirit, by reason of the unity of essence. Hence we must understand that in the text quoted, the term *no one* is not the same as *no man*, which the word itself would seem to signify (for the person of the Father could not be excepted), but is taken according to the usual way of speaking in a distributive sense, to mean any rational nature.

REPLY OBJ. 3: The exclusive diction does not exclude what enters into the concept of the term to which it is adjoined, if they do not differ in suppositum, as part and universal. But the Son differs in suppositum from the Father; and so there is no parity.

REPLY OBJ. 4: We do not say absolutely that the Son alone is Most High; but that He alone is Most High *with the Holy Spirit, in the glory of God the Father.*

QUESTION 32

THE KNOWLEDGE OF THE DIVINE PERSONS

Consequenter inquirendum est de cognitione divinarum personarum. Et circa hoc quaeruntur quatuor.

Primo, utrum per rationem naturalem possint cognosci divinae personae.

Secundo, utrum sint aliquae notiones divinis personis attribuendae.

Tertio, de numero notionum.

Quarto, utrum liceat diversimode circa notiones opinari.

We proceed to inquire concerning the knowledge of the divine persons; and this involves four points of inquiry:

(1) Whether the divine persons can be known by natural reason?

(2) Whether notions are to be attributed to the divine persons?

(3) The number of the notions.

(4) Whether we may lawfully have various contrary opinions of these notions?

Article 1

Whether the Trinity of the Divine Persons Can Be Known by Natural Reason?

AD PRIMUM SIC PROCEDITUR. Videtur quod Trinitas divinarum personarum possit per naturalem rationem cognosci. Philosophi enim non devenerunt in Dei cognitionem nisi per rationem naturalem, inveniuntur autem a philosophis multa dicta de Trinitate personarum. Dicit enim Aristoteles, in I de caelo et mundo, per hunc numerum, scilicet ternarium, *adhibuimus nos ipsos magnificare Deum unum, eminentem proprietatibus eorum quae sunt creata.* Augustinus etiam dicit, VII Confes., ibi legi, scilicet in libris Platonicorum, *non quidem his verbis, sed hoc idem omnino, multis et multiplicibus suaderi rationibus, quod in principio erat verbum, et verbum erat apud Deum, et Deus erat verbum,* et huiusmodi quae ibi sequuntur, in quibus verbis distinctio divinarum personarum traditur. Dicitur etiam in Glossa Rom. I, et Exod. VIII, quod magi Pharaonis defecerunt in tertio signo, idest in notitia tertiae personae, scilicet spiritus sancti, et sic ad minus duas cognoverunt. Trismegistus etiam dixit, *monas genuit monadem, et in se suum reflexit ardorem,* per quod videtur generatio filii, et spiritus sancti processio intimari. Cognitio ergo divinarum personarum potest per rationem naturalem haberi.

PRAETEREA, Ricardus de sancto Victore dicit, in libro de Trin., *credo sine dubio quod ad quamcumque explanationem veritatis, non modo probabilia, imo etiam necessaria argumenta non desint.* Unde etiam ad probandum Trinitatem personarum, aliqui induxerunt rationem ex infinitate bonitatis divinae, quae seipsam infinite communicat in processione divinarum personarum. Quidam vero per hoc, quod *nullius boni sine consortio potest esse iucunda possessio.* Augustinus vero procedit ad manifestandum Trinitatem personarum, ex

OBJECTION 1: It would seem that the trinity of the divine persons can be known by natural reason. For philosophers came to the knowledge of God not otherwise than by natural reason. Now we find that they said many things about the trinity of persons, for Aristotle says (*De Coelo et Mundo* i, 2): *Through this number*—namely, three—*we bring ourselves to acknowledge the greatness of one God, surpassing all things created.* And Augustine says (*Confess.* vii, 9): *I have read in their works, not in so many words, but enforced by many and various reasons, that in the beginning was the Word, and the Word was with God, and the Word was God,* and so on; in which passage the distinction of persons is laid down. We read, moreover, in a gloss on Rom. 1 and Ex. 8 that the magicians of Pharaoh failed in the third sign—that is, as regards knowledge of a third person—i.e., of the Holy Spirit—and thus it is clear that they knew at least two persons. Likewise Trismegistus says: *The monad begot a monad, and reflected upon itself its own heat.* By which words the generation of the Son and procession of the Holy Spirit seem to be indicated. Therefore knowledge of the divine persons can be obtained by natural reason.

OBJ. 2: Further, Richard St. Victor says (*De Trin.* i, 4): *I believe without doubt that probable and even necessary arguments can be found for any explanation of the truth.* So even to prove the Trinity some have brought forward a reason from the infinite goodness of God, who communicates Himself infinitely in the procession of the divine persons; while some are moved by the consideration that *no good thing can be joyfully possessed without partnership.* Augustine proceeds (*De Trin.* x, 4; x, 11, 12) to prove the trinity of persons by the procession of the word and of

processione verbi et amoris in mente nostra, quam viam supra secuti sumus. Ergo per rationem naturalem potest cognosci Trinitas personarum.

PRAETEREA, superfluum videtur homini tradere quod humana ratione cognosci non potest. Sed non est dicendum quod traditio divina de cognitione Trinitatis sit superflua. Ergo Trinitas personarum ratione humana cognosci potest.

SED CONTRA est quod Hilarius dicit, in libro II de Trin., *non putet homo sua intelligentia generationis sacramentum posse consequi.* Ambrosius etiam dicit, *impossibile est generationis scire secretum, mens deficit, vox silet.* Sed per originem generationis et processionis distinguitur Trinitas in personis divinis, ut ex supra dictis patet. Cum ergo illud homo non possit scire et intelligentia consequi, ad quod ratio necessaria haberi non potest, sequitur quod Trinitas personarum per rationem cognosci non possit.

RESPONDEO dicendum quod impossibile est per rationem naturalem ad cognitionem Trinitatis divinarum personarum pervenire. Ostensum est enim supra quod homo per rationem naturalem in cognitionem Dei pervenire non potest nisi ex creaturis. Creaturae autem ducunt in Dei cognitionem, sicut effectus in causam. Hoc igitur solum ratione naturali de Deo cognosci potest, quod competere ei necesse est secundum quod est omnium entium principium, et hoc fundamento usi sumus supra in consideratione Dei. Virtus autem creativa Dei est communis toti Trinitati, unde pertinet ad unitatem essentiae, non ad distinctionem personarum. Per rationem igitur naturalem cognosci possunt de Deo ea quae pertinent ad unitatem essentiae, non autem ea quae pertinent ad distinctionem personarum. Qui autem probare nititur Trinitatem personarum naturali ratione, fidei dupliciter derogat. Primo quidem, quantum ad dignitatem ipsius fidei, quae est ut sit de rebus invisibilibus, quae rationem humanam excedunt. Unde apostolus dicit, ad Heb. XI, quod fides est de non apparentibus. Et apostolus dicit, I Cor. II, *sapientiam loquimur inter perfectos, sapientiam vero non huius saeculi, neque principum huius saeculi; sed loquimur Dei sapientiam in mysterio, quae abscondita est.* Secundo, quantum ad utilitatem trahendi alios ad fidem. Cum enim aliquis ad probandam fidem inducit rationes quae non sunt cogentes, cedit in irrisionem infidelium, credunt enim quod huiusmodi rationibus innitamur, et propter eas credamus.

Quae igitur fidei sunt, non sunt tentanda probare nisi per auctoritates, his qui auctoritates suscipiunt. Apud alios vero, sufficit defendere non esse impossibile quod praedicat fides. Unde Dionysius dicit, II cap. de Div. Nom., *si aliquis est qui totaliter eloquiis resistit, longe erit a nostra philosophia; si autem ad veritatem eloquiorum,* scilicet sacrorum, *respicit, hoc et nos canone utimur.*

love in our own mind; and we have followed him in this (Q. 27, AA. 1, 3). Therefore the trinity of persons can be known by natural reason.

OBJ. 3: Further, it seems to be superfluous to teach what cannot be known by natural reason. But it ought not to be said that the divine tradition of the Trinity is superfluous. Therefore the trinity of persons can be known by natural reason.

ON THE CONTRARY, Hilary says (*De Trin.* i), *Let no man think to reach the sacred mystery of generation by his own mind.* And Ambrose says (*De Fide* ii, 5), *It is impossible to know the secret of generation. The mind fails, the voice is silent.* But the trinity of the divine persons is distinguished by origin of generation and procession (Q. 30, A. 2). Since, therefore, man cannot know, and with his understanding grasp that for which no necessary reason can be given, it follows that the trinity of persons cannot be known by reason.

I ANSWER THAT, It is impossible to attain to the knowledge of the Trinity by natural reason. For, as above explained (Q. 12, AA. 4, 12), man cannot obtain the knowledge of God by natural reason except from creatures. Now creatures lead us to the knowledge of God, as effects do to their cause. Accordingly, by natural reason we can know of God that only which of necessity belongs to Him as the principle of things, and we have cited this fundamental principle in treating of God as above (Q. 12, A. 12). Now, the creative power of God is common to the whole Trinity; and hence it belongs to the unity of the essence, and not to the distinction of the persons. Therefore, by natural reason we can know what belongs to the unity of the essence, but not what belongs to the distinction of the persons. Whoever, then, tries to prove the trinity of persons by natural reason, derogates from faith in two ways. First, as regards the dignity of faith itself, which consists in its being concerned with invisible things, that exceed human reason; wherefore the Apostle says that *faith is of things that appear not* (Heb 11:1), and the same Apostle says also, *We speak wisdom among the perfect, but not the wisdom of this world, nor of the princes of this world; but we speak the wisdom of God in a mystery which is hidden* (1 Cor 2:6, 7). Second, as regards the utility of drawing others to the faith. For when anyone in the endeavor to prove the faith brings forward reasons which are not cogent, he falls under the ridicule of the unbelievers: since they suppose that we stand upon such reasons, and that we believe on such grounds.

Therefore, we must not attempt to prove what is of faith, except by authority alone, to those who receive the authority; while as regards others it suffices to prove that what faith teaches is not impossible. Hence it is said by Dionysius (*Div. Nom.* ii): *Whoever wholly resists the word, is far off from our philosophy; whereas if he regards the truth of the word*—i.e., *the sacred word, we too follow this rule.*

AD PRIMUM ergo dicendum quod philosophi non cognoverunt mysterium Trinitatis divinarum personarum per propria, quae sunt paternitas, filiatio et processio; secundum illud apostoli, I ad Cor. II, *loquimur Dei sapientiam, quam nemo principum huius saeculi cognovit,* idest philosophorum, secundum Glossam. Cognoverunt tamen quaedam essentialia attributa quae appropriantur personis, sicut potentia patri, sapientia filio, bonitas spiritui sancto, ut infra patebit. Quod ergo Aristoteles dicit, *per hunc numerum adhibuimus nos ipsos* etc., non est sic intelligendum, quod ipse poneret ternarium numerum in divinis, sed vult dicere quod antiqui utebantur ternario numero in sacrificiis et orationibus, propter quandam ternarii numeri perfectionem. In libris etiam Platonicorum invenitur *in principio erat verum,* non secundum quod verbum significat personam genitam in divinis, sed secundum quod per verbum intelligitur ratio idealis, per quam Deus omnia condidit, quae filio appropriatur. Et licet appropriata tribus personis cognoscerent, dicuntur tamen in tertio signo defecisse, idest in cognitione tertiae personae, quia a bonitate, quae spiritui sancto appropriatur, deviaverunt, dum cognoscentes Deum, non sicut Deum glorificaverunt, ut dicitur Rom. I. Vel, quia ponebant Platonici unum primum ens, quod etiam dicebant esse patrem totius universitatis rerum, consequenter ponebant aliam substantiam sub eo, quam vocabant mentem vel paternum intellectum, in qua erant rationes omnium rerum, sicut Macrobius recitat super somnium Scipionis, non autem ponebant aliquam substantiam tertiam separatam, quae videretur spiritui sancto respondere. Sic autem nos non ponimus patrem et filium, secundum substantiam differentes, sed hoc fuit error Origenis et Arii. Sequentium in hoc Platonicos. Quod vero Trismegistus dixit, *monas monadem genuit, et in se suum reflexit ardorem,* non est referendum ad generationem filii vel processionem spiritus sancti, sed ad productionem mundi, nam unus Deus produxit unum mundum propter sui ipsius amorem.

AD SECUNDUM dicendum quod ad aliquam rem dupliciter inducitur ratio. Uno modo, ad probandum sufficienter aliquam radicem, sicut in scientia naturali inducitur ratio sufficiens ad probandum quod motus caeli semper sit uniformis velocitatis. Alio modo inducitur ratio, non quae sufficienter probet radicem, sed quae radici iam positae ostendat congruere consequentes effectus, sicut in astrologia ponitur ratio excentricorum et epicyclorum ex hoc quod, hac positione facta, possunt salvari apparentia sensibilia circa motus caelestes, non tamen ratio haec est sufficienter probans, quia etiam forte alia positione facta salvari possent. Primo ergo modo potest induci ratio ad probandum Deum esse unum, et similia. Sed secundo modo se habet ratio quae inducitur ad manifestationem Trinitatis, quia scilicet, Trinitate posita, congruunt huiusmodi rationes; non tamen ita

REPLY OBJ. 1: The philosophers did not know the mystery of the trinity of the divine persons by its proper attributes, such as paternity, filiation, and procession, according to the Apostle's words, *We speak the wisdom of God which none of the princes of the world*—i.e., the philosophers—'knew' (1 Cor 2:6). Nevertheless, they knew some of the essential attributes appropriated to the persons, as power to the Father, wisdom to the Son, goodness to the Holy Spirit; as will later on appear. So, when Aristotle said, *By this number,* etc., we must not take it as if he affirmed a threefold number in God, but that he wished to say that the ancients used the threefold number in their sacrifices and prayers on account of some perfection residing in the number three. In the Platonic books also we find, *In the beginning was the word,* not as meaning the Person begotten in God, but as meaning the ideal type whereby God made all things, and which is appropriated to the Son. And although they knew these were appropriated to the three persons, yet they are said to have failed in the third sign—that is, in the knowledge of the third person, because they deviated from the goodness appropriated to the Holy Spirit, in that knowing God *they did not glorify Him as God* (Rom 1); or, because the Platonists asserted the existence of one Primal Being whom they also declared to be the father of the universe, they consequently maintained the existence of another substance beneath him, which they called *mind* or the *paternal intellect,* containing the idea of all things, as Macrobius relates (Som. Scip. iv). They did not, however, assert the existence of a third separate substance which might correspond to the Holy Spirit. So also we do not assert that the Father and the Son differ in substance, which was the error of Origen and Arius, who in this followed the Platonists. When Trismegistus says, *Monad begot monad,* etc., this does not refer to the generation of the Son, or to the procession of the Holy Spirit, but to the production of the world. For one God produced one world by reason of His love for Himself.

REPLY OBJ. 2: Reason may be employed in two ways to establish a point: first, for the purpose of furnishing sufficient proof of some principle, as in natural science, where sufficient proof can be brought to show that the movement of the heavens is always of uniform velocity. Reason is employed in another way, not as furnishing a sufficient proof of a principle, but as confirming an already established principle, by showing the congruity of its results, as in astrology the theory of eccentrics and epicycles is considered as established, because thereby the sensible appearances of the heavenly movements can be explained; not, however, as if this proof were sufficient, forasmuch as some other theory might explain them. In the first way, we can prove that God is one; and the like. In the second way, reasons avail to prove the Trinity; as, when assumed to be true, such reasons confirm it. We must not, however, think that

quod per has rationes sufficienter probetur Trinitas personarum. Et hoc patet per singula. Bonitas enim infinita Dei manifestatur etiam in productione creaturarum, quia infinitae virtutis est ex nihilo producere. Non enim oportet, si infinita bonitate se communicat, quod aliquid infinitum a Deo procedat, sed secundum modum suum recipiat divinam bonitatem. Similiter etiam quod dicitur, quod *sine consortio non potest esse iucunda possessio alicuius boni*, locum habet quando in una persona non invenitur perfecta bonitas; unde indiget, ad plenam iucunditatis bonitatem, bono alicuius alterius consociati sibi. Similitudo autem intellectus nostri non sufficienter probat aliquid de Deo, propter hoc quod intellectus non univoce invenitur in Deo et in nobis. Et inde est quod Augustinus, super Ioan., dicit quod per fidem venitur ad cognitionem, et non e converso.

AD TERTIUM dicendum quod cognitio divinarum personarum fuit necessaria nobis dupliciter. Uno modo, ad recte sentiendum de creatione rerum. Per hoc enim quod dicimus Deum omnia fecisse verbo suo, excluditur error ponentium Deum produxisse res ex necessitate naturae. Per hoc autem quod ponimus in eo processionem amoris, ostenditur quod Deus non propter aliquam indigentiam creaturas produxit, neque propter aliquam aliam causam extrinsecam; sed propter amorem suae bonitatis. Unde et Moyses, postquam dixerat, in principio creavit Deus caelum et terram, subdit, dixit Deus, fiat lux, ad manifestationem divini verbi; et postea dixit, vidit Deus lucem, quod esset bona, ad ostendendum approbationem divini amoris; et similiter in aliis operibus. Alio modo, et principalius, ad recte sentiendum de salute generis humani, quae perficitur per filium incarnatum, et per donum spiritus sancti.

the trinity of persons is adequately proved by such reasons. This becomes evident when we consider each point; for the infinite goodness of God is manifested also in creation, because to produce from nothing is an act of infinite power. For if God communicates Himself by His infinite goodness, it is not necessary that an infinite effect should proceed from God: but that according to its own mode and capacity it should receive the divine goodness. Likewise, when it is said that joyous possession of good requires partnership, this holds in the case of one not having perfect goodness: hence it needs to share some other's good, in order to have the goodness of complete happiness. Nor is the image in our mind an adequate proof in the case of God, forasmuch as the intellect is not in God and ourselves univocally. Hence, Augustine says (*Tract.* xxvii. in Joan.) that by faith we arrive at knowledge, and not conversely.

REPLY OBJ. 3: There are two reasons why the knowledge of the divine persons was necessary for us. It was necessary for the right idea of creation. The fact of saying that God made all things by His Word excludes the error of those who say that God produced things by necessity. When we say that in Him there is a procession of love, we show that God produced creatures not because He needed them, nor because of any other extrinsic reason, but on account of the love of His own goodness. So Moses, when he had said, *In the beginning God created heaven and earth*, subjoined, *God said, Let there be light*, to manifest the divine Word; and then said, *God saw the light that it was good*, to show proof of the divine love. The same is also found in the other works of creation. In another way, and chiefly, that we may think rightly concerning the salvation of the human race, accomplished by the Incarnate Son, and by the gift of the Holy Spirit.

Article 2

Whether There Are Notions in God?

AD SECUNDUM SIC PROCEDITUR. Videtur quod non sint ponendae notiones in divinis. Dicit enim Dionysius, in I cap. de Div. Nom., quod *non est audendum dicere aliquid de Deo, praeter ea quae nobis ex sacris eloquiis sunt expressa.* Sed de notionibus nulla fit mentio in eloquiis sacrae Scripturae. Ergo non sunt ponendae notiones in divinis.

PRAETEREA, quidquid ponitur in divinis, aut pertinet ad unitatem essentiae, aut ad Trinitatem personarum. Sed notiones non pertinent ad unitatem essentiae, nec ad Trinitatem personarum. De notionibus enim neque praedicantur ea quae sunt essentiae, non enim dicimus quod paternitas sit sapiens vel creet, neque etiam ea quae sunt personae; non enim dicimus quod paternitas

OBJECTION 1: It would seem that in God there are no notions. For Dionysius says (*Div. Nom.* i): *We must not dare to say anything of God but what is taught to us by the Holy Scripture.* But Holy Scripture does not say anything concerning notions. Therefore there are none in God.

OBJ. 2: Further, all that exists in God concerns the unity of the essence or the trinity of the persons. But the notions do not concern the unity of the essence, nor the trinity of the persons; for neither can what belongs to the essence be predicated of the notions: for instance, we do not say that paternity is wise or creates; nor can what belongs to the persons be so predicated; for example, we do not say that

generet et filiatio generetur. Ergo non sunt ponendae notiones in divinis.

PRAETEREA, in simplicibus non sunt ponenda aliqua abstracta, quae sint principia cognoscendi, quia cognoscuntur seipsis. Sed divinae personae sunt simplicissimae. Ergo non sunt ponendae in divinis personis notiones.

SED CONTRA est quod dicit Ioannes Damascenus, differentiam hypostaseon, idest personarum, in tribus proprietatibus, *idest paternali et filiali et processionali, recognoscimus.* Sunt ergo ponendae proprietates et notiones in divinis.

RESPONDEO dicendum quod Praepositivus, attendens simplicitatem personarum, dixit non esse ponendas proprietates et notiones in divinis, et sicubi inveniantur, exponit abstractum pro concreto, sicut enim consuevimus dicere, rogo benignitatem tuam, idest te benignum, ita cum dicitur in divinis paternitas, intelligitur Deus pater.

Sed, sicut ostensum est supra, divinae simplicitati non praeiudicat quod in divinis utamur nominibus concretis et abstractis. Quia secundum quod intelligimus, sic nominamus. Intellectus autem noster non potest pertingere ad ipsam simplicitatem divinam, secundum quod in se est consideranda, et ideo secundum modum suum divina apprehendit et nominat, idest secundum quod invenitur in rebus sensibilibus, a quibus cognitionem accipit. In quibus, ad significandum simplices formas, nominibus abstractis utimur, ad significandum vero res subsistentes, utimur nominibus concretis. Unde et divina, sicut supra dictum est, ratione simplicitatis, per nomina abstracta significamus, ratione vero subsistentiae et complementi, per nomina concreta.

Oportet autem non solum nomina essentialia in abstracto et in concreto significare, ut cum dicimus deitatem et Deum, vel sapientiam et sapientem; sed etiam personalia, ut dicamus paternitatem et patrem.

Ad quod duo praecipue nos cogunt. Primo quidem, haereticorum instantia. Cum enim confiteamur patrem et filium et spiritum sanctum esse unum Deum et tres personas, quaerentibus quo sunt unus Deus, et quo sunt tres personae, sicut respondetur quod sunt essentia vel deitate unum, ita oportuit esse aliqua nomina abstracta, quibus responderi possit personas distingui. Et huiusmodi sunt proprietates vel notiones in abstracto significatae, ut paternitas et filiatio. Et ideo essentia significatur in divinis ut quid, persona vero ut quis, proprietas autem ut quo.

Secundo, quia una persona invenitur in divinis referri ad duas personas, scilicet persona patris ad personam filii et personam spiritus sancti. Non autem una relatione, quia sic sequeretur quod etiam filius et Spiritus Sanctus una et eadem relatione referrentur ad patrem; et sic, cum

paternity begets, nor that filiation is begotten. Therefore there do not exist notions in God.

OBJ. 3: Further, we do not require to presuppose any abstract notions as principles of knowing things which are devoid of composition: for they are known of themselves. But the divine persons are supremely simple. Therefore we are not to suppose any notions in God.

ON THE CONTRARY, Damascene says (*De Fide Orth.* iii, 5): *We recognize difference of hypostases, in the three properties; i.e., in the paternal, the filial, and the processional.* Therefore we must admit properties and notions in God.

I ANSWER THAT, Prepositivus, considering the simplicity of the persons, said that in God there were no properties or notions, and wherever there were mentioned, he propounded the abstract for the concrete. For as we are accustomed to say, *I beseech your kindness*—i.e., you who are kind—so when we speak of paternity in God, we mean God the Father.

But, as shown above (Q. 3, A. 3, ad 1), the use of concrete and abstract names in God is not in any way repugnant to the divine simplicity; forasmuch as we always name a thing as we understand it. Now, our intellect cannot attain to the absolute simplicity of the divine essence, considered in itself; and therefore, our human intellect apprehends and names divine things, according to its own mode, that is, in so far as they are found in sensible objects, whence its knowledge is derived. In these things we use abstract terms to signify simple forms; and to signify subsistent things we use concrete terms. Hence also we signify divine things, as above stated, by abstract names, to express their simplicity; whereas, to express their subsistence and completeness, we use concrete names.

But not only must essential names be signified in the abstract and in the concrete, as when we say Deity and God; or wisdom and wise; but the same applies to the personal names, so that we may say paternity and Father.

Two chief motives for this can be cited. The first arises from the obstinacy of heretics. For since we confess the Father, the Son, and the Holy Spirit to be one God and three persons, to those who ask: *Whereby are They one God? and whereby are They three persons?* as we answer that They are one in essence or deity; so there must also be some abstract terms whereby we may answer that the persons are distinguished; and these are the properties or notions signified by an abstract term, as paternity and filiation. Therefore the divine essence is signified as *What*; and the person as *Who*; and the property as *Whereby.*

The second motive is because one person in God is related to two persons—namely, the person of the Father to the person of the Son and the person of the Holy Spirit. This is not, however, by one relation; otherwise it would follow that the Son also and the Holy Spirit would be related

sola relatio in divinis multiplicet Trinitatem, sequeretur quod filius et Spiritus Sanctus non essent duae personae. Neque potest dici, ut Praepositivus dicebat, quod sicut Deus uno modo se habet ad creaturas, cum tamen creaturae diversimode se habeant ad ipsum, sic pater una relatione refertur ad filium et ad spiritum sanctum, cum tamen illi duo duabus relationibus referantur ad patrem. Quia cum ratio specifica relativi consistat in hoc quod ad aliud se habet, necesse est dicere quod duae relationes non sunt diversae secundum speciem, si ex opposito una relatio eis correspondeat, oportet enim aliam speciem relationis esse domini et patris, secundum diversitatem filiationis et servitutis. Omnes autem creaturae sub una specie relationis referuntur ad Deum, ut sunt creaturae ipsius, filius autem et Spiritus Sanctus non secundum relationes unius rationis referuntur ad patrem, unde non est simile.

Et iterum, in Deo non requiritur relatio realis ad creaturam, ut supra dictum est, relationes autem rationis in Deo multiplicare non est inconveniens. Sed in patre oportet esse relationem realem qua refertur ad filium et spiritum sanctum, unde secundum duas relationes filii et spiritus sancti quibus referuntur ad patrem, oportet intelligi duas relationes in patre, quibus referatur ad filium et spiritum sanctum. Unde, cum non sit nisi una patris persona, necesse fuit seorsum significari relationes in abstracto, quae dicuntur proprietates et notiones.

AD PRIMUM ergo dicendum quod, licet de notionibus non fiat mentio in sacra Scriptura, fit tamen mentio de personis, in quibus intelliguntur notiones, sicut abstractum in concreto.

AD SECUNDUM dicendum quod notiones significantur in divinis, non ut res, sed ut rationes quaedam quibus cognoscuntur personae; licet ipsae notiones vel relationes realiter sint in Deo, ut supra dictum est. Et ideo ea quae habent ordinem aliquem ad actum aliquem essentialem vel personalem, non possunt dici de notionibus, quia hoc repugnat modo significandi ipsarum. Unde non possumus dicere quod paternitas generet vel creet, sit sapiens vel intelligens. Essentialia vero quae non habent ordinem ad aliquem actum, sed removent conditiones creaturae a Deo possunt praedicari de notionibus, possumus enim dicere quod paternitas est aeterna vel immensa, vel quodcumque huiusmodi. Et similiter, propter identitatem rei, possunt substantiva personalia et essentialia praedicari de notionibus, possumus enim dicere quod paternitas est Deus, et paternitas est pater.

AD TERTIUM dicendum quod, licet personae sint simplices, tamen absque praeiudicio simplicitatis possunt propriae rationes personarum in abstracto significari, ut dictum est.

to the Father by one and the same relation. Thus, since relation alone multiplies the Trinity, it would follow that the Son and the Holy Spirit would not be two persons. Nor can it be said with Prepositivus that as God is related in one way to creatures, while creatures are related to Him in diverse ways, so the Father is related by one relation to the Son and to the Holy Spirit; whereas these two persons are related to the Father by two relations. For, since the very specific idea of a relation is that it refers to another, it must be said that two relations are not specifically different if but one opposite relation corresponds to them. For the relation of lord and father must differ according to the difference of filiation and servitude. Now, all creatures are related to God as His creatures by one specific relation. But the Son and the Holy Spirit are not related to the Father by one and the same kind of relation. Hence there is no parity.

Further, in God there is no need to admit any real relation to the creature (Q. 28, A. 1, 3); while there is no reason against our admitting in God, many logical relations. But in the Father there must be a real relation to the Son and to the Holy Spirit. Hence, corresponding to the two relations of the Son and of the Holy Spirit, whereby they are related to the Father, we must understand two relations in the Father, whereby He is related to the Son and to the Holy Spirit. Hence, since there is only one Person of the Father, it is necessary that the relations should be separately signified in the abstract; and these are what we mean by properties and notions.

REPLY OBJ. 1: Although the notions are not mentioned in Holy Scripture, yet the persons are mentioned, comprising the idea of notions, as the abstract is contained in the concrete.

REPLY OBJ. 2: In God the notions have their significance not after the manner of realities, but by way of certain ideas whereby the persons are known; although in God these notions or relations are real, as stated above (Q. 28, A. 1). Therefore whatever has order to any essential or personal act, cannot be applied to the notions; forasmuch as this is against their mode of signification. Hence we cannot say that paternity begets, or creates, or is wise, or is intelligent. The essentials, however, which are not ordered to any act, but simply remove created conditions from God, can be predicated of the notions; for we can say that paternity is eternal, or immense, or such like. So also on account of the real identity, substantive terms, whether personal or essential, can be predicated of the notions; for we can say that paternity is God, and that paternity is the Father.

REPLY OBJ. 3: Although the persons are simple, still without prejudice to their simplicity, the proper ideas of the persons can be abstractedly signified, as above explained.

Article 3

Whether There Are Five Notions?

AD TERTIUM SIC PROCEDITUR. Videtur quod non sint quinque notiones. Propriae enim notiones personarum sunt relationes quibus distinguuntur. Sed relationes in divinis non sunt nisi quatuor, ut supra dictum est. Ergo et notiones sunt tantum quatuor.

PRAETEREA, propter hoc quod in divinis est una essentia, dicitur Deus unus, propter hoc autem quod sunt tres personae, dicitur Deus trinus. Si ergo in divinis sunt quinque notiones, dicetur quinus, quod est inconveniens.

PRAETEREA, si, tribus personis existentibus in divinis, sunt quinque notiones, oportet quod in aliqua personarum sint aliquae notiones duae vel plures; sicut in persona patris ponitur innascibilitas et paternitas et communis spiratio. Aut igitur istae tres notiones differunt re, aut non. Si differunt re, sequitur quod persona patris sit composita ex pluribus rebus. Si autem differunt ratione tantum, sequitur quod una earum possit de alia praedicari, ut dicamus quod, sicut bonitas divina est eius sapientia propter indifferentiam rei, ita communis spiratio sit paternitas, quod non conceditur. Igitur non sunt quinque notiones.

SED CONTRA, videtur quod sint plures. Quia sicut pater a nullo est, et secundum hoc accipitur notio quae dicitur innascibilitas, ita a spiritu sancto non est alia persona. Et secundum hoc oportebit accipere sextam notionem.

PRAETEREA, sicut patri et filio commune est quod ab eis procedat Spiritus Sanctus, ita commune est filio et spiritui sancto quod procedant a patre. Ergo, sicut una notio ponitur communis patri et filio, ita debet poni una notio communis filio et spiritui sancto.

RESPONDEO dicendum quod notio dicitur id quod est propria ratio cognoscendi divinam personam. Divinae autem personae multiplicantur secundum originem. Ad originem autem pertinet a quo alius, et qui ab alio, et secundum hos duos modos potest innotescere persona. Igitur persona patris non potest innotescere per hoc quod sit ab alio, sed per hoc quod a nullo est, et sic ex hac parte eius notio est innascibilitas. Sed inquantum aliquis est ab eo, innotescit dupliciter. Quia inquantum filius est ab eo, innotescit notione paternitatis, inquantum autem Spiritus Sanctus est ab eo, innotescit notione communis spirationis. Filius autem potest innotescere per hoc quod est ab alio nascendo, et sic innotescit per filiationem. Et per hoc quod est alius ab eo, scilicet Spiritus Sanctus, et per hoc innotescit eodem modo sicut et pater, scilicet communi spiratione. Spiritus sanctus autem innotescere potest per hoc quod est ab alio vel ab aliis, et sic

OBJECTION 1: It would seem that there are not five notions. For the notions proper to the persons are the relations whereby they are distinguished from each other. But the relations in God are only four (Q. 28, A. 4). Therefore the notions are only four in number.

OBJ. 2: Further, as there is only one essence in God, He is called one God, and because in Him there are three persons, He is called the Trine God. Therefore, if in God there are five notions, He may be called quinary; which cannot be allowed.

OBJ. 3: Further, if there are five notions for the three persons in God, there must be in some one person two or more notions, as in the person of the Father there is innascibility and paternity, and common spiration. Either these three notions really differ, or not. If they really differ, it follows that the person of the Father is composed of several things. But if they differ only logically, it follows that one of them can be predicated of another, so that we can say that as the divine goodness is the same as the divine wisdom by reason of the common reality, so common spiration is paternity; which is not to be admitted. Therefore there are not five notions.

OBJ. 4: On the contrary, It seems that there are more; because as the Father is from no one, and therefrom is derived the notion of innascibility; so from the Holy Spirit no other person proceeds. And in this respect there ought to be a sixth notion.

OBJ. 5: Further, as the Father and the Son are the common origin of the Holy Spirit, so it is common to the Son and the Holy Spirit to proceed from the Father. Therefore, as one notion is common to the Father and the Son, so there ought to be one notion common to the Son and to the Holy Spirit.

I ANSWER THAT, A notion is the proper idea whereby we know a divine Person. Now the divine persons are multiplied by reason of their origin: and origin includes the idea of someone from whom another comes, and of someone that comes from another, and by these two modes a person can be known. Therefore the Person of the Father cannot be known by the fact that He is from another; but by the fact that He is from no one; and thus the notion that belongs to Him is called *innascibility*. As the source of another, He can be known in two ways, because as the Son is from Him, the Father is known by the notion of *paternity*; and as the Holy Spirit is from Him, He is known by the notion of *common spiration*. The Son can be known as begotten by another, and thus He is known by *filiation*; and also by another person proceeding from Him, the Holy Spirit, and thus He is known in the same way as the Father is known, by *common spiration*. The Holy Spirit can be known by the fact that He

innotescit processione. Non autem per hoc quod alius sit ab eo, quia nulla divina persona procedit ab eo.

Sunt igitur quinque notiones in divinis, scilicet innascibilitas, paternitas, filiatio, communis spiratio et processio. Harum autem tantum quatuor sunt relationes, nam innascibilitas non est relatio nisi per reductionem, ut infra dicetur. Quatuor autem tantum proprietates sunt, nam communis spiratio non est proprietas, quia convenit duabus personis. Tres autem sunt notiones personales, idest constituentes personas, scilicet paternitas, filiatio et processio, nam communis spiratio et innascibilitas dicuntur notiones personarum, non autem personales, ut infra magis patebit.

AD PRIMUM ergo dicendum quod praeter quatuor relationes oportet ponere aliam notionem, ut dictum est.

AD SECUNDUM dicendum quod essentia in divinis significatur ut res quaedam; et similiter personae significantur ut res quaedam sed notiones significantur ut rationes notificantes personas. Et ideo, licet dicatur Deus unus propter unitatem essentiae, et trinus propter Trinitatem personarum; non tamen dicitur quinus propter quinque notiones.

AD TERTIUM dicendum quod, cum sola oppositio relativa faciat pluralitatem realem in divinis, plures proprietates unius personae, cum non opponantur ad invicem relative, non differunt realiter. Nec tamen de invicem praedicantur, quia significantur ut diversae rationes personarum. Sicut etiam non dicimus quod attributum potentiae sit attributum scientiae, licet dicamus quod scientia sit potentia.

AD QUARTUM dicendum quod, cum persona importet dignitatem, ut supra dictum est, non potest accipi notio aliqua spiritus sancti ex hoc quod nulla persona est ab ipso. Hoc enim non pertinet ad dignitatem ipsius; sicut pertinet ad auctoritatem patris quod sit a nullo.

AD QUINTUM dicendum quod filius et Spiritus Sanctus non conveniunt in uno speciali modo existendi a patre; sicut pater et filius conveniunt in uno speciali modo producendi spiritum sanctum. Id autem quod est principium innotescendi, oportet esse aliquid speciale. Et ideo non est simile.

is from another, or from others; thus He is known by *procession*; but not by the fact that another is from Him, as no divine person proceeds from Him.

Therefore, there are Five notions in God: *innascibility*, *paternity*, *filiation*, *common spiration*, and *procession*. Of these only four are relations, for *innascibility* is not a relation, except by reduction, as will appear later (Q. 33, A. 4, ad 3). Four only are properties. For *common spiration* is not a property; because it belongs to two persons. Three are personal notions—i.e., constituting persons, *paternity*, *filiation*, and *procession*. *Common spiration* and *innascibility* are called notions of Persons, but not personal notions, as we shall explain further on (Q. 40, A. 1, ad 1).

REPLY OBJ. 1: Besides the four relations, another notion must be admitted, as above explained.

REPLY OBJ. 2: The divine essence is signified as a reality; and likewise the persons are signified as realities; whereas the notions are signified as ideas notifying the persons. Therefore, although God is one by unity of essence, and trine by trinity of persons, nevertheless He is not quinary by the five notions.

REPLY OBJ. 3: Since the real plurality in God is founded only on relative opposition, the several properties of one Person, as they are not relatively opposed to each other, do not really differ. Nor again are they predicated of each other, because they are different ideas of the persons; as we do not say that the attribute of power is the attribute of knowledge, although we do say that knowledge is power.

REPLY OBJ. 4: Since Person implies dignity, as stated above (Q. 19, A. 3), we cannot derive a notion of the Holy Spirit from the fact that no person is from Him. For this does not belong to His dignity, as it belongs to the authority of the Father that He is from no one.

REPLY OBJ. 5: The Son and the Holy Spirit do not agree in one special mode of existence derived from the Father; as the Father and the Son agree in one special mode of producing the Holy Spirit. But the principle on which a notion is based must be something special; thus no parity of reasoning exists.

Article 4

Whether It Is Lawful to Have Various Contrary Opinions of Notions?

AD QUARTUM SIC PROCEDITUR. Videtur quod non liceat contrarie opinari de notionibus. Dicit enim Augustinus, in I de Trin., quod *non erratur alicubi periculosius quam in materia Trinitatis*, ad quam certum est notiones pertinere. Sed contrariae opiniones non possunt esse

OBJECTION 1: It would seem that it is not lawful to have various contrary opinions of the notions. For Augustine says (*De Trin.* i, 3): *No error is more dangerous than any as regards the Trinity*: to which mystery the notions assuredly belong. But contrary opinions must be in some way

absque errore. Ergo contrarie opinari circa notiones non licet.

PRAETEREA, per notiones cognoscuntur personae, ut dictum est. Sed circa personas non licet contrarie opinari. Ergo nec circa notiones.

SED CONTRA, articuli fidei non sunt de notionibus. Ergo circa notiones licet sic vel aliter opinari.

RESPONDEO dicendum quod ad fidem pertinet aliquid dupliciter. Uno modo, directe; sicut ea quae nobis sunt principaliter divinitus tradita, ut Deum esse trinum et unum, filium Dei esse incarnatum, et huiusmodi. Et circa haec opinari falsum, hoc ipso inducit haeresim, maxime si pertinacia adiungatur. Indirecte vero ad fidem pertinent ea ex quibus consequitur aliquid contrarium fidei; sicut si quis diceret Samuelem non fuisse filium Elcanae; ex hoc enim sequitur Scripturam divinam esse falsam. Circa huiusmodi ergo absque periculo haeresis aliquis falsum potest opinari, antequam consideretur, vel determinatum sit, quod ex hoc sequitur aliquid contrarium fidei, et maxime si non pertinaciter adhaereat. Sed postquam manifestum est, et praecipue si sit per Ecclesiam determinatum, quod ex hoc sequitur aliquid contrarium fidei, in hoc errare non esset absque haeresi. Et propter hoc, multa nunc reputantur haeretica, quae prius non reputabantur, propter hoc quod nunc est magis manifestum quid ex eis sequatur.

Sic igitur dicendum est quod circa notiones aliqui absque periculo haeresis contrarie sunt opinati, non intendentes sustinere aliquid contrarium fidei. Sed si quis falsum opinaretur circa notiones, considerans quod ex hoc sequatur aliquid contrarium fidei, in haeresim laberetur.

ET PER HOC patet responsio ad obiecta.

erroneous. Therefore it is not right to have contrary opinions of the notions.

OBJ. 2: Further, the persons are known by the notions. But no contrary opinion concerning the persons is to be tolerated. Therefore neither can there be about the notions.

ON THE CONTRARY, The notions are not articles of faith. Therefore different opinions of the notions are permissible.

I ANSWER THAT, Anything is of faith in two ways; directly, where any truth comes to us principally as divinely taught, as the trinity and unity of God, the Incarnation of the Son, and the like; and concerning these truths a false opinion of itself involves heresy, especially if it be held obstinately. A thing is of faith, indirectly, if the denial of it involves as a consequence something against faith; as for instance if anyone said that Samuel was not the son of Elcana, for it follows that the divine Scripture would be false. Concerning such things anyone may have a false opinion without danger of heresy, before the matter has been considered or settled as involving consequences against faith, and particularly if no obstinacy be shown; whereas when it is manifest, and especially if the Church has decided that consequences follow against faith, then the error cannot be free from heresy. For this reason many things are now considered as heretical which were formerly not so considered, as their consequences are now more manifest.

So we must decide that anyone may entertain contrary opinions about the notions, if he does not mean to uphold anything at variance with faith. If, however, anyone should entertain a false opinion of the notions, knowing or thinking that consequences against the faith would follow, he would lapse into heresy.

BY WHAT HAS BEEN SAID all the objections may be solved.

QUESTION 33

THE PERSON OF THE FATHER

Consequenter considerandum est de personis in speciali. Et primo de persona patris. Circa quam quaeruntur quatuor.

Primo, utrum patri competat esse principium.

Secundo, utrum persona patris proprie significetur hoc nomine pater.

Tertio, utrum per prius dicatur in divinis pater secundum quod sumitur personaliter, quam secundum quod sumitur essentialiter.

Quarto, utrum sit proprium patri esse ingenitum.

We now consider the persons singly; and first, the Person of the Father, concerning Whom there are four points of inquiry:

(1) Whether the Father is the Principle?

(2) Whether the person of the Father is properly signified by this name *Father*?

(3) Whether *Father* in God is said personally before it is said essentially?

(4) Whether it belongs to the Father alone to be unbegotten?

Article 1

Whether It Belongs to the Father to Be the Principle?

AD PRIMUM SIC PROCEDITUR. Videtur quod pater non possit dici principium filii vel spiritus sancti. Principium enim et causa idem sunt, secundum philosophum. Sed non dicimus patrem esse causam filii. Ergo non debet dici quod sit eius principium.

PRAETEREA, principium dicitur respectu principiati. Si igitur pater est principium filii, sequitur filium esse principiatum, et per consequens esse creatum. Quod videtur esse erroneum.

PRAETEREA, nomen principii a prioritate sumitur. Sed in divinis non est prius et posterius, ut Athanasius dicit. Ergo in divinis non debemus uti nomine principii.

SED CONTRA est quod dicit Augustinus, in IV de Trin., *pater est principium totius deitatis.*

RESPONDEO dicendum quod hoc nomen principium nihil aliud significat quam id a quo aliquid procedit, omne enim a quo aliquid procedit quocumque modo, dicimus esse principium; et e converso. Cum ergo pater sit a quo procedit alius, sequitur quod pater est principium.

AD PRIMUM ergo dicendum quod Graeci utuntur in divinis indifferenter nomine causae, sicut et nomine principii, sed Latini doctores non utuntur nomine causae, sed solum nomine principii. Cuius ratio est, quia principium communius est quam causa, sicut causa communius quam elementum, primus enim terminus, vel etiam prima pars rei dicitur principium, sed non causa. Quanto autem aliquod nomen est communius,

OBJECTION 1: It would seem that the Father cannot be called the principle of the Son, or of the Holy Spirit. For principle and cause are the same, according to the Philosopher (*Metaph.* iv). But we do not say that the Father is the cause of the Son. Therefore we must not say that He is the principle of the Son.

OBJ. 2: Further, a principle is so called in relation to the thing principled. So if the Father is the principle of the Son, it follows that the Son is a person principled, and is therefore created; which appears false.

OBJ. 3: Further, the word principle is taken from priority. But in God there is no *before* and *after*, as Athanasius says. Therefore in speaking of God we ought not to used the term principle.

ON THE CONTRARY, Augustine says (*De Trin.* iv, 20), *The Father is the Principle of the whole Deity.*

I ANSWER THAT, The word *principle* signifies only that whence another proceeds: since anything whence something proceeds in any way we call a principle; and conversely. As the Father then is the one whence another proceeds, it follows that the Father is a principle.

REPLY OBJ. 1: The Greeks use the words *cause* and *principle* indifferently, when speaking of God; whereas the Latin Doctors do not use the word *cause*, but only *principle*. The reason is because *principle* is a wider term than *cause*; as *cause* is more common than *element*. For the first term of a thing, as also the first part, is called the principle, but not the cause. Now the wider a term is, the more suitable it is to use as regards God (Q. 13, A. 11), because the more

tanto convenientius assumitur in divinis, ut supra dictum est, quia nomina, quanto magis specialia sunt, tanto magis determinant modum convenientem creaturae. Unde hoc nomen causa videtur importare diversitatem substantiae, et dependentiam alicuius ab altero; quam non importat nomen principii. In omnibus enim causae generibus, semper invenitur distantia inter causam et id cuius est causa, secundum aliquam perfectionem aut virtutem. Sed nomine principii utimur etiam in his quae nullam huiusmodi differentiam habent, sed solum secundum quendam ordinem, sicut cum dicimus punctum esse principium lineae, vel etiam cum dicimus primam partem lineae esse principium lineae.

AD SECUNDUM dicendum quod apud Graecos invenitur de filio vel spiritu sancto dici quod principientur. Sed hoc non est in usu doctorum nostrorum. Quia licet attribuamus patri aliquid auctoritatis ratione principii, nihil tamen ad subiectionem vel minorationem quocumque modo pertinens, attribuimus filio vel spiritui sancto, ut vitetur omnis erroris occasio. Secundum quem modum Hilarius dicit, IX de Trin., *donantis auctoritate pater maior est; sed minor non est filius, cui unum esse donatur.*

AD TERTIUM dicendum quod, licet hoc nomen principium, quantum ad id a quo imponitur ad significandum, videatur a prioritate sumptum; non tamen significat prioritatem, sed originem. Non enim idem est quod significat nomen, et a quo nomen imponitur, ut supra dictum est.

REPLY OBJ. 2: It is the custom with the Greeks to say that the Son and the Holy Spirit are principled. This is not, however, the custom with our Doctors; because, although we attribute to the Father something of authority by reason of His being the principle, still we do not attribute any kind of subjection or inferiority to the Son, or to the Holy Spirit, to avoid any occasion of error. In this way, Hilary says (*De Trin.* ix): *By authority of the Giver, the Father is the greater; nevertheless the Son is not less to Whom oneness of nature is give.*

REPLY OBJ. 3: Although this word principle, as regards its derivation, seems to be taken from priority, still it does not signify priority, but origin. For what a term signifies, and the reason why it was imposed, are not the same thing, as stated above (Q. 13, A. 8).

special terms are, the more they determine the mode adapted to the creature. Hence this term *cause* seems to mean diversity of substance, and dependence of one from another; which is not implied in the word *principle*. For in all kinds of causes there is always to be found between the cause and the effect a distance of perfection or of power: whereas we use the term *principle* even in things which have no such difference, but have only a certain order to each other; as when we say that a point is the principle of a line; or also when we say that the first part of a line is the principle of a line.

Article 2

Whether This Name Father Is Properly the Name of a Divine Person?

AD SECUNDUM SIC PROCEDITUR. Videtur quod hoc nomen pater non sit proprie nomen divinae personae. Hoc enim nomen pater significat relationem. Persona autem est substantia individua. Non ergo hoc nomen pater est proprie nomen significativum personae.

PRAETEREA, generans communius est quam pater, nam omnis pater est generans, sed non e converso. Sed nomen communius magis proprie dicitur in divinis, ut dictum est. Ergo magis proprium nomen est personae divinae generans et genitor, quam pater.

PRAETEREA, nihil quod secundum metaphoram dicitur, potest esse nomen proprium alicuius. Sed verbum metaphorice apud nos dicitur genitum vel proles, et per consequens ille cuius est verbum, metaphorice dicitur pater. Non ergo principium verbi in divinis potest proprie dici pater.

PRAETEREA, omne quod proprie dicitur in divinis, per prius dicitur de Deo quam de creaturis. Sed

OBJECTION 1: It would seem that this name *Father* is not properly the name of a divine person. For the name *Father* signifies relation. Moreover *person* is an individual substance. Therefore this name *Father* is not properly a name signifying a Person.

OBJ. 2: Further, a begetter is more common than father; for every father begets; but it is not so conversely. But a more common term is more properly applied to God, as stated above (Q. 13, A. 11). Therefore the more proper name of the divine person is begetter and genitor than Father.

OBJ. 3: Further, a metaphorical term cannot be the proper name of anyone. But the word is by us metaphorically called begotten, or offspring; and consequently, he of whom is the word, is metaphorically called father. Therefore the principle of the Word in God is not properly called Father.

OBJ. 4: Further, everything which is said properly of God, is said of God first before creatures. But generation

generatio per prius videtur dici de creaturis quam de Deo, verior enim ibi videtur esse generatio, ubi aliquid procedit ab alio distinctum non secundum relationem tantum, sed etiam secundum essentiam. Ergo nomen patris, quod a generatione sumitur, non videtur esse proprium alicuius divinae personae.

Sed contra est quod dicitur in Psalmo, *ipse invocabit me, pater meus es tu.*

Respondeo dicendum quod nomen proprium cuiuslibet personae significat id per quod illa persona distinguitur ab omnibus aliis. Sicut enim de ratione hominis est anima et corpus, ita de intellectu huius hominis est haec anima et hoc corpus, ut dicitur in VII Metaphys.; his autem hic homo ab omnibus aliis distinguitur. Id autem per quod distinguitur persona patris ab omnibus aliis, est paternitas. Unde proprium nomen personae patris est hoc nomen pater, quod significat paternitatem.

Ad primum ergo dicendum quod apud nos relatio non est subsistens persona, et ideo hoc nomen pater, apud nos, non significat personam, sed relationem personae. Non autem est ita in divinis, ut quidam falso opinati sunt, nam relatio quam significat hoc nomen pater, est subsistens persona. Unde supra dictum est quod hoc nomen persona in divinis significat relationem ut subsistentem in divina natura.

Ad secundum dicendum quod, secundum philosophum, in II de anima, denominatio rei maxime debet fieri a perfectione et fine. Generatio autem significat ut in fieri, sed paternitas significat complementum generationis. Et ideo potius est nomen divinae personae pater, quam generans vel genitor.

Ad tertium dicendum quod verbum non est aliquid subsistens in natura humana, unde non proprie potest dici genitum vel filius. Sed verbum divinum est aliquid subsistens in natura divina, unde proprie, et non metaphorice, dicitur filius, et eius principium, pater.

Ad quartum dicendum quod nomen generationis et paternitatis, sicut et alia nomina quae proprie dicuntur in divinis, per prius dicuntur de Deo quam de creaturis, quantum ad rem significatam, licet non quantum ad modum significandi. Unde et apostolus dicit, ad Ephes. III, *flecto genua mea ad patrem domini nostri Iesu Christi, ex quo omnis paternitas in caelo et in terra nominatur.* Quod sic apparet. Manifestum est enim quod generatio accipit speciem a termino, qui est forma generati. Et quanto haec fuerit propinquior formae generantis, tanto verior et perfectior est generatio; sicut generatio univoca est perfectior quam non univoca, nam de ratione generantis est, quod generet sibi simile secundum formam. Unde hoc ipsum quod in generatione divina est eadem numero forma generantis et geniti, in rebus autem creatis non est eadem numero, sed specie tantum, ostendit

appears to apply to creatures before God; because generation seems to be truer when the one who proceeds is distinct from the one whence it proceeds, not only by relation but also by essence. Therefore the name *Father* taken from generation does not seem to be the proper name of any divine person.

On the contrary, It is said (Ps 88:27): *He shall cry out to me: Thou art my Father.*

I answer that, The proper name of any person signifies that whereby the person is distinguished from all other persons. For as body and soul belong to the nature of man, so to the concept of this particular man belong this particular soul and this particular body; and by these is this particular man distinguished from all other men. Now it is paternity which distinguishes the person of the Father from all other persons. Hence this name *Father*, whereby paternity is signified, is the proper name of the person of the Father.

Reply Obj. 1: Among us relation is not a subsisting person. So this name *father* among us does not signify a person, but the relation of a person. In God, however, it is not so, as some wrongly thought; for in God the relation signified by the name *Father* is a subsisting person. Hence, as above explained (Q. 29, A. 4), this name *person* in God signifies a relation subsisting in the divine nature.

Reply Obj. 2: According to the Philosopher (*De Anima* ii, 49), a thing is denominated chiefly by its perfection, and by its end. Now generation signifies something in process of being made, whereas paternity signifies the complement of generation; and therefore the name *Father* is more expressive as regards the divine person than genitor or begettor.

Reply Obj. 3: In human nature the word is not a subsistence, and hence is not properly called begotten or son. But the divine Word is something subsistent in the divine nature; and hence He is properly and not metaphorically called Son, and His principle is called Father.

Reply Obj. 4: The terms *generation* and *paternity* like the other terms properly applied to God, are said of God before creatures as regards the thing signified, but not as regards the mode of signification. Hence also the Apostle says, *I bend my knee to the Father of my Lord Jesus Christ, from whom all paternity in heaven and on earth is named* (Eph 3:14). This is explained thus. It is manifest that generation receives its species from the term which is the form of the thing generated; and the nearer it is to the form of the generator, the truer and more perfect is the generation; as univocal generation is more perfect than non-univocal, for it belongs to the essence of a generator to generate what is like itself in form. Hence the very fact that in the divine generation the form of the Begetter and Begotten is numerically the same, whereas in creatures it is not numerically, but only specifically, the same, shows that generation, and

quod generatio, et per consequens paternitas, per prius sit in Deo quam in creaturis. Unde hoc ipsum quod in divinis est distinctio geniti a generante secundum relationem tantum, ad veritatem divinae generationis et paternitatis pertinet.

consequently paternity, is applied to God before creatures. Hence the very fact that in God a distinction exists of the Begotten from the Begetter as regards relation only, belongs to the truth of the divine generation and paternity.

Article 3

Whether This Name Father Is Applied to God, First As a Personal Name?

AD TERTIUM SIC PROCEDITUR. Videtur quod hoc nomen pater non dicatur in divinis per prius secundum quod personaliter sumitur. Commune enim, secundum intellectum, est prius proprio. Sed hoc nomen pater, secundum quod personaliter sumitur, est proprium personae patris, secundum vero quod sumitur essentialiter est commune toti Trinitati, nam toti Trinitati dicimus pater noster. Ergo per prius dicitur pater essentialiter sumptum, quam personaliter.

PRAETEREA, in his quae sunt eiusdem rationis, non est praedicatio per prius et posterius. Sed paternitas et filiatio secundum unam rationem videntur dici secundum quod persona divina est pater filii, et secundum quod tota Trinitas est pater noster vel creaturae, cum, secundum Basilium, accipere sit commune creaturae et filio. Ergo non per prius dicitur pater in divinis secundum quod sumitur essentialiter, quam secundum quod sumitur personaliter.

PRAETEREA, inter ea quae non dicuntur secundum rationem unam, non potest esse comparatio. Sed filius comparatur creaturae in ratione filiationis vel generationis, secundum illud Coloss. I, *qui est imago Dei invisibilis, primogenitus omnis creaturae.* Ergo non per prius dicitur in divinis paternitas personaliter sumpta, quam essentialiter; sed secundum rationem eandem.

SED CONTRA est quod aeternum prius est temporali. Ab aeterno autem Deus est pater filii, ex tempore autem pater est creaturae. Ergo per prius dicitur paternitas in Deo respectu filii, quam respectu creaturae.

RESPONDEO dicendum quod per prius dicitur nomen de illo in quo salvatur tota ratio nominis perfecte, quam de illo in quo salvatur secundum aliquid, de hoc enim dicitur quasi per similitudinem ad id in quo perfecte salvatur, quia omnia imperfecta sumuntur a perfectis. Et inde est quod hoc nomen leo per prius dicitur de animali in quo tota ratio leonis salvatur, quod proprie dicitur leo, quam de aliquo homine in quo invenitur aliquid de ratione leonis, ut puta audacia vel fortitudo, vel aliquid huiusmodi, de hoc enim per similitudinem dicitur.

OBJECTION 1: It would seem that this name *Father* is not applied to God, first as a personal name. For in the intellect the common precedes the particular. But this name *Father* as a personal name, belongs to the person of the Father; and taken in an essential sense it is common to the whole Trinity; for we say *Our Father* to the whole Trinity. Therefore *Father* comes first as an essential name before its personal sense.

OBJ. 2: Further, in things of which the concept is the same there is no priority of predication. But paternity and filiation seem to be of the same nature, according as a divine person is Father of the Son, and the whole Trinity is our Father, or the creature's; since, according to Basil (*Hom. xv, De Fide*), to receive is common to the creature and to the Son. Therefore *Father* in God is not taken as an essential name before it is taken personally.

OBJ. 3: Further, it is not possible to compare things which have not a common concept. But the Son is compared to the creature by reason of filiation or generation, according to Col. 1:15: *Who is the image of the invisible God, the first-born of every creature.* Therefore paternity taken in a personal sense is not prior to, but has the same concept as, paternity taken essentially.

ON THE CONTRARY, The eternal comes before the temporal. But God is the Father of the Son from eternity; while He is the Father of the creature in time. Therefore paternity in God is taken in a personal sense as regards the Son, before it is so taken as regards the creature.

I ANSWER THAT, A name is applied to that wherein is perfectly contained its whole signification, before it is applied to that which only partially contains it; for the latter bears the name by reason of a kind of similitude to that which answers perfectly to the signification of the name; since all imperfect things are taken from perfect things. Hence this name *lion* is applied first to the animal containing the whole nature of a lion, and which is properly so called, before it is applied to a man who shows something of a lion's nature, as courage, or strength, or the like; and of whom it is said by way of similitude.

Manifestum est autem ex praemissis quod perfecta ratio paternitatis et filiationis invenitur in Deo patre et Deo filio, quia patris et filii una est natura et gloria. Sed in creatura filiatio invenitur respectu Dei, non secundum perfectam rationem, cum non sit una natura creatoris et creaturae; sed secundum aliqualem similitudinem. Quae quanto perfectior fuerit, tanto propinquius acceditur ad veram filiationis rationem. Dicitur enim Deus alicuius creaturae pater, propter similitudinem vestigii tantum, utpote irrationalium creaturarum; secundum illud Iob XXXVIII, *quis est pluviae pater? Aut quis genuit stillas roris?* Alicuius vero creaturae, scilicet rationalis, secundum similitudinem imaginis; secundum illud Deut. XXXII, *nonne ipse est pater tuus, qui possedit et fecit et creavit te?* Aliquorum vero est pater secundum similitudinem gratiae, qui etiam dicuntur filii adoptivi, secundum quod ordinantur ad haereditatem aeternae gloriae per munus gratiae acceptum; secundum illud Rom. VIII, *ipse spiritus reddit testimonium spiritui nostro, quod sumus filii Dei; si autem filii, et haeredes.* Aliquorum vero secundum similitudinem gloriae, prout iam gloriae haereditatem possident; secundum illud Rom. V, *gloriamur in spe gloriae filiorum Dei.* Sic igitur patet quod per prius paternitas dicitur in divinis secundum quod importatur respectus personae ad personam, quam secundum quod importatur respectus Dei ad creaturam.

AD PRIMUM ergo dicendum quod communia absolute dicta, secundum ordinem intellectus nostri, sunt priora quam propria, quia includuntur in intellectu propriorum, sed non e converso; in intellectu enim personae patris intelligitur Deus, sed non convertitur. Sed communia quae important respectum ad creaturam, per posterius dicuntur quam propria quae important respectus personales, quia persona procedens in divinis, procedit ut principium productionis creaturarum. Sicut enim verbum conceptum in mente artificis, per prius intelligitur procedere ab artifice quam artificiatum, quod producitur ad similitudinem verbi concepti in mente; ita per prius procedit filius a patre quam creatura, de qua nomen filiationis dicitur secundum quod aliquid participat de similitudine filii; ut patet per illud quod dicitur Rom. VIII, *quos praescivit, et praedestinavit fieri conformes imaginis filii eius.*

AD SECUNDUM dicendum quod accipere dicitur esse commune creaturae et filio, non secundum univocationem, sed secundum similitudinem quandam remotam, ratione cuius dicitur primogenitus creaturae. Unde in auctoritate inducta subditur, *ut sit ipse primogenitus in multis fratribus,* postquam dixerat conformes fieri aliquos imaginis filii Dei. Sed filius Dei naturaliter habet quoddam singulare prae aliis, scilicet habere per naturam id quod accipit; ut idem Basilius dicit. Et secundum hoc dicitur unigenitus, ut patet Ioan. I, *unigenitus, qui est in sinu patris, ipse nobis enarravit.*

Now it is manifest from the foregoing (Q. 27, A. 2; Q. 28, A. 4), that the perfect idea of paternity and filiation is to be found in God the Father, and in God the Son, because one is the nature and glory of the Father and the Son. But in the creature, filiation is found in relation to God, not in a perfect manner, since the Creator and the creature have not the same nature; but by way of a certain likeness, which is the more perfect the nearer we approach to the true idea of filiation. For God is called the Father of some creatures, by reason only of a trace, for instance of irrational creatures, according to Job 38:28: *Who is the father of the rain? or who begot the drops of dew?* Of some, namely, the rational creature (He is the Father), by reason of the likeness of His image, according to Deut. 32:6: *Is He not thy Father, who possessed, and made, and created thee?* And of others He is the Father by similitude of grace, and these are also called adoptive sons, as ordained to the heritage of eternal glory by the gift of grace which they have received, according to Rom. 8:16, 17: *The Spirit Himself gives testimony to our spirit that we are the sons of God; and if sons, heirs also.* Lastly, He is the Father of others by similitude of glory, forasmuch as they have obtained possession of the heritage of glory, according to Rom. 5:2: *We glory in the hope of the glory of the sons of God.* Therefore it is plain that *paternity* is applied to God first, as importing regard of one Person to another Person, before it imports the regard of God to creatures.

REPLY OBJ. 1: Common terms taken absolutely, in the order of our intelligence, come before proper terms; because they are included in the understanding of proper terms; but not conversely. For in the concept of the person of the Father, God is understood; but not conversely. But common terms which import relation to the creature come after proper terms which import personal relations; because the person proceeding in God proceeds as the principle of the production of creatures. For as the word conceived in the mind of the artist is first understood to proceed from the artist before the thing designed, which is produced in likeness to the word conceived in the artist's mind; so the Son proceeds from the Father before the creature, to which the name of filiation is applied as it participates in the likeness of the Son, as is clear from the words of Rom. 8:29: *Whom He foreknew and predestined to be made conformable to the image of His Son.*

REPLY OBJ. 2: To *receive* is said to be common to the creature and to the Son not in a univocal sense, but according to a certain remote similitude whereby He is called the First Born of creatures. Hence the authority quoted subjoins: *That He may be the First Born among many brethren,* after saying that some were conformed to the image of the Son of God. But the Son of God possesses a position of singularity above others, in having by nature what He receives, as Basil also declares (*Hom.* xv De Fide); hence He is called the only begotten (John 1:18): *The only begotten Who is in the bosom of the Father, He hath declared unto us.*

ET PER HOC patet solutio ad tertium.

FROM THIS appears the Reply to the Third Objection.

Article 4

Whether It Is Proper to the Father to Be Unbegotten?

AD QUARTUM SIC PROCEDITUR. Videtur quod esse ingenitum non sit patri proprium. Omnis enim proprietas ponit aliquid in eo cuius est proprietas. Sed ingenitus nihil ponit in patre, sed removet tantum. Ergo non significat proprietatem patris.

PRAETEREA, ingenitum aut dicitur privative, aut negative. Si negative, tunc quidquid non est genitum, potest dici ingenitum. Sed Spiritus Sanctus non est genitus, neque etiam essentia divina. Ergo ingenitum etiam eis convenit, et sic non est proprium patri. Si autem privative sumatur, cum omnis privatio significet imperfectionem in privato, sequitur quod persona patris sit imperfecta. Quod est impossibile.

PRAETEREA, ingenitus in divinis non significat relationem, quia non dicitur relative, significat ergo substantiam. Ingenitus igitur et genitus secundum substantiam differunt. Filius autem, qui est genitus, non differt a patre secundum substantiam. Pater ergo non debet dici ingenitus.

PRAETEREA, proprium est quod uni soli convenit. Sed cum sint plures ab alio procedentes in divinis, nihil videtur prohibere quin etiam sint plures ab alio non existentes. Non igitur est proprium patri esse ingenitum.

PRAETEREA, sicut pater est principium personae genitae, ita et personae procedentis. Si ergo propter oppositionem quam habet ad personam genitam, proprium patris ponitur esse quod sit ingenitus; etiam proprium eius debet poni quod sit improcessibilis.

SED CONTRA est quod dicit Hilarius, IV de Trin.: *est unus ab uno*, scilicet ab ingenito genitus, *proprietate videlicet in unoquoque et innascibilitatis et originis*.

RESPONDEO dicendum quod, sicut in creaturis invenitur principium primum et principium secundum, ita in personis divinis, in quibus non est prius et posterius, invenitur principium non de principio, quod est pater, et principium a principio, quod est filius.

In rebus autem creatis aliquod principium primum innotescit dupliciter, uno quidem modo, inquantum est principium primum per hoc quod habet relationem ad ea quae ab ipso sunt; alio modo, inquantum est primum principium per hoc quod non est ab alio. Sic igitur et pater innotescit quidem paternitate et communi spiratione, per respectum ad personas ab eo procedentes,

OBJECTION 1: It would seem that it is not proper to the Father to be unbegotten. For every property supposes something in that of which it is the property. But *unbegotten* supposes nothing in the Father; it only removes something. Therefore it does not signify a property of the Father.

OBJ. 2: Further, Unbegotten is taken either in a privative, or in a negative sense. If in a negative sense, then whatever is not begotten can be called unbegotten. But the Holy Spirit is not begotten; neither is the divine essence. Therefore to be unbegotten belongs also to the essence; thus it is not proper to the Father. But if it be taken in a privative sense, as every privation signifies imperfection in the thing which is the subject of privation, it follows that the Person of the Father is imperfect; which cannot be.

OBJ. 3: Further, in God, *unbegotten* does not signify relation, for it is not used relatively. Therefore it signifies substance; therefore unbegotten and begotten differ in substance. But the Son, Who is begotten, does not differ from the Father in substance. Therefore the Father ought not to be called unbegotten.

OBJ. 4: Further, property means what belongs to one alone. Since, then, there are more than one in God proceeding from another, there is nothing to prevent several not receiving their being from another. Therefore the Father is not alone unbegotten.

OBJ. 5: Further, as the Father is the principle of the person begotten, so is He of the person proceeding. So if by reason of his opposition to the person begotten, it is proper to the Father to be unbegotten it follows that it is proper to Him also to be unproceeding.

ON THE CONTRARY, Hilary says (*De Trin.* iv): *One is from one—that is, the Begotten is from the Unbegotten—namely, by the property in each one respectively of innascibility and origin.*

I ANSWER THAT, As in creatures there exist a first and a secondary principle, so also in the divine Persons, in Whom there is no before or after, is formed the principle not from a principle, Who is the Father; and the principle from a principle, Who is the Son.

Now in things created a first principle is known in two ways; in one way as the first principle, by reason of its having a relation to what proceeds from itself; in another way, inasmuch as it is a first principle by reason of its not being from another. Thus therefore the Father is known both by paternity and by common spiration, as regards the persons proceeding from Himself. But as the principle, not

inquantum autem est principium non de principio, innotescit per hoc, quod non est ab alio, quod pertinet ad proprietatem innascibilitatis, quam significat hoc nomen ingenitus.

AD PRIMUM ergo dicendum quod quidam dicunt quod innascibilitas, quam significat hoc nomen ingenitus, secundum quod est proprietas patris, non dicitur tantum negative; sed importat vel utrumque simul, scilicet quod pater a nullo est, et quod est principium aliorum; vel importat universalem auctoritatem; vel etiam fontalem plenitudinem. Sed hoc non videtur verum. Quia sic innascibilitas non esset alia proprietas a paternitate et spiratione, sed includeret eas, sicut includitur proprium in communi, nam fontalitas et auctoritas nihil aliud significant in divinis quam principium originis. Et ideo dicendum est, secundum Augustinum, V de Trin., quod ingenitus negationem generationis passivae importat, dicit enim quod *tantum valet quod dicitur ingenitus, quantum valet quod dicitur non filius.* Nec propter hoc sequitur quod ingenitus non debeat poni propria notio patris, quia prima et simplicia per negationes notificantur; sicut dicimus punctum esse cuius pars non est.

AD SECUNDUM dicendum quod ingenitum quandoque sumitur negative tantum. Et secundum hoc Hieronymus dicit spiritum sanctum esse ingenitum, idest non genitum. Alio modo potest dici ingenitum aliquo modo privative, non tamen aliquam imperfectionem importat. Multipliciter enim dicitur privatio. Uno modo, quando aliquid non habet quod natum est haberi ab alio, etiamsi ipsum non sit natum habere illud, sicut si lapis dicatur res mortua, quia caret vita, quam quaedam res natae sunt habere. Alio modo dicitur privatio, quando aliquid non habet quod natum est haberi ab aliquo sui generis; sicut si talpa dicatur caeca. Tertio modo, quando ipsum non habet quod natum est habere, et hoc modo privatio imperfectionem importat. Sic autem ingenitum non dicitur privative de patre, sed secundo modo, prout scilicet aliquod suppositum divinae naturae non est genitum, cuius tamen naturae aliquod suppositum est genitum. Sed secundum hanc rationem, etiam de spiritu sancto potest dici ingenitum. Unde ad hoc quod sit proprium soli patri, oportet ulterius in nomine ingeniti intelligere, quod conveniat alicui personae divinae quae sit principium alterius personae; ut sic intelligatur importare negationem in genere principii personaliter dicti in divinis. Vel, ut intelligatur in nomine ingeniti, quod omnino non sit ab alio, et non solum quod non sit ab alio per generationem. Sic enim nec spiritui sancto convenit esse ingenitum, qui est ab alio per processionem ut persona subsistens, nec etiam divinae essentiae, de qua potest dici quod est in filio vel in spiritu sancto ab alio, scilicet a patre.

from a principle He is known by the fact that He is not from another; and this belongs to the property of innascibility, signified by this word *unbegotten.*

REPLY OBJ. 1: Some there are who say that innascibility, signified by the word *unbegotten*, as a property of the Father, is not a negative term only, but either that it means both these things together—namely, that the Father is from no one, and that He is the principle of others; or that it imports universal authority, or also His plenitude as the source of all. This, however, does not seem true, because thus innascibility would not be a property distinct from paternity and spiration; but would include them as the proper is included in the common. For source and authority signify in God nothing but the principle of origin. We must therefore say with Augustine (*De Trin.* v, 7) that *unbegotten* imports the negation of passive generation. For he says that *unbegotten* has the same meaning as *not a son.* Nor does it follow that *unbegotten* is not the proper notion of the Father; for primary and simple things are notified by negations; as, for instance, a point is defined as what has no part.

REPLY OBJ. 2: *Unbegotten* is taken sometimes in a negative sense only, and in that sense Jerome says that *the Holy Spirit is unbegotten*, that is, He is not begotten. Otherwise *unbegotten* may be taken in a kind of privative sense, but not as implying any imperfection. For privation can be taken in many ways; in one way when a thing has not what naturally belongs to another, even though it is not of its own nature to have it; as, for instance, if a stone be called a dead thing, as wanting life, which naturally belongs to some other things. In another sense, privation is so called when something has not what naturally belongs to some members of its genus; as for instance when a mole is called blind. In a third sense privation means the absence of what something ought to have; in which sense, privation imports an imperfection. In this sense, *unbegotten* is not attributed to the Father as a privation, but it may be so attributed in the second sense, meaning that a certain person of the divine nature is not begotten, while some person of the same nature is begotten. In this sense the term *unbegotten* can be applied also to the Holy Spirit. Hence to consider it as a term proper to the Father alone, it must be further understood that the name *unbegotten* belongs to a divine person as the principle of another person; so that it be understood to imply negation in the genus of principle taken personally in God. Or that there be understood in the term *unbegotten* that He is not in any way derived from another; and not only that He is not from another by way only of generation. In this sense the term *unbegotten* does not belong at all to the Holy Spirit, Who is from another by procession, as a subsisting person; nor does it belong to the divine essence, of which it may be said that it is in the Son or in the Holy Spirit from another—namely, from the Father.

AD TERTIUM dicendum quod, secundum Damascenum, ingenitum uno modo significat idem quod increatum, et sic secundum substantiam dicitur; per hoc enim differt substantia creata ab increata. Alio modo significat id quod non est genitum. Et sic relative dicitur, eo modo quo negatio reducitur ad genus affirmationis, sicut non homo ad genus substantiae, et non album ad genus qualitatis. Unde, cum genitum in divinis relationem importet, ingenitum etiam ad relationem pertinet. Et sic non sequitur quod pater ingenitus distinguatur a filio genito secundum substantiam; sed solum secundum relationem, inquantum scilicet relatio filii negatur de patre.

AD QUARTUM dicendum quod, sicut in quolibet genere oportet ponere unum primum, ita in divina natura oportet ponere unum principium quod non sit ab alio, quod ingenitum dicitur. Ponere igitur duos innascibiles, est ponere duos deos, et duas naturas divinas. Unde Hilarius dicit, in libro de synodis, *cum unus Deus sit, duo innascibiles esse non possunt*. Et hoc praecipue quia, si essent duo innascibiles, unus eorum non esset ab alio, et sic non distinguerentur oppositione relativa oporteret igitur quod distinguerentur diversitate naturae.

AD QUINTUM dicendum quod proprietas patris prout non est ab alio, potius significatur per remotionem nativitatis filii, quam per remotionem processionis spiritus sancti. Tum quia processio spiritus sancti non habet nomen speciale, ut supra dictum est. Tum quia etiam ordine naturae praesupponit generationem filii. Unde, remoto a patre quod non sit genitus, cum tamen sit principium generationis, sequitur consequenter quod non sit procedens processione spiritus sancti, quia Spiritus Sanctus non est generationis principium, sed a genito procedens.

REPLY OBJ. 3: According to Damascene (*De Fide Orth.* ii, 9), *unbegotten* in one sense signifies the same as *uncreated*; and thus it applies to the substance, for thereby does the created substance differ from the uncreated. In another sense it signifies what is not begotten, and in this sense it is a relative term; just as negation is reduced to the genus of affirmation, as *not man* is reduced to the genus of substance, and *not white* to the genus of quality. Hence, since *begotten* implies relation in God, *unbegotten* belongs also to relation. Thus it does not follow that the Father unbegotten is substantially distinguished from the Son begotten; but only by relation; that is, as the relation of Son is denied of the Father.

REPLY OBJ. 4: In every genus there must be something first; so in the divine nature there must be some one principle which is not from another, and which we call *unbegotten*. To admit two innascibles is to suppose the existence of two Gods, and two divine natures. Hence Hilary says (*De Synod.*): *As there is one God, so there cannot be two innascibles*. And this especially because, did two innascibles exist, one would not be from the other, and they would not be distinguished by relative opposition: therefore they would be distinguished from each other by diversity of nature.

REPLY OBJ. 5: The property of the Father, whereby He is not from another, is more clearly signified by the removal of the nativity of the Son, than by the removal of the procession of the Holy Spirit; both because the procession of the Holy Spirit has no special name, as stated above (Q. 27, A. 4, ad 3), and because also in the order of nature it presupposes the generation of the Son. Hence, it being denied of the Father that He is begotten, although He is the principle of generation, it follows, as a consequence, that He does not proceed by the procession of the Holy Spirit, because the Holy Spirit is not the principle of generation, but proceeds from the person begotten.

QUESTION 34

THE PERSON OF THE SON

Deinde considerandum est de persona filii. Attribuuntur autem tria nomina filio, scilicet filius, verbum et imago. Sed ratio filii ex ratione patris consideratur. Unde restat considerandum de verbo et imagine.

Circa verbum quaeruntur tria.

Primo, utrum verbum dicatur essentialiter in divinis, vel personaliter.

Secundo, utrum sit proprium nomen filii.

Tertio, utrum in nomine verbi importetur respectus ad creaturas.

We next consider the person of the Son. Three names are attributed to the Son—namely, *Son*, *Word*, and *Image*. The idea of Son is gathered from the idea of Father. Hence it remains for us to consider Word and Image.

Concerning Word there are three points of inquiry:

(1) Whether Word is an essential term in God, or a personal term?

(2) Whether it is the proper name of the Son?

(3) Whether in the name of Word is expressed relation to creatures?

Article 1

Whether Word in God Is a Personal Name?

AD PRIMUM SIC PROCEDITUR. Videtur quod verbum in divinis non sit nomen personale. Nomina enim personalia proprie dicuntur in divinis, ut pater et filius. Sed verbum metaphorice dicitur in divinis, ut Origenes dicit, super Ioannem. Ergo verbum non est personale in divinis.

PRAETEREA, secundum Augustinum, in libro de Trin., *verbum est notitia cum amore.* Et secundum Anselmum, in Monol., *dicere summo spiritui nihil aliud est quam cogitando intueri.* Sed notitia et cogitatio et intuitus in divinis essentialiter dicuntur. Ergo verbum non dicitur personaliter in divinis.

PRAETEREA, de ratione verbi est quod dicatur. Sed, secundum Anselmum, sicut pater est intelligens, et filius est intelligens, et Spiritus Sanctus est intelligens; ita pater est dicens, filius est dicens, et Spiritus Sanctus est dicens. Et similiter quilibet eorum dicitur. Ergo nomen verbi essentialiter dicitur in divinis, et non personaliter.

PRAETEREA, nulla persona divina est facta. Sed verbum Dei est aliquid factum, dicitur enim in Psalmo CXLVIII, *ignis, grando, nix, glacies, spiritus procellarum, quae faciunt verbum eius.* Ergo verbum non est nomen personale in divinis.

SED CONTRA est quod dicit Augustinus, in VII de Trin., *sicut filius refertur ad patrem, ita et verbum ad id cuius est verbum.* Sed filius est nomen personale, quia relative dicitur. Ergo et verbum.

RESPONDEO dicendum quod nomen verbi in divinis, si proprie sumatur, est nomen personale, et nullo modo essentiale.

OBJECTION 1: It would seem that *Word* in God is not a personal name. For personal names are applied to God in a proper sense, as Father and Son. But Word is applied to God metaphorically, as Origen says on (John 1:1), *In the beginning was the Word.* Therefore *Word* is not a personal name in God.

OBJ. 2: Further, according to Augustine (*De Trin.* ix, 10), *The Word is knowledge with love*; and according to Anselm (*Monol.* lx), *To speak is to the Supreme Spirit nothing but to see by thought.* But knowledge and thought, and sight, are essential terms in God. Therefore Word is not a personal term in God.

OBJ. 3: Further, it is essential to word to be spoken. But, according to Anselm (*Monol.* lix), as the Father is intelligent, the Son is intelligent, and the Holy Spirit is intelligent, so the Father speaks, the Son speaks, and the Holy Spirit speaks; and likewise, each one of them is spoken. Therefore, the name Word is used as an essential term in God, and not in a personal sense.

OBJ. 4: Further, no divine person is made. But the Word of God is something made. For it is said, *Fire, hail, snow, ice, the storms which do His Word* (Ps 148:8). Therefore the Word is not a personal name in God.

ON THE CONTRARY, Augustine says (*De Trin.* vii, 11): *As the Son is related to the Father, so also is the Word to Him Whose Word He is.* But the Son is a personal name, since it is said relatively. Therefore so also is Word.

I ANSWER THAT, The name of Word in God, if taken in its proper sense, is a personal name, and in no way an essential name.

Ad cuius evidentiam, sciendum est quod verbum tripliciter quidem in nobis proprie dicitur, quarto autem modo, dicitur improprie sive figurative. Manifestius autem et communius in nobis dicitur verbum quod voce profertur. Quod quidem ab interiori procedit quantum ad duo quae in verbo exteriori inveniuntur, scilicet vox ipsa, et significatio vocis. Vox enim significat intellectus conceptum, secundum philosophum, in libro I Periherm., et iterum vox ex imaginatione procedit, ut in libro de anima dicitur. Vox autem quae non est significativa, verbum dici non potest. Ex hoc ergo dicitur verbum vox exterior, quia significat interiorem mentis conceptum. Sic igitur primo et principaliter interior mentis conceptus verbum dicitur, secundario vero, ipsa vox interioris conceptus significativa, tertio vero, ipsa imaginatio vocis verbum dicitur. Et hos tres modos verbi ponit Damascenus, in I libro, cap. XIII, dicens quod *verbum dicitur naturalis intellectus motus, secundum quem movetur et intelligit et cogitat, velut lux et splendor*, quantum ad primum, rursus *verbum est quod non verbo profertur, sed in corde pronuntiatur*, quantum ad tertium, rursus *etiam verbum est Angelus*, idest nuntius, *intelligentiae*, quantum ad secundum. Dicitur autem figurative quarto modo verbum, id quod verbo significatur vel efficitur, sicut consuevimus dicere, hoc est verbum quod dixi tibi, vel quod mandavit rex, demonstrato aliquo facto quod verbo significatum est vel simpliciter enuntiantis, vel etiam imperantis.

Dicitur autem proprie verbum in Deo, secundum quod verbum significat conceptum intellectus. Unde Augustinus dicit, in XV de Trin., *quisquis potest intelligere verbum, non solum antequam sonet, verum etiam antequam sonorum eius imagines cogitatione involvantur, iam potest videre aliquam verbi illius similitudinem, de quo dictum est, in principio erat verbum*. Ipse autem conceptus cordis de ratione sua habet quod ab alio procedat, scilicet a notitia concipientis. Unde verbum, secundum quod proprie dicitur in divinis, significat aliquid ab alio procedens, quod pertinet ad rationem nominum personalium in divinis, eo quod personae divinae distinguuntur secundum originem, ut dictum est. Unde oportet quod nomen verbi, secundum quod proprie in divinis accipitur, non sumatur essentialiter, sed personaliter tantum.

AD PRIMUM ergo dicendum quod Ariani, quorum fons Origenes invenitur, posuerunt filium alium a patre esse in diversitate substantiae. Unde conati sunt, cum filius Dei verbum dicitur, astruere non esse proprie dictum; ne, sub ratione verbi procedentis, cogerentur fateri filium Dei non esse extra substantiam patris; nam verbum interius sic a dicente procedit, quod in ipso manet. Sed necesse est, si ponitur verbum Dei metaphorice

To see how this is true, we must know that our own word taken in its proper sense has a threefold meaning; while in a fourth sense it is taken improperly or figuratively. The clearest and most common sense is when it is said of the word spoken by the voice; and this proceeds from an interior source as regards two things found in the exterior word—that is, the vocal sound itself, and the signification of the sound. For, according to the Philosopher (*Peri Herm.* i), vocal sound signifies the concept of the intellect. Again the vocal sound proceeds from the signification or the imagination, as stated in *De Anima* ii, text 90. The vocal sound, which has no signification cannot be called a word: wherefore the exterior vocal sound is called a word from the fact the it signifies the interior concept of the mind. Therefore it follows that, first and chiefly, the interior concept of the mind is called a word; secondarily, the vocal sound itself, signifying the interior concept, is so called; and third, the imagination of the vocal sound is called a word. Damascene mentions these three kinds of words (*De Fide Orth.* i, 17), saying that *word* is called *the natural movement of the intellect, whereby it is moved, and understands, and thinks, as light and splendor*; which is the first kind. *Again*, he says, *the word is what is not pronounced by a vocal word, but is uttered in the heart*; which is the third kind. *Again*, also, *the word is the angel*—that is, the messenger *of intelligence*; which is the second kind. Word is also used in a fourth way figuratively for that which is signified or effected by a word; thus we are wont to say, *This is the word I have said*, or *which the king has commanded*, alluding to some deed signified by the word either by way of assertion or of command.

Now word is taken strictly in God, as signifying the concept of the intellect. Hence Augustine says (*De Trin.* xv, 10): *Whoever can understand the word, not only before it is sounded, but also before thought has clothed it with imaginary sound, can already see some likeness of that Word of Whom it is said: In the beginning was the Word.* The concept itself of the heart has of its own nature to proceed from something other than itself—namely, from the knowledge of the one conceiving. Hence *Word*, according as we use the term strictly of God, signifies something proceeding from another; which belongs to the nature of personal terms in God, inasmuch as the divine persons are distinguished by origin (Q. 27, AA. 3, 4, 5). Hence the term *Word*, according as we use the term strictly of God, is to be taken as said not essentially, but personally.

REPLY OBJ. 1: The Arians, who sprang from Origen, declared that the Son differed in substance from the Father. Hence, they endeavored to maintain that when the Son of God is called the Word, this is not to be understood in a strict sense; lest the idea of the Word proceeding should compel them to confess that the Son of God is of the same substance as the Father. For the interior word proceeds in such a manner from the one who pronounces

dictum, quod ponatur verbum Dei proprie dictum. Non enim potest aliquid metaphorice verbum dici, nisi ratione manifestationis, quia vel manifestat sicut verbum, vel est verbo manifestatum. Si autem est manifestatum verbo, oportet ponere verbum quo manifestetur. Si autem dicitur verbum quia exterius manifestat, ea quae exterius manifestant, non dicuntur verba nisi inquantum significant interiorem mentis conceptum, quem aliquis etiam per exteriora signa manifestat. Etsi ergo verbum aliquando dicatur metaphorice in divinis, tamen oportet ponere verbum proprie dictum, quod personaliter dicatur.

AD SECUNDUM dicendum quod nihil eorum quae ad intellectum pertinent, personaliter dicitur in divinis, nisi solum verbum, solum enim verbum significat aliquid ab alio emanans. Id enim quod intellectus in concipiendo format, est verbum. Intellectus autem ipse, secundum quod est per speciem intelligibilem in actu, consideratur absolute. Et similiter intelligere, quod ita se habet ad intellectum in actu, sicut esse ad ens in actu, non enim intelligere significat actionem ab intelligente exeuntem, sed in intelligente manentem. Cum ergo dicitur quod verbum est notitia, non accipitur notitia pro actu intellectus cognoscentis, vel pro aliquo eius habitu, sed pro eo quod intellectus concipit cognoscendo. Unde et Augustinus dicit quod verbum est sapientia genita, quod nihil aliud est quam ipsa conceptio sapientis, quae etiam pari modo notitia genita dici potest. Et per eundem modum potest intelligi quod dicere Deo sit cogitando intueri, inquantum scilicet intuitu cogitationis divinae concipitur verbum Dei. Cogitationis tamen nomen Dei verbo proprie non convenit, dicit enim Augustinus, XV de Trin., *ita dicitur illud verbum Dei, ut cogitatio non dicatur; ne aliquid esse quasi volubile credatur in Deo, quod nunc accipiat formam ut verbum sit, eamque dimittere possit, atque informiter quodammodo volutari.* Cogitatio enim proprie in inquisitione veritatis consistit, quae in Deo locum non habet. Cum vero intellectus iam ad formam veritatis pertingit, non cogitat, sed perfecte veritatem contemplatur. Unde Anselmus improprie accipit cogitationem pro contemplatione.

AD TERTIUM dicendum quod, sicut, proprie loquendo, verbum dicitur personaliter in divinis et non essentialiter, ita et dicere. Unde, sicut verbum non est commune patri et filio et spiritui sancto, ita non est verum quod pater et filius et Spiritus Sanctus sint unus dicens. Unde Augustinus dicit, VII de Trin., *dicens illo coaeterno verbo non singulus intelligitur in divinis.* Sed dici convenit cuilibet personae, dicitur enim non solum verbum sed res quae verbo intelligitur vel significatur. Sic ergo uni soli personae in divinis convenit dici eo modo quo dicitur verbum, eo vero modo quo dicitur res in verbo intellecta, cuilibet personae convenit dici. Pater enim,

it, as to remain within him. But supposing Word to be said metaphorically of God, we must still admit Word in its strict sense. For if a thing be called a word metaphorically, this can only be by reason of some manifestation; either it makes something manifest as a word, or it is manifested by a word. If manifested by a word, there must exist a word whereby it is manifested. If it is called a word because it exteriorly manifests, what it exteriorly manifests cannot be called word except in as far as it signifies the interior concept of the mind, which anyone may also manifest by exterior signs. Therefore, although Word may be sometimes said of God metaphorically, nevertheless we must also admit Word in the proper sense, and which is said personally.

REPLY OBJ. 2: Nothing belonging to the intellect can be applied to God personally, except word alone; for word alone signifies that which emanates from another. For what the intellect forms in its conception is the word. Now, the intellect itself, according as it is made actual by the intelligible species, is considered absolutely; likewise the act of understanding which is to the actual intellect what existence is to actual being; since the act of understanding does not signify an act going out from the intelligent agent, but an act remaining in the agent. Therefore when we say that word is knowledge, the term knowledge does not mean the act of a knowing intellect, or any one of its habits, but stands for what the intellect conceives by knowing. Hence also Augustine says (*De Trin.* vii, 1) that the Word is *begotten wisdom*; for it is nothing but the concept of the Wise One; and in the same way It can be called *begotten knowledge*. Thus can also be explained how *to speak* is in God *to see by thought*, forasmuch as the Word is conceived by the gaze of the divine thought. Still the term *thought* does not properly apply to the Word of God. For Augustine says (*De Trin.* xv, 16): *Therefore do we speak of the Word of God, and not of the Thought of God, lest we believe that in God there is something unstable, now assuming the form of Word, now putting off that form and remaining latent and as it were formless.* For thought consists properly in the search after the truth, and this has no place in God. But when the intellect attains to the form of truth, it does not think, but perfectly contemplates the truth. Hence Anselm (*Monol.* lx) takes *thought* in an improper sense for *contemplation*.

REPLY OBJ. 3: As, properly speaking, Word in God is said personally, and not essentially, so likewise is to *speak*. Hence, as the Word is not common to the Father, Son, and Holy Spirit, so it is not true that the Father, Son, and Holy Spirit are one speaker. So Augustine says (*De Trin.* vii, 1): *He who speaks in that co-eternal Word is understood as not alone in God, but as being with that very Word, without which, forsooth, He would not be speaking.* On the other hand, *to be spoken* belongs to each Person, for not only is the word spoken, but also the thing understood or signified by the word. Therefore in this manner to one person alone in God does it belong to be spoken in the same way as a word

intelligendo se et filium et spiritum sanctum, et omnia alia quae eius scientia continentur, concipit verbum, ut sic tota Trinitas verbo dicatur, et etiam omnis creatura; sicut intellectus hominis verbo quod concipit intelligendo lapidem, lapidem dicit. Anselmus vero improprie accepit dicere pro intelligere. Quae tamen differunt. Nam intelligere importat solam habitudinem intelligentis ad rem intellectam; in qua nulla ratio originis importatur, sed solum informatio quaedam in intellectu nostro, prout intellectus noster fit in actu per formam rei intellectae. In Deo autem importat omnimodam identitatem, quia in Deo est omnino idem intellectus et intellectum, ut supra ostensum est. Sed dicere importat principaliter habitudinem ad verbum conceptum nihil enim est aliud dicere quam proferre verbum. Sed mediante verbo importat habitudinem ad rem intellectam, quae in verbo prolato manifestatur intelligenti. Et sic sola persona quae profert verbum, est dicens in divinis, cum tamen singula personarum sit intelligens et intellecta, et per consequens verbo dicta.

AD QUARTUM dicendum quod verbum sumitur ibi figurative, prout significatum vel effectus verbi dicitur verbum. Sic enim creaturae dicuntur facere verbum Dei, inquantum exequuntur effectum aliquem, ad quem ordinantur ex verbo concepto divinae sapientiae, sicut aliquis dicitur facere verbum regis, dum facit opus ad quod ex verbo regis instigatur.

is spoken; whereas in the way whereby a thing is spoken as being understood in the word, it belongs to each Person to be spoken. For the Father, by understanding Himself, the Son, and the Holy Spirit, and all other things comprised in this knowledge, conceives the Word; so that thus the whole Trinity is *spoken* in the Word; and likewise also all creatures: as the intellect of a man by the word he conceives in the act of understanding a stone, speaks a stone. Anselm took the term *speak* improperly for the act of understanding; whereas they really differ from each other; for *to understand* means only the habitude of the intelligent agent to the thing understood, in which habitude no trace of origin is conveyed, but only a certain information of our intellect; forasmuch as our intellect is made actual by the form of the thing understood. In God, however, it means complete identity, because in God the intellect and the thing understood are altogether the same, as was proved above (Q. 14, AA. 4, 5). Whereas to *speak* means chiefly the habitude to the word conceived; for *to speak* is nothing but to utter a word. But by means of the word it imports a habitude to the thing understood which in the word uttered is manifested to the one who understands. Thus, only the Person who utters the Word is *speaker* in God, although each Person understands and is understood, and consequently is spoken by the Word.

REPLY OBJ. 4: The term *word* is there taken figuratively, as the thing signified or effected by word is called word. For thus creatures are said to do the word of God, as executing any effect, whereto they are ordained from the word conceived of the divine wisdom; as anyone is said to do the word of the king when he does the work to which he is appointed by the king's word.

Article 2

Whether Word Is the Son's Proper Name?

AD SECUNDUM SIC PROCEDITUR. Videtur quod verbum non sit proprium nomen filii. Filius enim est persona subsistens in divinis. Sed verbum non significat rem subsistentem, ut in nobis patet. Ergo verbum non potest esse proprium nomen personae filii.

PRAETEREA, verbum prolatione quadam procedit a dicente. Si ergo filius est proprie verbum, non procedit a patre nisi per modum prolationis. Quod est haeresis Valentini, ut patet per Augustinum, in libro de haeresibus.

PRAETEREA, omne nomen proprium alicuius personae significat proprietatem aliquam eius. Si igitur verbum sit proprium nomen filii, significabit aliquam proprietatem eius. Et sic erunt plures proprietates in divinis quam supra enumeratae sunt.

OBJECTION 1: It would seem that *Word* is not the proper name of the Son. For the Son is a subsisting person in God. But word does not signify a subsisting thing, as appears in ourselves. Therefore word cannot be the proper name of the person of the Son.

OBJ. 2: Further, the word proceeds from the speaker by being uttered. Therefore if the Son is properly the word, He proceeds from the Father, by way only of utterance; which is the heresy of Valentine; as appears from Augustine (*De Haeres.* xi).

OBJ. 3: Further, every proper name of a person signifies some property of that person. Therefore, if the Word is the Son's proper name, it signifies some property of His; and thus there will be several more properties in God than those above mentioned.

PRAETEREA, quicumque intelligit, intelligendo concipit verbum. Sed filius intelligit. Ergo filii est aliquod verbum. Et sic non est proprium filii esse verbum.

PRAETEREA, Hebr. I dicitur de filio, *portans omnia verbo virtutis suae*, ex quo Basilius accipit quod Spiritus Sanctus sit verbum filii. Non est ergo proprium filii esse verbum.

SED CONTRA est quod Augustinus dicit, VI de Trin., *verbum solus filius accipitur.*

RESPONDEO dicendum quod verbum proprie dictum in divinis personaliter accipitur, et est proprium nomen personae filii. Significat enim quandam emanationem intellectus, persona autem quae procedit in divinis secundum emanationem intellectus, dicitur filius, et huiusmodi processio dicitur generatio, ut supra ostensum est. Unde relinquitur quod solus filius proprie dicatur verbum in divinis.

AD PRIMUM ergo dicendum quod in nobis non est idem esse et intelligere, unde illud quod habet in nobis esse intelligibile, non pertinet ad naturam nostram. Sed esse Dei est ipsum eius intelligere, unde verbum Dei non est aliquod accidens in ipso, vel aliquis effectus eius; sed pertinet ad ipsam naturam eius. Et ideo oportet quod sit aliquid subsistens, quia quidquid est in natura Dei, subsistit. Et ideo Damascenus dicit quod *verbum Dei est substantiale, et in hypostasi ens, reliqua vero verba*, scilicet nostra, *virtutes sunt animae.*

AD SECUNDUM dicendum quod non propter hoc error Valentini est damnatus, quia filium dixit prolatione natum, ut Ariani calumniabantur, sicut Hilarius refert, VI de Trin., sed propter varium modum prolationis quem posuit, sicut patet per Augustinum in libro de haeresibus.

AD TERTIUM dicendum quod in nomine verbi eadem proprietas importatur quae in nomine filii, unde dicit Augustinus, *eo dicitur verbum, quo filius.* Ipsa enim nativitas filii, quae est proprietas personalis eius, diversis nominibus significatur, quae filio attribuuntur ad exprimendum diversimode perfectionem eius. Nam ut ostendatur connaturalis patri, dicitur filius; ut ostendatur coaeternus, dicitur splendor; ut ostendatur omnino similis, dicitur imago; ut ostendatur immaterialiter genitus, dicitur verbum. Non autem potuit unum nomen inveniri, per quod omnia ista designarentur.

AD QUARTUM dicendum quod eo modo convenit filio esse intelligentem, quo convenit ei esse Deum, cum intelligere essentialiter dicatur in divinis, ut dictum est. Est autem filius Deus genitus, non autem generans Deus. Unde est quidem intelligens, non ut producens verbum, sed ut verbum procedens; prout scilicet in Deo verbum procedens secundum rem non differt ab intellectu divino, sed relatione sola distinguitur a principio verbi.

OBJ. 4: Further, whoever understands conceives a word in the act of understanding. But the Son understands. Therefore some word belongs to the Son; and consequently to be Word is not proper to the Son.

OBJ. 5: Further, it is said of the Son (Heb 1:3): *Bearing all things by the word of His power*; whence Basil infers (*Cont. Eunom.* v, 11) that the Holy Spirit is the Son's Word. Therefore to be Word is not proper to the Son.

ON THE CONTRARY, Augustine says (*De Trin.* vi, 11): *By Word we understand the Son alone.*

I ANSWER THAT, *Word*, said of God in its proper sense, is used personally, and is the proper name of the person of the Son. For it signifies an emanation of the intellect: and the person Who proceeds in God, by way of emanation of the intellect, is called the Son; and this procession is called generation, as we have shown above (Q. 27, A. 2). Hence it follows that the Son alone is properly called Word in God.

REPLY OBJ. 1: *To be* and *to understand* are not the same in us. Hence that which in us has intellectual being, does not belong to our nature. But in God *to be* and *to understand* are one and the same: hence the Word of God is not an accident in Him, or an effect of His; but belongs to His very nature. And therefore it must needs be something subsistent; for whatever is in the nature of God subsists; and so Damascene says (*De Fide Orth.* i, 18) that *the Word of God is substantial and has a hypostatic being; but other words are activities of the soul.*

REPLY OBJ. 2: The error of Valentine was condemned, not as the Arians pretended, because he asserted that the Son was born by being uttered, as Hilary relates (*De Trin.* vi); but on account of the different mode of utterance proposed by its author, as appears from Augustine (*De Haeres.* xi).

REPLY OBJ. 3: In the term *Word* the same property is comprised as in the name Son. Hence Augustine says (*De Trin.* vii, 11): *Word and Son express the same.* For the Son's nativity, which is His personal property, is signified by different names, which are attributed to the Son to express His perfection in various ways. To show that He is of the same nature as the Father, He is called the Son; to show that He is co-eternal, He is called the Splendor; to show that He is altogether like, He is called the Image; to show that He is begotten immaterially, He is called the Word. All these truths cannot be expressed by only one name.

REPLY OBJ. 4: To be intelligent belongs to the Son, in the same way as it belongs to Him to be God, since to understand is said of God essentially, as stated above (Q. 14, AA. 2, 4). Now the Son is God begotten, and not God begetting; and hence He is intelligent, not as producing a Word, but as the Word proceeding; forasmuch as in God the Word proceeding does not differ really from the divine intellect, but is distinguished from the principle of the Word only by relation.

AD QUINTUM dicendum quod, cum de filio dicitur, portans omnia verbo virtutis suae, verbum figurate accipitur pro effectu verbi. Unde Glossa ibi dicit quod verbum sumitur pro imperio; inquantum scilicet ex effectu virtutis verbi est quod res conserventur in esse, sicut ex effectu virtutis verbi est quod res producantur in esse. Quod vero Basilius interpretatur verbum pro spiritu sancto, improprie et figurate locutus est, prout verbum alicuius dici potest omne illud quod est manifestativum eius, ut sic ea ratione dicatur Spiritus Sanctus verbum filii, quia manifestat filium.

REPLY OBJ. 5: When it is said of the Son, *Bearing all things by the word of His power; word* is taken figuratively for the effect of the Word. Hence a gloss says that *word* is here taken to mean command; inasmuch as by the effect of the power of the Word, things are kept in being, as also by the effect of the power of the Word things are brought into being. Basil speaks widely and figuratively in applying Word to the Holy Spirit; in the sense perhaps that everything that makes a person known may be called his word, and so in that way the Holy Spirit may be called the Son's Word, because He manifests the Son.

Article 3

Whether the Name Word Imports Relation to Creatures?

AD TERTIUM SIC PROCEDITUR. Videtur quod in nomine verbi non importetur respectus ad creaturam. Omne enim nomen connotans effectum in creatura, essentialiter in divinis dicitur. Sed verbum non dicitur essentialiter, sed personaliter, ut dictum est. Ergo verbum non importat respectum ad creaturam.

PRAETEREA, quae important respectum ad creaturas, dicuntur de Deo ex tempore, ut dominus et creator. Sed verbum dicitur de Deo ab aeterno. Ergo non importat respectum ad creaturam.

PRAETEREA, verbum importat respectum ad id a quo procedit. Si ergo importat respectum ad creaturam, sequitur quod procedat a creatura.

PRAETEREA, ideae sunt plures secundum diversos respectus ad creaturas. Si igitur verbum importat respectum ad creaturas, sequitur quod in Deo non sit unum verbum tantum, sed plura.

PRAETEREA, si verbum importat respectum ad creaturam, hoc non est nisi inquantum creaturae cognoscuntur a Deo. Sed Deus non solum cognoscit entia, sed etiam non entia. Ergo in verbo importabitur respectus ad non entia, quod videtur falsum.

SED CONTRA est quod dicit Augustinus, in libro octoginta trium quaest., quod *in nomine verbi significatur non solum respectus ad patrem, sed etiam ad illa quae per verbum facta sunt operativa potentia.*

RESPONDEO dicendum quod in verbo importatur respectus ad creaturam. Deus enim, cognoscendo se, cognoscit omnem creaturam. Verbum autem in mente conceptum, est repraesentativum omnis eius quod actu intelligitur. Unde in nobis sunt diversa verba, secundum diversa quae intelligimus. Sed quia Deus uno actu et se et omnia intelligit, unicum verbum eius est expressivum non solum patris, sed etiam creaturarum.

OBJECTION 1: It would seem that the name 'Word' does not import relation to creatures. For every name that connotes some effect in creatures, is said of God essentially. But Word is not said essentially, but personally. Therefore Word does not import relation to creatures.

OBJ. 2: Further, whatever imports relation to creatures is said of God in time; as *Lord* and *Creator*. But Word is said of God from eternity. Therefore it does not import relation to the creature.

OBJ. 3: Further, Word imports relation to the source whence it proceeds. Therefore, if it imports relation to the creature, it follows that the Word proceeds from the creature.

OBJ. 4: Further, ideas (in God) are many according to their various relations to creatures. Therefore if Word imports relation to creatures, it follows that in God there is not one Word only, but many.

OBJ. 5: Further, if Word imports relation to the creature, this can only be because creatures are known by God. But God does not know beings only; He knows also nonbeings. Therefore in the Word are implied relations to nonbeings; which appears to be false.

ON THE CONTRARY, Augustine says (QQ. lxxxiii, qu. 63), that *the name Word signifies not only relation to the Father, but also relation to those beings which are made through the Word, by His operative power.*

I ANSWER THAT, Word implies relation to creatures. For God by knowing Himself, knows every creature. Now the word conceived in the mind is representative of everything that is actually understood. Hence there are in ourselves different words for the different things which we understand. But because God by one act understands Himself and all things, His one only Word is expressive not only of the Father, but of all creatures.

Et sicut Dei scientia Dei quidem est cognoscitiva tantum, creaturarum autem cognoscitiva et factiva; ita verbum Dei eius quod in Deo patre est, est expressivum tantum, creaturarum vero est expressivum et operativum. Et propter hoc dicitur in Psalmo XXXII, *dixit, et facta sunt*; quia in verbo importatur ratio factiva eorum quae Deus facit.

AD PRIMUM ergo dicendum quod in nomine personae includitur etiam natura oblique, nam persona est rationalis naturae individua substantia. In nomine igitur personae divinae, quantum ad relationem personalem, non importatur respectus ad creaturam, sed importatur in eo quod pertinet ad naturam. Nihil tamen prohibet, inquantum includitur in significatione eius essentia, quod importetur respectus ad creaturam, sicut enim proprium est filio quod sit filius, ita proprium est ei quod sit genitus Deus, vel genitus creator. Et per hunc modum importatur relatio ad creaturam in nomine verbi.

AD SECUNDUM dicendum quod, cum relationes consequantur actiones, quaedam nomina important relationem Dei ad creaturam, quae consequitur actionem Dei in exteriorem effectum transeuntem, sicut creare et gubernare, et talia dicuntur de Deo ex tempore. Quaedam vero relationem quae consequitur actionem non transeuntem in exteriorem effectum, sed manentem in agente, ut scire et velle, et talia non dicuntur de Deo ex tempore. Et huiusmodi relatio ad creaturam importatur in nomine verbi. Nec est verum quod nomina importantia relationem Dei ad creaturas, omnia dicantur ex tempore, sed sola illa nomina quae important relationem consequentem actionem Dei in exteriorem effectum transeuntem, ex tempore dicuntur.

AD TERTIUM dicendum quod creaturae non cognoscuntur a Deo per scientiam a creaturis acceptam, sed per essentiam suam. Unde non oportet quod a creaturis procedat verbum, licet verbum sit expressivum creaturarum.

AD QUARTUM dicendum quod nomen ideae principaliter est impositum ad significandum respectum ad creaturam, et ideo pluraliter dicitur in divinis, neque est personale. Sed nomen verbi principaliter impositum est ad significandam relationem ad dicentem, et ex consequenti ad creaturas, inquantum Deus, intelligendo se, intelligit omnem creaturam. Et propter hoc in divinis est unicum tantum verbum, et personaliter dictum.

AD QUINTUM dicendum quod eo modo quo scientia Dei est non entium, et verbum Dei est non entium, quia non est aliquid minus in verbo Dei quam in scientia Dei, ut Augustinus dicit. Sed tamen verbum est entium ut expressivum et factivum, non entium autem, ut expressivum et manifestativum.

And as the knowledge of God is only cognitive as regards God, whereas as regards creatures, it is both cognitive and operative, so the Word of God is only expressive of what is in God the Father, but is both expressive and operative of creatures; and therefore it is said (Ps 32:9): *He spake, and they were made*; because in the Word is implied the operative idea of what God makes.

REPLY OBJ. 1: The nature is also included indirectly in the name of the person; for person is an individual substance of a rational nature. Therefore the name of a divine person, as regards the personal relation, does not imply relation to the creature, but it is implied in what belongs to the nature. Yet there is nothing to prevent its implying relation to creatures, so far as the essence is included in its meaning: for as it properly belongs to the Son to be the Son, so it properly belongs to Him to be God begotten, or the Creator begotten; and in this way the name Word imports relation to creatures.

REPLY OBJ. 2: Since the relations result from actions, some names import the relation of God to creatures, which relation follows on the action of God which passes into some exterior effect, as to create and to govern; and the like are applied to God in time. But others import a relation which follows from an action which does not pass into an exterior effect, but abides in the agent—as to know and to will: such are not applied to God in time; and this kind of relation to creatures is implied in the name of the Word. Nor is it true that all names which import the relation of God to creatures are applied to Him in time; but only those names are applied in time which import relation following on the action of God passing into exterior effect.

REPLY OBJ. 3: Creatures are known to God not by a knowledge derived from the creatures themselves, but by His own essence. Hence it is not necessary that the Word should proceed from creatures, although the Word is expressive of creatures.

REPLY OBJ. 4: The name of Idea is imposed chiefly to signify relation to creatures; and therefore it is applied in a plural sense to God; and it is not said personally. But the name of Word is imposed chiefly to signify the speaker, and consequently, relation to creatures, inasmuch as God, by understanding Himself, understands every creature; and so there is only one Word in God, and that is a personal one.

REPLY OBJ. 5: God's knowledge of non-beings and God's Word about non-beings are the same; because the Word of God contains no less than does the knowledge of God, as Augustine says (*De Trin.* xv, 14). Nevertheless the Word is expressive and operative of beings, but is expressive and manifestive of non-beings.

QUESTION 35

IMAGE

Deinde quaeritur de imagine. Et circa hoc quaeruntur duo.

Primo, utrum imago in divinis dicatur personaliter.
Secundo, utrum sit proprium filii.

We next inquire concerning the image: about which there are two points of inquiry:

(1) Whether Image in God is said personally?
(2) Whether this name belongs to the Son alone?

Article 1

Whether Image in God Is Said Personally?

AD PRIMUM SIC PROCEDITUR. Videtur quod imago non dicatur personaliter in divinis. Dicit enim Augustinus, in libro de fide ad Petrum, *una est sanctae Trinitatis divinitas et imago, ad quam factus est homo*. Igitur imago dicitur essentialiter, et non personaliter.

PRAETEREA, Hilarius dicit, in libro de Synod., quod *imago est eius rei ad quam imaginatur, species indifferens*. Sed species, sive forma, in divinis dicitur essentialiter. Ergo et imago.

PRAETEREA, imago ab imitando dicitur, in quo importatur prius et posterius. Sed in divinis personis nihil est prius et posterius ergo imago non potest esse nomen personale in divinis.

SED CONTRA est quod dicit Augustinus, *quid est absurdius quam imaginem ad se dici?* Ergo imago in divinis relative dicitur. Et sic est nomen personale.

RESPONDEO dicendum quod de ratione imaginis est similitudo. Non tamen quaecumque similitudo sufficit ad rationem imaginis; sed similitudo quae est in specie rei, vel saltem in aliquo signo speciei. Signum autem speciei in rebus corporeis maxime videtur esse figura, videmus enim quod diversorum animalium secundum speciem, sunt diversae figurae, non autem diversi colores. Unde, si depingatur color alicuius rei in pariete, non dicitur esse imago, nisi depingatur figura. Sed neque ipsa similitudo speciei sufficit vel figurae; sed requiritur ad rationem imaginis origo, quia, ut Augustinus dicit in libro octoginta trium quaest., *unum ovum non est imago alterius, quia non est de illo expressum*. Ad hoc ergo quod vere aliquid sit imago, requiritur quod ex alio procedat simile ei in specie, vel saltem in signo speciei. Ea vero quae processionem sive originem important in divinis, sunt personalia. Unde hoc nomen imago est nomen personale.

AD PRIMUM ergo dicendum quod imago proprie dicitur quod procedit ad similitudinem alterius. Illud

OBJECTION 1: It would seem that image is not said personally of God. For Augustine (*Fulgentius, De Fide ad Petrum* i) says, *The Godhead of the Holy Trinity and the Image whereunto man is made are one*. Therefore Image is said of God essentially, and not personally.

OBJ. 2: Further, Hilary says (*De Synod.*): *An image is a like species of that which it represents*. But species or form is said of God essentially. Therefore so also is Image.

OBJ. 3: Further, Image is derived from imitation, which implies *before* and *after*. But in the divine persons there is no *before* and *after*. Therefore Image cannot be a personal name in God.

ON THE CONTRARY, Augustine says (*De Trin.* vii, 1): *What is more absurd than to say that an image is referred to itself?* Therefore the Image in God is a relation, and is thus a personal name.

I ANSWER THAT, Image includes the idea of similitude. Still, not any kind of similitude suffices for the notion of image, but only similitude of species, or at least of some specific sign. In corporeal things the specific sign consists chiefly in the figure. For we see that the species of different animals are of different figures; but not of different colors. Hence if the color of anything is depicted on a wall, this is not called an image unless the figure is likewise depicted. Further, neither the similitude of species or of figure is enough for an image, which requires also the idea of origin; because, as Augustine says (QQ. lxxxiii, qu. 74): *One egg is not the image of another, because it is not derived from it*. Therefore for a true image it is required that one proceeds from another like to it in species, or at least in specific sign. Now whatever imports procession or origin in God, belongs to the persons. Hence the name *Image* is a personal name.

REPLY OBJ. 1: Image, properly speaking, means whatever proceeds forth in likeness to another. That to the

autem ad cuius similitudinem aliquid procedit, proprie dicitur exemplar, improprie vero imago. Sic tamen Augustinus utitur nomine imaginis, cum dicit divinitatem sanctae Trinitatis esse imaginem ad quam factus est homo.

AD SECUNDUM dicendum quod species, prout ponitur ab Hilario in definitione imaginis, importat formam deductam in aliquo ab alio. Hoc enim modo imago dicitur esse species alicuius, sicuti id quod assimilatur alicui, dicitur forma eius, inquantum habet formam illi similem.

AD TERTIUM dicendum quod imitatio in divinis personis non significat posterioritatem, sed solam assimilationem.

likeness of which anything proceeds, is properly speaking called the exemplar, and is improperly called the image. Nevertheless Augustine uses the name of Image in this sense when he says that the divine nature of the Holy Trinity is the Image to whom man was made.

REPLY OBJ. 2: Species, as mentioned by Hilary in the definition of image, means the form derived from one thing to another. In this sense image is said to be the species of anything, as that which is assimilated to anything is called its form, inasmuch as it has a like form.

REPLY OBJ. 3: Imitation in God does not signify posteriority, but only assimilation.

Article 2

Whether the Name of Image Is Proper to the Son?

AD SECUNDUM SIC PROCEDITUR. Videtur quod nomen imaginis non sit proprium filio. Quia, ut dicit Damascenus, Spiritus Sanctus est imago filii. Non est ergo proprium filii.

PRAETEREA, de ratione imaginis est similitudo cum expressione, ut Augustinus dicit, in libro octoginta trium quaest. Sed hoc convenit spiritui sancto, procedit enim ab alio secundum modum similitudinis. Ergo Spiritus Sanctus est imago. Et ita non est proprium filii quod sit imago.

PRAETEREA, homo etiam dicitur imago Dei, secundum illud I ad Cor. XI, *vir non debet velare caput suum, quoniam imago et gloria Dei est.* Ergo non est proprium filio.

SED CONTRA est quod Augustinus dicit, VI de Trin., quod *solus filius est imago patris.*

RESPONDEO dicendum quod doctores Graecorum communiter dicunt spiritum sanctum esse imaginem patris et filii. Sed doctores Latini soli filio attribuunt nomen imaginis, non enim invenitur in canonica Scriptura nisi de filio. Dicitur enim Coloss. I, *qui est imago Dei invisibilis, primogenitus creaturae*; et ad Hebr. I, *qui cum sit splendor gloriae, et figura substantiae eius.*

Huius autem rationem assignant quidam ex hoc, quod filius convenit cum patre non solum in natura, sed etiam in notione principii, spiritus autem sanctus non convenit cum filio nec cum patre in aliqua notione. Sed hoc non videtur sufficere. Quia sicut secundum relationes non attenditur in divinis neque aequalitas neque inaequalitas, ut Augustinus dicit; ita neque similitudo, quae requiritur ad rationem imaginis. Unde alii dicunt quod Spiritus Sanctus non potest dici imago filii, quia

OBJECTION 1: It would seem that the name of Image is not proper to the Son; because, as Damascene says (*De Fide Orth.* i, 18), *The Holy Spirit is the Image of the Son.* Therefore Image does not belong to the Son alone.

OBJ. 2: Further, similitude in expression belongs to the nature of an image, as Augustine says (QQ. lxxxiii, qu. 74). But this belongs to the Holy Spirit, Who proceeds from another by way of similitude. Therefore the Holy Spirit is an Image; and so to be Image does not belong to the Son alone.

OBJ. 3: Further, man is also called the image of God, according to 1 Cor. 11:7, *The man ought not to cover his head, for he is the image and the glory of God.* Therefore Image is not proper to the Son.

ON THE CONTRARY, Augustine says (*De Trin.* vi, 2): *The Son alone is the Image of the Father.*

I ANSWER THAT, The Greek Doctors commonly say that the Holy Spirit is the Image of both the Father and of the Son; but the Latin Doctors attribute the name Image to the Son alone. For it is not found in the canonical Scripture except as applied to the Son; as in the words, *Who is the Image of the invisible God, the firstborn of creatures* (Col 1:15) and again: *Who being the brightness of His glory, and the figure of His substance* (Heb 1:3).

Some explain this by the fact that the Son agrees with the Father, not in nature only, but also in the notion of principle: whereas the Holy Spirit agrees neither with the Son, nor with the Father in any notion. This, however, does not seem to suffice. Because as it is not by reason of the relations that we consider either equality or inequality in God, as Augustine says (*De Trin.* v, 6), so neither (by reason thereof do we consider) that similitude which is essential to image. Hence others say that the Holy Spirit cannot be called the

imaginis non est imago. Neque etiam imago patris, quia etiam imago refertur immediate ad id cuius est imago; Spiritus Sanctus autem refertur ad patrem per filium. Neque etiam est imago patris et filii, quia sic esset una imago duorum, quod videtur impossibile. Unde relinquitur quod Spiritus Sanctus nullo modo sit imago. Sed hoc nihil est. Quia pater et filius sunt unum principium spiritus sancti, ut infra dicetur, unde nihil prohibet sic patris et filii, inquantum sunt unum, esse unam imaginem; cum etiam homo totius Trinitatis sit una imago.

Et ideo aliter dicendum est quod, sicut Spiritus Sanctus, quamvis sua processione accipiat naturam patris, sicut et filius, non tamen dicitur natus; ita, licet accipiat speciem similem patris, non dicitur imago. Quia filius procedit ut verbum, de cuius ratione est similitudo speciei ad id a quo procedit; non autem de ratione amoris; quamvis hoc conveniat amori qui est Spiritus Sanctus, inquantum est amor divinus.

AD PRIMUM ergo dicendum quod Damascenus et alii doctores Graecorum communiter utuntur nomine imaginis pro perfecta similitudine.

AD SECUNDUM dicendum quod, licet Spiritus Sanctus sit similis patri et filio, non tamen sequitur quod sit imago, ratione iam dicta.

AD TERTIUM dicendum quod imago alicuius dupliciter in aliquo invenitur. Uno modo, in re eiusdem naturae secundum speciem, ut imago regis invenitur in filio suo. Alio modo, in re alterius naturae, sicut imago regis invenitur in denario. Primo autem modo, filius est imago patris, secundo autem modo dicitur homo imago Dei. Et ideo ad designandam in homine imperfectionem imaginis, homo non solum dicitur imago, sed ad imaginem, per quod motus quidam tendentis in perfectionem designatur. Sed de filio Dei non potest dici quod sit ad imaginem, quia est perfecta patris imago.

Image of the Son, because there cannot be an image of an image; nor of the Father, because again the image must be immediately related to that which it is the image; and the Holy Spirit is related to the Father through the Son; nor again is He the Image of the Father and the Son, because then there would be one image of two; which is impossible. Hence it follows that the Holy Spirit is in no way an Image. But this is no proof: for the Father and the Son are one principle of the Holy Spirit, as we shall explain further on (Q. 36, A. 4). Hence there is nothing to prevent there being one Image of the Father and of the Son, inasmuch as they are one; since even man is one image of the whole Trinity.

Therefore we must explain the matter otherwise by saying that, as the Holy Spirit, although by His procession He receives the nature of the Father, as the Son also receives it, nevertheless is not said to be *born*; so, although He receives the likeness of the Father, He is not called the Image; because the Son proceeds as word, and it is essential to word to be like species with that whence it proceeds; whereas this does not essentially belong to love, although it may belong to that love which is the Holy Spirit, inasmuch as He is the divine love.

REPLY OBJ. 1: Damascene and the other Greek Doctors commonly employ the term image as meaning a perfect similitude.

REPLY OBJ. 2: Although the Holy Spirit is like to the Father and the Son, still it does not follow that He is the Image, as above explained.

REPLY OBJ. 3: The image of a thing may be found in something in two ways. In one way it is found in something of the same specific nature; as the image of the king is found in his son. In another way it is found in something of a different nature, as the king's image on the coin. In the first sense the Son is the Image of the Father; in the second sense man is called the image of God; and therefore in order to express the imperfect character of the divine image in man, man is not simply called the image, but *to the image*, whereby is expressed a certain movement of tendency to perfection. But it cannot be said that the Son of God is *to the image*, because He is the perfect Image of the Father.

QUESTION 36

THE PERSON OF THE HOLY SPIRIT

Post haec considerandum est de his quae pertinent ad personam spiritus sancti. Qui quidem non solum dicitur Spiritus Sanctus, sed etiam amor et donum Dei.

Circa nomen ergo spiritus sancti quaeruntur quatuor.

Primo, utrum hoc nomen Spiritus Sanctus sit proprium alicuius divinae personae.

Secundo, utrum illa persona divina quae Spiritus Sanctus dicitur, procedat a patre et filio.

Tertio, utrum procedat a patre per filium.

Quarto, utrum pater et filius sint unum principium spiritus sancti.

We proceed to treat of what belongs to the person of the Holy Spirit, Who is called not only the Holy Spirit, but also the Love and Gift of God.

Concerning the name *Holy Spirit* there are four points of inquiry:

(1) Whether this name, *Holy Spirit*, is the proper name of one divine Person?

(2) Whether that divine person Who is called the Holy Spirit, proceeds from the Father and the Son?

(3) Whether He proceeds from the Father through the Son?

(4) Whether the Father and the Son are one principle of the Holy Spirit?

Article 1

Whether This Name Holy Spirit Is the Proper Name of One Divine Person?

AD PRIMUM SIC PROCEDITUR. Videtur quod hoc nomen Spiritus Sanctus non sit proprium nomen alicuius divinae personae. Nullum enim nomen commune tribus personis, est proprium alicuius personae. Sed hoc nomen Spiritus Sanctus est commune tribus personis. Ostendit enim Hilarius, VIII de Trin., in spiritu Dei aliquando significari patrem, ut cum dicitur, *spiritus domini super me*; aliquando significari filium, ut cum dicit filius, *in spiritu Dei eiicio Daemonia*, naturae suae potestate eiicere se Daemonia demonstrans; aliquando spiritum sanctum, ut ibi, *effundam de spiritu meo super omnem carnem*. Ergo hoc nomen Spiritus Sanctus non est proprium alicuius divinae personae.

PRAETEREA, nomina divinarum personarum ad aliquid dicuntur, ut Boetius dicit, in libro de Trin. Sed hoc nomen Spiritus Sanctus non dicitur ad aliquid. Ergo hoc nomen non est proprium divinae personae.

PRAETEREA, quia filius est nomen alicuius divinae personae, non potest dici filius huius vel illius. Dicitur autem spiritus huius vel illius hominis. Ut enim habetur Num. XI, *dixit dominus ad Moysen, auferam de spiritu tuo, tradamque eis*; et IV Reg. II, *requievit spiritus Eliae super Elisaeum*. Ergo Spiritus Sanctus non videtur esse proprium nomen alicuius divinae personae.

SED CONTRA est quod dicitur I Ioan. ult., *tres sunt qui testimonium dant in caelo, pater, verbum et Spiritus Sanctus*. Ut autem Augustinus dicit, VII de Trin., *cum*

OBJECTION 1: It would seem that this name, *Holy Spirit*, is not the proper name of one divine person. For no name which is common to the three persons is the proper name of any one person. But this name of *Holy Spirit* is common to the three persons; for Hilary (*De Trin.* viii) shows that the *Spirit of God* sometimes means the Father, as in the words of Isa. 61:1: *The Spirit of the Lord is upon me*; and sometimes the Son, as when the Son says: *In the Spirit of God I cast out devils* (Matt 12:28), showing that He cast out devils by His own natural power; and that sometimes it means the Holy Spirit, as in the words of Joel 2:28: *I will pour out of My Spirit over all flesh*. Therefore this name *Holy Spirit* is not the proper name of a divine person.

OBJ. 2: Further, the names of the divine persons are relative terms, as Boethius says (*De Trin.*). But this name *Holy Spirit* is not a relative term. Therefore this name is not the proper name of a divine Person.

OBJ. 3: Further, because the Son is the name of a divine Person He cannot be called the Son of this or of that. But the spirit is spoken of as of this or that man, as appears in the words, *The Lord said to Moses, I will take of thy spirit and will give to them* (Num 11:17) and also *The Spirit of Elias rested upon Eliseus* (4 Kgs 2:15). Therefore *Holy Spirit* does not seem to be the proper name of a divine Person.

ON THE CONTRARY, It is said (1 John 5:7): *There are three who bear witness in heaven, the Father, the Word, and the Holy Spirit*. As Augustine says (*De Trin.* vii, 4): *When we*

quaeritur, quid tres? Dicimus, tres personae. Ergo Spiritus Sanctus est nomen divinae personae.

Respondeo dicendum quod, cum sint duae processiones in divinis, altera earum, quae est per modum amoris, non habet proprium nomen, ut supra dictum est. Unde et relationes quae secundum huiusmodi processionem accipiuntur, innominatae sunt, ut etiam supra dictum est. Propter quod et nomen personae hoc modo procedentis, eadem ratione, non habet proprium nomen. Sed sicut sunt accommodata aliqua nomina, ex usu loquentium, ad significandum praedictas relationes, cum nominamus eas nomine processionis et spirationis, quae, secundum proprietatem significationis, magis videntur significare actus notionales quam relationes; ita ad significandum divinam personam quae procedit per modum amoris, accommodatum est, ex usu Scripturae, hoc nomen Spiritus Sanctus. Et huius quidem convenientiae ratio sumi potest ex duobus. Primo quidem, ex ipsa communitate eius quod dicitur Spiritus Sanctus. Ut enim Augustinus dicit, XV de Trin., *quia Spiritus Sanctus communis est ambobus, id vocatur ipse proprie quod ambo communiter, nam et pater est spiritus, et filius est spiritus; et pater est sanctus, et filius est sanctus.* Secundo vero, ex propria significatione. Nam nomen spiritus, in rebus corporeis, impulsionem quandam et motionem significare videtur, nam flatum et ventum spiritum nominamus. Est autem proprium amoris, quod moveat et impellat voluntatem amantis in amatum. Sanctitas vero illis rebus attribuitur, quae in Deum ordinantur. Quia igitur persona divina procedit per modum amoris quo Deus amatur, convenienter Spiritus Sanctus nominatur.

Ad primum ergo dicendum quod hoc quod dico Spiritus Sanctus, prout sumitur in virtute duarum dictionum, commune est toti Trinitati. Quia nomine spiritus significatur immaterialitas divinae substantiae, spiritus enim corporeus invisibilis est, et parum habet de materia; unde omnibus substantiis immaterialibus et invisibilibus hoc nomen attribuimus. Per hoc vero quod dicitur sanctus, significatur puritas divinae bonitatis. Si autem accipiatur hoc quod dico Spiritus Sanctus, in vi unius dictionis, sic ex usu Ecclesiae est accommodatum ad significandam unam trium personarum, scilicet quae procedit per modum amoris, ratione iam dicta.

Ad secundum dicendum quod, licet hoc quod dico Spiritus Sanctus, relative non dicatur, tamen pro relativo ponitur, inquantum est accommodatum ad significandam personam sola relatione ab aliis distinctam. Potest tamen intelligi etiam in nomine aliqua relatio, si spiritus intelligatur quasi spiratus.

Ad tertium dicendum quod in nomine filii intelligitur sola relatio eius qui est a principio, ad principium, sed in nomine patris intelligitur relatio principii; et similiter in nomine spiritus, prout importat quandam vim motivam. Nulli autem creaturae competit

ask, Three what? we say, *Three persons.* Therefore the Holy Spirit is the name of a divine person.

I **answer that,** While there are two processions in God, one of these, the procession of love, has no proper name of its own, as stated above (Q. 27, A. 4, ad 3). Hence the relations also which follow from this procession are without a name (Q. 28, A. 4): for which reason the Person proceeding in that manner has not a proper name. But as some names are accommodated by the usual mode of speaking to signify the aforesaid relations, as when we use the names of procession and spiration, which in the strict sense more fittingly signify the notional acts than the relations; so to signify the divine Person, Who proceeds by way of love, this name *Holy Spirit* is by the use of scriptural speech accommodated to Him. The appropriateness of this name may be shown in two ways. First, from the fact that the person who is called *Holy Spirit* has something in common with the other Persons. For, as Augustine says (*De Trin.* xv, 17; v, 11), *Because the Holy Spirit is common to both, He Himself is called that properly which both are called in common. For the Father also is a spirit, and the Son is a spirit; and the Father is holy, and the Son is holy.* Second, from the proper signification of the name. For the name spirit in things corporeal seems to signify impulse and motion; for we call the breath and the wind by the term spirit. Now it is a property of love to move and impel the will of the lover towards the object loved. Further, holiness is attributed to whatever is ordered to God. Therefore because the divine person proceeds by way of the love whereby God is loved, that person is most properly named *The Holy Spirit.*

Reply Obj. 1: The expression Holy Spirit, if taken as two words, is applicable to the whole Trinity: because by 'spirit' the immateriality of the divine substance is signified; for corporeal spirit is invisible, and has but little matter; hence we apply this term to all immaterial and invisible substances. And by adding the word *holy* we signify the purity of divine goodness. But if Holy Spirit be taken as one word, it is thus that the expression, in the usage of the Church, is accommodated to signify one of the three persons, the one who proceeds by way of love, for the reason above explained.

Reply Obj. 2: Although this name *Holy Spirit* does not indicate a relation, still it takes the place of a relative term, inasmuch as it is accommodated to signify a Person distinct from the others by relation only. Yet this name may be understood as including a relation, if we understand the Holy Spirit as being breathed.

Reply Obj. 3: In the name Son we understand that relation only which is of something from a principle, in regard to that principle: but in the name *Father* we understand the relation of principle; and likewise in the name of Spirit inasmuch as it implies a moving power. But to no creature

esse principium respectu alicuius divinae personae, sed e converso. Et ideo potest dici pater noster, et spiritus noster, non tamen potest dici filius noster.

does it belong to be a principle as regards a divine person; but rather the reverse. Therefore we can say *our Father*, and *our Spirit*; but we cannot say *our Son*.

Article 2

Whether the Holy Spirit Proceeds from the Son?

Ad secundum sic proceditur. Videtur quod Spiritus Sanctus non procedat a filio. Quia secundum Dionysium, *non est audendum dicere aliquid de substantiali divinitate, praeter ea quae divinitus nobis ex sacris eloquiis sunt expressa.* Sed in Scriptura sacra non exprimitur quod Spiritus Sanctus a filio procedat, sed solum quod procedat a patre; ut patet Ioann. XV, *spiritum veritatis, qui a patre procedit.* Ergo Spiritus Sanctus non procedit a filio.

Praeterea, in symbolo Constantinopolitanae synodi sic legitur, *credimus in spiritum sanctum, dominum et vivificantem, ex patre procedentem, cum patre et filio adorandum et glorificandum.* Nullo igitur modo debuit addi in symbolo nostro quod Spiritus Sanctus procedat a filio, sed videntur esse anathematis rei, qui hoc addiderunt.

Praeterea, Damascenus dicit, *spiritum sanctum ex patre dicimus, et spiritum patris nominamus, ex filio autem spiritum sanctum non dicimus, spiritum vero filii nominamus.* Ergo Spiritus Sanctus non procedit a filio.

Praeterea, nihil procedit ab eo in quo quiescit. Sed Spiritus Sanctus quiescit in filio. Dicitur enim in legenda beati Andreae, *pax vobis, et universis qui credunt in unum Deum patrem, et in unum filium eius, unicum dominum nostrum Iesum Christum, et in unum spiritum sanctum, procedentem ex patre, et in filio permanentem.* Ergo Spiritus Sanctus non procedit a filio.

Praeterea, filius procedit ut verbum. Sed spiritus noster in nobis non videtur procedere a verbo nostro. Ergo nec Spiritus Sanctus procedit a filio.

Praeterea, Spiritus Sanctus perfecte procedit a patre. Ergo superfluum est dicere quod procedit a filio.

Praeterea, *in perpetuis non differt esse et posse,* ut dicitur in III Physic.; et multo minus in divinis. Sed Spiritus Sanctus potest distingui a filio, etiam si ab eo non procedat. Dicit enim Anselmus, in libro de processione spiritus sancti, *habent utique a patre esse filius et Spiritus Sanctus, sed diverso modo, quia alter nascendo, et alter procedendo, ut alii sint per hoc ab invicem.* Et postea subdit, *nam si per aliud non essent plures filius et Spiritus*

Objection 1: It would seem that the Holy Spirit does not proceed from the Son. For as Dionysius says (*Div. Nom.* i): *We must not dare to say anything concerning the substantial Divinity except what has been divinely expressed to us by the sacred oracles.* But in the Sacred Scripture we are not told that the Holy Spirit proceeds from the Son; but only that He proceeds from the Father, as appears from John 15:26: *The Spirit of truth, Who proceeds from the Father.* Therefore the Holy Spirit does not proceed from the Son.

Obj. 2: Further, in the creed of the council of Constantinople (*Can.* vii) we read: *We believe in the Holy Spirit, the Lord and Life-giver, who proceeds from the Father; with the Father and the Son to be adored and glorified.* Therefore it should not be added in our Creed that the Holy Spirit proceeds from the Son; and those who added such a thing appear to be worthy of anathema.

Obj. 3: Further, Damascene says (*De Fide Orth.* i): *We say that the Holy Spirit is from the Father, and we name Him the spirit of the Father; but we do not say that the Holy Spirit is from the Son, yet we name Him the Spirit of the Son.* Therefore the Holy Spirit does not proceed from the Son.

Obj. 4: Further, nothing proceeds from that wherein it rests. But the Holy Spirit rests in the Son; for it is said in the legend of St. Andrew: *Peace be to you and to all who believe in the one God the Father, and in His only Son our Lord Jesus Christ, and in the one Holy Spirit proceeding from the Father, and abiding in the Son.* Therefore the Holy Spirit does not proceed from the Son.

Obj. 5: Further, the Son proceeds as the Word. But our breath does not seem to proceed in ourselves from our word. Therefore the Holy Spirit does not proceed from the Son.

Obj. 6: Further, the Holy Spirit proceeds perfectly from the Father. Therefore it is superfluous to say that He proceeds from the Son.

Obj. 7: Further *the actual and the possible do not differ in things perpetual* (*Phys.* iii, 32), and much less so in God. But it is possible for the Holy Spirit to be distinguished from the Son, even if He did not proceed from Him. For Anselm says (*De Process. Spir. Sancti,* ii): *The Son and the Holy Spirit have their Being from the Father; but each in a different way; one by Birth, the other by Procession, so that they are thus distinct from one another.* And further on he says: *For even*

Sanctus, per hoc solum essent diversi. Ergo Spiritus Sanctus distinguitur a filio, ab eo non existens.

SED CONTRA est quod dicit Athanasius, *Spiritus Sanctus a patre et filio, non factus, nec creatus, nec genitus, sed procedens.*

RESPONDEO dicendum quod necesse est dicere spiritum sanctum a filio esse. Si enim non esset ab eo, nullo modo posset ab eo personaliter distingui. Quod ex supra dictis patet. Non enim est possibile dicere quod secundum aliquid absolutum divinae personae ab invicem distinguantur, quia sequeretur quod non esset trium una essentia; quidquid enim in divinis absolute dicitur, ad unitatem essentiae pertinet. Relinquitur ergo quod solum relationibus divinae personae ab invicem distinguantur. Relationes autem personas distinguere non possunt, nisi secundum quod sunt oppositae. Quod ex hoc patet, quia pater habet duas relationes, quarum una refertur ad filium, et alia ad spiritum sanctum; quae tamen, quia non sunt oppositae, non constituunt duas personas, sed ad unam personam patris tantum pertinent. Si ergo in filio et in spiritu sancto non esset invenire nisi duas relationes quibus uterque refertur ad patrem, illae relationes non essent ad invicem oppositae; sicut neque duae relationes quibus pater refertur ad illos. Unde, sicut persona patris est una, ita sequeretur quod persona filii et spiritus sancti esset una, habens duas relationes oppositas duabus relationibus patris. Hoc autem est haereticum, cum tollat fidem Trinitatis. Oportet ergo quod filius et Spiritus Sanctus ad invicem referantur oppositis relationibus. Non autem possunt esse in divinis aliae relationes oppositae nisi relationes originis, ut supra probatum est. Oppositae autem relationes originis accipiuntur secundum principium, et secundum quod est a principio. Relinquitur ergo quod necesse est dicere vel filium esse a spiritu sancto, quod nullus dicit, vel spiritum sanctum esse a filio, quod nos confitemur.

Et huic quidem consonat ratio processionis utriusque. Dictum enim est supra quod filius procedit per modum intellectus, ut verbum; Spiritus Sanctus autem per modum voluntatis, ut amor. Necesse est autem quod amor a verbo procedat, non enim aliquid amamus, nisi secundum quod conceptione mentis apprehendimus. Unde et secundum hoc manifestum est quod Spiritus Sanctus procedit a filio.

Ipse etiam ordo rerum hoc docet. Nusquam enim hoc invenimus, quod ab uno procedant plura absque ordine, nisi in illis solum quae materialiter differunt; sicut unus faber producit multos cultellos materialiter ab invicem distinctos, nullum ordinem habentes ad invicem. Sed in rebus in quibus non est sola materialis distinctio,

if for no other reason were the Son and the Holy Spirit distinct, this alone would suffice. Therefore the Holy Spirit is distinct from the Son, without proceeding from Him.

ON THE CONTRARY, Athanasius says: *The Holy Spirit is from the Father and the Son; not made, nor created, nor begotten, but proceeding.*

I ANSWER THAT, It must be said that the Holy Spirit is from the Son. For if He were not from Him, He could in no wise be personally distinguished from Him; as appears from what has been said above (Q. 28, A. 3; Q. 30, A. 2). For it cannot be said that the divine Persons are distinguished from each other in any absolute sense; for it would follow that there would not be one essence of the three persons: since everything that is spoken of God in an absolute sense, belongs to the unity of essence. Therefore it must be said that the divine persons are distinguished from each other only by the relations. Now the relations cannot distinguish the persons except forasmuch as they are opposite relations; which appears from the fact that the Father has two relations, by one of which He is related to the Son, and by the other to the Holy Spirit; but these are not opposite relations, and therefore they do not make two persons, but belong only to the one person of the Father. If therefore in the Son and the Holy Spirit there were two relations only, whereby each of them were related to the Father, these relations would not be opposite to each other, as neither would be the two relations whereby the Father is related to them. Hence, as the person of the Father is one, it would follow that the person of the Son and of the Holy Spirit would be one, having two relations opposed to the two relations of the Father. But this is heretical since it destroys the Faith in the Trinity. Therefore the Son and the Holy Spirit must be related to each other by opposite relations. Now there cannot be in God any relations opposed to each other, except relations of origin, as proved above (Q. 28, A. 4). And opposite relations of origin are to be understood as of a *principle*, and of what is *from the principle*. Therefore we must conclude that it is necessary to say that either the Son is from the Holy Spirit; which no one says; or that the Holy Spirit is from the Son, as we confess.

Furthermore, the order of the procession of each one agrees with this conclusion. For it was said above (Q. 27, AA. 2, 4; Q. 28, A. 4), that the Son proceeds by the way of the intellect as Word, and the Holy Spirit by way of the will as Love. Now love must proceed from a word. For we do not love anything unless we apprehend it by a mental conception. Hence also in this way it is manifest that the Holy Spirit proceeds from the Son.

We derive a knowledge of the same truth from the very order of nature itself. For we nowhere find that several things proceed from one without order except in those which differ only by their matter; as for instance one smith produces many knives distinct from each other materially, with no order to each other; whereas in things in which

semper invenitur in multitudine productorum aliquis ordo. Unde etiam in ordine creaturarum productarum, decor divinae sapientiae manifestatur. Si ergo ab una persona patris procedunt duae personae, scilicet filius et Spiritus Sanctus, oportet esse aliquem ordinem eorum ad invicem. Nec potest aliquis ordo alius assignari, nisi ordo naturae, quo alius est ex alio. Non est igitur possibile dicere quod filius et Spiritus Sanctus sic procedant a patre, quod neuter eorum procedat ab alio, nisi quis poneret in eis materialem distinctionem, quod est impossibile.

Unde etiam ipsi Graeci processionem spiritus sancti aliquem ordinem habere ad filium intelligunt. Concedunt enim spiritum sanctum esse spiritum filii, et esse a patre per filium. Et quidam eorum dicuntur concedere quod sit a filio, vel profluat ab eo, non tamen quod procedat. Quod videtur vel ex ignorantia, vel ex protervia esse. Quia si quis recte consideret, inveniet processionis verbum inter omnia quae ad originem qualemcumque pertinent, communissimum esse. Utimur enim eo ad designandum qualemcumque originem; sicut quod linea procedit a puncto, radius a sole, rivus a fonte; et similiter in quibuscumque aliis. Unde ex quocumque alio ad originem pertinente, potest concludi quod Spiritus Sanctus procedit a filio.

AD PRIMUM ergo dicendum quod de Deo dicere non debemus quod in sacra Scriptura non invenitur vel per verba, vel per sensum. Licet autem per verba non inveniatur in sacra Scriptura quod Spiritus Sanctus procedit a filio, invenitur tamen quantum ad sensum; et praecipue ubi dicit filius, Ioan. XVI, de spiritu sancto loquens, *ille me clarificabit, quia de meo accipiet.* Regulariter etiam in sacra Scriptura tenendum est, quod id quod de patre dicitur, oportet de filio intelligi, etiam si dictio exclusiva addatur, nisi solum in illis in quibus pater et filius secundum oppositas relationes distinguuntur. Cum enim dominus, Matth. XI, dicit, *nemo novit filium nisi pater,* non excluditur quin filius seipsum cognoscat. Sic igitur cum dicitur quod Spiritus Sanctus a patre procedit, etiam si adderetur quod a solo patre procedit, non excluderetur inde filius, quia quantum ad hoc quod est esse principium spiritus sancti, non opponuntur pater et filius; sed solum quantum ad hoc, quod hic est pater et ille filius.

AD SECUNDUM dicendum quod in quolibet Concilio institutum fuit symbolum aliquod, propter errorem aliquem qui in Concilio damnabatur. Unde sequens Concilium non faciebat aliud symbolum quam primum, sed id quod implicite continebatur in primo symbolo, per aliqua addita explanabatur contra haereses insurgentes. Unde in determinatione Chalcedonensis synodi dicitur, quod illi qui fuerunt congregati in Concilio

there is not only a material distinction we always find that some order exists in the multitude produced. Hence also in the order of creatures produced, the beauty of the divine wisdom is displayed. So if from the one Person of the Father, two persons proceed, the Son and the Holy Spirit, there must be some order between them. Nor can any other be assigned except the order of their nature, whereby one is from the other. Therefore it cannot be said that the Son and the Holy Spirit proceed from the Father in such a way as that neither of them proceeds from the other, unless we admit in them a material distinction; which is impossible.

Hence also the Greeks themselves recognize that the procession of the Holy Spirit has some order to the Son. For they grant that the Holy Spirit is the Spirit *of the Son*; and that He is from the Father *through the Son*. Some of them are said also to concede that *He is from the Son*; or that *He flows from the Son*, but not that He proceeds; which seems to come from ignorance or obstinacy. For a just consideration of the truth will convince anyone that the word procession is the one most commonly applied to all that denotes origin of any kind. For we use the term to describe any kind of origin; as when we say that a line proceeds from a point, a ray from the sun, a stream from a source, and likewise in everything else. Hence, granted that the Holy Spirit originates in any way from the Son, we can conclude that the Holy Spirit proceeds from the Son.

REPLY OBJ. 1: We ought not to say about God anything which is not found in Holy Scripture either explicitly or implicitly. But although we do not find it verbally expressed in Holy Scripture that the Holy Spirit proceeds from the Son, still we do find it in the sense of Scripture, especially where the Son says, speaking of the Holy Spirit, *He will glorify Me, because He shall receive of Mine* (John 16:14). It is also a rule of Holy Scripture that whatever is said of the Father, applies to the Son, although there be added an exclusive term; except only as regards what belongs to the opposite relations, whereby the Father and the Son are distinguished from each other. For when the Lord says, *No one knoweth the Son, but the Father*, the idea of the Son knowing Himself is not excluded. So therefore when we say that the Holy Spirit proceeds from the Father, even though it be added that He proceeds from the Father alone, the Son would not thereby be at all excluded; because as regards being the principle of the Holy Spirit, the Father and the Son are not opposed to each other, but only as regards the fact that one is the Father, and the other is the Son.

REPLY OBJ. 2: In every council of the Church a symbol of faith has been drawn up to meet some prevalent error condemned in the council at that time. Hence subsequent councils are not to be described as making a new symbol of faith; but what was implicitly contained in the first symbol was explained by some addition directed against rising heresies. Hence in the decision of the council of Chalcedon it is declared that those who were congregated together in

Constantinopolitano, doctrinam de spiritu sancto tradiderunt, non quod minus esset in praecedentibus (qui apud Nicaeam congregati sunt), inferentes; *sed intellectum eorum adversus haereticos declarantes.* Quia igitur in tempore antiquorum Conciliorum nondum exortus fuerat error dicentium spiritum sanctum non procedere a filio; non fuit necessarium quod hoc explicite poneretur. Sed postea, insurgente errore quorundam, in quodam Concilio in Occidentalibus partibus congregato, expressum fuit auctoritate Romani pontificis; cuius auctoritate etiam antiqua Concilia congregabantur et confirmabantur. Continebatur tamen implicite in hoc ipso quod dicebatur Spiritus Sanctus a patre procedere.

AD TERTIUM dicendum quod spiritum sanctum non procedere a filio, primo fuit a Nestorianis introductum; ut patet in quodam symbolo Nestorianorum damnato in Ephesina synodo. Et hunc errorem secutus fuit Theodoretus Nestorianus, et plures post ipsum; inter quos fuit etiam Damascenus. Unde in hoc eius sententiae non est standum. Quamvis a quibusdam dicatur quod Damascenus, sicut non confitetur spiritum sanctum esse a filio, ita etiam non negat, ex vi illorum verborum.

AD QUARTUM dicendum quod per hoc quod Spiritus Sanctus dicitur quiescere vel manere in filio, non excluditur quin ab eo procedat, quia et filius in patre manere dicitur, cum tamen a patre procedat. Dicitur etiam Spiritus Sanctus in filio quiescere, vel sicut amor amantis quiescit in amato; vel quantum ad humanam naturam Christi, propter id quod scriptum est, Ioan. I, *super quem videris spiritum descendentem, et manentem super eum, hic est qui baptizat.*

AD QUINTUM dicendum quod verbum in divinis non accipitur secundum similitudinem verbi vocalis, a quo non procedit spiritus, quia sic tantum metaphorice diceretur, sed secundum similitudinem verbi mentalis, a quo amor procedit.

AD SEXTUM dicendum quod per hoc quod Spiritus Sanctus perfecte procedit a patre, non solum non superfluum est dicere quod Spiritus Sanctus procedat a filio; sed omnino necessarium. Quia una virtus est patris et filii; et quidquid est a patre, necesse est esse a filio, nisi proprietati filiationis repugnet. Non enim filius est a seipso, licet sit a patre.

AD SEPTIMUM dicendum quod Spiritus Sanctus distinguitur personaliter a filio in hoc, quod origo unius distinguitur ab origine alterius. Sed ipsa differentia originis est per hoc, quod filius est solum a patre, Spiritus Sanctus vero a patre et filio. Non enim aliter processiones distinguerentur, sicut supra ostensum est.

the council of Constantinople, handed down the doctrine about the Holy Spirit, not implying that there was anything wanting in the doctrine of their predecessors who had gathered together at Nicaea, but explaining what those fathers had understood of the matter. Therefore, because at the time of the ancient councils the error of those who said that the Holy Spirit did not proceed from the Son had not arisen, it was not necessary to make any explicit declaration on that point; whereas, later on, when certain errors rose up, in another council assembled in the west, the matter was explicitly defined by the authority of the Roman Pontiff, by whose authority also the ancient councils were summoned and confirmed. Nevertheless the truth was contained implicitly in the belief that the Holy Spirit proceeds from the Father.

REPLY OBJ. 3: The Nestorians were the first to introduce the error that the Holy Spirit did not proceed from the Son, as appears in a Nestorian creed condemned in the council of Ephesus. This error was embraced by Theodoric the Nestorian, and several others after him, among whom was also Damascene. Hence, in that point his opinion is not to be held. Although, too, it has been asserted by some that while Damascene did not confess that the Holy Spirit was from the Son, neither do those words of his express a denial thereof.

REPLY OBJ. 4: When the Holy Spirit is said to rest or abide in the Son, it does not mean that He does not proceed from Him; for the Son also is said to abide in the Father, although He proceeds from the Father. Also the Holy Spirit is said to rest in the Son as the love of the lover abides in the beloved; or in reference to the human nature of Christ, by reason of what is written: *On whom thou shalt see the Spirit descending and remaining upon Him, He it is who baptizes* (John 1:33).

REPLY OBJ. 5: The Word in God is not taken after the similitude of the vocal word, whence the breath does not proceed; for it would then be only metaphorical; but after the similitude of the mental word, whence proceeds love.

REPLY OBJ. 6: For the reason that the Holy Spirit proceeds from the Father perfectly, not only is it not superfluous to say He proceeds from the Son, but rather it is absolutely necessary. Forasmuch as one power belongs to the Father and the Son; and because whatever is from the Father, must be from the Son unless it be opposed to the property of filiation; for the Son is not from Himself, although He is from the Father.

REPLY OBJ. 7: The Holy Spirit is distinguished from the Son, inasmuch as the origin of one is distinguished from the origin of the other; but the difference itself of origin comes from the fact that the Son is only from the Father, whereas the Holy Spirit is from the Father and the Son; for otherwise the processions would not be distinguished from each other, as explained above, and in Q. 27.

Article 3

Whether the Holy Spirit Proceeds from the Father Through the Son?

AD TERTIUM SIC PROCEDITUR. Videtur quod Spiritus Sanctus non procedat a patre per filium. Quod enim procedit ab aliquo per aliquem, non procedit ab eo immediate. Si igitur Spiritus Sanctus procedit a patre per filium, non procedit a patre immediate. Quod videtur inconveniens.

PRAETEREA, si Spiritus Sanctus procedit a patre per filium, non procedit a filio nisi propter patrem. Sed propter quod unumquodque, et illud magis. Ergo magis procedit a patre quam a filio.

PRAETEREA, filius habet esse per generationem. Si igitur Spiritus Sanctus est a patre per filium, sequitur quod prius generetur filius, et postea procedat Spiritus Sanctus. Et sic processio spiritus sancti non est aeterna. Quod est haereticum.

PRAETEREA, cum aliquis dicitur per aliquem operari, potest e converso dici, sicut enim dicimus quod rex operatur per ballivum, ita potest dici quod ballivus operatur per regem. Sed nullo modo dicimus quod filius spiret spiritum sanctum per patrem. Ergo nullo modo potest dici quod pater spiret spiritum sanctum per filium.

SED CONTRA est quod Hilarius dicit, in libro de Trin., *conserva hanc, oro, fidei meae religionem, ut semper obtineam patrem, scilicet te; et filium tuum una tecum adorem; et spiritum sanctum tuum, qui est per unigenitum tuum, promerear.*

RESPONDEO dicendum quod in omnibus locutionibus in quibus dicitur aliquis per aliquem operari, haec praepositio per designat in causali aliquam causam seu principium illius actus. Sed cum actio sit media inter faciens et factum, quandoque illud causale cui adiungitur haec praepositio per, est causa actionis secundum quod exit ab agente. Et tunc est causa agenti quod agat; sive sit causa finalis, sive formalis, sive effectiva vel motiva, finalis quidem, ut si dicamus quod artifex operatur per cupiditatem lucri; formalis vero, ut si dicamus quod operatur per artem suam; motiva vero, si dicamus quod operatur per imperium alterius. Quandoque vero dictio causalis cui adiungitur haec praepositio per, est causa actionis secundum quod terminatur ad factum; ut cum dicimus, artifex operatur per martellum. Non enim significatur quod martellus sit causa artifici quod agat, sed quod sit causa artificiato ut ab artifice procedat; et quod hoc ipsum habeat ab artifice. Et hoc est quod quidam dicunt, quod haec praepositio per quandoque notat auctoritatem in recto, ut cum dicitur, rex operatur per

OBJECTION 1: It would seem that the Holy Spirit does not proceed from the Father through the Son. For whatever proceeds from one through another, does not proceed immediately. Therefore, if the Holy Spirit proceeds from the Father through the Son, He does not proceed immediately; which seems to be unfitting.

OBJ. 2: Further, if the Holy Spirit proceeds from the Father through the Son, He does not proceed from the Son, except on account of the Father. But *whatever causes a thing to be such is yet more so.* Therefore He proceeds more from the Father than from the Son.

OBJ. 3: Further, the Son has His being by generation. Therefore if the Holy Spirit is from the Father through the Son, it follows that the Son is first generated and afterwards the Holy Spirit proceeds; and thus the procession of the Holy Spirit is not eternal, which is heretical.

OBJ. 4: Further, when anyone acts through another, the same may be said conversely. For as we say that the king acts through the bailiff, so it can be said conversely that the bailiff acts through the king. But we can never say that the Son spirates the Holy Spirit through the Father. Therefore it can never be said that the Father spirates the Holy Spirit through the Son.

ON THE CONTRARY, Hilary says (*De Trin.* xii): *Keep me, I pray, in this expression of my faith, that I may ever possess the Father—namely Thyself: that I may adore Thy Son together with Thee: and that I may deserve Thy Holy Spirit, who is through Thy Only Begotten.*

I ANSWER THAT, Whenever one is said to act through another, this preposition *through* points out, in what is covered by it, some cause or principle of that act. But since action is a mean between the agent and the thing done, sometimes that which is covered by the preposition *through* is the cause of the action, as proceeding from the agent; and in that case it is the cause of why the agent acts, whether it be a final cause or a formal cause, whether it be effective or motive. It is a final cause when we say, for instance, that the artisan works through love of gain. It is a formal cause when we say that he works through his art. It is a motive cause when we say that he works through the command of another. Sometimes, however, that which is covered by this preposition *through* is the cause of the action regarded as terminated in the thing done; as, for instance, when we say, the artisan acts through the mallet, for this does not mean that the mallet is the cause why the artisan acts, but that it is the cause why the thing made proceeds from the artisan, and that it has even this effect from the artisan. This is why it is sometimes said that this preposition *through*

ballivum, quandoque autem in obliquo, ut cum dicitur, ballivus operatur per regem.

Quia igitur filius habet a patre quod ab eo procedat Spiritus Sanctus, potest dici quod pater per filium spirat spiritum sanctum; vel quod Spiritus Sanctus procedat a patre per filium, quod idem est.

Ad primum ergo dicendum quod in qualibet actione est duo considerare, scilicet suppositum agens, et virtutem qua agit; sicut ignis calefacit calore. Si igitur in patre et filio consideretur virtus qua spirant spiritum sanctum, non cadit ibi aliquod medium, quia haec virtus est una et eadem. Si autem considerentur ipsae personae spirantes, sic, cum Spiritus Sanctus communiter procedat a patre et filio, invenitur Spiritus Sanctus immediate a patre procedere, inquantum est ab eo; et mediate, inquantum est a filio. Et sic dicitur procedere a patre per filium. Sicut etiam Abel processit immediate ab Adam, inquantum Adam fuit pater eius; et mediate, inquantum Eva fuit mater eius, quae processit ab Adam; licet hoc exemplum materialis processionis ineptum videatur ad significandam immaterialem processionem divinarum personarum.

Ad secundum dicendum quod, si filius acciperet a patre aliam virtutem numero ad spirandum spiritum sanctum, sequeretur quod esset sicut causa secunda et instrumentalis, et sic magis procederet a patre quam a filio. Sed una et eadem numero virtus spirativa est in patre et filio, et ideo aequaliter procedit ab utroque. Licet aliquando dicatur principaliter vel proprie procedere de patre, propter hoc quod filius habet hanc virtutem a patre.

Ad tertium dicendum quod, sicut generatio filii est coaeterna generanti, unde non prius fuit pater quam gigneret filium; ita processio spiritus sancti est coaeterna suo principio. Unde non fuit prius filius genitus, quam Spiritus Sanctus procederet, sed utrumque aeternum est.

Ad quartum dicendum quod, cum aliquis dicitur per aliquid operari, non semper recipitur conversio, non enim dicimus quod martellus operetur per fabrum. Dicimus autem quod ballivus operatur per regem, quia ballivi est agere, cum sit dominus sui actus. Martelli autem non est agere, sed solum agi, unde non designatur nisi ut instrumentum. Dicitur autem ballivus operari per regem, quamvis haec praepositio per denotet medium, quia, quanto suppositum est prius in agendo, tanto virtus eius est immediatior effectui, quia virtus causae primae coniungit causam secundam suo effectui, unde et prima principia dicuntur immediata in demonstrativis scientiis. Sic igitur, inquantum ballivus est medius secundum ordinem suppositorum agentium, dicitur rex operari

sometimes denotes direct authority, as when we say, the king works through the bailiff; and sometimes indirect authority, as when we say, the bailiff works through the king.

Therefore, because the Son receives from the Father that the Holy Spirit proceeds from Him, it can be said that the Father spirates the Holy Spirit through the Son, or that the Holy Spirit proceeds from the Father through the Son, which has the same meaning.

Reply Obj. 1: In every action two things are to be considered, the suppositum acting, and the power whereby it acts; as, for instance, fire heats through heat. So if we consider in the Father and the Son the power whereby they spirate the Holy Spirit, there is no mean, for this is one and the same power. But if we consider the persons themselves spirating, then, as the Holy Spirit proceeds both from the Father and from the Son, the Holy Spirit proceeds from the Father immediately, as from Him, and mediately, as from the Son; and thus He is said to proceed from the Father through the Son. So also did Abel proceed immediately from Adam, inasmuch as Adam was his father; and mediately, as Eve was his mother, who proceeded from Adam; although, indeed, this example of a material procession is inept to signify the immaterial procession of the divine persons.

Reply Obj. 2: If the Son received from the Father a numerically distinct power for the spiration of the Holy Spirit, it would follow that He would be a secondary and instrumental cause; and thus the Holy Spirit would proceed more from the Father than from the Son; whereas, on the contrary, the same spirative power belongs to the Father and to the Son; and therefore the Holy Spirit proceeds equally from both, although sometimes He is said to proceed principally or properly from the Father, because the Son has this power from the Father.

Reply Obj. 3: As the begetting of the Son is co-eternal with the begetter (and hence the Father does not exist before begetting the Son), so the procession of the Holy Spirit is co-eternal with His principle. Hence, the Son was not begotten before the Holy Spirit proceeded; but each of the operations is eternal.

Reply Obj. 4: When anyone is said to work through anything, the converse proposition is not always true. For we do not say that the mallet works through the carpenter; whereas we can say that the bailiff acts through the king, because it is the bailiff's place to act, since he is master of his own act, but it is not the mallet's place to act, but only to be made to act, and hence it is used only as an instrument. The bailiff is, however, said to act through the king, although this preposition *through* denotes a medium, for the more a suppositum is prior in action, so much the more is its power immediate as regards the effect, inasmuch as the power of the first cause joins the second cause to its effect. Hence also first principles are said to be immediate in the demonstrative sciences. Therefore, so far as the bailiff

per ballivum, secundum ordinem vero virtutum, dicitur ballivus operari per regem, quia virtus regis facit quod actio ballivi consequatur effectum. Ordo autem non attenditur inter patrem et filium quantum ad virtutem; sed solum quantum ad supposita. Et ideo dicitur quod pater spirat per filium, et non e converso.

is a medium according to the order of the subject's acting, the king is said to work through the bailiff; but according to the order of powers, the bailiff is said to act through the king, forasmuch as the power of the king gives the bailiff's action its effect. Now there is no order of power between Father and Son, but only order of 'supposita'; and hence we say that the Father spirates through the Son; and not conversely.

Article 4

Whether the Father and the Son Are One Principle of the Holy Spirit?

AD QUARTUM SIC PROCEDITUR. Videtur quod pater et filius non sint unum principium spiritus sancti. Quia Spiritus Sanctus non videtur a patre et filio procedere inquantum sunt unum, neque in natura, quia Spiritus Sanctus sic etiam procederet a seipso, qui est unum cum eis in natura; neque etiam inquantum sunt unum in aliqua proprietate, quia una proprietas non potest esse duorum suppositorum, ut videtur. Ergo Spiritus Sanctus procedit a patre et filio ut sunt plures. Non ergo pater et filius sunt unum principium spiritus sancti.

PRAETEREA, cum dicitur, pater et filius sunt unum principium spiritus sancti, non potest ibi designari unitas personalis, quia sic pater et filius essent una persona. Neque etiam unitas proprietatis, quia si propter unam proprietatem pater et filius sunt unum principium spiritus sancti, pari ratione, propter duas proprietates pater videtur esse duo principia filii et spiritus sancti; quod est inconveniens. Non ergo pater et filius sunt unum principium spiritus sancti.

PRAETEREA, filius non magis convenit cum patre quam Spiritus Sanctus. Sed Spiritus Sanctus et pater non sunt unum principium respectu alicuius divinae personae. Ergo neque pater et filius.

PRAETEREA, si pater et filius sunt unum principium spiritus sancti aut unum quod est pater; aut unum quod non est pater. Sed neutrum est dare, quia si unum quod est pater, sequitur quod filius sit pater; si unum quod non est pater, sequitur quod pater non est pater. Non ergo dicendum est quod pater et filius sint unum principium spiritus sancti.

PRAETEREA, si pater et filius sunt unum principium spiritus sancti videtur e converso dicendum quod unum principium spiritus sancti sit pater et filius. Sed haec videtur esse falsa, quia hoc quod dico principium, oportet quod supponat vel pro persona patris, vel pro persona

OBJECTION 1: It would seem that the Father and the Son are not one principle of the Holy Spirit. For the Holy Spirit does not proceed from the Father and the Son as they are one; not as they are one in nature, for the Holy Spirit would in that way proceed from Himself, as He is one in nature with Them; nor again inasmuch as they are united in any one property, for it is clear that one property cannot belong to two subjects. Therefore the Holy Spirit proceeds from the Father and the Son as distinct from one another. Therefore the Father and the Son are not one principle of the Holy Spirit.

OBJ. 2: Further, in this proposition *the Father and the Son are one principle of the Holy Spirit*, we do not designate personal unity, because in that case the Father and the Son would be one person; nor again do we designate the unity of property, because if one property were the reason of the Father and the Son being one principle of the Holy Spirit, similarly, on account of His two properties, the Father would be two principles of the Son and of the Holy Spirit, which cannot be admitted. Therefore the Father and the Son are not one principle of the Holy Spirit.

OBJ. 3: Further, the Son is not one with the Father more than is the Holy Spirit. But the Holy Spirit and the Father are not one principle as regards any other divine person. Therefore neither are the Father and the Son.

OBJ. 4: Further, if the Father and the Son are one principle of the Holy Spirit, this one is either the Father or it is not the Father. But we cannot assert either of these positions because if the one is the Father, it follows that the Son is the Father; and if the one is not the Father, it follows that the Father is not the Father. Therefore we cannot say that the Father and the Son are one principle of the Holy Spirit.

OBJ. 5: Further, if the Father and the Son are one principle of the Holy Spirit, it seems necessary to say, conversely, that the one principle of the Holy Spirit is the Father and the Son. But this seems to be false; for this word *principle* stands either for the person of the Father, or for the person

filii; et utroque modo est falsa. Ergo etiam haec est falsa, pater et filius sunt unum principium spiritus sancti.

PRAETEREA, unum in substantia facit idem. Si igitur pater et filius sunt unum principium spiritus sancti, sequitur quod sint idem principium. Sed hoc a multis negatur. Ergo non est concedendum quod pater et filius sint unum principium spiritus sancti.

PRAETEREA, pater et filius et Spiritus Sanctus, quia sunt unum principium creaturae, dicuntur esse unus creator. Sed pater et filius non sunt unus spirator, sed duo spiratores, ut a multis dicitur. Quod etiam consonat dictis Hilarii, qui dicit, in II de Trin., quod *Spiritus Sanctus a patre et filio auctoribus confitendus est.* Ergo pater et filius non sunt unum principium spiritus sancti.

SED CONTRA est quod Augustinus dicit, in V de Trin., quod pater et filius non sunt duo principia, sed unum principium spiritus sancti.

RESPONDEO dicendum quod pater et filius in omnibus unum sunt, in quibus non distinguit inter eos relationis oppositio. Unde, cum in hoc quod est esse principium spiritus sancti, non opponantur relative, sequitur quod pater et filius sunt unum principium spiritus sancti.

Quidam tamen dicunt hanc esse impropriam, pater et filius sunt unum principium spiritus sancti. Quia cum hoc nomen principium, singulariter acceptum, non significet personam, sed proprietatem, dicunt quod sumitur adiective, et quia adiectivum non determinatur per adiectivum, non potest convenienter dici quod pater et filius sint unum principium spiritus sancti, nisi unum intelligatur quasi adverbialiter positum, ut sit sensus, sunt unum principium, idest uno modo. Sed simili ratione posset dici pater duo principia filii et spiritus sancti, idest duobus modis. Dicendum est ergo quod, licet hoc nomen principium significet proprietatem, tamen significat eam per modum substantivi, sicut hoc nomen pater vel filius etiam in rebus creatis. Unde numerum accipit a forma significata, sicut et alia substantiva. Sicut igitur pater et filius sunt unus Deus, propter unitatem formae significatae per hoc nomen Deus; ita sunt unum principium spiritus sancti, propter unitatem proprietatis significatae in hoc nomine principium.

AD PRIMUM ergo dicendum quod, si attendatur virtus spirativa, Spiritus Sanctus procedit a patre et filio inquantum sunt unum in virtute spirativa, quae quodammodo significat naturam cum proprietate, ut infra dicetur. Neque est inconveniens unam proprietatem esse in duobus suppositis, quorum est una natura. Si vero considerentur supposita spirationis, sic Spiritus Sanctus procedit a patre et filio ut sunt plures, procedit enim ab eis ut amor unitivus duorum.

of the Son; and in either sense it is false. Therefore this proposition also is false, that the Father and the Son are one principle of the Holy Spirit.

OBJ. 6: Further, unity in substance makes identity. So if the Father and the Son are the one principle of the Holy Spirit, it follows that they are the same principle; which is denied by many. Therefore we cannot grant that the Father and the Son are one principle of the Holy Spirit.

OBJ. 7: Further, the Father, Son and Holy Spirit are called one Creator, because they are the one principle of the creature. But the Father and the Son are not one, but two Spirators, as many assert; and this agrees also with what Hilary says (*De Trin.* ii) that *the Holy Spirit is to be confessed as proceeding from Father and Son as authors.* Therefore the Father and the Son are not one principle of the Holy Spirit.

ON THE CONTRARY, Augustine says (*De Trin.* v, 14) that the Father and the Son are not two principles, but one principle of the Holy Spirit.

I ANSWER THAT, The Father and the Son are in everything one, wherever there is no distinction between them of opposite relation. Hence since there is no relative opposition between them as the principle of the Holy Spirit it follows that the Father and the Son are one principle of the Holy Spirit.

Some, however, assert that this proposition is incorrect: *The Father and the Son are one principle of the Holy Spirit,* because, they declare, since the word *principle* in the singular number does not signify *person,* but *property,* it must be taken as an adjective; and forasmuch as an adjective cannot be modified by another adjective, it cannot properly be said that the Father and the Son are one principle of the Holy Spirit unless one be taken as an adverb, so that the meaning should be: They are one principle—that is, in one and the same way. But then it might be equally right to say that the Father is two principles of the Son and of the Holy Spirit—namely, in two ways. Therefore, we must say that, although this word *principle* signifies a property, it does so after the manner of a substantive, as do the words *father* and *son* even in things created. Hence it takes its number from the form it signifies, like other substantives. Therefore, as the Father and the Son are one God, by reason of the unity of the form that is signified by this word *God*; so they are one principle of the Holy Spirit by reason of the unity of the property that is signified in this word *principle.*

REPLY OBJ. 1: If we consider the spirative power, the Holy Spirit proceeds from the Father and the Son as they are one in the spirative power, which in a certain way signifies the nature with the property, as we shall see later (ad 7). Nor is there any reason against one property being in two supposita that possess one common nature. But if we consider the supposita of the spiration, then we may say that the Holy Spirit proceeds from the Father and the Son, as distinct; for He proceeds from them as the unitive love of both.

AD SECUNDUM dicendum quod, cum dicitur, pater et filius sunt unum principium spiritus sancti, designatur una proprietas, quae est forma significata per nomen. Non tamen sequitur quod propter plures proprietates possit dici pater plura principia, quia implicaretur pluralitas suppositorum.

AD TERTIUM dicendum quod secundum relativas proprietates non attenditur in divinis similitudo vel dissimilitudo, sed secundum essentiam. Unde, sicut pater non est similior sibi quam filio, ita nec filius similior patri quam Spiritus Sanctus.

AD QUARTUM dicendum quod haec duo, scilicet, pater et filius sunt unum principium quod est pater, aut, unum principium quod non est pater, non sunt contradictorie opposita. Unde non est necesse alterum eorum dare. Cum enim dicimus, pater et filius sunt unum principium, hoc quod dico principium, non habet determinatam suppositionem, imo confusam pro duabus personis simul. Unde in processu est fallacia figurae dictionis, a confusa suppositione ad determinatam.

AD QUINTUM dicendum quod haec etiam est vera, unum principium spiritus sancti est pater et filius. Quia hoc quod dico principium non supponit pro una persona tantum, sed indistincte pro duabus, ut dictum est.

AD SEXTUM dicendum quod convenienter potest dici quod pater et filius sunt idem principium, secundum quod ly principium supponit confuse et indistincte pro duabus personis simul.

AD SEPTIMUM dicendum quod quidam dicunt quod pater et filius, licet sint unum principium spiritus sancti, sunt tamen duo spiratores, propter distinctionem suppositorum, sicut etiam duo spirantes, quia actus referuntur ad supposita. Nec est eadem ratio de hoc nomine creator. Quia Spiritus Sanctus procedit a patre et filio ut sunt duae personae distinctae, ut dictum est, non autem creatura procedit a tribus personis ut sunt personae distinctae, sed ut sunt unum in essentia. Sed videtur melius dicendum quod, quia spirans adiectivum est, spirator vero substantivum, possumus dicere quod pater et filius sunt duo spirantes, propter pluralitatem suppositorum; non autem duo spiratores, propter unam spirationem. Nam adiectiva nomina habent numerum secundum supposita, substantiva vero a seipsis, secundum formam significatam. Quod vero Hilarius dicit, quod *Spiritus Sanctus est a patre et filio auctoribus*, exponendum est quod ponitur substantivum pro adiectivo.

REPLY OBJ. 2: In the proposition *the Father and the Son are one principle of the Holy Spirit*, one property is designated which is the form signified by the term. It does not thence follow that by reason of the several properties the Father can be called several principles, for this would imply in Him a plurality of subjects.

REPLY OBJ. 3: It is not by reason of relative properties that we speak of similitude or dissimilitude in God, but by reason of the essence. Hence, as the Father is not more like to Himself than He is to the Son; so likewise neither is the Son more like to the Father than is the Holy Spirit.

REPLY OBJ. 4: These two propositions, *The Father and the Son are one principle which is the Father*, or, *one principle which is not the Father*, are not mutually contradictory; and hence it is not necessary to assert one or other of them. For when we say the Father and the Son are one principle, this word *principle* has not determinate supposition but rather it stands indeterminately for two persons together. Hence there is a fallacy of *figure of speech* as the argument concludes from the indeterminate to the determinate.

REPLY OBJ. 5: This proposition is also true:—*The one principle of the Holy Spirit is the Father and the Son*; because the word *principle* does not stand for one person only, but indistinctly for the two persons as above explained.

REPLY OBJ. 6: There is no reason against saying that the Father and the Son are the same principle, because the word *principle* stands confusedly and indistinctly for the two Persons together.

REPLY OBJ. 7: Some say that although the Father and the Son are one principle of the Holy Spirit, there are two spirators, by reason of the distinction of supposita, as also there are two spirating, because acts refer to subjects. Yet this does not hold good as to the name *Creator*; because the Holy Spirit proceeds from the Father and the Son as from two distinct persons, as above explained; whereas the creature proceeds from the three persons not as distinct persons, but as united in essence. It seems, however, better to say that because spirating is an adjective, and spirator a substantive, we can say that the Father and the Son are two spirating, by reason of the plurality of the supposita but not two spirators by reason of the one spiration. For adjectival words derive their number from the supposita but substantives from themselves, according to the form signified. As to what Hilary says, that *the Holy Spirit is from the Father and the Son as His authors*, this is to be explained in the sense that the substantive here stands for the adjective.

QUESTION 37

THE NAME LOVE

Deinde quaeritur de nomine amoris. Et circa hoc quaeruntur duo.

Primo, utrum sit proprium nomen spiritus sancti.

Secundo, utrum pater et filius diligant se spiritu sancto.

We now inquire concerning the name *Love*, on which arise two points of inquiry:

(1) Whether it is the proper name of the Holy Spirit?

(2) Whether the Father and the Son love each other by the Holy Spirit?

Article 1

Whether Love Is the Proper Name of the Holy Spirit?

AD PRIMUM SIC PROCEDITUR. Videtur quod amor non sit proprium nomen spiritus sancti. Dicit enim Augustinus, XV de Trin., *nescio cur, sicut sapientia dicitur et pater et filius et Spiritus Sanctus, et simul omnes non tres sed una sapientia, non ita et caritas dicatur pater et filius et Spiritus Sanctus, et simul omnes una caritas*. Sed nullum nomen quod de singulis personis praedicatur et de omnibus in communi singulariter, est nomen proprium alicuius personae. Ergo hoc nomen amor non est proprium spiritus sancti.

PRAETEREA, Spiritus Sanctus est persona subsistens. Sed amor non significatur ut persona subsistens, sed ut actio quaedam ab amante transiens in amatum. Ergo amor non est proprium nomen spiritus sancti.

PRAETEREA, amor est nexus amantium, quia secundum Dionysium, IV cap. de Div. Nom., est *quaedam vis unitiva*. Sed nexus est medium inter ea quae connectit, non autem aliquid ab eis procedens. Cum igitur Spiritus Sanctus procedat a patre et filio, sicut ostensum est, videtur quod non sit amor aut nexus patris et filii.

PRAETEREA, cuiuslibet amantis est aliquis amor. Sed Spiritus Sanctus est amans. Ergo eius est aliquis amor. Si igitur Spiritus Sanctus est amor, erit amor amoris, et spiritus a spiritu. Quod est inconveniens.

SED CONTRA est quod Gregorius dicit, in homilia Pentecostes, *ipse Spiritus Sanctus est amor*.

RESPONDEO dicendum quod nomen amoris in divinis sumi potest et essentialiter et personaliter. Et secundum quod personaliter sumitur, est proprium nomen spiritus sancti; sicut verbum est proprium nomen filii.

Ad cuius evidentiam, sciendum est quod, cum in divinis, ut supra ostensum est, sint duae processiones, una per modum intellectus, quae est processio verbi; alia per modum voluntatis, quae est processio amoris, quia prima est nobis magis nota, ad singula significanda quae

OBJECTION 1: It would seem that *Love* is not the proper name of the Holy Spirit. For Augustine says (*De Trin.* xv, 17): *As the Father, Son and Holy Spirit are called Wisdom, and are not three Wisdoms, but one; I know not why the Father, Son and Holy Spirit should not be called Charity, and all together one Charity*. But no name which is predicated in the singular of each person and of all together, is a proper name of a person. Therefore this name, *Love*, is not the proper name of the Holy Spirit.

OBJ. 2: Further, the Holy Spirit is a subsisting person, but love is not used to signify a subsisting person, but rather an action passing from the lover to the beloved. Therefore Love is not the proper name of the Holy Spirit.

OBJ. 3: Further, Love is the bond between lovers, for as Dionysius says (*Div. Nom.* iv): *Love is a unitive force*. But a bond is a medium between what it joins together, not something proceeding from them. Therefore, since the Holy Spirit proceeds from the Father and the Son, as was shown above (Q. 36, A. 2), it seems that He is not the Love or bond of the Father and the Son.

OBJ. 4: Further, Love belongs to every lover. But the Holy Spirit is a lover: therefore He has love. So if the Holy Spirit is Love, He must be love of love, and spirit from spirit; which is not admissible.

ON THE CONTRARY, Gregory says (*Hom. xxx, in Pentecost.*): *The Holy Spirit Himself is Love*.

I ANSWER THAT, The name Love in God can be taken essentially and personally. If taken personally it is the proper name of the Holy Spirit; as Word is the proper name of the Son.

To see this we must know that since as shown above (Q. 27, AA. 2, 3, 4, 5), there are two processions in God, one by way of the intellect, which is the procession of the Word, and another by way of the will, which is the procession of Love; forasmuch as the former is the more known to us, we

in ea considerari possunt, sunt magis propria nomina adinventa; non autem in processione voluntatis. Unde et quibusdam circumlocutionibus utimur ad significandam personam procedentem, et relationes etiam quae accipiuntur secundum hanc processionem, et processionis et spirationis nominibus nominantur, ut supra dictum est, quae tamen sunt magis nomina originis quam relationis, secundum proprietatem vocabuli. Et tamen similiter utramque processionem considerari oportet. Sicut enim ex hoc quod aliquis rem aliquam intelligit, provenit quaedam intellectualis conceptio rei intellectae in intelligente, quae dicitur verbum; ita ex hoc quod aliquis rem aliquam amat, provenit quaedam impressio, ut ita loquar, rei amatae in affectu amantis, secundum quam amatum dicitur esse in amante, sicut et intellectum in intelligente. Ita quod, cum aliquis seipsum intelligit et amat, est in seipso non solum per identitatem rei, sed etiam ut intellectum in intelligente, et amatum in amante. Sed ex parte intellectus, sunt vocabula adinventa ad significandum respectum intelligentis ad rem intellectam, ut patet in hoc quod dico intelligere, et sunt etiam alia vocabula adinventa ad significandum processum intellectualis conceptionis, scilicet ipsum dicere, et verbum. Unde in divinis intelligere solum essentialiter dicitur, quia non importat habitudinem ad verbum procedens, sed verbum personaliter dicitur, quia significat id quod procedit, ipsum vero dicere dicitur notionaliter, quia importat habitudinem principii verbi ad verbum ipsum. Ex parte autem voluntatis, praeter diligere et amare, quae important habitudinem amantis ad rem amatam, non sunt aliqua vocabula imposita, quae important habitudinem ipsius impressionis vel affectionis rei amatae, quae provenit in amante ex hoc quod amat, ad suum principium, aut e converso. Et ideo, propter vocabulorum inopiam, huiusmodi habitudines significamus vocabulis amoris et dilectionis; sicut si verbum nominaremus intelligentiam conceptam, vel sapientiam genitam.

Sic igitur, inquantum in amore vel dilectione non importatur nisi habitudo amantis ad rem amatam, amor et diligere essentialiter dicuntur, sicut intelligentia et intelligere. Inquantum vero his vocabulis utimur ad exprimendam habitudinem eius rei quae procedit per modum amoris, ad suum principium, et e converso; ita quod per amorem intelligatur amor procedens, et per diligere intelligatur spirare amorem procedentem, sic amor est nomen personae, et diligere vel amare est verbum notionale, sicut dicere vel generare.

AD PRIMUM ergo dicendum quod Augustinus loquitur de caritate, secundum quod essentialiter sumitur in divinis, ut dictum est.

AD SECUNDUM dicendum quod intelligere et velle et amare, licet significentur per modum actionum

have been able to apply more suitable names to express our various considerations as regards that procession, but not as regards the procession of the will. Hence, we are obliged to employ circumlocution as regards the person Who proceeds, and the relations following from this procession which are called *procession* and *spiration*, as stated above (Q. 27, A. 4, ad 3), and yet express the origin rather than the relation in the strict sense of the term. Nevertheless we must consider them in respect of each procession simply. For as when a thing is understood by anyone, there results in the one who understands a conception of the object understood, which conception we call word; so when anyone loves an object, a certain impression results, so to speak, of the thing loved in the affection of the lover; by reason of which the object loved is said to be in the lover; as also the thing understood is in the one who understands; so that when anyone understands and loves himself he is in himself, not only by real identity, but also as the object understood is in the one who understands, and the thing loved is in the lover. As regards the intellect, however, words have been found to describe the mutual relation of the one who understands the object understood, as appears in the word *to understand*; and other words are used to express the procession of the intellectual conception—namely, *to speak*, and *word*. Hence in God, *to understand* is applied only to the essence; because it does not import relation to the Word that proceeds; whereas *Word* is said personally, because it signifies what proceeds; and the term *to speak* is a notional term as importing the relation of the principle of the Word to the Word Himself. On the other hand, on the part of the will, with the exception of the words *dilection* and *love*, which express the relation of the lover to the object loved, there are no other terms in use, which express the relation of the impression or affection of the object loved, produced in the lover by fact that he loves—to the principle of that impression, or *vice versa*. And therefore, on account of the poverty of our vocabulary, we express these relations by the words *love* and *dilection*: just as if we were to call the Word *intelligence conceived*, or *wisdom begotten*.

It follows that so far as love means only the relation of the lover to the object loved, *love* and *to love* are said of the essence, as *understanding* and *to understand*; but, on the other hand, so far as these words are used to express the relation to its principle, of what proceeds by way of love, and *vice versa*, so that by *love* is understood the *love proceeding*, and by *to love* is understood *the spiration of the love proceeding*, in that sense *love* is the name of the person and *to love* is a notional term, as *to speak* and *to beget*.

REPLY OBJ. 1: Augustine is there speaking of charity as it means the divine essence, as was said above (here and Q. 24, A. 2, ad 4).

REPLY OBJ. 2: Although to understand, and to will, and to love signify actions passing on to their objects,

transeuntium in obiecta, sunt tamen actiones manentes in agentibus, ut supra dictum est; ita tamen quod in ipso agente important habitudinem quandam ad obiectum. Unde amor, etiam in nobis, est aliquid manens in amante, et verbum cordis manens in dicente; tamen cum habitudine ad rem verbo expressam, vel amatam. Sed in Deo, in quo nullum est accidens, plus habet, quia tam verbum quam amor est subsistens. Cum ergo dicitur quod Spiritus Sanctus est amor patris in filium, vel in quidquam aliud, non significatur aliquid transiens in alium; sed solum habitudo amoris ad rem amatam; sicut et in verbo importatur habitudo verbi ad rem verbo expressam.

AD TERTIUM dicendum quod Spiritus Sanctus dicitur esse nexus patris et filii, inquantum est amor, quia, cum pater amet unica dilectione se et filium, et e converso, importatur in spiritu sancto, prout est amor, habitudo patris ad filium, et e converso, ut amantis ad amatum. Sed ex hoc ipso quod pater et filius se mutuo amant, oportet quod mutuus amor, qui est Spiritus Sanctus, ab utroque procedat. Secundum igitur originem, Spiritus Sanctus non est medius, sed tertia in Trinitate persona. Secundum vero praedictam habitudinem, est medius nexus duorum, ab utroque procedens.

AD QUARTUM dicendum quod, sicut filio, licet intelligat, non tamen sibi competit producere verbum, quia intelligere convenit ei ut verbo procedenti; ita, licet Spiritus Sanctus amet, essentialiter accipiendo, non tamen convenit ei quod spiret amorem, quod est diligere notionaliter sumptum; quia sic diligit essentialiter ut amor procedens, non ut a quo procedit amor.

nevertheless they are actions that remain in the agents, as stated above (Q. 14, A. 4), yet in such a way that in the agent itself they import a certain relation to their object. Hence, love also in ourselves is something that abides in the lover, and the word of the heart is something abiding in the speaker; yet with a relation to the thing expressed by word, or loved. But in God, in whom there is nothing accidental, there is more than this; because both Word and Love are subsistent. Therefore, when we say that the Holy Spirit is the Love of the Father for the Son, or for something else; we do not mean anything that passes into another, but only the relation of love to the beloved; as also in the Word is imported the relation of the Word to the thing expressed by the Word.

REPLY OBJ. 3: The Holy Spirit is said to be the bond of the Father and Son, inasmuch as He is Love; because, since the Father loves Himself and the Son with one Love, and conversely, there is expressed in the Holy Spirit, as Love, the relation of the Father to the Son, and conversely, as that of the lover to the beloved. But from the fact that the Father and the Son mutually love one another, it necessarily follows that this mutual Love, the Holy Spirit, proceeds from both. As regards origin, therefore, the Holy Spirit is not the medium, but the third person in the Trinity; whereas as regards the aforesaid relation He is the bond between the two persons, as proceeding from both.

REPLY OBJ. 4: As it does not belong to the Son, though He understands, to produce a word, for it belongs to Him to understand as the word proceeding; so in like manner, although the Holy Spirit loves, taking Love as an essential term, still it does not belong to Him to spirate love, which is to take love as a notional term; because He loves essentially as love proceeding; but not as the one whence love proceeds.

Article 2

Whether the Father and the Son Love Each Other by the Holy Spirit?

AD SECUNDUM SIC PROCEDITUR. Videtur quod pater et filius non diligant se spiritu sancto. Augustinus enim, in VII de Trin., probat quod pater non est sapiens sapientia genita. Sed sicut filius est sapientia genita, ita Spiritus Sanctus est amor procedens, ut dictum est. Ergo pater et filius non diligunt se amore procedente, qui est Spiritus Sanctus.

PRAETEREA, cum dicitur, pater et filius diligunt se spiritu sancto, hoc verbum diligere aut sumitur essentialiter, aut notionaliter. Sed non potest esse vera secundum quod sumitur essentialiter, quia pari ratione posset dici quod pater intelligit filio. Neque etiam secundum quod

OBJECTION 1: It would seem that the Father and the Son do not love each other by the Holy Spirit. For Augustine (*De Trin.* vii, 1) proves that the Father is not wise by the Wisdom begotten. But as the Son is Wisdom begotten, so the Holy Spirit is the Love proceeding, as explained above (Q. 27, A. 3). Therefore the Father and the Son do not love Themselves by the Love proceeding, which is the Holy Spirit.

OBJ. 2: Further, in the proposition, *The Father and the Son love each other by the Holy Spirit*, this word *love* is to be taken either essentially or notionally. But it cannot be true if taken essentially, because in the same way we might say that *the Father understands by the Son*; nor, again, if it is

sumitur notionaliter, quia pari ratione posset dici quod pater et filius spirant spiritu sancto, vel quod pater generat filio. Ergo nullo modo haec est vera, pater et filius diligunt se spiritu sancto.

PRAETEREA, eodem amore pater diligit filium, et se, et nos. Sed pater non diligit se spiritu sancto. Quia nullus actus notionalis reflectitur super principium actus, non enim potest dici quod pater generat se, vel spirat se. Ergo etiam non potest dici quod diligat se spiritu sancto, secundum quod diligere sumitur notionaliter. Item, amor quo diligit nos, non videtur esse Spiritus Sanctus, quia importatur respectus ad creaturam, et ita ad essentiam pertinet. Ergo et haec est falsa, pater diligit filium spiritu sancto.

SED CONTRA est quod Augustinus dicit, VI de Trin., quod *Spiritus Sanctus est quo genitus a generante diligitur, genitoremque suum diligit.*

RESPONDEO dicendum quod circa hanc quaestionem difficultatem affert quod, cum dicitur, pater diligit filium spiritu sancto, cum ablativus construatur in habitudine alicuius causae, videtur quod Spiritus Sanctus sit principium diligendi patri et filio; quod est omnino impossibile.

Et ideo quidam dixerunt hanc esse falsam, pater et filius diligunt se spiritu sancto. Et dicunt hanc esse retractatam ab Augustino in suo simili, cum scilicet retractavit istam, pater est sapiens sapientia genita. Quidam vero dicunt quod est propositio impropria; et est sic exponenda, pater diligit filium spiritu sancto, idest amore essentiali, qui appropriatur spiritui sancto. Quidam vero dixerunt quod ablativus iste construitur in habitudine signi, ut sit sensus, Spiritus Sanctus est signum quod pater diligat filium, inquantum scilicet procedit ab eis ut amor. Quidam vero dixerunt quod ablativus iste construitur in habitudine causae formalis, quia Spiritus Sanctus est amor, quo formaliter pater et filius se invicem diligunt. Quidam vero dixerunt quod construitur in habitudine effectus formalis. Et isti propinquius ad veritatem accesserunt.

Unde ad huius evidentiam, sciendum est quod, cum res communiter denominentur a suis formis, sicut album ab albedine, et homo ab humanitate; omne illud a quo aliquid denominatur, quantum ad hoc habet habitudinem formae. Ut si dicam, iste est indutus vestimento, iste ablativus construitur in habitudine causae formalis, quamvis non sit forma. Contingit autem aliquid denominari per id quod ab ipso procedit, non solum sicut agens actione; sed etiam sicut ipso termino actionis, qui est effectus, quando ipse effectus in intellectu actionis includitur. Dicimus enim quod ignis est calefaciens calefactione, quamvis calefactio non sit calor, qui

taken notionally, for then, in like manner, it might be said that *the Father and the Son spirate by the Holy Spirit*, or that *the Father generates by the Son*. Therefore in no way is this proposition true: *The Father and the Son love each other by the Holy Spirit*.

OBJ. 3: Further, by the same love the Father loves the Son, and Himself, and us. But the Father does not love Himself by the Holy Spirit; for no notional act is reflected back on the principle of the act; since it cannot be said that the *Father begets Himself*, or that *He spirates Himself*. Therefore, neither can it be said that *He loves Himself by the Holy Spirit*, if *to love* is taken in a notional sense. Again, the love wherewith He loves us is not the Holy Spirit; because it imports a relation to creatures, and this belongs to the essence. Therefore this also is false: *The Father loves the Son by the Holy Spirit*.

ON THE CONTRARY, Augustine says (*De Trin.* vi, 5): *The Holy Spirit is He whereby the Begotten is loved by the one begetting and loves His Begetter*.

I ANSWER THAT, A difficulty about this question is objected to the effect that when we say, *the Father loves the Son by the Holy Spirit*, since the ablative is construed as denoting a cause, it seems to mean that the Holy Spirit is the principle of love to the Father and the Son; which cannot be admitted.

In view of this difficulty some have held that it is false, that *the Father and the Son love each other by the Holy Spirit*; and they add that it was retracted by Augustine when he retracted its equivalent to the effect that *the Father is wise by the Wisdom begotten*. Others say that the proposition is inaccurate and ought to be expounded as that *the Father loves the Son by the Holy Spirit*—that is, *by His essential Love*, which is appropriated to the Holy Spirit. Others further say that this ablative should be construed as importing a sign, so that it means, *the Holy Spirit is the sign that the Father loves the Son*; inasmuch as the Holy Spirit proceeds from them both, as Love. Others, again, say that this ablative must be construed as importing the relation of formal cause, because the Holy Spirit is the love whereby the Father and the Son formally love each other. Others, again, say that it should be construed as importing the relation of a formal effect; and these approach nearer to the truth.

To make the matter clear, we must consider that since a thing is commonly denominated from its forms, as *white* from whiteness, and *man* from humanity; everything whence anything is denominated, in this particular respect stands to that thing in the relation of form. So when I say, *This man is clothed with a garment*, the ablative is to be construed as having relation to the formal cause, although the garment is not the form. Now it may happen that a thing may be denominated from that which proceeds from it, not only as an agent is from its action, but also as from the term itself of the action—that is, the effect, when the effect itself is included in the idea of the action. For we say that fire

est forma ignis, sed actio ab igne procedens, et dicimus quod arbor est florens floribus, quamvis flores non sint forma arboris, sed quidam effectus ab ipsa procedentes. Secundum hoc ergo dicendum quod, cum diligere in divinis dupliciter sumatur, essentialiter scilicet et notionaliter; secundum quod essentialiter sumitur, sic pater et filius non diligunt se spiritu sancto, sed essentia sua. Unde Augustinus dicit, in XV de Trin., *quis audet dicere patrem nec se nec filium nec spiritum sanctum diligere nisi per spiritum sanctum?* Et secundum hoc procedunt primae opiniones. Secundum vero quod notionaliter sumitur, sic diligere nihil est aliud quam spirare amorem; sicut dicere est producere verbum, et florere est producere flores. Sicut ergo dicitur arbor florens floribus, ita dicitur pater dicens verbo vel filio, se et creaturam, et pater et filius dicuntur diligentes spiritu sancto, vel amore procedente, et se et nos.

AD PRIMUM ergo dicendum quod esse sapientem vel intelligentem in divinis non sumitur nisi essentialiter, et ideo non potest dici quod pater sit sapiens vel intelligens filio. Sed diligere sumitur non solum essentialiter, sed etiam notionaliter. Et secundum hoc, possumus dicere quod pater et filius diligunt se spiritu sancto, ut dictum est.

AD SECUNDUM dicendum quod, quando in intellectu alicuius actionis importatur determinatus effectus, potest denominari principium actionis et ab actione et ab effectu; sicut possumus dicere quod arbor est florens floritione, et floribus. Sed quando in actione non includitur determinatus effectus, tunc non potest principium actionis denominari ab effectu, sed solum ab actione, non enim dicimus quod arbor producit florem flore, sed productione floris. In hoc igitur quod dico spirat vel generat, importatur actus notionalis tantum. Unde non possumus dicere quod pater spiret spiritu sancto, vel generet filio. Possumus autem dicere quod pater dicit verbo, tanquam persona procedente, et dicit dictione, tanquam actu notionali, quia dicere importat determinatam personam procedentem, cum dicere sit producere verbum. Et similiter diligere, prout notionaliter sumitur, est producere amorem. Et ideo potest dici quod pater diligit filium spiritu sancto, tanquam persona procedente, et ipsa dilectione, tanquam actu notionali.

AD TERTIUM dicendum quod pater non solum filium, sed etiam se et nos diligit spiritu sancto. Quia, ut dictum est diligere, prout notionaliter sumitur, non solum importat productionem divinae personae, sed etiam personam productam per modum amoris, qui habet habitudinem ad rem dilectam. Unde, sicut pater dicit se et omnem creaturam verbo quod genuit, inquantum verbum genitum sufficienter repraesentat patrem et omnem creaturam; ita diligit se et omnem creaturam spiritu

warms by heating, although heating is not the heat which is the form of the fire, but is an action proceeding from the fire; and we say that a tree flowers with the flower, although the flower is not the tree's form, but is the effect proceeding from the form. In this way, therefore, we must say that since in God *to love* is taken in two ways, essentially and notionally, when it is taken essentially, it means that the Father and the Son love each other not by the Holy Spirit, but by their essence. Hence Augustine says (*De Trin.* xv, 7): *Who dares to say that the Father loves neither Himself, nor the Son, nor the Holy Spirit, except by the Holy Spirit?* The opinions first quoted are to be taken in this sense. But when the term Love is taken in a notional sense it means nothing else than *to spirate love*; just as to speak is to produce a word, and to flower is to produce flowers. As therefore we say that a tree flowers by its flower, so do we say that the Father, by the Word or the Son, speaks Himself, and His creatures; and that the Father and the Son love each other and us, by the Holy Spirit, or by Love proceeding.

REPLY OBJ. 1: To be wise or intelligent is taken only essentially in God; therefore we cannot say that *the Father is wise or intelligent by the Son.* But to love is taken not only essentially, but also in a notional sense; and in this way, we can say that the Father and the Son love each other by the Holy Spirit, as was above explained.

REPLY OBJ. 2: When the idea of an action includes a determined effect, the principle of the action may be denominated both from the action, and from the effect; so we can say, for instance, that a tree flowers by its flowering and by its flower. When, however, the idea of an action does not include a determined effect, then in that case, the principle of the action cannot be denominated from the effect, but only from the action. For we do not say that the tree produces the flower by the flower, but by the production of the flower. So when we say, *spirates* or *begets*, this imports only a notional act. Hence we cannot say that the Father spirates by the Holy Spirit, or begets by the Son. But we can say that the Father speaks by the Word, as by the Person proceeding, *and speaks by the speaking*, as by a notional act; forasmuch as *to speak* imports a determinate person proceeding; since *to speak* means to produce a word. Likewise to love, taken in a notional sense, means to produce love; and so it can be said that the Father loves the Son by the Holy Spirit, as by the person proceeding, and by Love itself as a notional act.

REPLY OBJ. 3: The Father loves not only the Son, but also Himself and us, by the Holy Spirit; because, as above explained, to love, taken in a notional sense, not only imports the production of a divine person, but also the person produced, by way of love, which has relation to the object loved. Hence, as the Father speaks Himself and every creature by His begotten Word, inasmuch as the Word *begotten* adequately represents the Father and every creature; so He loves Himself and every creature by the Holy Spirit,

sancto, inquantum Spiritus Sanctus procedit ut amor bonitatis primae, secundum quam pater amat se et omnem creaturam. Et sic etiam patet quod respectus importatur ad creaturam et in verbo et in amore procedente, quasi secundario; inquantum scilicet veritas et bonitas divina est principium intelligendi et amandi omnem creaturam.

inasmuch as the Holy Spirit proceeds as the love of the primal goodness whereby the Father loves Himself and every creature. Thus it is evident that relation to the creature is implied both in the Word and in the proceeding Love, as it were in a secondary way, inasmuch as the divine truth and goodness are a principle of understanding and loving all creatures.

QUESTION 38

THE NAME GIFT

Consequenter quaeritur de dono. Et circa hoc quaeruntur duo.

Primo, utrum donum possit esse nomen personale.

Secundo, utrum sit proprium spiritus sancti.

There now follows the consideration of the Gift; concerning which there are two points of inquiry:

(1) Whether *Gift* can be a personal name?

(2) Whether it is the proper name of the Holy Spirit?

Article 1

Whether Gift Is a Personal Name?

AD PRIMUM SIC PROCEDITUR. Videtur quod donum non sit nomen personale. Omne enim nomen personale importat aliquam distinctionem in divinis. Sed nomen doni non importat aliquam distinctionem in divinis, dicit enim Augustinus, XV de Trin., quod *Spiritus Sanctus ita datur sicut Dei donum, ut etiam seipsum det sicut Deus.* Ergo donum non est nomen personale.

PRAETEREA, nullum nomen personale convenit essentiae divinae. Sed essentia divina est donum quod pater dat filio, ut patet per Hilarium, IX de Trin. Ergo donum non est nomen personale.

PRAETEREA, secundum Damascenum, nihil est subiectum aut serviens in divinis personis. Sed donum importat quandam subiectionem et ad eum cui datur, et ad eum a quo datur. Ergo donum non est nomen personale.

PRAETEREA, donum importat respectum ad creaturam, et ita videtur de Deo dici ex tempore. Sed nomina personalia dicuntur de Deo ab aeterno, ut pater et filius. Ergo donum non est nomen personale.

SED CONTRA est quod Augustinus dicit, XV de Trin., *sicut corpus carnis nihil aliud est quam caro, sic donum spiritus sancti nihil aliud est quam Spiritus Sanctus.* Sed Spiritus Sanctus est nomen personale. Ergo et donum.

RESPONDEO dicendum quod in nomine doni importatur aptitudo ad hoc quod donetur. Quod autem donatur, habet habitudinem et ad id a quo datur, et ad id cui datur, non enim daretur ab aliquo nisi esset eius; et ad hoc alicui datur, ut eius sit. Persona autem divina dicitur esse alicuius, vel secundum originem, sicut filius est patris; vel inquantum ab aliquo habetur. Habere autem dicimur id quo libere possumus uti vel frui, ut volumus. Et per hunc modum divina persona non potest haberi nisi a rationali creatura Deo coniuncta. Aliae autem creaturae moveri quidem possunt a divina persona; non tamen sic quod in potestate earum sit frui divina persona, et uti effectu eius. Ad quod quandoque pertingit

OBJECTION 1: It would seem that *Gift* is not a personal name. For every personal name imports a distinction in God. But the name of *Gift* does not import a distinction in God; for Augustine says (*De Trin.* xv, 19): that *the Holy Spirit is so given as God's Gift, that He also gives Himself as God.* Therefore *Gift* is not a personal name.

OBJ. 2: Further, no personal name belongs to the divine essence. But the divine essence is the Gift which the Father gives to the Son, as Hilary says (*De Trin.* ix). Therefore *Gift* is not a personal name.

OBJ. 3: Further, according to Damascene (*De Fide Orth.* iv, 19) there is no subjection nor service in the divine persons. But gift implies a subjection both as regards him to whom it is given, and as regards him by whom it is given. Therefore *Gift* is not a personal name.

OBJ. 4: Further, *Gift* imports relation to the creature, and it thus seems to be said of God in time. But personal names are said of God from eternity; as *Father*, and *Son*. Therefore *Gift* is not a personal name.

ON THE CONTRARY, Augustine says (*De Trin.* xv, 19): *As the body of flesh is nothing but flesh; so the gift of the Holy Spirit is nothing but the Holy Spirit.* But the Holy Spirit is a personal name; so also therefore is *Gift*.

I ANSWER THAT, The word *gift* imports an aptitude for being given. And what is given has an aptitude or relation both to the giver and to that to which it is given. For it would not be given by anyone, unless it was his to give; and it is given to someone to be his. Now a divine person is said to belong to another, either by origin, as the Son belongs to the Father; or as possessed by another. But we are said to possess what we can freely use or enjoy as we please: and in this way a divine person cannot be possessed, except by a rational creature united to God. Other creatures can be moved by a divine person, not, however, in such a way as to be able to enjoy the divine person, and to use the effect thereof. The rational creature does sometimes attain

rationalis creatura; ut puta cum sic fit particeps divini verbi et procedentis amoris, ut possit libere Deum vere cognoscere et recte amare. Unde sola creatura rationalis potest habere divinam personam. Sed ad hoc quod sic eam habeat, non potest propria virtute pervenire, unde oportet quod hoc ei desuper detur; hoc enim dari nobis dicitur, quod aliunde habemus. Et sic divinae personae competit dari, et esse donum.

AD PRIMUM ergo dicendum quod nomen doni importat distinctionem personalem, secundum quod donum dicitur esse alicuius per originem. Et tamen Spiritus Sanctus dat seipsum, inquantum est sui ipsius, ut potens se uti, vel potius frui; sicut et homo liber dicitur esse sui ipsius. Et hoc est quod Augustinus dicit, super Ioan., *quid tam tuum est quam tu?* Vel dicendum, et melius, quod donum oportet esse aliquo modo dantis. Sed hoc esse huius dicitur multipliciter. Uno modo, per modum identitatis, sicut dicit Augustinus super Ioan., et sic donum non distinguitur a dante, sed ab eo cui datur. Et sic dicitur quod Spiritus Sanctus dat se. Alio modo dicitur aliquid esse alicuius ut possessio vel servus, et sic oportet quod donum essentialiter distinguatur a dante. Et sic donum Dei est aliquid creatum. Tertio modo dicitur hoc esse huius per originem tantum, et sic filius est patris, et Spiritus Sanctus utriusque. Inquantum ergo donum hoc modo dicitur esse dantis, sic distinguitur a dante personaliter, et est nomen personale.

AD SECUNDUM dicendum quod essentia dicitur esse donum patris primo modo, quia essentia est patris per modum identitatis.

AD TERTIUM dicendum quod donum, secundum quod est nomen personale in divinis, non importat subiectionem, sed originem tantum, in comparatione ad dantem. In comparatione vero ad eum cui datur, importat liberum usum vel fruitionem, ut dictum est.

AD QUARTUM dicendum quod donum non dicitur ex eo quod actu datur, sed inquantum habet aptitudinem ut possit dari. Unde ab aeterno divina persona dicitur donum, licet ex tempore detur. Nec tamen per hoc quod importatur respectus ad creaturam, oportet quod sit essentiale, sed quod aliquid essentiale in suo intellectu includatur, sicut essentia includitur in intellectu personae, ut supra dictum est.

thereto; as when it is made partaker of the divine Word and of the Love proceeding, so as freely to know God truly and to love God rightly. Hence the rational creature alone can possess the divine person. Nevertheless in order that it may possess Him in this manner, its own power avails nothing: hence this must be given it from above; for that is said to be given to us which we have from another source. Thus a divine person can *be given*, and can be a *gift*.

REPLY OBJ. 1: The name *Gift* imports a personal distinction, in so far as gift imports something belonging to another through its origin. Nevertheless, the Holy Spirit gives Himself, inasmuch as He is His own, and can use or rather enjoy Himself; as also a free man belongs to himself. And as Augustine says (*In Joan. Tract.* xxix): *What is more yours than yourself?* Or we might say, and more fittingly, that a gift must belong in a way to the giver. But the phrase, *this is this one's*, can be understood in several senses. In one way it means identity, as Augustine says (In Joan. Tract. xxix); and in that sense *gift* is the same as *the giver*, but not the same as the one to whom it is given. The Holy Spirit gives Himself in that sense. In another sense, a thing is another's as a possession, or as a slave; and in that sense gift is essentially distinct from the giver; and the gift of God so taken is a created thing. In a third sense, *this is this one's* through its origin only; and in this sense the Son is the Father's; and the Holy Spirit belongs to both. Therefore, so far as gift in this way signifies the possession of the giver, it is personally distinguished from the giver, and is a personal name.

REPLY OBJ. 2: The divine essence is the Father's gift in the first sense, as being the Father's by way of identity.

REPLY OBJ. 3: Gift as a personal name in God does not imply subjection, but only origin, as regards the giver; but as regards the one to whom it is given, it implies a free use, or enjoyment, as above explained.

REPLY OBJ. 4: Gift is not so called from being actually given, but from its aptitude to be given. Hence the divine person is called Gift from eternity, although He is given in time. Nor does it follow that it is an essential name because it imports relation to the creature; but that it includes something essential in its meaning; as the essence is included in the idea of person, as stated above (Q. 34, A. 3).

Article 2

Whether Gift Is the Proper Name of the Holy Spirit?

AD SECUNDUM SIC PROCEDITUR. Videtur quod donum non sit proprium nomen spiritus sancti. Donum enim dicitur ex eo quod datur. Sed, sicut dicitur Isa. IX, *filius datus est nobis.* Ergo esse donum convenit filio, sicut spiritui sancto.

PRAETEREA, omne nomen proprium alicuius personae significat aliquam eius proprietatem. Sed hoc nomen donum non significat proprietatem aliquam spiritus sancti. Ergo donum non est proprium nomen spiritus sancti.

PRAETEREA, Spiritus Sanctus potest dici spiritus alicuius hominis, ut supra dictum est. Sed non potest dici donum alicuius hominis, sed solum donum Dei. Ergo donum non est proprium nomen spiritus sancti.

SED CONTRA est quod Augustinus dicit, in IV de Trin., *sicut natum esse est filio a patre esse, ita spiritui sancto donum Dei esse est a patre et filio procedere.* Sed Spiritus Sanctus sortitur proprium nomen inquantum procedit a patre et filio. Ergo et donum est proprium nomen spiritus sancti.

RESPONDEO dicendum quod donum, secundum quod personaliter sumitur in divinis, est proprium nomen spiritus sancti.

Ad cuius evidentiam, sciendum est quod donum proprie est datio irreddibilis, secundum philosophum, idest quod non datur intentione retributionis, et sic importat gratuitam donationem. Ratio autem gratuitae donationis est amor, ideo enim damus gratis alicui aliquid, quia volumus ei bonum. Primum ergo quod damus ei, est amor quo volumus ei bonum. Unde manifestum est quod amor habet rationem primi doni, per quod omnia dona gratuita donantur. Unde, cum Spiritus Sanctus procedat ut amor, sicut iam dictum est, procedit in ratione doni primi. Unde dicit Augustinus, XV de Trin., quod *per donum quod est Spiritus Sanctus, multa propria dona dividuntur membris Christi.*

AD PRIMUM ergo dicendum quod, sicut filius, quia procedit per modum verbi, quod de ratione sua habet quod sit similitudo sui principii dicitur proprie imago, licet etiam Spiritus Sanctus sit similis patri; ita etiam Spiritus Sanctus, quia a patre procedit ut amor, dicitur proprie donum, licet etiam filius detur. Hoc enim ipsum quod filius datur, est ex patris amore, secundum illud Ioan. III, *sic Deus dilexit mundum, ut filium suum unigenitum daret.*

AD SECUNDUM dicendum quod in nomine doni importatur quod sit dantis per originem. Et sic importatur proprietas originis spiritus sancti, quae est processio.

OBJECTION 1: It would seem that Gift is not the proper name of the Holy Spirit. For the name Gift comes from being given. But, as Isaiah says (9:16): *A Son is given to us.* Therefore to be Gift belongs to the Son, as well as to the Holy Spirit.

OBJ. 2: Further, every proper name of a person signifies a property. But this word Gift does not signify a property of the Holy Spirit. Therefore Gift is not a proper name of the Holy Spirit.

OBJ. 3: Further, the Holy Spirit can be called the spirit of a man, whereas He cannot be called the gift of any man, but *God's Gift* only. Therefore Gift is not the proper name of the Holy Spirit.

ON THE CONTRARY, Augustine says (*De Trin.* iv, 20): *As 'to be born' is, for the Son, to be from the Father, so, for the Holy Spirit, 'to be the Gift of God' is to proceed from Father and Son.* But the Holy Spirit receives His proper name from the fact that He proceeds from Father and Son. Therefore Gift is the proper name of the Holy Spirit.

I ANSWER THAT, Gift, taken personally in God, is the proper name of the Holy Spirit.

In proof of this we must know that a gift is properly an unreturnable giving, as Aristotle says (*Topic.* iv, 4)—i.e., a thing which is not given with the intention of a return—and it thus contains the idea of a gratuitous donation. Now, the reason of donation being gratuitous is love; since therefore do we give something to anyone gratuitously forasmuch as we wish him well. So what we first give him is the love whereby we wish him well. Hence it is manifest that love has the nature of a first gift, through which all free gifts are given. So since the Holy Spirit proceeds as love, as stated above (Q. 27, A. 4; Q. 37, A. 1), He proceeds as the first gift. Hence Augustine says (*De Trin.* xv, 24): *By the gift, which is the Holy Spirit, many particular gifts are portioned out to the members of Christ.*

REPLY OBJ. 1: As the Son is properly called the Image because He proceeds by way of a word, whose nature it is to be the similitude of its principle, although the Holy Spirit also is like to the Father; so also, because the Holy Spirit proceeds from the Father as love, He is properly called Gift, although the Son, too, is given. For that the Son is given is from the Father's love, according to the words, *God so loved the world, as to give His only begotten Son* (John 3:16).

REPLY OBJ. 2: The name Gift involves the idea of belonging to the Giver through its origin; and thus it imports the property of the origin of the Holy Spirit—that is, His procession.

AD TERTIUM dicendum quod donum, antequam detur, est tantum dantis, sed postquam datur, est eius cui datur. Quia igitur donum non importat dationem in actu, non potest dici quod sit donum hominis; sed donum Dei dantis. Cum autem iam datum est, tunc hominis est vel spiritus vel datum.

REPLY OBJ. 3: Before a gift is given, it belongs only to the giver; but when it is given, it is his to whom it is given. Therefore, because *Gift* does not import the actual giving, it cannot be called a gift of man, but the Gift of God giving. When, however, it has been given, then it is the spirit of man, or a gift bestowed on man.

QUESTION 39

THE PERSONS IN RELATION TO THE ESSENCE

Post ea quae de personis divinis absolute tractata sunt, considerandum restat de personis in comparatione ad essentiam, et ad proprietates, et ad actus notionales; et de comparatione ipsarum ad invicem.

Quantum igitur ad primum horum, octo quaeruntur.

Primo, utrum essentia in divinis sit idem quod persona.

Secundo, utrum dicendum sit quod tres personae sunt unius essentiae.

Tertio, utrum nomina essentialia praedicanda sint de personis in plurali vel in singulari.

Quarto, utrum adiectiva notionalia, aut verba vel participia, praedicari possint de nominibus essentialibus concretive acceptis.

Quinto, utrum praedicari possint de nominibus essentialibus in abstracto acceptis.

Sexto, utrum nomina personarum praedicari possint de nominibus essentialibus concretis.

Septimo, utrum essentialia attributa sint approprianda personis.

Octavo, quod attributum cuique personae debeat appropriari.

Those things considered which belong to the divine persons absolutely, we next treat of what concerns the person in reference to the essence, to the properties, and to the notional acts; and of the comparison of these with each other.

As regards the first of these, there are eight points of inquiry:

(1) Whether the essence in God is the same as the person?

(2) Whether we should say that the three persons are of one essence?

(3) Whether essential names should be predicated of the persons in the plural, or in the singular?

(4) Whether notional adjectives, or verbs, or participles, can be predicated of the essential names taken in a concrete sense?

(5) Whether the same can be predicated of essential names taken in the abstract?

(6) Whether the names of the persons can be predicated of concrete essential names?

(7) Whether essential attributes can be appropriated to the persons?

(8) Which attributes should be appropriated to each person?

Article 1

Whether in God the Essence Is the Same As the Person?

AD PRIMUM SIC PROCEDITUR. Videtur quod in divinis essentia non sit idem quod persona. In quibuscumque enim essentia est idem quod persona seu suppositum, oportet quod sit tantum unum suppositum unius naturae, ut patet in omnibus substantiis separatis, eorum enim quae sunt idem re, unum multiplicari non potest, quin multiplicetur et reliquum. Sed in divinis est una essentia et tres personae, ut ex supra dictis patet. Ergo essentia non est idem quod persona.

PRAETEREA, affirmatio et negatio simul et semel non verificantur de eodem. Sed affirmatio et negatio verificantur de essentia et persona, nam persona est distincta, essentia vero non est distincta. Ergo persona et essentia non sunt idem.

PRAETEREA, nihil subiicitur sibi ipsi. Sed persona subiicitur essentiae, unde suppositum vel hypostasis nominatur. Ergo persona non est idem quod essentia.

OBJECTION 1: It would seem that in God the essence is not the same as person. For whenever essence is the same as person or suppositum, there can be only one suppositum of one nature, as is clear in the case of all separate substances. For in those things which are really one and the same, one cannot be multiplied apart from the other. But in God there is one essence and three persons, as is clear from what is above expounded (Q. 28, A. 3; Q. 30, A. 2). Therefore essence is not the same as person.

OBJ. 2: Further, simultaneous affirmation and negation of the same things in the same respect cannot be true. But affirmation and negation are true of essence and of person. For person is distinct, whereas essence is not. Therefore person and essence are not the same.

OBJ. 3: Further, nothing can be subject to itself. But person is subject to essence; whence it is called suppositum or *hypostasis*. Therefore person is not the same as essence.

SED CONTRA est quod Augustinus dicit, VII de Trin., *cum dicimus personam patris, non aliud dicimus quam substantiam patris.*

RESPONDEO dicendum quod considerantibus divinam simplicitatem, quaestio ista in manifesto habet veritatem. Ostensum est enim supra quod divina simplicitas hoc requirit, quod in Deo sit idem essentia et suppositum; quod in substantiis intellectualibus nihil est aliud quam persona. Sed difficultatem videtur ingerere quod, multiplicatis personis divinis, essentia retinet unitatem. Et quia, ut Boetius dicit, *relatio multiplicat personarum Trinitatem,* posuerunt aliqui hoc modo in divinis differre essentiam et personam, quo et relationes dicebant esse assistentes, considerantes in relationibus solum quod ad alterum sunt, et non quod res sunt. Sed, sicut supra ostensum est, sicut relationes in rebus creatis accidentaliter insunt, ita in Deo sunt ipsa essentia divina. Ex quo sequitur quod in Deo non sit aliud essentia quam persona secundum rem; et tamen quod personae realiter ab invicem distinguantur. Persona enim, ut dictum est supra, significat relationem, prout est subsistens in natura divina. Relatio autem, ad essentiam comparata, non differt re, sed ratione tantum, comparata autem ad oppositam relationem, habet, virtute oppositionis, realem distinctionem. Et sic remanet una essentia, et tres personae.

AD PRIMUM ergo dicendum quod in creaturis non potest esse distinctio suppositorum per relationes, sed oportet quod sit per essentialia principia, quia relationes non sunt subsistentes in creaturis. In divinis autem relationes sunt subsistentes, et ideo, secundum quod habent oppositionem ad invicem, possunt distinguere supposita. Neque tamen distinguitur essentia, quia relationes ipsae non distinguuntur ab invicem secundum quod sunt realiter idem cum essentia.

AD SECUNDUM dicendum quod, inquantum essentia et persona in divinis differunt secundum intelligentiae rationem, sequitur quod aliquid possit affirmari de uno, quod negatur de altero, et per consequens quod, supposito uno, non supponatur alterum.

AD TERTIUM dicendum quod rebus divinis nomina imponimus secundum modum rerum creatarum, ut supra dictum est. Et quia naturae rerum creatarum individuantur per materiam, quae subiicitur naturae speciei, inde est quod individua dicuntur subiecta, vel supposita, vel hypostases. Et propter hoc etiam divinae personae supposita vel hypostases nominantur, non quod ibi sit aliqua suppositio vel subiectio secundum rem.

ON THE CONTRARY, Augustine says (*De Trin.* vi, 7): *When we say the person of the Father we mean nothing else but the substance of the Father.*

I ANSWER THAT, The truth of this question is quite clear if we consider the divine simplicity. For it was shown above (Q. 3, A. 3) that the divine simplicity requires that in God essence is the same as suppositum, which in intellectual substances is nothing else than person. But a difficulty seems to arise from the fact that while the divine persons are multiplied, the essence nevertheless retains its unity. And because, as Boethius says (*De Trin.* i), *relation multiplies the Trinity of persons,* some have thought that in God essence and person differ, forasmuch as they held the relations to be *adjacent;* considering only in the relations the idea of *reference to another,* and not the relations as realities. But as it was shown above (Q. 28, A. 2) in creatures relations are accidental, whereas in God they are the divine essence itself. Thence it follows that in God essence is not really distinct from person; and yet that the persons are really distinguished from each other. For person, as above stated (Q. 29, A. 4), signifies relation as subsisting in the divine nature. But relation as referred to the essence does not differ therefrom really, but only in our way of thinking; while as referred to an opposite relation, it has a real distinction by virtue of that opposition. Thus there are one essence and three persons.

REPLY OBJ. 1: There cannot be a distinction of suppositum in creatures by means of relations, but only by essential principles; because in creatures relations are not subsistent. But in God relations are subsistent, and so by reason of the opposition between them they distinguish the supposita; and yet the essence is not distinguished, because the relations themselves are not distinguished from each other so far as they are identified with the essence.

REPLY OBJ. 2: As essence and person in God differ in our way of thinking, it follows that something can be denied of the one and affirmed of the other; and therefore, when we suppose the one, we need not suppose the other.

REPLY OBJ. 3: Divine things are named by us after the way of created things, as above explained (Q. 13, AA. 1, 3). And since created natures are individualized by matter which is the subject of the specific nature, it follows that individuals are called *subjects,* supposita, or *hypostases.* So the divine persons are named supposita or *hypostases,* but not as if there really existed any real *supposition* or *subjection.*

Article 2

Whether It Must Be Said That the Three Persons Are of One Essence?

AD SECUNDUM SIC PROCEDITUR. Videtur quod non sit dicendum tres personas esse unius essentiae. Dicit enim Hilarius, in libro de Synod., quod pater et filius et Spiritus Sanctus *sunt quidem per substantiam tria, per consonantiam vero unum.* Sed substantia Dei est eius essentia. Ergo tres personae non sunt unius essentiae.

PRAETEREA, non est affirmandum aliquid de divinis, quod auctoritate Scripturae sacrae non est expressum, ut patet per Dionysium, I cap. de Div. Nom. Sed nunquam in Scriptura sacra exprimitur quod pater et filius et Spiritus Sanctus sunt unius essentiae. Ergo hoc non est asserendum.

PRAETEREA, natura divina est idem quod essentia. Sufficeret ergo dicere quod tres personae sunt unius naturae.

PRAETEREA, non consuevit dici quod persona sit essentiae, sed magis quod essentia sit personae. Ergo neque convenienter videtur dici quod tres personae sunt unius essentiae.

PRAETEREA, Augustinus dicit quod non dicimus tres personas esse ex una essentia, ne intelligatur in divinis aliud esse essentia et persona. Sed sicut praepositiones sunt transitivae, ita et obliqui. Ergo, pari ratione, non est dicendum quod tres personae sunt unius essentiae.

PRAETEREA, id quod potest esse erroris occasio, non est in divinis dicendum. Sed cum dicuntur tres personae unius essentiae vel substantiae datur erroris occasio. Quia, ut Hilarius dicit, in libro de Synod., *una substantia patris et filii praedicata, aut unum qui duas nuncupationes habeat, subsistentem significat; aut divisam unam substantiam duas imperfectas fecisse substantias; aut tertiam priorem substantiam, quae a duobus et usurpata sit et assumpta.* Non est ergo dicendum tres personas esse unius substantiae.

SED CONTRA est quod Augustinus dicit, in libro II contra Maximinum, quod hoc nomen homousion, quod in Concilio Nicaeno adversus Arianos firmatum est, idem significat quod tres personas esse unius essentiae.

RESPONDEO dicendum quod, sicut supra dictum est, intellectus noster res divinas nominat, non secundum modum earum, quia sic eas cognoscere non potest; sed secundum modum in rebus creatis inventum. Et quia in rebus sensibilibus, a quibus intellectus noster scientiam capit, natura alicuius speciei per materiam individuatur; et sic natura se habet ut forma, individuum autem ut suppositum formae, propter hoc etiam in divinis, quantum ad modum significandi, essentia significatur ut forma trium personarum. Dicimus autem in rebus creatis formam quamcumque esse eius cuius est forma; sicut

OBJECTION 1: It would seem not right to say that the three persons are of one essence. For Hilary says (*De Synod.*) that the Father, Son and Holy Spirit *are indeed three by substance, but one in harmony.* But the substance of God is His essence. Therefore the three persons are not of one essence.

OBJ. 2: Further, nothing is to be affirmed of God except what can be confirmed by the authority of Holy Writ, as appears from Dionysius (*Div. Nom.* i). Now Holy Writ never says that the Father, Son and Holy Spirit are of one essence. Therefore this should not be asserted.

OBJ. 3: Further, the divine nature is the same as the divine essence. It suffices therefore to say that the three persons are of one nature.

OBJ. 4: Further, it is not usual to say that the person is of the essence; but rather that the essence is of the person. Therefore it does not seem fitting to say that the three persons are of one essence.

OBJ. 5: Further, Augustine says (*De Trin.* vii, 6) that we do not say that the three persons are *from one essence*, lest we should seem to indicate a distinction between the essence and the persons in God. But prepositions which imply transition, denote the oblique case. Therefore it is equally wrong to say that the three persons are *of one essence*.

OBJ. 6: Further, nothing should be said of God which can be occasion of error. Now, to say that the three persons are of one essence or substance, furnishes occasion of error. For, as Hilary says (*De Synod.*): *One substance predicated of the Father and the Son signifies either one subsistent, with two denominations; or one substance divided into two imperfect substances; or a third prior substance taken and assumed by the other two.* Therefore it must not be said that the three persons are of one substance.

ON THE CONTRARY, Augustine says (*Contra Maxim.* iii) that the word homoousion, which the Council of Nicaea adopted against the Arians, means that the three persons are of one essence.

I ANSWER THAT, As above explained (Q. 13, AA. 1, 2), divine things are named by our intellect, not as they really are in themselves, for in that way it knows them not; but in a way that belongs to things created. And as in the objects of the senses, whence the intellect derives its knowledge, the nature of the species is made individual by the matter, and thus the nature is as the form, and the individual is the suppositum of the form; so also in God the essence is taken as the form of the three persons, according to our mode of signification. Now in creatures we say that every form belongs to that whereof it is the form; as

sanitatem vel pulchritudinem hominis alicuius. Rem autem habentem formam non dicimus esse formae, nisi cum adiectione alicuius adiectivi, quod designat illam formam, ut cum dicimus, ista mulier est egregiae formae, iste homo est perfectae virtutis. Et similiter, quia in divinis, multiplicatis personis, non multiplicatur essentia, dicimus unam essentiam esse trium personarum; et tres personas unius essentiae, ut intelligantur isti genitivi construi in designatione formae.

AD PRIMUM ergo dicendum quod substantia sumitur pro hypostasi; et non pro essentia.

AD SECUNDUM dicendum quod, licet tres personas esse unius essentiae non inveniatur in sacra Scriptura per haec verba, invenitur tamen quantum ad hunc sensum, sicut ibi, *ego et pater unum sumus*; et, *ego in patre, et pater in me est*. Et per multa alia haberi potest idem.

AD TERTIUM dicendum quod, quia natura designat principium actus, essentia vero ab essendo dicitur, possunt dici aliqua unius naturae, quae conveniunt in aliquo actu, sicut omnia calefacientia, sed unius essentiae dici non possunt, nisi quorum est unum esse. Et ideo magis exprimitur unitas divina per hoc quod dicitur quod tres personae sunt unius essentiae, quam si diceretur quod sunt unius naturae.

AD QUARTUM dicendum quod forma, absolute accepta, consuevit significari ut eius cuius est forma, ut virtus Petri. E converso autem, res habens formam aliquam non consuevit significari ut eius, nisi cum volumus determinare sive designare formam. Et tunc requiruntur duo genitivi, quorum unus significet formam, et alius determinationem formae, ut si dicatur, Petrus est magnae virtutis, vel etiam requiritur unus genitivus habens vim duorum genitivorum, ut cum dicitur, vir sanguinum est iste, idest effusor multi sanguinis. Quia igitur essentia divina significatur ut forma respectu personae, convenienter essentia personae dicitur. Non autem e converso, nisi aliquid addatur ad designationem essentiae; ut si dicatur quod pater est persona divinae essentiae, vel quod tres personae sunt unius essentiae.

AD QUINTUM dicendum quod haec praepositio ex vel de non designat habitudinem causae formalis, sed magis habitudinem causae efficientis vel materialis. Quae quidem causae in omnibus distinguuntur ab his quorum sunt causae, nihil enim est sua materia, neque aliquid est suum principium activum. Aliquid tamen est sua forma, ut patet in omnibus rebus immaterialibus. Et ideo per hoc quod dicimus tres personas unius essentiae, significando essentiam in habitudine formae, non ostenditur aliud esse essentia quam persona, quod ostenderetur, si diceremus tres personas ex eadem essentia.

AD SEXTUM dicendum quod, sicut Hilarius dicit, in libro de Synod., *male sanctis rebus praeiudicatur, si, quia*

the health and beauty of a man belongs to the man. But we do not say of that which has a form, that it belongs to the form, unless some adjective qualifies the form; as when we say: *That woman is of a handsome figure*, or: *This man is of perfect virtue*. In like manner, as in God the persons are multiplied, and the essence is not multiplied, we speak of one essence of the three persons, and three persons of the one essence, provided that these genitives be understood as designating the form.

REPLY OBJ. 1: Substance is here taken for the *hypostasis*, and not for the essence.

REPLY OBJ. 2: Although we may not find it declared in Holy Writ in so many words that the three persons are of one essence, nevertheless we find it so stated as regards the meaning; for instance, *I and the Father are one* (John 10:30), and *I am in the Father, and the Father in Me* (John 10:38); and there are many other texts of the same import.

REPLY OBJ. 3: Because *nature* designates the principle of action while *essence* comes from being, things may be said to be of one nature which agree in some action, as all things which give heat; but only those things can be said to be of *one essence* which have one being. So the divine unity is better described by saying that the three persons are *of one essence*, than by saying they are *of one nature*.

REPLY OBJ. 4: Form, in the absolute sense, is wont to be designated as belonging to that of which it is the form, as we say *the virtue of Peter*. On the other hand, the thing having form is not wont to be designated as belonging to the form except when we wish to qualify or designate the form. In which case two genitives are required, one signifying the form, and the other signifying the determination of the form, as, for instance, when we say, *Peter is of great virtue*, or else one genitive must have the force of two, as, for instance, *he is a man of blood*—that is, he is a man who sheds much blood. So, because the divine essence signifies a form as regards the person, it may properly be said that the essence is of the person; but we cannot say the converse, unless we add some term to designate the essence; as, for instance, the Father is a person of the *divine essence*; or, the three persons are *of one essence*.

REPLY OBJ. 5: The preposition *from* or *out of* does not designate the habitude of a formal cause, but rather the habitude of an efficient or material cause; which causes are in all cases distinguished from those things of which they are the causes. For nothing can be its own matter, nor its own active principle. Yet a thing may be its own form, as appears in all immaterial things. So, when we say, *three persons of one essence*, taking essence as having the habitude of form, we do not mean that essence is different from person, which we should mean if we said, *three persons from the same essence*.

REPLY OBJ. 6: As Hilary says (*De Synod.*): *It would be prejudicial to holy things, if we had to do away with them,*

non sanctae a quibusdam habentur, esse non debeant. Sic, si male intelligitur homousion, quid ad me bene intelligentem? Sit ergo una substantia ex naturae genitae proprietate, non sit autem ex portione, aut ex unione, aut ex communione.

just because some do not think them holy. So if some misunderstand homoousion, what is that to me, if I understand it rightly? . . . The oneness of nature does not result from division, or from union or from community of possession, but from one nature being proper to both Father and Son.

Article 3

Whether Essential Names Should Be Predicated in the Singular of the Three Persons?

AD TERTIUM SIC PROCEDITUR. Videtur quod nomina essentialia, ut hoc nomen Deus, non praedicentur singulariter de tribus personis, sed pluraliter. Sicut enim homo significatur ut habens humanitatem, ita Deus significatur ut habens deitatem. Sed tres personae sunt tres habentes deitatem. Ergo tres personae sunt tres dii.

PRAETEREA, Gen. I, ubi dicitur, *in principio creavit Deus caelum et terram*, Hebraica veritas habet Elohim, quod potest interpretari dii, sive iudices. Et hoc dicitur propter pluralitatem personarum. Ergo tres personae sunt plures dii, et non unus Deus.

PRAETEREA, hoc nomen res, cum absolute dicatur, videtur ad substantiam pertinere. Sed hoc nomen pluraliter praedicatur de tribus personis, dicit enim Augustinus, in libro de Doctr. Christ., *res quibus fruendum est, sunt pater et filius et Spiritus Sanctus.* Ergo et alia nomina essentialia pluraliter praedicari possunt de tribus personis.

PRAETEREA, sicut hoc nomen Deus significat habentem deitatem, ita hoc nomen persona significat subsistentem in natura aliqua intellectuali. Sed dicimus tres personas. Ergo, eadem ratione, dicere possumus tres deos.

SED CONTRA est quod dicitur Deut. VI, *audi, Israel, dominus Deus tuus, Deus unus est.*

RESPONDEO dicendum quod nominum essentialium quaedam significant essentiam substantive, quaedam vero adiective. Ea quidem quae substantive essentiam significant, praedicantur de tribus personis singulariter tantum, et non pluraliter, quae vero adiective essentiam significant, praedicantur de tribus personis in plurali. Cuius ratio est, quia nomina substantiva significant aliquid per modum substantiae, nomina vero adiectiva significant aliquid per modum accidentis, quod inhaeret subiecto. Substantia autem, sicut per se habet esse, ita per se habet unitatem vel multitudinem, unde et singularitas vel pluralitas nominis substantivi attenditur secundum formam significatam per nomen. Accidentia autem, sicut esse habent in subiecto, ita ex subiecto suscipiunt unitatem et multitudinem, et ideo in adiectivis attenditur singularitas et pluralitas secundum supposita. In creaturis autem non invenitur una forma in pluribus

OBJECTION 1: It would seem that essential names, as the name *God*, should not be predicated in the singular of the three persons, but in the plural. For as *man* signifies *one that has humanity*, so God signifies *one that has Godhead*. But the three persons are three who have Godhead. Therefore the three persons are *three Gods*.

OBJ. 2: Further, Gen. 1:1, where it is said, *In the beginning God created heaven and earth*, the Hebrew original has *Elohim*, which may be rendered *Gods* or *Judges*: and this word is used on account of the plurality of persons. Therefore the three persons are *several Gods*, and not *one* God.

OBJ. 3: Further, this word *thing* when it is said absolutely, seems to belong to substance. But it is predicated of the three persons in the plural. For Augustine says (*De Doctr. Christ.* i, 5): *The things that are the objects of our future glory are the Father, Son and Holy Spirit*. Therefore other essential names can be predicated in the plural of the three persons.

OBJ. 4: Further, as this word *God* signifies *a being who has Deity*, so also this word *person* signifies a being subsisting in an intellectual nature. But we say there are three persons. So for the same reason we can say there are *three Gods*.

ON THE CONTRARY, It is said (Deut 6:4): *Hear, O Israel, the Lord thy God is one God.*

I ANSWER THAT, Some essential names signify the essence after the manner of substantives; while others signify it after the manner of adjectives. Those which signify it as substantives are predicated of the three persons in the singular only, and not in the plural. Those which signify the essence as adjectives are predicated of the three persons in the plural. The reason of this is that substantives signify something by way of substance, while adjectives signify something by way of accident, which adheres to a subject. Now just as substance has existence of itself, so also it has of itself unity or multitude; wherefore the singularity or plurality of a substantive name depends upon the form signified by the name. But as accidents have their existence in a subject, so they have unity or plurality from their subject; and therefore the singularity and plurality of adjectives depends upon their supposita. In creatures, one form does not exist in several supposita except by unity of order, as

suppositis nisi unitate ordinis, ut forma multitudinis ordinatae. Unde nomina significantia talem formam, si sint substantiva, praedicantur de pluribus in singulari, non autem si sint adiectiva. Dicimus enim quod multi homines sunt collegium vel exercitus aut populus, dicimus tamen quod plures homines sunt collegiati. In divinis autem essentia divina significatur per modum formae, ut dictum est quae quidem simplex est et maxime una, ut supra ostensum est. Unde nomina significantia divinam essentiam substantive, singulariter, et non pluraliter, de tribus personis praedicantur. Haec igitur est ratio quare Socratem et Platonem et Ciceronem dicimus tres homines; patrem autem et filium et spiritum sanctum non dicimus tres deos, sed unum Deum, quia in tribus suppositis humanae naturae sunt tres humanitates; in tribus autem personis est una divina essentia. Ea vero quae significant essentiam adiective, praedicantur pluraliter de tribus, propter pluralitatem suppositorum. Dicimus enim tres existentes vel tres sapientes, aut tres aeternos et increatos et immensos, si adiective sumantur. Si vero substantive sumantur, dicimus unum increatum, immensum et aeternum, ut Athanasius dicit.

AD PRIMUM ergo dicendum quod, licet Deus significet habentem deitatem, est tamen alius modus significandi, nam Deus dicitur substantive, sed habens deitatem dicitur adiective. Unde, licet sint tres habentes deitatem, non tamen sequitur quod sint tres dii.

AD SECUNDUM dicendum quod diversae linguae habent diversum modum loquendi. Unde, sicut propter pluralitatem suppositorum Graeci dicunt tres hypostases, ita et in Hebraeo dicitur pluraliter Elohim. Nos autem non dicimus pluraliter neque deos neque substantias, ne pluralitas ad substantiam referatur.

AD TERTIUM dicendum quod hoc nomen res est de transcendentibus. Unde, secundum quod pertinet ad relationem, pluraliter praedicatur in divinis, secundum vero quod pertinet ad substantiam, singulariter praedicatur. Unde Augustinus dicit ibidem quod eadem Trinitas quaedam summa res est.

AD QUARTUM dicendum quod forma significata per hoc nomen persona, non est essentia vel natura, sed personalitas. Unde, cum sint tres personalitates, idest tres personales proprietates, in patre et filio et spiritu sancto, non singulariter, sed pluraliter praedicatur de tribus.

the form of an ordered multitude. So if the names signifying such a form are substantives, they are predicated of many in the singular, but otherwise if they adjectives. For we say that many men are a college, or an army, or a people; but we say that many men are collegians. Now in God the divine essence is signified by way of a form, as above explained (A. 2), which, indeed, is simple and supremely one, as shown above (Q. 3, A. 7; Q. 11, A. 4). So, names which signify the divine essence in a substantive manner are predicated of the three persons in the singular, and not in the plural. This, then, is the reason why we say that Socrates, Plato and Cicero are *three men*; whereas we do not say the Father, Son and Holy Spirit are *three Gods*, but *one God*; forasmuch as in the three supposita of human nature there are three humanities, whereas in the three divine Persons there is but one divine essence. On the other hand, the names which signify essence in an adjectival manner are predicated of the three persons plurally, by reason of the plurality of supposita. For we say there are three *existent* or three *wise* beings, or three *eternal*, *uncreated*, and *immense* beings, if these terms are understood in an adjectival sense. But if taken in a substantive sense, we say *one uncreated, immense, eternal being*, as Athanasius declares.

REPLY OBJ. 1: Though the name *God* signifies a being having Godhead, nevertheless the mode of signification is different. For the name *God* is used substantively; whereas *having Godhead* is used adjectively. Consequently, although there are *three having Godhead*, it does not follow that there are three Gods.

REPLY OBJ. 2: Various languages have diverse modes of expression. So as by reason of the plurality of supposita the Greeks said *three hypostases*, so also in Hebrew *Elohim* is in the plural. We, however, do not apply the plural either to *God* or to *substance*, lest plurality be referred to the substance.

REPLY OBJ. 3: This word *thing* is one of the transcendentals. Whence, so far as it is referred to relation, it is predicated of God in the plural; whereas, so far as it is referred to the substance, it is predicated in the singular. So Augustine says, in the passage quoted, that *the same Trinity is a thing supreme*.

REPLY OBJ. 4: The form signified by the word *person* is not essence or nature, but personality. So, as there are three personalities—that is, three personal properties in the Father, Son and Holy Spirit—it is predicated of the three, not in the singular, but in the plural.

Article 4

Whether the Concrete Essential Names Can Stand for the Person?

AD QUARTUM SIC PROCEDITUR. Videtur quod nomina essentialia concretiva non possunt supponere pro persona, ita quod haec sit vera, Deus genuit Deum. Quia, ut sophistae dicunt, terminus singularis idem significat et supponit. Sed hoc nomen Deus videtur esse terminus singularis, cum pluraliter praedicari non possit, ut dictum est. Ergo, cum significet essentiam, videtur quod supponat pro essentia, et non pro persona.

PRAETEREA, terminus in subiecto positus non restringitur per terminum positum in praedicato, ratione significationis; sed solum ratione temporis consignificati. Sed cum dico, Deus creat, hoc nomen Deus supponit pro essentia. Ergo cum dicitur, Deus genuit, non potest iste terminus Deus, ratione praedicati notionalis, supponere pro persona.

PRAETEREA, si haec est vera, Deus genuit, quia pater generat; pari ratione haec erit vera, Deus non generat, quia filius non generat. Ergo est Deus generans, et Deus non generans. Et ita videtur sequi quod sint duo dii.

PRAETEREA, si Deus genuit Deum, aut se Deum, aut alium Deum. Sed non se Deum, quia, ut Augustinus dicit, in I de Trin., *nulla res generat seipsam.* Neque alium Deum, quia non est nisi unus Deus. Ergo haec est falsa, Deus genuit Deum.

PRAETEREA, si Deus genuit Deum, aut Deum qui est Deus pater, aut Deum qui non est Deus pater. Si Deum qui est Deus pater, ergo Deus pater est genitus. Si Deum qui non est Deus pater, ergo Deus est qui non est Deus pater, quod est falsum. Non ergo potest dici quod Deus genuit Deum.

SED CONTRA est quod in symbolo dicitur Deum de Deo.

RESPONDEO dicendum quod quidam dixerunt quod hoc nomen Deus, et similia, proprie secundum suam naturam supponunt pro essentia, sed ex adiuncto notionali trahuntur ad supponendum pro persona. Et haec opinio processisse videtur ex consideratione divinae simplicitatis, quae requirit quod in Deo idem sit habens et quod habetur, et sic habens deitatem, quod significat hoc nomen Deus, est idem quod deitas. Sed in proprietatibus locutionum, non tantum attendenda est res significata; sed etiam modus significandi. Et ideo, quia hoc nomen Deus significat divinam essentiam ut in habente ipsam, sicut hoc nomen homo humanitatem significat in supposito; alii melius dixerunt quod hoc nomen Deus ex modo significandi habet ut proprie possit supponere pro persona, sicut et hoc nomen homo. Quandoque ergo hoc nomen Deus supponit pro essentia, ut cum dicitur, Deus creat, quia hoc praedicatum competit subiecto ratione

OBJECTION 1: It would seem that the concrete, essential names cannot stand for the person, so that we can truly say *God begot God.* For, as the logicians say, *a singular term signifies what it stands for.* But this name *God* seems to be a singular term, for it cannot be predicated in the plural, as above explained (A. 3). Therefore, since it signifies the essence, it stands for essence, and not for person.

OBJ. 2: Further, a term in the subject is not modified by a term in the predicate, as to its signification; but only as to the sense signified in the predicate. But when I say, *God creates,* this name *God* stands for the essence. So when we say *God begot,* this term *God* cannot by reason of the notional predicate, stand for person.

OBJ. 3: Further, if this be true, *God begot,* because the Father generates; for the same reason this is true, *God does not beget,* because the Son does not beget. Therefore there is God who begets, and there is God who does not beget; and thus it follows that there are two Gods.

OBJ. 4: Further, if *God begot God,* He begot either God, that is Himself, or another God. But He did not beget God, that is Himself; for, as Augustine says (*De Trin.* i, 1), *nothing begets itself.* Neither did He beget another God; as there is only one God. Therefore it is false to say, *God begot God.*

OBJ. 5: Further, if *God begot God,* He begot either God who is the Father, or God who is not the Father. If God who is the Father, then God the Father was begotten. If God who is not the Father, then there is a God who is not God the Father: which is false. Therefore it cannot be said that *God begot God.*

ON THE CONTRARY, In the Creed it is said, *God of God.*

I ANSWER THAT, Some have said that this name *God* and the like, properly according to their nature, stand for the essence, but by reason of some notional adjunct are made to stand for the Person. This opinion apparently arose from considering the divine simplicity, which requires that in God, He *who possesses* and *what is possessed* be the same. So He who possesses Godhead, which is signified by the name God, is the same as Godhead. But when we consider the proper way of expressing ourselves, the mode of signification must be considered no less than the thing signified. Hence as this word *God* signifies the divine essence as in Him Who possesses it, just as the name *man* signifies humanity in a subject, others more truly have said that this word *God,* from its mode of signification, can, in its proper sense, stand for person, as does the word *man.* So this word *God* sometimes stands for the essence, as when we say *God creates;* because this predicate is attributed to the subject by

formae significatae, quae est deitas. Quandoque vero supponit personam, vel unam tantum, ut cum dicitur, Deus generat; vel duas, ut cum dicitur Deus spirat; vel tres, ut cum dicitur, *regi saeculorum immortali, invisibili, soli Deo* etc., I Tim. I.

AD PRIMUM ergo dicendum quod hoc nomen Deus, licet conveniat cum terminis singularibus in hoc, quod forma significata non multiplicatur; convenit tamen cum terminis communibus in hoc, quod forma significata invenitur in pluribus suppositis. Unde non oportet quod semper supponat pro essentia quam significat.

AD SECUNDUM dicendum quod obiectio illa procedit contra illos qui dicebant quod hoc nomen Deus non habet naturalem suppositionem pro persona.

AD TERTIUM dicendum quod aliter se habet hoc nomen Deus ad supponendum pro persona, et hoc nomen homo. Quia enim forma significata per hoc nomen homo, idest humanitas, realiter dividitur in diversis suppositis, per se supponit pro persona; etiamsi nihil addatur quod determinet ipsum ad personam, quae est suppositum distinctum. Unitas autem sive communitas humanae naturae non est secundum rem, sed solum secundum considerationem, unde iste terminus homo non supponit pro natura communi, nisi propter exigentiam alicuius additi, ut cum dicitur, homo est species. Sed forma significata per hoc nomen Deus, scilicet essentia divina, est una et communis secundum rem. Unde per se supponit pro natura communi, sed ex adiuncto determinatur eius suppositio ad personam. Unde cum dicitur, Deus generat, ratione actus notionalis supponit hoc nomen Deus pro persona patris. Sed cum dicitur, Deus non generat, nihil additur quod determinet hoc nomen ad personam filii, unde datur intelligi quod generatio repugnet divinae naturae. Sed si addatur aliquid pertinens ad personam filii, vera erit locutio; ut si dicatur, Deus genitus non generat. Unde etiam non sequitur, est Deus generans et est Deus non generans, nisi ponatur aliquid pertinens ad personas; ut puta si dicamus, pater est Deus generans, et filius est Deus non generans. Et ita non sequitur quod sint plures dii, quia pater et filius sunt unus Deus, ut dictum est.

AD QUARTUM dicendum quod haec est falsa, pater genuit se Deum, quia ly se, cum sit reciprocum, refert idem suppositum. Neque est contrarium quod Augustinus dicit, ad maximum, quod *Deus pater genuit alterum se.* Quia ly se vel est casus ablativi; ut sit sensus, genuit alterum a se. Vel facit relationem simplicem, et sic refert identitatem naturae, sed est impropria vel emphatica locutio, ut sit sensus, genuit alterum simillimum sibi. Similiter et haec est falsa, genuit alium Deum. Quia licet filius sit alius a patre, ut supra dictum est, non tamen est dicendum quod sit alius Deus, quia intelligeretur quod hoc adiectivum alius poneret rem suam circa substantivum

reason of the form signified—that is, Godhead. But sometimes it stands for the person, either for only one, as when we say, *God begets,* or for two, as when we say, *God spirates;* or for three, as when it is said: *To the King of ages, immortal, invisible, the only God,* etc. (1 Tim 1:17).

REPLY OBJ. 1: Although this name *God* agrees with singular terms as regards the form signified not being multiplied; nevertheless it agrees also with general terms so far as the form signified is to be found in several supposita. So it need not always stand for the essence it signifies.

REPLY OBJ. 2: This holds good against those who say that the word *God* does not naturally stand for person.

REPLY OBJ. 3: The word *God* stands for the person in a different way from that in which this word *man* does; for since the form signified by this word *man*—that is, humanity—is really divided among its different subjects, it stands of itself for the person, even if there is no adjunct determining it to the person—that is, to a distinct subject. The unity or community of the human nature, however, is not a reality, but is only in the consideration of the mind. Hence this term *man* does not stand for the common nature, unless this is required by some adjunct, as when we say, *man is a species;* whereas the form signified by the name *God*—that is, the divine essence—is really one and common. So of itself it stands for the common nature, but by some adjunct it may be restricted so as to stand for the person. So, when we say, *God generates,* by reason of the notional act this name *God* stands for the person of the Father. But when we say, *God does not generate,* there is no adjunct to determine this name to the person of the Son, and hence the phrase means that generation is repugnant to the divine nature. If, however, something be added belonging to the person of the Son, this proposition, for instance, *God begotten does not beget,* is true. Consequently, it does not follow that there exists a *God generator,* and a *God not generator;* unless there be an adjunct pertaining to the persons; as, for instance, if we were to say, *the Father is God the generator* and 'the Son is God the non-generator' and so it does not follow that there are many Gods; for the Father and the Son are one God, as was said above (A. 3).

REPLY OBJ. 4: This is false, *the Father begot God, that is Himself,* because the word *Himself,* as a reciprocal term, refers to the same suppositum. Nor is this contrary to what Augustine says (*Ep. lxvi ad Maxim.*) that *God the Father begot another self,* forasmuch as the word *se* is either in the ablative case, and then it means *He begot another from Himself,* or it indicates a single relation, and thus points to identity of nature. This is, however, either a figurative or an emphatic way of speaking, so that it would really mean, *He begot another most like to Himself.* Likewise also it is false to say, *He begot another God,* because although the Son is another than the Father, as above explained (Q. 31, A. 2),

quod est Deus; et sic significaretur distinctio deitatis. Quidam tamen concedunt istam, genuit alium Deum, ita quod ly alius sit substantivum, et ly Deus appositive construatur cum eo. Sed hic est improprius modus loquendi, et evitandus, ne detur occasio erroris.

AD QUINTUM dicendum quod haec est falsa, Deus genuit Deum qui est Deus pater, quia, cum ly pater appositive construatur cum ly Deus, restringit ipsum ad standum pro persona patris; ut sit sensus, genuit Deum qui est ipse pater, et sic pater esset genitus, quod est falsum. Unde negativa est vera, genuit Deum qui non est Deus pater. Si tamen intelligeretur constructio non esse appositiva, sed aliquid esse interponendum; tunc e converso affirmativa esset vera, et negativa falsa; ut sit sensus, genuit Deum qui est Deus qui est pater. Sed haec est extorta expositio. Unde melius est quod simpliciter affirmativa negetur, et negativa concedatur. Praepositivus tamen dixit quod tam negativa quam affirmativa est falsa. Quia hoc relativum qui in affirmativa potest referre suppositum, sed in negativa refert et significatum et suppositum. Unde sensus affirmativae est, quod esse Deum patrem conveniat personae filii. Negativae vero sensus est, quod esse Deum patrem non tantum removeatur a persona filii, sed etiam a divinitate eius sed hoc irrationabile videtur, cum, secundum philosophum, de eodem de quo est affirmatio, possit etiam esse negatio.

nevertheless it cannot be said that He is *another God*; forasmuch as this adjective *another* would be understood to apply to the substantive God; and thus the meaning would be that there is a distinction of Godhead. Yet this proposition *He begot another God* is tolerated by some, provided that *another* be taken as a substantive, and the word *God* be construed in apposition with it. This, however, is an inexact way of speaking, and to be avoided, for fear of giving occasion to error.

REPLY OBJ. 5: To say, *God begot God Who is God the Father*, is wrong, because since the word *Father* is construed in apposition to *God*, the word *God* is restricted to the person of the Father; so that it would mean, *He begot God, Who is Himself the Father*; and then the Father would be spoken of as begotten, which is false. Wherefore the negative of the proposition is true, *He begot God Who is not God the Father*. If however, we understand these words not to be in apposition, and require something to be added, then, on the contrary, the affirmative proposition is true, and the negative is false; so that the meaning would be, *He begot God Who is God Who is the Father*. Such a rendering however appears to be forced, so that it is better to say simply that the affirmative proposition is false, and the negative is true. Yet Prepositivus said that both the negative and affirmative are false, because this relative *Who* in the affirmative proposition can be referred to the suppositum; whereas in the negative it denotes both the thing signified and the suppositum. Whence, in the affirmative the sense is that *to be God the Father* is befitting to the person of the Son; and in the negative sense is that *to be God the Father*, is to be removed from the Son's divinity as well as from His personality. This, however, appears to be irrational; since, according to the Philosopher (*Peri Herm.* ii), what is open to affirmation, is open also to negation.

Article 5

Whether Abstract Essential Names Can Stand for the Person?

AD QUINTUM SIC PROCEDITUR. Videtur quod nomina essentialia in abstracto significata possint supponere pro persona, ita quod haec sit vera, essentia generat essentiam. Dicit enim Augustinus, VII de Trin., *pater et filius sunt una sapientia, quia una essentia; et singillatim sapientia de sapientia, sicut essentia de essentia.*

PRAETEREA, generatis nobis vel corruptis, generantur vel corrumpuntur ea quae in nobis sunt. Sed filius generatur. Ergo, cum essentia divina sit in filio, videtur quod essentia divina generetur.

PRAETEREA, idem est Deus et essentia divina, ut ex supra dictis patet. Sed haec est vera, Deus generat Deum,

OBJECTION 1: It would seem that abstract essential names can stand for the person, so that this proposition is true, *Essence begets essence*. For Augustine says (*De Trin.* vii, i, 2): *The Father and the Son are one Wisdom, because they are one essence; and taken singly Wisdom is from Wisdom, as essence from essence.*

OBJ. 2: Further, generation or corruption in ourselves implies generation or corruption of what is within us. But the Son is generated. Therefore since the divine essence is in the Son, it seems that the divine essence is generated.

OBJ. 3: Further, God and the divine essence are the same, as is clear from what is above explained (Q. 3, A. 3).

sicut dictum est. Ergo haec est vera, essentia generat essentiam.

PRAETEREA, de quocumque praedicatur aliquid, potest supponere pro illo. Sed essentia divina est pater. Ergo essentia potest supponere pro persona patris. Et sic essentia generat.

PRAETEREA, essentia est res generans, quia est pater, qui est generans. Si igitur essentia non sit generans, erit essentia res generans et non generans, quod est impossibile.

PRAETEREA, Augustinus dicit, in IV de Trin., *pater est principium totius deitatis*. Sed non est principium nisi generando vel spirando. Ergo pater generat vel spirat deitatem.

SED CONTRA est quod Augustinus dicit, in I de Trin., quod *nulla res generat seipsam*. Sed si essentia generat essentiam, non generat nisi seipsam, cum nihil sit in Deo, quod distinguatur a divina essentia. Ergo essentia non generat essentiam.

RESPONDEO dicendum quod circa hoc erravit abbas Ioachim, asserens quod, sicut dicitur, Deus genuit Deum, ita potest dici quod essentia genuit essentiam; considerans quod, propter divinam simplicitatem, non est aliud Deus quam divina essentia. Sed in hoc deceptus fuit, quia ad veritatem locutionum, non solum oportet considerare res significatas, sed etiam modum significandi ut dictum est. Licet autem, secundum re, sit idem Deus quod deitas, non tamen est idem modus significandi utrobique. Nam hoc nomen Deus, quia significat divinam essentiam ut in habente, ex modo suae significationis naturaliter habet quod possit supponere pro persona, et sic ea quae sunt propria personarum, possunt praedicari de hoc nomine Deus, ut dicatur quod Deus est genitus vel generans, sicut dictum est. Sed hoc nomen essentia non habet ex modo suae significationis quod supponat pro persona, quia significat essentiam ut formam abstractam. Et ideo ea quae sunt propria personarum, quibus ab invicem distinguuntur, non possunt essentiae attribui, significaretur enim quod esset distinctio in essentia divina, sicut est distinctio in suppositis.

AD PRIMUM ergo dicendum quod, ad exprimendam unitatem essentiae et personae, sancti doctores aliquando expressius locuti sunt quam proprietas locutionis patiatur. Unde huiusmodi locutiones non sunt extendendae, sed exponendae, ut scilicet nomina abstracta exponantur per concreta, vel etiam per nomina personalia, ut, cum dicitur, essentia de essentia, vel sapientia de sapientia, sit sensus, filius, qui est essentia et sapientia, est de patre, qui est essentia et sapientia. In his tamen nominibus abstractis est quidam ordo attendendus, quia ea quae pertinent ad actum, magis propinque se habent ad personas, quia actus sunt suppositorum. Unde minus

But, as was shown, it is true to say that *God begets God.* Therefore this is also true: *Essence begets essence.*

OBJ. 4: Further, a predicate can stand for that of which it is predicated. But the Father is the divine essence; therefore essence can stand for the person of the Father. Thus the essence begets.

OBJ. 5: Further, the essence is *a thing begetting*, because the essence is the Father who is begetting. Therefore if the essence is not begetting, the essence will be *a thing begetting*, and *not begetting*: which cannot be.

OBJ. 6: Further, Augustine says (*De Trin.* iv, 20): *The Father is the principle of the whole Godhead.* But He is principle only by begetting or spirating. Therefore the Father begets or spirates the Godhead.

ON THE CONTRARY, Augustine says (*De Trin.* i, 1): *Nothing begets itself.* But if the essence begets the essence, it begets itself only, since nothing exists in God as distinguished from the divine essence. Therefore the essence does not beget essence.

I ANSWER THAT, Concerning this, the abbot Joachim erred in asserting that as we can say *God begot God,* so we can say *Essence begot essence*: considering that, by reason of the divine simplicity, God is nothing else but the divine essence. In this he was wrong, because if we wish to express ourselves correctly, we must take into account not only the thing which is signified, but also the mode of its signification as above stated (A. 4). Now although *God* is really the same as *Godhead,* nevertheless the mode of signification is not in each case the same. For since this word *God* signifies the divine essence in Him that possesses it, from its mode of signification it can of its own nature stand for person. Thus the things which properly belong to the persons, can be predicated of this word, *God,* as, for instance, we can say *God is begotten* or is *Begetter,* as above explained (A. 4). The word *essence,* however, in its mode of signification, cannot stand for Person, because it signifies the essence as an abstract form. Consequently, what properly belongs to the persons whereby they are distinguished from each other, cannot be attributed to the essence. For that would imply distinction in the divine essence, in the same way as there exists distinction in the supposita.

REPLY OBJ. 1: To express unity of essence and of person, the holy Doctors have sometimes expressed themselves with greater emphasis than the strict propriety of terms allows. Whence instead of enlarging upon such expressions we should rather explain them: thus, for instance, abstract names should be explained by concrete names, or even by personal names; as when we find *essence from essence*; or *wisdom from wisdom*; we should take the sense to be, the Son who is essence and wisdom, is from the Father who is essence and wisdom. Nevertheless, as regards these abstract names a certain order should be observed, forasmuch as what belongs to action is more nearly allied to the persons because actions belong to supposita. So *nature*

impropria est ista, natura de natura, vel sapientia de sapientia, quam essentia de essentia.

AD SECUNDUM dicendum quod in creaturis generatum non accipit naturam eandem numero quam generans habet, sed aliam numero, quae incipit in eo esse per generationem de novo, et desinit esse per corruptionem, et ideo generatur et corrumpitur per accidens. Sed Deus genitus eandem naturam numero accipit quam generans habet. Et ideo natura divina in filio non generatur, neque per se neque per accidens.

AD TERTIUM dicendum quod, licet Deus et divina essentia sint idem secundum rem, tamen, ratione alterius modi significandi, oportet loqui diversimode de utroque.

AD QUARTUM dicendum quod essentia divina praedicatur de patre per modum identitatis, propter divinam simplicitatem, nec tamen sequitur quod possit supponere pro patre, propter diversum modum significandi. Ratio autem procederet in illis, quorum unum praedicatur de altero sicut universale de particulari.

AD QUINTUM dicendum quod haec est differentia inter nomina substantiva et adiectiva, quia nomina substantiva ferunt suum suppositum, adiectiva vero non, sed rem significatam ponunt circa substantivum. Unde sophistae dicunt quod nomina substantiva supponunt; adiectiva vero non supponunt, sed copulant. Nomina igitur personalia substantiva possunt de essentia praedicari, propter identitatem rei, neque sequitur quod proprietas personalis distinctam determinet essentiam; sed ponitur circa suppositum importatum per nomen substantivum. Sed notionalia et personalia adiectiva non possunt praedicari de essentia, nisi aliquo substantivo adiuncto. Unde non possumus dicere quod essentia est generans. Possumus tamen dicere quod essentia est res generans, vel Deus generans, si res et Deus supponant pro persona, non autem si supponant pro essentia. Unde non est contradictio, si dicatur quod essentia est res generans, et res non generans, quia primo res tenetur pro persona, secundo pro essentia.

AD SEXTUM dicendum quod deitas, inquantum est una in pluribus suppositis, habet quandam convenientiam cum forma nominis collectivi. Unde cum dicitur, pater est principium totius deitatis, potest sumi pro universitate personarum; inquantum scilicet, in omnibus personis divinis, ipse est principium. Nec oportet quod sit principium sui ipsius, sicut aliquis de populo dicitur rector totius populi, non tamen sui ipsius. Vel potest dici quod est principium totius deitatis, non quia eam generet et spiret, sed quia eam, generando et spirando, communicat.

from nature, and *wisdom from wisdom* are less inexact than *essence from essence*.

REPLY OBJ. 2: In creatures the one generated has not the same nature numerically as the generator, but another nature, numerically distinct, which commences to exist in it anew by generation, and ceases to exist by corruption, and so it is generated and corrupted accidentally; whereas God begotten has the same nature numerically as the begetter. So the divine nature in the Son is not begotten either directly or accidentally.

REPLY OBJ. 3: Although God and the divine essence are really the same, nevertheless, on account of their different mode of signification, we must speak in a different way about each of them.

REPLY OBJ. 4: The divine essence is predicated of the Father by mode of identity by reason of the divine simplicity; yet it does not follow that it can stand for the Father, its mode of signification being different. This objection would hold good as regards things which are predicated of another as the universal of a particular.

REPLY OBJ. 5: The difference between substantive and adjectival names consist in this, that the former carry their subject with them, whereas the latter do not, but add the thing signified to the substantive. Whence logicians are wont to say that the substantive is considered in the light of suppositum, whereas the adjective indicates something added to the suppositum. Therefore substantive personal terms can be predicated of the essence, because they are really the same; nor does it follow that a personal property makes a distinct essence; but it belongs to the suppositum implied in the substantive. But notional and personal adjectives cannot be predicated of the essence unless we add some substantive. We cannot say that the *essence is begetting*; yet we can say that the *essence is a thing begetting*, or that it is *God begetting*, if *thing* and God stand for person, but not if they stand for essence. Consequently there exists no contradiction in saying that *essence is a thing begetting*, and *a thing not begetting*; because in the first case *thing* stands for person, and in the second it stands for the essence.

REPLY OBJ. 6: So far as Godhead is one in several supposita, it agrees in a certain degree with the form of a collective term. So when we say, *the Father is the principle of the whole Godhead*, the term Godhead can be taken for all the persons together, inasmuch as it is the principle in all the divine persons. Nor does it follow that He is His own principle; as one of the people may be called the ruler of the people without being ruler of himself. We may also say that He is the principle of the whole Godhead; not as generating or spirating it, but as communicating it by generation and spiration.

Article 6

Whether the Persons Can Be Predicated of the Essential Terms?

AD SEXTUM SIC PROCEDITUR. Videtur quod personae non possint praedicari de nominibus essentialibus concretis, ut dicatur, Deus est tres personae, vel est Trinitas. Haec enim est falsa, homo est omnis homo, quia pro nullo suppositorum verificari potest, neque enim Socrates est omnis homo, neque Plato, neque aliquis alius. Sed similiter ista, Deus est Trinitas, pro nullo suppositorum naturae divinae verificari potest, neque enim pater est Trinitas, neque filius, neque Spiritus Sanctus. Ergo haec est falsa, Deus est Trinitas.

PRAETEREA, inferiora non praedicantur de suis superioribus nisi accidentali praedicatione, ut cum dico, animal est homo, accidit enim animali esse hominem. Sed hoc nomen Deus se habet ad tres personas sicut commune ad inferiora, ut Damascenus dicit. Ergo videtur quod nomina personarum non possint praedicari de hoc nomine Deus, nisi accidentaliter.

SED CONTRA est quod Augustinus dicit, in sermone de fide, *credimus unum Deum unam esse divini nominis Trinitatem.*

RESPONDEO dicendum quod, sicut iam dictum est, licet nomina personalia vel notionalia adiectiva non possint praedicari de essentia; tamen substantiva possunt, propter realem identitatem essentiae et personae. Essentia autem divina non solum idem est realiter cum una persona, sed cum tribus. Unde et una persona, et duae, et tres possunt de essentia praedicari; ut si dicamus, essentia est pater et filius et Spiritus Sanctus. Et quia hoc nomen Deus per se habet quod supponat pro essentia, ut dictum est, ideo, sicut haec est vera, essentia est tres personae, ita haec est vera, Deus est tres personae.

AD PRIMUM ergo dicendum quod, sicut supra dictum est, hoc nomen homo per se habet supponere pro persona; sed ex adiuncto habet quod stet pro natura communi. Et ideo haec est falsa, homo est omnis homo, quia pro nullo supposito verificari potest. Sed hoc nomen Deus per se habet quod stet pro essentia. Unde, licet pro nullo suppositorum divinae naturae haec sit vera, Deus est Trinitas, est tamen vera pro essentia. Quod non attendens, Porretanus eam negavit.

AD SECUNDUM dicendum quod, cum dicitur, Deus vel divina essentia est pater, est praedicatio per identitatem, non autem sicut inferioris de superiori, quia in divinis non est universale et singulare. Unde, sicut est per se ista, pater est Deus, ita et ista, Deus est pater; et nullo modo per accidens.

OBJECTION 1: It would seem that the persons cannot be predicated of the concrete essential names; so that we can say for instance, *God is three persons*; or *God is the Trinity*. For it is false to say, *man is every man*, because it cannot be verified as regards any particular subject. For neither Socrates, nor Plato, nor anyone else is every man. In the same way this proposition, *God is the Trinity*, cannot be verified of any one of the supposita of the divine nature. For the Father is not the Trinity; nor is the Son; nor is the Holy Spirit. So to say, *God is the Trinity*, is false.

OBJ. 2: Further, the lower is not predicated of the higher except by accidental predication; as when I say, *animal is man*; for it is accidental to animal to be man. But this name *God* as regards the three persons is as a general term to inferior terms, as Damascene says (*De Fide Orth.* iii, 4). Therefore it seems that the names of the persons cannot be predicated of this name *God*, except in an accidental sense.

ON THE CONTRARY, Augustine says, in his sermon on Faith, *We believe that one God is one divinely named Trinity.*

I ANSWER THAT, As above explained (A. 5), although adjectival terms, whether personal or notional, cannot be predicated of the essence, nevertheless substantive terms can be so predicated, owing to the real identity of essence and person. The divine essence is not only really the same as one person, but it is really the same as the three persons. Whence, one person, and two, and three, can be predicated of the essence as if we were to say, *The essence is the Father, and the Son, and the Holy Spirit*. And because this word *God* can of itself stand for the essence, as above explained (A. 4, ad 3), hence, as it is true to say, *The essence is the three persons*; so likewise it is true to say, *God is the three persons*.

REPLY OBJ. 1: As above explained this term *man* can of itself stand for person, whereas an adjunct is required for it to stand for the universal human nature. So it is false to say, *Man is every man*; because it cannot be verified of any particular human subject. On the contrary, this word *God* can of itself be taken for the divine essence. So, although to say of any of the supposita of the divine nature, *God is the Trinity*, is untrue, nevertheless it is true of the divine essence. This was denied by Porretanus because he did not take note of this distinction.

REPLY OBJ. 2: When we say, *God*, or *the divine essence is the Father*, the predication is one of identity, and not of the lower in regard to a higher species: because in God there is no universal and singular. Hence, as this proposition, *The Father is God* is of itself true, so this proposition *God is the Father* is true of itself, and by no means accidentally.

Article 7

Whether the Essential Names Should Be Appropriated to the Persons?

AD SEPTIMUM SIC PROCEDITUR. Videtur quod nomina essentialia non sint approprianda personis. Quod enim potest vergere in errorem fidei, vitandum est in divinis, quia, ut Hieronymus dicit, *ex verbis inordinate prolatis incurritur haeresis.* Sed ea quae sunt communia tribus personis appropriare alicui, potest vergere in errorem fidei, quia potest intelligi quod vel illi tantum personae conveniant cui appropriantur; vel quod magis conveniant ei quam aliis. Ergo essentialia attributa non sunt approprianda personis.

PRAETEREA, essentialia attributa, in abstracto significata, significant per modum formae. Sed una persona non se habet ad aliam ut forma, cum forma ab eo cuius est forma, supposito non distinguatur. Ergo essentialia attributa, maxime in abstracto significata, non debent appropriari personis.

PRAETEREA, proprium prius est appropriato, proprium enim est de ratione appropriati. Sed essentialia attributa, secundum modum intelligendi, sunt priora personis, sicut commune est prius proprio. Ergo essentialia attributa non debent esse appropriata.

SED CONTRA est quod apostolus dicit, I Cor. I, *Christum, Dei virtutem et Dei sapientiam.*

RESPONDEO dicendum quod, ad manifestationem fidei, conveniens fuit essentialia attributa personis appropriari. Licet enim Trinitas personarum demonstratione probari non possit, ut supra dictum est, convenit tamen ut per aliqua magis manifesta declaretur. Essentialia vero attributa sunt nobis magis manifesta secundum rationem, quam propria personarum, quia ex creaturis, ex quibus cognitionem accipimus, possumus per certitudinem devenire in cognitionem essentialium attributorum; non autem in cognitionem personalium proprietatum, ut supra dictum est. Sicut igitur similitudine vestigii vel imaginis in creaturis inventa utimur ad manifestationem divinarum personarum, ita et essentialibus attributis. Et haec manifestatio personarum per essentialia attributa, appropriatio nominatur.

Possunt autem manifestari personae divinae per essentialia attributa dupliciter. Uno modo, per viam similitudinis, sicut ea quae pertinent ad intellectum, appropriantur filio, qui procedit per modum intellectus ut verbum. Alio modo, per modum dissimilitudinis, sicut potentia appropriatur patri, ut Augustinus dicit, quia apud nos patres solent esse propter senectutem infirmi; ne tale aliquid suspicemur in Deo.

OBJECTION 1: It would seem that the essential names should not be appropriated to the persons. For whatever might verge on error in faith should be avoided in the treatment of divine things; for, as Jerome says, *careless words involve risk of heresy.* But to appropriate to any one person the names which are common to the three persons, may verge on error in faith; for it may be supposed either that such belong only to the person to whom they are appropriated or that they belong to Him in a fuller degree than to the others. Therefore the essential attributes should not be appropriated to the persons.

OBJ. 2: Further, the essential attributes expressed in the abstract signify by mode of form. But one person is not as a form to another; since a form is not distinguished in subject from that of which it is the form. Therefore the essential attributes, especially when expressed in the abstract, are not to be appropriated to the persons.

OBJ. 3: Further, property is prior to the appropriated, for property is included in the idea of the appropriated. But the essential attributes, in our way of understanding, are prior to the persons; as what is common is prior to what is proper. Therefore the essential attributes are not to be appropriated to the persons.

ON THE CONTRARY, the Apostle says: *Christ the power of God and the wisdom of God* (1 Cor 1:24).

I ANSWER THAT, For the manifestation of our faith it is fitting that the essential attributes should be appropriated to the persons. For although the trinity of persons cannot be proved by demonstration, as was above expounded (Q. 32, A. 1), nevertheless it is fitting that it be declared by things which are more known to us. Now the essential attributes of God are more clear to us from the standpoint of reason than the personal properties; because we can derive certain knowledge of the essential attributes from creatures which are sources of knowledge to us, such as we cannot obtain regarding the personal properties, as was above explained (Q. 32, A. 1). As, therefore, we make use of the likeness of the trace or image found in creatures for the manifestation of the divine persons, so also in the same manner do we make use of the essential attributes. And such a manifestation of the divine persons by the use of the essential attributes is called *appropriation.*

The divine person can be manifested in a twofold manner by the essential attributes; in one way by similitude, and thus the things which belong to the intellect are appropriated to the Son, Who proceeds by way of intellect, as Word. In another way by dissimilitude; as power is appropriated to the Father, as Augustine says, because fathers by reason of old age are sometimes feeble; lest anything of the kind be imagined of God.

Ad primum ergo dicendum quod essentialia attributa non sic appropriantur personis ut eis esse propria asserantur, sed ad manifestandum personas per viam similitudinis vel dissimilitudinis, ut dictum est. Unde nullus error fidei sequitur, sed magis manifestatio veritatis.

Ad secundum dicendum quod, si sic appropriarentur essentialia attributa personis, quod essent eis propria, sequeretur quod una persona se haberet ad aliam in habitudine formae. Quod excludit Augustinus, in VII de Trin., ostendens quod pater non est sapiens sapientia quam genuit, quasi solus filius sit sapientia; ut sic pater et filius simul tantum possint dici sapiens, non autem pater sine filio. Sed filius dicitur sapientia patris, quia est sapientia de patre sapientia, uterque enim per se est sapientia, et simul ambo una sapientia. Unde pater non est sapiens sapientia quam genuit, sed sapientia quae est sua essentia.

Ad tertium dicendum quod, licet essentiale attributum, secundum rationem propriam, sit prius quam persona, secundum, modum intelligendi; tamen, inquantum habet rationem appropriati, nihil prohibet proprium personae esse prius quam appropriatum. Sicut color posterior est corpore, inquantum est corpus, prius tamen est naturaliter corpore albo, inquantum est album.

Reply Obj. 1: The essential attributes are not appropriated to the persons as if they exclusively belonged to them; but in order to make the persons manifest by way of similitude, or dissimilitude, as above explained. So, no error in faith can arise, but rather manifestation of the truth.

Reply Obj. 2: If the essential attributes were appropriated to the persons as exclusively belonging to each of them, then it would follow that one person would be as a form as regards another; which Augustine altogether repudiates (*De Trin.* vi, 2), showing that the Father is wise, not by Wisdom begotten by Him, as though only the Son were Wisdom; so that the Father and the Son together only can be called wise, but not the Father without the Son. But the Son is called the Wisdom of the Father, because He is Wisdom from the Father Who is Wisdom. For each of them is of Himself Wisdom; and both together are one Wisdom. Whence the Father is not wise by the wisdom begotten by Him, but by the wisdom which is His own essence.

Reply Obj. 3: Although the essential attribute is in its proper concept prior to person, according to our way of understanding; nevertheless, so far as it is appropriated, there is nothing to prevent the personal property from being prior to that which is appropriated. Thus color is posterior to body considered as body, but is naturally prior to *white body*, considered as white.

Article 8

Whether the Essential Attributes Are Appropriated to the Persons in a Fitting Manner by the Holy Doctors?

Ad octavum sic proceditur. Videtur quod inconvenienter a sacris doctoribus sint essentialia personis attributa. Dicit enim Hilarius, in II de Trin., *aeternitas est in patre, species in imagine, usus in munere.* In quibus verbis ponit tria nomina propria personarum, scilicet nomen patris; et nomen imaginis, quod est proprium filio, ut supra dictum est; et nomen muneris, sive doni, quod est proprium spiritus sancti, ut supra habitum est. Ponit etiam tria appropriata, nam aeternitatem appropriat patri, speciem filio, usum spiritui sancto. Et videtur quod irrationabiliter. Nam aeternitas importat durationem essendi, species vero est essendi principium, usus vero ad operationem pertinere videtur. Sed essentia et operatio nulli personae appropriari inveniuntur. Ergo inconvenienter videntur ista appropriata personis.

Praeterea, Augustinus in I de Doctr. Christ., sic dicit, *in patre est unitas, in filio aequalitas, in spiritu sancto unitatis aequalitatisque concordia.* Et videtur quod inconvenienter. Quia una persona non denominatur formaliter per id quod appropriatur alteri, non enim

Objection 1: It would seem that the essential attributes are appropriated to the persons unfittingly by the holy doctors. For Hilary says (*De Trin.* ii): *Eternity is in the Father, the species in the Image; and use is in the Gift.* In which words he designates three names proper to the persons: the name of the *Father*, the name *Image* proper to the Son (Q. 35, A. 2), and the name *Bounty* or *Gift*, which is proper to the Holy Spirit (Q. 38, A. 2). He also designates three appropriated terms. For he appropriates *eternity* to the Father, species to the Son, and *use* to the Holy Spirit. This he does apparently without reason. For *eternity* imports duration of existence; species, the principle of existence; and 'use' belongs to the operation. But essence and operation are not found to be appropriated to any person. Therefore the above terms are not fittingly appropriated to the persons.

Obj. 2: Further, Augustine says (*De Doctr. Christ.* i, 5): *Unity is in the Father, equality in the Son, and in the Holy Spirit is the concord of equality and unity.* This does not, however, seem fitting; because one person does not receive formal denomination from what is appropriated to another.

est sapiens pater sapientia genita, ut dictum est. Sed, sicut ibidem subditur, *tria haec unum omnia sunt propter patrem, aequalia omnia propter filium, connexa omnia propter spiritum sanctum.* Non ergo convenienter appropriantur personis.

ITEM, secundum Augustinum, patri attribuitur potentia, filio sapientia, spiritui sancto bonitas. Et videtur hoc esse inconveniens. Nam virtus ad potentiam pertinet. Virtus autem invenitur appropriari filio, secundum illud I ad Cor. I, *Christum, Dei virtutem*; et etiam spiritui sancto, secundum illud Luc. VI, *virtus de illo exibat, et sanabat omnes.* Non ergo potentia patri est approprianda.

ITEM, Augustinus, in libro de Trin., dicit, *non confuse accipiendum est quod ait apostolus, ex ipso, et per ipsum, et in ipso—ex ipso dicens propter patrem; per ipsum propter filium; in ipso propter spiritum sanctum.* Sed videtur quod inconvenienter. Quia per hoc quod dicit in ipso, videtur importari habitudo causae finalis, quae est prima causarum. Ergo ista habitudo causae deberet appropriari patri, qui est principium non de principio.

ITEM, invenitur veritas appropriari filio, secundum illud Ioan. XIV, *ego sum via, veritas et vita.* Et similiter liber vitae, secundum illud Psalmi XXXIX, *in capite libri scriptum est de me,* Glossa, idest apud patrem, qui est caput meum. Et similiter hoc quod dico, qui est, quia super illud Isa. LXV, *ecce ego, ad gentes,* dicit Glossa, *filius loquitur, qui dixit Moysi, ego sum qui sum.* Sed videtur quod propria sint filii, et non appropriata. *Nam veritas,* secundum Augustinum, in libro de vera religione, *est summa similitudo principii, absque omni dissimilitudine,* et sic videtur quod proprie conveniat filio, qui habet principium. Liber etiam vitae videtur proprium aliquid esse, quia significat ens ab alio, omnis enim liber ab aliquo scribitur. Hoc etiam ipsum qui est videtur esse proprium filio. Quia si, cum Moysi dicitur, ego sum qui sum, loquitur Trinitas, ergo Moyses poterat dicere, ille qui est pater et filius et Spiritus Sanctus, misit me ad vos. Ergo et ulterius dicere poterat, ille qui est pater et filius et Spiritus Sanctus, misit me ad vos, demonstrando certam personam. Hoc autem est falsum, quia nulla persona est pater et filius et Spiritus Sanctus. Non ergo potest esse commune Trinitati, sed est proprium filii.

RESPONDEO dicendum quod intellectus noster, qui ex creaturis in Dei cognitionem manuducitur, oportet quod Deum consideret secundum modum quem ex creaturis assumit. In consideratione autem alicuius creaturae, quatuor per ordinem nobis occurrunt. Nam primo, consideratur res ipsa absolute, inquantum est ens quoddam. Secunda autem consideratio rei est, inquantum est una. Tertia consideratio rei est, secundum quod

For the Father is not wise by the wisdom begotten, as above explained (Q. 37, A. 2, ad 1). But, as he subjoins, *All these three are one by the Father; all are equal by the Son, and all united by the Holy Spirit.* The above, therefore, are not fittingly appropriated to the Persons.

OBJ. 3: Further, according to Augustine, to the Father is attributed *power*, to the Son *wisdom*, to the Holy Spirit *goodness*. Nor does this seem fitting; for *strength* is part of power, whereas strength is found to be appropriated to the Son, according to the text, *Christ the strength of God* (1 Cor 1:24). So it is likewise appropriated to the Holy Spirit, according to the words, *strength came out from Him and healed all* (Luke 6:19). Therefore power should not be appropriated to the Father.

OBJ. 4: Likewise Augustine says (*De Trin.* vi, 10): *What the Apostle says, 'From Him, and by Him, and in Him,' is not to be taken in a confused sense.* And (*Contra Maxim.* ii) *'from Him' refers to the Father, 'by Him' to the Son, 'in Him' to the Holy Spirit.* This, however, seems to be incorrectly said; for the words *in Him* seem to imply the relation of final cause, which is first among the causes. Therefore this relation of cause should be appropriated to the Father, Who is *the principle from no principle.*

OBJ. 5: Likewise, Truth is appropriated to the Son, according to John 14:6, *I am the Way, the Truth, and the Life*; and likewise *the book of life*, according to Ps. 39:9, *In the beginning of the book it is written of Me*, where a gloss observes, *that is, with the Father Who is My head*, also this word *Who is*; because on the text of Isaias, *Behold I go to the Gentiles* (65:1), a gloss adds, *The Son speaks Who said to Moses, I am Who am.* These appear to belong to the Son, and are not appropriated. For *truth*, according to Augustine (*De Vera Relig.* 36), *is the supreme similitude of the principle without any dissimilitude.* So it seems that it properly belongs to the Son, Who has a principle. Also the *book of life* seems proper to the Son, as signifying *a thing from another*; for every book is written by someone. This also, *Who is*, appears to be proper to the Son; because if when it was said to Moses, *I am Who am*, the Trinity spoke, then Moses could have said, *He Who is Father, Son, and Holy Spirit, and the Holy Spirit sent me to you*, so also he could have said further, *He Who is the Father, and the Son, and the Holy Spirit sent me to you*, pointing out a certain person. This, however, is false; because no person is Father, Son and Holy Spirit. Therefore it cannot be common to the Trinity, but is proper to the Son.

I ANSWER THAT, Our intellect, which is led to the knowledge of God from creatures, must consider God according to the mode derived from creatures. In considering any creature four points present themselves to us in due order. First, the thing itself taken absolutely is considered as a being. Second, it is considered as one. Third, its intrinsic power of operation and causality is considered. The fourth point of consideration embraces its relation to

inest ei virtus ad operandum et ad causandum. Quarta autem consideratio rei est, secundum habitudinem quam habet ad causata. Unde haec etiam quadruplex consideratio circa Deum nobis occurrit.

Secundum igitur primam considerationem, qua consideratur absolute Deus secundum esse suum, sic sumitur appropriatio Hilarii, secundum quam aeternitas appropriatur patri, species filio, usus spiritui sancto. Aeternitas enim, inquantum significat esse non principiatum, similitudinem habet cum proprio patris, qui est principium non de principio. Species autem, sive pulchritudo, habet similitudinem cum propriis filii. Nam ad pulchritudinem tria requiruntur. Primo quidem, integritas sive perfectio, quae enim diminuta sunt, hoc ipso turpia sunt. Et debita proportio sive consonantia. Et iterum claritas, unde quae habent colorem nitidum, pulchra esse dicuntur.

Quantum igitur ad primum, similitudinem habet cum proprio filii, inquantum est filius habens in se vere et perfecte naturam patris. Unde, ad hoc innuendum, Augustinus in sua expositione dicit, ubi, scilicet in filio, summa et prima vita est, et cetera.

Quantum vero ad secundum, convenit cum proprio filii, inquantum est imago expressa patris. Unde videmus quod aliqua imago dicitur esse pulchra, si perfecte repraesentat rem, quamvis turpem. Et hoc tetigit Augustinus cum dicit, ubi est tanta convenientia, et prima aequalitas, et cetera.

Quantum vero ad tertium, convenit cum proprio filii, inquantum est verbum, quod quidem lux est, et splendor intellectus, ut Damascenus dicit. Et hoc tangit Augustinus cum dicit, *tanquam verbum perfectum cui non desit aliquid, et ars quaedam omnipotentis Dei*, et cetera.

Usus autem habet similitudinem cum propriis spiritus sancti, largo modo accipiendo usum, secundum quod uti comprehendit sub se etiam frui; prout uti est assumere aliquid in facultatem voluntatis, et frui est cum gaudio uti, ut Augustinus, X de Trin., dicit. Usus ergo quo pater et filius se invicem fruuntur, convenit cum proprio spiritus sancti, inquantum est amor. Et hoc est quod Augustinus dicit, *illa dilectio, delectatio, felicitas vel beatitudo, usus ab illo appellatus est*. Usus vero quo nos fruimur Deo, similitudinem habet cum proprio spiritus sancti, inquantum est donum. Et hoc ostendit Augustinus cum dicit, *est in Trinitate Spiritus Sanctus, genitoris genitique suavitas, ingenti largitate atque ubertate nos perfundens*. Et sic patet quare aeternitas, species et usus personis attribuantur vel approprientur, non autem essentia vel operatio. Quia in ratione horum, propter sui communitatem, non invenitur aliquid similitudinem habens cum propriis personarum.

Secunda vero consideratio Dei est, inquantum consideratur ut unus. Et sic Augustinus patri appropriat

its effects. Hence this fourfold consideration comes to our mind in reference to God.

According to the first point of consideration, whereby we consider God absolutely in His being, the appropriation mentioned by Hilary applies, according to which *eternity* is appropriated to the Father, species to the Son, *use* to the Holy Spirit. For *eternity* as meaning a *being* without a principle, has a likeness to the property of the Father, Who is *a principle without a principle*. Species or beauty has a likeness to the property of the Son. For beauty includes three conditions, *integrity* or *perfection*, since those things which are impaired are by the very fact ugly; due *proportion* or *harmony*; and lastly, *brightness* or *clarity*, whence things are called beautiful which have a bright color.

The first of these has a likeness to the property of the Son, inasmuch as He as Son has in Himself truly and perfectly the nature of the Father. To insinuate this, Augustine says in his explanation (*De Trin.* vi, 10): *Where—that is, in the Son—there is supreme and primal life*, etc.

The second agrees with the Son's property, inasmuch as He is the express Image of the Father. Hence we see that an image is said to be beautiful, if it perfectly represents even an ugly thing. This is indicated by Augustine when he says (*De Trin.* vi, 10), *Where there exists wondrous proportion and primal equality*, etc.

The third agrees with the property of the Son, as the Word, which is the light and splendor of the intellect, as Damascene says (*De Fide Orth.* iii, 3). Augustine alludes to the same when he says (*De Trin.* vi, 10): *As the perfect Word, not wanting in anything, and, so to speak, the art of the omnipotent God*, etc.

Use has a likeness to the property of the Holy Spirit; provided the *use* be taken in a wide sense, as including also the sense of *to enjoy*; according as *to use* is to employ something at the beck of the will, and *to enjoy* means to use joyfully, as Augustine says (*De Trin.* x, 11). So *use*, whereby the Father and the Son enjoy each other, agrees with the property of the Holy Spirit, as Love. This is what Augustine says (*De Trin.* vi, 10): *That love, that delectation, that felicity or beatitude, is called use by him* (Hilary). But the *use* by which we enjoy God, is likened to the property of the Holy Spirit as the Gift; and Augustine points to this when he says (*De Trin.* vi, 10): *In the Trinity, the Holy Spirit, the sweetness of the Begettor and the Begotten, pours out upon us mere creatures His immense bounty and wealth*. Thus it is clear how *eternity*, species, and *use* are attributed or appropriated to the persons, but not essence or operation; because, being common, there is nothing in their concept to liken them to the properties of the Persons.

The second consideration of God regards Him as *one*. In that view Augustine (*De Doctr. Christ.* i, 5) appropriates

unitatem, filio aequalitatem, spiritui sancto concordiam sive connexionem. Quae quidem tria unitatem importare manifestum est, sed differenter. Nam unitas dicitur absolute, non praesupponens aliquid aliud. Et ideo appropriatur patri, qui non praesupponit aliquam personam, cum sit principium non de principio. Aequalitas autem importat unitatem in respectu ad alterum, nam aequale est quod habet unam quantitatem cum alio. Et ideo aequalitas appropriatur filio, qui est principium de principio. Connexio autem importat unitatem aliquorum duorum. Unde appropriatur spiritui sancto, inquantum est a duobus. Ex quo etiam intelligi potest quod dicit Augustinus, *tria esse unum propter patrem, aequalia propter filium, connexa propter spiritum sanctum.* Manifestum est enim quod illi attribuitur unumquodque, in quo primo invenitur, sicut omnia inferiora dicuntur vivere propter animam vegetabilem, in qua primo invenitur ratio vitae in istis inferioribus. Unitas autem statim invenitur in persona patris, etiam, per impossibile, remotis aliis personis. Et ideo aliae personae a patre habent unitatem. Sed remotis aliis personis, non invenitur aequalitas in patre, sed statim, posito filio, invenitur aequalitas. Et ideo dicuntur omnia aequalia propter filium, non quod filius sit principium aequalitatis patri; sed quia, nisi esset patri aequalis filius, pater aequalis non posset dici. Aequalitas enim eius primo consideratur ad filium, hoc enim ipsum quod Spiritus Sanctus patri aequalis est, a filio habet. Similiter, excluso spiritu sancto, qui est duorum nexus, non posset intelligi unitas connexionis inter patrem et filium. Et ideo dicuntur omnia esse connexa propter spiritum sanctum, quia, posito spiritu sancto, invenitur unde pater et filius possint dici connexi.

SECUNDUM VERO TERTIAM considerationem, qua in Deo sufficiens virtus consideratur ad causandum, sumitur tertia appropriatio, scilicet potentiae, sapientiae et bonitatis. Quae quidem appropriatio fit et secundum rationem similitudinis, si consideretur quod in divinis personis est, et secundum rationem dissimilitudinis, si consideretur quod in creaturis est. Potentia enim habet rationem principii. Unde habet similitudinem cum patre caelesti, qui est principium totius divinitatis. Deficit autem interdum patri terreno, propter senectutem. Sapientia vero similitudinem habet cum filio caelesti, inquantum est verbum, quod nihil aliud est quam conceptus sapientiae. Deficit autem interdum filio terreno, propter temporis paucitatem. Bonitas autem, cum sit ratio et obiectum amoris, habet similitudinem cum spiritu divino, qui est amor. Sed repugnantiam habere videtur ad spiritum terrenum, secundum quod importat violentam quandam impulsionem; prout dicitur Isa. XXV, *spiritus robustorum quasi turbo impellens parietem.* Virtus autem appropriatur filio et spiritui sancto, non secundum

unity to the Father, *equality* to the Son, *concord* or *union* to the Holy Spirit. It is manifest that these three imply unity, but in different ways. For *unity* is said absolutely, as it does not presuppose anything else; and for this reason it is appropriated to the Father, to Whom any other person is not presupposed since He is the *principle without principle.* *Equality* implies unity as regards another; for that is equal which has the same quantity as another. So equality is appropriated to the Son, Who is the *principle from a principle.* *Union* implies the unity of two; and is therefore appropriated to the Holy Spirit, inasmuch as He proceeds from two. And from this we can understand what Augustine means when he says (*De Doctr. Christ.* i, 5) that *The Three are one, by reason of the Father; They are equal by reason of the Son; and are united by reason of the Holy Spirit.* For it is clear that we trace a thing back to that in which we find it first: just as in this lower world we attribute life to the vegetative soul, because therein we find the first trace of life. Now *unity* is perceived at once in the person of the Father, even if by an impossible hypothesis, the other persons were removed. So the other persons derive their unity from the Father. But if the other persons be removed, we do not find equality in the Father, but we find it as soon as we suppose the Son. So, all are equal by reason of the Son, not as if the Son were the principle of equality in the Father, but that, without the Son equal to the Father, the Father could not be called equal; because His equality is considered first in regard to the Son: for that the Holy Spirit is equal to the Father, is also from the Son. Likewise, if the Holy Spirit, Who is the union of the two, be excluded, we cannot understand the oneness of the union between the Father and the Son. So all are connected by reason of the Holy Spirit; because given the Holy Spirit, we find whence the Father and the Son are said to be united.

According to the third consideration, which brings before us the adequate power of God in the sphere of causality, there is said to be a third kind of appropriation, of *power, wisdom,* and *goodness.* This kind of appropriation is made both by reason of similitude as regards what exists in the divine persons, and by reason of dissimilitude if we consider what is in creatures. For *power* has the nature of a principle, and so it has a likeness to the heavenly Father, Who is the principle of the whole Godhead. But in an earthly father it is wanting sometimes by reason of old age. *Wisdom* has likeness to the heavenly Son, as the Word, for a word is nothing but the concept of wisdom. In an earthly son this is sometimes absent by reason of lack of years. *Goodness,* as the nature and object of love, has likeness to the Holy Spirit; but seems repugnant to the earthly spirit, which often implies a certain violent impulse, according to Isa. 25:4: *The spirit of the strong is as a blast beating on the wall. Strength* is appropriated to the Son and to the Holy Spirit, not as denoting the power itself of a thing, but as sometimes used

quod virtus dicitur ipsa potentia rei, sed secundum quod interdum virtus dicitur id quod a potentia rei procedit, prout dicimus aliquod virtuosum factum esse virtutem alicuius agentis.

Secundum vero quartam considerationem, prout consideratur Deus in habitudine ad suos effectus, sumitur illa appropriatio ex quo, per quem, et in quo. Haec enim praepositio ex importat quandoque quidem habitudinem causae materialis, quae locum non habet in divinis, aliquando vero habitudinem causae efficientis. Quae quidem competit Deo ratione suae potentiae activae, unde et appropriatur patri, sicut et potentia. Haec vero praepositio per designat quidem quandoque causam mediam; sicut dicimus quod faber operatur per martellum. Et sic ly per quandoque non est appropriatum, sed proprium filii, secundum illud Ioan. I, *omnia per ipsum facta sunt*; non quia filius sit instrumentum, sed quia ipse est principium de principio. Quandoque vero designat habitudinem formae per quam agens operatur; sicut dicimus quod artifex operatur per artem. Unde, sicut sapientia et ars appropriantur filio, ita et ly per quem. Haec vero praepositio in denotat proprie habitudinem continentis. Continet autem Deus res dupliciter. Uno modo, secundum suas similitudines; prout scilicet res dicuntur esse in Deo, inquantum sunt in eius scientia. Et sic hoc quod dico in ipso, esset appropriandum filio. Alio vero modo continentur res a Deo, inquantum Deus sua bonitate eas conservat et gubernat, ad finem convenientem adducendo. Et sic ly in quo appropriatur spiritui sancto, sicut et bonitas. Nec oportet quod habitudo causae finalis, quamvis sit prima causarum, approprietur patri, qui est principium non de principio, quia personae divinae, quarum pater est principium, non procedunt ut ad finem, cum quaelibet illarum sit ultimus finis; sed naturali processione, quae magis ad rationem naturalis potentiae pertinere videtur.

Ad illud vero quod de aliis quaeritur, dicendum quod veritas, cum pertineat ad intellectum, ut supra dictum est, appropriatur filio, non tamen est proprium eius. Quia veritas, ut supra dictum est, considerari potest prout est in intellectu, vel prout est in re. Sicut igitur intellectus et res essentialiter sumpta sunt essentialia et non personalia, ita et veritas. Definitio autem Augustini inducta, datur de veritate secundum quod appropriatur filio. Liber autem vitae in recto quidem importat notitiam, sed in obliquo vitam, est enim, ut supra dictum est, notitia Dei de his qui habituri sunt vitam aeternam. Unde appropriatur filio, licet vita approprietur spiritui sancto, inquantum importat quendam interiorem motum, et sic convenit cum proprio spiritus sancti, inquantum est amor. Esse autem scriptum ab alio, non est de ratione libri inquantum est liber; sed inquantum est quoddam artificiatum. Unde non importat originem,

to express that which proceeds from power; for instance, we say that the strong work done by an agent is its strength.

According to the fourth consideration, i.e., God's relation to His effects, there arises appropriation of the expression *from Whom, by Whom, and in Whom*. For this preposition *from* sometimes implies a certain relation of the material cause; which has no place in God; and sometimes it expresses the relation of the efficient cause, which can be applied to God by reason of His active power; hence it is appropriated to the Father in the same way as power. The preposition *by* sometimes designates an intermediate cause; thus we may say that a smith works *by* a hammer. Hence the word *by* is not always appropriated to the Son, but belongs to the Son properly and strictly, according to the text, *All things were made by Him* (John 1:3); not that the Son is an instrument, but as *the principle from a principle*. Sometimes it designates the habitude of a form *by* which an agent works; thus we say that an artificer works by his art. Hence, as wisdom and art are appropriated to the Son, so also is the expression *by Whom*. The preposition *in* strictly denotes the habitude of one containing. Now, God contains things in two ways: in one way by their similitudes; thus things are said to be in God, as existing in His knowledge. In this sense the expression *in Him* should be appropriated to the Son. In another sense things are contained in God forasmuch as He in His goodness preserves and governs them, by guiding them to a fitting end; and in this sense the expression *in Him* is appropriated to the Holy Spirit, as likewise is *goodness*. Nor need the habitude of the final cause (though the first of causes) be appropriated to the Father, Who is *the principle without a principle*: because the divine persons, of Whom the Father is the principle, do not proceed from Him as towards an end, since each of Them is the last end; but They proceed by a natural procession, which seems more to belong to the nature of a natural power.

Regarding the other points of inquiry, we can say that since *truth* belongs to the intellect, as stated above (Q. 16, A. 1), it is appropriated to the Son, without, however, being a property of His. For truth can be considered as existing in the thought or in the thing itself. Hence, as intellect and thing in their essential meaning, are referred to the essence, and not to the persons, so the same is to be said of truth. The definition quoted from Augustine belongs to truth as appropriated to the Son. The *book of life* directly means knowledge but indirectly it means life. For, as above explained (Q. 24, A. 1), it is God's knowledge regarding those who are to possess eternal life. Consequently, it is appropriated to the Son; although life is appropriated to the Holy Spirit, as implying a certain kind of interior movement, agreeing in that sense with the property of the Holy Spirit as Love. To be written by another is not of the essence of a book considered as such; but this belongs to it only

neque est personale, sed appropriatum personae. Ipsum autem qui est appropriatur personae filii, non secundum propriam rationem, sed ratione adiuncti, inquantum scilicet in locutione Dei ad Moysen, praefigurabatur liberatio humani generis, quae facta est per filium. Sed tamen, secundum quod ly qui sumitur relative, posset referre interdum personam filii, et sic sumeretur personaliter, ut puta si dicatur, filius est genitus qui est; sicut et Deus genitus personale est. Sed infinite sumptum est essentiale. Et licet hoc pronomen iste, grammatice loquendo, ad aliquam certam personam videatur pertinere; tamen quaelibet res demonstrabilis, grammatice loquendo, persona dici potest, licet secundum rei naturam non sit persona; dicimus enim iste lapis, et iste asinus. Unde et, grammatice loquendo, essentia divina, secundum quod significatur et supponitur per hoc nomen Deus, potest demonstrari hoc pronomine iste; secundum illud Exod. XV, *iste Deus meus, et glorificabo eum.*

as a work produced. So this does not imply origin; nor is it personal, but an appropriation to a person. The expression *Who is* is appropriated to the person of the Son, not by reason of itself, but by reason of an adjunct, inasmuch as, in God's word to Moses, was prefigured the delivery of the human race accomplished by the Son. Yet, forasmuch as the word *Who* is taken in a relative sense, it may sometimes relate to the person of the Son; and in that sense it would be taken personally; as, for instance, were we to say, *The Son is the begotten 'Who is,'* inasmuch as *God begotten is personal.* But taken indefinitely, it is an essential term. And although the pronoun *this* seems grammatically to point to a particular person, nevertheless everything that we can point to can be grammatically treated as a person, although in its own nature it is not a person; as we may say, *this stone*, and *this ass*. So, speaking in a grammatical sense, so far as the word *God* signifies and stands for the divine essence, the latter may be designated by the pronoun *this*, according to Ex. 15:2: *This is my God, and I will glorify Him.*

QUESTION 40

PERSONS COMPARED TO RELATIONS OR PROPERTIES

Deinde quaeritur de personis in comparatione ad relationes sive proprietates. Et quaeruntur quatuor.

Primo, utrum relatio sit idem quod persona.

Secundo, utrum relationes distinguant et constituant personas.

Tertio, utrum, abstractis per intellectum relationibus a personis, remaneant hypostases distinctae.

Quarto, utrum relationes, secundum intellectum, praesupponant actus personarum, vel e converso.

We now consider the persons in connection with the relations, or properties; and there are four points of inquiry:

(1) Whether relation is the same as person?

(2) Whether the relations distinguish and constitute the persons?

(3) Whether mental abstraction of the relations from the persons leaves the hypostases distinct?

(4) Whether the relations, according to our mode of understanding, presuppose the acts of the persons, or contrariwise?

Article 1

Whether Relation Is the Same As Person?

AD PRIMUM SIC PROCEDITUR. Videtur quod in divinis non sit idem relatio quod persona. Quaecumque enim sunt idem, multiplicato uno eorum, multiplicatur et aliud. Sed contingit in una persona esse plures relationes, sicut in persona patris est paternitas et communis spiratio, et iterum unam relationem in duabus personis esse, sicut communis spiratio est in patre et filio. Ergo relatio non est idem quod persona.

PRAETEREA, nihil est in seipso, secundum philosophum, in IV Physic. Sed relatio est in persona. Nec potest dici quod ratione identitatis, quia sic esset etiam in essentia. Ergo relatio sive proprietas et persona non sunt idem in divinis.

PRAETEREA, quaecumque sunt idem, ita se habent, quod quidquid praedicatur de uno, praedicatur et de alio. Non autem quidquid praedicatur de persona, praedicatur de proprietate. Dicimus enim quod pater generat, sed non dicimus quod paternitas sit generans. Ergo proprietas non est idem quod persona in divinis.

SED CONTRA, in divinis non differt quod est et quo est, ut habetur a Boetio in libro de Hebd. Sed pater paternitate est pater. Ergo pater idem est quod paternitas. Et eadem ratione aliae proprietates idem sunt cum personis.

RESPONDEO dicendum quod circa hoc aliqui diversimode opinati sunt. Quidam enim dixerunt proprietates neque esse personas, neque in personis. Qui fuerunt moti ex modo significandi relationum, quae quidem non significant ut in aliquo, sed magis ut ad aliquid. Unde

OBJECTION 1: It would seem that in God relation is not the same as person. For when things are identical, if one is multiplied the others are multiplied. But in one person there are several relations; as in the person of the Father there is paternity and common spiration. Again, one relation exists in two person, as common spiration in the Father and in the Son. Therefore relation is not the same as person.

OBJ. 2: Further, according to the Philosopher (*Phys.* iv, text. 24), nothing is contained by itself. But relation is in the person; nor can it be said that this occurs because they are identical, for otherwise relation would be also in the essence. Therefore relation, or property, is not the same as person in God.

OBJ. 3: Further, when several things are identical, what is predicated of one is predicated of the others. But all that is predicated of a Person is not predicated of His property. For we say that the Father begets; but not that the paternity is begetting. Therefore property is not the same as person in God.

ON THE CONTRARY, in God *what is* and *whereby it is* are the same, according to Boethius (*De Hebdom.*). But the Father is Father by paternity. In the same way, the other properties are the same as the persons.

I ANSWER THAT, Different opinions have been held on this point. Some have said that the properties are not the persons, nor in the persons; and these have thought thus owing to the mode of signification of the relations, which do not indeed signify existence *in* something, but rather

dixerunt relationes esse assistentes, sicut supra expositum est. Sed quia relatio, secundum quod est quaedam res in divinis, est ipsa essentia; essentia autem idem est quod persona, ut ex dictis patet; oportet quod relatio sit idem quod persona.

Hanc igitur identitatem alii considerantes, dixerunt proprietates quidem esse personas, non autem in personis, quia non ponebant proprietates in divinis nisi secundum modum loquendi, ut supra dictum est. Necesse est autem ponere proprietates in divinis, ut supra ostendimus. Quae quidem significantur in abstracto, ut quaedam formae personarum. Unde, cum de ratione formae sit, quod sit in eo cuius est forma, oportet dicere proprietates esse in personis, et eas tamen esse personas; sicut essentiam esse in Deo dicimus, quae tamen est Deus.

AD PRIMUM ergo dicendum quod persona et proprietas sunt idem re, differunt tamen secundum rationem. Unde non oportet quod, multiplicato uno, multiplicetur reliquum. Considerandum tamen est quod, propter divinam simplicitatem, consideratur duplex realis identitas in divinis eorum quae differunt in rebus creatis. Quia enim divina simplicitas excludit compositionem formae et materiae, sequitur quod in divinis idem est abstractum et concretum, ut deitas et Deus. Quia vero divina simplicitas excludit compositionem subiecti et accidentis, sequitur quod quidquid attribuitur Deo, est eius essentia, et propter hoc sapientia et virtus idem sunt in Deo, quia ambo sunt in divina essentia. Et secundum hanc duplicem rationem identitatis, proprietas in divinis est idem cum persona. Nam proprietates personales sunt idem cum personis, ea ratione qua abstractum est idem cum concreto. Sunt enim ipsae personae subsistentes; ut paternitas est ipse pater, et filiatio filius, et processio Spiritus Sanctus. Proprietates autem non personales sunt idem cum personis secundum aliam rationem identitatis, qua omne illud quod attribuitur Deo, est eius essentia. Sic igitur communis spiratio est idem cum persona patris et cum persona filii, non quod sit una persona per se subsistens; sed, sicut una essentia est in duabus personis, ita et una proprietas, ut supra dictum est.

AD SECUNDUM dicendum quod proprietates dicuntur esse in essentia, per modum identitatis tantum. In personis autem dicuntur esse per modum identitatis, non quidem secundum rem tantum, sed quantum ad modum significandi, sicut forma in supposito. Et ideo proprietates determinant et distinguunt personas, non autem essentiam.

AD TERTIUM dicendum quod participia et verba notionalia significant actus notionales. Actus autem suppositorum sunt. Proprietates autem non significantur ut supposita, sed ut formae suppositorum. Et ideo modus

existence *towards* something. Whence, they styled the relations *assistant*, as above explained (Q. 28, A. 2). But since relation, considered as really existing in God, is the divine essence Itself, and the essence is the same as person, as appears from what was said above (Q. 39, A. 1), relation must necessarily be the same as person.

Others, therefore, considering this identity, said that the properties were indeed the persons; but not *in* the persons; for, they said, there are no properties in God except in our way of speaking, as stated above (Q. 32, A. 2). We must, however, say that there are properties in God; as we have shown (Q. 32, A. 2). These are designated by abstract terms, being forms, as it were, of the persons. So, since the nature of a form requires it to be *in* that of which it is the form, we must say that the properties are in the persons, and yet that they are the persons; as we say that the essence is in God, and yet is God.

REPLY OBJ. 1: Person and property are really the same, but differ in concept. Consequently, it does not follow that if one is multiplied, the other must also be multiplied. We must, however, consider that in God, by reason of the divine simplicity, a twofold real identity exists as regards what in creatures are distinct. For, since the divine simplicity excludes the composition of matter and form, it follows that in God the abstract is the same as the concrete, as *Godhead* and *God*. And as the divine simplicity excludes the composition of subject and accident, it follows that whatever is attributed to God, is His essence Itself; and so, wisdom and power are the same in God, because they are both in the divine essence. According to this twofold identity, property in God is the same as person. For personal properties are the same as the persons because the abstract and the concrete are the same in God; since they are the subsisting persons themselves, as paternity is the Father Himself, and filiation is the Son, and procession is the Holy Spirit. But the non-personal properties are the same as the persons according to the other reason of identity, whereby whatever is attributed to God is His own essence. Thus, common spiration is the same as the person of the Father, and the person of the Son; not that it is one self-subsisting person; but that as there is one essence in the two persons, so also there is one property in the two persons, as above explained (Q. 30, A. 2).

REPLY OBJ. 2: The properties are said to be in the essence, only by mode of identity; but in the persons they exist by mode of identity, not merely in reality, but also in the mode of signification; as the form exists in its subject. Thus the properties determine and distinguish the persons, but not the essence.

REPLY OBJ. 3: Notional participles and verbs signify the notional acts: and acts belong to a suppositum. Now, properties are not designated as supposita, but as forms of supposita. And so their mode of signification is against

significandi repugnat, ut participia et verba notionalia de proprietatibus praedicentur.

notional participles and verbs being predicated of the properties.

Article 2

Whether the Persons Are Distinguished by the Relations?

Ad secundum sic procedo. Videtur quod personae non distinguantur per relationes. Simplicia enim seipsis distinguuntur. Sed personae divinae sunt maxime simplices. Ergo distinguuntur seipsis, et non relationibus.

Praeterea, nulla forma distinguitur nisi secundum suum genus, non enim album a nigro distinguitur nisi secundum qualitatem. Sed hypostasis significat individuum in genere substantiae. Non ergo relationibus hypostases distingui possint.

Praeterea, absolutum est prius quam relativum. Sed prima distinctio est distinctio divinarum personarum. Ergo divinae personae non distinguuntur relationibus.

Praeterea, id quod praesupponit distinctionem, non potest esse primum distinctionis principium. Sed relatio praesupponit distinctionem, cum in eius definitione ponatur, esse enim relativi est ad aliud se habere. Ergo primum principium distinctivum in divinis non potest esse relatio.

Sed contra est quod Boetius dicit, in libro de Trin., *quod sola relatio multiplicat Trinitatem divinarum personarum.*

Respondeo dicendum quod in quibuscumque pluribus invenitur aliquid commune, oportet quaerere aliquid distinctivum. Unde, cum tres personae conveniant secundum essentiae unitatem, necesse est quaerere aliquid quo distinguantur, ad hoc quod plures sint. Inveniuntur autem in divinis personis duo secundum quae differunt, scilicet origo, et relatio. Quae quidem quamvis re non differant, differunt tamen secundum modum significandi, nam origo significatur per modum actus, ut generatio; relatio vero per modum formae, ut paternitas.

Quidam igitur, attendentes quod relatio consequitur actum, dixerunt quod hypostases in divinis distinguuntur per originem; ut dicamus quod pater distinguitur a fi-[X]lio, inquantum ille generat et hic est genitus. Relationes autem sive proprietates manifestant consequenter hypostasum sive personarum distinctiones, sicut et in creaturis proprietates manifestant distinctiones individuorum, quae fiunt per materialia principia.

Sed hoc non potest stare, propter duo. Primo quidem, quia ad hoc quod aliqua duo distincta intelligantur, necesse est eorum distinctionem intelligi per

Objection 1: It would seem that the persons are not distinguished by the relations. For simple things are distinct by themselves. But the persons are supremely simple. Therefore they are distinguished by themselves, and not by the relation.

Obj. 2: Further, a form is distinguished only in relation to its genus. For white is distinguished from black only by quality. But *hypostasis* signifies an individual in the genus of substance. Therefore the hypostases cannot be distinguished by relations.

Obj. 3: Further, what is absolute comes before what is relative. But the distinction of the divine persons is the primary distinction. Therefore the divine persons are not distinguished by the relations.

Obj. 4: Further, whatever presupposes distinction cannot be the first principle of distinction. But relation presupposes distinction, which comes into its definition; for a relation is essentially what is towards another. Therefore the first distinctive principle in God cannot be relation.

On the contrary, Boethius says (*De Trin.*): *Relation alone multiplies the Trinity of the divine persons.*

I answer that, In whatever multitude of things is to be found something common to all, it is necessary to seek out the principle of distinction. So, as the three persons agree in the unity of essence, we must seek to know the principle of distinction whereby they are several. Now, there are two principles of difference between the divine persons, and these are *origin* and *relation*. Although these do not really differ, yet they differ in the mode of signification; for *origin* is signified by way of act, as *generation*; and *relation* by way of the form, as *paternity*.

Some, then, considering that relation follows upon act, have said that the divine hypostases are distinguished by origin, so that we may say that the Father is distinguished from the Son, inasmuch as the former begets and the latter is begotten. Further, that the relations, or the properties, make known the distinctions of the hypostases or persons as resulting therefrom; as also in creatures the properties manifest the distinctions of individuals, which distinctions are caused by the material principles.

This opinion, however, cannot stand—for two reasons. First, because, in order that two things be understood as distinct, their distinction must be understood as resulting

aliquid intrinsecum utrique; sicut in rebus creatis vel per materiam, vel per formam. Origo autem alicuius rei non significatur ut aliquid intrinsecum, sed ut via quaedam a re vel ad rem, sicut generatio significatur ut via quaedam ad rem genitam, et ut progrediens a generante. Unde non potest esse quod res genita et generans distinguantur sola generatione, sed oportet intelligere tam in generante quam in genito ea quibus ab invicem distinguuntur. In persona autem divina non est aliud intelligere nisi essentiam et relationem sive proprietatem. Unde, cum in essentia conveniant, relinquitur quod per relationes personae ab invicem distinguantur. Secundo, quia distinctio in divinis personis non est sic intelligenda, quasi aliquid commune dividatur, quia essentia communis remanet indivisa, sed oportet quod ipsa distinguentia constituant res distinctas. Sic autem relationes vel proprietates distinguunt vel constituunt hypostases vel personas, inquantum sunt ipsae personae subsistentes, sicut paternitas est pater, et filiatio est filius, eo quod in divinis non differt abstractum et concretum. Sed contra rationem originis est, quod constituat hypostasim vel personam. Quia origo active significata, significatur ut progrediens a persona subsistente, unde praesupponit eam. Origo autem passive significata, ut nativitas, significatur ut via ad personam subsistentem; et nondum ut eam constituens.

Unde melius dicitur quod personae seu hypostases distinguantur relationibus, quam per originem. Licet enim distinguantur utroque modo, tamen prius et principalius per relationes, secundum modum intelligendi. Unde hoc nomen pater non solum significat proprietatem, sed etiam hypostasim, sed hoc nomen genitor, vel generans, significat tantum proprietatem. Quia hoc nomen pater significat relationem, quae est distinctiva et constitutiva hypostasis, hoc autem nomen generans, vel genitus, significat originem, quae non est distinctiva et constitutiva hypostasis.

AD PRIMUM ergo dicendum quod personae sunt ipsae relationes subsistentes. Unde non repugnat simplicitati divinarum personarum, quod relationibus distinguantur.

AD SECUNDUM dicendum quod personae divinae non distinguuntur in esse in quo subsistunt, neque in aliquo absoluto, sed solum secundum id quod ad aliquid dicuntur. Unde ad earum distinctionem sufficit relatio.

AD TERTIUM dicendum quod quanto distinctio prior est, tanto propinquior est unitati. Et ideo debet esse minima. Et ideo distinctio personarum non debet esse nisi per id quod minimum distinguit, scilicet per relationem.

AD QUARTUM dicendum quod relatio praesupponit distinctionem suppositorum, quando est accidens, sed si

from something intrinsic to both; thus in things created it results from their matter or their form. Now origin of a thing does not designate anything intrinsic, but means the way from something, or to something; as generation signifies the way to a thing generated, and as proceeding from the generator. Hence it is not possible that what is generated and the generator should be distinguished by generation alone; but in the generator and in the thing generated we must presuppose whatever makes them to be distinguished from each other. In a divine person there is nothing to presuppose but essence, and relation or property. Whence, since the persons agree in essence, it only remains to be said that the persons are distinguished from each other by the relations. Second: because the distinction of the divine persons is not to be so understood as if what is common to them all is divided, because the common essence remains undivided; but the distinguishing principles themselves must constitute the things which are distinct. Now the relations or the properties distinguish or constitute the hypostases or persons, inasmuch as they are themselves the subsisting persons; as paternity is the Father, and filiation is the Son, because in God the abstract and the concrete do not differ. But it is against the nature of origin that it should constitute hypostasis or person. For origin taken in an active sense signifies proceeding from a subsisting person, so that it presupposes the latter; while in a passive sense origin, as *nativity*, signifies the way to a subsisting person, and as not yet constituting the person.

It is therefore better to say that the persons or hypostases are distinguished rather by relations than by origin. For, although in both ways they are distinguished, nevertheless in our mode of understanding they are distinguished chiefly and first by relations; whence this name *Father* signifies not only a property, but also the hypostasis; whereas this term *Begetter* or *Begetting* signifies property only; forasmuch as this name *Father* signifies the relation which is distinctive and constitutive of the hypostasis; and this term *Begetter* or *Begotten* signifies the origin which is not distinctive and constitutive of the hypostasis.

REPLY OBJ. 1: The persons are the subsisting relations themselves. Hence it is not against the simplicity of the divine persons for them to be distinguished by the relations.

REPLY OBJ. 2: The divine persons are not distinguished as regards being, in which they subsist, nor in anything absolute, but only as regards something relative. Hence relation suffices for their distinction.

REPLY OBJ. 3: The more prior a distinction is, the nearer it approaches to unity; and so it must be the least possible distinction. So the distinction of the persons must be by that which distinguishes the least possible; and this is by relation.

REPLY OBJ. 4: Relation presupposes the distinction of the subjects, when it is an accident; but when the relation

relatio sit subsistens, non praesupponit, sed secum fert distinctionem. Cum enim dicitur quod relativi esse est ad aliud se habere, per ly aliud intelligitur correlativum, quod non est prius, sed simul natura.

is subsistent, it does not presuppose, but brings about distinction. For when it is said that relation is by nature to be towards another, the word *another* signifies the correlative which is not prior, but simultaneous in the order of nature.

Article 3

Whether the Hypostases Remain If the Relations Are Mentally Abstracted from the Persons?

AD TERTIUM SIC PROCEDITUR. Videtur quod, abstractis per intellectum proprietatibus seu relationibus a personis, adhuc remaneant hypostases. Id enim ad quod aliquid se habet ex additione, potest intelligi remoto eo quod sibi additur, sicut homo se habet ad animal ex additione, et potest intelligi animal remoto rationali. Sed persona se habet ex additione ad hypostasim, est enim persona hypostasis proprietate distincta ad dignitatem pertinente. Ergo, remota proprietate personali a persona, intelligitur hypostasis.

PRAETEREA, pater non ab eodem habet quod sit pater, et quod sit aliquis. Cum enim paternitate sit pater, si paternitate esset aliquis, sequeretur quod filius, in quo non est paternitas, non esset aliquis. Remota ergo per intellectum paternitate a patre, adhuc remanet quod sit aliquis; quod est esse hypostasim. Ergo, remota proprietate a persona, remanet hypostasis.

PRAETEREA, Augustinus dicit, V de Trin., *non hoc est dicere ingenitum, quod est dicere patrem, quia etsi filium non genuisset, nihil prohiberet eum dicere ingenitum.* Sed si filium non genuisset, non inesset ei paternitas. Ergo, remota paternitate, adhuc remanet hypostasis patris ut ingenita.

SED CONTRA est quod Hilarius dicit, IV de Trin., *nihil habet filius nisi natum.* Nativitate autem est filius. Ergo, remota filiatione, non remanet hypostasis filii. Et eadem ratio est de aliis personis.

RESPONDEO dicendum quod duplex fit abstractio per intellectum. Una quidem, secundum quod universale abstrahitur a particulari, ut animal ab homine. Alia vero, secundum quod forma abstrahitur a materia; sicut forma circuli abstrahitur per intellectum ab omni materia sensibili. Inter has autem abstractiones haec est differentia, quod in abstractione quae fit secundum universale et particulare, non remanet id a quo fit abstractio, remota enim ab homine differentia rationali, non remanet in intellectu homo, sed solum animal. In abstractione vero quae attenditur secundum formam et materiam, utrumque manet in intellectu, abstrahendo enim formam circuli ab aere, remanet seorsum in intellectu nostro et intellectus circuli et intellectus aeris. Quamvis

OBJECTION 1: It would seem that the hypostases remain if the properties or relations are mentally abstracted from the persons. For that to which something is added, may be understood when the addition is taken away; as man is something added to animal which can be understood if rational be taken away. But person is something added to hypostasis; for person is *a hypostasis distinguished by a property of dignity.* Therefore, if a personal property be taken away from a person, the hypostasis remains.

OBJ. 2: Further, that the Father is Father, and that He is someone, are not due to the same reason. For as He is the Father by paternity, supposing He is some one by paternity, it would follow that the Son, in Whom there is not paternity, would not be *someone.* So when paternity is mentally abstracted from the Father, He still remains *someone*—that is, a hypostasis. Therefore, if property be removed from person, the hypostasis remains.

OBJ. 3: Further, Augustine says (*De Trin.* v, 6): *Unbegotten is not the same as Father; for if the Father had not begotten the Son, nothing would prevent Him being called unbegotten.* But if He had not begotten the Son, there would be no paternity in Him. Therefore, if paternity be removed, there still remains the hypostasis of the Father as unbegotten.

ON THE CONTRARY, Hilary says (*De Trin.* iv): *The Son has nothing else than birth.* But He is Son by *birth.* Therefore, if filiation be removed, the Son's hypostasis no more remains; and the same holds as regards the other persons.

I ANSWER THAT, Abstraction by the intellect is twofold—when the universal is abstracted from the particular, as animal abstracted from man; and when the form is abstracted from the matter, as the form of a circle is abstracted by the intellect from any sensible matter. The difference between these two abstractions consists in the fact that in the abstraction of the universal from the particular, that from which the abstraction is made does not remain; for when the difference of rationality is removed from man, the man no longer remains in the intellect, but animal alone remains. But in the abstraction of the form from the matter, both the form and the matter remain in the intellect; as, for instance, if we abstract the form of a circle from brass, there remains in our intellect separately the understanding

autem in divinis non sit universale neque particulare, nec forma et materia, secundum rem; tamen, secundum modum significandi, invenitur aliqua similitudo horum in divinis; secundum quem modum Damascenus dicit quod *commune est substantia, particulare vero hypostasis.* Si igitur loquamur de abstractione quae fit secundum universale et particulare, remotis proprietatibus, remanet in intellectu essentia communis, non autem hypostasis patris, quae est quasi particulare.

Si vero loquamur secundum modum abstractionis formae a materia, remotis proprietatibus non personalibus, remanet intellectus hypostasum et personarum, sicut, remoto per intellectum a patre quod sit ingenitus vel spirans, remanet hypostasis vel persona patris.

Sed remota proprietate personali per intellectum, tollitur intellectus hypostasis. Non enim proprietates personales sic intelliguntur advenire hypostasibus divinis, sicut forma subiecto praeexistenti, sed ferunt secum sua supposita, inquantum sunt ipsae personae subsistentes, sicut paternitas est ipse pater, hypostasis enim significat aliquid distinctum in divinis, cum hypostasis sit substantia individua. Cum igitur relatio sit quae distinguit hypostases et constituit eas, ut dictum est, relinquitur quod, relationibus personalibus remotis per intellectum, non remaneant hypostases. Sed, sicut dictum est, aliqui dicunt quod hypostases in divinis non distinguuntur per relationes, sed per solam originem; ut intelligatur pater esse hypostasis quaedam per hoc, quod non est ab alio; filius autem per hoc, quod est ab alio per generationem. Sed relationes advenientes quasi proprietates ad dignitatem pertinentes, constituunt rationem personae, unde et personalitates dicuntur. Unde, remotis huiusmodi relationibus per intellectum, remanent quidem hypostases, sed non personae.

Sed hoc non potest esse, propter duo. Primo, quia relationes distinguunt et constituunt hypostases, ut ostensum est. Secundo, quia omnis hypostasis naturae rationalis est persona, ut patet per definitionem Boetii, dicentis quod *persona est rationalis naturae individua substantia.* Unde, ad hoc quod esset hypostasis et non persona, oporteret abstrahi ex parte naturae rationalitatem; non autem ex parte personae proprietatem.

AD PRIMUM ergo dicendum quod persona non addit supra hypostasim proprietatem distinguentem absolute, sed proprietatem distinguentem ad dignitatem pertinentem, totum enim hoc est accipiendum loco unius differentiae. Ad dignitatem autem pertinet proprietas distinguens, secundum quod intelligitur subsistens in natura rationali. Unde, remota proprietate distinguente a persona, non remanet hypostasis, sed remaneret, si tolleretur rationalitas naturae. Tam enim persona quam

both of a circle, and of brass. Now, although there is no universal nor particular in God, nor form and matter, in reality; nevertheless, as regards the mode of signification there is a certain likeness of these things in God; and thus Damascene says (*De Fide Orth.* iii, 6) that *substance is common and hypostasis is particular.* So, if we speak of the abstraction of the universal from the particular, the common universal essence remains in the intellect if the properties are removed; but not the hypostasis of the Father, which is, as it were, a particular.

But as regards the abstraction of the form from the matter, if the non-personal properties are removed, then the idea of the hypostases and persons remains; as, for instance, if the fact of the Father's being unbegotten or spirating be mentally abstracted from the Father, the Father's hypostasis or person remains.

If, however, the personal property be mentally abstracted, the idea of the hypostasis no longer remains. For the personal properties are not to be understood as added to the divine hypostases, as a form is added to a pre-existing subject: but they carry with them their own supposita, inasmuch as they are themselves subsisting persons; thus paternity is the Father Himself. For hypostasis signifies something distinct in God, since hypostasis means an individual substance. So, as relation distinguishes and constitutes the hypostases, as above explained (A. 2), it follows that if the personal relations are mentally abstracted, the hypostases no longer remain. Some, however, think, as above noted, that the divine hypostases are not distinguished by the relations, but only by origin; so that the Father is a hypostasis as not from another, and the Son is a hypostasis as from another by generation. And that the consequent relations which are to be regarded as properties of dignity, constitute the notion of a person, and are thus called *personal properties.* Hence, if these relations are mentally abstracted, the hypostasis, but not the persons, remain.

But this is impossible, for two reasons: first, because the relations distinguish and constitute the hypostases, as shown above (A. 2); second, because every hypostasis of a rational nature is a person, as appears from the definition of Boethius (*De Duab. Nat.*) that, *person is the individual substance of a rational nature.* Hence, to have hypostasis and not person, it would be necessary to abstract the rationality from the nature, but not the property from the person.

REPLY OBJ. 1: Person does not add to hypostasis a distinguishing property absolutely, but a distinguishing property of dignity, all of which must be taken as the difference. Now, this distinguishing property is one of dignity precisely because it is understood as subsisting in a rational nature. Hence, if the distinguishing property be removed from the person, the hypostasis no longer remains; whereas it would remain were the rationality of the nature removed; for both person and hypostasis are individual substances.

hypostasis est substantia individua, unde in divinis de ratione utriusque est relatio distinguens.

Ad secundum dicendum quod paternitate pater non solum est pater, sed est persona, et est quis sive hypostasis. Nec tamen sequitur quod filius non sit quis sive hypostasis; sicut non sequitur quod non sit persona.

Ad tertium dicendum quod intentio Augustini non fuit dicere quod hypostasis patris remaneat ingenita, remota paternitate, quasi innascibilitas constituat et distinguat hypostasim patris, hoc enim esse non potest, cum ingenitum nihil ponat, sed negative dicatur, ut ipsemet dicit. Sed loquitur in communi, quia non omne ingenitum est pater. Remota ergo paternitate, non remanet in divinis hypostasis patris, ut distinguitur ab aliis personis; sed ut distinguitur a creaturis, sicut Iudaei intelligunt.

Consequently, in God the distinguishing relation belongs essentially to both.

Reply Obj. 2: By paternity the Father is not only Father, but is a person, and is *someone*, or a hypostasis. It does not follow, however, that the Son is not *someone* or a hypostasis; just as it does not follow that He is not a person.

Reply Obj. 3: Augustine does not mean to say that the hypostasis of the Father would remain as unbegotten, if His paternity were removed, as if innascibility constituted and distinguished the hypostasis of the Father; for this would be impossible, since *being unbegotten* says nothing positive and is only a negation, as he himself says. But he speaks in a general sense, forasmuch as not every unbegotten being is the Father. So, if paternity be removed, the hypostasis of the Father does not remain in God, as distinguished from the other persons, but only as distinguished from creatures; as the Jews understand it.

Article 4

Whether the Properties Presuppose the Notional Acts?

Ad quartum sic proceditur. Videtur quod actus notionales praeintelligantur proprietatibus. Dicit enim Magister, XXVII dist. I Sent., quod *semper pater est, quia genuit semper filium.* Et ita videtur quod generatio, secundum intellectum, praecedat paternitatem.

Praeterea, omnis relatio praesupponit, in intellectu, id supra quod fundatur; sicut aequalitas quantitatem. Sed paternitas est relatio fundata super actione quae est generatio. Ergo paternitas praesupponit generationem.

Praeterea, sicut se habet generatio activa ad paternitatem, ita se habet nativitas ad filiationem. Sed filiatio praesupponit nativitatem, ideo enim filius est, quia natus est. Ergo et paternitas praesupponit generationem.

Sed contra, generatio est operatio personae patris. Sed paternitas constituit personam patris. Ergo prius est, secundum intellectum, paternitas quam generatio.

Respondeo dicendum quod, secundum illos qui dicunt quod proprietates non distinguunt et constituunt hypostases, sed manifestant hypostases distinctas et constitutas, absolute dicendum est quod relationes, secundum modum intelligendi, consequuntur actus notionales; ut dici possit simpliciter quod quia generat, est pater. Sed supponendo quod relationes distinguant et constituant hypostases in divinis, oportet distinctione uti. Quia origo significatur in divinis active et passive, active quidem, sicut generatio attribuitur patri, et spiratio, sumpta pro actu notionali, attribuitur patri et filio; passive autem, sicut nativitas attribuitur filio, et processio

Objection 1: It would seem that the notional acts are understood before the properties. For the Master of the Sentences says (*Sent.* i, D, xxvii) that *the Father always is, because He is ever begetting the Son.* So it seems that generation precedes paternity in the order of intelligence.

Obj. 2: Further, in the order of intelligence every relation presupposes that on which it is founded; as equality presupposes quantity. But paternity is a relation founded on the action of generation. Therefore paternity presupposes generation.

Obj. 3: Further, active generation is to paternity as nativity is to filiation. But filiation presupposes nativity; for the Son is so called because He is born. Therefore paternity also presupposes generation.

On the contrary, Generation is the operation of the person of the Father. But paternity constitutes the person of the Father. Therefore in the order of intelligence, paternity is prior to generation.

I answer that, According to the opinion that the properties do not distinguish and constitute the hypostases in God, but only manifest them as already distinct and constituted, we must absolutely say that the relations in our mode of understanding follow upon the notional acts, so that we can say, without qualifying the phrase, that *because He begets, He is the Father.* A distinction, however, is needed if we suppose that the relations distinguish and constitute the divine hypostases. For origin has in God an active and passive signification—active, as generation is attributed to the Father, and spiration, taken for the notional act, is attributed to the Father and the Son; passive, as nativity

spiritui sancto. Origines enim passive significatae, simpliciter praecedunt, secundum intellectum, proprietates personarum procedentium, etiam personales, quia origo passive significata, significatur ut via ad personam proprietate constitutam. Similiter et origo active significata, prior est, secundum intellectum, quam relatio personae originantis quae non est personalis, sicut actus notionalis spirationis, secundum intellectum, praecedit proprietatem relativam innominatam communem patri et filio. Sed proprietas personalis patris potest considerari dupliciter. Uno modo, ut est relatio, et sic iterum, secundum intellectum, praesupponit actum notionalem; quia relatio, inquantum huiusmodi, fundatur super actum. Alio modo, secundum quod est constitutiva personae, et sic oportet quod praeintelligatur relatio actui notionali, sicut persona agens praeintelligitur actioni.

AD PRIMUM ergo dicendum quod, cum Magister dicit quod quia generat est pater, accipit nomen patris secundum quod designat relationem tantum, non autem secundum quod significat personam subsistentem. Sic enim oporteret e converso dicere quod quia pater est, generat.

AD SECUNDUM dicendum quod obiectio illa procedit de paternitate, secundum quod est relatio, et non secundum quod est constitutiva personae.

AD TERTIUM dicendum quod nativitas est via ad personam filii, et ideo, secundum intellectum, praecedit filiationem, etiam secundum quod est constitutiva personae filii. Sed generatio activa significatur ut progrediens a persona patris, et ideo praesupponit proprietatem personalem patris.

is attributed to the Son, and procession to the Holy Spirit. For, in the order of intelligence, origin, in the passive sense, simply precedes the personal properties of the person proceeding; because origin, as passively understood, signifies the way to a person constituted by the property. Likewise, origin signified actively is prior in the order of intelligence to the non-personal relation of the person originating; as the notional act of spiration precedes, in the order of intelligence, the unnamed relative property common to the Father and the Son. The personal property of the Father can be considered in a twofold sense: first, as a relation; and thus again in the order of intelligence it presupposes the notional act, for relation, as such, is founded upon an act: second, according as it constitutes the person; and thus the notional act presupposes the relation, as an action presupposes a person acting.

REPLY OBJ. 1: When the Master says that *because He begets, He is Father*, the term *Father* is taken as meaning relation only, but not as signifying the subsisting person; for then it would be necessary to say conversely that because He is Father He begets.

REPLY OBJ. 2: This objection avails of paternity as a relation, but not as constituting a person.

REPLY OBJ. 3: Nativity is the way to the person of the Son; and so, in the order of intelligence, it precedes filiation, even as constituting the person of the Son. But active generation signifies a proceeding from the person of the Father; wherefore it presupposes the personal property of the Father.

QUESTION 41

PERSONS COMPARED TO NOTIONAL ACTS

Deinde considerandum est de personis in comparatione ad actus notionales. Et circa hoc quaeruntur sex.

Primo, utrum actus notionales sint attribuendi personis.

Secundo, utrum huiusmodi actus sint necessarii vel voluntarii.

Tertio, utrum, secundum huiusmodi actus, persona procedat de nihilo, vel de aliquo.

Quarto, utrum in divinis sit ponere potentiam respectu actuum notionalium.

Quinto, quid significet huiusmodi potentia.

Sexto, utrum actus notionalis ad plures personas terminari possit.

We now consider the persons in reference to the notional acts, concerning which six points of inquiry arise:

(1) Whether the notional acts are to be attributed to the persons?

(2) Whether these acts are necessary, or voluntary?

(3) Whether as regards these acts, a person proceeds from nothing or from something?

(4) Whether in God there exists a power as regards the notional acts?

(5) What this power means?

(6) Whether several persons can be the term of one notional act?

Article 1

Whether the Notional Acts Are to Be Attributed to the Persons?

AD PRIMUM SIC PROCEDITUR. Videtur quod actus notionales non sint personis attribuendi. Dicit enim Boetius, in libro de Trin., quod *omnia genera, cum quis in divinam vertit praedicationem, in divinam mutantur substantiam, exceptis relativis.* Sed actio est unum de decem generibus. Si igitur actio aliqua Deo attribuitur, ad eius essentiam pertinebit, et non ad notionem.

PRAETEREA, Augustinus dicit, V de Trin., *omne quod de Deo dicitur, aut dicitur secundum substantiam, aut secundum relationem.* Sed ea quae ad substantiam pertinent, significantur per essentialia attributa, quae vero ad relationem, per nomina personarum et per nomina proprietatum. Non sunt ergo, praeter haec, attribuendi personis notionales actus.

PRAETEREA, proprium actionis est ex se passionem inferre. Sed in divinis non ponimus passiones. Ergo neque actus notionales ibi ponendi sunt.

SED CONTRA est quod Augustinus dicit, in libro de fide ad Petrum, *proprium patris est, quod filium genuit.* Sed generatio actus quidam est. Ergo actus notionales ponendi sunt in divinis.

RESPONDEO dicendum quod in divinis personis attenditur distinctio secundum originem. Origo autem convenienter designari non potest nisi per aliquos actus. Ad designandum igitur ordinem originis in divinis personis, necessarium fuit attribuere personis actus notionales.

OBJECTION 1: It would seem that the notional acts are not to be attributed to the persons. For Boethius says (*De Trin.*): *Whatever is predicated of God, of whatever genus it be, becomes the divine substance, except what pertains to the relation.* But action is one of the ten genera. Therefore any action attributed to God belongs to His essence, and not to a notion.

OBJ. 2: Further, Augustine says (*De Trin.* v, 4,5) that, *everything which is said of God, is said of Him as regards either His substance, or relation.* But whatever belongs to the substance is signified by the essential attributes; and whatever belongs to the relations, by the names of the persons, or by the names of the properties. Therefore, in addition to these, notional acts are not to be attributed to the persons.

OBJ. 3: Further, the nature of action is of itself to cause passion. But we do not place passions in God. Therefore neither are notional acts to be placed in God.

ON THE CONTRARY, Augustine (*Fulgentius, De Fide ad Petrum* ii) says: *It is a property of the Father to beget the Son.* Therefore notional acts are to be placed in God.

I ANSWER THAT, In the divine persons distinction is founded on origin. But origin can be properly designated only by certain acts. Wherefore, to signify the order of origin in the divine persons, we must attribute notional acts to the persons.

Ad primum ergo dicendum quod omnis origo designatur per aliquem actum. Duplex autem ordo originis attribui Deo potest. Unus quidem, secundum quod creatura ab eo progreditur, et hoc commune est tribus personis. Et ideo actiones quae attribuuntur Deo ad designandum processum creaturarum ab ipso, ad essentiam pertinent. Alius autem ordo originis in divinis attenditur secundum processionem personae a persona. Unde actus designantes huius originis ordinem, notionales dicuntur, quia notiones personarum sunt personarum habitudines ad invicem, ut ex dictis patet.

Ad secundum dicendum quod actus notionales secundum modum significandi tantum differunt a relationibus personarum; sed re sunt omnino idem. Unde Magister dicit, in I Sent., XXVI dist., quod *generatio et nativitas aliis nominibus dicuntur paternitas et filiatio.* Ad cuius evidentiam, attendendum est quod primo coniicere potuimus originem alicuius ab alio, ex motu, quod enim aliqua res a sua dispositione removeretur per motum, manifestum fuit hoc ab aliqua causa accidere. Et ideo actio, secundum primam nominis impositionem, importat originem motus, sicut enim motus, prout est in mobili ab aliquo, dicitur passio; ita origo ipsius motus, secundum quod incipit ab alio et terminatur in id quod movetur, vocatur actio. Remoto igitur motu, actio nihil aliud importat quam ordinem originis, secundum quod a causa aliqua vel principio procedit in id quod est a principio. Unde, cum in divinis non sit motus, actio personalis producentis personam, nihil aliud est quam habitudo principii ad personam quae est a principio. Quae quidem habitudines sunt ipsae relationes vel notiones. Quia tamen de divinis et intelligibilibus rebus loqui non possumus nisi secundum modum rerum sensibilium, a quibus cognitionem accipimus; et in quibus actiones et passiones, inquantum motum implicant, aliud sunt a relationibus quae ex actionibus et passionibus consequuntur, oportuit seorsum significari habitudines personarum per modum actus, et seorsum per modum relationum. Et sic patet quod sunt idem secundum rem, sed differunt solum secundum modum significandi.

Ad tertium dicendum quod actio, secundum quod importat originem motus, infert ex se passionem, sic autem non ponitur actio in divinis personis. Unde non ponuntur ibi passiones, nisi solum grammatice loquendo, quantum ad modum significandi; sicut patri attribuimus generare, et filio generari.

Reply Obj. 1: Every origin is designated by an act. In God there is a twofold order of origin: one, inasmuch as the creature proceeds from Him, and this is common to the three persons; and so those actions which are attributed to God to designate the proceeding of creatures from Him, belong to His essence. Another order of origin in God regards the procession of person from person; wherefore the acts which designate the order of this origin are called notional; because the notions of the persons are the mutual relations of the persons, as is clear from what was above explained (Q. 32, A. 2).

Reply Obj. 2: The notional acts differ from the relations of the persons only in their mode of signification; and in reality are altogether the same. Whence the Master says that *generation and nativity in other words are paternity and filiation (Sent.* i, D, xxvi). To see this, we must consider that the origin of one thing from another is first inferred from movement: for that anything be changed from its disposition by movement evidently arises from some cause. Hence action, in its primary sense, means origin of movement; for, as movement derived from another into a mobile object, is called *passion*, so the origin of movement itself as beginning from another and terminating in what is moved, is called *action*. Hence, if we take away movement, action implies nothing more than order of origin, in so far as action proceeds from some cause or principle to what is from that principle. Consequently, since in God no movement exists, the personal action of the one producing a person is only the habitude of the principle to the person who is from the principle; which habitudes are the relations, or the notions. Nevertheless we cannot speak of divine and intelligible things except after the manner of sensible things, whence we derive our knowledge, and wherein actions and passions, so far as these imply movement, differ from the relations which result from action and passion, and therefore it was necessary to signify the habitudes of the persons separately after the manner of act, and separately after the manner of relations. Thus it is evident that they are really the same, differing only in their mode of signification.

Reply Obj. 3: Action, so far as it means origin of movement, naturally involves passion; but action in that sense is not attributed to God. Whence, passions are attributed to Him only from a grammatical standpoint, and in accordance with our manner of speaking, as we attribute *to beget* with the Father, and to the Son *to be begotten.*

Article 2

Whether the Notional Acts Are Voluntary?

Ad secundum sic proceditur. Videtur quod actus notionales sint voluntarii. Dicit enim Hilarius, in libro de Synod., *non naturali necessitate ductus, pater genuit filium.*

Praeterea, apostolus, Coloss. I, *transtulit nos in regnum filii dilectionis suae.* Dilectio autem voluntatis est. Ergo filius genitus est a patre, voluntate.

Praeterea, nihil magis est voluntarium quam amor. Sed Spiritus Sanctus procedit a patre et filio ut amor. Ergo procedit voluntarie.

Praeterea, filius procedit per modum intellectus, ut verbum. Sed omne verbum procedit a dicente per voluntatem. Ergo filius procedit a patre per voluntatem, et non per naturam.

Praeterea, quod non est voluntarium, est necessarium. Si igitur pater non genuit filium voluntate, videtur sequi quod necessitate genuerit. Quod est contra Augustinum, in libro ad Orosium.

Sed contra est quod Augustinus dicit, in eodem libro, quod *neque voluntate genuit pater filium, neque necessitate.*

Respondeo dicendum quod, cum dicitur aliquid esse vel fieri voluntate, dupliciter potest intelligi. Uno modo, ut ablativus designet concomitantiam tantum, sicut possum dicere quod ego sum homo mea voluntate, quia scilicet volo me esse hominem. Et hoc modo potest dici quod pater genuit filium voluntate, sicut et est voluntate Deus, quia vult se esse Deum, et vult se generare filium. Alio modo sic, quod ablativus importet habitudinem principii, sicut dicitur quod artifex operatur voluntate, quia voluntas est principium operis. Et secundum hunc modum, dicendum est quod Deus pater non genuit filium voluntate; sed voluntate produxit creaturam. Unde in libro de Synod. dicitur, *si quis voluntate Dei, tanquam unum aliquid de creaturis, filium factum dicat, anathema sit.* Et huius ratio est, quia voluntas et natura secundum hoc differunt in causando, quia natura determinata est ad unum; sed voluntas non est determinata ad unum. Cuius ratio est, quia effectus assimilatur formae agentis per quam agit. Manifestum est autem quod unius rei non est nisi una forma naturalis, per quam res habet esse, unde quale ipsum est, tale facit. Sed forma per quam voluntas agit, non est una tantum, sed sunt plures, secundum quod sunt plures rationes intellectae, unde quod voluntate agitur, non est tale quale est agens, sed quale vult et intelligit illud esse agens. Eorum igitur voluntas principium est, quae possunt sic vel aliter esse. Eorum autem quae non possunt nisi sic esse, principium natura est. Quod autem potest sic vel aliter esse, longe

Objection 1: It would seem that the notional acts are voluntary. For Hilary says (*De Synod.*): *Not by natural necessity was the Father led to beget the Son.*

Obj. 2: Further, the Apostle says, *He transferred us to the kingdom of the Son of His love* (Col 1:13). But love belongs to the will. Therefore the Son was begotten of the Father by will.

Obj. 3: Further, nothing is more voluntary than love. But the Holy Spirit proceeds as Love from the Father and the Son. Therefore He proceeds voluntarily.

Obj. 4: Further, the Son proceeds by mode of the intellect, as the Word. But every word proceeds by the will from a speaker. Therefore the Son proceeds from the Father by will, and not by nature.

Obj. 5: Further, what is not voluntary is necessary. Therefore if the Father begot the Son, not by the will, it seems to follow that He begot Him by necessity; and this is against what Augustine says (*Ad Orosium qu.* vii).

On the contrary, Augustine says, in the same book, that, *the Father begot the Son neither by will, nor by necessity.*

I answer that, When anything is said to be, or to be made by the will, this can be understood in two senses. In one sense, the ablative designates only concomitance, as I can say that I am a man by my will—that is, I will to be a man; and in this way it can be said that the Father begot the Son by will; as also He is God by will, because He wills to be God, and wills to beget the Son. In the other sense, the ablative imports the habitude of a principle as it is said that the workman works by his will, as the will is the principle of his work; and thus in that sense it must be said the God the Father begot the Son, not by His will; but that He produced the creature by His will. Whence in the book De Synod., it is said: *If anyone say that the Son was made by the Will of God, as a creature is said to be made, let him be anathema.* The reason of this is that will and nature differ in their manner of causation, in such a way that nature is determined to one, while the will is not determined to one; and this because the effect is assimilated to the form of the agent, whereby the latter acts. Now it is manifest that of one thing there is only one natural form whereby it exists; and hence such as it is itself, such also is its work. But the form whereby the will acts is not only one, but many, according to the number of ideas understood. Hence the quality of the will's action does not depend on the quality of the agent, but on the agent's will and understanding. So the will is the principle of those things which may be this way or that way; whereas of those things which can be only in one way, the principle is nature. What, however, can exist in different

est a natura divina, sed hoc pertinet ad rationem creaturae, quia Deus est per se necesse esse, creatura autem est facta ex nihilo. Et ideo Ariani, volentes ad hoc deducere quod filius sit creatura, dixerunt quod pater genuit filium voluntate, secundum quod voluntas designat principium. Nobis autem dicendum est quod pater genuit filium non voluntate, sed natura. Unde Hilarius dicit, in libro de Synod., *omnibus creaturis substantiam Dei voluntas attulit; sed naturam filio dedit ex impassibili ac non nata substantia perfecta nativitas. Talia enim cuncta creata sunt, qualia Deus esse voluit, filius autem, natus ex Deo, talis subsistit, qualis et Deus est.*

AD PRIMUM ergo dicendum quod auctoritas illa inducitur contra illos qui a generatione filii etiam concomitantiam paternae voluntatis removebant, dicentes sic eum natura genuisse filium, ut inde voluntas generandi ei non adesset, sicut nos multa naturali necessitate contra voluntatem patimur, ut mortem, senectutem, et huiusmodi defectus. Et hoc patet per praecedentia et subsequentia. Sic enim ibi dicitur, *non enim, nolente patre, vel coactus pater, vel naturali necessitate inductus cum nollet, genuit filium.*

AD SECUNDUM dicendum quod apostolus nominat Christum filium dilectionis Dei, inquantum est a Deo superabundanter dilectus, non quod dilectio sit principium generationis filii.

AD TERTIUM dicendum quod etiam voluntas, inquantum est natura quaedam, aliquid naturaliter vult; sicut voluntas hominis naturaliter tendit ad beatitudinem. Et similiter Deus naturaliter vult et amat seipsum. Sed circa alia a se, voluntas Dei se habet ad utrumque quodammodo, ut dictum est. Spiritus autem sanctus procedit ut amor, inquantum Deus amat seipsum. Unde naturaliter procedit, quamvis per modum voluntatis procedat.

AD QUARTUM dicendum quod etiam in conceptionibus intellectualibus fit reductio ad prima, quae naturaliter intelliguntur. Deus autem naturaliter intelligit seipsum. Et secundum hoc, conceptio verbi divini est naturalis.

AD QUINTUM dicendum quod necessarium dicitur aliquid per se, et per aliud. Per aliud quidem dupliciter. Uno modo, sicut per causam agentem et cogentem, et sic necessarium dicitur quod est violentum. Alio modo, sicut per causam finalem, sicut dicitur aliquid esse necessarium in his quae sunt ad finem, inquantum sine hoc non potest esse finis, vel bene esse. Et neutro istorum modorum divina generatio est necessaria, quia Deus non est propter finem, neque coactio cadit in ipsum. Per se autem dicitur aliquid necessarium, quod non potest non esse. Et sic Deum esse est necessarium. Et hoc modo patrem generare filium est necessarium.

ways is far from the divine nature, whereas it belongs to the nature of a created being; because God is of Himself necessary being, whereas a creature is made from nothing. Thus, the Arians, wishing to prove the Son to be a creature, said that the Father begot the Son by will, taking will in the sense of principle. But we, on the contrary, must assert that the Father begot the Son, not by will, but by nature. Wherefore Hilary says (*De Synod.*): *The will of God gave to all creatures their substance: but perfect birth gave the Son a nature derived from a substance impassible and unborn. All things created are such as God willed them to be; but the Son, born of God, subsists in the perfect likeness of God.*

REPLY OBJ. 1: This saying is directed against those who did not admit even the concomitance of the Father's will in the generation of the Son, for they said that the Father begot the Son in such a manner by nature that the will to beget was wanting; just as we ourselves suffer many things against our will from natural necessity—as, for instance, death, old age, and like ills. This appears from what precedes and from what follows as regards the words quoted, for thus we read: *Not against His will, nor as it were, forced, nor as if He were led by natural necessity did the Father beget the Son.*

REPLY OBJ. 2: The Apostle calls Christ the Son of the love of God, inasmuch as He is superabundantly loved by God; not, however, as if love were the principle of the Son's generation.

REPLY OBJ. 3: The will, as a natural faculty, wills something naturally, as man's will naturally tends to happiness; and likewise God naturally wills and loves Himself; whereas in regard to things other than Himself, the will of God is in a way, undetermined in itself, as above explained (Q. 19, A. 3). Now, the Holy Spirit proceeds as Love, inasmuch as God loves Himself, and hence He proceeds naturally, although He proceeds by mode of will.

REPLY OBJ. 4: Even as regards the intellectual conceptions of the mind, a return is made to those first principles which are naturally understood. But God naturally understands Himself, and thus the conception of the divine Word is natural.

REPLY OBJ. 5: A thing is said to be necessary *of itself*, and *by reason of another*. Taken in the latter sense, it has a twofold meaning: first, as an efficient and compelling cause, and thus necessary means what is violent; second, it means a final cause, when a thing is said to be necessary as the means to an end, so far as without it the end could not be attained, or, at least, so well attained. In neither of these ways is the divine generation necessary; because God is not the means to an end, nor is He subject to compulsion. But a thing is said to be necessary *of itself* which cannot but be: in this sense it is necessary for God to be; and in the same sense it is necessary that the Father beget the Son.

Article 3

Whether the Notional Acts Proceed from Something?

AD TERTIUM SIC PROCEDITUR. Videtur quod actus notionales non sint de aliquo. Quia si pater generat filium de aliquo, aut de seipso, aut de aliquo alio. Si de aliquo alio, cum id de quo aliquid generatur, sit in eo quod generatur, sequitur quod aliquid alienum a patre sit in filio. Quod est contra Hilarium, VII de Trin., ubi dicit, *nihil in his diversum est vel alienum.* Si autem filium generat pater de seipso, id autem de quo aliquid generatur, si sit permanens, recipit eius praedicationem quod generatur; sicut dicimus quod homo est albus, quia homo permanet, cum de non albo fit albus, sequitur igitur quod pater vel non permaneat, genito filio, vel quod pater sit filius, quod est falsum. Non ergo pater generat filium de aliquo, sed de nihilo.

PRAETEREA, id de quo aliquid generatur, est principium eius quod generatur. Si ergo pater generat filium de essentia vel natura sua sequitur quod essentia vel natura patris sit principium filii. Sed non principium materiale, quia materia locum in divinis non habet. Ergo est principium quasi activum, sicut generans est principium geniti. Et ita sequitur quod essentia generet, quod supra improbatum est.

PRAETEREA, Augustinus dicit quod tres personae non sunt ex eadem essentia, quia non est aliud essentia et persona. Sed persona filii non est aliud ab essentia patris. Ergo filius non est de essentia patris.

PRAETEREA, omnis creatura est ex nihilo. Sed filius in Scripturis dicitur creatura, dicitur enim Eccli. XXIV, ex ore sapientiae genitae, *ego ex ore altissimi prodii, primogenita ante omnem creaturam*; et postea ex ore eiusdem sapientiae dicitur, *ab initio, et ante saecula, creata sum.* Ergo filius non est genitus ex aliquo, sed ex nihilo. Et similiter potest obiici de spiritu sancto, propter hoc quod dicitur, Zac. XII *dixit dominus, extendens caelum et fundans terram, et creans spiritum hominis in eo*; et Amos IV, secundum aliam litteram, *ego formans montes, et creans spiritum.*

SED CONTRA est quod Augustinus dicit, in libro de fide ad Petrum, *pater Deus de sua natura sine initio genuit filium sibi aequalem.*

RESPONDEO dicendum quod filius non est genitus de nihilo, sed de substantia patris. Ostensum est enim supra quod paternitas, et filiatio, et nativitas, vere et proprie est in divinis. Hoc autem interest inter generationem veram,

OBJECTION 1: It would seem that the notional acts do not proceed from anything. For if the Father begets the Son from something, this will be either from Himself or from something else. If from something else, since that whence a thing is generated exists in what is generated, it follows that something different from the Father exists in the Son, and this contradicts what is laid down by Hilary (*De Trin.* vii) that, *In them nothing diverse or different exists.* If the Father begets the Son from Himself, since again that whence a thing is generated, if it be something permanent, receives as predicate the thing generated therefrom—just as we say, *The man is white*, since the man remains, when from not white he is made white—it follows that either the Father does not remain after the Son is begotten, or that the Father is the Son, which is false. Therefore the Father does not beget the Son from something, but from nothing.

OBJ. 2: Further, that whence anything is generated is the principle regarding what is generated. So if the Father generate the Son from His own essence or nature, it follows that the essence or nature of the Father is the principle of the Son. But it is not a material principle, because in God nothing material exists; and therefore it is, as it were, an active principle, as the begetter is the principle of the one begotten. Thus it follows that the essence generates, which was disproved above (Q. 39, A. 5).

OBJ. 3: Further, Augustine says (*De Trin.* vii, 6) that the three persons are not from the same essence; because the essence is not another thing from person. But the person of the Son is not another thing from the Father's essence. Therefore the Son is not from the Father's essence.

OBJ. 4: Further, every creature is from nothing. But in Scripture the Son is called a creature; for it is said (Sir 24:5), in the person of the Wisdom begotten, 'I came out of the mouth of the Most High, the first-born before all creatures': and further on (Sir 24:14) it is said as uttered by the same Wisdom, *From the beginning, and before the world was I created.* Therefore the Son was not begotten from something, but from nothing. Likewise we can object concerning the Holy Spirit, by reason of what is said (Zech 12:1): *Thus saith the Lord Who stretcheth forth the heavens, and layeth the foundations of the earth, and formeth the spirit of man within him*; and (Amos 4:13) according to another version: *I Who form the earth, and create the spirit.*

ON THE CONTRARY, Augustine (*Fulgentius, De Fide ad Petrum* i, 1) says: *God the Father, of His nature, without beginning, begot the Son equal to Himself.*

I ANSWER THAT, The Son was not begotten from nothing, but from the Father's substance. For it was explained above (Q. 27, A. 2; Q. 33, AA. 2 ,3) that paternity, filiation and nativity really and truly exist in God. Now, this is the

per quam aliquis procedit ut filius, et factionem, quod faciens facit aliquid de exteriori materia, sicut scamnum facit artifex de ligno; homo autem generat filium de seipso. Sicut autem artifex creatus facit aliquid ex materia, ita Deus facit ex nihilo, ut infra ostendetur, non quod nihilum cedat in substantiam rei, sed quia ab ipso tota substantia rei producitur, nullo alio praesupposito. Si ergo filius procederet a patre ut de nihilo existens, hoc modo se haberet ad patrem ut artificiatum ad artificem, quod manifestum est nomen filiationis proprie habere non posse, sed solum secundum aliquam similitudinem. Unde relinquitur quod, si filius Dei procederet a patre quasi existens ex nihilo, non esset vere et proprie filius. Cuius contrarium dicitur I Ioan. ult., *ut simus in vero filio eius Iesu Christo.* Filius igitur Dei verus non est ex nihilo, nec factus, sed tantum genitus.

Si qui autem ex nihilo a Deo facti filii Dei dicantur, hoc erit metaphorice, secundum aliqualem assimilationem ad eum qui vere filius est. Unde, inquantum solus est verus et naturalis Dei filius, dicitur unigenitus, secundum illud Ioan. I *unigenitus, qui est in sinu patris, ipse enarravit.* Inquantum vero per assimilationem ad ipsum alii dicuntur filii adoptivi, quasi metaphorice dicitur esse primogenitus, secundum illud Rom. VIII, *quos praescivit, et praedestinavit conformes fieri imaginis filii sui, ut sit ipse primogenitus in multis fratribus.* Relinquitur ergo quod Dei filius sit genitus de substantia patris. Aliter tamen quam filius hominis. Pars enim substantiae hominis generantis transit in substantiam geniti. Sed divina natura impartibilis est. Unde necesse est quod pater, generando filium, non partem naturae in ipsum transfuderit, sed totam naturam ei communicaverit, remanente distinctione solum secundum originem, ut ex dictis patet.

Ad primum ergo dicendum quod, cum filius dicitur natus de patre, haec praepositio de significat principium generans consubstantiale; non autem principium materiale. Quod enim producitur de materia, fit per transmutationem illius de quo producitur, in aliquam formam; divina autem essentia non est transmutabilis, neque alterius formae susceptiva.

Ad secundum dicendum quod, cum dicitur filius genitus de essentia patris, secundum expositionem Magistri, V dist. I Sent., designat habitudinem principii quasi activi, ubi sic exponit, *filius est genitus de essentia patris, idest de patre essentia*; propter hoc quod Augustinus, XV libro de Trin., dicit, *tale est quod dico, de patre essentia, ac si expressius dicerem, de patris essentia.*

difference between true *generation*, whereby one proceeds from another as a son, and *making*, that the maker makes something out of external matter, as a carpenter makes a bench out of wood, whereas a man begets a son from himself. Now, as a created workman makes a thing out of matter, so God makes things out of nothing, as will be shown later on (Q. 45, A. 1), not as if this nothing were a part of the substance of the thing made, but because the whole substance of a thing is produced by Him without anything else whatever presupposed. So, were the Son to proceed from the Father as out of nothing, then the Son would be to the Father what the thing made is to the maker, whereto, as is evident, the name of filiation would not apply except by a kind of similitude. Thus, if the Son of God proceeds from the Father out of nothing, He could not be properly and truly called the Son, whereas the contrary is stated (1 John 5:20): *That we may be in His true Son Jesus Christ.* Therefore the true Son of God is not from nothing; nor is He made, but begotten.

That certain creatures made by God out of nothing are called sons of God is to be taken in a metaphorical sense, according to a certain likeness of assimilation to Him Who is the true Son. Whence, as He is the only true and natural Son of God, He is called the *only begotten*, according to John 1:18, *The only begotten Son, Who is in the bosom of the Father, He hath declared Him*; and so as others are entitled sons of adoption by their similitude to Him, He is called the *first begotten*, according to Rom. 8:29: *Whom He foreknew He also predestined to be made conformable to the image of His Son, that He might be the first born of many brethren.* Therefore the Son of God is begotten of the substance of the Father, but not in the same way as man is born of man; for a part of the human substance in generation passes into the substance of the one begotten, whereas the divine nature cannot be parted; whence it necessarily follows that the Father in begetting the Son does not transmit any part of His nature, but communicates His whole nature to Him, the distinction only of origin remaining as explained above (Q. 40, A. 2).

Reply Obj. 1: When we say that the Son was born of the Father, the preposition *of* designates a consubstantial generating principle, but not a material principle. For that which is produced from matter, is made by a change of form in that whence it is produced. But the divine essence is unchangeable, and is not susceptive of another form.

Reply Obj. 2: When we say the Son is begotten of the essence of the Father, as the Master of the Sentences explains (*Sent.* i, D, v), this denotes the habitude of a kind of active principle, and as he expounds, *the Son is begotten of the essence of the Father*—that is, of the Father Who is essence; and so Augustine says (*De Trin.* xv, 13): *When I say of the Father Who is essence, it is the same as if I said more explicitly, of the essence of the Father.*

Sed hoc non videtur sufficere ad sensum huiusmodi locutionis. Possumus enim dicere quod creatura est ex Deo essentia, non tamen quod sit ex essentia Dei. Unde aliter dici potest quod haec praepositio de semper denotat consubstantialitatem. Unde non dicimus quod domus sit de aedificatore, cum non sit causa consubstantialis. Possumus autem dicere quod aliquid sit de aliquo, quocumque modo illud significetur ut principium consubstantiale, sive illud sit principium activum, sicut filius dicitur esse de patre; sive sit principium materiale, sicut cultellus dicitur esse de ferro; sive sit principium formale, in his dumtaxat in quibus ipsae formae sunt subsistentes, et non advenientes alteri; possumus enim dicere quod Angelus aliquis est de natura intellectuali. Et per hunc modum dicimus quod filius est genitus de essentia patris; inquantum essentia patris, filio per generationem communicata, in eo subsistit.

AD TERTIUM dicendum quod, cum dicitur, filius est genitus de essentia patris, additur aliquid respectu cuius potest salvari distinctio. Sed cum dicitur quod tres personae sunt de essentia divina, non ponitur aliquid respectu cuius possit importari distinctio per praepositionem significata. Et ideo non est simile.

AD QUARTUM dicendum quod, cum dicitur, sapientia est creata, potest intelligi, non de sapientia quae est filius Dei, sed de sapientia creata, quam Deus indidit creaturis, dicitur enim Eccli. I, *ipse creavit eam*, scilicet sapientiam, *spiritu sancto, et effudit illam super omnia opera sua.* Neque est inconveniens quod in uno contextu locutionis loquatur Scriptura de sapientia genita et creata, quia sapientia creata est participatio quaedam sapientiae increatae. Vel potest referri ad naturam creatam assumptam a filio, ut sit sensus, ab initio et ante saecula creata sum, idest, praevisa sum creaturae uniri. Vel, per hoc quod sapientia creata et genita nuncupatur, modus divinae generationis nobis insinuatur. In generatione enim, quod generatur accipit naturam generantis, quod perfectionis est, in creatione vero, creans non mutatur, sed creatum non recipit naturam creantis. Dicitur ergo filius simul creatus et genitus, ut ex creatione accipiatur immutabilitas patris, et ex generatione unitas naturae in patre et filio. Et sic exponitur intellectus huius Scripturae ab Hilario, in libro de Synod. Auctoritates autem inductae non loquuntur de spiritu sancto, sed de spiritu creato; qui quandoque dicitur ventus, quandoque aer, quandoque flatus hominis, quandoque etiam anima, vel quaecumque substantia invisibilis.

This, however, is not enough to explain the real meaning of the words. For we can say that the creature is from God Who is essence; but not that it is from the essence of God. So we may explain them otherwise, by observing that the preposition *of* always denotes consubstantiality. We do not say that a house is *of* the builder, since he is not the consubstantial cause. We can say, however, that something is *of* another, if this is its consubstantial principle, no matter in what way it is so, whether it be an active principle, as the son is said to be *of* the father, or a material principle, as a knife is *of* iron; or a formal principle, but in those things only in which the forms are subsisting, and not accidental to another, for we can say that an angel is *of* an intellectual nature. In this way, then, we say that the Son is begotten 'of' the essence of the Father, inasmuch as the essence of the Father, communicated by generation, subsists in the Son.

REPLY OBJ. 3: When we say that the Son is begotten of the essence of the Father, a term is added which saves the distinction. But when we say that the three persons are 'of' the divine essence, there is nothing expressed to warrant the distinction signified by the preposition, so there is no parity of argument.

REPLY OBJ. 4: When we say *Wisdom was created*, this may be understood not of Wisdom which is the Son of God, but of created wisdom given by God to creatures: for it is said, *He created her in the Holy Spirit, and He poured her out over all His works* (Sir 1:9, 10). Nor is it inconsistent for Scripture in one text to speak of the Wisdom begotten and wisdom created, for wisdom created is a kind of participation of the uncreated Wisdom. The saying may also be referred to the created nature assumed by the Son, so that the sense be, *From the beginning and before the world was I made*—that is, I was foreseen as united to the creature. Or the mention of wisdom as both created and begotten insinuates into our minds the mode of the divine generation; for in generation what is generated receives the nature of the generator and this pertains to perfection; whereas in creation the Creator is not changed, but the creature does not receive the Creator's nature. Thus the Son is called both created and begotten, in order that from the idea of creation the immutability of the Father may be understood, and from generation the unity of nature in the Father and the Son. In this way Hilary expounds the sense of this text of Scripture (*De Synod.*). The other passages quoted do not refer to the Holy Spirit, but to the created spirit, sometimes called wind, sometimes air, sometimes the breath of man, sometimes also the soul, or any other invisible substance.

Article 4

Whether in God There Is a Power in Respect of the Notional Acts?

AD QUARTUM SIC PROCEDITUR. Videtur quod in divinis non sit potentia respectu actuum notionalium. Omnis enim potentia est vel activa, vel passiva. Sed neutra hic competere potest, potentia enim passiva in Deo non est, ut supra ostensum est; potentia vero activa non competit uni personae respectu alterius, cum personae divinae non sint factae, ut ostensum est. Ergo in divinis non est potentia ad actus notionales.

PRAETEREA, potentia dicitur ad possibile. Sed divinae personae non sunt de numero possibilium, sed de numero necessariorum. Ergo respectu actuum notionalium, quibus divinae personae procedunt, non debet poni potentia in divinis.

PRAETEREA, filius procedit ut verbum, quod est conceptio intellectus, spiritus autem sanctus procedit ut amor, qui pertinet ad voluntatem. Sed potentia in Deo dicitur per comparationem ad effectus, non autem per comparationem ad intelligere et velle, ut supra habitum est. Ergo in divinis non debet dici potentia per comparationem ad actus notionales.

SED CONTRA est quod dicit Augustinus, contra Maximinum haereticum, *si Deus pater non potuit generare filium sibi aequalem, ubi est omnipotentia Dei patris?* Est ergo in divinis potentia respectu actuum notionalium.

RESPONDEO dicendum quod, sicut ponuntur actus notionales in divinis, ita necesse est ibi ponere potentiam respectu huiusmodi actuum, cum potentia nihil aliud significet quam principium alicuius actus. Unde, cum patrem intelligamus ut principium generationis, et patrem et filium ut principium spirationis, necesse est quod patri attribuamus potentiam generandi, et patri et filio potentiam spirandi. Quia potentia generandi significat id quo generans generat, omne autem generans generat aliquo, unde in omni generante oportet ponere potentiam generandi, et in spirante potentiam spirandi.

AD PRIMUM ergo dicendum quod, sicut secundum actus notionales non procedit aliqua persona ut facta, ita neque potentia ad actus notionales dicitur in divinis per respectum ad aliquam personam factam, sed solum per respectum ad personam procedentem.

AD SECUNDUM dicendum quod possibile, secundum quod necessario opponitur, sequitur potentiam passivam, quae non est in divinis. Unde neque in divinis est aliquid possibile per modum istum, sed solum secundum quod possibile continetur sub necessario. Sic autem dici potest quod, sicut Deum esse est possibile, sic filium generari est possibile.

AD TERTIUM dicendum quod potentia significat principium. Principium autem distinctionem importat

OBJECTION 1: It would seem that in God there is no power in respect of the notional acts. For every kind of power is either active or passive; neither of which can be here applied, there being in God nothing which we call passive power, as above explained (Q. 25, A. 1); nor can active power belong to one person as regards another, since the divine persons were not made, as stated above (A. 3). Therefore in God there is no power in respect of the notional acts.

OBJ. 2: Further, the object of power is what is possible. But the divine persons are not regarded as possible, but necessary. Therefore, as regards the notional acts, whereby the divine persons proceed, there cannot be power in God.

OBJ. 3: Further, the Son proceeds as the word, which is the concept of the intellect; and the Holy Spirit proceeds as love, which belongs to the will. But in God power exists as regards effects, and not as regards intellect and will, as stated above (Q. 25, A. 1). Therefore, in God power does not exist in reference to the notional acts.

ON THE CONTRARY, Augustine says (*Contra Maxim.* iii, 1): *If God the Father could not beget a co-equal Son, where is the omnipotence of God the Father?* Power therefore exists in God regarding the notional acts.

I ANSWER THAT, As the notional acts exist in God, so must there be also a power in God regarding these acts; since power only means the principle of act. So, as we understand the Father to be principle of generation; and the Father and the Son to be the principle of spiration, we must attribute the power of generating to the Father, and the power of spiration to the Father and the Son; for the power of generation means that whereby the generator generates. Now every generator generates by something. Therefore in every generator we must suppose the power of generating, and in the spirator the power of spirating.

REPLY OBJ. 1: As a person, according to notional acts, does not proceed as if made; so the power in God as regards the notional acts has no reference to a person as if made, but only as regards the person as proceeding.

REPLY OBJ. 2: Possible, as opposed to what is necessary, is a consequence of a passive power, which does not exist in God. Hence, in God there is no such thing as possibility in this sense, but only in the sense of possible as contained in what is necessary; and in this latter sense it can be said that as it is possible for God to be, so also is it possible that the Son should be generated.

REPLY OBJ. 3: Power signifies a principle: and a principle implies distinction from that of which it is the principle.

ab eo cuius est principium. Consideratur autem duplex distinctio in his quae dicuntur de Deo, una secundum rem, alia secundum rationem tantum. Secundum rem quidem, Deus distinguitur per essentiam a rebus quarum est per creationem principium, sicut una persona distinguitur ab alia, cuius est principium, secundum actum notionalem. Sed actio ab agente non distinguitur in Deo nisi secundum rationem tantum, alioquin actio esset accidens in Deo. Et ideo respectu illarum actionum secundum quas aliquae res procedunt distinctae a Deo, vel essentialiter vel personaliter, potest Deo attribui potentia, secundum propriam rationem principii. Et ideo, sicut potentiam ponimus creandi in Deo, ita possumus ponere potentiam generandi vel spirandi. Sed intelligere et velle non sunt tales actus qui designent processionem alicuius rei a Deo distinctae, vel essentialiter vel personaliter. Unde respectu horum actuum, non potest salvari ratio potentiae in Deo, nisi secundum modum intelligendi et significandi tantum; prout diversimode significatur in Deo intellectus et intelligere, cum tamen ipsum intelligere Dei sit eius essentia, non habens principium.

Now we must observe a double distinction in things said of God: one is a real distinction, the other is a distinction of reason only. By a real distinction, God by His essence is distinct from those things of which He is the principle by creation: just as one person is distinct from the other of which He is principle by a notional act. But in God the distinction of action and agent is one of reason only, otherwise action would be an accident in God. And therefore with regard to those actions in respect of which certain things proceed which are distinct from God, either personally or essentially, we may ascribe power to God in its proper sense of principle. And as we ascribe to God the power of creating, so we may ascribe the power of begetting and of spirating. But *to understand* and *to will* are not such actions as to designate the procession of something distinct from God, either essentially or personally. Wherefore, with regard to these actions we cannot ascribe power to God in its proper sense, but only after our way of understanding and speaking: inasmuch as we designate by different terms the intellect and the act of understanding in God, whereas in God the act of understanding is His very essence which has no principle.

Article 5

Whether the Power of Begetting Signifies a Relation, and Not the Essence?

AD QUINTUM SIC PROCEDITUR. Videtur quod potentia generandi vel spirandi significet relationem, et non essentiam. Potentia enim significat principium, ut ex eius definitione patet, dicitur enim potentia activa esse principium agendi, ut patet in V Metaphys. Sed principium in divinis respectu personae dicitur notionaliter. Ergo potentia in divinis non significat essentiam, sed relationem.

PRAETEREA, in divinis non differt posse et agere. Sed generatio in divinis significat relationem. Ergo et potentia generandi.

PRAETEREA, ea quae significant essentiam in divinis, communia sunt tribus personis. Sed potentia generandi non est communis tribus personis, sed propria patri. Ergo non significat essentiam.

SED CONTRA est quod, sicut Deus potest generare filium, ita et vult. Sed voluntas generandi significat essentiam. Ergo et potentia generandi.

RESPONDEO dicendum quod quidam dixerunt quod potentia generandi significat relationem in divinis. Sed hoc esse non potest. Nam illud proprie dicitur potentia in quocumque agente, quo agens agit. Omne autem producens aliquid per suam actionem, producit sibi simile quantum ad formam qua agit sicut homo genitus est similis generanti in natura humana, cuius virtute pater

OBJECTION 1: It would seem that the power of begetting, or of spirating, signifies the relation and not the essence. For power signifies a principle, as appears from its definition: for active power is the principle of action, as we find in *Metaph.* v, text 17. But in God, principle in regard to Person is said notionally. Therefore, in God, power does not signify essence but relation.

OBJ. 2: Further, in God, the power to act and 'to act' are not distinct. But in God, begetting signifies relation. Therefore, the same applies to the power of begetting.

OBJ. 3: Further, terms signifying the essence in God, are common to the three persons. But the power of begetting is not common to the three persons, but proper to the Father. Therefore it does not signify the essence.

ON THE CONTRARY, As God has the power to beget the Son, so also He wills to beget Him. But the will to beget signifies the essence. Therefore, also, the power to beget.

I ANSWER THAT, Some have said that the power to beget signifies relation in God. But this is not possible. For in every agent, that is properly called power, by which the agent acts. Now, everything that produces something by its action, produces something like itself, as to the form by which it acts; just as man begotten is like his begetter in his human nature, in virtue of which the father has the power

potest generare hominem. Illud ergo est potentia generativa in aliquo generante, in quo genitum similatur generanti.

Filius autem Dei similatur patri gignenti in natura divina. Unde natura divina in patre, est potentia generandi in ipso. Unde et Hilarius dicit, in V de Trin., *nativitas Dei non potest eam ex qua profecta est, non tenere naturam; nec enim aliud quam Deus subsistit, quod non aliunde quam de Deo subsistit.*

Sic igitur dicendum est quod potentia generandi principaliter significat divinam essentiam, ut Magister dicit, VII dist. I Sent.; non autem tantum relationem. Nec etiam essentiam inquantum est idem relationi, ut significet ex aequo utrumque. Licet enim paternitas ut forma patris significetur, est tamen proprietas personalis, habens se ad personam patris, ut forma individualis ad aliquod individuum creatum. Forma autem individualis, in rebus creatis, constituit personam generantem, non autem est quo generans generat, alioquin Socrates generaret Socratem. Unde neque paternitas potest intelligi ut quo pater generat, sed ut constituens personam generantis, alioquin pater generaret patrem. Sed id quo pater generat, est natura divina, in qua sibi filius assimilatur. Et secundum hoc Damascenus dicit quod generatio est opus naturae, non sicut generantis, sed sicut eius quo generans generat. Et ideo potentia generandi significat in recto naturam divinam, sed in obliquo relationem.

Ad primum ergo dicendum quod potentia non significat ipsam relationem principii, alioquin esset in genere relationis, sed significat id quod est principium; non quidem sicut agens dicitur principium, sed sicut id quo agens agit, dicitur principium agens autem distinguitur a facto, et generans a generato, sed id quo generans generat, est commune genito et generanti; et tanto perfectius, quanto perfectior fuerit generatio. Unde, cum divina generatio sit perfectissima, id quo generans generat, est commune genito et generanti, et idem numero, non solum specie, sicut in rebus creatis. Per hoc ergo quod dicimus quod essentia divina est principium quo generans generat, non sequitur quod essentia divina distinguatur; sicut sequeretur, si diceretur quod essentia divina generat.

Ad secundum dicendum quod sic est idem in divinis potentia generandi cum generatione, sicut essentia divina cum generatione et paternitate est idem re, sed non ratione.

Ad tertium dicendum quod, cum dico potentiam generandi, potentia significatur in recto, et generatio in obliquo; sicut si dicerem essentiam patris. Unde quantum ad essentiam quae significatur, potentia generandi

to beget a man. In every begetter, therefore, that is the power of begetting in which the begotten is like the begetter.

Now the Son of God is like the Father, who begets Him, in the divine nature. Wherefore the divine nature in the Father is in Him the power of begetting. And so Hilary says (*De Trin.* v): *The birth of God cannot but contain that nature from which it proceeded; for He cannot subsist other than God, Who subsists from no other source than God.*

We must therefore conclude that the power of begetting signifies principally the divine essence as the Master says (*Sent.* i, D, vii), and not the relation only. Nor does it signify the essence as identified with the relation, so as to signify both equally. For although paternity is signified as the form of the Father, nevertheless it is a personal property, being in respect to the person of the Father, what the individual form is to the individual creature. Now the individual form in things created constitutes the person begetting, but is not that by which the begetter begets, otherwise Socrates would beget Socrates. So neither can paternity be understood as that by which the Father begets, but as constituting the person of the Father, otherwise the Father would beget the Father. But that by which the Father begets is the divine nature, in which the Son is like to Him. And in this sense Damascene says (*De Fide Orth.* i, 18) that generation is the *work of nature*, not of nature generating, but of nature, as being that by which the generator generates. And therefore the power of begetting signifies the divine nature directly, but the relation indirectly.

Reply Obj. 1: Power does not signify the relation itself of a principle, for thus it would be in the genus of relation; but it signifies that which is a principle; not, indeed, in the sense in which we call the agent a principle, but in the sense of being that by which the agent acts. Now the agent is distinct from that which it makes, and the generator from that which it generates: but that by which the generator generates is common to generated and generator, and so much more perfectly, as the generation is more perfect. Since, therefore, the divine generation is most perfect, that by which the Begetter begets, is common to Begotten and Begetter by a community of identity, and not only of species, as in things created. Therefore, from the fact that we say that the divine essence *is the principle by which the Begetter begets*, it does not follow that the divine essence is distinct (from the Begotten): which would follow if we were to say that the divine essence begets.

Reply Obj. 2: As in God, the power of begetting is the same as the act of begetting, so the divine essence is the same in reality as the act of begetting or paternity; although there is a distinction of reason.

Reply Obj. 3: When I speak of the *power of begetting*, power is signified directly, generation indirectly: just as if I were to say, the *essence of the Father*. Wherefore in respect of the essence, which is signified, the power of

communis est tribus personis, sed quantum ad notionem quae connotatur, propria est personae patris.

begetting is common to the three persons: but in respect of the notion that is connoted, it is proper to the person of the Father.

Article 6

Whether Several Persons Can Be the Term of One Notional Act?

Ad sextum sic proceditur. Videtur quod actus notionalis ad plures personas terminari possit, ita quod sint plures personae genitae vel spiratae in divinis. Cuicumque enim inest potentia generandi, potest generare. Sed filio inest potentia generandi. Ergo potest generare. Non autem seipsum. Ergo alium filium. Ergo possunt esse plures filii in divinis.

Praeterea, Augustinus dicit, contra Maximinum, *filius non genuit creatorem. Neque enim non potuit, sed non oportuit.*

Praeterea, Deus pater est potentior ad generandum quam pater creatus. Sed unus homo potest generare plures filios. Ergo et Deus, praecipue cum potentia patris, uno filio generato, non diminuatur.

Sed contra est quod in divinis non differt esse et posse. Si igitur in divinis possent esse plures filii, essent plures filii. Et ita essent plures personae quam tres in divinis, quod est haereticum.

Respondeo dicendum quod, sicut Athanasius dicit, *in divinis est tantum unus pater, unus filius, unus Spiritus Sanctus.* Cuius quidem ratio quadruplex assignari potest.

Prima quidem ex parte relationum, quibus solum personae distinguuntur. Cum enim personae divinae sint ipsae relationes subsistentes, non possent esse plures patres vel plures filii in divinis, nisi essent plures paternitates et plures filiationes. Quod quidem esse non posset nisi secundum materialem rerum distinctionem, formae enim unius speciei non multiplicantur nisi secundum materiam, quae in divinis non est. Unde in divinis non potest esse nisi una tantum filiatio subsistens; sicut et albedo subsistens non posset esse nisi una.

Secunda vero ex modo processionum. Quia Deus omnia intelligit et vult uno et simplici actu. Unde non potest esse nisi una persona procedens per modum verbi, quae est filius; et una tantum per modum amoris, quae est Spiritus Sanctus.

Tertia ratio sumitur ex modo procedendi. Quia personae ipsae procedunt naturaliter, ut dictum est, natura autem determinatur ad unum.

Quarta ex perfectione divinarum personarum. Ex hoc enim est perfectus filius, quod tota filiatio divina in

Objection 1: It would seem that a notional act can be directed to several Persons, so that there may be several Persons begotten or spirated in God. For whoever has the power of begetting can beget. But the Son has the power of begetting. Therefore He can beget. But He cannot beget Himself: therefore He can beget another son. Therefore there can be several Sons in God.

Obj. 2: Further, Augustine says (*Contra Maxim.* iii, 12): *The Son did not beget a Creator: not that He could not, but that it behoved Him not.*

Obj. 3: Further, God the Father has greater power to beget than has a created father. But a man can beget several sons. Therefore God can also: the more so that the power of the Father is not diminished after begetting the Son.

On the contrary, In God *that which is possible*, and *that which is* do not differ. If, therefore, in God it were possible for there to be several Sons, there would be several Sons. And thus there would be more than three Persons in God; which is heretical.

I answer that, As Athanasius says, in God there is only *one Father, one Son, one Holy Spirit.* For this four reasons may be given.

The first reason is in regard to the relations by which alone are the Persons distinct. For since the divine Persons are the relations themselves as subsistent, there would not be several Fathers, or several Sons in God, unless there were more than one paternity, or more than one filiation. And this, indeed, would not be possible except owing to a material distinction: since forms of one species are not multiplied except in respect of matter, which is not in God. Wherefore there can be but one subsistent filiation in God: just as there could be but one subsistent whiteness.

The second reason is taken from the manner of the processions. For God understands and wills all things by one simple act. Wherefore there can be but one person proceeding after the manner of word, which person is the Son; and but one person proceeding after the manner of love, which person is the Holy Spirit.

The third reason is taken from the manner in which the persons proceed. For the persons proceed naturally, as we have said (A. 2), and nature is determined to one.

The fourth reason is taken from the perfection of the divine persons. For this reason is the Son perfect, that the

eo continetur, et quod est tantum unus filius. Et similiter dicendum est de aliis personis.

AD PRIMUM ergo dicendum quod, quamvis simpliciter concedendum sit quod potentiam quam habet pater, habeat filius; non tamen concedendum est quod filius habeat potentiam generandi, si generandi sit gerundivum verbi activi, ut sit sensus quod filius habeat potentiam ad generandum. Sicut, licet idem esse sit patris et filii, non tamen convenit filio esse patrem, propter notionale adiunctum. Si tamen hoc quod dico generandi, sit gerundivum verbi passivi, potentia generandi est in filio, idest ut generetur. Et similiter si sit gerundivum verbi impersonalis, ut sit sensus, potentia generandi, idest qua ab aliqua persona generatur.

AD SECUNDUM dicendum quod Augustinus in verbis illis non intendit dicere quod filius posset generare filium, sed quod hoc non est ex impotentia filii, quod non generet, ut infra patebit.

AD TERTIUM dicendum quod immaterialitas et perfectio divina requirit ut non possint esse plures filii in divinis, sicut dictum est. Unde quod non sint plures filii, non est ex impotentia patris ad generandum.

entire divine filiation is contained in Him, and that there is but one Son. The argument is similar in regard to the other persons.

REPLY OBJ. 1: We can grant, without distinction, that the Son has the same power as the Father; but we cannot grant that the Son has the power *generandi* thus taking *generandi* as the gerund of the active verb, so that the sense would be that the Son has the *power to beget.* Just as, although Father and Son have the same being, it does not follow that the Son is the Father, by reason of the notional term added. But if the word *generandi* is taken as the gerundive of the passive verb, the power *generandi* is in the Son—that is, the power of being begotten. The same is to be said if it be taken as the gerundive of an impersonal verb, so that the sense be *the power of generation*—that is, a power by which it is generated by some person.

REPLY OBJ. 2: Augustine does not mean to say by those words that the Son could beget a Son: but that if He did not, it was not because He could not, as we shall see later on (Q. 42, A. 6, ad 3).

REPLY OBJ. 3: Divine perfection and the total absence of matter in God require that there cannot be several Sons in God, as we have explained. Wherefore that there are not several Sons is not due to any lack of begetting power in the Father.

QUESTION 42

EQUALITY AND LIKENESS AMONG THE DIVINE PERSONS

Deinde considerandum est de comparatione personarum ad invicem. Et primo, quantum ad aequalitatem et similitudinem; secundo, quantum ad missionem.

Circa primum quaeruntur sex.

Primo, utrum aequalitas locum habeat in divinis personis.

Secundo, utrum persona procedens sit aequalis ei a qua procedit, secundum aeternitatem.

Tertio, utrum sit aliquis ordo in divinis personis.

Quarto utrum personae divinae sint aequales secundum magnitudinem.

Quinto, utrum una earum sit in alia.

Sexto, utrum sint aequales secundum potentiam.

We now have to consider the persons as compared to one another: first, with regard to equality and likeness; second, with regard to mission.

Concerning the first there are six points of inquiry.

(1) Whether there is equality among the divine persons?

(2) Whether the person who proceeds is equal to the one from Whom He proceeds in eternity?

(3) Whether there is any order among the divine persons?

(4) Whether the divine persons are equal in greatness?

(5) Whether the one divine person is in another?

(6) Whether they are equal in power?

Article 1

Whether There Is Equality in God?

AD PRIMUM SIC PROCEDITUR. Videtur quod aequalitas non competat divinis personis. Aequalitas enim attenditur secundum unum in quantitate, ut patet per philosophum, V Metaphys. In divinis autem personis non invenitur neque quantitas continua intrinseca, quae dicitur magnitudo; neque quantitas continua extrinseca, quae dicitur locus et tempus; neque secundum quantitatem discretam invenitur in eis aequalitas, quia duae personae sunt plures quam una. Ergo divinis personis non convenit aequalitas.

PRAETEREA, divinae personae sunt unius essentiae, ut supra dictum est. Essentia autem significatur per modum formae. Convenientia autem in forma non facit aequalitatem, sed similitudinem. Ergo in divinis personis est dicenda similitudo, et non aequalitas.

PRAETEREA, in quibuscumque invenitur aequalitas, illa sunt sibi invicem aequalia, quia aequale dicitur aequali aequale. Sed divinae personae non possunt sibi invicem dici aequales. Quia, ut Augustinus dicit, VI de Trin., *imago, si perfecte implet illud cuius est imago, ipsa coaequatur ei, non illud imagini suae.* Imago autem patris est filius, et sic pater non est aequalis filio. Non ergo in divinis personis invenitur aequalitas.

PRAETEREA, aequalitas relatio quaedam est. Sed nulla relatio est communis omnibus personis, cum

OBJECTION 1: It would seem that equality is not becoming to the divine persons. For equality is in relation to things which are one in quantity as the Philosopher says (*Metaph.* v, 20). But in the divine persons there is no quantity, neither continuous intrinsic quantity, which we call size, nor continuous extrinsic quantity, which we call place and time. Nor can there be equality by reason of discrete quantity, because two persons are more than one. Therefore equality is not becoming to the divine persons.

OBJ. 2: Further, the divine persons are of one essence, as we have said (Q. 39, A. 2). Now essence is signified by way of form. But agreement in form makes things to be alike, not to be equal. Therefore, we may speak of likeness in the divine persons, but not of equality.

OBJ. 3: Further, things wherein there is to be found equality, are equal to one another, for equality is reciprocal. But the divine persons cannot be said to be equal to one another. For as Augustine says (*De Trin.* vi, 10): *If an image answers perfectly to that whereof it is the image, it may be said to be equal to it; but that which it represents cannot be said to be equal to the image.* But the Son is the image of the Father; and so the Father is not equal to the Son. Therefore equality is not to be found among the divine persons.

OBJ. 4: Further, equality is a relation. But no relation is common to the three persons; for the persons are distinct

secundum relationes personae ab invicem distinguantur. Non ergo aequalitas divinis personis convenit.

SED CONTRA est quod Athanasius dicit, quod *tres personae coaeternae sibi sunt et coaequales.*

RESPONDEO dicendum quod necesse est ponere aequalitatem in divinis personis. Quia secundum philosophum, in X Metaphys., aequale dicitur quasi per negationem minoris et maioris. Non autem possumus in divinis personis ponere aliquid maius et minus, quia, ut Boetius dicit, in libro de Trin., eos differentia, scilicet deitatis, comitatur, *qui vel augent vel minuunt, ut Ariani, qui gradibus meritorum Trinitatem variantes distrahunt, atque in pluralitatem deducunt.* Cuius ratio est, quia inaequalium non potest esse una quantitas numero. Quantitas autem in divinis non est aliud quam eius essentia. Unde relinquitur quod, si esset aliqua inaequalitas in divinis personis, quod non esset in eis una essentia, et sic non essent tres personae unus Deus, quod est impossibile. Oportet igitur aequalitatem ponere in divinis personis.

AD PRIMUM ergo dicendum quod duplex est quantitas. Una scilicet quae dicitur quantitas molis, vel quantitas dimensiva, quae in solis rebus corporalibus est, unde in divinis personis locum non habet. Sed alia est quantitas virtutis, quae attenditur secundum perfectionem alicuius naturae vel formae, quae quidem quantitas designatur secundum quod dicitur aliquid magis vel minus calidum, inquantum est perfectius vel minus perfectum in caliditate. Huiusmodi autem quantitas virtualis attenditur primo quidem in radice, idest in ipsa perfectione formae vel naturae, et sic dicitur magnitudo spiritualis, sicut dicitur magnus calor propter suam intensionem et perfectionem. Et ideo dicit Augustinus, VI de Trin., quod *in his quae non mole magna sunt, hoc est maius esse, quod est melius esse,* nam melius dicitur quod perfectius est. Secundo autem attenditur quantitas virtualis in effectibus formae. Primus autem effectus formae est esse, nam omnis res habet esse secundum suam formam. Secundus autem effectus est operatio, nam omne agens agit per suam formam. Attenditur igitur quantitas virtualis et secundum esse, et secundum operationem, secundum esse quidem, inquantum ea quae sunt perfectioris naturae, sunt maioris durationis; secundum operationem vero, inquantum ea quae sunt perfectioris naturae, sunt magis potentia ad agendum. Sic igitur, ut Augustinus dicit, in libro de fide ad Petrum, aequalitas intelligitur in patre et filio et spiritu sancto, *inquantum nullus horum aut praecedit aeternitate, aut excedit magnitudine, aut superat potestate.*

AD SECUNDUM dicendum quod ubi attenditur aequalitas secundum quantitatem virtualem, aequalitas includit in se similitudinem, et aliquid plus, quia excludit excessum. Quaecumque enim communicant in una forma, possunt dici similia, etiamsi inaequaliter illam formam participant, sicut si dicatur aer esse similis igni

by reason of the relations. Therefore equality is not becoming to the divine persons.

ON THE CONTRARY, Athanasius says that *the three persons are co-eternal and co-equal to one another.*

I ANSWER THAT, We must needs admit equality among the divine persons. For, according to the Philosopher (*Metaph.* x, 15, 16, 17), equality signifies the negation of greater or less. Now we cannot admit anything greater or less in the divine persons; for as Boethius says (*De Trin.* i): *They must needs admit a difference who speak of either increase or decrease, as the Arians do, who sunder the Trinity by distinguishing degrees as of numbers, thus involving a plurality.* Now the reason of this is that unequal things cannot have the same quantity. But quantity, in God, is nothing else than His essence. Wherefore it follows, that if there were any inequality in the divine persons, they would not have the same essence; and thus the three persons would not be one God; which is impossible. We must therefore admit equality among the divine persons.

REPLY OBJ. 1: Quantity is twofold. There is quantity of *bulk* or dimensive quantity, which is to be found only in corporeal things, and has, therefore, no place in God. There is also quantity of *virtue,* which is measured according to the perfection of some nature or form: to this sort of quantity we allude when we speak of something as being more, or less, hot; forasmuch as it is more, or less, perfect in heat. Now this virtual quantity is measured first by its source—that is, by the perfection of that form or nature: such is the greatness of spiritual things, just as we speak of great heat on account of its intensity and perfection. And so Augustine says (*De Trin.* vi, 18) that *in things which are great, but not in bulk, to be greater is to be better,* for the more perfect a thing is the better it is. Second, virtual quantity is measured by the effects of the form. Now the first effect of form is being, for everything has being by reason of its form. The second effect is operation, for every agent acts through its form. Consequently virtual quantity is measured both in regard to being and in regard to action: in regard to being, forasmuch as things of a more perfect nature are of longer duration; and in regard to action, forasmuch as things of a more perfect nature are more powerful to act. And so as Augustine (*Fulgentius, De Fide ad Petrum* i) says: *We understand equality to be in the Father, Son and Holy Spirit, inasmuch as no one of them either precedes in eternity, or excels in greatness, or surpasses in power.*

REPLY OBJ. 2: Where we have equality in respect of virtual quantity, equality includes likeness and something besides, because it excludes excess. For whatever things have a common form may be said to be alike, even if they do not participate in that form equally, just as the air may be said to be like fire in heat; but they cannot be said to be

in calore, sed non possunt dici aequalia, si unum altero perfectius formam illam participet. Et quia non solum una est natura patris et filii, sed etiam aeque perfecte est in utroque, ideo non solum dicimus filium esse similem patri, ut excludatur error Eunomii; sed etiam dicimus aequalem, ut excludatur error Arii.

Ad tertium dicendum quod aequalitas vel similitudo dupliciter potest significari in divinis, scilicet per nomina et per verba. Secundum quidem quod significatur per nomina, mutua aequalitas dicitur in divinis personis et similitudo, filius enim est aequalis et similis patri, et e converso. Et hoc ideo, quia essentia divina non magis est patris quam filii, unde, sicut filius habet magnitudinem patris, quod est esse eum aequalem patri, ita pater habet magnitudinem filii, quod est esse eum aequalem filio. Sed quantum ad creaturas, ut Dionysius dicit, IX cap. de Div. Nom., *non recipitur conversio aequalitatis et similitudinis*. Dicuntur enim causata similia causis, inquantum habent formam causarum, sed non e converso, quia forma principaliter est in causa, et secundario in causato.

Sed verba significant aequalitatem cum motu. Et licet motus non sit in divinis, est tamen ibi accipere. Quia igitur filius accipit a patre unde est aequalis ei, et non e converso, propter hoc dicimus quod filius coaequatur patri, et non e converso.

Ad quartum dicendum quod in divinis personis nihil est considerare nisi essentiam, in qua communicant, et relationes, in quibus distinguuntur. Aequalitas autem utrumque importat, scilicet distinctionem personarum, quia nihil sibi ipsi dicitur aequale; et unitatem essentiae, quia ex hoc personae sunt sibi invicem aequales, quod sunt unius magnitudinis et essentiae. Manifestum est autem quod idem ad seipsum non refertur aliqua relatione reali. Nec iterum una relatio refertur ad aliam per aliquam aliam relationem, cum enim dicimus quod paternitas opponitur filiationi, oppositio non est relatio media inter paternitatem et filiationem. Quia utroque modo relatio multiplicaretur in infinitum. Et ideo aequalitas et similitudo in divinis personis non est aliqua realis relatio distincta a relationibus personalibus, sed in suo intellectu includit et relationes distinguentes personas, et essentiae unitatem. Et propterea Magister dicit, in XXXI dist. I Sent., quod *in his appellatio tantum est relativa*.

equal if one participates in the form more perfectly than another. And because not only is the same nature in both Father and Son, but also is it in both in perfect equality, therefore we say not only that the Son is like to the Father, in order to exclude the error of Eunomius, but also that He is equal to the Father to exclude the error of Arius.

Reply Obj. 3: Equality and likeness in God may be designated in two ways—namely, by nouns and by verbs. When designated by nouns, equality in the divine persons is mutual, and so is likeness; for the Son is equal and like to the Father, and conversely. This is because the divine essence is not more the Father's than the Son's. Wherefore, just as the Son has the greatness of the Father, and is therefore equal to the Father, so the Father has the greatness of the Son, and is therefore equal to the Son. But in reference to creatures, Dionysius says (*Div. Nom.* ix): *Equality and likeness are not mutual*. For effects are said to be like their causes, inasmuch as they have the form of their causes; but not conversely, for the form is principally in the cause, and secondarily in the effect.

But verbs signify equality with movement. And although movement is not in God, there is something that receives. Since, therefore, the Son receives from the Father, this, namely, that He is equal to the Father, and not conversely, for this reason we say that the Son is equalled to the Father, but not conversely.

Reply Obj. 4: In the divine persons there is nothing for us to consider but the essence which they have in common and the relations in which they are distinct. Now equality implies both—namely, distinction of persons, for nothing can be said to be equal to itself; and unity of essence, since for this reason are the persons equal to one another, that they are of the same greatness and essence. Now it is clear that the relation of a thing to itself is not a real relation. Nor, again, is one relation referred to another by a further relation: for when we say that paternity is opposed to filiation, opposition is not a relation mediating between paternity and filiation. For in both these cases relation would be multiplied indefinitely. Therefore equality and likeness in the divine persons is not a real relation distinct from the personal relations: but in its concept it includes both the relations which distinguish the persons, and the unity of essence. For this reason the Master says (*Sent.* i, D, xxxi) that in these *it is only the terms that are relative*.

Article 2

Whether the Person Proceeding Is Co-eternal with His Principle, As the Son with the Father?

AD SECUNDUM SIC PROCEDITUR. Videtur quod persona procedens non sit coaeterna suo principio, ut filius patri. Arius enim duodecim modos generationis assignat. Primus modus est iuxta fluxum lineae a puncto, ubi deest aequalitas simplicitatis. Secundus modus est iuxta emissionem radiorum a sole, ubi deest aequalitas naturae. Tertius modus est iuxta characterem, seu impressionem a sigillo, ubi deest consubstantialitas et potentiae efficientia. Quartus modus est iuxta immissionem bonae voluntatis a Deo, ubi etiam deest consubstantialitas. Quintus modus est iuxta exitum accidentis a substantia, sed accidenti deest subsistentia. Sextus modus est iuxta abstractionem speciei a materia, sicut sensus accipit speciem a re sensibili, ubi deest aequalitas simplicitatis spiritualis. Septimus modus est iuxta excitationem voluntatis a cogitatione, quae quidem excitatio temporalis est. Octavus modus est iuxta transfigurationem, ut ex aere fit imago, quae materialis est. Nonus modus est motus a movente, et hic etiam ponitur effectus et causa. Decimus modus est iuxta eductionem specierum a genere, qui non competit in divinis, quia pater non praedicatur de filio sicut genus de specie. Undecimus modus est iuxta ideationem, ut arca exterior ab ea quae est in mente. Duodecimus modus est iuxta nascentiam, ut homo est a patre, ubi est prius et posterius secundum tempus. Patet ergo quod in omni modo quo aliquid est ex altero, aut deest aequalitas naturae, aut aequalitas durationis. Si igitur filius est a patre, oportet dicere vel eum esse minorem patre, aut posteriorem, aut utrumque.

PRAETEREA, omne quod est ex altero, habet principium. Sed nullum aeternum habet principium. Ergo filius non est aeternus, neque Spiritus Sanctus.

PRAETEREA, omne quod corrumpitur, desinit esse. Ergo omne quod generatur, incipit esse, ad hoc enim generatur, ut sit. Sed filius est genitus a patre. Ergo incipit esse, et non est coaeternus patri.

PRAETEREA, si filius genitus est a patre, aut semper generatur, aut est dare aliquod instans suae generationis. Si semper generatur; dum autem aliquid est in generari, est imperfectum, sicut patet in successivis, quae sunt semper in fieri, ut tempus et motus, sequitur quod filius semper sit imperfectus; quod est inconveniens. Est ergo dare aliquod instans generationis filii. Ante illud ergo instans filius non erat.

SED CONTRA est quod Athanasius dicit, quod *totae tres personae coaeternae sibi sunt.*

RESPONDEO dicendum quod necesse est dicere filium esse coaeternum patri. Ad cuius evidentiam,

OBJECTION 1: It would seem that the person proceeding is not co-eternal with His principle, as the Son with the Father. For Arius gives twelve modes of generation. The first mode is like the issue of a line from a point; wherein is wanting equality of simplicity. The second is like the emission of rays from the sun; wherein is absent equality of nature. The third is like the mark or impression made by a seal; wherein is wanting consubstantiality and executive power. The fourth is the infusion of a good will from God; wherein also consubstantiality is wanting. The fifth is the emanation of an accident from its subject; but the accident has no subsistence. The sixth is the abstraction of a species from matter, as sense receives the species from the sensible object; wherein is wanting equality of spiritual simplicity. The seventh is the exciting of the will by knowledge, which excitation is merely temporal. The eighth is transformation, as an image is made of brass; which transformation is material. The ninth is motion from a mover; and here again we have effect and cause. The tenth is the taking of species from genera; but this mode has no place in God, for the Father is not predicated of the Son as the genus of a species. The eleventh is the realization of an idea, as an external coffer arises from the one in the mind. The twelfth is birth, as a man is begotten of his father; which implies priority and posteriority of time. Thus it is clear that equality of nature or of time is absent in every mode whereby one thing is from another. So if the Son is from the Father, we must say that He is less than the Father, or later than the Father, or both.

OBJ. 2: Further, everything that comes from another has a principle. But nothing eternal has a principle. Therefore the Son is not eternal; nor is the Holy Spirit.

OBJ. 3: Further, everything which is corrupted ceases to be. Hence everything generated begins to be; for the end of generation is existence. But the Son is generated by the Father. Therefore He begins to exist, and is not co-eternal with the Father.

OBJ. 4: Further, if the Son be begotten by the Father, either He is always being begotten, or there is some moment in which He is begotten. If He is always being begotten, since, during the process of generation, a thing must be imperfect, as appears in successive things, which are always in process of becoming, as time and motion, it follows that the Son must be always imperfect, which cannot be admitted. Thus there is a moment to be assigned for the begetting of the Son, and before that moment the Son did not exist.

ON THE CONTRARY, Athanasius declares that *all the three persons are co-eternal with each other.*

I ANSWER THAT, We must say that the Son is co-eternal with the Father. In proof of which we must consider that

considerandum est quod aliquid ex principio existens posterius esse suo principio, potest contingere ex duobus, uno modo, ex parte agentis; alio modo, ex parte actionis. Ex parte agentis quidem, aliter in agentibus voluntariis, aliter in agentibus naturalibus. In agentibus quidem voluntariis, propter electionem temporis, sicut enim in agentis voluntarii potestate est eligere formam quam effectui conferat, ut supra dictum est, ita in eius potestate est eligere tempus in quo effectum producat. In agentibus autem naturalibus hoc contingit, quia agens aliquod non a principio habet perfectionem virtutis naturaliter ad agendum, sed ei advenit post aliquod tempus; sicut homo non a principio generare potest. Ex parte autem actionis, impeditur ne id quod est a principio simul sit cum suo principio, propter hoc quod actio est successiva. Unde, dato quod aliquod agens tali actione agere inciperet statim cum est, non statim eodem instanti esset effectus, sed in instanti ad quod terminatur actio. Manifestum est autem secundum praemissa, quod pater non generat filium voluntate, sed natura. Et iterum, quod natura patris ab aeterno perfecta fuit. Et iterum, quod actio qua pater producit filium, non est successiva, quia sic filius Dei successive generaretur, et esset eius generatio materialis et cum motu, quod est impossibile. Relinquitur ergo quod filius fuit, quandocumque fuit pater. Et sic filius est coaeternus patri, et similiter Spiritus Sanctus utrique.

AD PRIMUM ergo dicendum quod, sicut Augustinus dicit, in libro de verbis domini, nullus modus processionis alicuius creaturae perfecte repraesentat divinam generationem, unde oportet ex multis modis colligere similitudinem, ut quod deest ex uno, aliqualiter suppleatur ex altero. Et propter hoc dicitur in synodo Ephesina, *coexistere semper coaeternum patri filium, splendor tibi denuntiet, impassibilitatem nativitatis ostendat verbum; consubstantialitatem filii nomen insinuet.* Inter omnia tamen expressius repraesentat processio verbi ab intellectu, quod quidem non est posterius eo a quo procedit; nisi sit talis intellectus qui exeat de potentia in actum, quod in Deo dici non potest.

AD SECUNDUM dicendum quod aeternitas excludit principium durationis, sed non principium originis.

AD TERTIUM dicendum quod omnis corruptio est mutatio quaedam, et ideo omne quod corrumpitur, incipit non esse, et desinit esse. Sed generatio divina non est transmutatio, ut dictum est supra. Unde filius semper generatur, et pater semper generat.

AD QUARTUM dicendum quod in tempore aliud est quod est indivisibile, scilicet instans; et aliud est quod est durans, scilicet tempus. Sed in aeternitate ipsum nunc indivisibile est semper stans, ut supra dictum est. Generatio vero filii non est in nunc temporis, aut in tempore, sed in aeternitate. Et ideo, ad significandum praesentialitatem et permanentiam aeternitatis, potest dici quod

for a thing which proceeds from a principle to be posterior to its principle may be due to two reasons: one on the part of the agent, and the other on the part of the action. On the part of the agent this happens differently as regards free agents and natural agents. In free agents, on account of the choice of time; for as a free agent can choose the form it gives to the effect, as stated above (Q. 41, A. 2), so it can choose the time in which to produce its effect. In natural agents, however, the same happens from the agent not having its perfection of natural power from the very first, but obtaining it after a certain time; as, for instance, a man is not able to generate from the very first. Considered on the part of action, anything derived from a principle cannot exist simultaneously with its principle when the action is successive. So, given that an agent, as soon as it exists, begins to act thus, the effect would not exist in the same instant, but in the instant of the action's termination. Now it is manifest, according to what has been said (Q. 41, A. 2), that the Father does not beget the Son by will, but by nature; and also that the Father's nature was perfect from eternity; and again that the action whereby the Father produces the Son is not successive, because thus the Son would be successively generated, and this generation would be material, and accompanied with movement; which is quite impossible. Therefore we conclude that the Son existed whensoever the Father existed and thus the Son is co-eternal with the Father, and likewise the Holy Spirit is co-eternal with both.

REPLY OBJ. 1: As Augustine says (De Verbis Domini, Serm. 38), no mode of the procession of any creature perfectly represents the divine generation. Hence we need to gather a likeness of it from many of these modes, so that what is wanting in one may be somewhat supplied from another; and thus it is declared in the council of Ephesus: *Let Splendor tell thee that the co-eternal Son existed always with the Father; let the Word announce the impassibility of His birth; let the name Son insinuate His consubstantiality.* Yet, above them all the procession of the word from the intellect represents it more exactly; the intellectual word not being posterior to its source except in an intellect passing from potentiality to act; and this cannot be said of God.

REPLY OBJ. 2: Eternity excludes the principle of duration, but not the principle of origin.

REPLY OBJ. 3: Every corruption is a change; and so all that corrupts begins not to exist and ceases to be. The divine generation, however, is not changed, as stated above (Q. 27, A. 2). Hence the Son is ever being begotten, and the Father is always begetting.

REPLY OBJ. 4: In time there is something indivisible— namely, the instant; and there is something else which endures—namely, time. But in eternity the indivisible *now* stands ever still, as we have said above (Q. 10, A. 2, ad 1; A. 4, ad 2). But the generation of the Son is not in the *now* of time, or in time, but in eternity. And so to express the presentiality and permanence of eternity, we can say that

semper nascitur, ut Origenes dixit. Sed, ut Gregorius et Augustinus dicunt, melius est quod dicatur semper natus, ut ly semper designet permanentiam aeternitatis, et ly natus perfectionem geniti. Sic ergo filius nec imperfectus est, neque erat quando non erat, ut Arius dixit.

He is ever being born, as Origen said (*Hom.* in Joan. i). But as Gregory and Augustine said, it is better to say *ever born*, so that *ever* may denote the permanence of eternity, and *born* the perfection of the only Begotten. Thus, therefore, neither is the Son imperfect, nor *was there a time when He was not*, as Arius said.

Article 3

Whether in the Divine Persons There Exists an Order of Nature?

AD TERTIUM SIC PROCEDITUR. Videtur quod in divinis personis non sit ordo naturae. Quidquid enim in divinis est, vel est essentia vel persona vel notio. Sed ordo naturae non significat essentiam, neque est aliqua personarum aut notionum. Ergo ordo naturae non est in divinis.

PRAETEREA, in quibuscumque est ordo naturae, unum est prius altero, saltem secundum naturam et intellectum. Sed in divinis personis nihil est prius et posterius, ut Athanasius dicit. Ergo in divinis personis non est ordo naturae.

PRAETEREA, quidquid ordinatur, distinguitur. Sed natura in divinis non distinguitur. Ergo non ordinatur. Ergo non est ibi ordo naturae.

PRAETEREA, natura divina est eius essentia. Sed non dicitur in divinis ordo essentiae. Ergo neque ordo naturae.

SED CONTRA, ubicumque est pluralitas sine ordine, ibi est confusio. Sed in divinis personis non est confusio, ut Athanasius dicit. Ergo est ibi ordo.

RESPONDEO dicendum quod ordo semper dicitur per comparationem ad aliquod principium. Unde sicut dicitur principium multipliciter, scilicet secundum situm, ut punctus, secundum intellectum, ut principium demonstrationis, et secundum causas singulas; ita etiam dicitur ordo. In divinis autem dicitur principium secundum originem, absque prioritate, ut supra dictum est. Unde oportet ibi esse ordinem secundum originem, absque prioritate. Et hic vocatur ordo naturae, secundum Augustinum, *non quo alter sit prius altero, sed quo alter est ex altero.*

AD PRIMUM ergo dicendum quod ordo naturae significat notionem originis in communi, non autem in speciali.

AD SECUNDUM dicendum quod in rebus creatis, etiam cum id quod est a principio sit suo principio coaevum secundum durationem, tamen principium est prius secundum naturam et intellectum, si consideretur id quod est principium. Sed si considerentur ipsae

OBJECTION 1: It would seem that among the divine persons there does not exist an order of nature. For whatever exists in God is the essence, or a person, or a notion. But the order of nature does not signify the essence, nor any of the persons, or notions. Therefore there is no order of nature in God.

OBJ. 2: Further, wherever order of nature exists, there one comes before another, at least, according to nature and intellect. But in the divine persons there exists neither priority nor posteriority, as declared by Athanasius. Therefore, in the divine persons there is no order of nature.

OBJ. 3: Further, wherever order exists, distinction also exists. But there is no distinction in the divine nature. Therefore it is not subject to order; and order of nature does not exist in it.

OBJ. 4: Further, the divine nature is the divine essence. But there is no order of essence in God. Therefore neither is there of nature.

ON THE CONTRARY, Where plurality exists without order, confusion exists. But in the divine persons there is no confusion, as Athanasius says. Therefore in God order exists.

I ANSWER THAT, Order always has reference to some principle. Wherefore since there are many kinds of principle—namely, according to site, as a point; according to intellect, as the principle of demonstration; and according to each individual cause—so are there many kinds of order. Now principle, according to origin, without priority, exists in God as we have stated (Q. 33, A. 1): so there must likewise be order according to origin, without priority; and this is called 'the order of nature': in the words of Augustine (*Contra Maxim.* iv): *Not whereby one is prior to another, but whereby one is from another.*

REPLY OBJ. 1: The order of nature signifies the notion of origin in general, not a special kind of origin.

REPLY OBJ. 2: In things created, even when what is derived from a principle is co-equal in duration with its principle, the principle still comes first in the order of nature and reason, if formally considered as principle. If, however, we consider the relations of cause and effect, or

relationes causae et causati, et principii et principiati, manifestum est quod relativa sunt simul natura et intellectu, inquantum unum est in definitione alterius. Sed in divinis ipsae relationes sunt subsistentes personae in una natura. Unde neque ex parte naturae, neque ex parte relationum, una persona potest esse prior alia, neque etiam secundum naturam et intellectum.

AD TERTIUM dicendum quod ordo naturae dicitur, non quod ipsa natura ordinetur, sed quod ordo in divinis personis attenditur secundum naturalem originem.

AD QUARTUM dicendum quod natura quodammodo importat rationem principii, non autem essentia. Et ideo ordo originis melius nominatur ordo naturae, quam ordo essentiae.

of the principle and the thing proceeding therefrom, it is clear that the things so related are simultaneous in the order of nature and reason, inasmuch as the one enters the definition of the other. But in God the relations themselves are the persons subsisting in one nature. So, neither on the part of the nature, nor on the part the relations, can one person be prior to another, not even in the order of nature and reason.

REPLY OBJ. 3: The order of nature means not the ordering of nature itself, but the existence of order in the divine Persons according to natural origin.

REPLY OBJ. 4: Nature in a certain way implies the idea of a principle, but essence does not; and so the order of origin is more correctly called the order of nature than the order of essence.

Article 4

Whether the Son Is Equal to the Father in Greatness?

AD QUARTUM SIC PROCEDITUR. Videtur quod filius non sit aequalis patri in magnitudine. Dicit enim ipse, Ioan. XIV, *pater maior me est*; et apostolus, I Cor. XV, *ipse filius subiectus erit illi qui sibi subiecit omnia.*

PRAETEREA, paternitas pertinet ad dignitatem patris. Sed paternitas non convenit filio. Ergo non quidquid dignitatis habet pater, habet filius. Ergo non est aequalis patri in magnitudine.

PRAETEREA, ubicumque est totum et pars, plures partes sunt aliquid maius quam una tantum vel pauciores; sicut tres homines sunt aliquid maius quam duo vel unus. Sed in divinis videtur esse totum universale et pars, nam sub relatione vel notione plures notiones continentur. Cum igitur in patre sint tres notiones, in filio autem tantum duae, videtur quod filius non sit aequalis patri.

SED CONTRA est quod dicitur Philip. II, *non rapinam arbitratus est esse se aequalem Deo.*

RESPONDEO dicendum quod necesse est dicere filium esse aequalem patri in magnitudine. Magnitudo enim Dei non est aliud quam perfectio naturae ipsius. Hoc autem est de ratione paternitatis et filiationis, quod filius per generationem pertingat ad habendam perfectionem naturae quae est in patre, sicut et pater. Sed quia in hominibus generatio est transmutatio quaedam exeuntis de potentia in actum, non statim a principio homo filius est aequalis patri generanti; sed per debitum incrementum ad aequalitatem perducitur, nisi aliter eveniat propter defectum principii generationis. Manifestum est autem ex dictis quod in divinis est proprie et vere paternitas et filiatio. Nec potest dici quod virtus Dei

OBJECTION 1: It would seem that the Son is not equal to the Father in greatness. For He Himself said (John 14:28): *The Father is greater than I*; and the Apostle says (1 Cor 15:28): *The Son Himself shall be subject to Him that put all things under Him.*

OBJ. 2: Further, paternity is part of the Father's dignity. But paternity does not belong to the Son. Therefore the Son does not possess all the Father's dignity; and so He is not equal in greatness to the Father.

OBJ. 3: Further, wherever there exist a whole and a part, many parts are more than one only, or than fewer parts; as three men are more than two, or than one. But in God a universal whole exists, and a part; for under relation or notion, several notions are included. Therefore, since in the Father there are three notions, while in the Son there are only two, the Son is evidently not equal to the Father.

ON THE CONTRARY, It is said (Phil 2:6): *He thought it not robbery to be equal with God.*

I ANSWER THAT, The Son is necessarily equal to the Father in greatness. For the greatness of God is nothing but the perfection of His nature. Now it belongs to the very nature of paternity and filiation that the Son by generation should attain to the possession of the perfection of the nature which is in the Father, in the same way as it is in the Father Himself. But since in men generation is a certain kind of transmutation of one proceeding from potentiality to act, it follows that a man is not equal at first to the father who begets him, but attains to equality by due growth, unless owing to a defect in the principle of generation it should happen otherwise. From what precedes (Q. 27, A. 2; Q. 33, AA. 2 ,3), it is evident that in God there exist real

patris fuerit defectiva in generando; neque quod Dei filius successive et per transmutationem ad perfectionem pervenerit. Unde necesse est dicere quod ab aeterno fuerit patri aequalis in magnitudine. Unde et Hilarius dicit, in libro de Synod., *tolle corporum infirmitates, tolle conceptus initium, tolle dolores et omnem humanam necessitatem, omnis filius secundum naturalem nativitatem aequalitas patris est, quia est et similitudo naturae.*

AD PRIMUM ergo dicendum quod verba illa intelliguntur dicta de Christo secundum humanam naturam, in qua minor est patre, et ei subiectus. Sed secundum naturam divinam, aequalis est patri. Et hoc est quod Athanasius dicit; *aequalis patri secundum divinitatem, minor patre secundum humanitatem.* Vel, secundum Hilarium, in IX libro de Trin., *donantis auctoritate pater maior est, sed minor non est cui unum esse donatur.* Et in libro de Synod. dicit quod subiectio filii naturae pietas est, idest recognitio auctoritatis paternae, subiectio autem ceterorum, creationis infirmitas.

AD SECUNDUM dicendum quod aequalitas attenditur secundum magnitudinem. Magnitudo autem in divinis significat perfectionem naturae, ut dictum est, et ad essentiam pertinet. Et ideo aequalitas in divinis, et similitudo, secundum essentialia attenditur, nec potest secundum distinctionem relationum inaequalitas vel dissimilitudo dici. Unde Augustinus dicit, contra Maximinum, *originis quaestio est quid de quo sit; aequalitatis autem, qualis aut quantus sit.* Paternitas igitur est dignitas patris, sicut et essentia patris, nam dignitas absolutum est, et ad essentiam pertinet. Sicut igitur eadem essentia quae in patre est paternitas, in filio est filiatio; ita eadem dignitas quae in patre est paternitas, in filio est filiatio. Vere ergo dicitur quod quidquid dignitatis habet pater, habet filius. Nec sequitur, paternitatem habet pater, ergo paternitatem habet filius. Mutatur enim quid in ad aliquid, eadem enim est essentia et dignitas patris et filii, sed in patre est secundum relationem dantis, in filio secundum relationem accipientis.

AD TERTIUM dicendum quod relatio in divinis non est totum universale, quamvis de pluribus relationibus praedicetur, quia omnes relationes sunt unum secundum essentiam et esse, quod repugnat rationi universalis, cuius partes secundum esse distinguuntur. Et similiter persona, ut supra dictum est, non est universale in divinis. Unde neque omnes relationes sunt maius aliquid quam una tantum; nec omnes personae maius aliquid quam una tantum; quia tota perfectio divinae naturae est in qualibet personarum.

true paternity and filiation. Nor can we say that the power of generation in the Father was defective, nor that the Son of God arrived at perfection in a successive manner and by change. Therefore we must say that the Son was eternally equal to the Father in greatness. Hence, Hilary says (*De Synod.* Can. 27): *Remove bodily weakness, remove the beginning of conception, remove pain and all human shortcomings, then every son, by reason of his natural nativity, is the father's equal, because he has a like nature.*

REPLY OBJ. 1: These words are to be understood of Christ's human nature, wherein He is less than the Father, and subject to Him; but in His divine nature He is equal to the Father. This is expressed by Athanasius, *Equal to the Father in His Godhead; less than the Father in humanity*: and by Hilary (*De Trin.* ix): *By the fact of giving, the Father is greater; but He is not less to Whom the same being is given*; and (*De Synod.*): *The Son subjects Himself by His inborn piety*—that is, by His recognition of paternal authority; whereas *creatures are subject by their created weakness.*

REPLY OBJ. 2: Equality is measured by greatness. In God greatness signifies the perfection of nature, as above explained (A. 1, ad 1), and belongs to the essence. Thus equality and likeness in God have reference to the essence; nor can there be inequality or dissimilitude arising from the distinction of the relations. Wherefore Augustine says (*Contra Maxim.* iii, 13), *The question of origin is, Who is from whom? but the question of equality is, Of what kind, or how great, is he?* Therefore, paternity is the Father's dignity, as also the Father's essence: since dignity is something absolute, and pertains to the essence. As, therefore, the same essence, which in the Father is paternity, in the Son is filiation, so the same dignity which, in the Father is paternity, in the Son is filiation. It is thus true to say that the Son possesses whatever dignity the Father has; but we cannot argue—*the Father has paternity, therefore the Son has paternity*, for there is a transition from substance to relation. For the Father and the Son have the same essence and dignity, which exist in the Father by the relation of giver, and in the Son by relation of receiver.

REPLY OBJ. 3: In God relation is not a universal whole, although it is predicated of each of the relations; because all the relations are one in essence and being, which is irreconcilable with the idea of universal, the parts of which are distinguished in being. Person likewise is not a universal term in God as we have seen above (Q. 30, A. 4). Wherefore all the relations together are not greater than only one; nor are all the persons something greater than only one; because the whole perfection of the divine nature exists in each person.

Article 5

Whether the Son Is in the Father, and Conversely?

AD QUINTUM SIC PROCEDITUR. Videtur quod filius non sit in patre, et e converso. Philosophus enim, in IV Physic., ponit octo modos essendi aliquid in aliquo; et secundum nullum horum filius est in patre, aut e converso, ut patet discurrenti per singulos modos. Ergo filius non est in patre, nec e converso.

PRAETEREA, nihil quod exivit ab aliquo, est in eo. Sed filius ab aeterno exivit a patre, secundum illud Micheae V, *egressus eius ab initio, a diebus aeternitatis.* Ergo filius non est in patre.

PRAETEREA, unum oppositorum non est in altero. Sed filius et pater opponuntur relative. Ergo unus non potest esse in alio.

SED CONTRA est quod dicitur Ioan. XIV, *ego in patre, et pater in me est.*

RESPONDEO dicendum quod in patre et filio tria est considerare, scilicet essentiam, relationem et originem; et secundum quodlibet istorum filius est in patre, et e converso. Secundum essentiam enim pater est in filio, quia pater est sua essentia, et communicat suam essentiam filio, non per aliquam suam transmutationem, unde sequitur quod, cum essentia patris sit in filio, quod in filio sit pater. Et similiter, cum filius sit sua essentia, sequitur quod sit in patre, in quo est eius essentia. Et hoc est quod Hilarius dicit, V de Trin., *naturam suam, ut ita dicam, sequitur immutabilis Deus, immutabilem gignens Deum. Subsistentem ergo in eo Dei naturam intelligimus, cum in Deo Deus insit.* Secundum etiam relationes, manifestum est quod unum oppositorum relative est in altero secundum intellectum. Secundum originem etiam manifestum est quod processio verbi intelligibilis non est ad extra, sed manet in dicente. Id etiam quod verbo dicitur, in verbo continetur. Et eadem ratio est de spiritu sancto.

AD PRIMUM ergo dicendum quod ea quae in creaturis sunt, non sufficienter repraesentant ea quae Dei sunt. Et ideo secundum nullum eorum modorum quos philosophus enumerat, filius est in patre, aut e converso. Accedit tamen magis ad hoc modus ille, secundum quem aliquid dicitur esse in principio originante, nisi quod deest unitas essentiae, in rebus creatis, inter principium et id quod est a principio.

AD SECUNDUM dicendum quod exitus filii a patre est secundum modum processionis interioris, prout verbum exit a corde, et manet in eo. Unde exitus iste in divinis est secundum solam distinctionem relationum, non secundum essentialem aliquam distantiam.

OBJECTION 1: It would seem that the Son and the Father are not in each other. For the Philosopher (*Phys.* iv, text. 23) gives eight modes of one thing existing in another, according to none of which is the Son in the Father, or conversely; as is patent to anyone who examines each mode. Therefore the Son and the Father are not in each other.

OBJ. 2: Further, nothing that has come out from another is within. But the Son from eternity came out from the Father, according to Mic. 5:2: *His going forth is from the beginning, from the days of eternity.* Therefore the Son is not in the Father.

OBJ. 3: Further, one of two opposites cannot be in the other. But the Son and the Father are relatively opposed. Therefore one cannot be in the other.

ON THE CONTRARY, It is said (John 14:10): *I am in the Father, and the Father is in Me.*

I ANSWER THAT, There are three points of consideration as regards the Father and the Son; the essence, the relation and the origin; and according to each the Son and the Father are in each other. The Father is in the Son by His essence, forasmuch as the Father is His own essence and communicates His essence to the Son not by any change on His part. Hence it follows that as the Father's essence is in the Son, the Father Himself is in the Son; likewise, since the Son is His own essence, it follows that He Himself is in the Father in Whom is His essence. This is expressed by Hilary (*De Trin.* v), *The unchangeable God, so to speak, follows His own nature in begetting an unchangeable subsisting God. So we understand the nature of God to subsist in Him, for He is God in God.* It is also manifest that as regards the relations, each of two relative opposites is in the concept of the other. Regarding origin also, it is clear that the procession of the intelligible word is not outside the intellect, inasmuch as it remains in the utterer of the word. What also is uttered by the word is therein contained. And the same applies to the Holy Spirit.

REPLY OBJ. 1: What is contained in creatures does not sufficiently represent what exists in God; so according to none of the modes enumerated by the Philosopher, are the Son and the Father in each other. The mode the most nearly approaching to the reality is to be found in that whereby something exists in its originating principle, except that the unity of essence between the principle and that which proceeds therefrom is wanting in things created.

REPLY OBJ. 2: The Son's going forth from the Father is by mode of the interior procession whereby the word emerges from the heart and remains therein. Hence this going forth in God is only by the distinction of the relations, not by any kind of essential separation.

AD TERTIUM dicendum quod pater et filius opponuntur secundum relationes, non autem secundum essentiam. Et tamen oppositorum relative unum est in altero, ut dictum est.

REPLY OBJ. 3: The Father and the Son are relatively opposed, but not essentially; while, as above explained, one relative opposite is in the other.

Article 6

Whether the Son Is Equal to the Father in Power?

AD SEXTUM SIC PROCEDITUR. Videtur quod filius non sit aequalis patri secundum potentiam. Dicitur enim Ioan. V, *non potest filius a se facere quidquam, nisi quod viderit patrem facientem.* Pater autem a se potest facere. Ergo pater maior est filio secundum potentiam.

PRAETEREA, maior est potentia eius qui praecipit et docet, quam eius qui obedit et audit. Sed pater mandat filio, secundum illud Ioan. XIV, *sicut mandatum dedit mihi pater, sic facio.* Pater etiam docet filium, secundum illud Ioan. V, *pater diligit filium, et omnia demonstrat ei quae ipse facit.* Similiter et filius audit, secundum illud Ioan. V, *sicut audio, iudico.* Ergo pater est maioris potentiae quam filius.

PRAETEREA, ad omnipotentiam patris pertinet quod possit filium generare sibi aequalem, dicit enim Augustinus, in libro contra Maximin., *si non potuit generare sibi aequalem, ubi est omnipotentia Dei patris?* Sed filius non potest generare filium, ut supra ostensum est. Non ergo quidquid pertinet ad omnipotentiam patris, potest filius. Et ita non est ei in potestate aequalis.

SED CONTRA est quod dicitur Ioan. V, *quaecumque pater facit, haec et filius similiter facit.*

RESPONDEO dicendum quod necesse est dicere quod filius est aequalis patri in potestate. Potentia enim agendi consequitur perfectionem naturae, videmus enim in creaturis quod quanto aliquid habet perfectiorem naturam, tanto est maioris virtutis in agendo. Ostensum est autem supra quod ipsa ratio divinae paternitatis et filiationis exigit quod filius sit aequalis patri in magnitudine, idest in perfectione naturae. Unde relinquitur quod filius sit aequalis patri in potestate. Et eadem ratio est de spiritu sancto respectu utriusque.

AD PRIMUM ergo dicendum quod in hoc quod dicitur quod *filius non potest a se facere quidquam*, non subtrahitur filio aliqua potestas quam habeat pater; cum statim subdatur quod *quaecumque pater facit, filius similiter facit.* Sed ostenditur quod filius habet potestatem a patre, a quo habet naturam. Unde dicit Hilarius, IX de Trin., *naturae divinae haec unitas est, ut ita per se agat filius, quod non a se agat.*

OBJECTION 1: It would seem that the Son is not equal to the Father in power. For it is said (John 5:19): *The Son cannot do anything of Himself but what He seeth the Father doing.* But the Father can act of Himself. Therefore the Father's power is greater than the Son's.

OBJ. 2: Further, greater is the power of him who commands and teaches than of him who obeys and hears. But the Father commands the Son according to John 14:31: *As the Father gave Me commandment so do I.* The Father also teaches the Son: *The Father loveth the Son, and showeth Him all things that Himself doth* (John 5:20). Also, the Son hears: *As I hear, so I judge* (John 5:30). Therefore the Father has greater power than the Son.

OBJ. 3: Further, it belongs to the Father's omnipotence to be able to beget a Son equal to Himself. For Augustine says (*Contra Maxim.* iii, 7), *Were He unable to beget one equal to Himself, where would be the omnipotence of God the Father?* But the Son cannot beget a Son, as proved above (Q. 41, A. 6). Therefore the Son cannot do all that belongs to the Father's omnipotence; and hence He is not equal to Him power.

ON THE CONTRARY, It is said (John 5:19): *Whatsoever things the Father doth, these the Son also doth in like manner.*

I ANSWER THAT, The Son is necessarily equal to the Father in power. Power of action is a consequence of perfection in nature. In creatures, for instance, we see that the more perfect the nature, the greater power is there for action. Now it was shown above (A. 4) that the very notion of the divine paternity and filiation requires that the Son should be the Father's equal in greatness—that is, in perfection of nature. Hence it follows that the Son is equal to the Father in power; and the same applies to the Holy Spirit in relation to both.

REPLY OBJ. 1: The words, *the Son cannot of Himself do anything*, do not withdraw from the Son any power possessed by the Father, since it is immediately added, *Whatsoever things the Father doth, the Son doth in like manner*; but their meaning is to show that the Son derives His power from the Father, of Whom He receives His nature. Hence, Hilary says (*De Trin.* ix), *The unity of the divine nature implies that the Son so acts of Himself, that He does not act by Himself.*

AD SECUNDUM dicendum quod in demonstratione patris et auditione filii, non intelligitur nisi quod pater communicat scientiam filio, sicut et essentiam. Et ad idem potest referri mandatum patris, per hoc quod ab aeterno dedit ei scientiam et voluntatem agendorum, eum generando. Vel potius referendum est ad Christum secundum humanam naturam.

AD TERTIUM dicendum quod, sicut eadem essentia quae in patre est paternitas, in filio est filiatio; ita eadem est potentia qua pater generat, et qua filius generatur. Unde manifestum est quod quidquid potest pater, potest filius. Non tamen sequitur quod possit generare, sed mutatur quid in ad aliquid, nam generatio significat relationem in divinis. Habet ergo filius eandem omnipotentiam quam pater, sed cum alia relatione. Quia pater habet eam ut dans, et hoc significatur, cum dicitur quod potest generare. Filius autem habet eam ut accipiens, et hoc significatur, cum dicitur quod potest generari.

REPLY OBJ. 2: The Father's *showing* and the Son's *hearing* are to be taken in the sense that the Father communicates knowledge to the Son, as He communicates His essence. The command of the Father can be explained in the same sense, as giving Him from eternity knowledge and will to act, by begetting Him. Or, better still, this may be referred to Christ in His human nature.

REPLY OBJ. 3: As the same essence is paternity in the Father, and filiation in the Son: so by the same power the Father begets, and the Son is begotten. Hence it is clear that the Son can do whatever the Father can do; yet it does not follow that the Son can beget; for to argue thus would imply transition from substance to relation, for generation signifies a divine relation. So the Son has the same omnipotence as the Father, but with another relation; the Father possessing power as *giving* signified when we say that He is able to beget; while the Son possesses the power of *receiving*, signified by saying that He can be begotten.

QUESTION 43

THE MISSION OF THE DIVINE PERSONS

Deinde considerandum de missione divinarum personarum. Et circa hoc quaeruntur octo.

Primo, utrum alicui divinae personae conveniat mitti.

Secundo, utrum missio sit aeterna, vel temporalis tantum.

Tertio, secundum quid divina persona invisibiliter mittatur.

Quarto, utrum cuilibet personae conveniat mitti.

Quinto, utrum invisibiliter mittatur tam filius, quam Spiritus Sanctus.

Sexto, ad quos fiat missio invisibilis.

Septimo, de missione visibili.

Octavo, utrum aliqua persona mittat seipsam, visibiliter aut invisibiliter.

We next consider the mission of the divine persons, concerning which there are eight points of inquiry:

(1) Whether it is suitable for a divine person to be sent?

(2) Whether mission is eternal, or only temporal?

(3) In what sense a divine person is invisibly sent?

(4) Whether it is fitting that each person be sent?

(5) Whether both the Son and the Holy Spirit are invisibly sent?

(6) To whom the invisible mission is directed?

(7) Of the visible mission.

(8) Whether any person sends Himself visibly or invisibly?

Article 1

Whether a Divine Person Can Be Properly Sent?

AD PRIMUM SIC PROCEDITUR. Videtur quod personae divinae non conveniat mitti. Missus enim minor est mittente. Sed una persona divina non est minor alia. Ergo una persona non mittitur ab alia.

PRAETEREA, omne quod mittitur, separatur a mittente, unde Hieronymus dicit, super Ezechiel., *quod coniunctum est, et in corpore uno copulatum, mitti non potest.* Sed in divinis personis nihil est separabile, ut Hilarius dicit. Ergo una persona non mittitur ab alia.

PRAETEREA, quicumque mittitur, ab aliquo loco discedit, et ad aliquem locum de novo vadit. Hoc autem divinae personae non convenit, cum ubique sit. Ergo divinae personae non convenit mitti.

SED CONTRA est quod dicitur Ioan. VIII, *non sum ego solus, sed ego et qui misit me, pater.*

RESPONDEO dicendum quod in ratione missionis duo importantur, quorum unum est habitudo missi ad eum a quo mittitur; aliud est habitudo missi ad terminum ad quem mittitur. Per hoc autem quod aliquis mittitur, ostenditur processio quaedam missi a mittente; vel secundum imperium, sicut dominus mittit servum; vel secundum consilium, ut si consiliarius mittere dicatur regem ad bellandum; vel secundum originem, ut si dicatur quod flos emittitur ab arbore. Ostenditur etiam habitudo ad terminum ad quem mittitur, ut aliquo modo

OBJECTION 1: It would seem that a divine person cannot be properly sent. For one who is sent is less than the sender. But one divine person is not less than another. Therefore one person is not sent by another.

OBJ. 2: Further, what is sent is separated from the sender; hence Jerome says, commenting on Ezech. 16:53: *What is joined and tied in one body cannot be sent.* But in the divine persons there is nothing that is separable, as Hilary says (*De Trin.* vii). Therefore one person is not sent by another.

OBJ. 3: Further, whoever is sent, departs from one place and comes anew into another. But this does not apply to a divine person, Who is everywhere. Therefore it is not suitable for a divine person to be sent.

ON THE CONTRARY, It is said (John 8:16): *I am not alone, but I and the Father that sent Me.*

I ANSWER THAT, the notion of mission includes two things: the habitude of the one sent to the sender; and that of the one sent to the end whereto he is sent. Anyone being sent implies a certain kind of procession of the one sent from the sender: either according to command, as the master sends the servant; or according to counsel, as an adviser may be said to send the king to battle; or according to origin, as a tree sends forth its flowers. The habitude to the term to which he is sent is also shown, so that in some way he begins to be present there: either because in no way

ibi esse incipiat; vel quia prius ibi omnino non erat quo mittitur; vel quia incipit ibi aliquo modo esse, quo prius non erat. Missio igitur divinae personae convenire potest, secundum quod importat ex una parte processionem originis a mittente; et secundum quod importat ex alia parte novum modum existendi in aliquo. Sicut filius dicitur esse missus a patre in mundum, secundum quod incoepit esse in mundo visibiliter per carnem assumptam, et tamen ante in mundo erat, ut dicitur Ioan. I.

AD PRIMUM ergo dicendum quod missio importat minorationem in eo qui mittitur, secundum quod importat processionem a principio mittente aut secundum imperium, aut secundum consilium, quia imperans est maior, et consilians est sapientior. Sed in divinis non importat nisi processionem originis; quae est secundum aequalitatem, ut supra dictum est.

AD SECUNDUM dicendum quod illud quod sic mittitur ut incipiat esse ubi prius nullo modo erat, sua missione localiter movetur, unde oportet quod loco separetur a mittente. Sed hoc non accidit in missione divinae personae, quia persona divina missa, sicut non incipit esse ubi prius non fuerat, ita nec desinit esse ubi fuerat. Unde talis missio est sine separatione; sed habet solam distinctionem originis.

AD TERTIUM dicendum quod obiectio illa procedit de missione quae fit secundum motum localem; quae non habet locum in divinis.

was he present before in the place whereto he is sent, or because he begins to be there in some way in which he was not there hitherto. Thus the mission of a divine person is a fitting thing, as meaning in one way the procession of origin from the sender, and as meaning a new way of existing in another; thus the Son is said to be sent by the Father into the world, inasmuch as He began to exist visibly in the world by taking our nature; whereas *He was* previously *in the world* (John 1:1).

REPLY OBJ. 1: Mission implies inferiority in the one sent, when it means procession from the sender as principle, by command or counsel; forasmuch as the one commanding is the greater, and the counsellor is the wiser. In God, however, it means only procession of origin, which is according to equality, as explained above (Q. 42, AA. 4, 6).

REPLY OBJ. 2: What is so sent as to begin to exist where previously it did not exist, is locally moved by being sent; hence it is necessarily separated locally from the sender. This, however, has no place in the mission of a divine person; for the divine person sent neither begins to exist where he did not previously exist, nor ceases to exist where He was. Hence such a mission takes place without a separation, having only distinction of origin.

REPLY OBJ. 3: This objection rests on the idea of mission according to local motion, which is not in God.

Article 2

Whether Mission Is Eternal, or Only Temporal?

AD SECUNDUM SIC PROCEDITUR. Videtur quod missio possit esse aeterna. Dicit enim Gregorius, eo mittitur filius, quo generatur. Sed generatio filii est aeterna. Ergo et missio.

PRAETEREA, cuicumque convenit aliquid temporaliter, illud mutatur. Sed persona divina non mutatur. Ergo missio divinae personae non est temporalis, sed aeterna.

PRAETEREA, missio processionem importat. Sed processio divinarum personarum est aeterna. Ergo et missio.

SED CONTRA est quod dicitur Galat. IV, *cum venit plenitudo temporis, misit Deus filium suum.*

RESPONDEO dicendum quod in his quae important originem divinarum personarum, est quaedam differentia attendenda. Quaedam enim in sui significatione important solam habitudinem ad principium, ut processio et exitus. Quaedam vero, cum habitudine ad principium, determinant processionis terminum. Quorum quaedam determinant terminum aeternum, sicut generatio et

OBJECTION 1: It would seem that mission can be eternal. For Gregory says (*Hom. xxvi, in Ev.*), *The Son is sent as He is begotten.* But the Son's generation is eternal. Therefore mission is eternal.

OBJ. 2: Further, a thing is changed if it becomes something temporally. But a divine person is not changed. Therefore the mission of a divine person is not temporal, but eternal.

OBJ. 3: Further, mission implies procession. But the procession of the divine persons is eternal. Therefore mission is also eternal.

ON THE CONTRARY, It is said (Gal 4:4): *When the fullness of the time was come, God sent His Son.*

I ANSWER THAT, A certain difference is to be observed in all the words that express the origin of the divine persons. For some express only relation to the principle, as *procession* and *going forth*. Others express the term of procession together with the relation to the principle. Of these some express the eternal term, as *generation* and *spiration*; for generation is the procession of the divine person into the

spiratio, nam generatio est processio divinae personae in naturam divinam; et spiratio, passive accepta, importat processionem amoris subsistentis. Quaedam vero, cum habitudine ad principium, important terminum temporalem, sicut missio et datio, mittitur enim aliquid ad hoc ut sit in aliquo, et datur ad hoc quod habeatur; personam autem divinam haberi ab aliqua creatura, vel esse novo modo existendi in ea, est quoddam temporale.

Unde missio et datio in divinis dicuntur temporaliter tantum. Generatio autem et spiratio solum ab aeterno. Processio autem et exitus dicuntur in divinis et aeternaliter et temporaliter, nam filius ab aeterno processit ut sit Deus; temporaliter autem ut etiam sit homo, secundum missionem visibilem; vel etiam ut sit in homine, secundum invisibilem missionem.

AD PRIMUM ergo dicendum quod Gregorius loquitur de generatione temporali filii, non a patre, sed a matre. Vel, quia ex hoc ipso filius habet quod possit mitti, quod est ab aeterno genitus.

AD SECUNDUM dicendum quod divinam personam esse novo modo in aliquo, vel ab aliquo haberi temporaliter, non est propter mutationem divinae personae, sed propter mutationem creaturae, sicut et Deus temporaliter dicitur dominus, propter mutationem creaturae.

AD TERTIUM dicendum quod missio non solum importat processionem a principio, sed determinat processionis terminum temporalem. Unde missio solum est temporalis. Vel, missio includit processionem aeternam, et aliquid addit, scilicet temporalem effectum, habitudo enim divinae personae ad suum principium non est nisi ab aeterno. Unde gemina dicitur processio, aeterna scilicet et temporalis, non propter hoc quod habitudo ad principium geminetur, sed geminatio est ex parte termini temporalis et aeterni.

divine nature, and passive spiration is the procession of the subsisting love. Others express the temporal term with the relation to the principle, as *mission* and *giving*. For a thing is sent that it may be in something else, and is given that it may be possessed; but that a divine person be possessed by any creature, or exist in it in a new mode, is temporal.

Hence *mission* and *giving* have only a temporal significance in God; but *generation* and *spiration* are exclusively eternal; whereas *procession* and *giving*, in God, have both an eternal and a temporal signification: for the Son may proceed eternally as God; but temporally, by becoming man, according to His visible mission, or likewise by dwelling in man according to His invisible mission.

REPLY OBJ. 1: Gregory speaks of the temporal generation of the Son, not from the Father, but from His mother; or it may be taken to mean that He could be sent because eternally begotten.

REPLY OBJ. 2: That a divine person may newly exist in anyone, or be possessed by anyone in time, does not come from change of the divine person, but from change in the creature; as God Himself is called Lord temporally by change of the creature.

REPLY OBJ. 3: Mission signifies not only procession from the principle, but also determines the temporal term of the procession. Hence mission is only temporal. Or we may say that it includes the eternal procession, with the addition of a temporal effect. For the relation of a divine person to His principle must be eternal. Hence the procession may be called a twin procession, eternal and temporal, not that there is a double relation to the principle, but a double term, temporal and eternal.

Article 3

Whether the Invisible Mission of the Divine Person Is Only According to the Gift of Sanctifying Grace?

AD TERTIUM SIC PROCEDITUR. Videtur quod missio invisibilis divinae personae non sit solum secundum donum gratiae gratum facientis. Divinam enim personam mitti, est ipsam donari. Si igitur divina persona mittitur solum secundum dona gratiae gratum facientis, non donabitur ipsa persona divina, sed solum dona eius. Quod est error dicentium spiritum sanctum non dari, sed eius dona.

PRAETEREA, haec praepositio secundum denotat habitudinem alicuius causae. Sed persona divina est causa quod habeatur donum gratiae gratum facientis, et non e converso; secundum illud Rom. V, *caritas Dei diffusa est in cordibus nostris per spiritum sanctum, qui*

OBJECTION 1: It would seem that the invisible mission of the divine person is not only according to the gift of sanctifying grace. For the sending of a divine person means that He is given. Hence if the divine person is sent only according to the gift of sanctifying grace, the divine person Himself will not be given, but only His gifts; and this is the error of those who say that the Holy Spirit is not given, but that His gifts are given.

OBJ. 2: Further, this preposition, *according to*, denotes the habitude of some cause. But the divine person is the cause why the gift of sanctifying grace is possessed, and not conversely, according to Rom. 5:5, *the charity of God is poured forth in our hearts by the Holy Spirit, Who is given to*

datus est nobis. Ergo inconvenienter dicitur quod persona divina secundum dona gratiae gratum facientis mittatur.

PRAETEREA, Augustinus dicit, IV de Trin., quod *filius, cum ex tempore mente percipitur, mitti dicitur.* Sed filius cognoscitur non solum per gratiam gratum facientem, sed etiam per gratiam gratis datam, sicut per fidem et per scientiam. Non ergo persona divina mittitur secundum solam gratiam gratum facientem.

PRAETEREA, Rabanus dicit quod Spiritus Sanctus datus est apostolis ad operationem miraculorum. Hoc autem non est donum gratiae gratum facientis, sed gratiae gratis datae. Ergo persona divina non solum datur secundum gratiam gratum facientem.

SED CONTRA est quod Augustinus dicit, XV de Trin., quod *Spiritus Sanctus procedit temporaliter ad sanctificandam creaturam.* Missio autem est temporalis processio. Cum igitur sanctificatio creaturae non sit nisi per gratiam gratum facientem, sequitur quod missio divinae personae non sit nisi per gratiam gratum facientem.

RESPONDEO dicendum quod divinae personae convenit mitti, secundum quod novo modo existit in aliquo; dari autem, secundum quod habetur ab aliquo. Neutrum autem horum est nisi secundum gratiam gratum facientem.

Est enim unus communis modus quo Deus est in omnibus rebus per essentiam, potentiam et praesentiam, sicut causa in effectibus participantibus bonitatem ipsius. Super istum modum autem communem, est unus specialis, qui convenit creaturae rationali, in qua Deus dicitur esse sicut cognitum in cognoscente et amatum in amante. Et quia, cognoscendo et amando, creatura rationalis sua operatione attingit ad ipsum Deum, secundum istum specialem modum Deus non solum dicitur esse in creatura rationali, sed etiam habitare in ea sicut in templo suo. Sic igitur nullus alius effectus potest esse ratio quod divina persona sit novo modo in rationali creatura, nisi gratia gratum faciens. Unde secundum solam gratiam gratum facientem, mittitur et procedit temporaliter persona divina.

Similiter illud solum habere dicimur, quo libere possumus uti vel frui. Habere autem potestatem fruendi divina persona, est solum secundum gratiam gratum facientem. Sed tamen in ipso dono gratiae gratum facientis, Spiritus Sanctus habetur, et inhabitat hominem. Unde ipsemet Spiritus Sanctus datur et mittitur.

AD PRIMUM ergo dicendum quod per donum gratiae gratum facientis perficitur creatura rationalis, ad hoc quod libere non solum ipso dono creato utatur, sed ut ipsa divina persona fruatur. Et ideo missio invisibilis fit secundum donum gratiae gratum facientis, et tamen ipsa persona divina datur.

us. Therefore it is improperly said that the divine person is sent according to the gift of sanctifying grace.

OBJ. 3: Further, Augustine says (*De Trin.* iv, 20) that *the Son, when temporally perceived by the mind, is sent.* But the Son is known not only by sanctifying grace, but also by gratuitous grace, as by faith and knowledge. Therefore the divine person is not sent only according to the gift of sanctifying grace.

OBJ. 4: Further, Rabanus says that the Holy Spirit was given to the apostles for the working of miracles. This, however, is not a gift of sanctifying grace, but a gratuitous grace. Therefore the divine person is not given only according to the gift of sanctifying grace.

ON THE CONTRARY, Augustine says (*De Trin.* iii, 4) that *the Holy Spirit proceeds temporally for the creature's sanctification.* But mission is a temporal procession. Since then the creature's sanctification is by sanctifying grace, it follows that the mission of the divine person is only by sanctifying grace.

I ANSWER THAT, The divine person is fittingly sent in the sense that He exists newly in any one; and He is given as possessed by anyone; and neither of these is otherwise than by sanctifying grace.

For God is in all things by His essence, power and presence, according to His one common mode, as the cause existing in the effects which participate in His goodness. Above and beyond this common mode, however, there is one special mode belonging to the rational nature wherein God is said to be present as the object known is in the knower, and the beloved in the lover. And since the rational creature by its operation of knowledge and love attains to God Himself, according to this special mode God is said not only to exist in the rational creature but also to dwell therein as in His own temple. So no other effect can be put down as the reason why the divine person is in the rational creature in a new mode, except sanctifying grace. Hence, the divine person is sent, and proceeds temporally only according to sanctifying grace.

Again, we are said to possess only what we can freely use or enjoy: and to have the power of enjoying the divine person can only be according to sanctifying grace. And yet the Holy Spirit is possessed by man, and dwells within him, in the very gift itself of sanctifying grace. Hence the Holy Spirit Himself is given and sent.

REPLY OBJ. 1: By the gift of sanctifying grace the rational creature is perfected so that it can freely use not only the created gift itself, but enjoy also the divine person Himself; and so the invisible mission takes place according to the gift of sanctifying grace; and yet the divine person Himself is given.

AD SECUNDUM dicendum quod gratia gratum faciens disponit animam ad habendam divinam personam, et significatur hoc, cum dicitur quod Spiritus Sanctus datur secundum donum gratiae. Sed tamen ipsum donum gratiae est a spiritu sancto, et hoc significatur, cum dicitur quod *caritas Dei diffunditur in cordibus nostris per spiritum sanctum.*

AD TERTIUM dicendum quod, licet per aliquos effectus filius cognosci possit a nobis, non tamen per aliquos effectus nos inhabitat, vel etiam habetur a nobis.

AD QUARTUM dicendum quod operatio miraculorum est manifestativa gratiae gratum facientis, sicut et donum prophetiae, et quaelibet gratia gratis data. Unde I Cor. XII, gratia gratis data nominatur *manifestatio spiritus.* Sic igitur apostolis dicitur datus Spiritus Sanctus ad operationem miraculorum, quia data est eis gratia gratum faciens cum signo manifestante. Si autem daretur solum signum gratiae gratum facientis sine gratia, non diceretur dari simpliciter Spiritus Sanctus; nisi forte cum aliqua determinatione, secundum quod dicitur quod alicui datur spiritus propheticus vel miraculorum, inquantum a spiritu sancto habet virtutem prophetandi vel miracula faciendi.

REPLY OBJ. 2: Sanctifying grace disposes the soul to possess the divine person; and this is signified when it is said that the Holy Spirit is given according to the gift of grace. Nevertheless the gift itself of grace is from the Holy Spirit; which is meant by the words, *the charity of God is poured forth in our hearts by the Holy Spirit.*

REPLY OBJ. 3: Although the Son can be known by us according to other effects, yet neither does He dwell in us, nor is He possessed by us according to those effects.

REPLY OBJ. 4: The working of miracles manifests sanctifying grace as also does the gift of prophecy and any other gratuitous graces. Hence gratuitous grace is called the *manifestation of the Spirit* (1 Cor 12:7). So the Holy Spirit is said to be given to the apostles for the working of miracles, because sanctifying grace was given to them with the outward sign. Were the sign only of sanctifying grace given to them without the grace itself, it would not be simply said that the Holy Spirit was given, except with some qualifying term; just as we read of certain ones receiving the gift of the spirit of prophecy, or of miracles, as having from the Holy Spirit the power of prophesying or of working miracles.

Article 4

Whether the Father Can Be Fittingly Sent?

AD QUARTUM SIC PROCEDITUR. Videtur quod etiam patri conveniat mitti. Mitti enim divinam personam est ipsam dari. Sed pater dat seipsum, cum haberi non possit, nisi se ipso donante. Ergo potest dici quod pater mittat seipsum.

PRAETEREA, persona divina mittitur secundum inhabitationem gratiae. Sed per gratiam tota Trinitas inhabitat in nobis, secundum illud Ioan. XIV, *ad eum veniemus, et mansionem apud eum faciemus.* Ergo quaelibet divinarum personarum mittitur.

PRAETEREA, quidquid convenit alicui personae, convenit omnibus, praeter notiones et personas. Sed missio non significat aliquam personam, neque etiam notionem, cum sint tantum quinque notiones, ut supra dictum est. Ergo cuilibet personae divinae convenit mitti.

SED CONTRA est quod Augustinus dicit, in II libro de Trin., quod *solus pater nunquam legitur missus.*

RESPONDEO dicendum quod missio in sui ratione importat processionem ab alio; et in divinis, secundum originem, ut supra dictum est. Unde, cum pater non sit ab alio, nullo modo convenit sibi mitti; sed solum filio et spiritui sancto, quibus convenit esse ab alio.

OBJECTION 1: It would seem that it is fitting also that the Father should be sent. For being sent means that the divine person is given. But the Father gives Himself since He can only be possessed by His giving Himself. Therefore it can be said that the Father sends Himself.

OBJ. 2: Further, the divine person is sent according to the indwelling of grace. But by grace the whole Trinity dwells in us according to John 14:23: *We will come to him and make Our abode with him.* Therefore each one of the divine persons is sent.

OBJ. 3: Further, whatever belongs to one person, belongs to them all, except the notions and persons. But mission does not signify any person; nor even a notion, since there are only five notions, as stated above (Q. 32, A. 3). Therefore every divine person can be sent.

ON THE CONTRARY, Augustine says (*De Trin.* ii, 3), *The Father alone is never described as being sent.*

I ANSWER THAT, The very idea of mission means procession from another, and in God it means procession according to origin, as above expounded. Hence, as the Father is not from another, in no way is it fitting for Him to be sent; but this can only belong to the Son and to the Holy Spirit, to Whom it belongs to be from another.

AD PRIMUM ergo dicendum quod si dare importet liberalem communicationem alicuius, sic pater dat seipsum, inquantum se liberaliter communicat creaturae ad fruendum. Si vero importet auctoritatem dantis respectu eius quod datur, sic non convenit dari in divinis nisi personae quae est ab alio; sicut nec mitti.

AD SECUNDUM dicendum quod, licet effectus gratiae sit etiam a patre, qui inhabitat per gratiam, sicut et filius et Spiritus Sanctus; quia tamen non est ab alio, non dicitur mitti. Et hoc est quod dicit Augustinus, IV de Trin., quod *pater, cum in tempore a quoquam cognoscitur, non dicitur missus, non enim habet de quo sit, aut ex quo procedat.*

AD TERTIUM dicendum quod missio, inquantum importat processionem a mittente, includit in sui significatione notionem, non quidem in speciali, sed in generali, prout esse ab alio est commune duabus notionibus.

REPLY OBJ. 1: In the sense of *giving* as a free bestowal of something, the Father gives Himself, as freely bestowing Himself to be enjoyed by the creature. But as implying the authority of the giver as regards what is given, *to be given* only applies in God to the Person Who is from another; and the same as regards *being sent*.

REPLY OBJ. 2: Although the effect of grace is also from the Father, Who dwells in us by grace, just as the Son and the Holy Spirit, still He is not described as being sent, for He is not from another. Thus Augustine says (*De Trin.* iv, 20) that *The Father, when known by anyone in time, is not said to be sent; for there is no one whence He is, or from whom He proceeds.*

REPLY OBJ. 3: Mission, meaning procession from the sender, includes the signification of a notion, not of a special notion, but in general; thus *to be from another* is common to two of the notions.

Article 5

Whether It Is Fitting for the Son to Be Sent Invisibly?

AD QUINTUM SIC PROCEDITUR. Videtur quod filio non conveniat invisibiliter mitti. Missio enim invisibilis divinae personae attenditur secundum dona gratiae. Sed omnia dona gratiae pertinent ad spiritum sanctum, secundum illud I Cor. XII, *omnia operatur unus atque idem spiritus.* Ergo invisibiliter non mittitur nisi Spiritus Sanctus.

PRAETEREA, missio divinae personae fit secundum gratiam gratum facientem. Sed dona quae pertinent ad perfectionem intellectus, non sunt dona gratiae gratum facientis, cum sine caritate possint haberi, secundum illud I ad Cor. XIII, *si habuero prophetiam, et noverim mysteria omnia, et omnem scientiam, et si habuero omnem fidem, ita ut montes transferam, caritatem autem non habeam, nihil sum.* Cum ergo filius procedat ut verbum intellectus, videtur quod non conveniat sibi invisibiliter mitti.

PRAETEREA, missio divinae personae est quaedam processio, ut dictum est. Sed alia est processio filii, alia spiritus sancti. Ergo et alia missio, si uterque mittitur. Et sic altera earum superflueret, cum una sit sufficiens ad sanctificandam creaturam.

SED CONTRA est quod Sap. IX dicitur de divina sapientia, *mitte illam de caelis sanctis tuis, et a sede magnitudinis tuae.*

RESPONDEO dicendum quod per gratiam gratum facientem tota Trinitas inhabitat mentem, secundum illud Ioan. XIV, *ad eum veniemus, et mansionem apud eum faciemus.* Mitti autem personam divinam ad aliquem per

OBJECTION 1: It would seem that it is not fitting for the Son to be sent invisibly. For invisible mission of the divine person is according to the gift of grace. But all gifts of grace belong to the Holy Spirit, according to 1 Cor. 12:11: *One and the same Spirit worketh all things.* Therefore only the Holy Spirit is sent invisibly.

OBJ. 2: Further, the mission of the divine person is according to sanctifying grace. But the gifts belonging to the perfection of the intellect are not gifts of sanctifying grace, since they can be held without the gift of charity, according to 1 Cor. 13:2: *If I should have prophecy, and should know all mysteries, and all knowledge, and if I should have all faith so that I could move mountains, and have not charity, I am nothing.* Therefore, since the Son proceeds as the word of the intellect, it seems unfitting for Him to be sent invisibly.

OBJ. 3: Further, the mission of the divine person is a procession, as expounded above (AA. 1, 4). But the procession of the Son and of the Holy Spirit differ from each other. Therefore they are distinct missions if both are sent; and then one of them would be superfluous, since one would suffice for the creature's sanctification.

ON THE CONTRARY, It is said of divine Wisdom (Wis 9:10): *Send her from heaven to Thy Saints, and from the seat of Thy greatness.*

I ANSWER THAT, The whole Trinity dwells in the mind by sanctifying grace, according to John 14:23: *We will come to him, and will make Our abode with him.* But that a divine person be sent to anyone by invisible grace signifies both

invisibilem gratiam, significat novum modum inhabitandi illius personae, et originem eius ab alia. Unde, cum tam filio quam spiritui sancto conveniat et inhabitare per gratiam et ab alio esse, utrique convenit invisibiliter mitti. Patri autem licet conveniat inhabitare per gratiam, non tamen sibi convenit ab alio esse; et per consequens nec mitti.

AD PRIMUM ergo dicendum quod, licet omnia dona, inquantum dona sunt, attribuantur spiritui sancto, quia habet rationem primi doni, secundum quod est amor, ut supra dictum est; aliqua tamen dona, secundum proprias rationes, attribuuntur per quandam appropriationem filio, scilicet illa quae pertinent ad intellectum et secundum illa dona attenditur missio filii. Unde Augustinus dicit, IV de Trin., quod *tunc invisibiliter filius cuiquam mittitur, cum a quoquam cognoscitur atque percipitur.*

AD SECUNDUM dicendum quod anima per gratiam conformatur Deo. Unde ad hoc quod aliqua persona divina mittatur ad aliquem per gratiam, oportet quod fiat assimilatio illius ad divinam personam quae mittitur per aliquod gratiae donum. Et quia Spiritus Sanctus est amor, per donum caritatis anima spiritui sancto assimilatur, unde secundum donum caritatis attenditur missio spiritus sancti. Filius autem est verbum, non qualecumque, sed spirans amorem, unde Augustinus dicit, in IX libro de Trin., *verbum quod insinuare intendimus, cum amore notitia est.* Non igitur secundum quamlibet perfectionem intellectus mittitur filius, sed secundum talem instructionem intellectus, qua prorumpat in affectum amoris, ut dicitur Ioan. VI, *omnis qui audivit a patre, et didicit, venit ad me*; et in Psalm., *in meditatione mea exardescet ignis.* Et ideo signanter dicit Augustinus quod *filius mittitur, cum a quoquam cognoscitur atque percipitur,* perceptio enim experimentalem quandam notitiam significat. Et haec proprie dicitur sapientia, quasi sapida scientia, secundum illud Eccli. VI, *sapientia doctrinae secundum nomen eius est.*

AD TERTIUM dicendum quod, cum missio importet originem personae missae et inhabitationem per gratiam, ut supra dictum est, si loquamur de missione quantum ad originem, sic missio filii distinguitur a missione spiritus sancti, sicut et generatio a processione. Si autem quantum ad effectum gratiae, sic communicant duae missiones in radice gratiae, sed distinguuntur in effectibus gratiae, qui sunt illuminatio intellectus, et inflammatio affectus. Et sic manifestum est quod una non potest esse sine alia, quia neutra est sine gratia gratum faciente, nec una persona separatur ab alia.

that this person dwells in a new way within him and that He has His origin from another. Hence, since both to the Son and to the Holy Spirit it belongs to dwell in the soul by grace, and to be from another, it therefore belongs to both of them to be invisibly sent. As to the Father, though He dwells in us by grace, still it does not belong to Him to be from another, and consequently He is not sent.

REPLY OBJ. 1: Although all the gifts, considered as such, are attributed to the Holy Spirit, forasmuch as He is by His nature the first Gift, since He is Love, as stated above (Q. 38, A. 1), some gifts nevertheless, by reason of their own particular nature, are appropriated in a certain way to the Son, those, namely, which belong to the intellect, and in respect of which we speak of the mission of the Son. Hence Augustine says (*De Trin.* iv, 20) that *The Son is sent to anyone invisibly, whenever He is known and perceived by anyone.*

REPLY OBJ. 2: The soul is made like to God by grace. Hence for a divine person to be sent to anyone by grace, there must needs be a likening of the soul to the divine person Who is sent, by some gift of grace. Because the Holy Spirit is Love, the soul is assimilated to the Holy Spirit by the gift of charity: hence the mission of the Holy Spirit is according to the mode of charity. Whereas the Son is the Word, not any sort of word, but one Who breathes forth Love. Hence Augustine says (*De Trin.* ix 10): *The Word we speak of is knowledge with love.* Thus the Son is sent not in accordance with every and any kind of intellectual perfection, but according to the intellectual illumination, which breaks forth into the affection of love, as is said (John 6:45): *Everyone that hath heard from the Father and hath learned, cometh to Me*, and (Ps 38:4): *In my meditation a fire shall flame forth.* Thus Augustine plainly says (*De Trin.* iv, 20): *The Son is sent, whenever He is known and perceived by anyone.* Now perception implies a certain experimental knowledge; and this is properly called wisdom, as it were a sweet knowledge, according to Ecclus. 6:23: *The wisdom of doctrine is according to her name.*

REPLY OBJ. 3: Since mission implies the origin of the person Who is sent, and His indwelling by grace, as above explained (A. 1), if we speak of mission according to origin, in this sense the Son's mission is distinguished from the mission of the Holy Spirit, as generation is distinguished from procession. If we consider mission as regards the effect of grace, in this sense the two missions are united in the root which is grace, but are distinguished in the effects of grace, which consist in the illumination of the intellect and the kindling of the affection. Thus it is manifest that one mission cannot be without the other, because neither takes place without sanctifying grace, nor is one person separated from the other.

Article 6

Whether the Invisible Mission Is to All Who Participate Grace?

AD SEXTUM SIC PROCEDITUR. Videtur quod missio invisibilis non fiat ad omnes qui sunt participes gratiae. Patres enim veteris testamenti gratiae participes fuerunt. Sed ad illos non videtur fuisse facta missio invisibilis, dicitur enim Ioan. VII, *nondum erat spiritus datus, quia nondum erat Iesus glorificatus.* Ergo missio invisibilis non fit ad omnes qui sunt participes gratiae.

PRAETEREA, profectus in virtute non est nisi per gratiam. Sed missio invisibilis non videtur attendi secundum profectum virtutis, quia profectus virtutis videtur esse continuus, cum caritas semper aut proficiat aut deficiat; et sic missio esset continua. Ergo missio invisibilis non fit ad omnes participes gratiae.

PRAETEREA, Christus et beati plenissime habent gratiam. Sed ad eos non videtur fieri missio, quia missio fit ad aliquid distans; Christus autem, secundum quod homo, et omnes beati perfecte sunt uniti Deo. Non ergo ad omnes participes gratiae fit missio invisibilis.

PRAETEREA, sacramenta novae legis continent gratiam. Nec tamen ad ea dicitur fieri missio invisibilis. Non ergo ad omnia quae habent gratiam, fit missio invisibilis.

SED CONTRA est quod, secundum Augustinum, missio invisibilis fit ad sanctificandam creaturam. Omnis autem creatura habens gratiam sanctificatur. Ergo ad omnem creaturam huiusmodi fit missio invisibilis.

RESPONDEO dicendum quod, sicut supra dictum est, missio de sui ratione importat quod ille qui mittitur vel incipiat esse ubi prius non fuit, sicut accidit in rebus creatis; vel incipiat esse ubi prius fuit, sed quodam modo novo, secundum quod missio attribuitur divinis personis. Sic ergo in eo ad quem fit missio, oportet duo considerare, scilicet inhabitationem gratiae, et innovationem quandam per gratiam. Ad omnes ergo fit missio invisibilis, in quibus haec duo inveniuntur.

AD PRIMUM ergo dicendum quod missio invisibilis est facta ad patres veteris testamenti. Unde dicit Augustinus, IV de Trin., quod secundum quod filius mittitur invisibiliter, *fit in hominibus aut cum hominibus; hoc autem antea factum est in patribus et prophetis.* Quod ergo dicitur, nondum erat datus spiritus, intelligitur de illa datione cum signo visibili, quae facta est in die Pentecostes.

AD SECUNDUM dicendum quod etiam secundum profectum virtutis, aut augmentum gratiae, fit missio invisibilis. Unde Augustinus dicit, IV de Trin., quod *tunc cuiquam mittitur filius, cum a quoquam cognoscitur atque percipitur, quantum cognosci et percipi potest pro captu vel proficientis in Deum, vel perfectae in Deo animae rationalis.* Sed tamen secundum illud augmentum

OBJECTION 1: It would seem that the invisible mission is not to all who participate grace. For the Fathers of the Old Testament had their share of grace. Yet to them was made no invisible mission; for it is said (John 7:39): *The Spirit was not yet given, because Jesus was not yet glorified.* Therefore the invisible mission is not to all partakers in grace.

OBJ. 2: Further, progress in virtue is only by grace. But the invisible mission is not according to progress in virtue; because progress in virtue is continuous, since charity ever increases or decreases; and thus the mission would be continuous. Therefore the invisible mission is not to all who share in grace.

OBJ. 3: Further, Christ and the blessed have fullness of grace. But mission is not to them, for mission implies distance, whereas Christ, as man, and all the blessed are perfectly united to God. Therefore the invisible mission is not to all sharers in grace.

OBJ. 4: Further, the Sacraments of the New Law contain grace, and it is not said that the invisible mission is sent to them. Therefore the invisible mission is not to all that have grace.

ON THE CONTRARY, According to Augustine (*De Trin.* iii, 4; xv, 27), the invisible mission is for the creature's sanctification. Now every creature that has grace is sanctified. Therefore the invisible mission is to every such creature.

I ANSWER THAT, As above stated (AA. 3, 4 ,5), mission in its very meaning implies that he who is sent either begins to exist where he was not before, as occurs to creatures; or begins to exist where he was before, but in a new way, in which sense mission is ascribed to the divine persons. Thus, mission as regards the one to whom it is sent implies two things, the indwelling of grace, and a certain renewal by grace. Thus the invisible mission is sent to all in whom are to be found these two conditions.

REPLY OBJ. 1: The invisible mission was directed to the Old Testament Fathers, as appears from what Augustine says (*De Trin.* iv, 20), that the invisible mission of the Son *is in man and with men. This was done in former times with the Fathers and the Prophets.* Thus the words, *the Spirit was not yet given,* are to be applied to that giving accompanied with a visible sign which took place on the day of Pentecost.

REPLY OBJ. 2: The invisible mission takes place also as regards progress in virtue or increase of grace. Hence Augustine says (*De Trin.* iv, 20), that *the Son is sent to each one when He is known and perceived by anyone, so far as He can be known and perceived according to the capacity of the soul, whether journeying towards God, or united perfectly to Him.* Such invisible mission, however, chiefly occurs as regards

gratiae praecipue missio invisibilis attenditur, quando aliquis proficit in aliquem novum actum, vel novum statum gratiae, ut puta cum aliquis proficit in gratiam miraculorum aut prophetiae, vel in hoc quod ex fervore caritatis exponit se martyrio, aut abrenuntiat his quae possidet, aut quodcumque opus arduum aggreditur.

AD TERTIUM dicendum quod ad beatos est facta missio invisibilis in ipso principio beatitudinis. Postmodum autem ad eos fit missio invisibilis, non secundum intensionem gratiae, sed secundum quod aliqua mysteria eis revelantur de novo, quod est usque ad diem iudicii. Quod quidem augmentum attenditur secundum extensionem gratiae ad plura se extendentis. Ad Christum autem fuit facta invisibilis missio in principio suae conceptionis, non autem postea, cum a principio suae conceptionis fuerit plenus omni sapientia et gratia.

AD QUARTUM dicendum quod gratia est in sacramentis novae legis instrumentaliter, sicut forma artificiati est in instrumentis artis, secundum quendam decursum ab agente in patiens. Missio autem non dicitur fieri nisi respectu termini. Unde missio divinae personae non fit ad sacramenta, sed ad eos qui per sacramenta gratiam suscipiunt.

anyone's proficiency in the performance of a new act, or in the acquisition of a new state of grace; as, for example, the proficiency in reference to the gift of miracles or of prophecy, or in the fervor of charity leading a man to expose himself to the danger of martyrdom, or to renounce his possessions, or to undertake any arduous work.

REPLY OBJ. 3: The invisible mission is directed to the blessed at the very beginning of their beatitude. The invisible mission is made to them subsequently, not by *intensity* of grace, but by the further revelation of mysteries; which goes on till the day of judgment. Such an increase is by the *extension* of grace, because it extends to a greater number of objects. To Christ the invisible mission was sent at the first moment of His conception; but not afterwards, since from the beginning of His conception He was filled with all wisdom and grace.

REPLY OBJ. 4: Grace resides instrumentally in the sacraments of the New Law, as the form of a thing designed resides in the instruments of the art designing, according to a process flowing from the agent to the passive object. But mission is only spoken of as directed to its term. Hence the mission of the divine person is not sent to the sacraments, but to those who receive grace through the sacraments.

Article 7

Whether It Is Fitting for the Holy Spirit to Be Sent Visibly?

AD SEPTIMUM SIC PROCEDITUR. Videtur quod spiritui sancto non conveniat visibiliter mitti. Filius enim, secundum quod visibiliter missus est in mundum, dicitur esse minor patre. Sed nunquam legitur Spiritus Sanctus minor patre. Ergo spiritui sancto non convenit visibiliter mitti.

PRAETEREA, missio visibilis attenditur secundum aliquam creaturam visibilem assumptam, sicut missio filii secundum carnem. Sed Spiritus Sanctus non assumpsit aliquam creaturam visibilem. Unde non potest dici quod in aliquibus creaturis visibilibus sit alio modo quam in aliis, nisi forte sicut in signo; sicut est etiam in sacramentis, et in omnibus figuris legalibus. Non ergo Spiritus Sanctus visibiliter mittitur, vel oportet dicere quod secundum omnia huiusmodi, eius missio visibilis attenditur.

PRAETEREA, quaelibet creatura visibilis est effectus demonstrans totam Trinitatem. Non ergo per illas creaturas visibiles magis mittitur Spiritus Sanctus quam alia persona.

PRAETEREA, filius visibiliter est missus secundum dignissimam visibilium creaturarum, scilicet secundum naturam humanam. Si igitur Spiritus Sanctus visibiliter

OBJECTION 1: It would seem that the Holy Spirit is not fittingly sent in a visible manner. For the Son as visibly sent to the world is said to be less than the Father. But the Holy Spirit is never said to be less than the Father. Therefore the Holy Spirit is not fittingly sent in a visible manner.

OBJ. 2: Further, the visible mission takes place by way of union to a visible creature, as the Son's mission according to the flesh. But the Holy Spirit did not assume any visible creature; and hence it cannot be said that He exists otherwise in some creatures than in others, unless perhaps as in a sign, as He is also present in the sacraments, and in all the figures of the law. Thus the Holy Spirit is either not sent visibly at all, or His visible mission takes place in all these things.

OBJ. 3: Further, every visible creature is an effect showing forth the whole Trinity. Therefore the Holy Spirit is not sent by reason of those visible creatures more than any other person.

OBJ. 4: Further, the Son was visibly sent by reason of the noblest kind of creature—namely, the human nature.

mittitur, debuit mitti secundum aliquas creaturas rationales.

PRAETEREA, quae visibiliter fiunt divinitus, dispensantur per ministerium Angelorum, ut Augustinus dicit, III de Trin. Si ergo aliquae species visibiles apparuerunt, hoc factum fuit per Angelos. Et sic ipsi Angeli mittuntur, et non Spiritus Sanctus.

PRAETEREA, si Spiritus Sanctus visibiliter mittatur, hoc non est nisi ad manifestandum invisibilem missionem, quia invisibilia per visibilia manifestantur. Ergo ad quem missio invisibilis facta non fuit, nec missio visibilis fieri debuit, et ad omnes ad quos fit missio invisibilis, sive in novo sive in veteri testamento, missio visibilis fieri debet, quod patet esse falsum. Non ergo Spiritus Sanctus visibiliter mittitur.

SED CONTRA est quod dicitur Matth. III, quod Spiritus Sanctus descendit super dominum baptizatum in specie columbae.

RESPONDEO dicendum quod Deus providet omnibus secundum uniuscuiusque modum. Est autem modus connaturalis hominis, ut per visibilia ad invisibilia manuducatur, ut ex supra dictis patet, et ideo invisibilia Dei oportuit homini per visibilia manifestari. Sicut igitur seipsum Deus, et processiones aeternas personarum, per creaturas visibiles, secundum aliqua indicia, hominibus quodammodo demonstravit; ita conveniens fuit ut etiam invisibiles missiones divinarum personarum secundum aliquas visibiles creaturas manifestarentur.

Aliter tamen filius et Spiritus Sanctus. Nam spiritui sancto, inquantum procedit ut amor, competit esse sanctificationis donum, filio autem, inquantum est spiritus sancti principium, competit esse sanctificationis huius auctorem. Et ideo filius visibiliter missus est tanquam sanctificationis auctor, sed Spiritus Sanctus tanquam sanctificationis indicium.

AD PRIMUM ergo dicendum quod filius creaturam visibilem in qua apparuit, in unitatem personae assumpsit, sic ut quod de illa creatura dicitur, de filio Dei dici possit. Et sic, ratione naturae assumptae, filius dicitur minor patre. Sed Spiritus Sanctus non assumpsit creaturam visibilem in qua apparuit, in unitatem personae, ut quod illi convenit, de illo praedicetur. Unde non potest dici minor patre propter visibilem creaturam.

AD SECUNDUM dicendum quod missio visibilis spiritus sancti non attenditur secundum visionem imaginariam, quae est visio prophetica. Quia, ut Augustinus dicit, II de Trin., *visio prophetica non est exhibita corporeis oculis per formas corporeas, sed in spiritu per spirituales corporum imagines, columbam vero illam et ignem oculis viderunt quicumque viderunt. Neque iterum sic se habuit Spiritus Sanctus ad huiusmodi species, sicut filius ad*

Therefore if the Holy Spirit is sent visibly, He ought to be sent by reason of rational creatures.

OBJ. 5: Further, whatever is done visibly by God is dispensed by the ministry of the angels; as Augustine says (*De Trin.* iii, 4,5,9). So visible appearances, if there have been any, came by means of the angels. Thus the angels are sent, and not the Holy Spirit.

OBJ. 6: Further, the Holy Spirit being sent in a visible manner is only for the purpose of manifesting the invisible mission; as invisible things are made known by the visible. So those to whom the invisible mission was not sent, ought not to receive the visible mission; and to all who received the invisible mission, whether in the New or in the Old Testament, the visible mission ought likewise to be sent; and this is clearly false. Therefore the Holy Spirit is not sent visibly.

ON THE CONTRARY, It is said (Matt 3:16) that, when our Lord was baptized, the Holy Spirit descended upon Him in the shape of a dove.

I ANSWER THAT, God provides for all things according to the nature of each thing. Now the nature of man requires that he be led to the invisible by visible things, as explained above (Q. 12, A. 12). Wherefore the invisible things of God must be made manifest to man by the things that are visible. As God, therefore, in a certain way has demonstrated Himself and His eternal processions to men by visible creatures, according to certain signs; so was it fitting that the invisible missions also of the divine persons should be made manifest by some visible creatures.

This mode of manifestation applies in different ways to the Son and to the Holy Spirit. For it belongs to the Holy Spirit, Who proceeds as Love, to be the gift of sanctification; to the Son as the principle of the Holy Spirit, it belongs to be the author of this sanctification. Thus the Son has been sent visibly as the author of sanctification; the Holy Spirit as the sign of sanctification.

REPLY OBJ. 1: The Son assumed the visible creature, wherein He appeared, into the unity of His person, so that whatever can be said of that creature can be said of the Son of God; and so, by reason of the nature assumed, the Son is called less than the Father. But the Holy Spirit did not assume the visible creature, in which He appeared, into the unity of His person; so that what is said of it cannot be predicated of Him. Hence He cannot be called less than the Father by reason of any visible creature.

REPLY OBJ. 2: The visible mission of the Holy Spirit does not apply to the imaginary vision which is that of prophecy; because as Augustine says (*De Trin.* ii, 6): *The prophetic vision is not displayed to corporeal eyes by corporeal shapes, but is shown in the spirit by the spiritual images of bodies. But whoever saw the dove and the fire, saw them by their eyes. Nor, again, has the Holy Spirit the same relation to these images that the Son has to the rock, because*

petram (quia dicitur, petra erat Christus). Illa enim petra iam erat in creatura, et per actionis modum nuncupata est nomine Christi, quem significabat, sed illa columba et ignis ad haec tantum significanda repente extiterunt. Sed videntur esse similia flammae illi quae in rubo apparuit Moysi, et illi columnae quam populus in eremo sequebatur, et fulgoribus ac tonitruis quae fiebant cum lex daretur in monte, ad hoc enim rerum illarum corporalis extitit species, ut aliquid significaret, atque praeteriret. Sic igitur patet quod missio visibilis neque attenditur secundum visiones propheticas, quae fuerunt imaginariae, et non corporales, neque secundum signa sacramentalia veteris et novi testamenti, in quibus quaedam res praeexistentes assumuntur ad aliquid significandum. Sed Spiritus Sanctus visibiliter dicitur esse missus, inquantum fuit monstratus in quibusdam creaturis, sicut in signis, ad hoc specialiter factis.

AD TERTIUM dicendum quod, licet illas creaturas visibiles tota Trinitas operata sit, tamen factae sunt ad demonstrandum specialiter hanc vel illam personam. Sicut enim diversis nominibus significantur pater et filius et Spiritus Sanctus, ita etiam diversis rebus significari potuerunt; quamvis inter eos nulla sit separatio aut diversitas.

AD QUARTUM dicendum quod personam filii declarari oportuit ut sanctificationis auctorem, ut dictum est, et ideo oportuit quod missio visibilis filii fieret secundum naturam rationalem, cuius est agere, et cui potest competere sanctificare. Indicium autem sanctificationis esse potuit quaecumque alia creatura. Neque oportuit quod creatura visibilis ad hoc formata, esset assumpta a spiritu sancto in unitatem personae, cum non assumeretur ad aliquid agendum, sed ad indicandum tantum. Et propter hoc etiam non oportuit quod duraret, nisi quandiu perageret officium suum.

AD QUINTUM dicendum quod illae creaturae visibiles formatae sunt ministerio Angelorum, non tamen ad significandum personam Angeli, sed ad significandam personam spiritus sancti. Quia igitur Spiritus Sanctus erat in illis creaturis visibilibus sicut signatum in signo, propter hoc secundum eas Spiritus Sanctus visibiliter mitti dicitur, et non Angelus.

AD SEXTUM dicendum quod non est de necessitate invisibilis missionis, ut semper manifestetur per aliquod signum visibile exterius, sed, sicut dicitur I Cor. XII, *manifestatio spiritus datur alicui ad utilitatem*, scilicet Ecclesiae. Quae quidem utilitas est, ut per huiusmodi visibilia signa fides confirmetur et propagetur. Quod quidem principaliter factum est per Christum et per apostolos, secundum illud Hebr. II, *cum initium accepisset enarrari per dominum, ab eis qui audierunt in nos confirmata est.*

Et ideo specialiter debuit fieri missio visibilis spiritus sancti ad Christum et ad apostolos, et ad aliquos primitivos sanctos, in quibus quodammodo Ecclesia fundabatur,

it is said, 'The rock was Christ' (1 Cor 10:4). For that rock was already created, and after the manner of an action was named Christ, Whom it typified; whereas the dove and the fire suddenly appeared to signify only what was happening. They seem, however, to be like to the flame of the burning bush seen by Moses and to the column which the people followed in the desert, and to the lightning and thunder issuing forth when the law was given on the mountain. For the purpose of the bodily appearances of those things was that they might signify, and then pass away. Thus the visible mission is neither displayed by prophetic vision, which belongs to the imagination, and not to the body, nor by the sacramental signs of the Old and New Testament, wherein certain pre-existing things are employed to signify something. But the Holy Spirit is said to be sent visibly, inasmuch as He showed Himself in certain creatures as in signs especially made for that purpose.

REPLY OBJ. 3: Although the whole Trinity makes those creatures, still they are made in order to show forth in some special way this or that person. For as the Father, Son and Holy Spirit are signified by diverse names, so also can They each one be signified by different things; although neither separation nor diversity exists amongst Them.

REPLY OBJ. 4: It was necessary for the Son to be declared as the author of sanctification, as explained above. Thus the visible mission of the Son was necessarily made according to the rational nature to which it belongs to act, and which is capable of sanctification; whereas any other creature could be the sign of sanctification. Nor was such a visible creature, formed for such a purpose, necessarily assumed by the Holy Spirit into the unity of His person, since it was not assumed or used for the purpose of action, but only for the purpose of a sign; and so likewise it was not required to last beyond what its use required.

REPLY OBJ. 5: Those visible creatures were formed by the ministry of the angels, not to signify the person of an angel, but to signify the Person of the Holy Spirit. Thus, as the Holy Spirit resided in those visible creatures as the one signified in the sign, on that account the Holy Spirit is said to be sent visibly, and not as an angel.

REPLY OBJ. 6: It is not necessary that the invisible mission should always be made manifest by some visible external sign; but, as is said (1 Cor 12:7)—'the manifestation of the Spirit is given to every man unto profit'—that is, of the Church. This utility consists in the confirmation and propagation of the faith by such visible signs. This has been done chiefly by Christ and by the apostles, according to Heb. 2:3, *which having begun to be declared by the Lord, was confirmed unto us by them that heard.*

Thus in a special sense, a mission of the Holy Spirit was directed to Christ, to the apostles, and to some of the early saints on whom the Church was in a way founded;

ita tamen quod visibilis missio facta ad Christum, demonstraret missionem invisibilem non tunc, sed in principio suae conceptionis, ad eum factam. Facta autem est missio visibilis ad Christum, in Baptismo quidem sub specie columbae, quod est animal fecundum, ad ostendendum in Christo auctoritatem donandi gratiam per spiritualem regenerationem, unde vox patris intonuit, *hic est filius meus dilectus*, ut ad similitudinem unigeniti alii regenerarentur. In transfiguratione vero, sub specie nubis lucidae, ad ostendendam exuberantiam doctrinae, unde dictum est, *ipsum audite*. Ad apostolos autem, sub specie flatus, ad ostendendam potestatem ministerii in dispensatione sacramentorum, unde dictum est eis, *quorum remiseritis peccata, remittuntur eis*. Sed sub linguis igneis, ad ostendendum officium doctrinae, unde dicitur quod *coeperunt loqui variis linguis*. Ad patres autem veteris testamenti, missio visibilis spiritus sancti fieri non debuit quia prius debuit perfici missio visibilis filii quam spiritus sancti, cum Spiritus Sanctus manifestet filium, sicut filius patrem. Fuerunt tamen factae visibiles apparitiones divinarum personarum patribus veteris testamenti. Quae quidem missiones visibiles dici non possunt, quia non fuerunt factae, secundum Augustinum, ad designandum inhabitationem divinae personae per gratiam, sed ad aliquid aliud manifestandum.

in such a manner, however, that the visible mission made to Christ should show forth the invisible mission made to Him, not at that particular time, but at the first moment of His conception. The visible mission was directed to Christ at the time of His baptism by the figure of a dove, a fruitful animal, to show forth in Christ the authority of the giver of grace by spiritual regeneration; hence the Father's voice spoke, *This is My beloved Son* (Matt 3:17), that others might be regenerated to the likeness of the only Begotten. The Transfiguration showed it forth in the appearance of a bright cloud, to show the exuberance of doctrine; and hence it was said, *Hear ye Him* (Matt 17:5). To the apostles the mission was directed in the form of breathing to show forth the power of their ministry in the dispensation of the sacraments; and hence it was said, *Whose sins you shall forgive, they are forgiven* (John 20:23): and again under the sign of fiery tongues to show forth the office of teaching; whence it is said that, *they began to speak with diverse tongues* (Acts 2:4). The visible mission of the Holy Spirit was fittingly not sent to the fathers of the Old Testament, because the visible mission of the Son was to be accomplished before that of the Holy Spirit; since the Holy Spirit manifests the Son, as the Son manifests the Father. Visible apparitions of the divine persons were, however, given to the Fathers of the Old Testament which, indeed, cannot be called visible missions; because, according to Augustine (*De Trin.* ii, 17), they were not sent to designate the indwelling of the divine person by grace, but for the manifestation of something else.

Article 8

Whether a Divine Person Is Sent Only by the Person Whence He Proceeds Eternally?

AD OCTAVUM SIC PROCEDITUR. Videtur quod nulla persona divina mittatur nisi ab ea a qua procedit aeternaliter. Quia, sicut dicit Augustinus, IV de Trin., *pater a nullo mittitur, quia a nullo est*. Si ergo aliqua persona divina mittitur ab alia, oportet quod sit ab illa.

PRAETEREA, mittens habet auctoritatem respectu missi. Sed respectu divinae personae non potest haberi auctoritas nisi secundum originem. Ergo oportet quod divina persona quae mittitur, sit a persona mittente.

PRAETEREA, si persona divina potest mitti ab eo a quo non est, nihil prohibebit dicere quod Spiritus Sanctus detur ab homine, quamvis non sit ab eo. Quod est contra Augustinum, XV de Trin. Ergo divina persona non mittitur nisi ab ea a qua est.

SED CONTRA est quod filius mittitur a spiritu sancto, secundum illud Isaiae XLVIII, *et nunc misit me dominus*

OBJECTION 1: It would seem that a divine person is sent only by the one whence He proceeds eternally. For as Augustine says (*De Trin.* iv), *The Father is sent by no one because He is from no one.* Therefore if a divine person is sent by another, He must be from that other.

OBJ. 2: Further, the sender has authority over the one sent. But there can be no authority as regards a divine person except from origin. Therefore the divine person sent must proceed from the one sending.

OBJ. 3: Further, if a divine person can be sent by one whence He does not proceed, then the Holy Spirit may be given by a man, although He proceeds not from him; which is contrary to what Augustine says (*De Trin.* xv). Therefore the divine person is sent only by the one whence He proceeds.

ON THE CONTRARY, The Son is sent by the Holy Spirit, according to Isa. 48:16, *Now the Lord God hath sent Me and His Spirit.* But the Son is not from the Holy Spirit.

Deus, et spiritus eius. Filius autem non est a spiritu sancto. Ergo persona divina mittitur ab ea a qua non est.

RESPONDEO dicendum quod circa hoc inveniuntur aliqui diversimode locuti esse. Secundum quosdam enim, persona divina non mittitur nisi ab eo a quo est aeternaliter. Et secundum hoc, cum dicitur filius Dei missus a spiritu sancto, referendum est hoc ad humanam naturam, secundum quam missus est ad praedicandum a spiritu sancto. Augustinus autem dicit, II de Trin., quod filius mittitur et a se et a spiritu sancto; et Spiritus Sanctus etiam mittitur et a se et a filio, ut sic mitti in divinis non conveniat cuilibet personae, sed solum personae ab alio existenti; mittere autem conveniat cuilibet personae.

Utrumque autem habet aliquo modo veritatem. Quia cum dicitur aliqua persona mitti, designatur et ipsa persona ab alio existens, et effectus visibilis aut invisibilis, secundum quem missio divinae personae attenditur. Si igitur mittens designetur ut principium personae quae mittitur, sic non quaelibet persona mittit, sed solum illa cui convenit esse principium illius personae. Et sic filius mittitur tantum a patre, Spiritus Sanctus autem a patre et filio. Si vero persona mittens intelligatur esse principium effectus secundum quem attenditur missio, sic tota Trinitas mittit personam missam. Non autem propter hoc homo dat spiritum sanctum, quia nec effectum gratiae potest causare.

ET PER HOC patet solutio ad obiecta.

Therefore a divine person is sent by one from Whom He does not proceed.

I ANSWER THAT, There are different opinions on this point. Some say that the divine person is sent only by the one whence He proceeds eternally; and so, when it is said that the Son of God is sent by the Holy Spirit, this is to be explained as regards His human nature, by reason of which He was sent to preach by the Holy Spirit. Augustine, however, says (*De Trin.* ii, 5) that the Son is sent by Himself, and by the Holy Spirit; and the Holy Spirit is sent by Himself, and by the Son; so that to be sent in God does not apply to each person, but only to the person proceeding from another, whereas to send belongs to each person.

There is some truth in both of these opinions; because when a person is described as being sent, the person Himself existing from another is designated, with the visible or invisible effect, applicable to the mission of the divine person. Thus if the sender be designated as the principle of the person sent, in this sense not each person sends, but that person only Who is the principle of that person who is sent; and thus the Son is sent only by the Father; and the Holy Spirit by the Father and the Son. If, however, the person sending is understood as the principle of the effect implied in the mission, in that sense the whole Trinity sends the person sent. This reason does not prove that a man can send the Holy Spirit, forasmuch as man cannot cause the effect of grace.

THE ANSWERS to the objections appear from the above.

QUESTION 44

THE PROCESSION OF CREATURES FROM GOD

Post considerationem divinarum personarum, considerandum restat de processione creaturarum a Deo. Erit autem haec consideratio tripartita, ut primo consideretur de productione creaturarum; secundo, de earum distinctione; tertio, de conservatione et gubernatione.

Circa primum tria sunt consideranda, primo quidem, quae sit prima causa entium; secundo, de modo procedendi creaturarum a prima causa; tertio vero, de principio durationis rerum.

Circa primum quaeruntur quatuor.

Primo, utrum Deus sit causa efficiens omnium entium.

Secundo, utrum materia prima sit creata a Deo, vel sit principium ex aequo coordinatum ei.

Tertio, utrum Deus sit causa exemplaris rerum, vel sint alia exemplaria praeter ipsum.

Quarto, utrum ipse sit causa finalis rerum.

After treating of the procession of the divine persons, we must consider the procession of creatures from God. This consideration will be threefold: (1) of the production of creatures; (2) of the distinction between them; (3) of their preservation and government.

Concerning the first point there are three things to be considered: (1) the first cause of beings; (2) the mode of procession of creatures from the first cause; (3) the principle of the duration of things.

Under the first head there are four points of inquiry:

(1) Whether God is the efficient cause of all beings?

(2) Whether primary matter is created by God, or is an independent coordinate principle with Him?

(3) Whether God is the exemplar cause of beings or whether there are other exemplar causes?

(4) Whether He is the final cause of things?

Article 1

Whether It Is Necessary That Every Being Be Created by God?

AD PRIMUM SIC PROCEDITUR. Videtur quod non sit necessarium omne ens esse creatum a Deo. Nihil enim prohibet inveniri rem sine eo quod non est de ratione rei, sicut hominem sine albedine. Sed habitudo causati ad causam non videtur esse de ratione entium quia sine hac possunt aliqua entia intelligi. Ergo sine hac possunt esse. Ergo nihil prohibet esse aliqua entia non creata a Deo.

PRAETEREA, ad hoc aliquid indiget causa efficiente, ut sit. Ergo quod non potest non esse, non indiget causa efficiente. Sed nullum necessarium potest non esse, quia quod necesse est esse, non potest non esse. Cum igitur multa sint necessaria in rebus, videtur quod non omnia entia sint a Deo.

PRAETEREA, quorumcumque est aliqua causa, in his potest fieri demonstratio per causam illam. Sed in mathematicis non fit demonstratio per causam agentem, ut per philosophum patet, in III Metaphys. Non igitur omnia entia sunt a Deo sicut a causa agente.

SED CONTRA est quod dicitur Rom. XI, *ex ipso, et per ipsum, et in ipso sunt omnia.*

RESPONDEO dicendum quod necesse est dicere omne quod quocumque modo est, a Deo esse. Si enim

OBJECTION 1: It would seem that it is not necessary that every being be created by God. For there is nothing to prevent a thing from being without that which does not belong to its essence, as a man can be found without whiteness. But the relation of the thing caused to its cause does not appear to be essential to beings, for some beings can be understood without it; therefore they can exist without it; and therefore it is possible that some beings should not be created by God.

OBJ. 2: Further, a thing requires an efficient cause in order to exist. Therefore whatever cannot but exist does not require an efficient cause. But no necessary thing can not exist, because whatever necessarily exists cannot but exist. Therefore as there are many necessary things in existence, it appears that not all beings are from God.

OBJ. 3: Further, whatever things have a cause, can be demonstrated by that cause. But in mathematics, demonstration is not made by the efficient cause, as appears from the Philosopher (*Metaph.* iii, 3); therefore not all beings are from God as from their efficient cause.

ON THE CONTRARY, It is said (Rom 11:36): *Of Him, and by Him, and in Him are all things.*

I ANSWER THAT, It must be said that every being in any way existing is from God. For whatever is found in anything

451

aliquid invenitur in aliquo per participationem, necesse est quod causetur in ipso ab eo cui essentialiter convenit; sicut ferrum fit ignitum ab igne. Ostensum est autem supra, cum de divina simplicitate ageretur, quod Deus est ipsum esse per se subsistens. Et iterum ostensum est quod esse subsistens non potest esse nisi unum, sicut si albedo esset subsistens, non posset esse nisi una, cum albedines multiplicentur secundum recipientia. Relinquitur ergo quod omnia alia a Deo non sint suum esse, sed participant esse. Necesse est igitur omnia quae diversificantur secundum diversam participationem essendi, ut sint perfectius vel minus perfecte, causari ab uno primo ente, quod perfectissime est.

Unde et Plato dixit quod necesse est ante omnem multitudinem ponere unitatem. Et Aristoteles dicit, in II Metaphys., quod id quod est maxime ens et maxime verum, est causa omnis entis et omnis veri, sicut id quod maxime calidum est, est causa omnis caliditatis.

AD PRIMUM ergo dicendum quod, licet habitudo ad causam non intret definitionem entis quod est causatum, tamen sequitur ad ea qua sunt de eius ratione, quia ex hoc quod aliquid per participationem est ens, sequitur quod sit causatum ab alio. Unde huiusmodi ens non potest esse, quin sit causatum; sicut nec homo, quin sit risibile. Sed quia esse causatum non est de ratione entis simpliciter, propter hoc invenitur aliquod ens non causatum.

AD SECUNDUM dicendum quod ex hac ratione quidam moti fuerunt ad ponendum quod id quod est necessarium non habeat causam, ut dicitur in VIII Physic. Sed hoc manifeste falsum apparet in scientiis demonstrativis, in quibus principia necessaria sunt causae conclusionum necessariarum. Et ideo dicit Aristoteles, in V Metaphys., quod sunt quaedam necessaria quae habent causam suae necessitatis. Non ergo propter hoc solum requiritur causa agens, quia effectus potest non esse, sed quia effectus non esset, si causa non esset. Haec enim conditionalis est vera, sive antecedens et consequens sint possibilia, sive impossibilia.

AD TERTIUM dicendum quod mathematica accipiuntur ut abstracta secundum rationem, cum tamen non sint abstracta secundum esse. Unicuique autem competit habere causam agentem, secundum quod habet esse. Licet igitur ea quae sunt mathematica habeant causam agentem, non tamen secundum habitudinem quam habent ad causam agentem, cadunt sub consideratione mathematici. Et ideo in scientiis mathematicis non demonstratur aliquid per causam agentem.

by participation, must be caused in it by that to which it belongs essentially, as iron becomes ignited by fire. Now it has been shown above (Q. 3, A. 4) when treating of the divine simplicity that God is the essentially self-subsisting Being; and also it was shown (Q. 11, AA. 3, 4) that subsisting being must be one; as, if whiteness were self-subsisting, it would be one, since whiteness is multiplied by its recipients. Therefore all beings apart from God are not their own being, but are beings by participation. Therefore it must be that all things which are diversified by the diverse participation of being, so as to be more or less perfect, are caused by one First Being, Who possesses being most perfectly.

Hence Plato said (*Parmen.* xxvi) that unity must come before multitude; and Aristotle said (*Metaph.* ii, 4) that whatever is greatest in being and greatest in truth, is the cause of every being and of every truth; just as whatever is the greatest in heat is the cause of all heat.

REPLY OBJ. 1: Though the relation to its cause is not part of the definition of a thing caused, still it follows, as a consequence, on what belongs to its essence; because from the fact that a thing has being by participation, it follows that it is caused. Hence such a being cannot be without being caused, just as man cannot be without having the faculty of laughing. But, since to be caused does not enter into the essence of being as such, therefore is it possible for us to find a being uncaused.

REPLY OBJ. 2: This objection has led some to say that what is necessary has no cause (*Phys.* viii, 46). But this is manifestly false in the demonstrative sciences, where necessary principles are the causes of necessary conclusions. And therefore Aristotle says (*Metaph.* v, 6), that there are some necessary things which have a cause of their necessity. But the reason why an efficient cause is required is not merely because the effect is not necessary, but because the effect might not be if the cause were not. For this conditional proposition is true, whether the antecedent and consequent be possible or impossible.

REPLY OBJ. 3: The science of mathematics treats its object as though it were something abstracted mentally, whereas it is not abstract in reality. Now, it is becoming that everything should have an efficient cause in proportion to its being. And so, although the object of mathematics has an efficient cause, still, its relation to that cause is not the reason why it is brought under the consideration of the mathematician, who therefore does not demonstrate that object from its efficient cause.

Article 2

Whether Primary Matter Is Created by God?

AD SECUNDUM SIC PROCEDITUR. Videtur quod materia prima non sit creata a Deo. Omne enim quod fit, componitur ex subiecto et ex aliquo alio, ut dicitur in I Physic. Sed materiae primae non est aliquod subiectum. Ergo materia prima non potest esse facta a Deo.

PRAETEREA, actio et passio dividuntur contra se invicem. Sed sicut primum principium activum est Deus, ita primum principium passivum est materia. Ergo Deus et materia prima sunt duo principia contra se invicem divisa, quorum neutrum est ab alio.

PRAETEREA, omne agens agit sibi simile, et sic, cum omne agens agat inquantum est actu, sequitur quod omne factum aliquo modo sit in actu. Sed materia prima est tantum in potentia, inquantum huiusmodi. Ergo contra rationem materiae primae est, quod sit facta.

SED CONTRA est quod dicit Augustinus, XII Confess., *duo fecisti, domine, unum prope te*, scilicet Angelum, *aliud prope nihil*, scilicet materiam primam.

RESPONDEO dicendum quod antiqui philosophi paulatim, et quasi pedetentim, intraverunt in cognitionem veritatis. A principio enim, quasi grossiores existentes, non existimabant esse entia nisi corpora sensibilia. Quorum qui ponebant in eis motum, non considerabant motum nisi secundum aliqua accidentia, ut puta secundum raritatem et densitatem, congregationem et segregationem. Et supponentes ipsam substantiam corporum increatam, assignabant aliquas causas huiusmodi accidentalium transmutationum, ut puta amicitiam, litem, intellectum, aut aliquid huiusmodi. Ulterius vero procedentes, distinxerunt per intellectum inter formam substantialem et materiam, quam ponebant increatam; et perceperunt transmutationem fieri in corporibus secundum formas essentiales. Quarum transmutationum quasdam causas universaliores ponebant, ut obliquum circulum, secundum Aristotelem, vel ideas, secundum Platonem. Sed considerandum est quod materia per formam contrahitur ad determinatam speciem; sicut substantia alicuius speciei per accidens ei adveniens contrahitur ad determinatum modum essendi, ut homo contrahitur per album. Utrique igitur consideraverunt ens particulari quadam consideratione, vel inquantum est hoc ens, vel inquantum est tale ens. Et sic rebus causas agentes particulares assignaverunt. Et ulterius aliqui erexerunt se ad considerandum ens inquantum est ens, et consideraverunt causam rerum, non solum secundum quod sunt haec vel talia, sed secundum quod sunt entia.

Hoc igitur quod est causa rerum inquantum sunt entia, oportet esse causam rerum, non solum secundum

OBJECTION 1: It would seem that primary matter is not created by God. For whatever is made is composed of a subject and of something else (*Phys.* i, 62). But primary matter has no subject. Therefore primary matter cannot have been made by God.

OBJ. 2: Further, action and passion are opposite members of a division. But as the first active principle is God, so the first passive principle is matter. Therefore God and primary matter are two principles divided against each other, neither of which is from the other.

OBJ. 3: Further, every agent produces its like, and thus, since every agent acts in proportion to its actuality, it follows that everything made is in some degree actual. But primary matter is only in potentiality, formally considered in itself. Therefore it is against the nature of primary matter to be a thing made.

ON THE CONTRARY, Augustine says (*Confess.* xii, 7), *Two things hast Thou made, O Lord; one nigh unto Thyself*—viz. angels—*the other nigh unto nothing*—viz. primary matter.

I ANSWER THAT, The ancient philosophers gradually, and as it were step by step, advanced to the knowledge of truth. At first being of grosser mind, they failed to realize that any beings existed except sensible bodies. And those among them who admitted movement, did not consider it except as regards certain accidents, for instance, in relation to rarefaction and condensation, by union and separation. And supposing as they did that corporeal substance itself was uncreated, they assigned certain causes for these accidental changes, as for instance, affinity, discord, intellect, or something of that kind. An advance was made when they understood that there was a distinction between the substantial form and matter, which latter they imagined to be uncreated, and when they perceived transmutation to take place in bodies in regard to essential forms. Such transmutations they attributed to certain universal causes, such as the oblique circle, or ideas, according to Plato. But we must take into consideration that matter is contracted by its form to a determinate species, as a substance, belonging to a certain species, is contracted by a supervening accident to a determinate mode of being; for instance, man by whiteness. Each of these opinions, therefore, considered *being* under some particular aspect, either as *this* or as *such*; and so they assigned particular efficient causes to things. Then others there were who arose to the consideration of *being*, as being, and who assigned a cause to things, not as *these*, or as *such*, but as *beings*.

Therefore whatever is the cause of things considered as beings, must be the cause of things, not only according as

quod sunt talia per formas accidentales, nec secundum quod sunt haec per formas substantiales, sed etiam secundum omne illud quod pertinet ad esse illorum quocumque modo. Et sic oportet ponere etiam materiam primam creatam ab universali causa entium.

AD PRIMUM ergo dicendum quod philosophus in I Physic. loquitur de fieri particulari, quod est de forma in formam, sive accidentalem sive substantialem nunc autem loquimur de rebus secundum emanationem earum ab universali principio essendi. A qua quidem emanatione nec materia excluditur, licet a primo modo factionis excludatur.

AD SECUNDUM dicendum quod passio est effectus actionis. Unde et rationabile est quod primum principium passivum sit effectus primi principii activi, nam omne imperfectum causatur a perfecto. Oportet enim primum principium esse perfectissimum, ut dicit Aristoteles, in XII Metaphys.

AD TERTIUM dicendum quod ratio illa non ostendit quod materia non sit creata, sed quod non sit creata sine forma. Licet enim omne creatum sit in actu, non tamen est actus purus. Unde oportet quod etiam illud quod se habet ex parte potentiae, sit creatum, si totum quod ad esse ipsius pertinet, creatum est.

they are *such* by accidental forms, nor according as they are *these* by substantial forms, but also according to all that belongs to their being at all in any way. And thus it is necessary to say that also primary matter is created by the universal cause of things.

REPLY OBJ. 1: The Philosopher (*Phys.* i, 62), is speaking of *becoming* in particular—that is, from form to form, either accidental or substantial. But here we are speaking of things according to their emanation from the universal principle of being; from which emanation matter itself is not excluded, although it is excluded from the former mode of being made.

REPLY OBJ. 2: Passion is an effect of action. Hence it is reasonable that the first passive principle should be the effect of the first active principle, since every imperfect thing is caused by one perfect. For the first principle must be most perfect, as Aristotle says (*Metaph.* xii, 40).

REPLY OBJ. 3: The reason adduced does not show that matter is not created, but that it is not created without form; for though everything created is actual, still it is not pure act. Hence it is necessary that even what is potential in it should be created, if all that belongs to its being is created.

Article 3

Whether the Exemplar Cause Is Anything Besides God?

AD TERTIUM SIC PROCEDITUR. Videtur quod causa exemplaris sit aliquid praeter Deum. Exemplatum enim habet similitudinem exemplaris. Sed creaturae longe sunt a divina similitudine. Non ergo Deus est causa exemplaris earum.

PRAETEREA, omne quod est per participationem, reducitur ad aliquid per se existens, ut ignitum ad ignem, sicut iam dictum est. Sed quaecumque sunt in sensibilibus rebus, sunt solum per participationem alicuius speciei, quod ex hoc patet, quod in nullo sensibilium invenitur solum id quod ad rationem speciei pertinet, sed adiunguntur principiis speciei principia individuantia. Oportet ergo ponere ipsas species per se existentes, ut per se hominem, et per se equum, et huiusmodi. Et haec dicuntur exemplaria. Sunt igitur exemplaria res quaedam extra Deum.

PRAETEREA, scientiae et definitiones sunt de ipsis speciebus, non secundum quod sunt in particularibus, quia particularium non est scientia nec definitio. Ergo sunt quaedam entia, quae sunt entia vel species non in singularibus. Et haec dicuntur exemplaria. Ergo idem quod prius.

OBJECTION 1: It would seem that the exemplar cause is something besides God. For the effect is like its exemplar cause. But creatures are far from being like God. Therefore God is not their exemplar cause.

OBJ. 2: Further, whatever is by participation is reduced to something self-existing, as a thing ignited is reduced to fire, as stated above (A. 1). But whatever exists in sensible things exists only by participation of some species. This appears from the fact that in all sensible species is found not only what belongs to the species, but also individuating principles added to the principles of the species. Therefore it is necessary to admit self-existing species, as for instance, a per se man, and a per se horse, and the like, which are called the exemplars. Therefore exemplar causes exist besides God.

OBJ. 3: Further, sciences and definitions are concerned with species themselves, but not as these are in particular things, because there is no science or definition of particular things. Therefore there are some beings, which are beings or species not existing in singular things, and these are called exemplars. Therefore the same conclusion follows as above.

PRAETEREA, hoc idem videtur per Dionysium, qui dicit, V cap. de Div. Nom., quod *ipsum secundum se esse, prius est eo quod est per se vitam esse, et eo quod est per se sapientiam esse.*

SED CONTRA est quod exemplar est idem quod idea. Sed ideae, secundum quod Augustinus libro octoginta trium quaest. dicit, *sunt formae principales, quae divina intelligentia continentur.* Ergo exemplaria rerum non sunt extra Deum.

RESPONDEO dicendum quod Deus est prima causa exemplaris omnium rerum. Ad cuius evidentiam, considerandum est quod ad productionem alicuius rei ideo necessarium est exemplar, ut effectus determinatam formam consequatur, artifex enim producit determinatam formam in materia, propter exemplar ad quod inspicit, sive illud sit exemplar ad quod extra intuetur, sive sit exemplar interius mente conceptum. Manifestum est autem quod ea quae naturaliter fiunt, determinatas formas consequuntur. Haec autem formarum determinatio oportet quod reducatur, sicut in primum principium, in divinam sapientiam, quae ordinem universi excogitavit, qui in rerum distinctione consistit. Et ideo oportet dicere quod in divina sapientia sunt rationes omnium rerum, quas supra diximus ideas, id est formas exemplares in mente divina existentes. Quae quidem licet multiplicentur secundum respectum ad res, tamen non sunt realiter aliud a divina essentia, prout eius similitudo a diversis participari potest diversimode. Sic igitur ipse Deus est primum exemplar omnium. Possunt etiam in rebus creatis quaedam aliorum exemplaria dici, secundum quod quaedam sunt ad similitudinem aliorum, vel secundum eandem speciem, vel secundum analogiam alicuius imitationis.

AD PRIMUM ergo dicendum quod, licet creaturae non pertingant ad hoc quod sint similes Deo secundum suam naturam, similitudine speciei, ut homo genitus homini generanti; attingunt tamen ad eius similitudinem secundum repraesentationem rationis intellectae a Deo, ut domus quae est in materia, domui quae est in mente artificis.

AD SECUNDUM dicendum quod de ratione hominis est quod sit in materia, et sic non potest inveniri homo sine materia. Licet igitur hic homo sit per participationem speciei, non tamen potest reduci ad aliquid existens per se in eadem specie; sed ad speciem superexcedentem, sicut sunt substantiae separatae. Et eadem ratio est de aliis sensibilibus.

AD TERTIUM dicendum quod, licet quaelibet scientia et definitio sit solum entium, non tamen oportet quod res eundem modum habeant in essendo, quem intellectus habet in intelligendo. Nos enim, per virtutem intellectus agentis, abstrahimus species universales a particularibus conditionibus, non tamen oportet

OBJ. 4: Further, this likewise appears from Dionysius, who says (*Div. Nom.* v) that self-subsisting being is before self-subsisting life, and before self-subsisting wisdom.

ON THE CONTRARY, The exemplar is the same as the idea. But ideas, according to Augustine (QQ. 83, qu. 46), are *the master forms, which are contained in the divine intelligence.* Therefore the exemplars of things are not outside God.

I ANSWER THAT, God is the first exemplar cause of all things. In proof whereof we must consider that if for the production of anything an exemplar is necessary, it is in order that the effect may receive a determinate form. For an artificer produces a determinate form in matter by reason of the exemplar before him, whether it is the exemplar beheld externally, or the exemplar interiorly conceived in the mind. Now it is manifest that things made by nature receive determinate forms. This determination of forms must be reduced to the divine wisdom as its first principle, for divine wisdom devised the order of the universe, which order consists in the variety of things. And therefore we must say that in the divine wisdom are the types of all things, which types we have called ideas—i.e., exemplar forms existing in the divine mind (Q. 15, A. 1). And these ideas, though multiplied by their relations to things, in reality are not apart from the divine essence, according as the likeness to that essence can be shared diversely by different things. In this manner therefore God Himself is the first exemplar of all things. Moreover, in things created one may be called the exemplar of another by the reason of its likeness thereto, either in species, or by the analogy of some kind of imitation.

REPLY OBJ. 1: Although creatures do not attain to a natural likeness to God according to similitude of species, as a man begotten is like to the man begetting, still they do attain to likeness to Him, forasmuch as they represent the divine idea, as a material house is like to the house in the architect's mind.

REPLY OBJ. 2: It is of a man's nature to be in matter, and so a man without matter is impossible. Therefore although this particular man is a man by participation of the species, he cannot be reduced to anything self-existing in the same species, but to a superior species, such as separate substances. The same applies to other sensible things.

REPLY OBJ. 3: Although every science and definition is concerned only with beings, still it is not necessary that a thing should have the same mode in reality as the thought of it has in our understanding. For we abstract universal ideas by force of the active intellect from the particular conditions; but it is not necessary that the universals

quod universalia praeter particularia subsistant, ut particularium exemplaria.

AD QUARTUM dicendum quod, sicut dicit Dionysius, XI cap. de Div. Nom., per se vitam et per se sapientiam quandoque nominat ipsum Deum, quandoque virtutes ipsis rebus datas, non autem quasdam subsistentes res, sicut antiqui posuerunt.

should exist outside the particulars in order to be their exemplars.

REPLY OBJ. 4: As Dionysius says (*Div. Nom.* iv), by *self-existing life and self-existing wisdom* he sometimes denotes God Himself, sometimes the powers given to things themselves; but not any self-subsisting things, as the ancients asserted.

Article 4

Whether God Is the Final Cause of All Things?

AD QUARTUM SIC PROCEDITUR. Videtur quod Deus non sit causa finalis omnium. Agere enim propter finem videtur esse alicuius indigentis fine. Sed Deus nullo est indigens. Ergo non competit sibi agere propter finem.

PRAETEREA, finis generationis et forma generati et agens non incidunt in idem numero, ut dicitur in II Physic., quia finis generationis est forma generati. Sed Deus est primum agens omnium. Non ergo est causa finalis omnium.

PRAETEREA, finem omnia appetunt. Sed Deum non omnia appetunt, quia neque omnia ipsum cognoscunt. Deus ergo non est omnium finis.

PRAETEREA, finalis causa est prima causarum. Si igitur Deus sit causa agens et causa finalis, sequitur quod in eo sit prius et posterius. Quod est impossibile.

SED CONTRA est quod dicitur Prov. XVI, *universa propter semetipsum operatus est dominus.*

RESPONDEO dicendum quod omne agens agit propter finem, alioquin ex actione agentis non magis sequeretur hoc quam illud, nisi a casu. Est autem idem finis agentis et patientis, inquantum huiusmodi, sed aliter et aliter, unum enim et idem est quod agens intendit imprimere, et quod patiens intendit recipere. Sunt autem quaedam quae simul agunt et patiuntur, quae sunt agentia imperfecta, et his convenit quod etiam in agendo intendant aliquid acquirere. Sed primo agenti, qui est agens tantum, non convenit agere propter acquisitionem alicuius finis; sed intendit solum communicare suam perfectionem, quae est eius bonitas. Et unaquaeque creatura intendit consequi suam perfectionem, quae est similitudo perfectionis et bonitatis divinae. Sic ergo divina bonitas est finis rerum omnium.

AD PRIMUM ergo dicendum quod agere propter indigentiam non est nisi agentis imperfecti, quod natum est agere et pati. Sed hoc Deo non competit. Et ideo ipse solus est maxime liberalis, quia non agit propter suam utilitatem, sed solum propter suam bonitatem.

OBJECTION 1: It would seem that God is not the final cause of all things. For to act for an end seems to imply need of the end. But God needs nothing. Therefore it does not become Him to act for an end.

OBJ. 2: Further, the end of generation, and the form of the thing generated, and the agent cannot be identical (*Phys.* ii, 70), because the end of generation is the form of the thing generated. But God is the first agent producing all things. Therefore He is not the final cause of all things.

OBJ. 3: Further, all things desire their end. But all things do not desire God, for all do not even know Him. Therefore God is not the end of all things.

OBJ. 4: Further, the final cause is the first of causes. If, therefore, God is the efficient cause and the final cause, it follows that before and after exist in Him; which is impossible.

ON THE CONTRARY, It is said (Prov 16:4): *The Lord has made all things for Himself.*

I ANSWER THAT, Every agent acts for an end: otherwise one thing would not follow more than another from the action of the agent, unless it were by chance. Now the end of the agent and of the patient considered as such is the same, but in a different way respectively. For the impression which the agent intends to produce, and which the patient intends to receive, are one and the same. Some things, however, are both agent and patient at the same time: these are imperfect agents, and to these it belongs to intend, even while acting, the acquisition of something. But it does not belong to the First Agent, Who is agent only, to act for the acquisition of some end; He intends only to communicate His perfection, which is His goodness; while every creature intends to acquire its own perfection, which is the likeness of the divine perfection and goodness. Therefore the divine goodness is the end of all things.

REPLY OBJ. 1: To act from need belongs only to an imperfect agent, which by its nature is both agent and patient. But this does not belong to God, and therefore He alone is the most perfectly liberal giver, because He does not act for His own profit, but only for His own goodness.

AD SECUNDUM dicendum quod forma generati non est finis generationis nisi inquantum est similitudo formae generantis, quod suam similitudinem communicare intendit. Alioquin forma generati esset nobilior generante, cum finis sit nobilior his quae sunt ad finem.

AD TERTIUM dicendum quod omnia appetunt Deum ut finem, appetendo quodcumque bonum, sive appetitu intelligibili, sive sensibili, sive naturali, qui est sine cognitione, quia nihil habet rationem boni et appetibilis, nisi secundum quod participat Dei similitudinem.

AD QUARTUM dicendum quod, cum Deus sit causa efficiens, exemplaris et finalis omnium rerum, et materia prima sit ab ipso, sequitur quod primum principium omnium rerum sit unum tantum secundum rem. Nihil tamen prohibet in eo considerari multa secundum rationem, quorum quaedam prius cadunt in intellectu nostro quam alia.

REPLY OBJ. 2: The form of the thing generated is not the end of generation, except inasmuch as it is the likeness of the form of the generator, which intends to communicate its own likeness; otherwise the form of the thing generated would be more noble than the generator, since the end is more noble than the means to the end.

REPLY OBJ. 3: All things desire God as their end, when they desire some good thing, whether this desire be intellectual or sensible, or natural, i.e., without knowledge; because nothing is good and desirable except forasmuch as it participates in the likeness to God.

REPLY OBJ. 4: Since God is the efficient, the exemplar and the final cause of all things, and since primary matter is from Him, it follows that the first principle of all things is one in reality. But this does not prevent us from mentally considering many things in Him, some of which come into our mind before others.

QUESTION 45

CREATION

Deinde quaeritur de modo emanationis rerum a primo principio, qui dicitur creatio. De qua quaeruntur octo.

Primo, quid sit creatio.

Secundo, utrum Deus possit aliquid creare.

Tertio, utrum creatio sit aliquod ens in rerum natura.

Quarto, cui competit creari.

Quinto, utrum solius Dei sit creare.

Sexto, utrum commune sit toti Trinitati, aut proprium alicuius personae.

Septimo, utrum vestigium aliquod Trinitatis sit in rebus creatis.

Octavo, utrum opus creationis admisceatur in operibus naturae et voluntatis.

The next question concerns the mode of the emanation of things from the First Principle, and this is called creation, and includes eight points of inquiry:

(1) What is creation?

(2) Whether God can create anything?

(3) Whether creation is anything in the very nature of things?

(4) To what things it belongs to be created?

(5) Whether it belongs to God alone to create?

(6) Whether creation is common to the whole Trinity, or proper to any one Person?

(7) Whether any trace of the Trinity is to be found in created things?

(8) Whether the work of creation is mingled with the works of nature and of the will?

Article 1

Whether to Create Is to Make Something from Nothing?

AD PRIMUM SIC PROCEDITUR. Videtur quod creare non sit ex nihilo aliquid facere. Dicit enim Augustinus, contra adversarium legis et prophetarum, *facere est quod omnino non erat, creare vero est ex eo quod iam erat educendo aliquid constituere.*

PRAETEREA, nobilitas actionis et motus ex terminis consideratur. Nobilior igitur est actio quae ex bono in bonum est, et ex ente in ens, quam quae est ex nihilo in aliquid. Sed creatio videtur esse nobilissima actio, et prima inter omnes actiones. Ergo non est ex nihilo in aliquid, sed magis ex ente in ens.

PRAETEREA, haec praepositio ex importat habitudinem alicuius causae, et maxime materialis; sicut cum dicimus quod statua fit ex aere. Sed nihil non potest esse materia entis, nec aliquo modo causa eius. Ergo creare non est ex nihilo aliquid facere.

SED CONTRA est quod super illud Gen. I, *in principio creavit Deus caelum* etc., dicit Glossa quod *creare est aliquid ex nihilo facere.*

RESPONDEO dicendum quod, sicut supra dictum est, non solum oportet considerare emanationem alicuius entis particularis ab aliquo particulari agente, sed etiam emanationem totius entis a causa universali, quae est Deus, et hanc quidem emanationem designamus nomine creationis. Quod autem procedit secundum emanationem particularem, non praesupponitur emanationi,

OBJECTION 1: It would seem that to create is not to make anything from nothing. For Augustine says (*Contra Adv. Leg. et Proph.* i): *To make concerns what did not exist at all; but to create is to make something by bringing forth something from what was already.*

OBJ. 2: Further, the nobility of action and of motion is considered from their terms. Action is therefore nobler from good to good, and from being to being, than from nothing to something. But creation appears to be the most noble action, and first among all actions. Therefore it is not from nothing to something, but rather from being to being.

OBJ. 3: Further, the preposition *from* imports relation of some cause, and especially of the material cause; as when we say that a statue is made from brass. But *nothing* cannot be the matter of being, nor in any way its cause. Therefore to create is not to make something from nothing.

ON THE CONTRARY, On the text of Gen. 1, *In the beginning God created*, etc., the gloss has, *To create is to make something from nothing.*

I ANSWER THAT, As said above (Q. 44, A. 2), we must consider not only the emanation of a particular being from a particular agent, but also the emanation of all being from the universal cause, which is God; and this emanation we designate by the name of creation. Now what proceeds by particular emanation, is not presupposed to that emanation; as when a man is generated, he was not before,

459

sicut, si generatur homo, non fuit prius homo, sed homo fit ex non homine, et album ex non albo. Unde, si consideretur emanatio totius entis universalis a primo principio, impossibile est quod aliquod ens praesupponatur huic emanationi. Idem autem est nihil quod nullum ens. Sicut igitur generatio hominis est ex non ente quod est non homo, ita creatio, quae est emanatio totius esse, est ex non ente quod est nihil.

AD PRIMUM ergo dicendum quod Augustinus aequivoce utitur nomine creationis, secundum quod creari dicuntur ea quae in melius reformantur, ut cum dicitur aliquis creari in episcopum. Sic autem non loquimur hic de creatione, sed sicut dictum est.

AD SECUNDUM dicendum quod mutationes accipiunt speciem et dignitatem non a termino a quo, sed a termino ad quem. Tanto ergo perfectior et prior est aliqua mutatio, quanto terminus ad quem illius mutationis est nobilior et prior; licet terminus a quo, qui opponitur termino ad quem, sit imperfectior. Sicut generatio simpliciter est nobilior et prior quam alteratio, propter hoc quod forma substantialis est nobilior quam forma accidentalis, tamen privatio substantialis formae, quae est terminus a quo in generatione, est imperfectior quam contrarium, quod est terminus a quo in alteratione. Et similiter creatio est perfectior et prior quam generatio et alteratio, quia terminus ad quem est tota substantia rei. Id autem quod intelligitur ut terminus a quo, est simpliciter non ens.

AD TERTIUM dicendum quod, cum dicitur aliquid ex nihilo fieri, haec praepositio ex non designat causam materialem, sed ordinem tantum; sicut cum dicitur, ex mane fit meridies, idest, post mane fit meridies. Sed intelligendum est quod haec praepositio ex potest includere negationem importatam in hoc quod dico nihil, vel includi ab ea. Si primo modo, tunc ordo remanet affirmatus, et ostenditur ordo eius, quod est ad non esse praecedens. Si vero negatio includat praepositionem, tunc ordo negatur, et est sensus, fit ex nihilo, idest non fit ex aliquo; sicut si dicatur, iste loquitur de nihilo, quia non loquitur de aliquo. Et utroque modo verificatur, cum dicitur ex nihilo aliquid fieri. Sed primo modo, haec praepositio ex importat ordinem, ut dictum est, secundo modo, importat habitudinem causae materialis, quae negatur.

but man is made from *not-man*, and white from *not-white*. Hence if the emanation of the whole universal being from the first principle be considered, it is impossible that any being should be presupposed before this emanation. For nothing is the same as no being. Therefore as the generation of a man is from the *not-being* which is *not-man*, so creation, which is the emanation of all being, is from the *not-being* which is *nothing*.

REPLY OBJ. 1: Augustine uses the word creation in an equivocal sense, according as to be created signifies improvement in things; as when we say that a bishop is created. We do not, however, speak of creation in that way here, but as it is described above.

REPLY OBJ. 2: Changes receive species and dignity, not from the term wherefrom, but from the term whereto. Therefore a change is more perfect and excellent when the term whereto of the change is more noble and excellent, although the term wherefrom, corresponding to the term whereto, may be more imperfect: thus generation is simply nobler and more excellent than alteration, because the substantial form is nobler than the accidental form; and yet the privation of the substantial form, which is the term wherefrom in generation, is more imperfect than the contrary, which is the term wherefrom in alteration. Similarly creation is more perfect and excellent than generation and alteration, because the term whereto is the whole substance of the thing; whereas what is understood as the term wherefrom is simply not-being.

REPLY OBJ. 3: When anything is said to be made from nothing, this preposition *from* does not signify the material cause, but only order; as when we say, *from morning comes midday*—i.e., after morning is midday. But we must understand that this preposition *from* can comprise the negation implied when I say the word *nothing*, or can be included in it. If taken in the first sense, then we affirm the order by stating the relation between what is now and its previous non-existence. But if the negation includes the preposition, then the order is denied, and the sense is, *It is made from nothing*—i.e., *it is not made from anything*—as if we were to say, *He speaks of nothing*, because he does not speak of anything. And this is verified in both ways, when it is said, that anything is made from nothing. But in the first way this preposition *from* implies order, as has been said in this reply. In the second sense, it imports the material cause, which is denied.

Article 2

Whether God Can Create Anything?

AD SECUNDUM SIC PROCEDITUR. Videtur quod Deus non possit aliquid creare. Quia secundum philosophum, I Physic., antiqui philosophi acceperunt ut communem conceptionem animi, ex nihilo nihil fieri. Sed potentia Dei non se extendit ad contraria primorum principiorum; utpote quod Deus faciat quod totum non sit maius sua parte, vel quod affirmatio et negatio sint simul vera. Ergo Deus non potest aliquid ex nihilo facere, vel creare.

PRAETEREA, si creare est aliquid ex nihilo facere, ergo creari est aliquid fieri. Sed omne fieri est mutari. Ergo creatio est mutatio. Sed omnis mutatio est ex subiecto aliquo, ut patet per definitionem motus, nam motus est actus existentis in potentia. Ergo est impossibile aliquid a Deo ex nihilo fieri.

PRAETEREA, quod factum est, necesse est aliquando fieri. Sed non potest dici quod illud quod creatur, simul fiat et factum sit, quia in permanentibus, quod fit, non est, quod autem factum est, iam est; simul ergo aliquid esset et non esset. Ergo, si aliquid fit, fieri eius praecedit factum esse. Sed hoc non potest esse, nisi praeexistat subiectum in quo sustentetur ipsum fieri. Ergo impossibile est aliquid fieri ex nihilo.

PRAETEREA, infinitam distantiam non est pertransire. Sed infinita distantia est inter ens et nihil. Ergo non contingit ex nihilo aliquid fieri.

SED CONTRA est quod dicitur Gen. I, *in principio creavit Deus caelum et terram.*

RESPONDEO dicendum quod non solum non est impossibile a Deo aliquid creari, sed necesse est ponere a Deo omnia creata esse, ut ex praemissis habetur. Quicumque enim facit aliquid ex aliquo, illud ex quo facit praesupponitur actioni eius, et non producitur per ipsam actionem, sicut artifex operatur ex rebus naturalibus, ut ex ligno et aere, quae per artis actionem non causantur, sed causantur per actionem naturae. Sed et ipsa natura causat res naturales quantum ad formam, sed praesupponit materiam. Si ergo Deus non ageret nisi ex aliquo praesupposito, sequeretur quod illud praesuppositum non esset causatum ab ipso. Ostensum est autem supra quod nihil potest esse in entibus quod non sit a Deo, qui est causa universalis totius esse. Unde necesse est dicere quod Deus ex nihilo res in esse producit.

AD PRIMUM ergo dicendum quod antiqui philosophi, sicut supra dictum est, non consideraverunt nisi

OBJECTION 1: It would seem that God cannot create anything, because, according to the Philosopher (*Phys.* i, 34), the ancient philosophers considered it as a commonly received axiom that *nothing is made from nothing.* But the power of God does not extend to the contraries of first principles; as, for instance, that God could make the whole to be less than its part, or that affirmation and negation are both true at the same time. Therefore God cannot make anything from nothing, or create.

OBJ. 2: Further, if to create is to make something from nothing, to be created is to be made. But to be made is to be changed. Therefore creation is change. But every change occurs in some subject, as appears by the definition of movement: for movement is the act of what is in potentiality. Therefore it is impossible for anything to be made out of nothing by God.

OBJ. 3: Further, what has been made must have at some time been becoming. But it cannot be said that what is created, at the same time, is becoming and has been made, because in permanent things what is becoming, is not, and what has been made, already is: and so it would follow that something would be, and not be, at the same time. Therefore when anything is made, its becoming precedes its having been made. But this is impossible, unless there is a subject in which the becoming is sustained. Therefore it is impossible that anything should be made from nothing.

OBJ. 4: Further, infinite distance cannot be crossed. But infinite distance exists between being and nothing. Therefore it does not happen that something is made from nothing.

ON THE CONTRARY, It is said (Gen 1:1): *In the beginning God created heaven and earth.*

I ANSWER THAT, Not only is it not impossible that anything should be created by God, but it is necessary to say that all things were created by God, as appears from what has been said (Q. 44, A. 1). For when anyone makes one thing from another, this latter thing from which he makes is presupposed to his action, and is not produced by his action; thus the craftsman works from natural things, as wood or brass, which are caused not by the action of art, but by the action of nature. So also nature itself causes natural things as regards their form, but presupposes matter. If therefore God did only act from something presupposed, it would follow that the thing presupposed would not be caused by Him. Now it has been shown above (Q. 44, AA. 1, 2), that nothing can be, unless it is from God, Who is the universal cause of all being. Hence it is necessary to say that God brings things into being from nothing.

REPLY OBJ. 1: Ancient philosophers, as is said above (Q. 44, A. 2), considered only the emanation of particular

emanationem effectuum particularium a causis particularibus, quas necesse est praesupponere aliquid in sua actione, et secundum hoc erat eorum communis opinio, ex nihilo nihil fieri. Sed tamen hoc locum non habet in prima emanatione ab universali rerum principio.

AD SECUNDUM dicendum quod creatio non est mutatio nisi secundum modum intelligendi tantum. Nam de ratione mutationis est, quod aliquid idem se habeat aliter nunc et prius, nam quandoque est idem ens actu, aliter se habens nunc et prius, sicut in motibus secundum quantitatem et qualitatem et ubi; quandoque vero est idem ens in potentia tantum, sicut in mutatione secundum substantiam, cuius subiectum est materia. Sed in creatione, per quam producitur tota substantia rerum, non potest accipi aliquid idem aliter se habens nunc et prius, nisi secundum intellectum tantum; sicut si intelligatur aliqua res prius non fuisse totaliter, et postea esse. Sed cum actio et passio conveniant in substantia motus, et differant solum secundum habitudines diversas, ut dicitur in III Physic., oportet quod, subtracto motu, non remaneant nisi diversae habitudines in creante et creato. Sed quia modus significandi sequitur modum intelligendi, ut dictum est, creatio significatur per modum mutationis, et propter hoc dicitur quod creare est ex nihilo aliquid facere. Quamvis facere et fieri magis in hoc conveniant quam mutare et mutari, quia facere et fieri important habitudinem causae ad effectum et effectus ad causam, sed mutationem ex consequenti.

AD TERTIUM dicendum quod in his quae fiunt sine motu, simul est fieri et factum esse, sive talis factio sit terminus motus, sicut illuminatio (nam simul aliquid illuminatur et illuminatum est); sive non sit terminus motus, sicut simul formatur verbum in corde et formatum est. Et in his, quod fit, est, sed cum dicitur fieri, significatur ab alio esse, et prius non fuisse. Unde, cum creatio sit sine motu, simul aliquid creatur et creatum est.

AD QUARTUM dicendum quod obiectio illa procedit ex falsa imaginatione, ac si sit aliquod infinitum medium inter nihilum et ens, quod patet esse falsum. Procedit autem falsa haec imaginatio ex eo quod creatio significatur ut quaedam mutatio inter duos terminos existens.

effects from particular causes, which necessarily presuppose something in their action; whence came their common opinion that *nothing is made from nothing*. But this has no place in the first emanation from the universal principle of things.

REPLY OBJ. 2: Creation is not change, except according to a mode of understanding. For change means that the same something should be different now from what it was previously. Sometimes, indeed, the same actual thing is different now from what it was before, as in motion according to quantity, quality and place; but sometimes it is the same being only in potentiality, as in substantial change, the subject of which is matter. But in creation, by which the whole substance of a thing is produced, the same thing can be taken as different now and before only according to our way of understanding, so that a thing is understood as first not existing at all, and afterwards as existing. But as action and passion coincide as to the substance of motion, and differ only according to diverse relations (*Phys.* iii, 20, 21), it must follow that when motion is withdrawn, only diverse relations remain in the Creator and in the creature. But because the mode of signification follows the mode of understanding as was said above (Q. 13, A. 1), creation is signified by mode of change; and on this account it is said that to create is to make something from nothing. And yet *to make* and *to be made* are more suitable expressions here than *to change* and *to be changed*, because *to make* and *to be made* import a relation of cause to the effect, and of effect to the cause, and imply change only as a consequence.

REPLY OBJ. 3: In things which are made without movement, to become and to be already made are simultaneous, whether such making is the term of movement, as illumination (for a thing is being illuminated and is illuminated at the same time) or whether it is not the term of movement, as the word is being made in the mind and is made at the same time. In these things what is being made, is; but when we speak of its being made, we mean that it is from another, and was not previously. Hence since creation is without movement, a thing is being created and is already created at the same time.

REPLY OBJ. 4: This objection proceeds from a false imagination, as if there were an infinite medium between nothing and being; which is plainly false. This false imagination comes from creation being taken to signify a change existing between two forms.

Article 3

Whether Creation Is Anything in the Creature?

AD TERTIUM SIC PROCEDITUR. Videtur quod creatio non sit aliquid in creatura. Sicut enim creatio passive accepta attribuitur creaturae, ita creatio active accepta attribuitur creatori. Sed creatio active accepta non est aliquid in creatore, quia sic sequeretur quod in Deo esset aliquid temporale. Ergo creatio passive accepta non est aliquid in creatura.

PRAETEREA, nihil est medium inter creatorem et creaturam. Sed creatio significatur ut medium inter utrumque, non enim est creator, cum non sit aeterna; neque creatura, quia oporteret eadem ratione aliam ponere creationem qua ipsa crearetur, et sic in infinitum. Creatio ergo non est aliquid.

PRAETEREA, si creatio est aliquid praeter substantiam creatam, oportet quod sit accidens eius. Omne autem accidens est in subiecto. Ergo res creata esset subiectum creationis. Et sic idem esset subiectum creationis et terminus. Quod est impossibile, quia subiectum prius est accidente, et conservat accidens; terminus autem posterius est actione et passione cuius est terminus, et eo existente cessat actio et passio. Igitur ipsa creatio non est aliqua res.

SED CONTRA, maius est fieri aliquid secundum totam substantiam, quam secundum formam substantialem vel accidentalem. Sed generatio simpliciter vel secundum quid, qua fit aliquid secundum formam substantialem vel accidentalem, est aliquid in generato. Ergo multo magis creatio, qua fit aliquid secundum totam substantiam, est aliquid in creato.

RESPONDEO dicendum quod creatio ponit aliquid in creato secundum relationem tantum. Quia quod creatur, non fit per motum vel per mutationem. Quod enim fit per motum vel mutationem, fit ex aliquo praeexistenti, quod quidem contingit in productionibus particularibus aliquorum entium; non autem potest hoc contingere in productione totius esse a causa universali omnium entium, quae est Deus. Unde Deus, creando, producit res sine motu. Subtracto autem motu ab actione et passione, nihil remanet nisi relatio, ut dictum est. Unde relinquitur quod creatio in creatura non sit nisi relatio quaedam ad creatorem, ut ad principium sui esse; sicut in passione quae est cum motu, importatur relatio ad principium motus.

AD PRIMUM ergo dicendum quod creatio active significata significat actionem divinam, quae est eius essentia cum relatione ad creaturam. Sed relatio in Deo ad creaturam non est realis, sed secundum rationem

OBJECTION 1: It would seem that creation is not anything in the creature. For as creation taken in a passive sense is attributed to the creature, so creation taken in an active sense is attributed to the Creator. But creation taken actively is not anything in the Creator, because otherwise it would follow that in God there would be something temporal. Therefore creation taken passively is not anything in the creature.

OBJ. 2: Further, there is no medium between the Creator and the creature. But creation is signified as the medium between them both: since it is not the Creator, as it is not eternal, nor is it the creature, because in that case it would be necessary for the same reason to suppose another creation to create it, and so on to infinity. Therefore creation is not anything in the creature.

OBJ. 3: Further, if creation is anything besides the created substance, it must be an accident belonging to it. But every accident is in a subject. Therefore a thing created would be the subject of creation, and so the same thing would be the subject and also the term of creation. This is impossible, because the subject is before the accident, and preserves the accident; while the term is after the action and passion whose term it is, and as soon as it exists, action and passion cease. Therefore creation itself is not any thing.

ON THE CONTRARY, It is greater for a thing to be made according to its entire substance, than to be made according to its substantial or accidental form. But generation taken simply, or relatively, whereby anything is made according to the substantial or the accidental form, is something in the thing generated. Therefore much more is creation, whereby a thing is made according to its whole substance, something in the thing created.

I ANSWER THAT, Creation places something in the thing created according to relation only; because what is created, is not made by movement, or by change. For what is made by movement or by change is made from something pre-existing. And this happens, indeed, in the particular productions of some beings, but cannot happen in the production of all being by the universal cause of all beings, which is God. Hence God by creation produces things without movement. Now when movement is removed from action and passion, only relation remains, as was said above (A. 2, ad 2). Hence creation in the creature is only a certain relation to the Creator as to the principle of its being; even as in passion, which implies movement, is implied a relation to the principle of motion.

REPLY OBJ. 1: Creation signified actively means the divine action, which is God's essence, with a relation to the creature. But in God relation to the creature is not a real relation, but only a relation of reason; whereas the relation

tantum. Relatio vero creaturae ad Deum est relatio realis, ut supra dictum est, cum de divinis nominibus ageretur.

AD SECUNDUM dicendum quod, quia creatio significatur ut mutatio, sicut dictum est; mutatio autem media quodammodo est inter movens et motum, ideo etiam creatio significatur ut media inter creatorem et creaturam. Tamen creatio passive accepta est in creatura, et est creatura. Neque tamen oportet quod alia creatione creetur, quia relationes, cum hoc ipsum quod sunt, ad aliquid dicantur, non referuntur per aliquas alias relationes, sed per seipsas; sicut etiam supra dictum est, cum de aequalitate personarum ageretur.

AD TERTIUM dicendum quod creationis, secundum quod significatur ut mutatio, creatura est terminus, sed secundum quod vere est relatio, creatura est eius subiectum, et prius ea in esse, sicut subiectum accidente. Sed habet quandam rationem prioritatis ex parte obiecti ad quod dicitur, quod est principium creaturae. Neque tamen oportet quod, quandiu creatura sit, dicatur creari, quia creatio importat habitudinem creaturae ad creatorem cum quadam novitate seu incoeptione.

of the creature to God is a real relation, as was said above (Q. 13, A. 7) in treating of the divine names.

REPLY OBJ. 2: Because creation is signified as a change, as was said above (A. 2, ad 2), and change is a kind of medium between the mover and the moved, therefore also creation is signified as a medium between the Creator and the creature. Nevertheless passive creation is in the creature, and is a creature. Nor is there need of a further creation in its creation; because relations, or their entire nature being referred to something, are not referred by any other relations, but by themselves; as was also shown above (Q. 42, A. 1, ad 4), in treating of the equality of the Persons.

REPLY OBJ. 3: The creature is the term of creation as signifying a change, but is the subject of creation, taken as a real relation, and is prior to it in being, as the subject is to the accident. Nevertheless creation has a certain aspect of priority on the part of the object to which it is directed, which is the beginning of the creature. Nor is it necessary that as long as the creature is it should be created; because creation imports a relation of the creature to the Creator, with a certain newness or beginning.

Article 4

Whether to Be Created Belongs to Composite and Subsisting Things?

AD QUARTUM SIC PROCEDITUR. Videtur quod creari non sit proprium compositorum et subsistentium. Dicitur enim in libro de causis, *prima rerum creatarum est esse*. Sed esse rei creatae non est subsistens. Ergo creatio proprie non est subsistentis et compositi.

PRAETEREA, quod creatur est ex nihilo. Composita autem non sunt ex nihilo, sed ex suis componentibus. Ergo compositis non convenit creari.

PRAETEREA, illud proprie producitur per primam emanationem, quod supponitur in secunda, sicut res naturalis per generationem naturalem, quae supponitur in operatione artis. Sed illud quod supponitur in generatione naturali, est materia. Ergo materia est quae proprie creatur, et non compositum.

SED CONTRA est quod dicitur Gen. I, *in principio creavit Deus caelum et terram*. Caelum autem et terra sunt res compositae subsistentes. Ergo horum proprie est creatio.

RESPONDEO dicendum quod creari est quoddam fieri, ut dictum est. Fieri autem ordinatur ad esse rei. Unde illis proprie convenit fieri et creari, quibus convenit esse. Quod quidem convenit proprie subsistentibus, sive sint simplicia, sicut substantiae separatae; sive sint composita, sicut substantiae materiales. Illi enim proprie

OBJECTION 1: It would seem that to be created does not belong to composite and subsisting things. For in the book *De Causis* (prop. iv), it is said, *The first of creatures is being*. But the being of a thing created is not subsisting. Therefore creation properly speaking does not belong to subsisting and composite things.

OBJ. 2: Further, whatever is created is from nothing. But composite things are not from nothing, but are the result of their own component parts. Therefore composite things are not created.

OBJ. 3: Further, what is presupposed in the second emanation is properly produced by the first: as natural generation produces the natural thing, which is presupposed in the operation of art. But the thing supposed in natural generation is matter. Therefore matter, and not the composite, is, properly speaking, that which is created.

ON THE CONTRARY, It is said (Gen 1:1): *In the beginning God created heaven and earth*. But heaven and earth are subsisting composite things. Therefore creation belongs to them.

I ANSWER THAT, To be created is, in a manner, to be made, as was shown above (Q. 44, A. 2, ad 2, 3). Now, to be made is directed to the being of a thing. Hence to be made and to be created properly belong to whatever being belongs to; which, indeed, belongs properly to subsisting things, whether they are simple things, as in the case

convenit esse, quod habet esse; et hoc est subsistens in suo esse. Formae autem et accidentia, et alia huiusmodi, non dicuntur entia quasi ipsa sint, sed quia eis aliquid est; ut albedo ea ratione dicitur ens, quia ea subiectum est album. Unde, secundum philosophum, accidens magis proprie dicitur entis quam ens. Sicut igitur accidentia et formae, et huiusmodi, quae non subsistunt, magis sunt coexistentia quam entia; ita magis debent dici concreata quam creata. Proprie vero creata sunt subsistentia.

AD PRIMUM ergo dicendum quod, cum dicitur, prima rerum creatarum est esse, ly esse non importat subiectum creatum; sed importat propriam rationem obiecti creationis. Nam ex eo dicitur aliquid creatum, quod est ens, non ex eo quod est hoc ens, cum creatio sit emanatio totius esse ab ente universali, ut dictum est. Et est similis modus loquendi, sicut si diceretur quod primum visibile est color, quamvis illud quod proprie videtur, sit coloratum.

AD SECUNDUM dicendum quod creatio non dicit constitutionem rei compositae ex principiis praeexistentibus, sed compositum sic dicitur creari, quod simul cum omnibus suis principiis in esse producitur.

AD TERTIUM dicendum quod ratio illa non probat quod sola materia creetur; sed quod materia non sit nisi ex creatione. Nam creatio est productio totius esse, et non solum materiae.

of separate substances, or composite, as in the case of material substances. For being belongs to that which has being—that is, to what subsists in its own being. But forms and accidents and the like are called beings, not as if they themselves were, but because something is by them; as whiteness is called a being, inasmuch as its subject is white by it. Hence, according to the Philosopher (*Metaph.* vii, 2), accident is more properly said to be *of a being* than *a being*. Therefore, as accidents and forms and the like non-subsisting things are to be said to co-exist rather than to exist, so they ought to be called rather *concreated* than *created* things; whereas, properly speaking, created things are subsisting beings.

REPLY OBJ. 1: In the proposition *The first of created things is being*, the word *being* does not refer to the subject of creation, but to the proper concept of the object of creation. For a created thing is called created because it is a being, not because it is *this* being, since creation is the emanation of all being from the Universal Being, as was said above (A. 1). We use a similar way of speaking when we say that *the first visible thing is color*, although, strictly speaking, the thing colored is what is seen.

REPLY OBJ. 2: Creation does not mean the building up of a composite thing from pre-existing principles; but it means that the *composite* is created so that it is brought into being at the same time with all its principles.

REPLY OBJ. 3: This reason does not prove that matter alone is created, but that matter does not exist except by creation; for creation is the production of the whole being, and not only matter.

Article 5

Whether It Belongs to God Alone to Create?

AD QUINTUM SIC PROCEDITUR. Videtur quod non solius Dei sit creare. Quia secundum philosophum, perfectum est quod potest sibi simile facere. Sed creaturae immateriales sunt perfectiores creaturis materialibus, quae faciunt sibi simile, ignis enim generat ignem, et homo generat hominem. Ergo substantia immaterialis potest facere substantiam sibi similem. Sed substantia immaterialis non potest fieri nisi per creationem, cum non habeat materiam ex qua fiat. Ergo aliqua creatura potest creare.

PRAETEREA, quanto maior est resistentia ex parte facti, tanto maior virtus requiritur in faciente. Sed plus resistit contrarium quam nihil. Ergo maioris virtutis est aliquid facere ex contrario, quod tamen creatura facit; quam aliquid facere ex nihilo. Multo magis igitur creatura hoc facere potest.

OBJECTION 1: It would seem that it does not belong to God alone to create, because, according to the Philosopher (*De Anima* ii, 34), what is perfect can make its own likeness. But immaterial creatures are more perfect than material creatures, which nevertheless can make their own likeness, for fire generates fire, and man begets man. Therefore an immaterial substance can make a substance like to itself. But immaterial substance can be made only by creation, since it has no matter from which to be made. Therefore a creature can create.

OBJ. 2: Further, the greater the resistance is on the part of the thing made, so much the greater power is required in the maker. But a *contrary* resists more than *nothing*. Therefore it requires more power to make (something) from its contrary, which nevertheless a creature can do, than to make a thing from nothing. Much more therefore can a creature do this.

PRAETEREA, virtus facientis consideratur secundum mensuram eius quod fit. Sed ens creatum est finitum, ut supra probatum est, cum de Dei infinitate ageretur. Ergo ad producendum per creationem aliquid creatum, non requiritur nisi virtus finita. Sed habere virtutem finitam non est contra rationem creaturae. Ergo non est impossibile creaturam creare.

SED CONTRA est quod Augustinus dicit, in III de Trin., quod neque boni neque mali Angeli possunt esse creatores alicuius rei. Multo minus igitur aliae creaturae.

RESPONDEO dicendum quod satis apparet in primo aspectu, secundum praemissa, quod creare non potest esse propria actio nisi solius Dei. Oportet enim universaliores effectus in universaliores et priores causas reducere. Inter omnes autem effectus, universalissimum est ipsum esse. Unde oportet quod sit proprius effectus primae et universalissimae causae, quae est Deus. Unde etiam dicitur libro de causis, quod *neque intelligentia vel anima nobilis dat esse, nisi inquantum operatur operatione divina*. Producere autem esse absolute, non inquantum est hoc vel tale, pertinet ad rationem creationis. Unde manifestum est quod creatio est propria actio ipsius Dei.

Contingit autem quod aliquid participet actionem propriam alicuius alterius, non virtute propria, sed instrumentaliter, inquantum agit in virtute alterius; sicut aer per virtutem ignis habet calefacere et ignire. Et secundum hoc, aliqui opinati sunt quod, licet creatio sit propria actio universalis causae, tamen aliqua inferiorum causarum inquantum agit in virtute primae causae, potest creare. Et sic posuit Avicenna quod prima substantia separata, creata a Deo, creat aliam post se, et substantiam orbis, et animam eius; et quod substantia orbis creat materiam inferiorum corporum. Et secundum hunc etiam modum Magister dicit, in V dist. IV Sent., quod Deus potest creaturae communicare potentiam creandi, ut creet per ministerium, non propria auctoritate.

Sed hoc esse non potest. Quia causa secunda instrumentalis non participat actionem causae superioris, nisi inquantum per aliquid sibi proprium dispositive operatur ad effectum principalis agentis. Si igitur nihil ibi ageret secundum illud quod est sibi proprium, frustra adhiberetur ad agendum, nec oporteret esse determinata instrumenta determinatarum actionum. Sic enim videmus quod securis, scindendo lignum, quod habet ex proprietate suae formae, producit scamni formam, quae est effectus proprius principalis agentis. Illud autem quod est proprius effectus Dei creantis, est illud quod praesupponitur omnibus aliis, scilicet esse absolute. Unde non potest aliquid operari dispositive et instrumentaliter ad hunc effectum, cum creatio non sit ex aliquo praesupposito, quod possit disponi per actionem instrumentalis agentis. Sic igitur impossibile est quod alicui creaturae

OBJ. 3: Further, the power of the maker is considered according to the measure of what is made. But created being is finite, as we proved above when treating of the infinity of God (Q. 7, AA. 2, 3, 4). Therefore only a finite power is needed to produce a creature by creation. But to have a fi-⊠ nite power is not contrary to the nature of a creature. Therefore it is not impossible for a creature to create.

ON THE CONTRARY, Augustine says (*De Trin.* iii, 8) that neither good nor bad angels can create anything. Much less therefore can any other creatures.

I ANSWER THAT, It sufficiently appears at the first glance, according to what precedes (A. 1), that to create can be the action of God alone. For the more universal effects must be reduced to the more universal and prior causes. Now among all effects the most universal is being itself: and hence it must be the proper effect of the first and most universal cause, and that is God. Hence also it is said (*De Causis* prop., iii) that *neither intelligence nor the soul gives us being, except inasmuch as it works by divine operation*. Now to produce being absolutely, not as this or that being, belongs to creation. Hence it is manifest that creation is the proper act of God alone.

It happens, however, that something participates the proper action of another, not by its own power, but instrumentally, inasmuch as it acts by the power of another; as air can heat and ignite by the power of fire. And so some have supposed that although creation is the proper act of the universal cause, still some inferior cause, acting by the power of the first cause, can create. And thus Avicenna asserted that the first separate substance created by God created another after itself, and the substance of the world and its soul; and that the substance of the world creates the matter of inferior bodies. And in the same manner the Master says (*Sent.* iv, D, 5) that God can communicate to a creature the power of creating, so that the latter can create ministerially, not by its own power.

But such a thing cannot be, because the secondary instrumental cause does not participate the action of the superior cause, except inasmuch as by something proper to itself it acts dispositively to the effect of the principal agent. If therefore it effects nothing, according to what is proper to itself, it is used to no purpose; nor would there be any need of certain instruments for certain actions. Thus we see that a saw, in cutting wood, which it does by the property of its own form, produces the form of a bench, which is the proper effect of the principal agent. Now the proper effect of God creating is what is presupposed to all other effects, and that is absolute being. Hence nothing else can act dispositively and instrumentally to this effect, since creation is not from anything presupposed, which can be disposed by the action of the instrumental agent. So therefore it is

conveniat creare, neque virtute propria, neque instrumentaliter sive per ministerium.

Et hoc praecipue inconveniens est dici de aliquo corpore, quod creet, cum nullum corpus agat nisi tangendo vel movendo; et sic requirit in sua actione aliquid praeexistens, quod possit tangi et moveri; quod est contra rationem creationis.

AD PRIMUM ergo dicendum quod aliquod perfectum participans aliquam naturam, facit sibi simile, non quidem producendo absolute illam naturam, sed applicando eam ad aliquid. Non enim hic homo potest esse causa naturae humanae absolute, quia sic esset causa sui ipsius, sed est causa quod natura humana sit in hoc homine generato. Et sic praesupponit in sua actione determinatam materiam per quam est hic homo. Sed sicut hic homo participat humanam naturam, ita quodcumque ens creatum participat, ut ita dixerim, naturam essendi, quia solus Deus est suum esse, ut supra dictum est. Nullum igitur ens creatum potest producere aliquod ens absolute, nisi inquantum esse causat in hoc, et sic oportet quod praeintelligatur id per quod aliquid est hoc, actioni qua facit sibi simile. In substantia autem immateriali non potest praeintelligi aliquid per quod sit haec, quia est haec per suam formam, per quam habet esse, cum sint formae subsistentes. Igitur substantia immaterialis non potest producere aliam substantiam immaterialem sibi similem, quantum ad esse eius; sed quantum ad perfectionem aliquam superadditam; sicut si dicamus quod superior Angelus illuminat inferiorem, ut Dionysius dicit. Secundum quem modum etiam in caelestibus est paternitas, ut ex verbis apostoli patet, Ephes. III, *ex quo omnis paternitas in caelo et in terra nominatur*. Et ex hoc etiam evidenter apparet quod nullum ens creatum potest causare aliquid, nisi praesupposito aliquo. Quod repugnat rationi creationis.

AD SECUNDUM dicendum quod ex contrario fit aliquid per accidens, ut dicitur in I Physic., per se autem fit aliquid ex subiecto, quod est in potentia. Contrarium igitur resistit agenti, inquantum impedit potentiam ab actu in quem intendit reducere agens, sicut ignis intendit reducere materiam aquae in actum sibi similem, sed impeditur per formam et dispositiones contrarias, quibus quasi ligatur potentia ne reducatur in actum. Et quanto magis fuerit potentia ligata, tanto requiritur maior virtus in agente ad reducendam materiam in actum. Unde multo maior potentia requiritur in agente, si nulla potentia praeexistat. Sic ergo patet quod multo maioris virtutis est facere aliquid ex nihilo, quam ex contrario.

AD TERTIUM dicendum quod virtus facientis non solum consideratur ex substantia facti, sed etiam ex modo faciendi, maior enim calor non solum magis, sed etiam citius calefacit. Quamvis igitur creare aliquem effectum finitum non demonstret potentiam infinitam, tamen

impossible for any creature to create, either by its own power or instrumentally—that is, ministerially.

And above all it is absurd to suppose that a body can create, for no body acts except by touching or moving; and thus it requires in its action some pre-existing thing, which can be touched or moved, which is contrary to the very idea of creation.

REPLY OBJ. 1: A perfect thing participating any nature, makes a likeness to itself, not by absolutely producing that nature, but by applying it to something else. For an individual man cannot be the cause of human nature absolutely, because he would then be the cause of himself; but he is the cause of human nature being in the man begotten; and thus he presupposes in his action a determinate matter whereby he is an individual man. But as an individual man participates human nature, so every created being participates, so to speak, the nature of being; for God alone is His own being, as we have said above (Q. 7, AA. 1, 2). Therefore no created being can produce a being absolutely, except forasmuch as it causes *being* in *this*: and so it is necessary to presuppose that whereby a thing is this thing, before the action whereby it makes its own likeness. But in an immaterial substance it is not possible to presuppose anything whereby it is this thing; because it is what it is by its form, whereby it has being, since it is a subsisting form. Therefore an immaterial substance cannot produce another immaterial substance like to itself as regards its being, but only as regards some added perfection; as we may say that a superior angel illuminates an inferior, as Dionysius says (*Coel. Hier.* iv, x). In this way even in heaven there is paternity, as the Apostle says (Eph 3:15): *From whom all paternity in heaven and on earth is named.* From which evidently appears that no created being can cause anything, unless something is presupposed; which is against the very idea of creation.

REPLY OBJ. 2: A thing is made from its contrary indirectly (*Phys.* i, 43), but directly from the subject which is in potentiality. And so the contrary resists the agent, inasmuch as it impedes the potentiality from the act which the agent intends to induce, as fire intends to reduce the matter of water to an act like to itself, but is impeded by the form and contrary dispositions, whereby the potentiality (of the water) is restrained from being reduced to act; and the more the potentiality is restrained, the more power is required in the agent to reduce the matter to act. Hence a much greater power is required in the agent when no potentiality pre-exists. Thus therefore it appears that it is an act of much greater power to make a thing from nothing, than from its contrary.

REPLY OBJ. 3: The power of the maker is reckoned not only from the substance of the thing made, but also from the mode of its being made; for a greater heat heats not only more, but quicker. Therefore although to create a finite effect does not show an infinite power, yet to create it from

creare ipsum ex nihilo demonstrat potentiam infinitam. Quod ex praedictis patet. Si enim tanto maior virtus requiritur in agente, quanto potentia est magis remota ab actu, oportet quod virtus agentis ex nulla praesupposita potentia, quale agens est creans, sit infinita, quia nulla proportio est nullius potentiae ad aliquam potentiam, quam praesupponit virtus agentis naturalis, sicut et non entis ad ens. Et quia nulla creatura habet simpliciter potentiam infinitam, sicut neque esse infinitum, ut supra probatum est, relinquitur quod nulla creatura possit creare.

nothing does show an infinite power: which appears from what has been said (ad 2). For if a greater power is required in the agent in proportion to the distance of the potentiality from the act, it follows that the power of that which produces something from no presupposed potentiality is infinite, because there is no proportion between *no potentiality* and the potentiality presupposed by the power of a natural agent, as there is no proportion between *not being* and *being*. And because no creature has simply an infinite power, any more than it has an infinite being, as was proved above (Q. 7, A. 2), it follows that no creature can create.

Article 6

Whether to Create Is Proper to Any Person?

AD SEXTUM SIC PROCEDITUR. Videtur quod creare sit proprium alicuius personae. Quod enim est prius, est causa eius quod est post; et perfectum imperfecti. Sed processio divinae personae est prior quam processio creaturae, et magis perfecta, quia divina persona procedit in perfecta similitudine sui principii, creatura vero in imperfecta. Ergo processiones divinarum personarum sunt causa processionis rerum. Et sic creare est proprium personae.

PRAETEREA, personae divinae non distinguuntur ab invicem nisi per suas processiones et relationes. Quidquid igitur differenter attribuitur divinis personis, hoc convenit eis secundum processiones et relationes personarum. Sed causalitas creaturarum diversimode attribuitur divinis personis, nam in symbolo fidei patri attribuitur quod sit creator omnium visibilium et invisibilium; filio autem attribuitur quod per eum omnia facta sunt; sed spiritui sancto, quod sit dominus et vivificator. Causalitas ergo creaturarum convenit personis secundum processiones et relationes.

PRAETEREA, si dicatur quod causalitas creaturae attenditur secundum aliquod attributum essentiale quod appropriatur alicui personae, hoc non videtur sufficiens. Quia quilibet effectus divinus causatur a quolibet attributo essentiali, scilicet potentia, bonitate et sapientia, et sic non magis pertinet ad unum quam ad aliud. Non deberet ergo aliquis determinatus modus causalitatis attribui uni personae magis quam alii, nisi distinguerentur in creando secundum relationes et processiones.

SED CONTRA est quod dicit Dionysius, II cap. de Div. Nom., quod communia totius divinitatis sunt omnia causalia.

RESPONDEO dicendum quod creare est proprie causare sive producere esse rerum. Cum autem omne agens

OBJECTION 1: It would seem that to create is proper to some Person. For what comes first is the cause of what is after; and what is perfect is the cause of what is imperfect. But the procession of the divine Person is prior to the procession of the creature: and is more perfect, because the divine Person proceeds in perfect similitude of its principle; whereas the creature proceeds in imperfect similitude. Therefore the processions of the divine Persons are the cause of the processions of things, and so to create belongs to a Person.

OBJ. 2: Further, the divine Persons are distinguished from each other only by their processions and relations. Therefore whatever difference is attributed to the divine Persons belongs to them according to the processions and relations of the Persons. But the causation of creatures is diversely attributed to the divine Persons; for in the Creed, to the Father is attributed that *He is the Creator of all things visible and invisible*; to the Son is attributed that by Him *all things were made*; and to the Holy Spirit is attributed that He is *Lord and Life-giver*. Therefore the causation of creatures belongs to the Persons according to processions and relations.

OBJ. 3: Further, if it be said that the causation of the creature flows from some essential attribute appropriated to some one Person, this does not appear to be sufficient; because every divine effect is caused by every essential attribute—viz. by power, goodness and wisdom—and thus does not belong to one more than to another. Therefore any determinate mode of causation ought not to be attributed to one Person more than to another, unless they are distinguished in creating according to relations and processions.

ON THE CONTRARY, Dionysius says (*Div. Nom.* ii) that all things caused are the common work of the whole Godhead.

I ANSWER THAT, To create is, properly speaking, to cause or produce the being of things. And as every agent

agat sibi simile, principium actionis considerari potest ex actionis effectu, ignis enim est qui generat ignem. Et ideo creare convenit Deo secundum suum esse, quod est eius essentia, quae est communis tribus personis. Unde creare non est proprium alicui personae, sed commune toti Trinitati.

Sed tamen divinae personae secundum rationem suae processionis habent causalitatem respectu creationis rerum. Ut enim supra ostensum est, cum de Dei scientia et voluntate ageretur, Deus est causa rerum per suum intellectum et voluntatem, sicut artifex rerum artificiatarum. Artifex autem per verbum in intellectu conceptum, et per amorem suae voluntatis ad aliquid relatum, operatur. Unde et Deus pater operatus est creaturam per suum verbum, quod est filius; et per suum amorem, qui est Spiritus Sanctus. Et secundum hoc processiones personarum sunt rationes productionis creaturarum, inquantum includunt essentialia attributa, quae sunt scientia et voluntas.

AD PRIMUM ergo dicendum quod processiones divinarum personarum sunt causa creationis sicut dictum est.

AD SECUNDUM dicendum quod, sicut natura divina, licet sit communis tribus personis, ordine tamen quodam eis convenit, inquantum filius accipit naturam divinam a patre, et Spiritus Sanctus ab utroque; ita etiam et virtus creandi, licet sit communis tribus personis, ordine tamen quodam eis convenit; nam filius habet eam a patre, et Spiritus Sanctus ab utroque. Unde creatorem esse attribuitur patri, ut ei qui non habet virtutem creandi ab alio. De filio autem dicitur per quem omnia facta sunt, inquantum habet eandem virtutem, sed ab alio, nam haec praepositio per solet denotare causam mediam, sive principium de principio. Sed spiritui sancto, qui habet eandem virtutem ab utroque, attribuitur quod dominando gubernet, et vivificet quae sunt creata a patre per filium. Potest etiam huius attributionis communis ratio accipi ex appropriatione essentialium attributorum. Nam, sicut supra dictum est, patri appropriatur potentia, quae maxime manifestatur in creatione, et ideo attribuitur patri creatorem esse. Filio autem appropriatur sapientia, per quam agens per intellectum operatur, et ideo dicitur de filio, per quem omnia facta sunt. Spiritui sancto autem appropriatur bonitas, ad quam pertinet gubernatio deducens res in debitos fines, et vivificatio, nam vita in interiori quodam motu consistit, primum autem movens est finis et bonitas.

AD TERTIUM dicendum quod, licet quilibet effectus Dei procedat ex quolibet attributorum, tamen reducitur unusquisque effectus ad illud attributum, cum quo habet convenientiam secundum propriam rationem, sicut

produces its like, the principle of action can be considered from the effect of the action; for it must be fire that generates fire. And therefore to create belongs to God according to His being, that is, His essence, which is common to the three Persons. Hence to create is not proper to any one Person, but is common to the whole Trinity.

Nevertheless the divine Persons, according to the nature of their procession, have a causality respecting the creation of things. For as was said above (Q. 14, A. 8; Q. 19, A. 4), when treating of the knowledge and will of God, God is the cause of things by His intellect and will, just as the craftsman is the cause of the things made by his craft. Now the craftsman works through the word conceived in his mind, and through the love of his will regarding some object. Hence also God the Father made the creature through His Word, which is His Son; and through His Love, which is the Holy Spirit. And so the processions of the Persons are the type of the productions of creatures inasmuch as they include the essential attributes, knowledge and will.

REPLY OBJ. 1: The processions of the divine Persons are the cause of creation, as above explained.

REPLY OBJ. 2: As the divine nature, although common to the three Persons, still belongs to them in a kind of order, inasmuch as the Son receives the divine nature from the Father, and the Holy Spirit from both: so also likewise the power of creation, whilst common to the three Persons, belongs to them in a kind of order. For the Son receives it from the Father, and the Holy Spirit from both. Hence to be the Creator is attributed to the Father as to Him Who does not receive the power of creation from another. And of the Son it is said (John 1:3), *Through Him all things were made*, inasmuch as He has the same power, but from another; for this preposition *through* usually denotes a mediate cause, or *a principle from a principle*. But to the Holy Spirit, Who has the same power from both, is attributed that by His sway He governs, and quickens what is created by the Father through the Son. Again, the reason for this particular appropriation may be taken from the common notion of the appropriation of the essential attributes. For, as above stated (Q. 39, A. 8, ad 3), to the Father is appropriated power which is chiefly shown in creation, and therefore it is attributed to Him to be the Creator. To the Son is appropriated wisdom, through which the intellectual agent acts; and therefore it is said: *Through Whom all things were made*. And to the Holy Spirit is appropriated goodness, to which belong both government, which brings things to their proper end, and the giving of life—for life consists in a certain interior movement; and the first mover is the end, and goodness.

REPLY OBJ. 3: Although every effect of God proceeds from each attribute, each effect is reduced to that attribute with which it is naturally connected; thus the order of things is reduced to *wisdom*, and the justification of the

ordinatio rerum ad sapientiam, et iustificatio impii ad misericordiam et bonitatem se superabundanter diffundentem. Creatio vero, quae est productio ipsius substantiae rei, reducitur ad potentiam.

sinner to *mercy* and *goodness* poured out super-abundantly. But creation, which is the production of the very substance of a thing, is reduced to *power*.

Article 7

Whether in Creatures Is Necessarily Found a Trace of the Trinity?

AD SEPTIMUM SIC PROCEDITUR. Videtur quod in creaturis non sit necesse inveniri vestigium Trinitatis. Per sua enim vestigia unumquodque investigari potest. Sed Trinitas personarum non potest investigari ex creaturis, ut supra habitum est. Ergo vestigia Trinitatis non sunt in creatura.

PRAETEREA, quidquid in creatura est, creatum est. Si igitur vestigium Trinitatis invenitur in creatura secundum aliquas proprietates suas, et omne creatum habet vestigium Trinitatis, oportet in unaquaque illarum inveniri etiam vestigium Trinitatis, et sic in infinitum.

PRAETEREA, effectus non repraesentat nisi suam causam. Sed causalitas creaturarum pertinet ad naturam communem, non autem ad relationes, quibus personae distinguuntur et numerantur. Ergo in creatura non invenitur vestigium Trinitatis, sed solum unitatis essentiae.

SED CONTRA est quod Augustinus dicit, VI de Trin., quod *Trinitatis vestigium in creatura apparet.*

RESPONDEO dicendum quod omnis effectus aliqualiter repraesentat suam causam, sed diversimode. Nam aliquis effectus repraesentat solam causalitatem causae, non autem formam eius, sicut fumus repraesentat ignem, et talis repraesentatio dicitur esse repraesentatio vestigii; vestigium enim demonstrat motum alicuius transeuntis, sed non qualis sit. Aliquis autem effectus repraesentat causam quantum ad similitudinem formae eius, sicut ignis generatus ignem generantem, et statua Mercurii Mercurium, et haec est repraesentatio imaginis. Processiones autem divinarum personarum attenduntur secundum actus intellectus et voluntatis, sicut supra dictum est, nam filius procedit ut verbum intellectus, Spiritus Sanctus ut amor voluntatis. In creaturis igitur rationalibus, in quibus est intellectus et voluntas, invenitur repraesentatio Trinitatis per modum imaginis, inquantum invenitur in eis verbum conceptum et amor procedens.

Sed in creaturis omnibus invenitur repraesentatio Trinitatis per modum vestigii, inquantum in qualibet creatura inveniuntur aliqua quae necesse est reducere in divinas personas sicut in causam. Quaelibet enim creatura subsistit in suo esse, et habet formam per quam determinatur ad speciem, et habet ordinem ad aliquid

OBJECTION 1: It would seem that in creatures there is not necessarily found a trace of the Trinity. For anything can be traced through its traces. But the trinity of persons cannot be traced from the creatures, as was above stated (Q. 32, A. 1). Therefore there is no trace of the Trinity in creatures.

OBJ. 2: Further, whatever is in creatures is created. Therefore if the trace of the Trinity is found in creatures according to some of their properties, and if everything created has a trace of the Trinity, it follows that we can find a trace of the Trinity in each of these (properties): and so on to infinitude.

OBJ. 3: Further, the effect represents only its own cause. But the causality of creatures belongs to the common nature, and not to the relations whereby the Persons are distinguished and numbered. Therefore in the creature is to be found a trace not of the Trinity but of the unity of essence.

ON THE CONTRARY, Augustine says (*De Trin.* vi, 10), that *the trace of the Trinity appears in creatures.*

I ANSWER THAT, Every effect in some degree represents its cause, but diversely. For some effects represent only the causality of the cause, but not its form; as smoke represents fire. Such a representation is called a *trace*: for a trace shows that someone has passed by but not who it is. Other effects represent the cause as regards the similitude of its form, as fire generated represents fire generating; and a statue of Mercury represents Mercury; and this is called the representation of *image*. Now the processions of the divine Persons are referred to the acts of intellect and will, as was said above (Q. 27). For the Son proceeds as the word of the intellect; and the Holy Spirit proceeds as love of the will. Therefore in rational creatures, possessing intellect and will, there is found the representation of the Trinity by way of image, inasmuch as there is found in them the word conceived, and the love proceeding.

But in all creatures there is found the trace of the Trinity, inasmuch as in every creature are found some things which are necessarily reduced to the divine Persons as to their cause. For every creature subsists in its own being, and has a form, whereby it is determined to a species, and has relation to something else. Therefore as it is a created

aliud. Secundum igitur quod est quaedam substantia creata, repraesentat causam et principium, et sic demonstrat personam patris, qui est principium non de principio. Secundum autem quod habet quandam formam et speciem, repraesentat verbum; secundum quod forma artificiati est ex conceptione artificis. Secundum autem quod habet ordinem, repraesentat spiritum sanctum, inquantum est amor, quia ordo effectus ad aliquid alterum est ex voluntate creantis. Et ideo dicit Augustinus, in VI Lib. de Trin., quod vestigium Trinitatis invenitur in unaquaque creatura, secundum quod unum aliquid est, et secundum quod aliqua specie formatur, et secundum quod quendam ordinem tenet. Et ad haec etiam reducuntur illa tria, numerus, pondus et mensura, quae ponuntur Sap. XI, nam mensura refertur ad substantiam rei limitatam suis principiis, numerus ad speciem, pondus ad ordinem. Et ad haec etiam reducuntur alia tria quae ponit Augustinus, modus species et ordo. Et ea quae ponit in libro octoginta trium quaest. quod constat, quod discernitur, quod congruit, constat enim aliquid per suam substantiam, discernitur per formam, congruit per ordinem. Et in idem de facili reduci possunt quaecumque sic dicuntur.

AD PRIMUM ergo dicendum quod repraesentatio vestigii attenditur secundum appropriata, per quem modum ex creaturis in Trinitatem divinarum personarum veniri potest, ut dictum est.

AD SECUNDUM dicendum quod creatura est res proprie subsistens, in qua est praedicta tria invenire. Neque oportet quod in quolibet eorum quae ei insunt, haec tria inveniantur, sed secundum ea vestigium rei subsistenti attribuitur.

AD TERTIUM dicendum quod etiam processiones personarum sunt causa et ratio creationis aliquo modo, ut dictum est.

substance, it represents the cause and principle; and so in that manner it shows the Person of the Father, Who is the *principle from no principle*. According as it has a form and species, it represents the Word as the form of the thing made by art is from the conception of the craftsman. According as it has relation of order, it represents the Holy Spirit, inasmuch as He is love, because the order of the effect to something else is from the will of the Creator. And therefore Augustine says (*De Trin.* vi 10) that the trace of the Trinity is found in every creature, according *as it is one individual*, and according *as it is formed by a species*, and according as it *has a certain relation of order*. And to these also are reduced those three, *number, weight,* and *measure,* mentioned in the Book of Wisdom (9:21). For *measure* refers to the substance of the thing limited by its principles, *number* refers to the species, *weight* refers to the order. And to these three are reduced the other three mentioned by Augustine (*De Nat. Boni* iii), *mode,* species, and *order,* and also those he mentions (QQ. 83, qu. 18): *that which exists; whereby it is distinguished; whereby it agrees.* For a thing exists by its substance, is distinct by its form, and agrees by its order. Other similar expressions may be easily reduced to the above.

REPLY OBJ. 1: The representation of the trace is to be referred to the appropriations: in which manner we are able to arrive at a knowledge of the trinity of the divine persons from creatures, as we have said (Q. 32, A. 1).

REPLY OBJ. 2: A creature properly speaking is a thing self-subsisting; and in such are the three above-mentioned things to be found. Nor is it necessary that these three things should be found in all that exists in the creature; but only to a subsisting being is the trace ascribed in regard to those three things.

REPLY OBJ. 3: The processions of the persons are also in some way the cause and type of creation; as appears from the above (A. 6).

Article 8

Whether Creation Is Mingled with Works of Nature and Art?

AD OCTAVUM SIC PROCEDITUR. Videtur quod creatio admisceatur in operibus naturae et artis. In qualibet enim operatione naturae et artis producitur aliqua forma. Sed non producitur ex aliquo, cum non habeat materiam partem sui. Ergo producitur ex nihilo. Et sic in qualibet operatione naturae et artis est creatio.

PRAETEREA, effectus non est potior sua causa. Sed in rebus naturalibus non invenitur aliquid agens nisi forma accidentalis, quae est forma activa vel passiva. Non ergo per operationem naturae producitur forma substantialis. Relinquitur igitur quod sit per creationem.

OBJECTION 1: It would seem that creation is mingled in works of nature and art. For in every operation of nature and art some form is produced. But it is not produced from anything, since matter has no part in it. Therefore it is produced from nothing; and thus in every operation of nature and art there is creation.

OBJ. 2: Further, the effect is not more powerful than its cause. But in natural things the only agent is the accidental form, which is an active or a passive form. Therefore the substantial form is not produced by the operation of nature; and therefore it must be produced by creation.

PRAETEREA, natura facit sibi simile. Sed quaedam inveniuntur generata in natura non ab aliquo sibi simili, sicut patet in animalibus generatis per putrefactionem. Ergo eorum forma non est a natura, sed a creatione. Et eadem ratio est de aliis.

PRAETEREA, quod non creatur, non est creatura. Si igitur in his quae sunt a natura non adiungatur creatio, sequitur quod ea quae sunt a natura, non sunt creaturae. Quod est haereticum.

SED CONTRA est quod Augustinus, super Gen. ad Lit., distinguit opus propagationis, quod est opus naturae, ab opere creationis.

RESPONDEO dicendum quod haec dubitatio inducitur propter formas. Quas quidam posuerunt non incipere per actionem naturae, sed prius in materia extitisse, ponentes latitationem formarum. Et hoc accidit eis ex ignorantia materiae, quia nesciebant distinguere inter potentiam et actum, quia enim formae praeexistunt in materia in potentia, posuerunt eas simpliciter praeexistere. Alii vero posuerunt formas dari vel causari ab agente separato, per modum creationis. Et secundum hoc cuilibet operationi naturae adiungitur creatio. Sed hoc accidit eis ex ignorantia formae. Non enim considerabant quod forma naturalis corporis non est subsistens, sed quo aliquid est, et ideo, cum fieri et creari non conveniat proprie nisi rei subsistenti, sicut supra dictum est, formarum non est fieri neque creari, sed concreata esse. Quod autem proprie fit ab agente naturali, est compositum, quod fit ex materia.

Unde in operibus naturae non admiscetur creatio, sed praesupponitur ad operationem naturae.

AD PRIMUM ergo dicendum quod formae incipiunt esse in actu, compositis factis, non quod ipsae fiant per se, sed per accidens tantum.

AD SECUNDUM dicendum quod qualitates activae in natura agunt in virtute formarum substantialium. Et ideo agens naturale non solum producit sibi simile secundum qualitatem, sed secundum speciem.

AD TERTIUM dicendum quod ad generationem animalium imperfectorum sufficit agens universale, quod est virtus caelestis, cui assimilantur non secundum speciem, sed secundum analogiam quandam, neque oportet dicere quod eorum formae creantur ab agente separato. Ad generationem vero animalium perfectorum non sufficit agens universale, sed requiritur agens proprium, quod est generans univocum.

AD QUARTUM dicendum quod operatio naturae non est nisi ex praesuppositione principiorum creatorum, et sic ea quae per naturam fiunt, creaturae dicuntur.

OBJ. 3: Further, in nature like begets like. But some things are found generated in nature by a thing unlike to them; as is evident in animals generated through putrefaction. Therefore the form of these is not from nature, but by creation; and the same reason applies to other things.

OBJ. 4: Further, what is not created, is not a creature. If therefore in nature's productions there were not creation, it would follow that nature's productions are not creatures; which is heretical.

ON THE CONTRARY, Augustine (*Super Gen.* v, 6,14,15) distinguishes the work of propagation, which is a work of nature, from the work of creation.

I ANSWER THAT, The doubt on this subject arises from the forms which, some said, do not come into existence by the action of nature, but previously exist in matter; for they asserted that forms are latent. This arose from ignorance concerning matter, and from not knowing how to distinguish between potentiality and act. For because forms pre-exist in matter, *in potentiality*, they asserted that they pre-exist *simply*. Others, however, said that the forms were given or caused by a separate agent by way of creation; and accordingly, that to each operation of nature is joined creation. But this opinion arose from ignorance concerning form. For they failed to consider that the form of the natural body is not subsisting, but is that by which a thing is. And therefore, since to be made and to be created belong properly to a subsisting thing alone, as shown above (A. 4), it does not belong to forms to be made or to be created, but to be *concreated*. What, indeed, is properly made by the natural agent is the *composite*, which is made from matter.

Hence in the works of nature creation does not enter, but is presupposed to the work of nature.

REPLY OBJ. 1: Forms begin to be actual when the composite things are made, not as though they were made *directly*, but only *indirectly*.

REPLY OBJ. 2: The active qualities in nature act by virtue of substantial forms: and therefore the natural agent not only produces its like according to quality, but according to species.

REPLY OBJ. 3: For the generation of imperfect animals, a universal agent suffices, and this is to be found in the celestial power to which they are assimilated, not in species, but according to a kind of analogy. Nor is it necessary to say that their forms are created by a separate agent. However, for the generation of perfect animals the universal agent does not suffice, but a proper agent is required, in the shape of a univocal generator.

REPLY OBJ. 4: The operation of nature takes place only on the presupposition of created principles; and thus the products of nature are called creatures.

QUESTION 46

THE BEGINNING OF THE DURATION OF CREATURES

Consequenter considerandum est de principio durationis rerum creatarum. Et circa hoc quaeruntur tria.

Primo, utrum creaturae semper fuerint.

Secundo, utrum eas incoepisse sit articulus fidei.

Tertio, quomodo Deus dicatur in principio caelum et terram creasse.

Next must be considered the beginning of the duration of creatures, about which there are three points for treatment:

(1) Whether creatures always existed?
(2) Whether that they began to exist is an article of Faith?
(3) How God is said to have created heaven and earth in the beginning?

Article 1

Whether the Universe of Creatures Always Existed?

Ad primum sic proceditur. Videtur quod universitas creaturarum, quae mundi nomine nuncupatur, non incoeperit, sed fuerit ab aeterno. Omne enim quod incoepit esse, antequam fuerit, possibile fuit ipsum esse, alioquin impossibile fuisset ipsum fieri. Si ergo mundus incoepit esse, antequam inciperet, possibile fuit ipsum esse. Sed quod possibile est esse, est materia, quae est in potentia ad esse, quod est per formam, et ad non esse, quod est per privationem. Si ergo mundus incoepit esse, ante mundum fuit materia. Sed non potest esse materia sine forma, materia autem mundi cum forma, est mundus. Fuit ergo mundus antequam esse inciperet, quod est impossibile.

Praeterea, nihil quod habet virtutem ut sit semper, quandoque est et quandoque non est, quia ad quantum se extendit virtus alicuius rei, tandiu est. Sed omne incorruptibile habet virtutem ut sit semper, non enim virtutem habet ad determinatum durationis tempus. Nullum ergo incorruptibile quandoque est et quandoque non est. Sed omne quod incipit esse, quandoque est et quandoque non est. Nullum ergo incorruptibile incipit esse. Sed multa sunt in mundo incorruptibilia, ut corpora caelestia, et omnes substantiae intellectuales. Ergo mundus non incoepit esse.

Praeterea, nullum ingenitum incoepit esse. Sed philosophus probat in I Physic., quod materia est ingenita; et in I de caelo et mundo, quod caelum est ingenitum. Non ergo universitas rerum incoepit esse.

Praeterea, vacuum est ubi non est corpus, sed possibile est esse. Sed si mundus incoepit esse, ubi nunc est corpus mundi, prius non fuit aliquod corpus, et

Objection 1: It would seem that the universe of creatures, called the world, had no beginning, but existed from eternity. For everything which begins to exist, is a possible being before it exists: otherwise it would be impossible for it to exist. If therefore the world began to exist, it was a possible being before it began to exist. But possible being is matter, which is in potentiality to existence, which results from a form, and to non-existence, which results from privation of form. If therefore the world began to exist, matter must have existed before the world. But matter cannot exist without form: while the matter of the world with its form is the world. Therefore the world existed before it began to exist: which is impossible.

Obj. 2: Further, nothing which has power to be always, sometimes is and sometimes is not; because so far as the power of a thing extends so long it exists. But every incorruptible thing has power to be always; for its power does not extend to any determinate time. Therefore no incorruptible thing sometimes is, and sometimes is not: but everything which has a beginning at some time is, and at some time is not; therefore no incorruptible thing begins to exist. But there are many incorruptible things in the world, as the celestial bodies and all intellectual substances. Therefore the world did not begin to exist.

Obj. 3: Further, what is unbegotten has no beginning. But the Philosopher (*Phys.* i, 82) proves that matter is unbegotten, and also (*De Coelo et Mundo* i, 20) that the heaven is unbegotten. Therefore the universe did not begin to exist.

Obj. 4: Further, a vacuum is where there is not a body, but there might be. But if the world began to exist, there was first no body where the body of the world now is; and

tamen poterat ibi esse, alioquin nunc ibi non esset. Ergo ante mundum fuit vacuum, quod est impossibile.

Praeterea, nihil de novo incipit moveri, nisi per hoc quod movens vel mobile aliter se habet nunc quam prius. Sed quod aliter se habet nunc quam prius, movetur. Ergo ante omnem motum de novo incipientem, fuit aliquis motus. Motus ergo semper fuit. Ergo et mobile, quia motus non est nisi in mobili.

Praeterea, omne movens aut est naturale, aut est voluntarium. Sed neutrum incipit movere, nisi aliquo motu praeexistente. Natura enim semper eodem modo operatur. Unde, nisi praecedat aliqua immutatio vel in natura moventis vel in mobili, non incipiet a movente naturali esse motus, qui non fuit prius. Voluntas autem absque sui immutatione retardat facere quod proponit, sed hoc non est nisi per aliquam immutationem quam imaginatur, ad minus ex parte ipsius temporis. Sicut qui vult facere domum cras, et non hodie, expectat aliquid futurum cras, quod hodie non est; et ad minus expectat quod dies hodiernus transeat, et crastinus adveniat; quod sine mutatione non est, quia tempus est numerus motus. Relinquitur ergo quod ante omnem motum de novo incipientem, fuit alius motus. Et sic idem quod prius.

Praeterea, quidquid est semper in principio et semper in fine, nec incipere nec desinere potest, quia quod incipit, non est in suo fine; quod autem desinit, non est in suo principio. Sed tempus semper est in suo principio et fine, quia nihil est temporis nisi nunc, quod est finis praeteriti, et principium futuri. Ergo tempus nec incipere nec desinere potest. Et per consequens nec motus, cuius numerus tempus est.

Praeterea, Deus aut est prior mundo natura tantum, aut duratione. Si natura tantum, ergo, cum Deus sit ab aeterno, et mundus est ab aeterno. Si autem est prior duratione; prius autem et posterius in duratione constituunt tempus, ergo ante mundum fuit tempus; quod est impossibile.

Praeterea, posita causa sufficienti, ponitur effectus, causa enim ad quam non sequitur effectus, est causa imperfecta, indigens alio ad hoc quod effectus sequatur. Sed Deus est sufficiens causa mundi; et finalis, ratione suae bonitatis; et exemplaris, ratione suae sapientiae; et effectiva, ratione suae potentiae; ut ex superioribus patet. Cum ergo Deus sit ab aeterno, et mundus fuit ab aeterno.

Praeterea, cuius actio est aeterna, et effectus aeternus. Sed actio Dei est eius substantia, quae est aeterna. Ergo et mundus est aeternus.

Sed contra est quod dicitur Ioan. XVII, *clarifica me, pater, apud temetipsum, claritate quam habui priusquam mundus fieret*; et Proverb. VIII, *dominus possedit*

yet it could be there, otherwise it would not be there now. Therefore before the world there was a vacuum; which is impossible.

Obj. 5: Further, nothing begins anew to be moved except through either the mover or the thing moved being otherwise than it was before. But what is otherwise now than it was before, is moved. Therefore before every new movement there was a previous movement. Therefore movement always was; and therefore also the thing moved always was, because movement is only in a movable thing.

Obj. 6: Further, every mover is either natural or voluntary. But neither begins to move except by some pre-existing movement. For nature always moves in the same manner: hence unless some change precede either in the nature of the mover, or in the movable thing, there cannot arise from the natural mover a movement which was not there before. And the will, without itself being changed, puts off doing what it proposes to do; but this can be only by some imagined change, at least on the part of time. Thus he who wills to make a house tomorrow, and not today, awaits something which will be tomorrow, but is not today; and at least awaits for today to pass, and for tomorrow to come; and this cannot be without change, because time is the measure of movement. Therefore it remains that before every new movement, there was a previous movement; and so the same conclusion follows as before.

Obj. 7: Further, whatever is always in its beginning, and always in its end, cannot cease and cannot begin; because what begins is not in its end, and what ceases is not in its beginning. But time always is in its beginning and end, because there is no time except *now* which is the end of the past and the beginning of the future. Therefore time cannot begin or end, and consequently neither can movement, the measure of what is time.

Obj. 8: Further, God is before the world either in the order of nature only, or also by duration. If in the order of nature only, therefore, since God is eternal, the world also is eternal. But if God is prior by duration, since what is prior and posterior in duration constitutes time, it follows that time existed before the world, which is impossible.

Obj. 9: Further, if there is a sufficient cause, there is an effect; for a cause to which there is no effect is an imperfect cause, requiring something else to make the effect follow. But God is the sufficient cause of the world; being the final cause, by reason of His goodness, the exemplar cause by reason of His wisdom, and the efficient cause, by reason of His power, as appears from the above (Q. 44, AA. 2, 3, 4). Since therefore God is eternal, the world is also eternal.

Obj. 10: Further, eternal action postulates an eternal effect. But the action of God is His substance, which is eternal. Therefore the world is eternal.

On the contrary, It is said (John 17:5), *Glorify Me, O Father, with Thyself with the glory which I had before the world was*; and (Prov 8:22), *The Lord possessed Me in*

me in initio viarum suarum, antequam quidquam face-ret a principio.

RESPONDEO dicendum nihil praeter Deum ab ae-terno fuisse. Et hoc quidem ponere non est impossibile. Ostensum est enim supra quod voluntas Dei est causa rerum. Sic ergo aliqua necesse est esse, sicut necesse est Deum velle illa, cum necessitas effectus ex necessita-te causae dependeat, ut dicitur in V Metaphys. Osten-sum est autem supra quod, absolute loquendo, non est necesse Deum velle aliquid nisi seipsum. Non est ergo necessarium Deum velle quod mundus fuerit semper. Sed eatenus mundus est, quatenus Deus vult illum esse, cum esse mundi ex voluntate Dei dependeat sicut ex sua causa. Non est igitur necessarium mundum semper esse. Unde nec demonstrative probari potest.

Nec rationes quas ad hoc Aristoteles inducit, sunt demonstrativae simpliciter, sed secundum quid, scilicet ad contradicendum rationibus antiquorum, ponentium mundum incipere secundum quosdam modos in verita-te impossibiles. Et hoc apparet ex tribus. Primo quidem, quia tam in VIII Physic. quam in I de caelo, praemit-tit quasdam opiniones, ut Anaxagorae et Empedoclis et Platonis, contra quos rationes contradictorias inducit. Secundo, quia, ubicumque de hac materia loquitur, in-ducit testimonia antiquorum, quod non est demonstra-toris, sed probabiliter persuadentis. Tertio, quia expresse dicit in I Lib. Topic., quod quaedam sunt problemata dialectica, de quibus rationes non habemus, ut utrum mundus sit aeternus.

AD PRIMUM ergo dicendum quod, antequam mun-dus esset, possibile fuit mundum esse, non quidem se-cundum potentiam passivam, quae est materia; sed secundum potentiam activam Dei. Et etiam secundum quod dicitur aliquid absolute possibile, non secundum aliquam potentiam sed ex sola habitudine terminorum, qui sibi non repugnant; secundum quod possibile oppo-nitur impossibili, ut patet per philosophum, in V Meta-phys.

AD SECUNDUM dicendum quod illud quod habet virtutem ut sit semper ex quo habet illam virtutem, non quandoque est et quandoque non est, sed antequam ha-beret illam virtutem, non fuit.

Unde haec ratio, quae ponitur ab Aristotele in I de caelo, non concludit simpliciter quod incorruptibilia non incoeperunt esse, sed quod non incoeperunt esse per modum naturalem, quo generabilia et corruptibilia incipiunt esse.

AD TERTIUM dicendum quod Aristoteles, in I Phy-sic., probat materiam esse ingenitam, per hoc quod non habet subiectum de quo sit. In I autem de caelo et mundo, probat caelum ingenitum, quia non habet con-trarium ex quo generetur. Unde patet quod per utrum-que non concluditur nisi quod materia et caelum non

the beginning of His ways, before He made anything from the beginning.

I ANSWER THAT, Nothing except God can be eternal. And this statement is far from impossible to uphold: for it has been shown above (Q. 19, A. 4) that the will of God is the cause of things. Therefore things are necessary, ac-cording as it is necessary for God to will them, since the necessity of the effect depends on the necessity of the cause (*Metaph.* v, 6). Now it was shown above (Q. 19, A. 3), that, absolutely speaking, it is not necessary that God should will anything except Himself. It is not therefore necessary for God to will that the world should always exist; but the world exists forasmuch as God wills it to exist, since the be-ing of the world depends on the will of God, as on its cause. It is not therefore necessary for the world to be always; and hence it cannot be proved by demonstration.

Nor are Aristotle's reasons (*Phys.* viii) simply, but rela-tively, demonstrative—viz. in order to contradict the rea-sons of some of the ancients who asserted that the world began to exist in some quite impossible manner. This ap-pears in three ways. First, because, both in *Phys.* viii and in *De Coelo* i, text 101, he premises some opinions, as those of Anaxagoras, Empedocles and Plato, and brings forward reasons to refute them. Second, because wherever he speaks of this subject, he quotes the testimony of the an-cients, which is not the way of a demonstrator, but of one persuading of what is probable. Third, because he expressly says (*Topic.* i, 9), that there are dialectical problems, about which we have nothing to say from reason, as, *whether the world is eternal.*

REPLY OBJ. 1: Before the world existed it was possi-ble for the world to be, not, indeed, according to a passive power which is matter, but according to the active power of God; and also, according as a thing is called absolutely pos-sible, not in relation to any power, but from the sole habi-tude of the terms which are not repugnant to each other; in which sense possible is opposed to impossible, as appears from the Philosopher (*Metaph.* v, 17).

REPLY OBJ. 2: Whatever has power always to be, from the fact of having that power, cannot sometimes be and sometimes not be; but before it received that power, it did not exist.

Hence this reason which is given by Aristotle (*De Coelo* i, 120) does not prove simply that incorruptible things never began to exist; but that they did not begin by the natural mode whereby things generated and corrupt-ible begin.

REPLY OBJ. 3: Aristotle (*Phys.* i, 82) proves that matter is unbegotten from the fact that it has not a subject from which to derive its existence; and (*De Coelo et Mundo* i, 20) he proves that heaven is ungenerated, forasmuch as it has no contrary from which to be generated. Hence it appears that no conclusion follows either way, except that matter

incoeperunt per generationem, ut quidam ponebant, praecipue de caelo. Nos autem dicimus quod materia et coelum producta sunt in esse per creationem, ut ex dictis patet.

AD QUARTUM dicendum quod ad rationem vacui non sufficit in quo nihil est, sed requiritur quod sit spatium capax corporis, in quo non sit corpus, ut patet per Aristotelem, in IV Physic. Nos autem dicimus non fuisse locum aut spatium ante mundum.

AD QUINTUM dicendum quod primus motor semper eodem modo se habuit primum autem mobile non semper eodem modo se habuit, quia incoepit esse, cum prius non fuisset. Sed hoc non fuit per mutationem, sed per creationem, quae non est mutatio, ut supra dictum est. Unde patet quod haec ratio, quam ponit Aristoteles in VIII Physic., procedit contra eos qui ponebant mobilia aeterna, sed motum non aeternum; ut patet ex opinionibus Anaxagorae et Empedoclis. Nos autem ponimus, ex quo mobilia incoeperunt, semper fuisse motum.

AD SEXTUM dicendum quod primum agens est agens voluntarium. Et quamvis habuit voluntatem aeternam producendi aliquem effectum, non tamen produxit aeternum effectum. Nec est necesse quod praesupponatur aliqua mutatio, nec etiam propter imaginationem temporis. Aliter enim est intelligendum de agente particulari, quod praesupponit aliquid, et causat alterum, et aliter de agente universali, quod producit totum. Sicut agens particulare producit formam, et praesupponit materiam, unde oportet quod formam inducat secundum proportionem ad debitam materiam. Unde rationabiliter in ipso consideratur quod inducit formam in talem materiam et non in aliam, ex differentia materiae ad materiam. Sed hoc non rationabiliter consideratur in Deo, qui simul producit formam et materiam, sed consideratur rationabiliter in eo, quod ipse producit materiam congruam formae et fini. Agens autem particulare praesupponit tempus, sicut et materiam. Unde rationabiliter consideratur in eo, quod agit in tempore posteriori et non in priori, secundum imaginationem successionis temporis post tempus. Sed in agente universali, quod producit rem et tempus, non est considerare quod agat nunc et non prius, secundum imaginationem temporis post tempus, quasi tempus praesupponatur eius actioni, sed considerandum est in eo, quod dedit effectui suo tempus quantum voluit, et secundum quod conveniens fuit ad suam potentiam demonstrandam. Manifestius enim mundus ducit in cognitionem divinae potentiae creantis, si mundus non semper fuit, quam si semper fuisset, omne enim quod non semper fuit, manifestum est habere causam; sed non ita manifestum est de eo quod semper fuit.

AD SEPTIMUM dicendum quod, sicut dicitur in IV Physic., prius et posterius est in tempore, secundum

and heaven did not begin by generation, as some said, especially about heaven. But we say that matter and heaven were produced into being by creation, as appears above (Q. 44, A. 1, ad 2).

REPLY OBJ. 4: The notion of a vacuum is not only *in which is nothing*, but also implies a space capable of holding a body and in which there is not a body, as appears from Aristotle (*Phys.* iv, 60). Whereas we hold that there was no place or space before the world was.

REPLY OBJ. 5: The first mover was always in the same state: but the first movable thing was not always so, because it began to be whereas hitherto it was not. This, however, was not through change, but by creation, which is not change, as said above (Q. 45, A. 2, ad 2). Hence it is evident that this reason, which Aristotle gives (*Phys.* viii), is valid against those who admitted the existence of eternal movable things, but not eternal movement, as appears from the opinions of Anaxagoras and Empedocles. But we hold that from the moment that movable things began to exist movement also existed.

REPLY OBJ. 6: The first agent is a voluntary agent. And although He had the eternal will to produce some effect, yet He did not produce an eternal effect. Nor is it necessary for some change to be presupposed, not even on account of imaginary time. For we must take into consideration the difference between a particular agent, that presupposes something and produces something else, and the universal agent, who produces the whole. The particular agent produces the form, and presupposes the matter; and hence it is necessary that it introduce the form in due proportion into a suitable matter. Hence it is correct to say that it introduces the form into such matter, and not into another, on account of the different kinds of matter. But it is not correct to say so of God Who produces form and matter together: whereas it is correct to say of Him that He produces matter fitting to the form and to the end. Now, a particular agent presupposes time just as it presupposes matter. Hence it is correctly described as acting in time *after* and not in time *before*, according to an imaginary succession of time after time. But the universal agent who produces the thing and time also, is not correctly described as acting now, and not before, according to an imaginary succession of time succeeding time, as if time were presupposed to His action; but He must be considered as giving time to His effect as much as and when He willed, and according to what was fitting to demonstrate His power. For the world leads more evidently to the knowledge of the divine creating power, if it was not always, than if it had always been; since everything which was not always manifestly has a cause; whereas this is not so manifest of what always was.

REPLY OBJ. 7: As is stated (*Phys.* iv, 99), *before* and *after* belong to time, according as they are in movement. Hence

quod prius et posterius est in motu. Unde principium et finis accipienda sunt in tempore, sicut et in motu. Supposita autem aeternitate motus, necesse est quod quodlibet momentum in motu acceptum sit principium et terminus motus, quod non oportet, si motus incipiat. Et eadem ratio est de nunc temporis. Et sic patet quod ratio illa instantis nunc, quod semper sit principium et finis temporis, praesupponit aeternitatem temporis et motus. Unde Aristoteles hanc rationem inducit, in VIII Physic., contra eos qui ponebant aeternitatem temporis, sed negabant aeternitatem motus.

Ad octavum dicendum quod Deus est prior mundo duratione. Sed ly prius non designat prioritatem temporis, sed aeternitatis. Vel dicendum quod designat aeternitatem temporis imaginati, et non realiter existentis. Sicut, cum dicitur, supra caelum nihil est, ly supra designat locum imaginatum tantum, secundum quod possibile est imaginari dimensionibus caelestis corporis dimensiones alias superaddi.

Ad nonum dicendum quod, sicut effectus sequitur a causa agente naturaliter secundum modum suae formae, ita sequitur ab agente per voluntatem secundum formam ab eo praeconceptam et definitam, ut ex superioribus patet. Licet igitur Deus ab aeterno fuerit sufficiens causa mundi, non tamen oportet quod ponatur mundus ab eo productus, nisi secundum quod est in praedefinitione suae voluntatis; ut scilicet habeat esse post non esse, ut manifestius declaret suum auctorem.

Ad decimum dicendum quod, posita actione, sequitur effectus secundum exigentiam formae quae est principium actionis. In agentibus autem per voluntatem, quod conceptum est et praedefinitum, accipitur ut forma quae est principium actionis. Ex actione igitur Dei aeterna non sequitur effectus aeternus, sed qualem Deus voluit, ut scilicet haberet esse post non esse.

beginning and end in time must be taken in the same way as in movement. Now, granted the eternity of movement, it is necessary that any given moment in movement be a beginning and an end of movement; which need not be if movement be a beginning. The same applies to the *now* of time. Thus it appears that the idea of the instant *now*, as being always the beginning and end of time, presupposes the eternity of time and movement. Hence Aristotle brings forward this reason (*Phys.* viii, 10) against those who asserted the eternity of time, but denied the eternity of movement.

Reply Obj. 8: God is prior to the world by priority of duration. But the word *prior* signifies priority not of time, but of eternity. Or we may say that it signifies the eternity of imaginary time, and not of time really existing; thus, when we say that above heaven there is nothing, the word *above* signifies only an imaginary place, according as it is possible to imagine other dimensions beyond those of the heavenly body.

Reply Obj. 9: As the effect follows from the cause that acts by nature, according to the mode of its form, so likewise it follows from the voluntary agent, according to the form preconceived and determined by the agent, as appears from what was said above (Q. 19, A. 4; Q. 41, A. 2). Therefore, although God was from eternity the sufficient cause of the world, we should not say that the world was produced by Him, except as preordained by His will—that is, that it should have being after not being, in order more manifestly to declare its author.

Reply Obj. 10: Given the action, the effect follows according to the requirement of the form, which is the principle of action. But in agents acting by will, what is conceived and preordained is to be taken as the form, which is the principle of action. Therefore from the eternal action of God an eternal effect did not follow; but such an effect as God willed: an effect, to wit, which has being after not being.

Article 2

Whether It Is an Article of Faith That the World Began?

Ad secundum sic proceditur. Videtur quod mundum incoepisse non sit articulus fidei, sed conclusio demonstrabilis. Omne enim factum habet principium suae durationis. Sed demonstrative probari potest quod Deus sit causa effectiva mundi, et hoc etiam probabiliores philosophi posuerunt. Ergo demonstrative probari potest quod mundus incoeperit.

Praeterea, si necesse est dicere quod mundus factus est a Deo, aut ergo ex nihilo, aut ex aliquo. Sed non ex aliquo, quia sic materia mundi praecessisset mundum;

Objection 1: It would seem that it is not an article of faith but a demonstrable conclusion that the world began. For everything that is made has a beginning of its duration. But it can be proved demonstratively that God is the effective cause of the world; indeed this is asserted by the more approved philosophers. Therefore it can be demonstratively proved that the world began.

Obj. 2: Further, if it is necessary to say that the world was made by God, it must therefore have been made from nothing or from something. But it was not made from

contra quod procedunt rationes Aristotelis ponentis caelum ingenitum. Ergo oportet dicere quod mundus sit factus ex nihilo. Et sic habet esse post non esse. Ergo oportet quod esse incoeperit.

PRAETEREA, omne quod operatur per intellectum, a quodam principio operatur, ut patet in omnibus artificibus. Sed Deus est agens per intellectum. Ergo a quodam principio operatur mundus igitur, qui est eius effectus, non fuit semper.

PRAETEREA, manifeste apparet artes aliquas, et habitationes regionum, ex determinatis temporibus incoepisse. Sed hoc non esset, si mundus semper fuisset. Mundum igitur non semper fuisse manifestum est.

PRAETEREA, certum est nihil Deo aequari posse. Sed si mundus semper fuisset, aequipararetur Deo in duratione. Ergo certum est non semper mundum fuisse.

PRAETEREA, si mundus semper fuit, infiniti dies praecesserunt diem istum. Sed infinita non est pertransire. Ergo nunquam fuisset perventum ad hunc diem, quod est manifeste falsum.

PRAETEREA, si mundus fuit aeternus, et generatio fuit ab aeterno. Ergo unus homo genitus est ab alio in infinitum. Sed pater est causa efficiens filii, ut dicitur in II Physic. Ergo in causis efficientibus est procedere in infinitum, quod improbatur in II Metaphys.

PRAETEREA, si mundus et generatio semper fuit, infiniti homines praecesserunt. Sed anima hominis est immortalis. Ergo infinitae animae humanae nunc essent actu, quod est impossibile. Ergo ex necessitate sciri potest quod mundus incoeperit; et non sola fide tenetur.

SED CONTRA, fidei articuli demonstrative probari non possunt, quia *fides de non apparentibus est*, ut dicitur ad Hebr. XI. Sed Deum esse creatorem mundi, sic quod mundus incoeperit esse, est articulus fidei, dicimus enim, credo in unum Deum et cetera. Et iterum, Gregorius dicit, in Homil. I in Ezech., quod Moyses prophetizavit de praeterito, dicens *in principio creavit Deus caelum et terram*; in quo novitas mundi traditur. Ergo novitas mundi habetur tantum per revelationem. Et ideo non potest probari demonstrative.

RESPONDEO dicendum quod mundum non semper fuisse, sola fide tenetur, et demonstrative probari non potest, sicut et supra de mysterio Trinitatis dictum est. Et huius ratio est, quia novitas mundi non potest demonstrationem recipere ex parte ipsius mundi. Demonstrationis enim principium est quod quid est. Unumquodque autem, secundum rationem suae speciei, abstrahit ab hic et nunc, propter quod dicitur quod universalia sunt

something; otherwise the matter of the world would have preceded the world; against which are the arguments of Aristotle (*De Coelo* i), who held that heaven was ungenerated. Therefore it must be said that the world was made from nothing; and thus it has being after not being. Therefore it must have begun.

OBJ. 3: Further, everything which works by intellect works from some principle, as appears in all kinds of craftsmen. But God acts by intellect: therefore His work has a principle. The world, therefore, which is His effect, did not always exist.

OBJ. 4: Further, it appears manifestly that certain arts have developed, and certain countries have begun to be inhabited at some fixed time. But this would not be the case if the world had been always. Therefore it is manifest that the world did not always exist.

OBJ. 5: Further, it is certain that nothing can be equal to God. But if the world had always been, it would be equal to God in duration. Therefore it is certain that the world did not always exist.

OBJ. 6: Further, if the world always was, the consequence is that infinite days preceded this present day. But it is impossible to pass through an infinite medium. Therefore we should never have arrived at this present day; which is manifestly false.

OBJ. 7: Further, if the world was eternal, generation also was eternal. Therefore one man was begotten of another in an infinite series. But the father is the efficient cause of the son (*Phys.* ii, 5). Therefore in efficient causes there could be an infinite series, which is disproved (*Metaph.* ii, 5).

OBJ. 8: Further, if the world and generation always were, there have been an infinite number of men. But man's soul is immortal: therefore an infinite number of human souls would actually now exist, which is impossible. Therefore it can be known with certainty that the world began, and not only is it known by faith.

ON THE CONTRARY, The articles of faith cannot be proved demonstratively, because *faith is of things that appear not* (Heb 11:1). But that God is the Creator of the world: hence that the world began, is an article of faith; for we say, *I believe in one God*, etc. And again, Gregory says (*Hom. i in Ezech.*), that Moses prophesied of the past, saying, *In the beginning God created heaven and earth*: in which words the newness of the world is stated. Therefore the newness of the world is known only by revelation; and therefore it cannot be proved demonstratively.

I ANSWER THAT, By faith alone do we hold, and by no demonstration can it be proved, that the world did not always exist, as was said above of the mystery of the Trinity (Q. 32, A. 1). The reason of this is that the newness of the world cannot be demonstrated on the part of the world itself. For the principle of demonstration is the essence of a thing. Now everything according to its species is abstracted from *here* and *now*; whence it is said that

ubique et semper. Unde demonstrari non potest quod homo, aut caelum, aut lapis non semper fuit. Similiter etiam neque ex parte causae agentis, quae agit per voluntatem. Voluntas enim Dei ratione investigari non potest, nisi circa ea quae absolute necesse est Deum velle, talia autem non sunt quae circa creaturas vult, ut dictum est. Potest autem voluntas divina homini manifestari per revelationem, cui fides innititur. Unde mundum incoepisse est credibile, non autem demonstrabile vel scibile. Et hoc utile est ut consideretur, ne forte aliquis, quod fidei est demonstrare praesumens, rationes non necessarias inducat, quae praebeant materiam irridendi infidelibus, existimantibus nos propter huiusmodi rationes credere quae fidei sunt.

Ad primum ergo dicendum quod, sicut dicit Augustinus, XI de Civ. Dei, philosophorum ponentium aeternitatem mundi, duplex fuit opinio. Quidam enim posuerunt quod substantia mundi non sit a Deo. Et horum est intollerabilis error; et ideo ex necessitate refellitur. Quidam autem sic posuerunt mundum aeternum, quod tamen mundum a Deo factum dixerunt. *Non enim mundum temporis volunt habere, sed suae creationis initium, ut quodam modo vix intelligibili semper sit factus. Id autem quomodo intelligant, invenerunt,* ut idem dicit in X de Civ. Dei. *Sicut enim, inquiunt, si pes ex aeternitate semper fuisset in pulvere, semper subesset vestigium, quod a calcante factum nemo dubitaret; sic et mundus semper fuit, semper existente qui fecit.* Et ad hoc intelligendum, considerandum est quod causa efficiens quae agit per motum, de necessitate praecedit tempore suum effectum, quia effectus non est nisi in termino actionis, agens autem omne oportet esse principium actionis. Sed si actio sit instantanea, et non successiva, non est necessarium faciens esse prius facto duratione; sicut patet in illuminatione. Unde dicunt quod non sequitur ex necessitate, si Deus est causa activa mundi, quod sit prior mundo duratione, quia creatio, qua mundum produxit, non est mutatio successiva, ut supra dictum est.

Ad secundum dicendum quod illi qui ponerent mundum aeternum, dicerent mundum factum a Deo ex nihilo, non quod factus sit post nihilum, secundum quod nos intelligimus per nomen creationis; sed quia non est factus de aliquo. Et sic etiam non recusant aliqui eorum creationis nomen, ut patet ex Avicenna in sua metaphysica.

Ad tertium dicendum quod illa est ratio Anaxagorae, quae ponitur in III Physic. Sed non de necessitate concludit, nisi de intellectu qui deliberando investigat quid agendum sit, quod est simile motui. Talis autem est intellectus humanus, sed non divinus, ut supra patet.

Ad quartum dicendum quod ponentes aeternitatem mundi, ponunt aliquam regionem infinities esse

universals are everywhere and always. Hence it cannot be demonstrated that man, or heaven, or a stone were not always. Likewise neither can it be demonstrated on the part of the efficient cause, which acts by will. For the will of God cannot be investigated by reason, except as regards those things which God must will of necessity; and what He wills about creatures is not among these, as was said above (Q. 19, A. 3). But the divine will can be manifested by revelation, on which faith rests. Hence that the world began to exist is an object of faith, but not of demonstration or science. And it is useful to consider this, lest anyone, presuming to demonstrate what is of faith, should bring forward reasons that are not cogent, so as to give occasion to unbelievers to laugh, thinking that on such grounds we believe things that are of faith.

Reply Obj. 1: As Augustine says (*De Civ. Dei* xi, 4), the opinion of philosophers who asserted the eternity of the world was twofold. For some said that the substance of the world was not from God, which is an intolerable error; and therefore it is refuted by proofs that are cogent. Some, however, said that the world was eternal, although made by God. For they hold that the world has a beginning, not of time, but of creation, so that in a certain hardly intelligible way it was always made. *And they try to explain their meaning thus* (*De Civ. Dei* x, 31): for as, if the foot were always in the dust from eternity, there would always be a footprint which without doubt was caused by him who trod on it, so also the world always was, because its Maker always existed. To understand this we must consider that the efficient cause, which acts by motion, of necessity precedes its effect in time; because the effect is only in the end of the action, and every agent must be the principle of action. But if the action is instantaneous and not successive, it is not necessary for the maker to be prior to the thing made in duration as appears in the case of illumination. Hence they say that it does not follow necessarily if God is the active cause of the world, that He should be prior to the world in duration; because creation, by which He produced the world, is not a successive change, as was said above (Q. 45, A. 2).

Reply Obj. 2: Those who would say that the world was eternal, would say that the world was made by God from nothing; not that it was made after nothing, according to what we understand by the word creation, but that it was not made from anything; and so also some of them do not reject the word creation, as appears from Avicenna (*Metaph.* ix, 4).

Reply Obj. 3: This is the argument of Anaxagoras (as quoted in *Phys.* viii, 15). But it does not lead to a necessary conclusion, except as to that intellect which deliberates in order to find out what should be done, which is like movement. Such is the human intellect, but not the divine intellect (Q. 14, AA. 7, 12).

Reply Obj. 4: Those who hold the eternity of the world hold that some region was changed an infinite number of

mutatam de inhabitabili in habitabilem, et e converso. Et similiter ponunt quod artes, propter diversas corruptiones et accidentia, infinities fuerunt inventae, et iterum corruptae. Unde Aristoteles dicit, in libro Meteor., quod ridiculum est ex huiusmodi particularibus mutationibus opinionem accipere de novitate mundi totius.

AD QUINTUM dicendum quod, etsi mundus semper fuisset, non tamen parificaretur Deo in aeternitate, ut dicit Boetius, in fine de Consolat., quia esse divinum est esse totum simul, absque successione; non autem sic est de mundo.

AD SEXTUM dicendum quod transitus semper intelligitur a termino in terminum. Quaecumque autem praeterita dies signetur, ab illa usque ad istam sunt finiti dies, qui pertransiri poterunt. Obiectio autem procedit ac si, positis extremis, sint media infinita.

AD SEPTIMUM dicendum quod in causis efficientibus impossibile est procedere in infinitum per se; ut puta si causae quae per se requiruntur ad aliquem effectum, multiplicarentur in infinitum; sicut si lapis moveretur a baculo, et baculus a manu, et hoc in infinitum. Sed per accidens in infinitum procedere in causis agentibus non reputatur impossibile; ut puta si omnes causae quae in infinitum multiplicantur, non teneant ordinem nisi unius causae, sed earum multiplicatio sit per accidens; sicut artifex agit multis martellis per accidens, quia unus post unum frangitur. Accidit ergo huic martello, quod agat post actionem alterius martelli. Et similiter accidit huic homini, inquantum generat, quod sit generatus ab alio, generat enim inquantum homo, et non inquantum est filius alterius hominis; omnes enim homines generantes habent gradum unum in causis efficientibus, scilicet gradum particularis generantis. Unde non est impossibile quod homo generetur ab homine in infinitum. Esset autem impossibile, si generatio huius hominis dependeret ab hoc homine, et a corpore elementari, et a sole, et sic in infinitum.

AD OCTAVUM dicendum quod hanc rationem ponentes aeternitatem mundi multipliciter effugiunt quidam enim non reputant impossibile esse infinitas animas actu; ut patet in metaphysica Algazelis, dicentis hoc esse infinitum per accidens. Sed hoc improbatum est superius. Quidam vero dicunt animam corrumpi cum corpore. Quidam vero quod ex omnibus animabus remanet una tantum. Alii vero, ut Augustinus dicit, posuerunt propter hoc circuitum animarum; ut scilicet animae separatae a corporibus, post determinata temporum curricula, iterum redirent ad corpora. De quibus omnibus in sequentibus est agendum. Considerandum tamen quod haec ratio particularis est. Unde posset dicere aliquis quod mundus fuit aeternus, vel saltem aliqua creatura, ut Angelus; non autem homo. Nos autem intendimus universaliter, an aliqua creatura fuerit ab aeterno.

times, from being uninhabitable to being inhabitable and *vice versa*, and likewise they hold that the arts, by reason of various corruptions and accidents, were subject to an infinite variety of advance and decay. Hence Aristotle says (*Meteor.* i) that it is absurd from such particular changes to hold the opinion of the newness of the whole world.

REPLY OBJ. 5: Even supposing that the world always was, it would not be equal to God in eternity, as Boethius says (*De Consol.* v, 6); because the divine Being is all being simultaneously without succession; but with the world it is otherwise.

REPLY OBJ. 6: Passage is always understood as being from term to term. Whatever bygone day we choose, from it to the present day there is a finite number of days which can be passed through. The objection is founded on the idea that, given two extremes, there is an infinite number of mean terms.

REPLY OBJ. 7: In efficient causes it is impossible to proceed to infinity per se—thus, there cannot be an infinite number of causes that are per se required for a certain effect; for instance, that a stone be moved by a stick, the stick by the hand, and so on to infinity. But it is not impossible to proceed to infinity accidentally as regards efficient causes; for instance, if all the causes thus infinitely multiplied should have the order of only one cause, their multiplication being accidental, as an artificer acts by means of many hammers accidentally, because one after the other may be broken. It is accidental, therefore, that one particular hammer acts after the action of another; and likewise it is accidental to this particular man as generator to be generated by another man; for he generates as a man, and not as the son of another man. For all men generating hold one grade in efficient causes—viz. the grade of a particular generator. Hence it is not impossible for a man to be generated by man to infinity; but such a thing would be impossible if the generation of this man depended upon this man, and on an elementary body, and on the sun, and so on to infinity.

REPLY OBJ. 8: Those who hold the eternity of the world evade this reason in many ways. For some do not think it impossible for there to be an actual infinity of souls, as appears from the Metaphysics of Algazel, who says that such a thing is an accidental infinity. But this was disproved above (Q. 7, A. 4). Some say that the soul is corrupted with the body. And some say that of all souls only one will remain. But others, as Augustine says, asserted on this account a circuit of souls—viz. that souls separated from their bodies return again thither after a course of time; a fuller consideration of which matters will be given later (Q. 75, A. 2; Q. 118, A. 6). But be it noted that this argument considers only a particular case. Hence one might say that the world was eternal, or at least some creature, as an angel, but not man. But we are considering the question in general, as to whether any creature can exist from eternity.

Article 3

Whether the Creation of Things Was in the Beginning of Time?

Ad tertium sic proceditur. Videtur quod creatio rerum non fuit in principio temporis. Quod enim non est in tempore, non est in aliquo temporis. Sed creatio rerum non fuit in tempore, per creationem enim rerum substantia in esse producta est; tempus autem non mensurat substantiam rerum, et praecipue incorporalium. Ergo creatio non fuit in principio temporis.

Praeterea, philosophus probat quod omne quod fit, fiebat, et sic omne fieri habet prius et posterius. In principio autem temporis, cum sit indivisibile, non est prius et posterius. Ergo, cum creari sit quoddam fieri, videtur quod res non sint creatae in principio temporis.

Praeterea, ipsum etiam tempus creatum est. Sed non potest creari in principio temporis, cum tempus sit divisibile, principium autem temporis indivisibile. Non ergo creatio rerum fuit in principio temporis.

Sed contra est quod Gen. I dicitur, *in principio creavit Deus caelum et terram.*

Respondeo dicendum quod illud verbum Genes. I, *in principio creavit Deus caelum et terram*, tripliciter exponitur, ad excludendum tres errores. Quidam enim posuerunt mundum semper fuisse, et tempus non habere principium. Et ad hoc excludendum, exponitur, in principio, scilicet temporis. Quidam vero posuerunt duo esse creationis principia, unum bonorum, aliud malorum. Et ad hoc excludendum, exponitur, in principio, idest in filio. Sicut enim principium effectivum appropriatur patri, propter potentiam, ita principium exemplare appropriatur filio, propter sapientiam, ut sicut dicitur, omnia in sapientia fecisti, ita intelligatur Deum omnia fecisse in principio, idest in filio; secundum illud apostoli ad Coloss. I, in ipso, scilicet filio, condita sunt universa. Alii vero dixerunt corporalia esse creata a Deo mediantibus creaturis spiritualibus. Et ad hoc excludendum, exponitur, in principio creavit Deus caelum et terram, idest ante omnia. Quatuor enim ponuntur simul creata, scilicet caelum Empyreum, materia corporalis (quae nomine terrae intelligitur), tempus, et natura angelica.

Ad primum ergo dicendum quod non dicuntur in principio temporis res esse creatae, quasi principium temporis sit creationis mensura sed quia simul cum tempore caelum et terra creata sunt.

Ad secundum dicendum quod verbum illud philosophi intelligitur de fieri quod est per motum, vel quod est terminus motus. Quia cum in quolibet motu sit accipere prius et posterius, ante quodcumque signum in motu signato, dum scilicet aliquid est in moveri et fieri,

Objection 1: It would seem that the creation of things was not in the beginning of time. For whatever is not in time, is not of any part of time. But the creation of things was not in time; for by the creation the substance of things was brought into being; and time does not measure the substance of things, and especially of incorporeal things. Therefore creation was not in the beginning of time.

Obj. 2: Further, the Philosopher proves (*Phys.* vi, 40) that everything which is made, was being made; and so to be made implies a *before* and *after*. But in the beginning of time, since it is indivisible, there is no *before* and *after*. Therefore, since to be created is a kind of *being made*, it appears that things were not created in the beginning of time.

Obj. 3: Further, even time itself is created. But time cannot be created in the beginning of time, since time is divisible, and the beginning of time is indivisible. Therefore, the creation of things was not in the beginning of time.

On the contrary, It is said (Gen 1:1): *In the beginning God created heaven and earth.*

I answer that, The words of Genesis, *In the beginning God created heaven and earth*, are expounded in a threefold sense in order to exclude three errors. For some said that the world always was, and that time had no beginning; and to exclude this the words *In the beginning* are expounded—viz. *of time*. And some said that there are two principles of creation, one of good things and the other of evil things, against which *In the beginning* is expounded—'in the Son.' For as the efficient principle is appropriated to the Father by reason of power, so the exemplar principle is appropriated to the Son by reason of wisdom, in order that, as it is said (Ps 103:24), *Thou hast made all things in wisdom*, it may be understood that God made all things in the beginning—that is, in the Son; according to the word of the Apostle (Col 1:16), *In Him*—viz. the Son—*were created all things*. But others said that corporeal things were created by God through the medium of spiritual creation; and to exclude this it is expounded thus: *In the beginning*—i.e., before all things—'God created heaven and earth.' For four things are stated to be created together—viz. the empyrean heaven, corporeal matter, by which is meant the earth, time, and the angelic nature.

Reply Obj. 1: Things are said to be created in the beginning of time, not as if the beginning of time were a measure of creation, but because together with time heaven and earth were created.

Reply Obj. 2: This saying of the Philosopher is understood *of being made* by means of movement, or as the term of movement. Because, since in every movement there is *before* and *after*, before any one point in a given movement—that is, whilst anything is in the process of being

est accipere prius, et etiam aliquid post ipsum, quia quod est in principio motus, vel in termino, non est in moveri. Creatio autem neque est motus neque terminus motus, ut supra dictum est. Unde sic aliquid creatur, quod non prius creabatur.

AD TERTIUM dicendum quod nihil fit nisi secundum quod est. Nihil autem est temporis nisi nunc. Unde non potest fieri nisi secundum aliquod nunc, non quia in ipso primo nunc sit tempus, sed quia ab eo incipit tempus.

moved and made, there is a *before* and also an *after*, because what is in the beginning of movement or in its term is not in *being moved*. But creation is neither movement nor the term of movement, as was said above (Q. 45, AA. 2, 3). Hence a thing is created in such a way that it was not being created before.

REPLY OBJ. 3: Nothing is made except as it exists. But nothing exists of time except *now*. Hence time cannot be made except according to some *now*; not because in the first *now* is time, but because from it time begins.

QUESTION 47

THE DISTINCTION OF THINGS IN GENERAL

Post productionem creaturarum in esse, considerandum est de distinctione earum. Erit autem haec consideratio tripartita. Nam primo considerabimus de distinctione rerum in communi; secundo, de distinctione boni et mali; tertio, de distinctione spiritualis et corporalis creaturae.

Circa primum quaeruntur tria.

Primo, de ipsa rerum multitudine seu distinctione.

Secundo, de earum inaequalitate.

Tertio, de unitate mundi.

After considering the production of creatures, we come to the consideration of the distinction of things. This consideration will be threefold—first, of the distinction of things in general; second, of the distinction of good and evil; third, of the distinction of the spiritual and corporeal creature.

Under the first head, there are three points of inquiry:

(1) The multitude or distinction of things.

(2) Their inequality.

(3) The unity of the world.

Article 1

Whether the Multitude and Distinction of Things Come from God?

AD PRIMUM SIC PROCEDITUR. Videtur quod rerum multitudo et distinctio non sit a Deo. Unum enim semper natum est unum facere. Sed Deus est maxime unus, ut ex praemissis patet. Ergo non producit nisi unum effectum.

PRAETEREA, exemplatum assimilatur suo exemplari. Sed Deus est causa exemplaris sui effectus, ut supra dictum est. Ergo, cum Deus sit unus, effectus eius est unus tantum, et non distinctus.

PRAETEREA, ea quae sunt ad finem, proportionantur fini. Sed finis creaturae est unus, scilicet divina bonitas, ut supra ostensum est. Ergo effectus Dei non est nisi unus.

SED CONTRA est quod dicitur Gen. I, quod *Deus distinxit lucem a tenebris, et divisit aquas ab aquis*. Ergo distinctio et multitudo rerum est a Deo.

RESPONDEO dicendum quod causam distinctionis rerum multipliciter aliqui assignaverunt. Quidam enim attribuerunt eam materiae, vel soli, vel simul cum agente. Soli quidem materiae, sicut Democritus, et omnes antiqui naturales, ponentes solam causam materialem, secundum quos distinctio rerum provenit a casu, secundum motum materiae. Materiae vero et agenti simul distinctionem et multitudinem rerum attribuit Anaxagoras, qui posuit intellectum distinguentem res, extrahendo quod erat permixtum in materia.

Sed hoc non potest stare propter duo. Primo quidem, quia supra ostensum est quod etiam ipsa materia a Deo creata est. Unde oportet et distinctionem, si qua est ex

OBJECTION 1: It would seem that the multitude and distinction of things does not come from God. For one naturally always makes one. But God is supremely one, as appears from what precedes (Q. 11, A. 4). Therefore He produces but one effect.

OBJ. 2: Further, the representation is assimilated to its exemplar. But God is the exemplar cause of His effect, as was said above (Q. 44, A. 3). Therefore, as God is one, His effect is one only, and not diverse.

OBJ. 3: Further, the means are proportional to the end. But the end of the creation is one—viz. the divine goodness, as was shown above (Q. 44, A. 4). Therefore the effect of God is but one.

ON THE CONTRARY, It is said (Gen 1:4, 7) that God *divided the light from the darkness*, and *divided waters from waters*. Therefore the distinction and multitude of things is from God.

I ANSWER THAT, The distinction of things has been ascribed to many causes. For some attributed the distinction to matter, either by itself or with the agent. Democritus, for instance, and all the ancient natural philosophers, who admitted no cause but matter, attributed it to matter alone; and in their opinion the distinction of things comes from chance according to the movement of matter. Anaxagoras, however, attributed the distinction and multitude of things to matter and to the agent together; and he said that the intellect distinguishes things by extracting what is mixed up in matter.

But this cannot stand, for two reasons. First, because, as was shown above (Q. 44, A. 2), even matter itself was created by God. Hence we must reduce whatever distinction

parte materiae, in altiorem causam reducere. Secundo, quia materia est propter formam, et non e converso. Distinctio autem rerum est per formas proprias. Non ergo distinctio est in rebus propter materiam, sed potius e converso in materia creata est difformitas, ut esset diversis formis accommodata.

Quidam vero attribuerunt distinctionem rerum secundis agentibus. Sicut Avicenna, qui dixit quod Deus, intelligendo se, produxit intelligentiam primam, in qua, quia non est suum esse, ex necessitate incidit compositio potentiae et actus, ut infra patebit. Sic igitur prima intelligentia, inquantum intelligit causam primam, produxit secundam intelligentiam; inquantum autem intelligit se secundum quod est in potentia, produxit corpus caeli, quod movet; inquantum vero intelligit se secundum illud quod habet de actu, produxit animam caeli.

Sed hoc non potest stare propter duo. Primo quidem, quia supra ostensum est quod creare solius Dei est. Unde ea quae non possunt causari nisi per creationem, a solo Deo producuntur, et haec sunt omnia quae non subiacent generationi et corruptioni. Secundo, quia secundum hanc positionem, non proveniret ex intentione primi agentis universitas rerum, sed ex concursu multarum causarum agentium. Tale autem dicimus provenire a casu. Sic igitur complementum universi, quod in diversitate rerum consistit, esset a casu, quod est impossibile.

Unde dicendum est quod distinctio rerum et multitudo est ex intentione primi agentis, quod est Deus. Produxit enim res in esse propter suam bonitatem communicandam creaturis, et per eas repraesentandam. Et quia per unam creaturam sufficienter repraesentari non potest, produxit multas creaturas et diversas, ut quod deest uni ad repraesentandam divinam bonitatem, suppleatur ex alia, nam bonitas quae in Deo est simpliciter et uniformiter, in creaturis est multipliciter et divisim. Unde perfectius participat divinam bonitatem, et repraesentat eam, totum universum, quam alia quaecumque creatura.

Et quia ex divina sapientia est causa distinctionis rerum, ideo Moyses dicit res esse distinctas verbo Dei, quod est conceptio sapientiae. Et hoc est quod dicitur Gen. I, *dixit Deus, fiat lux. Et divisit lucem a tenebris.*

AD PRIMUM ergo dicendum quod agens per naturam agit per formam per quam est, quae unius tantum est una, et ideo non agit nisi unum. Agens autem voluntarium, quale est Deus, ut supra ostensum est, agit per formam intellectam. Cum igitur Deum multa

comes from matter to a higher cause. Second, because matter is for the sake of the form, and not the form for the matter, and the distinction of things comes from their proper forms. Therefore the distinction of things is not on account of the matter; but rather, on the contrary, created matter is formless, in order that it may be accommodated to different forms.

Others have attributed the distinction of things to secondary agents, as did Avicenna, who said that God by understanding Himself, produced the first intelligence; in which, forasmuch as it was not its own being, there is necessarily composition of potentiality and act, as will appear later (Q. 50, A. 3). And so the first intelligence, inasmuch as it understood the first cause, produced the second intelligence; and in so far as it understood itself as in potentiality it produced the heavenly body, which causes movement, and inasmuch as it understood itself as having actuality it produced the soul of the heavens.

But this opinion cannot stand, for two reasons. First, because it was shown above (Q. 45, A. 5) that to create belongs to God alone, and hence what can be caused only by creation is produced by God alone—viz. all those things which are not subject to generation and corruption. Second, because, according to this opinion, the universality of things would not proceed from the intention of the first agent, but from the concurrence of many active causes; and such an effect we can describe only as being produced by chance. Therefore, the perfection of the universe, which consists of the diversity of things, would thus be a thing of chance, which is impossible.

Hence we must say that the distinction and multitude of things come from the intention of the first agent, who is God. For He brought things into being in order that His goodness might be communicated to creatures, and be represented by them; and because His goodness could not be adequately represented by one creature alone, He produced many and diverse creatures, that what was wanting to one in the representation of the divine goodness might be supplied by another. For goodness, which in God is simple and uniform, in creatures is manifold and divided and hence the whole universe together participates the divine goodness more perfectly, and represents it better than any single creature whatever.

And because the divine wisdom is the cause of the distinction of things, therefore Moses said that things are made distinct by the word of God, which is the concept of His wisdom; and this is what we read in Gen. 1:3, 4: *God said: Be light made . . . And He divided the light from the darkness.*

REPLY OBJ. 1: The natural agent acts by the form which makes it what it is, and which is only one in one thing; and therefore its effect is one only. But the voluntary agent, such as God is, as was shown above (Q. 19, A. 4), acts by an intellectual form. Since, therefore, it is not against God's unity

intelligere non repugnet unitati et simplicitati ipsius, ut supra ostensum est, relinquitur quod, licet sit unus, possit multa facere.

AD SECUNDUM dicendum quod ratio illa teneret de exemplato quod perfecte repraesentat exemplar, quod non multiplicatur nisi materialiter. Unde imago increata, quae est perfecta, est una tantum. Sed nulla creatura repraesentat perfecte exemplar primum, quod est divina essentia. Et ideo potest per multa repraesentari. Et tamen secundum quod ideae dicuntur exemplaria, pluralitati rerum correspondet in mente divina pluralitas idearum.

AD TERTIUM dicendum quod in speculativis medium demonstrationis, quod perfecte demonstrat conclusionem, est unum tantum, sed media probabilia sunt multa. Et similiter in operativis, quando id quod est ad finem adaequat, ut ita dixerim, finem, non requiritur quod sit nisi unum tantum. Sed creatura non sic se habet ad finem qui est Deus. Unde oportuit creaturas multiplicari.

and simplicity to understand many things, as was shown above (Q. 15, A. 2), it follows that, although He is one, He can make many things.

REPLY OBJ. 2: This reason would apply to the representation which reflects the exemplar perfectly, and which is multiplied by reason of matter only; hence the uncreated image, which is perfect, is only one. But no creature represents the first exemplar perfectly, which is the divine essence; and, therefore, it can be represented by many things. Still, according as ideas are called exemplars, the plurality of ideas corresponds in the divine mind to the plurality of things.

REPLY OBJ. 3: In speculative things the medium of demonstration, which demonstrates the conclusion perfectly, is one only; whereas probable means of proof are many. Likewise when operation is concerned, if the means be equal, so to speak, to the end, one only is sufficient. But the creature is not such a means to its end, which is God; and hence the multiplication of creatures is necessary.

Article 2

Whether the Inequality of Things Is from God?

AD SECUNDUM SIC PROCEDITUR. Videtur quod inaequalitas rerum non sit a Deo. Optimi enim est optima adducere. Sed inter optima unum non est maius altero. Ergo Dei, qui est optimus, est omnia aequalia facere.

PRAETEREA, aequalitas est effectus unitatis, ut dicitur in V Metaphys. Sed Deus est unus. Ergo fecit omnia aequalia.

PRAETEREA, iustitiae est inaequalia inaequalibus dare. Sed Deus est iustus in omnibus operibus suis. Cum ergo operationi eius, qua esse rebus communicat, non praesupponatur aliqua inaequalitas rerum, videtur quod fecerit omnia aequalia.

SED CONTRA est quod dicitur Eccli. XXXIII, *quare dies diem superat, et iterum lux lucem, et annus annum, sol solem? A domini scientia separata sunt.*

RESPONDEO dicendum quod Origenes, volens excludere positionem ponentium distinctionem in rebus ex contrarietate principiorum boni et mali, posuit a Deo a principio omnia creata esse aequalia. Dicit enim quod Deus primo creavit creaturas rationales tantum, et omnes aequales, in quibus primo exorta est inaequalitas ex libero arbitrio, quibusdam conversis in Deum secundum magis et minus, quibusdam etiam secundum magis et minus a Deo aversis. Illae igitur rationales creaturae quae ad Deum per liberum arbitrium conversae

OBJECTION 1: It would seem that the inequality of things is not from God. For it belongs to the best to produce the best. But among things that are best, one is not greater than another. Therefore, it belongs to God, Who is the Best, to make all things equal.

OBJ. 2: Further, equality is the effect of unity (*Metaph.* v, 20). But God is one. Therefore, He has made all things equal.

OBJ. 3: Further, it is the part of justice to give unequal to unequal things. But God is just in all His works. Since, therefore, no inequality of things is presupposed to the operation whereby He gives being to things, it seems that He has made all things equal.

ON THE CONTRARY, It is said (Sir 33:7): *Why does one day excel another, and one light another, and one year another year, one sun another sun?. By the knowledge of the Lord they were distinguished.*

I ANSWER THAT, When Origen wished to refute those who said that the distinction of things arose from the contrary principles of good and evil, he said that in the beginning all things were created equal by God. For he asserted that God first created only the rational creatures and all equal; and that inequality arose in them from free-will, some being turned to God more and some less, and others turned more and others less away from God. And so those rational creatures which were turned to God by free-will, were promoted to the order of angels according to the

sunt, promotae sunt ad diversos ordines Angelorum, pro diversitate meritorum. Illae autem quae aversae sunt a Deo, sunt corporibus alligatae diversis, secundum diversitatem peccati, et hanc causam dicit esse creationis et diversitatis corporum. Sed secundum hoc, universitas corporalium creaturarum non esset propter bonitatem Dei communicandam creaturis, sed ad puniendum peccatum. Quod est contra illud quod dicitur Gen. I, *vidit Deus cuncta quae fecerat, et erant valde bona*. Et ut Augustinus dicit, XI de Civ. Dei, *quid stultius dici potest, quam istum solem, ut in uno mundo unus esset, non decori pulchritudinis, vel saluti rerum corporalium consuluisse artificem Deum; sed hoc potius evenisse, quia una anima sic peccaverat? Ac per hoc, si centum animae peccassent, centum soles haberet hic mundus.*

Et ideo dicendum est quod, sicut sapientia Dei est causa distinctionis rerum, ita et inaequalitatis. Quod sic patet. Duplex enim distinctio invenitur in rebus, una formalis, in his quae differunt specie; alia vero materialis, in his quae differunt numero tantum. Cum autem materia sit propter formam, distinctio materialis est propter formalem. Unde videmus quod in rebus incorruptibilibus non est nisi unum individuum unius speciei, quia species sufficienter conservatur in uno, in generabilibus autem et corruptibilibus, sunt multa individua unius speciei, ad conservationem speciei. Ex quo patet quod principalior est distinctio formalis quam materialis. Distinctio autem formalis semper requirit inaequalitatem, quia, ut dicitur in VIII Metaphys., formae rerum sunt sicut numeri, in quibus species variantur per additionem vel subtractionem unitatis. Unde in rebus naturalibus gradatim species ordinatae esse videntur, sicut mixta perfectiora sunt elementis, et plantae corporibus mineralibus, et animalia plantis, et homines aliis animalibus; et in singulis horum una species perfectior aliis invenitur. Sicut ergo divina sapientia causa est distinctionis rerum propter perfectionem universi, ita et inaequalitatis. Non enim esset perfectum universum, si tantum unus gradus bonitatis inveniretur in rebus.

AD PRIMUM ergo dicendum quod optimi agentis est producere totum effectum suum optimum, non tamen quod quamlibet partem totius faciat optimam simpliciter, sed optimam secundum proportionem ad totum, tolleretur enim bonitas animalis, si quaelibet pars eius oculi haberet dignitatem. Sic igitur et Deus totum universum constituit optimum, secundum modum creaturae, non autem singulas creaturas, sed unam alia meliorem. Et ideo de singulis creaturis dicitur Gen. I, *vidit Deus lucem quod esset bona*, et similiter de singulis, sed de omnibus simul dicitur, *vidit Deus cuncta quae fecerat, et erant valde bona*.

diversity of merits. And those who were turned away from God were bound down to bodies according to the diversity of their sin; and he said this was the cause of the creation and diversity of bodies. But according to this opinion, it would follow that the universality of bodily creatures would not be the effect of the goodness of God as communicated to creatures, but it would be for the sake of the punishment of sin, which is contrary to what is said: *God saw all the things that He had made, and they were very good* (Gen 1:31). And, as Augustine says (*De Civ. Dei* ii, 3): *What can be more foolish than to say that the divine Architect provided this one sun for the one world, not to be an ornament to its beauty, nor for the benefit of corporeal things, but that it happened through the sin of one soul; so that, if a hundred souls had sinned, there would be a hundred suns in the world?*

Therefore it must be said that as the wisdom of God is the cause of the distinction of things, so the same wisdom is the cause of their inequality. This may be explained as follows. A twofold distinction is found in things; one is a formal distinction as regards things differing specifically; the other is a material distinction as regards things differing numerically only. And as the matter is on account of the form, material distinction exists for the sake of the formal distinction. Hence we see that in incorruptible things there is only one individual of each species, forasmuch as the species is sufficiently preserved in the one; whereas in things generated and corruptible there are many individuals of one species for the preservation of the species. Whence it appears that formal distinction is of greater consequence than material. Now, formal distinction always requires inequality, because as the Philosopher says (*Metaph.* viii, 10), the forms of things are like numbers in which species vary by addition or subtraction of unity. Hence in natural things species seem to be arranged in degrees; as the mixed things are more perfect than the elements, and plants than minerals, and animals than plants, and men than other animals; and in each of these one species is more perfect than others. Therefore, as the divine wisdom is the cause of the distinction of things for the sake of the perfection of the universe, so it is the cause of inequality. For the universe would not be perfect if only one grade of goodness were found in things.

REPLY OBJ. 1: It is part of the best agent to produce an effect which is best in its entirety; but this does not mean that He makes every part of the whole the best absolutely, but in proportion to the whole; in the case of an animal, for instance, its goodness would be taken away if every part of it had the dignity of an eye. Thus, therefore, God also made the universe to be best as a whole, according to the mode of a creature; whereas He did not make each single creature best, but one better than another. And therefore we find it said of each creature, *God saw the light that it was good* (Gen 1:4); and in like manner of each one of the rest. But of all together it is said, *God saw all the things that He had made, and they were very good* (Gen 1:31).

Ad secundum dicendum quod primum quod procedit ab unitate, est aequalitas; et deinde procedit multiplicitas. Et ideo a patre, cui, secundum Augustinum, appropriatur unitas, processit filius, cui appropriatur aequalitas; et deinde creatura, cui competit inaequalitas. Sed tamen etiam a creaturis participatur quaedam aequalitas, scilicet proportionis.

Ad tertium dicendum quod ratio illa est quae movit Origenem, sed non habet locum nisi in retributione praemiorum, quorum inaequalitas debetur inaequalibus meritis. Sed in constitutione rerum non est inaequalitas partium per quamcumque inaequalitatem praecedentem vel meritorum vel etiam dispositionis materiae; sed propter perfectionem totius. Ut patet etiam in operibus artis, non enim propter hoc differt tectum a fundamento, quia habet diversam materiam; sed ut sit domus perfecta ex diversis partibus, quaerit artifex diversam materiam, et faceret eam si posset.

Reply Obj. 2: The first effect of unity is equality; and then comes multiplicity; and therefore from the Father, to Whom, according to Augustine (*De Doctr. Christ.* i, 5), is appropriated unity, the Son proceeds, to Whom is appropriated equality, and then from Him the creature proceeds, to which belongs inequality; but nevertheless even creatures share in a certain equality—namely, of proportion.

Reply Obj. 3: This is the argument that persuaded Origen: but it holds only as regards the distribution of rewards, the inequality of which is due to unequal merits. But in the constitution of things there is no inequality of parts through any preceding inequality, either of merits or of the disposition of the matter; but inequality comes from the perfection of the whole. This appears also in works done by art; for the roof of a house differs from the foundation, not because it is made of other material; but in order that the house may be made perfect of different parts, the artificer seeks different material; indeed, he would make such material if he could.

Article 3

Whether There Is Only One World?

Ad tertium sic proceditur. Videtur quod non sit unus mundus tantum, sed plures. Quia, ut Augustinus dicit, in libro octoginta trium quaest., inconveniens est dicere quod Deus sine ratione res creavit. Sed ea ratione qua creavit unum, potuit creare multos, cum eius potentia non sit limitata ad unius mundi creationem, sed est infinita, ut supra ostensum est. Ergo Deus plures mundos produxit.

Praeterea, natura facit quod melius est, et multo magis Deus. Sed melius esset esse plures mundos quam unum, quia plura bona paucioribus meliora sunt. Ergo plures mundi facti sunt a Deo.

Praeterea, omne quod habet formam in materia, potest multiplicari secundum numerum, manente eadem specie, quia multiplicatio secundum numerum est ex materia. Sed mundus habet formam in materia, sicut enim cum dico homo, significo formam, cum autem dico hic homo, significo formam in materia; ita, cum dicitur mundus, significatur forma, cum autem dicitur hic mundus, significatur forma in materia. Ergo nihil prohibet esse plures mundos.

Sed contra est quod dicitur Ioan. I, *mundus per ipsum factus est*; ubi singulariter mundum nominavit, quasi uno solo mundo existente.

Respondeo dicendum quod ipse ordo in rebus sic a Deo creatis existens, unitatem mundi manifestat. Mundus enim iste unus dicitur unitate ordinis, secundum quod quaedam ad alia ordinantur. Quaecumque

Objection 1: It would seem that there is not only one world, but many. Because, as Augustine says (QQ. 83, qu. 46), it is unfitting to say that God has created things without a reason. But for the same reason He created one, He could create many, since His power is not limited to the creation of one world; but rather it is infinite, as was shown above (Q. 25, A. 2). Therefore God has produced many worlds.

Obj. 2: Further, nature does what is best and much more does God. But it is better for there to be many worlds than one, because many good things are better than a few. Therefore many worlds have been made by God.

Obj. 3: Further, everything which has a form in matter can be multiplied in number, the species remaining the same, because multiplication in number comes from matter. But the world has a form in matter. Thus as when I say *man* I mean the form, and when I say *this man*, I mean the form in matter; so when we say *world*, the form is signified, and when we say *this world*, the form in the matter is signified. Therefore there is nothing to prevent the existence of many worlds.

On the contrary, It is said (John 1:10): *The world was made by Him*, where the world is named as one, as if only one existed.

I answer that, The very order of things created by God shows the unity of the world. For this world is called one by the unity of order, whereby some things are ordered to others. But whatever things come from God, have

autem sunt a Deo, ordinem habent ad invicem et ad ipsum Deum, ut supra ostensum est. Unde necesse est quod omnia ad unum mundum pertineant. Et ideo illi potuerunt ponere plures mundos, qui causam mundi non posuerunt aliquam sapientiam ordinantem, sed casum; ut Democritus, qui dixit ex concursu atomorum factum esse hunc mundum, et alios infinitos.

AD PRIMUM ergo dicendum quod haec ratio est quare mundus est unus, quia debent omnia esse ordinata uno ordine, et ad unum. Propter quod Aristoteles, in XII Metaphys., ex unitate ordinis in rebus existentis concludit unitatem Dei gubernantis. Et Plato ex unitate exemplaris probat unitatem mundi, quasi exemplati.

AD SECUNDUM dicendum quod nullum agens intendit pluralitatem materialem ut finem, quia materialis multitudo non habet certum terminum, sed de se tendit in infinitum; infinitum autem repugnat rationi finis. Cum autem dicitur plures mundos esse meliores quam unum, hoc dicitur secundum multitudinem materialem. Tale autem melius non est de intentione Dei agentis, quia eadem ratione dici posset quod, si fecisset duos, melius esset quod essent tres; et sic in infinitum.

AD TERTIUM dicendum quod mundus constat ex sua tota materia. Non enim est possibile esse aliam terram quam istam, quia omnis terra ferretur naturaliter ad hoc medium, ubicumque esset. Et eadem ratio est de aliis corporibus quae sunt partes mundi.

relation of order to each other, and to God Himself, as shown above (Q. 11, A. 3; Q. 21, A. 1). Hence it must be that all things should belong to one world. Therefore those only can assert that many worlds exist who do not acknowledge any ordaining wisdom, but rather believe in chance, as Democritus, who said that this world, besides an infinite number of other worlds, was made from a casual concourse of atoms.

REPLY OBJ. 1: This reason proves that the world is one because all things must be arranged in one order, and to one end. Therefore from the unity of order in things Aristotle infers (*Metaph.* xii, 52) the unity of God governing all; and Plato (*Tim.*), from the unity of the exemplar, proves the unity of the world, as the thing designed.

REPLY OBJ. 2: No agent intends material plurality as the end forasmuch as material multitude has no certain limit, but of itself tends to infinity, and the infinite is opposed to the notion of end. Now when it is said that many worlds are better than one, this has reference to material order. But the best in this sense is not the intention of the divine agent; forasmuch as for the same reason it might be said that if He had made two worlds, it would be better if He had made three; and so on to infinity.

REPLY OBJ. 3: The world is composed of the whole of its matter. For it is not possible for there to be another earth than this one, since every earth would naturally be carried to this central one, wherever it was. The same applies to the other bodies which are part of the world.

QUESTION 48

THE DISTINCTION OF THINGS IN PARTICULAR

Deinde considerandum est de distinctione rerum in speciali. Et primo, de distinctione boni et mali; deinde de distinctione spiritualis et corporalis creaturae.

Circa primum, quaerendum est de malo; et de causa mali.

Circa malum quaeruntur sex.

Primo, utrum malum sit natura aliqua.

Secundo, utrum malum inveniatur in rebus.

Tertio, utrum bonum sit subiectum mali.

Quarto, utrum malum totaliter corrumpat bonum.

Quinto, de divisione mali per poenam et culpam.

Sexto, quid habeat plus de ratione mali, utrum poena vel culpa.

We must now consider the distinction of things in particular; and first the distinction of good and evil; and then the distinction of the spiritual and corporeal creatures.

Concerning the first, we inquire into evil and its cause.

Concerning evil, six points are to be considered:

(1) Whether evil is a nature?

(2) Whether evil is found in things?

(3) Whether good is the subject of evil?

(4) Whether evil totally corrupts good?

(5) The division of evil into pain and fault.

(6) Whether pain, or fault, has more the nature of evil?

Article 1

Whether Evil Is a Nature?

AD PRIMUM SIC PROCEDITUR. Videtur quod malum sit natura quaedam. Quia omne genus est natura quaedam. Sed malum est quoddam genus, dicitur enim in praedicamentis, quod *bonum et malum non sunt in genere, sed sunt genera aliorum.* Ergo malum est natura quaedam.

PRAETEREA, omnis differentia constitutiva alicuius speciei est natura quaedam. Malum autem est differentia constitutiva in moralibus, differt enim specie malus habitus a bono, ut liberalitas ab illiberalitate. Ergo malum significat naturam quandam.

PRAETEREA, utrumque contrariorum est natura quaedam. Sed malum et bonum non opponuntur ut privatio et habitus, sed ut contraria, ut probat philosophus, in praedicamentis, per hoc quod inter bonum et malum est aliquid medium, et a malo potest fieri reditus ad bonum. Ergo malum significat naturam quandam.

PRAETEREA, quod non est, non agit. Sed malum agit, quia corrumpit bonum. Ergo malum est quoddam ens, et natura quaedam.

PRAETEREA, ad perfectionem universitatis rerum non pertinet nisi quod est ens et natura quaedam. Sed malum pertinet ad perfectionem universitatis rerum, dicit enim Augustinus, in Enchirid., quod *ex omnibus consistit universitatis admirabilis pulchritudo; in qua etiam illud quod malum dicitur, bene ordinatum, et suo loco positum, eminentius commendat bona.* Ergo malum est natura quaedam.

OBJECTION 1: It would seem that evil is a nature. For every genus is a nature. But evil is a genus; for the Philosopher says (*Praedic.* x) that *good and evil are not in a genus, but are genera of other things.* Therefore evil is a nature.

OBJ. 2: Further, every difference which constitutes a species is a nature. But evil is a difference constituting a species of morality; for a bad habit differs in species from a good habit, as liberality from illiberality. Therefore evil signifies a nature.

OBJ. 3: Further, each extreme of two contraries is a nature. But evil and good are not opposed as privation and habit, but as contraries, as the Philosopher shows (*Praedic.* x) by the fact that between good and evil there is a medium, and from evil there can be a return to good. Therefore evil signifies a nature.

OBJ. 4: Further, what is not, acts not. But evil acts, for it corrupts good. Therefore evil is a being and a nature.

OBJ. 5: Further, nothing belongs to the perfection of the universe except what is a being and a nature. But evil belongs to the perfection of the universe of things; for Augustine says (*Enchir.* 10, 11) that the *admirable beauty of the universe is made up of all things. In which even what is called evil, well ordered and in its place, is the eminent commendation of what is good.* Therefore evil is a nature.

SED CONTRA est quod Dionysius dicit, IV cap. de Div. Nom., *malum non est existens neque bonum.*

RESPONDEO dicendum quod unum oppositorum cognoscitur per alterum, sicut per lucem tenebra. Unde et quid sit malum, oportet ex ratione boni accipere. Diximus autem supra quod bonum est omne id quod est appetibile, et sic, cum omnis natura appetat suum esse et suam perfectionem, necesse est dicere quod esse et perfectio cuiuscumque naturae rationem habeat bonitatis. Unde non potest esse quod malum significet quoddam esse, aut quandam formam seu naturam. Relinquitur ergo quod nomine mali significetur quaedam absentia boni. Et pro tanto dicitur quod malum neque est existens nec bonum, quia cum ens, inquantum huiusmodi, sit bonum, eadem est remotio utrorumque.

AD PRIMUM ergo dicendum quod Aristoteles ibi loquitur secundum opinionem Pythagoricorum, qui malum existimabant esse naturam quandam, et ideo ponebant bonum et malum genera. Consuevit enim Aristoteles, et praecipue in libris logicalibus, ponere exempla quae probabilia erant suo tempore, secundum opinionem aliquorum philosophorum. Vel dicendum, sicut dicit philosophus in X Metaphys., quod *prima contrarietas est habitus et privatio,* quia scilicet in omnibus contrariis salvatur, cum semper unum contrariorum sit imperfectum respectu alterius, ut nigrum respectu albi, et amarum respectu dulcis. Et pro tanto bonum et malum dicuntur genera, non simpliciter, sed contrariorum, quia sicut omnis forma habet rationem boni, ita omnis privatio, inquantum huiusmodi, habet rationem mali.

AD SECUNDUM dicendum quod bonum et malum non sunt differentiae constitutivae nisi in moralibus, quae recipiunt speciem ex fine, qui est obiectum voluntatis, a qua moralia dependent. Et quia bonum habet rationem finis, ideo bonum et malum sunt differentiae specificae in moralibus; bonum per se, sed malum inquantum est remotio debiti finis. Nec tamen remotio debiti finis constituit speciem in moralibus, nisi secundum quod adiungitur fini indebito, sicut neque in naturalibus invenitur privatio formae substantialis, nisi adiuncta alteri formae. Sic igitur malum quod est differentia constitutiva in moralibus, est quoddam bonum adiunctum privationi alterius boni, sicut finis intemperati est, non quidem carere bono rationis, sed delectabile sensus absque ordine rationis. Unde malum, inquantum malum, non est differentia constitutiva; sed ratione boni adiuncti.

ET PER HOC etiam patet responsio ad tertium. Nam ibi philosophus loquitur de bono et malo, secundum quod inveniuntur in moralibus. Sic enim inter bonum et malum invenitur medium, prout bonum dicitur quod est ordinatum; malum autem, quod non solum est deordinatum, sed etiam nocivum alteri. Unde dicit philosophus in IV Ethic., quod prodigus vanus quidem est,

ON THE CONTRARY, Dionysius says (*Div. Nom.* iv), *Evil is neither a being nor a good.*

I ANSWER THAT, One opposite is known through the other, as darkness is known through light. Hence also what evil is must be known from the nature of good. Now, we have said above that good is everything appetible; and thus, since every nature desires its own being and its own perfection, it must be said also that the being and the perfection of any nature is good. Hence it cannot be that evil signifies being, or any form or nature. Therefore it must be that by the name of evil is signified the absence of good. And this is what is meant by saying that *evil is neither a being nor a good.* For since being, as such, is good, the absence of one implies the absence of the other.

REPLY OBJ. 1: Aristotle speaks there according to the opinion of Pythagoreans, who thought that evil was a kind of nature; and therefore they asserted the existence of the genus of good and evil. For Aristotle, especially in his logical works, brings forward examples that in his time were probable in the opinion of some philosophers. Or, it may be said that, as the Philosopher says (*Metaph.* iv, 6), *the first kind of contrariety is habit and privation,* as being verified in all contraries; since one contrary is always imperfect in relation to another, as black in relation to white, and bitter in relation to sweet. And in this way good and evil are said to be genera not simply, but in regard to contraries; because, as every form has the nature of good, so every privation, as such, has the nature of evil.

REPLY OBJ. 2: Good and evil are not constitutive differences except in morals, which receive their species from the end, which is the object of the will, the source of all morality. And because good has the nature of an end, therefore good and evil are specific differences in moral things; good in itself, but evil as the absence of the due end. Yet neither does the absence of the due end by itself constitute a moral species, except as it is joined to the undue end; just as we do not find the privation of the substantial form in natural things, unless it is joined to another form. Thus, therefore, the evil which is a constitutive difference in morals is a certain good joined to the privation of another good; as the end proposed by the intemperate man is not the privation of the good of reason, but the delight of sense without the order of reason. Hence evil is not a constitutive difference as such, but by reason of the good that is annexed.

REPLY OBJ. 3: This appears from the above. For the Philosopher speaks there of good and evil in morality. Because in that respect, between good and evil there is a medium, as good is considered as something rightly ordered, and evil as a thing not only out of right order, but also as injurious to another. Hence the Philosopher says (*Ethic.* iv, i) that a *prodigal man is foolish, but not evil.* And from this

sed non malus. Ab hoc etiam malo quod est secundum morem, contingit fieri reditum ad bonum; non autem ex quocumque malo. Non enim ex caecitate fit reditus ad visionem, cum tamen caecitas sit malum quoddam.

AD QUARTUM dicendum quod aliquid agere dicitur tripliciter. Uno modo, formaliter, eo modo loquendi quo dicitur albedo facere album. Et sic malum, etiam ratione ipsius privationis, dicitur corrumpere bonum, quia est ipsa corruptio vel privatio boni. Alio modo dicitur aliquid agere effective, sicut pictor dicitur facere album parietem. Tertio modo, per modum causae finalis, sicut finis dicitur efficere, movendo efficientem. His autem duobus modis malum non agit aliquid per se, idest secundum quod est privatio quaedam, sed secundum quod ei bonum adiungitur, nam omnis actio est ab aliqua forma, et omne quod desideratur ut finis, est perfectio aliqua. Et ideo, ut Dionysius dicit, IV cap. de Div. Nom., *malum non agit neque desideratur nisi virtute boni adiuncti; per se autem est infinitum, et praeter voluntatem et intentionem.*

AD QUINTUM dicendum quod, sicut supra dictum est, partes universi habent ordinem ad invicem, secundum quod una agit in alteram, et est finis alterius et exemplar. Haec autem, ut dictum est, non possunt convenire malo, nisi ratione boni adiuncti. Unde malum neque ad perfectionem universi pertinet, neque sub ordine universi concluditur, nisi per accidens, idest ratione boni adiuncti.

evil in morality, there may be a return to good, but not from any sort of evil, for from blindness there is no return to sight, although blindness is an evil.

REPLY OBJ. 4: A thing is said to act in a threefold sense. In one way, formally, as when we say that whiteness makes white; and in that sense evil considered even as a privation is said to corrupt good, forasmuch as it is itself a corruption or privation of good. In another sense a thing is said to act effectively, as when a painter makes a wall white. Third, it is said in the sense of the final cause, as the end is said to effect by moving the efficient cause. But in these two ways evil does not effect anything of itself, that is, as a privation, but by virtue of the good annexed to it. For every action comes from some form; and everything which is desired as an end, is a perfection. And therefore, as Dionysius says (*Div. Nom.* iv): *Evil does not act, nor is it desired, except by virtue of some good joined to it: while of itself it is nothing definite, and beside the scope of our will and intention.*

REPLY OBJ. 5: As was said above, the parts of the universe are ordered to each other, according as one acts on the other, and according as one is the end and exemplar of the other. But, as was said above, this can only happen to evil as joined to some good. Hence evil neither belongs to the perfection of the universe, nor does it come under the order of the same, except accidentally, that is, by reason of some good joined to it.

Article 2

Whether Evil Is Found in Things?

AD SECUNDUM SIC PROCEDITUR. Videtur quod malum non inveniatur in rebus. Quidquid enim invenitur in rebus, vel est ens aliquod, vel privatio entis alicuius, quod est non ens. Sed Dionysius dicit, IV cap. de Div. Nom., quod *malum distat ab existente, et adhuc plus distat a non existente.* Ergo malum nullo modo invenitur in rebus.

PRAETEREA, ens et res convertuntur. Si ergo malum est ens in rebus, sequitur quod malum sit res quaedam. Quod est contra praedicta.

PRAETEREA, *albius est quod est nigro impermixtius,* ut dicitur in III libro Topic. Aristotelis. Ergo et melius est quod est malo impermixtius. Sed Deus facit semper quod melius est, multo magis quam natura. Ergo in rebus a Deo conditis nihil malum invenitur.

SED CONTRA est quod secundum hoc removerentur omnes prohibitiones et poenae, quae non sunt nisi malorum.

OBJECTION 1: It would seem that evil is not found in things. For whatever is found in things, is either something, or a privation of something, that is a *not-being*. But Dionysius says (*Div. Nom.* iv) that *evil is distant from existence, and even more distant from non-existence.* Therefore evil is not at all found in things.

OBJ. 2: Further, *being* and *thing* are convertible. If therefore evil is a being in things, it follows that evil is a thing, which is contrary to what has been said (A. 1).

OBJ. 3: Further, *the white unmixed with black is the most white,* as the Philosopher says (*Topic.* iii, 4). Therefore also the good unmixed with evil is the greater good. But God makes always what is best, much more than nature does. Therefore in things made by God there is no evil.

ON THE CONTRARY, On the above assumptions, all prohibitions and penalties would cease, for they exist only for evils.

RESPONDEO dicendum quod, sicut supra dictum est, perfectio universi requirit inaequalitatem esse in rebus, ut omnes bonitatis gradus impleantur. Est autem unus gradus bonitatis ut aliquid ita bonum sit, quod nunquam deficere possit. Alius autem gradus bonitatis est, ut sic aliquid bonum sit, quod a bono deficere possit. Qui etiam gradus in ipso esse inveniuntur, quaedam enim sunt, quae suum esse amittere non possunt, ut incorporalia; quaedam vero sunt, quae amittere possunt, ut corporalia.

Sicut igitur perfectio universitatis rerum requirit ut non solum sint entia incorruptibilia, sed etiam corruptibilia; ita perfectio universi requirit ut sint quaedam quae a bonitate deficere possint; ad quod sequitur ea interdum deficere. In hoc autem consistit ratio mali, ut scilicet aliquid deficiat a bono. Unde manifestum est quod in rebus malum invenitur, sicut et corruptio, nam et ipsa corruptio malum quoddam est.

AD PRIMUM ergo dicendum quod malum distat et ab ente simpliciter, et non ente simpliciter, quia neque est sicut habitus, neque sicut pura negatio, sed sicut privatio.

AD SECUNDUM dicendum quod, sicut dicitur in V Metaphys., ens dupliciter dicitur. Uno modo, secundum quod significat entitatem rei, prout dividitur per decem praedicamenta, et sic convertitur cum re. Et hoc modo, nulla privatio est ens, unde nec malum. Alio modo dicitur ens, quod significat veritatem propositionis, quae in compositione consistit, cuius nota est hoc verbum est, et hoc est ens quo respondetur ad quaestionem an est. Et sic caecitatem dicimus esse in oculo, vel quamcumque aliam privationem. Et hoc modo etiam malum dicitur ens. Propter huius autem distinctionis ignorantiam, aliqui, considerantes quod aliquae res dicuntur malae, vel quod malum dicitur esse in rebus, crediderunt quod malum esset res quaedam.

AD TERTIUM dicendum quod Deus et natura, et quodcumque agens, facit quod melius est in toto; sed non quod melius est in unaquaque parte, nisi per ordinem ad totum, ut supra dictum est. Ipsum autem totum quod est universitas creaturarum, melius et perfectius est, si in eo sint quaedam quae a bono deficere possunt, quae interdum deficiunt, Deo hoc non impediente. Tum quia providentiae non est naturam destruere, sed salvare, ut Dionysius dicit, IV cap. de Div. Nom., ipsa autem natura rerum hoc habet, ut quae deficere possunt, quandoque deficiant. Tum quia, ut dicit Augustinus in Enchirid., Deus est adeo potens, quod etiam potest bene facere de malis. Unde multa bona tollerentur, si Deus nullum malum permitteret esse. Non enim generaretur ignis, nisi corrumperetur aer; neque conservaretur vita leonis, nisi occideretur asinus; neque etiam laudaretur iustitia vindicans, et patientia sufferens, si non esset iniquitas.

I ANSWER THAT, As was said above (Q. 47, AA. 1, 2), the perfection of the universe requires that there should be inequality in things, so that every grade of goodness may be realized. Now, one grade of goodness is that of the good which cannot fail. Another grade of goodness is that of the good which can fail in goodness, and this grade is to be found in existence itself; for some things there are which cannot lose their existence, as incorruptible things, while some there are which can lose it, as things corruptible.

As, therefore, the perfection of the universe requires that there should be not only beings incorruptible, but also corruptible beings; so the perfection of the universe requires that there should be some which can fail in goodness, and thence it follows that sometimes they do fail. Now it is in this that evil consists, namely, in the fact that a thing fails in goodness. Hence it is clear that evil is found in things, as corruption also is found; for corruption is itself an evil.

REPLY OBJ. 1: Evil is distant both from simple being and from simple *not-being*, because it is neither a habit nor a pure negation, but a privation.

REPLY OBJ. 2: As the Philosopher says (*Metaph.* v, 14), being is twofold. In one way it is considered as signifying the entity of a thing, as divisible by the ten *predicaments*; and in that sense it is convertible with thing, and thus no privation is a being, and neither therefore is evil a being. In another sense being conveys the truth of a proposition which unites together subject and attribute by a copula, notified by this word *is*; and in this sense being is what answers to the question, *Does it exist?* and thus we speak of blindness as being in the eye; or of any other privation. In this way even evil can be called a being. Through ignorance of this distinction some, considering that things may be evil, or that evil is said to be in things, believed that evil was a positive thing in itself.

REPLY OBJ. 3: God and nature and any other agent make what is best in the whole, but not what is best in every single part, except in order to the whole, as was said above (Q. 47, A. 2). And the whole itself, which is the universe of creatures, is all the better and more perfect if some things in it can fail in goodness, and do sometimes fail, God not preventing this. This happens, first, because *it belongs to Providence not to destroy, but to save nature*, as Dionysius says (*Div. Nom.* iv); but it belongs to nature that what may fail should sometimes fail; second, because, as Augustine says (*Enchir.* 11), *God is so powerful that He can even make good out of evil*. Hence many good things would be taken away if God permitted no evil to exist; for fire would not be generated if air was not corrupted, nor would the life of a lion be preserved unless the ass were killed. Neither would avenging justice nor the patience of a sufferer be praised if there were no injustice.

Article 3

Whether Evil Is in Good As in Its Subject?

AD TERTIUM SIC PROCEDITUR. Videtur quod malum non sit in bono sicut in subiecto. Omnia enim bona sunt existentia. Sed Dionysius dicit, IV cap. de Div. Nom., quod *malum non est existens, neque in existentibus*. Ergo malum non est in bono sicut in subiecto.

PRAETEREA, malum non est ens, bonum vero est ens. Sed non ens non requirit ens, in quo sit sicut in subiecto. Ergo nec malum requirit bonum, in quo sit sicut in subiecto.

PRAETEREA, unum contrariorum non est subiectum alterius. Sed bonum et malum sunt contraria. Ergo malum non est in bono sicut in subiecto.

PRAETEREA, id in quo est albedo sicut in subiecto, dicitur esse album. Ergo et id in quo est malum sicut in subiecto, est malum. Si ergo malum sit in bono sicut in subiecto, sequitur quod bonum sit malum, contra id quod dicitur Isai. V, *vae, qui dicitis malum bonum, et bonum malum.*

SED CONTRA est quod Augustinus dicit, in Enchirid., quod malum non est nisi in bono.

RESPONDEO dicendum quod, sicut dictum est, malum importat remotionem boni. Non autem quaelibet remotio boni malum dicitur. Potest enim accipi remotio boni et privative, et negative. Remotio igitur boni negative accepta, mali rationem non habet, alioquin sequeretur quod ea quae nullo modo sunt, mala essent; et iterum quod quaelibet res esset mala, ex hoc quod non habet bonum alterius rei, utpote quod homo esset malus, quia non habet velocitatem capreae, vel fortitudinem leonis. Sed remotio boni privative accepta, malum dicitur, sicut privatio visus caecitas dicitur.

Subiectum autem privationis et formae est unum et idem, scilicet ens in potentia, sive sit ens in potentia simpliciter, sicut materia prima, quae est subiectum formae substantialis et privationis oppositae; sive sit ens in potentia secundum quid et in actu simpliciter, ut corpus diaphanum, quod est subiectum tenebrarum et lucis. Manifestum est autem quod forma per quam aliquid est actu, perfectio quaedam est, et bonum quoddam, et sic omne ens in actu, bonum quoddam est. Et similiter omne ens in potentia, inquantum huiusmodi, bonum quoddam est, secundum quod habet ordinem ad bonum, sicut enim est ens in potentia, ita et bonum in potentia. Relinquitur ergo quod subiectum mali sit bonum.

AD PRIMUM ergo dicendum quod Dionysius intelligit malum non esse in existentibus sicut partem, aut sicut proprietatem naturalem alicuius existentis.

AD SECUNDUM dicendum quod non ens negative acceptum non requirit subiectum. Sed privatio est negatio

OBJECTION 1: It would seem that evil is not in good as its subject. For good is something that exists. But Dionysius says (*Div. Nom.* iv, 4) that *evil does not exist, nor is it in that which exists.* Therefore, evil is not in good as its subject.

OBJ. 2: Further, evil is not a being; whereas good is a being. But *non-being* does not require being as its subject. Therefore, neither does evil require good as its subject.

OBJ. 3: Further, one contrary is not the subject of another. But good and evil are contraries. Therefore, evil is not in good as in its subject.

OBJ. 4: Further, the subject of whiteness is called white. Therefore also the subject of evil is evil. If, therefore, evil is in good as in its subject, it follows that good is evil, against what is said (Isa 5:20): *Woe to you who call evil good, and good evil!*

ON THE CONTRARY, Augustine says (*Enchiridion* 14) that *evil exists only in good.*

I ANSWER THAT, As was said above (A. 1), evil imports the absence of good. But not every absence of good is evil. For absence of good can be taken in a privative and in a negative sense. Absence of good, taken negatively, is not evil; otherwise, it would follow that what does not exist is evil, and also that everything would be evil, through not having the good belonging to something else; for instance, a man would be evil who had not the swiftness of the roe, or the strength of a lion. But the absence of good, taken in a privative sense, is an evil; as, for instance, the privation of sight is called blindness.

Now, the subject of privation and of form is one and the same—viz. being in potentiality, whether it be being in absolute potentiality, as primary matter, which is the subject of the substantial form, and of privation of the opposite form; or whether it be being in relative potentiality, and absolute actuality, as in the case of a transparent body, which is the subject both of darkness and light. It is, however, manifest that the form which makes a thing actual is a perfection and a good; and thus every actual being is a good; and likewise every potential being, as such, is a good, as having a relation to good. For as it has being in potentiality, so has it goodness in potentiality. Therefore, the subject of evil is good.

REPLY OBJ. 1: Dionysius means that evil is not in existing things as a part, or as a natural property of any existing thing.

REPLY OBJ. 2: *Not-being*, understood negatively, does not require a subject; but privation is negation in a subject,

in subiecto, ut dicitur in IV Metaphys., et tale non ens est malum.

AD TERTIUM dicendum quod malum non est sicut in subiecto in bono quod ei opponitur, sed in quodam alio bono, subiectum enim caecitatis non est visus, sed animal. Videtur tamen, ut Augustinus dicit, hic fallere dialecticorum regula, quae dicit contraria simul esse non posse. Hoc tamen intelligendum est secundum communem acceptionem boni et mali, non autem secundum quod specialiter accipitur hoc bonum et hoc malum. Album autem et nigrum, dulce et amarum, et huiusmodi contraria, non accipiuntur nisi specialiter, quia sunt in quibusdam generibus determinatis. Sed bonum circuit omnia genera, unde unum bonum potest simul esse cum privatione alterius boni.

AD QUARTUM dicendum quod propheta imprecatur vae illis qui dicunt id quod est bonum, secundum quod est bonum, esse malum. Hoc autem non sequitur ex praemissis, ut per praedicta patet.

as the Philosopher says (*Metaph.* iv, 4), and such *not-being* is an evil.

REPLY OBJ. 3: Evil is not in the good opposed to it as in its subject, but in some other good, for the subject of blindness is not *sight*, but *animal*. Yet, it appears, as Augustine says (*Enchiridion* 13), that the rule of dialectics here fails, where it is laid down that contraries cannot exist together. But this is to be taken as referring to good and evil in general, but not in reference to any particular good and evil. For white and black, sweet and bitter, and the like contraries, are only considered as contraries in a special sense, because they exist in some determinate genus; whereas good enters into every genus. Hence one good can coexist with the privation of another good.

REPLY OBJ. 4: The prophet invokes woe to those who say that good as such is evil. But this does not follow from what is said above, as is clear from the explanation given.

Article 4

Whether Evil Corrupts the Whole Good?

AD QUARTUM SIC PROCEDITUR. Videtur quod malum corrumpat totum bonum. Unum enim contrariorum totaliter corrumpitur per alterum. Sed bonum et malum sunt contraria. Ergo malum potest corrumpere totum bonum.

PRAETEREA, Augustinus dicit, in Enchirid., quod *malum nocet inquantum adimit bonum.* Sed bonum est sibi simile et uniforme. Ergo totaliter tollitur per malum.

PRAETEREA, malum, quandiu est, nocet et aufert bonum. Sed illud a quo semper aliquid aufertur, quandoque consumitur, nisi sit infinitum; quod non potest dici de aliquo bono creato. Ergo malum consumit totaliter bonum.

SED CONTRA est quod Augustinus dicit, in Enchirid., quod *malum non potest totaliter consumere bonum.*

RESPONDEO dicendum quod malum non potest totaliter consumere bonum. Ad cuius evidentiam, considerandum est quod est triplex bonum. Quoddam, quod per malum totaliter tollitur, et hoc est bonum oppositum malo; sicut lumen totaliter per tenebras tollitur, et visus per caecitatem. Quoddam vero bonum est, quod nec totaliter tollitur per malum, nec diminuitur, scilicet bonum quod est subiectum mali; non enim per tenebras aliquid de substantia aeris diminuitur. Quoddam vero bonum est, quod diminuitur quidem per malum, sed non totaliter tollitur, et hoc bonum est habilitas subiecti ad actum.

OBJECTION 1: It would seem that evil corrupts the whole good. For one contrary is wholly corrupted by another. But good and evil are contraries. Therefore evil corrupts the whole good.

OBJ. 2: Further, Augustine says (*Enchiridion* 12) that *evil hurts inasmuch as it takes away good.* But good is all of a piece and uniform. Therefore it is wholly taken away by evil.

OBJ. 3: Further, evil, as long as it lasts, hurts, and takes away good. But that from which something is always being removed, is at some time consumed, unless it is infinite, which cannot be said of any created good. Therefore evil wholly consumes good.

ON THE CONTRARY, Augustine says (*Enchiridion* 12) that *evil cannot wholly consume good.*

I ANSWER THAT, Evil cannot wholly consume good. To prove this we must consider that good is threefold. One kind of good is wholly destroyed by evil, and this is the good opposed to evil, as light is wholly destroyed by darkness, and sight by blindness. Another kind of good is neither wholly destroyed nor diminished by evil, and that is the good which is the subject of evil; for by darkness the substance of the air is not injured. And there is also a kind of good which is diminished by evil, but is not wholly taken away; and this good is the aptitude of a subject to some actuality.

Diminutio autem huius boni non est accipienda per subtractionem, sicut est diminutio in quantitatibus, sed per remissionem, sicut est diminutio in qualitatibus et formis. Remissio autem huius habilitatis est accipienda e contrario intensioni ipsius. Intenditur enim huiusmodi habilitas per dispositiones quibus materia praeparatur ad actum; quae quanto magis multiplicantur in subiecto, tanto habilius est ad recipiendum perfectionem et formam. Et e contrario remittitur per dispositiones contrarias; quae quanto magis multiplicatae sunt in materia, et magis intensae, tanto magis remittitur potentia ad actum.

Si igitur contrariae dispositiones in infinitum multiplicari et intendi non possunt, sed usque ad certum terminum, neque habilitas praedicta in infinitum diminuitur vel remittitur. Sicut patet in qualitatibus activis et passivis elementorum, frigiditas enim et humiditas, per quae diminuitur sive remittitur habilitas materiae ad formam ignis, non possunt multiplicari in infinitum. Si vero dispositiones contrariae in infinitum multiplicari possunt, et habilitas praedicta in infinitum diminuitur vel remittitur. Non tamen totaliter tollitur, quia semper manet in sua radice, quae est substantia subiecti. Sicut si in infinitum interponantur corpora opaca inter solem et aerem, in infinitum diminuetur habilitas aeris ad lumen, nunquam tamen totaliter tollitur, manente aere, qui secundum naturam suam est diaphanus. Similiter in infinitum potest fieri additio in peccatis, per quae semper magis ac magis minuitur habilitas animae ad gratiam, quae quidem peccata sunt quasi obstacula interposita inter nos et Deum secundum illud Isaiae LIX, *peccata nostra diviserunt inter nos et Deum*. Neque tamen tollitur totaliter ab anima praedicta habilitas, quia consequitur naturam ipsius.

AD PRIMUM ergo dicendum quod bonum quod opponitur malo, totaliter tollitur, sed alia bona non totaliter tolluntur, ut dictum est.

AD SECUNDUM dicendum quod habilitas praedicta est media inter subiectum et actum. Unde ex ea parte qua attingit actum, diminuitur per malum, sed ex ea parte qua tenet se cum subiecto, remanet. Ergo, licet bonum in se sit simile, tamen, propter comparationem eius ad diversa, non totaliter tollitur, sed in parte.

AD TERTIUM dicendum quod quidam, imaginantes diminutionem boni praedicti ad similitudinem diminutionis quantitatis, dixerunt quod, sicut continuum dividitur in infinitum, facta divisione secundum eandem proportionem (ut puta quod accipiatur medium medii, vel tertium tertii), sic in proposito accidit. Sed haec ratio hic locum non habet. Quia in divisione in qua semper servatur eadem proportio, semper subtrahitur minus et minus, minus enim est medium medii quam medium totius. Sed secundum peccatum non de necessitate minus

The diminution, however, of this kind of good is not to be considered by way of subtraction, as diminution in quantity, but rather by way of remission, as diminution in qualities and forms. The remission likewise of this habitude is to be taken as contrary to its intensity. For this kind of aptitude receives its intensity by the dispositions whereby the matter is prepared for actuality; which the more they are multiplied in the subject the more is it fitted to receive its perfection and form; and, on the contrary, it receives its remission by contrary dispositions which, the more they are multiplied in the matter, and the more they are intensified, the more is the potentiality remitted as regards the actuality.

Therefore, if contrary dispositions cannot be multiplied and intensified to infinity, but only to a certain limit, neither is the aforesaid aptitude diminished or remitted infinitely, as appears in the active and passive qualities of the elements; for coldness and humidity, whereby the aptitude of matter to the form of fire is diminished or remitted, cannot be infinitely multiplied. But if the contrary dispositions can be infinitely multiplied, the aforesaid aptitude is also infinitely diminished or remitted; yet, nevertheless, it is not wholly taken away, because its root always remains, which is the substance of the subject. Thus, if opaque bodies were interposed to infinity between the sun and the air, the aptitude of the air to light would be infinitely diminished, but still it would never be wholly removed while the air remained, which in its very nature is transparent. Likewise, addition in sin can be made to infinitude, whereby the aptitude of the soul to grace is more and more lessened; and these sins, indeed, are like obstacles interposed between us and God, according to Isa. 59:2: *Our sins have divided between us and God*. Yet the aforesaid aptitude of the soul is not wholly taken away, for it belongs to its very nature.

REPLY OBJ. 1: The good which is opposed to evil is wholly taken away; but other goods are not wholly removed, as said above.

REPLY OBJ. 2: The aforesaid aptitude is a medium between subject and act. Hence, where it touches act, it is diminished by evil; but where it touches the subject, it remains as it was. Therefore, although good is like to itself, yet, on account of its relation to different things, it is not wholly, but only partially taken away.

REPLY OBJ. 3: Some, imagining that the diminution of this kind of good is like the diminution of quantity, said that just as the continuous is infinitely divisible, if the division be made in an ever same proportion (for instance, half of half, or a third of a third), so is it in the present case. But this explanation does not avail here. For when in a division we keep the same proportion, we continue to subtract less and less; for half of half is less than half of the whole. But a second sin does not necessarily diminish the above

diminuit de habilitate praedicta, quam praecedens, sed forte aut aequaliter, aut magis.

Dicendum est ergo quod, licet ista habilitas sit quoddam finitum, diminuitur tamen in infinitum, non per se, sed per accidens, secundum quod contrariae dispositiones etiam in infinitum augentur, ut dictum est.

mentioned aptitude less than a preceding sin, but perchance either equally or more.

Therefore it must be said that, although this aptitude is a finite thing, still it may be so diminished infinitely, not per se, but accidentally; according as the contrary dispositions are also increased infinitely, as explained above.

Article 5

Whether Evil Is Adequately Divided into Pain and Fault?

AD QUINTUM SIC PROCEDITUR. Videtur quod malum insufficienter dividatur per poenam et culpam. Omnis enim defectus malum quoddam esse videtur. Sed in omnibus creaturis est quidam defectus, quod se in esse conservare non possunt, qui tamen nec poena nec culpa est. Non ergo sufficienter malum dividitur per poenam et culpam.

PRAETEREA, in rebus irrationalibus non invenitur culpa nec poena. Invenitur tamen in eis corruptio et defectus, quae ad rationem mali pertinent. Ergo non omne malum est poena vel culpa.

PRAETEREA, tentatio quoddam malum est. Nec tamen est culpa, quia tentatio cui non consentitur, *non est peccatum, sed materia exercendae virtutis*, ut dicitur in Glossa II Cor. XII. Nec etiam poena, quia tentatio praecedit culpam, poena autem subsequitur. Insufficienter ergo malum dividitur per poenam et culpam.

SED CONTRA, videtur quod divisio sit superflua. Ut enim Augustinus dicit, in Enchirid., malum dicitur quia nocet. Quod autem nocet, poenale est. Omne ergo malum sub poena continetur.

RESPONDEO dicendum quod malum, sicut supra dictum est, est privatio boni, quod in perfectione et actu consistit principaliter et per se. Actus autem est duplex, primus, et secundus. Actus quidem primus est forma et integritas rei, actus autem secundus est operatio. Contingit ergo malum esse dupliciter. Uno modo, per subtractionem formae, aut alicuius partis, quae requiritur ad integritatem rei; sicut caecitas malum est, et carere membro. Alio modo, per subtractionem debitae operationis; vel quia omnino non est; vel quia debitum modum et ordinem non habet. Quia vero bonum simpliciter est obiectum voluntatis, malum, quod est privatio boni, secundum specialem rationem invenitur in creaturis rationalibus habentibus voluntatem. Malum igitur quod est per subtractionem formae vel integritatis rei, habet rationem poenae; et praecipue supposito quod omnia divinae providentiae et iustitiae subdantur, ut supra ostensum est, de ratione enim poenae est, quod sit contraria voluntati. Malum autem quod consistit in subtractione debitae operationis in rebus voluntariis, habet

OBJECTION 1: It would seem that evil is not adequately divided into pain and fault. For every defect is a kind of evil. But in all creatures there is the defect of not being able to preserve their own existence, which nevertheless is neither a pain nor a fault. Therefore evil is inadequately divided into pain and fault.

OBJ. 2: Further, in irrational creatures there is neither fault nor pain; but, nevertheless, they have corruption and defect, which are evils. Therefore not every evil is a pain or a fault.

OBJ. 3: Further, temptation is an evil, but it is not a fault; for *temptation which involves no consent, is not a sin, but an occasion for the exercise of virtue*, as is said in a gloss on 2 Cor. 12; nor is it a pain; because temptation precedes the fault, and the pain follows afterwards. Therefore, evil is not sufficiently divided into pain and fault.

ON THE CONTRARY, It would seem that this division is superfluous: for, as Augustine says (*Enchiridion* 12), a thing is evil *because it hurts*. But whatever hurts is penal. Therefore every evil comes under pain.

I ANSWER THAT, Evil, as was said above (A. 3), is the privation of good, which chiefly and of itself consists in perfection and act. Act, however, is twofold; first, and second. The first act is the form and integrity of a thing; the second act is its operation. Therefore evil also is twofold. In one way it occurs by the subtraction of the form, or of any part required for the integrity of the thing, as blindness is an evil, as also it is an evil to be wanting in any member of the body. In another way evil exists by the withdrawal of the due operation, either because it does not exist, or because it has not its due mode and order. But because good in itself is the object of the will, evil, which is the privation of good, is found in a special way in rational creatures which have a will. Therefore the evil which comes from the withdrawal of the form and integrity of the thing, has the nature of a pain; and especially so on the supposition that all things are subject to divine providence and justice, as was shown above (Q. 22, A. 2); for it is of the very nature of a pain to be against the will. But the evil which consists in the subtraction of the due operation in voluntary things has

rationem culpae. Hoc enim imputatur alicui in culpam, cum deficit a perfecta actione, cuius dominus est secundum voluntatem. Sic igitur omne malum in rebus voluntariis consideratum vel est poena vel culpa.

Ad primum ergo dicendum quod, quia malum privatio est boni, et non negatio pura, ut dictum est supra; non omnis defectus boni est malum, sed defectus boni quod natum est et debet haberi. Defectus enim visionis non est malum in lapide, sed in animali, quia contra rationem lapidis est, quod visum habeat. Similiter etiam contra rationem creaturae est, quod in esse conservetur a seipsa, quia idem dat esse et conservat. Unde iste defectus non est malum creaturae.

Ad secundum dicendum quod poena et culpa non dividunt malum simpliciter; sed malum in rebus voluntariis.

Ad tertium dicendum quod tentatio, prout importat provocationem ad malum, semper malum culpae est in tentante. Sed in eo qui tentatur, non est proprie, nisi secundum quod aliqualiter immutatur, sic enim actio agentis est in patiente. Secundum autem quod tentatus immutatur ad malum a tentante, incidit in culpam.

Ad quartum dicendum quod de ratione poenae est, quod noceat agenti in seipso. Sed de ratione culpae est, quod noceat agenti in sua actione. Et sic utrumque sub malo continetur, secundum quod habet rationem nocumenti.

the nature of a fault; for this is imputed to anyone as a fault to fail as regards perfect action, of which he is master by the will. Therefore every evil in voluntary things is to be looked upon as a pain or a fault.

Reply Obj. 1: Because evil is the privation of good, and not a mere negation, as was said above (A. 3), therefore not every defect of good is an evil, but the defect of the good which is naturally due. For the want of sight is not an evil in a stone, but it is an evil in an animal; since it is against the nature of a stone to see. So, likewise, it is against the nature of a creature to be preserved in existence by itself, because existence and conservation come from one and the same source. Hence this kind of defect is not an evil as regards a creature.

Reply Obj. 2: Pain and fault do not divide evil absolutely considered, but evil that is found in voluntary things.

Reply Obj. 3: Temptation, as importing provocation to evil, is always an evil of fault in the tempter; but in the one tempted it is not, properly speaking, a fault; unless through the temptation some change is wrought in the one who is tempted; for thus is the action of the agent in the patient. And if the tempted is changed to evil by the tempter he falls into fault.

Reply Obj. 4: In answer to the opposite argument, it must be said that the very nature of pain includes the idea of injury to the agent in himself, whereas the idea of fault includes the idea of injury to the agent in his operation; and thus both are contained in evil, as including the idea of injury.

Article 6

Whether Pain Has the Nature of Evil More Than Fault Has?

Ad sextum sic proceditur. Videtur quod habeat plus de ratione mali poena quam culpa. Culpa enim se habet ad poenam, ut meritum ad praemium. Sed praemium habet plus de ratione boni quam meritum, cum sit finis eius. Ergo poena plus habet de ratione mali quam culpa.

Praeterea, illud est maius malum, quod opponitur maiori bono. Sed poena, sicut dictum est, opponitur bono agentis, culpa autem bono actionis. Cum ergo melius sit agens quam actio, videtur quod peius sit poena quam culpa.

Praeterea, ipsa privatio finis poena quaedam est, quae dicitur carentia visionis divinae. Malum autem culpae est per privationem ordinis ad finem. Ergo poena est maius malum quam culpa.

Sed contra, sapiens artifex inducit minus malum ad vitandum maius; sicut medicus praecidit membrum,

Objection 1: It would seem that pain has more of evil than fault. For fault is to pain what merit is to reward. But reward has more good than merit, as its end. Therefore pain has more evil in it than fault has.

Obj. 2: Further, that is the greater evil which is opposed to the greater good. But pain, as was said above (A. 5), is opposed to the good of the agent, while fault is opposed to the good of the action. Therefore, since the agent is better than the action, it seems that pain is worse than fault.

Obj. 3: Further, the privation of the end is a pain consisting in forfeiting the vision of God; whereas the evil of fault is privation of the order to the end. Therefore pain is a greater evil than fault.

On the contrary, A wise workman chooses a less evil in order to prevent a greater, as the surgeon cuts off a limb

ne corrumpatur corpus. Sed Dei sapientia infert poenam ad vitandam culpam. Ergo culpa est maius malum quam poena.

RESPONDEO dicendum quod culpa habet plus de ratione mali quam poena, et non solum quam poena sensibilis, quae consistit in privatione corporalium bonorum, cuiusmodi poenas plures intelligunt; sed etiam universaliter accipiendo poenam, secundum quod privatio gratiae vel gloriae poenae quaedam sunt.

Cuius est duplex ratio. Prima quidem est, quia ex malo culpae fit aliquis malus, non autem ex malo poenae; secundum illud Dionysii, IV cap. de Div. Nom., *puniri non est malum, sed fieri poena dignum.* Et hoc ideo est quia, cum bonum simpliciter consistat in actu, et non in potentia, ultimus autem actus est operatio, vel usus quarumcumque rerum habitarum; bonum hominis simpliciter consideratur in bona operatione, vel bono usu rerum habitarum. Utimur autem rebus omnibus per voluntatem. Unde ex bona voluntate, qua homo bene utitur rebus habitis, dicitur homo bonus; et ex mala, malus. Potest enim qui habet malam voluntatem, etiam bono quod habet, male uti; sicut si grammaticus voluntarie incongrue loquatur. Quia ergo culpa consistit in deordinato actu voluntatis, poena vero in privatione alicuius eorum quibus utitur voluntas; perfectius habet rationem mali culpa quam poena.

Secunda ratio sumi potest ex hoc, quod Deus est auctor mali poenae, non autem mali culpae. Cuius ratio est, quia malum poenae privat bonum creaturae, sive accipiatur bonum creaturae aliquid creatum, sicut caecitas privat visum; sive sit bonum increatum, sicut per carentiam visionis divinae tollitur creaturae bonum increatum. Malum vero culpae opponitur proprie ipsi bono increato, contrariatur enim impletioni divinae voluntatis, et divino amori quo bonum divinum in seipso amatur; et non solum secundum quod participatur a creatura. Sic igitur patet quod culpa habet plus de ratione mali quam poena.

AD PRIMUM ergo dicendum quod, licet culpa terminetur ad poenam, sicut meritum ad praemium, tamen culpa non intenditur propter poenam, sicut meritum propter praemium, sed potius e converso poena inducitur ut vitetur culpa. Et sic culpa est peius quam poena.

AD SECUNDUM dicendum quod ordo actionis, qui tollitur per culpam, est perfectius bonum agentis, cum sit perfectio secunda, quam bonum quod tollitur per poenam, quod est perfectio prima.

AD TERTIUM dicendum quod non est comparatio culpae ad poenam sicut finis et ordinis ad finem, quia utrumque potest privari aliquo modo et per culpam, et per poenam. Sed per poenam quidem, secundum quod ipse homo removetur a fine, et ab ordine ad finem, per

to save the whole body. But divine wisdom inflicts pain to prevent fault. Therefore fault is a greater evil than pain.

I ANSWER THAT, Fault has the nature of evil more than pain has; not only more than pain of sense, consisting in the privation of corporeal goods, which kind of pain appeals to most men; but also more than any kind of pain, thus taking pain in its most general meaning, so as to include privation of grace or glory.

There is a twofold reason for this. The first is that one becomes evil by the evil of fault, but not by the evil of pain, as Dionysius says (*Div. Nom.* iv): *To be punished is not an evil; but it is an evil to be made worthy of punishment.* And this because, since good absolutely considered consists in act, and not in potentiality, and the ultimate act is operation, or the use of something possessed, it follows that the absolute good of man consists in good operation, or the good use of something possessed. Now we use all things by the act of the will. Hence from a good will, which makes a man use well what he has, man is called good, and from a bad will he is called bad. For a man who has a bad will can use ill even the good he has, as when a grammarian of his own will speaks incorrectly. Therefore, because the fault itself consists in the disordered act of the will, and the pain consists in the privation of something used by the will, fault has more of evil in it than pain has.

The second reason can be taken from the fact that God is the author of the evil of pain, but not of the evil of fault. And this is because the evil of pain takes away the creature's good, which may be either something created, as sight, destroyed by blindness, or something uncreated, as by being deprived of the vision of God, the creature forfeits its uncreated good. But the evil of fault is properly opposed to uncreated good; for it is opposed to the fulfilment of the divine will, and to divine love, whereby the divine good is loved for itself, and not only as shared by the creature. Therefore it is plain that fault has more evil in it than pain has.

REPLY OBJ. 1: Although fault results in pain, as merit in reward, yet fault is not intended on account of the pain, as merit is for the reward; but rather, on the contrary, pain is brought about so that the fault may be avoided, and thus fault is worse than pain.

REPLY OBJ. 2: The order of action which is destroyed by fault is the more perfect good of the agent, since it is the second perfection, than the good taken away by pain, which is the first perfection.

REPLY OBJ. 3: Pain and fault are not to be compared as end and order to the end; because one may be deprived of both of these in some way, both by fault and by pain; by pain, accordingly as a man is removed from the end and from the order to the end; by fault, inasmuch as this

culpam vero, secundum quod ista privatio pertinet ad actionem, quae non ordinatur ad finem debitum.

privation belongs to the action which is not ordered to its due end.

QUESTION 49

THE CAUSE OF EVIL

Consequenter quaeritur de causa mali. Et circa hoc quaeruntur tria.

Primo, utrum bonum possit esse causa mali.

Secundo, utrum summum bonum, quod est Deus, sit causa mali.

Tertio, utrum sit aliquod summum malum, quod sit prima causa omnium malorum.

We next inquire into the cause of evil. Concerning this there are three points of inquiry:

(1) Whether good can be the cause of evil?

(2) Whether the supreme good, God, is the cause of evil?

(3) Whether there be any supreme evil, which is the first cause of all evils?

Article 1

Whether Good Can Be the Cause of Evil?

AD PRIMUM SIC PROCEDITUR. Videtur quod bonum non possit esse causa mali. Dicitur enim Matth. VII, *non potest arbor bona malos fructus facere.*

PRAETEREA, unum contrariorum non potest esse causa alterius. Malum autem est contrarium bono. Ergo bonum non potest esse causa mali.

PRAETEREA, effectus deficiens non procedit nisi a causa deficiente. Sed malum, si causam habeat, est effectus deficiens. Ergo habet causam deficientem. Sed omne deficiens malum est. Ergo causa mali non est nisi malum.

PRAETEREA, Dionysius dicit, IV cap. de Div. Nom., quod malum non habet causam. Ergo bonum non est causa mali.

SED CONTRA est quod Augustinus dicit, contra Iulianum, *non fuit omnino unde oriri posset malum, nisi ex bono.*

RESPONDEO dicendum quod necesse est dicere quod omne malum aliqualiter causam habeat. Malum enim est defectus boni quod natum est et debet haberi. Quod autem aliquid deficiat a sua naturali et debita dispositione, non potest provenire nisi ex aliqua causa trahente rem extra suam dispositionem, non enim grave movetur sursum nisi ab aliquo impellente, nec agens deficit in sua actione nisi propter aliquod impedimentum. Esse autem causam non potest convenire nisi bono, quia nihil potest esse causa nisi inquantum est ens; omne autem ens, inquantum huiusmodi, bonum est.

Et si consideremus speciales rationes causarum, agens et forma et finis perfectionem quandam important, quae pertinet ad rationem boni, sed et materia, inquantum est potentia ad bonum, habet rationem boni. Et quidem quod bonum sit causa mali per modum causae materialis, iam ex praemissis patet, ostensum est enim

OBJECTION 1: It would seem that good cannot be the cause of evil. For it is said (Matt 7:18): *A good tree cannot bring forth evil fruit.*

OBJ. 2: Further, one contrary cannot be the cause of another. But evil is the contrary to good. Therefore good cannot be the cause of evil.

OBJ. 3: Further, a deficient effect can proceed only from a deficient cause. But evil is a deficient effect. Therefore its cause, if it has one, is deficient. But everything deficient is an evil. Therefore the cause of evil can only be evil.

OBJ. 4: Further, Dionysius says (*Div. Nom.* iv) that evil has no cause. Therefore good is not the cause of evil.

ON THE CONTRARY, Augustine says (*Contra Julian.* i, 9): *There is no possible source of evil except good.*

I ANSWER THAT, It must be said that every evil in some way has a cause. For evil is the absence of the good, which is natural and due to a thing. But that anything fail from its natural and due disposition can come only from some cause drawing it out of its proper disposition. For a heavy thing is not moved upwards except by some impelling force; nor does an agent fail in its action except from some impediment. But only good can be a cause; because nothing can be a cause except inasmuch as it is a being, and every being, as such, is good.

And if we consider the special kinds of causes, we see that the agent, the form, and the end, import some kind of perfection which belongs to the notion of good. Even matter, as a potentiality to good, has the nature of good. Now, that good is the cause of evil by way of the material cause was shown above (Q. 48, A. 3). For it was shown that good

quod bonum est subiectum mali. Causam autem formalem malum non habet, sed est magis privatio formae. Et similiter nec causam finalem, sed magis est privatio ordinis ad finem debitum; non solum enim finis habet rationem boni, sed etiam utile, quod ordinatur ad finem. Causam autem per modum agentis habet malum, non autem per se, sed per accidens.

Ad cuius evidentiam, sciendum est quod aliter causatur malum in actione, et aliter in effectu. In actione quidem causatur malum propter defectum alicuius principiorum actionis, vel principalis agentis, vel instrumentalis, sicut defectus in motu animalis potest contingere vel propter debilitatem virtutis motivae, ut in pueris; vel propter solam ineptitudinem instrumenti, ut in claudis. Malum autem in re aliqua, non tamen in proprio effectu agentis, causatur quandoque ex virtute agentis; quandoque autem ex defectu ipsius, vel materiae. Ex virtute quidem vel perfectione agentis, quando ad formam intentam ab agente sequitur ex necessitate alterius formae privatio; sicut ad formam ignis sequitur privatio formae aeris vel aquae. Sicut ergo, quanto ignis fuerit perfectior in virtute, tanto perfectius imprimit formam suam, ita etiam tanto perfectius corrumpit contrarium, unde malum et corruptio aeris et aquae, est ex perfectione ignis. Sed hoc est per accidens, quia ignis non intendit privare formam aquae, sed inducere formam propriam; sed hoc faciendo, causat et illud per accidens. Sed si sit defectus in effectu proprio ignis, puta quod deficiat a calefaciendo, hoc est vel propter defectum actionis, qui redundat in defectum alicuius principii, ut dictum est; vel ex indispositione materiae, quae non recipit actionem ignis agentis. Sed et hoc ipsum quod est esse deficiens, accidit bono, cui per se competit agere. Unde verum est quod malum secundum nullum modum habet causam nisi per accidens. Sic autem bonum est causa mali.

AD PRIMUM ergo dicendum quod, sicut Augustinus dicit, contra Iulian., *arborem malam appellat dominus voluntatem malam, et arborem bonam, voluntatem bonam.* Ex voluntate autem bona non producitur actus moralis malus, cum ex ipsa voluntate bona iudicetur actus moralis bonus. Sed tamen ipse motus malae voluntatis causatur a creatura rationali, quae bona est. Et sic est causa mali.

AD SECUNDUM dicendum quod bonum non causat illud malum quod est sibi contrarium, sed quoddam aliud, sicut bonitas ignis causat malum aquae; et homo bonus secundum suam naturam, causat malum actum secundum morem. Et hoc ipsum per accidens est, ut dictum est. Invenitur autem quod etiam unum

is the subject of evil. But evil has no formal cause, rather is it a privation of form; likewise, neither has it a final cause, but rather is it a privation of order to the proper end; since not only the end has the nature of good, but also the useful, which is ordered to the end. Evil, however, has a cause by way of an agent, not directly, but accidentally.

In proof of this, we must know that evil is caused in the action otherwise than in the effect. In the action, evil is caused by reason of the defect of some principle of action, either of the principal or the instrumental agent; thus the defect in the movement of an animal may happen by reason of the weakness of the motive power, as in the case of children, or by reason only of the ineptitude of the instrument, as in the lame. On the other hand, evil is caused in a thing, but not in the proper effect of the agent, sometimes by the power of the agent, sometimes by reason of a defect, either of the agent or of the matter. It is caused by reason of the power or perfection of the agent when there necessarily follows on the form intended by the agent the privation of another form; as, for instance, when on the form of fire there follows the privation of the form of air or of water. Therefore, as the more perfect the fire is in strength, so much the more perfectly does it impress its own form, so also the more perfectly does it corrupt the contrary. Hence that evil and corruption befall air and water comes from the perfection of the fire: but this is accidental; because fire does not aim at the privation of the form of water, but at the bringing in of its own form, though by doing this it also accidentally causes the other. But if there is a defect in the proper effect of the fire—as, for instance, that it fails to heat—this comes either by defect of the action, which implies the defect of some principle, as was said above, or by the indisposition of the matter, which does not receive the action of the fire, the agent. But this very fact that it is a deficient being is accidental to good to which of itself it belongs to act. Hence it is true that evil in no way has any but an accidental cause; and thus is good the cause of evil.

REPLY OBJ. 1: As Augustine says (*Contra Julian.* i): *The Lord calls an evil will the evil tree, and a good will a good tree.* Now, a good will does not produce a morally bad act, since it is from the good will itself that a moral act is judged to be good. Nevertheless the movement itself of an evil will is caused by the rational creature, which is good; and thus good is the cause of evil.

REPLY OBJ. 2: Good does not cause that evil which is contrary to itself, but some other evil: thus the goodness of the fire causes evil to the water, and man, good as to his nature, causes an act morally evil. And, as explained above (Q. 19, A. 9), this is by accident. Moreover, it does happen sometimes that one contrary causes another by accident:

contrariorum causat aliud per accidens, sicut frigidum exterius ambiens calefacit, inquantum calor retrahitur ad interiora.

AD TERTIUM dicendum quod malum habet causam deficientem aliter in rebus voluntariis, et naturalibus. Agens enim naturale producit effectum suum talem quale ipsum est, nisi impediatur ab aliquo extrinseco, et hoc ipsum est quidam defectus eius. Unde nunquam sequitur malum in effectu, nisi praeexistat aliquod aliud malum in agente vel materia, sicut dictum est. Sed in rebus voluntariis, defectus actionis a voluntate actu deficiente procedit, inquantum non subiicit se actu suae regulae. Qui tamen defectus non est culpa, sed sequitur culpa ex hoc quod cum tali defectu operatur.

AD QUARTUM dicendum quod malum non habet causam per se, sed per accidens tantum, ut dictum est.

for instance, the exterior surrounding cold heats (the body) through the concentration of the inward heat.

REPLY OBJ. 3: Evil has a deficient cause in voluntary things otherwise than in natural things. For the natural agent produces the same kind of effect as it is itself, unless it is impeded by some exterior thing; and this amounts to some defect belonging to it. Hence evil never follows in the effect, unless some other evil pre-exists in the agent or in the matter, as was said above. But in voluntary things the defect of the action comes from the will actually deficient, inasmuch as it does not actually subject itself to its proper rule. This defect, however, is not a fault, but fault follows upon it from the fact that the will acts with this defect.

REPLY OBJ. 4: Evil has no direct cause, but only an accidental cause, as was said above.

Article 2

Whether the Supreme Good, God, Is the Cause of Evil?

AD SECUNDUM SIC PROCEDITUR. Videtur quod summum bonum, quod est Deus, sit causa mali. Dicitur enim Isai. XLV, *ego dominus, et non est alter Deus, formans lucem et creans tenebras, faciens pacem et creans malum.* Et Amos III, *si erit malum in civitate, quod dominus non fecerit.*

PRAETEREA, effectus causae secundae reducitur in causam primam. Bonum autem est causa mali, ut dictum est. Cum igitur omnis boni causa sit Deus, ut supra ostensum est, sequitur quod etiam omne malum sit a Deo.

PRAETEREA, sicut dicitur in II Physic., idem est causa salutis navis, et periculi. Sed Deus est causa salutis omnium rerum. Ergo est ipse causa omnis perditionis et mali.

SED CONTRA est quod dicit Augustinus, in libro octoginta trium quaest., quod *Deus non est auctor mali, quia non est causa tendendi ad non esse.*

RESPONDEO dicendum quod, sicut ex dictis patet, malum quod in defectu actionis consistit, semper causatur ex defectu agentis. In Deo autem nullus defectus est, sed summa perfectio, ut supra ostensum est. Unde malum quod in defectu actionis consistit, vel quod ex defectu agentis causatur, non reducitur in Deum sicut in causam.

Sed malum quod in corruptione rerum aliquarum consistit, reducitur in Deum sicut in causam. Et hoc patet tam in naturalibus quam in voluntariis. Dictum est enim quod aliquod agens, inquantum sua virtute producit aliquam formam ad quam sequitur corruptio et defectus, causat sua virtute illam corruptionem et defectum.

OBJECTION 1: It would seem that the supreme good, God, is the cause of evil. For it is said (Isa 45:5,7): *I am the Lord, and there is no other God, forming the light, and creating darkness, making peace, and creating evil.* And Amos 3:6, *Shall there be evil in a city, which the Lord hath not done?*

OBJ. 2: Further, the effect of the secondary cause is reduced to the first cause. But good is the cause of evil, as was said above (A. 1). Therefore, since God is the cause of every good, as was shown above (Q. 2, A. 3; Q. 6, AA. 1, 4), it follows that also every evil is from God.

OBJ. 3: Further, as is said by the Philosopher (*Phys.* ii, 30), the cause of both safety and danger of the ship is the same. But God is the cause of the safety of all things. Therefore He is the cause of all perdition and of all evil.

ON THE CONTRARY, Augustine says (QQ. 83, qu. 21) that *God is not the author of evil because He is not the cause of tending to not-being.*

I ANSWER THAT, As appears from what was said (A. 1), the evil which consists in the defect of action is always caused by the defect of the agent. But in God there is no defect, but the highest perfection, as was shown above (Q. 4, A. 1). Hence, the evil which consists in defect of action, or which is caused by defect of the agent, is not reduced to God as to its cause.

But the evil which consists in the corruption of some things is reduced to God as the cause. And this appears as regards both natural things and voluntary things. For it was said (A. 1) that some agent, inasmuch as it produces by its power a form to which follows corruption and defect, causes by its power that corruption and defect. But it is

Manifestum est autem quod forma quam principaliter Deus intendit in rebus creatis, est bonum ordinis universi. Ordo autem universi requirit, ut supra dictum est, quod quaedam sint quae deficere possint, et interdum deficiant. Et sic Deus, in rebus causando bonum ordinis universi, ex consequenti, et quasi per accidens, causat corruptiones rerum; secundum illud quod dicitur I Reg. II, *dominus mortificat et vivificat*. Sed quod dicitur Sap. I, quod *Deus mortem non fecit*, intelligitur quasi per se intentam. Ad ordinem universi pertinet etiam ordo iustitiae, qui requirit ut peccatoribus poena inferatur. Et secundum hoc, Deus est auctor mali quod est poena, non autem mali quod est culpa, ratione supra dicta.

AD PRIMUM ergo dicendum quod auctoritates illae loquuntur de malo poenae, non autem de malo culpae.

AD SECUNDUM dicendum quod effectus causae secundae deficientis reducitur in causam primam non deficientem, quantum ad id quod habet entitatis et perfectionis, non autem quantum ad id quod habet de defectu. Sicut quidquid est motus in claudicatione, causatur a virtute motiva; sed quod est obliquitatis in ea, non est ex virtute motiva, sed ex curvitate cruris. Et similiter quidquid est entitatis et actionis in actione mala, reducitur in Deum sicut in causam, sed quod est ibi defectus, non causatur a Deo, sed ex causa secunda deficiente.

AD TERTIUM dicendum quod submersio navis attribuitur nautae ut causae, ex eo quod non agit quod requiritur ad salutem navis. Sed Deus non deficit ab agendo quod est necessarium ad salutem. Unde non est simile.

manifest that the form which God chiefly intends in things created is the good of the order of the universe. Now, the order of the universe requires, as was said above (Q. 22, A. 2, ad 2; Q. 48, A. 2), that there should be some things that can, and do sometimes, fail. And thus God, by causing in things the good of the order of the universe, consequently and as it were by accident, causes the corruptions of things, according to 1 Kings 2:6: *The Lord killeth and maketh alive.* But when we read that *God hath not made death* (Wis 1:13), the sense is that God does not will death for its own sake. Nevertheless the order of justice belongs to the order of the universe; and this requires that penalty should be dealt out to sinners. And so God is the author of the evil which is penalty, but not of the evil which is fault, by reason of what is said above.

REPLY OBJ. 1: These passages refer to the evil of penalty, and not to the evil of fault.

REPLY OBJ. 2: The effect of the deficient secondary cause is reduced to the first non-deficient cause as regards what it has of being and perfection, but not as regards what it has of defect; just as whatever there is of motion in the act of limping is caused by the motive power, whereas what there is of obliqueness in it does not come from the motive power, but from the curvature of the leg. And, likewise, whatever there is of being and action in a bad action, is reduced to God as the cause; whereas whatever defect is in it is not caused by God, but by the deficient secondary cause.

REPLY OBJ. 3: The sinking of a ship is attributed to the sailor as the cause, from the fact that he does not fulfill what the safety of the ship requires; but God does not fail in doing what is necessary for the safety of all. Hence there is no parity.

Article 3

Whether There Be One Supreme Evil Which Is the Cause of Every Evil?

AD TERTIUM SIC PROCEDITUR. Videtur quod sit unum summum malum, quod sit causa omnis mali. Contrariorum enim effectuum contrariae sunt causae. Sed in rebus invenitur contrarietas, secundum illud Eccli. XXXIII, *contra malum bonum est, et contra vitam mors; sic et contra virum iustum peccator*. Ergo sunt contraria principia, unum boni, et aliud mali.

PRAETEREA, si unum contrariorum est in rerum natura, et reliquum, ut dicitur in II de caelo et mundo. Sed summum bonum est in rerum natura, quod est causa omnis boni, ut supra ostensum est. Ergo est et summum malum ei oppositum, causa omnis mali.

PRAETEREA, sicut in rebus invenitur bonum et melius, ita malum et peius. Sed bonum et melius dicuntur

OBJECTION 1: It would seem that there is one supreme evil which is the cause of every evil. For contrary effects have contrary causes. But contrariety is found in things, according to Ecclus. 33:15: *Good is set against evil, and life against death; so also is the sinner against a just man.* Therefore there are many contrary principles, one of good, the other of evil.

OBJ. 2: Further, if one contrary is in nature, so is the other. But the supreme good is in nature, and is the cause of every good, as was shown above (Q. 2, A. 3; Q. 6, AA. 2, 4). Therefore, also, there is a supreme evil opposed to it as the cause of every evil.

OBJ. 3: Further, as we find good and better things, so we find evil and worse. But good and better are so considered

per respectum ad optimum. Ergo malum et peius dicuntur per respectum ad aliquod summum malum.

PRAETEREA, omne quod est per participationem, reducitur ad illud quod est per essentiam. Sed res quae sunt malae apud nos, non sunt malae per essentiam, sed per participationem. Ergo est invenire aliquod summum malum per essentiam, quod est causa omnis mali.

PRAETEREA, omne quod est per accidens, reducitur ad illud quod est per se. Sed bonum est causa mali per accidens. Ergo oportet ponere aliquod summum malum, quod sit causa malorum per se. Neque potest dici quod malum non habeat causam per se, sed per accidens tantum, quia sequeretur quod malum non esset ut in pluribus, sed ut in paucioribus.

PRAETEREA, malum effectus reducitur ad malum causae, quia effectus deficiens est a causa deficiente, sicut supra dictum est. Sed hoc non est procedere in infinitum. Ergo oportet ponere unum primum malum, quod sit causa omnis mali.

SED CONTRA est quod summum bonum est causa omnis entis, ut supra ostensum est. Ergo non potest esse aliquod principium ei oppositum, quod sit causa malorum.

RESPONDEO dicendum quod ex praedictis patet non esse unum primum principium malorum, sicut est unum primum principium bonorum.

Primo quidem, quia primum principium bonorum est per essentiam bonum, ut supra ostensum est. Nihil autem potest esse per suam essentiam malum, ostensum est enim quod omne ens, inquantum est ens, bonum est; et quod malum non est nisi in bono ut in subiecto.

Secundo, quia primum bonorum principium est summum et perfectum bonum, quod praehabet in se omnem bonitatem, ut supra ostensum est. Summum autem malum esse non potest, quia, sicut ostensum est, etsi malum semper diminuat bonum, nunquam tamen illud potest totaliter consumere; et sic, semper remanente bono, non potest esse aliquid integre et perfecte malum. Propter quod philosophus dicit, in IV Ethic., quod *si malum integrum sit, seipsum destruet*, quia destructo omni bono (quod requiritur ad integritatem mali), subtrahitur etiam ipsum malum, cuius subiectum est bonum.

Tertio, quia ratio mali repugnat rationi primi principii. Tum quia omne malum causatur ex bono, ut supra ostensum est. Tum quia malum non potest esse causa nisi per accidens, et sic non potest esse prima causa, quia causa per accidens est posterior ea quae est per se, ut patet in II Physic.

Qui autem posuerunt duo prima principia, unum bonum et alterum malum, ex eadem radice in hunc errorem inciderunt, ex qua et aliae extraneae positiones antiquorum ortum habuerunt, quia scilicet non consideraverunt causam universalem totius entis, sed particulares

in relation to what is best. Therefore evil and worse are so considered in relation to some supreme evil.

OBJ. 4: Further, everything participated is reduced to what is essential. But things which are evil among us are evil not essentially, but by participation. Therefore we must seek for some supreme essential evil, which is the cause of every evil.

OBJ. 5: Further, whatever is accidental is reduced to that which is per se. But good is the accidental cause of evil. Therefore, we must suppose some supreme evil which is the per se cause of evils. Nor can it be said that evil has no per se cause, but only an accidental cause; for it would then follow that evil would not exist in the many, but only in the few.

OBJ. 6: Further, the evil of the effect is reduced to the evil of the cause; because the deficient effect comes from the deficient cause, as was said above (AA. 1, 2). But we cannot proceed to infinity in this matter. Therefore, we must suppose one first evil as the cause of every evil.

ON THE CONTRARY, The supreme good is the cause of every being, as was shown above (Q. 2, A. 3; Q. 6, A. 4). Therefore there cannot be any principle opposed to it as the cause of evils.

I ANSWER THAT, It appears from what precedes that there is no one first principle of evil, as there is one first principle of good.

First, indeed, because the first principle of good is essentially good, as was shown above (Q. 6, AA. 3, 4). But nothing can be essentially bad. For it was shown above that every being, as such, is good (Q. 5, A. 3); and that evil can exist only in good as in its subject (Q. 48, A. 3).

Second, because the first principle of good is the highest and perfect good which pre-contains in itself all goodness, as shown above (Q. 6, A. 2). But there cannot be a supreme evil; because, as was shown above (Q. 48, A. 4), although evil always lessens good, yet it never wholly consumes it; and thus, while good ever remains, nothing can be wholly and perfectly bad. Therefore, the Philosopher says (*Ethic*. iv, 5) that *if the wholly evil could be, it would destroy itself*; because all good being destroyed (which it need be for something to be wholly evil), evil itself would be taken away, since its subject is good.

Third, because the very nature of evil is against the idea of a first principle; both because every evil is caused by good, as was shown above (A. 1), and because evil can be only an accidental cause, and thus it cannot be the first cause, for the accidental cause is subsequent to the direct cause.

Those, however, who upheld two first principles, one good and the other evil, fell into this error from the same cause, whence also arose other strange notions of the ancients; namely, because they failed to consider the universal cause of all being, and considered only the particular

tantum causas particularium effectuum. Propter hoc enim, si aliquid invenerunt esse nocivum alicui rei per virtutem suae naturae, aestimaverunt naturam illius rei esse malam, puta si quis dicat naturam ignis esse malam, quia combussit domum alicuius pauperis. Iudicium autem de bonitate alicuius rei non est accipiendum secundum ordinem ad aliquid particulare; sed secundum seipsum, et secundum ordinem ad totum universum, in quo quaelibet res suum locum ordinatissime tenet, ut ex dictis patet.

Similiter etiam, quia invenerunt duorum particularium effectuum contrariorum duas causas particulares contrarias, nesciverunt reducere causas particulares contrarias in causam universalem communem. Et ideo usque ad prima principia contrarietatem in causis esse iudicaverunt. Sed cum omnia contraria conveniant in uno communi, necesse est in eis, supra causas contrarias proprias, inveniri unam causam communem, sicut supra qualitates contrarias elementorum invenitur virtus corporis caelestis. Et similiter supra omnia quae quocumque modo sunt, invenitur unum primum principium essendi, ut supra ostensum est.

AD PRIMUM ergo dicendum quod contraria conveniunt in genere uno, et etiam conveniunt in ratione essendi. Et ideo, licet habeant causas particulares contrarias, tamen oportet devenire ad unam primam causam communem.

AD SECUNDUM dicendum quod privatio et habitus nata sunt fieri circa idem. Subiectum autem privationis est ens in potentia, ut dictum est. Unde, cum malum sit privatio boni, ut ex dictis patet, illi bono opponitur cui adiungitur potentia, non autem summo bono, quod est actus purus.

AD TERTIUM dicendum quod unumquodque intenditur secundum propriam rationem. Sicut autem forma est perfectio quaedam, ita privatio est quaedam remotio. Unde omnis forma et perfectio et bonum per accessum ad terminum perfectum intenditur, privatio autem et malum per recessum a termino. Unde non dicitur malum et peius per accessum ad summum malum, sicut dicitur bonum et melius per accessum ad summum bonum.

AD QUARTUM dicendum quod nullum ens dicitur malum per participationem, sed per privationem participationis. Unde non oportet fieri reductionem ad aliquid quod sit per essentiam malum.

AD QUINTUM dicendum quod malum non potest habere causam nisi per accidens, ut supra ostensum est. Unde impossibile est fieri reductionem ad aliquid quod sit per se causa mali. Quod autem dicitur, quod malum est ut in pluribus, simpliciter falsum est. Nam generabilia et corruptibilia, in quibus solum contingit esse malum naturae, sunt modica pars totius universi. Et

causes of particular effects. For on that account, if they found a thing hurtful to something by the power of its own nature, they thought that the very nature of that thing was evil; as, for instance, if one should say that the nature of fire was evil because it burnt the house of a poor man. The judgment, however, of the goodness of anything does not depend upon its order to any particular thing, but rather upon what it is in itself, and on its order to the whole universe, wherein every part has its own perfectly ordered place, as was said above (Q. 47, A. 2, ad 1).

Likewise, because they found two contrary particular causes of two contrary particular effects, they did not know how to reduce these contrary particular causes to the universal common cause; and therefore they extended the contrariety of causes even to the first principles. But since all contraries agree in something common, it is necessary to search for one common cause for them above their own contrary proper causes; as above the contrary qualities of the elements exists the power of a heavenly body; and above all things that exist, no matter how, there exists one first principle of being, as was shown above (Q. 2, A. 3).

REPLY OBJ. 1: Contraries agree in one genus, and they also agree in the nature of being; and therefore, although they have contrary particular causes, nevertheless we must come at last to one first common cause.

REPLY OBJ. 2: Privation and habit belong naturally to the same subject. Now the subject of privation is a being in potentiality, as was said above (Q. 48, A. 3). Hence, since evil is privation of good, as appears from what was said above (Q. 48, AA. 1, 2, 3), it is opposed to that good which has some potentiality, but not to the supreme good, who is pure act.

REPLY OBJ. 3: Increase in intensity is in proportion to the nature of a thing. And as the form is a perfection, so privation removes a perfection. Hence every form, perfection, and good is intensified by approach to the perfect term; but privation and evil by receding from that term. Hence a thing is not said to be evil and worse, by reason of access to the supreme evil, in the same way as it is said to be good and better, by reason of access to the supreme good.

REPLY OBJ. 4: No being is called evil by participation, but by privation of participation. Hence it is not necessary to reduce it to any essential evil.

REPLY OBJ. 5: Evil can only have an accidental cause, as was shown above (A. 1). Hence reduction to any *per se* cause of evil is impossible. And to say that evil is in the greater number is simply false. For things which are generated and corrupted, in which alone can there be natural evil, are the smaller part of the whole universe. And again, in every species the defect of nature is in the smaller

iterum in unaquaque specie defectus naturae accidit ut in paucioribus. In solis autem hominibus malum videtur esse ut in pluribus, quia bonum hominis secundum sensum non est hominis inquantum homo, idest secundum rationem; plures autem sequuntur sensum quam rationem.

Ad sextum dicendum quod in causis mali non est procedere in infinitum, sed est reducere omnia mala in aliquam causam bonam, ex qua sequitur malum per accidens.

number. In man alone does evil appear as in the greater number; because the good of man as regards the senses is not the good of man as man—that is, in regard to reason; and more men seek good in regard to the senses than good according to reason.

Reply Obj. 6: In the causes of evil we do not proceed to infinity, but reduce all evils to some good cause, whence evil follows accidentally.